League Express

LEAGUE
Publications Ltd

RUGBY LEAGUE
2014-2015
Into the unknown

League Publications Ltd

First published in Great Britain in 2014 by
League Publications Ltd
Wellington House
Briggate
Brighouse
West Yorkshire HD6 1DN

Copyright © League Publications Ltd

A CIP catalogue record for this book is available from the British Library
ISBN 978-1-901347-31-9

Designed and Typeset by League Publications Limited
Printed by H Charlesworth & Co Ltd, Wakefield

Contributing Editor
Tim Butcher

Statistics, production and design
Daniel Spencer

Contributors
Malcolm Andrews
Matt Anniss
Neil Barraclough
Andrew Belt
Aaron Bower
Martin Butcher
Michael Butcher
Phil Caplan
Paul Clarke
John Cox
John Davidson
Paul English
Steve Fox
Ian Golden
Ryan Gould
Adam Gray
Roger Halstead
Phil Hodgson
Steve Hossack
Andrew Jackson
Chris Jackson
Gareth Jones
Steve Kilmartin
David Kuzio
Lorraine Marsden
Tom Marsden

Steve Mascord
Paddy McAteer
Keith McGhie
Joe Mills
David Parkinson
Joseph Pearson
Ian Rigg
Mike Rylance
Martyn Sadler
David Saffer
Steve Slater
Pete Stephenson
James Stott
Ben Turner
Gareth Walker
Jordan Walker
John Walsh
James Whaling
Joe Whitley
Ricky Wilby
Gavin Wilson
Ian Wilson

Pictures
Rugby League Photos
RLA Images
Action Photographics,
Australia
RLPix
Glenn Ashley
Bob Brough
Gordon Clayton
Paul Clayton
Paul English
Steve Gaunt
Peter Green
Magi Haroun
Richard Land
Ian Lovell
Allan McKenzie
Mike McKenzie
John Rushworth
Mal Walker
Bill Watkinson

CONTENTS

Acknowledgments	7	**4. International 2014**	**107**
Introduction	8	Four Nations	108
		Other Internationals	117
1. The 2014 Season	**11**	Season Down Under	121
December 2013	12		
January	14	**5. World Cup 2013**	**135**
February	16	World Cup 2013 - Statistical review	135
March	23	World Cup 2013 - In Colour	145
April	32		
May	38	**6. Statistical review 2014**	**161**
June	46	Super League Players 1996-2014	163
July	53	Super League XIX club by club	185
August	59	Super League XIX round by round	214
September	67	Super League XIX Opta Analysis	232
Super League Play-offs	71	Championship 2014 club by club	243
Super League award winners	77	Championship 2014	
		round by round	258
2. Championships 2014	**79**	Championship One 2014 club by club	275
Championship Season	80	Championship One 2014	
Championship One Season	101	round by round	285
Championship Play-offs	104	Challenge Cup 2014	
		round by round	294
3. 2014 Season - In Colour	**81**	Super League 2015 Fixtures	300
Personalities of 2014	81	Championship 2015 Fixtures	302
Paul Wellens	81	League One 2015 Fixtures	303
Joe Burgess	82	Grand Final History	305
Daryl Clark	83	Longest serving players 2014	315
Paul Rowley	84	2014 Statistical round-up	316
Sam Burgess	85		

ACKNOWLEDGEMENTS

Rugby League 2014-2015 is the 19th of League Publications Ltd's annual series of Rugby League Yearbooks.

In compiling this historical record of the Rugby League year, we rely on the hard work and dedication of all the contributors to *Rugby Leaguer & Rugby League Express* and *Rugby League World* magazine. Without their efforts this yearbook would not be possible.

We are able to include some wonderful action photography provided by, in particular RLphotos.com, Action Photographics in Sydney, Magi Haroun, Steve Jones and Peter Morley of RLAImages.

Thanks also to the Rugby Football League for their help during the year, and to the historians and statisticians at clubs who help to keep us on our toes.

Acknowledgement also to the Rothmans Yearbook 1999, compiled by Ray Fletcher, the British Rugby Records Book from London Publications, and to the club officials, and some supporters, who helped us verify records.

The comprehensive statistical review was put together meticulously, as always, by Daniel Spencer, who also designed the book.

Invaluable contributions once again from Gareth Walker and Malcolm Andrews, who wrote the Championship and NRL/State of Origin sections. Thanks also to Opta Sportdata, who compiled the Opta Index Analysis in our thought-provoking statistical section.

TIM BUTCHER
Contributing Editor

INTRODUCTION

At the end of the year 2014 the sport of Rugby League was about to change, as it had done so many times over the past century and a half.

The sport has felt itself compelled to wrestle with its own appeal, and since the Northern Union was formed in 1895 to change its structure on many occasions. 2015 was to bring change again, with a far from unanimous approval of the re-structuring.

The top two divisions of the Rugby League will both have 12 instead of 14 teams in 2015, and after 23 rounds will split into three divisions of eight, each playing seven league fixtures, and each with their own points and play-off systems.

The approaching change had repercussions in 2014. It meant that two teams had to be relegated from Super League, with none promoted from the Kingstone Championship, from which five clubs were relegated to accommodate the two relegated clubs and the one promoted from Championship One (Hunslet Hawks earning that right in a golden-point Grand Final win over Oldham).

The new structure is planned to provide a safer and securer way for clubs to face promotion into Super League and the second tier will include at least two full-time clubs in the relegated pair, Bradford and London. To many it appears a gamble.

With the emphasis on relegation, without promotion, it is unsurprising that attendances fell in 2014. It was hardly an ideal way to build on the optimism that was engendered by the 2013 Rugby League World Cup held in England, Wales, Ireland and France. The crowd of 74,468 for the final at Old Trafford, Manchester between Australia and New Zealand was the best attended international Rugby League match of all time, the 28 matches of the tournament were watched by over 450,000 people and 67,545 people packed Wembley Stadium for the 'Big Hit' semi-finals.

RFL chief executive Nigel Wood's claim that 'RLWC2013 has lit the blue touch paper for every arm of the sport and it is my hope that everyone involved in Rugby League at every level makes the most of the opportunities that now exist for them' sadly fell flat.

After the bonanza of the World Cup, England didn't have another international game until the end of October 2014, and that was in Brisbane in the Four Nations opener. Spectators who had thrilled to England's rousing performance against New Zealand at Wembley the previous year didn't get one single chance to see their team in live action again this year.

Wood's appointment to the chairmanship of the Rugby League International Federation will hopefully at last provide the spark for the growth of international Rugby League.

The 2014 Four Nations itself will have helped the cause, not because New Zealand won it in a magnificent final with Australia, or because England, whose coach Steve McNamara spent the season as an assistant coach at Sydney Roosters, were more competitive than they have been for many years, but thanks to the super performances of Samoa, who were within an inch of beating both England and New Zealand in the group games. The potential for the growth of Rugby League on the back of international competition was hopefully starting to dawn on the game's power brokers.

James Graham and Sam Tomkins lead out England before the Four Nations clash with New Zealand

The highly promising performances by England had many observers forecasting a renaissance in national fortunes on the back of a new breed of young English players. A handful of them starred in the Australian NRL competition in 2014. The rest honed their game in probably the most competitive Super League to date in 2014. The ups and downs of Super League XIX made the outcome impossible to predict, even going into the play-off stages.

Eventual League Leaders and Champions St Helens looked totally unstoppable right up to Easter, blipped mid-season, were cruelled by injuries at the season end, but despite losing their three first-choice halfbacks, and coach Nathan Brown's announcement six days before the Grand Final that he was leaving, managed to win the title. The 2013 Champions Wigan looked to have peaked at just the right time but fell just short as their prop Ben Flower became the first player to be sent off in a Super League Grand Final in the most dramatic of season climaxes.

Castleford Tigers were expected to have a better year in 2014, but at times Tigers fans must have been pinching themselves as, under Coach of the Year Daryl Powell, they finished fourth in the table and runners-up in the Challenge Cup, with hooker Daryl Clark named Steve Prescott Man of Steel, and going on to establish himself as a genuine international-class player in the Four Nations.

Leeds Rhinos won the Challenge Cup for the first time in 15 years and, after a five-match losing league run at the end of the season could only finish sixth. But no-one was writing off their chances of completing the double, even up to their last-second elimination by Catalans Dragons at Headingley.

Introduction

Warrington Wolves were expected to have a season of transition after the enforced retirement of the enigmatic Lee Briers in the close season last year, but they were only denied a Grand Final place when Albert Goldthorpe Rookie of the Year Joe Burgess scored in the last seconds of their Qualifying Semi-final at Wigan. Huddersfield Giants, League Leaders in 2013, stumbled through the early part of the season, at one point languishing in 10th place, but eventually finished fourth, going into the play-offs on the back of a seven-match unbeaten run. Their captain, Danny Brough was the winner of the Albert Goldthorpe Medal for the third time.

The Dragons went on from their first ever win at Headingley to edge the Giants at the John Smith's Stadium until they fell at the last hurdle at St Helens. And this was the side that had lost their first five games of the season and appeared to be in a downward spiral.

Widnes Vikings made up the top-eight to reach the play-offs for the first time in their history, a sign of their steady progression under the six-year licensing experiment, in its last year in 2014.

After 27 rounds there were four points between the top eight and the chasing pack, with five of the bottom six having a change of coach mid-season. The only exception was Hull FC, who stuck by Lee Radford in an inconsistent year. Supporters of neighbours Hull KR suffered a similar season and jettisoned Craig Sandercock; whereas Wakefield coach Richard Agar decided he had had enough after some traumatic times. Salford Red Devils had a colourful year, moving Brian Noble upstairs without his knowledge and chairman Marwan Koukash becoming one of several club chairmen to be fined by the Rugby Football League for speaking his mind.

The two relegated clubs, Bradford and London, also finished the season with different coaches and suffered horrible years, hardly surprising as their off-field troubles at the end of the 2013 season had them some way behind everyone else before a ball was kicked.

It might be hard for the fans of the Bulls and the Broncos to accept, but it all made for a fantastic season that featured some superb sport.

And a mention too to Leigh Centurions, who lost only one Championship game all season, as well as giving Leeds a serious run for their money in the Challenge Cup. Leigh won the Championship Grand Final against Featherstone in exciting fashion. It was a great occasion but, for the time being, it was the last Championship Grand Final because of the new league structure. Well, after all, this is Rugby League.

The League Express Yearbook contains the full story of the domestic year, the Australian NRL season, and match facts for all Super League, Challenge Cup games involving professional teams, Championship and Championship One game. Every player who has played Super League is also listed along with those players to have made their debuts this year. We have also selected five individuals who we judge to have made the biggest impact on Rugby League in 2014. There are scoring and attendance records for every club and a list of every club's longest serving player. There is also full colour coverage of the 2013 World Cup. League Publications publishes the weekly newspaper Rugby Leaguer & Rugby League Express, as well as the monthly glossy magazine Rugby League World and the UK's most popular website 'totalrl.com'.

TIM BUTCHER
Contributing Editor

1
THE 2014 SEASON

DECEMBER 2013
World Horizons

Rugby League World Cup 2013 Tournament Director Nigel Wood hailed the tournament staged in England, Wales, Ireland and France as the start of a boom period for international Rugby League. 'The success of the tournament provides the Rugby League International Federation with the resources to move the sport forward and we will be putting in place structures that ensure the legacy of RLWC2013 around the world is lasting and positive,' said Wood, who was also chief executive of the Rugby Football League.

'RLWC2013 has lit the blue touch paper for every arm of the sport and it is my hope that everyone involved in Rugby League at every level makes the most of the opportunities that now exist for them.'

The crowd of 74,468 for the final at Old Trafford, Manchester between Australia and New Zealand was the best attended international Rugby League match of all time and the 28 matches of the tournament were watched by over 450,000 people. 67,545 people packed Wembley Stadium for the 'Big Hit' semi-finals.

Johnathan Thurston was voted the man of the match in the World Cup Final, as Australia registered a convincing 34-2 victory over New Zealand to win the World Cup for the tenth time, with a record World Cup Final margin. After edging England 28-20 in the opening game in Cardiff, the Kangaroos played the last 404 minutes of the tournament without having their line breached again.

England were knocked out by New Zealand in the semi-final, losing 20-18 to a last-second Shaun Johnson try and conversion in one of the great games of all time. The details of the tournament can be found later in this book.

England's exit brought the future of head coach Steve McNamara into question but the RFL confirmed that he would be continuing in the role, despite the fact that he was to be based in Sydney in 2014, as an assistant to former Catalan Dragons coach Trent Robinson, under a two-year contract, at NRL Premiers Sydney Roosters.

The RFL denied a story that broke out in a Sydney newspaper suggesting that England or Great Britain would take on Australian rugby union's Wallabies in a hybrid code game at Wembley Stadium in December 2014.

The World Cup had engrossed Rugby League and non-Rugby League supporters alike and had diverted attention from a growing row that had developed over the restructuring of the top two divisions. The RFL had proposed a structure comprising two divisions of 12 teams that would split into three groups for the last seven weeks of the season, as a convoluted way of re-introducing promotion and relegation. Red Hall bosses had portrayed it as a done deal but just before the World Cup a group of six top Super League clubs - Wigan, Warrington, Hull FC, Hull KR, Catalans and Huddersfield - had walked out of a meting to ratify the proposal and had raised concerns over the governance and commercial performance of Super League, which was effectively controlled by the RFL.

One complicating factor was the unclear future of London Broncos. At the start of December Broncos chief executive Gus Mackay said that the club would go into financial administration within ten days to ward off their main creditors, HMRC and the owners of their Roehampton training facility. The RFL was still hoping to broker a deal between the

Broncos' owner David Hughes and Tony Kleanthous, the owner of Barnet Football Club, after a proposed deal between the two men fell through at the end of November. After two weeks the Broncos agreed a two-year ground share with Barnet FC. The announcement was the culmination of six months of talks amid speculation that the Broncos' long-term Chairman and benefactor Hughes was looking to wind down his commitment to the club. Hughes was set to remain in charge of the Londoners during the 2014 season, with Kleanthous expected to assume control for 2015. In addition to playing their home games at The Hive, the Broncos were to switch their training to Barnet's former ground, Underhill.

The uncertainty meant that on the field the Broncos are some way behind their Super League rivals, with 16 players having left the club since the end of the 2013 season, and just a dozen predominantly home-grown players currently signed.

The future of Bradford Bulls was once again clouded. Chairman Mark Moore and his fellow directors Ian Watt and Andrew Calvert, who all took up their positions in October, announced they were to stand down immediately from their roles. Their decision meant that OK Bulls Ltd, the company set up by Omar Khan that owned the Bulls, now had no directors, although the three changed their minds the same week.

Problems arose when Khan agreed to sell the company jointly to former Bulls director Ryan Whitcut and Moore for £300,000. It was followed by a demand from Khan for the company to repay loans he had made to it. Whitcut had resigned from the board on 8th November, after he had failed to satisfy the RFL that he was a fit and proper person to be a director of a Super League club. However, prior to his departure he had negotiated a loan of £180,000 from Safeguard Security Ltd, secured by a debenture against the Bulls' assets. Khan was reportedly pursuing legal proceedings against Whitcut and Moore. The matter was unresolved as the year ended, although players and staff received their salaries for December. Several star names we predicted to leave the Bulls.

There were no money worries at Salford Red Devils, whose owner Dr Marwan Koukash again urged the RFL to lift the Super League salary cap so he could attempt to sign Sonny Bill Williams, despite him having already signed a contract extension at Sydney Roosters. Another player joined the Red Devils as Harrison Hansen transferred from Wigan after a nine-year stint with the Warriors. The 28-year-old penned a four-year-deal at the AJ Bell Stadium.

The latest Active People survey, published by Sport England, showed an increase in the number of people playing Rugby League over the previous year. Rugby League was unique in that no other team sport registered an increase across that 12-month period.

Despite the success of Scotland in reaching the quarter-finals of the World Cup, it was announced that the RFL was to withdraw funding from the Scotland Rugby League, with the body's two permanent employees being made redundant.

There was also bad news for Catalans Dragons, who were fined £2,000 by the RFL for failing to control their fans in the home, on the road, fixture against Hull KR in June. The Dragons snatched victory in Toulouse with a late try but were found guilty of not carrying out a sufficient investigation into their crowd, which was deemed to have 'verbally abused and intimidated match officials'.

Super League clubs were finalising their recruitment. Jordan Rankin, the youngest player ever to make an NRL appearance, signed for Hull FC. Castleford announced the signing of Irish international halfback Liam Finn from local rivals Featherstone Rovers. The 30-year-old scored 1,484 points during his two spells with Rovers. England hooker James Roby committed himself to St Helens for the next five years.

Three Boxing Day friendlies took place, two of them ending in draws. Paul Aiton made his first outing for the Rhinos against the club that had to sell him to help solve a financial shortfall, Wakefield Trinity, and played his part in an entertaining 18-18 draw for a holiday crowd of 8,909 spectators. Just down the road at the Mend-a-Hose Jungle, Castleford Tigers and Halifax finished all square at 30-30. Batley Bulldogs won at Dewsbury Rams 10-4. And on the last Sunday of the year Warrington Wolves recorded a 36-32 victory over Widnes Vikings.

JANUARY
The numbers game

A rift between the Rugby Football League and some Super League clubs over the future of league structures was seemingly healed on Friday 17th January when the Super League clubs voted by a majority of 13-0, with one abstention from the Catalans Dragons, to reduce the size of Super League from 14 to 12 clubs in 2015. They then voted by a much smaller majority of 7-6, with the Catalans again abstaining, for a move to a controversial new structure of two leagues of 12 clubs playing 23 rounds of fixtures, before splitting into three leagues of eight clubs playing seven rounds of fixtures. The six clubs that voted against the new league structure were Huddersfield, Hull FC, Hull KR, Salford, Warrington and Wigan.

The proponents of the new system claimed it would make movement between Super League and the Championship easier for clubs to manage than it would with a more conventional promotion and relegation system. The financial distribution to the clubs still had to be worked out.

The previous Tuesday the Super League clubs had held a meeting to discuss the governance of their competition, with the six 'rebel' clubs proposing a Super League Board of Directors that would still include the RFL Chairman and Chief Executive, but in future three other members - a Super League Chief Executive, a Super League Sales & Marketing Director and an external independent non-executive director.

In May, Blake Solly, the RFL's Director of Standards and Licensing was appointed to the new post of General Manager of Super League and Richard Bowker CBE became the new non-executive independent director of Super League (Europe).

A week after the January agreement, the RFL signed a new broadcasting contract with BSkyB to cover domestic and international Rugby League for the five-year period from 2017 to 2021 for a total value of £200 million. Income from the new deal was to flow almost immediately, with every club in Super League set to be boosted by an immediate payment of £300,000, and with a further payment of £100,000 to each of the clubs' charitable foundations in July. The monies were brought forward to facilitate the change to the changed structure from 2015.

The new contract was negotiated by RFL chief executive Nigel Wood and he described it as a 'game changer' for the sport. The value of the Sky contract had risen from £127 million for the current five-year deal (2012 to 2016) to £200 million, although it did include coverage of the Championship competitions from 2015 and international Rugby League from 2018 onwards.

Wigan Chairman Ian Lenagan described the new deal as 'a dreadful commercial decision to be agreeing in 2014, with three years still to go on Super League's current deal, a new deal for Super League TV rights for the five future years at only a 30% increase and without going out to tender and allowing BT Sport to compete.'

Speaking at Salford's pre-season launch at Media City, Red Devils owner Marwan Koukash said of the new Sky deal: 'All right, we've got more money – bloody £300,000 per year. Will it let us increase the salary cap? No. I tell you what it will do – it will allow us to stabilise some of the clubs. But imagine a salary cap of £1.8m in a few years time. It will drive our best talent to bloody [rugby] union or the NRL [Australia's National Rugby League]. That's what it's going to do.'

Koukash was found to be in breach of RFL operational rule D1.8 (c) by 'engaging in conduct which is prejudicial to the interests of the game' and fined a thousand pounds.

An immediate fall out from the deal was that Premier Sports, a subscription channel that had rights to broadcast the NRL and State of Origin from Australia, pulled out of covering the 2014 Kingstone Press Championship after learning that they would no longer be covering the competition in 2015.

Criticism wasn't universal. St Helens chairman Eamonn McManus insisted the game was in its rudest health for a long time.

Independent energy supplier First Utility became the title sponsor of Super League for the next three years after two years without a title sponsor. Koukash was similarly scathing over that deal. 'Supposedly wonderful news, but we will be lucky if we get £30-40,000. We are securing better deals than that ourselves as a club.'

Johnathan Thurston was confirmed as the winner of the 2013 Rugby League World Golden Boot, with the award reflecting his performances as the outstanding player of the 2013 Rugby League World Cup.

Thurston also won the Golden Boot in 2011, and he became only the third player to win it twice, after Andrew Johns (1999 and 2001) and Darren Lockyer (2003 and 2006).

Huddersfield captain and Albert Goldthorpe Medal winner Danny Brough was voted Super League player of the year for 2013 by League Express readers, while double-winning Wigan coach Shaun Wane was voted Super League Coach of the Year in the annual Readers' Poll.

Bradford Bulls Chairman Mark Moore said there was no longer 'an appetite to make player sales' at his club. Moore was speaking a day after the club's former operating company, OK Bulls Ltd, was placed into administration, before later being purchased by a new company, Bradford Bulls 2014 Ltd, and before the Bulls suffered an embarrassing 66-10 friendly defeat by Castleford Tigers at Odsal.

London Broncos signed former England hooker Scott Moore from the North Queensland Cowboys and Melbourne Storm fullback or winger Denny Solomona. Former Penrith, South Sydney and Cronulla prop Ben Ross denied on Twitter that he was to come out of retirement and sign for London after a Broncos press release said they had agreed a deal with him.

Hull KR pulled the plug on their two Papua New Guinean signings - prop forward Enoch Maki and second-rower Francis Paniu, who both represented the Kumuls in the World Cup - because of lengthy delays in obtaining visas.

St Helens unveiled new signing, giant prop Mose Masoe, who had starred for Samoa in the World Cup, although an ankle injury disrupted his pre-season and he would miss the start of the competition.

Wakefield Trinity head coach Richard Agar said he wasn't going to panic after the Wildcats had to have their team photo taken without key players Pita Godinet, Matt Ryan and Scott Anderson, who were still awaiting visas. The Wildcats were also hit with the news from the local council that they would have to operate with a reduced ground capacity of 5,333 for the start of the season.

There were a raft of friendlies, although some fell foul of the wettest January since records began. Testimonial matches for Wakefield's Andy Raleigh and former Wigan star Paul Prescott had to be postponed because of waterlogged pitches at Wakefield and Workington respectively, where Huddersfield and Wigan were scheduled to be the respective visitors.

Salford Red Devils overcame Leigh Centurions 26-16 at a cold and wet Leigh Sports Village, while Catalans Dragons edged their two home warm-ups, by 16-12 over London and 18-16 against Widnes. Hull FC beat Hull KR at home by 20-12. And Wigan beat St Helens at Langtree Park 28-16 in James Roby's Testimonial

And Leeds coach Brian McDermott compared Jamie Peacock to some of the game's greatest ever prop forwards, claiming he was 'one in a million'. Peacock signed a new deal with the Rhinos until the end of 2015, just weeks shy of his 39th birthday.

FEBRUARY
Red alert

Round 1

Wigan Warriors and Huddersfield Giants got the 2014 season off to a wonderful start on the first Friday night of February, in a game brought forward a week to allow Wigan to fly down under for the first World Club Challenge to be held in Australia since 1994.

The Giants registered a 24-8 victory in front of over 16,640 people at the DW Stadium, Jermaine McGillvary scoring a hat-trick of tries. The Giants, winners of the League Leaders' Shield in 2013, led 12-0 at half-time, a Brett Ferres try and two from winger McGillvary putting them in control.

Tries from Iain Thornley and Joe Burgess in the first eleven minutes of the second half brought Wigan back into contention at 12-8, but Danny Brough's short kick-off regained possession for the Giants and led almost immediately to McGillvary's third try. A late effort from the outstanding Scott Grix sealed the visitors' victory.

Wigan, playing their first competitive match since the departure of star fullback Sam Tomkins to New Zealand Warriors, were without prolific winger Josh Charnley because of a groin injury and then lost influential captain Sean O'Loughlin to a thigh problem shortly before kick-off.

New Wigan fullback Matty Bowen was put on report, for a late high tackle on Giants fullback Grix as he kicked through, to mark a frustrating Super League debut, although he was not charged by the RFL.

The Giants also suffered injury blows. Forward Larne Patrick was stretchered off the field with 53 seconds remaining in the first half with a knee ligament injury. In the second half, hooker Shaun Lunt went down with an ankle problem.

The game drew a peak audience of 350,000 viewers to Sky Sports 1.

Wakefield's new signings from the NRL - Brisbane Broncos prop Scott Anderson, Parramatta Eels second-rower Matt Ryan, and New Zealand Warriors halfback Pita Godinet - joined up with the Wildcats' squad after they finally received their visas. However, centre Lee Smith was set to complete a transfer to rugby union side Newcastle Falcons.

The problems at Bradford Bulls were far from over. The club had faced several months of uncertainty about its ownership, culminating in OK Bulls Ltd, the club's former holding company owned by Omar Khan, being placed into administration on January 31.

The club was bought by a new company, Bradford Bulls 2014 Ltd, with directors Mark Moore, Ian Watt and Andrew Calvert taking shares in the new company, but operating under a 28-day temporary Super League licence

The club was also facing a possible exodus of some of its players under the Transfer of Undertakings (Protection of Employment) Regulations 2006, which allowed employees to leave unilaterally where there is a change of ownership of a business. Garreth Carvell had declared he was no longer a Bulls player and negotiated with Hull FC for a new contract. A London-based businessman said he was preparing to make an offer to buy the Bulls.

The club also lost Jarrod Sammut to Wakefield Trinity Wildcats, although in Sammut's case it was an amicable transfer, whereas the current Bradford directors were threatening to sue Carvell for what they claimed was a breach of contract.

Warrington celebrated their tenth anniversary at the Halliwell Jones Stadium in front of a bumper crowd in the Thursday night TV game - a new slot on Sky Sports - in the round one-proper opener. It was by no means a perfect anniversary as St Helens thrashed them 38-8.

Saints coach Nathan Brown praised stand-off Gary Wheeler, whose career had been blighted by injuries, but was selected ahead of New Zealand international Lance Hohaia. The 24-year-old justified his pick with sharp passing and evasive running and partnered Saints' new recruit from down under, Luke Walsh, in the halfbacks. Saints also handed a debut to former Wakefield forward Kyle Amor, although Samoan powerhouse Mose Masoe was still to make his bow because of an ankle injury.

Walsh marshalled his side with great aplomb, deploying an impressive kicking game and some polished handling skills, kicking eight from eight goals and scoring a late try from an interception to cap a perfect debut.

Questions had been asked about the Wolves' ability to manage without Lee Briers, who had been forced to retire with a neck injury in the off-season. Coach Tony Smith admitted his side's kicking game was as bad as it could be.

That weekend all eyes were on Salford Red Devils and their big-money team. At half-time of their home Sunday game, things were seamlessly going to plan as they led Wakefield 18-0 in front of 7,102 people, the biggest ever Rugby League crowd at the new stadium. Halfbacks Rangi Chase and Tim Smith combined to orchestrate a fluent attack and forwards Harrison Hansen and Gareth Hock led a fearsome defence. With a 5-1 penalty count in their favour, nothing looked like stopping Salford. The only blemish in an impressive first half was a seemingly innocuous injury to Chase, who was forced off on 19 minutes with a leg complaint after completing a covering tackle.

But the half-time break helped the Wildcats. On their return, Wakefield piled on 14 points in 17 minutes, with the penalty count squaring up, to trail the Red Devils by just four. But the Wildcats - a strong tip for relegation - could not find the final score to record what would have been a dramatic comeback win.

Wakefield had six players on debut, but the complete Salford starting 13 were making their club debut.

In the Friday TV game, new Hull FC head coach Lee Radford admitted that there was much work still to be done after his side held on for a 36-34 home win to secure a seventh consecutive victory over Catalans Dragons at the KC Stadium.

Catalans scrum-half Thomas Bosc missed a last-minute conversion that would have tied the scores after the Dragons, who had led 16-12 at the break came back from being 36-22 down heading into the closing stages.

Zeb Taia got the comeback rolling with 12 minutes left and Ben Crooks' reply for Hull wasn't enough to kill off the Dragons. Three tries in the last five minutes, from Damien Cardace, Morgan Escaré and Zeb Taia, had Hull fans biting their nails. Jordan Rankin impressed on debut for Hull.

On the Sunday, former Hull FC stalwart Tom Briscoe bagged a hat-trick on his Leeds' Super League debut as they defeated Hull KR 34-6 at a sold-out Craven Park, now known as the KC Lightstream Stadium. England centre Kallum Watkins was at the heart of all Briscoe's tries in a superb display. Hull KR still had a slim chance at 18-6 down just past

the hour mark, but when Danny McGuire picked up a loose ball and raced home the game was sealed for Leeds. The Robins would be without winger David Hodgson for six to eight weeks after he picked up a knee ligament injury.

London Broncos were expected to get a hiding at Widnes on the same day, with their collection of young Londoners and loan players and that is exactly what happened as the Vikings showed little mercy in an impressive 64-10 thrashing. Denis Betts was quick to pay tribute to new signing Danny Tickle after he recorded a 24-point haul on debut, in what was a Super League record win for the Vikings. The 64-10 triumph eclipsed the 58-24 win over Salford the previous season and saw Tickle kick ten goals from eleven attempts, several of them from the touchline. Tormentor-in-chief was Vikings skipper for the day Kevin Brown who bagged a hat-trick of tries and was the architect of numerous others.

Also on the Sunday, a late points surge ensured Castleford started Super League XIX with an impressive 36-18 win at Bradford, as they piled further misery on a beleaguered Bulls outfit. The game was very much in the balance heading into the final quarter, with the Bulls more than playing their part in a compelling contest. However, the Tigers came good when it mattered, with three late tries in 14 second-half minutes. Kirk Dixon's try and six goals took him past the 1,000 points mark for the Tigers.

Wigan coach Shaun Wane was delighted with the performance of a predominantly young side that enjoyed a resounding 46-22 win over New Zealand Warriors the previous Wednesday, just two days after arriving on the long flight from England. Wigan scored 30 unanswered points in the second half, with teenage rookie winger Joe Burgess scoring four tries and Dominic Manfredi scoring a spectacular length-of-the-field effort.

* That weekend, in front of a full house of around 45,000 each day at Eden Park, North Queensland Cowboys beat Brisbane 16-7 in the final of the Auckland Nines. It was revealed that Rugby League Nines was to feature in the build-up to this year's Commonwealth Games in Glasgow as an unofficial exhibition sport, with a view to be included in the next games.

World Club Challenge

Wigan coach Shaun Wane vowed to get his side back in the World Club Challenge and avenge their disappointing showing in Sydney where they went down 36-14 at the Allianz Stadium to the Roosters in the first World Club Challenge match in Australia for 20 years.

Wigan failed to live up to their own high expectations. Australian Test centre Michael Jennings became the first player to score a hat-trick in the World Club Challenge, while winger Josh Charnley, on his 100th appearance, touched down twice in the second half as Wigan fought back from an 18-0 half-time deficit.

A blistering opening 23 minutes saw the Roosters take the game away from Wigan, with Jennings scoring either side of a close-range Sam Moa try.

Jennings completed his hat-trick in the second half after teenage wing Joe Burgess scored Wigan's first points. Although the Warriors hit back with Charnley's tries it wasn't enough, as the Roosters crossed twice more, with Jared Waerea-Hargreaves and Shaun Kenny-Dowall sealing the victory.

Roosters coach Trent Robinson felt the sport could have done more to help draw a bigger crowd. A total of 31,515 people turned up, despite an almost total lack of pre-match promotion for the game.

Sydney Roosters' Sonny Bill Williams closes down Wigan's Dan Sarginson

The former Catalans Dragons coach said: 'How much time and effort did we put in to preparing this as a competition?

'Our focus was on the Nines. There wasn't a huge amount of advertising or preparation this event, and yet over 31,000 people turned up. We underestimated the crowd and we underestimated the occasion to Australian fans. We could easily make this a huge event.

'This is the important one. We need to support our code. There should have been 42 or 43 thousand there.

'Souths and St George played in the Charity Shield two hours before we played. Have this as a standalone game and make a big thing about it and you fill the stadium. We need a better effort than that.'

WORLD CLUB CHALLENGE

Saturday 22nd February 2014

SYDNEY ROOSTERS 36 WIGAN WARRIORS 14

ROOSTERS: 1 Anthony Minichiello (C); 5 Shaun Kenny-Dowall; 4 Mitchell Aubusson; 3 Michael Jennings; 2 Daniel Tupou; 6 James Maloney; 7 Mitchell Pearce; 8 Jared Waerea-Hargreaves; 9 Jake Friend; 10 Sam Moa; 11 Boyd Cordner; 12 Sonny Bill Williams; 13 Frank-Paul Nuuausala. Subs (all used): 14 Daniel Mortimer; 15 Aidan Guerra; 16 Dylan Napa; 17 Remi Casty.
Tries: Jennings (3, 23, 48), Moa (14), Waerea-Hargreaves (63), Kenny-Dowall (73); **Goals:** Maloney 6/6.
WARRIORS: 1 Matt Bowen; 2 Josh Charnley; 3 Darrell Goulding; 23 Dan Sarginson; 32 Joe Burgess; 6 Blake Green; 7 Matty Smith; 10 Ben Flower; 9 Michael McIlorum; 16 Gil Dudson; 14 Jack Hughes; 12 Liam Farrell; 13 Sean O'Loughlin (C). Subs (all used): 8 Scott Taylor; 22 Eddy Pettybourne; 17 Dominic Crosby; 25 John Bateman (D).
Tries: Burgess (44), Charnley (53, 59); **Goals:** Smith 1/3.
On report:
Pettybourne (38) - alleged high tackle on Kenny-Dowall. **Rugby Leaguer & League Express Men of the Match:** *Roosters:* Michael Jennings; *Warriors:* Sean O'Loughlin. **Penalty count:** 6-5; **Half-time:** 18-0;
Referees: Ben Cummins & Gerard Sutton;
Attendance: 31,515 *(at Allianz Stadium, Sydney).*

Round 2

Bradford Bulls, with the prospect of a points deduction for going into administration at the end of January and two teams to be relegated at the end of the season, struck a blow when they won away in the Thursday TV game at Wakefield, another side tipped to struggle, by 23-10.

Both sides had only a four-day turnaround and, on a muddy pitch, it wasn't the game of the season. Bulls coach Francis Cummins labelled the short turn-around as 'ridiculous', but his side's first win of 2014 as 'priceless'.

A lot was said before the game about the eve-of-season defection of Bradford's star halfback Jarrod Sammut to Wakefield. But, although the Australian-born Maltese international showed glimpses of his unorthodox inspirational qualities after coming off of the bench, it was another debutant, Luke George, who scored the early second-half try that first gave the Bulls breathing space in a battling affair that, until then, could have gone either way.

Bradford captain Matt Diskin never took a backward step, while the equally industrious Luke Gale kicked effectively to ensure Trinity frequently needed to attack from deep in their own territory. The Bulls suffered the worst possible start when new stand-off Lee Gaskell suffered knee ligament damage in almost the first tackle of the game and limped off shortly afterwards. The following week Wakefield centre Dean Collis was banned for two games for dangerous contact.

Young hooker Adam O'Brien's opportunist try from dummy half on 65 minutes put two scores between the sides and Gale kicked the field goal three minutes from time that ended Wakefield's chances for good.

Off the field, things were looking up for Bradford, with the new board of directors set to meet the RFL that week to ratify ownership of the club.

London Broncos were billed as relegation certainties, although they had started to recruit from down under, signing St George Illawarra pair Josh Drinkwater and Atelea Vea, and former Catalans centre Ben Farrar and prop Nick Slyney from Brisbane. Leeds Rhinos players Alex Foster, 20, Thomas Minns and James Duckworth, both 19, who joined at the start of the season on loan, signed for the club for the rest of the 2014 campaign.

Their first game at their new home, The Hive, in north London should have been a bumper celebration but a crowd of only 1,246 turned out on the Saturday afternoon to see Salford Red Devils record their second win, by 44-18, Theo Fages and Harrison Hansen both scoring try doubles. Standing in for the injured Rangi Chase, Fages grasped his opportunity well, making a number of inroads into the home defence to go with his try brace. Alongside him, Tim Smith was also influential at halfback, setting up two first-half tries and scoring one himself. Hansen was excellent in the back row, while coach Brian Noble was quick to highlight the contributions of Tommy Lee and Lama Tasi alongside him in the pack.

It meant a second straight win for the most talked-about club in Super League at the start of 2014, setting up a televised top-of-the-table clash with St Helens perfectly for the following Thursday night.

St Helens had defeated Hull FC 34-22 the night before, with the two teams playing for the Steve Prescott Cup over both league games that season. Saints and Hull FC fans turned out to pay tribute to Prescott, an iconic player at both clubs, and the footbridge linking St Helens town centre to Langtree Park was named 'The Steve Prescott Bridge' at a special ceremony before the game. And a tribute to Prescott was shown on the big screen at half-time.

St Helens ran in five second-half tries. Mickey Paea and Richard Whiting tries gave Hull a 10-6 half-time lead. But scores from Sia Soliola, Jonny Lomax and James Roby, who also scored a first-half try for Saints, put the hosts in command. Gareth Ellis crossed as

Hull hit back, but Tommy Makinson and Mark Percival touched down to make the game safe before Danny Houghton's consolation.

On the same Friday night, Leeds beat Warrington 18-12 at Headingley to also make it two wins from two. Wolves coach Tony Smith was upbeat about his side's performance despite falling to a second successive defeat. He reserved special praise for one of his two debutants, former Featherstone forward Anthony England - who had been brought out of the Championship in similar fashion to England international Chris Hill - and former Oldham St Annes winger Gene Ormsby.

Tom Briscoe scored a sensational try in the lead up to the break that finally capitalised on an opening 40 minutes of Rhinos dominance, after Joel Monaghan had opened the scoring and Zak Hardaker had levelled. Hardaker was the architect with a wonderful flat pass as Briscoe appeared in midfield, stepping Stefan Ratchford and palming off chasing back Ben Currie for a memorable 70-metre score.

After Hardaker brought off a miraculous tackle on Stefan Ratchford to stop him scoring, Leeds survived five sets during which Michael Monaghan was denied, before Danny McGuire's thrust brought relief that Hardaker capitalised on just before the hour. McGuire was brought down on the last, Stevie Ward – back after ten months out with a shoulder injury – smuggled the ball back and Hardaker, spotting a gap, darted over on an angled run, Kevin Sinfield with the extras.

There was still a thrilling finish after Ben Westwood crawled under the posts on 73 minutes after Sinfield had missed with a field-goal attempt. In Warrington's last attack, in the final throes, Hardaker just got to Richie Myler as he tore for the line.

Kallum Watkins, in his 100th game, was for the second week running, in great form.

On the Sunday, Huddersfield boss Paul Anderson launched a verbal attack on his players after they gave up a 12-point lead to draw with Hull Kingston Rovers. The Giants led 24-12 with just two minutes left, and were seemingly cruising towards a second consecutive victory. However, late scores from Josh Hodgson and Omari Caro meant the points were shared at the John Smith's Stadium.

Castleford shared top spot after a 32-6 home win over Catalans. Justin Carney closed the contest with a hat-trick, and had another touchdown ruled out by referee Tim Roby for a forward pass, to edge the man-of-the-match award ahead of the likes of hooker Daryl Clark, centre Michael Shenton and halfbacks Liam Finn and Marc Sneyd. Jordan Tansey's try five minutes into the second period gave the Tigers a 12-point buffer which Catalans were never going to overhaul.

The Dragons prop Julian Bousquet was suspended for four matches later that week after being put on report for a 'cannon-ball tackle' on Tansey. Scott Dureau, playing his first game of the season after missing the defeat at Hull because of a fall-out with coach Laurent Frayssinous, suffered a biceps injury.

FIRST UTILITY SUPER LEAGUE TABLE
Sunday 23rd February

	P	W	D	L	F	A	D	PTS
Castleford Tigers	2	2	0	0	68	24	44	4
St Helens	2	2	0	0	72	30	42	4
Leeds Rhinos	2	2	0	0	52	18	34	4
Salford Red Devils	2	2	0	0	62	32	30	4
Huddersfield Giants	2	1	1	0	48	32	16	3
Widnes Vikings	1	1	0	0	64	10	54	2
Bradford Bulls	2	1	0	1	41	46	-5	2
Hull FC	2	1	0	1	58	68	-10	2
Hull Kingston Rovers	2	0	1	1	30	58	-28	1
Wigan Warriors	1	0	0	1	8	24	-16	0
Wakefield T Wildcats	2	0	0	2	24	41	-17	0
Catalan Dragons	2	0	0	2	40	68	-28	0
Warrington Wolves	2	0	0	2	20	56	-36	0
London Broncos	2	0	0	2	28	108	-80	0

The last week of February proved eventful off the field.

First, at a meeting of Super League, the clubs rejected, by a majority of 7-5, the adoption of a marquee player signing outside the salary cap, which was designed to try and halt the exodus to the NRL and other sports of League's top players.

Salford, Wigan, Warrington, Leeds and Widnes voted for the proposal, which would have seen one player in any club's squad valued at £100,000 per annum, regardless of what his actual salary might be. There was no proposed restriction on the nationality of

21

a marquee player and clubs could even keep the identity of their marquee player confidential, if they wished.

Things got messier at the Bradford Bulls. The RFL announced a six-point deduction in a press release, which was quickly followed by a press release from the three directors attempting to take over the club, Mark Moore, Andrew Calvert and Ian Watt, saying they were withdrawing their bid to buy the Bulls from the administrator. They also demanded the RFL withdraw their press release and make a public apology for its contents, which they claim had damaged their reputations.

As well as the points deduction the RFL was to place the Bulls' licence into 'special measures'.

RFL Chief Operating Officer Ralph Rimmer issued his own press release, making several assertions aimed at the former directors, claiming they were 'disingenuous', that the problems were of their own making, and that the RFL had no confidence in their business plans.

The Bulls were now being managed by the administrator David Wilson, who on Saturday 1 March announced the sale of prop forward Nick Scruton to Wakefield.

TETLEY'S CHALLENGE CUP - ROUND 1

Saturday 1st February 2014
Askam 8 British Army 12
Blackbrook 4 Egremont Rangers 10
Castleford Lock Lane 14 Normanton Knights 15
Hull Dockers 76 Bristol Sonics 0
Kells 24 Wigan St Judes 16
Leeds Metropolitan University 44 Millom 16
Leigh Miners Rangers 12 Hunslet Warriors 10
Myton Warriors 24 East Hull 22
Pilkington Recs 46 Aberdeen Warriors 5
RAF 38 Dewsbury Celtic 10
Royal Navy 4 Walney Central 24
Skirlaugh 10 Rochdale Mayfield 16
South West London Chargers 12 Torfaen Tigers 6
Underbank Rangers 30 East Leeds 34 *(after extra-time)*
Wath Brow Hornets 18 Halton Simms Cross 0
Widnes St Maries 16 Wigan St Patricks 42
Woolston Rovers 6 Elland 20
York Acorn 12 Siddal 16

Sunday 2nd February 2014
Loughborough University 24 Great Britain Police 38

Saturday 8th February 2014
Oulton Raiders 16 West Hull 22
Saddleworth Rangers 18 Milford Marlins 20
Shaw Cross Sharks 12 Thatto Heath Crusaders 16

TETLEY'S CHALLENGE CUP - ROUND 2

Saturday 22nd February 2014
East Leeds 28 Leeds Metropolitan University 16
Hull Dockers 42 Siddal 8
Kells 26 Leigh Miners Rangers 12
Normanton Knights 44 RAF 10
Pilkington Recs 38 Myton Warriors 0
Rochdale Mayfield 28 Wigan St Patricks 36
South West London Chargers 6 Milford Marlins 24
Walney Central 16 Egremont Rangers 28
Wath Brow Hornets 12 Elland 6
West Hull 28 Thatto Heath Crusaders 18

Sunday 23rd February 2014
Great Britain Police 30 British Army 34 *(after golden point extra-time)*

MARCH
Beware the Tiger

Round 3

Bradford knocked another two points off their six-point penalty with a 25-12 Sunday, home win over the team predicted to face the drop at the end of 2014, London Broncos. The victory was assured only after Tom Olbison's try in the last minute, Luke Gale's field goal four minutes before having put seven points between the two teams. Two league points on the back of the previous week's victory at Wakefield gave hope to the Bulls' survival chances. But a crowd of 5,410 emphasised the Bulls' current plight, despite some observers' claim that the threat of relegation would increase excitement and crowds. The Broncos had Aussies, halfback Josh Drinkwater and prop Nick Slyney, on debut.

There was absolutely no threat of relegation for St Helens, who continued their whirlwind start to the season with a 38-0 Thursday-night hammering of Salford Red Devils on their own patch. Saints were again fast and precise in attack, where Luke Walsh continued to pull the strings and their young threequarter line took full advantage. They were powered up front by Kyle Amor and Alex Walmsley, who had both started the season in rampaging form. Lance Hohaia was given a chance to shine after Gary Wheeler was ruled out with a dead leg suffered in training the previous Wednesday.

The Red Devils started the night without Rangi Chase, still nursing a leg injury from the round-one victory over Wakefield, and before the end Gareth Hock was limping off with an ankle problem. Reds coach Brian Noble said: 'The honeymoon period is over. We've been feeling quite good about ourselves, but now it's important we get down to the nitty gritty of some tough practise. You certainly can't mask what needs to be done.'

Salford only trailed 12-0 at half-time, but in truth could have been 30 points behind. To their credit they battled on manfully, but the toll of the defensive effort they put in before the break was always likely to tell. Mark Percival's stunning long-range try 11 minutes into the second half finally broke the Devils' resistance for good, and from then on there was no way back for the hosts.

Devils owner Marwan Koukash was tweeting his apologies within five minutes of full time, promising: 'We won't play this bad again.'

Leeds and surprise packages Castleford and Widnes also remained 100 per cent after round three.

The Rhinos continued their superb recent form in Perpignan and ran away with the Friday-night game after the opening 30 minutes to beat the Dragons 40-12. Kevin Sinfield scored a personal tally of 16 points, as the England captain turned in a man of the match performance against the Dragons, whose squad was decimated with injury and suspension, with hooker Ian Henderson breaking his arm in the game. Rhinos winger Ryan Hall scored twice to catapult himself into Super League's all-time top 10 tryscorers list. The 26-year-old overtook St Helens legend Keiron Cunningham with his 139th four-pointer.

In the Friday TV game, the Tigers registered an emphatic 30-10 win at Hull KR, themselves still without a win. Richard Owen celebrated his return to the Tigers side with a hat-trick of tries on his first appearance of the year, but it was the halfback combination

of Liam Finn and Marc Sneyd that orchestrated the Tigers' impressive performance.

After falling behind to an early James Green try, Castleford led at the interval 18-10 from a first-half brace from Owen and a Frankie Mariano touchdown. The Robins never recovered, as they lacked any real conviction in attack due to a solid defensive effort from their counterparts.

In contrast, the Tigers took their chances well and when Oliver Holmes stormed over with 12 minutes remaining the game was over as a contest. Owen completed his treble in the dying embers of the game, which had the travelling support bouncing and singing in the new North Stand.

The Vikings, without the injured Kevin Brown, maintained their two-game winning start to the season by way of a dramatic – and controversial – late try on the Friday evening against a Huddersfield side that conceded a two-score advantage in the closing minutes for the second time in six days. The Giants this time did not even secure a draw as they lost 22-20 after leading 20-12, thanks to tries in the final minutes by Widnes pair Joe Mellor and Rhys Hanbury.

The Giants chose on three occasions to take penalty kicks at goal rather than press for tries in the second half and Danny Brough booted over two of the three efforts for 12-20. But Widnes weathered the storm and were still within striking distance as the superb Mellor set up a grandstand finish with a 20-metre gallop to the posts after scooping up a Chris Bailey knock on.

Then came the sensational winning score. A Widnes backline move looked to be running out of room at the left corner but Jack Owens somehow smuggled the football away to allow Hanbury to claim his second try. The three officials on the spot debated for what seemed like an eternity before Robert Hicks sparked scenes of Vikings jubilation by signalling a try.

On the Sunday, Warrington ground out their first win of the season, by 18-16, in a scrappy affair at a wet and windy Halliwell Jones Stadium but they were made to work hard for it by a Hull FC side that refused to throw in the towel. Makeshift fullback Stefan Ratchford was inspirational for the Wolves, scoring the opening try and kicking three of his four shots on goal.

The previous season's grand finalists went into the break with a comfortable 18-6 lead, with both teams struggling to finish off their attacking opportunities. But in the second 40 it was Hull who looked sharper, pulling within two points of the Wire with just two minutes left on the clock after a Fetuli Talanoa try.

Wigan captain Sean O'Loughlin ensured there was no World Club Challenge hangover as the much-changed Warriors eased past a depleted and still win-less Wakefield side, who debuted 17-year old Jordan Crowther in the forwards, at DW Stadium. Warriors coach Shaun Wane retained just nine players from the defeat to Sydney Roosters, and also lost O'Loughlin, Michael McIlorum and Blake Green during the game.

All three were withdrawn as precautions, but by that time two tries from O'Loughlin had already ensured the two points were staying in Wigan. Wane also hailed the performance of John Bateman, while his back-row partner Liam Farrell came up with some significant contributions and halfbacks Green and Matty Smith both caught the eye. A purple patch of five first-half tries in the space of 17 minutes laid the foundations for the 46-24 victory. Ben Flower's 50th minute try ended any hopes of an unlikely Wildcats comeback.

Round 4

When the Super League clubs decided to reduce their competition by two clubs they didn't envisage that Catalans Dragons might be one of the clubs to be relegated. But that prospect raised its head when the Dragons made it four losses from four matches with a 56-14 thrashing at previously win-less Wakefield on the Sunday of round 4.

Coach Laurent Frayssinous said decisions would be made quickly on the future of the club's playing squad after a woeful performance he described as embarrassing, revealing that he didn't speak to his players at full-time. The Dragons were missing Ian Henderson, Scott Dureau, Ben Pomeroy, Vincent Duport, Damien Cardace and Olivier Elima for the match at the Rapid Solicitors Stadium. And Brent Webb was substituted on 28 minutes after an error-strewn opening period. The fullback did not return to the field for the rest of the game.

Owner Bernard Guasch ordered the team home from a planned stay in England for crisis talks and stalwart forward Jamal Fakir was dropped to reserve grade later that week, but refused to play.

Wakefield were on form, Taulima Tautai scoring two tries and opening up the Dragons defence at will. Jarrod Sammut controlled proceedings with his excellent kicking game and pin-point passing, and it was a bomb and then a steal three minutes before the break that really settled the game in Wakefield's favour. The halfback chased his own kick, ripped the ball free from a Catalans runner and then found Reece Lyne out wide for the winger to cross for his second try.

Fellow outpost club London Broncos, with former hot prospect from Melbourne, Denny Solomona, on debut were starting to show improvement, leading Warrington 16-6 after a half an hour of their Sunday game at the Hive. But it was 16-14 at half-time and the Wolves scored 30-unanswered points in the second half for their second win of the season, by 44-16.

Joel Monaghan missed the game with a swollen knee and replacement Rhys Evans grabbed four tries. Chris Hill led the forward charge and Richie Myler made hay on the back of it.

Bradford Bulls were still two points behind the win-less pair of London and Catalans after a 44-16 defeat at Hull FC on the Friday. Jamie Shaul bagged a brace of tries and turned in another eye-catching performance but it was Hull's forward pack, led superbly by Joe Westerman, which laid the platform and inspired the victory. Tom Lineham was carried from the field with two minutes to go with a broken leg.

Hull KR were still chasing their first win of the season after a 38-18 defeat at St Helens. Saints coach Nathan Brown was able to welcome back Gary Wheeler from a dead leg and there was a debut for Samoan Mose Masoe, who had finally recovered from an ankle injury to make his Super League bow at Langtree Park. Craig Sandercock had Aussie front-rowers Michael Weyman and Justin Poore back from suspension. But Alex Walmsley turned out to be the best front rower on show, not for the first time in 2014. Two tries in the last ten minutes of the first half from Kevin Larroyer and Greg Eden got the Robins back to 12-all at the break. But Saints eased away with five more tries in the second half.

Saints were top on points difference, but Castleford were still up with them after their fourth win, a sensational 36-31 home success over champions Wigan on the Sunday afternoon.

The Tigers, after having seen an early 16-point lead slip away, had battled back to lead 30-24 for much of the closing quarter but, in the last few minutes, had looked destined to have nothing to show for a monumental effort.

Wigan, after having seen Castleford centre Michael Channing (playing on the wing following the withdrawal of Kirk Dixon with a suspected broken jaw) have two late tries ruled out - one for a forward pass and another for obstruction - worked their way downfield where a bomb by scrum-half Matty Smith led to winger Josh Charnley pouncing in the corner.

Smith, who had only landed two goals from five previous attempts, was not fancied to land the levelling goal from the touchline – his attempt, however, sailed sweetly between the sticks to restore parity.

Matters got worse for the Tigers, who had themselves ignored a number of field-goal opportunities when, in the next set - and in the final minute – Smith edged Wigan ahead

with a one-pointer from 30 metres out.

Castleford not only retrieved possession at the restart, but grabbed a sensational winning try by fullback Luke Dorn, who shot over from a telling pass by stand-off Marc Sneyd. Sneyd added the conversion – his sixth from seven attempts – to bring the curtain down on a rousing display.

Leeds were now a point adrift after a 12-12 draw at Huddersfield on the Friday, the Giants' second draw in four games.

For a while Leeds had looked likely winners after withstanding almost an hour of pressure before Kevin Sinfield's penalty gave them a two-point lead going into the final 15 minutes. But Joe Wardle, out on the wing after Jodie Broughton had been withdrawn with a knee injury just moments before, produced a spectacular left-handed finish to edge the Giants ahead for the first time with only eleven minutes to go.

Danny Brough's touchline conversion gave the hosts a four-point advantage, but that was wiped out three minutes later when Danny McGuire broke clear and combined with Paul Aiton to make valuable metres. Leeds had the numbers on the right, and executed to perfection when Zak Hardaker's offload put Kallum Watkins over.

Sinfield could have won it, only for his conversion attempt to miss and set up a frantic finish as both sides looked for the match-winning field goal. Brough and McGuire both struck efforts that went wide, Sinfield hit the post and Brough mis-kicked one final desperate attempt before time ran out on a fantastic clash.

Kevin Brown returned for Widnes in the Thursday night TV game as the Vikings kept up their 100 per cent record with a 32-18 win over Salford. Brown scored two tries as the Vikings came back from 18-14 down. A superb second-half performance from scrum-half Joe Mellor helped his team secure a sixth consecutive Super League victory since the previous August.

* That week the RFL agreed to re-name the Man of Steel award in honour of former St Helens, Hull FC and Wakefield fullback Steve Prescott, who died at the end of 2013 after a seven-year battle with stomach cancer after raising thousands of pound for charity in a personal crusade.

Round 5

St Helens captain Paul Wellens led his team out against the Catalans Dragons on the Friday night of round five to become only the fourth player in the summer era to hit 500 career appearances.

Wellens had played 465 games for St Helens since his debut against Halifax in 1998, and represented Great Britain in 20 Tests, England in eleven games and Lancashire on four occasions. He joined Leeds Rhinos captain Kevin Sinfield in reaching the landmark entirely in the summer era, Salford's Adrian Morley and former Leeds favourite Keith Senior having reached it after starting their careers before the start of Super League.

Saints maintained their 100 per cent start to the season with a 40-22 win, despite the in-game loss to injury of three key figures - playmaker Luke Walsh, centre Jordan Turner and second rower Sia Soliola, all before the 45th minute. But with Jonny Lomax, James Roby and Jon Wilkin all stepping up to the plate, they ensured that a 24-0 lead didn't slip away to keep their early place at the top of Super League.

The win-less Dragons regrouped well and, with Leon Pryce leading the side from stand-off and Benjamin Garcia, an Avignon junior who had honed his game in Brisbane Broncos under-20s, and Eloi Pelissier impressive in the pack, they saw this performance as a platform for the rest of the campaign.

Having patiently waited for four rounds to be given his chance, Leeds winger Ben Jones-Bishop, who had turned down a loan move to Wakefield, made a statement of intent with the Rhinos' first two tries in their 38-4 win over Widnes at Headingley on the Friday

night, in a clash of two unbeaten sides. With Ryan Hall rested, Jones-Bishop came in on the right with Tom Briscoe switching wings.

It was only 10-0 at the break but Leeds regained the kick-off to the second half, judging the strong wind superbly, and within three minutes Kallum Watkins was over for their third try and the Rhinos were dominant for the rest of the game.

Castleford's bubble showed little sign of bursting as they edged another Sunday afternoon thriller at Wheldon Road, known this year as the Mend-a-Hose Jungle, beating Hull FC 19-16.

Hull went into the last six minutes 16-12 ahead and, with Castleford lacking something of the sparkle that had secured them a last-gasp win over Wigan seven days earlier, looked capable of taking the spoils. But a raid by fullback Jordan Tansey – brought in to replace the previous week's match-winner, Luke Dorn – led to captain-centre Michael Shenton bursting through from 40 metres. Shenton found Frankie Mariano on his shoulder, and the substitute raced away for a levelling score.

Marc Sneyd, whose reputation was growing by the week, coolly slotted over the conversion from 20 metres to the side of the posts, to complete a 100 per cent record with the boot and give his side the lead and four minutes later the Salford-loanee fired a one-pointer to stretch the score to 19-16.

The Broncos suffered another heavy defeat on the Saturday as they went down at home 50-22 to an impressive Wakefield. Richie Mathers profited from Wakefield's all-round superiority with a four-try haul.

Iain Thornley grabbed his first hat-trick for Wigan on the Friday as Wigan beat Hull KR 34-20 at the DW Stadium. Warriors captain Sean O'Loughlin missed his second game in succession with a shoulder problem. Wigan raced into an 8-0 lead, with Thornley and Matty Bowen going over the whitewash, but it was again looking like Wigan's lack of a goalkicker was going to be costly as Matty Smith missed both conversion attempts.

With the start they had it looked like Wigan would win the game at a canter, but three tries in less than 15 minutes through Jamie Langley, Liam Salter and Kris Welham put the Robins in the box seat.

Thornley's second try of the half reduced the deficit to two points, but poor defensive reads from the double winners allowed Ben Cockayne to extend the Robins lead to 20-14 at half-time.

But the Warriors kept the Robins scoreless in the second 40 minutes. Second-half tries from Liam Farrell, Ben Flower and Thornley's third saw Wigan home, with Smith eventually finding his kicking form by slotting over four from four more attempts.

Salford, still missing Rangi Chase, suffered their third straight defeat, this time a 28-12 home reverse to Warrington. Three tries in an eight-minute spell midway through the first half from Chris Bridge, Mickey Higham and Gene Ormsby set Warrington on their way and further scores after the break from Joel Monaghan and Roy Asotasi, plus four goals from Stefan Ratchford, cemented the win.

Salford, who spent long spells camped deep in their own half, never really got back in touch despite scoring three times themselves through on-debut loan winger from Wigan Dominic Manfredi (twice) and Greg Johnson.

RFL officials and the administrator of Bradford Bulls were due to meet on the following Monday to discuss five separate bids received to buy the club, one from Mandy Koukash, wife of Salford owner Marwan Koukash. The Koukash family attended the game against Huddersfield Giants at the Provident Stadium on the Sunday to witness the Bulls crash to a 66-18 reverse. Mrs Koukash gave a thumbs-up to the Odsal crowd and didn't appear to be deterred by the heavy scale of the defeat.

The rampant Giants scored twelve tries, with Scott Grix, Jermaine McGillvary, Joe Wardle and Ukuma Ta'ai all grabbing braces.

Dr Koukash was fined £1,000 the previous week by the RFL for a breach of RFL rules, for comments he made on the social media website Twitter and for using foul and/or abusive language at Salford's pre-season media launch at MediaCityUK.

Round 6

Salford Red Devils coach Brian Noble praised his players after they secured a pressure-relieving win over Castleford at the AJ Bell Stadium on the Sunday of round 6. Salford won the match 23-16, their first victory since February 22, and ended the Tigers' perfect start to the season.

Rangi Chase returned from the injury he suffered in the round-one win over Wakefield and was one of the stars for Salford, kicking the match-winning field goal with seven minutes left on the clock to put the Red Devils seven points in front. Andrew Dixon scored two of the Salford tries.

In the Thursday TV game at Halliwell Jones Stadium, Wigan took a major step to eradicating lingering doubts about their pack by producing a fearsome first 30 minutes and then grinding out a solid 12-4 win in a rematch of last year's Grand Final.

The Warriors' young forwards, missing their two most influential men in Sean O'Loughlin and Michael McIlorum, met their sternest test head on and delivered against a strong Wolves pack.

A try in each half for the visitors – from the outstanding Liam Farrell in the 12th minute and Blake Green in the 50th minute – secured the points, but Wigan were comfortable winners. Twice in the first half they had tries ruled out, while Warrington consistently failed to offer anything in attack. The hosts' only try came through Gene Ormsby's interception midway through the second half, and they never looked capable of building on that to launch a late comeback.

St Helens marched on with their sixth straight win of the season but they had to come from 12 points behind at Wakefield to maintain their 100 per cent winning start.

The Wildcats had threatened to take control when tries either side of half-time had them 16-4 ahead. But the depleted table toppers, with Luke Walsh out injured and guided by stand-in halfback Jon Wilkin, responded with four scores in less than a quarter of an hour to emerge from their toughest test yet.

Trinity boss Richard Agar questioned the consistency of referee Tim Roby as his team's impressive recent revival - two wins, scoring 106 points - was halted. 'I felt the game was refereed differently in the first half to the second,' said Agar, who claimed that referees chief Steve Ganson had entered the officials dressing room at half-time and 'given him (referee Roby) a good old dressing down'.

Leeds retained their unbeaten record on the Friday night with a predictable 54-6 romp over the outclassed London Broncos at Headingley. London, against a side that rested Kevin Sinfield for the first time since 2009 and Tom Briscoe and were without Joel Moon, Jamie Peacock, Brett Delaney and Ryan Bailey, were never in contention from the moment the kick-off was allowed to bounce for a drop-out. Tottenham-born fullback Iliess Macani shone for them, twice saving tries along with a potential 40/20 and running the ball strongly and bravely.

Ryan Hall celebrated a new five-year deal with a hat-trick, Zak Hardaker ran great lines, and stand-in skipper Rob Burrow, on his 350th Super League appearance, was uncontainable.

Catalans Dragons looked to have turned the corner after their first win, a 30-14 home victory over Huddersfield Giants, Eloi Pelissier, in for the whole game with Ian Henderson nursing a broken arm, the catalyst, and Louis Anderson scoring two tries in a dominant pack performance.

Widnes Vikings head coach Denis Betts pointed to the progression his side had made since the club's return to Super League in 2012, as their impressive start to 2014 continued.

It was now four wins from five in Super League XIX for the Vikings, with a hugely impressive defensive showing the backbone of a 7-0 whitewash of Hull FC on the Sunday,

Salford's Rangi Chase lands the winning field goal against former club Castleford

the Vikings having suffered two heavy losses in their previous two visits to the KC Stadium.

The only try of a rain-affected game came after just one minute. Jordan Rankin, in at fullback for the injured Jamie Shaul, dropped the ball on his very first carry after a routine kick return, which set the platform for the afternoon for Hull. That error created an opportunity for Widnes to strike, and Patrick Ah Van charged his way over to nudge the Vikings in front. An Ah Van penalty just after the hour mark and a Tom Gilmore field goal four minutes from time were the only other scores, with Hull bombing plenty of chances.

Hull coach Lee Radford claimed his side were in a crisis. Radford's comments came after his Chairman Adam Pearson claimed in the matchday programme that the two-match suspension of Mickey Paea by the RFL for dangerous contact in the defeat at Castleford the week before was 'ludicrous', and he compared the judiciary panel to popular TV show 'Strictly Come Dancing'. He was later fined 1,000 pounds by the RFL for his comments.

Over the river on the same rain-soaked afternoon, Hull KR were nilling Bradford, to register their first win of the season, 16-0. The heavens opened in Hull an hour before kick-off and showers poured down throughout the game making the playing conditions very wet, cold and heavy under foot.

Right from Ben Cockayne's kick-off the game quickly descended into a battle up the middle and the Rovers' pack soon got on top. Justin Poore and Mick Weyman laid the platform in the first half, which saw the home side lead 12-0 at the break courtesy of tries from Omari Caro and Kris Keating.

A scrappy, error ridding second half followed, with just Kevin Larroyer's solitary try

29

on the hour mark securing a valuable two points for the Robins.

Coincidentally, the Robins' chairman Neil Hudgell was also later fined a thousand pounds for claiming the RFL disciplinary was 'not fit for purpose' after prop Weyman copped a three-match ban for a dangerous tackle in the win.

The long-running saga over ownership of the Bradford Bulls looked set to come to a conclusion, with London-based businessman Richard Lamb seemingly set to take control of the club. Lamb was the public face of a consortium made up largely of property developers, with former Bulls player and chief executive Abi Ekoku also linked to the bid. Proof of the consortium's ability to provide funding within the required deadline had not been forthcoming.

Round 7

St Helens' understrength side defied all expectations and Leeds' vast experience to record a last-gasp 14-10 win at Langtree Park in the Friday TV game. Captain Paul Wellens marked a record-equalling 413th Super League appearance by producing two of the defining moments in an enthralling clash, including the break and offload that put Tommy Makinson over for his first try 15 minutes from time. But it was the effort of Saints' youngsters, and the 78th minute match-winning score from Makinson, that lifted the roof off the new stadium.

Leeds' old guard of Kevin Sinfield, Rob Burrow, Danny McGuire and Jamie Peacock, having each enjoyed a decade of success, looked set to prove too strong for the spirited Saints. Peacock was a colossus as he had been all season, racking up 247 metres and 44 tackles, while Sinfield's kicking game was his best.

Saints opted to start Greg Richards in the front row ahead of Anthony Laffranchi. Laffranchi was by far the most experienced of Saints' interchange options. With Joe Greenwood, Luke Thompson and debutant Andre Savelio making up the rest of the numbers that meant Leeds, even without injured Paul Aiton, were pre-match favourites.

McGuire's 250th career try had put Leeds ahead in the first half and the Rhinos dominated the opening quarter in a manner that suggested the hosts would surely collapse at some stage. But brave St Helens roared back, led by James Roby's tireless efforts and brilliant contributions from Jonny Lomax and Lance Hohaia.

It was 10-all with three minutes to go, Sinfield having missed a field-goal attempt, when Saints had possession on halfway. Hohaia chipped the defence, Lomax ran onto the ball and measured a perfect kick to the right corner. Makinson had time to collect the dribbling ball safely and squeeze into the corner as the stadium erupted.

It was later revealed second-rower Jamie Jones-Buchanan played 25 minutes with a torn biceps muscle before withdrawing at half-time.

Castleford Tigers got back on track with a dominant 54-6 win at London in the Thursday TV game, Michael Shenton and Justin Carney collecting two tries each. The Broncos had parted company with chief executive Gus Mackay in the week.

Widnes, on the Sunday, had a much tougher task at home to Bradford, eventually holding out for a 22-18 win, Kevin Brown scoring two tries.

The Vikings were pushed all the way by a resurgent Bradford side that almost treated their new owner Marc Green to a remarkable first-up victory in a thrilling contest. But Danny Tickle landed a couple of difficult kicks that, in the final reckoning, were enough to earn his team the win.

Green, best known as the chairman of a Leeds-based security firm, took over the club the previous week, having injected cash into the Bulls through a debenture at the end of August the previous year. Earlier in 2014 he used his debenture to protect the club from being closed down via a winding-up order.

Green appointed Steve Ferres, a former Bradford player who spent several years with the RFL mainly working with struggling clubs, as managing director, to work

alongside Robbie Hunter-Paul, who remained as chief executive.

Wigan did it tough on the Friday night at home to the rejuvenated Catalans, a breakaway try from Matty Bowen seeing them get out of jail and record a 22-16 win. Wigan only led once in the game and the lead came in the 79th minute.

The Dragons raced into a 10-0 lead inside the opening 10 minutes with tries from Morgan Escaré and Ben Pomeroy, but Bowen's first of the night saw the Warriors trail 10-4 at the break.

Escaré's first try was an absolute beauty. Matty Smith put up a towering bomb which was misjudged by Mathias Pala, which allowed Escaré to sweep up. Escaré, with the help of Leon Pryce and Eloi Pelissier, cut through Wigan's right-side defence before Escaré finished off to score. Escaré extended Catalan's lead to 12 points but tries from Josh Charnley and Liam Farrell looked like earning Wigan just a point – until Bowen had the final say of an absorbing game.

Scotland World Cup star Matty Russell celebrated his first Super League start for Warrington with a starring role as the Wolves maintained their astonishing recent stranglehold over Huddersfield at the John Smith's Stadium. Russell scored a try and repeatedly threatened to rip the Giants apart as the Wolves came from ten points behind with five tries and 29 unanswered second-half points to finish 33-14 winners.

Warrington had now won the last ten meetings between the sides, dating back to April 2011, even triumphing on all four occasions when the side's clashed during the Giant's League Leaders Shield success in 2013.

With just a Rhys Evans try to show for their first-half efforts and trailing 14-4 at the break thanks to Scott Grix and Jodie Broughton tries, the Wolves responded with further touchdowns from Richie Myler, Ben Westwood, man of the match Russell, Gene Ormsby and Joel Monaghan as the tenacious tackling home team ran out of steam towards the end.

On the same Sunday afternoon, Hull KR dominated opposition on their home patch for the second week running as they completely dismantled Wakefield, winning 44-6.

Both sides were looking to make the play-offs in September, but after slow starts the Wildcats and the Robins both desperately needed two points at the KC Lightstream Stadium. It was the home side who took the game by the scruff of the neck in the end, despite playing against the wrong side of the penalty count. Omari Caro, Josh Hodgson and Kris Welham each scored try braces.

Salford Red Devils' inconsistent season continued at Hull FC where they lost 30-8 on the Friday night. Lee Radford has asked for a response from his players from the lacklustre performance against Widnes and he certainly got one. Jacob Miller returned to the side to make his first appearance of the season alongside Richard Horne in the halves and the Australian scored a try and turned in a man-of-the-match display which inspired the victory.

After an opening onslaught from the Devils, Hull weathered the storm to lead at the interval 12-4 courtesy of tries from Miller and Jamie Shaul. The Black and

FIRST UTILITY SUPER LEAGUE TABLE
Sunday 30th March

	P	W	D	L	F	A	D	PTS
St Helens	7	7	0	0	226	96	130	14
Castleford Tigers	7	6	0	1	223	110	113	12
Leeds Rhinos	7	5	1	1	206	66	140	11
Widnes Vikings	6	5	0	1	151	104	47	10
Wigan Warriors	6	4	0	2	153	124	29	8
Warrington Wolves	7	4	0	3	147	126	21	8
Hull FC	7	3	0	4	164	136	28	6
Huddersfield Giants	7	2	2	3	174	147	27	6
Salford Red Devils	7	3	0	4	123	176	-53	6
Hull Kingston Rovers	7	2	1	4	138	166	-28	5
Wakefield T Wildcats	7	2	0	5	176	191	-15	4
Catalan Dragons	7	1	0	6	134	240	-106	2
London Broncos	7	0	0	7	90	335	-245	0
Bradford Bulls *	7	2	0	5	118	206	-88	-2

* Deducted six points for entering administration

Whites then scored twice in the first five minutes of the second period through Ben Crooks and Horne to give them a 20 point margin they defended with vigour, with the exception of a Junior Sa'u try from the visitors. Liam Watts rounded off the impressive win when he crossed in the final minute.

APRIL
Saints stumble

Challenge Cup Round 4

Bradford Bulls' new owner and chairman Marc Green made his first media appearance at the start of April and claimed that planning for relegation was 'Plan Z'. The Bulls still had two Super League points to make up from their six-point deduction - although an appeal was in the pipeline - but the first weekend of the month saw the diversion of the Tetley's Challenge Cup and an easy passage at home to Championship One (third tier) side Oldham by 60-6.

There were no major shocks in a fourth round that had an unusually high number of all-Super League ties.

Ryan Hall grabbed two tries on his 200th appearance for Leeds in a 60-6 hammering of Wakefield at Rapid Solicitors Stadium. Wakefield were blown away by a spell of five tries in 13 first-half minutes, and if anything, the scoreline could have been wider.

Warrington edged through to the fifth round after a 28-24 victory in a tight and hugely entertaining contest at Hull KR. The Wolves recovered from 12-0 down in the first half to pull to within four points before the break. Rovers struggled to dominate the game in the second half as they had in the first, with the Wolves, Richard Myler the key man, edging the game late on.

London were eliminated by 40-24 at Catalans, with Leon Pryce the standout.

The Sunday afternoon BBC TV game provided plenty of controversy, with St Helens winning 17-16 at Huddersfield thanks to a last-minute Luke Walsh field goal. But Giants captain Danny Brough was convinced his fourth drop-goal attempt a minute earlier had been successful, only for referee Phil Bentham to rule it had gone wide, well above the top of the uprights. Coach Paul Anderson questioned why Bentham did not refer the kick to video official Ian Smith, venting his rage on a television in the Giants' media room, pulling it from its socket and leaving it upside down on a table rather than simply turning it off, before letting rip with his post-match press conference. 'It was absolutely over,' he said.

Brett Ferres was dismissed for a spear tackle on Jonny Lomax in the 64th minute. Huddersfield led 16-8 at the time, but conceded nine points while they were down to twelve men as St Helens booked their place in the next round. Ferres was banned the following Tuesday for five games and made a public apology to Lomax.

There had also been great drama at Hull FC on the Thursday night as Rangi Chase's 88th minute golden-point field-goal clinched a dramatic win for the Salford Red Devils. In

a breathtaking contest that see-sawed throughout, it looked as if Hull had done enough when they led 36-30 with five minutes remaining. But, when Francis Meli went over to complete his hat-trick, with 66 left seconds on the clock, it was left to Jake Mullaney to ensure the game went into extra time. The Australian fullback, who had been 100 per cent successful with his kicking all night, held his nerve to nail the conversion from the touchline to bring the scores level.

Despite the win, less than a week after a thrashing by Hull in the league, on the Friday morning Marwan Koukash announced on Twitter that Wigan assistant and Wales coach Iestyn Harris would be taking over as head coach the following Monday on a contract until the end of the 2016 season, with Brian Noble offered the position of director of football. Noble expressed his surprise, taking over a week to refuse the offer and consult his lawyers.

Round 8

Jamie Peacock reached the landmark of 500 career games when he stepped out for Leeds' home game against Wakefield on the Friday night, and marked the occasion by scoring a try.

Peacock was quick to quash speculation that an 'unofficial' Great Britain game he played in down under didn't count towards his 500-game career, claiming: 'Whenever you play for Great Britain it is a game; and when you're getting bashed about and tackled it is a game as far as I'm concerned, so the record counts!' Ian Kirke made his 200th Rhinos appearance.

Leeds beat the Wildcats handsomely for the second week running, the left-sided pairing of Joel Moon, who later moved to stand-off, and especially Ryan Hall near unstoppable. The Rhinos raced to an 18-point lead. Wakefield looked to have stemmed the flow, defending three consecutive drop outs. But some trickery from Moon just before the break to send in Carl Ablett took the game away from the Wildcats.

Wakefield lost Ali Lauitiiti to a serious knee injury in the fifth minute while he set up the first real chance of the game when lively Jarrod Sammut was held up by Tom Briscoe.

The win put Leeds second but they were still chasing St Helens at the top, an astounding 30-28 win at high-flying Castleford in the Friday TV game keeping up their 100 per cent record. Astounding because they trailed 24-6 at half-time and 28-14 with only 12 minutes to go.

Hooker James Roby, fullback Jonny Lomax, scrum-half Luke Walsh and loose forward Josh Jones became increasingly effective as the Saints maintained their 100 per cent record with the help of three unanswered tries, including a Paul Wellens effort that took him past 1,000 career points, in the last 12 minutes. Adam Swift's try two minutes from the close was the first time St Helens had been in front.

Wellens' introduction at half-time transformed the contest, and he had now made more Super League appearances than any other player, with 414 appearances since making his debut in 1998, taking over the mantle from Keith Senior. He was, though, only one appearance ahead of Leeds captain Kevin Sinfield.

All the games in England, apart from the Thursday TV game between Hull and Huddersfield, were played on the Friday night in preparation for Easter, and at the DW Stadium, Wigan struggled to boss the League's whipping boys, London Broncos.

Tries from Jamie O'Callaghan and Mike McMeeken gave London a shock but deserved 10-0 lead as Wigan failed to get going for a good 30 minutes. The champions finally got some joy in the 26th minute when Tony Clubb went over against his former club, before further tries from another former Bronco, Dan Sarginson and Iain Thornley saw the Warriors lead 16-10.

It took the Warriors 23 minutes after the break before they breached the London line through Clubb again. The Broncos fell away and made too many errors and further tries to Sarginson, Thornley and Matty Bowen sealed the points with a 36-14 victory.

Hull FC bounced back from their gut-wrenching Cup exit in style with a comfortable

30-6 home victory over a downcast-looking Huddersfield side, which sank into tenth spot in the league. Props Mickey Paea and Garreth Carvell laid the foundations as the Airlie Birds scored four unanswered tries after the first quarter, establishing a 20-point lead they never relinquished.

A short four-day turnaround looked to have taken its toll on Huddersfield as they were outmatched in every department. Fetuli Talanoa, Richard Whiting, Jordan Rankin and Danny Houghton all crossed the whitewash in an opening 20 minutes that saw the Black and Whites hold a 20-6 half-time lead, with the only response from the Giants a Jodie Broughton try on the half-hour mark. Hull kept the Giants at bay in the second half with strong defence and added further tries through Jacob Miller and Dean Hadley to round off proceedings.

It was a bumper night for the city of Hull as Hull KR travelled to Warrington and avenged their Cup exit the week before with a 25-12 win. Prop Michael Weyman scored his first and second tries for the club in a low-scoring affair marked by strong defence from both sides. It took either team 35 minutes to finally get on the scoreboard through Weyman's first and the Robins eventually proved too good for Wolves in the second half. Travis Burns' field goal with 15 minutes left on the clock to put the Robins 13 points ahead was the nail in the coffin for Warrington.

The Wolves, the previous year's Grand Finalists, had now won four and lost four of their eight Super League fixtures.

Hull KR Chairman Neil Hudgell said he would appeal against the fine of £1,000 imposed by the RFL for his criticism of the RFL disciplinary process after Rovers prop Justin Poore was suspended for three matches for a tackle in the Robins' 16-0 win over Bradford in March, when he claimed the governing body's match review panel was 'not fit for purpose'. Hull FC Chairman Adam Pearson was also fined the same amount by the RFL for similar comments, but decided not to appeal against the verdict. The appeal failed anyway.

New head coach Iestyn Harris, after his first game in charge, was content that Salford took a small step towards the play-off zone with an ultimately comfortable 38-24 victory at Bradford. The Red Devils led 22-6 at half-time and as the game wore on Rangi Chase became an increasing headache for the Bulls' tiring defence with an opportunist try and a hand in several others. Bulls stand-off Lee Gaskell made his return after six games out with a knee injury.

Catalans Dragons hailed their match with Widnes Vikings as a great success, after they moved the kick-off forward to 3.30pm on the Saturday to enable fans of both the Dragons and the Perpignan rugby union team, USAP, to take in the Super League clash and the union game straight after.

The Dragons were rewarded with an attendance of 9,588, and they provided the crowd with an exciting performance in hot conditions to defeat the Vikings 42-20. It was more like the Catalans of old but Thomas Bosc and Morgan Escaré's inability to convert their tries kept the Vikings in the game. It wasn't until Elliott Whitehead's hat-trick try on the hour mark that the game was secure for the Catalans.

Round 9

Craig Hall's field goal, with 30 seconds remaining, clinched a dramatic 21-20 win for Hull KR in the Hull derby at KC Lightstream Stadium on the Thursday night of the Easter weekend. It was a fourth successive Super League victory for the Robins, who were without the influential Kris Keating, with Travis Burns stepping up to the fore.

Hull got their noses in front early in the opening quarter through a Jordan Rankin try but the Robins hit back to lead at the break 10-4 after Kevin Larroyer and Michael Weyman crossed the whitewash. Hull drew level almost immediately after the restart through Josh Bowden, before a brace from Graeme Horne gave Rovers a 10-point lead heading into the final third. But the Black and Whites fought their way back into

contention when tries from Danny Houghton and Fetuli Talanoa brought the scores back level at 20 apiece.

When Burns missed a field-goal attempt with a minute-and-a-half remaining it looked as though the spoils would be shared, but a mistake by Hull led to Rovers finding their way back in the visitors' red zone and this time Hall stepped up to slot home the winning one-pointer.

In the other Thursday-night derby, Rob Burrow celebrated his 400th appearance for the club - only the twelfth player to make 400 appearances for Leeds - with the ninth and final Rhinos try, while Ryan Hall claimed a hat-trick in a 46-6 success over the Bulls at Provident Stadium, Odsal. The Rhinos made a devastating start, carving out four tries and a 20-point lead within the opening quarter of an hour, and they finished strongly too.

On the same night, London Broncos were 28-4 down to the Catalans at the Hive before coming back to 28-22 with three late converted tries. Tries from Zeb Taia, Michael Oldfield and William Barthau - all converted by Thomas Bosc - put the Dragons 18-0 up before Mason Caton-Brown hit back. But Eloi Pelissier and Vincent Duport then scored to open a 24-point lead.

Caton-Brown's second try sparked the Broncos fightback, but further scores from Nesi Mataitonga and Denny Solomona came too late.

Warrington Wolves fullback Matty Russell celebrated a new four-year contract with the club by helping them to an impressive 44-6 home win over local rivals Widnes Vikings on a sun-drenched Good Friday afternoon. Chris Bridge's try late in the first half extended the lead to 24-0 and snuffed out any remote chance of a Widnes recovery.

The Tigers returned to winning ways with a 43-20 victory at struggling Wakefield. Five first-half tries had helped the Tigers into a 26-12 interval lead, with Daryl Clark at the centre of everything the Tigers did well, helping himself to two smart tries.

Danny Brough starred with an 18-point haul as Huddersfield picked up their first Super League win in four as they outclassed the disappointing Red Devils at the AJ Bell Stadium. Leading 18-0 before the game was even 15 minutes old, the Giants rarely looked troubled, with winger Aaron Murphy bagging a hat-trick of tries.

In the big TV blockbuster, Wigan halted Saints' unbeaten record with a 33-14 win at Langtree Park. The opening ten minutes were all square, with Sean O'Loughlin and Tommy Makinson trading tries. But the Warriors hit a purple patch midway through the first half, with Dan Sarginson and Liam Farrell touching down to put Wigan 18-6 in front. But Makinson's second and another for Jordan Turner saw Saints hit back to trail by four points, only for Matty Smith to extend that to six on the stroke of half-time.

Two quick tries in the second half for Farrell and youngster Joe Burgess set the platform for Wigan's victory, before a late field goal from Smith sealed the points.

There was one negative for Wigan, with their joint top-try scorer Iain Thornley set to miss most of the rest of the season due to a shoulder injury he suffered after five minutes of a game played out in front of a capacity crowd.

Round 10

With the possibility that the RFL was to abandon playing two games over the Easter weekend, St Helens supporters were left wishing that limiting the weekend to one round of games had already been established as their side was knocked off the top of the table on the Monday.

With Wigan having ended Saints' whirlwind start to Super League XIX on Good Friday, on Easter Monday Widnes recorded their first ever home win over their close rivals in the Super League era, by 40-26. Kevin Brown was influential as Rhys Hanbury's brace added to tries from Willie Isa, Alex Gerrard, Paddy Flynn, Chris Dean and MacGraff Leuluai to seal victory.

Saints - without regulars such as Jonny Lomax and Luke Walsh - responded through

April

Sia Soliola, Mose Masoe, Paul Wellens, Tommy Makinson and Lance Hohaia.

Leeds Rhinos went top after a 32-4 home win over Salford.

With stand-in skipper Rangi Chase at times imperious while also at his most exasperating, three times giving away penalties in possession for running behind his bemused runners, Salford were in, and even shaded, the contest up until the closing quarter hour. But Leeds' committed defence was characterised by holding the Red Devils up four times over their line, allied to a stunning counterpunch, with three length-of-the-field tries in the second half for their destructive backs.

Castleford went second as they hammered Warrington at home 40-6. Ashley Gibson and Richard Owen were brought in to the threequarters but, despite the reshuffle, it was business as usual for the Tigers, for whom captain Michael Shenton claimed a hat-trick. Stand-off Marc Sneyd directed the side to fine effect and landed six goals from seven attempts, including three from the touchline to add to Warrington's woes.

Catalans Dragons maintained their excellent recent form with a ground-out 37-24 home win against Hull KR. Leon Pryce was instrumental as the Dragons won their fourth consecutive home game in League and Cup after a disastrous start to the season. Thomas Bosc's penalty goal eleven minutes from time opened up a 12-point advantage for the Dragons and the game was safe.

Huddersfield Giants also made it a perfect Easter, beating Wakefield at home by 36-16, Shaun Lunt the outstanding player. The Giants led at the break with tries from Jodie Broughton, Michael Lawrence, Ukuma Ta'ai and Leroy Cudjoe, while Jarrod Sammut and Lucas Walshaw replied. Jason Chan and Lunt made sure of the points after half-time as Danny Brough kicked all six conversions. Jon Molloy crossed for Wakefield, who had now lost their last six games.

Hull looked a class above London in a 40-4 home win and, had the heavens not opened mid-way through the first half, the winning margin could have been considerably greater. Tries from Jamie Shaul, Ben Crooks, Jordan Thompson and Jordan Rankin gave their side a 22-0 lead at the interval that set the pattern for the game.

Shaul and Rankin completed their doubles in the second half, which also saw Jacob Miller complete the scoring for the Black and Whites as Crooks celebrated his return to the side with a try and six goals. The only riposte for the visitors, who did not lack effort, was a Mason Caton-Brown try just before the hour mark.

Ryan Hampshire collected a personal tally of 24 points as Wigan made it a memorable Easter with a 15-try hammering of Bradford Bulls in an 84-6 home win. The young fullback, who was filling the shoes of Matty Bowen, crossed for two tries and kicked eight goals as the champions made light work of Super League's bottom club.

Hampshire was unplayable all afternoon and had a hand in several scores as the Super League champions ran in a total of 15 tries in a forgettable afternoon for the Bulls. Nine of those tries came in the first half, with Blake Green, Anthony Gelling, Sean O'Loughlin, Liam Farrell, Jack Hughes and Sam Powell adding to Hampshire's two.

Gelling added his second, with John Bateman, Dom Manfredi, Darrell Goulding, George Williams, Blake Green and Gil Dudson also crossing as the Warriors inflicted the worst ever Super League defeat in Bradford's history.

Wigan had won at Hull KR a year previously on Easter Monday by exactly the same scoreline.

FIRST UTILITY SUPER LEAGUE TABLE
Monday 21st April

	P	W	D	L	F	A	D	PTS
Leeds Rhinos	10	8	1	1	326	82	244	17
Castleford Tigers	10	8	0	2	334	166	168	16
St Helens	10	8	0	2	296	197	99	16
Wigan Warriors	9	7	0	2	306	158	148	14
Widnes Vikings	9	6	0	3	217	216	1	12
Hull FC	10	5	0	5	254	167	87	10
Huddersfield Giants	10	4	2	4	258	215	43	10
Warrington Wolves	10	5	0	5	209	197	12	10
Hull Kingston Rovers	10	4	1	5	208	235	-27	9
Catalan Dragons	10	4	0	6	241	306	-65	8
Salford Red Devils	10	4	0	6	187	274	-87	8
Wakefield T Wildcats	10	2	0	8	218	312	-94	4
London Broncos	10	0	0	10	130	439	-309	0
Bradford Bulls *	10	2	0	8	154	374	-220	-2

* Deducted six points for entering administration

Challenge Cup Round 5

Leeds winger Ryan Hall served up a virtuoso performance as his side overcame St Helens 32-12 at Headingley Carnegie Stadium in the BBCTV game on Saturday afternoon. Tries from Zak Hardaker, who got two, Joel Moon, Danny McGuire and Jamie Peacock saw off Saints, with Kevin Sinfield landing six goals.

Saints responded with Adam Swift and Josh Jones tries, both converted by Luke Walsh, who struggled throughout with an elbow problem, while Leeds saw hooker Rob Burrow forced off with a broken collarbone. Saints were also dealt an injury blow, as in-form prop Kyle Amor was ruled out for at least three months with a serious knee injury.

Widnes Vikings booked their place in the last eight with a 30-20 win at Salford, after surviving an almighty scare in the final moments of a match they somehow came close to losing. Denis Betts' side held a 24-8 advantage with seven minutes remaining but quickfire tries from Lama Tasi and Gareth Hock put the hosts within striking distance.

Then after Francis Meli was bundled into touch with a minute remaining, Salford still had one last throw of the dice when they were awarded a scrum with three seconds on the clock. They were 80 metres from Widnes's line, but looked capable of keeping the ball alive after the hooter had sounded until Tony Puletua lost possession and Lloyd White raced away to claim the visitors' fifth score.

In the other all-Super League clash, a 20-point haul from Jamie Foster helped his Bulls side stage a staggering fightback to beat Catalans at home by 33-20, and earn a place in the Challenge Cup quarter-finals for the first time since 2010.

The Super League's basement side looked like lamely succumbing to another defeat when they conceded three tries in an error-strewn opening 13 minutes. But Bradford, with another former St Helens player, Lee Gaskell, in great form, responded with gusto, scoring five tries and 30 unanswered points in less than half an hour either side of half-time.

Keighley won at Swinton by exactly the same scoreline, 33-20, a Daley Williams try 13 minutes from time finally seeing the Paul March-inspired Cougars home.

Wigan, Warrington and Castleford had few problems in seeing off Kingstone Press Championship teams in home ties. Wigan beat Hunslet 52-8, featuring a first-half hat-trick from Matt Bowen; Chris Bridge, playing at stand-off, scored four tries, notching 36 points in total, kicking 10 out of his 12 conversion attempts as the Wolves beat Doncaster 68-nil; and Castleford knocked out Sheffield Eagles by 60-16, Justin Carney scoring four tries.

MAY
Bulls appeal

Round 11

Wigan's eight-game winning run came to an end at Headingley on the first Friday night of May in a blood-and-thunder game that ended 28-12 in Leeds' favour. Wigan captain Sean O'Loughlin was a late withdrawal before the match with a strained groin and Leeds coped better with the injury absence of both hookers, Paul Aiton and Rob Burrow. Chris Clarkson filled the void admirably as the Rhinos shot into a 10-0 lead after 12 minutes with tries to Danny McGuire and Zak Hardaker before Tony Clubb barged over to get Wigan back to 10-6.

Two Leeds tries in seven minutes either side of half-time took the wind out of Wigan's sails and the try that broke the contest two minutes into the second half summed up the Rhinos' clinical edge. The dangerous Matty Bowen and John Bateman had been held out close to the home line in the first meaningful set of the second half and, within a wink of an eye, Leeds struck.

On the last tackle, Kallum Watkins showed determination to chase and recover his own high kick coupled with the strength to wrestle out of the cover and dump the ball backwards to keep it alive. Jamie Peacock, to the satisfaction of the video ref who checked for a knock-on, shipped it on to McGuire who found Carl Ablett. He gave Joel Moon space and the Aussie's left-footed grubber to the corner sat up perfectly for Ryan Hall to time his gather and dive to perfection, to go over in the corner. Kevin Sinfield landed the touchline conversion and sent Leeds on the path to maintain their top-of-the-table spot.

That week Leeds coach Brian McDermott insisted that Ben Jones-Bishop would not be sent out on loan from Headingley, despite being left out of the side recently.

St Helens were still within a point of Leeds after their 48-18 home win over London the night before ended a three-match losing streak. Nathan Brown's side racked up nine different scorers in a match they were never in danger of losing, but at times their attack looked disorganised and struggled to find fluency.

Luke Walsh's class was an important part of Saints' success, but the victory was built on the efforts of front-rowers Alex Walmsley and Louie McCarthy-Scarsbrook, who were dominant during their spells in the middle.

The Broncos already looked certain to be one of the two clubs relegated at the end of the season, though coach Tony Rea insisted the club would continue to operate even if it did.

On the Sunday, Castleford lost a bit of ground after being edged as a Danny Brough field goal late in the second half sealed a thrilling 29-28 win for Huddersfield at the John Smith's Stadium.

The Giants came back from a 12-0 deficit early in the first 40 minutes to score three tries in a row and then withstand a late Castleford charge to secure their fifth win of the season. A Brough 40/20 just before the hour mark was pivotal, as it set up Aaron Murphy

to touch down on the left to give the Giants some much-needed breathing space at 28-16 after the conversion. But Jake Webster and Daryl Clark tries levelled at 28-all going into the last nine minutes before Brough potted the one-pointer after 75 minutes.

The Catalans were building momentum at home and on the Saturday they beat Salford 37-24, although it was far from plain sailing. The Red Devils, despite trailing 16-0 after the first quarter of the game, roared back into contention and led at the interval. However individual mistakes led to the Dragons running away with the game late on.

Morgan Escaré stole the headlines again with his hat-trick and the battle of the stand-offs between Leon Pryce and Rangi Chase was one to savour. Salford led 24-22 after Gareth Hock's try after 50 minutes. But Pryce's try just after the hour took the Dragons home.

The Red Devils, who that week had announced the signing of Kiwi international fullback Kevin Locke on a three-year contract starting in 2015, were on eight league points now looking over their shoulder at Wakefield, who registered their third win, a shock, Sunday afternoon 23-16 success at Hull FC. The Wildcats overturned a 16-0 deficit and produced a tenacious comeback to claim their first league victory in six outings. Jarrod Sammut's try with the scores locked at 16-apiece, with six minutes to go, clinched the spoils for the plucky visitors who scored 23 unanswered second-half points in a clichéd game of two halves.

Hull had led 12-0 at the interval courtesy of tries from Danny Houghton and Jordan Rankin and looked to be cruising to victory when Ben Crooks' try put them 16-0 to the good 10 minutes after the re-start. But the game then sparked into life just before the hour mark when Richie Mathers pulled one back for the visitors.

Then a fight broke out between Wakefield's on-loan winger Chris Riley and his opposite Jason Crookes which saw them both shown a yellow card. The fracas seemed to lift the Wildcats and they responded with two tries in three minutes that evened up the scores and set up a tense final quarter. After Sammut claimed the match-winner it was left to Paul Sykes to rub salt into the wounded Hull side when he slotted home a one-pointer to rubber stamp a much-needed Wakefield win.

It was a barren day for Hull as, over on the east side, Widnes produced an excellent comeback to thwart Hull KR by 34-29 at the KC Lightstream Stadium, with a hat-trick by Kevin Brown proving instrumental.

The Vikings dominated the first half as they built up an 18-6 lead that shocked the Robins into life. Two quick-fire tries before the break closed the gap to two points. And Rovers looked on the verge of victory when Travis Burns dropped a goal to make it 29-22 with 15 minutes left in the game.

However, Widnes came back from the dead to shock Rovers with two tries in the last eight minutes, from captain Jon Clarke and Brown, to usurp the home side and pick up yet another win, their first at Hull KR in 21 years.

Warrington Wolves suffered their sixth defeat in eleven games as they slipped to a shock 34-28 defeat at Bradford, a result which saw them clinging on to their top-eight spot on points difference.

It was Bradford's first win over the Wolves since June 2009 and lifted them off the bottom of the table for the first time since February - when they were docked six points for entering administration - and out of the negative points tally.

Lee Gaskell was magnificent for Bradford at fullback, and another former St Helens junior, Jamie Foster's penalty minutes from time gave Bradford a six-point cushion, which couldn't be clawed back.

* *That week RFL chief executive Nigel Wood was selected as the new Chairman of the Rugby League International Federation at its executive meeting in Sydney.*

Round 12

London Broncos had a new head coach in Joey Grima going into round 12. Grima, who joined the Broncos in February as an assistant, was promoted to the top job after the sudden exit of Tony Rea. The original plan was for Grima to assist Rea in 2014 and take over as head coach the following year.

There was little change in fortunes at The Hive on the Saturday as Huddersfield Giants recovered from a 16-10 half-time deficit to make it four league wins on the bounce with a 30-16 success. The Giants' formidable forwards were forced to play big minutes after fullback Jake Connor, making his first appearance of 2014, and winger Jermaine McGillvary went down with ankle injuries during the early stages and there were some superb performances from two-try Ukuma Ta'ai, Michael Lawrence and Eorl Crabtree, whilst Leroy Cudjoe stepped in well at the back.

With Josh Drinkwater and Hull FC junior James Cunningham pulling the strings, the still point-less Broncos put in their best showing of the season. But two Giants tries in the first three minutes of the second half broke them.

On the same day in an exciting encounter at AJ Bell Stadium, Martin Gleeson's 64th minute try gave Salford Red Devils a share of the spoils in a 16-all draw with Hull KR and ended their four-match losing streak. Both sides had late opportunities to win the game, with an ambitious 40-metre field-goal attempt from Rangi Chase hitting the crossbar, and Hull KR turning down a kickable penalty attempt, to the frustration of their coach Craig Sandercock.

Match Commissioner David Campbell was twice called onto the pitch after referee Phil Bentham reported objects being thrown onto the field, one from each end of the ground. A third incident saw a supporter attempt to get onto the pitch before being led away by stewards.

The draw kept Salford one point ahead of Wakefield who had stunned Widnes at the Select Security Stadium, Paul Sykes' 79th minute try - which proved to be the last play of the game - gaining a 24-18 win for the Wildcats.

The touchdown came with the scores tied at 18-18 and after a passage of play in which both sides had a couple of failed one-point efforts. The home defence assumed that Sykes, too, would attempt a drop goal but instead he ghosted in from 20 metres to the delight of his teammates and the travelling support.

Warrington put their shock loss at Bradford behind them with a comprehensive dismantling of a lacklustre Catalans Dragons at the Halliwell Jones Stadium. The Wolves secured the dominant 42-10 victory on the back of an impressive defence and a much-improved kicking game displayed by Chris Bridge and Stefan Ratchford. In a match marked by a number of handling errors, by both teams, but especially by the visitors, Catalans were well below par and only troubled Warrington in the dying stages.

The Dragons took 66 minutes to finally get on the scoreboard but it was just a consolation as the Wolves virtually had the game wrapped up after taking a 24-0 lead at half-time.

Leeds maintained their one-point lead at the top of the table in testing, rain-swept conditions with a seventh successive victory, winning at Castleford by 22-14 in the Thursday TV game. It was tough as the Rhinos battled back from 8-0 down in the early stages, and from being 14-12 adrift at the break.

Two Leeds tries in a seven-minute spell early in the second half effectively put the game, in very wet conditions, beyond Castleford. Leeds centre Kallum Watkins grabbed two tries and provided the final passes for winger Ben Jones-Bishop's brace.

Frustrated Tigers boss Daryl Powell was forced to ponder two successive defeats for the first time in 2014, after the previous Sunday's one-point reverse at Huddersfield Giants. And the fact that Castleford had only four days' rest before what was billed as the

biggest league fixture between the sides in 40 years, with Leeds having six days to prepare after having played Wigan the previous Friday, clearly riled him.

Wigan took the opportunity to overtake the Tigers into third spot with a 44-16 Friday-night win at Hull FC. Stand-in fullback Dan Sarginson claimed a hat-trick as Wigan's youngsters cruised to a comfortable win. Tries from Sarginson, Anthony Gelling and Jack Hughes, along with the boot of Matty Smith, gave Wigan a commanding 20-6 half-time lead. And, when Joe Burgess crossed shortly after the re-start the game was effectively over as a contest.

Sarginson completed his treble with a second-half brace and there were further tries from Dominic Manfredi and a second from Gelling. Hull's only reply were touchdowns from Jamie Shaul and Fetuli Talanoa, which added to Gareth Ellis's first-half effort.

The Airlie Birds, whose defeat was their third at home this season, now faced two months away from the KC Stadium while the pitch was re-laid.

Saints moved back to within a point of league leaders Leeds as they ran in nine tries and Luke Walsh added seven conversions in a thumping 50-0 home win over Bradford in wet and windy conditions. Walsh also scored a try for a personal tally of 18 points, while there was a brace for Jon Wilkin and other touchdowns for Jonny Lomax, Tom Makinson, Adam Swift, Sia Soliola, Louie McCarthy-Scarsbrook and James Roby.

* Blake Solly, the RFL's current Director of Standards and Licensing was appointed to the new post of General Manager of Super League, whose clubs agreed to appoint Richard Bowker CBE, as the new non-executive independent director of Super League (Europe).

Round 13 - Magic Weekend

A record crowd of 64,552 witnessed a sun-lit weekend of Rugby League at the Etihad Stadium in Manchester.

The crowd of 36,339 that watched four matches on the Saturday was the biggest for a single day at Magic Weekend, whilst 28,214 people filed through the turnstiles for the three fixtures on Sunday.

The previous record attendance at Magic Weekend was 63,716 in 2012, when the crowd of 32,953 on the Sunday was the previous high for a single day.

The London-Catalans opening game set the tone for some tight contests. Broncos scrum-half Josh Drinkwater missed a late conversion to tie the scores in the Broncos' 24-22 loss. The Broncos looked on track for their first win of the season, after 12 Super League games in 2014 without a victory. Drinkwater, one of London's best performers in the defeat, scored a crucial solo try in the 73rd minute and had a conversion opportunity to equal the scores at 24-all. But the Australian halfback hooked his attempt to the left and, despite a late flurry from the Broncos in the final seconds, the Dragons held on for the win. Elliott Whitehead scored two tries and ran the Catalans right edge.

Widnes overcame the loss of playmakers Danny Craven and Jon Clarke to leave Salford coach Iestyn Harris without a win in six games. In an entertaining, see-saw clash, stand-off Kevin Brown produced another influential display and had a hand in five of the Vikings' six tries in a 30-24 win, in a game that was only settled when winger Paddy Flynn crossed on 78 minutes.

With scrum-half Joe Mellor already sidelined, Widnes lost Craven in the opening minute after he was stretchered off following an awkward collision with the rampaging Gareth Hock's knee. Clarke was also withdrawn inside the first quarter with a calf injury,

Huddersfield's Jodie Broughton races away from Bradford's Elliot Kear on the way to scoring

but the Vikings adapted well to see off a gutsy effort from the Red Devils, who led at various points in the game.

The Hull derby was another beauty, with Rovers gaining a 38-24 victory thanks to tries from on-loan St Helens winger Ade Gardner and co-captain Josh Hodgson in the last ten minutes, Hull FC having 12 men after Jason Crookes was sent off in the 48th minute for a high tackle on Liam Salter.

Albert Goldthorpe Medal leader Travis Burns inspired the victory with an all-round leading performance as Salter and Gardner both claimed a brace of tries.

The Saturday finale was another cracker with Wigan gaining an 18-14 victory against Leeds Rhinos. Wigan coach Shaun Wane claimed it was 'the best win ever' as the injury ravaged champions harassed the Rhinos off their game. Captain Sean O'Loughlin was still missing and hadn't featured since the victory over Bradford Bulls on Easter Monday.

It was fiery from the off and Michael McIlorum, Ryan Bailey and John Bateman were sin-binned in the 25th minute after a huge flare-up. By then Wigan were already winning 8-0 after a remarkable try scored by Anthony Gelling that came from a kick towards the right corner by Matty Smith. Gelling jumped for the ball and knocked it forward, before catching it again and overcoming an attempted tackle by Zak Hardaker.

The Rhinos came back strongly in the final quarter of the game, with tries by Carl Ablett and Ryan Hall, before Joel Moon looked to have touched down at the end of the game for a try that would have won it for Leeds. But Moon nudged the ball forward when he tried to catch it and it rebounded off Wigan's Dominic Manfredi before he touched it down. The video refs ruled no try.

The three Sunday games weren't quite as close.

Castleford Tigers totally outplayed Wakefield in a 50-12 win. In a one-sided match that Castleford had in the bag at half-time, the Tigers, with 22-point Marc Sneyd running riot, ran out convincing winners to record their first victory in their past three games. Wakefield centre Dean Collis sustained a knee injury which kept him sidelined for most of the season.

Huddersfield's recent run of form continued as they stormed past a hapless Bradford Bulls outfit 54-16 to make it five wins in succession. The Bulls had only one recognised prop on the field in Adam Sidlow and coach Francis Cummins reiterated that he was proud of his side, who matched the Giants for long periods of the first half before being ultimately outclassed.

Danny Brough was as mercurial and pivotal as ever, laying on plenty of points for the Giants - as well as grabbing 22, with nine perfect conversions, himself.

In the final game, Warrington - boosted by the return of skipper Ben Westwood after several weeks out with a calf injury and with Stefan Ratchford leading the Wolves round the field - ran in eight tries in a 41-24 win over St Helens.

Saints coach Nathan Brown was cryptic in his analysis. 'It wouldn't have mattered if we won the game or not,' he said. 'Why have teams like Wigan and Warrington dominated us for the last four years? Players here who have won trophies know why. We have an issue we need to address at the club, both players and staff.'

The Saints defeat meant Leeds stayed a point clear at the top but both Castleford and Wigan made up ground.

Round 14

As a host of veterans looked on on heritage night, St Helens produced a polished seven-try display in the rain to beat the Giants 41-22.

Saints, with nine first-team regulars unavailable through injury, defeated an almost full-strength Giants side, unbeaten for five games, to stay in second place in the Super League table, with Samoan star Mose Masoe having his best game for the club and captain Paul Wellens reverting to fullback in the absence of the injured Jonny Lomax.

St Helens shot into an 18-0 lead after 13 minutes, with three tries, including one to gamestar Wellens, and Jon Wilkin's 43rd minute try ultimately put the brake on any thoughts of a Giants comeback, with Huddersfield's young winger Ben Blackmore getting a brace of tries.

Torrential rain meant lots of dropped ball at Headingley where leaders Leeds bounced back from the Magic Weekend defeat to Wigan with a 20-6 win over Hull FC. The loss was the fourth on the bounce for Hull but in skipper Gareth Ellis – finally making his return to Headingley Carnegie 15 months late - they had the commanding player on the field; with Joe Westerman showing flashes of his continuing good form in 2014.

The Airlie Birds were broken twice with kicks on the back of a ricochet and fumble and fell victim to a dropped ball, their defensive efforts throughout the campaign to date meaning that, despite their lower than expected position, they maintained a positive points difference.

There were three debutants. Rhinos' 18-year-old rake Robbie Ward was on hand to snap up Kirk Yeaman's double loss of a Danny McGuire grubber to poach a try nine minutes from time.

A year younger, Hull winger Callum Lancaster, called up after Ben Crooks failed a late fitness test, dealt capably with everything that was thrown at him and, although blowing after very limited game time with London Irish, Setaimata Sa was heavily involved off the bench in the second half for the black and whites.

Castleford stayed third on points difference as they overturned a half-time deficit after the returning two-try Luke Dorn inspired them to a fantastic 34-22 home win against Widnes. The Tigers trailed 12-10 at half-time but Daryl Clark's score with eight minutes left confirmed that the points would be heading to the Tigers, after a stunning second-half showing.

That week, Salford Chairman Marwan Koukash had confirmed that on-loan, boom Cas scrum-half Marc Sneyd would definitely be returning to the Red Devils on an extended contract at the end of the season.

May

On the Thursday night, Matty Smith guided a young side as Wigan shrugged off their injury crisis to grind out a hard-fought 25-4 win at Salford Red Devils in a rain-affected slugfest. Salford had two tries ruled out, with Francis Meli denied for obstruction and Gareth Hock for a double movement, while Ryan Hampshire and Dan Sarginson both had efforts denied for obstruction for the Warriors. Wigan's third try of the night from Joe Burgess pushed the Warriors out to 18-0 and after that Salford had no chance of producing a fight-back.

Catalans Dragons maintained their excellent home form with a resounding 46-4 victory over the Bulls, in a game they led throughout after scoring after only 45 seconds. Two-try gamestar Morgan Escaré's second try two minutes after the interval ended any doubts that Bradford could get back into the game and ensured a fifth consecutive home victory for the Catalans.

Bradford were still above bottom side London on points difference after the Broncos' 48-16 defeat at Hull KR. Josh Hodgson, Ade Gardner and Craig Hall all scored a brace apiece as Rovers ran in nine tries to the plucky visitors' three. Kevin Larroyer's sixth try of the season, on the hour, opened the floodgates and was the first of five unanswered tries for the Rovers that secured victory.

Gamestar Ben Currie scored twice before the break and killed off Wakefield's hopes with more than half of the game still to play as Warrington recorded a one-sided 36-4 victory at the Rapid Solicitors Stadium. Currie was Warrington's most eye-catching presence, but there were solid efforts too from Chris Hill and Stefan Ratchford.

Round 15

Bradford Bulls secured a crucial 20-12 home win over Wakefield Trinity on the last Sunday of May to move into positive league points, and within six points of the Wildcats in 12th position. With the appeal against their six-point deduction for going into administration due that week, it could have turned out to be a significant result.

Wakefield had not won at Odsal in their previous seven attempts, dating back to September 2006, and tries from Adrian Purtell (two) and Tom Olbison, all created by Luke Gale, who added four goals from five attempts, earned the fired up Bulls a 16-0 half-time advantage.

Although Trinity turned around the momentum after the break, with two tries from Matt Ryan resulting, and were perhaps unlucky not to draw closer earlier as Richard Mathers had a score contentiously ruled out just after the hour, they were kept at arm's length by a brace of Gale penalties and too many handling errors.

Wakefield prop Richard Moore was sin-binned following a fight with Elliot Kear, which resulted in his side being reduced to 12 men for ten minutes, though the Bradford winger wasn't given a yellow card. Moore got one match and Kear no further action after taking an early guilty plea.

The following Tuesday, Richard Agar stepped down as Wakefield head coach and was replaced by his assistant, James Webster.

London head coach Joey Grima was left frustrated after his team suffered several injuries and were on the wrong side of a heavy penalty count in recording their 15th loss of the season. Hull FC beat the Broncos 50-12 at the Hive on the Saturday, with London hooker Scott Moore sent off just before half-time for a high shot on Hull's teenage winger Callum Lancaster. London lost both of their fullbacks during the game, with Ben Farrar picking up a hamstring injury and Nesi Mataitonga injuring his ankle.

Joe Westerman was Hull's best and along with Lancaster scored two tries in what was Hull's first away win of Super League XIX.

Leaders Leeds fell to a 24-6 defeat at Warrington, who registered their fourth straight win. Led by hooker Michael Monaghan, who that week had revealed he would retire at the end of the season, the Wolves were without Ben Westwood, who had been suspended

for three games for a dangerous tackle against the Wildcats the previous week. Chris Bridge was in great form at stand-off and when he scored his second try and added the conversion on 34 minutes, the Wolves had an 18-point lead that proved to be insurmountable for Leeds.

The following Tuesday, Carl Ablett was suspended for two games, after being found guilty of kicking Joel Monaghan's face as he scored the clinching try in the 73rd minute.

Rhinos fullback Zak Hardaker was also due to face disciplinary action after TV footage caught him making a homophobic comment at referee James Child, although he later claimed he was aiming his words at Michael Monaghan.

The result meant St Helens went back to the top after beating Salford at home on the same night by 32-12. Captain Paul Wellens grabbed a try in each half, laid on another for Gary Wheeler and provided calm leadership throughout. Lance Hohaia's try on 30 minutes put St Helens three scores clear before the break, and there was no way back for Salford.

On the Sunday, Castleford, playing in a style that matched the scorching conditions and with hooker Daryl Clark in great form again, ripped Hull KR apart in a 54-12 home win.

Hull KR, who had prop Michael Weyman sent off on 62 minutes for alleged dissent at a time when Castleford had established a 40-6 lead, had no answer to the Tigers attack, which led to 11 home tries - three from Luke Dorn - being registered. Rovers could draw few positives from the afternoon other than scoring the last try, when winger Wayne Ulugia intercepted a pass by home prop Grant Millington to speed over from 40 metres.

Weyman was banned for two games, but that was lifted on appeal, the Aussie prop successfully arguing his comments were aimed at a teammate and not the referee.

Catalans Dragons, with Leon Pryce at his best, made nonsense of their previously poor form on the road in 2014 to earn a valuable point in an absorbing 26-all draw at Widnes. Twice they led by a ten-point margin and were only denied the win by a late converted try from young Vikings halfback Tom Gilmore.

Huddersfield showed their Championship credentials by overcoming an early 12-0 deficit to fight back and beat Wigan in the Thursday night TV game 31-22, despite the return of Warriors captain Sean O'Loughlin.

Tries by Joe Wardle either side of half-time had the Giants 24-12 up and Danny Brough's field goal minutes after gave the Warriors too much to make up.

That week Wigan announced they had signed Wakefield forward Taulima Tautai from 2015.

FIRST UTILITY SUPER LEAGUE TABLE
Sunday 1st June

	P	W	D	L	F	A	D	PTS
St Helens	15	12	0	3	491	290	201	24
Leeds Rhinos	15	11	1	3	416	156	260	23
Castleford Tigers	15	11	0	4	514	263	251	22
Wigan Warriors	14	10	0	4	427	251	176	20
Warrington Wolves	15	9	0	6	380	275	105	18
Huddersfield Giants	15	8	2	5	424	338	86	18
Widnes Vikings	14	8	1	5	347	353	-6	17
Catalan Dragons	15	7	1	7	384	424	-40	15
Hull Kingston Rovers	15	6	2	7	351	379	-28	14
Hull FC	15	6	0	9	366	304	62	12
Salford Red Devils	15	4	1	10	267	414	-147	9
Wakefield T Wildcats	15	4	0	11	293	452	-159	8
Bradford Bulls *	15	4	0	11	228	564	-336	2
London Broncos	15	0	0	15	214	639	-425	0

* Deducted six points for entering administration

JUNE
Wolves prowl

Challenge Cup Quarter Finals

Championship leaders Leigh had been unbeaten in their first 13 league matches but that run was expected to come to an abrupt end at Headingley on the first Friday of June. The Centurions did eventually lose, by 25-12 to the Rhinos, but only after a truly memorable Cup tie. Leigh came within seven minutes of an almighty upset, with heroes in Tom Spencer, Sam Barlow, Martyn Ridyard and Tom Armstrong.

The difference in the end proved to be split-second decision making under extreme pressure. With the scores tied at 12-all, as they had been from just after the half hour, Leigh had two opportunities to take a stranglehold.

First Ryan Brierley handled twice, linking with Barlow and, with an overlap on the right, Tommy Goulden elected to kick for the corner, his boot too strong to uncover a hovering Jonny Pownall. Eight minutes later, after Robbie Ward had had the ball stolen bringing it away looking for desperate relief, Sean Penkywicz's pass went behind his support runners to the left, Tom Briscoe swooping to carry the ball to safety.

After a run from Kallum Watkins and, on the last, with everyone expecting a drop goal, Robbie Ward shot through the gap to the posts and the semi-final deal was effectively done.

The evening before had been more one-sided, with Widnes Vikings strolling to a 56-6 victory over Keighley, Tom Gilmore finishing with a hat-trick of tries.

Denis Betts went with the strongest possible combination from his injury-hit squad whereas Cougars coach Paul March – who watched the game on TV in a nearby pub due to a two-month stadium ban for abusing officials – chose to give season debuts to half-a-dozen players with an eye on forthcoming league fixtures - five Championship clubs were due to be relegated at the end of the season to accommodate the new league structure.

Any notions that the home side might be given a run for their money were quashed in the first ten minutes as the Vikings built up a 16-0 lead.

Warrington Wolves set up a mouth-watering semi-final date with Leeds, as they cantered past a hapless Bradford outfit 46-10 at Odsal to ease into the last four. Led by the outstanding Stefan Ratchford - playing out of position at loose forward - the Wolves were too hot to handle, as they advanced to their third consecutive Challenge Cup semi-final.

High-flying Castleford beat Wigan at the DW Stadium on the Saturday 16-4.

There was only one try in the first 40 minutes,

with James Clare going over in the left corner, but as on numerous occasions in 2014, the major talking point was the obstruction rule. The Tigers had an earlier effort by Luke Dorn ruled out by the video referee, but he gave the green light for Clare's try, with many people confused about the rulings.

Shaun Wane must have delivered a roasting at half-time as Wigan came back out full of energy and attacking options, but it took until the 63rd minute for them to get on the scoresheet.

From then on it looked as though they would kick on and take advantage of a tiring Castleford, but it was the Tigers who finished the stronger with tries from Kirk Dixon and Lee Jewitt to seal a memorable win.

The last team to beat Wigan on home soil in the Challenge Cup had been Castleford in 1986 - and they went on to win the trophy.

Round 16

Bradford Bulls' Super League status was left in a precarious position after the six-point deduction by the RFL was confirmed on appeal by an independent panel, although the club's board was to decide within the next ten days whether to take any further action.

The Bulls, now lay eight points behind Wakefield after their 46-18 defeat at Salford on the Sunday. Rangi Chase, who scored 22 points from two tries and seven goals, produced a dazzling first-half performance to ease any lingering relegation hopes that Salford might have had while pushing Bradford one step closer to the drop.

Chase was virtually untouchable in a blistering opening spell by the Red Devils that saw them race in a commanding 24-0 lead after less than 13 minutes. With centre Junior Sa'u and back-rower Gareth Hock terrorising the right side of Bradford's defence, Salford looked every inch the play-off contenders that they were expected to be at the start of the season.

Kevin Locke was due to join Salford on a three-year contract from November but having failed to break into the NZ Warriors' team in 2014, would now arrive as soon as he got a visa.

New Wakefield coach James Webster watched his side come from behind at home on the Friday night to beat London Broncos 18-10 and further distance themselves from the relegation zone. The Wildcats were woeful in a rain-lashed opening 40 minutes and trailed 10-4 but responded to Webster's half-time team talk with 14 unanswered points after the break.

The Broncos' big pack totally dominated the opening stanza, but Trinity surprisingly struck first when Danny Kirmond powered his way over, although Paul Sykes failed to master the slippery conditions and missed the conversion

London levelled in almost farcical circumstances as a hopeful Iliess Macani kick ricocheted back from Wakefield's defence for Macani to touch down. The visitors struck again almost immediately, launched by a stirring Atelea Vea break down the middle, with Nesi Mataitonga's kick, this time a short stab infield, creating a try for Thomas Minns.

The forward-thrusting Broncos forced no fewer than four goal-line drop outs with the Wildcats rarely getting out of their own half in the first half. But Tim Smith, back on loan from Salford where he hadn't settled, did enough to get Wakefield to the win, creating tries for Daniel Smith and Matt Ryan.

Castleford Tigers coach Daryl Powell signed a new five-year contract to the end of 2019 in the wake of the Cup win at Wigan, but in the repeat fixture on the Friday night, this time in the league, the Warriors hammered the Tigers 46-6.

The Tigers had outclassed the Warriors less than a week earlier, but this time Wigan led 22-0 at the break thanks to tries from Dominic Manfredi, Matty Bowen, Jordan James and Joe Burgess. Further tries from Liam Farrell, Michael McIlorum and a second for

47

June

Burgess saw them cruise to victory

The win moved Wigan to within two points of leaders St Helens, who crashed to a 42-0 defeat in Perpignan. Saints failed to cope with the stifling conditions that saw the temperature still in the 30s at kick-off. There was a hat-trick for winger Michael Oldfield and Thomas Bosc registered his 1,000th Super League point for the club

To further increase St Helen' woes, fullback Jonny Lomax suffered a season-ending injury as he left the field in the 64th minute. Lomax was returning a Catalans kick as his knee buckled under him and he fell to the floor.

Meanwhile Scott Dureau, the 2012 Albert Goldthorpe Medal winner, was de-registered by the Dragons to accommodate new signing from St George Illawarra, Sam Williams.

Leeds missed the chance to hit the top of the table as they lost at home 24-22 to Huddersfield. Playing behind a big mobile pack, augmented by a large, roving bench, Danny Brough orchestrated brilliantly, and his kicking – including two 40/20s – was game defining.

It was a heart-stopping finish as Leeds had a Harlem Globetrotters type 'try' that started in their own half ruled out on the last play of the game.

At the end of the move, Tom Briscoe and Brough jostled for the ball after Joel Moon's preceding kick bounced into the in-goal on the right. Briscoe got there first, but the video referee ruled he had pushed Brough.

Hull FC registered their first back-to-back win of 2014 with a stunning 56-6 victory at Widnes on the Friday night, with 17-year-old winger Callum Lancaster getting a hat-trick. With Gareth Ellis the stand-out player on the night, two quickfire Hull tries in as many minutes approaching the hour mark took the score from 6-20 to 6-32 and ended any prospect of a Widnes comeback.

Warrington head coach Tony Smith agreed an extended contract until November 2016, taking on a Director of Rugby role, with former Wakefield coach Richard Agar becoming the first-team coach on a two-year contract.

On the Friday night the Wolves made it five consecutive wins in the Super League with a determined 34-4 away victory over a gritty Hull KR side.

Joel Monaghan scored a brace as the Wolves backed up their Challenge Cup quarter-final win at Bradford five days earlier and continued their resurgence to form. Nothing separated the two sides as the game remained scoreless during a scrappy opening half-an-hour, but two punishing 10-minute spells from the Wolves at the end of each half secured the spoils for the visitors.

Tries from Gene Ormsby, Stefan Ratchford and Monaghan's first gave Warrington an 18-0 lead at the interval. Rovers hit back through Graeme Horne early in the second period, but it would be their only score of the match despite plenty of effort.

Warrington ended the game as they finished the first 40 minutes with another clinical 10-minute spell that put the game to bed. Ben Evans claimed the game-clincher before Ryan Atkins went over and Monaghan added to his first-half effort with the final try of the game.

Leeds fullback Zak Hardaker received a five-match ban after being found guilty of homophobic abuse. Hardaker, who was represented by his club's legal team, was charged with a grade E offence, which carried a suspension of between four and eight matches, after his offensive comments were spotted on television during Leeds' 24-6 defeat by Warrington 11 days before.

The 22-year-old had issued an apology for his comments, admitting he used inappropriate language and insisted it had been aimed at the Warrington captain Michael Monaghan, rather than the referee James Child.

Round 2

Wigan went to the top of the table for the first time in 2014, beating Widnes 48-4 in a Wednesday night game re-arranged from the start of the season because of the World Club Challenge.

The Warriors led 32-4 at half-time and despite Josh Charnley grabbing four first-half tries he was still not the biggest news of the day as Wigan announced the re-signing of Joel Tomkins at the break on a four-and-a-half year contract.

Wigan opened the scoring after 31 seconds when Liam Farrell raced clear following good work from Sean O'Loughlin and Dan Sarginson. Widnes did get back in the game with a try from Paddy Flynn, but Charnley and O'Loughlin traded scores before the winger stole the show with three more tries in a 10-minute period to put the Super League champions out of sight at the break.

Charnley - back in action for the first time since picking up a knee injury in April - added a fifth after the turnaround and Liam Farrell added a second before his brother Connor, on debut as was Callum Wright, got in on the act. Widnes had conceded over a century of points in two matches.

Michael McIlorum was ruled out for two months with a broken arm.

Round 17

Wigan's spell at the top of the table lasted only a few days as they were downed 36-28 at in-form Wakefield the following Sunday. Danny Washbrook and Reece Lyne scored decisive late tries for Wakefield, who had won both games under new head coach James Webster and were now 10 points above the relegation zone.

The Wildcats had led 24-18 at half-time, captain Danny Kirmond among their four first-half try scorers. Liam Farrell scored two of Wigan's five tries as the Warriors dropped to third in the table

After the hammering at Catalans, St Helens produced their best display of the season to return to the Super League summit with a 38-16 Sunday afternoon win over Castleford. Inspired by Luke Walsh and Paul Wellens, Saints quickly returned to winning ways, leading 22-4 by the half-time break.

Leeds were back in second after two successive defeats with a 38-28 win at Widnes. Leeds dummy-half Paul Aiton was back on duty after long spell out with illness as Danny McGuire scored a try in each half and captain Kevin Sinfield added 14 points. The Vikings had come from 10 points down to lead 16-10 at half-time thanks to three quick tries from Chris Dean, Rhys Hanbury and Patrick Ah Van.

Zak Hardaker was serving the first of a five-match ban for homophobic abuse.

The Wolves were the form side at this stage of the season, although they weren't at their best in a 36-20 home win over Salford. The Red Devils were fully in the contest for most of the game, only for handling errors and ill-discipline to prove crucial in the final quarter. They conceded five straight penalties after closing the gap to six points with Niall Evalds' first try and that saw the game drift away.

Huddersfield survived a mild second-half scare to record an eighth win in nine games, a 38-22 home victory over London Broncos. Jermaine McGillvary and Joe Wardle both claimed a brace as the Giants ran in seven tries while Danny Brough added five conversions to condemn the bottom-of-the-table Broncos to a record extending 17th successive league defeat since the start of a Super League season.

With the Broncos almost certainly relegated, players started to secure their futures with other Super League clubs, hooker Scott Moore set to join Castleford Tigers for the next season to replace the departing Daryl Clark, rumoured to be Warrington-bound.

Catalans blew away leaders St Helens the previous weekend, but their 20-16 home

win over Hull FC was much more hard fought. The Dragons looked in control on another scorching Perpignan day, leading 20-4 on the hour, but the Airlie Birds, with 2013 Albert Goldthorpe Rookie of the Year Tom Lineham playing his first game since breaking an ankle in round 4, pulled the deficit back to four points with Kirk Yeaman and Jamie Shaul tries to set up a tense last 15 minutes.

Hull were missing prop Liam Watts, who had mis-laid his passport and was unable to travel to France.

Hull KR moved two points above Hull FC and within a point of eighth-placed Widnes with a 44-18 Friday night win at Bradford, for whom time was running out in the bid to save their Super League life.

In a week where head coach Francis Cummins was sacked, the smallest league crowd at Odsal all season were treated to an eventually dejected performance from the Bulls, who were being coached on a interim basis by captain Matt Diskin. With the Robins leading 18-6 at the break, Craig Hall's score within seconds of the second half beginning was a real hammer blow, and set the tone for the remainder of the match.

The Robins were missing Jonathan Walker and Wayne Ulugia, stood down by coach Craig Sandercock for unspecified disciplinary reasons. And co-captain Josh Hodgson had been linked with a move to the NRL's Canberra Raiders in a week when he was fined £500, suspended to the end of 2015, for making an offensive gesture to supporters during the Magic Weekend fixture with Hull FC at the Etihad Stadium in May.

Round 18

St Helens remained top of the Super League ladder with a stunning defensive performance to beat Wigan Warriors 16-12 on their home turf. Saints gained a measure of revenge for the Good Friday hammering by tackling their hearts out in a game that saw both teams score three tries.

The score was 4-4 at the break with a try apiece as Joe Burgess put the champions ahead following good work from Sam Powell before Tommy Makinson levelled matters thanks to an amazing offload from Mark Flanagan.

After the break, tries from Paul Wellens and Makinson saw Nathan Brown's men get home on the back of an outstanding defensive display. Josh Charnley managed to grab a second-half double and Wigan almost won at the death after back-to-back penalties, but St Helens' defensive line was not going to break.

The Warriors brought back captain Sean O'Loughlin, Matty Bowen, Burgess, Charnley and John Bateman after their defeat against Wakefield, although Liam Farrell was suspended for a dangerous tackle in that game.

Despite the win, after the game in which Saints were on the wrong end of an 11-5 penalty count, coach Brown accused his counterpart Shaun Wane of putting pressure on referees. 'Absolute disgrace. Absolute garbage, that's all I want to say about that,' was Wane's immediate reaction.

Apart from the penalty count the big negative for St Helens was the loss of scrum-half Luke Walsh, who came off after 20 minutes with a back injury.

Catalans Dragons came the closest they had ever done to victory on the sole ground they had never won at, Headingley, a nerveless Liam Sutcliffe penalty – standing in for Kevin Sinfield - as the hooter sounded snatching a 32-31 Leeds win in the most dramatic fashion.

It was only the second time in the contest the hosts were ahead, Joel Moon's second score intercepting Leon Pryce's pass in the 65th minute the first, the Dragons having only themselves to blame in a French farce finish.

Daryl Millard's try from a majestic round-the-man pass from Pryce and a superb touchline conversion for the highly impressive Sam Williams on full debut had levelled and Morgan Escaré – again magnificent throughout – with a field goal four minutes from

St Helens' Tom Makinson fends off Wigan's Josh Charnley

time looked to have secured history.

But from the short kick-off Jason Baitieri grabbed a ball that had not gone ten metres to give away a needless penalty and, with Leeds having seemingly butchered their last chance with a poor final set; when running down the clock, Ben Pomeroy ran behind Zeb Taia to hand Sutcliffe the hero's chance, as Leeds remained with a point of leaders St Helens.

The Dragons had been forced to back down from their intention to wear a pink polka dot playing strip that celebrated the Tour de France 'King of the Mountains'. The massively hyped start to the race was due to take place the following weekend in Leeds, but Tour officials threatened them with legal action for a breach of copyright.

Meanwhile the Dragons that week had agreed to allow former Albert Goldthorpe Medal winner Scott Dureau to head to Australia to join Sydney Roosters, who were coached by former Dragons coach Trent Robinson, on loan for the rest of the season.

Bradford Bulls appointed former playing great James Lowes as head coach but the chances of the Bulls retaining their Super League status decreased further as they fell 50-24 at Warrington in his first game in charge.

For the attack-minded Wolves, Stefan Ratchford produced an influential display throughout, while halfback partner Gareth O'Brien capped an impressive performance with two tries as he stood in for the rested Chris Bridge. Warrington scored 22 points in less than 10 minutes at the start of the second half to take the game away from Bradford.

Bulls Chairman Marc Green was still hoping to have a decision made by the High Court about the possible restoration of the six points taken from the club by the RFL earlier that season, and confirmed by an independent tribunal two weeks before.

Warrington were still outside the top four on points difference as Castleford beat Salford at home on a wet Saturday by 14-10. Down 10-8 against third-bottom Red Devils with just seconds left on the clock, Jake Webster came up with a crucial play - created by the mercurial Daryl Clark - to end a mini-blip after defeats to Wigan and St Helens.

June

Devils coach Iestyn Harris, who gave a debut to midweek signing, former Cas man Josh Griffin, declared emphatically that the best team lost. London centre Mason Caton-Brown had signed a two-and-a-half-year deal but didn't play.

Castleford, Wigan and Warrington were also joined on 24 league points by Huddersfield who had edged Hull KR on the Thursday night at the KC Lightstream Stadium by 26-22, the Giants' fourth consecutive victory. Two second-half tries from Larne Patrick sealed the win after the scores were at a 16-16 deadlock going into half-time.

A breathtaking first 40 minutes produced plenty of entertainment and proved a real see-saw affair as both sides scored three tries apiece. David Hodgson, Kris Welham and Ade Gardner crossed for the Robins to which Leroy Cudjoe, Ukuma Ta'ai and Eorl Crabtree, in turn, responded for the visitors.

Patrick's second try with just over 10 minutes remaining looked to have put the game to bed but David Hodgson went over to complete his double in the final minute to bring the Rovers to within four points of the Giants. However, with only 22 seconds remaining when Rovers got the ball back, it was too little, too late, and Huddersfield came away with the spoils.

Widnes went three points clear of Hull KR into the top eight with a 42-24 win at London. Kevin Brown was in unstoppable form, with Rhys Hanbury and Paddy Flynn each scoring two tries.

Joe Westerman marked his 200th career appearance with a last-minute conversion to deny Wakefield the chance to claim a double over Hull and, with it, three wins on the bounce for the first time in 2014, the game ending in a 20-all draw.

Trinity had snatched the lead for the first time just seven minutes earlier through a Nick Scruton try but Kirk Yeaman's second try of the game gave loose forward Westerman, who hadn't missed a game for Hull since May 2013, the chance to snatch a dramatic point for the visitors.

Australian halfback Jordan Rankin was back in his homeland on compassionate leave, and Hull coach Lee Radford plunged 18-year old Jordan Abdull in at the deep end for his debut, while restoring Liam Watts to the line-up after the passport troubles that prevented him getting to France the previous week.

FIRST UTILITY SUPER LEAGUE TABLE
Sunday 29th June

	P	W	D	L	F	A	D	PTS
St Helens	18	14	0	4	545	360	185	28
Leeds Rhinos	18	13	1	4	508	239	269	27
Wigan Warriors	18	12	0	6	561	313	248	24
Castleford Tigers	18	12	0	6	550	357	193	24
Warrington Wolves	18	12	0	6	500	323	177	24
Huddersfield Giants	18	11	2	5	512	404	108	24
Catalan Dragons	18	9	1	8	477	472	5	19
Widnes Vikings	18	9	1	8	427	519	-92	19
Hull Kingston Rovers	18	7	2	9	421	457	-36	16
Hull FC	18	7	1	10	458	350	108	15
Wakefield T Wildcats	18	6	1	11	367	510	-143	13
Salford Red Devils	18	5	1	12	343	482	-139	11
Bradford Bulls *	18	4	0	14	288	704	-416	2
London Broncos	18	0	0	18	270	737	-467	0

* Deducted six points for entering administration

* On the last Saturday of June, Papua New Guinea were crowned Commonwealth Rugby League champions after defeating tournament favourites Australia in a thrilling final at Cumbernauld, near Glasgow.

The Papuans came out on top in the eight-team, under-19s tournament, after going through their pool games undefeated against England, Canada and Jamaica, and then booking a place in the final with a 12-6 semi-final win over Wales.

There were plans to make Rugby League Nines and exhibition sport at the next Commonwealth Games, due to be staged in the Gold Coast, Australia in 2018.

JULY
Down and out

Round 19

The battle at the top of the table heated up after the first weekend in July. In the Friday TV game at Wakefield, on-loan Richard Owen's last-gasp touchdown maintained new coach James Webster's unbeaten record since taking over at the helm from Richard Agar at the beginning of June, as the Wildcats beat Leeds 14-10. Richard Mathers scored a try and then helped create the late winner to end a run of five straight defeats against his home-town club.

The Rhinos were depleted but the Wildcats themselves were missing skipper Danny Kirmond, Scott Anderson, Ali Lauitiiti and Dean Collis, and were twice forced to come from behind.

Salford-bound Ben Jones-Bishop almost produced a second long-range effort late on, but Owen's brilliant tackle forced him towards the touchline, and then, as Wakefield tried to respond, the ball came loose on halfway and Danny McGuire thought he'd sealed matters by racing over, only for video replays to reveal a knock-on from Ryan Hall. Trinity refused to lie down and, with barely two minutes remaining, Tim Smith set Mathers going forward on the blind side and Owen slid in at the corner to send the home crowd wild.

Then on the Sunday, Hull KR embarrassed table-topping St Helens by 40-10 as a dominant second-half performance and 26 unanswered points saw the Robins pull away and give interim coach Chris Chester a win in his first game in charge.

Rovers moved to within a point of the play-off places at the end of a week of upheaval, with Craig Sandercock having been removed from the position of head coach just three days earlier. Starting left centre Craig Hall was also signed by Wakefield the previous Friday, and the Hull-born man showed his quality with a scintillating hat-trick.

The Vikings were now in the Robins' sights after a 40-20 home defeat by Castleford on the Thursday night. The key moment was a disallowed long-range interception try by Patrick Ah Van, who went under the posts after running almost the length of the field for what appeared to be a score that would have levelled the game at 22-22. But it was ruled out on touch judge Robert Hicks' call, with Castleford being awarded a penalty for offside.

The disallowed Ah Van 'score' was followed by frenzied Widnes pressure that was relieved in an instant by Daryl Clark's inspired power-play try, and the competition's form hooker scored another as Castleford - who had led 18-0 after ten minutes - finished strongly.

Warrington produced a solid performance to spoil Hull FC's homecoming - their first game at the KC Stadium since 9th May - as the Wolves secured their eighth consecutive win in the Super League, by 24-18, despite a hat-trick from the Airlie Birds' teenage-wing sensation Callum Lancaster.

Lancaster took his season tally to eight tries in just four appearances but the 17-year-old's efforts proved to be in vain as the Wolves crossed on four occasions through Stefan Ratchford, Ryan Atkins, Ben Harrison and Gene Ormsby, tries that clinched a hard-earned victory for the visitors in the tricky, wet conditions.

July

That week, Hull FC announced the signings of a new halfback pairing for 2015 in Leon Pryce, from Catalans, and Salford's Marc Sneyd, who had starred in his season-long loan spell at Castleford.

Wigan ran out 58-6 winners at London Broncos, with halfback Matty Smith kicking two 40/20s, controlling the game magnificently and slotting nine conversions from ten attempts. Josh Charnley grabbed a hat-trick to continue his impressive run of scoring since his return from injury. The England flyer had racked up ten tries in four appearances.

On the Saturday, with Kevin Locke and Mason Caton-Brown highly impressive on debut and Rangi Chase pulling the strings from stand-off, the Red Devils overcame the 60th minute dismissal of Lama Tasi to sweep Huddersfield aside at the John Smith's Stadium by 36-10.

For the second week running the Catalans were in a tight finish, but this time came out as winners as former Bull Elliott Whitehead's last-ditch score gave them a 32-30 win at Bradford. Whitehead's try levelled the game up at 30-30, and Sam Williams' conversion ultimately won the points for the Dragons.

At a meeting of Super League clubs in the week after round 19, the clubs decided to defer a decision to introduce a marquee player outside the salary cap. The move's main proponent, Salford chairman Marwan Koukash, publicly declared a personal vote of no confidence in the RFL's running of Super League Europe, calling for control of Super League to be handed over to the member clubs.

* That week it was announced that Coventry Bears would enter the Championship One competition in 2015.

Round 20

London Broncos' relegation was confirmed after they were beaten 72-12 at Warrington. The winless Broncos had no answers on a sunny Sunday at the Halliwell Jones Stadium, as the Wolves racked up 13 tries and notched their ninth win in a row in a very one-sided affair. It was the Broncos' 20th consecutive loss in 2014.

Warrington were missing Stefan Ratchford, Trent Waterhouse, Michael Monaghan and Roy Asotasi, and fielding 18-year old debutant Toby King in the centres, but still far too strong for the beleaguered Broncos. Joel Monaghan, playing in the centre, scored four tries and prop Chris Hill got three.

The big win was enough to take the Wolves into fourth on points difference above Castleford. A 44-30 home win over the Giants maintained the Tigers' challenge for top spot, with last year's League Leaders Huddersfield now four points adrift of the leading group of five.

The Giants were without playmaker-in-chief Danny Brough and fullback Scott Grix through injury and lacked an effective kicking game. Castleford had recovered from 12-4 down in the early stages to lead 32-12 shortly after half-time, only to find themselves pegged back to eight points by the hour-mark. And the result could have been different if Giants' winger Jodie Broughton hadn't had a subsequent length-of-the-field touchdown ruled out by video referee Ben Thaler for putting a foot in touch en route to the tryline.

Both Catalans and Widnes in seventh and eighth positions were pulled back to the chasing pack.

The Vikings suffered a Thursday-night 12-10 defeat at Wakefield. The Wildcats looked certain winners when Nick Scruton put them 12-4 up just before the hour, but a howler from fullback Richie Mathers gifted Stefan Marsh an easy try in the corner and set up a frantic finale. Mathers was under no pressure to collect Joe Mellor's kick, but he waited for the ball to go out, it didn't and Marsh picked his pocket with 12 minutes to go.

Widnes piled forward in search of a dramatic winner, only to run out of time in a

tense finish. And the sound of the hooter had Wakefield celebrating a win that gave their play-off hopes a major boost.

Vikings coach Denis Betts was left bemused when referee Ben Thaler appeared to assure Widnes players that the video referee would check to see whether Richard Moore was offside in the build-up to Tim Smith's second-half try. Betts and Widnes supporters thought he was.

The Catalans fell 37-16 at home to Wigan, who took advantage of an undisciplined show from the Dragons as referee James Child felt the heat not only from the searing temperatures in Perpignan, but also from the hostile Catalan crowd, which booed him constantly from the 30-minute mark.

But the Catalans only had themselves to blame. Warriors coach Shaun Wane praised referee Child who sent Catalan duo Jason Baitieri and Benjamin Garcia to the sin bin during a run of five consecutive penalties conceded in a three-minute period in the second half. Ten minutes swung the game in Wigan's favour, from Matty Bowen putting Wigan 14 points in front just before the break to Joe Burgess's 49th-minute try making the difference 26 points.

Bowen was superb for the Warriors at the back, making line-breaks, creating tries and scoring two himself.

Rob Burrow became the Super League's eighth all-time leading try scorer as Leeds beat Hull KR 30-6 at home to stay second. After no score in the first half, Burrow - it took until almost an hour for the game's first try - who had been out of action since breaking his collarbone at the end of April, darted over from dummy half to equal Pat Richards' impressive tally and he wrapped the game up with his 148th all-time try. Liam Sutcliffe, Carl Ablett and Danny McGuire also went over for the hosts, with Josh Hodgson replying for Hull KR. Kevin Sinfield, also returning after two games out with a strained back, kicked five goals from five attempts.

Leeds remained a point behind leaders St Helens, who won 46-22 at home against Bradford on the same Friday night. Saints, with two-try captain Paul Wellens outstanding and having been on the end of a sound defeat at Hull KR themselves just five days earlier, threatened to completely run away with matters when they led 40-0 after 50 minutes.

But, inspired by Luke Gale, Bradford then scored four unanswered tries to give new coach James Lowes some positives as the Bulls' relegation moved closer.

The following Monday after a meeting of the club's directors the Bulls abandoned their legal challenge to the decision of the independent tribunal that confirmed a six-points deduction for going into administration.

Bradford were now 13 points behind Salford with seven games to go after the Red Devils' 35-22 home win over Hull FC, which drew them level on points in the table.

The Red Devils, missing Kevin Locke who failed a fitness test, were sitting pretty at 19-0 when, with Jordan Rankin in the sin bin, Josh Griffin converted his own try on 53 minutes. But Kirk Yeaman and Jamie Shaul tries had the deficit down to seven points and that made for a nervous last five minutes for Salford before Mason Caton-Brown scored his second try to seal the win.

Round 21

Bradford's relegation was confirmed with their 52-26 Sunday afternoon defeat at Huddersfield Giants. The Giants were forced to come from behind three times during an error-strewn first half but two tries in the last four minutes earned them a slightly unreflective 26-16 lead at the break and they kicked on from there.

Brett Ferres produced a forceful display which helped create a couple and scored one of the tries that condemned his former club to Championship rugby in 2015, while Jermaine McGillvary grabbed a hat-trick of tries.

Widnes upset the odds with a first home win since Easter Monday, a 28-14 success

over neighbours Warrington. The Wolves came into the game on the back of a ten-game winning streak, whilst the Vikings were struggling to cling on to their top-eight place after a poor run of form.

Jack Owens' try around the hour mark steadied Widnes nerves after two quick Wolves tries had threatened a comeback.

Catalans' play-off place was also looking more secure after their 40-6 home win over Wakefield, despite them missing Vincent Duport and Greg Mounis due to suspensions.

The Dragons were 28-0 up at the break as the Wildcats' five-match unbeaten streak came to a crashing halt, with Elliott Whitehead once again a standout as he finished with three tries.

The play-off hopes of Hull FC and Hull KR both took a dent.

On the Friday night, George Williams was the star of the star of the show as he guided Wigan Warriors to their third consecutive win, completely outclassing Hull FC by 56-10.

The Super League champions got off to a dream start with a superb individual try from Lewis Tierney inside the first five minutes. But despite many thinking the floodgates would open, the visitors soon found themselves back in the game.

It did not take long for Hull, who were far from at full strength and had 18-year-old Skirlaugh product Jack Logan making his debut at centre, to draw level through Fetuli Talanoa. But further tries from Josh Charnley, Williams and Matty Smith in a blistering ten-minute period put Wigan 22-4 in front at half-time.

Williams caused Hull plenty of problems and managed to complete his hat-trick in the second half as Wigan cruised to victory, scoring ten tries in total.

Salford moved to within four points of the play-off spots after they took advantage of Hull KR's poor second-half indiscipline at KC Lightstream Stadium with a 38-18 win.

Rovers started the game the brighter and they went into the break leading 12-4. But Salford came out in the second half with renewed vigour as the Rangi Chase-inspired Red Devils opened up a ten-point lead. Travis Burns then took exception to standard kick charge pressure from Salford's Tommy Lee, before the Australian proceeded to throw a flurry of punches Lee's way. Tempers boiled over before Burns was eventually sent to the sin bin by referee James Child. Rovers looked lost without their star man from there, as the Reds ran in three more tries, from Theo Fages, Josh Griffin and Greg Johnson, to embarrass the hosts.

St Helens kept their top spot after a 58-16 win at London. Mark Percival bagged his side's first try on the way to a 22-point haul as Saints' pack, led by Alex Walmsley, dominated from start to finish. The highlight of the game was a length-of-the-field effort from the outstanding Sia Soliola.

The game of the round had come on the Thursday night at Headingley as Leeds and Castleford ended all square at 24-all.

It was a great game and will be remembered for the 72nd-minute send-off of Leeds captain Kevin Sinfield, for the first time in his professional career. With Leeds holding a slender six-point lead, the margin never more throughout, they forced a drop-out – the only one of the game. But from the restart, Danny McGuire's pass was spilled by Carl Ablett and within in a flash Andy Lynch had swept up and slipped an offload to the recalled Luke Dorn, whose electrifying running into space had been a feature throughout. Sinfield did well to wrap Dorn up before he hit high gear, with the pair then becoming entangled.

An angry exchange of words took place between the protagonists, but there was no doubting the lead with the head by Sinfield, and that it was deserving of a red card. Sinfield copped a two-match ban the following Tuesday.

With mouths still open and the ground agog, Cas won two more penalties for Justin Carney being pulled back on a Liam Finn kick-chase and then a ball steal by Ablett on Weller Hauraki. On the back of the mounting tide, Lee Jewitt sent in Grant Millington with a perfectly-timed pass. Marc Sneyd, who was back at stand-off, levelled the scores with the conversion.

Bradford celebrate a memorable victory over Wigan

Round 22

Bradford Bulls had slipped out of Super League the week before but produced an astounding 16-8 home win over Wigan - who had beaten them 84-6 on Easter Monday - on the last Sunday of July.

Lee Gaskell completed a week in which he signed a new deal at the club by putting in a superb performance, with his excellent kicking game having a disappointing Wigan defence in knots on several occasions.

It looked more likely there would be a repeat of the Easter Monday riot in the opening exchanges, as Wigan drew first blood with a well-worked try. Matty Bowen's wide pass caught Danny Williams off guard, and Dom Manfredi outpaced Brett Kearney to break the deadlock.

However, with the half-hour mark approaching, Williams grabbed his first try in Bulls colours off the back of a slick handling move, before Joe Arundel danced in under the sticks.

Halfway through the second half Bradford struck a potentially telling blow. After another penalty gifted the Bulls field possession, they pounced when Matty Blythe finished excellently in the corner after some great work from Gaskell and Arundel. Gale missed the kick though, leaving Wigan still in the hunt to get back into the contest. But even though Manfredi scored his and Wigan's second try just six minutes later, the improbable comeback never happened.

The defeat left Wigan four points adrift of leaders St Helens, who had beaten Widnes 42-22 on the Friday, with Tommy Makinson finishing with a hat-trick. But Saints paid a heavy price for their win, losing playmaker Luke Walsh for the season with a broken ankle during a devastating five-minute second-half spell. The Australian maestro had helped his side forge a 32-0 lead after just 45 minutes and Saints seemed set to run up a cricket score.

Widnes, though, had other ideas, running in three tries from Cameron Phelps, two, and Stefan Marsh, who surged 80 metres for a stunning score that closed the gap to just 16 points.

Walsh, whose season had already been punctuated by a series of niggling injuries, was stretchered from the field following an accidental collision, with his dream of taking Saints all the way to the Grand Final in tatters. Jonny Lomax was already out for the rest of the season due to a knee injury suffered in Perpignan in June.

Warrington suffered their second loss in a row as Wakefield shocked them at the Halliwell Jones Stadium by 40-26. James Webster registered his first away victory since taking charge of the Wildcats as they moved within two points of the play-off places, in a fitting response to the previous week's humbling in the south of France. On-loan Chris Riley scored a hat-trick of tries against his parent club as Richie Mathers' try on 73 minutes finally took the game away from the Wolves.

Which meant that Huddersfield's 38-16 home success over Catalans the day before had brought them level on points with Warrington. Danny Brough had a hand in everything the Giants did, his kicking game was superb and he put the Giants on the front foot throughout the game.

Jermaine McGillvary, Kyle Wood and Aaron Murphy tries put the hosts in control before Eloi Pelissier's score made it 14-6 at the break. McGillvary added his second as Joe Wardle grabbed a second-half brace. Morgan Escaré and Michael Oldfield tries made little difference as Brett Ferres ran in the Giants' seventh try.

Victory all but cemented Huddersfield's place in the top six as they move five points clear of the Dragons in seventh place.

A 77th minute try from James Clare salvaged an 18-all draw for Castleford at the KC Stadium after it looked like Hull were heading for their first win in six games. A clinical 12-minute spell from the Tigers ensured they came away with a point for the second week running, after their previous week's draw against Leeds. Hull had been the dominant side for the majority of the game and they led throughout. But Marc Sneyd's try twelve minutes from time gave the Tigers a glimmer of hope and started their resurgence.

Clare, who came into the side to replace the rested Justin Carney, grabbed the first of his brace with five minutes remaining to reduce Castleford's deficit to just four points.

When the winger went over two minutes after his first, it was left to Sneyd to clinch the win. But the halfback, who was a major thorn in his future employee's side all evening, failed with his conversion attempt from the touchline and the spoils were shared.

For Hull, it was another disappointing conclusion to a game that should have been closed out when they went 18-4 up shortly after the start of the second half.

Hull KR obliterated London Broncos 62-10 on a sweltering Saturday in the capital, capitalising on Widnes's defeat on Friday to move back within one point of eighth place. Particularly impressive for Rovers was the combination of playmaking duo Travis Burns and Greg Eden, the latter having returned from two weeks on loan at Gateshead Thunder. Eden was safe under the high ball, ran in a hat-trick of classy tries and had a hand in just as many.

Zak Hardaker scored a try and kicked three conversions, with Kevin Sinfield out suspended, as Leeds beat Salford away by 22-18 to move up to second in the table. After Junior Sa'u's try put the hosts ahead, Leeds responded with quick tries by Hardaker and Kallum Watkins, before Theo Fages made it 12-12 at half-time.

Carl Ablett and Stevie Ward opened up a 10-point lead for Leeds with two tries within eight minutes of the restart. Jordan Walne went over to set up a tense finish, but Leeds held on for 22 scoreless minutes.

FIRST UTILITY SUPER LEAGUE TABLE
Sunday 27th July

	P	W	D	L	F	A	D	PTS
St Helens	22	17	0	5	703	460	243	34
Leeds Rhinos	22	15	2	5	598	303	295	32
Wigan Warriors	22	15	0	7	720	361	359	30
Castleford Tigers	22	14	2	6	676	449	227	30
Warrington Wolves	22	14	0	8	636	421	215	28
Huddersfield Giants	22	13	2	7	642	526	116	28
Catalan Dragons	22	11	1	10	581	583	-2	23
Widnes Vikings	22	10	1	11	507	629	-122	21
Hull Kingston Rovers	22	9	2	11	547	545	2	20
Wakefield T Wildcats	22	9	1	12	441	600	-159	19
Salford Red Devils	22	8	1	13	470	554	-84	17
Hull FC	22	7	2	13	526	483	43	16
Bradford Bulls *	22	5	0	17	382	842	-460	4
London Broncos	22	0	0	22	314	987	-673	0

* Deducted six points for entering administration

AUGUST
Rhinos up for the Cup

Round 23

A dominant second-half performance earned Widnes a vital 28-10 home win over Hull KR in the race for a top-eight place. The Vikings had gone into the game only a point clear of the Robins but a three-point gap had now opened up.

Widnes pivot Kevin Brown was an injury doubt leading up to the game but he proved the key figure yet again. The Vikings led 10-4 at the break, with Jack Owens and Chris Dean touching down either side of Kris Keating's try. Joe Mellor and Brown both went over within five minutes of the restart before Jason Chan pulled one back for Rovers. But Stefan Marsh and Rhys Hanbury both scored, the latter spectacularly on 67 minutes to stretch the Vikings lead to 28-10 and effectively seal the result.

The other challengers for the eighth spot, Wakefield and Salford all lost ground.

The on-form Red Devils' trip to Wigan for the Thursday night TV game was a let down as Anthony Gelling scored his first ever hat-trick for Wigan and Matty Smith collected a personal haul of 17 points as the Warriors bounced back to winning ways in a 45-4 win.

The opening 30 minutes of the first half were evenly matched with just one score – Matty Bowen's finger nail being the difference – but the Red Devils seemed to switch off. Two tries in three minutes from Gelling and Josh Charnley put Wigan 16-0 up at the break.

Gelling's second try after the break put the game out of Salford's reach and when the visitors did manage to score it just provoked the champions as they ran in late tries from Gelling, George Williams, Tony Clubb and Smith to make sure Niall Evalds' reply was scant consolation.

Joel Tomkins came on from the bench for his first game since returning from rugby union.

Wakefield's play-off hopes were dealt a body blow by Huddersfield on the Sunday after they crashed to a first home defeat, by 36-18, under coach James Webster.

The Wildcats never recovered from a dismal first half after which they trailed a rampant Huddersfield 32-0 and, although they produced a revival, they were now four points behind eighth-placed Widnes with four games left. Shaun Lunt's first game back after eight weeks out with injury was a special one. The number 9 scored one try, set up two others and was influential behind a strong forward pack.

Hull FC still had faint play-off hopes after their first win in seven games as they beat the league leaders St Helens 19-12 at the KC Stadium. Richard Horne, who had announced that this season would be his last in a playing capacity at Hull, returned from injury and scored a try that levelled the scores after Tom Makinson had put the visitors in front inside the opening five minutes.

Horne was involved in the build-up to Hull's second try and his organisational play was the difference throughout. Tom Lineham eventually burrowed over to give the home side a 12-4 lead at the interval. The scores were tied once more when Paul Wellens crossed 10-minutes after the restart, scoring a try that saw the fullback surpass 1,000 career points for Saints.

However, Mickey Paea crashed over on the hour to reinstate his side's lead and Joe Westerman kicked a penalty and field goal in the closing stages that sealed a much-needed Hull FC win. It meant St Helens had missed their chance to extend their lead at the top of the table to four points.

Leeds missed their chance to go top on the same Friday night as they were stunned by the Bulls at Headingley. Lee Gaskell scored a try four minutes from time to help the relegated side to a memorable 20-14 derby victory.

Danny Williams ran in the Bulls' first points before Mitch Achurch responded to make it 4-4 at the break. Gamestar Luke Gale and Brett Delaney then traded converted tries before a Gale penalty edged the visitors ahead again, only for Luke Briscoe to grab a Rhinos try before Gaskell's score and Gale's fourth goal sealed victory.

Castleford joined Leeds and Wigan in joint second spot. Justin Carney crashed over for three first-half tries in an ultimately comfortable 64-18 home victory over a gallant Broncos outfit, that led 12-6 after 20 minutes, but was still seeking a first league win in 2014. Carney later copped a two-match ban for a dangerous throw.

Michael Monaghan, returning from injury, was the difference between the two teams as Warrington edged Catalans 26-24 in rain-soaked Perpignan. The game was never safe for the Wolves right up to the final moments and it wasn't until Ben Pomeroy knocked on in the closing seconds as the Catalans looked to launch one last attack that Warrington knew they would be heading home with the two points.

Challenge Cup Semi-Finals

Leeds captain Kevin Sinfield returned from his two-game suspension to steer the Rhinos to the Challenge Cup final after a 24-16 win over Warrington Wolves at Langtree Park, St Helens.

There were enormous stats from Jamie Peacock, while Sinfield's game management was superb and Carl Ablett was everywhere. But the vital cog in the Leeds performance was Danny McGuire, who was scheming throughout, defensively sound and had a hand in three of the Rhinos' four tries.

The Wolves had a bad start. On their second set of six their fullback Matty Russell, running the ball out of defence, charged straight into his teammate Ben Harrison to concede a penalty for obstruction.

Sinfield kicked the two points, and then Stefan Ratchford put the kick-off straight out on the full, conceding a second penalty and giving the Rhinos vital field position.

The Rhinos then subjected Warrington to a constant bombardment, gaining two goal-line drop-outs, right up to the point at which Ablett got almost to the line but was unable to touch down after seven minutes.

The first half carried on with the Wolves making errors and the Rhinos gradually pulling further ahead with two fine tries by Ryan Hall. For the first he got around Joel Monaghan to sneak the ball down just inside the corner flag. His second try came from a beautiful pass by McGuire, who spotted the Wolves' defence moving away from the touchline. Hall took the ball brilliantly, taking the ball above his head.

The Wolves tried valiantly to get back into the game in the second half but they never managed to close the gap to less than eight points. The killer blow came with 13 minutes to go and eight points the margin. Warrington swept the ball wide but Simon Grix spilt it on half way. In a flash Tom Briscoe stepped in and was able to fend off Rhys Evans in cantering to the posts for the vital score.

On the Sunday afternoon at the Leigh Sports Village, Castleford Tigers' 28-6 victory against Widnes Vikings saw them book a date at Wembley for the first time since 1992.

It was a wet and windy afternoon, and the Tigers were in complete control, never really allowing the Vikings a sniff after establishing a 14-0 half-time lead. They were 10-0 up after only eight minutes after tries to Liam Finn and Daryl Clark, who was always a

handful for the Widnes defence. Kirk Dixon's try just after the half-hour mark made it 14-0.

Back-up hooker Jamie Ellis sealed the match in Castleford's favour seven minutes after half-time when he caught the Vikings napping. Marc Sneyd added the conversion to that score and to Jake Webster's try, also kicking a penalty in between. Jack Owens' try and conversion five minutes from time was irrelevant.

The only blot for Cas was an injury to Craig Huby. Huby looked almost certain to miss the Challenge Cup final in two weeks time after suffering a dislocated elbow in the first half.

The match was marred by a small pitch invasion at the end of the game when more than 50 Vikings fans ran on to the field after full-time. Stewards and police struggled to contain the louts, who unsuccessfully tried to incite the Castleford supporters.

Round 24

St Helens took a significant step towards clinching the League Leaders' Shield on the Friday night as their patched-up side eventually wore down dogged Wakefield, winning 40-16.

Shorn of the creative Luke Walsh, Jonny Lomax, Lance Hohaia and Jon Wilkin, who had finally been written off with a shoulder injury he suffered against Salford at the end of May despite playing on until the win in London on 19th July, Saints adapted their playing style, with Jordan Turner operating as their main pivot despite being named at loose forward.

Turner was the standout along with back-rowers Sia Soliola and Louie McCarthy-Scarsbrook, and two-try debutant fullback Shannon McDonnell. Tries to Soliola and McDonnell in the space of five second-half minutes took the game away from the Wildcats.

Saints were three points clear now as Wigan drew 14-all at Hull KR in the Thursday TV game.

Rovers were the best team and dominated for large periods, and it looked like they were heading for a much-needed victory when they led 14-4 after 73 minutes. But the champions showed all their quality by fighting right until the death. When Wigan skipper Sean O'Loughlin crossed with seven minutes left, it gave the visitors a glimmer of hope.

Wigan came close twice more, but Rovers scrambled well and clung on until one final assault from the visitors saw Anthony Gelling carve through the tired Hull KR defence and send Josh Charnley into the corner. Matty Smith could have clinched the win, but his conversion attempt from the right-hand touch-line sailed wide.

For Hull KR, Jason Chan worked overtime, scored a try and set up another four-pointer, and there were tireless efforts from Neville Costigan and Josh Hodgson, who had announced that week he would be joining Canberra Raiders at the end of the season.

Leeds also fell off the pace, as the Rhinos conceded London Broncos' first victory of the season, when they went down 40-36 at The Hive on Sunday.

The Rhinos dominated for the first 60 minutes of the game, and played themselves into what appeared to be an unassailable position just after half-time when they were 30-8 up. But 18-year-old Joe Keyes stepped in to the lead role, steering his team around confidently, executing a skilful, defensive kicking game, and scoring three tries, including

a sensational match winner.

It wasn't quite over. When Kallum Watkins screamed down the right edge after the hooter sounded, it seemed Broncos hearts would be broken. After Watkins held off three defenders over 70 metres and dived over to score, the touch judge raised his flag, deeming the England centre to have stepped into touch during his breathtaking run.

Warrington moved level with the Rhinos after a 48-10 home win over Wembley-bound Castleford Tigers.

Tigers coach Daryl Powell rested many of his top stars, making eight changes and handing first-team debuts to academy products Brad Day and Will Maher. Justin Carney was missing through suspension, while Craig Huby was out with a dislocated elbow.

The Tigers were 18-0 behind after tries from Ryan Atkins, Gareth O'Brien and Chris Bridge but got off the mark just before the break through James Clare and Oliver Holmes tries.

But two tries from Rhys Evans and one each for Anthony England, Stefan Ratchford and Joel Monaghan took the Wolves home.

There were four teams level in third on 32 points - Leeds, Warrington, Castleford and Huddersfield, who registered their fourth victory in a row with a penalty-ridden 28-14 win over Widnes at the John Smith's Stadium. After a tight first half, the Giants closed out the match with three tries in the second period to run away 28-14 victors.

Salford defeated Catalans Dragons 34-22 on the Friday night. Rangi Chase, Kevin Locke and Theo Fages all combined superbly for the home team and their 22-4 lead flattered the Catalans. Tony Puletua's try on the hour mark gave the Devils an unassailable 24-point lead heading into the final quarter.

Bradford had been rejuvenated since their relegation and registered their third straight win, a 34-28 home success over Hull FC. In wet conditions, Jamie Shaul and Gareth Ellis gave the visitors a 12-0 lead, but 28 unanswered points put Bradford, with Lee Gaskell once again outstanding, in control.

Jamie Foster and Joe Arundel went over before half-time, while Adam Sidlow, Arundel and Jay Pitts, another loanee from Hull, crossed after the interval. Ellis scored a second but Danny Addy made it safe for the Bulls, Setaimata Sa and Tom Lineham replying for Hull.

After one win from their last eight games, the Airlie Birds' play-off hopes were shot to pieces.

Challenge Cup Final

Leeds Rhinos avoided their seventh successive Challenge Cup Final defeat since winning the Cup in 1999 by toppling local rivals Castleford Tigers 23-10 with a highly polished performance at Wembley. Coach Brian McDermott admitted there was a 'sense of relief and elation' after they finally ended their 15-year Cup drought.

Two-try Ryan Hall won the Lance Todd Trophy to become the sixth Leeds player to pick up the award, following in the footsteps of current teammate Kevin Sinfield, Gary Connolly, Leroy Rivett, Steve Pitchford and Jeff Stevenson. Hall finished two votes ahead of Danny McGuire in the voting, with Rob Burrow, Sinfield and Zak Hardaker also collecting votes.

Leeds were clinical from the off, taking the lead after just five minutes - a lead they would never surrender throughout the remaining 75 minutes.

Leeds' Ryan Hall mobbed after scoring his first try against Castleford at Wembley

The Tigers were predicted to be affected by the occasion and on their first attack a wide move ended with the ball going to ground. And then Andy Lynch turned the ball over in their second set of the game, and the pendulum was immediately swung in the Rhinos' favour. They made the pressure count, too; after a repeat set on Castleford's line, Hardaker and Kallum Watkins sent Tom Briscoe into the right corner before Sinfield converted superbly.

The Tigers hit back though when Daryl Clark collected Marc Sneyd's clever reverse grubber kick to twist and turn his way over the line. However, Sneyd's relatively easy conversion was missed, leaving the Tigers two points behind.

TETLEY'S CHALLENGE CUP FINAL

Saturday 23rd August 2014

CASTLEFORD TIGERS 10 LEEDS RHINOS 23

TIGERS: 6 Luke Dorn; 2 Kirk Dixon; 4 Jake Webster; 3 Michael Shenton (C); 5 Justin Carney; 7 Marc Sneyd; 26 Liam Finn; 8 Andy Lynch; 14 Daryl Clark; 10 Craig Huby; 16 Oliver Holmes; 12 Weller Hauraki; 13 Nathan Massey. Subs (all used): 18 Frankie Mariano; 19 Scott Wheeldon; 20 Jamie Ellis; 32 Lee Jewitt.
Tries: Clark (12), Holmes (47); **Goals:** Sneyd 0/1, Finn 1/1.
RHINOS: 1 Zak Hardaker; 20 Tom Briscoe; 3 Kallum Watkins; 4 Joel Moon; 5 Ryan Hall; 13 Kevin Sinfield (C); 6 Danny McGuire; 8 Kylie Leuluai; 7 Rob Burrow; 10 Jamie Peacock; 15 Brett Delaney; 12 Carl Ablett; 11 Jamie Jones-Buchanan. Subs (all used): 9 Paul Aiton; 16 Ryan Bailey; 17 Ian Kirke; 21 Liam Sutcliffe.
Tries: T Briscoe (5), McGuire (17), Hall (25, 67);
Goals: Sinfield 3/4; **Field goal:** McGuire (77).
Rugby Leaguer & League Express Men of the Match:
Tigers: Lee Jewitt; *Rhinos:* Danny McGuire.
Penalty count: 2-2; **Half-time:** 4-16; **Referee:** Phil Bentham;
Attendance: 77,914 *(at Wembley Stadium).*

And five minutes later McGuire, on the run, scored a sensational try by claiming Rob Burrow's high kick out of dummy half before Luke Dorn could get off the ground, touching down to stretch Leeds' lead.

Hall's first try came as Burrow's pass from acting-half and McGuire's bullet pass created a one-on-one against Castleford winger Kirk Dixon. Dixon attempted to stop Hall, but it wasn't to be as the Leeds winger himself grabbed hold of Dixon's shirt, leaving the Castleford man struggling as his momentum went backwards. Hall powered over the top of Dixon for what was his 198th career try.

Sneyd was withdrawn for Jamie Ellis, and Cas looked rusty going forward, with the Leeds pack and the Rhinos' kicking game strangling the life out of them. They at least avoided conceding another try before the hooter, but the Rhinos were in complete control at half-time, leading 16-4.

Seven minutes after the turnaround the Tigers grabbed a lifeline as Cas captain Michael Shenton danced around Watkins and tore away, before offloading on the inside to the supporting Oliver Holmes, who raced in under the sticks.

Liam Finn's conversion brought the gap to just six and, with half an hour left, the result was very much in the balance. But Hall turned the momentum of the clash completely on its head with 13 minutes remaining. It was all about Hall's power once more. He had swapped positions with Joel Moon and was effectively the Leeds centre, but, more importantly, it left him facing Finn.

Paul Aiton's wide ball gave Hall the one-on-one on Finn and his brute strength won that battle. He then stepped inside Jake Webster and by the time the covering defence came across he was already on his way to his 199th try.

It was a telling blow. Shenton again came close by tapping through a kick into open field - but the Rhinos scrambled well. And with three minutes left the result was long confirmed, as McGuire put over a field goal, despite suffering a rib injury five minutes earlier.

Round 25

Lance Hohaia's field goal, seven minutes from time, ensured St Helens were guaranteed a top-two finish and, almost certainly, the League Leaders' shield after a 13-12 win at Leeds.

With 18 minutes left to play, and despite having been a man up after the dismissal of Rhinos centre Joel Moon, for a shoulder charge in the 22nd minute on Mark Percival, it seemed unlikely that the visitors would be set for their first silverware for six years.

Still ten points in arrears, the half-time margin, after depleted Leeds, who showed three changes from their Challenge Cup winning 17 but chose to use only two substitutes, had put in a tremendously gutsy display, Saints rallied to avenge a one-point loss in last season's Headingley Carnegie eliminator.

It ensured Nathan Brown's men a double over the Rhinos in 2014. And the turnaround in fortunes was best summed up by Louie McCarthy-Scarsbrook, Jordan Turner and Hohaia, who was back from a month out.

Back-rower McCarthy-Scarsbrook was moved to centre for a period to cover for Percival and was found grasping when Leeds protégé Liam Sutcliffe, starting at scrum-half, stepped him for the hosts' sole try during their rampant first-half dominance.

But LMS always made himself available, running hard, strong and often to lead the revival. And he atoned with a 62nd minute touchdown of his own that was a momentum changer.

Turner, from loose forward, always posed a silky danger but his missed, relatively straightforward conversion to McCarthy-Scarsbrook's try looked costly, only for his brilliant 40/20 soon afterwards to set the position for relentless James Roby's equalising score.

Second-placed Castleford posted an impressive 32-18 victory over a Bulls side that

Wigan's Sean O'Loughlin and John Bateman move in to halt Widnes' Alex Gerrard

went into the contest on the back of three successive wins.

The Tigers had to do it the hard way, with already-relegated Bradford blasting back superbly from 24-6 down at the interval to only six points adrift, on the back of a hat-trick by stand-off Lee Gaskell, before Castleford hooker Daryl Clark settled home nerves with an 80-metre solo score on 64 minutes.

That touchdown, converted by stand-off Marc Sneyd, proved to be pivotal – and there was no way back for the Bulls when, with less than three minutes remaining, the Tigers were awarded a penalty close to the visitors' posts.

Castleford's default position that season would normally be to run the ball. Instead Sneyd went for goal in the knowledge that, at that stage, a 14-point gap would be impossible for Bradford to overhaul.

Widnes Vikings registered a famous 24-10 Friday-night away win over champions Wigan Warriors. Kevin Brown was in sensational form, having a hand in all three tries as Widnes moved a step closer to securing a play-off place.

For the majority of the first half Widnes outclassed Wigan. They could have extended their lead on a number of occasions, but two tries in four minutes from Dom Manfredi and Josh Charnley narrowed the gap to just 14-10 at the break.

It was a strange half because Wigan, who were second best for the best part of half an hour, almost levelled matters as Charnley was held up inches short as the hooter sounded.

There was only one try in the second half, with Patrick Ah Van grabbing his second try. It was the boot of Tickle that did all the damage, with a conversion and two more penalties securing the points against a Warriors team looking out of sorts.

It meant Wigan dropped into third with the Vikings four points clear of Hull KR in eighth.

August

Hull KR, with Chris Chester appointed as head coach on a permanent basis on a three-year contract, were humbled across the city by Hull FC, who ran out 28-0 winners, the first time since October 1957 that Rovers had been held to zero in a derby.

Last season's Albert Goldthorpe Rookie of the Year, Tom Lineham, helped himself to a double, including a length-of-the-field try. Hull were clinical in attack, but it was their impenetrable defence that was the difference, and it was led by the relentless efforts of their skipper Gareth Ellis.

The hosts held a well-deserved 12-0 lead at the interval. Fetuli Talanoa opened the scoring after just 10 minutes, and that advantage was extended when Setaimata Sa crashed over with a quarter of the game gone. Jordan Rankin's penalty goal topped a fine first 40 minutes from Hull.

Rovers tried in vain to get themselves back into contention, but Hull simply weathered a 10-minute spell with some more determined defence after the restart. And when Lineham grabbed his first try, the result was only heading one way. Jordan Thompson stretched the lead when he found his way over, and Lineham's 90-metre interception was the icing on the cake.

Salford's top-eight hopes ended at Wakefield with 'what a waste of money' ringing in their ears behind their own posts as loanee Tim Smith, starring for the Wildcats, tormented his parent club in a 42-6 home win.

Smith was allowed to feature against his own club, and made them pay for their decision with a hand in five tries as the Wildcats completely out-enthused and out-played the Red Devils. Wakefield were now level with Hull KR.

In Perpignan, Morgan Escaré's first-half hat-trick demolished London's hopes of back-to-back wins and a 46-6 scoreline gave a glimpse of the Dragons' potential play-off strength.

The Broncos arrived in the south of France buoyant after their first win of the season. But unfortunately for London, the conditions did not help them. The home side made the most of a trailing wind, as well as humid conditions that caused London's Mike McMeeken to leave the field in the second half with heat exhaustion.

The game of the round was the Thursday night TV game at the Halliwell Jones Stadium, with the Wolves and Giants ending all square at 24-all.

The Giants looked in complete control when leading 23-6, largely thanks to an imperious performance from Danny Brough, before Warrington ran in 18 unanswered points to take the lead, with Brough's late field goal earning Huddersfield a share of the spoils.

It was a night of individual accolades for Brough. As well as passing Iestyn Harris's points tally in Super League to move up to eighth on the all-time points scorers list, he also opened up a commanding lead in the Albert Goldthorpe Medal table with just two rounds remaining. Brough was already the only man in the history of the award to win it twice.

FIRST UTILITY SUPER LEAGUE TABLE
Sunday 31st August

	P	W	D	L	F	A	D	PTS
St Helens	25	19	0	6	768	507	261	38
Castleford Tigers	25	16	2	7	782	533	249	34
Wigan Warriors	25	16	1	8	789	403	386	33
Warrington Wolves	25	16	1	8	734	479	255	33
Huddersfield Giants	25	15	3	7	730	582	148	33
Leeds Rhinos	25	15	2	8	660	376	284	32
Catalan Dragons	25	12	1	12	673	647	26	25
Widnes Vikings	25	12	1	12	573	677	-104	25
Hull Kingston Rovers	25	9	3	13	571	615	-44	21
Wakefield T Wildcats	25	10	1	14	517	682	-165	21
Hull FC	25	9	2	14	601	529	72	20
Salford Red Devils	25	9	1	15	514	663	-149	19
Bradford Bulls *	25	7	0	18	454	916	-462	8
London Broncos	25	1	0	24	376	1133	-757	2

* Deducted six points for entering administration

SEPTEMBER
Vikings make the cut

Round 26

Widnes Vikings secured their first ever place in the Super League play-offs by putting on a second-half masterclass to defeat already-relegated Bradford at Odsal by 32-12.

The final score looked anything but possible as the game reached half-time. Bradford had built up a strong position, despite a blistering start by the visitors, rallying to lead 12-8 at the break. But in the second half the Vikings scored 24 unanswered points to blow away the Bulls. Centre Stefan Marsh collected three tries, his third on 69 minutes sealing the result.

Catalans Dragons also secured their place in the play-offs, and ended any hope of Hull KR making the final eight, after running out convincing 32-14 winners at the KC Lightstream Stadium. Michael Oldfield claimed a hat-trick and Sam Williams bagged a brace.

The Dragons held a slender 12-10 lead at the interval, courtesy of an Oldfield double that was sandwiched in-between Liam Salter's opener and 18-year-old debutant Macauley Hallett's try. Jason Chan put the home side in front when he crossed shortly after the restart, but Williams' first reinstalled the visitors' lead.

The game was in the balance until a ruthless final spell saw the Dragons cross three times through Oldfield's third, Williams' second and a customary try from Morgan Escaré.

The League Leaders trophy, the destiny of which seemed a formality a week earlier, was back in the melting pot after Warrington Wolves gave their best performance of the season when they beat St Helens 39-12 at Langtree Park in the Thursday night TV game.

And on the back of the Wolves' forward domination, halves Richie Myler and Gareth O'Brien, plus outstanding fullback Matty Russell, had a field day.

Joel Monaghan crossed twice for the visitors to bring up his century of tries in the competition, though victory came at a price for Tony Smith's side as they lost Simon Grix to a broken ankle and Ben Westwood with a torn calf.

Castleford had to win on the Sunday to be the only side who could overtake St Helens and they did, beating Wakefield at home by 26-22. Wakefield recovered from 26-10 adrift early in the final quarter to pull within just four points and it was only a magnificent rearguard effort by the Tigers that saved it.

The Tigers stormed into a 22-0 lead just after the hour mark but Ali Lauitiiti inspired a remarkable fightback for the visitors. Lee Gilmour and Richard Owen, both playing on loan from Castleford, scored tries against their parent club to help set up a tense finish before the Tigers were able to finally complete a third win of the season over their near neighbours.

Danny Brough retained his hold on the Albert Goldthorpe Medal, with one round of Super League fixtures still remaining. Brough, who won the Albert Goldthorpe Medal in 2008 and 2013, and was the reigning Man of Steel, clinched the Medal when he was awarded three points for his performance in the Giants' 38-28 victory against Hull FC at

the John Smith's Stadium.

Hull led 18-4 after a lacklustre opening half-hour from Huddersfield, and were still two scores ahead before a spell of four tries in 13 second-half minutes, inspired by Brough, helped see the Giants home, in Luke Robinson's 350th career game.

Salford, with try hat-tricks to Josh Griffin and Greg Johnson blew away London Broncos 58-26.

On the Friday night, Wigan sent Leeds Rhinos crashing to their fourth consecutive Super League defeat at the DW Stadium in front of Super League's biggest crowd of the season.

The defending champions led 14-0 at the break after frustrating the Rhinos in defence and showing more enthusiasm in attack as they look to kick on and defend their Super League title.

Joe Burgess grabbed the opening try on his return from injury, while a gift of a score for Matty Smith put them 12-0 in front before the scrum-half added a penalty on the hooter to take the champions to half-time 14-0 ahead.

Leeds hit back straight after the break with a try to Liam Sutcliffe that put them well and truly back in the contest. But Wigan defended well in the second half and eventually sealed victory in the last ten minutes.

Rhinos fullback Zak Hardaker went into the match under a cloud after a second accusation of homophobic abuse surfaced in the wake of the club's defeat to St Helens. Hardaker, who was banned for five matches for the use of homophobic language in June, allegedly blew a kiss and made a comment towards Saints player Mark Flanagan during that game.

The RFL had employed the services of a lip reader to attempt to determine exactly what was said. The Rhinos released a statement on the issue, in which chief executive Gary Hetherington described the situation as: 'a witch-hunt by the RFL towards Zak Hardaker'.

The investigation against Hardaker was dropped two weeks later. However Hetherington was subsequently charged with improper conduct and fined by the RFL for his comments.

Round 27

St Helens finally won the League Leaders' Shield on the last Saturday of the regular season, despite losing their last game 24 hours earlier.

On the Friday night, Saints lost 17-16 to the Giants at the John Smith's Stadium, but, the day after, their only possible challengers to the top spot, Castleford Tigers, went down 28-6 to the Catalans Dragons in Perpignan.

Forced to go into the Giants' vital season finale without talismanic stand-off Danny Brough, Huddersfield coach Paul Anderson opted to switch Jake Connor, the 19-year-old former Siddal junior, from fullback to stand-off. The Academy international repaid his coach's faith with an outstanding performance that paved the road to success in a bruising encounter, which the visitors had begun to boss until the sending off of Alex Walmsley just prior to the half-hour mark, with Saints leading 10-0 at the time through Tommy Makinson and James Roby tries. Walmsley went in late and high on Luke Robinson, and was promptly shown a straight red card, getting a one-match suspension the following Tuesday.

Leroy Cudjoe's late field goal secured Huddersfield a fourth-placed finish after tries from Connor, Shaun Lunt and Cudjoe put the home side 16-10 in front, only for Lance Hohaia's try on 60 minutes to level it.

Saints would play the Tigers at Langtree Park in the qualifying play-off, with Wigan hosting Huddersfield, themselves on a seven-match undefeated run dating back to 11 July, at the DW Stadium.

Richard Horne brought down the curtain on his career after Hull FC's victory over Leeds

Wigan had secured second spot with a grinding 24-20 home win over Warrington in the Thursday TV game. The reigning champions produced a brilliant second-half comeback to wipe out an 18-4 half-time deficit. Two tries from Joel Monaghan and one from Richie Myler, all converted by Stefan Ratchford, put the Wolves in charge. But a Josh Charnley double and tries from Joe Burgess and Blake Green earned Wigan a thrilling victory.

In Perpignan, a first-half double from Morgan Escaré helped Catalans Dragons deny Castleford, who looked drained by the heat, a first top-of-the-table finish in their history with a resounding 28-6 triumph.

Tigers fans travelled in numbers, determined to see their team end their remarkable regular season with a win. But the Dragons had other intentions, looking to head into the play-offs on the back of three consecutive victories.

Richard Horne brought down the curtain on his 16-year career on the Friday night at the KC Stadium, having played over 350 games for Hull FC after making his debut as a fresh faced 16-year-old in 1999.

And the 32-year-old, who was to take up a role on the under-19s and first-team coaching staff at Hull, got a rousing reception from the Hull fans after playing a key role in their 24-19 victory over Leeds.

The Airlie Birds scored 20 unanswered points in the final quarter after the visitors looked to be cruising with a 19-4 lead.

Tom Lineham's try had seemed set to give the hosts a first-half-lead but Carl Ablett's score, along with Kevin Sinfield's conversation and field goal, gave Leeds a 7-4 interval advantage. Danny McGuire and Ryan Hall went over after the break as the Rhinos looked in control with a 15-point lead.

Gareth Ellis started the fight back with his try on the hour. Fetuli Talanoa crossed shortly after, and that was followed by a late brace from 19-year-old centre Jack Logan, whose double sealed an unlikely victory. It was a fifth straight league defeat for the Rhinos.

September

Salford ended a campaign that had fallen well below expectations on a relative high, with an accomplished 36-6 home win over a Widnes side resting a host of key figures ahead of the play-offs.

Vikings coach Denis Betts chose to leave out Kevin Brown, Rhys Hanbury, Jon Clarke and Danny Tickle among others. Rangi Chase scored one try and created three others, Junior Sa'u was a constant menace out wide and scored twice himself, while Kevin Locke showed more flashes of brilliance that hinted at a brighter future ahead for the Red Devils.

Hull Kingston Rovers finished their season in style in ninth position with a one-sided 42-18 victory at Wakefield, after leading 36-0 four minutes into the second half.

Omari Caro had a memorable final game for the club, bagging a hat-trick of tries, as did fullback Greg Eden, who scored two and set up a third ahead of an anticipated switch to Brisbane Broncos in the NRL.

In the last-weekend battle of the two relegated sides, Bradford beat London away 46-36. With 25 minutes to play, the hosts were in a winning position at 30-16. But an all-in brawl reignited the Bulls' fire and spurred them on to victory as former Harlequins man Luke Gale tormented his old club, scoring four tries. Gale's fourth try of the match, three minutes from time, proved decisive.

Off the field, news broke that former head coach Francis Cummins was suing the Bulls for wrongful dismissal following his sacking on 16th June. Cummins had had signed a three-year contract following his appointment in September 2012 and had been unable to get a compensation agreement with the club.

FIRST UTILITY SUPER LEAGUE - FINAL TABLE
Sunday 14th September

	P	W	D	L	F	A	D	PTS
St Helens	27	19	0	8	796	563	233	38
Wigan Warriors	27	18	1	8	834	429	405	37
Huddersfield Giants	27	17	3	7	785	626	159	37
Castleford Tigers	27	17	2	8	814	583	231	36
Warrington Wolves	27	17	1	9	793	515	278	35
Leeds Rhinos	27	15	2	10	685	421	264	32
Catalan Dragons	27	14	1	12	733	667	66	29
Widnes Vikings	27	13	1	13	611	725	-114	27
Hull Kingston Rovers	27	10	3	14	627	665	-38	23
Salford Red Devils	27	11	1	15	608	695	-87	23
Hull FC	27	10	2	15	653	586	67	22
Wakefield T Wildcats	27	10	1	16	557	750	-193	21
Bradford Bulls *	27	8	0	19	512	984	-472	10
London Broncos	27	1	0	26	438	1237	-799	2

* Deducted six points for entering administration

SUPER LEAGUE PLAY-OFFS
Saints on high

Week One - Qualifying Play-offs

WIGAN WARRIORS 57 HUDDERSFIELD GIANTS 4

Champions Wigan completely outclassed Huddersfield Giants in a 10-try demolition.

The Warriors laid siege on the Giants line in the opening quarter, but they only had a Matty Smith penalty to show for their efforts until two tries in as many minutes rewarded Wigan for their constant pressure.

Josh Charnley claimed the first following a great cut-out ball from Matty Bowen; then Smith added another in their next set to put the hosts 12-0 ahead. Further scores from Tony Clubb and Liam Farrell before the break saw the Warriors hold a comfortable lead of 24-0 at half-time.

The Giants did manage to get on the score sheet two minutes after the break with Leroy Cudjoe going over, but three tries in the space of seven minutes, from Joel Tomkins, his first since his return to the club, Dan Sarginson and Bowen put the Warriors well clear.

Wigan refused to see out the game conservatively, with further tries for Charnley, Sean O'Loughlin and Joe Burgess, Smith potting a field goal in the last seconds.

ST HELENS 41 CASTLEFORD TIGERS 0

James Roby inspired St Helens to an emphatic victory against the Tigers.

The platform was laid in a ruthless first 40 minutes by the Saints. The opening score was a classic Roby try as he stepped out of dummy-half before crashing over from close range to nudge Saints in front. Saints' kicking game was at its best in the opening half hour - despite the absences of Jonny Lomax, Jon Wilkin and Luke Walsh. It paid dividends on 25 minutes, with Roby dancing in for his second of the night.

At the half-time hooter, Jordan Turner - who had enjoyed an excellent first 40 minutes - kicked over a field goal to make it 13-0.

Within just six minutes of the restart, Roby's clever pass sent Turner through a huge gap for another try. And just before the hour mark a stray pass from Liam Finn could only find the opposition, and Adam Swift picked up superbly before racing home from 70 metres out. Mark Percival converted his fourth goal of the evening and, at 25-0, that was it.

Tommy Makinson, Kyle Amor and Mose Masoe added more tries after Cas skipper Michael Shenton was sin-binned for obstruction.

Week One - Elimination Play-offs

WARRINGTON WOLVES 22 WIDNES VIKINGS 19

Joel Monaghan's hat-trick helped Warrington recover from an 18-point deficit in a thrilling play-off derby at the Halliwell Jones Stadium on the Saturday.

The key performer was right centre Chris Bridge, who provided the final pass for all three Joel Monaghan tries, and was a constant source of danger. Kevin Brown inspired Widnes to their commanding 18-0 lead, and they were still leading 19-6 at half-time. Widnes crossed twice in the opening nine minutes in near identical circumstances.

Twice Brown kicked neatly behind Rhys Evans, where Paddy Flynn touched down after lengthy video referee analysis on both occasions. Danny Tickle kicked two difficult conversions for an early and unexpected 12-0 lead.

Tickle missed a kickable penalty following Bridge's high tackle on Danny Galea. But, in the ensuing set of six, Rhys Hanbury escaped Richie Myler's tackle and then stepped past Matt Russell for a terrific individual try.

Bridge sent Joel Monaghan over for his first. Stefan Ratchford converted from out wide, only for Brown to extend the lead to 13 points with a field goal just before the hooter.

But the Wolves scored twice more in the opening eight minutes of the second half through Monaghan's second and Rhys Evans to narrow the gap to three points.

By the hour mark Warrington were ahead for the first time courtesy of some Bridge magic. The centre took Ben Currie's offload, beat both Stefan Marsh and Patrick Ah Van, and put Monaghan away for a hat-trick try that Ratchford converted for 22-19.

There was some late drama, including a bad facial injury to Russell after a tackle from MacGraff Leuluai. Russell was rushed straight to hospital. Luckily the only damage was lost teeth.

LEEDS RHINOS 20 CATALAN DRAGONS 24

Halfback Sam Williams snatched a dramatic late try on the Saturday evening as Catalans Dragons earned their first ever win at Headingley.

Winger Tom Briscoe's misfortune determined the outcome, as he spilled a Kevin Sinfield pass out of dummy half on his own line as the clock wound down, allowing Canberra-bound Williams to pounce and Thomas Bosc to convert.

Carl Ablett went over for the Rhinos before Williams grabbed his first try. Benjamin Garcia's superb pass to put Mounis into the clear, and he found Williams for a fine score.

A converted Kallum Watkins try - the centre and Briscoe twice hacking on after Morgan Escaré inexplicably lost the ball - and Zak Hardaker's earlier penalty put the Challenge Cup holders 14-6 up at the break. But second-half tries from Zeb Taia and Louis Anderson had the Dragons ahead 18-14.

It appeared the Dragons had cracked with 13 minutes left, when Vincent Duport lost possession 25 metres out from his own line with his side clinging to that four-point lead after a fine third quarter.

On the back of it – and Leeds' best passage of inter-play – Jamie Jones-Buchanan romped over, Sinfield – who had supplied the money ball at the end of the glorious ten-man move – converting to make it 20-18. The Rhinos looked home and hosed, until Briscoe's blooper.

Week Two - Preliminary Semi-Finals

CASTLEFORD TIGERS 14 WARRINGTON WOLVES 30

Stefan Ratchford celebrated a new four-year contract by giving a man-of-the-match performance in the Wolves' hard-fought win at Castleford on the Thursday night, leaving them 80 minutes away from a third consecutive Old Trafford appearance.

Warrington players wore black armbands in homage to former player Greg Mackey, who died of cancer that week. Lacking Ben Westwood, Simon Grix and Matty Russell through injury, the Wolves led 10-4 at the break, Ryan Atkins and Joel Monaghan grabbing tries either side of Jamie Ellis's for Cas.

After a Ratchford penalty goal, Luke Dorn gave the Tigers hope with a second-half try before a stunning try sparked by Ratchford, who burst through from his own half, feeding the supporting Richie Myler out of the tackle, sunk the Tigers. Myler, in turn, found fellow halfback Gareth O'Brien on his shoulder for a great try.

Rhys Evans went over for the Wolves and Joel Monaghan scored a second to complete the win before Michael Shenton crossed for a late consolation.

Ratchford also kicked five goals, including two penalties, as Castleford finished strongly, their supporters giving them a rousing send-off.

HUDDERSFIELD GIANTS 16 CATALAN DRAGONS 18

On the Friday night the Giants, despite the return of captain Danny Brough, were the second play-off victims of the never-say-die Dragons.

One half of the John Smith's Stadium was plunged into darkness following a power cut, putting the game into serious doubt until 20 minutes before kick-off. Catalans' travel commitments and the TV broadcasters' needs meant the match started under just two working floodlights and the main stand was closed.

Thomas Bosc's conversion of Ben Pomeroy's 70th minute try settled a close contest, with Brough spearheading a much improved Giants showing.

The two sides were level 10-10 at half-time, Jodie Broughton and Aaron Murphy tries countered by Catalans' Daryl Millard and Michael Oldfield.

Brough's measured grubber saw Luke Robinson ground millimetres before the dead ball line for what looked like the crucial try, until Pomeroy's effort, after Elliott Whitehead had palmed on a high kick to the corner, sealed the win. Bosc was faced with a tough conversion but the French international showed nerves of steel to slot the goal.

St Helens selected Catalans in the 'ClubCall', with Warrington set to visit to holders Wigan.

Week Three - Qualifying Semi-Finals

ST HELENS 30 CATALAN DRAGONS 12

St Helens won their way back to Old Trafford for the first time in three years, aiming to end their eight-year wait for another Super League trophy.

The League Leaders' Shield winners fell behind early to a Dragons try, but St Helens then crossed for five unanswered tries to knock out the gutsy French side

Catalans drew first blood in the 21st minute, Morgan Escaré scrambling over after what appeared to be a forward pass from Thomas Bosc.

With the scores tied at 6-6 after Jordan Turner's barge-over try, St Helens went ahead at a pivotal time three minutes before half-time when Adam Swift raced 40 metres past a clearly unfit Escaré.

Seven minutes after the break, Willie Manu was the final beneficiary of a flowing 55-metre move before Escaré went off with a hip injury, and with him went Catalan's hopes.

Mose Masoe carried several Dragons players on his back for a fine try and Mark Percival rounded things off, going straight up the middle and beating three defenders to touch down.

The exhausted Catalans, after three weeks of play-off travel, did not lie down in the final 17 minutes, with Michael Oldfield scoring a consolation try.

The next day, St Helens coach Nathan Brown announced he would be leaving the club at the end of the season and returning home to Australia for family reasons.

WIGAN WARRIORS 16 WARRINGTON WOLVES 12

A Joe Burgess try with just over 60 seconds of the game remaining saw Wigan make it back-to-back Super League Grand Finals after a tough, hard semi-final.

The Warriors dominated the opening 25 minutes and camped out on Warrington's line, but only had a Joel Tomkins try, off a Blake Green break and two Matty Smith goals to show for their efforts.

The last 15 minutes of the half belonged to the Wolves. As tempers started to get heated, they were the ones who kept their cool and Joel Monaghan went over before the interval after Richie Myler's pass had accidentally bounced forward off James Laithwaite's head.

Warrington took a 10-8 lead six minutes into the second half when Gareth O'Brien followed up his own hopeful high kick that Matty Bowen allowed to bounce.

An unconverted one-handed score from Anthony Gelling put the Warriors back in front before a Stefan Ratchford penalty made it 12-12.

Matty Smith, twice, Gareth O'Brien and Myler all missed field goals and the game was heading into golden-point extra time until Sean O'Loughlin used all his experience to keep cool on the blindside to send Burgess over for the winner.

Super League Grand Final

St Helens ended a five-match losing run at Old Trafford to lift the Super League trophy for the first time since 2006 in one of the most dramatic Grand Finals.

After 90 explosive seconds of the 2014 decider, the destiny of the game had been decided. Within minutes, Wigan prop Ben Flower was trending on Twitter after he punched Lance Hohaia and followed that up with another punch as the Saints halfback lay on the ground. Referee Phil Bentham had absolutely no option but to send the Wales prop from the field, with Hohaia being led into the changing rooms shortly after for a concussion check. The Kiwi returned to the bench before half-time, but he never returned to the field of play.

FIRST UTILITY SUPER LEAGUE GRAND FINAL

Saturday 11th October 2014

ST HELENS 14 WIGAN WARRIORS 6

SAINTS: 17 Paul Wellens (C); 2 Tom Makinson; 22 Mark Percival; 4 Josh Jones; 5 Adam Swift; 15 Mark Flanagan; 6 Lance Hohaia; 16 Kyle Amor; 9 James Roby; 8 Mose Masoe; 10 Louie McCarthy-Scarsbrook; 11 Iosia Soliola; 3 Jordan Turner. Subs (all used): 28 Luke Thompson; 13 Willie Manu; 18 Alex Walmsley; 27 Greg Richards.
Tries: Soliola (54), Makinson (69); **Goals:** Percival 3/3.
WARRIORS: 1 Matt Bowen; 2 Josh Charnley; 5 Anthony Gelling; 23 Dan Sarginson; 32 Joe Burgess; 6 Blake Green; 7 Matty Smith; 10 Ben Flower; 19 Sam Powell; 17 Dominic Crosby; 11 Joel Tomkins; 12 Liam Farrell; 13 Sean O'Loughlin (C). Subs (all used): 22 Eddy Pettybourne; 24 Tony Clubb; 25 John Bateman; 27 George Williams.
Try: Burgess (40); **Goals:** Smith 1/3.
Dismissal: Flower (2) - punching Hohaia.
Rugby Leaguer & League Express Men of the Match:
Saints: James Roby; *Warriors:* Liam Farrell.
Penalty count: 9-7; **Half-time:** 2-6; **Referee:** Phil Bentham; **Attendance:** 70,102 *(at Old Trafford, Manchester).*

Flower's place in the Hall of Shame was assured as the first man ever to be sent off in a Super League Grand Final. There was some provocation. He pushed Hohaia in the back chasing a kick and Hohaia flew at him with his forearms after Flower had knocked on trying to pick the ball up. The Saints man took an early guilty plea for a one-match ban. Flower was suspended for six months.

Flower's send off meant that Wigan, defending their title and hot pre-match favourites, played just about the whole game with 12 men. But it also meant that St Helens were deprived of their one halfback still standing. The fact that St Helens had reached the Grand Final was an achievement.

Luke Walsh (who broke his leg and damaged ankle ligaments in the 44-22 win at Widnes in July), Jonny Lomax (knee injury sustained at Catalans in June) and Jon Wilkin

St Helens' Tom Makinson celebrates scoring a crucial try against Wigan in the Grand Final

(dislocated shoulder suffered in May) had all been missing for weeks. Fullback Shannon McDonnell, a late-season draft, was also out with a broken jaw.

The result was, despite the one-man advantage, Saints' attack stuttered and stumbled through most of the match, and Wigan led 6-2 at half-time thanks to a Joe Burgess try just before the hooter.

James Roby was named Harry Sunderland Trophy winner as the man of the match after a huge effort over 80 minutes and played a big part in a more composed final 30 minutes that won the game.

Roby was run close by captain Paul Wellens, winger Tommy Makinson and their departing forward Sia Soliola. Soliola brought Saints back into the game when he forced his way over from a Roby pass after 53 minutes.

Super League Play-offs

Four minutes later Makinson pulled off an extraordinary try-saving tackle on Liam Farrell when the Wigan star looked certain to score after he had turned Makinson inside out.

And a few minutes later Makinson jumped to take a superb Wellens bomb, beating Matty Bowen and Matty Smith to the ball, and touched it down amid scenes of great joy among the Saints fans behind the posts.

Wigan had also suffered an injury blow with Michael McIlorum ruled out with a facial injury suffered in the Qualifying Semi-final win over Warrington. George Williams, not named in the 19-man squad in midweek, came onto the bench as Sam Powell moved up to the starting dummy-half spot.

Old Trafford was a sea of red and white as Mark Percival kicked off on a dry crisp night. Dom Crosby returned the ball and was smashed by Soliola and Kyle Amor, but on the next tackle Mose Masoe came over the top on Anthony Gelling and gave away a penalty.

Two minutes after Flower found his place in history and Hohaia had exited, we were given an indication that Saints' lack of creativity would prevent them taking advantage of the numbers.

Jordan Turner's raking kick was knocked on cold by Matt Bowen to give them position. They had a 'four on two' to the left of the Wigan red zone but stand-in halfback Mark Flanagan chose to grubber to the posts and in the scramble the ball was collected by Wigan.

Three times, stand-in centre Louie McCarthy-Scarsbrook was forced to the touchline and hurried passes went to ground. The closest Saints got was when Masoe and the highly impressive teenager Luke Thompson had tilts for the line, and when the video referee was employed to check whether Josh Jones had his back in touch when he tried to pass infield. He had.

Wigan's attack looked much the slicker, with the usual suspects of Matty Smith, Blake Green and Sean O'Loughlin creating overlaps, and Gelling getting Charnley away down the right with a beautiful one-handed drop pass. Liam Farrell was running his blood to water.

Smith gave them a 2-0 lead after 14 minutes with a penalty goal from 25 metres out after Adam Swift's great kick return ended with him running too close to McCarthy-Scarsbrook and an obstruction was ruled.

Smith got Gelling away down the right and a Green break and offload to O'Loughlin confirmed Wigan had the attacking advantage. Percival dropped Smith's bomb backwards but managed to regather. Wellens' kick on halfway went straight into touch and then Jones ran behind Makinson to concede another penalty

When, on 29 minutes, Green held on too long to the legs of James Roby 12 metres out, it was a gift St Helens couldn't turn down, and Percival obliged with the penalty goal to level at 2-2.

Roby was injecting himself more and more into the game but it was Wigan who would go into half-time in the lead. After Jones went close for the first video ruling, McCarthy-Scarsbrook was penalised for a ball steal on O'Loughlin and then Wigan won a scrum near Saints' line.

With 19 seconds left on the clock, Burgess was sent clear into the left corner, Green supplying the money ball after evading Wellens. Crucially, Smith missed the goal.

St Helens need more composure to win the game, and though they continued to misfire after the break, they eventually found it, though not around the edges.

Sub Eddie Pettybourne knocked on in Wellens' tackle 22 metres out. Turner's pass went behind the runners on the left but Saints retained possession. On the fourth tackle Roby, within sight of the line, ran right and his pass to Soliola sent the increasingly influential Kiwi crashing through Williams' tackle, the try given the green light by the video referee. Percival's goal from the right of the sticks gave his side a precious 8-6 lead.

Wigan almost retook the lead within two minutes after a Turner bomb was defused by Burgess. O'Loughlin put Farrell through the left channel from halfway and the back-rower turned Makinson inside out as he looked a scorer. But Makinson got back to make the try- and possibly game-saving tackle. Wigan moved the ball right and should have scored, but John Bateman could not collect Bowen's offload on the line.

Smith had a chance to level after Wigan had kept the ball alive after a Crosby offload. Charnley was held down by Jones 10 metres out but Smith hooked the kick left of posts.

Six minutes later, Makinson made the game safe for Saints when he rose to collect Wellens' crossfield bomb and rolled over in the tackle of Smith and Bowen by the post protector for the definitive try. An easy conversion for Percival made the gap eight points.

Wigan had a good go at chipping away the lead, but Saints' excellent defence, which had earned their passage to the Grand Final wasn't going to break again.

SUPER LEAGUE XIX AWARDS

STEVE PRESCOTT
MAN OF STEEL
Daryl Clark
(Castleford Tigers)

YOUNG PLAYER OF THE YEAR
Daryl Clark (Castleford Tigers)

COACH OF THE YEAR
Daryl Powell (Castleford Tigers)

CLUB OF THE YEAR
Widnes Vikings

TOP TRY SCORER
Joel Monaghan (Warrington Wolves)
for scoring 28 regular season tries

TOP METRE MAKER
Matthew Russell (Warrington Wolves)
for making 3,546 regular season metres

TOP TACKLER
James Roby (St Helens)
for making 1,054 regular season tackles

MIKE GREGORY SPIRIT OF RUGBY LEAGUE AWARD
Terry Flanagan (Rugby League Cares)

SUPER LEAGUE DREAM TEAM
(previous appearances in italics)
1 Zak Hardaker (Leeds Rhinos) *Debut*
2 Ryan Hall (Leeds Rhinos) *2009, 2010, 2012*
3 Michael Shenton (Castleford Tigers) *Debut*
4 Kallum Watkins (Leeds Rhinos) *Debut*
5 Tom Makinson (St Helens) *Debut*
6 Kevin Brown (Widnes Vikings) *Debut*
7 Matty Smith (Wigan Warriors) *2013*
8 Jamie Peacock (Leeds Rhinos)
2000, 2001, 2002, 2003, 2005, 2007, 2008, 2009, 2013
9 Daryl Clark (Castleford Tigers) *Debut*
10 Chris Hill (Warrington Wolves) *2012*
11 Elliott Whitehead (Catalan Dragons) *Debut*
12 Carl Ablett (Leeds Rhinos) *Debut*
13 Sean O'Loughlin (Wigan Warriors)
2010, 2011, 2012, 2013

ALBERT GOLDTHORPE
MEDAL
Danny Brough
(Huddersfield Giants)

ALBERT GOLDTHORPE
ROOKIE OF THE YEAR
Joe Burgess
(Wigan Warriors)

2
CHAMPIONSHIPS 2014

CHAMPIONSHIP SEASON
Year of the Centurion

LEIGH CENTURIONS dominated the Kingstone Press Championship from the first kick-off to the Grand Final hooter, earning a host of accolades and admirers along the way.

Paul Rowley's side came within one match of the perfect Championship campaign, with their 24-16 mid-July loss at Doncaster the only blemish on an otherwise impeccable record.

They also shook eventual Challenge Cup winners Leeds Rhinos to their boots in the quarter-finals, and were level with the Super League giants going into the final stages of an absorbing quarter-final clash at Headingley.

It all added up to what was statistically the most successful season in the club's long history, and which culminated in a Grand Final win against Featherstone that showcased both the attacking flair and steely grit that characterised a year to remember.

Honours and awards were plentiful. Stand-off Martyn Ridyard was crowned Championship Player of the Year, while his halfback partner Ryan Brierley saw his 43 tries in all competitions rewarded with a second consecutive Young Player prize.

The pair were joined in the Championship All Stars team by a remarkable total of six teammates - Tom Armstrong, Liam Kay, Jacob Emmett, Bob Beswick, Matt Sarsfield and Sam Barlow. The likes of Tommy Goulden, Sean Penkywicz and Tom Spencer could also have been in - virtually the entire squad made an impression at some point.

Perhaps the only surprise was that Rowley missed out on the Coach of the Year to Paul Cooke - but he can still look back with fondness on overseeing what was a remarkable season for his hometown club.

FEATHERSTONE ROVERS eventually fought their way to second place in the table and the Grand Final after a far from straight forward year.

The club would undoubtedly have settled for both midway through the campaign when a change of coach and murmurs of financial uncertainty disrupted what had promised to be a big season at the Big Fellas Stadium.

It started with John Bastian in charge following Daryl Powell's exit to Castleford, and included a host of new faces as Rovers looked to move towards a new era.

But although Featherstone were rarely out of the top two, Bastian had left by early May and was replaced by Andy Hay. The former Castleford and Leeds back-rower had to contend with on-going off-field issues and a host of serious injuries, but a late-season win at Halifax in what was dubbed the "quarter of a million pound match" helped them eventually secure second, despite an ensuing home loss to Sheffield and major scare against Keighley.

They then found their best form of the season in accounting for Fax and the Eagles in the play-offs, only to fall short in the Grand Final against Leigh despite playing their part in an entertaining game.

Winger Will Sharp - who ended the season at fullback - was their only representative in the All Stars team after finishing as top try scorer, with Greg Worthington, James Mendeika, Jason Crookes, Ian Hardman and Andy Kain also reaching double figures.

Steve Crossley, Andy Ellis and Gareth Moore also had their moments, but arguably the most promising factor of the season was the emergence of youngsters like Shaun Pick and Luke Teasdale, and the continued development of Jack Bussey. *continued on page 97*

St Helens were hardly dark horses for the Super League title at the beginning of 2014 and they started like a whirlwind, not dropping a single league point until round nine in mid-April.

New halfback Luke Walsh was key to the hot start, but he suffered some niggling injuries until his season was finally ended when he broke his leg at Widnes in July. Which was a big problem for coach Nathan Brown, with Walsh's replacements at scrum-half, Jonny Lomax and Jon Wilkin already ruled out for the rest of the season.

Incredibly, Saints went on to win both the League Leaders trophy and the Super League title.

Brown had talked many times during the year about trying to re-establish the winning culture that had brought so much success to St Helens. He mentioned the names that refused to contemplate not winning.

One of those names was that of Paul Wellens, whose leadership whether at fullback or in the middle of the park had seen Saints through many a close scrape.

After making his first-team debut in 1998, Wellens passed the 500-career-game mark in 2014 and made a record-equalling 10th Grand Final appearance in St Helens' 14-6 win over Wigan.

His club roll of honour now includes five Super League Championship rings and five Challenge Cup winners medals, the Man of Steel in 2006, the Harry Sunderland Trophy in the same year and the Lance Todd Trophy in 2007, jointly, and 2008.

Paul
Wellens
St Helens

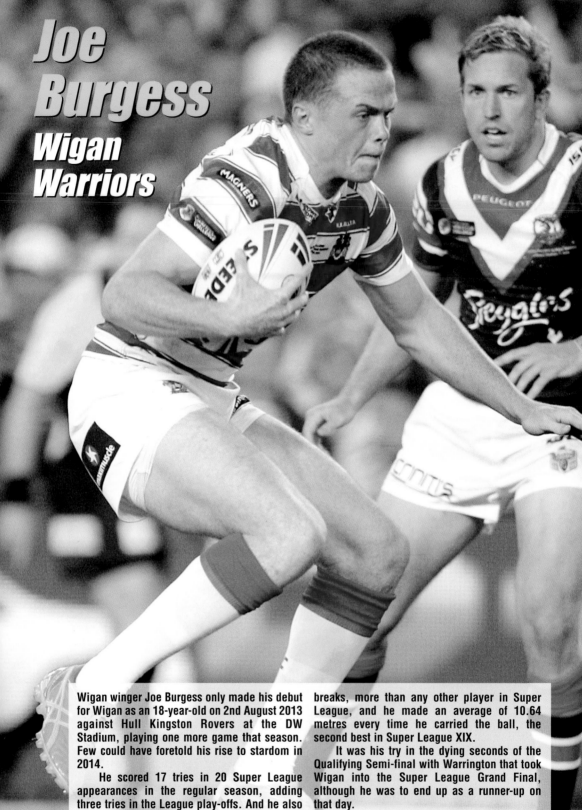

Joe Burgess
Wigan Warriors

Wigan winger Joe Burgess only made his debut for Wigan as an 18-year-old on 2nd August 2013 against Hull Kingston Rovers at the DW Stadium, playing one more game that season. Few could have foretold his rise to stardom in 2014.

He scored 17 tries in 20 Super League appearances in the regular season, adding three tries in the League play-offs. And he also scored four tries in three Challenge Cup appearances, and he scored one try in Wigan's 36-14 World Club Challenge defeat against Sydney Roosters in February.

In the regular season he made 27 clean breaks, more than any other player in Super League, and he made an average of 10.64 metres every time he carried the ball, the second best in Super League XIX.

It was his try in the dying seconds of the Qualifying Semi-final with Warrington that took Wigan into the Super League Grand Final, although he was to end up as a runner-up on that day.

It was enough to see him selected in the England squad for the Four Nations.

And he capped off an unforgettable 2014 by being named as the Albert Goldthorpe Rookie of the Year.

Daryl Clark

Castleford Tigers & England

Castleford Tigers enjoyed a wondrous season in 2014, getting to Wembley for the first time since 1992, and coming within one game of finishing top of the table.

Coach Daryl Powell, who took over the reins mid-season in 2013, manufactured Super League's surprise package as a host of players enjoyed excellent form in the cause of the black and amber.

None more so than local hooker Daryl Clark, who stood out in game after game after game for the Tigers and at end of 2014 was named Steve Prescott Man of Steel and the Super League's Young Player of the Year.

After the Tigers' 23-10 defeat to Leeds in the Challenge Cup final, the club announced that Clark would be heading to Warrington Wolves for 2015. It was a blow for Cas fans and coach Powell, but the Tigers revealed the deal had been done a year before when the club was financially struggling.

Clark became the third player in the 37-year history of the Man of Steel awards to claim both individual titles after Leeds hooker David Ward in 1977 and Widnes centre Joe Lydon in 1984.

The 21-year-old fully deserved his place in the England Four Nations squad and with his first touch of the ball in England shirt, when he came off the bench against Samoa, created a wonderful try for his clubmate Michael Shenton in trademark style. Daryl Clark certainly made an impact in 2014.

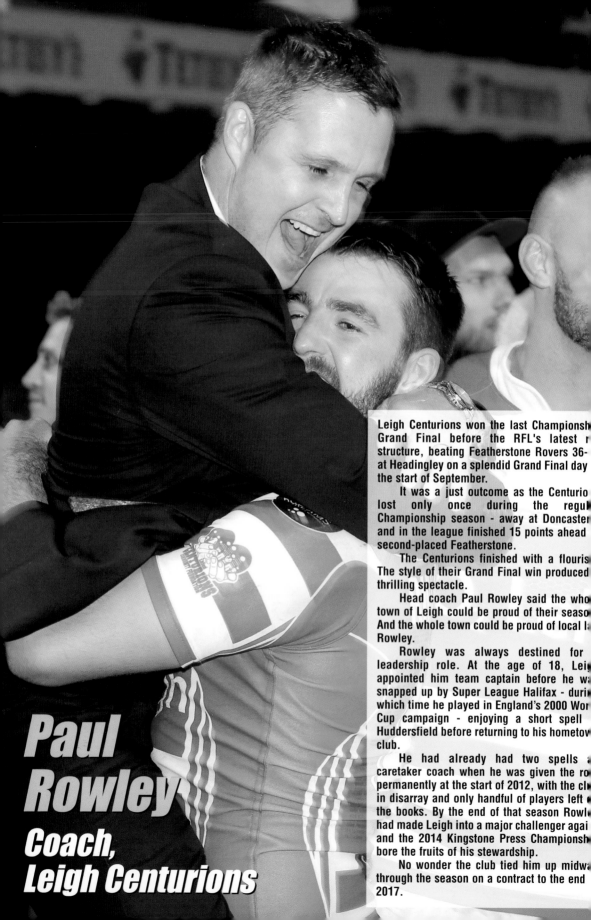

Paul Rowley

Coach, Leigh Centurions

Leigh Centurions won the last Championsh
Grand Final before the RFL's latest r
structure, beating Featherstone Rovers 36-
at Headingley on a splendid Grand Final day
the start of September.

It was a just outcome as the Centurio
lost only once during the regul
Championship season - away at Doncaster
and in the league finished 15 points ahead
second-placed Featherstone.

The Centurions finished with a flouris
The style of their Grand Final win produced
thrilling spectacle.

Head coach Paul Rowley said the who
town of Leigh could be proud of their seaso
And the whole town could be proud of local l
Rowley.

Rowley was always destined for
leadership role. At the age of 18, Lei
appointed him team captain before he w
snapped up by Super League Halifax - duri
which time he played in England's 2000 Wor
Cup campaign - enjoying a short spell
Huddersfield before returning to his hometov
club.

He had already had two spells
caretaker coach when he was given the ro
permanently at the start of 2012, with the cl
in disarray and only handful of players left
the books. By the end of that season Rowl
had made Leigh into a major challenger agai
and the 2014 Kingstone Press Championsh
bore the fruits of his stewardship.

No wonder the club tied him up midwa
through the season on a contract to the end
2017.

am Burgess made history in his final game of ugby League before heading to rugby union becoming the first non-Australian player er to win the Clive Churchill Medal, which s been awarded to the best player in the ustralian Grand Final since 1986.

He played a key role in South Sydney's 0-6 victory over Canterbury Bulldogs at dney's ANZ Stadium as Russell Crowe's uths won the competition for the first time nce 1971.

Astoundingly, he suffered a broken eekbone in the first minute of the game, hen he was on the wrong end of an accidental ead clash with Canterbury's England prop rward James Graham.

But he played on, drawing comparisons ith South Sydney hero John Sattler, who layed on with a broken jaw in the 1971 Grand inal.

Burgess burst into tears near the end of he game in front of a record crowd of 83,833 fter playing alongside his brothers Tom and eorge in a convincing victory.

By the end of 2014, the Burgess brothers nd former St Helens prop Graham had proven hemselves high up amongst the best forwards n the world. It would be a pity if Sam Burgess idn't return to Rugby League one day.

Sam Burgess
South Sydney Rabbitohs

2014 SEASON REVIEW

LEFT: Alex Walmsley celebrates with Luke Walsh as St Helens edge Huddersfield

ROUND 4

LEFT: Daryl Millard gets a pass away during Catalans' narro win against London

TETLEY'S CHALLENGE CUP

RIGHT: Gareth Hock meets Lloyd White and Chris Dean head on as Widnes down Salford

ROUND 5

LEFT: Danny McGuire scores Leeds' winning try against St Helens

LEFT: Weller Hauraki halted during Castleford's win at Wigan

QUARTER FINALS

ABOVE: Catalan Dragons celebrate a memorable victory over Leeds

ABOVE: Brett Delaney and Paul Aiton tackle Warrington's Paul Wood as Leeds reach Wembley

SEMI-FINALS

ABOVE: Rhys Hanbury takes on Jake Webster and Liam Finn as Castleford sweep past Widnes

first:utility SUPER LEAGUE

MAGIC WEEKEND

ABOVE: Roy Asotasi driven back as Warrington prove too strong for St Helens

ABOVE: Tempers flare during a thrilling encounter as Wigan hold off Leeds

BELOW: Joe Burgess scores Wigan's last-gasp winning try against Warrington

RIGHT: Hull KR's Ade Gardner scores during the Robins' derby victory against Hull FC

first:utility SUPER LEAGUE

PLAY-OFFS

LEFT: Warrington's Joel Monaghan races away as the Wolves eliminate Widnes

RIGHT: Castleford's Daryl Clark shows off the Steve Prescott Man of Steel award

ABOVE: Michael Oldfield flies in to score as Catalan Dragons battle past Huddersfield

RUGBY LEAGUE
WORLD CLUB
CHALLENGE

RIGHT: Eddy Pettybourne and Dylan Napa collide head on

ABOVE: The Roosters front row - Jared Waerea-Hargreaves, Jake Friend and Sam Moa - get to grips with Ben Flower

SYDNEY ROOSTERS 36
WIGAN WARRIORS 14

LEFT: The victorious Sydney Roosters team celebrate their World Club Challenge win against Wigan

CASTLEFORD TIGERS 10
LEEDS RHINOS 23

ABOVE: Party time in the Rhinos' dressing room as Leeds end their long wait for a Challenge Cup Final win

TETLEY'S CHALLENGE CUP

FINAL

ABOVE: Kallum Watkins bursts past Michael Shenton as Justin Carney looks on

LEFT: Oliver Holmes beats Danny McGuire on the way to scoring his try

Kingstone Press CHAMPIONSHIPS

FEATHERSTONE ROVERS 12
LEIGH CENTURIONS 36

TOP: Leigh Centurions, Championship Grand Final winners

ABOVE: Ian Hardman gives chase as Gregg McNally makes a break

ABOVE: Thomas Coyle mobbed by teammates after landing the Hawks' golden point field goal

BELOW: Oldham's Lewis Palfrey tries to escape the clutches of Richard Moore

HUNSLET HAWKS 17
OLDHAM 16

RIGHT: John Oakes and Michael Haley celebrate Hunslet's promotion

CHAMPIONSHIP 1 GRAND FINAL

LEFT: Paul Wellens shows his delight at Saints' Grand Final victory

ST HELENS 14
WIGAN WARRIORS.....................6

ABOVE: Mark Percival beats Joe Burgess to a high ball

first:utility
SUPER LEAGUE
GRAND FINAL

BELOW: Flashpoint as the players clash following Ben Flower's attack on a grounded Lance Hohaia

RIGHT: Ben Flower leaves the Old Trafford pitch after being dismissed

LEFT: New South Wales captain Paul Gallen celebrates the Blues' first State of Origin series win since 2005

TOP: Queensland's Corey Parker brought down during Origin III

RIGHT: Sam Tagataese offloads during Samoa's victory against Fiji

LEFT: Australia's Cameron Smith gets a kick away under pressure from New Zealand's Simon Mannerin

BELOW: Jonathan Walke scores against France as Scotland earn a place in the 2016 Four Nations

HOLDEN STATE OF ORIGIN

FOUR NATIONS QUALIFIER

ANZAC TEST

EUROPEAN CUP

CANTERBURY BULLDOGS.............6
SOUTH SYDNEY RABBITOHS 30

ABOVE: A battered, bruised and emotional Sam Burgess bows out from South Sydney in style, following the Rabbitohs' Grand Final win

ABOVE: Canterbury's James Graham drives forward

NRL
TELSTRA
PREMIERSHIP

GRAND FINAL 2014
SYDNEY

ABOVE: South Sydney celebrate the end of the club's long wait for a Premiership title

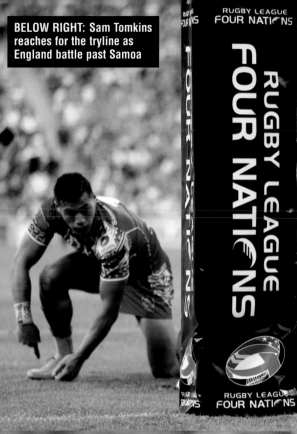

BELOW RIGHT: Sam Tomkins reaches for the tryline as England battle past Samoa

ABOVE: Daryl Clark takes on Australia's Daly Cherry-Evans during an agonising defeat for England

LEFT: Shaun Johnson looks to break free during a big New Zealand win against Australia

RUGBY LEAGUE
OUR NATIONS

ABOVE: Matty Smith tackled by Shaun Kenny-Dowall as New Zealand deny England

RIGHT: Issac Luke brought down by Frank Pritchard and Pita Godinet as New Zealand edge Samoa

BELOW: Greg Inglis dives over for a try during Australia's victory against Samoa

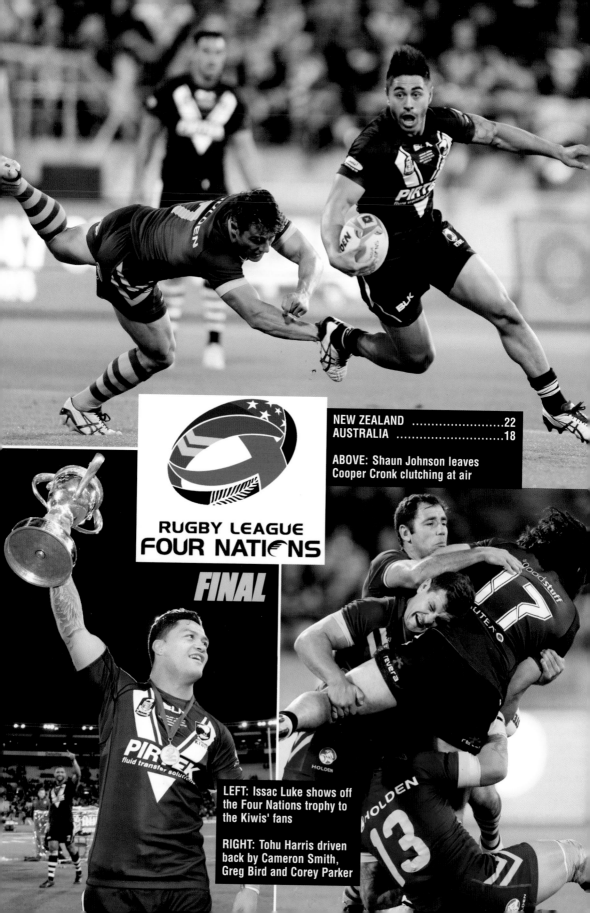

RUGBY LEAGUE
FOUR NATIONS
FINAL

NEW ZEALAND 22
AUSTRALIA 18

ABOVE: Shaun Johnson leaves Cooper Cronk clutching at air

LEFT: Issac Luke shows off the Four Nations trophy to the Kiwis' fans

RIGHT: Tohu Harris driven back by Cameron Smith, Greg Bird and Corey Parker

continued from page 80

HALIFAX finished the year outside their target of the top two, leading to a change in coach when Richard Marshall replaced Karl Harrison.

The timing of Harrison's exit - with one league game left - was a surprise, and some felt that having worked under a smaller budget than some other rivals, he was harshly treated. But ultimately he paid the price for losing a host of close matches over the course of the season.

On several occasions Fax fell foul of late tries, and they also let match-winning situations against champions Leigh slip both home and away.

By the time a sluggish start cost them the crucial match against Featherstone in mid-August, the writing was on the wall for Harrison, with captain Scott Murrell overseeing the final three matches of the season, including play-off defeats to Rovers again and a 0-25 home reversal to Dewsbury.

Murrell was probably Fax's most consistent performer in a campaign that lacked exactly that for the most part, though prop Luke Ambler and back-rower Ross Divorty never allowed their efforts to waver in the pack.

DONCASTER provided the surprise package of the Championship season, continuing their progress of recent years to secure a fourth-placed finish under rookie coach Paul Cooke.

The former Hull FC and Hull KR playmaker was again the Dons' talisman on the field as well, securing a Player of the Year nomination to go alongside his Coach of the Year award, voted for by his peers.

He oversaw a year of consistency from a largely unheralded squad, which nonetheless had a host of heroes in it.

Outside backs Dave Scott, Tom Hodson and Stewart Sanderson gave Cooke's side a cutting edge out wide, while in the pack Mike Emmett, Kyle Kesik and Craig Robinson were reliable performers.

The mid-season arrival of the experienced Steve Snitch gave the Dons a significant push towards the end of the year, and scrum-half Richard Wilkinson emerged as a genuine prospect.

The season hit a major high when they became the only team to beat Leigh in July, raising hopes that they could also make an impact in the play-offs.

But by the time they came round Cooke's relatively small squad, despite help from dual registration partners Hull FC, was dwindling in numbers and they lost to the Centurions and Sheffield on consecutive weekends.

That certainly should not detract from what was an excellent 2014 for one of the competition's best-run clubs.

SHEFFIELD EAGLES paid the price for a sluggish start, and although they recovered well to earn an unlikely Grand Final shot, they were forced to relinquish the title they had held for the previous two seasons.

Mark Aston's side were as low as ninth when they lost to Leigh in mid-July, and talk suddenly centred around a possible relegation fight rather than their usual play-off charge.

But the Eagles - playing for one season at the far from ideal Owlerton Stadium - found their feet late in the campaign, and lost just one of their last nine league games, in what turned out to be a controversial clash with Batley due to the Bulldogs' use of ineligible dual registration player Jacob Fairbank.

That defeat ultimately cost them a top-four spot, but they still looked potential Grand Finalists when accounting for Batley and Doncaster in the play-offs, only to finally come up short at Featherstone the following week.

Quentin Laulu-Togagae and Menzie Yere might not quite have scaled the heights of 2013, but they still finished with 34 and 19 tries respectively, with Scott Turner also bagging 26.

Sheffield's most consistent performer was winger Misi Taulapapa, who never dropped his performance levels, and the reliable Michael Knowles and Mitchell Stringer helped keep things together in what was a smaller squad than in previous years.

DEWSBURY RAMS continued their progress under coach Glenn Morrison, and ended the season just one game short of the Grand Final.

They had their moments too in that qualifying semi-final against champions Leigh, asking plenty of questions of the Centurions in a 33-22 defeat, to illustrate the strides they made in 2014.

That came despite losing influential playmaker Aaron Brown for the full season after just six league appearances, with his absence covered by the form of Anthony Thackeray.

The experienced playmaker earned a nomination for the Championship Player of the Year award and scored an outstanding 28 tries in 29 appearances, terrorising defences on a weekly basis.

Shane Grady's 16 tries earned him a place in the All Stars team, and Morrison was also regularly full of praise for the likes of Rob Spicer, Scott Hale and Tom Hemingway for their contributions.

Outside back Dale Morton and evergreen forward Tommy Gallagher also reached double figures in the try-scoring stakes.

WORKINGTON TOWN were the form team in the competition for a spell in mid-season when coach Phil Veivers oversaw a run of seven straight victories.

That sequence turned a campaign of relegation struggle into one heading for the play-offs, and was the culmination of a steady improvement implemented by Coach of the Year nominee Veivers after he took over just three games into the year.

Initially Town suffered a host of narrow defeats, and when they went down 18-10 at Halifax in mid-June they were languishing in 11th.

But victory against all odds versus Featherstone the following Sunday - Town were so low on numbers that conditioner Matt Johnson had to play on the wing - proved to be a real turning point, and they lost just two more league matches, including a gutsy effort at Leigh.

The play-offs proved a step too far as a depleted team was thrashed 50-6 at Dewsbury, but Veivers has inspired a new feel-good factor at Derwent Park and they would start 2015 full of hope.

The Phillips brothers Callum and especially All Stars member Brett again made significant contributions, along with Young Player of the Year nominee Liam McAvoy, who was little short of a revelation in the pack.

BATLEY BULLDOGS played out a year of inconsistency and controversy that ultimately finished on a major high as they avoided relegation on the final day.

Coach John Kear did not shy away from the inability to string a lengthy run of form together, something that ensured they were constantly flitting between the play-offs and looking over their shoulders.

When they were initially docked two points for fielding the ineligible Jacob Fairbank in their win at Sheffield, relegation looked a distinct possibility for a club that had made the Grand Final in 2013.

But the Bulldogs regrouped, and with chairman Kevin Nicholas's diligent research uncovering similar breaches of the rules last season and leading to those points being reinstated, and Kear overseeing a late campaign revival, Batley survived by the skin of their teeth by beating Doncaster on the last day.

Fullback Miles Greenwood was their best performer, finishing with 22 tries and a place in the All Stars team.

Winger Alex Brown was the only other player to reach double figures for crossing the whitewash, with fellow strike players Johnny Campbell and Ayden Faal missing considerable chunks of the year - in Campbell's case all of it - after breaking the sport's gambling rules.

WHITEHAVEN's rollercoaster year finally finished on a high when they escaped relegation by the finest of margins on the final day of the season.

Dave Woods' side comfortably fulfilled their part of the equation by winning 44-18 at Swinton, but they still needed a dramatic late Ben Blackmore try for Featherstone to send Keighley Cougars down.

It wasn't enough to save Woods' job - he parted company with the club soon after and was replaced by Steve Deakin for 2015.

But the Australian had at least preserved Haven's hard-earned Championship status, albeit in a far from straight forward manner. A mid-season run of five wins from six had the Cumbrians as high as seventh at one point, with hope of looking up rather than down.

But just two wins in the next eight plunged them into the dog fight at the bottom, one they only just emerged from after three victories in their last four games.

Dual registration prop Carl Forster was one of their more consistent performers, earning a Young Player of the Year nomination, while the back row of Lee Doran, Lee Mitchell and Scott McAvoy all sprung to the fore when it mattered most.

KEIGHLEY COUGARS supporters will need a long time to forget the 2014 season - and mainly for all the wrong reasons.

Paul March's side saw their Championship status slip away when Featherstone's Ben Blackmore scored a late try on the final day of the season to condemn them to relegation.

But that told only half the story - Cougars supporters and officials were infuriated when Batley and Doncaster were reinstated the points deducted for fielding ineligible dual registration players. Had those penalties stood, Keighley, who didn't break any such rule, would have survived.

That led to a lengthy and very public challenge to the RFL over the way the decision was reached, and left a bad taste in the mouth of supporters not only at Cougar Park but across the game.

When the dust eventually settled, coach March - who himself was handed a hotly disputed two-month stadium ban for abusing a match official, something he still denies - was forced to look towards life back in Championship One.

March will feel his squad should have survived regardless, but defeats in their final three matches cost them dearly.

NORTH WALES CRUSADERS brought in a number of high-profile recruits for life in the Championship, but it didn't prove to be enough despite a largely competitive year.

Two of those captures, Mark Offerdahl and Michael Platt, didn't finish the season with the club, while coach Clive Griffiths moved upstairs midway through the campaign to be replaced by Anthony Murray.

He eventually ended up as the club's permanent replacement after a long spell as caretaker, and will be hoping to oversee a quick-fire recovery following a season that fell just short of the required standards at the higher level.

It started with two wins from three, against Barrow and Swinton - but that was as good as it got and Crusaders were in the relegation places from early May onwards.

A 34-0 win at Whitehaven in late April also heralded promise that was never fulfilled.

Fullback Tommy Johnson and back-rower Steve Wild were near ever-presents in a side whose run of eight straight defeats from June to August ultimately cost them their Championship place.

ROCHDALE HORNETS were only out of the relegation places for one weekend on their return to the Championship, though survival was always going to be tough for the supporter-owned club.

Victory over Swinton in May - a third win on the trot - briefly raised hopes that coach Ian Talbot could inspire an against-the-odds battle against the drop with limited resources.

Championship Season

But Rochdale's small squad - supplemented by loan signings and the dual registration partnership with St Helens - soon caught up with them, though they were rarely heavily beaten and competed fully for the most part.

The season high probably came with a dramatic home win over high-flying Featherstone in July, which ended a run of eight consecutive defeats that had all but condemned them to relegation.

Still, the club remained true to its strict financial guidelines, and they made enough promising signings for 2015 to suggest that an immediate return is not out of the question.

The link with Saints saw five members of their Super League Grand Final-winning side make appearances for Hornets during the year, though only on a sporadic basis.

Instead it was left to Hornets stalwarts such as Paul Crook, Wayne English and John Cookson to hold the side together during the difficult times.

SWINTON LIONS started the season miles behind most of their peers in terms of preparation, with uncertainty over the club's future giving coach Ian Watson and his assistant Marlon Billy a matter of weeks to put a team together.

That they did so - and managed to be competitive for the most part - was of great credit to them, and Watson remains a Lions favourite despite leaving mid-season for a full-time coaching role with local rivals Salford.

Like neighbours Rochdale, they threatened an unlikely play-offs push early on when an exciting home win over Dewsbury lifted them temporarily to ninth in April.

A run of three straight wins in June re-ignited that hope, but they lost their remaining 10 matches, with John Duffy taking over from Watson and helping a patched-up squad complete the season. Hooker Andy Ackers was one of the finds of the season from Warrington, and also agreed to remain with the Lions after scoring nine tries in 25 appearances in 2014.

BARROW RAIDERS finished bottom of the Championship pile after an eventful campaign under coaches Anthony Murray and then Bobbie Goulding.

Murray started the season following the departure of Darren Holt and brought a number of new signings in, several of whom contributed to a shock early win at Sheffield.

But Murray stepped down from the role after just four matches in charge due to personal reasons, and was quickly replaced by former Great Britain international Goulding.

Among the changes he made was to instigate a comeback for himself at the age of 42, which started with a home win over Rochdale in which he set up the winning try.

Less memorable was a red card at home to Doncaster the following week after an altercation with a touch-judge, and Goulding featured just once again - away at Leigh - as his side faltered as the season unfolded.

Goulding turned down the offer of a new contract towards the end of the season, and the Raiders looked to rebuild again under popular local coach Paul Crarey, who returned for a second spell in charge.

CHAMPIONSHIP AWARDS

Martyn Ridyard

PLAYER OF THE YEAR
Martyn Ridyard
(Leigh Centurions)

YOUNG PLAYER OF THE YEAR
Ryan Brierley
(Leigh Centurions)

COACH OF THE YEAR
Paul Cooke
(Doncaster)

CLUB OF THE YEAR
Leigh Centurions

RUGBY LEAGUE WORLD TEAM OF THE YEAR
1 Miles Greenwood (Batley Bulldogs)
2 Liam Kay (Leigh Centurions)
3 Tom Armstrong (Leigh Centurions)
4 Shane Grady (Dewsbury Rams)
5 Will Sharp (Featherstone Rovers)
6 Martyn Ridyard (Leigh Centurions)
7 Ryan Brierley (Leigh Centurions)
8 Luke Ambler (Halifax)
9 Sean Penkywicz (Leigh Centurions)
10 Tom Spencer (Leigh Centurions)
11 Brett Phillips (Workington Town)
12 Liam McAvoy (Workington Town)
13 Sam Barlow (Leigh Centurions)

CHAMPIONSHIP ONE SEASON
Hawks take flight

HUNSLET HAWKS overcame a number of stutters during an enthralling Kingstone Press Championship One season to eventually earn promotion back to the higher level.

Those stumbles included three defeats to eventual League Leaders York, a home loss to Gloucestershire All Golds in June, and a play-off defeat to Oldham.

But all those were forgotten when halfback Thomas Coyle slotted the all-important golden point extra time drop goal to beat the Roughyeds 17-16 in the Headingley Grand Final.

It meant that Barry Eaton's squad - tipped to be the strongest before the start of the season - achieved their ultimate objective of restoring their Championship status.

Coyle produced a superb man of the match performance when it mattered most, after an influential season in general alongside the evergreen David March, who played both hooker and loose forward.

The Hawks' sole representative in the Championship One All Stars side was veteran centre Danny Maun, while fullback Jimmy Watson capped an impressive year as top try scorer with 16. Two late-season additions had a significant impact - winger Gavin Duffy crossed 15 times in just 12 appearances while on loan from Keighley, while prop Richard Moore produced some huge 80-minute efforts in the closing stages of the campaign.

YORK CITY KNIGHTS ended the season as League Leaders, and with the Player of the Year, Young Player, Coach and seven All Stars members in their ranks. But the ultimate prize eluded them after they faltered in the play-offs.

Hooker Jack Lee was crowned Championship One Player of the Year, and was joined in the All Stars team by joint Young Player winners Ben Reynolds and James Saltonstall, plus Ben Dent, Pat Smith, Jack Aldous and Colton Roche.

Gary Thornton was also named Coach of the Year as recognition for his part in the Knights finishing top.

But by the time the Championship awards night was held, York were out of the Grand Final race and the unfortunate Thornton was out of a job, with his contract not renewed.

Along the seven All Stars players, Ed Smith, Ryan Mallinder and promising centre Greg Minikin were others to catch the eye at different stages of the season.

For **OLDHAM**, the season finished in heartbreakingly familiar circumstances - Grand Final defeat.

For the sixth time in eight seasons the Roughyeds failed to win promotion in the season-defining game, having also lost the 2001 NFP Grand Final.

But the nature of their 2014 setback was arguably the toughest to take of all, as Thomas Coyle's late field goal saw them lose to Hunslet in golden-point extra-time.

Having beaten both the Hawks and York away from home in the play-offs, it was a difficult loss for coach Scott Naylor to stomach, especially as he had been inexplicably overlooked by his peers for even a nomination for the Coach of the Year.

Championship One Season

Winger Mo Agoro did earn some recognition for the club in the Young Player category, while Jon Ford and Josh Crowley made the All Stars team.

Crowley and Danny Langtree again formed an ultra-consistent second row partnership, while Ford continued to be a potent weapon out wide on dual registration from Salford.

GATESHEAD THUNDER developed consistently over the course of the season under rookie coach Stanley Gene and finished the campaign in a highly creditable fourth place.

They recorded seven more wins than their 2013 return, including six from seven late in the season - their only setback being a four-point loss at League Leaders York.

Thunder also progressed to the second weekend of the play-offs by edging out Hemel Stags in golden point extra-time, only for the following week to prove one step too far against eventual champions Hunslet.

But overall this was a season of definite progression, and Gene - who had been in charge as part of the partnership with Hull KR - was rewarded with a permanent contract and a Coach of the Year nomination.

Alongside the Papua New Guinean legend, ever-consistent skipper and top try scorer Jason Payne was nominated for the Player of the Year award and dual registration scrum-half Matty Beharrell for the Young Player.

The club came under the ownership of rugby union club Newcastle Falcons during the season, and started 2015 with high hopes of further development both on and off the field.

HEMEL STAGS replicated their impressive debut campaign finish of fifth place and fell agonisingly short in their play-off game at Gateshead.

That match was not without its controversy either, with the Stags objecting to a late Sunday afternoon kick-off time that left them short of numbers. But the overall view of their 2014 season had to be one of satisfaction.

Again they proved that they can compete fully under coach Troy Perkins, not least against Grand Finalists Oldham, who they beat at home and drew with away.

Perkins had a backbone to his side that included Australian outside back James Cameron, impressive signing Jy-Mel Coleman and experienced prop Dominic Maloney, who was their sole representative in the All Stars team.

James Hill finished as top try scorer with 13 in 19 matches, while Michael Brown, James Howitt and the goal kicking Barry-John Swindells also played their part.

When **GLOUCESTERSHIRE ALL GOLDS** beat Hunslet and York in the space of three weeks in June, they were justifiably being touted as potential Grand Finalists.

It was part of a stirring mid-season run under coach Steve McCormack that also included a narrow loss to Oldham and eye-catching away win at London Skolars.

But eventually McCormack ran out of numbers and the All Golds' play-off charge faltered, though there was still much to admire in their 2014 season.

Having finished bottom in their debut campaign the year earlier, they showed significant ambition in appointing Scotland coach McCormack when Brad Hepi left mid-season.

The signings of experienced hooker Craig Cook, Rochdale outside back Sam Te'o and South Wales back-rower James Tutuila further emphasised the point.

But injuries hit McCormack hard, and he also felt the travelling from his north west home was becoming too much, leading to him stepping down towards the end of the campaign. Still, he left a squad with potential in place, with experienced playmaker Danny Thomas, the strong-running Phil Cowburn and hard-working Brendan Smith among their most consistent.

For **LONDON SKOLARS**, a seventh placed finish was undoubtedly a disappointment.

Having lost a number of key players from the 2013 side that came level on points with third-placed Rochdale, it was always going to be something of a transitional campaign.

But Skolars just never really got going from the moment that they lost their opening fixture at relative neighbours Oxford.

Ironically, that first weekend was the only time they were in the top five all year, and a return of just five wins saw Joe Mbu's squad take a step backwards.

But they were keen to regroup ahead of the sport's restructuring, and desperate to ensure that their progress of recent seasons was not undone.

There were still a number of players to come out of the season with credit, with top try scorer Mufaro Mvududu's performances earning him a move to Championship side Hunslet.

OXFORD also fell below their 2013 mark of sixth, although that should be tempered by the fact that they won two more games in their second season.

That included arguably the best win in their short history to date when they beat York away 24-16 in April, raising hopes that they could make the play-offs again.

That didn't eventuate, but six other wins and a final day draw against Hemel showed that Oxford were far from easy beats under coach Tony Benson.

He should also be commended for moving towards a more locally-based side in 2014, and that approach took a step further when Benson left at the end of the campaign with the club cutting down on travelling costs.

Fullback or centre Sean Morris enjoyed another good season and finished as top try scorer with 17 in as many games, with consistent forward Alex Thompson the next in line with 11 in all competitions.

SOUTH WALES SCORPIONS were always likely wooden spoonists after a close season in which the club was in danger of going out of existence.

That left rookie coach Mike Grady with little time to prepare a hugely inexperienced squad - he later told Rugby League World that for the first three weeks in charge there were no players, no training and no equipment.

That led to a couple of early heavy defeats, most notably to York and London Skolars, but for the most part Grady's fledgling side were competitive.

And by early June they had completely turned the tables on Skolars, beating them 46-18 at Enfield to snap a near year-long losing run.

They would beat Skolars again in July, and although they finished some way off their nearest competitors Oxford, their largely Welsh team had much to build on from their 2014 base.

Grady was rewarded for his efforts in keeping the squad going with a Coach of the Year nomination from his peers, while hooker Connor Farrer went a step better.

Alongside his Young Player of the Year nomination he earned selection for the full Welsh side in the European Championship, and Grady was among those to tip the teenager for a Super League future.

CHAMPIONSHIP ONE AWARDS

PLAYER OF THE YEAR
Jack Lee (York City Knights)

YOUNG PLAYER OF THE YEAR
Ben Reynolds
(York City Knights) and
James Saltonstall
(York City Knights)

COACH OF THE YEAR
Gary Thornton
(York City Knights)

CLUB OF THE YEAR
Gloucestershire All Golds

Jack Lee

RUGBY LEAGUE WORLD TEAM OF THE YEAR
1 James Haynes (York City Knights)
2 Mo Agoro (Oldham)
3 Danny Maun (Hunslet Hawks)
4 James Saltonstall (York City Knights)
5 Gavin Duffy (Hunslet Hawks)
6 Pat Smith (York City Knights)
7 Ben Reynolds (York City Knights)
8 Jason Boults (Oldham)
9 David March (Hunslet Hawks)
10 Richard Moore (Hunslet Hawks)
11 Danny Langtree (Oldham)
12 Josh Crowley (Oldham)
13 Jason Payne (Gateshead Thunder)

CHAMPIONSHIP PLAY-OFFS
Love-Leigh

Leigh Centurions' unstoppable march to the Grand Final began with an accomplished win over a Doncaster side that was still fully in the contest at half-time. Only Ryan Brierley's 38th minute try had stretched the score to 24-14 at the break, but the Centurions broke clear after the restart, with Brierley completing his double and centres Michael Platt and Tom Armstrong both touching down twice to put them within 80 minutes of Headingley.

That was the same scenario for Featherstone after Andy Hay's improving side proved too strong for Halifax and ran out 34-16 winners at the Big Fellas Stadium. Gareth Moore was the key man, kicking five goals, scoring a try and having a hand in several others to finish with 14 points. Fax, with captain Scott Murrell in charge following the exit of coach Karl Harrison, had led 16-12 at half-time, only to falter after the break.

Sheffield Eagles and Batley Bulldogs were still locked in a scoreless arm wrestle with 11 minutes remaining, before a late flurry from Mark Aston's side saw them home in their elimination play-off. The game was played at Doncaster's Keepmoat Stadium, and late tries to Etu Uaisele (2) and Quentin Laulu-Togagae eventually saw the Eagles home in what was a repeat of the 2013 Grand Final.

Workington Town saw their strong season finish on a low, as Phil Veivers' depleted ranks were completely overrun 50-6 by Dewsbury. Player of the Year nominee Anthony Thackerary scored a hat-trick in a dominant display by the Rams.

They moved up another level the following week, with Thackeray influential again as they stunned Halifax 25-0 at the Shay. Thackeray scored two more tries with Sam Wood and Tommy Gallagher also touching down in an emphatic win.

The other elimination semi-final that weekend saw Sheffield maintain hopes of a fourth straight Grand Final when they eased past tired Doncaster 58-24. The Dons were hardly helped by the 27th minute dismissal of Liam Cunningham for kicking, and Laulu-Togagae added another double to his collection in a comfortable win.

That set up a trip to Featherstone as Sheffield looked to regain their title for a third straight year, but with Moore again in fine form, a flying Rovers start was central to their 21-12 win. Moore was among the scorers as they raced into a 21-0 half-time lead that proved too much for the Eagles to overcome, and booked a first Grand Final appearance since 2012.

Elsewhere, Leigh took a step closer fulfilling their own destiny by eventually overcoming gutsy Dewsbury 33-22. Winger Adam Higson scored a hat-trick, with his third try on the hour proving enough to see them home.

Championship Grand Final

Leigh Centurions coach Paul Rowley saw his side cap an unforgettable season by beating Featherstone in the Kingstone Press Championship Grand Final 36-12.

The Centurions had dominated the competition all season, and although Rovers briefly rocked them with a stirring third-quarter comeback, Rowley's team had too much know-how and class for their opponents.

The game had the potential to become the most one-sided Grand Final yet at this level when three converted tries put the Centurions 18-0 ahead.

But Andy Hay's Featherstone regrouped well, and had Luke Teasdale's try been awarded just after the hour mark they would have been back within two points.

Instead, clinical Leigh powered home with further tries to Adam Higson, Sam Barlow and the prolific Ryan Brierley, putting the perfect seal on a near-perfect campaign.

Rowley said: "We are ambitious like all clubs - we want to reach the promised land of Super League but so does everybody else.

"We want to cement our place in the top 16 of Rugby League and improve steadily.

"This group has probably got five years together and with a few key additions each year we are not far off. I think some Super League clubs would worry if they got us in a Cup game next year. The club has made the move to full-time for next year to try and aid that progression. We are a capable outfit."

Stand-off Martyn Ridyard completed a memorable personal year by winning the Tom Bergin Trophy as man of the match, just days after being announced as the Championship Player of the Year.

Other try scorers were Matt Sarsfield, Gregg McNally and Tom Armstrong, with Will Sharp replying twice for a gallant, if out-gunned Featherstone side.

Rovers coach Hay said: "I was disappointed with the first half, most of the players were.

"We gave them a big start and you can't afford to do that to a side like Leigh. I thought some of our senior players were a bit off the mark.

"We regrouped at half-time. They weren't that far away from us and in the second half we got on a roll. But that disallowed try knocked us. It was a bit controversial and it gave Leigh a leg up. We ran out of a bit of steam in the end."

Championship One Play-offs

Hemel Stags' season finished in heart-breaking fashion as Matty Beharrell's golden-point field goal saw Gateshead Thunder edge them out 15-14 in a dramatic elimination play-off at Kingston Park. Hemel had objected to the late afternoon kick-off time, but showed little sign of disappointment during the game, with Jy-Mel Coleman's try on the hour mark helping to send the match into added time. There, dual-registration halfback Beharrell took just three minutes to slot over the decisive point to end Hemel's hopes.

Oldham began their journey to the Grand Final with another one-point win at Hunslet Hawks, with back-rower Josh Crowley the unlikely hero. His kick right on the half-time hooter made it 12-7 to Hunslet, and that single point proved to be the difference as Oldham scored three tries in 16 second half minutes to book a clash with York the following week.

KINGSTONE PRESS CHAMPIONSHIP GRAND FINAL

Sunday 5th October 2014

FEATHERSTONE ROVERS 12 LEIGH CENTURIONS 36

ROVERS: 2 Will Sharp; 35 Jason Crookes; 1 Ian Hardman; 18 Jamie Cording; 36 Ben Blackmore; 23 Andy Kain; 7 Gareth Moore; 8 Steve Crossley; 9 Andy Ellis; 13 Matt James; 31 Shaun Pick; 11 James Lockwood; 12 Tim Spears. Subs (all used): 30 Luke Teasdale; 6 Jack Bussey; 42 Chris Annakin; 10 Keegan Hirst.
Tries: Sharp (27, 51); **Goals:** Moore 2/2.
Sin bin: Crookes (68) - high tackle on Armstrong.
CENTURIONS: 1 Gregg McNally; 22 Adam Higson; 34 Michael Platt; 4 Tom Armstrong; 15 Liam Kay; 6 Martyn Ridyard; 7 Ryan Brierley; 29 Jake Emmitt; 14 Sean Penkywicz; 10 Oliver Wilkes; 11 Matt Sarsfield; 30 Kurt Haggerty; 13 Sam Barlow. Subs (all used): 9 Bob Beswick; 18 Jamie Acton; 16 Martin Aspinwall; 33 Jonathan Walker.
Tries: Sarsfield (5), McNally (17), Armstrong (22), Higson (65), Barlow (70), Brierley (80); **Goals:** Ridyard 6/8.
Sin bin: Penkywicz (68) - retaliation.
Rugby Leaguer & League Express Men of the Match:
Rovers: Jack Bussey; *Centurions:* Tom Armstrong.
Penalty count: 6-8; **Half-time:** 6-20;
Referee: Matthew Thomason; **Attendance:** 9,164
(at Headingley Carnegie, Leeds).

Championship Play-offs

Then, Scott Naylor's side needed no such narrow margins as an outstanding performance at the Huntington Stadium saw them run out 31-12 winners. The Roughyeds were 24-0 up at the break and George Tyson's 69th minute try put paid to any faint hopes of a late Knights comeback, booking Oldham a Grand Final place at Headingley in the process.

Elsewhere Hunslet were proving far too strong for Gateshead as Barry Eaton's side ran out 50-6 winners at the South Leeds Stadium. Loan winger Gavin Duffy, fullback Jimmy Watson and hooker Liam Hood all helped themselves to try doubles in a one-sided win that ended with two Thunder players in the sin bin for dissent.

That set up a final eliminator between regular season top two York and Hunslet, and for the first time in four 2014 matches the Hawks emerged as winners, 32-24. Gary Thornton's Knights had actually led 12-0 at the break and seemed perfectly placed for the Grand Final. But six second-half Hunslet tries, including two more to the influential Hood, sent the Hawks to face Oldham instead.

Championship One Grand Final

Halfback Thomas Coyle was Hunslet Hawks' hero as he kept his cool to slot the decisive field goal and break Oldham hearts yet again.

Coyle took just under five minutes of golden point extra-time to come up with the winner against his former club and book promotion to the Championship.

It ended an enthralling clash between two well-matched sides, with the Roughyeds having won two of the three previous meetings by the same solitary point margin.

But they came up short yet again when it mattered most, losing a sixth Grand Final at this level in the last eight years.

Coyle was named man of the match and coach Barry Eaton said: "In extra-time we talked about keeping our composure and if a drop goal presents itself take it, but if we get an opportunity to score a try go for it.

"Young Liam Hood made a break – and he was outstanding for us – and Danny Ansell showed great composure to not risk the kick when he was under pressure. Danny showed great composure to find Tom, who had put himself in a fantastic position and we got the win. But credit to Oldham. They wouldn't go away and that made it a fantastic spectacle."

The Roughyeds had been 10-6 ahead at the break after an exciting if error-strewn opening 40 minutes.

Their halfback Steve Roper had opened the scoring only for Jimmy Watson to respond, before Dale Bloomfield's try put Oldham ahead at half-time.

But the Hawks took control after the restart, with James Duckworth and Coyle scoring in the space of nine minutes to help them into a six-point lead.

That lasted until the 74th minute when Danny Langtree's gutsy effort and Roper's conversion levelled the scores again, only for the Roughyeds to suffer another difficult defeat in extra-time.

Coach Scott Naylor said: "It was outstanding effort, (but) dumb rugby.

"We lost because we didn't have enough ball and, at a guess, I would say we spent 75 per cent of the game in our own half. I knew it would be close, but we didn't play anything like as well as we can play, and we came close to getting away with it.

"Neutrals will say it was a brilliant game, but to me it was a game I didn't want to watch - a game of Hunslet attack and Oldham defence."

KINGSTONE PRESS CHAMPIONSHIP ONE GRAND FINAL

Sunday 5th October 2014

HUNSLET HAWKS 17 OLDHAM 16
(after golden point extra-time)

HAWKS: 2 Jimmy Watson; 36 Gavin Duffy; 4 Danny Maun; 3 Lee Brickwood; 37 James Duckworth; 6 Thomas Coyle; 20 Danny Ansell; 38 Richard Moore; 9 David March; 10 James Houston; 11 John Oakes; 12 Aaron Lyons; 31 Luke Briscoe. Subs (all used): 27 Liam Hood; 8 Michael Haley; 1 Stuart Kain; 40 Luke Hardbottle.
Tries: Watson (22), Duckworth (45), T Coyle (53);
Goals: March 2/3; **Field goal:** T Coyle (85).
OLDHAM: 4 Steven Nield; 29 Adam Clay; 21 David Cookson; 25 Jonathan Ford; 5 Dale Bloomfield; 6 Lewis Palfrey; 26 Steve Roper; 8 Phil Joy; 30 Gareth Owen; 10 Jason Boults; 11 Josh Crowley; 12 Danny Langtree; 22 Liam Thompson. Subs (all used): 19 Michael Ward; 28 Nathan Mason; 16 Kenny Hughes; 20 George Tyson.
Tries: Roper (5), Bloomfield (31), Langtree (74);
Goals: Roper 2/3.
Rugby Leaguer & League Express Men of the Match:
Hawks: Liam Hood; *Oldham:* Jonathan Ford.
Penalty count: 4-3; **Half-time:** 6-10; **Referee:** Joe Cobb.
(at Headingley Carnegie, Leeds).

4
INTERNATIONAL YEAR

FOUR NATIONS
Flying Kiwis

The year after the 2013 World Cup, which had illustrated the rich promise of international Rugby League, was a barren one for games between the top nations.

England's preparations for the Four Nations tournament to be held down under paled against those in the build-up years to the World Cup. The annual mid-season game against the Exiles was dropped after three years.

England coach Steve McNamara spent 2014 as an assistant coach at Sydney Roosters in the NRL but the lack of a lead-in didn't seem to affect England's performance much.

England enjoyed only one win - against the Pacific Nations qualifier Samoa, who beat Fiji 32-16 in Sydney in May to qualify - but lost against Australia and New Zealand in very close games they could have won.

New Zealand won the tournament with a 22-18 win over Australia in Wellington, with the competitiveness of Samoa in their first two games adding a different dimension to this year's tournament.

Wigan Warriors skipper Sean O'Loughlin, who replaced Kevin Sinfield after his international retirement earlier that summer, captained England.

England train-on squad *(June)*: Carl Ablett (Leeds Rhinos), Kyle Amor (St Helens), John Bateman (Wigan Warriors), Chris Bridge (Warrington Wolves), Tom Briscoe (Leeds Rhinos), Joe Burgess (Wigan Warriors), Josh Charnley (Wigan Warriors), Daryl Clark (Castleford Tigers), Leroy Cudjoe (Huddersfield Giants), Liam Farrell (Wigan Warriors), Brett Ferres (Huddersfield Giants), Ryan Hall (Leeds Rhinos), Zak Hardaker (Leeds Rhinos), Chris Hill (Warrington Wolves), Josh Hodgson (Hull Kingston Rovers), Craig Huby (Castleford Tigers), Jamie Jones-Buchanan (Leeds Rhinos), Jonny Lomax (St Helens), Tom Makinson (St Helens), Michael McIlorum (Wigan Warriors), Richard Myler (Warrington Wolves), Sean O'Loughlin (Wigan Warriors), Stefan Ratchford (Warrington Wolves), James Roby (St Helens), Dan Sarginson (Wigan Warriors), Michael Shenton (Castleford Tigers), Kevin Sinfield (Leeds Rhinos), Matty Smith (Wigan Warriors), Scott Taylor (Wigan Warriors), Alex Walmsley (St Helens), Kallum Watkins (Leeds Rhinos), Joe Westerman (Hull FC), Ben Westwood (Warrington Wolves), Elliott Whitehead (Catalan Dragons).

FOUR NATIONS SQUADS

AUSTRALIA: Greg Bird (Gold Coast Titans), Daly Cherry-Evans (Manly Sea Eagles), Boyd Cordner (Sydney Roosters), Cooper Cronk (Melbourne Storm), Robbie Farah (Wests Tigers), Aidan Guerra (Sydney Roosters), Ryan Hoffman (Melbourne Storm), Ben Hunt (Brisbane Broncos), Greg Inglis (South Sydney Rabbitohs), Josh Jackson (Canterbury Bulldogs), Michael Jennings (Sydney Roosters), Alex Johnston (South Sydney Rabbitohs), David Klemmer (Canterbury Bulldogs), Josh Mansour (Penrith Panthers), Sione Mata'utia (Newcastle Knights), Matt Moylan (Penrith Panthers), Josh Papalii (Canberra Raiders), Corey Parker (Brisbane Broncos), Beau Scott (Newcastle Knights), Cameron Smith (Melbourne Storm) (C), Sam Thaiday (Brisbane Broncos), Daniel Tupou (Sydney Roosters), Dylan Walker (South Sydney Rabbitohs), Aaron Woods (Wests Tigers).

Billy Slater and Johnathan Thurston were missing through injury, along with the suspended Paul Gallen. Matt Moylan was added to the squad following the withdrawal of Jarryd Hayne, who went to the USA to try his hand in the NFL.

ENGLAND: George Burgess (South Sydney Rabbitohs), Joe Burgess (Wigan Warriors), Tom Burgess (South Sydney Rabbitohs), Josh Charnley (Wigan Warriors), Daryl Clark (Castleford Tigers), Michael Cooper (St George Illawarra Dragons), Liam Farrell (Wigan Warriors), Brett Ferres (Huddersfield Giants), James Graham (Canterbury Bulldogs), Ryan Hall (Leeds Rhinos), Zak Hardaker (Leeds Rhinos), Chris Hill (Warrington Wolves), Josh Hodgson (Hull Kingston Rovers), Sean O'Loughlin (Wigan Warriors) (C), Stefan Ratchford (Warrington Wolves), Dan Sarginson (Wigan Warriors), Michael Shenton (Castleford Tigers), Matty Smith (Wigan Warriors), Sam Tomkins (New Zealand Warriors), Kallum Watkins (Leeds Rhinos), Joe Westerman (Hull FC), Elliott Whitehead (Catalan Dragons), Gareth Widdop (St George Illawarra Dragons).

NEW ZEALAND: Gerard Beale (St George Illawarra Dragons), Adam Blair (Wests Tigers), Jesse Bromwich (Melbourne Storm), Lewis Brown (Penrith Panthers), Greg Eastwood (Canterbury Bulldogs), Sosaia Feki (Cronulla Sharks), Kieran Foran (Manly Sea Eagles), Tohu Harris (Melbourne Storm), Siliva Havili (New Zealand Warriors), Peta Hiku (Manly Sea Eagles), Josh Hoffman (Brisbane Broncos), Shaun Johnson (New Zealand Warriors), Shaun Kenny-Dowall (Sydney Roosters), Thomas Leuluai (New Zealand Warriors), Issac Luke (South Sydney Rabbitohs), Simon Mannering (New Zealand Warriors) (C), Suaia Matagi (New Zealand Warriors), Jason Nightingale (St George Illawarra Dragons), Kevin Proctor (Melbourne Storm), Jason Taumalolo (North Queensland Cowboys), Martin Taupau (Wests Tigers), Bodene Thompson (Wests Tigers), Manu Vatuvei (New Zealand Warriors), Dean Whare (Penrith Panthers).

Sam Moa withdrew due to family reasons and was replaced by Bodene Thompson. Dallin Watene-Zelezniak withdrew due to injury and was replaced by Josh Hoffman.

SAMOA: Leeson Ah Mau (St George Illawarra Dragons), David Fa'alogo (Newcastle Knights) (C), Pita Godinet (Wakefield Trinity Wildcats), Tim Lafai (Canterbury Bulldogs), Joseph Leilua (Newcastle Knights), Ricky Leutele (Cronulla Sharks), Isaac Liu (Sydney Roosters), Dunamis Lui (Manly Sea Eagles), Reni Maitua (Canterbury Bulldogs), Penani Manumalealii (Cronulla Sharks), Mose Masoe (St Helens), Peter Mata'utia (St George Illawarra Dragons), Josh McGuire (Brisbane Broncos), Tautau Moga (North Queensland Cowboys), Dominique Peyroux (New Zealand Warriors), Frank Pritchard (Canterbury Bulldogs), Ben Roberts (Melbourne Storm), Jesse Sene-Lefao (Manly Sea Eagles), Tim Simona (Wests Tigers), Michael Sio (New Zealand Warriors), Kyle Stanley (St George Illawarra Dragons), Sauaso Sue (Wests Tigers), Sam Tagataese (Cronulla Sharks), Daniel Vidot (Brisbane Broncos), Antonio Winterstein (North Queensland Cowboys).

Jesse Sene-Lefao was added to the squad as a replacement for Suaia Matagi - who had also been named by New Zealand and opted to play for the Kiwis.

The squad included 13 survivors from the 2013 Rugby League World Cup. Wigan's Joel Tomkins, who returned to Rugby League in the late summer following a three-year stint in rugby union, was included alongside his brother Sam.

Wigan had the biggest representation with seven players. James Roby, Wigan's Michael McIlorum and Warrington's Ben Westwood were not considered because of surgery at the end of the domestic season. Sam Burgess did not take part after signing for Bath rugby union.

England achieved their main objective in the first game of the 2014 Four Nations tournament, after a rip-roaring Test match played in 30-degree heat, the first game of a double-header at Suncorp Stadium in Brisbane.

Gareth Widdop was a steadying hand, as was debutant halfback partner Matty Smith, after two dummy-half tries from Wakefield's Pita Godinet had put Samoa into a two-point lead just after the hour mark. It was Smith's two bombs that got England back into the ascendancy, creating tries for the two Tomkins brothers, before Samoa mounted a mighty comeback, with Antonio Winterstein's unconverted try making for a nervous and exciting last nine minutes. In the end, Widdop's six out of six goals were the difference between the two teams.

New England captain Sean O'Loughlin was out with a quad injury, and Steve McNamara gave England debuts to four players - Smith, Daryl Clark, Joe Westerman and Josh Hodgson.

Samoa were fielding a top-quality side after having comfortably won a qualification match with Fiji in April. They were ferocious right from the off, with their pace and power in the backs testing England's defensive resolve many times.

England's four-point lead was fortunate after an error-strewn first half saw them cough up possession time after time. It was nil-all when Daryl Clark came off the bench in the 21st minute. With his first ever touch of the ball in an England shirt, Clark created a try in trademark fashion. It was a try made in Castleford as Man of Steel Clark shot out of dummy-half

FOUR NATIONS - GAME ONE

Saturday 25th October 2014

ENGLAND 32 SAMOA 26

ENGLAND: 1 Sam Tomkins (New Zealand Warriors); 2 Josh Charnley (Wigan Warriors); 3 Kallum Watkins (Leeds Rhinos); 4 Michael Shenton (Castleford Tigers); 5 Ryan Hall (Leeds Rhinos); 6 Gareth Widdop (St George Illawarra Dragons); 7 Matty Smith (Wigan Warriors); 8 George Burgess (South Sydney Rabbitohs); 9 Josh Hodgson (Hull Kingston Rovers); 10 James Graham (Canterbury Bulldogs) (C); 11 Liam Farrell (Wigan Warriors); 12 Joel Tomkins (Wigan Warriors); 13 Joe Westerman (Hull FC). Subs (all used): 14 Daryl Clark (Castleford Tigers); 15 Brett Ferres (Huddersfield Giants); 16 Tom Burgess (South Sydney Rabbitohs); 17 Chris Hill (Warrington Wolves).
Tries: Shenton (21), Watkins (33), Farrell (46), J Tomkins (64), S Tomkins (68); **Goals:** Widdop 6/6.
SAMOA: 1 Tim Simona (Wests Tigers); 5 Daniel Vidot (Brisbane Broncos); 4 Joseph Leilua (Newcastle Knights); 3 Ricky Leutele (Cronulla Sharks); 2 Antonio Winterstein (North Queensland Cowboys); 6 Ben Roberts (Melbourne Storm); 7 Kyle Stanley (St George Illawarra Dragons); 8 Sam Tagataese (Cronulla Sharks); 9 Michael Sio (New Zealand Warriors); 10 David Fa'alogo (Newcastle Knights) (C); 11 Frank Pritchard (Canterbury Bulldogs); 12 Leeson Ah Mau (St George Illawarra Dragons); 13 Josh McGuire (Brisbane Broncos). Subs (all used): 14 Pita Godinet (Wakefield Trinity Wildcats); 15 Jesse Sene-Lefao (Manly Sea Eagles); 16 Isaac Liu (Sydney Roosters); 17 Mose Masoe (St Helens).
Tries: Liu (25), Vidot (30), Godinet (55, 61), Winterstein (71);
Goals: Stanley 2/3, Roberts 1/2.
Rugby Leaguer & League Express Men of the Match:
England: Chris Hill; *Samoa:* Joseph Leilua.
Penalty count: 9-6; **Half-time:** 14-10; **Referee:** Gerard Sutton (Australia).

FOUR NATIONS - GAME TWO

Saturday 25th October 2014

AUSTRALIA 12 NEW ZEALAND 30

AUSTRALIA: 1 Greg Inglis (South Sydney Rabbitohs); 2 Josh Mansour (Penrith Panthers); 3 Michael Jennings (Sydney Roosters); 4 Dylan Walker (South Sydney Rabbitohs); 5 Daniel Tupou (Sydney Roosters); 6 Daly Cherry-Evans (Manly Sea Eagles); 7 Cooper Cronk (Melbourne Storm); 8 Aaron Woods (Wests Tigers); 9 Cameron Smith (Melbourne Storm) (C); 10 Sam Thaiday (Brisbane Broncos); 11 Beau Scott (Newcastle Knights); 12 Ryan Hoffman (Melbourne Storm); 13 Greg Bird (Gold Coast Titans). Subs (all used): 14 Robbie Farah (Wests Tigers); 15 Aidan Guerra (Sydney Roosters); 16 Josh Papalii (Canberra Raiders); 17 Corey Parker (Brisbane Broncos).
Tries: Scott (2), Inglis (21); **Goals:** Smith 2/2.
NEW ZEALAND: 1 Peta Hiku (Manly Sea Eagles); 2 Jason Nightingale (St George Illawarra Dragons); 3 Dean Whare (Penrith Panthers); 4 Dean Whare (Penrith Panthers); 19 Gerard Beale (St George Illawarra Dragons); 6 Kieran Foran (Manly Sea Eagles); 7 Shaun Johnson (New Zealand Warriors); 8 Jesse Bromwich (Melbourne Storm); 9 Thomas Leuluai (New Zealand Warriors); 10 Adam Blair (Wests Tigers); 11 Simon Mannering (New Zealand Warriors) (C); 12 Kevin Proctor (Melbourne Storm); 13 Jason Taumalolo (North Queensland Cowboys). Subs (all used): 14 Lewis Brown (Penrith Panthers); 15 Greg Eastwood (Canterbury Bulldogs); 16 Martin Taupau (Wests Tigers); 17 Tohu Harris (Melbourne Storm).
Tries: Proctor (17), Brown (29), Johnson (47), Whare (51), Nightingale (68); **Goals:** Johnson 5/5.
Rugby Leaguer & League Express Men of the Match:
Australia: Aaron Woods; *New Zealand:* Shaun Johnson.
Penalty count: 4-5; **Half-time:** 12-12; **Referee:** Phil Bentham (England).

Attendance: 47,813 *(at Suncorp Stadium, Brisbane).*

after Liam Farrell produced a quick play-the-ball 45 metres out. Up the middle went Clark and on his inside was his Tigers captain Michael Shenton to take the pass and race in. Widdop's conversion opened a six-point gap.

But Josh McGuire threw a deft pass for Isaac Lui to barge his way through four defenders to score to have the pro-Samoa crowd roaring, with Kyle Stanley's conversion

levelling the scores. An upset then looked well in the offing as another Brisbane player Daniel Vidot crossed in the corner after Stanley and Joey Leilua wriggled out of tackles and slipped offloads.

But Smith's quick hands to Sam Tomkins as Ben Roberts rushed up got Kallum Watkins clear through the right channel, for Widdop's fine conversion to put England two points up. Widdop kicked a last-second penalty from under the posts, after Smith and Widdop each forced a goal-line drop-out, for a dangerous tackle on Clark, for a score of 14-10 at the break.

England took control when Brett Ferres released Josh Charnley on half way with a peach of a miss-pass. Charnley was closed down, but the ball was worked left sweetly by Clark and Smith before Widdop, with Sam Tomkins running wide out the back, hit Farrell with a short ball and the Wigan second rower was through and over. At 20-10 it looked safe, but it wasn't. Godinet's two tries, and a conversion apiece to Stanley and Roberts put Samoa 22-20 up.

Within three minutes England were back on the attack and Smith put up a last-tackle bomb. Shenton challenged Tim Simona, the ball hit the fullback on the chest and the video referee decided it bounced backwards for Joel Tomkins to collect and have a free run for the line. The partisan crowd didn't like it one bit.

And they didn't like it when, four minutes later, England scored another scrappy try when Sam Tomkins was the first up for another Smith bomb to the left of the posts. The ball brushed his chest as he kept his hands out of the way and, although Stanley managed to grab his shorts as he went for the line, Tomkins' long arm reached out to plant the ball. Widdop converted both tries and at 32-22 it looked over again.

On 71 minutes, Winterstein was over on the left after Pritchard caught Stanley's bomb and offloaded back, with McGuire's long pass giving Winterstein the space. Crucially, Roberts missed the kick and a six-point gap remained.

In the second game at Suncorp, an injury-riddled Australian squad was given a rugby lesson by the Kiwis, ending a winning streak of 16 Tests over the past four seasons.

The two sides had been locked at 12-12 at the interval, but it was one-way traffic in the second half, with New Zealand running out 30-12 victors.

The Kiwis now had the luxury of the return of inspirational hooker Issac Luke from the two-week suspension that also cost him a place in South Sydney's drought-breaking Grand Final success. And the knowledge that all their remaining matches would be played on home soil.

Aussie playmaker Daly Cherry-Evans, injured, and fullback Greg Inglis, suffering from a virus, were missing for the second half, forcing a wholesale reshuffle of the Australian attack.

There was no indication of how the match was going to unfold in the early action. With a crisp pass Cherry-Evans had Beau Scott across the whitewash in less than two minutes.

The Kiwis should have been quickly back in the equation. But the normally reliable Jason Nightingale lost control of the ball when attempting an acrobatic touchdown after gathering a wonderful cut-out pass from Kieran Foran.

It wasn't long before the Kiwis did make it over the whitewash. Big Kevin Proctor stormed through some paper-thin defence and Shaun Johnson levelled with the conversion.

After some good lead-up work by Corey Parker and Josh Papalii, who had just arrived

on the pitch, Greg Inglis charged from dummy half to plant the ball down next to the right hand post.

The Aussies were in front again but it didn't take long for the Kiwis to fight back, with Penrith's utility star Lewis Brown showing his versatility, dummying his way past several defenders. The conversion meant the two sides were all tied up on the scoreboard at half-time.

When Shaun Johnson put in a beautiful grubber kick early in the second half and regathered, the Kiwis were in front. And there was no looking back. They went further into the lead when Dean Whare won the leap for the ball off a bomb four minutes later.

Winger Gerard Beale missed the chance to extend the deficit when he was denied because debutant loose forward Jason Taumalolo had made a shoulder-charge on Cooper Cronk as Beale was heading for the line. But Nightingale then rubbed salt in the wound with a late try.

The Kiwis, impressive the previous weekend against Australia, snatched victory over the Samoans in Whangarei with a try five minutes from full-time to remain unbeaten in the tournament.

With Samoa holding on for grim death at 12-10, the New Zealanders dug deep for one last effort. Scrum-half Shaun Johnson was determined to take on the defensive line. As Samoa scrambled to keep the Kiwis at bay, the ball spun through the hands of Jason Nightingale, Issac Luke and captain Simon Mannering before finding Shaun Kenny-Dowall, who waltzed past the tiring defenders.

Samoa refused to give up, despite the fact there were fewer than four minutes remaining after the restart.

And in the shadow of full-time Newcastle centre Joey Leilua surged 50 metres but did not have enough support

FOUR NATIONS - GAME THREE

Saturday 1st November 2014

NEW ZEALAND 14 SAMOA 12

NEW ZEALAND: 1 Peta Hiku (Manly Sea Eagles); 2 Jason Nightingale (St George Illawarra Dragons); 3 Dean Whare (Penrith Panthers); 4 Shaun Kenny-Dowall (Sydney Roosters); 5 Manu Vatuvei (New Zealand Warriors); 6 Kieran Foran (Many Sea Eagles); 7 Shaun Johnson (New Zealand Warriors); 8 Jesse Bromwich (Melbourne Storm); 9 Issac Luke (South Sydney Rabbitohs); 10 Adam Blair (Wests Tigers); 11 Simon Mannering (New Zealand Warriors) (C); 12 Kevin Proctor (Melbourne Storm); 13 Jason Taumalolo (North Queensland Cowboys). Subs (all used): 14 Lewis Brown (Penrith Panthers); 15 Suaia Matagi (New Zealand Warriors); 16 Martin Taupau (Wests Tigers); 17 Tohu Harris (Melbourne Storm).
Tries: Foran (10), Nightingale (63), Kenny-Dowall (75);
Goals: Johnson 1/3.
SAMOA: 1 Tim Simona (Wests Tigers); 20 Tautau Moga (North Queensland Cowboys); 3 Tim Lafai (Canterbury Bulldogs); 4 Joseph Leilua (Newcastle Knights); 5 Daniel Vidot (Brisbane Broncos); 6 Ben Roberts (Melbourne Storm); 7 Kyle Stanley (St George Illawarra Dragons); 8 Isaac Liu (Sydney Roosters); 16 Sauaso Sue (Wests Tigers); 10 David Fa'alogo (Newcastle Knights) (C); 11 Frank Pritchard (Canterbury Bulldogs); 12 Leeson Ah Mau (St George Illawarra Dragons); 13 Josh McGuire (Brisbane Broncos). Subs (all used): 9 Pita Godinet (Wakefield Trinity Wildcats); 14 Dunamis Lui (Manly Sea Eagles); 17 Mose Masoe (St Helens); 18 Dominique Peyroux (New Zealand Warriors).
Tries: Moga (5), Vidot (17), Leilua (44); **Goals:** Lafai 0/3.
Rugby Leaguer & League Express Men of the Match:
New Zealand: Shaun Johnson; *Samoa:* Joseph Leilua.
Penalty count: 10-7; **Half-time:** 6-8; **Referee:** Henry Perenara (New Zealand); **Attendance:** 16,912 *(at Toll Stadium, Whangarei).*

for a fairytale finish, with the siren sounding as, still full of spirit, he rose to play the ball.

The Samoans were shattered. For the second straight weekend, the minnows had been beaten by goal-kicking after scoring the same number tries as two of the sport's three heavyweights, England and New Zealand.

New Zealand welcomed back Luke after his two-match suspension. And he led the pre-game Haka with gusto.

The underdogs showed the spirit that had shocked the England players seven days earlier. Cowboys winger Tautau Moga intercepted a loose pass from Peta Hiku and ran 80 metres to score, leaving Johnson in his wake.

Within four minutes the New Zealanders had struck back. Luke found a gap in the Samoan defence and sent Keiran Foran under the posts.

The Samoans were not to be denied. Some quick hands from Pita Godinet, who had just come off the bench, and Kyle Stanley gave stand-off Ben Roberts some room to put in a kick along the turf. Bruising Brisbane Broncos left winger Daniel Vidot was on hand to touch down.

Seven minutes before the break Manu Vatuvei looked to have scored in his return to the New Zealand Test side, pouncing on a grubber from Hiku. But, in a controversial decision, it was ruled Whare had obstructed substitute Dominique Peyroux as he

attempted a tackle in the lead-up action.

In the second half, Samoa continued the brutal play that characterised their performance in the first 40 minutes. Josh McGuire, unwanted by the Australians, was held up over the line. And from the very next ruck, Newcastle centre Leilua forced his way over, handing out a solid left-hand fend to Kenny-Dowall in the process.

Sadly for the Samoans, like the previous two tries, it was scored wide out and Tim Lafai again missed the conversion.

Eventually the concerted New Zealand attack took its toll, and Nightingale dived over in the right-hand corner. Johnson missed the conversion and the home side trailed 12-10, setting up the exciting conclusion.

England were denied a try in the closing minute of the Melbourne clash in which a defeat would have seen Australia miss the final of a major competition for the first time in 60 years.

The Australians were leading by four points when their fullback Greg Inglis flicked a rolling ball from Liam Farrell's grubber behind his tryline a millisecond before flying England winger Ryan Hall lunged. There seemed little doubt that Inglis had saved the day until slow-motion replays indicated Hall may have ever so slightly forced it with an out-stretched finger. The English players were convinced it was a try.

Australian video referee Bernard Sutton ruled Hall's hand had touched the ball while it was rising and there was no downward pressure.

Such a controversy was always on the cards when the tournament organisers scrapped the idea of neutral referees for the weekend matches, giving the one involving the Kiwis to New Zealander Henry Perenara and Australia's game against England to the local referee Gerard Sutton.

Both teams - and the referee and officials - wore commemorative strips to celebrate the 100th anniversary of the 'Rorke's Drift' Test match between Australia and England in 1914, in which 10 Englishmen held off the Australians to win the Ashes series.

Australia took the lead, when, from deep, stand-off Daly Cherry-Evans turned the ball back inside to Greg Bird, coming through at full pace. And centre Michael Jennings was there in support. But he went close to bombing the try, taking his left hand off the ball as he forced it behind the tryline with his right forearm.

There was some brave work that kept the Aussies at bay midway through the half. Sam Tomkins took a bomb and - cool, calm and collected - he passed behind his own line to Dan Sarginson, who fed Ryan Hall, who made some great ground up the left wing.

A few minutes later Hall broke through, up the centre, setting up Daryl Clark, who couldn't find two unmarked players in support on his left. But he was saved from embarrassment by a penalty when Greg Inglis dragged him across the sideline. From the subsequent play, Kallum Watkins was across the whitewash and Gareth Widdop's successful conversion edged England in front for the first time.

Then, with a second set of six, Hall increased the lead, dancing past Sione Mata'utia and Inglis after a superb one-handed back-flick from debutant Sarginson, brought in to make his debut in place of Michael Shenton. Then James Graham started a move that

FOUR NATIONS - GAME FOUR

Sunday 2nd November 2014

AUSTRALIA 16 ENGLAND 12

AUSTRALIA: 1 Greg Inglis (South Sydney Rabbitohs); 2 Josh Mansour (Penrith Panthers); 3 Michael Jennings (Sydney Roosters); 4 Dylan Walker (South Sydney Rabbitohs); 5 Sione Mata'utia (Newcastle Knights); 6 Daly Cherry-Evans (Manly Sea Eagles); 7 Cooper Cronk (Melbourne Storm); 8 Aaron Woods (Wests Tigers); 9 Cameron Smith (Melbourne Storm) (C); 10 Sam Thaiday (Brisbane Broncos); 11 Beau Scott (Newcastle Knights); 12 Greg Bird (Gold Coast Titans); 13 Corey Parker (Brisbane Broncos). Subs (all used): 14 Boyd Cordner (Sydney Roosters); 18 Ben Hunt (Brisbane Broncos); 19 David Klemmer (Canterbury Bulldogs); 20 Josh Papalii (Canberra Raiders). **Tries:** Jennings (15), Hunt (56), Inglis (63); **Goals:** Smith 2/3. **On report:** Bird (10) - alleged dangerous challenge on O'Loughlin.
ENGLAND: 1 Sam Tomkins (New Zealand Warriors); 2 Josh Charnley (Wigan Warriors); 3 Kallum Watkins (Leeds Rhinos); 4 Dan Sarginson (Wigan Warriors); 5 Ryan Hall (Leeds Rhinos); 6 Gareth Widdop (St George Illawarra Dragons); 7 Matty Smith (Wigan Warriors); 8 George Burgess (South Sydney Rabbitohs); 9 Josh Hodgson (Hull Kingston Rovers); 10 James Graham (Canterbury Bulldogs); 11 Liam Farrell (Wigan Warriors); 12 Joel Tomkins (Wigan Warriors); 19 Sean O'Loughlin (Wigan Warriors) (C). Subs (all used): 14 Daryl Clark (Castleford Tigers); 15 Brett Ferres (Huddersfield Giants); 16 Tom Burgess (South Sydney Rabbitohs); 17 Chris Hill (Warrington Wolves). **Tries:** Watkins (28), Hall (33); **Goals:** Widdop 2/2. **On report:** Farrell (7) - alleged dangerous challenge on Inglis; O'Loughlin (8) - alleged trip on Smith. **Rugby Leaguer & League Express Men of the Match:** *Australia:* Cameron Smith; *England:* Ryan Hall. **Penalty count:** 8-5; **Half-time:** 4-12; **Referee:** Gerard Sutton (Australia); **Attendance:** 20,585 *(at AAMI Park, Melbourne).*

went most of the length of the pitch before Widdop put the ball down. Still, England were sitting pretty at the break with a 12-4 lead.

England continued where they had left off once play resumed. And within a couple of minutes they went close to scoring again after some frantic offloads, only to have the move break down because of a forward pass.

When the Aussies took play the length of the field for Inglis to claim a try, they were disappointed, too, because of an obstruction by Boyd Cordner.

Ben Hunt was thrown into the fray 13 minutes after the interval. He replaced Sam Thaiday, which meant there was an extra halfback in action.

The decision paid an instant dividend. One of those playmakers, Cameron Smith, found the narrowest of gaps to put in a low kick on the line and Hunt scored just three minutes after coming on. Then Cherry-Evans sliced through some ordinary defence and turned the ball back inside for Inglis to score the try he was denied earlier.

It all built up to the dramatic finish.

Shaun Johnson was the key man in swinging a fabulous Test match the Kiwis' way, the first to be played in New Zealand's Deep South in Dunedin since 1928.

England - with Daryl Clark starting, Josh Hodgson dropped, and Elliott Whitehead coming off the bench for his full England debut on 24 minutes - had to win by 10 points to assure themselves of a place in the final. But at the end of the Kiwis' first set Johnson put up a high bomb into the right corner and Jason Nightingale rose above Ryan Hall to collect and, after a bit of a juggle, turn and plant the ball down for a try before two minutes were up. Johnson converted for a 6-0 lead.

A superbly executed move to the left saw Sean O'Loughlin, Gareth Widdop and Sam Tomkins link before Dan Sarginson

FOUR NATIONS - GAME FIVE

Saturday 8th November 2014

NEW ZEALAND 16 ENGLAND 14

NEW ZEALAND: 1 Peta Hiku (Manly Sea Eagles); 2 Jason Nightingale (St George Illawarra Dragons); 4 Dean Whare (Penrith Panthers); 3 Shaun Kenny-Dowall (Sydney Roosters); 5 Manu Vatuvei (New Zealand Warriors); 6 Kieran Foran (Many Sea Eagles); 7 Shaun Johnson (New Zealand Warriors); 8 Jesse Bromwich (Melbourne Storm); 14 Thomas Leuluai (New Zealand Warriors); 10 Adam Blair (Wests Tigers); 11 Simon Mannering (New Zealand Warriors) (C); 12 Kevin Proctor (Melbourne Storm); 13 Jason Taumalolo (North Queensland Cowboys). Subs (all used): 9 Issac Luke (South Sydney Rabbitohs); 15 Greg Eastwood (Canterbury Bulldogs); 16 Martin Taupau (Wests Tigers); 17 Tohu Harris (Melbourne Storm).
Tries: Nightingale (2, 30), Vatuvei (45); **Goals:** Johnson 2/3.
ENGLAND: 1 Sam Tomkins (New Zealand Warriors); 2 Josh Charnley (Wigan Warriors); 3 Kallum Watkins (Leeds Rhinos); 18 Dan Sarginson (Wigan Warriors); 5 Ryan Hall (Leeds Rhinos); 6 Gareth Widdop (St George Illawarra Dragons); 7 Matty Smith (Wigan Warriors); 8 George Burgess (South Sydney Rabbitohs); 14 Daryl Clark (Castleford Tigers); 10 James Graham (Canterbury Bulldogs); 11 Liam Farrell (Wigan Warriors); 12 Joel Tomkins (Wigan Warriors); 19 Sean O'Loughlin (Wigan Warriors) (C). Subs (all used): 15 Brett Ferres (Huddersfield Giants); 16 Tom Burgess (South Sydney Rabbitohs); 17 Chris Hill (Warrington Wolves); 20 Elliott Whitehead (Catalan Dragons).
Tries: Hall (7, 56), Charnley (25); **Goals:** Widdop 1/3.
On report: J Tomkins (73) - alleged fighting.
Rugby Leaguer & League Express Men of the Match:
New Zealand: Shaun Johnson; *England:* Sam Tomkins.
Penalty count: 8-6; **Half-time:** 12-8; **Referee:** Phil Bentham (England); **Attendance:** 15,836 *(at Forsyth Barr Stadium, Dunedin).*

gave the killer pass to send Ryan Hall into the left corner. Widdop's touchline kick hit the post and bounced out.

England took the lead on 25 minutes. This time the miss-move was to the right and Widdop and Matty Smith combined to hit O'Loughlin, whose perfect pass gave Josh Charnley just enough room to get on the outside of Manu Vatuvei and into the right corner. Widdop's conversion looked perfect, but it hit the far post again and bounced out. England's lead was only two points when it could so easily have been six.

Just before the half-hour mark, the Kiwis did 'an England' with a structured attack to the right and it took a clever piece of footwork from Dean Whare to step the on-rushing Ryan Hall and deliver the pass for the head-bandaged Nightingale to grab his second try.

Four Nations

Johnson nailed the touchline kick.

Within two minutes of the turnaround, England looked to have levelled. They were lucky to regain possession when a Johnson bomb was allowed to bounce. But within seconds Charnley was away down the right and when the ball was moved swiftly left, Hall was in at the corner, Sarginson creating the space. The referee called a try but sent it to video and in slow-motion Hall had clearly dropped the ball as he tried to ground it one-handed in Nightingale's tackle.

New Zealand responded in clinical fashion. Johnson trapped Sam Tomkins in-goal after a great Nightingale break from deep. And when they attacked left, captain Simon Mannering supplied the last pass that sent Vatuvei into the corner. Johnson missed the conversion, but the 10-point England win was looking unlikely with an eight-point arrear.

The Kiwis' offload game out of the tackle looked like strangling England, but a wonderful attack from their own half should have gained immediate reward. Graham found O'Loughlin with a smart inside ball at the ruck and the captain then looped a pass behind the defender to Daryl Clark. Clark tore away, bumped off Peta Hiku, fed George Burgess, who passed back to Clark, who looped a pass around the man to Widdop, who was closed down.

From the play-the-ball England moved right, and a try was begging when Brett Ferres knocked on Smith's pass on the half-volley. But six minutes later England were back in the game when the ball was moved left after Hiku dropped a Smith bomb and Sarginson's pass gave Hall enough room to this time get the ball down in the corner. Widdop did kick this one from the touchline.

It was the end of the scoring but, as both teams felt the pace of the game, in no way the end of the thrills especially a frantic last two minutes.

Kallum Watkins got around Shaun Kenny-Dowall and sent Charnley racing away on his inside, but he had his foot on the line when he delivered the pass. Then Widdop intercepted Johnson's grubber and tore away 40 metres. England kept the ball alive as though their lives depended on it and, with seconds left, got a penalty for offside when Vatuvei dropped Graham's bomb.

A draw was no good to England and they moved the ball left, only for Graham to lose possession as Adam Blair sprinted up.

In the first Test ever played in Wollongong, the Australians needed a win or draw to qualify for the final against the Kiwis, while Samoa needed to win by at least nine points. As it turned out it was a one-sided contest, with Australia hammering the Samoans who had given their all when almost beating both England and New Zealand.

It did not take long for the Australians to get on the scoreboard. Greg Inglis chimed into the backline just inside his own half, gave young winger Sione Mata'utia a bit of room to put down the accelerator and, as the defence eventually got to the rookie, Cooper Cronk was in support to touch down

Brisbane Broncos' connection set up the next try – Sam Thaiday flung an overhead pass to his club captain Corey Parker, who gave Inglis a clear run for the line. Inglis had scored in every 2014 Test in which he had played.

The Samoans were their own worst enemies, conceding stupid penalties when they were in attacking positions. But the first time they showed composure, the Samoans struck back, fullback Tim Simona ducking under a tackle to score near the left-hand post. Tim Lafai's conversion had the Pacific islanders back in the equation.

Samoa were almost in a second time two minutes later but Inglis managed to hold up Wakefield's Pita Godinet. There was a subsequent scuffle, but the Samoans could not capitalise on their penalty.

Then, after a charge-down by Greg Bird, a burst from Michael Jennings and another penalty against Joey Leilua, the Australians were ready to pounce. They did through Inglis.

No sooner had play resumed than Australia scored again. Stand-off Daly Cherry-Evans ran 70 metres down the left flank to score. Then it was the turn of rookie Canterbury prop David Klemmer for Australia to go to the break with a 22-point lead.

Samoa refused to throw in the towel and soon after resumption of play in the second half Castleford-bound stand-off Ben Roberts danced his way past a couple of would-be defenders to score and ease a little of the pain.

Australia had more trouble scoring in the second half, with the first try not coming until the 62nd minute when Cronk was across the whitewash once more just moments after he was cleaned up in a suspect tackle by St Helens' Mose Masoe.

Samoa still refused to capitulate. Lafai was bundled into touch in the left-hand corner before captain David Fa'alogo touched down.

Australia pulled away. Big Josh Papalii surged over, bouncing off four Samoans trying desperately to stop him. Then, with less than 90 seconds remaining on the clock, Penrith winger Josh Mansour rubbed salt in the wound by scoring his first Test try.

New Zealand stamped themselves as the world's best with a thrilling victory in the final of the Four Nations Tournament in windy Wellington, making amends for the humiliation of their 34-2 thrashing by Australia in the World Cup final at Old Trafford 12 months before.

It was 61 years since New Zealand had won consecutive Tests against the traditional Trans-Tasman rival in the same series or competition.

Scrum-half Shaun Johnson was a stand-out man of the match, continuing his great recent form by scoring a superb solo try and setting up one of two tries for winger Manu Vatuvei. But after Vatuvei's second effort it was a nail-biting conclusion, with substitute Ben Hunt touching down for Australia's third try before winger Sione Mata'utia was denied what could have proved to be a winning try with 15 seconds remaining on the clock.

There had been a forward pass from centre Dylan Walker to the teenager. Luckily it was the

---

FOUR NATIONS - GAME SIX

Sunday 9th November 2014

AUSTRALIA 44 SAMOA 18

AUSTRALIA: 1 Greg Inglis (South Sydney Rabbitohs); 2 Josh Mansour (Penrith Panthers); 3 Michael Jennings (Sydney Roosters); 4 Dylan Walker (South Sydney Rabbitohs); 5 Sione Mata'utia (Newcastle Knights); 6 Daly Cherry-Evans (Manly Sea Eagles); 7 Cooper Cronk (Melbourne Storm); 8 Aaron Woods (Wests Tigers); 9 Cameron Smith (Melbourne Storm) (C); 10 Josh Papalii (Canberra Raiders); 11 Sam Thaiday (Brisbane Broncos); 12 Greg Bird (Gold Coast Titans); 13 Corey Parker (Brisbane Broncos). Subs (all used): 14 Boyd Cordner (Sydney Roosters); 18 Ben Hunt (Brisbane Broncos); 19 David Klemmer (Canterbury Bulldogs); 21 Josh Jackson (Canterbury Bulldogs). **Tries:** Cronk (2, 62), Inglis (10, 25), Cherry-Evans (30), Klemmer (33), Papalii (76), Mansour (79); **Goals:** Smith 4/6, Cherry-Evans 2/2.
SAMOA: 1 Tim Simona (Wests Tigers); 2 Antonio Winterstein (North Queensland Cowboys); 3 Tim Lafai (Canterbury Bulldogs); 4 Joseph Leilua (Newcastle Knights); 5 Daniel Vidot (Brisbane Broncos); 6 Ben Roberts (Melbourne Storm); 7 Kyle Stanley (St George Illawarra Dragons); 8 Isaac Liu (Sydney Roosters); 13 Josh McGuire (Brisbane Broncos); 10 David Fa'alogo (Newcastle Knights) (C); 11 Frank Pritchard (Canterbury Bulldogs); 12 Leeson Ah Mau (St George Illawarra Dragons); 17 Mose Masoe (St Helens). Subs (all used): 9 Pita Godinet (Wakefield Trinity Wildcats); 14 Dunamis Lui (Manly Sea Eagles); 15 Reni Maitua (Canterbury Bulldogs); 16 Sauaso Sue (Wests Tigers). **Tries:** Simona (19), Roberts (46), Fa'alogo (70); **Goals:** Lafai 3/3.
Rugby Leaguer & League Express Men of the Match:
Australia: Greg Inglis; *Samoa:* Josh McGuire.
Penalty count: 10-8; **Half-time:** 28-6; **Referee:** Gerard Sutton (Australia); **Attendance:** 18,456 *(at WIN Stadium, Wollongong).*

FOUR NATIONS - FINAL STANDINGS								
	P	W	D	L	F	A	Diff	PTS
New Zealand	3	3	0	0	60	38	22	6
Australia	3	2	0	1	72	60	12	4
England	3	1	0	2	58	58	0	2
Samoa	3	0	0	3	56	90	-34	0

neutral referee Phil Bentham from England who ruled on the pass on the advice of his touch judge, preventing any accusations of favouritism.

The Kiwis had first use of the ball, the set of six tackles finishing with a stirring run by captain Simon Mannering.

When Australia got the ball they went close to scoring. However the bounce of the ball was not complimentary to winger Josh Mansour. A couple of minutes later the Aussies went close again, with Corey Parker held up over the line after a clever offload from Cameron Smith.

Eventually the Australians got a bit of luck. Cooper Cronk put up a bomb. Kiwi centre Dean Whare got his fingertips to the ball but pushed it straight to opposing centre Michael Jennings who was delighted to touch down for the first try of the night.

FOUR NATIONS - FINAL

Saturday 15th November 2014

NEW ZEALAND 22 AUSTRALIA 18

NEW ZEALAND: 1 Peta Hiku (Manly Sea Eagles); 2 Jason Nightingale (St George Illawarra Dragons); 3 Shaun Kenny-Dowall (Sydney Roosters); 4 Dean Whare (Penrith Panthers); 5 Manu Vatuvei (New Zealand Warriors); 6 Kieran Foran (Manly Sea Eagles); 7 Shaun Johnson (New Zealand Warriors); 8 Jesse Bromwich (Melbourne Storm); 9 Issac Luke (South Sydney Rabbitohs); 10 Adam Blair (Wests Tigers); 11 Simon Mannering (New Zealand Warriors) (C); 12 Kevin Proctor (Melbourne Storm); 13 Jason Taumalolo (North Queensland Cowboys). Subs (all used): 14 Lewis Brown (Penrith Panthers); 15 Greg Eastwood (Canterbury Bulldogs); 16 Martin Taupau (Wests Tigers); 17 Tohu Harris (Melbourne Storm).
Tries: Nightingale (23), Vatuvei (34, 63), Johnson (58);
Goals: Johnson 3/5.
AUSTRALIA: 1 Greg Inglis (South Sydney Rabbitohs); 2 Josh Mansour (Penrith Panthers); 3 Michael Jennings (Sydney Roosters); 4 Dylan Walker (South Sydney Rabbitohs); 5 Sione Mata'utia (Newcastle Knights); 6 Daly Cherry-Evans (Manly Sea Eagles); 7 Cooper Cronk (Melbourne Storm); 8 Aaron Woods (Wests Tigers); 9 Cameron Smith (Melbourne Storm) (C); 10 Josh Papalii (Canberra Raiders); 11 Sam Thaiday (Brisbane Broncos); 12 Greg Bird (Gold Coast Titans); 13 Corey Parker (Brisbane Broncos). Subs (all used): 14 Boyd Cordner (Sydney Roosters); 18 Ben Hunt (Brisbane Broncos); 19 Josh Jackson (Canterbury Bulldogs); 20 David Klemmer (Canterbury Bulldogs).
Tries: Jennings (11), Mata'utia (42), Hunt (76); **Goals:** Smith 3/3.
Rugby Leaguer & League Express Men of the Match:
New Zealand: Shaun Johnson; *Australia:* Michael Jennings.
Penalty count: 3-6; **Half-time:** 14-6; **Referee:** Phil Bentham (England); **Attendance:** 25,183 *(at Westpac Stadium, Wellington).*

The Kiwis refused to knuckle under. Shaun Kenny-Dowall made a burst of around 40 metres before the ball raced across the backline for Nightingale to score in the right corner. Johnson's successful conversion levelled the scores.

The Kiwis were never behind again from that moment on.

Within five minutes, New Zealand were close to scoring once more as Keiran Foran was held up over the tryline. It mattered not as they were awarded a penalty for a high tackle in the lead-up and Johnson edged the home side ahead by two.

Johnson's kicks were causing chaos in the swirling wind. But then he put on a display of dancing and prancing that mesmerised his opponents before flinging a long pass to Vatuvei. And 'The Beast', after collecting on the half volley, was over for his 19th try, equalling the New Zealand Test record of Nigel Vagana.

The Kiwis, capitalising on more than 60 per cent of possession, went to the interval with a handy 14-6 lead.

Once play resumed for the second half, Australia struck back with a controversial try to Mata'utia. The New Zealanders claimed a decoy took out Foran. But referee Bentham and video official Bernard Sutton disagreed. Moments later, Martin Taupau, arguably New Zealand's best forward, suffered a neck injury and was carried off.

But Johnson's brilliance lit up the arena. He raced from 45 metres out and past Daly Cherry-Evans before brushing off Greg Inglis to score. His conversion attempt bounced off the woodwork. Nevertheless the Kiwis were ahead by six.

When Vatuvei stormed through Mata'utia and across the line for his second try, after wonderful early work by Foran and fullback Peta Hiku, the home side were looking good, at 22-12

Hunt gave Australia a last sniff of victory with just over three minutes to play. He sent the ball right via Cronk to Dylan Walker, whose back-flick sent Mata'utia down the wing. He found Cronk on his inside, and, as he was tackled, a speculative back pass was gobbled up by Hunt for the try in the right corner.

With four points in it, the Aussies looked like they would snatch it. A penalty gave them field position. Jennings darted across the field to the right heading for Walker and Mata'utia. But it was all in vain because of the forward pass picked up by the touch judge.

OTHER INTERNATIONALS
Scotland the brave

Alitalia European Cup

ALITALIA EUROPEAN CUP - FINAL STANDINGS								
	P	W	D	L	F	A	Diff	PTS
Scotland	3	2	0	1	89	60	29	4
France	3	2	0	1	92	66	26	4
Ireland	3	2	0	1	72	51	21	4
Wales	3	0	0	3	54	130	-76	0

Scotland claimed the European Championship and a spot in the 2016 Four Nations after a dramatic final weekend of action in November as they finished equal on league points with France and Ireland, with a better points difference of three over France, and eight over Ireland.

An understrength Wales team, weakened by the withdrawals of a host of Super League stars because of the wedding of Wigan's Gil Dudson, finished without a win.

When it came to the final weekend of the round-robin, either of the three top teams could have won it.

But after Ireland's inability to beat Wales by 41 points at Wrexham on the Sunday, it was Scotland who claimed top spot, despite losing 22-38 to France in Galashiels on the Friday night. They had earned the right to face off against England, Australia and New Zealand in two years' time, with a three-Test tour by New Zealand scheduled for 2015.

Scotland were staring into the abyss at half-time at Galashiels, trailing France 38-6 at the break, before eventually scoring enough points to ensure they remained top heading into the final game of the tournament.

France coach Richard Agar said: "The tournament has a massive prize at the end of it, and for it to be settled on points difference is a shame. Perhaps there should be a final at the end of it for the two teams at the top. The tournament has been pretty well supported and, for such a massive prize, a final is perhaps the way to give the tournament a little bit more credibility."

Scotland scrum-half and captain Danny Brough was selected as the player of the tournament.

Ireland's Shannon McDonnell makes a break against Wales

Other Internationals

ALITALIA EUROPEAN CUP

Friday 17th October 2014

SCOTLAND 42 WALES 18

SCOTLAND: 1 Oscar Thomas (London Broncos); 2 Dave Scott (Doncaster); 3 Ben Hellewell (Featherstone Rovers); 4 Joe Wardle (Huddersfield Giants); 5 Alex Hurst (Tweed Heads Seagulls); 6 Danny Brough (Huddersfield Giants) (C); 7 Nathan Massey (Canterbury Bulldogs); 8 Adam Walker (Hull Kingston Rovers); 9 Danny Addy (Bradford Bulls); 10 Ben Kavanagh (Widnes Vikings); 11 Brett Phillips (Workington Town); 12 Corbyn Kilday (Wakefield Trinity Wildcats); 13 Sonny Esslemont (Hull Kingston Rovers). Subs (all used): 14 Callum Phillips (Workington Town); 15 Josh Barlow (Swinton Lions); 16 Jonathan Walker (Leigh Centurions); 17 Louis Senter (Halifax).
Tries: Brough (12), Thomas (16), Kilday (27), J Walker (46), Scott (48, 61), C Phillips (51), B Phillips (69); **Goals:** Brough 5/8.
WALES: 1 Tom Hughes (Coventry Bears); 3 Yannic Parker (Oxford); 8 Kyle Scrivens (South Wales Scorpions); 11 Christiaan Roets (North Wales Crusaders); 19 Rhys Williams (Central Queensland Capras); 6 Ollie Olds (Ipswich Jets); 10 Peter Lupton (Workington Town) (C); 13 Daniel Fleming (Castleford Tigers); 16 Ricky Hough (Gateshead Thunder); 12 Matt Barron (Gateshead Thunder); 9 Phil Carleton (South Wales Scorpions); 7 Ashley Bateman (South Wales Scorpions); 22 Joe Burke (Barrow Raiders). Subs (all used): 5 Connor Farrer (South Wales Scorpions); 24 Morgan Evans (South Wales Scorpions); 15 Izaak Duffy (Gloucestershire All Golds); 21 Lewis Reece (Toowoomba Clydesdales).
Tries: Williams (10), Roets (39), Lupton (43), Farrer (75);
Goals: Hough 0/2, Reece 1/2.
Rugby Leaguer & League Express Men of the Match:
Scotland: Danny Brough; *Wales:* Connor Farrer.
Penalty count: 9-7; **Half-time:** 16-8; **Referee:** James Child (England);
Attendance: 2,036 *(at Derwent Park, Workington)*.

Saturday 18th October 2014

IRELAND 22 FRANCE 12

IRELAND: 1 Shannon McDonnell (St Helens); 2 Callum Mulkeen (Oxford); 3 Haydn Peacock (Carcassonne); 4 Michael Platt (Leigh Centurions); 5 Casey Dunne (Athboy Longhorns); 6 Callum Casey (Halifax); 7 Ben Johnston (Halifax); 8 Rob Mulhern (Leeds Rhinos); 9 Bob Beswick (Leigh Centurions) (C); 10 Luke Ambler (Halifax); 11 Elliott Cosgrove (Keighley Cougars); 12 Joshua Toole (Illawarra Cutters); 13 Will Hope (Sheffield Eagles). Subs (all used): 14 Jobe Murphy (Dewsbury Rams); 15 Sean Hesketh (Keighley Cougars); 16 Wayne Kelly (Belfast Met Scholars); 17 Matty Hadden (Oxford).
Tries: McDonnell (7, 47), Peacock (31, 54), Murphy (80); **Goals:** Dunne 1/5.
FRANCE: 1 Tony Maurel (Toulouse Olympique); 2 Mathias Pala (Catalan Dragons); 3 Jean-Philippe Baile (Catalan Dragons); 4 Damien Cardace (Catalan Dragons); 5 Frederic Vaccari (Palau Broncos); 6 Theo Fages (Salford Red Devils); 7 William Barthau (Catalan Dragons); 8 Jamal Fakir (Lezignan); 9 Eloi Pelissier (Catalan Dragons); 10 Mickael Simon (Catalan Dragons); 11 Kevin Larroyer (Hull Kingston Rovers); 12 Benjamin Garcia (Catalan Dragons); 13 Jason Baitieri (Catalan Dragons) (C). Subs (all used): 14 Remy Marginet (Palau Broncos); 15 Aaron Wood (Toulouse Olympique); 16 Julian Bousquet (Catalan Dragons); 17 Antoni Maria (Catalan Dragons).
Tries: Larroyer (59), Pelissier (70); **Goals:** Marginet 2/2.
Rugby Leaguer & League Express Men of the Match:
Ireland: Bob Beswick; *France:* Remy Marginet.
Penalty count: 11-5; **Half-time:** 8-0; **Referee:** Ben Thaler (England);
Attendance: 1,428 *(at Tallaght Stadium, Dublin)*.

Saturday 25th October 2014

FRANCE 42 WALES 22

FRANCE: 1 Mathias Pala (Catalan Dragons); 2 Clement Soubeyras (Carcassonne); 3 Aurelien Decarnin (Villeneuve); 4 Damien Cardace (Catalan Dragons); 5 Frederic Vaccari (Palau Broncos); 6 Theo Fages (Salford Red Devils); 7 Remy Marginet (Palau Broncos); 8 Jamal Fakir (Lezignan); 9 John Boudebza (Lezignan); 10 Mickael Simon (Catalan Dragons); 11 Kevin Larroyer (Hull Kingston Rovers); 12 Benjamin Garcia (Catalan Dragons); 13 Jason Baitieri (Catalan Dragons) (C). Subs (all used): 14 Eloi Pelissier (Catalan Dragons); 15 Jean-Philippe Baile (Catalan Dragons); 16 Julian Bousquet (Catalan Dragons); 17 Aaron Wood (Toulouse Olympique).
Tries: Soubeyras (6), Fages (18), Baile (34), Pala (37, 51), Marginet (41, 52); **Goals:** Marginet 7/7.
WALES: 1 Tom Hughes (Coventry Bears); 3 Dalton Grant (Barrow Raiders); 8 Kyle Scrivens (South Wales Scorpions); 11 Christiaan Roets (North Wales Crusaders); 19 Rhys Williams (Central Queensland Capras); 10 Peter Lupton (Workington Town) (C); 6 Ollie Olds (Ipswich Jets); 13 Daniel Fleming (Castleford Tigers); 5 Connor Farrer (South Wales Scorpions); 12 Matt Barron (Gateshead Thunder); 21 Lewis Reece (Toowoomba Clydesdales); 16 Ricky Hough (Gateshead Thunder); 7 Matty Fozard (St Helens). Subs (all used): 14 Owain Griffiths (North Wales Crusaders); 17 Paul Emanuelli (South Wales Scorpions); 24 Morgan Evans (South Wales Scorpions); 15 Izaak Duffy (Gloucestershire All Golds).
Tries: Fleming (9), Fozard (47), Williams (65), Roets (69); **Goals:** Reece 3/4.
Rugby Leaguer & League Express Men of the Match:
France: Remy Marginet; *Wales:* Daniel Fleming.
Penalty count: 5-1; **Half-time:** 24-6; **Referee:** Tim Roby (England);
Attendance: 5,225 *(at Stadium Municipal d'Albi)*.

IRELAND 4 SCOTLAND 25

IRELAND: 1 Shannon McDonnell (St Helens); 2 Callum Mulkeen (Oxford); 3 Haydn Peacock (Carcassonne); 4 Stuart Littler (Rochdale Hornets); 5 Casey Dunne (Athboy Longhorns); 6 Callum Casey (Halifax); 7 James Toole (Tweed Heads Seagulls); 8 Rob Mulhern (Leeds Rhinos); 9 Bob Beswick (Leigh Centurions) (C); 10 Luke Ambler (Halifax); 11 Jobe Murphy (Dewsbury Rams); 12 Joshua Toole (Illawarra Cutters); 13 Will Hope (Sheffield Eagles). Subs (all used): 14 Wayne Kelly (Belfast Met Scholars); 15 Sean Hesketh (Keighley Cougars); 16 Graham O'Keeffe (Oxford); 17 Matty Hadden (Oxford).
Try: James Toole (73); **Goals:** Dunne 0/1.
SCOTLAND: 1 Oscar Thomas (London Broncos); 2 Dave Scott (Doncaster); 3 Ben Hellewell (Featherstone Rovers); 4 Joe Wardle (Huddersfield Giants); 5 Alex Hurst (Tweed Heads Seagulls); 6 Danny Brough (Huddersfield Giants) (C); 7 Nathan Massey (Canterbury Bulldogs); 8 Adam Walker (Hull Kingston Rovers); 9 Danny Addy (Bradford Bulls); 10 Ben Kavanagh (Widnes Vikings); 11 Corbyn Kilday (Wakefield Trinity Wildcats); 12 Brett Phillips (Workington Town); 13 Sonny Esslemont (Hull Kingston Rovers). Subs (all used): 14 Callum Phillips (Workington Town); 15 Joe McClean (Gloucestershire All Golds); 16 Josh Barlow (Swinton Lions); 17 Louis Senter (Halifax).
Tries: C Phillips (39), Hurst (48), Addy (68), Thomas (77);
Goals: Brough 4/4; **Field goal:** Brough (63).
Rugby Leaguer & League Express Men of the Match:
Ireland: Will Hope; *Scotland:* Adam Walker.
Penalty count: 8-10; **Half-time:** 0-6;
Referee: Richard Silverwood (England); **Attendance:** 1,342
(at Tallaght Stadium, Dublin).

Friday 31st October 2014

SCOTLAND 22 FRANCE 38

SCOTLAND: 1 Oscar Thomas (London Broncos); 2 Dave Scott (Doncaster); 3 Ben Hellewell (Featherstone Rovers); 4 Joe Wardle (Huddersfield Giants); 5 Alex Hurst (Tweed Heads Seagulls); 6 Danny Brough (Huddersfield Giants) (C); 7 Nathan Massey (Canterbury Bulldogs); 8 Adam Walker (Hull Kingston Rovers); 9 Danny Addy (Bradford Bulls); 10 Jonathan Walker (Leigh Centurions); 11 Sonny Esslemont (Hull Kingston Rovers); 12 Corbyn Kilday (Wakefield Trinity Wildcats); 13 Ben Kavanagh (Widnes Vikings). Subs (all used): 14 Callum Phillips (Workington Town); 15 Josh Barlow (Swinton Lions); 16 Harvey Burnett (London Broncos); 17 Louis Senter (Halifax).
Tries: Kavanagh (3), Hellewell (63), A Walker (73), J Walker (76);
Goals: Brough 3/4.
FRANCE: 1 Mathias Pala (Catalan Dragons); 2 Tony Gigot (Avignon); 3 Jean-Philippe Baile (Catalan Dragons); 4 Aurelien Decarnin (Villeneuve); 5 Frederic Vaccari (Palau Broncos); 6 Theo Fages (Salford Red Devils); 7 Remy Marginet (Palau Broncos); 8 Jamal Fakir (Lezignan); 9 Eloi Pelissier (Catalan Dragons); 10 Mickael Simon (Catalan Dragons); 11 Kevin Larroyer (Hull Kingston Rovers); 12 Benjamin Garcia (Catalan Dragons); 13 Jason Baitieri (Catalan Dragons) (C). Subs (all used): 14 John Boudebza (Lezignan); 15 Aaron Wood (Toulouse Olympique); 16 Julian Bousquet (Catalan Dragons); 17 Antoni Maria (Catalan Dragons).
Tries: Marginet (15, 21, 27), Baitieri (17), Pelissier (25), Decarnin (34), Gigot (39); **Goals:** Marginet 5/7.
Rugby Leaguer & League Express Men of the Match:
Scotland: Danny Brough; *France:* Remy Marginet.
Penalty count: 7-6; **Half-time:** 6-38;
Referee: Richard Silverwood (England); **Attendance:** 1,432
(at Netherdale, Galashiels).

Sunday 2nd November 2014

WALES 14 IRELAND 46

WALES: 1 Tom Hughes (Coventry Bears); 3 Dalton Grant (Barrow Raiders); 21 Lewis Reece (Toowoomba Clydesdales); 11 Christiaan Roets (North Wales Crusaders); 19 Rhys Williams (Central Queensland Capras); 6 Ollie Olds (Ipswich Jets); 10 Peter Lupton (Workington Town) (C); 30 Byron Smith (Batley Bulldogs); 18 Matty Fozard (St Helens); 12 Matt Barron (Gateshead Thunder); 31 Ricky Hough (Gateshead Thunder); 7 Ashley Bateman (South Wales Scorpions); 13 Daniel Fleming (Castleford Tigers). Subs (all used): 22 Joe Burke (Barrow Raiders); 5 Connor Farrer (South Wales Scorpions); 24 Morgan Evans (South Wales Scorpions); 17 Paul Emanuelli (South Wales Scorpions).
Tries: Williams (46), Grant (63), Hughes (79);
Goals: Reece 1/2, Emanuelli 0/1.
IRELAND: 1 Shannon McDonnell (St Helens); 2 Brad Hargreaves (Wigan St Patricks); 3 Haydn Peacock (Carcassonne); 4 Stuart Littler (Rochdale Hornets); 5 Casey Dunne (Athboy Longhorns); 6 Ben Johnston (Halifax); 7 Liam Finn (Castleford Tigers); 8 Rob Mulhern (Leeds Rhinos); 9 Bob Beswick (Leigh Centurions) (C); 10 Luke Ambler (Halifax); 11 Will Hope (Sheffield Eagles); 12 Joshua Toole (Illawarra Cutters); 13 Callum Casey (Halifax). Subs (all used): 14 Jobe Murphy (Dewsbury Rams); 15 Sean Hesketh (Keighley Cougars); 16 James Toole (Tweed Heads Seagulls); 17 Matty Hadden (Oxford).
Tries: Hope (3), Hargreaves (11, 29, 50), Casey (16), Finn (37), Peacock (72), Dunne (76); **Goals:** Finn 7/8.
Rugby Leaguer & League Express Men of the Match:
Wales: Byron Smith; *Ireland:* Liam Finn.
Penalty count: 7-10; **Half-time:** 0-28; **Referee:** Ben Thaler (England);
Attendance: 1,293 *(at Glyndwr University Racecourse Stadium, Wrexham)*.

Anzac Test

Australia edged to a 16th straight victory, by 30-18 against an understrength New Zealand side at the Sydney Football Stadium on Friday evening, 2 May.

The game had been written off as a waste of time by the Australian media. But the 25,000-plus people that turned out were treated to a true Test match. The Kiwis led 18-12 at half-time before being overhauled in the second half by a ruthless Kangaroos side.

The Kiwis were well worth their lead at half-time, gained despite a 5-1 penalty count against them. But the vast experience of the Australians won through with 18-unanswered points, as the greenness of the Kiwis meant they were unable to replicate their incisiveness of the opening 40 minutes.

Coach Stephen Kearney had copped some flak for leaving out the experience of Jared Waerea-Hargreaves, but his side's front row was the main reason for their first-half dominance.

Melbourne's Jesse Bromwich ran 135 metres from 17 carries, as well as making 37 tackles. Former Hull FC prop Sam Moa made 129 metres from 14 runs, which was also more than any Australian player except Paul Gallen (188 metres). In the centres, Dean Whare kept Greg Inglis under wraps for most of the night, although the bullocking centre's 61st minute try gave Australia the lead for the final time.

Shaun Johnson was his mercurial self, though the Kiwis lacked another halfback of the like of Cooper Cronk and Johnathan Thurston, who never wavered. Nor did skipper Cameron Smith, whose controlled kicking game and leadership were the key to victory.

Smith's grubber in-goal and Nate Myles' tackle that trapped Shaun Johnson set up Inglis's 61st minute try. Cronk finished off the try-scoring with seven minutes left.

ANZAC TEST
Friday 2nd May 2014

AUSTRALIA 30 NEW ZEALAND 18

AUSTRALIA: 1 Billy Slater (Melbourne Storm); 2 Darius Boyd (Newcastle Knights); 3 Greg Inglis (South Sydney Rabbitohs); 4 Josh Morris (Canterbury Bulldogs); 5 Brett Morris (St George Illawarra Dragons); 6 Johnathan Thurston (North Queensland Cowboys); 7 Cooper Cronk (Melbourne Storm); 8 Matthew Scott (North Queensland Cowboys); 9 Cameron Smith (Melbourne Storm) (C); 16 Nate Myles (Gold Coast Titans); 11 Greg Bird (Gold Coast Titans); 12 Boyd Cordner (Sydney Roosters); 13 Paul Gallen (Cronulla Sharks). Subs (all used): 14 Daly Cherry-Evans (Manly Sea Eagles); 15 Matt Gillett (Brisbane Broncos); 10 James Tamou (North Queensland Cowboys); 17 Corey Parker (Brisbane Broncos).
Tries: Bird (12), B Morris (17, 52), Inglis (61), Cronk (73);
Goals: Thurston 5/5.
NEW ZEALAND: 1 Peta Hiku (Manly Sea Eagles); 2 Roger Tuivasa-Sheck (Sydney Roosters); 3 Dean Whare (Penrith Panthers); 4 Gerard Beale (St George Illawarra Dragons); 5 Jason Nightingale (St George Illawarra Dragons); 17 Tohu Harris (Melbourne Storm); 7 Shaun Johnson (New Zealand Warriors); 8 Jesse Bromwich (Melbourne Storm); 9 Ben Henry (New Zealand Warriors); 10 Sam Moa (Sydney Roosters); 11 Simon Mannering (New Zealand Warriors) (C); 12 Kevin Proctor (Melbourne Storm); 13 Adam Blair (Wests Tigers). Subs (all used): 6 Isaac John (Penrith Panthers); 14 Siliva Havili (New Zealand Warriors); 15 Martin Taupau (Wests Tigers); 16 Greg Eastwood (Canterbury Bulldogs).
Tries: Bromwich (6), Harris (22), Moa (27); **Goals:** Johnson 3/3.
Rugby Leaguer & League Express Men of the Match:
Australia: Cameron Smith; *New Zealand:* Sam Moa.
Penalty count: 8-4; **Half-time:** 12-18;
Referee: Shayne Hayne (Australia); **Attendance:** 25,529
(at Allianz Stadium, Sydney).

Commonwealth Nines

Papua New Guinea became the Commonwealth Rugby League Champions after defeating tournament favourites Australia 22-8 in a thrilling final at Cumbernauld, near Glasgow.

The two-day tournament was played as an exhibition sport for the Commonwealth Games, officially endorsed by the Commonwealth Games Federation and featured under 19s teams from eight nations, with Australia represented by the Sydney Roosters SG Ball winning team.

The Papuans came out on top in the eight-team tournament after going through their pool games undefeated against England, Canada and Jamaica, and then booking a place in the final with a 12-6 semi-final win over Wales.

The Papuan players were presented with gold medals, while the Welsh came third in the tournament after beating Canada in the bronze medal game.

England came sixth in the tournament, suffering a shock defeat to Canada in their pool game, and then losing to Scotland in the game to decide the fifth-placed team.

COMMONWEALTH NINES
Friday 27th June 2014
POOL A: Australia 26 Jamaica 4; Wales 18 Scotland 6; Australia 34 Wales 10; Scotland 4 Jamaica 0; Wales 34 Jamaica 0; Scotland 18 Australia 18
POOL B: Papua New Guinea 22 South Africa 8; Canada 24 England 4; Canada 24 South Africa 16; Papua New Guinea 16 England 10; Papua New Guinea 26 Canada 6; England 22 South Africa 6

Saturday 28th June 2014
PLAY-OFFS: England 24 Jamaica 8; Scotland 34 South Africa 6
SEVENTH/EIGHTH: Jamaica 12 South Africa 4
FIFTH/SIXTH: Scotland 14 England 4
SEMI-FINALS: Australia 20 Canada 0; Papua New Guinea 12 Wales 6
BRONZE MEDAL: Wales 20 Canada 8
FINAL: Papua New Guinea 22 Australia 8

(all at Broadwood Stadium, Glasgow)

Four Nations Qualifier

Toa Samoa earned the right to compete in the 2014 Four Nations with a 32-16 win on the first Saturday of May, gaining revenge for their World Cup quarter-final defeat to the Batis after coming back from a 16-6 deficit just before half-time.

Key to the outcome was the 35th minute facial injury to former Sheffield halfback Aaron Groom, who was led off never to return. Fiji desperately lacked direction in the second half, with winger Lote Tuqiri, in his first Test for Fiji since 2000, trying in vain to create and control.

Samoa forced three goal-line drop outs in the first ten minutes. Cronulla's Penani Manumalealii benefitted from the pressure when he scored the first of his hat-trick, side-stepping through and under the posts straight from a scrum.

From then on it looked like Fiji would repeat their World Cup dominance over Samoa as three tries - from Kevin Naiqama, Tuqiri and James Storer - took them clear, two converted by Tuqiri.

But Samoa got one back when Manumalealii wrapped around and took an offload from sub Sam Tagataese to reduce the margin to 16-12 at half-time.

The Samoans got off to a flyer in the second half and took the lead when Sharks prop Tagataese - who was later red carded for a head butt on Kane Evans - broke 40 metres and his quick play the ball allowed Manumalealii to scoot in for his hat-trick try. Krisnan Inu's conversion and a penalty shortly after gave Samoa a four-point lead.

Further tries from Warriors utility Carlos Tuimavave and Daniel Vidot sealed it.

FOUR NATIONS QUALIFIER

Saturday 3rd May 2014

FIJI 16 SAMOA 32

FIJI: 1 Kevin Naiqama (Penrith Panthers); 5 Eto Nabuli (Penrith Panthers); 4 Lote Tuqiri (South Sydney Rabbitohs); 3 Semi Waqavatu (Parramatta Eels); 2 Marika Koroibete (Wests Tigers); 6 Alipate Noilea (Illawarra Cutters); 7 Aaron Groom (Asquith Magpies); 8 Ashton Sims (North Queensland Cowboys); 9 James Storer (Illawarra Cutters); 10 Kane Evans (Sydney Roosters); 11 Vitale Roqica (Cronulla Sharks); 12 Peni Botiki (Illawarra Cutters); 13 Korbin Sims (Newcastle Knights). Subs (all used): 18 Petero Civoniceva (unattached) (C); 15 Reagan Campbell-Gillard (Penrith Panthers); 16 Osea Sadrau (Carcassonne); 17 Atunaisa Turagaiviu (Fiji Police).
Tries: Naiqama (16), Storer (27), Tuqiri (30); **Goals:** Tuqiri 2/3.
SAMOA: 1 Peter Mata'utia (St George Illawarra Dragons); 2 Daniel Vidot (Brisbane Broncos); 4 Krisnan Inu (Canterbury Bulldogs); 3 Ricky Leutele (Cronulla Sharks); 5 Young Tonumaipea (Melbourne Storm); 6 Reni Maitua (Canterbury Bulldogs); 7 Penani Manumalealii (Cronulla Sharks); 17 Suaia Matagi (New Zealand Warriors); 9 Michael Sio (New Zealand Warriors); 10 David Fa'alogo (Newcastle Knights) (C); 11 Leeson Ah Mau (St George Illawarra Dragons); 12 Dominique Peyroux (New Zealand Warriors); 13 Isaac Liu (Sydney Roosters). Subs (all used): 18 Carlos Tuimavave (New Zealand Warriors); 15 Dunamis Lui (Manly Sea Eagles); 16 Jesse Sene-Lefao (Manly Sea Eagles); 8 Sam Tagataese (Cronulla Sharks).
Tries: Manumalealii (13, 38, 44), Tuimavave (54), Vidot (64); **Goals:** Inu 6/6.
Rugby Leaguer & League Express Men of the Match: *Fiji:* Lote Tuqiri; *Samoa:* Penani Manumalealii.
Penalty count: 4-10; **Half-time:** 16-12;
Referee: Ashley Klein (Australia); **Attendance:** 9,063
(at Sportingbet Stadium, Penrith).

EUROPEAN CHAMPIONSHIP B - 2014-2015

Saturday 17th May 2014
Serbia 40 Ukraine 14
(at Zeleznicar Stadium, Nis)
Saturday 24th May 2014
Russia 20 Ukraine 18
(at Vereya Stadium, Vereya)
Saturday 21st June 2014
Russia 20 Serbia 6
(at Nara Stadium, Narofominsk)
Saturday 5th July 2014
Italy 54 Ukraine 12
(at Stadio comunale di Teglio Veneto, Gemona)
Saturday 26th July 2014
Italy 22 Russia 18
(at Stadio comunale di Teglio Veneto, Gemona)
Saturday 20th September 2014
Serbia 45 Italy 6
(at Makis Stadium, Belgrade)

STANDINGS (halfway stage)

	P	W	D	L	F	A	Diff	PTS
Serbia	3	2	0	1	91	40	51	4
Russia	3	2	0	1	62	46	16	4
Italy	3	2	0	1	82	75	7	4
Ukraine	3	0	0	3	44	118	-74	0

EUROPEAN CHAMPIONSHIP C

Thursday 26th June 2014
Malta 18 Greece 32
(at FC Melita, Pembroke)
Saturday 12th July 2014
Czech Republic 8 Malta 34
(at Havlichkuv Brod)
Saturday 11th October 2014
Greece 68 Czech Republic 16
(at Gloritsa Field, Aspropyrgos, Athens)

(Greece were the winners)

NORDIC CUP

Saturday 28th June 2014
Norway 10 Denmark 16 *(Oslo)*
Saturday 16th August 2014
Denmark 44 Sweden 6 *(Lyngby)*
Saturday 30th August 2014
Sweden 24 Norway 12 *(Lund)*

(Denmark were the winners)

BALKANS CUP

Grand Final
Sunday 19th October 2014
Greece 50 Serbia 22
(at Makis Stadium, Belgrade)
Third-place play-off
Sunday 19th October 2014
Bosnia/Herzegovina 32 Hungary 6
(at Makis Stadium, Belgrade)

COLONIAL CUP

Saturday 9th August 2014
Canada 52 USA 14 *(Toronto)*

OTHER INTERNATIONALS

Saturday 18th January 2014
Latin Heat 0 Philippines 114
(Bycroft Oval, Runaway Bay, Gold Coast)
Thursday 30th January 2014
Thailand 46 Japan 10 *(Redfern Oval, Sydney)*
Sunday 25th May 2014
Belgium 10 Spain 12 *(Neder-Over-Heembeek)*
Sunday 1st June 2014
Latin Heat 6 Thailand 16 *(Windsor)*
Sunday 8th June 2014
Spain 54 Belgium 10
(Campo de Rugby la Pelosa, Valencia)

Saturday 5th July 2014
Ghana 10 GB Student Pioneers 48 *(Legon)*
Sunday 6th July 2014
Ghana 4 GB Student Pioneers 46 *(Accra)*
Sunday 13th July 2014
Ghana 6 GB Student Pioneers 34 *(Accra)*

Saturday 21st June 2014
Canada 18 Royal Air Force 40
(Lamport Stadium, Toronto)
Saturday 5th July 2014
Canada 12 England Lionhearts 34
(Lamport Stadium, Toronto)

Saturday 19th July 2014
United States 18 Samoa 12 *(Honolulu)*
Saturday 19th July 2014
Belgium 6 England Colleges 72 *(Brussels)*
Saturday 19th July 2014
Canada 24 Jamaica 20 *(Toronto)*

Saturday 4th October 2014
Niue 36 Philippines 22 *(Wentworthville)*
Saturday 11th October 2014
Philippines 32 Vanuatu 16 *(Espiritu Santo)*
Sunday 19th October 2014
Latin Heat 4 Portugal 6 *(Rose Bay)*
Sunday 19th October 2014
Papua New Guinea 32 Tonga 18 *(Lae)*
Sunday 19th October 2014
Lebanon 28 Fiji 40 *(Cronulla)*

Sunday 12th October 2014
Papua New Guinea PMXIII 16 Australia PMXIII 34
(Kokopo)

SEASON DOWN UNDER
Pure Blockbuster

South Sydney owner Russell Crowe knew all about Hollywood scripts that defy the imagination. The Oscar winner was used to the mind-boggling and the bizarre, stories that tug at the heart-strings, incidents that put the cynics into damage control. The good, the bad, the unbelievable.

He got it all in 2014 as his beloved Rabbitohs swept aside four-and-a-half decades of disappointment for their staunch fans – not the least being Crowe himself. The fans had stayed true through thick and thin. Down but not out! And on a crisp Sunday evening in October they got their just reward. Some 83,833 jammed the former Olympic arena, the most for any sporting event since the seating was reconfigured after the balmy days of 2000 Olympiad and the subsequent 2001 NRL Grand Final. And millions more watched live coverage on television as Souths wore down the Canterbury Bulldogs 30-6.

They had waited a long time for another Premiership to add to the record 20 won by the Rabbitohs in the past.

Is it any wonder that England Test forward Sam Burgess, with a cheekbone and eye socket fractured in the first five seconds of the action, had tears running from his swollen, black right eye? It wasn't pain, although the throbbing would have laid low a lesser mortal. The tears were of joy. He later admitted that adrenaline had got him through the game.

It was way back in 1971 that the 'Pride of the League' had won its most recent Premiership. In the meantime the bean-counters kicked them out of the competition, and only a grass-roots rebellion forced a change of attitude.

Burgess hadn't been born back then, but he clearly understood: "My face is a bit of a mess. But it is something that can never be taken away from me." It was a fitting way to finish his Rugby League career before defecting to rugby union back in England.

Coach Michael Maguire hardly needed words to explain the feelings of Burgess and his teammates: "The boys believed this was going to be our year. And the memories will last forever."

Actually, despite the lopsided final score, the Bulldogs were still in the equation when trailing by just 14-6 midway through the second half. But they couldn't compete with Sam Burgess, his two brothers George and Tom, and the 14 other Rabbitohs, who saw the agony Sam was experiencing and lifted accordingly.

Both sides were without their key playmakers. Souths lost Kiwi Test hooker Issac Luke to a two-match ban for a dangerous lifting tackle made on the Roosters' Sonny Bill Williams the previous weekend, while Bulldogs' firebrand captain Mick Ennis was laid low by two fractures in his left foot. Rookies were drafted in as replacements by their respective coaches. Souths used Fiji Bati World Cup hooker Apisai Koroisau, with just 17 senior appearances to his credit and Moses Mbye, with only nine NRL games under his belt, was the Canterbury choice. Mbye was gallant, making no less than 46 tackles.

England World Cup prop James Graham and NSW Origin scrum-half Trent Hodkinson took over as Canterbury's co-skippers. However it was Graham who harangued his teammates before kick-off. As everyone expected!

121

Souths got a bonus when the bell that rang half-time and full-time at the Rabbitohs' first season games in 1908 was rung again before the Grand Final. How did it affect the Bulldogs? Well, Souths may have had their team song – the Battle Hymn of the Republic (with changed words) – ringing out. But the Canterbury players made the Rabbitohs wait for them to make an appearance on the pitch. A long wait and one that earned the Bulldogs a hefty $20,000 fine for what were clearly delaying tactics.

It was one of the most fiery starts in recent Grand Final history. In the very first tackle of the evening Sam Burgess rushed out of a head clash with Graham – pointing at his right cheekbone. There was nothing illegal – but Big Sam was obviously badly injured. In shades of past heroics, most notably Souths captain John Sattler playing through the 1970 Grand Final with his jaw shattered in three places, Burgess shrugged it all off and continued as if it was no more than a mere scratch. In doing so, he became the first British player to win the Clive Churchill Medal as man of the match and ensured himself a place in Rugby League folklore.

In the sixth minute the veteran Lote Tuqiri was across the whitewash but was denied a try after video replays showed a high tackle by Souths half Adam Reynolds had forced the ball from the grasp of Canterbury's Kiwi international Sam Perrett.

Eventually the nil-all deadlock was broken when exciting young Rabbitohs stand-off Luke Keary sent a crisp pass to left winger Alex Johnston, who was over in the corner in a flash for his 21st try in 17 appearances during the season. The most by any NRL player in 2014.

Dale Finucane was lucky not to have been dispatched to the sin bin for a professional foul when raking the ball from Sam Burgess. And the Rabbitohs opted for two points to extend the lead, which they kept until the break.

Graham had been off but returned when needed. Within two minutes of his running back onto the pitch he sent a kick along the ground and Tony 'T-Rex' Williams pounced to score. Hodkinson, who had not kicked for goal the previous weekend for fear of aggravating a leg injury, added the extras and the scores were all locked up with half an hour remaining. But not for long. A few minutes later George Burgess stormed some 20 metres to score between the uprights and restore the Rabbitohs' six-point buffer. Two penalty goal attempts, one missed and the other perfectly placed, added two points to the Souths' score.

As the clocked ticked down, Souths had a bit of luck to score again. But fortune favours the brave and rookie centre Kirisome Auva'a was across the line. Two more tries – to Reynolds and Greg Inglis – rubbed salt into the wound.

What would happen in 2015 with Sam Burgess playing for Bath in the other rugby code. Crowe summed it up succinctly: "It will be more of the same. You know Madge [Maguire]. We'll start again."

Fifteen other clubs must start again, too. But they have to start from behind the Rabbitohs.

Here's how the clubs fared during the season.

SOUTH SYDNEY RABBITOHS (Premiers)

Private ownership of Rugby League teams is not always a formula to success – as had been proven many a time in Britain and more recently in the NRL with Newcastle. But no one could argue with what had happened at Redfern since Hollywood's Russell Crowe took over. To think the NRL showed South Sydney the door in 1999. But 'people power' forced them to be welcomed back after a two-season hiatus. And in 2014 it all paid off.

One only has to look at the statistics to see just how dominant they were as they wiped away the disappointment of falling in the penultimate weekend in both 2012 and 2013. The most tackle breaks of any club in the NRL (more than 29 per game), the most metres gained from dummy-half runs (135), one of only four clubs to score more than 100 tries, the fewest number of tries conceded (63) and the fewest points conceded per game (an average of 15).

How Crowe must have been chuckling over his lunch in England while filming Robin Hood in which he persuaded Sam Burgess to join the Rabbitohs. He got not only Sam, but his three brothers, George, Tom and Luke, too. And, of course, the steadying influence of their mother, Julie. Sam (an average of 180 metres in runs and 35 tackles per game) and George (152 metres and 27 tackles) with the other two not far behind. The Burgess inspiration on their teammates also counted.

Suddenly Souths had some of the best Test representatives in the world. Greg Inglis, Alex Johnston, Dylan Walker, Lote Tuqiri, Issac Luke, the Burgess brothers. There will be a few more who could be knocking on the door in the next couple of years, too. The halves Adam Reynolds and Luke Keary, Kirisome Auva'a, Kyle Turner, Apisai Koroisau and Junior Kangaroos captain Cameron McInnes.

And don't forget the pair at the helm, coach Michael Maguire and skipper John Sutton.

Glory, Glory to South Sydney. The Pride of the League!

CANTERBURY BULLDOGS (2nd)

The yo-yo record of Canterbury continued. Cellar-dwellers in 2010 and 2011, runners-up in 2012, then beaten on the first weekend of the play-offs 12 months later. In 2014 the Bulldogs made it through to the Grand Final only to come up against an emotionally-charged South Sydney. The Bulldogs' cause was hardly helped by losing six of their last eight games in the regular season, costing them a spot in the top four. This meant they could not afford to lose a single game in the play-offs.

After a solid victory in Melbourne over the Storm, they returned to Sydney where two vital field goals by NSW Origin scrum-half Trent Hodkinson gave them narrowest of victories over Manly. As full time approached, he snapped the first to put the Bulldogs ahead 17-16. Then after a Daly Cherry-Evans equaliser sent the game into golden-point extra time, Hodkinson calmly booted the one-point winner. The Bulldogs then accounted for Penrith to reach the season finale.

The stand-out star was England World Cup prop James Graham. It was hard for the xenophobic Australian sports writers and broadcasters to admit he was best front-rower in the world … but they did. He averaged more than 150 metres in bullocking runs in each match and 36 tackles. But he was not alone in a fine Canterbury line-up. There were his fellow forwards, not the least the Graham 'look-alike' Aiden Tolman (145 metres and 32 tackles). And what about the halves Hodkinson and Josh Reynolds, who also helped New South Wales to a drought-breaking State of Origin series success?

Centre Josh Morris turned out for Australia in the Anzac Test against the Kiwis, who included on the bench his Canterbury teammate Greg Eastwood. Morris will be joined at the Bulldogs in 2015 by his twin brother Brett from the Dragons.

Utility Reni Maitua and centre Krisnan Inu (before he left for French rugby union) helped Toa Samoa to win the final spot in the Four Nations Tournament, Inu kicking six goals in the 32-16 victory in the May qualifier. Graham was one of the first picked for the England squad in the Four Nations, young Canterbury forwards Josh Jackson and David Klemmer made the Australian squad for the tournament, Eastwood was in the Kiwi squad, while Frank Pritchard joined Maitua for Samoa.

In 2015, their 70th anniversary year, Canterbury were to play a celebration match at their first home ground – Belmore Oval.

SYDNEY ROOSTERS (3rd/Minor Premiers)

Once again the difficulty in winning back-to-back Premierships was made patently clear when the Sydney Roosters were beaten on the penultimate weekend of the finals' series. The subsequent champions, South Sydney, reversed the result from the final round of the regular season in which the Roosters had clinched the Minor Premiership with a 22-18 victory.

It was a sad end to the 15-season career of Roosters captain and former Golden Boot winner Anthony Minichiello, who then hung up his boots after a club record 302 appearances for the Tricolours. His 17 tries took his career tally to another record of 139, well clear of the 104 by Bill Mullins, the only other Rooster to have topped the century.

Much of the success of the club was built on the efforts of their halves Mitchell Pearce and James Maloney. Arguably, Pearce had the best year since he broke into the senior ranks in 2007 after captaining the Australian Schoolboys on their tour of Britain and France the previous year. Maloney shared the honours with Johnathan Thurston (North Queensland) as the top NRL points-scorer of 2014.

Backrower Boyd Cordner (Australia) and centre Roger Tuivasa-Sheck and prop Sam Moa (both New Zealand) clashed in the Anzac Test, pitting the two Trans-Tasman nations against each other. Moa was joined by Shaun Kenny-Dowall in the Kiwis' Four Nations squad, while winger Daniel Tupou, centre Michael Jennings, Cordner and Aidan Guerra were in Australia's ranks.

Cook Islands World Cup youngster Dylan Napa shaped as a star of the future, and was rewarded for a fine season with a spot in the Prime Minister's XIII that accounted for a spirited Papua New Guinea Kumuls outfit.

Before the NRL season kicked off the Roosters thrashed Wigan Warriors 36-14 to take out the World Club Challenge.

PENRITH PANTHERS (4th)

The Panthers were the surprise packets of the 2014 season. Most experts predicted they would finish in the middle of the Premiership hopefuls. But, after a slow start to the season before being plagued by a rash of injuries, they came home under a wet sail to finish equal third (fourth on points-difference) on the NRL Ladder.

On the opening weekend of the play-offs they managed a remarkable victory. Born-again Penrith captain Jamie Soward snapped a field goal with just 10 seconds left on the clock to snatch a one-point victory over the Minor Premiers, Sydney Roosters. And, in doing so, he saved the NRL from embarrassment after officials had controversially allowed the Roosters' James Maloney to kick a conversion that had previously locked up the scores - even though he wasn't on the pitch when the try was scored. On the preliminary finals weekend the Panthers encountered the Bulldogs at their savage best and went down 18-12.

Soward was the club's best performer, holding his teammates together as injury after injury decimated their ranks. Almost as impressive was Papua New Guinea-born James Segeyaro, who was named Dally M Hooker of the Year and young fullback Matt Moylan, whose efforts earned him a spot in the Prime Minister's XIII which beat the Kumuls and then in Australia's squad for the Four Nations Tournament.

Stand-off Isaac John came off the bench for the Kiwis in the Anzac Test before being struck down by a season-ending Achilles tendon tear. Centre Dean Whare was in the Kiwis squads for both the mid-season Test and the Four Nations while utility Lewis Brown returned for the latter.

MANLY SEA EAGLES (5th)

Off-field dissension cost Manly dearly. Many of the players were unhappy that the board had not made a decent offer to stalwart Glenn Stewart for 2015. The decision was blamed on the salary cap, with extra money needed to fight off scavengers from other clubs trying to lure the halfbacks Daly Cherry-Evans and Kieran Foran away from Brookvale.

Glenn Stewart eventually signed for South Sydney. Fellow international backrower Anthony Watmough was allowed to move to Parramatta before his current contract had ended. There were other high-profile names said to be unhappy but veteran forward Willie Mason signed in November. Manly would be the 34-year-old's sixth club.

The rumblings of discontent eventually showed on the pitch, with Manly late in the season favourites to take out the Minor Premiership but losing three of their final home-and-away games to miss out on the equivalent of the northern hemisphere's League Leaders Trophy on points-difference. The Sea Eagles then suffered successive losses to the eventual Grand Final sides, Souths and Canterbury in the first two weeks of the play-offs.

Before the wheels fell off, Cherry-Evans (Australia) and Peta Hiku (New Zealand) played in the Anzac Test and Manly's Rookie of the Year Jesse Sene-Lefao helped Toa Samoa to a shock victory over Fiji in the Four Nations qualifier.

Cherry-Evans, Hiku and Sene-Lefao backed up for the Four Nations with Foran as the Kiwis stand-off and Dunamis Lui was chosen in the back row for Samoa.

NORTH QUEENSLAND COWBOYS (6th)

One can only wonder how the Cowboys would have fared without the inspirational Johnathan Thurston. He was one of the stand-out stars of the NRL season, sharing the Dally M Medal as Player of the Year. It was his third Dally M Medal, having previously won it in 2005 and 2007. JT was also awarded the Provan-Summons Medal as the People's Choice, voted by the fans. He was also the official man of the match in the Anzac Test against the Kiwis, and topped the NRL pointscoring with 234. As well as scoring 11 tries he helped set up no less than 31 others.

For the third straight year the Cowboys were controversially bundled out of the NRL finals series – but this time the referees seemed to have got it correct. The Cowboys trailed the Sydney Roosters by 30-0 after as many minutes in their semi-final before staging a remarkable comeback to level the scores 16 minutes into the second half. Stand-off James Maloney edged the Roosters ahead with a field goal five minutes before the full-time siren before Thurston touched down with 64 seconds remaining on the clock. However he was denied what could have been the winning try by a faint knock-on in the lead-up.

"Look I am still filthy, we just lost a final…it is a bitter pill to swallow but the start is what put us under the pump," Thurston said.

"To be down 30-0 after 30 minutes, it is pretty tough to claw back."

Thurston was joined by forwards Matt Scott and James Tamou in the Anzac Test. But injury kept them all out of the Four Nations Tournament. Tongan World Cup star Jason Taumalolo was chosen in the Kiwis Four Nations squad and threequarters Tautau Moga and Antonio Winterstein for Samoa.

MELBOURNE STORM (7th)

Once again the play of the Melbourne Storm revolved around their big three – Cameron Smith, Cooper Cronk and Billy Slater. But it was not enough for them to overcome the eventual runners-up Canterbury Bulldogs in the first weekend of the play-offs.

The Origin Series was hardly kind to Melbourne, with the trio all suffering injuries in the first encounter, forcing Cronk out for seven matches with a broken arm and Slater for two with an ankle injury. Smith carried his own ankle problem for the rest of the season.

The clinical coaching of Craig Bellamy paid off once again, with the Storm completing 78 per cent of their sets of six tackles, the best figures in the NRL. They also made the least amount of errors in the Premiership, fewer than eight per game. Smith led by example, with not a single handling error all season.

The 'Three Musketeers' turned out for Australia in the Anzac Test, while Kevin Proctor and Tohu Harris were in the Kiwis squad for that May clash, the latter in the unfamiliar role of stand-off.

Smith and Cronk were in Australia's Four Nations squad, while Proctor and Harris were joined by prop Jesse Bromwich for New Zealand and Castleford-bound stand-off Ben Roberts for Samoa.

Among those joining the Storm in 2015 was Wigan stand-off Blake Green. It would be his fourth NRL club.

BRISBANE BRONCOS (8th)

A lack of consistency cost Brisbane dearly – and ultimately led to the demise of coach Anthony Griffin. Five times the Broncos lost games in the shadow of full time. Victory in those encounters would have had them up at the top of the table instead of just scraping into the play-offs on points-difference.

The news that pioneer Wayne Bennett would be back at the helm in 2015 didn't help the young players who obviously worried about their future under the super-coach.

But there were some bright spots, not the least being the coming of age after his apprenticeship as a hooker on the bench of scrum-half Ben Hunt. His 'show and go' was arguably the best in the NRL and earned him fourth spot in the voting for the Dally M Medal as NRL Player of the Year. He followed that up with a fine display for the Prime Minister's XIII against Papua New Guinea and a spot in Australia's squad for the Four Nations Tournament. Also in the squad were veteran forwards Sam Thaiday and Corey Parker.

Parker and Matt Gillett both played for Australia in the Anzac Test against the Kiwis. Prop Josh McGuire, unwanted by Australia, and winger Daniel Vidot were both chosen for Toa Samoa in the Four Nations.

Test winger/fullback Darius Boyd was following Bennett back to the Broncos. He would be joined by the talented Canberra fullback-cum-stand-off Anthony Milford, who paired with Hunt in the Prime Minister's XIII match. As if they hadn't got enough fullbacks already, another to link with the Broncos in 2015 would be Hull KR's Greg Eden.

And look out for young Junior Kangaroos prop Joe Ofahengaue in 2015. He has yet to make his senior debut, but made the most metres by any player from any club in the NRL Under-20s during the 2014 season.

NEW ZEALAND WARRIORS (9th)

Rarely has there been such a pre-season focus on one player as there was on the Auckland signing from Old Blighty, fullback Sam Tomkins. Unfairly, he was hailed as the Messiah. And when, naturally, enough he took time to get used to the ways of his new club there was a media outcry. Not only did the Warriors lose five of their first seven encounters, they sacked their coach Matt Elliott amid a boardroom squabble and Kiwi Test fullback Kevin Locke realised he was no longer wanted and headed for Salford in the Super League.

But things eventually turned around under new coach Andrew McFadden, especially when Tomkins developed a wonderful combination with New Zealand Test No 7 Shaun Johnson. The forwards rallied under the leadership of Simon Mannering and Tongan World Cup centre Konrad Hurrell emerged as a monster to be feared by opponents. But the Warriors missed out on what looked to be a spot in the play-offs after losing three of their last four matches.

Manu Vatuvei topped the club's tryscoring lists for the ninth straight season. Johnson, Mannering, Siliva Havili and Ben Henry were in the beaten Kiwis line-up for the Anzac Test. The first three were joined by Vatuvei and former Wigan half Thomas Leuluai in the Kiwis Four Nations squad while utility stars Dominique Peyroux and Michael Sio were chosen in the Toa Samoa side.

The fourth Under-20s Grand Final appearance in the past five years will help the Warriors' future depth of talent.

PARRAMATTA EELS (10th)

Under new coach Brad Arthur, the Eels discarded the wooden spoon that they had held for the previous two seasons, and they only missed out on a spot in the play-offs through points-difference. But their season can only be seen as a failure. They were poised to play in the finals but lost in their final two outings to the lowly rated Knights and Raiders, after beating one of the Premiership favourites Manly and pushing the Bulldogs to the limit.

They relied too much on the talents of Jarryd Hayne, who ultimately shared the Dally M Medal as NRL Player of the Year with the Cowboys' Johnathan Thurston. When Hayne was in full flight, so, too, were the Eels. He scored 20 tries in 21 appearances, the most of any player from any club in the home-and-away matches. But the NRL fraternity as a whole was shocked when at the end of the season, Hayne knocked back an offer of $6.75 million to extend his contract and try for a possible new career in American Football.

Hayne's departure gave Arthur the spare cash to plug some holes. Manly back-rower Anthony Watmough, South's centre Beau Champion and Hull FC outside back Ben Crooks were moving to Parramatta.

During the year, Fijian winger Semi Radradra emerged as a real cult figure, scoring 19 tries in 24 appearances, running an average of 140 metres per game.

Scrum-half Ryan Matterson and loose forward Kelepi Tanginoa were chosen for the Junior Kangaroos in 2014. Also waiting to make a name for himself in the future was giant second-rower Tepai Moeroa, who earned a record nine caps for the Australian Schoolboys in rugby union during 2012 and 2013. The barnstorming 18-year-old made his NRL debut in 2014.

ST GEORGE ILLAWARRA DRAGONS (11th)

When the Dragons won their first three matches, hopes were high. But those dreams quickly disintegrated with seven losses in their next eight games. Head coach Steve Price was shown the door and there was talk about luring former mentor Wayne Bennett back. Eventually interim coach Paul 'Mary' McGregor was given the job of rebuilding the shattered Dragons structure.

McGregor, a former captain and stalwart of St George Illawarra, would need some clever recruiting. But he already had arguably the best buy of the 2014 season, England international stand-off Gareth Widdop, who stepped out of the shadows of the Melbourne Storm's 'Three Musketeers' – Billy Slater, Cooper Cronk and Cameron Smith – to become a true star in his own right, finishing a close-up fourth in the voting for the Dally M Medal. He formed a fine combination with Benji Marshall, back in Rugby League after a failed dalliance in the Rah-Rah ranks. 'Bad Boy' Josh Dugan seemed to be back on the straight and narrow but the Dragons still needed some experienced forwards.

The St George Illawarra club was well represented in the Test arena. Widdop and prop Mike Cooper were in England's Four Nations squad. Winger Brett Morris scored two tries in Australia's 30-18 victory over the Kiwis in the Anzac Test, while fellow three-quarters Gerard Beale and Jason Nightingale were on the beaten side. The Kiwis pair backed up for the Four Nations Tournament. But Morris left the club to join his twin brother Josh at Canterbury. Peter Mata'utia was at fullback and Leeson Ah Mau in the back row when Samoa surprised Fiji in the Four Nations qualifier. The two retained their spots in the squad for the tournament itself and were joined by half Kyle Stanley.

Centre Euan Aitken, an Australian Schoolboys representative in 2013, and utility star Jack Bird were chosen for the Junior Kangaroos. But Bird was to line up with Cronulla in 2015.

NEWCASTLE KNIGHTS (12th)

It was a tumultuous year in Newcastle. Even before a ball had been kicked, the Knights' new signing, Russell Packer was jailed for two years for an unprovoked assault on a stranger in a central Sydney street.

Then, in only Round Three, talented young forward Alex McKinnon broke his neck in a match against Melbourne, leaving him to life in a wheelchair. The injury led to an outpouring of emotion throughout the game. A weekend in July was set aside as the 'Rise For Alex' Round in which more than $1.1 million was raised to help in his rehabilitation.

In May, the Knights' mining magnate patron Nathan Tinkler quit the club following major losses in various companies not associated with Rugby League.

Finally, in July, Wayne Bennett announced he would end his stint as coach at the end of the season after three years in the job. He planned to return to the Brisbane Broncos, where he had won six Premierships. Rick Stone was appointed as his successor. Ironically it was Stone who was pushed aside when Bennett took over in Newcastle. Stone can take heart from the fact that the Knights won eight of their final 11 games in 2014.

Darius Boyd, who was released by Newcastle to go with his long-time mentor Bennett to Brisbane, took his international record for Australia to 17 Tests in the Anzac clash with the Kiwis.

Beau Scott forced his way back into the Australian squad for the Four Nations Tournament after a break of a couple of years. In the same competition threequarter Sione Mata'utia, after starring for the Prime Minister's XIII against the PNG Kumuls, became the youngest player to represent Australia in the history of Rugby League (at 18 years and 129 days old). He had played just seven senior games for Newcastle (scoring seven tries) but would have made many more senior appearances but for NRL rule denying that chance to anyone younger than 18. David Fa'alogo was captain of Toa Samoa in the Four Nations and was joined by fellow-Knight Joey Leilua.

Jake Mamo, who made his senior debut during the year, was chosen as a winger for the Junior Kangaroos for the end-of-season clash with the Junior Kiwis.

WESTS TIGERS (13th)

It was a turbulent season for Wests Tigers. Once again they suffered a rash of injuries. But the real problems were off the pitch, where the NRL hierarchy was forced to intervene and restructure the board. The NRL imposed three independent board members including two women and stripped the Balmain representatives of voting rights because of money owed to the merged entity.

But the ruling body didn't move quickly enough. On the eve of a vital match against St George in July, while there were still hopes of making the finals, an anonymous club official leaked the news that coach Michael Potter was going to be sacked immediately after the Dragons encounter. Outraged fans prevented the move – but only temporarily, with Potter shown the door in September after the disillusioned players suffered several massive defeats including 28-6 at the hands of Melbourne, 64-6 by the Cowboys and 48-4 by the Roosters. Canterbury thrashed the Tigers 30-10.

Former Wests Magpie Jason Taylor would hold the coaching reins in 2015 and he had a ready-made side of young talent headed by Dally M Rookie of the Year, Luke Brooks, and his half partner Mitchell Moses as well as rookie Test prop Aaron Woods. There is also the steadying influence of veterans Robbie Farah and Pat Richards.

GOLD COAST TITANS (14th)

When the Titans snatched a two-point victory over the Storm in Melbourne in early April they were on top of the NRL Ladder and the world seemed to be their oyster. Bt they soon found out that Premierships are never won in Round Five. As they lost a host of players to injuries and suspension it was downhill from then on and for a while it looked as if they were going to swap from first to worst. At one stage they were missing 17 players from their senior squad – a massive 60 per cent.

It was all very well to point out that they were able to blood some young stars, but the success or otherwise of this will not be known for another 12 months. Centre James Roberts was one. The 'enfant terrible', sacked by both South Sydney and Penrith, accepted the lifeline offered to him on the Gold Coast.

The rapid slip down the ladder had its consequences. John Cartwright, coach since the current Gold Coast outfit was admitted to the big league in 2007, jumped before he was pushed, handing over the reins to Neil Henry.

Heading off from Robina was another original Titan, honest backrower Mark Minichiello, set to play out his career in Super League with Hull FC. And ex-Test prop Luke 'Bull' Bailey decided to hang up his boots after 15 seasons in the NRL.

On the other hand Kiwis World Cup fullback Josh Hoffman would be in the Titan ranks in 2015.

Titans co-captains Greg Bird and Nate Myles were in the Australian side that beat New Zealand in the Anzac Test and Bird backed up for the Four Nations Tournament.

CANBERRA RAIDERS (15th)

The arrival of Ricky Stuart as coach of the Raiders had little effect. Only victories in their final three home-and-away games prevented the former Test coach claiming the dubious record of successive wooden spoons with two different clubs (his Eels' outfit had finished last in 2013).

Three times they had more than 50 points scored against them, including once on successive weekends (twice to the Warriors and the other time to the Sea Eagles). Their big problem was finding a halfback combination – and stalwart captain Terry Campese was eventually given his leave-pass from the senior squad. Sadly for Canberra fans, his successful replacement, Samoan World Cup star Anthony Milford, was off to Brisbane next season. But scrum-half Mitchell Cornish looked a likely prospect.

Josh Papalii made Australia's Four Nations squad, centre Jack Wighton turned out for the Prime Minister's XIII against the Papua New Guinea Kumuls and two young fellow Canberra backrowers, Patrick Mago and Tevita Pangai, were chosen for the Junior Kangaroos.

CRONULLA SHARKS (16th)

What a wretched years for the Sharks. Almost everything that could go wrong did! The Federal Government drug investigation dragged on … and on … and on. Coach Shane Flanagan was banned for 12 months before many of their stars, including captain Paul Gallen and vice-captain Wade Graham, pleaded guilty to taking prohibited substances in 2011. They accepted the guilty pleas in order to avoid lengthy disqualifications. Talented stand-off Todd Carney was sacked over a grossly offensive mobile-phone video of him urinating in his own mouth. And interim coach Peter Sharp quit. Chief executive Steve Noyce was sacked and Gallen was asked to explain why he should not be fined $50,000 and banned from Test duty in 2015 for an obscene rant about the NRL hierarchy on social media

But what is it they say about every cloud having a silver lining. Despite their lowly status on the NRL Premiership race, the Sharks managed to pull off several upsets against the top sides.

Gallen won the Wally Lewis Medal for his role in leading New South Wales to victory in the State of Origin Series. Backrower Graham came of age, stepping into Gallen's shoes when the Blues skipper missed matches through injury. Michael Gordon enhanced his reputation at fullback. Centre Ricky Leutele helped Toa Samoa snare a spot in the Four Nations Tournament, while scrum-half Penani Manumalealii was called into the squad once there. Winger Sosia Feki made the Kiwis' line-up.

Exciting winger Valentine Holmes made an impact late in the season and was rewarded with a call-up to the Junior Kangaroos.

SEASON DOWN UNDER - ROUND-UP

NRL PREMIERSHIP FINALS SERIES

QUALIFYING FINALS

Friday 12th September 2014

Manly Sea Eagles 24...South Sydney Rabbitohs 40
(at Allianz Stadium, Sydney)

Saturday 13th September 2014

Sydney Roosters 18 ....Penrith Panthers 19

ELIMINATION FINALS

Saturday 13th September 2014

North Queensland Cowboys 32 ....Brisbane Broncos 20

Sunday 14th September 2014

Melbourne Storm 4 ....Canterbury Bulldogs 28

SEMI-FINALS

Friday 19th September 2014

Sydney Roosters 31.......................................North Queensland Cowboys 30

Saturday 20th September 2014

Manly Sea Eagles 17 ....Canterbury Bulldogs 18
(at Allianz Stadium, Sydney)

PRELIMINARY FINALS

Friday 26th September 2014

South Sydney Rabbitohs 32 ....Sydney Roosters 22

Saturday 27th September 2014

Penrith Panthers 12...Canterbury Bulldogs 18
(at ANZ Stadium, Sydney)

GRAND FINAL

Sunday 5th October 2014

CANTERBURY BULLDOGS 6 SOUTH SYDNEY RABBITOHS 30

BULLDOGS: 1 Sam Perrett; 2 Corey Thompson; 3 Josh Morris; 4 Tim Lafai; 5 Mitch Brown; 6 Josh Reynolds; 7 Trent Hodkinson (C); 8 Aiden Tolman; 9 Moses Mbye; 10 James Graham (C); 11 Josh Jackson; 12 Tony Williams; 13 Greg Eastwood. Subs (all used): 14 Tim Browne; 15 Dale Finucane; 16 David Klemmer; 17 Frank Pritchard.
Try: Williams (49); **Goals:** Hodkinson 1/1.
On report: Reynolds (72) - alleged high tackle.
RABBITOHS: 1 Greg Inglis; 2 Alex Johnston; 3 Dylan Walker; 4 Kirisome Auva'a; 5 Lote Tuqiri; 6 Luke Keary; 7 Adam Reynolds; 8 George Burgess; 9 Apisai Koroisau; 10 David Tyrrell; 11 Ben Te'o; 12 John Sutton (C); 13 Sam Burgess. Subs (all used): 14 Jason Clark; 15 Kyle Turner; 16 Chris McQueen; 17 Tom Burgess.
Tries: Johnston (20), G Burgess (56), Auva'a (73), Reynolds (76), Inglis (79); **Goals:** Reynolds 5/7, S Burgess 0/1.
On report: T Burgess (68) - alleged shoulder charge.
Rugby Leaguer & League Express Men of the Match:
Bulldogs: James Graham; *Rabbitohs:* Sam Burgess.
Clive Churchill Medal (Man of the Match):
Sam Burgess (South Sydney Rabbitohs).
Half-time: 0-6; **Referees:** Shayne Hayne & Gerard Sutton;
Attendance: 83,833 *(at ANZ Stadium, Sydney)*.

FINAL NRL PREMIERSHIP TABLE

	P	W	D	L	B	F	A	D	Pts
Sydney Roosters	24	16	0	8	2	615	385	230	36
Manly Sea Eagles	24	16	0	8	2	502	399	103	36
South Sydney Rabbitohs	24	15	0	9	2	585	361	224	34
Penrith Panthers	24	15	0	9	2	506	426	80	34
North Queensland Cowboys	24	14	0	10	2	596	406	190	32
Melbourne Storm	24	14	0	10	2	536	460	76	32
Canterbury Bulldogs	24	13	0	11	2	446	439	7	30
Brisbane Broncos	24	12	0	12	2	549	456	93	28
New Zealand Warriors	24	12	0	12	2	571	491	80	28
Parramatta Eels	24	12	0	12	2	477	580	-103	28
St George Illawarra Dragons	24	11	0	13	2	469	528	-59	26
Newcastle Knights	24	10	0	14	2	463	571	-108	24
Wests Tigers	24	10	0	14	2	420	631	-211	24
Gold Coast Titans	24	9	0	15	2	372	538	-166	22
Canberra Raiders	24	8	0	16	2	466	623	-157	20
Cronulla Sharks	24	5	0	19	2	334	613	-279	14

TOP POINTSCORERS

James Maloney	Sydney Roosters	234
Johnathan Thurston	North Queensland Cowboys	234
Adam Reynolds	South Sydney Rabbitohs	205
Jarrod Croker	Canberra Raiders	202
Jamie Lyon	Manly Sea Eagles	170

TOP TRYSCORERS

Alex Johnston	South Sydney Rabbitohs	21
Jarryd Hayne	Parramatta Eels	20
Semi Radradra Waqavatu		
	Parramatta Eels	19
Jarrod Croker	Canberra Raiders	18
Sisa Waqa	Melbourne Storm	18

HOLDEN CUP GRAND FINAL *(Under-20s)*
Sunday 5th October 2014

Brisbane Broncos 32..New Zealand Warriors 34
(at ANZ Stadium, Sydney)

QUEENSLAND CUP GRAND FINAL
Sunday 28th September 2014

Easts Tigers 4 ....Northern Pride 36
(at Suncorp Stadium, Brisbane)

NEW SOUTH WALES CUP GRAND FINAL
Sunday 28th September 2014

Newcastle Knights 12 ....Penrith Panthers 48
(at Allianz Stadium, Sydney)

NRL STATE CHAMPIONSHIP *(Queensland Premiers v NSW Premiers)*
Sunday 5th October 2014

Northern Pride 32 ....Penrith Panthers 28
(at ANZ Stadium, Sydney)

DALLY M AWARDS
Dally M Medal (Player of the Year): Jarryd Hayne (Parramatta Eels)
& Johnathan Thurston (North Queensland Cowboys)
Provan-Summons Medal (People's Choice):
Johnathan Thurston (North Queensland Cowboys)
Coach of the Year: Ivan Cleary (Penrith Panthers)
Captain of the Year: Jamie Lyon (Manly Sea Eagles)
Representative Player of the Year: Jarryd Hayne (Parramatta Eels)
Rookie of the Year: Luke Brooks (Wests Tigers)
Holden Cup Player of the Year (Under-20s): Kane Elgey (Gold Coast Titans)

State of Origin

It took nine long years – but the Queensland State of Origin dynasty finally ended in 2014. With narrow victories in the first two encounters the Blues managed what had had been denied them year after year after year. They held off a Maroons second-half fight-back to register the first NSW win in any opening match played in the Queensland capital since 2003 before scoring the only try of the evening in a dour encounter at Homebush for a two-point victory and an unbeatable 2-0 lead in the series. It mattered not that the Queenslanders gave them the mother of all hidings in the third game.

"I've thought about this every day for so many years," said a relieved NSW coach Laurie Daley. "We kept banging on the door, 'til we broke through. We've been trying for so many years." And one of Daley's stars, fullback Jarryd Hayne agreed: "It's been a long time coming. We've come so close so many times."

However the tribal warfare is set to resume in 2015 with the Maroons brimming with confidence after their superb Origin III performance. As their coach Mal Meninga noted after ruling the roost for so many years: "It [the series loss] is bitter-sweet. I am proud of the boys and the pride they showed in the jumper. We have a bright future, don't worry."

The win by New South Wales in the opening clash came on the back of an inspirational display by fullback Hayne and some courageous defence by the NSW players, many of them shrugging off awful injuries which would have seen them hauled off the pitch in a match of lesser importance. Daley hailed it the greatest State of Origin triumph of his entire career, in which as a player he was involved in five series victories: "I was extremely proud. We had no ball, some of the other things were against us, but jeez I was proud. We had a truckload of injuries … serious injuries … blokes that battled away. They should have come off in the first half but courageously stayed out there because we needed them to be there. I hope everyone talks about that, because I know in the past it's always the opposition they've spoken about. But our boys … wow!"

STATE OF ORIGIN - GAME I
Wednesday 28th May 2014
QUEENSLAND 8 NEW SOUTH WALES 12

QUEENSLAND: 1 Billy Slater (Melbourne Storm); 2 Darius Boyd (Newcastle Knights); 3 Greg Inglis (South Sydney Rabbitohs); 4 Justin Hodges (Brisbane Broncos); 5 Brent Tate (North Queensland Cowboys); 6 Johnathan Thurston (North Queensland Cowboys); 7 Cooper Cronk (Melbourne Storm); 8 Matthew Scott (North Queensland Cowboys); 9 Cameron Smith (Melbourne Storm) (C); 10 Nate Myles (Gold Coast Titans); 18 Chris McQueen (South Sydney Rabbitohs)*; 12 Matt Gillett (Brisbane Broncos); 13 Corey Parker (Brisbane Broncos). Subs (all used): 14 Daly Cherry-Evans (Manly Sea Eagles); 15 Ben Te'o (South Sydney Rabbitohs); 16 Aidan Guerra (Sydney Roosters); 17 Josh Papalii (Canberra Raiders).
Arthur Beetson's number 11 shirt was rested for the 100th Origin match.
Tries: Boyd (5, 56); **Goals:** Thurston 0/2.
NEW SOUTH WALES: 1 Jarryd Hayne (Parramatta Eels); 2 Brett Morris (St George Illawarra Dragons); 3 Michael Jennings (Sydney Roosters); 4 Josh Morris (Canterbury Bulldogs); 5 Daniel Tupou (Sydney Roosters); 6 Josh Reynolds (Canterbury Bulldogs); 7 Trent Hodkinson (Canterbury Bulldogs); 8 Aaron Woods (Wests Tigers); 9 Robbie Farah (Wests Tigers); 10 James Tamou (North Queensland Cowboys); 11 Beau Scott (Newcastle Knights); 12 Ryan Hoffman (Melbourne Storm); 13 Paul Gallen (Cronulla Sharks) (C). Subs (all used): 14 Anthony Watmough (Manly Sea Eagles); 15 Trent Merrin (St George Illawarra Dragons); 16 Luke Lewis (Cronulla Sharks); 17 Tony Williams (Canterbury Bulldogs).
Tries: B Morris (18), Hayne (32); **Goals:** Hodkinson 2/4.
On report: Reynolds (28) - alleged dangerous challenge on Tate.
Rugby Leaguer & League Express Men of the Match:
Queensland: Nate Myles; *New South Wales:* Jarryd Hayne.
Half-time: 4-10; **Referees:** Shayne Hayne & Ben Cummins; **Attendance:** 52,111 *(at Suncorp Stadium, Brisbane).*

Meninga was beaten but not bowed: "There was no bad player. I thought we did enough to win, but NSW defensively were outstanding."

Hayne was a stand-out man of the match, making 170 metres in 23 runs that included two line-breaks and nine tackle busts. He paid the price, explaining after the game: "At the end I was on my knees and I couldn't feel my legs." But he recovered to back up for Origin II. NSW captain Paul Gallen ran him close for the best on the pitch, with 25 runs for 175 metres and 32 bone-crushing tackles.

The Queenslanders started on fire and winger Darius Boyd was across the stripe after less than five minutes, leaving World Cup star Brett Morris floundering in his wake. But Morris was to more than make up for this miss later in the game.

Cooper Cronk left after nine minutes with a broken left arm. He was replaced in the Queensland line-up by the exciting young Manly scrum-half Daly Cherry-Evans. But it was a defining moment as so many of the Maroons' tactics had been devised around Cronk's combination with stand-off Johnathan Thurston, fullback Billy Slater and dummy half Cameron Smith. And Cherry-Evans' kicking game was not up to its usual near perfection and it was not until the second half that the well-oiled Maroons' machine began to click into gear.

The Blues struck back when Hayne created an overlap for Brett Morris to score the try that levelled the scores. But there was a real worry when it was realised he had dislocated his left shoulder in the process. However this was an Origin match and, despite excruciating pain, it was quickly pushed back into place for Morris to carry on. Nevertheless it was to end his 2014 Origin series.

A penalty goal from Trent Hodkinson edged the NSW side ahead.

Moments later NSW stand-off Josh Reynolds was placed on report for a dangerous tackle in which he cart-wheeled Brett Tate into the turf. Beau Scott was also involved in the tackle. Reynolds was charged with a dangerous throw but managed to persuade the

131

judiciary to downgrade the charge and escaped suspension. Scott also missed any ban with an early guilty plea. After the game, the normally placid Tate was furious: "I have never been more frightened in all my life. My legs were shaking for the next 10 minutes. I was legitimately shaken up about it. I didn't know where I was. You can't have it in our game. It has to stop."

Late in the half, the Blues' danger man Hayne extended the lead with a remarkable try in which, when tackled by Thurston, he did a back-flip to force the ball behind his right shoulder. This sent the visitors to break ahead 10-4.

The intensity lifted soon after half-time … and how!

Some 16 minutes into the second spell, Thurston showed some of the typical brilliance that won him his second Golden Boot in 2013. He darted to attract several would-be defenders before sending on to Greg Inglis who gave Boyd a clear run to the left corner for his second try of the night.

For the rest of the evening it was only inspirational defence by the NSW players that kept the Maroons at bay as, time after time, they launched attacks on the tryline.

The best was an effort from the battle-scarred Brett Morris. Boyd looked certain to snare a hat-trick when he surged towards the left-hand corner. However he didn't figure on the big heart of Morris. The Dragons winger hurled himself at Boyd and smashed him into touch just centimetres from the tryline.

Gallen best summed what lay ahead: "It's just a matter of doing it again down in Sydney. They will get better. We have to get better. It's one win, it's not the series."

The second interstate clash, at the stadium that was home of the 2000 Sydney Olympics, was even more nail-biting than the first. The Blues won by just two points. And they scored the only try of the evening ten minutes from time.

Scrum-half Hodkinson ran the ball for only the second time in the match, catching the Maroons' defence unawares. His subsequent conversion gave New South Wales a 6-4 victory.

It hardly mattered that there was a controversial penalty on the halfway line after the Hodkinson try that denied the Maroons a chance of an immediate reply, nor the fact that the Queenslanders were missing their key playmaker Cronk, out with the broken arm suffered two weeks earlier. It was a case of the Blues outplaying their opponents, grinding them out of contention.

"We just wanted to win more than them … and it showed," said NSW captain (and arguably the best player on the pitch) Gallen. He certainly showed how much he wanted victory, making some 220 metres in 25 bullocking runs, as well as 35 crunching tackles.

From the kick-off both sides threw caution to the wind and, after a couple of early scuffles set the mood for the night, Thurston put the visitors ahead 2-nil. After grafting by both sides, the Queenslanders got another a penalty within kicking distance when New Zealand-born James Tamou used a forearm on his Cowboys' teammate and co-captain Thurston, who was lying prone on the turf. Thurston's goal gave him a new Origin scoring record of 162, a point more than the previous best tally, set back in 1994 by the

---

STATE OF ORIGIN - GAME II

Wednesday 18th June 2014

NEW SOUTH WALES 6 QUEENSLAND 4

NEW SOUTH WALES: 1 Jarryd Hayne (Parramatta Eels); 2 Will Hopoate (Parramatta Eels); 4 Josh Dugan (St George Illawarra Dragons); 3 Michael Jennings (Sydney Roosters); 5 Daniel Tupou (Sydney Roosters); 6 Josh Reynolds (Canterbury Bulldogs); 7 Trent Hodkinson (Canterbury Bulldogs); 8 Paul Gallen (Cronulla Sharks) (C); 9 Robbie Farah (Wests Tigers); 10 Aaron Woods (Wests Tigers); 11 Beau Scott (Newcastle Knights); 12 Ryan Hoffman (Melbourne Storm); 13 Greg Bird (Gold Coast Titans). Subs (all used): 14 James Tamou (North Queensland Cowboys); 15 Anthony Watmough (Manly Sea Eagles); 16 Trent Merrin (St George Illawarra Dragons); 17 Luke Lewis (Cronulla Sharks).
Try: Hodkinson (70); **Goals:** Hodkinson 1/1.
On report: Watmough (41) - alleged dangerous challenge on Myles; Reynolds (78) - alleged use of the head.
QUEENSLAND: 1 Billy Slater (Melbourne Storm); 5 Brent Tate (North Queensland Cowboys); 4 Justin Hodges (Brisbane Broncos); 3 Greg Inglis (South Sydney Rabbitohs); 2 Darius Boyd (Newcastle Knights); 6 Johnathan Thurston (North Queensland Cowboys); 7 Daly Cherry-Evans (Manly Sea Eagles); 8 Matthew Scott (North Queensland Cowboys); 9 Cameron Smith (Melbourne Storm) (C); 10 Nate Myles (Gold Coast Titans); 11 Aidan Guerra (Sydney Roosters); 12 Matt Gillett (Brisbane Broncos); 13 Sam Thaiday (Brisbane Broncos). Subs (all used): 14 Jacob Lillyman (New Zealand Warriors); 15 Ben Te'o (South Sydney Rabbitohs); 16 Chris McQueen (South Sydney Rabbitohs); 17 Dave Taylor (Gold Coast Titans).
Goals: Thurston 2/2.
On report: Thurston (78) - alleged use of the head.
Rugby Leaguer & League Express Men of the Match:
New South Wales: Paul Gallen; *Queensland:* Nate Myles.
Half-time: 0-4; **Referees:** Shayne Hayne & Ben Cummins; **Attendance:** 83,421 *(at ANZ Stadium, Sydney)*.

---

current Maroons coach Meninga.

In the shadow of half-time the Queenslanders almost pulled of the first try of the night. There was a long run by centre Justin Hodges, carving up the NSW defences. Cherry-Evans continued the action before putting in a short kick behind the tryline. It was only a desperation response from Reynolds that prevented what looked to be a certain try.

Both sides lifted in the second spell, with some wonderful, exciting Rugby League, although Anthony Watmough was placed on report for a spear tackle on Nate Myles. This subsequently saw the NSW back-rower suspended for four matches, including Origin III.

Sam Thaiday looked to have scored in the 50th minute. However, video replays showed Hayne had stripped the ball loose and, although Thaiday regathered and fell on the ball as he swept across the tryline, he was ruled not to have had full control. Moments later NSW tacklers rolled Brent Tate over on the tryline, preventing him from grounding the ball.

The Maroons suffered a huge setback when Tate left the field with a career-ending leg injury after a tackle from Ryan Hoffman in the 57th minute. This forced a major reshuffle with forward Chris McQueen moving to the right wing. The 32-year-old Tate had to undergo knee reconstruction – the fourth such surgery in his career – and he realised it was time to bring down the curtain on a career that saw him make 239 senior appearances for the Brisbane Broncos, New Zealand Warriors and the Cowboys, 26 Tests for Australia and 23 games for Queensland.

As the clock wound down both Robbie Farah and Greg Bird were grassed short of the Queensland line. Then, after the Maroons had successfully defended five straight sets of six tackles, Hodkinson managed to find the narrowest of gaps between Cherry-Evans and Ben Te'o to score the match-winning try. It was then that the Blues got a reprieve. From the restart the ball was deemed to have gone out on the full even though replays seemed to show it had touched NSW prop Aaron Woods on the way through.

Tempers were frayed and there were a few spiteful incidents in the shadow of full-time. But in the end it was obvious – Queensland's eight-year Origin reign was over.

Meninga questioned several refereeing decisions but was gracious in defeat: "We live and breathe by those decisions every week. I'm not going to offer any excuses. I'm so proud of these players. What they've achieved over the years has been fantastic and will probably never be repeated again."

Queensland ensured there would not be a clean-sweep of the Origin series with an emphatic 32-8 hammering of their southern rivals in Brisbane. The Maroons took the lead with the first try of the night, a minute before half-time, and were then never headed, scoring five tries to one. Had it not been for some heroic defence by the NSW Blues the score could well have topped the half-century.

But in New South Wales the media ignored the final score, preferring to point out that the Brisbane encounter was never going to alter the status of the final series result.

"Queensland might have won on Wednesday night, but who cares?" sniffed Dean Ritchie of the Sydney Daily Telegraph. "The Maroons might have come good ... with a 32-8 win, but history will say this is the year NSW became the dominant state in Rugby League again. Nothing can take the gloss off what Laurie Daley, Paul Gallen and their team have achieved in this series. In the process, they have knocked some of the cockiness from Queensland."

Of course, there was no cockiness in the gracious words of Meninga and captain Cam Smith. "New South Wales played extremely well. They deserved the Origin shield," Smith said. "It was a hard fought series. Hopefully we will be back bigger and better next year."

Indeed, players from both sides showed they didn't regard Origin III as a 'nothing' match.

Some great work by NSW winger James McManus and stand-off Reynolds, who rolled

Inglis before stripping him of the ball over the stripe, saved what looked like a certain try in the sixth minute. The same pair then held up Thurston before Maroons second-rower Aidan Guerra was across the line. But the video referees controversially overruled the on-pitch officials and disallowed a possible Queensland try.

So close was the tussle that the Blues decided to accept two points from a Hodkinson penalty goal in the 23rd minute. The NSW players had to dig deep in defence to keep the Maroons at bay – holding up both Boyd and Inglis within the space of two minutes.

However, the defensive line eventually cracked. As the half-time break loomed large Cherry-Evans, thrown into the fray after half-an-hour, swerved his way through a gap near the halfway line, kicked ahead and Smith was perfectly placed to run onto the bouncing ball and score. The move sent the Queenslanders to the interval with a 6-2 lead.

The Maroons' spirits could only have been further lifted at half-time when Queenslanders from their eight-year reign were presented to the 50,155 fans. Then, just after the resumption for the second half, the mastery of two Origin greats sent Queensland further ahead – Hodges creating a try for Slater. Thurston extended the lead with a penalty goal after a dangerous tackle on Myles.

Nevertheless, the Blues struck back midway though the half with a try to Canberra's Josh Dugan. They were back in the equation, trailing 14-8.

It was all in vain. With nine minutes remaining the Maroons rejected the chance to take a penalty attempt which, if successful, would have put them in front by eight – and went for a possible try. Thurston sent a long pass for Boyd to score and JT's conversion put Queensland ahead by 20-8. It meant that Boyd joined Inglis as the top tryscorer in Origin history (with 15 each). Tries to Guerra and Cronk late in the action proved to be the icing on the cake.

Four players were charged by the judiciary after the Origin encounter. All opted for an early guilty plea to avoid heavier sentences. Reynolds was suspended for three matches for a shoulder charge on Will Chambers. Bird was outed for two games for the dangerous throw on Myles. Ben Te'o was given a one-match ban for dangerous contact with kicker Hodkinson and Myles escaped suspension for dangerous contact on Bird with an elbow. The incidents involving Bird and Myles within the space of two minutes were quite bizarre, considering the two players were co-captains of the Gold Coast Titans.

State against state … Mate against mate!

* Gallen was awarded the Wally Lewis Medal as Man of the Series and Thurston took his Origin points-scoring record to 174.

STATE OF ORIGIN - GAME III

Wednesday 9th July 2014

QUEENSLAND 32 NEW SOUTH WALES 8

QUEENSLAND: 1 Billy Slater (Melbourne Storm); 2 Darius Boyd (Newcastle Knights); 3 Greg Inglis (South Sydney Rabbitohs); 4 Justin Hodges (Brisbane Broncos); 5 Will Chambers (Melbourne Storm); 6 Johnathan Thurston (North Queensland Cowboys); 7 Cooper Cronk (Melbourne Storm); 8 Jacob Lillyman (New Zealand Warriors); 9 Cameron Smith (Melbourne Storm) (C); 10 Nate Myles (Gold Coast Titans); 11 Aidan Guerra (Sydney Roosters); 12 Sam Thaiday (Brisbane Broncos); 13 Corey Parker (Brisbane Broncos). Subs (all used): 14 Daly Cherry-Evans (Manly Sea Eagles); 15 Ben Te'o (South Sydney Rabbitohs); 16 Matt Gillett (Brisbane Broncos); 17 Dave Taylor (Gold Coast Titans). **Tries:** Smith (39), Slater (43), Boyd (71), Guerra (74), Cronk (77); **Goals:** Thurston 6/6. **On report:** Te'o (22) - alleged late challenge on Hodkinson; Myles (60) - alleged use of the elbow on Bird. **NEW SOUTH WALES:** 1 Jarryd Hayne (Parramatta Eels); 2 James McManus (Newcastle Knights); 3 Josh Dugan (St George Illawarra Dragons); 4 Josh Morris (Canterbury Bulldogs); 5 Daniel Tupou (Sydney Roosters); 6 Josh Reynolds (Canterbury Bulldogs); 7 Trent Hodkinson (Canterbury Bulldogs); 8 Paul Gallen (Cronulla Sharks) (C); 9 Robbie Farah (Wests Tigers); 10 Aaron Woods (Wests Tigers); 11 Beau Scott (Newcastle Knights); 12 Ryan Hoffman (Melbourne Storm); 13 Greg Bird (Gold Coast Titans). Subs (all used): 14 Trent Merrin (St George Illawarra Dragons); 15 Boyd Cordner (Sydney Roosters); 16 James Tamou (North Queensland Cowboys); 17 Luke Lewis (Cronulla Sharks). **Try:** Dugan (61); **Goals:** Hodkinson 2/2. **On report:** Reynolds (33) - alleged shoulder charge on Chambers. **Rugby Leaguer & League Express Men of the Match:** *Queensland:* Corey Parker; *New South Wales:* Paul Gallen. **Half-time:** 6-2; **Referees:** Ben Cummins & Gerard Sutton; **Attendance:** 50,155 *(at Suncorp Stadium, Brisbane).*

Wally Lewis Medal (Man of the Series): Paul Gallen (New South Wales).

WORLD CUP 2013
Statistical review

World Cup 2013 - Statistical review

GROUP A

Saturday 26th October 2013

ENGLAND 20 AUSTRALIA 28

ENGLAND: 1 Sam Tomkins (Wigan Warriors); 2 Josh Charnley (Wigan Warriors); 3 Kallum Watkins (Leeds Rhinos); 4 Leroy Cudjoe (Huddersfield Giants); 5 Ryan Hall (Leeds Rhinos); 6 Rangi Chase (Castleford Tigers); 7 Kevin Sinfield (Leeds Rhinos) (C); 8 Chris Hill (Warrington Wolves); 9 James Roby (St Helens); 10 George Burgess (South Sydney Rabbitohs); 11 Brett Ferres (Huddersfield Giants); 12 Ben Westwood (Warrington Wolves); 13 Sam Burgess (South Sydney Rabbitohs). Subs (all used): 14 Gareth Widdop (Melbourne Storm); 15 Carl Ablett (Leeds Rhinos); 16 Tom Burgess (South Sydney Rabbitohs); 17 Lee Mossop (Wigan Warriors).
Tries: Hall (8), Cudjoe (20), G Burgess (51), Charnley (76);
Goals: Sinfield 2/4.
On report: S Burgess (63) - alleged high tackle on Thaiday.
AUSTRALIA: 1 Billy Slater (Melbourne Storm); 2 Brett Morris (St George Illawarra Dragons); 3 Brent Tate (North Queensland Cowboys); 4 Greg Inglis (South Sydney Rabbitohs); 5 Darius Boyd (Newcastle Knights); 6 Johnathan Thurston (North Queensland Cowboys); 7 Cooper Cronk (Melbourne Storm); 8 Matthew Scott (North Queensland Cowboys); 9 Cameron Smith (Melbourne Storm) (C); 10 James Tamou (North Queensland Cowboys); 11 Greg Bird (Gold Coast Titans); 12 Sam Thaiday (Brisbane Broncos); 13 Paul Gallen (Cronulla Sharks). Subs (all used): 14 Robbie Farah (Wests Tigers); 15 Andrew Fifita (Cronulla Sharks); 16 Luke Lewis (Cronulla Sharks); 17 Corey Parker (Brisbane Broncos).
Tries: Thurston (27), Bird (37), Slater (40), B Morris (44), Boyd (71);
Goals: Thurston 4/6.
Rugby Leaguer & League Express Men of the Match:
England: George Burgess; *Australia:* Johnathan Thurston.
Penalty count: 7-12; **Half-time:** 10-18; **Referee:** Henry Perenara (New Zealand); **Attendance:** 45,052 (at Millennium Stadium, Cardiff).

Monday 28th October 2013

FIJI 32 IRELAND 14

FIJI: 1 Kevin Naiqama (Newcastle Knights); 5 Akuila Uate (Newcastle Knights); 4 Wes Naiqama (Penrith Panthers); 3 Sisa Waqa (Melbourne Storm); 2 Marika Koroibete (Wests Tigers); 6 Alipate Noilea (Collegians); 7 Aaron Groom (Asquith Magpies); 8 Ashton Sims (North Queensland Cowboys); 9 James Storer (Collegians); 10 Petero Civoniceva (Redcliffe Dolphins) (C); 11 Tariq Sims (North Queensland Cowboys); 12 Jayson Bukuya (Cronulla Sharks); 13 Korbin Sims (Newcastle Knights). Subs (all used): 14 Apisai Koroisau (South Sydney Rabbitohs); 15 Eloni Vunakece (Toulouse Olympique); 16 Kane Evans (Sydney Roosters); 17 Vitale Roqica (Cronulla Sharks).
Tries: Uate (10, 64, 73), K Naiqama (13), T Sims (52), K Sims (67);
Goals: W Naiqama 4/7.
Sin bin: Vunakece (35) - high tackle.
IRELAND: 1 Scott Grix (Huddersfield Giants); 2 Damien Blanch (Catalan Dragons); 3 Stuart Littler (Leigh Centurions); 4 Apirana Pewhairangi (Parramatta Eels); 5 Pat Richards (Wigan Warriors); 6 James Mendeika (Warrington Wolves); 7 Liam Finn (Featherstone Rovers) (C); 8 Brett White (Canberra Raiders); 9 Rory Kostjasyn (North Queensland Cowboys); 10 Eamon O'Carroll (Widnes Vikings); 11 Tyrone McCarthy (Warrington Wolves); 12 Dave Allen (Widnes Vikings); 13 Ben Currie (Warrington Wolves). Subs (all used): 14 Bob Beswick (Leigh Centurions); 15 James Hasson (Manly Sea Eagles); 16 Kurt Haggerty (Barrow Raiders); 17 Anthony Mullally (Huddersfield Giants).
Tries: McCarthy (23), Blanch (77), Hasson (80); **Goals:** Richards 1/3.
Rugby Leaguer & League Express Men of the Match:
Fiji: Akuila Uate; *Ireland:* Brett White.
Penalty count: 5-13; **Half-time:** 12-4; **Referee:** Phil Bentham (England); **Attendance:** 8,872 (at Spotland, Rochdale).

Saturday 2nd November 2013

ENGLAND 42 IRELAND 0

ENGLAND: 1 Sam Tomkins (Wigan Warriors); 2 Tom Briscoe (Hull FC); 3 Kallum Watkins (Leeds Rhinos); 4 Leroy Cudjoe (Huddersfield Giants); 5 Ryan Hall (Leeds Rhinos); 6 Rangi Chase (Castleford Tigers); 7 Kevin Sinfield (Leeds Rhinos) (C); 8 Chris Hill (Warrington Wolves); 9 James Roby (St Helens); 10 George Burgess (South Sydney Rabbitohs); 11 Brett Ferres (Huddersfield Giants); 12 Ben Westwood (Warrington Wolves); 13 Sean O'Loughlin (Wigan Warriors). Subs (all used): 14 Gareth Widdop (Melbourne Storm); 15 Carl Ablett (Leeds Rhinos); 16 Tom Burgess (South Sydney Rabbitohs); 17 James Graham (Canterbury Bulldogs).
Tries: Hall (3, 13, 22), Briscoe (17, 19), Ferres (24), Watkins (57), Chase (69); **Goals:** Sinfield 4/7, Widdop 1/1.
IRELAND: 1 James Mendeika (Warrington Wolves); 2 Damien Blanch (Catalan Dragons); 3 Stuart Littler (Leigh Centurions); 4 Apirana Pewhairangi (Parramatta Eels); 5 Pat Richards (Wigan Warriors); 6 Ben Currie (Warrington Wolves); 7 Liam Finn (Featherstone Rovers) (C); 8 Brett White (Canberra Raiders); 9 Rory Kostjasyn (North Queensland Cowboys); 10 James Hasson (Manly Sea Eagles); 11 Simon Finnigan (Leigh Centurions); 12 Dave Allen (Widnes Vikings); 13 Tyrone McCarthy (Warrington Wolves). Subs (all used): 14 Bob Beswick (Leigh Centurions); 15 Luke Ambler (Halifax); 16 Danny Bridge (Warrington Wolves); 17 Anthony Mullally (Huddersfield Giants).
Rugby Leaguer & League Express Men of the Match:
England: Sam Tomkins; *Ireland:* Luke Ambler.
Penalty count: 10-6; **Half-time:** 30-0; **Referee:** Thierry Alibert (France); **Attendance:** 24,375 (at John Smith's Stadium, Huddersfield).

AUSTRALIA 34 FIJI 2

AUSTRALIA: 1 Greg Inglis (South Sydney Rabbitohs); 2 Jarryd Hayne (Parramatta Eels); 3 Josh Morris (Canterbury Bulldogs); 4 Michael Jennings (Sydney Roosters); 5 Darius Boyd (Newcastle Knights); 6 Johnathan Thurston (North Queensland Cowboys); 7 Daly Cherry-Evans (Manly Sea Eagles); 8 Matthew Scott (North Queensland Cowboys); 9 Cameron Smith (Melbourne Storm) (C); 10 James Tamou (North Queensland Cowboys); 11 Luke Lewis (Cronulla Sharks); 12 Josh Papalii (Canberra Raiders); 13 Nate Myles (Gold Coast Titans). Subs (all used): 14 Boyd Cordner (Sydney Roosters); 15 Robbie Farah (Wests Tigers); 16 Andrew Fifita (Cronulla Sharks); 17 Paul Gallen (Cronulla Sharks).
Tries: Papalii (15), Boyd (21), Jennings (31), J Morris (44), Cherry-Evans (56), Lewis (66); **Goals:** Thurston 5/6.
FIJI: 1 Kevin Naiqama (Newcastle Knights); 5 Akuila Uate (Newcastle Knights); 3 Sisa Waqa (Melbourne Storm); 4 Daryl Millard (Catalan Dragons); 2 Marika Koroibete (Wests Tigers); 6 Alipate Noilea (Collegians); 7 Aaron Groom (Asquith Magpies); 8 Ashton Sims (North Queensland Cowboys); 9 James Storer (Collegians); 10 Petero Civoniceva (Redcliffe Dolphins) (C); 11 Tariq Sims (North Queensland Cowboys); 12 Jayson Bukuya (Cronulla Sharks); 13 Korbin Sims (Newcastle Knights). Subs (all used): 14 Apisai Koroisau (South Sydney Rabbitohs); 15 Eloni Vunakece (Toulouse Olympique); 16 Kane Evans (Sydney Roosters); 17 Vitale Roqica (Cronulla Sharks).
Goals: Noilea 1/1.
Rugby Leaguer & League Express Men of the Match:
Australia: Johnathan Thurston; *Fiji:* Aaron Groom.
Penalty count: 5-6; **Half-time:** 16-2; **Referee:** Richard Silverwood (England); **Attendance:** 14,137 (at Langtree Park, St Helens).

Saturday 9th November 2013

ENGLAND 34 FIJI 12

ENGLAND: 1 Sam Tomkins (Wigan Warriors); 2 Tom Briscoe (Hull FC); 3 Kallum Watkins (Leeds Rhinos); 4 Leroy Cudjoe (Huddersfield Giants); 5 Ryan Hall (Leeds Rhinos); 6 Rangi Chase (Castleford Tigers); 7 Kevin Sinfield (Leeds Rhinos) (C); 8 Sam Burgess (South Sydney Rabbitohs); 9 Michael McIlorum (Wigan Warriors); 10 James Graham (Canterbury Bulldogs); 11 Brett Ferres (Huddersfield Giants); 12 Ben Westwood (Warrington Wolves); 13 Sean O'Loughlin (Wigan Warriors). Subs (all used): 14 Rob Burrow (Leeds Rhinos); 15 Liam Farrell (Wigan Warriors); 16 Chris Hill (Warrington Wolves); 17 George Burgess (South Sydney Rabbitohs).
Tries: Westwood (38), S Burgess (41), Ferres (44), Hall (49, 56), Burrow (53); **Goals:** Sinfield 5/6.
On report: Westwood (75) - alleged use of the forearm on T Sims.
FIJI: 1 Kevin Naiqama (Newcastle Knights); 2 Marika Koroibete (Wests Tigers); 4 Wes Naiqama (Penrith Panthers); 3 Daryl Millard (Catalan Dragons); 5 Semi Waqavatu (Parramatta Eels); 6 Ryan Millard (Burwood United); 7 Aaron Groom (Asquith Magpies); 8 Ashton Sims (North Queensland Cowboys); 9 James Storer (Collegians); 10 Petero Civoniceva (Redcliffe Dolphins) (C); 11 Tariq Sims (North Queensland Cowboys); 12 Jayson Bukuya (Cronulla Sharks); 13 Korbin Sims (Newcastle Knights). Subs (all used): 15 Eloni Vunakece (Toulouse Olympique); 16 Peni Botiki (Saru Dragons); 17 Vitale Roqica (Cronulla Sharks); 18 Kane Evans (Sydney Roosters).
Tries: Vunakece (34), Waqavatu (72); **Goals:** W Naiqama 2/2.
On report: K Sims (19) - alleged dangerous challenge on Graham.
Rugby Leaguer & League Express Men of the Match:
England: Sam Burgess; *Fiji:* Tariq Sims.
Penalty count: 10-7; **Half-time:** 6-6; **Referee:** Ben Cummins (Australia); **Attendance:** 25,114 (at Kingston Communications Stadium, Hull).

IRELAND 0 AUSTRALIA 50

IRELAND: 1 Scott Grix (Huddersfield Giants); 2 Damien Blanch (Catalan Dragons); 3 Stuart Littler (Leigh Centurions); 4 Joshua Toole (St George Illawarra Dragons); 5 Pat Richards (Wigan Warriors); 6 James Mendeika (Warrington Wolves); 7 Liam Finn (Featherstone Rovers) (C); 8 Brett White (Canberra Raiders); 9 Rory Kostjasyn (North Queensland Cowboys); 10 Anthony Mullally (Huddersfield Giants); 11 Tyrone McCarthy (Warrington Wolves); 12 Dave Allen (Widnes Vikings); 13 Simon Finnigan (Leigh Centurions). Subs (all used): 14 Bob Beswick (Leigh Centurions); 15 James Hasson (Manly Sea Eagles); 16 Ben Currie (Warrington Wolves); 17 Luke Ambler (Halifax).
AUSTRALIA: 1 Billy Slater (Melbourne Storm); 5 Jarryd Hayne (Parramatta Eels); 4 Brent Tate (North Queensland Cowboys); 3 Josh Morris (Canterbury Bulldogs); 2 Brett Morris (St George Illawarra Dragons); 6 Daly Cherry-Evans (Manly Sea Eagles); 7 Cooper Cronk (Melbourne Storm); 8 Paul Gallen (Cronulla Sharks); 9 Cameron Smith (Melbourne Storm) (C); 10 James Tamou (North Queensland Cowboys); 11 Greg Bird (Gold Coast Titans); 12 Sam Thaiday (Brisbane Broncos); 13 Nate Myles (Gold Coast Titans). Subs (all used): 14 Boyd Cordner (Sydney Roosters); 15 Robbie Farah (Wests Tigers); 16 Andrew Fifita (Cronulla Sharks); 17 Corey Parker (Brisbane Broncos).
Tries: Hayne (1, 72), Cronk (11, 57), Bird (30), B Morris (31), Slater (39), Cherry-Evans (59), Fifita (64); **Goals:** Smith 3/5, Parker 4/4.
Rugby Leaguer & League Express Men of the Match:
Ireland: Brett White; *Australia:* Daly Cherry-Evans.
Penalty count: 2-12; **Half-time:** 0-26; **Referee:** Phil Bentham (England); **Attendance:** 5,021 (at Thomond Park, Limerick).

AUSTRALIA

	CLUB	D.O.B.	APP(S)	T	G	FG	PTS
Greg Bird	Gold Coast Titans	10/2/84	5	2	0	0	8
Darius Boyd	Newcastle Knights	17/7/87	5	4	0	0	16
Daly Cherry-Evans	Manly Sea Eagles	20/2/89	2(3)	2	0	0	8
Boyd Cordner	Sydney Roosters	9/6/92	(2)	0	0	0	0
Cooper Cronk	Melbourne Storm	5/12/83	5	5	0	0	20
Robbie Farah	Wests Tigers	23/1/84	(3)	0	0	0	0
Andrew Fifita	Cronulla Sharks	28/6/89	(6)	2	0	0	8
Paul Gallen	Cronulla Sharks	14/8/81	5(1)	0	0	0	0
Jarryd Hayne	Parramatta Eels	15/2/88	5	9	0	0	36
Greg Inglis	South Sydney Rabbitohs 15/1/87		5	2	0	0	8
Michael Jennings	Sydney Roosters	20/4/88	1	1	0	0	4
Luke Lewis	Cronulla Sharks	11/8/83	1(1)	1	0	0	4
Brett Morris	St George Illawarra Dragons 23/8/86		5	9	0	0	36
Josh Morris	Canterbury Bulldogs 23/8/86		2	1	0	0	4
Nate Myles	Gold Coast Titans	24/6/85	2	0	0	0	0
Josh Papalii	Canberra Raiders	13/5/92	1(3)	2	0	0	8
Corey Parker	Brisbane Broncos	5/5/82	(5)	0	4	0	8
Matthew Scott	North Queensland Cowboys 30/7/85		5	0	0	0	0
Billy Slater	Melbourne Storm	18/6/83	4	4	0	0	16
Cameron Smith	Melbourne Storm	18/6/83	6	1	3	0	10
James Tamou	North Queensland Cowboys 13/12/88		6	1	0	0	4
Brent Tate	North Queensland Cowboys 3/3/82		3	0	0	0	0
Sam Thaiday	Brisbane Broncos	12/6/85	5	0	0	0	0
Johnathan Thurston	North Queensland Cowboys 25/4/83		5	2	33	0	74

ENGLAND

	CLUB	D.O.B.	APP(S)	T	G	FG	PTS
Carl Ablett	Leeds Rhinos	19/12/85	(2)	0	0	0	0
Tom Briscoe	Hull FC	19/3/90	2	2	0	0	8
George Burgess	South Sydney Rabbitohs 21/4/92		2(3)	1	0	0	4
Sam Burgess	South Sydney Rabbitohs 14/12/88		4	2	0	0	8
Tom Burgess	South Sydney Rabbitohs 21/4/92		(2)	0	0	0	0
Rob Burrow	Leeds Rhinos	26/9/82	(2)	1	0	0	4
Josh Charnley	Wigan Warriors	26/6/91	3	3	0	0	12
Rangi Chase	Castleford Tigers	11/4/86	4	1	0	0	4
Leroy Cudjoe	Huddersfield Giants	7/4/88	5	1	0	0	4
Liam Farrell	Wigan Warriors	2/7/90	(2)	0	0	0	0
Brett Ferres	Huddersfield Giants	17/4/86	4(1)	3	0	0	12
James Graham	Canterbury Bulldogs	10/9/85	3(1)	0	0	0	0
Ryan Hall	Leeds Rhinos	27/11/87	5	8	0	0	32
Zak Hardaker	Leeds Rhinos	17/10/91	0	0	0	0	0
Chris Hill	Warrington Wolves	3/11/87	3(2)	0	0	0	0
Michael McIlorum	Wigan Warriors	10/1/88	2	0	0	0	0
Lee Mossop	Wigan Warriors	17/1/89	(1)	0	0	0	0
Sean O'Loughlin	Wigan Warriors	24/11/82	4	2	0	0	8
James Roby	St Helens	22/11/85	3(1)	0	0	0	0
Kevin Sinfield	Leeds Rhinos	12/9/80	5	0	19	0	38
Sam Tomkins	Wigan Warriors	23/3/89	5	0	0	0	0
Kallum Watkins	Leeds Rhinos	12/3/91	5	2	0	0	8
Ben Westwood	Warrington Wolves	25/7/81	5	1	0	0	4
Gareth Widdop	Melbourne Storm	12/3/89	1(2)	0	1	0	2

Zak Hardaker withdrew from the squad 'due to personal issues' (4/11/13) and was not replaced

FIJI

	CLUB	D.O.B.	APP(S)	T	G	FG	PTS
Peni Botiki	Saru Dragons	30/1/89	(1)	0	0	0	0
Jayson Bukuya	Cronulla Sharks	21/4/89	5	0	0	0	0
Petero Civoniceva	Redcliffe Dolphins	21/4/76	5	0	0	0	0
Kane Evans	Sydney Roosters	9/1/92	(5)	0	0	0	0
Aaron Groom	Asquith Magpies	23/6/87	5	1	0	0	4
Ilisavani Jegesa	Nabua Broncos	22/11/88	0	0	0	0	0
Marika Koroibete	Wests Tigers	26/7/92	5	0	0	0	0
Apisai Koroisau	South Sydney Rabbitohs 7/11/92		(4)	0	0	0	0
Daryl Millard	Catalan Dragons	20/2/85	4	0	0	0	0
Ryan Millard	Burwood United	13/3/87	1	0	0	0	0
Kevin Naiqama	Newcastle Knights	4/2/89	5	1	0	0	4
Wes Naiqama	Penrith Panthers	19/10/82	4	1	11	0	26
Kaliova Nauqe	Fassifern Bombers	7/5/85	0	0	0	0	0
Alipate Noilea	Collegians	21/2/83	2	0	1	0	2
Tikiko Noke	Lautoka Crushers	15/9/94	0	0	0	0	0
Vitale Roqica	Cronulla Sharks	13/2/91	(5)	1	0	0	4
Ashton Sims	North Queensland Cowboys 26/2/85		5	0	0	0	0
Korbin Sims	Newcastle Knights	2/1/92	3	1	0	0	4
Tariq Sims	North Queensland Cowboys 9/2/90		5	1	0	0	4
James Storer	Collegians	16/2/82	5	0	0	0	0
Akuila Uate	Newcastle Knights	6/10/87	4	3	0	0	12
Eloni Vunakece	Toulouse Olympique	27/5/87	2(3)	1	0	0	4
Sisa Waqa	Melbourne Storm	29/4/86	4	0	0	0	0
Semi Waqavatu	Parramatta Eels	13/6/92	1(2)	1	0	0	4

IRELAND

	CLUB	D.O.B.	APP(S)	T	G	FG	PTS
Dave Allen	Widnes Vikings	15/9/85	3	0	0	0	0
Luke Ambler	Halifax	18/12/89	(2)	0	0	0	0
Bob Beswick	Leigh Centurions	8/12/84	(3)	0	0	0	0
Damien Blanch	Catalan Dragons	24/5/83	3	1	0	0	4
Danny Bridge	Warrington Wolves	4/1/93	(1)	0	0	0	0
Ben Currie	Warrington Wolves	15/7/94	2(1)	0	0	0	0
Liam Finn	Featherstone Rovers	2/11/83	3	0	0	0	0
Simon Finnigan	Leigh Centurions	8/12/81	2	0	0	0	0
Scott Grix	Huddersfield Giants	1/5/84	2	0	0	0	0
Matty Hadden	Oxford	7/6/90	0	0	0	0	0
Kurt Haggerty	Barrow Raiders	8/1/89	(1)	0	0	0	0
James Hasson	Manly Sea Eagles	1/5/92	1(2)	1	0	0	4
Rory Kostjasyn	North Queensland Cowboys 6/6/87		3	0	0	0	0
Stuart Littler	Leigh Centurions	19/2/79	3	0	0	0	0
Tyrone McCarthy	Warrington Wolves	21/4/88	3	1	0	0	4
James Mendeika	Warrington Wolves	16/12/91	3	0	0	0	0
Anthony Mullally	Huddersfield Giants	28/6/91	1(2)	0	0	0	0
Eamon O'Carroll	Widnes Vikings	13/6/87	1	0	0	0	0
Apirana Pewhairangi	Parramatta Eels	19/3/92	2	0	0	0	0
Pat Richards	Wigan Warriors	27/2/82	3	0	1	0	2
Colton Roche	Sheffield Eagles	23/6/93	0	0	0	0	0
Joshua Toole	St George Illawarra Dragons 11/9/89		1	0	0	0	0
Brett White	Canberra Raiders	8/4/82	3	0	0	0	0

GROUP A - FINAL STANDINGS

	P	W	D	L	F	A	Diff	PTS
Australia	3	3	0	0	112	22	90	6
England	3	2	0	1	96	40	56	4
Fiji	3	1	0	2	46	82	-36	2
Ireland	3	0	0	3	14	124	-110	0

World Cup 2013 - Statistical review

GROUP B

FRANCE 9 PAPUA NEW GUINEA 8

FRANCE: 1 Morgan Escare (Catalan Dragons); 5 Clint Greenshields (North Queensland Cowboys); 3 Jean-Philippe Baile (Catalan Dragons); 4 Vincent Duport (Catalan Dragons); 2 Frederic Vaccari (Catalan Dragons); 6 Thomas Bosc (Catalan Dragons); 7 William Barthau (Catalan Dragons); 15 Jamal Fakir (Catalan Dragons); 9 Eloi Pelissier (Catalan Dragons); 10 Remi Casty (Catalan Dragons); 11 Kevin Larroyer (Catalan Dragons); 12 Sebastien Raguin (St Esteve); 13 Gregory Mounis (Catalan Dragons). Subs (all used): 14 Theo Fages (Salford City Reds); 8 Olivier Elima (Catalan Dragons) (C); 16 Benjamin Garcia (Catalan Dragons); 17 Mickael Simon (Catalan Dragons).
Try: Bosc (6); **Goals:** Bosc 2/2; **Field goal:** Barthau (64).
PAPUA NEW GUINEA: 1 David Mead (Gold Coast Titans); 5 Nene McDonald (Sydney Roosters); 4 Isreal Eliab (Port Moresby Vipers); 3 Menzie Yere (Sheffield Eagles); 2 Josiah Abavu (Port Moresby Vipers); 6 Ray Thompson (North Queensland Cowboys); 7 Ase Boas (Rabaul Gurias); 8 Mark Mexico (Lae Tigers); 9 Paul Aiton (Wakefield Trinity Wildcats); 10 Enoch Maki (Mendi Muruks); 11 Dion Aiye (Rabaul Gurias); 12 Jason Chan (Huddersfield Giants); 13 Neville Costigan (Newcastle Knights) (C). Subs (all used): 14 Charlie Wabo (Mendi Muruks); 15 Richard Kambo (Port Moresby Vipers); 16 Jessie Joe Nandye (Whitehaven); 17 Larsen Marabe (Orange CYMS).
Tries: McDonald (17), Abavu (42); **Goals:** Mead 0/3.
On report: Aiton (76) - alleged dangerous challenge on Escare.
Rugby Leaguer & League Express Men of the Match:
France: William Barthau; *Papua New Guinea:* Neville Costigan.
Penalty count: 4-5; **Half-time:** 6-4; **Referee:** Ben Cummins (Australia); **Attendance:** 7,481 *(at MS3 Craven Park, Hull).*

NEW ZEALAND 42 SAMOA 24

NEW ZEALAND: 1 Josh Hoffman (Brisbane Broncos); 2 Roger Tuivasa-Sheck (Sydney Roosters); 3 Dean Whare (Penrith Panthers); 4 Bryson Goodwin (South Sydney Rabbitohs); 5 Manu Vatuvei (New Zealand Warriors); 6 Kieran Foran (Manly Sea Eagles); 7 Shaun Johnson (New Zealand Warriors); 8 Jared Waerea-Hargreaves (Sydney Roosters); 9 Issac Luke (South Sydney Rabbitohs); 15 Sam Moa (Sydney Roosters); 11 Frank Pritchard (Canterbury Bulldogs); 12 Sonny Bill Williams (Sydney Roosters); 13 Simon Mannering (New Zealand Warriors) (C). Subs (all used): 14 Elijah Taylor (New Zealand Warriors); 10 Jesse Bromwich (Melbourne Storm); 16 Sam Kasiano (Canterbury Bulldogs); 17 Frank-Paul Nuuausala (Sydney Roosters).
Tries: Hoffman (11), Mannering (15, 22), Tuivasa-Sheck (18), Vatuvei (42, 49, 73), Luke (46); **Goals:** Johnson 5/8.
SAMOA: 1 Anthony Milford (Canberra Raiders); 5 Daniel Vidot (St George Illawarra Dragons); 4 Joseph Leilua (Newcastle Knights); 3 Junior Sa'u (Melbourne Storm); 2 Antonio Winterstein (North Queensland Cowboys); 6 Reni Maitua (Parramatta Eels); 7 Ben Roberts (Parramatta Eels); 8 David Fa'alogo (Newcastle Knights); 9 Pita Godinet (New Zealand Warriors); 10 Suaia Matagi (New Zealand Warriors); 11 Iosia Soliola (St Helens) (C); 12 Frank Winterstein (Widnes Vikings); 13 Sauaso Sue (Wests Tigers). Subs (all used): 14 Penani Manumalealii (Cronulla Sharks); 15 Leeson Ah Mau (St George Illawarra Dragons); 16 Mark Taufua (Cronulla Sharks); 17 Mose Masoe (Penrith Panthers).
Tries: Roberts (39), Leilua (52), Manumalealii (56), Matagi (61), A Winterstein (65); **Goals:** Milford 2/5.
Rugby Leaguer & League Express Men of the Match:
New Zealand: Kieran Foran; *Samoa:* Joseph Leilua.
Penalty count: 8-4; **Half-time:** 22-4; **Referee:** Richard Silverwood (England); **Attendance:** 14,965 *(at Halliwell Jones Stadium, Warrington).*

FRANCE 0 NEW ZEALAND 48

FRANCE: 1 Morgan Escare (Catalan Dragons); 5 Cyril Stacul (Lezignan); 3 Jean-Philippe Baile (Catalan Dragons); 4 Vincent Duport (Catalan Dragons); 2 Frederic Vaccari (Catalan Dragons); 6 Thomas Bosc (Catalan Dragons); 7 Theo Fages (Salford City Reds); 8 Olivier Elima (Catalan Dragons) (C); 9 Kane Bentley (Toulouse Olympique); 10 Remi Casty (Catalan Dragons); 11 Kevin Larroyer (Catalan Dragons); 12 Sebastien Raguin (St Esteve); 13 Andrew Bentley (Toulouse Olympique). Subs (all used): 14 Gregory Mounis (Catalan Dragons); 15 Jamal Fakir (Catalan Dragons); 16 Benjamin Garcia (Catalan Dragons); 17 Mickael Simon (Catalan Dragons).
NEW ZEALAND: 1 Kevin Locke (New Zealand Warriors); 5 Roger Tuivasa-Sheck (Sydney Roosters); 4 Krisnan Inu (Canterbury Bulldogs); 3 Bryson Goodwin (South Sydney Rabbitohs); 2 Jason Nightingale (St George Illawarra Dragons); 6 Kieran Foran (Manly Sea Eagles); 7 Shaun Johnson (New Zealand Warriors); 8 Ben Matulino (New Zealand Warriors); 9 Issac Luke (South Sydney Rabbitohs); 10 Jared Waerea-Hargreaves (Sydney Roosters); 11 Frank Pritchard (Canterbury Bulldogs); 12 Alex Glenn (Brisbane Broncos); 13 Simon Mannering (New Zealand Warriors) (C). Subs (all used): 14 Elijah Taylor (New Zealand Warriors); 15 Sam Kasiano (Canterbury Bulldogs); 16 Frank-Paul Nuuausala (Sydney Roosters); 17 Greg Eastwood (Canterbury Bulldogs).
Tries: Inu (4), Goodwin (25), Nuuausala (38, 75), Johnson (51, 56), Eastwood (65), Tuivasa-Sheck (80); **Goals:** Johnson 8/8.
Rugby Leaguer & League Express Men of the Match:
France: Olivier Elima; *New Zealand:* Shaun Johnson.
Penalty count: 7-8; **Half-time:** 0-18; **Referee:** Phil Bentham (England); **Attendance:** 17,518 *(at Parc des Sports, Avignon).*

PAPUA NEW GUINEA 4 SAMOA 38

PAPUA NEW GUINEA: 1 David Mead (Gold Coast Titans); 5 Nene McDonald (Sydney Roosters); 4 Isreal Eliab (Port Moresby Vipers); 3 Menzie Yere (Sheffield Eagles); 2 Josiah Abavu (Port Moresby Vipers); 6 Dion Aiye (Rabaul Gurias); 7 Ray Thompson (North Queensland Cowboys); 8 Mark Mexico (Lae Tigers); 9 Paul Aiton (Wakefield Trinity Wildcats); 10 Larsen Marabe (Orange CYMS); 11 Jessie Joe Nandye (Whitehaven); 12 Jason Chan (Huddersfield Giants); 13 Neville Costigan (Newcastle Knights) (C). Subs (all used): 14 Charlie Wabo (Mendi Muruks); 15 Richard Kambo (Port Moresby Vipers); 16 Jason Tali (Mount Hagen Eagles); 17 Enoch Maki (Mendi Muruks).
Try: Nandye (46); **Goals:** Eliab 0/1.
SAMOA: 1 Anthony Milford (Canberra Raiders); 5 Daniel Vidot (St George Illawarra Dragons); 4 Joseph Leilua (Newcastle Knights); 3 Tim Lafai (Canterbury Bulldogs); 2 Antonio Winterstein (North Queensland Cowboys); 6 Penani Manumalealii (Cronulla Sharks); 7 Ben Roberts (Parramatta Eels); 8 David Fa'alogo (Newcastle Knights); 9 Pita Godinet (New Zealand Warriors); 10 Suaia Matagi (New Zealand Warriors); 11 Iosia Soliola (St Helens) (C); 12 Leeson Ah Mau (St George Illawarra Dragons); 13 Sauaso Sue (Wests Tigers). Subs (all used): 14 Michael Sio (New Zealand Warriors); 15 Junior Moors (Melbourne Storm); 16 Mark Taufua (Cronulla Sharks); 17 Mose Masoe (Penrith Panthers).
Tries: Matagi (2), A Winterstein (9, 25, 78), Godinet (15), Roberts (38), Sue (61); **Goals:** Milford 5/7.
Rugby Leaguer & League Express Men of the Match:
Papua New Guinea: Jessie Joe Nandye; *Samoa:* Anthony Milford.
Penalty count: 7-9; **Half-time:** 0-28; **Referee:** Shayne Hayne (Australia); **Attendance:** 6,871 *(at MS3 Craven Park, Hull).*

NEW ZEALAND 56 PAPUA NEW GUINEA 10

NEW ZEALAND: 1 Josh Hoffman (Brisbane Broncos); 2 Roger Tuivasa-Sheck (Sydney Roosters); 3 Dean Whare (Penrith Panthers); 4 Bryson Goodwin (South Sydney Rabbitohs); 5 Manu Vatuvei (New Zealand Warriors); 6 Kieran Foran (Manly Sea Eagles); 7 Shaun Johnson (New Zealand Warriors) (C); 8 Ben Matulino (New Zealand Warriors); 9 Issac Luke (South Sydney Rabbitohs); 10 Jesse Bromwich (Melbourne Storm); 11 Alex Glenn (Brisbane Broncos); 12 Sonny Bill Williams (Sydney Roosters); 13 Elijah Taylor (New Zealand Warriors). Subs (all used): 14 Sam Moa (Sydney Roosters); 15 Sam Kasiano (Canterbury Bulldogs); 16 Frank-Paul Nuuausala (Sydney Roosters); 17 Thomas Leuluai (New Zealand Warriors).
Tries: Goodwin (2), Tuivasa-Sheck (7, 11), Williams (15, 26, 40), Nuuausala (30), Whare (50, 56), Taylor (68); **Goals:** Johnson 8/10.
PAPUA NEW GUINEA: 1 David Mead (Gold Coast Titans); 5 Nene McDonald (Sydney Roosters); 4 Francis Paniu (Rabaul Gurias); 3 Menzie Yere (Sheffield Eagles); 2 Josiah Abavu (Port Moresby Vipers); 6 Ray Thompson (North Queensland Cowboys); 7 Dion Aiye (Rabaul Gurias); 8 Neville Costigan (Newcastle Knights) (C); 9 Charlie Wabo (Mendi Muruks); 10 Joe Bruno (Rabaul Gurias); 11 Jessie Joe Nandye (Whitehaven); 12 Jason Chan (Huddersfield Giants); 13 Sebastian Pandia (Port Moresby Vipers). Subs (all used): 14 Wellington Albert (Lae Tigers); 15 Paul Aiton (Wakefield Trinity Wildcats); 16 Jason Tali (Mount Hagen Eagles); 17 Mark Mexico (Lae Tigers).
Tries: Aiye (41), Albert (78); **Goals:** Paniu 1/2.
Rugby Leaguer & League Express Men of the Match:
New Zealand: Sonny Bill Williams; *Papua New Guinea:* Menzie Yere.
Penalty count: 6-9; **Half-time:** 40-0; **Referee:** Ashley Klein (Australia); **Attendance:** 18,180 *(at Headingley Carnegie, Leeds).*

FRANCE 6 SAMOA 22

FRANCE: 1 Morgan Escare (Catalan Dragons); 5 Clint Greenshields (North Queensland Cowboys); 3 Jean-Philippe Baile (Catalan Dragons); 4 Vincent Duport (Catalan Dragons); 2 Frederic Vaccari (Catalan Dragons); 6 Thomas Bosc (Catalan Dragons); 7 William Barthau (Catalan Dragons); 8 Jamal Fakir (Catalan Dragons); 9 Eloi Pelissier (Catalan Dragons); 10 Remi Casty (Catalan Dragons) (C); 11 Kevin Larroyer (Catalan Dragons); 12 Sebastien Raguin (St Esteve); 13 Gregory Mounis (Catalan Dragons). Subs (all used): 14 Tony Gigot (Avignon); 15 Antoni Maria (Catalan Dragons); 16 Benjamin Garcia (Catalan Dragons); 17 Mickael Simon (Catalan Dragons).
Try: Escare (31); **Goals:** Bosc 1/1.
SAMOA: 1 Anthony Milford (Canberra Raiders); 5 Daniel Vidot (St George Illawarra Dragons); 4 Joseph Leilua (Newcastle Knights); 3 Tim Lafai (Canterbury Bulldogs); 2 Antonio Winterstein (North Queensland Cowboys); 11 Iosia Soliola (St Helens) (C); 7 Ben Roberts (Parramatta Eels); 8 David Fa'alogo (Newcastle Knights); 9 Michael Sio (New Zealand Warriors); 10 Suaia Matagi (New Zealand Warriors); 14 Tony Puletua (St Helens); 12 Leeson Ah Mau (St George Illawarra Dragons); 13 Sauaso Sue (Wests Tigers). Subs (all used): 6 Pita Godinet (New Zealand Warriors); 15 Junior Moors (Melbourne Storm); 16 Mark Taufua (Cronulla Sharks); 17 Mose Masoe (Penrith Panthers).
Tries: Vidot (4), Milford (46), Godinet (61), Moors (74); **Goals:** Milford 3/4.
Sin bin: Masoe (26) - shoulder charge on Bosc.
On report: Ah Mau (13) - alleged late challenge on Barthau; Sue (14) - alleged late challenge on Barthau; Roberts (38) - alleged dangerous challenge; Sue (58) - alleged trip on Barthau.
Rugby Leaguer & League Express Men of the Match:
France: Eloi Pelissier; *Samoa:* Anthony Milford.
Penalty count: 14-9; **Half-time:** 6-6; **Referee:** Henry Perenara (New Zealand); **Attendance:** 11,576 *(at Stade Gilbert Brutus, Perpignan).*

FRANCE

	CLUB	D.O.B.	APP(S)	T	G	FG	PTS
Jean-Philippe Baile	Catalan Dragons	7/6/87	4	0	0	0	0
William Barthau	Catalan Dragons	30/1/90	3	0	0	1	1
Andrew Bentley	Toulouse Olympique	13/5/85	1	0	0	0	0
Kane Bentley	Toulouse Olympique	16/4/87	2	0	0	0	0
Thomas Bosc	Catalan Dragons	5/8/83	4	1	4	0	12
Damien Cardace	Catalan Dragons	16/10/92	1	0	0	0	0
Remi Casty	Catalan Dragons	5/2/85	4	0	0	0	0
Vincent Duport	Catalan Dragons	15/12/87	4	1	0	0	4
Olivier Elima	Catalan Dragons	19/5/83	2(1)	0	0	0	0
Morgan Escare	Catalan Dragons	18/10/91	4	1	0	0	4
Theo Fages	Salford City Reds	23/8/94	1(1)	0	0	0	0
Jamal Fakir	Catalan Dragons	30/8/82	3(1)	0	0	0	0
Benjamin Garcia	Catalan Dragons	5/4/93	(3)	0	0	0	0
Tony Gigot	Avignon	27/12/90	(1)	0	0	0	0
Clint Greenshields	North Queensland Cowboys	11/1/82	3	0	0	0	0
Younes Khattabi	Carcassonne	28/3/84	(1)	0	0	0	0
Kevin Larroyer	Catalan Dragons	19/6/89	3	0	0	0	0
Antoni Maria	Catalan Dragons	21/3/87	(2)	0	0	0	0
Gregory Mounis	Catalan Dragons	18/1/85	3(1)	0	0	0	0
Eloi Pelissier	Catalan Dragons	18/6/91	2(1)	0	0	0	0
Sebastien Raguin	St Esteve	14/2/79	4	0	0	0	0
Mickael Simon	Catalan Dragons	2/4/87	(4)	0	0	0	0
Cyril Stacul	Lezignan	12/10/84	1	0	0	0	0
Frederic Vaccari	Catalan Dragons	7/11/87	3	0	0	0	0

NEW ZEALAND

	CLUB	D.O.B.	APP(S)	T	G	FG	PTS
Jesse Bromwich	Melbourne Storm	3/5/89	4(1)	1	0	0	4
Greg Eastwood	Canterbury Bulldogs	10/3/87	(1)	1	0	0	4
Kieran Foran	Manly Sea Eagles	13/7/90	6	0	0	0	0
Alex Glenn	Brisbane Broncos	31/8/88	2(2)	0	0	0	0
Bryson Goodwin	South Sydney Rabbitohs	30/12/85	6	4	0	0	16
Josh Hoffman	Brisbane Broncos	10/3/88	2	1	0	0	4
Krisnan Inu	Canterbury Bulldogs	17/3/87	1	1	0	0	4
Shaun Johnson	New Zealand Warriors	9/9/90	6	4	30	0	76
Sam Kasiano	Canterbury Bulldogs	21/9/90	(5)	0	0	0	0
Thomas Leuluai	New Zealand Warriors	22/6/85	(1)	0	0	0	0
Kevin Locke	New Zealand Warriors	4/4/89	4	0	0	0	0
Issac Luke	South Sydney Rabbitohs	29/5/87	6	1	0	0	4
Simon Mannering	New Zealand Warriors	28/8/86	5	2	0	0	8
Ben Matulino	New Zealand Warriors	3/1/89	3(2)	0	0	0	0
Sam Moa	Sydney Roosters	14/6/86	1(2)	0	0	0	0
Jason Nightingale	St George Illawarra Dragons	20/9/86	2	0	0	0	0
Frank-Paul Nuuausala	Sydney Roosters	13/2/87	(6)	3	0	0	12
Frank Pritchard	Canterbury Bulldogs	3/11/83	3	1	0	0	4
Elijah Taylor	New Zealand Warriors	27/2/90	3(3)	1	0	0	4
Roger Tuivasa-Sheck	Sydney Roosters	15/6/93	6	8	0	0	32
Manu Vatuvei	New Zealand Warriors	4/3/86	4	4	0	0	16
Jared Waerea-Hargreaves	Sydney Roosters	20/1/89	4(1)	0	0	0	0
Dean Whare	Penrith Panthers	22/1/90	5	2	0	0	8
Sonny Bill Williams	Sydney Roosters	3/8/85	5	3	0	0	12

PAPUA NEW GUINEA

	CLUB	D.O.B.	APP(S)	T	G	FG	PTS
Josiah Abavu	Port Moresby Vipers	21/8/87	3	1	0	0	4
Paul Aiton	Wakefield Trinity Wildcats	29/5/85	2(1)	0	0	0	0
Dion Aiye	Rabaul Gurias	6/11/87	3	1	0	0	4
Wellington Albert	Lae Tigers	3/9/93	(1)	1	0	0	4
Ase Boas	Rabaul Gurias	26/12/88	1	0	0	0	0
Joe Bruno	Rabaul Gurias	25/5/85	1	0	0	0	0
Jason Chan	Huddersfield Giants	26/1/84	3	0	0	0	0
Neville Costigan	Newcastle Knights	16/3/85	3	0	0	0	0
Isreal Eliab	Port Moresby Vipers	16/1/91	2	0	0	0	0
Richard Kambo	Port Moresby Vipers	19/5/83	(2)	0	0	0	0
Roger Laka	Mendi Muruks	23/3/88	0	0	0	0	0
Enoch Maki	Mendi Muruks	9/12/89	1(1)	0	0	0	0
Larsen Marabe	Orange CYMS	9/6/86	1(1)	0	0	0	0
Nene McDonald	Sydney Roosters	11/5/94	3	1	0	0	4
David Mead	Gold Coast Titans	4/11/88	3	0	0	0	0
Mark Mexico	Lae Tigers	21/5/89	2(1)	0	0	0	0
Jessie Joe Nandye	Whitehaven	22/8/85	2(1)	1	0	0	4
Sebastian Pandia	Port Moresby Vipers	12/10/90	1	0	0	0	0
Francis Paniu	Rabaul Gurias	9/9/89	1	0	1	0	2
Jason Tali	Mount Hagen Eagles	7/7/87	(2)	0	0	0	0
Ray Thompson	North Queensland Cowboys	20/1/90	3	0	0	0	0
Charlie Wabo	Mendi Muruks	19/9/83	1(2)	0	0	0	0
Menzie Yere	Sheffield Eagles	24/10/83	3	0	0	0	0

SAMOA

	CLUB	D.O.B.	APP(S)	T	G	FG	PTS
Leeson Ah Mau	St George Illawarra Dragons	20/12/89	2(1)	0	0	0	0
David Fa'alogo	Newcastle Knights	4/9/80	4	0	0	0	0
Pita Godinet	New Zealand Warriors	21/12/87	2(2)	2	0	0	8
Harrison Hansen	Wigan Warriors	26/10/85	0	0	0	0	0
Faleniu Iosi	Letava Bulldogs	-	0	0	0	0	0
Tim Lafai	Canterbury Bulldogs	27/5/91	3	0	0	0	0
Joseph Leilua	Newcastle Knights	12/12/91	4	1	0	0	4
Reni Maitua	Parramatta Eels	11/6/82	1	0	0	0	0
Penani Manumalealii	Cronulla Sharks	14/6/82	2(1)	1	0	0	4
Mose Masoe	Penrith Panthers	17/5/89	(4)	0	0	0	0
Suaia Matagi	New Zealand Warriors	23/3/88	4	2	0	0	8
Anthony Milford	Canberra Raiders	11/7/94	4	1	10	0	24
Junior Moors	Melbourne Storm	30/7/86	(3)	1	0	0	4
Tony Puletua	St Helens	25/6/79	2	0	0	0	0
Edward Purcell	Akarana Falcons	-	0	0	0	0	0
Ben Roberts	Parramatta Eels	8/7/85	4	2	0	0	8
Junior Sa'u	Melbourne Storm	18/4/87	1	0	0	0	0
Michael Sio	New Zealand Warriors	16/5/93	2(1)	0	0	0	0
Iosia Soliola	St Helens	4/8/86	4	0	0	0	0
Sauaso Sue	Wests Tigers	20/4/92	4	1	0	0	4
Mark Taufua	Cronulla Sharks	24/10/81	(4)	0	0	0	0
Ionatana Tino	Parkes Spacemen	-	0	0	0	0	0
Daniel Vidot	St George Illawarra Dragons	8/2/90	4	1	0	0	4
Antonio Winterstein	North Queensland Cowboys	30/5/88	4	5	0	0	20
Frank Winterstein	Widnes Vikings	17/12/86	1	0	0	0	0

Tony Puletua replaced Reni Maitua due to injury. Harrison Hansen and Frank Winterstein withdrew from the squad, also due to injury (5/11/13)

GROUP B - FINAL STANDINGS

	P	W	D	L	F	A	Diff	PTS
New Zealand	3	3	0	0	146	34	112	6
Samoa	3	2	0	1	84	52	32	4
France	3	1	0	2	15	78	-63	2
Papua New Guinea	3	0	0	3	22	103	-81	0

World Cup 2013 - Statistical review

GROUP C

Tuesday 29th October 2013

SCOTLAND 26 TONGA 24

SCOTLAND: 1 Matthew Russell (Gold Coast Titans); 5 Brett Carter (Workington Town); 3 Ben Hellewell (Featherstone Rovers); 4 Kane Linnett (North Queensland Cowboys); 2 Alex Hurst (London Broncos); 6 Danny Brough (Huddersfield Giants) (C); 7 Peter Wallace (Brisbane Broncos); 8 Adam Walker (Hull Kingston Rovers); 9 Ian Henderson (Catalan Dragons); 10 Luke Douglas (Gold Coast Titans); 11 Danny Addy (Bradford Bulls); 12 Dale Ferguson (Huddersfield Giants); 13 Oliver Wilkes (Wakefield Trinity Wildcats). Subs (all used): 14 Ben Fisher (London Broncos); 15 Brett Phillips (Workington Town); 16 Mitchell Stringer (Sheffield Eagles); 17 Ben Kavanagh (Widnes Vikings).
Tries: Russell (14, 73), Fisher (32), Carter (38); **Goals:** Brough 5/6.
Sin bin: Linnett (79) - professional foul.
TONGA: 1 Glen Fisi'iahi (New Zealand Warriors); 5 Sosaia Feki (Cronulla Sharks); 3 Konrad Hurrell (New Zealand Warriors); 4 Jorge Taufua (Manly Sea Eagles); 2 Daniel Tupou (Sydney Roosters); 6 Samsoni Langi (Sydney Roosters); 7 Daniel Foster (Penrith Panthers); 8 Brent Kite (Manly Sea Eagles) (C); 9 Siliva Havili (New Zealand Warriors); 10 Fuifui Moimoi (Parramatta Eels); 11 Jason Taumalolo (North Queensland Cowboys); 12 Sika Manu (Penrith Panthers); 13 Willie Manu (St Helens). Subs (all used): 14 Nafe Seluini (Sydney Roosters); 15 Ben Murdoch-Masila (Wests Tigers); 16 Ukuma Ta'ai (Huddersfield Giants); 17 Mickey Paea (Hull Kingston Rovers).
Tries: Fisi'iahi (8), S Manu (41, 56), Seluini (50), W Manu (65);
Goals: Langi 2/5.
Rugby Leaguer & League Express Men of the Match:
Scotland: Danny Brough; *Tonga:* Sika Manu.
Penalty count: 11-9; **Half-time:** 20-4; **Referee:** Shayne Hayne (Australia); **Attendance:** 7,630 *(at Derwent Park, Workington)*.

Sunday 3rd November 2013

SCOTLAND 30 ITALY 30

SCOTLAND: 1 Matthew Russell (Gold Coast Titans); 5 Brett Carter (Workington Town); 3 Ben Hellewell (Featherstone Rovers); 4 Kane Linnett (North Queensland Cowboys); 2 Alex Hurst (London Broncos); 6 Danny Brough (Huddersfield Giants) (C); 7 Peter Wallace (Brisbane Broncos); 8 Adam Walker (Hull Kingston Rovers); 9 Ian Henderson (Catalan Dragons); 10 Luke Douglas (Gold Coast Titans); 11 Danny Addy (Bradford Bulls); 12 Dale Ferguson (Huddersfield Giants); 13 Ben Kavanagh (Widnes Vikings). Subs (all used): 14 Ben Fisher (London Broncos); 15 Brett Phillips (Workington Town); 16 Mitchell Stringer (Sheffield Eagles); 17 Oliver Wilkes (Wakefield Trinity Wildcats).
Tries: Russell (21), Linnett (25), Addy (41), Hellewell (50, 70);
Goals: Brough 5/6.
ITALY: 1 Anthony Minichiello (Sydney Roosters) (C); 2 Josh Mantellato (Newcastle Knights); 3 James Tedesco (Wests Tigers); 4 Aidan Guerra (Sydney Roosters); 5 Chris Centrone (North Sydney Bears); 6 Ben Falcone (Souths Logan Magpies); 7 Ryan Ghietti (Northern Pride); 8 Anthony Laffranchi (St Helens); 9 Dean Parata (Parramatta Eels); 10 Paul Vaughan (Canberra Raiders); 11 Mark Minichiello (Gold Coast Titans); 12 Cameron Ciraldo (Penrith Panthers); 13 Joel Riethmuller (North Queensland Cowboys). Subs (all used): 14 Kade Snowden (Newcastle Knights); 15 Ryan Tramonte (Windsor Wolves); 16 Brendan Santi (Wests Tigers); 17 Raymond Nasso (Avignon).
Tries: Ciraldo (32), Nasso (39, 46), Centrone (53), A Minichiello (59);
Goals: Mantellato 5/5.
Rugby Leaguer & League Express Men of the Match:
Scotland: Danny Brough; *Italy:* Cameron Ciraldo.
Penalty count: 7-9; **Half-time:** 14-12; **Referee:** Henry Perenara (New Zealand); **Attendance:** 7,280 *(at Derwent Park, Workington)*.

Sunday 10th November 2013

ITALY 0 TONGA 16

ITALY: 1 Anthony Minichiello (Sydney Roosters) (C); 5 Chris Centrone (North Sydney Bears); 3 James Tedesco (Wests Tigers); 4 Aidan Guerra (Sydney Roosters); 2 Josh Mantellato (Newcastle Knights); 6 Ben Falcone (Souths Logan Magpies); 7 Ryan Ghietti (Northern Pride); 8 Anthony Laffranchi (St Helens); 9 Dean Parata (Parramatta Eels); 10 Paul Vaughan (Canberra Raiders); 11 Mark Minichiello (Gold Coast Titans); 12 Cameron Ciraldo (Penrith Panthers); 13 Joel Riethmuller (North Queensland Cowboys). Subs (all used): 14 Kade Snowden (Newcastle Knights); 15 Ryan Tramonte (Windsor Wolves); 16 Brendan Santi (Wests Tigers); 17 Raymond Nasso (Avignon).
TONGA: 1 Nesiasi Mataitonga (Cronulla Sharks); 2 Daniel Tupou (Sydney Roosters); 3 Konrad Hurrell (New Zealand Warriors); 4 Mahe Fonua (Melbourne Storm); 5 Jorge Taufua (Manly Sea Eagles); 6 Samsoni Langi (Sydney Roosters); 7 Daniel Foster (Penrith Panthers); 8 Brent Kite (Manly Sea Eagles) (C); 9 Patrick Politoni (Cronulla Sharks); 10 Fuifui Moimoi (Parramatta Eels); 11 Ukuma Ta'ai (Huddersfield Giants); 12 Willie Manu (St Helens); 13 Mickey Paea (Hull Kingston Rovers). Subs (all used): 14 Nafe Seluini (Sydney Roosters); 15 Siosaia Vave (Parramatta Eels); 16 Peni Terepo (Parramatta Eels); 17 Siuatonga Likiliki (Newcastle Knights).
Tries: W Manu (46), Foster (64), Terepo (79); **Goals:** Langi 2/3, Kite 0/1.
Rugby Leaguer & League Express Men of the Match:
Italy: Anthony Minichiello; *Tonga:* Fuifui Moimoi.
Penalty count: 7-7; **Half-time:** 0-2; **Referee:** Ben Thaler (England); **Attendance:** 10,266 *(at The Shay, Halifax)*.

ITALY

	CLUB	D.O.B.	APP(S)	T	G	FG	PTS
Christophe Calegari	Lezignan	3/6/84	0	0	0	0	0
Gioele Celerino	North West Roosters	-	0	0	0	0	0
Chris Centrone	North Sydney Bears	24/7/91	3	2	0	0	8
Fabrizio Ciaurro	Brescia	20/1/89	0	0	0	0	0
Cameron Ciraldo	Penrith Panthers	30/10/84	3	1	0	0	4
Ben Falcone	Souths Logan Magpies		0	0	0	0	0
		11/7/88	3	0	0	0	0
Sam Gardel	Souths Logan Magpies						
		19/1/88	(1)	0	0	0	0
Ryan Ghietti	Northern Pride	22/7/89	3	0	0	0	0
Aidan Guerra	Sydney Roosters	25/2/85	3	2	0	0	8
Gavin Hiscox	Central Queensland Capras						
		24/8/88	0	0	0	0	0
Anthony Laffranchi	St Helens	16/11/80	3	0	0	0	0
Tim Maccan	Tweed Heads Seagulls						
		5/6/82	0	0	0	0	0
Josh Mantellato	Newcastle Knights	21/4/87	3	1	9	0	22
Anthony Minichiello	Sydney Roosters	24/5/80	3	1	0	0	4
Mark Minichiello	Gold Coast Titans	30/1/82	3	1	0	0	4
Raymond Nasso	Avignon	3/7/87	(3)	2	0	0	8
Dean Parata	Parramatta Eels	4/10/91	3	0	0	0	0
Joel Riethmuller	North Queensland Cowboys						
		9/5/85	3	0	0	0	0
James Saltonstall	Warrington Wolves	27/9/93	0	0	0	0	0
Brendan Santi	Wests Tigers	5/8/93	(3)	0	0	0	0
Kade Snowden	Newcastle Knights	31/12/86	2	0	0	0	0
James Tedesco	Wests Tigers	8/1/93	3	1	0	0	4
Ryan Tramonte	Windsor Wolves	12/3/82	(3)	0	0	0	0
Paul Vaughan	Canberra Raiders	23/4/91	3	0	0	0	0

SCOTLAND

	CLUB	D.O.B.	APP(S)	T	G	FG	PTS
Danny Addy	Bradford Bulls	15/1/91	4	1	0	0	4
Josh Barlow	Swinton Lions	15/5/91	0	0	0	0	0
Sam Barlow	Featherstone Rovers	7/3/88	(2)	0	0	0	0
Danny Brough	Huddersfield Giants	15/1/83	4	0	13	0	26
Brett Carter	Workington Town	9/7/88	2	1	0	0	4
Luke Douglas	Gold Coast Titans	12/5/86	4	1	0	0	4
Dale Ferguson	Huddersfield Giants	13/4/88	3	0	0	0	0
Ben Fisher	London Broncos	4/2/81	(2)	1	0	0	4
Ben Hellewell	Featherstone Rovers	30/1/92	4	2	0	0	8
Andrew Henderson	Sheffield Eagles	17/6/79	1(1)	0	0	0	0
Ian Henderson	Catalan Dragons	23/4/83	3	0	0	0	0
Alex Hurst	London Broncos	17/3/90	4	2	0	0	8
Ben Kavanagh	Widnes Vikings	4/9/86	3(1)	0	0	0	0
Kane Linnett	North Queensland Cowboys						
		11/1/89	3	1	0	0	4
Rhys Lovegrove	Hull Kingston Rovers						
		11/3/87	0	0	0	0	0
Brett Phillips	Workington Town	25/10/88	2(2)	1	0	0	4
Callum Phillips	Workington Town	19/2/92	0	0	0	0	0
Matthew Russell	Gold Coast Titans	6/6/93	4	4	0	0	16
Dave Scott	Doncaster	8/6/93	2	0	0	0	0
Mitchell Stringer	Sheffield Eagles	1/11/83	(3)	0	0	0	0
Alex Szostak	Sheffield Eagles	4/3/86	2	0	0	0	0
Adam Walker	Hull Kingston Rovers						
		20/2/91	4	0	0	0	0
Peter Wallace	Brisbane Broncos	16/10/85	4	0	0	0	0
Oliver Wilkes	Wakefield Trinity Wildcats						
		2/5/80	1(3)	0	0	0	0

TONGA

	CLUB	D.O.B.	APP(S)	T	G	FG	PTS
Sosaia Feki	Cronulla Sharks	5/9/91	1	0	0	0	0
Glen Fisi'iahi	New Zealand Warriors						
		2/12/90	2	2	0	0	8
Mahe Fonua	Melbourne Storm	24/12/92	2	0	0	0	0
Daniel Foster	Penrith Panthers	20/4/93	3	1	0	0	4
Sydney Havea	Liahona Old Boys	14/8/87	0	0	0	0	0
Siliva Havili	New Zealand Warriors						
		18/2/93	1	0	0	0	0
Konrad Hurrell	New Zealand Warriors						
		5/8/91	3	1	0	0	4
Brent Kite	Manly Sea Eagles	7/3/81	3	0	0	0	0
Samsoni Langi	Sydney Roosters	11/6/93	3	0	7	0	14
Siuatonga Likiliki	Newcastle Knights	10/4/90	(1)	0	0	0	0
Sika Manu	Penrith Panthers	22/1/87	2	2	0	0	8
Willie Manu	St Helens	20/3/80	2(1)	2	0	0	8
Nesiasi Mataitonga	Cronulla Sharks	25/2/93	1	0	0	0	0
Fuifui Moimoi	Parramatta Eels	26/9/79	3	0	0	0	0
Ben Murdoch-Masila	Wests Tigers	7/2/91	(1)	0	0	0	0
Mickey Paea	Hull Kingston Rovers						
		25/3/86	2(1)	0	0	0	0
Patrick Politoni	Cronulla Sharks	17/3/91	2	0	0	0	0
Nafe Seluini	Sydney Roosters	21/6/90	(3)	1	0	0	4
Ukuma Ta'ai	Huddersfield Giants	17/1/87	1(2)	0	0	0	0
Jorge Taufua	Manly Sea Eagles	23/10/91	3	0	0	0	0
Jason Taumalolo	North Queensland Cowboys						
		30/5/93	2	1	0	0	4
Peni Terepo	Parramatta Eels	21/11/91	(1)	1	0	0	4
Daniel Tupou	Sydney Roosters	17/6/91	3	1	0	0	4
Siosaia Vave	Parramatta Eels	23/9/89	(2)	0	0	0	0

GROUP D

Wednesday 30th October 2013

COOK ISLANDS 20 USA 32

COOK ISLANDS: 1 Drury Low (Canterbury Bulldogs); 5 Jordan Rapana (Canberra Raiders); 3 Anthony Gelling (Wigan Warriors); 4 Keith Lulia (Bradford Bulls); 2 Lulia Lulia (Shellharbour City Sharks); 6 Brad Takairangi (Gold Coasts Titans); 7 Isaac John (Penrith Panthers); 8 Dylan Napa (Sydney Roosters); 9 Daniel Fepuleai (North Sydney Bears); 10 Zane Tetavano (Newcastle Knights); 11 Zeb Taia (Catalan Dragons) (C); 12 Dominique Peyroux (New Zealand Warriors); 13 Tinirau Arona (Sydney Roosters). Subs (all used): 14 Sam Brunton (Mounties); 15 Sam Mataora (Canberra Raiders); 16 Tupou Sopoaga (Cronulla Sharks); 17 Adam Tangata (Mounties).
Tries: Takairangi (5), Low (37), L Lulia (47), Peyroux (62);
Goals: Rapana 2/4.
USA: 1 Kristian Freed (Connecticut Wildcats); 2 Bureta Faraimo (Mackay Cutters); 3 Lelauloto Tagaloa (Hawaii Chiefs); 4 Michael Garvey (Pennsylvania Bulls); 5 Matt Petersen (Cudgen Hornets); 6 Joseph Paulo (Parramatta Eels) (C); 7 Craig Priestly (Southampton Dragons); 15 Mark Offerdahl (Carcassonne); 9 Haveatama Luani (Wests Tigers); 10 Eddy Pettybourne (Wests Tigers); 11 Clint Newton (Penrith Panthers); 12 Matthew Shipway (South Newcastle); 13 Daniel Howard (Wentworthville Magpies). Subs (all used): 14 Tuisegasega Samoa (Redcliffe Dolphins); 16 Junior Paulo (Windsor Wolves); 16 Stephen Howard (Tuggeranong Bushrangers); 17 Les Soloai (Hawaii Chiefs).
Tries: Faraimo (15), Petersen (17), Joseph Paulo (41), Samoa (59), Offerdahl (72), Priestly (76); **Goals:** Joseph Paulo 4/8.
Rugby Leaguer & League Express Men of the Match:
Cook Islands: Lulia Lulia; *USA:* Mark Offerdahl.
Penalty count: 5-8; **Half-time:** 10-10; **Referee:** Ben Thaler (England);
Attendance: 7,247 *(at Memorial Stadium, Bristol).*

Sunday 3rd November 2013

WALES 16 USA 24

WALES: 1 Rhys Evans (Warrington Wolves); 2 Elliot Kear (Bradford Bulls); 3 Ian Webster (Central Queensland Capras); 4 Christiaan Roets (North Wales Crusaders); 5 Rhys Williams (Warrington Wolves); 6 Lloyd White (Widnes Vikings); 7 Matt Seamark (Wynnum Manly Seagulls); 8 Craig Kopczak (Huddersfield Giants) (C); 9 Neil Budworth (Moranbah Miners); 10 Jordan James (Salford City Reds); 11 Larne Patrick (Huddersfield Giants); 12 Tyson Frizell (St George Illawarra Dragons); 13 Ben Flower (Wigan Warriors). Subs (all used): 14 Gil Dudson (Wigan Warriors); 15 Ben Evans (Bradford Bulls); 16 Peter Lupton (Workington Town); 17 Anthony Walker (St Helens).
Tries: Roets (16, 76), Walker (77); **Goals:** White 2/3.
USA: 1 Kristian Freed (Connecticut Wildcats); 2 Bureta Faraimo (Mackay Cutters); 3 Lelauloto Tagaloa (Hawaii Chiefs); 4 Taylor Welch (Chicago Griffins); 5 Matt Petersen (Cudgen Hornets); 6 Joseph Paulo (Parramatta Eels) (C); 7 Craig Priestly (Southampton Dragons); 8 Mark Offerdahl (Carcassonne); 9 Haveatama Luani (Wests Tigers); 10 Eddy Pettybourne (Wests Tigers); 11 Clint Newton (Penrith Panthers); 12 Matthew Shipway (South Newcastle); 13 Daniel Howard (Wentworthville Magpies). Subs (all used): 14 Tuisegasega Samoa (Redcliffe Dolphins); 15 Roman Hifo (Mangere East Hawks); 16 Judah Lavulo (Cabramatta); 17 Les Soloai (Hawaii Chiefs).
Tries: Newton (21, 63), Petersen (34), Joseph Paulo (54), Samoa (60);
Goals: Joseph Paulo 2/5.
Rugby Leaguer & League Express Men of the Match:
Wales: Ben Evans; *USA:* Joseph Paulo.
Penalty count: 9-6; **Half-time:** 4-8; **Referee:** Ben Cummins (Australia);
Attendance: 8,019 *(at Glyndwr University Racecourse Stadium, Wrexham).*

Sunday 10th November 2013

WALES 24 COOK ISLANDS 28

WALES: 1 Elliot Kear (Bradford Bulls); 2 Christiaan Roets (North Wales Crusaders); 3 Rhodri Lloyd (Wigan Warriors); 4 Rhys Evans (Warrington Wolves); 5 Rob Massam (North Wales Crusaders); 6 Danny Jones (Keighley Cougars); 7 Peter Lupton (Workington Town); 8 Ben Flower (Wigan Warriors); 9 Neil Budworth (Moranbah Miners); 10 Jordan James (Salford City Reds); 11 Ross Divorty (Halifax); 12 Tyson Frizell (St George Illawarra Dragons); 13 Larne Patrick (Huddersfield Giants). Subs (all used): 14 Lloyd White (Widnes Vikings); 15 Craig Kopczak (Huddersfield Giants) (C); 16 Gil Dudson (Wigan Warriors); 17 Anthony Walker (St Helens).
Tries: Massam (14), White (51), Roets (60, 76), Lloyd (67);
Goals: Jones 1/4, White 1/1.
COOK ISLANDS: 1 Lulia Lulia (Shellharbour City Sharks); 5 Rea Pittman (Cronulla Sharks); 3 Brad Takairangi (Gold Coast Titans); 4 Keith Lulia (Bradford Bulls); 2 Christopher Taripo (Newton Jets); 6 Johnathon Ford (Toulouse Olympique); 7 Isaac John (Penrith Panthers); 8 Dylan Napa (Sydney Roosters); 9 Daniel Fepuleai (North Sydney Bears); 10 Zeb Taia (Catalan Dragons) (C); 11 Tupou Sopoaga (Cronulla Sharks); 12 Dominique Peyroux (New Zealand Warriors); 13 Tinirau Arona (Sydney Roosters). Subs (all used): 14 Sam Brunton (Mounties); 15 Anthony Gelling (Wigan Warriors); 16 Joseph Matapuku (North Sydney Bears); 17 Adam Tangata (Mounties).
Tries: Fepulea (8), K Lulia (31), John (40), Peyroux (45), Ford (73);
Goals: Taripo 4/5.
Rugby Leaguer & League Express Men of the Match:
Wales: Christiaan Roets; *Cook Islands:* Keith Lulia.
Penalty count: 5-7; **Half-time:** 4-16; **Referee:** Richard Silverwood (England); **Attendance:** 3,270 *(at The Gnoll, Neath).*

COOK ISLANDS

	CLUB	D.O.B.	APP(S)	T	G	FG	PTS
Tinirau Arona	Sydney Roosters	8/5/89	3	0	0	0	0
Sam Brunton	Mounties	20/2/90	(2)	0	0	0	0
Daniel Fepuleai	North Sydney Bears	25/11/88	3	1	0	0	4
Johnathon Ford	Toulouse Olympique	17/8/89	2	1	0	0	4
Anthony Gelling	Wigan Warriors	18/10/90	1(1)	0	0	0	0
Isaac John	Penrith Panthers	12/12/88	3	1	0	0	4
Drury Low	Canterbury Bulldogs	2/4/90	2	1	0	0	4
Keith Lulia	Bradford Bulls	17/6/87	3	1	0	0	4
Lulia Lulia	Shellharbour City Sharks	26/5/85	2	1	0	0	4
Hikule'o Malu	New Zealand Warriors	5/4/93	(1)	0	0	0	0
Sam Mataora	Canberra Raiders	20/10/90	(2)	0	0	0	0
Joseph Matapuku	North Sydney Bears	6/4/89	(2)	0	0	0	0
Dylan Napa	Sydney Roosters	13/11/92	3	0	0	0	0
Dominique Peyroux	New Zealand Warriors	21/1/89	3	2	0	0	8
Rea Pittman	Cronulla Sharks	14/2/93	1	0	0	0	0
Jordan Rapana	Canberra Raiders	5/8/89	2	0	2	0	4
Tupou Sopoaga	Cronulla Sharks	5/6/92	1(1)	0	0	0	0
Zeb Taia	Catalan Dragons	11/10/84	3	0	0	0	0
Brad Takairangi	Gold Coast Titans	14/6/89	3	1	0	0	4
Adam Tangata	Mounties	17/3/91	(3)	0	0	0	0
Christopher Taripo	Newtown Jets	19/2/92	2	3	6	0	24
Zane Tetavano	Newcastle Knights	4/11/90	2	0	0	0	0
Tyrone Viiga	Wentworthville Magpies	9/6/92	0	0	0	0	0

USA

	CLUB	D.O.B.	APP(S)	T	G	FG	PTS
Mark Cantoni	Dalby Devils	29/5/79	(1)	0	0	0	0
Bureta Faraimo	Mackay Cutters	16/7/90	4	1	0	0	4
Gabriel Farley	Southampton Dragons	1/5/94	0	0	0	0	0
Kristian Freed	Connecticut Wildcats	4/7/87	4	1	0	0	4
Michael Garvey	Pennsylvania Bulls	27/7/88	3	0	0	0	0
Roman Hifo	Mangere East Hawks	17/4/86	(3)	0	0	0	0
Daniel Howard	Wentworthville Magpies	13/12/84	4	0	0	0	0
Stephen Howard	Tuggeranong Bushrangers	13/1/87	(1)	0	0	0	0
Judah Lavulo	Cabramatta	1/2/91	(2)	0	0	0	0
Haveatama Luani	Wests Tigers	19/2/92	3(1)	0	0	0	0
David Marando	Belrose Eagles	2/5/84	(1)	0	0	0	0
Clint Newton	Penrith Panthers	18/6/81	4	2	0	0	8
Mark Offerdahl	Carcassonne	15/10/87	4	1	0	0	4
Joseph Paulo	Parramatta Eels	2/1/88	4	2	6	0	20
Junior Paulo	Windsor Wolves	8/9/83	(1)	0	0	0	0
Matt Petersen	Cudgen Hornets	27/3/80	4	2	0	0	8
Eddy Pettybourne	Wests Tigers	13/2/88	4	0	0	0	0
Craig Priestly	Southampton Dragons	8/1/87	4	1	0	0	4
Tuisegasega Samoa	Redcliffe Dolphins	29/4/83	1(3)	2	0	0	8
Matthew Shipway	South Newcastle	11/9/85	4	0	0	0	0
Les Soloai	Hawaii Chiefs	20/2/87	(3)	0	0	0	0
Lelauloto Tagaloa	Hawaii Chiefs	26/12/86	2	0	0	0	0
Taylor Welch	Chicago Griffins	1/11/89	3	1	0	0	4

WALES

	CLUB	D.O.B.	APP(S)	T	G	FG	PTS
Neil Budworth	Moranbah Miners	10/3/82	3	0	0	0	0
Ross Divorty	Halifax	27/11/88	1	0	0	0	0
Gil Dudson	Wigan Warriors	16/6/90	(3)	0	0	0	0
Jake Emmitt	Salford City Reds	4/10/88	(1)	0	0	0	0
Ben Evans	Bradford Bulls	30/10/92	1(1)	1	0	0	4
Rhys Evans	Warrington Wolves	30/10/92	3	0	0	0	0
Daniel Fleming	Castleford Tigers	8/7/92	0	0	0	0	0
Ben Flower	Wigan Warriors	19/10/87	3	0	0	0	0
Tyson Frizell	St George Illawarra Dragons	9/10/91	3	0	0	0	0
James Gurtjens	Norths Devils	28/4/86	0	0	0	0	0
Jordan James	Salford City Reds	24/5/80	2(1)	0	0	0	0
Danny Jones	Keighley Cougars	6/3/86	1	0	1	0	2
Elliot Kear	Bradford Bulls	29/11/88	3	1	0	0	4
Craig Kopczak	Huddersfield Giants	20/12/86	2(1)	0	0	0	0
Rhodri Lloyd	Wigan Warriors	22/7/93	2	2	0	0	8
Peter Lupton	Workington Town	7/3/82	1(2)	0	0	0	0
Rob Massam	North Wales Crusaders	29/11/87	1	1	0	0	4
Larne Patrick	Huddersfield Giants	3/11/88	3	0	0	0	0
Christiaan Roets	North Wales Crusaders	5/9/80	2	4	0	0	16
Matt Seamark	Wynnum Manly Seagulls	18/3/87	2	0	0	0	0
Anthony Walker	St Helens	28/12/91	(2)	1	0	0	4
Ian Webster	Central Queensland Capras	16/11/86	2	0	0	0	0
Lloyd White	Widnes Vikings	9/10/88	2(1)	1	5	0	14
Rhys Williams	Warrington Wolves	8/12/89	2	0	0	0	0

GROUP C/D

Saturday 26th October 2013

WALES 16 ITALY 32

WALES: 1 Rhys Evans (Warrington Wolves); 2 Elliot Kear (Bradford Bulls); 3 Rhodri Lloyd (Wigan Warriors); 4 Ian Webster (Central Queensland Capras); 5 Rhys Williams (Warrington Wolves); 6 Lloyd White (Widnes Vikings); 7 Matt Seamark (Wynnum Manly Seagulls); 8 Craig Kopczak (Huddersfield Giants) (C); 9 Neil Budworth (Moranbah Miners); 10 Ben Flower (Wigan Warriors); 11 Ben Evans (Bradford Bulls); 12 Tyson Frizell (St George Illawarra Dragons); 13 Larne Patrick (Huddersfield Giants). Subs (all used): 14 Gil Dudson (Wigan Warriors); 15 Peter Lupton (Workington Town); 16 Jordan James (Salford City Reds); 17 Jake Emmitt (Salford City Reds).
Tries: B Evans (15), Lloyd (38), Kear (43); **Goals:** White 2/3.
ITALY: 1 Anthony Minichiello (Sydney Roosters) (C); 2 Josh Mantellato (Newcastle Knights); 3 James Tedesco (Wests Tigers); 4 Aidan Guerra (Sydney Roosters); 5 Chris Centrone (North Sydney Bears); 6 Ben Falcone (Souths Logan Magpies); 7 Ryan Ghietti (Northern Pride); 8 Anthony Laffranchi (St Helens); 9 Dean Parata (Parramatta Eels); 10 Paul Vaughan (Canberra Raiders); 11 Mark Minichiello (Gold Coast Titans); 12 Cameron Ciraldo (Penrith Panthers); 13 Joel Riethmuller (North Queensland Cowboys). Subs (all used): 14 Raymond Nasso (Avignon); 15 Sam Gardel (Souths Logan Magpies); 16 Ryan Tramonte (Windsor Wolves); 17 Brendan Santi (Wests Tigers).
Tries: Guerra (9, 21), Mantellato (47), Tedesco (69), Centrone (72), M Minichiello (80); **Goals:** Mantellato 4/7.
Rugby Leaguer & League Express Men of the Match:
Wales: Elliot Kear; *Italy:* Aidan Guerra.
Penalty count: 4-10; **Half-time:** 12-14; **Referee:** Ashley Klein (Australia); **Attendance:** 45,052 *(at Millennium Stadium, Cardiff).*

Tuesday 5th November 2013

COOK ISLANDS 16 TONGA 22

COOK ISLANDS: 1 Drury Low (Canterbury Bulldogs); 5 Jordan Rapana (Canberra Raiders); 3 Brad Takairangi (Gold Coast Titans); 4 Keith Lulia (Bradford Bulls); 2 Christopher Taripo (Newtown Jets); 6 Johnathon Ford (Toulouse Olympique); 7 Isaac John (Penrith Panthers); 8 Dylan Napa (Sydney Roosters); 9 Daniel Fepuleai (North Sydney Bears); 10 Zane Tetavano (Newcastle Knights); 11 Dominique Peyroux (New Zealand Warriors); 12 Zeb Taia (Catalan Dragons) (C); 13 Tinirau Arona (Sydney Roosters). Subs (all used): 14 Hikule'o Malu (New Zealand Warriors); 15 Adam Tangata (Mounties); 16 Joseph Matapuku (North Sydney Bears); 17 Sam Mataora (Canberra Raiders).
Tries: Taripo (12, 19, 43); **Goals:** Taripo 2/3.
TONGA: 1 Glen Fisi'iahi (New Zealand Warriors); 2 Daniel Tupou (Sydney Roosters); 3 Konrad Hurrell (New Zealand Warriors); 4 Mahe Fonua (Melbourne Storm); 5 Jorge Taufua (Manly Sea Eagles); 6 Samsoni Langi (Sydney Roosters); 7 Daniel Foster (Penrith Panthers); 8 Brent Kite (Manly Sea Eagles) (C); 9 Patrick Politoni (Cronulla Sharks); 10 Fuifui Moimoi (Parramatta Eels); 11 Jason Taumalolo (North Queensland Cowboys); 12 Sika Manu (Penrith Panthers); 13 Mickey Paea (Hull Kingston Rovers). Subs (all used): 14 Nafe Seluini (Sydney Roosters); 15 Siosaia Vave (Parramatta Eels); 16 Willie Manu (St Helens); 17 Ukuma Ta'ai (Huddersfield Giants).
Tries: Fisi'iahi (7), Taumalolo (31), Hurrell (39), Taufua (61);
Goals: Langi 3/5.
Rugby Leaguer & League Express Men of the Match:
Cook Islands: Christopher Taripo; *Tonga:* Fuifui Moimoi.
Penalty count: 6-12; **Half-time:** 10-18; **Referee:** Ashley Klein (Australia); **Attendance:** 10,544 *(at Leigh Sports Village).*

Thursday 7th November 2013

SCOTLAND 22 USA 8

SCOTLAND: 1 Matthew Russell (Gold Coast Titans); 5 Dave Scott (Doncaster); 3 Ben Hellewell (Featherstone Rovers); 4 Danny Addy (Bradford Bulls); 2 Alex Hurst (London Broncos); 6 Danny Brough (Huddersfield Giants) (C); 7 Peter Wallace (Brisbane Broncos); 8 Adam Walker (Hull Kingston Rovers); 14 Andrew Henderson (Sheffield Eagles); 10 Luke Douglas (Gold Coast Titans); 11 Brett Phillips (Workington Town); 12 Dale Ferguson (Huddersfield Giants); 13 Ben Kavanagh (Widnes Vikings). Subs (all used): 15 Alex Szostak (Sheffield Eagles); 16 Mitchell Stringer (Sheffield Eagles); 17 Oliver Wilkes (Wakefield Trinity Wildcats); 18 Sam Barlow (Featherstone Rovers).
Tries: B Phillips (52), Russell (53), Douglas (63), Hurst (79);
Goals: Brough 3/4.
USA: 1 Kristian Freed (Connecticut Wildcats); 2 Bureta Faraimo (Mackay Cutters); 3 Taylor Welch (Chicago Griffins); 4 Michael Garvey (Pennsylvania Bulls); 5 Matt Petersen (Cudgen Hornets); 6 Joseph Paulo (Parramatta Eels) (C); 7 Craig Priestly (Southampton Dragons); 8 Mark Offerdahl (Carcassonne); 9 Tuisegasega Samoa (Redcliffe Dolphins); 10 Eddy Pettybourne (Wests Tigers); 11 Clint Newton (Penrith Panthers); 12 Matthew Shipway (South Newcastle); 13 Daniel Howard (Wentworthville Magpies). Subs (all used): 14 David Marando (Belrose Eagles); 15 Roman Hifo (Mangere East Hawks); 16 Haveatama Luani (Wests Tigers); 17 Judah Lavulo (Cabramatta).
Tries: Freed (7), Welch (23); **Goals:** Joseph Paulo 0/2.
On report: Luani (78) - alleged dangerous challenge.
Rugby Leaguer & League Express Men of the Match:
Scotland: Dale Ferguson; *USA:* Craig Priestly.
Penalty count: 11-5; **Half-time:** 0-8; **Referee:** Thierry Alibert (France); **Attendance:** 6,041 *(at AJ Bell Stadium, Salford).*

GROUP C - FINAL STANDINGS

	P	W	D	L	F	A	Diff	PTS
Scotland	3	2	1	0	78	62	16	5
Tonga	3	2	0	1	62	42	20	4
Italy	3	1	1	1	62	62	0	3

GROUP D - FINAL STANDINGS

	P	W	D	L	F	A	Diff	PTS
USA	3	2	0	1	64	58	6	4
Cook Islands	3	1	0	2	64	78	-14	2
Wales	3	0	0	3	56	84	-28	0

QUARTER FINALS

Friday 15th November 2013

NEW ZEALAND 40 SCOTLAND 4

NEW ZEALAND: 1 Kevin Locke (New Zealand Warriors); 2 Roger Tuivasa-Sheck (Sydney Roosters); 3 Dean Whare (Penrith Panthers); 4 Bryson Goodwin (South Sydney Rabbitohs); 5 Manu Vatuvei (New Zealand Warriors); 6 Kieran Foran (Manly Sea Eagles); 7 Shaun Johnson (New Zealand Warriors); 8 Ben Matulino (New Zealand Warriors); 9 Issac Luke (South Sydney Rabbitohs); 10 Jesse Bromwich (Melbourne Storm); 11 Frank Pritchard (Canterbury Bulldogs); 12 Sonny Bill Williams (Sydney Roosters); 13 Simon Mannering (New Zealand Warriors) (C). Subs (all used): 14 Elijah Taylor (New Zealand Warriors); 15 Jared Waerea-Hargreaves (Sydney Roosters); 16 Frank-Paul Nuuausala (Sydney Roosters); 17 Sam Moa (Sydney Roosters).
Tries: Goodwin (8, 71), Bromwich (15), Tuivasa-Sheck (20, 50), Pritchard (26), Johnson (30), Vatuvei (57); **Goals:** Johnson 4/8.
SCOTLAND: 1 Matthew Russell (Gold Coast Titans); 2 Dave Scott (Doncaster); 3 Ben Hellewell (Featherstone Rovers); 4 Kane Linnett (North Queensland Cowboys); 5 Alex Hurst (London Broncos); 6 Danny Brough (Huddersfield Giants) (C); 7 Peter Wallace (Brisbane Broncos); 8 Adam Walker (Hull Kingston Rovers); 9 Ian Henderson (Catalan Dragons); 10 Luke Douglas (Gold Coast Titans); 11 Danny Addy (Bradford Bulls); 12 Brett Phillips (Workington Town); 13 Ben Kavanagh (Widnes Vikings). Subs (all used): 14 Andrew Henderson (Sheffield Eagles); 15 Oliver Wilkes (Wakefield Trinity Wildcats); 16 Alex Szostak (Sheffield Eagles); 17 Sam Barlow (Featherstone Rovers).
Try: Hurst (65); **Goals:** Brough 0/1.
Rugby Leaguer & League Express Men of the Match:
New Zealand: Shaun Johnson; *Scotland:* Danny Brough.
Penalty count: 4-8; **Half-time:** 26-0; **Referee:** Ben Cummins (Australia); **Attendance:** 16,207 *(at Headingley Carnegie, Leeds).*

Saturday 16th November 2013

AUSTRALIA 62 USA 0

AUSTRALIA: 1 Billy Slater (Melbourne Storm); 2 Brett Morris (St George Illawarra Dragons); 3 Jarryd Hayne (Parramatta Eels); 4 Greg Inglis (South Sydney Rabbitohs); 5 Darius Boyd (Newcastle Knights); 6 Johnathan Thurston (North Queensland Cowboys); 7 Cooper Cronk (Melbourne Storm); 8 Matthew Scott (North Queensland Cowboys); 9 Cameron Smith (Melbourne Storm) (C); 10 James Tamou (North Queensland Cowboys); 11 Greg Bird (Gold Coast Titans); 12 Sam Thaiday (Brisbane Broncos); 13 Paul Gallen (Cronulla Sharks). Subs (all used): 14 Daly Cherry-Evans (Manly Sea Eagles); 15 Josh Papalii (Canberra Raiders); 16 Andrew Fifita (Cronulla Sharks); 17 Corey Parker (Brisbane Broncos).
Tries: Hayne (3, 57, 69, 79), Inglis (11, 51), B Morris (21, 25, 35, 39), Smith (23), Cronk (28); **Goals:** Thurston 7/12.
USA: 1 Kristian Freed (Connecticut Wildcats); 2 Bureta Faraimo (Mackay Cutters); 3 Taylor Welch (Chicago Griffins); 4 Michael Garvey (Pennsylvania Bulls); 5 Matt Petersen (Cudgen Hornets); 6 Joseph Paulo (Parramatta Eels) (C); 7 Craig Priestly (Southampton Dragons); 8 Mark Offerdahl (Carcassonne); 9 Haveatama Luani (Wests Tigers); 10 Eddy Pettybourne (Wests Tigers); 11 Clint Newton (Penrith Panthers); 12 Matthew Shipway (South Newcastle); 13 Daniel Howard (Wentworthville Magpies). Subs (all used): 14 Tuisegasega Samoa (Redcliffe Dolphins); 15 Roman Hifo (Mangere East Hawks); 16 Mark Cantoni (Dalby Devils); 17 Les Soloai (Hawaii Chiefs).
Rugby Leaguer & League Express Men of the Match:
Australia: Brett Morris; *USA:* Eddy Pettybourne.
Penalty count: 5-6; **Half-time:** 38-0.
Referee: Henry Perenara (New Zealand); **Attendance:** 5,762 *(at Glyndwr University Racecourse Stadium, Wrexham).*

ENGLAND 34 FRANCE 6

ENGLAND: 1 Sam Tomkins (Wigan Warriors); 2 Josh Charnley (Wigan Warriors); 3 Kallum Watkins (Leeds Rhinos); 4 Leroy Cudjoe (Huddersfield Giants); 5 Ryan Hall (Leeds Rhinos); 6 Rangi Chase (Castleford Tigers); 7 Kevin Sinfield (Leeds Rhinos) (C); 8 James Graham (Canterbury Bulldogs); 9 Michael McIlorum (Wigan Warriors); 10 Chris Hill (Warrington Wolves); 11 Sam Burgess (South Sydney Rabbitohs); 12 Ben Westwood (Warrington Wolves); 13 Sean O'Loughlin (Wigan Warriors). Subs (all used): 14 James Roby (St Helens); 15 George Burgess (South Sydney Rabbitohs); 16 Brett Ferres (Huddersfield Giants); 17 Liam Farrell (Wigan Warriors).
Tries: Charnley (11, 25), Hall (18, 28), O'Loughlin (46), Ferres (76); **Goals:** Sinfield 5/6.
Sin bin: Tomkins (73) - professional foul.
FRANCE: 1 Morgan Escare (Catalan Dragons); 2 Damien Cardace (Catalan Dragons); 3 Jean-Philippe Baile (Catalan Dragons); 4 Vincent Duport (Catalan Dragons); 5 Clint Greenshields (North Queensland Cowboys); 6 Thomas Bosc (Catalan Dragons); 7 William Barthau (Catalan Dragons); 8 Jamal Fakir (Catalan Dragons); 9 Kane Bentley (Toulouse Olympique); 10 Remi Casty (Catalan Dragons); 11 Olivier Elima (Catalan Dragons) (C); 12 Sebastien Raguin (St Esteve); 13 Gregory Mounis (Catalan Dragons). Subs (all used): 14 Eloi Pelissier (Catalan Dragons); 15 Younes Khattabi (Carcassonne); 16 Antoni Maria (Catalan Dragons); 17 Mickael Simon (Catalan Dragons).
Try: Duport (4); **Goals:** Bosc 1/1.
Rugby Leaguer & League Express Men of the Match:
England: James Graham; *France:* Eloi Pelissier.
Penalty count: 10-5; **Half-time:** 22-6; **Referee:** Ashley Klein (Australia); **Attendance:** 22,276 *(at DW Stadium, Wigan).*

Sunday 17th November 2013

FIJI 22 SAMOA 4

FIJI: 1 Kevin Naiqama (Newcastle Knights); 5 Akuila Uate (Newcastle Knights); 4 Wes Naiqama (Penrith Panthers); 3 Sisa Waqa (Melbourne Storm); 2 Marika Koroibete (Wests Tigers); 6 Daryl Millard (Catalan Dragons); 7 Aaron Groom (Asquith Magpies); 8 Ashton Sims (North Queensland Cowboys); 9 James Storer (Collegians); 10 Petero Civoniceva (Redcliffe Dolphins) (C); 11 Tariq Sims (North Queensland Cowboys); 12 Jayson Bukuya (Cronulla Sharks); 13 Eloni Vunakece (Toulouse Olympique). Subs (all used): 14 Apisai Koroisau (South Sydney Rabbitohs); 15 Vitale Roqica (Cronulla Sharks); 16 Kane Evans (Sydney Roosters); 17 Semi Waqavatu (Parramatta Eels).
Tries: Groom (4), W Naiqama (32), Roqica (78); **Goals:** W Naiqama 5/5.
SAMOA: 1 Anthony Milford (Canberra Raiders); 5 Daniel Vidot (St George Illawarra Dragons); 4 Joseph Leilua (Newcastle Knights); 3 Tim Lafai (Canterbury Bulldogs); 2 Antonio Winterstein (North Queensland Cowboys); 6 Penani Manumalealii (Cronulla Sharks); 7 Ben Roberts (Parramatta Eels); 8 David Fa'alogo (Newcastle Knights); 14 Michael Sio (New Zealand Warriors); 10 Suaia Matagi (New Zealand Warriors); 11 Iosia Soliola (St Helens) (C); 12 Tony Puletua (St Helens); 13 Sauaso Sue (Wests Tigers). Subs (all used): 9 Pita Godinet (New Zealand Warriors); 15 Junior Moors (Melbourne Storm); 16 Mark Taufua (Cronulla Sharks); 17 Mose Masoe (Penrith Panthers).
Try: A Winterstein (58); **Goals:** Milford 0/1.
On report: Lafai (69) - alleged high tackle on Bukuya.
Rugby Leaguer & League Express Men of the Match:
Fiji: Aaron Groom; *Samoa:* Iosia Soliola.
Penalty count: 7-10; **Half-time:** 14-0; **Referee:** Richard Silverwood (England); **Attendance:** 12,766 *(at Halliwell Jones Stadium, Warrington).*

SEMI-FINALS

Saturday 23rd November 2013

ENGLAND 18 NEW ZEALAND 20

ENGLAND: 1 Sam Tomkins (Wigan Warriors); 2 Josh Charnley (Wigan Warriors); 3 Kallum Watkins (Leeds Rhinos); 4 Leroy Cudjoe (Huddersfield Giants); 5 Ryan Hall (Leeds Rhinos); 6 Gareth Widdop (Melbourne Storm); 7 Kevin Sinfield (Leeds Rhinos) (C); 8 James Graham (Canterbury Bulldogs); 9 James Roby (St Helens); 10 Sam Burgess (South Sydney Rabbitohs); 11 Brett Ferres (Huddersfield Giants); 12 Ben Westwood (Warrington Wolves); 13 Sean O'Loughlin (Wigan Warriors). Subs: 14 Rob Burrow (Leeds Rhinos); 15 George Burgess (South Sydney Rabbitohs); 16 Chris Hill (Warrington Wolves); 17 Carl Ablett (Leeds Rhinos) (not used).
Tries: O'Loughlin (16), Watkins (58), S Burgess (67); **Goals:** Sinfield 3/4.
NEW ZEALAND: 1 Kevin Locke (New Zealand Warriors); 2 Roger Tuivasa-Sheck (Sydney Roosters); 3 Dean Whare (Penrith Panthers); 4 Bryson Goodwin (South Sydney Rabbitohs); 5 Jason Nightingale (St George Illawarra Dragons); 6 Kieran Foran (Manly Sea Eagles); 7 Shaun Johnson (New Zealand Warriors); 8 Jared Waerea-Hargreaves (Sydney Roosters); 9 Issac Luke (South Sydney Rabbitohs); 10 Jesse Bromwich (Melbourne Storm); 13 Simon Mannering (New Zealand Warriors) (C); 12 Sonny Bill Williams (Sydney Roosters); 17 Elijah Taylor (New Zealand Warriors). Subs (all used): 14 Frank-Paul Nuuausala (Sydney Roosters); 15 Sam Kasiano (Canterbury Bulldogs); 16 Ben Matulino (New Zealand Warriors); 19 Alex Glenn (Brisbane Broncos).
Tries: Tuivasa-Sheck (31, 44), Johnson (80); **Goals:** Johnson 4/5.
Rugby Leaguer & League Express Men of the Match:
England: Sam Burgess; *New Zealand:* Shaun Johnson.
Penalty count: 7-11; **Half-time:** 8-8; **Referee:** Ben Cummins (Australia).

AUSTRALIA 64 FIJI 0

AUSTRALIA: 1 Greg Inglis (South Sydney Rabbitohs); 2 Brett Morris (St George Illawarra Dragons); 4 Jarryd Hayne (Parramatta Eels); 3 Brent Tate (North Queensland Cowboys); 5 Darius Boyd (Newcastle Knights); 6 Johnathan Thurston (North Queensland Cowboys); 7 Cooper Cronk (Melbourne Storm); 8 Matthew Scott (North Queensland Cowboys); 9 Cameron Smith (Melbourne Storm) (C); 10 James Tamou (North Queensland Cowboys); 12 Sam Thaiday (Brisbane Broncos); 11 Greg Bird (Gold Coast Titans); 13 Paul Gallen (Cronulla Sharks). Subs (all used): 14 Daly Cherry-Evans (Manly Sea Eagles); 15 Josh Papalii (Canberra Raiders); 16 Andrew Fifita (Cronulla Sharks); 17 Corey Parker (Brisbane Broncos).
Tries: Thurston (9), Boyd (15, 59), Cronk (19), Hayne (22, 40, 69), Papalii (35), Tamou (54), B Morris (71), Fifita (80); **Goals:** Thurston 10/11.
FIJI: 1 Kevin Naiqama (Newcastle Knights); 5 Akuila Uate (Newcastle Knights); 4 Wes Naiqama (Penrith Panthers); 3 Sisa Waqa (Melbourne Storm); 2 Marika Koroibete (Wests Tigers); 6 Daryl Millard (Catalan Dragons); 7 Aaron Groom (Asquith Magpies); 8 Ashton Sims (North Queensland Cowboys); 9 James Storer (Collegians); 10 Petero Civoniceva (Redcliffe Dolphins) (C); 11 Tariq Sims (North Queensland Cowboys); 12 Jayson Bukuya (Cronulla Sharks); 13 Eloni Vunakece (Toulouse Olympique). Subs (all used): 14 Apisai Koroisau (South Sydney Rabbitohs); 15 Vitale Roqica (Cronulla Sharks); 16 Kane Evans (Sydney Roosters); 17 Semi Waqavatu (Parramatta Eels).
On report: W Naiqama (21) - alleged late challenge on Tate.
Rugby Leaguer & League Express Men of the Match:
Australia: Johnathan Thurston; *Fiji:* Aaron Groom.
Penalty count: 10-6; **Half-time:** 34-0; **Referee:** Richard Silverwood (England).

Attendance: 67,545 *(at Wembley Stadium).*

FINAL

Saturday 30th November 2013

AUSTRALIA 34 NEW ZEALAND 2

AUSTRALIA: 1 Billy Slater (Melbourne Storm); 2 Brett Morris (St George Illawarra Dragons); 4 Jarryd Hayne (Parramatta Eels); 3 Greg Inglis (South Sydney Rabbitohs); 5 Darius Boyd (Newcastle Knights); 6 Johnathan Thurston (North Queensland Cowboys); 7 Cooper Cronk (Melbourne Storm); 8 Matthew Scott (North Queensland Cowboys); 9 Cameron Smith (Melbourne Storm) (C); 10 James Tamou (North Queensland Cowboys); 11 Greg Bird (Gold Coast Titans); 12 Sam Thaiday (Brisbane Broncos); 13 Paul Gallen (Cronulla Sharks). Subs (all used): 14 Daly Cherry-Evans (Manly Sea Eagles); 15 Josh Papalii (Canberra Raiders); 16 Andrew Fifita (Cronulla Sharks); 17 Corey Parker (Brisbane Broncos).
Tries: Slater (19, 41), Cronk (30), B Morris (52, 72); **Goals:** Thurston 7/7.
NEW ZEALAND: 1 Kevin Locke (New Zealand Warriors); 2 Roger Tuivasa-Sheck (Sydney Roosters); 3 Dean Whare (Penrith Panthers); 4 Bryson Goodwin (South Sydney Rabbitohs); 5 Manu Vatuvei (New Zealand Warriors); 6 Kieran Foran (Manly Sea Eagles); 7 Shaun Johnson (New Zealand Warriors); 8 Jared Waerea-Hargreaves (Sydney Roosters); 9 Issac Luke (South Sydney Rabbitohs); 10 Jesse Bromwich (Melbourne Storm); 11 Simon Mannering (New Zealand Warriors) (C); 12 Sonny Bill Williams (Sydney Roosters); 13 Elijah Taylor (New Zealand Warriors). Subs (all used): 14 Frank-Paul Nuuausala (Sydney Roosters); 15 Sam Kasiano (Canterbury Bulldogs); 16 Ben Matulino (New Zealand Warriors); 17 Alex Glenn (Brisbane Broncos).
Goals: Johnson 1/1.
Rugby Leaguer & League Express Men of the Match:
Australia: Johnathan Thurston; *New Zealand:* Sonny Bill Williams.
Penalty count: 4-8; **Half-time:** 16-2; **Referee:** Richard Silverwood (England); **Attendance:** 74,468 *(at Old Trafford, Manchester).*

LEADING SCORERS

TRIES

1	Jarryd Hayne	Australia	9
	Brett Morris	Australia	9
3	Ryan Hall	England	8
	Roger Tuivasa-Sheck	New Zealand	8
5	Cooper Cronk	Australia	5
	Antonio Winterstein	Samoa	5

GOALS

1	Johnathan Thurston	Australia	33
2	Shaun Johnson	New Zealand	30
3	Kevin Sinfield	England	19
4	Danny Brough	Scotland	13
5	Wes Naiqama	Fiji	11

POINTS

			T	G	FG	Pts
1	Shaun Johnson	New Zealand	4	30	0	76
2	Johnathan Thurston	Australia	2	33	0	74
3	Kevin Sinfield	England	0	19	0	38
4	Jarryd Hayne	Australia	9	0	0	36
	Brett Morris	Australia	9	0	0	36

143

RUGBY LEAGUE
WORLD CUP
ENGLAND AND WALES 2013

The 2013 Rugby League World Cup produced bumper crowds and commercial success which contributed to a profit in excess of £3.7 million for the Rugby League International Federation.

Fourteen nations were involved in the 14th global tournament in four groups, with unbeaten Australia eventually winning their 10th World Cup with a commanding win over holders New Zealand in the final.

GROUP A

ABOVE: Fiji celebrate in the rain after defeating Ireland

Australia came top of Group A, through which three of the four teams qualified, thanks to their 28-20 win over England in the opening game of the tournament, at Cardiff's Millennium Stadium.

With the roof closed to enhance a spectacular opening ceremony, England, who had lost by one point to minnows Italy in a warm-up seven days previously, raced into a 10-0 lead after 20 minutes through tries to Ryan Hall and Leroy Cudjoe.

But by half-time Australia led 18-10, a try straight from a scrum by Billy Slater on the cusp of the break the killer.

England trailed by only six points going into the final quarter, but Sam Burgess and then younger brother Tom conceded penalties in the space of a minute for Johnathan Thurston to land a close-range penalty goal that put the Kangaroos two scores clear once more. Darius Boyd and Josh Charnley swapped tries in the last ten minutes. Charnley's effort from a dropped Billy Slater ball was the last try that Australia conceded in the 2013 World Cup.

On the following Monday, Akuila Uate scored three tries as the Fijians eventually overpowered the plucky Irish 32-14 on an emotional night in cold, wet Rochdale, in front of a full house at Spotland.

The Fijians, captained by Petero Civoniceva, were big, fast and physical. That Ireland were still in the contest in the 50th minute, when they trailed only 12-4, was testament to their spirit.

The result decided that Fiji would be progressing, with both nations still to play England and Australia.

England beat Ireland 42-0 at the John Smith's Stadium, Huddersfield the following Saturday and Fiji 34-12 the week after at KC Stadium, Hull, both in front of capacity crowds.

Against Ireland, England racked up eight unanswered tries – five of them in an 11-minute period midway through the first half during which Ireland appeared only to touch the ball when Pat Richards was lining up his next restart. Ryan Hall's hat-trick was the highlight.

Six tries against Fiji in an 18-minute spell started just before half-time by Ben Westwood's score produced the England win over Fiji, after falling behind to Eloni Vunakece's 34th-minute try.

Australia, meanwhile, were ruthless as they beat Fiji 34-2 at St Helens, although they lost Luke Lewis for the rest of the tournament after he collided with an advertising board behind the dead-ball line. Johnathan Thurston ran the show.

Thurston was rested the following Saturday as Rugby League broke new ground in Limerick, although the Aussies showed no mercy again in a 50-0 win over Ireland. His replacement, Daly Cherry-Evans was the gamestar.

ABOVE: Fiji's Petero Civoniceva looks for a way past Ireland's Ben Currie

RIGHT: Ireland's Simon Finnigan gets to grips with Australia's Daly Cherry-Evans

LEFT: England's Tom Briscoe crosses to score against Ireland

LEFT: Australia's Johnathan Thurston holds off England's Sam Tomkins to score during the opening game of the 2013 World Cup

ABOVE: England's Sam Burgess loses the ball under pressure from Fiji's Ashton Sims

RIGHT: The Fijian defence halts this Australian attack

BELOW: Australia and Fiji pray following their game at St Helens' Langtree Park

LEFT: France's Jamal Fakir looks to get past Papua New Guinea's Charlie Wabo

RIGHT: New Zealand's Roger Tuivasa-Sheck flies in to score against Samoa

LEFT: Samoa's Anthony Milford spots a gap in the Papua New Guinea defence

ABOVE: New Zealand's Sonny Bill Williams drives towards the Papua New Guinea tryline

GROUP B

New Zealand marched through Group B - from which three teams out of four qualified for the quarter-finals - to become some people's favourites to retain their world title.

In their first game of the first Sunday at the Halliwell Jones Stadium, they had to see off a spirited second-half Samoan comeback to eventually win 42-24. The Kiwis raced to a 22-0 lead at the 21-minute mark. By the time Manu Vatuvei scored their seventh try in the 48th minute it was 36-4 but then the Samoans hit back thanks to bullocking centre Joey Leilua.

Samoa then went on a 22-minute rampage and racked up 18 more points, seriously threatening to record a stunning victory. Momentum was with them and the Warrington crowd was strongly behind them, with huge roars greeting every Samoan run with the ball. But the miracle fight-back was not to be as Vatuvei sealed the win with eight minutes left.

France were no obstacle to the Kiwis in front of a sell-out crowd on a memorable Friday night in Avignon, scrum-half Shaun Johnson scoring two tries and eight goals from eight attempts. Despite the eventual 48-0 hammering the French crowd stayed on to cheer their home heroes from the field.

France had already secured the two points that would see them qualify with a 9-8 win over Papua New Guinea at Craven Park in Hull. But they could count themselves lucky. Having already missed two conversions during the game, the Kumuls' David Mead missed a 79th-minute penalty goal from 30 metres out and from in front of the posts, meaning the Kumuls lost despite out-scoring their opponents two tries to one. A field goal by halfback William Barthau eventually separated the sides.

The result meant the winner of the highly-anticipated PNG v Samoa game at the same venue eight days later was crucial. It turned out to be a very one-sided first half. Canberra Raiders teenage fullback Anthony Milford mesmerised and danced his way to the man of the match award as Samoa, despite missing injury-victims Harrison Hansen, Reni Maitua and Frank Winterstein, led 28-0 at half-time and went on to win 38-4. Cowboys winger Antonio Winterstein finished with a hat-trick on the left wing. With New Zealand left to play, the Kumuls were already eliminated after showing only glimpses of their exciting potential.

They lost their game with the Kiwis at Headingley on the following Friday by 58-10, with a crowd of over 18,000 demonstrating the strong appeal of the World Cup.

In a blistering first-half performance, the Kiwis killed the game off within 15 minutes, as four early tries set them on the way. Amongst the tries was a first-half hat-trick for Sonny Bill Williams.

That meant that the last game of all the group stages in Perpignan - again a sell-out crowd - between France and Samoa decided who would be second and third.

Samoa won the battle 22-4 as referee Henry Perenara had a testing night, placing no less than four Samoans on report. Anthony Milford had another superb game and the Samoans' quarter-final would be with Fiji, France having to play England.

LEFT: France's Remi Casty takes the ball up against Samoa

RIGHT: New Zealand's Kevin Locke defuses a bomb against France

GROUP C

Scotland emerged from what proved to be the tightest group in the tournament, with the outcome in the balance right to the end of the very last game between Tonga and Italy in Halifax.

On the first Tuesday night at Derwent Park, Workington, Matty Russell scored a late try as Scotland snatched a dramatic win over Tonga, who looked to have pulled off a stunning comeback.

Glen Fisi'iahi scored an early try for Tonga but Scotland dominated the rest of the opening half, touching down three times to lead 20-4 at the break. But the Tongans responded in dynamic fashion, scoring four unanswered tries after the restart to move into a 24-20 lead and Scotland looked buried by Willie Manu's converted try in the 65th minute. But Danny Brough's kick-off forced an error and Russell drove low to the line and squeezed the ball onto the stripe. Brough made the conversion look easy and the Scots were in front.

In the last minute all hell broke loose as the desperate Tongans charged forward. Sosaia Feki put in a dangerous kick, Scotland centre Kane Linnett was yellow carded, Mickey Paea was held up, and, on the hooter, Daniel Foster made one final lung-busting charge over the line. Brough threw himself into contact and Addy came in as second man to dislodge the ball. When the dust settled, the video referee ruled no try and Scotland had won.

On the following Sunday at the same venue, Scotland and Italy drew 30-all. Italy had already beaten Wales in a cross-group game on the first day of the tournament.

Italy went ahead for the first time when a lucky deflection arrived to captain Anthony Minichiello perfectly for him to touch down on the hour and Josh Mantellato converted for 30-26. But ten minutes later Brough chipped into space and threw himself for the regather. A quick play-the-ball set off a fantastic spell of passing with Brett Phillips sending Ben Hellewell in for his second with a perfect ball. Brough couldn't convert, and so the game was tied. And despite desperate field-goal attempts at both ends, that's how it stayed.

With Scotland winning their cross-code game against USA the following Thursday, Italy needed to beat Tonga at Halifax to make the quarter-finals, which would have been tough justice on unbeaten Scotland.

Tenacious Tonga prevailed in a tense and tight match at the Shay. Tonga went ahead on the stroke of half-time thanks to a Samisoni Langi penalty as just two points separated the two teams at the break.

The Tongans went further ahead on 46 minutes thanks to a barnstorming run from Willie Manu and halfback Daniel Foster extended the lead in the 63rd minute with a controversial try. After a brilliant run Foster crawled for the line and looked to have got the ball down with an Italy foot in the way. There was a hint of a double movement as well but referee Ben Thaler didn't refer it upstairs and awarded the try immediately.

Replacement Peni Terepo added the final score for the Tongans with another contentious try with less than two minutes left on the clock. Scotland were through.

RUGBY LEAGUE
WORLD CUP
ENGLAND AND WALES 2013

ABOVE: Italy's Raymond Nasso forces the ball over the Scotland tryline

BELOW: Tonga's Mickey Paea driven back by the Scottish defensive ranks

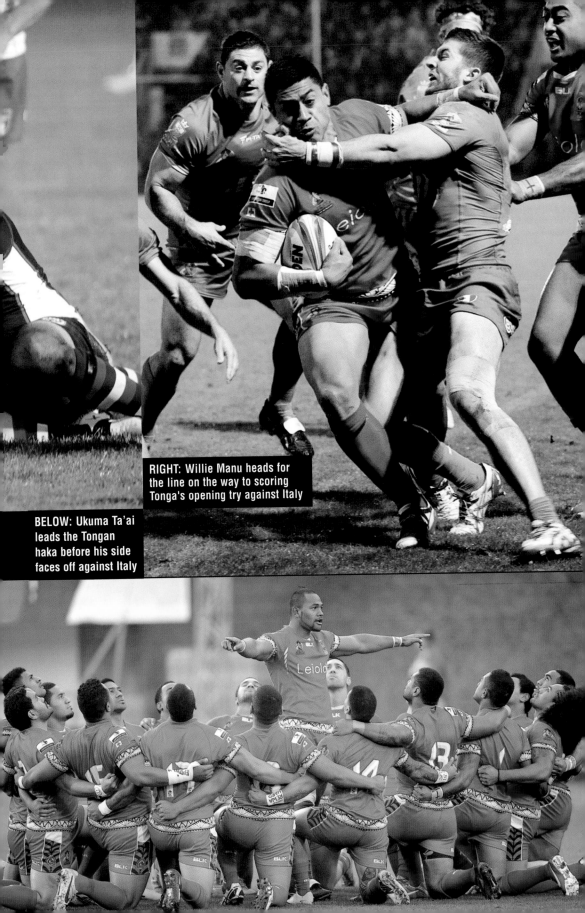

RIGHT: Willie Manu heads for the line on the way to scoring Tonga's opening try against Italy

BELOW: Ukuma Ta'ai leads the Tongan haka before his side faces off against Italy

LEFT: Italy's Josh Mantellato leaps to claim a high ball against Wales

LEFT: USA's Joseph Paulo dives over to score against Wales

LEFT: Tonga's Konrad Hurrell on the rampage against Cook Islands

ABOVE: The Cook Islands defence wraps up USA's Eddy Pettybourne

ABOVE: USA fullback Kristian Freed can't stop Scotland's Brett Phillips from scoring

RIGHT: Cook Islands' Isaac John takes on Wales duo Gil Dudson and Craig Kopczak

GROUP D

RUGBY LEAGUE
W⊕RLD CUP
ENGLAND AND WALES 2013

The US Tomahawks were the shock winners of the group based in the Wales and West, with the Welsh failing to register a single group point from their three games.

Wales opened with a cross-group game against Italy, played straight after the opener between England and Australia at the Millennium Stadium. Three tries in the last 11 minutes eventually blew the score out to 32-16 in favour of Italy, who had beaten England in a warm-up the week before. At the forefront of the victory was Sydney Roosters back-rower Aidan Guerra, playing at left centre, who scored two powerful tries in the first half to set the Italian advantage and then made the killer try for Chris Centrone on 72 minutes, when he was half stopped and as he hit the ground able to loop a brilliant pass outside to his winger.

The Cook Islands were the bookies favourites to win the group but the following Wednesday at Bristol, the USA, a cobbled together side consisting of domestic and lower league Australian-based players and with coach Terry Matterson appointed only days before after Brian Smith stood down, beat them 32-20 after a terrific game. It was only when the US went two tries up near the end that the game was safe.

The US Tomahawks then beat Wales 24-16 the following Sunday in Wrexham as Clint Newton's second and America's fifth try put the Tomahawks well out of reach, despite a late comeback from the Welsh.

The Cooks went out with honour at Leigh when they lost 22-16 to Tonga, with winger Chris Taripo scoring a brilliant hat-trick in defeat and then beat Wales in Neath on the last Sunday 28-24 in what was a dead rubber.

The USA had qualified when they went into their cross-group match with Scotland at Salford. They led 8-0 at half-time but with a 12-0 penalty count against them in the second half, eventually lost 22-8, with Gold Coast Titans prop Luke Douglas's 63rd-minute try sealing the game for the Bravehearts.

QUARTER FINALS

NEW ZEALAND 40 SCOTLAND 4

At Headingley on the Friday night, defending champions New Zealand set up a mouthwatering semi-final against England with another destructive first-half performance against Scotland.

Despite a fantastic effort from the Scots, who broke the first defence several times, the Kiwis dominated the game from the off, and it took them just eight minutes to break the deadlock, with a score of sheer quality. Some quick thinking and a dart from Isaac Luke sent Kevin Locke racing away, before he turned the ball onto Sonny Bill Williams, who put Bryson Goodwin over for the opening score of the night.

Goodwin and winger Roger Tuivasa-Sheck both scored two tries apiece, while Jesse Bromwich, Frank Pritchard, Shaun Johnson and Manu Vatuvei also crossed for the Kiwis. Alex Hurst grabbed a consolation try for Scotland.

AUSTRALIA 62 USA 0

The American dream came to a shuddering halt at Wrexham as the Kangaroos ran in twelve tries against the totally outclassed Tomahawks.

The Aussies forced a goal-line dropout after just one minute when Cameron Smith's kick-off rebounded off the crossbar and the Tomahawks were caught behind their own line. From the kick return the Kangaroos set the platform through James Tamou and Matthew Scott before Greg Inglis appeared in the right centre to produce a deft offload for Jarryd Hayne to glide in at the right corner to make it 4-0.

Hayne finished with four tries as did Brett Morris, who looked odds on after scoring them all in the first half to become the first man ever to score five tries in a World Cup game. Greg Inglis added two tries and Cameron Smith and Cooper Cronk also crossed.

ABOVE: Australia's Brett Morris races away to score against USA

ABOVE: England's Kevin Sinfield takes on France duo Morgan Escaré and Eloi Pelissier

BELOW RIGHT: New Zealand's Manu Vatuvei stretches out to score against Scotland

ENGLAND 34 FRANCE 6

England were far from convincing as they went through to the semi-finals at the expense of France.

Having struggled to score all tournament, registering just two tries in their three Group B games, France needed only four minutes to break England's line. They silenced the DW Stadium with a shock try down the blind side after Sebastien Raguin offloaded to Vincent Duport and the centre bundled his way over despite attempted tackles from Ben Westwood, Kevin Sinfield and Kallum Watkins.

But two tries each from wingers Josh Charnley and Ryan Hall helped England build a 22-6 half-time lead.

Wigan's Sean O'Loughlin and Huddersfield's Brett Ferres extended their advantage after the break.

FIJI 22 SAMOA 4

Samoa, heading into the match as slight favourites after an improving campaign, were out-classed and out-enthused by the brilliant Bati at Warrington.

Fiji were in control from the third minute when Akuila Uate made a brilliant dash. The Newcastle Knights winger drew Anthony Milford and found Aaron Groom on his left for Fiji's first try. Six minutes later, Wes Naiqama added two more points to Fiji's lead with a penalty after a David Fa'alogo shoulder charge.

The Bati were 14-0 ahead at half-time after Wes Naiqama's conversion of his own try.

After Antonio Winterstein's try just before the hour mark notched Samoa's first score, the game threatened to erupt several times in the second half, with the Samoans clearly frustrated. After Wes Naiqama kicked a penalty the Bati scored the try of the game. Uate attracted several defenders and gave a miracle offload to put Apisai Koroisau into space, and he put Vitale Junior through under the posts with a brilliant offload of his own as he fell. Naiqama converted the try to complete a five from five kicking performance.

ABOVE: Aaron Groom shows his delight at scoring Fiji's opening try against Samoa

RIGHT: Fiji's Marika Koroibete looks for a gap in the Samoan defence

SEMI-FINALS

ENGLAND 18 NEW ZEALAND 20

The first game of the "Big Hit' semi-final double header at Wembley was described by many as the greatest international game ever played.

Shaun Johnson scored a sensational last-minute try as defending champions New Zealand knocked out England.

England, 18-14 up, were seconds from victory when England skipper Kevin Sinfield tried to dash up off his own line to smother Johnson, whose side-stepping ability sent him to the line before he added the decisive conversion with the last kick of the match.

Sean O'Loughlin, Kallum Watkins and Sam Burgess had scored tries for England, while Roger Tuivasa-Sheck crossed twice for the Kiwis.

England, with Gareth Widdop preferred to Rangi Chase at stand-off, established an 8-0 lead after 25 minutes, James Graham passing to Sam Burgess just before the line and the South Sydney hero producing a brilliant offload for O'Loughlin. Sinfield converted and then kicked a penalty goal.

The Kiwis hit back with Dean Whare producing the outstanding pass of the tournament to feed Tuivasa-Sheck for a try. With the ball well over the touch line but his foot still in the air, Whare flung a bullet reverse pass back in-field that hit Tuivasa-Sheck and the winger gave Ryan Hall and Cudjoe no chance of stopping him. Johnson landed the conversion, and levelled the scores 90 seconds before half-time with a 35-metre penalty.

NZ had a 12-8 lead when Tuivasa-Sheck stepped past Widdop's despairing cover tackle and held off Cudjoe four minutes after half-time. Johnson missed the conversion, but kicked an easy penalty nine minutes later - New Zealand's fifth straight penalty of the second half.

England managed to bounce back. After Roby's grubber to the line earned a repeat set, Sinfield's pass hit Kallum Watkins, who was running a superb line, to narrow the gap down to two points.

On 67 minutes, James Roby's dart and offload to Sinfield allowed the captain to feed Sam Burgess after he cleverly got behind Johnson, and there was no stopping Burgess with a clear run from 20 metres out.

Sinfield's goal took England to 18-14 and that looked game, set and match - until there was 20 seconds left when Johnson's magic feet did the damage.

AUSTRALIA 64 FIJI 0

Australia were merciless towards the out-gunned Fijians in the second semi-final, registering 11 tries. Johnathan Thurston scored 24 points and received the official man of the match award, although that accolade could have gone to four or five of his teammates, such was the excellence of the Kangaroos.

Jarryd Hayne, who had starred for Fiji in the last World Cup, playing in the right centre, scored a hat-trick and would have had four if he hadn't sent his winger Brett Morris in for the Australians' penultimate try.

Kangaroos captain Cameron Smith acknowledged another immaculate defensive display, against a good Fiji side, that earned them a place in the following Saturday's World Cup final against holders New Zealand. His side had not conceded a try in four games since their 28-20 opening-day win over England.

ABOVE: A bloodied James Graham shows the pain of England's defeat to New Zealand

RIGHT: Australia's Josh Papalii crashes over to score against Fiji

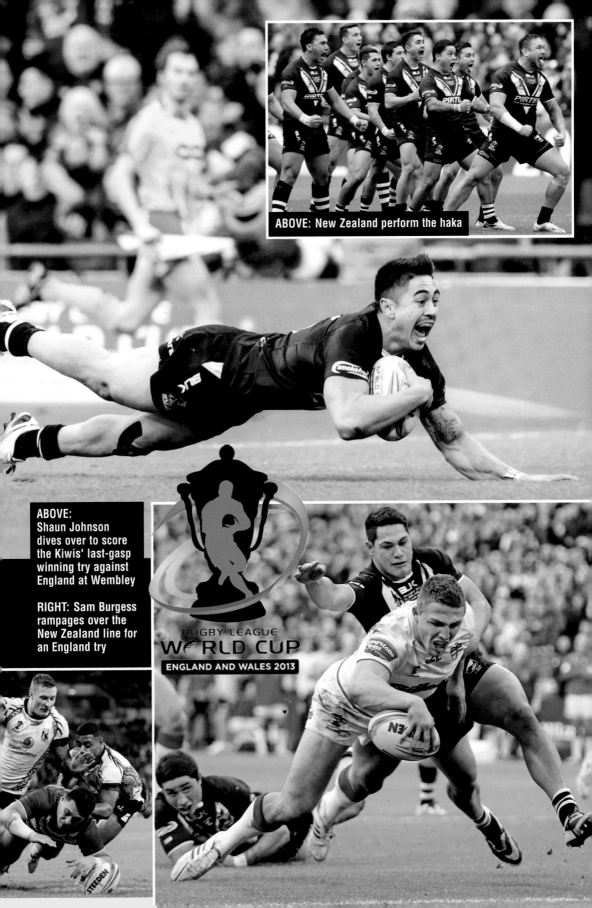

ABOVE: New Zealand perform the haka

ABOVE: Shaun Johnson dives over to score the Kiwis' last-gasp winning try against England at Wembley

RIGHT: Sam Burgess rampages over the New Zealand line for an England try

RUGBY LEAGUE
W RLD CUP
ENGLAND AND WALES 2013

BELOW: A packed house at Old Trafford gets ready to watch the 2013 World Cup Final

FINAL

ABOVE: Johnathan Thurston, Kangaroos coach Tim Sheens and captain Cameron Smith show off the World Cup

AUSTRALIA 34 NEW ZEALAND 2

"I can't remember the last time I played in such a complete game for an Australian side." Australia captain Cameron Smith summed it up succinctly after his side's dominating display against defending World Cup holders New Zealand at a sold-out Old Trafford, Manchester.

The Kiwis need to produce something special to break the Australian defence, which had not conceded a try in 324 minutes of rugby coming into the final. But they were unable to do that.

RUGBY LEAGUE
W⊕RLD CUP
ENGLAND AND WALES 2013

It was 2-2 as man of the match Johnathan Thurston and Shaun Johnson traded penalty goals until Billy Slater leapt to take Thurston's perfect kick across to the right of the posts and score the first try. Cooper Cronk was over next, scooping up a Darius Boyd mis-kick, and with Thurston kicking both conversions and another penalty, the Aussies led 16-2 at the break.

Within seconds of the start of the second half it was all over.

Alex Glenn had come off the bench when the Kiwis lost Roger Tuivasa-Sheck early on and slotted into the right centre, with Dean Whare moving to the wing. Thurston was able to exploit that when he called for the ball on the blindside and sprinted past Glenn before putting Boyd away down the left. On his inside was Slater who collected an imprecise pass to score his second try. Thurston made it 22-2.

ABOVE LEFT: Kiwi superstar Sonny Bill Williams reflects on defeat to Australia

LEFT: Brett Morris tumbles over the dead ball line after touching down for an Australian try

Australia sealed it with a super try as sub Josh Papalii sent a one-handed back flick out to release Brett Morris down the right. His inside pass was juggled with one hand by Jarryd Hayne who kicked forward for Morris to dive on the ball before crashing into the advertising hoardings.

To cap it, Hayne intercepted Sonny Bill Williams' long pass to the left and Morris took Hayne's low pass to finish under the sticks.

ABOVE: The opening ceremony of the 2013 World Cup in full swing

ABOVE: England fans in Wigan get behind their team at the Quarter Final against France

LEFT: A World Cup cheerleader entertains the crowd

ABOVE: Scotland coach Steve McCormack celebrates qualification for the last-eight with young fans at Salford, after victory against USA

6
STATISTICAL REVIEW

SUPER LEAGUE PLAYERS
1996-2014

Super League Players 1996-2014

PLAYER	CLUB	YEAR	APP	TRIES	GOALS	FG	PTS
Jordan Abdull	Hull	2014	6(1)	1	2	0	8
Carl Ablett	Leeds	2004,					
		2006-14	162(32)	47	0	0	188
	London	2005	3(2)	0	0	0	0
Darren Abram	Oldham	1996-97	25(2)	11	0	0	44
Mitch Achurch	Leeds	2013-14	13(27)	8	0	0	32
Brad Adams	Bradford	2014	1(1)	0	0	0	0
Darren Adams	Paris	1996	9(1)	1	0	0	4
Guy Adams	Huddersfield	1998	1(2)	0	0	0	0
Luke Adamson	Salford	2006-07,					
		2009-12	73(39)	11	1	0	46
Matt Adamson	Leeds	2002-04	54(8)	9	0	0	36
Phil Adamson	St Helens	1999	(1)	0	0	0	0
Toby Adamson	Salford	2010	(1)	0	0	0	0
Danny Addy	Bradford	2010-14	49(42)	13	7	0	66
Ade Adebisi	London	2004	(1)	0	0	0	0
Patrick Ah Van	Widnes	2012-14	50	39	54	0	264
	Bradford	2011	26	9	87	0	210
Jamie Ainscough	Wigan	2002-03	30(2)	18	0	0	72
Shaun Ainscough	Bradford	2011-12	27	15	0	0	60
	Wigan	2009-10	12	13	0	0	52
	Castleford	2010	7	4	0	0	16
Glen Air	London	1998-2001	57(13)	27	0	1	109
Paul Aiton	Leeds	2014	13(5)	0	0	0	0
	Wakefield	2012-13	43(2)	7	0	0	28
Makali Aizue	Hull KR	2007-09	18(32)	4	0	0	16
Darren Albert	St Helens	2002-05	105	77	0	0	308
Paul Alcock	Widnes	2003, 2005	1(7)	1	0	0	4
Neil Alexander	Salford	1998	(1)	0	0	0	0
Malcolm Alker	Salford	1997-2002,					
		2004-07,					
		2009-10	271(2)	40	0	1	161
Danny Allan	Leeds	2008-09	2(5)	0	0	0	0
Chris Allen	Castleford	1996	(1)	0	0	0	0
Dave Allen	Widnes	2012-14	50(13)	5	0	0	20
	Wigan	2003, 2005	6(15)	2	0	0	8
Gavin Allen	London	1996	10	0	0	0	0
John Allen	Workington	1996	20(1)	6	0	0	24
Ray Allen	London	1996	5(3)	3	0	0	12
Richard Allwood	Gateshead	1999	(4)	0	0	0	0
Sean Allwood	Gateshead	1999	3(17)	1	0	0	4
David Alstead	Warrington	2000-02	23(10)	3	0	0	12
Luke Ambler	Harlequins	2011	5(17)	1	0	0	4
	Leeds	2010	1(8)	1	0	0	4
Asa Amone	Halifax	1996-97	32(7)	10	0	0	40
Kyle Amor	St Helens	2014	17	4	0	0	16
	Wakefield	2011-13	51(23)	9	0	0	36
	Leeds	2010	(3)	0	0	0	0
Thibaut Ancely	Catalans	2011	(2)	0	0	0	0
Grant Anderson	Castleford	1996-97	15(6)	3	0	0	12
Louis Anderson	Catalans	2012-14	41(9)	16	0	0	64
	Warrington	2008-11	92	18	0	0	72
Paul Anderson	St Helens	2005-06	48(5)	7	1	0	30
	Bradford	1997-2004	74(104)	30	0	0	120
	Halifax	1996	5(1)	1	0	0	4
Paul Anderson	Sheffield	1999	3(7)	1	0	0	4
	St Helens	1996-98	2(28)	4	1	0	18
Scott Anderson	Wakefield	2014	19(1)	1	0	0	4
Vinnie Anderson	Salford	2011-12	33(3)	14	0	0	56
	Warrington	2007-10	57(19)	22	0	0	88
	St Helens	2005-06	28(14)	17	0	0	68
Phil Anderton	St Helens	2004	1	0	0	0	0
Chris Annakin	Wakefield	2013-14	1(19)	1	0	0	4
Eric Anselme	Leeds	2008	2(2)	2	0	0	8
	Halifax	1997	(2)	0	0	0	0
Mark Applegarth	Wakefield	2004-07	20(5)	3	0	0	12
Graham Appo	Warrington	2002-05	60(13)	35	80	0	300
	Huddersfield	2001	7	4	0	0	16
Anthony Armour	London	2005	11(7)	1	0	0	4
Colin Armstrong	Workington	1996	11(2)	1	0	0	4
Tom Armstrong	St Helens	2009-11	10(5)	9	0	0	36
Richard Armswood							
	Workington	1996	5(1)	1	0	0	4
Danny Arnold	Salford	2001-02	26(13)	13	0	0	52
	Huddersfield	1998-2000	55(7)	26	0	0	104
	Castleford	2000	(4)	0	0	0	0
	St Helens	1996-97	40(1)	33	0	0	132
Joe Arundel	Bradford	2014	9(3)	5	0	0	20
	Hull	2013-14	16	7	1	0	30
	Castleford	2008,					
		2010-12	35(4)	14	2	0	60
Craig Ashall	St Helens	2006	1	1	0	0	4
Nathan Ashe	St Helens	2011-13	6(4)	0	0	0	0
Chris Ashton	Wigan	2005-07	44(2)	25	2	0	104
Matty Ashurst	Salford	2012-14	65(7)	11	0	0	44
	St Helens	2009-11	12(39)	8	0	0	32
Roy Asotasi	Wakefield	2014	11(14)	2	0	0	8
Peter Aspinall	Huddersfield	2013	1(1)	0	0	0	0
Martin Aspinwall	Hull	2012	12(15)	0	0	0	0
	Castleford	2011	12(6)	2	0	0	8
	Huddersfield	2006-10	72(8)	22	0	0	88
	Wigan	2001-05	85(13)	27	0	0	108
Mark Aston	Sheffield	1996-99	67(6)	6	243	6	516

PLAYER	CLUB	YEAR	APP	TRIES	GOALS	FG	PTS
Paul Atcheson	Widnes	2002-04	16(35)	4	0	0	16
	St Helens	1998-2000	58(4)	18	0	0	72
	Oldham	1996-97	40	21	0	0	84
David Atkins	Huddersfield	2001	26(1)	4	0	0	16
Jordan Atkins	London	2014	13(1)	4	0	0	16
Ryan Atkins	Warrington	2010-14	133	88	0	0	352
	Wakefield	2006-09	86(2)	45	0	0	180
Josh Atkinson	Castleford	2012	2	0	0	0	0
Brad Attwood	Halifax	2003	(3)	0	0	0	0
Warren Ayres	Salford	1999	2(9)	1	2	0	8
Jerome Azema	Paris	1997	(1)	0	0	0	0
Marcus Bai	Bradford	2006	24	9	0	0	36
	Leeds	2004-05	57	42	0	0	168
David Baildon	Hull	1998-99	26(2)	4	0	0	16
Jean-Philippe Baile							
	Catalans	2008-14	62(16)	23	0	0	92
Andy Bailey	Hull	2004-05	2(8)	1	0	0	4
Chris Bailey	Huddersfield	2014	13(12)	5	0	0	20
	London	2012-13	41	14	0	0	56
	Harlequins	2011	24	3	0	0	12
Julian Bailey	Huddersfield	2003-04	47	13	0	0	52
Phil Bailey	Wigan	2007-10	84(4)	13	0	0	52
Ryan Bailey	Leeds	2002-14	171(102)	17	0	0	68
Jason Baitieri	Catalans	2011-14	66(24)	11	0	0	44
Simon Baldwin	Salford	2004-06	20(29)	3	0	0	12
	Sheffield	1999	7(15)	2	0	0	8
	Halifax	1996-98	41(15)	16	0	1	65
Jordan Baldwinson							
	Bradford	2014	2(4)	0	0	0	0
	Leeds	2013	(2)	0	0	0	0
Rob Ball	Wigan	1998-2000	3(4)	0	0	0	0
Paul Ballard	Celtic	2009	2	0	0	0	0
	Widnes	2005	3(1)	2	0	0	8
Darren Bamford	Salford	2005	2(1)	0	0	0	0
Michael Banks	Bradford	1998	(1)	0	0	0	0
Steve Bannister	Harlequins	2007	(6)	0	0	0	0
	St Helens	2006-07	(3)	0	0	0	0
Frederic Banquet	Paris	1996	16(2)	7	4	0	36
Lee Bardauskas	Castleford	1996-97	(2)	0	0	0	0
Craig Barker	Workington	1996	(2)	0	0	0	0
Dwayne Barker	Harlequins	2008	5(5)	1	0	0	4
	London	2004	3	1	0	0	4
	Hull	2003	(1)	0	0	0	0
Mark Barlow	Wakefield	2002	(1)	0	0	0	0
Danny Barnes	Halifax	1999	2	0	0	0	0
Richie Barnett	Salford	2007	7	4	0	0	16
	Warrington	2006-07	26(10)	15	0	0	60
	Hull	2004-05	21(5)	21	0	0	84
	Widnes	2005	4	2	0	0	8
Richie Barnett	Hull	2003-04	31(1)	17	0	0	68
	London	2001-02	31(4)	13	0	0	52
David Barnhill	Leeds	2000	20(8)	5	0	0	20
Trent Barrett	Wigan	2007-08	53(1)	22	0	4	92
Paul Barrow	Warrington	1996-97	1(10)	1	0	0	4
Scott Barrow	St Helens	1997-2000	9(13)	1	0	0	4
Steve Barrow	London	2000	2	0	0	0	0
	Hull	1998-99	4(17)	1	0	0	4
	Wigan	1996	(8)	3	0	0	12
William Barthau	Catalans	2010,					
		2012-14	13(3)	2	15	0	38
Ben Barton	Huddersfield	1998	1(6)	1	0	0	4
Danny Barton	Salford	2001	1	0	0	0	0
Wayne Bartrim	Castleford	2002-03	41(2)	9	157	0	350
Greg Barwick	London	1996-97	30(4)	21	110	2	306
David Bastian	Halifax	1996	(2)	0	0	0	0
Ashley Bateman	Celtic	2009	1	0	0	0	0
John Bateman	Wigan	2014	19(7)	4	0	0	16
	Bradford	2011-13	25(5)	7	0	0	28
David Bates	Castleford	2001-02	(4)	0	0	0	0
	Warrington	2001	1(2)	0	0	0	0
Sam Bates	Bradford	2014	(2)	0	0	0	0
Nathan Batty	Wakefield	2001	1(1)	0	0	0	0
Andreas Bauer	Hull KR	2007	10(2)	5	0	0	20
Russell Bawden	London	1996-97,					
		2002-04	50(49)	15	0	0	60
Neil Baxter	Salford	2001	1	0	0	0	0
Neil Baynes	Salford	1999-2002,					
		2004	84(19)	10	0	0	40
	Wigan	1996-98	(10)	1	0	0	4
Chris Beasley	Celtic	2009	15(5)	2	0	0	8
Chris Beattie	Catalans	2006	22(5)	3	0	0	12
Richard Beaumont							
	Hull KR	2011-13	1(16)	1	0	0	4
Robbie Beazley	London	1997-99	48(15)	13	0	0	52
Robbie Beckett	Halifax	2002	27	15	0	0	60
Matty Beharrell	Hull KR	2013	1	0	0	0	0
Dean Bell	Leeds	1996	1	1	0	0	4
Ian Bell	Hull	2003	(1)	0	0	0	0
Mark Bell	Wigan	1998	22	12	0	0	48
Paul Bell	Leeds	2000	1	0	0	0	0
Steven Bell	Catalans	2009-10	43	14	0	0	56
Troy Bellamy	Paris	1997	5(10)	0	0	0	0
Adrian Belle	Huddersfield	1998	10(2)	0	0	0	0
	Oldham	1996	19	8	0	0	32

PLAYER	CLUB	YEAR	APP	TRIES	GOALS	FG	PTS
Jamie Benn	Castleford	1998, 2000	3(8)	1	15	0	34
Andy Bennett	Warrington	1996	6(5)	1	0	0	4
Mike Bennett	St Helens	2000-08	74(70)	15	0	0	60
Andrew Bentley	Catalans	2007-10	9(15)	1	0	0	4
John Bentley	Huddersfield	1999	13(4)	3	0	0	12
	Halifax	1996, 1998	22(3)	24	0	0	96
Kane Bentley	Catalans	2007-10	11(19)	5	0	0	20
Phil Bergman	Paris	1997	20(1)	14	0	0	56
Shaun Berrigan	Hull	2008-10	60(8)	12	0	0	48
Joe Berry	Huddersfield	1998-99	25(14)	3	0	0	12
David Berthezene	Salford	2007	9(1)	0	0	0	0
	Catalans	2006-07	5(14)	0	0	0	0
Colin Best	Hull	2003-04	57	34	0	0	136
Roger Best	London	1997-98	1(5)	1	0	0	4
Bob Beswick	Wigan	2004-05	5(14)	2	0	0	8
Monty Betham	Wakefield	2006	26	2	0	0	8
Mike Bethwaite	Workington	1996	17(3)	1	0	0	4
Denis Betts	Wigan	1998-2001	82(24)	33	0	0	132
Cliff Beverley	Salford	2004-05	47(1)	14	0	0	56
Kyle Bibb	Wakefield	2008-10	1(24)	0	0	0	0
	Harlequins	2010	(2)	0	0	0	0
	Hull KR	2009	(2)	0	0	0	0
Adam Bibey	Widnes	2004	(1)	0	0	0	0
Ricky Bibey	Wakefield	2007-09	32(25)	1	0	0	4
	St Helens	2004	4(14)	0	0	0	0
	Wigan	2001-03	5(29)	0	0	0	0
Chris Birchall	Halifax	2002-03	24(22)	4	0	0	16
	Bradford	2000	(1)	0	0	0	0
Deon Bird	Castleford	2006	17(6)	5	0	0	20
	Widnes	2003-04	39(6)	9	0	0	36
	Wakefield	2002	10(1)	1	0	0	4
	Hull	2000-02	37(22)	20	0	0	80
	Gateshead	1999	19(3)	13	0	0	52
	Paris	1996-97	30	12	2	0	52
Greg Bird	Catalans	2009	20(2)	5	3	0	26
Mike Bishay	London	2013-14	7(11)	2	2	0	12
Nathan Blacklock	Hull	2005-06	44(3)	33	0	0	132
Ben Blackmore	Huddersfield	2013-14	3	4	0	0	16
	Castleford	2012	1	0	0	0	0
Richie Blackmore	Leeds	1997-2000	63	25	0	0	100
Anthony Blackwood							
	Crusaders	2010	1	0	0	0	0
	Celtic	2009	25	5	0	0	20
Jack Blagbrough	Huddersfield	2013	(1)	0	0	0	0
Luke Blake	Wakefield	2009	(2)	0	0	0	0
Matthew Blake	Wakefield	2003-04	1(5)	0	0	0	0
Steve Blakeley	Salford	1997-2002	103(5)	26	241	2	588
	Warrington	2000	4(3)	1	9	0	22
Richard Blakeway	Castleford	2002-04	1(14)	0	0	0	0
Damien Blanch	Catalans	2011-13	70	42	0	0	168
	Wakefield	2008-10	44(3)	31	0	0	124
	Castleford	2006	3(2)	0	0	0	0
Matt Blaymire	Wakefield	2007-11	96(3)	26	0	1	105
Ian Blease	Salford	1997	(1)	0	0	0	0
Jamie Bloem	Huddersfield	2003	18(4)	3	11	0	34
	Halifax	1998-2002	82(25)	25	100	2	302
Vea Bloomfield	Paris	1996	4(14)	3	0	0	12
Matty Blythe	Bradford	2013-14	24(6)	8	0	0	32
	Warrington	2007-12	28(27)	12	0	0	48
Ben Bolger	London	2012	2(7)	1	0	0	4
	Harlequins	2010-11	4(15)	0	0	0	0
Pascal Bomati	Paris	1996	17(1)	10	0	0	40
Simon Booth	Hull	1998-99	15(9)	2	0	0	8
	St Helens	1996-97	10(4)	1	0	0	4
Steve Booth	Huddersfield	1998-99	16(4)	2	3	0	14
Alan Boothroyd	Halifax	1997	2(3)	0	0	0	0
Thomas Bosc	Catalans	2006-14	167(4)	42	449	10	1076
John Boslem	Paris	1996	(5)	0	0	0	0
Liam Bostock	St Helens	2004	1	0	0	0	0
Liam Botham	Wigan	2005	5	0	0	0	0
	Leeds	2003-05	2(11)	4	0	0	16
	London	2004	6(2)	3	7	0	26
Frano Botica	Castleford	1996	21	5	84	2	190
Matthew Bottom	Leigh	2005	(1)	0	0	0	0
Hadj Boudebza	Paris	1996	(2)	0	0	0	0
David Boughton	Huddersfield	1999	26(1)	4	0	0	16
Julian Bousquet	Catalans	2012-14	15(16)	2	0	0	8
David Bouveng	Halifax	1997-99	66(2)	19	0	0	76
Josh Bowden	Hull	2012-14	14(22)	2	0	0	8
Matt Bowen	Wigan	2014	22	12	0	0	48
Tony Bowes	Huddersfield	1998	3(2)	0	0	0	0
Radney Bowker	London	2004	3	1	0	0	4
	St Helens	2001	(1)	0	0	0	0
David Boyle	Bradford	1999-2000	36(13)	15	0	1	61
Ryan Boyle	Castleford	2006, 2008-09, 2013-14	9(38)	4	0	0	16
	Salford	2010-14	57(14)	3	0	0	12
Andy Bracek	Crusaders	2011	(2)	0	0	0	0
	Warrington	2005-08	7(49)	7	0	0	28
	St Helens	2004	(1)	0	0	0	0
David Bradbury	Hudds-Sheff	2000	21(2)	1	0	0	4
	Salford	1997-99	23(10)	6	0	0	24
	Oldham	1996-97	19(6)	9	0	0	36
John Braddish	St Helens	2001-02	1(1)	0	3	0	6
Graeme Bradley	Bradford	1996-98	62(1)	29	0	0	116
Nick Bradley-Qalilawa							
	Harlequins	2006	27	6	0	0	24
	London	2005	28	19	0	0	76
Darren Bradstreet	London	1999-2000	1(3)	0	0	0	0
Dominic Brambani							
	Castleford	2004	2(2)	0	0	0	0
Liam Bretherton	Wigan	1999	(5)	2	0	0	8
	Warrington	1997	(2)	0	0	0	0
Johnny Brewer	Halifax	1996	4(2)	2	0	0	8
Chris Bridge	Warrington	2005-14	171(16)	87	245	1	839
	Bradford	2003-04	2(14)	4	6	0	28
Danny Bridge	Bradford	2014	4(4)	0	0	0	0
	Warrington	2013	(2)	0	0	0	0
Lee Briers	Warrington	1997-2013	365(12)	130	838	70	2266
	St Helens	1997	3	0	11	0	22
Carl Briggs	Salford	1999	8(5)	3	0	1	13
	Halifax	1996	5(3)	1	0	0	4
Kyle Briggs	Bradford	2011	6	4	0	0	16
	Harlequins	2011	3	0	0	0	0
Mike Briggs	Widnes	2002	1(2)	1	0	0	4
Luke Briscoe	Leeds	2014	(3)	1	0	0	4
	Wakefield	2014	2	0	0	0	0
Shaun Briscoe	Widnes	2012-13	11(2)	4	0	0	16
	Hull KR	2008-11	92	27	0	0	108
	Hull	2004-07	83(9)	50	0	0	200
	Wigan	2002-03	23(5)	11	0	0	44
Tom Briscoe	Leeds	2014	26	10	0	0	40
	Hull	2008-13	131(3)	83	0	0	332
Darren Britt	St Helens	2002-03	41	3	0	0	12
Gary Broadbent	Salford	1997-2002	117(2)	22	0	0	88
Paul Broadbent	Wakefield	2002	16(5)	0	0	0	0
	Hull	2000-01	40(9)	3	0	0	12
	Halifax	1999	26(1)	2	0	0	8
	Sheffield	1996-98	63(1)	6	0	0	24
Andrew Brocklehurst							
	Salford	2004-07	34(23)	5	0	0	20
	London	2004	12(6)	2	0	0	8
	Halifax	2001-03	37(8)	2	0	0	8
Justin Brooker	Wakefield	2001	25	9	0	0	36
	Bradford	2000	17(4)	11	0	0	44
Danny Brough	Huddersfield	2010-14	122(3)	31	447	9	1027
	Wakefield	2008-10	50(1)	14	174	4	408
	Castleford	2006	10	1	31	2	68
	Hull	2005-06	25(12)	3	85	1	183
Jodie Broughton	Huddersfield	2014	20	11	0	0	44
	Salford	2010-13	93	53	0	0	212
	Hull	2008-09	9(3)	6	0	0	24
Alex Brown	Hull KR	2013	16	9	0	0	36
	Huddersfield	2009	1	0	0	0	0
Darren Brown	Salford	1999-2001	47(9)	11	6	0	56
Gavin Brown	Leeds	1996-97	5(2)	1	2	0	8
Kevin Brown	Widnes	2013-14	43	22	1	1	91
	Huddersfield	2006-12	156	43	0	1	173
	Wigan	2003-06	46(18)	27	0	0	108
Lee Brown	Hull	1999	(1)	0	0	0	0
Michael Brown	Huddersfield	2008	(1)	0	0	0	0
Michael Brown	London	1996	(2)	0	0	0	0
Todd Brown	Paris	1996	8(1)	2	0	0	8
Adrian Brunker	Wakefield	1999	17	6	0	0	24
Lamont Bryan	Harlequins	2008-11	9(22)	2	0	0	8
Justin Bryant	Paris	1996	4(1)	0	0	0	0
	London	1996	(3)	1	0	0	4
Mark Bryant	London	2012-13	16(36)	3	1	0	14
	Crusaders	2010-11	42(8)	1	0	0	4
	Celtic	2009	23(3)	0	0	0	0
Austin Buchanan	Wakefield	2005-06	6	2	0	0	8
	London	2003	3(1)	2	0	0	8
Danny Buderus	Leeds	2009-11	57(14)	14	0	0	56
Neil Budworth	Celtic	2009	8(19)	0	0	0	0
	Harlequins	2006	2(19)	0	0	0	0
	London	2002-05	59(11)	4	1	0	18
James Bunyan	Huddersfield	1998-99	8(7)	2	0	0	8
Andy Burgess	Salford	1997	3(12)	0	0	0	0
Joe Burgess	Wigan	2013-14	25	21	0	0	84
Luke Burgess	Leeds	2008-11	10(63)	6	0	0	24
	Harlequins	2007	(3)	0	0	0	0
Sam Burgess	Bradford	2006-09	46(34)	14	5	0	66
Tom Burgess	Bradford	2011-12	1(41)	3	0	0	12
Greg Burke	Wigan	2013-14	9(13)	1	0	0	4
	Bradford	2014	(1)	0	0	0	0
Joe Burke	Crusaders	2011	(1)	0	0	0	0
Mike Burnett	Harlequins	2011	16(4)	1	0	0	4
	Hull	2008-10	13(21)	3	0	0	12
Darren Burns	Warrington	2002-04	66(6)	19	0	0	76
Gary Burns	Oldham	1996	6	1	0	0	4
Paul Burns	Workington	1996	5(2)	1	0	0	4
Travis Burns	Hull KR	2013-14	46	8	81	2	196
Rob Burrow	Leeds	2001-14	273(87)	148	126	5	849
Dean Busby	Warrington	1999-2002	34(34)	7	0	0	28
	Hull	1998	8(6)	0	0	0	0
	St Helens	1996-98	1(7)	1	0	0	4
Tom Bush	Leeds	2010	3(1)	1	0	0	4

PLAYER	CLUB	YEAR	APP	TRIES	GOALS	FG	PTS
Ikram Butt	London	1996	5(1)	0	0	0	0
Shane Byrne	Huddersfield	1998-99	1(5)	0	0	0	0
Todd Byrne	Hull	2008-09	20	4	0	0	16
Didier Cabestany	Paris	1996-97	20(6)	2	0	0	8
Hep Cahill	Widnes	2012-14	57(2)	3	0	0	12
	Crusaders	2011	16	2	0	0	8
Joel Caine	Salford	2004	24	8	13	0	58
	London	2003	6	4	1	0	18
Mark Calderwood	Harlequins	2011	13	2	0	0	8
	Hull	2009-10	23	6	0	0	24
	Wigan	2006-08	64	23	0	0	92
	Leeds	2001-05	117(9)	88	0	0	352
Mike Callan	Warrington	2002	(4)	0	0	0	0
Matt Calland	Huddersfield	2003	2	0	0	0	0
	Hull	1999	1	0	0	0	0
	Bradford	1996-98	44(5)	24	0	0	96
Dean Callaway	London	1999-2000	26(24)	12	0	0	48
Laurent Cambres	Paris	1996	(1)	0	0	0	0
Chris Campbell	Warrington	2000	7(1)	2	0	0	8
Liam Campbell	Wakefield	2005	(1)	0	0	0	0
Logan Campbell	Hull	1998-99, 2001	70(13)	14	0	0	56
	Castleford	2000	14(2)	3	0	0	12
	Workington	1996	7(1)	1	0	0	4
Blake Cannova	Widnes	2002	(1)	0	0	0	0
Phil Cantillon	Widnes	2002-03	27(21)	18	0	0	72
	Leeds	1997	(1)	0	0	0	0
Liam Carberry	Widnes	2014	(5)	0	0	0	0
Damien Cardace	Catalans	2012, 2014	13	9	0	0	36
Daryl Cardiss	Warrington	2003-04	23(2)	3	4	0	20
	Halifax	1999-2003	91(8)	39	4	0	164
	Wigan	1996-98	12(6)	4	0	0	16
Dale Cardoza	Warrington	2002	5	1	0	0	4
	Halifax	2001	3	1	0	0	4
	Huddersfield	2000-01	20(9)	11	0	0	44
	Sheffield	1998-99	11(7)	3	0	0	12
Paul Carige	Salford	1999	24(1)	7	0	0	28
Dane Carlaw	Catalans	2008-10	58(15)	9	0	0	36
Keal Carlile	Hull KR	2012-14	4(28)	1	0	0	4
	Huddersfield	2009, 2011	2(1)	1	0	0	4
	Bradford	2008	(1)	0	0	0	0
Jim Carlton	Huddersfield	1999	3(11)	2	0	0	8
George Carmont	Wigan	2008-12	136	71	0	0	284
Brian Carney	Warrington	2009	4	2	0	0	8
	Wigan	2001-05	91(10)	42	1	0	170
	Hull	2000	13(3)	7	0	0	28
	Gateshead	1999	3(2)	2	0	0	8
Justin Carney	Castleford	2013-14	40	38	0	0	152
Martin Carney	Warrington	1997	(1)	0	0	0	0
Omari Caro	Hull KR	2013-14	21	20	0	0	80
	London	2012	11	4	0	0	16
Paul Carr	Sheffield	1996-98	45(5)	15	0	0	60
Bernard Carroll	London	1996	2(1)	1	0	0	4
Mark Carroll	London	1998	15(3)	1	0	0	4
Tonie Carroll	Leeds	2001-02	42(2)	30	0	0	120
Darren Carter	Workington	1996	10(3)	0	1	0	2
Steve Carter	Widnes	2002	14(7)	4	0	0	16
John Cartwright	Salford	1997	9	0	0	0	0
Garreth Carvell	Castleford	2014	1(4)	1	0	0	4
	Hull	2001-08, 2014	75(84)	22	0	0	88
	Warrington	2009-13	77(40)	13	0	0	52
	Leeds	1997-2000	(4)	0	0	0	0
	Gateshead	1999	4(4)	1	0	0	4
Garen Casey	Salford	1999	13(5)	3	23	0	58
Ray Cashmere	Salford	2009-11	63(3)	5	0	0	20
Mick Cassidy	Widnes	2005	24	0	0	0	0
	Wigan	1996-2004	184(36)	30	0	0	120
Remi Casty	Catalans	2006-13	88(83)	18	0	0	72
Ned Catic	Castleford	2008	7(7)	3	0	0	12
	Wakefield	2006-07	17(29)	4	0	0	16
Mason Caton-Brown	Salford	2014	8	4	0	0	16
	London	2013-14	19	15	0	0	60
Chris Causey	Warrington	1997-99	(18)	1	0	0	4
Jason Cayless	St Helens	2006-09	62(9)	7	0	0	28
Arnaud Cervello	Paris	1996	4	4	0	0	16
Marshall Chalk	Celtic	2009	13	4	0	0	16
Gary Chambers	Warrington	1996-2000	65(28)	2	0	0	8
Pierre Chamorin	Paris	1996-97	27(3)	8	3	0	38
Alex Chan	Catalans	2006-08	59(19)	11	0	0	44
Jason Chan	Hull KR	2014	5(1)	3	0	0	12
	Huddersfield	2012-14	46(12)	9	0	0	36
	Crusaders	2010-11	48(1)	10	0	0	40
	Celtic	2009	17(6)	3	0	0	12
Joe Chandler	Leeds	2008	(1)	0	0	0	0
Michael Channing	Castleford	2013-14	17(2)	7	0	0	28
	London	2012-13	15(3)	2	0	0	8
Chris Chapman	Leeds	1999	(1)	0	0	0	0
Damien Chapman	London	1998	6(2)	3	4	1	21
David Chapman	Castleford	1996-98	24(6)	8	0	0	32
Jaymes Chapman	Halifax	2002-03	5(8)	1	0	0	4

PLAYER	CLUB	YEAR	APP	TRIES	GOALS	FG	PTS
Richard Chapman	Sheffield	1996	1	2	0	0	8
Chris Charles	Salford	2004-06	59(16)	6	140	0	304
	Castleford	2001	1(4)	1	0	0	4
Olivier Charles	Catalans	2007	2	2	0	0	8
Josh Charnley	Wigan	2010-14	102(2)	111	72	0	588
	Hull KR	2010	5	5	0	0	20
Lewis Charnock	St Helens	2013	1(1)	0	3	0	6
Rangi Chase	Salford	2014	23	7	13	2	56
	Castleford	2009-13	114(5)	38	0	3	155
Andy Cheetham	Huddersfield	1998-99	30	11	0	0	44
Kris Chesney	London	1998	1(2)	0	0	0	0
Chris Chester	Hull KR	2007-08	28(6)	4	0	0	16
	Hull	2002-06	67(25)	13	0	0	52
	Wigan	1999-2001	21(22)	5	0	0	20
	Halifax	1996-98	47(14)	16	15	1	95
Lee Chilton	Workington	1996	10(3)	6	0	0	24
Gary Christie	Bradford	1996-97	4(7)	1	0	0	4
James Clare	Castleford	2012-14	25	18	0	0	72
Daryl Clark	Castleford	2011-14	34(51)	31	0	0	124
Dean Clark	Leeds	1996	11(2)	3	0	0	12
Des Clark	St Helens	1999	4	0	0	0	0
	Halifax	1998-99	35(13)	6	0	0	24
Greg Clarke	Halifax	1997	1(1)	0	0	0	0
John Clarke	Oldham	1996-97	27(4)	5	0	0	20
Jon Clarke	Widnes	2012-14	59(1)	5	0	0	20
	Warrington	2001-11	217(25)	56	2	0	228
	London	2000-01	19(11)	2	0	0	8
	Wigan	1997-99	13(10)	3	0	0	12
Chris Clarkson	Leeds	2010-14	61(39)	9	0	0	36
Adam Clay	Salford	2011	2	3	0	0	12
Ryan Clayton	Castleford	2004, 2008-10	36(24)	5	0	0	20
	Salford	2006	3(8)	2	0	0	8
	Huddersfield	2005	4(6)	0	0	0	0
	Halifax	2000, 2002-03	28(12)	6	0	0	24
Gavin Clinch	Salford	2004	21(1)	1	0	1	5
	Halifax	1998-99, 2001-02	88(2)	26	45	5	199
	Hudds-Sheff	2000	18(2)	5	0	1	21
	Wigan	1999	10(2)	4	12	0	40
Joel Clinton	Hull KR	2010-12	42(14)	2	0	0	8
John Clough	Salford	2004-06	1(16)	0	0	0	0
Paul Clough	Widnes	2014	4(8)	1	0	0	4
	St Helens	2005-13	53(113)	16	0	0	64
Tony Clubb	Wigan	2014	8(13)	7	0	0	28
	London	2012-13	24(8)	7	0	0	28
	Harlequins	2006-11	100(11)	29	0	0	116
Bradley Clyde	Leeds	2001	7(5)	1	0	0	4
Michael Coady	Leeds	2010	1	1	0	0	4
Evan Cochrane	London	1996	5(1)	1	0	0	4
Ben Cockayne	Hull KR	2007-11, 2014	92(26)	30	0	0	120
	Wakefield	2012-13	54	28	2	0	116
Liam Colbon	Hull	2014	8	1	0	0	4
	London	2012-13	22	5	0	0	20
	Hull KR	2009-11	51	20	0	0	80
	Wigan	2004-05, 2007-08	37(14)	15	0	0	60
Anthony Colella	Huddersfield	2003	5(1)	2	0	0	8
Liam Coleman	Leigh	2005	1(4)	0	0	0	0
Andy Coley	Wigan	2008-11	100(10)	8	0	0	32
	Salford	2001-02, 2004-07	112(34)	34	0	0	136
Richard Colley	Bradford	2004	1	0	0	0	0
Steve Collins	Hull	2000	28	17	0	0	68
	Gateshead	1999	20(4)	13	0	0	52
Wayne Collins	Leeds	1997	21	3	0	0	12
Dean Collis	Wakefield	2012-14	54	26	0	0	104
Aurelien Cologni	Catalans	2006	4(1)	3	0	0	12
Gary Connolly	Widnes	2005	20	4	1	0	18
	Wigan	1996-2002, 2004	168(10)	70	5	0	290
	Leeds	2003-04	27	6	0	0	24
Jake Connor	Huddersfield	2013-14	9	7	2	0	32
Nathan Conroy	Bradford	2013-14	(4)	0	0	0	0
Matt Cook	London	2012-14	50(7)	8	0	0	32
	Hull KR	2010-11	9(16)	7	0	0	28
	Bradford	2005-09	11(52)	4	0	0	16
	Castleford	2008	2(1)	1	0	0	4
Mick Cook	Sheffield	1996	9(10)	2	0	0	8
Paul Cook	Huddersfield	1998-99	11(6)	2	13	0	34
	Bradford	1996-97	14(8)	7	38	1	105
Peter Cook	St Helens	2004	(1)	0	0	0	0
Paul Cooke	Wakefield	2010	16(1)	3	36	1	85
	Hull KR	2007-10	54(5)	8	76	2	186
	Hull	1999-2007	177(27)	32	333	4	798
Ben Cooper	Leigh	2005	25(1)	5	0	0	20
	Huddersfield	2000-01, 2003-04	28(12)	3	0	0	12
Michael Cooper	Warrington	2006-13	29(87)	6	0	0	24
	Castleford	2010	1(5)	2	0	0	8
Ged Corcoran	Halifax	2003	1(11)	0	0	0	0

PLAYER	CLUB	YEAR	APP	TRIES	GOALS	FG	PTS
Wayne Corcoran	Halifax	2003	4(2)	0	0	0	0
Jamie Cording	Huddersfield	2011-13	4(21)	5	0	0	20
Josh Cordoba	Hull	2009	8	1	0	0	4
Mark Corvo	Salford	2002	7(5)	0	0	0	0
Neville Costigan	Hull KR	2014	24	3	0	0	12
Brandon Costin	Huddersfield	2001, 2003-04	69	42	93	3	357
	Bradford	2002	20(1)	8	0	0	32
Wes Cotton	London	1997-98	12	3	0	0	12
Phil Coussons	Salford	1997	7(2)	3	0	0	12
Alex Couttet	Paris	1997	1	0	0	0	0
Nick Couttet	Paris	1997	1	0	0	0	0
Jamie Coventry	Castleford	1996	1	0	0	0	0
Jimmy Cowan	Oldham	1996-97	2(8)	0	0	0	0
Will Cowell	Warrington	1998-2000	6(8)	1	0	0	4
Neil Cowie	Wigan	1996-2001	116(27)	10	0	1	41
Danny Cowling	Wakefield	2012-13	2	0	0	0	0
Jordan Cox	Hull KR	2011-14	16(38)	4	0	0	16
Mark Cox	London	2003	(3)	0	0	0	0
James Coyle	Wigan	2005	2(3)	1	0	0	4
Thomas Coyle	Wigan	2008	2(1)	0	0	0	0
Eorl Crabtree	Huddersfield	2001, 2003-14	156(146)	44	0	0	176
Andy Craig	Halifax	1999	13(7)	1	3	0	10
	Wigan	1996	5(5)	2	0	0	8
Owen Craigie	Widnes	2005	15	7	0	2	30
Scott Cram	London	1999-2002	65(7)	4	0	0	16
Danny Craven	Widnes	2012-14	24(11)	5	3	1	27
Steve Craven	Hull	1998-2003	53(42)	4	0	0	16
Nicky Crellin	Workington	1996	(2)	0	0	0	0
Jason Critchley	Wakefield	2000	7(1)	4	0	0	16
	Castleford	1997-98	27(3)	11	0	0	44
Jason Croker	Catalans	2007-09	56(2)	11	0	1	45
Martin Crompton	Salford	1998-2000	30(6)	11	6	2	58
	Oldham	1996-97	36(1)	16	0	3	67
Paul Crook	Widnes	2005	2(2)	0	5	1	11
Paul Crook	Oldham	1996	4(9)	0	3	0	6
Jason Crookes	Hull	2013-14	15(1)	5	0	0	20
	Bradford	2009-12	25(1)	7	0	0	28
Ben Crooks	Hull	2012-14	42(3)	30	23	0	166
Lee Crooks	Castleford	1996-97	27(2)	2	14	0	36
Dominic Crosby	Wigan	2012-14	24(29)	2	0	0	8
Alan Cross	St Helens	1997	(2)	0	0	0	0
Ben Cross	Widnes	2012-13	27(1)	2	0	0	8
	Wigan	2011	(4)	0	0	0	0
	Leeds	2011	1(9)	0	0	0	0
Steve Crossley	Bradford	2010-11	(9)	1	0	0	4
Garret Crossman	Hull KR	2008	8(18)	0	0	0	0
Steve Crouch	Castleford	2004	4(1)	2	0	0	8
Kevin Crouthers	Warrington	2001-03	12(1)	4	0	0	16
	London	2000	6(4)	1	0	0	4
	Wakefield	1999	4(4)	1	0	0	4
	Bradford	1997-98	3(9)	2	0	0	8
Jordan Crowther	Wakefield	2014	(1)	0	0	0	0
Matt Crowther	Hull	2001-03	48	20	166	0	412
	Hudds-Sheff	2000	10(4)	5	22	0	64
	Sheffield	1996-99	43(4)	22	10	0	108
Heath Cruckshank							
	Halifax	2003	19(1)	0	0	0	0
	St Helens	2001	1(12)	0	0	0	0
Leroy Cudjoe	Huddersfield	2008-14	172(1)	79	57	1	431
Paul Cullen	Warrington	1996	19	3	0	0	12
Francis Cummins	Leeds	1996-2005	217(13)	120	26	2	534
James Cunningham							
	Hull	2012, 2014	(3)	0	0	0	0
	London	2014	10(7)	2	0	0	8
Keiron Cunningham							
	St Helens	1996-2010	357(24)	138	0	0	552
Liam Cunningham							
	Hull	2010	(1)	0	0	0	0
Ben Currie	Warrington	2012-14	20(29)	17	0	0	68
Andy Currier	Warrington	1996-97	(2)	1	0	0	4
Peter Cusack	Hull	2008-10	34(22)	3	0	0	12
Joe Dakuitoga	Sheffield	1996	6(3)	0	0	0	0
Matty Dale	Hull	2006, 2008	(7)	1	0	0	4
	Wakefield	2008	1(1)	0	0	0	0
Brett Dallas	Wigan	2000-06	156	89	0	0	356
Mark Dalle Cort	Celtic	2009	23	4	0	0	16
Paul Darbyshire	Warrington	1997	(6)	0	0	0	0
James Davey	Wakefield	2009-11	3(14)	1	0	0	4
Maea David	Hull	1998	1	0	0	0	0
Alex Davidson	Salford	2011, 2013	(3)	0	0	0	0
Paul Davidson	Halifax	2001-03	22(30)	10	0	0	40
	London	2000	6(10)	4	0	0	16
	St Helens	1998-99	27(16)	7	0	0	28
	Oldham	1996-97	17(18)	14	0	1	57
Ben Davies	Castleford	2011, 2013	3(4)	2	0	0	8
	Widnes	2012-13	10(15)	3	0	0	12
	Wigan	2010	(5)	0	0	0	0
Gareth Davies	Warrington	1996-97	1(6)	0	0	0	0
Geraint Davies	Celtic	2009	1	0	0	0	0
John Davies	Castleford	2010-12	1(6)	1	0	0	4
Jordan Davies	Salford	2013	2(3)	0	0	0	0
Wes Davies	Wigan	1998-2001	22(22)	11	0	0	44
Brad Davis	Castleford	1997-2000, 2004, 2006	102(3)	31	43	10	220
	Wakefield	2001-03	51(12)	15	22	5	109
Matty Dawson	St Helens	2014	19	6	0	0	24
	Huddersfield	2012-13	4	0	0	0	0
Brad Day	Castleford	2014	(1)	0	0	0	0
Matt Daylight	Hull	2000	17(1)	7	0	0	28
	Gateshead	1999	30	25	0	0	100
Michael De Vere	Huddersfield	2005-06	36	6	74	0	172
Paul Deacon	Wigan	2010-11	32(11)	4	14	0	44
	Bradford	1998-2009	258(43)	72	1029	23	2369
	Oldham	1997	(2)	0	0	0	0
Chris Dean	Widnes	2012-14	58(2)	14	0	0	56
	Wakefield	2011	20	8	0	0	32
	St Helens	2007-10	18(3)	9	0	0	36
Craig Dean	Halifax	1996-97	25(11)	12	1	1	51
Gareth Dean	London	2002	(4)	0	0	0	0
Yacine Dekkiche	Hudds-Sheff	2000	11(3)	3	0	0	12
Brett Delaney	Leeds	2010-14	112(4)	20	0	0	80
Jason Demetriou	Wakefield	2004-10	174(3)	50	2	0	204
	Widnes	2002-03	47(1)	15	1	0	62
Martin Dermott	Warrington	1997	1	0	0	0	0
David Despin	Paris	1996	(1)	0	0	0	0
Fabien Devecchi	Paris	1996-97	17(10)	2	0	0	8
Paul Devlin	Widnes	2002-04	32	16	0	0	64
Stuart Dickens	Salford	2005	4(5)	0	4	0	8
Matt Diskin	Bradford	2011-14	64(16)	11	0	0	44
	Leeds	2001-10	195(37)	40	0	0	160
Andrew Dixon	Salford	2013-14	34(2)	8	0	0	32
	St Helens	2009-12	19(41)	12	0	0	48
Kieran Dixon	London	2012-14	49(1)	32	2	0	132
Kirk Dixon	Castleford	2008-14	143(2)	63	267	0	786
	Hull	2004-06	13(4)	7	4	0	36
Paul Dixon	Sheffield	1996-97	5(9)	1	0	0	4
Gareth Dobson	Castleford	1998-2000	(10)	0	0	0	0
Michael Dobson	Hull KR	2008-13	142	51	500	11	1215
	Wigan	2006	14	5	61	0	142
	Catalans	2006	10	4	31	1	79
Michael Docherty	Hull	2000-01	(6)	0	0	0	0
Erjon Dollapi	London	2013-14	(18)	4	0	0	16
Sid Domic	Hull	2006-07	39(4)	15	0	0	60
	Wakefield	2004-05	48	30	0	0	120
	Warrington	2002-03	41(4)	17	0	0	68
Scott Donald	Leeds	2006-10	131	77	0	0	308
James Donaldson							
	Bradford	2009-14	38(35)	4	0	0	16
Glen Donkin	Hull	2002-03	(10)	1	0	0	4
Stuart Donlan	Castleford	2008	20	8	0	0	32
	Huddersfield	2004-06	59(3)	15	0	0	60
	Halifax	2001-03	65(2)	22	0	0	88
Jason Donohue	Bradford	1996	(4)	0	0	0	0
Jeremy Donougher							
	Bradford	1996-99	40(21)	13	0	0	52
Justin Dooley	London	2000-01	37(18)	2	0	0	8
Dane Dorahy	Halifax	2003	20	7	45	0	118
	Wakefield	2000-01	16(2)	4	19	1	55
Jamie Doran	Wigan	2014	(2)	0	0	0	0
Luke Dorn	Castleford	2008, 2014	45(1)	36	0	0	144
	London	2005, 2012-13	58(8)	42	0	0	168
	Harlequins	2006, 2009-11	83(1)	57	0	0	228
	Salford	2007	19(8)	11	0	0	44
Ewan Dowes	Hull	2003-11	169(51)	10	0	0	40
	Leeds	2001-03	1(9)	0	0	0	0
Adam Doyle	Warrington	1998	9(3)	4	0	0	16
Rod Doyle	Sheffield	1997-99	52(10)	10	0	0	40
Brad Drew	Huddersfield	2005-07, 2010	78(13)	18	13	1	99
	Wakefield	2008-09	27(9)	7	14	1	57
Josh Drinkwater	London	2014	23(1)	5	54	0	128
Damien Driscoll	Salford	2001	23(1)	1	0	0	4
James Duckworth							
	London	2014	3	0	0	0	0
	Leeds	2013	2	1	0	0	4
Gil Dudson	Wigan	2012-14	26(16)	2	0	0	8
	Crusaders	2011	3(7)	0	0	0	0
	Celtic	2009	(1)	0	0	0	0
Jason Duffy	Leigh	2005	3(1)	0	0	0	0
John Duffy	Leigh	2005	21	6	0	0	24
	Salford	2000	3(11)	0	1	1	3
	Warrington	1997-99	12(12)	0	0	0	0
Tony Duggan	Celtic	2009	4	3	0	0	12
Andrew Duncan	London	1997	2(4)	2	0	0	8
	Warrington	1997	(1)	0	0	0	0
Andrew Dunemann							
	Salford	2006	25	1	0	2	6
	Leeds	2003-05	76(4)	11	0	2	46
	Halifax	1999-2002	68	19	0	1	77
Matt Dunford	London	1997-98	18(20)	3	0	1	13
Vincent Duport	Catalans	2007-09, 2011-14	100(14)	51	0	0	204
Jamie Durbin	Widnes	2005	1	0	0	0	0
	Warrington	2003	(1)	0	0	0	0

Super League Players 1996-2014

PLAYER	CLUB	YEAR	APP	TRIES	GOALS	FG	PTS
Scott Dureau	Catalans	2011-14	62(1)	26	221	8	554
James Durkin	Paris	1997	(5)	0	0	0	0
Bernard Dwyer	Bradford	1996-2000	65(10)	14	0	0	56
Brad Dwyer	Warrington	2012-14	1(19)	3	0	0	12
	Huddersfield	2013	(6)	0	0	0	0
Luke Dyer	Crusaders	2010	23(1)	5	0	0	20
	Celtic	2009	21	6	0	0	24
	Hull KR	2007	26	13	0	0	52
	Castleford	2006	17(2)	5	0	0	20
Adam Dykes	Hull	2008	12	1	0	2	6
Jim Dymock	London	2001-04	94(1)	15	0	1	61
Leo Dynevor	London	1996	8(11)	5	7	0	34
Jason Eade	Paris	1997	9	4	0	0	16
Michael Eagar	Hull	2004-05	12	4	0	0	16
	Castleford	1999-2003	130(2)	60	0	0	240
	Warrington	1998	21	6	0	0	24
Kyle Eastmond	St Helens	2007-11	46(20)	35	117	3	377
Greg Eastwood	Leeds	2010	5(12)	1	0	0	4
Barry Eaton	Widnes	2002	25	2	49	4	110
	Castleford	2000	1(4)	0	3	0	6
Greg Ebrill	Salford	2002	15(6)	1	0	0	4
Cliff Eccles	Salford	1997-98	30(5)	1	0	0	4
Chris Eckersley	Warrington	1996	1	0	0	0	0
Greg Eden	Hull KR	2013-14	37	23	0	0	92
	Salford	2014	4	1	0	0	4
	Huddersfield	2012	24	8	0	0	32
	Castleford	2011	2	1	0	0	4
Steve Edmed	Sheffield	1997	15(1)	0	0	0	0
Mark Edmondson	Salford	2007	10(2)	0	0	0	0
	St Helens	1999-2005	27(75)	10	0	0	40
Diccon Edwards	Castleford	1996-97	10(5)	1	0	0	4
Grant Edwards	Castleford	2006	(2)	0	0	0	0
Max Edwards	Harlequins	2010	1	0	0	0	0
Peter Edwards	Salford	1997-98	35(2)	4	0	0	16
Shaun Edwards	London	1997-2000	32(8)	16	1	0	66
	Bradford	1998	8(2)	4	0	0	16
	Wigan	1996	17(3)	12	1	0	50
Danny Ekis	Halifax	2001	(1)	0	0	0	0
Abi Ekoku	Bradford	1997-98	21(4)	6	0	0	24
	Halifax	1996	15(1)	5	0	0	20
Shane Elford	Huddersfield	2007-08	26(1)	7	0	0	28
Olivier Elima	Catalans	2008-10, 2013-14	80(21)	33	0	0	132
	Bradford	2011-12	37(3)	12	0	0	48
	Wakefield	2003-07	40(47)	13	0	0	52
	Castleford	2002	(1)	1	0	0	4
Abderazak Elkhalouki							
	Paris	1997	(1)	0	0	0	0
George Elliott	Leeds	2011	1	0	0	0	0
Andy Ellis	Wakefield	2012	10	0	0	0	0
	Harlequins	2010-11	26(11)	8	0	0	32
Gareth Ellis	Hull	2013-14	37	11	0	0	44
	Leeds	2005-08	109	24	1	0	98
	Wakefield	1999-2004	86(17)	21	2	0	88
Jamie Ellis	Castleford	2012-14	36(8)	10	80	1	201
	Hull	2012	4(5)	1	0	0	4
	St Helens	2009	1(2)	0	1	0	2
Danny Ellison	Castleford	1998-99	7(16)	6	0	0	24
	Wigan	1996-97	15(1)	13	0	0	52
Andrew Emelio	Widnes	2005	22(2)	8	0	0	32
Jake Emmitt	Salford	2013	5(10)	0	0	0	0
	Castleford	2011-13	32(17)	0	0	0	0
	St Helens	2008-10	1(16)	1	0	0	4
Anthony England	Warrington	2014	10(11)	3	0	0	12
Patrick Entat	Paris	1996	22	2	0	0	8
Jason Erba	Sheffield	1997	1(4)	0	0	0	0
Morgan Escare	Catalans	2013-14	47	42	1	1	171
Ryan Esders	Harlequins	2009-10	9(11)	3	0	0	12
	Hull KR	2009	(1)	0	0	0	0
Sonny Esslemont	Hull KR	2014	(1)	0	0	0	0
Niall Evalds	Salford	2013-14	17(2)	9	0	0	36
Ben Evans	Warrington	2014	3(12)	2	0	0	8
	Bradford	2013	3(12)	1	0	0	4
James Evans	Castleford	2009-10	26(1)	13	0	0	52
	Bradford	2007-08	43(5)	20	0	0	80
	Wakefield	2006	6	3	0	0	12
	Huddersfield	2004-06	51	22	0	0	88
Paul Evans	Paris	1997	18	8	0	0	32
Rhys Evans	Warrington	2010-14	44(3)	26	0	0	104
Wayne Evans	London	2002	11(6)	2	0	0	8
Toby Everett	London	2014	(2)	0	0	0	0
Richie Eyres	Warrington	1997	2(5)	0	0	0	0
	Sheffield	1997	2(3)	0	0	0	0
Henry Fa'afili	Warrington	2004-07	90(1)	70	0	0	280
David Fa'alogo	Huddersfield	2010-12	38(16)	13	0	0	52
Sala Fa'alogo	Widnes	2004-05	8(15)	2	0	0	8
Richard Fa'aoso	Castleford	2006	10(15)	5	0	0	20
Maurie Fa'asavalu							
	St Helens	2004-10	5(137)	29	0	0	116
Bolouagi Fagborun							
	Huddersfield	2004-06	4(2)	1	0	0	4
Theo Fages	Salford	2013-14	41(2)	13	0	0	52
Esene Faimalo	Salford	1997-99	23(25)	2	0	0	8
	Leeds	1996	3(3)	0	0	0	0
Joe Faimalo	Salford	1998-2000	23(47)	7	0	0	28
	Oldham	1996-97	37(5)	7	0	0	28
Jacob Fairbank	Huddersfield	2011-14	10(3)	0	0	0	0
	Wakefield	2014	1(3)	0	0	0	0
	London	2013	4(1)	1	0	0	4
	Bradford	2013	(2)	0	0	0	0
Karl Fairbank	Bradford	1996	17(2)	4	0	0	16
David Fairleigh	St Helens	2001	26(1)	8	0	0	32
David Faiumu	Huddersfield	2008-14	38(108)	13	0	0	52
Jamal Fakir	Bradford	2014	5(8)	1	0	0	4
	Catalans	2006-14	55(100)	13	0	0	52
Jim Fallon	Leeds	1996	10	5	0	0	20
Ben Farrar	London	2014	22	1	0	0	4
	Catalans	2011	13	3	0	0	12
Danny Farrar	Warrington	1998-2000	76	13	0	0	52
Andy Farrell	Wigan	1996-2004	230	77	1026	16	2376
Anthony Farrell	Widnes	2002-03	24(22)	4	1	0	18
	Leeds	1997-2001	99(23)	18	0	0	72
	Sheffield	1996	14(5)	5	0	0	20
Connor Farrell	Wigan	2014	(2)	1	0	0	4
Craig Farrell	Hull	2000-01	1(3)	0	0	0	0
Liam Farrell	Wigan	2010-14	74(46)	51	0	0	204
Abraham Fatnowna							
	London	1997-98	7(2)	2	0	0	8
	Workington	1996	5	2	0	0	8
Sione Faumuina	Castleford	2009	18	1	0	0	4
	Hull	2005	3	1	0	0	4
Vince Fawcett	Wakefield	1999	13(1)	2	0	0	8
	Warrington	1998	4(7)	1	0	0	4
	Oldham	1997	5	3	0	0	12
Danny Fearon	Huddersfield	2001	(1)	0	0	0	0
	Halifax	1999-2000	5(6)	0	0	0	0
Chris Feather	Castleford	2009	1(23)	0	0	0	0
	Bradford	2007-08	7(20)	1	0	0	4
	Leeds	2003-04, 2006	16(35)	6	0	0	24
	Wakefield	2001-02, 2004-05	29(32)	9	0	0	36
Dom Feaunati	Leigh	2005	4	1	0	0	4
	St Helens	2004	10(7)	7	0	0	28
Adel Fellous	Hull	2008	1(2)	0	0	0	0
	Catalans	2006-07	16(22)	4	0	0	16
Luke Felsch	Hull	2000-01	46(6)	7	0	0	28
	Gateshead	1999	28(1)	2	0	0	8
Leon Felton	Warrington	2002	4(2)	0	0	0	0
	St Helens	2001	1(1)	0	0	0	0
Dale Ferguson	Bradford	2014	3(3)	0	0	0	0
	Huddersfield	2011-13	34(18)	13	0	0	52
	Hull KR	2013	3(1)	1	0	0	4
	Wakefield	2007-11	40(14)	12	0	0	48
Brett Ferres	Huddersfield	2012-14	58	24	0	0	96
	Castleford	2009-12	78(5)	26	0	0	104
	Wakefield	2007-08	36(2)	6	5	0	34
	Bradford	2005-06	18(17)	11	2	0	48
David Ferriol	Catalans	2007-12	72(55)	8	0	0	32
Jason Ferris	Leigh	2005	4	1	0	0	4
Jamie Field	Wakefield	1999-2006	133(59)	19	0	0	76
	Huddersfield	1998	15(5)	0	0	0	0
	Leeds	1996-97	3(11)	0	0	0	0
Mark Field	Wakefield	2003-07	28(7)	3	0	0	12
Jamie Fielden	London	2003	(1)	0	0	0	0
	Huddersfield	1998-2000	4(8)	0	0	0	0
Stuart Fielden	Huddersfield	2013	8(1)	0	0	0	0
	Wigan	2006-12	105(24)	2	0	0	8
	Bradford	1998-2006	142(78)	41	0	0	164
Lafaele Filipo	Workington	1996	15(4)	3	0	0	12
Salesi Finau	Warrington	1996-97	16(15)	8	0	0	32
Brett Finch	Wigan	2011-12	49(3)	16	0	0	64
Vinny Finigan	Bradford	2010	4(1)	4	0	0	16
Liam Finn	Castleford	2014	24	4	1	0	18
	Wakefield	2004	1(1)	0	1	0	2
	Halifax	2002-03	16(5)	2	30	1	69
Lee Finnerty	Halifax	2003	18(2)	5	2	0	24
Phil Finney	Warrington	1998	1	0	0	0	0
Simon Finnigan	Widnes	2003-05, 2012	56(24)	21	0	0	84
	Huddersfield	2009-10	22(5)	6	0	0	24
	Bradford	2008	14(13)	8	0	0	32
	Salford	2006-07	50	17	0	0	68
Matt Firth	Halifax	2000-01	12(2)	0	0	0	0
Andy Fisher	Wakefield	1999-2000	31(8)	4	0	0	16
Ben Fisher	London	2013	8(12)	1	0	0	4
	Catalans	2012	9(5)	1	0	0	4
	Hull KR	2007-11	78(46)	18	0	0	72
Craig Fitzgibbon	Hull	2010-11	42(1)	9	8	0	52
Daniel Fitzhenry	Hull KR	2008-09	36(11)	14	0	0	56
Karl Fitzpatrick	Salford	2004-07, 2009-10	89(11)	33	2	0	136
Mark Flanagan	St Helens	2012-14	27(27)	7	0	0	28
	Wigan	2009	3(7)	1	0	0	4
Chris Flannery	St Helens	2007-12	108(11)	32	0	0	128
Darren Fleary	Leigh	2005	24	1	0	0	4
	Huddersfield	2003-04	43(8)	4	0	0	16
	Leeds	1997-2002	98(9)	3	0	0	12

168

Super League Players 1996-2014

PLAYER	CLUB	YEAR	APP	TRIES	GOALS	FG	PTS
Daniel Fleming	Castleford	2013-14	(15)	1	0	0	4
Greg Fleming	London	1999-2001	64(1)	40	2	0	164
Adam Fletcher	Castleford	2006, 2008	16(7)	11	0	0	44
Bryan Fletcher	Wigan	2006-07	47(2)	14	0	0	56
Richard Fletcher	Castleford	2006	13(5)	3	4	0	20
	Hull	1999-2004	11(56)	5	0	0	20
Greg Florimo	Halifax	2000	26	6	4	0	32
	Wigan	1999	18(2)	7	1	0	30
Ben Flower	Wigan	2012-14	41(20)	9	0	0	36
	Crusaders	2010-11	10(23)	2	0	0	8
	Celtic	2009	2(15)	0	0	0	0
Jason Flowers	Salford	2004	6(1)	0	0	0	0
	Halifax	2002	24(4)	4	0	0	16
	Castleford	1996-2001	119(19)	33	0	1	133
Stuart Flowers	Castleford	1996	(3)	0	0	0	0
Adrian Flynn	Castleford	1996-97	19(2)	10	0	0	40
Paddy Flynn	Widnes	2012-14	62	34	0	0	136
Wayne Flynn	Sheffield	1997	3(5)	0	0	0	0
Adam Fogerty	Warrington	1998	4	0	0	0	0
	St Helens	1996	13	1	0	0	4
Liam Foran	Salford	2013	10(3)	1	0	0	4
Carl Forber	Leigh	2005	4	1	0	0	4
	St Helens	2004	1(1)	0	6	0	12
Paul Forber	Salford	1997-98	19(12)	4	0	0	16
Byron Ford	Hull KR	2007	13	6	0	0	24
James Ford	Castleford	2009	3(5)	1	0	0	4
Mike Ford	Castleford	1997-98	25(12)	5	0	3	23
	Warrington	1996	3	0	0	0	0
Jim Forshaw	Salford	1999	(1)	0	0	0	0
Mike Forshaw	Warrington	2004	20(1)	5	0	0	20
	Bradford	1997-2003	162(7)	32	0	0	128
	Leeds	1996	11(3)	5	0	0	20
Carl Forster	St Helens	2011-12, 2014	(4)	0	0	0	0
	London	2014	2(3)	0	0	0	0
Mark Forster	Warrington	1996-2000	102(1)	40	0	0	160
Alex Foster	London	2014	20	3	0	0	12
	Leeds	2013	(8)	1	0	0	4
David Foster	Halifax	2000-01	4(9)	0	0	0	0
Jamie Foster	Bradford	2013-14	32	12	111	0	270
	Hull	2012	9	5	45	0	110
	St Helens	2010-12	44(3)	30	201	0	522
Peter Fox	Wakefield	2007, 2012-14	85	44	0	0	176
	Hull KR	2008-11	95	52	0	0	208
Matty Fozard	St Helens	2014	1	0	0	0	0
Nick Fozzard	Castleford	2011	7(10)	0	0	0	0
	St Helens	2004-08, 2010	100(25)	7	0	0	28
	Hull KR	2009	18(4)	1	0	0	4
	Warrington	2002-03	43(11)	2	0	0	8
	Huddersfield	1998-2000	24(8)	2	0	0	8
	Leeds	1996-97	6(16)	3	0	0	12
David Fraisse	Workington	1996	8	0	0	0	0
Daniel Frame	Widnes	2002-05	100(6)	24	0	0	96
Paul Franze	Castleford	2006	2(1)	0	0	0	0
Laurent Frayssinous							
	Catalans	2006	14(2)	3	32	0	76
Andrew Frew	Halifax	2003	17	5	0	0	20
	Wakefield	2002	21	8	0	0	32
	Huddersfield	2001	26	15	0	0	60
Dale Fritz	Castleford	1999-2003	120(4)	9	0	0	36
Gareth Frodsham	St Helens	2008-09	1(9)	0	0	0	0
Liam Fulton	Huddersfield	2009	12(3)	4	0	0	16
David Furner	Leeds	2003-04	45	8	23	0	78
	Wigan	2001-02	51(2)	21	13	0	110
David Furness	Castleford	1996	(1)	0	0	0	0
Matt Gafa	Harlequins	2006-09	81	26	16	0	136
Luke Gale	Bradford	2012-14	56(2)	13	108	4	272
	Harlequins	2009-11	56(12)	18	86	3	247
Ben Galea	Hull	2013	12(2)	3	0	0	12
	Hull KR	2008-12	115(2)	33	0	0	132
Danny Galea	Widnes	2014	21(1)	2	0	0	8
Tommy Gallagher	Hull KR	2007	1(7)	0	0	0	0
	Widnes	2004	(6)	0	0	0	0
	London	2003	1(9)	1	0	0	4
Mark Gamson	Sheffield	1996	3	0	0	0	0
Jim Gannon	Hull KR	2007	7(16)	1	0	0	4
	Huddersfield	2003-06	79(14)	11	0	0	44
	Halifax	1999-2002	83(4)	14	0	0	56
Steve Garces	Salford	2001	(1)	0	0	0	0
Benjamin Garcia	Catalans	2013-14	(22)	2	0	0	8
Jean-Marc Garcia	Sheffield	1996-97	35(3)	22	0	0	88
Ade Gardner	Hull KR	2014	18	7	0	0	28
	St Helens	2002-13	236(12)	146	0	0	584
Matt Gardner	Harlequins	2009	6(3)	2	0	0	8
	Huddersfield	2006-07	22(3)	7	0	0	28
	Castleford	2004	1	1	0	0	4
Steve Gartland	Oldham	1996	1(1)	0	1	0	2
Daniel Gartner	Bradford	2001-03	74(1)	26	0	0	104
Dean Gaskell	Warrington	2002-05	58(1)	10	0	0	40
Lee Gaskell	Bradford	2014	21	5	0	0	20
	Salford	2013	17	8	0	2	36
	St Helens	2010-13	33(9)	14	12	1	81
George Gatis	Huddersfield	2008	5(5)	1	0	0	4
Richard Gay	Castleford	1996-2002	94(16)	39	0	0	156
Andrew Gee	Warrington	2000-01	33(1)	4	0	0	16
Anthony Gelling	Wigan	2012-14	43	26	0	0	104
Stanley Gene	Hull KR	2007-09	37(17)	9	0	0	36
	Bradford	2006	5(16)	8	0	0	32
	Huddersfield	2001, 2003-05	70(6)	27	0	0	108
	Hull	2000-01	5(23)	6	0	0	24
Steve Georgallis	Warrington	2001	5(1)	2	0	0	8
Luke George	Bradford	2014	9(1)	3	0	0	12
	Huddersfield	2012-13	28(2)	18	0	0	72
	Hull KR	2013	4	2	0	0	8
	Wakefield	2007-11	38(3)	24	0	0	96
Shaun Geritas	Warrington	1997	(5)	1	0	0	4
Alex Gerrard	Widnes	2012-14	24(19)	2	0	0	8
Anthony Gibbons	Leeds	1996	9(4)	2	0	1	9
David Gibbons	Leeds	1996	3(4)	2	0	0	8
Scott Gibbs	St Helens	1996	9	3	0	0	12
Ashley Gibson	Castleford	2014	6	1	0	0	4
	Salford	2010-13	77(4)	41	0	0	164
	Leeds	2005-09	25(7)	13	9	0	70
Damian Gibson	Castleford	2003-04	40(3)	5	0	0	20
	Salford	2002	28	3	0	0	12
	Halifax	1998-2001	104(1)	39	0	0	156
	Leeds	1997	18	3	0	0	12
Matt Gidley	St Helens	2007-10	105	40	6	0	172
Tony Gigot	London	2014	2	0	4	0	8
	Catalans	2010-11	9(13)	0	3	0	6
Ian Gildart	Oldham	1996-97	31(7)	0	0	0	0
Chris Giles	Widnes	2003-04	35	12	0	0	48
	St Helens	2002	(1)	0	0	0	0
Peter Gill	London	1996-99	75(6)	20	0	0	80
Carl Gillespie	Halifax	1996-99	47(36)	13	0	0	52
Michael Gillett	London	2001-02	23(21)	12	2	0	52
Simon Gillies	Warrington	1999	28	6	0	0	24
Tom Gilmore	Widnes	2012-14	7(1)	2	1	1	11
Lee Gilmour	Wakefield	2014	10(3)	2	0	0	8
	Castleford	2013	10(2)	0	0	0	0
	Huddersfield	2010-12	71(1)	17	0	0	68
	St Helens	2004-09	149(3)	41	0	0	164
	Bradford	2001-03	44(31)	20	0	0	80
	Wigan	1997-2000	44(39)	22	0	0	88
Marc Glanville	Leeds	1998-99	43(3)	5	0	0	20
Eddie Glaze	Castleford	1996	1	0	0	0	0
Paul Gleadhill	Leeds	1996	4	0	0	0	0
Ben Gledhill	Salford	2012-13	3(10)	1	0	0	4
	Wakefield	2010-11	(16)	0	0	0	0
Mark Gleeson	Warrington	2000-08	38(102)	12	0	0	48
Martin Gleeson	Salford	2013-14	26(1)	4	0	0	16
	Hull	2011	6	4	0	0	16
	Wigan	2009-11	46(1)	19	0	0	76
	Warrington	2005-09	110(1)	44	0	0	176
	St Helens	2002-04	56(1)	25	0	0	100
	Huddersfield	1999-2001	47(9)	18	0	0	72
Sean Gleeson	Hull KR	2013	6	0	0	0	0
	Salford	2011-12	35	14	0	0	56
	Wakefield	2007-10	67(6)	20	0	0	80
	Wigan	2005-06	3(3)	0	0	0	0
Jon Goddard	Hull KR	2007	20	2	0	0	8
	Castleford	2000-01	(2)	0	0	0	0
Richard Goddard	Castleford	1996-97	11(3)	2	10	0	28
Brad Godden	Leeds	1998-99	47	15	0	0	60
Pita Godinet	Wakefield	2014	12(10)	6	0	0	24
Wayne Godwin	Salford	2011-13	41(8)	6	0	0	24
	Bradford	2008-10	16(44)	9	0	0	36
	Hull	2007	3(13)	1	0	0	4
	Wigan	2005-06	9(38)	6	0	0	24
	Castleford	2001-04	30(33)	18	56	0	184
Jason Golden	London	2012	7(2)	1	0	0	4
	Harlequins	2009-11	34(12)	3	0	0	12
	Wakefield	2007-08	26(5)	1	0	0	4
Marvin Golden	Widnes	2003	4	1	0	0	4
	London	2001	17(2)	1	0	0	4
	Halifax	2000	20(2)	5	0	0	20
	Leeds	1996-99	43(11)	19	0	0	76
Ashton Golding	Leeds	2014	(1)	0	0	0	0
Brett Goldspink	Halifax	2000-02	64(5)	2	0	0	8
	Wigan	1999	6(16)	1	0	0	4
	St Helens	1998	19(4)	2	0	0	8
	Oldham	1997	13(2)	0	0	0	0
Lee Gomersall	Hull KR	2008	1	0	0	0	0
Luke Goodwin	London	1998	9(2)	3	1	1	15
	Oldham	1997	16(4)	10	17	2	76
Grant Gore	Widnes	2012-14	3(10)	1	0	0	4
Aaron Gorrell	Catalans	2007-08	23	6	14	0	52
Andy Gorski	Salford	2001-02	(2)	0	0	0	0
Cyrille Gossard	Catalans	2006-12	54(30)	5	0	0	20
Bobbie Goulding	Salford	2001-02	31(1)	2	56	4	124
	Wakefield	2000	12	3	25	3	65
	Huddersfield	1998-99	27(1)	3	65	4	146
	St Helens	1996-98	42(2)	9	210	4	460
Bobbie Goulding (Jnr)							
	Wakefield	2013	1(2)	0	1	0	2

Super League Players 1996-2014

PLAYER	CLUB	YEAR	APP	TRIES	GOALS	FG	PTS
Darrell Goulding	Wigan	2005-14	129(24)	68	0	0	272
	Salford	2009	9	5	0	0	20
Mick Govin	Leigh	2005	5(6)	4	0	0	16
Craig Gower	London	2012-14	40	7	24	0	76
David Gower	Salford	2006-07	(16)	0	0	0	0
Shane Grady	London	2013	5(4)	1	2	0	8
James Graham	St Helens	2003-11	132(63)	47	0	0	188
Nathan Graham	Bradford	1996-98	17(28)	4	0	1	17
Nick Graham	Wigan	2003	13(1)	2	0	0	8
Dalton Grant	Crusaders	2011	(1)	0	0	0	0
Jon Grayshon	Harlequins	2007-09	10(32)	4	0	0	16
	Huddersfield	2003-06	7(43)	5	0	0	20
Blake Green	Wigan	2013-14	42(1)	15	0	0	60
	Hull KR	2011-12	35	14	0	0	56
Brett Green	Gateshead	1999	10(2)	0	0	0	0
Chris Green	Hull	2012-14	12(27)	4	0	0	16
James Green	Hull KR	2012-14	2(31)	1	0	0	4
Toby Green	Huddersfield	2001	3(1)	1	0	0	4
Craig Greenhill	Castleford	2004	21(4)	1	0	0	4
	Hull	2002-03	56	3	2	0	16
Clint Greenshields							
	Catalans	2007-12	137	81	0	0	324
Brandon Greenwood							
	Halifax	1996	1	0	0	0	0
Gareth Greenwood							
	Huddersfield	2003	(1)	0	0	0	0
	Halifax	2002	1	0	0	0	0
James Greenwood							
	London	2014	10(5)	3	0	0	12
	Wigan	2013	(1)	0	0	0	0
Joe Greenwood	St Helens	2012-14	4(21)	5	0	0	20
Lee Greenwood	Huddersfield	2005	7	3	0	0	12
	London	2004-05	30(2)	19	0	0	76
	Halifax	2000-03	38(2)	17	0	0	68
	Sheffield	1999	1(1)	0	0	0	0
James Grehan	Castleford	2012	2(2)	0	0	0	0
Maxime Greseque							
	Wakefield	2007	2(1)	0	0	0	0
Mathieu Griffi	Catalans	2006-08	1(25)	0	0	0	0
Darrell Griffin	Salford	2013-14	29(11)	1	0	0	4
	Leeds	2012	8(19)	2	0	0	8
	Huddersfield	2007-11	65(60)	13	0	0	52
	Wakefield	2003-06	55(37)	9	3	0	42
George Griffin	London	2014	(19)	1	0	0	4
	Hull KR	2012-13	11(7)	0	0	0	0
Josh Griffin	Salford	2014	8	8	27	0	86
	Castleford	2012	20	13	1	0	54
	Wakefield	2011	17	5	21	0	62
	Huddersfield	2009	2	0	0	0	0
Jonathan Griffiths							
	Paris	1996	(4)	1	0	0	4
Andrew Grima	Workington	1996	2(9)	2	0	0	8
Tony Grimaldi	Hull	2000-01	56(1)	14	0	0	56
	Gateshead	1999	27(2)	10	0	0	40
Danny Grimley	Sheffield	1996	4(1)	1	0	0	4
Scott Grix	Huddersfield	2010-14	109(11)	46	32	0	248
	Wakefield	2008-09	39(3)	18	0	0	72
Simon Grix	Warrington	2006-14	133(25)	42	0	0	168
	Halifax	2003	2(4)	0	0	0	0
Brett Grogan	Gateshead	1999	14(7)	3	0	0	12
Brent Grose	Warrington	2003-07	134(1)	55	0	0	220
David Guasch	Catalans	2010	1	0	0	0	0
Joan Guasch	Catalans	2014	(4)	0	0	0	0
Renaud Guigue	Catalans	2006	14(4)	3	0	0	12
Jerome Guisset	Catalans	2006-10	102(23)	9	0	0	36
	Wigan	2005	20(2)	3	0	0	12
	Warrington	2000-04	59(65)	21	0	0	84
Awen Guttenbeil	Castleford	2008	19	0	0	0	0
Reece Guy	Oldham	1996	3(4)	0	0	0	0
Josh Guzdek	Hull KR	2013	1	1	0	0	4
Tom Haberecht	Castleford	2008	2(2)	1	0	0	4
Dean Hadley	Hull	2013-14	10(6)	3	0	0	12
Gareth Haggerty	Harlequins	2008-09	8(28)	6	0	0	24
	Salford	2004-07	1(93)	15	0	0	60
	Widnes	2002	1(2)	1	0	0	4
Kurt Haggerty	Widnes	2012	6(8)	2	0	0	8
Andy Haigh	St Helens	1996-98	20(16)	11	0	0	44
Scott Hale	St Helens	2011	(3)	1	0	0	4
Michael Haley	Leeds	2008	(1)	0	0	0	0
Carl Hall	Leeds	1996	7(2)	3	0	0	12
Craig Hall	Hull KR	2011-14	74(3)	38	41	2	236
	Hull	2007-10	59(9)	39	11	0	178
Glenn Hall	Bradford	2010	7(18)	2	0	0	8
Martin Hall	Halifax	1998	2(10)	0	0	0	0
	Hull	1999	7	0	0	0	0
	Castleford	1998	4	0	0	0	0
	Wigan	1996-97	31(5)	7	6	0	40
Ryan Hall	Leeds	2007-14	191(2)	153	0	0	612
Steve Hall	Widnes	2004	1	0	0	0	0
	London	2002-03	35(3)	10	0	0	40
	St Helens	1999-2001	36(22)	19	0	0	76
Graeme Hallas	Huddersfield	2001	1	0	0	0	0
	Hull	1998-99	30(10)	6	39	1	103
	Halifax	1996	11(4)	5	0	0	20
Macauley Hallett	Hull KR	2014	2	3	0	0	12
Dave Halley	Bradford	2007-10	63(12)	20	0	0	80
	Wakefield	2009	5	4	0	0	16
Danny Halliwell	Salford	2007	2(3)	0	0	0	0
	Leigh	2005	5	3	0	0	12
	Halifax	2000-03	17(8)	4	0	0	16
	Warrington	2002	9(1)	8	0	0	32
	Wakefield	2002	3	0	0	0	0
Colum Halpenny	Wakefield	2003-06	103(1)	36	0	0	144
	Halifax	2002	22	12	0	0	48
Jon Hamer	Bradford	1996	1	0	0	0	0
Andrew Hamilton	London	1997, 2003	1(20)	3	0	0	12
John Hamilton	St Helens	1998	3	0	0	0	0
Karle Hammond	Halifax	2002	10(2)	2	14	0	36
	Salford	2001	2(3)	1	0	0	4
	London	1999-2000	47	23	2	3	99
	St Helens	1996-98	58(8)	28	0	4	116
Ryan Hampshire	Wigan	2013-14	8(3)	4	12	0	40
Rhys Hanbury	Widnes	2012-14	72	46	34	1	253
	Crusaders	2010-11	26(1)	14	0	0	56
Anthony Hancock	Paris	1997	8(6)	1	0	0	4
Michael Hancock	Salford	2001-02	12(24)	7	0	0	28
Jordan Hand	St Helens	2013-14	(3)	0	0	0	0
Gareth Handford	Castleford	2001	7(2)	0	0	0	0
	Bradford	2000	1(1)	0	0	0	0
Paul Handforth	Castleford	2006	2(15)	2	1	0	10
	Wakefield	2000-04	17(44)	10	13	0	66
Ash Handley	Leeds	2014	1	0	0	0	0
Paddy Handley	Leeds	1996	1(1)	2	0	0	8
Dean Hanger	Warrington	1999	7(11)	3	0	0	12
	Huddersfield	1998	20(1)	5	0	0	20
Josh Hannay	Celtic	2009	17	2	24	0	56
Harrison Hansen	Salford	2014	21	5	0	0	20
	Wigan	2004-13	155(62)	39	0	0	156
Lee Hansen	Wigan	1997	10(5)	0	0	0	0
Shontayne Hape	Bradford	2003-08	123(2)	79	0	0	316
Lionel Harbin	Wakefield	2001	(1)	0	0	0	0
Zak Hardaker	Leeds	2011-14	92	45	30	0	240
Ian Hardman	Hull KR	2007	18	4	0	0	16
	St Helens	2003-07	32(11)	9	5	0	46
Jeff Hardy	Hudds-Sheff	2000	20(5)	6	0	1	25
	Sheffield	1999	22(4)	7	0	0	28
Spencer Hargrave							
	Castleford	1996-99	(6)	0	0	0	0
Bryn Hargreaves	Bradford	2011-12	45(5)	1	0	0	4
	St Helens	2007-10	53(44)	7	0	0	28
	Wigan	2004-06	16(12)	1	0	0	4
Lee Harland	Castleford	1996-2004	148(35)	20	0	0	80
Neil Harmon	Bradford	2003	13(3)	0	0	0	0
	Salford	2001	6(5)	0	0	0	0
	Bradford	1998-2000	15(13)	2	0	0	8
	Huddersfield	1998	12	1	0	0	4
	Leeds	1996	10	1	0	0	4
Ben Harris	Bradford	2005-07	70(4)	24	0	0	96
Iestyn Harris	Bradford	2004-08	109(11)	35	87	2	316
	Leeds	1997-2001	111(7)	57	490	6	1214
	Warrington	1996	16	4	63	2	144
Ben Harrison	Warrington	2007-14	107(52)	12	0	0	48
Karl Harrison	Hull	1999	26	2	0	0	8
	Halifax	1996-98	60(2)	2	0	0	8
Andrew Hart	London	2004	12(1)	2	0	0	8
Tim Hartley	Harlequins	2006	2	1	0	0	4
	Salford	2004-05	6(7)	5	0	0	20
Carlos Hassan	Bradford	1996	6(4)	2	0	0	8
Phil Hassan	Wakefield	2002	9(1)	0	0	0	0
	Halifax	2000-01	25(4)	3	0	0	12
	Salford	1998	15	2	0	0	8
	Leeds	1996-97	38(4)	12	0	0	48
Tom Haughey	Castleford	2006	1(3)	1	0	0	4
	London	2003-04	10(8)	1	0	0	4
	Wakefield	2001-02	5(11)	0	0	0	0
Simon Haughton	Wigan	1996-2002	63(46)	32	0	0	128
Solomon Haumono							
	Harlequins	2006	10(9)	6	0	0	24
	London	2005	24(5)	8	0	0	32
Weller Hauraki	Castleford	2013-14	50(2)	9	0	0	36
	Leeds	2011-12	8(17)	6	0	0	24
	Crusaders	2010	26(1)	11	0	0	44
Richie Hawkyard	Bradford	2007	1(2)	1	0	0	4
Andy Hay	Widnes	2003-04	50(2)	7	0	0	28
	Leeds	1997-2002	112(27)	43	0	0	172
	Sheffield	1996-97	17(3)	5	0	0	20
Adam Hayes	Hudds-Sheff	2000	2(1)	0	0	0	0
Joey Hayes	Salford	1999	9	2	0	0	8
	St Helens	1996-98	11(6)	7	0	0	28
James Haynes	Hull KR	2009	1	0	0	0	0
Mathew Head	Hull	2007	9(1)	1	0	1	5
Mitch Healey	Castleford	2001-03	68(1)	10	16	0	72
Daniel Heckenberg							
	Harlequins	2006-09	31(39)	4	0	0	16
Chris Heil	Hull KR	2012-13	4	2	0	0	8
Ricky Helliwell	Salford	1997-99	(2)	0	0	0	0
Tom Hemingway	Huddersfield	2005-09	7(7)	1	17	0	38
Bryan Henare	St Helens	2000-01	4(12)	1	0	0	4

PLAYER	CLUB	YEAR	APP	TRIES	GOALS	FG	PTS
Richard Henare	Warrington	1996-97	28(2)	24	0	0	96
Andrew Henderson							
	Castleford	2006, 2008	44(11)	4	0	0	16
Ian Henderson	Catalans	2011-14	91(8)	10	0	0	40
	Bradford	2005-07	33(37)	13	0	0	52
Kevin Henderson	Wakefield	2005-11	52(68)	9	0	0	36
	Leigh	2005	(1)	0	0	0	0
Adam Henry	Bradford	2014	23(1)	5	0	0	20
Mark Henry	Salford	2009-11	67	22	0	0	88
Brad Hepi	Castleford	1999, 2001	9(21)	3	0	0	12
	Salford	2000	3(5)	0	0	0	0
	Hull	1998	15(1)	3	0	0	12
Tyla Hepi	Hull KR	2013	(4)	0	0	0	0
Jon Hepworth	Castleford	2003-04	19(23)	7	8	0	44
	Leeds	2003	(1)	0	0	0	0
	London	2002	(2)	0	0	0	0
Marc Herbert	Bradford	2011	20	4	2	0	20
Aaron Heremaia	Hull	2012-14	27(37)	12	0	0	48
Maxime Herold	London	2014	(2)	0	0	0	0
Ian Herron	Hull	2000	9	1	17	0	38
	Gateshead	1999	25	4	105	0	226
Jason Hetherington							
	London	2001-02	37	9	0	0	36
Gareth Hewitt	Salford	1999	2(1)	0	0	0	0
Andrew Hick	Hull	2000	9(9)	1	0	0	4
	Gateshead	1999	12(5)	2	0	0	8
Jarrad Hickey	Wakefield	2011	(8)	2	0	0	8
Chris Hicks	Warrington	2008-10	72	56	119	0	462
Paul Hicks	Wakefield	1999	(1)	0	0	0	0
Darren Higgins	London	1998	5(6)	2	0	0	8
Iain Higgins	London	1997-98	1(7)	2	0	0	8
Liam Higgins	Wakefield	2011	4(12)	0	0	0	0
	Castleford	2008-10	42(32)	2	0	0	8
	Hull	2003-06	1(34)	0	0	0	0
Mick Higham	Warrington	2009-14	66(71)	32	0	0	128
	Wigan	2006-08	61(28)	13	0	0	52
	St Helens	2001-05	43(56)	32	0	0	128
Chris Highton	Warrington	1997	1(1)	0	0	0	0
David Highton	London	2004-05	21(24)	2	0	0	8
	Salford	2002	4(5)	2	0	0	8
	Warrington	1998-2001	18(14)	2	0	0	8
Paul Highton	Salford	1998-2002,					
		2004-07	114(80)	14	0	0	56
	Halifax	1996-97	12(18)	2	0	0	8
Andy Hill	Huddersfield	1999	(4)	0	0	0	0
	Castleford	1999	4(4)	0	0	0	0
Chris Hill	Warrington	2012-14	77(9)	12	0	0	48
	Leigh	2005	(1)	0	0	0	0
Danny Hill	Wigan	2006-07	1(10)	0	0	0	0
	Hull KR	2007	2	0	0	0	0
	Hull	2004-06	4(6)	0	0	0	0
Howard Hill	Oldham	1996-97	22(12)	4	0	0	16
John Hill	St Helens	2003	(1)	0	0	0	0
	Halifax	2003	1(2)	0	0	0	0
	Warrington	2001-02	(4)	0	0	0	0
Scott Hill	Harlequins	2007-08	41(2)	13	0	0	52
Mark Hilton	Warrington	1996-2000,					
		2002-06	141(40)	7	0	0	28
Ian Hindmarsh	Catalans	2006	25	3	0	0	12
Brendan Hlad	Castleford	2008	(3)	0	0	0	0
Andy Hobson	Widnes	2004	5(13)	0	0	0	0
	Halifax	1998-2003	51(85)	8	0	0	32
Gareth Hock	Salford	2014	13(1)	4	0	0	16
	Widnes	2013	15(2)	9	1	0	38
	Wigan	2003-09,					
		2011-12	126(43)	38	0	0	152
Tommy Hodgkinson							
	St Helens	2006	(1)	0	0	0	0
Andy Hodgson	Wakefield	1999	14(2)	2	1	0	10
	Bradford	1997-98	8(2)	4	0	0	16
Brett Hodgson	Warrington	2011-13	66	33	268	1	669
	Huddersfield	2009-10	45	13	166	0	384
David Hodgson	Hull KR	2012-14	51	31	0	0	124
	Huddersfield	2008-11	84	59	0	0	236
	Salford	2005-07	81	30	47	0	214
	Wigan	2000-04	90(19)	43	0	0	172
	Halifax	1999	10(3)	5	0	0	20
Elliot Hodgson	Huddersfield	2009	1	0	0	0	0
Josh Hodgson	Hull KR	2010-14	98(29)	35	0	0	140
	Hull	2009	(2)	0	0	0	0
Ryan Hoffman	Wigan	2011	28(1)	11	0	0	44
Darren Hogg	Wigan	1996	(1)	0	0	0	0
Michael Hogue	Paris	1997	5(7)	0	0	0	0
Lance Hohaia	St Helens	2012-14	61(7)	19	0	1	77
Chris Holden	Warrington	1996-97	2(1)	0	0	0	0
Daniel Holdsworth							
	Hull	2013	19	2	28	2	66
	Salford	2010-12	71	18	183	1	439
Stephen Holgate	Halifax	2000	1(10)	0	0	0	0
	Hull	1999	1	0	0	0	0
	Wigan	1997-98	11(26)	2	0	0	8
	Workington	1996	19	3	0	0	12
Martyn Holland	Wakefield	2000-03	52(3)	6	0	0	24
Oliver Holmes	Castleford	2010-14	73(19)	12	0	0	48

PLAYER	CLUB	YEAR	APP	TRIES	GOALS	FG	PTS
Tim Holmes	Widnes	2004-05	15(4)	0	0	0	0
Graham Holroyd	Huddersfield	2003	3(5)	0	0	0	0
	Salford	2000-02	40(11)	8	75	5	187
	Halifax	1999	24(2)	3	74	5	165
	Leeds	1996-98	40(26)	22	101	8	298
Dallas Hood	Wakefield	2003-04	18(9)	1	0	0	4
Liam Hood	Leeds	2012	1(4)	3	0	0	12
Jason Hooper	St Helens	2003-07	89(6)	35	30	0	200
Will Hope	Salford	2013	1(2)	0	0	0	0
Lee Hopkins	Harlequins	2006-07	44(3)	11	0	0	44
	London	2005	29	6	0	0	24
Sean Hoppe	St Helens	1999-2002	69(16)	32	0	0	128
Graeme Horne	Hull KR	2012-14	52(14)	14	0	0	56
	Huddersfield	2010-11	23(17)	11	0	0	44
	Hull	2003-09	49(74)	24	0	0	96
Richard Horne	Hull	1999-2014	341(16)	115	12	6	490
John Hough	Warrington	1996-97	9	2	0	0	8
Danny Houghton	Hull	2007-14	140(46)	25	0	0	100
Sylvain Houles	Wakefield	2003, 2005	8(1)	1	0	0	4
	London	2001-02	17(10)	11	0	0	44
	Hudds-Sheff	2000	5(2)	1	0	0	4
Harvey Howard	Wigan	2001-02	25(27)	1	0	0	4
	Bradford	1998	4(2)	1	0	0	4
	Leeds	1996	8	0	0	0	0
Kim Howard	London	1997	4(5)	0	0	0	0
Stuart Howarth	Salford	2012-14	25(12)	1	0	0	4
	St Helens	2013	14(1)	0	0	0	0
	Wakefield	2011	17(2)	1	0	0	4
Stuart Howarth	Workington	1996	(2)	0	0	0	0
David Howell	London	2012-13	24	5	0	0	20
	Harlequins	2008-11	76	26	0	0	104
Phil Howlett	Bradford	1999	5(1)	2	0	0	8
Craig Huby	Castleford	2003-04,					
		2006,					
		2008-14	130(57)	27	41	0	190
Ryan Hudson	Castleford	2002-04,					
		2009-12	138(12)	31	0	0	124
	Huddersfield	1998-99,					
		2007-08	51(22)	10	0	0	40
	Wakefield	2000-01	42(9)	11	0	1	45
Adam Hughes	Widnes	2002-05	89(2)	45	51	0	282
	Halifax	2001	8(8)	8	0	0	32
	Wakefield	1999-2000	43(3)	21	34	0	152
	Leeds	1996-97	4(5)	4	0	0	16
Ian Hughes	Sheffield	1996	9(8)	4	0	0	16
Jack Hughes	Wigan	2011-14	31(33)	9	0	0	36
Mark Hughes	Catalans	2006	23	9	0	0	36
Steffan Hughes	London	1999-2001	1(13)	1	0	0	4
David Hulme	Salford	1997-99	53(1)	5	0	0	20
	Leeds	1996	8(1)	2	0	0	8
Declan Hulme	Widnes	2013-14	3	2	0	0	8
Paul Hulme	Warrington	1996-97	23(1)	2	0	0	8
Gary Hulse	Widnes	2005	12(5)	2	0	0	8
	Warrington	2001-04	20(28)	8	0	1	33
Alan Hunte	Salford	2002	19(2)	9	0	0	36
	Warrington	1999-2001	83	49	0	0	196
	Hull	1998	21	7	0	0	28
	St Helens	1996-97	30(2)	28	0	0	112
Alex Hurst	London	2013	8(2)	2	0	0	8
Kieran Hyde	Wakefield	2010-11	11	4	4	0	24
Nick Hyde	Paris	1997	5(5)	1	0	0	4
Chaz I'Anson	Hull KR	2007-10	17(13)	3	0	0	12
Andy Ireland	Hull	1998-99	22(15)	0	0	0	0
	Bradford	1996	1	0	0	0	0
Kevin Iro	St Helens	1999-2001	76	39	0	0	156
	Leeds	1996	16	9	0	0	36
Willie Isa	Widnes	2012-14	36(26)	3	0	0	12
	Castleford	2011	7(2)	6	0	0	24
Andrew Isherwood							
	Wigan	1998-99	(5)	0	0	0	0
Olu Iwenofu	London	2000-01	2(1)	0	0	0	0
Chico Jackson	Hull	1999	(4)	0	0	0	0
Lee Jackson	Hull	2001-02	37(9)	12	1	0	50
	Leeds	1999-2000	28(24)	7	0	0	28
Michael Jackson	Sheffield	1998-99	17(17)	2	0	0	8
	Halifax	1996-97	27(6)	11	0	0	44
Paul Jackson	Castleford	2003-04,					
		2010-12	44(30)	5	0	0	20
	Huddersfield	1998,					
		2005-09	50(73)	4	0	0	16
	Wakefield	1999-2002	57(42)	2	0	0	8
Rob Jackson	Leigh	2005	20(3)	5	0	0	20
	London	2002-04	26(14)	9	0	0	36
Wayne Jackson	Halifax	1996-97	17(5)	2	0	0	8
Aled James	Crusaders	2011	1	0	0	0	0
	Celtic	2009	3(3)	0	0	0	0
	Widnes	2003	3	0	0	0	0
Andy James	Halifax	1996	(4)	0	0	0	0
Jordan James	Wigan	2006, 2014	3(18)	4	0	0	16
	Salford	2012-13	1(40)	6	0	0	24
	Crusaders	2010-11	5(24)	3	0	0	12
	Celtic	2009	17(4)	1	0	0	4
Matt James	Wakefield	2012	(4)	0	0	0	0
	Harlequins	2010	(2)	0	0	0	0
	Bradford	2006-09	1(23)	0	0	0	0

Super League Players 1996-2014

PLAYER	CLUB	YEAR	APP	TRIES	GOALS	FG	PTS
Pascal Jampy	Catalans	2006	4(7)	0	0	0	0
	Paris	1996-97	3(2)	0	0	0	0
Adam Janowski	Harlequins	2008	(1)	0	0	0	0
Ben Jeffries	Bradford	2008-09,					
		2011-12	76(3)	20	0	0	80
	Wakefield	2003-07,					
		2010-11	151(10)	70	20	6	326
Mick Jenkins	Hull	2000	24	2	0	0	8
	Gateshead	1999	16	3	0	0	12
Ed Jennings	London	1998-99	1(2)	0	0	0	0
Rod Jensen	Huddersfield	2007-08	26(3)	13	0	0	52
Anthony Jerram	Warrington	2007	(2)	0	0	0	0
Lee Jewitt	Castleford	2014	7(6)	0	0	0	0
	Salford	2007,					
		2009-13	32(62)	4	0	0	16
	Wigan	2005	(2)	0	0	0	0
Isaac John	Wakefield	2012	13	1	19	0	42
Andrew Johns	Warrington	2005	3	1	12	1	29
Matthew Johns	Wigan	2001	24	3	0	1	13
Andy Johnson	Salford	2004-05	8(26)	7	0	0	28
	Castleford	2002-03	32(16)	11	0	0	44
	London	2000-01	24(21)	12	0	0	48
	Huddersfield	1999	5	1	0	0	4
	Wigan	1996-99	24(20)	19	0	0	76
Bruce Johnson	Widnes	2004-05	(4)	0	0	0	0
Dallas Johnson	Catalans	2010	26	1	0	0	4
Greg Johnson	Salford	2014	20	10	0	0	40
	Wakefield	2011	12	2	0	0	8
Jason Johnson	St Helens	1997-99	2	0	0	0	0
Josh Johnson	Huddersfield	2013-14	6(6)	0	0	0	0
Mark Johnson	Salford	1999-2000	22(9)	16	0	0	64
	Hull	1998	10(1)	4	0	0	16
	Workington	1996	12	4	0	0	16
Nick Johnson	Hull KR	2012	1	0	0	0	0
Nick Johnson	London	2003	(1)	0	0	0	0
Paul Johnson	Crusaders	2011	6(4)	0	0	0	0
	Wakefield	2010	12(3)	4	0	0	16
	Warrington	2007-09	37(9)	17	0	0	68
	Bradford	2004-06	46(8)	19	0	0	76
	Wigan	1996-2003	74(46)	54	0	0	216
Paul Johnson	Widnes	2014	5(11)	0	0	0	0
	Hull	2013	3(16)	0	0	0	0
	Wakefield	2011-12	25(21)	6	0	0	24
	St Helens	2010	(2)	0	0	0	0
Richard Johnson	Bradford	2008	(2)	0	0	0	0
Ben Johnston	Castleford	2012	2	0	0	0	0
Ben Jones	Harlequins	2010	(2)	0	0	0	0
Chris Jones	Leigh	2005	1(1)	0	0	0	0
Danny Jones	Halifax	2003	1	0	0	0	0
David Jones	Oldham	1997	14(1)	5	0	0	20
Josh Jones	St Helens	2012-14	65(6)	18	0	0	72
Mark Jones	Warrington	1996	8(11)	2	0	0	8
Phil Jones	Leigh	2005	16	8	31	0	94
	Wigan	1999-2001	14(7)	6	25	0	74
Stacey Jones	Catalans	2006-07	39	11	43	3	133
Stephen Jones	Huddersfield	2005	(1)	0	0	0	0
Stuart Jones	Castleford	2009-12	69(27)	14	0	0	56
	Huddersfield	2004-08	96(22)	17	0	0	68
	St Helens	2003	(18)	2	0	0	8
	Wigan	2002	5(3)	1	0	0	4
Ben Jones-Bishop							
	Leeds	2008-09,					
		2011-14	70(2)	46	0	0	184
	Harlequins	2010	17	10	0	0	40
Jamie Jones-Buchanan							
	Leeds	1999-2014	226(62)	61	0	0	244
Tim Jonkers	Wigan	2006	3(1)	0	0	0	0
	Salford	2004-06	5(11)	0	0	0	0
	St Helens	1999-2004	41(64)	12	0	0	48
Darren Jordan	Wakefield	2003	(1)	0	0	0	0
Phil Joseph	Widnes	2013-14	10(30)	1	0	0	4
	Bradford	2012	(6)	0	0	0	0
	Huddersfield	2004	7(6)	0	0	0	0
Max Jowitt	Wakefield	2014	1	0	0	0	0
Warren Jowitt	Hull	2003	(2)	0	0	0	0
	Salford	2001-02	17(4)	2	0	0	8
	Wakefield	2000	19(3)	8	0	0	32
	Bradford	1996-99	13(25)	5	0	0	20
Chris Joynt	St Helens	1996-2004	201(14)	68	0	0	272
Gregory Kacala	Paris	1996	7	1	0	0	4
Andy Kain	Castleford	2004, 2006	9(7)	3	10	0	32
Antonio Kaufusi	Huddersfield	2014	15(2)	1	0	0	4
	Bradford	2014	4	0	0	0	0
	London	2012-13	44(5)	5	0	0	20
Mal Kaufusi	London	2004	1(3)	0	0	0	0
Ben Kavanagh	Widnes	2012-14	16(29)	0	0	0	0
Liam Kay	Wakefield	2012-13	4	4	0	0	16
Ben Kaye	Harlequins	2009-10	2(13)	0	0	0	0
	Leeds	2008	2(2)	1	0	0	4
Elliot Kear	Bradford	2012-14	53(2)	17	0	0	68
	Crusaders	2010-11	16(1)	4	0	0	16
	Celtic	2009	3	0	0	0	0
Brett Kearney	Bradford	2010-14	107	55	0	0	220
Stephen Kearney	Hull	2005	22(2)	5	0	0	20
Damon Keating	Wakefield	2002	7(17)	1	0	0	4
Kris Keating	Hull KR	2014	23	5	0	0	20
Shaun Keating	London	1996	1(3)	0	0	0	0
Mark Keenan	Workington	1996	3(4)	1	0	0	4
Jimmy Keinhorst	Leeds	2012-14	9(6)	6	0	0	24
	Wakefield	2014	7	1	0	0	4
Tony Kemp	Wakefield	1999-2000	15(5)	2	0	1	9
	Leeds	1996-98	23(2)	5	0	2	22
Damien Kennedy	London	2003	5(11)	1	0	0	4
Ian Kenny	St Helens	2004	(1)	0	0	0	0
Jason Kent	Leigh	2005	23	1	0	0	4
Liam Kent	Hull	2012-13	1(5)	0	0	0	0
Shane Kenward	Wakefield	1999	28	6	0	0	24
	Salford	1998	1	0	0	0	0
Jason Keough	Paris	1997	2	1	0	0	4
Keiran Kerr	Widnes	2005	6	2	0	0	8
Martin Ketteridge	Halifax	1996	7(5)	0	0	0	0
Ronnie Kettlewell	Warrington	1996	(1)	0	0	0	0
Joe Keyes	London	2014	7	5	0	0	20
Younes Khattabi	Catalans	2006-08	24(4)	10	0	0	40
David Kidwell	Warrington	2001-02	14(12)	9	0	0	36
Andrew King	London	2003	23(1)	15	0	0	60
Dave King	Huddersfield	1998-99	11(17)	2	0	0	8
George King	Warrington	2014	(2)	0	0	0	0
James King	Leigh	2005	5(7)	0	0	0	0
Kevin King	Wakefield	2005	8(1)	2	0	0	8
	Castleford	2004	(1)	0	0	0	0
Matt King	Warrington	2008-11	91	58	0	0	232
Paul King	Wakefield	2010-11	10(19)	0		1	1
	Hull	1999-2009	136(93)	20	0	1	81
Toby King	Warrington	2014	1	0	0	0	0
Andy Kirk	Wakefield	2005	6(3)	1	0	0	4
	Salford	2004	20	5	0	0	20
	Leeds	2001-02	4(4)	0	0	0	0
Ian Kirke	Leeds	2006-14	52(132)	10	0	0	40
John Kirkpatrick	London	2004-05	18(1)	5	0	0	20
	St Helens	2001-03	10(11)	10	0	0	40
	Halifax	2003	4	1	0	0	4
Danny Kirmond	Wakefield	2010,					
		2012-14	78(4)	27	0	0	108
	Huddersfield	2008-11	18(31)	9	0	0	36
Wayne Kitchin	Workington	1996	11(6)	3	17	1	47
Sione Kite	Widnes	2012	6(8)	1	0	0	4
Ian Knott	Leigh	2005	8(1)	2	0	0	8
	Wakefield	2002-03	34(5)	7	79	0	186
	Warrington	1996-2001	68(41)	24	18	0	132
Matt Knowles	Wigan	1996	(3)	0	0	0	0
Michael Knowles	Castleford	2006	(1)	0	0	0	0
Phil Knowles	Salford	1997	1	0	0	0	0
Simon Knox	Halifax	1999	(6)	0	0	0	0
	Salford	1998	1(1)	0	0	0	0
	Bradford	1996-98	9(19)	7	0	0	28
Toa Kohe-Love	Warrington	1996-2001,					
		2005-06	166(3)	90	0	0	360
	Bradford	2004	1(1)	0	0	0	0
	Hull	2002-03	42	19	0	0	76
Paul Koloi	Wigan	1997	1(2)	1	0	0	4
Craig Kopczak	Huddersfield	2013-14	39(15)	5	0	0	20
	Bradford	2006-12	32(83)	10	0	0	40
Michael Korkidas	Wakefield	2003-06,					
		2009-11	133(36)	15	0	0	60
	Huddersfield	2009	4(1)	1	0	0	4
	Castleford	2008	15(6)	1	0	0	4
	Salford	2007	26(1)	1	0	0	4
Nick Kouparitsas	Harlequins	2011	2(13)	1	0	0	4
Olsi Krasniqi	London	2012-14	28(34)	3	0	0	12
	Harlequins	2010-11	3(20)	1	0	0	4
David Krause	London	1996-97	22(1)	7	0	0	28
Ben Kusto	Huddersfield	2001	21(4)	9	0	1	37
Anthony Laffranchi							
	St Helens	2012-14	50(18)	19	0	0	76
James Laithwaite	Warrington	2013-14	14(12)	1	0	0	4
	Hull KR	2012	1(2)	1	0	0	4
Adrian Lam	Wigan	2001-04	105(2)	40	1	9	171
Callum Lancaster	Hull	2014	5	8	0	0	32
Mark Lane	Paris	1996	(2)	0	0	0	0
Allan Langer	Warrington	2000-01	47	13	4	0	60
Kevin Langer	London	1996	12(4)	2	0	0	8
Junior Langi	Salford	2005-06	27(7)	7	0	0	28
Chris Langley	Huddersfield	2000-01	18(1)	3	0	0	12
Gareth Langley	St Helens	2006	1	1	3	0	10
Jamie Langley	Hull KR	2014	6(5)	1	0	0	4
	Bradford	2002-13	182(57)	36	0	0	144
Kevin Larroyer	Hull KR	2014	19(5)	7	0	0	28
	Catalans	2012-13	10(9)	6	0	0	24
Andy Last	Hull	1999-2005	16(10)	4	0	0	16
Sam Latus	Hull KR	2010-13	34(3)	13	0	0	52
Epalahame Lauaki							
	Wigan	2012-13	14(16)	2	0	0	8
	Hull	2009-11	3(50)	4	0	0	16
Dale Laughton	Warrington	2002	15(1)	0	0	0	0
	Huddersfield	2000-01	36(2)	4	0	0	16
	Sheffield	1996-99	48(22)	5	0	0	20

PLAYER	CLUB	YEAR	APP	TRIES	GOALS	FG	PTS
Ali Lauitiiti	Wakefield	2012-14	43(20)	15	0	0	60
	Leeds	2004-11	64(117)	58	0	0	232
Jason Laurence	Salford	1997	1	0	0	0	0
Graham Law	Wakefield	1999-2002	34(30)	6	40	0	104
Neil Law	Wakefield	1999-2002	83	39	0	0	156
	Sheffield	1998	1(1)	1	0	0	4
Dean Lawford	Widnes	2003-04	17(1)	5	2	4	28
	Halifax	2001	1(1)	0	0	0	0
	Leeds	1997-2000	15(8)	2	3	0	14
	Huddersfield	1999	6(1)	0	6	1	13
	Sheffield	1996	9(5)	2	1	1	11
Johnny Lawless	Halifax	2001-03	73(1)	10	0	0	40
	Hudds-Sheff	2000	19(6)	3	0	0	12
	Sheffield	1996-99	76(4)	11	0	0	44
Michael Lawrence							
	Huddersfield	2007-14	139(15)	36	0	0	144
Adam Lawton	Widnes	2013-14	2(10)	5	0	0	20
Charlie Leaeno	Wakefield	2010	7(3)	2	0	0	8
Mark Leafa	Castleford	2008	5(9)	1	0	0	4
	Leigh	2005	28	2	0	0	8
Leroy Leapai	London	1996	2	0	0	0	0
Jim Leatham	Hull	1998-99	20(18)	4	0	0	16
	Leeds	1997	(1)	0	0	0	0
Andy Leathem	Warrington	1999	2(8)	0	0	0	0
	St Helens	1996-98	20(1)	1	0	0	4
Danny Lee	Gateshead	1999	16(2)	0	0	0	0
Jason Lee	Halifax	2001	10(1)	2	0	0	8
Mark Lee	Salford	1997-2000	25(11)	1	0	4	8
Robert Lee	Hull	1999	4(3)	0	0	0	0
Tommy Lee	Salford	2014	20(4)	2	0	0	8
	London	2013	16(4)	2	0	0	8
	Huddersfield	2012	11(7)	3	0	0	12
	Wakefield	2011	25	6	0	0	24
	Crusaders	2010	3(9)	0	0	0	0
	Hull	2005-09	44(27)	6	0	0	24
Kruise Leeming	Huddersfield	2013-14	(6)	2	0	0	8
Matthew Leigh	Salford	2000	(6)	0	0	0	0
Chris Leikvoll	Warrington	2004-07	72(18)	4	0	0	16
Jim Lenihan	Huddersfield	1999	19(1)	10	0	0	40
Mark Lennon	Celtic	2009	10(3)	1	8	0	20
	Hull KR	2007	11(4)	5	7	0	34
	Castleford	2001-03	30(21)	10	21	0	82
Tevita Leo-Latu	Wakefield	2006-10	28(49)	10	0	0	40
Gary Lester	Hull	1998-99	46	17	0	0	68
Stuart Lester	Wigan	1997	1(3)	0	0	0	0
Heath L'Estrange	Bradford	2010-13	56(35)	7	0	0	28
Afi Leuila	Oldham	1996-97	17(3)	2	0	0	8
Kylie Leuluai	Leeds	2007-14	175(33)	18	0	0	72
Macgraff Leuluai	Widnes	2012-14	30(25)	1	0	0	4
Phil Leuluai	Salford	2007,					
		2009-10	7(47)	3	0	0	12
Thomas Leuluai	Wigan	2007-12	167(1)	51	0	0	204
	Harlequins	2006	15(2)	6	0	0	24
	London	2005	20	13	0	0	52
Simon Lewis	Castleford	2001	4	3	0	0	12
Paul Leyland	St Helens	2006	1	0	0	0	0
Jon Liddell	Leeds	2001	1	0	0	0	0
Jason Lidden	Castleford	1997	15(1)	7	0	0	28
Danny Lima	Wakefield	2007	(3)	0	0	0	0
	Salford	2006	7(2)	0	0	0	0
	Warrington	2004-06	15(47)	9	0	0	36
Jeff Lima	Catalans	2014	19(5)	1	0	0	4
	Wigan	2011-12	24(29)	4	0	0	16
Tom Lineham	Hull	2012-14	39(1)	25	0	0	100
Harry Little	London	2013	2	0	0	0	0
Craig Littler	St Helens	2006	1	1	0	0	4
Stuart Littler	Salford	1998-2002,					
		2004-07,					
		2009-10	217(30)	65	0	0	260
Peter Livett	Workington	1996	3(1)	0	0	0	0
Rhodri Lloyd	Widnes	2014	(4)	0	0	0	0
	London	2013	2	0	0	0	0
	Wigan	2012-13	2(3)	0	0	0	0
Kevin Locke	Salford	2014	6	3	10	0	32
Jack Logan	Hull	2014	3	2	0	0	8
Scott Logan	Wigan	2006	10(11)	0	0	0	0
	Hull	2001-03	27(20)	5	0	0	20
Jamahl Lolesi	Huddersfield	2007-10	75(9)	27	0	0	108
Filimone Lolohea	Harlequins	2006	3(6)	0	0	0	0
	London	2005	8(15)	0	0	0	0
David Lomax	Huddersfield	2000-01	45(9)	4	0	0	16
	Paris	1997	19(2)	1	0	0	4
Jonny Lomax	St Helens	2009-14	105(2)	48	84	2	362
Dave Long	London	1999	(1)	0	0	0	0
Karl Long	London	2003	(1)	0	0	0	0
	Widnes	2002	4	1	0	0	4
Sean Long	Hull	2010-11	22	6	0	0	24
	St Helens	1997-2009	263(8)	126	826	20	2176
	Wigan	1996-97	1(5)	0	0	0	0
Davide Longo	Bradford	1996	1(3)	0	0	0	0
Gary Lord	Oldham	1996-97	28(12)	3	0	0	12
Paul Loughlin	Huddersfield	1998-99	34(2)	4	4	0	24
	Bradford	1996-97	36(4)	15	8	0	76
Rhys Lovegrove	Hull KR	2007-14	75(74)	19	0	0	76
Karl Lovell	Hudds-Sheff	2000	14	5	0	0	20
	Sheffield	1999	22(4)	8	0	0	32
Will Lovell	London	2012-14	16(16)	4	0	0	16
James Lowes	Bradford	1996-2003	205	84	2	2	342
Laurent Lucchese	Paris	1996	13(5)	2	0	0	8
Zebastian Luisi	Harlequins	2006-07	23(2)	4	0	0	16
	London	2004-05	21(1)	7	0	0	28
Keith Lulia	Bradford	2012-13	50	19	0	0	76
Shaun Lunt	Huddersfield	2009-14	70(38)	60	0	0	240
	Leeds	2012	10(9)	7	0	0	28
Peter Lupton	Crusaders	2010-11	37(9)	10	0	0	40
	Celtic	2009	16(4)	4	0	0	16
	Castleford	2006, 2008	40	11	0	0	44
	Hull	2003-06	19(26)	10	3	0	46
	London	2000-02	10(15)	2	2	0	12
Andy Lynch	Castleford	1999-2004, 2014	105(48)	16	0	0	64
	Hull	2012-13	39(14)	3	0	0	12
	Bradford	2005-11	159(29)	46	0	0	184
Reece Lyne	Wakefield	2013-14	34	13	0	0	52
	Hull	2010-11	11(1)	2	0	0	8
Jamie Lyon	St Helens	2005-06	54(1)	39	172	0	500
Iliess Macani	London	2013-14	12(3)	4	0	0	16
Duncan MacGillivray							
	Wakefield	2004-08	75(18)	6	0	0	24
Brad Mackay	Bradford	2000	24(2)	8	0	0	32
Graham Mackay	Hull	2002	27	18	24	0	120
	Bradford	2001	16(3)	12	1	0	50
	Leeds	2000	12(8)	10	2	0	44
Keiron Maddocks	Leigh	2005	1(3)	0	0	0	0
Steve Maden	Leigh	2005	23	9	0	0	36
	Warrington	2002	3	0	0	0	0
Mateaki Mafi	Warrington	1996-97	7(8)	7	0	0	28
Shaun Magennis	St Helens	2010-12	7(19)	3	0	0	12
Brendan Magnus	London	2000	3	1	0	0	4
Mark Maguire	London	1996-97	11(4)	7	13	0	54
Adam Maher	Hull	2000-03	88(4)	24	0	0	96
	Gateshead	1999	21(5)	3	0	0	12
Lee Maher	Leeds	1996	4(1)	0	0	0	0
Will Maher	Castleford	2014	(1)	0	0	0	0
Shaun Mahony	Paris	1997	5	0	0	0	0
Hutch Maiava	Hull	2007	(19)	1	0	0	4
David Maiden	Hull	2000-01	32(10)	11	0	0	44
	Gateshead	1999	5(16)	8	0	0	32
Craig Makin	Salford	1999-2001	24(20)	2	0	0	8
Tom Makinson	St Helens	2011-14	89(5)	60	75	0	390
Brady Malam	Wigan	2000	5(20)	1	0	0	4
Dominic Maloney	Hull	2009	(7)	0	0	0	0
Francis Maloney	Castleford	1998-99, 2003-04	71(7)	24	33	3	165
	Salford	2001-02	45(1)	26	5	0	114
	Wakefield	2000	11	1	1	0	6
	Oldham	1996-97	39(2)	12	91	2	232
Dominic Manfredi							
	Wigan	2013-14	13	11	0	0	44
	Salford	2014	1	2	0	0	8
George Mann	Warrington	1997	14(5)	1	0	0	4
	Leeds	1996	11(4)	2	0	0	8
Dane Manning	Leeds	2009	(1)	0	0	0	0
Misili Manu	Widnes	2005	1	0	0	0	0
Willie Manu	St Helens	2013-14	35(11)	9	0	0	36
	Hull	2007-12	133(18)	33	0	0	132
	Castleford	2006	19(4)	9	0	0	36
Manase Manuokafoa							
	Bradford	2012-14	49(21)	3	0	0	12
Darren Mapp	Celtic	2009	9(2)	1	0	0	4
David March	Wakefield	1999-2007	164(23)	34	126	0	388
Paul March	Wakefield	1999-2001, 2007	42(31)	17	23	0	114
	Huddersfield	2003-06	71(19)	17	36	1	141
Nick Mardon	London	1997-98	14	2	0	0	8
Thibaut Margalet	Catalans	2013-14	(2)	0	0	0	0
Remy Marginet	Catalans	2011	2	0	9	0	18
Antoni Maria	Catalans	2012-14	1(17)	0	0	0	0
Frankie Mariano	Castleford	2014	7(18)	5	0	0	20
	Wakefield	2011-13	41(12)	20	0	0	80
	Hull KR	2010	(3)	0	0	0	0
Oliver Marns	Halifax	1996-2002	54(19)	23	0	0	92
Paul Marquet	Warrington	2002	23(2)	0	0	0	0
Callum Marriott	Salford	2011	(1)	0	0	0	0
Iain Marsh	Salford	1998-2001	1(4)	0	0	0	0
Lee Marsh	Salford	2001-02	3(4)	0	0	0	0
Stefan Marsh	Widnes	2012-14	52	25	2	0	104
	Wigan	2010-11	12	3	0	0	12
Richard Marshall	Leigh	2005	4(16)	1	0	0	4
	London	2002-03	33(11)	1	0	0	4
	Huddersfield	2000-01	35(14)	1	0	0	4
	Halifax	1996-99	38(34)	2	0	0	8
Charlie Martin	Castleford	2013	(6)	0	0	0	0
Jason Martin	Paris	1997	15(2)	3	0	0	12
Scott Martin	Salford	1997-99	32(18)	8	0	0	32

Super League Players 1996-2014

PLAYER	CLUB	YEAR	APP	TRIES	GOALS	FG	PTS
Tony Martin	Hull	2012	10	1	0	0	4
	Crusaders	2010-11	40(1)	14	1	0	58
	Wakefield	2008-09	33	10	33	0	106
	London	1996-97, 2001-03	97(1)	36	170	1	485
Mick Martindale	Halifax	1996	(4)	0	0	0	0
Sebastien Martins	Catalans	2006, 2009-11	(21)	2	0	0	8
Tommy Martyn	St Helens	1996-2003	125(20)	87	63	12	486
Dean Marwood	Workington	1996	9(6)	0	22	0	44
Martin Masella	Warrington	2001	10(14)	5	0	0	20
	Wakefield	2000	14(8)	4	0	0	16
	Leeds	1997-1999	59(5)	1	0	0	4
Colin Maskill	Castleford	1996	8	1	1	0	6
Mose Masoe	St Helens	2014	10(17)	8	0	0	32
Keith Mason	Castleford	2006, 2013	11(6)	0	0	0	0
	Huddersfield	2006-12	118(14)	4	0	0	16
	St Helens	2003-05	33(23)	4	0	0	16
	Wakefield	2000-01	5(17)	0	0	0	0
Nathan Mason	Huddersfield	2013	(1)	0	0	0	0
Willie Mason	Hull KR	2011	6	1	0	0	4
Sammy Masselot	Wakefield	2011	(1)	0	0	0	0
Nathan Massey	Castleford	2008-14	41(50)	6	0	0	24
Nesiasi Mataitonga	London	2014	11(1)	1	0	0	4
Vila Matautia	St Helens	1996-2001	31(68)	9	0	0	36
Feleti Mateo	London	2005	4(10)	1	0	0	4
Barrie-Jon Mather	Castleford	1998, 2000-02	50(12)	21	0	0	84
Richard Mathers	Wakefield	2012-14	71	24	0	0	96
	Castleford	2011	21(1)	7	0	0	28
	Warrington	2002, 2009-10	42(3)	11	0	0	44
	Wigan	2008-09	23(1)	2	0	0	8
	Leeds	2002-06	85(2)	26	0	0	104
Jamie Mathiou	Leeds	1997-2001	31(82)	3	0	0	12
Terry Matterson	London	1996-98	46	15	90	6	246
Vic Mauro	Salford	2013	1(7)	1	0	0	4
Luke May	Harlequins	2009-10	(3)	0	0	0	0
Casey Mayberry	Halifax	2000	1(1)	0	0	0	0
Chris Maye	Halifax	2003	3(4)	0	0	0	0
Joe Mbu	Harlequins	2006-09	33(20)	3	0	0	12
	London	2003-05	29(19)	4	0	0	16
Danny McAllister	Gateshead	1999	3(3)	1	0	0	4
	Sheffield	1996-97	33(7)	10	0	0	40
John McAtee	St Helens	1996	2(1)	0	0	0	0
Nathan McAvoy	Bradford	1998-2002, 2007	83(31)	46	0	0	184
	Wigan	2006	15(2)	5	0	0	20
	Salford	1997-98, 2004-05	57(4)	18	0	0	72
Tyrone McCarthy	Warrington	2009-13	12(24)	2	0	0	8
	Wakefield	2011	2(5)	1	0	0	4
Louie McCarthy-Scarsbrook	St Helens	2011-14	60(51)	19	0	0	76
	Harlequins	2006-10	41(50)	17	0	0	68
Dave McConnell	London	2003	(4)	0	0	0	0
	St Helens	2001-02	3(2)	4	0	0	16
Robbie McCormack	Wigan	1998	24	2	0	0	8
Steve McCurrie	Leigh	2005	7(3)	1	0	0	4
	Widnes	2002-04	55(22)	10	0	0	40
	Warrington	1998-2001	69(26)	31	0	0	124
Barrie McDermott	Leeds	1996-2005	163(69)	28	0	0	112
Brian McDermott	Bradford	1996-2002	138(32)	33	0	0	132
Ryan McDonald	Widnes	2002-03	6(4)	0	0	0	0
Wayne McDonald	Huddersfield	2005-06	11(23)	1	0	0	4
	Wigan	2005	(4)	0	0	0	0
	Leeds	2002-05	34(47)	14	0	0	56
	St Helens	2001	7(11)	4	0	0	16
	Hull	2000	5(8)	4	0	0	16
	Wakefield	1999	9(17)	8	0	0	32
Shannon McDonnell	St Helens	2014	3	3	0	0	12
	Hull	2013	19	2	0	0	8
	Hull KR	2012	21	6	0	0	24
Craig McDowell	Huddersfield	2003	(1)	0	0	0	0
	Warrington	2002	(1)	0	0	0	0
	Bradford	2000	(1)	0	0	0	0
Wes McGibbon	Halifax	1999	1	0	0	0	0
Jermaine McGillvary	Huddersfield	2010-14	107	70	0	0	280
Dean McGilvray	Salford	2009-10	14	4	0	0	16
	St Helens	2006-08	5(1)	1	0	0	4
Billy McGinty	Workington	1996	1	0	0	0	0
Ryan McGoldrick	Salford	2013	19(1)	3	0	1	13
	Hull	2012	8	1	0	0	4
	Castleford	2006, 2008-12	129(5)	24	11	0	118
Kevin McGuinness	Salford	2004-07	63(3)	11	0	0	44
Casey McGuire	Catalans	2007-10	87(4)	27	0	0	108
Danny McGuire	Leeds	2001-14	265(37)	215	0	4	864
Gary McGuirk	Workington	1996	(4)	0	0	0	0
Michael McIlorum	Wigan	2007-14	106(52)	17	0	0	68
Richard McKell	Castleford	1997-98	22(7)	2	0	0	8
Chris McKenna	Bradford	2006-07	40(7)	7	0	0	28
	Leeds	2003-05	65(4)	18	0	0	72
Phil McKenzie	Workington	1996	4	0	0	0	0
Chris McKinney	Oldham	1996-97	4(9)	2	0	0	8
Wade McKinnon	Hull	2012	10	4	0	0	16
Mark McLinden	Harlequins	2006-08	46(1)	20	0	1	81
	London	2005	22(3)	8	0	0	32
Mike McMeeken	London	2012-14	25(9)	5	0	0	20
Shayne McMenemy	Hull	2003-07	80(8)	12	0	0	48
	Halifax	2001-03	63	11	0	0	44
Andy McNally	London	2004	5(3)	0	0	0	0
	Castleford	2001, 2003	2(5)	1	0	0	4
Gregg McNally	Huddersfield	2011	1	0	6	0	12
Steve McNamara	Huddersfield	2001, 2003	41(9)	3	134	1	281
	Wakefield	2000	15(2)	2	32	0	72
	Bradford	1996-99	90(3)	14	348	7	759
Paul McNicholas	Hull	2004-05	28(12)	4	0	0	16
Neil McPherson	Salford	1997	(1)	0	0	0	0
Shannan McPherson	Salford	2012-14	20(11)	0	0	0	0
Duncan McRae	London	1996	11(2)	3	0	1	13
Paul McShane	Wakefield	2014	24(2)	2	0	0	8
	Leeds	2009-13	17(38)	12	0	0	48
	Widnes	2012	6(5)	3	4	0	20
	Hull	2010	(4)	0	0	0	0
Derek McVey	St Helens	1996-97	28(4)	6	1	0	26
Dallas Mead	Warrington	1997	2	0	0	0	0
Robbie Mears	Leigh	2005	8(6)	0	0	0	0
	Leeds	2001	23	6	0	0	24
Paul Medley	Bradford	1996-98	6(35)	9	0	0	36
Francis Meli	Salford	2014	16	11	0	0	44
	St Helens	2006-13	194(1)	122	0	0	488
Vince Mellars	Wakefield	2012-13	21(5)	4	0	0	16
	Crusaders	2010-11	46	17	0	0	68
Chris Melling	London	2012-13	25(12)	5	2	0	24
	Harlequins	2007-11	100(11)	33	6	0	144
	Wigan	2004-05	8(2)	1	3	0	10
Alex Mellor	Bradford	2013-14	(10)	0	0	0	0
Joe Mellor	Widnes	2012-14	53	23	0	0	92
	Wigan	2012	1(1)	1	0	0	4
	Harlequins	2011	(1)	0	0	0	0
Paul Mellor	Castleford	2003-04	36(3)	18	0	0	72
James Mendeika	London	2013	4(2)	2	0	0	8
Craig Menkins	Paris	1997	4(5)	0	0	0	0
Luke Menzies	Hull KR	2008	(1)	0	0	0	0
Steve Menzies	Catalans	2011-13	61(6)	30	0	0	120
	Bradford	2009-10	52(1)	24	1	0	98
Gary Mercer	Castleford	2002	(1)	0	0	0	0
	Leeds	1996-97, 2001	40(2)	9	0	0	36
	Warrington	2001	18	2	0	0	8
	Halifax	1998-2001	73(2)	16	0	0	64
Tony Mestrov	London	1996-97, 2001	59(8)	4	0	0	16
	Wigan	1998-2000	39(39)	3	0	0	12
Keiran Meyer	London	1996	4	1	0	0	4
Brad Meyers	Bradford	2005-06	40(11)	13	0	0	52
Gary Middlehurst	Widnes	2004	(2)	0	0	0	0
Simon Middleton	Castleford	1996-97	19(3)	8	0	0	32
Constantine Mika	Hull KR	2012-13	45(4)	9	0	0	36
Daryl Millard	Catalans	2011-14	91	38	1	0	154
	Wakefield	2010-11	21(1)	11	0	0	44
Shane Millard	Wigan	2007	19(6)	3	0	0	12
	Leeds	2006	6(21)	3	0	0	12
	Widnes	2003-05	69	23	0	0	92
	London	1998-2001	72(14)	11	1	0	46
Jack Miller	Huddersfield	2013	1	0	1	0	2
Jacob Miller	Hull	2013-14	20	6	9	0	42
Grant Millington	Castleford	2012-14	50(18)	11	0	0	44
David Mills	Harlequins	2006-07, 2010	25(32)	2	0	0	8
	Hull KR	2008-09	20(11)	1	0	0	4
	Widnes	2002-05	17(77)	8	0	0	32
Lewis Mills	Celtic	2009	(4)	0	0	0	0
Adam Milner	Castleford	2010-14	61(28)	18	0	0	72
Lee Milner	Halifax	1999	(1)	0	0	0	0
Elliot Minchella	Leeds	2013-14	(6)	1	0	0	4
Thomas Minns	London	2014	23	6	0	0	24
	Leeds	2013	2(1)	1	0	0	4
John Minto	London	1996	13	4	0	0	16
Lee Mitchell	Castleford	2012	13(10)	2	0	0	8
	Warrington	2007-11	8(27)	4	0	0	16
	Harlequins	2011	11(1)	1	0	0	4
Sam Moa	Hull	2009-12	29(44)	6	0	0	24
Martin Moana	Salford	2004	6(3)	1	0	0	4
	Halifax	1996-2001, 2003	126(22)	62	0	1	249
	Wakefield	2002	19(2)	10	0	0	40
	Huddersfield	2001	3(3)	2	0	0	8

PLAYER	CLUB	YEAR	APP	TRIES	GOALS	FG	PTS
Adam Mogg	Catalans	2007-10	74	19	0	1	77
Jon Molloy	Wakefield	2013-14	3(11)	2	0	0	8
	Huddersfield	2011-12	2(1)	0	0	0	0
Steve Molloy	Huddersfield	2000-01	26(20)	3	0	0	12
	Sheffield	1998-99	32(17)	3	0	0	12
Chris Molyneux	Huddersfield	2000-01	1(18)	0	0	0	0
	Sheffield	1999	1(2)	0	0	0	0
Joel Monaghan	Warrington	2011-14	103	108	0	0	432
Michael Monaghan							
	Warrington	2008-14	143(28)	31	0	4	128
Joel Moon	Leeds	2013-14	49	23	0	0	92
	Salford	2012	17	9	0	0	36
Adrian Moore	Huddersfield	1998-99	1(4)	0	0	0	0
Danny Moore	London	2000	7	0	0	0	0
	Wigan	1998-99	49(3)	18	0	0	72
Gareth Moore	Wakefield	2011	5	1	14	1	33
Jason Moore	Workington	1996	(5)	0	0	0	0
Richard Moore	Wakefield	2007-10, 2014	52(57)	10	0	0	40
	Leeds	2012-13	3(27)	1	0	0	4
	Crusaders	2011	11(10)	1	0	0	4
	Leigh	2005	2(5)	0	0	0	0
	Bradford	2002-04	1(26)	0	0	0	0
	London	2002, 2004	5(9)	2	0	0	8
Scott Moore	London	2014	26	3	0	0	12
	Huddersfield	2009, 2012	29(7)	9	0	0	36
	Widnes	2012	3(3)	0	0	0	0
	St Helens	2004-07, 2010-11	29(37)	9	0	0	36
	Castleford	2008	11(5)	1	0	0	4
Dennis Moran	Wigan	2005-06	39	17	1	1	71
	London	2001-04	107(2)	74	2	5	305
Willie Morganson	Sheffield	1997-98	18(12)	5	3	0	26
Paul Moriarty	Halifax	1996	3(2)	0	0	0	0
Adrian Morley	Salford	2014	19(6)	2	0	0	8
	Warrington	2007-13	135(21)	8	0	0	32
	Bradford	2005	2(4)	0	0	0	0
	Leeds	1996-2000	95(14)	25	0	0	100
Chris Morley	Salford	1999	3(5)	0	0	0	0
	Warrington	1998	2(8)	0	0	0	0
	St Helens	1996-97	21(16)	4	0	0	16
Glenn Morrison	Wakefield	2010-11	43(1)	9	0	0	36
	Bradford	2007-09	48(2)	19	0	0	76
Iain Morrison	Hull KR	2007	5(6)	1	0	0	4
	Huddersfield	2003-05	11(23)	1	0	0	4
	London	2001	(1)	0	0	0	0
Dale Morton	Wakefield	2009-11	22(3)	8	5	0	42
Gareth Morton	Hull KR	2007	7(4)	3	23	0	58
	Leeds	2001-02	1(1)	0	0	0	0
Lee Mossop	Wigan	2008-13	55(40)	7	0	0	28
	Huddersfield	2009	1(4)	1	0	0	4
Aaron Moule	Salford	2006-07	45	17	0	0	68
	Widnes	2004-05	29	12	0	0	48
Wilfried Moulinec	Paris	1996	1	0	0	0	0
Gregory Mounis	Catalans	2006-14	141(77)	25	19	0	138
Mark Moxon	Huddersfield	1998-2001	20(5)	1	0	1	5
Rob Mulhern	Leeds	2014	(3)	0	0	0	0
Anthony Mullally	Huddersfield	2013-14	4(17)	4	0	0	16
	Bradford	2014	1(5)	0	0	0	0
	Widnes	2012	(9)	0	0	0	0
Jake Mullaney	Salford	2014	12	2	24	0	56
Brett Mullins	Leeds	2001	5(3)	1	0	0	4
Damian Munro	Widnes	2002	8(2)	1	0	0	4
	Halifax	1996-97	9(6)	8	0	0	32
Matt Munro	Oldham	1996-97	26(5)	8	0	0	32
Craig Murdock	Salford	2000	(2)	0	0	0	0
	Hull	1998-99	21(6)	8	0	2	34
	Wigan	1996-98	18(17)	14	0	0	56
Aaron Murphy	Huddersfield	2012-14	58	32	0	0	128
	Wakefield	2008-11	57(2)	12	0	0	48
Jack Murphy	Wigan	2012, 2014	3	1	0	0	4
	Salford	2013	10	3	1	0	14
Jamie Murphy	Crusaders	2011	(2)	0	0	0	0
Jobe Murphy	Bradford	2013	(4)	0	0	0	0
Justin Murphy	Catalans	2006-08	59	49	0	0	196
	Widnes	2004	5	1	0	0	4
Doc Murray	Warrington	1997	(2)	0	0	0	0
	Wigan	1997	6(2)	0	0	0	0
Scott Murrell	Hull KR	2007-12	114(24)	24	26	1	149
	Leeds	2005	(1)	0	0	0	0
	London	2004	3(3)	2	0	0	8
David Mycoe	Sheffield	1996-97	12(13)	1	0	0	4
Richard Myler	Warrington	2010-14	106(4)	59	1	1	239
	Salford	2009	18	11	0	0	44
Rob Myler	Oldham	1996-97	19(2)	6	0	0	24
Stephen Myler	Salford	2006	4(8)	1	15	0	34
	Widnes	2003-05	35(14)	8	74	0	180
Vinny Myler	Salford	2004	(4)	0	0	0	0
	Bradford	2003	(1)	0	0	0	0
Matt Nable	London	1997	2(2)	1	0	0	4
Brad Nairn	Workington	1996	14	4	0	0	16
Frank Napoli	London	2000	14(6)	2	0	0	8
Carlo Napolitano	Salford	2000	(3)	1	0	0	4

PLAYER	CLUB	YEAR	APP	TRIES	GOALS	FG	PTS
Stephen Nash	Castleford	2012	3(4)	0	0	0	0
	Salford	2007, 2009	2(18)	1	0	0	4
	Widnes	2005	4(1)	0	0	0	0
Curtis Naughton	Bradford	2013	1	0	0	0	0
Jim Naylor	Halifax	2000	7(6)	2	0	0	8
Scott Naylor	Salford	1997-98, 2004	30(1)	9	0	0	36
	Bradford	1999-2003	127(1)	51	0	0	204
Adam Neal	Salford	2010-13	17(28)	0	0	0	0
Mike Neal	Salford	1998	(1)	0	0	0	0
	Oldham	1996-97	6(4)	3	0	0	12
Jonathan Neill	Huddersfield	1998-99	20(11)	0	0	0	0
	St Helens	1996	1	0	0	0	0
Chris Nero	Salford	2011-13	31(16)	7	0	0	28
	Bradford	2008-10	65(5)	24	0	0	96
	Huddersfield	2004-07	97(8)	38	0	0	152
Jason Netherton	Hull KR	2007-14	60(74)	4	0	0	16
	London	2003-04	6	0	0	0	0
	Halifax	2002	2(3)	0	0	0	0
	Leeds	2001	(3)	0	0	0	0
Kirk Netherton	Castleford	2009-10	5(23)	3	0	0	12
	Hull KR	2007-08	9(15)	2	0	0	8
Paul Newlove	Castleford	2004	5	1	0	0	4
	St Helens	1996-2003	162	106	0	0	424
Richard Newlove	Wakefield	2003	17(5)	8	0	0	32
Clint Newton	Hull KR	2008-11	90(3)	37	0	0	148
Terry Newton	Wakefield	2010	(2)	0	0	0	0
	Bradford	2006-09	83(6)	26	0	0	104
	Wigan	2000-05	157(9)	62	0	0	248
	Leeds	1996-1999	55(14)	4	0	0	16
Gene Ngamu	Huddersfield	1999-2000	29(2)	9	67	0	170
Danny Nicklas	Hull	2010, 2012	2(8)	0	0	0	0
Sonny Nickle	St Helens	1999-2002	86(18)	14	0	0	56
	Bradford	1996-98	25(16)	9	0	0	36
Jason Nicol	Salford	2000-02	52(7)	11	0	0	44
Tawera Nikau	Warrington	2000-01	51	7	0	0	28
Rob Nolan	Hull	1998-99	20(11)	6	0	0	24
Paul Noone	Harlequins	2006	5(2)	0	0	0	0
	Warrington	2000-06	60(59)	12	20	0	88
Chris Norman	Halifax	2003	13(3)	2	0	0	8
Paul Norman	Oldham	1996	(1)	0	0	0	0
Andy Northey	St Helens	1996-97	8(17)	2	0	0	8
Danny Nutley	Castleford	2006	28	3	0	0	12
	Warrington	1998-2001	94(1)	3	0	0	12
Tony Nuttall	Oldham	1996-97	1(7)	0	0	0	0
Adam O'Brien	Bradford	2011-14	12(29)	6	0	0	24
Clinton O'Brien	Wakefield	2003	(2)	0	0	0	0
Gareth O'Brien	Warrington	2011-14	33(3)	12	38	0	124
	St Helens	2013	7	0	25	0	50
	Castleford	2013	2	0	0	1	1
	Widnes	2012	4	0	15	0	30
Sam Obst	Hull	2011	17(6)	6	0	0	24
	Wakefield	2005-11	100(28)	40	7	0	174
Jamie O'Callaghan							
	London	2012-14	44(2)	4	0	0	16
	Harlequins	2008-11	54(3)	12	0	0	48
Eamon O'Carroll	Widnes	2012-14	30(4)	1	0	0	4
	Hull	2012	1(9)	0	0	0	0
	Wigan	2006-11	2(59)	3	0	0	12
Matt O'Connor	Paris	1997	11(4)	1	26	2	58
Terry O'Connor	Widnes	2005	25	2	0	0	8
	Wigan	1996-2004	177(45)	9	0	0	36
Jarrod O'Doherty	Huddersfield	2003	26	3	0	0	12
David O'Donnell	Paris	1997	21	3	0	0	12
Luke O'Donnell	Huddersfield	2011-13	22(2)	2	0	0	8
Martin Offiah	Salford	2000-01	41	20	0	2	82
	London	1996-99	29(3)	21	0	0	84
	Wigan	1996	8	7	0	0	28
Mark O'Halloran	London	2004-05	34(3)	10	0	0	40
Ryan O'Hara	Hull KR	2012	8(7)	1	0	0	4
	Crusaders	2010-11	41(8)	3	0	0	12
	Celtic	2009	27	3	0	0	12
Hefin O'Hare	Huddersfield	2001, 2003-05	72(10)	27	0	0	108
Edwin Okanga-Ajwang							
	Salford	2013	2	0	0	0	0
Hitro Okesene	Hull	1998	21(1)	0	0	0	0
Anderson Okiwe	Sheffield	1997	1	0	0	0	0
Tom Olbison	Bradford	2009-14	55(26)	11	0	0	44
Michael Oldfield	Catalans	2014	29	22	0	0	88
Jamie Olejnik	Paris	1997	11	8	0	0	32
Aaron Ollett	Hull KR	2013-14	2(8)	0	0	0	0
Kevin O'Loughlin	Halifax	1997-98	2(4)	0	0	0	0
	St Helens	1997	(3)	0	0	0	0
Sean O'Loughlin	Wigan	2002-14	281(21)	64	3	2	264
Mark O'Meley	Hull	2010-13	70(13)	13	0	0	52
Jules O'Neill	Widnes	2003-05	57(3)	14	158	7	379
	Wakefield	2005	10(2)	2	4	0	16
	Wigan	2002-03	29(1)	12	72	0	192
Julian O'Neill	Widnes	2002-05	57(39)	3	0	0	12
	Wakefield	2001	24(1)	2	0	0	8
	St Helens	1997-2000	95(8)	5	0	0	20
Mark O'Neill	Hull KR	2007	17	5	0	0	20
	Leeds	2006	1(8)	0	0	0	0

175

PLAYER	CLUB	YEAR	APP	TRIES	GOALS	FG	PTS
Steve O'Neill	Gateshead	1999	1(1)	0	0	0	0
Tom O'Reilly	Warrington	2001-02	8(6)	1	0	0	4
Matt Orford	Bradford	2010	12	3	31	2	76
Gene Ormsby	Warrington	2014	19	12	0	0	48
Chris Orr	Huddersfield	1998	19(3)	2	0	0	8
Danny Orr	Castleford	1997-2003, 2011-12	197(23)	75	308	3	919
	Harlequins	2007-10	90(4)	13	96	0	244
	Wigan	2004-06	66(2)	18	12	0	96
Gareth Owen	Salford	2010, 2012-13	4(32)	6	0	0	24
Nick Owen	Leigh	2005	8(1)	1	11	0	26
Richard Owen	Wakefield	2014	14	6	0	0	24
	Castleford	2008-14	109(3)	57	0	0	228
Jack Owens	Widnes	2012-14	37(1)	18	62	0	196
Lopini Paea	Catalans	2011-14	41(41)	9	0	0	36
Mickey Paea	Hull	2014	19(5)	3	0	0	12
	Hull KR	2012-13	34(17)	5	0	0	20
Mathias Pala	Catalans	2011-14	24(1)	3	0	0	12
Iafeta Palea'aesina							
	Hull	2014	(21)	1	0	0	4
	Salford	2011-12	4(37)	3	0	0	12
	Wigan	2006-10	55(77)	16	0	0	64
Jason Palmada	Workington	1996	12	2	0	0	8
Junior Paramore	Castleford	1996	5(5)	3	0	0	12
Paul Parker	Hull	1999-2002	23(18)	9	0	0	36
Rob Parker	Castleford	2011	4(2)	2	0	0	8
	Salford	2009-11	23(14)	4	0	0	16
	Warrington	2006-08	10(56)	6	0	0	24
	Bradford	2000, 2002-05	19(76)	14	0	0	56
	London	2001	9	1	0	0	4
Wayne Parker	Halifax	1996-97	12(1)	0	0	0	0
Ian Parry	Warrington	2001	1	0	0	0	0
Jules Parry	Paris	1996	10(2)	0	0	0	0
Regis Pastre-Courtine							
	Paris	1996	4(3)	4	0	0	16
Cory Paterson	Hull KR	2013	15	7	0	0	28
Andrew Patmore	Oldham	1996	8(5)	3	0	0	12
Larne Patrick	Huddersfield	2009-14	25(102)	27	0	0	108
Luke Patten	Salford	2011-12	53	16	0	0	64
Henry Paul	Harlequins	2006-08	60(1)	8	94	2	222
	Bradford	1999-2001	81(5)	29	350	6	822
	Wigan	1996-98	60	37	23	0	194
Junior Paul	London	1996	3	1	0	0	4
Robbie Paul	Salford	2009	2(24)	2	0	0	8
	Huddersfield	2006-07	44(8)	7	0	0	28
	Bradford	1996-2005	198(31)	121	3	0	490
Jason Payne	Castleford	2006	1(1)	0	0	0	0
Danny Peacock	Bradford	1997-99	32(2)	15	0	0	60
Jamie Peacock	Leeds	2006-14	209(11)	22	0	0	88
	Bradford	1999-2005	163(25)	38	0	0	152
Martin Pearson	Wakefield	2001	21(1)	3	60	3	135
	Halifax	1997-98, 2000	55(6)	24	181	0	458
	Sheffield	1999	17(6)	9	36	2	110
Jacques Pech	Paris	1996	16	0	0	0	0
Mike Pechey	Warrington	1998	6(3)	2	0	0	8
Bill Peden	London	2003	21(3)	7	0	0	28
Adam Peek	Crusaders	2010-11	5(22)	1	0	0	4
	Celtic	2009	5(12)	3	0	0	12
Eloi Pelissier	Catalans	2011-14	14(79)	9	0	1	37
Dimitri Pelo	Catalans	2007-10	79	37	0	0	148
Sean Penkywicz	Huddersfield	2004-05	21(11)	7	0	0	28
	Halifax	2000-03	29(27)	8	0	0	32
Julian Penni	Salford	1998-99	4	0	0	0	0
Kevin Penny	Warrington	2006-09, 2014	41(1)	27	0	0	108
	Wakefield	2011	5	1	0	0	4
	Harlequins	2010	5	3	0	0	12
Lee Penny	Warrington	1996-2003	140(5)	54	0	0	216
Paul Penrice	Workington	1996	11(2)	2	0	0	8
Chris Percival	Widnes	2002-03	26	6	0	0	24
Mark Percival	St Helens	2013-14	26(1)	12	60	0	168
Apollo Perelini	St Helens	1996-2000	103(16)	27	0	0	108
Mark Perrett	Halifax	1996-97	15(4)	4	0	0	16
Josh Perry	St Helens	2011-13	32(9)	2	0	0	8
Shane Perry	Catalans	2009	8(8)	1	0	0	4
Adam Peters	Paris	1997	16(3)	0	0	0	0
Dominic Peters	London	1998-2003	58(11)	12	0	0	48
Mike Peters	Warrington	2000	2(12)	1	0	0	4
	Halifax	2000	1	0	0	0	0
Willie Peters	Widnes	2004	9	3	0	2	14
	Wigan	2000	29	15	5	6	76
	Gateshead	1999	27	11	1	6	52
Dave Petersen	Hull KR	2012	2(2)	1	0	0	4
Matt Petersen	Wakefield	2008-09	14	3	0	0	12
Adrian Petrie	Workington	1996	(1)	0	0	0	0
Eddy Pettybourne							
	Wigan	2014	1(15)	0	0	0	0
Cameron Phelps	Widnes	2012-14	54	20	2	0	84
	Hull	2011	19	2	0	0	8
	Wigan	2008-10	43(1)	14	4	0	64
Joe Philbin	Warrington	2014	(3)	0	0	0	0
Rowland Phillips	Workington	1996	22	1	0	0	4
Nathan Picchi	Leeds	1996	(1)	0	0	0	0
Ian Pickavance	Hull	1999	4(2)	2	0	0	8
	Huddersfield	1999	3(14)	0	0	0	0
	St Helens	1996-98	12(44)	6	0	0	24
James Pickering	Castleford	1999	1(19)	0	0	0	0
Steve Pickersgill	Widnes	2012-13	27(8)	1	0	0	4
	Warrington	2005-09	1(36)	0	0	0	0
Nick Pinkney	Salford	2000-02	64	29	0	0	116
	Halifax	1999	26(2)	13	0	0	52
	Sheffield	1997-98	33	10	0	0	40
Mikhail Piskunov	Paris	1996	1(1)	1	0	0	4
Darryl Pitt	London	1996	2(16)	4	0	1	17
Jay Pitts	Bradford	2014	15(1)	3	0	0	12
	Hull	2012-14	18(30)	1	0	0	4
	Leeds	2009-12	10(15)	2	0	0	8
	Wakefield	2008-09	9(8)	2	0	0	8
Andy Platt	Salford	1997-98	20(3)	1	0	0	4
Michael Platt	Salford	2001-02, 2014	4(1)	1	0	0	4
	Bradford	2007-13	121(6)	44	0	0	176
	Castleford	2006	26	7	0	0	28
Willie Poching	Leeds	2002-06	58(73)	44	0	0	176
	Wakefield	1999-2001	65(4)	20	0	0	80
Ben Pomeroy	Catalans	2014	27	6	0	0	24
Quentin Pongia	Wigan	2003-04	15(10)	0	0	0	0
Justin Poore	Hull KR	2014	7	0	0	0	0
	Wakefield	2013	23	1	0	0	4
Dan Potter	Widnes	2002-03	34(2)	6	0	0	24
	London	2001	1(3)	1	0	0	4
Craig Poucher	Hull	1999-2002	31(5)	5	0	0	20
Andy Powell	Wigan	2013	2(3)	1	0	0	4
Bryn Powell	Salford	2004	1(1)	0	0	0	0
Daio Powell	Sheffield	1999	13(1)	2	0	0	8
	Halifax	1997-98	30(3)	17	0	0	68
Daryl Powell	Leeds	1998-2000	49(30)	12	0	2	50
Sam Powell	Wigan	2012-14	23(13)	7	0	2	30
Karl Pratt	Bradford	2003-05	35(19)	18	0	0	72
	Leeds	1999-2002	62(12)	33	0	0	132
Paul Prescott	Wigan	2004-13	49(75)	4	0	0	16
Steve Prescott	Hull	1998-99, 2001-03	99	46	191	3	569
	Wakefield	2000	22(1)	3	13	0	38
	St Helens	1996-97	32	15	17	0	94
Lee Prest	Workington	1996	(1)	0	0	0	0
Gareth Price	Salford	2002	(2)	0	0	0	0
	London	2002	2(2)	3	0	0	12
	St Helens	1999	(11)	2	0	0	8
Gary Price	Wakefield	1999-2001	55(13)	11	0	0	44
Richard Price	Sheffield	1996	1(2)	0	0	0	0
Tony Priddle	Paris	1997	11(7)	3	0	0	12
Karl Pryce	Bradford	2003-06, 2012	47(19)	46	1	0	186
	Harlequins	2011	11(7)	12	0	0	48
	Wigan	2009-10	11(2)	12	0	0	48
Leon Pryce	Catalans	2012-14	72(2)	15	0	0	60
	St Helens	2006-11	133(3)	64	0	0	256
	Bradford	1998-2005	159(29)	86	0	0	344
Waine Pryce	Wakefield	2007	10(2)	4	0	0	16
	Castleford	2000-06	97(12)	49	0	0	196
Tony Puletua	Salford	2014	16(9)	3	0	0	12
	St Helens	2009-13	108(18)	39	0	0	156
Andrew Purcell	Castleford	2000	15(5)	3	0	0	12
	Hull	1999	27	4	0	0	16
Rob Purdham	Harlequins	2006-11	112(3)	18	131	1	335
	London	2002-05	53(15)	16	2	1	69
Adrian Purtell	Bradford	2012-14	45(1)	16	0	0	64
Luke Quigley	Catalans	2007	16(1)	1	0	0	4
Damien Quinn	Celtic	2009	20(1)	4	12	0	40
Scott Quinnell	Wigan	1996	6(3)	1	0	0	4
Florian Quintilla	Catalans	2008-09	1(4)	0	0	0	0
Lee Radford	Hull	1998, 2006-12	138(30)	23	1	0	94
	Bradford	1999-2005	79(65)	18	12	0	96
Kris Radlinski	Wigan	1996-2006	236(1)	134	1	0	538
Sebastien Raguin	Catalans	2007-12	103(22)	28	0	0	112
Adrian Rainey	Castleford	2002	4(7)	1	0	0	4
Andy Raleigh	Wakefield	2012-14	42(21)	9	0	0	36
	Huddersfield	2006-11	74(46)	13	0	0	52
Jean-Luc Ramondou							
	Paris	1996	1(1)	1	0	0	4
Chad Randall	London	2012-13	29(9)	4	0	0	16
	Harlequins	2006-11	141(2)	37	0	1	149
Craig Randall	Halifax	1999	8(11)	4	0	0	16
	Salford	1997-98	12(18)	4	0	0	16
Jordan Rankin	Hull	2014	19(3)	9	33	0	102
Scott Ranson	Oldham	1996-97	19(2)	7	0	0	28
Aaron Raper	Castleford	1999-2001	48(4)	4	2	1	21
Steve Rapira	Salford	2014	5(13)	0	0	0	0
Stefan Ratchford	Warrington	2012-14	74(6)	35	102	2	346
	Salford	2007, 2009-11	65(5)	23	20	0	132
Mike Ratu	Hull KR	2010	5	1	0	0	4
	Leeds	2007, 2009	1(5)	1	0	0	4

PLAYER	CLUB	YEAR	APP	TRIES	GOALS	FG	PTS
Paul Rauhihi	Warrington	2006-09	67(20)	10	0	0	40
Ben Rauter	Wakefield	2001	15(6)	4	0	0	16
Gareth Raynor	Bradford	2011	18	4	0	0	16
	Crusaders	2010	7	4	0	0	16
	Hull	2001-09	186	102	0	0	408
	Leeds	2000	(3)	0	0	0	0
Tony Rea	London	1996	22	4	0	0	16
Stuart Reardon	Crusaders	2011	25	11	0	0	44
	Bradford	2003-05, 2010	78(11)	37	0	0	148
	Warrington	2006-08	48	12	0	0	48
	Salford	2002	7(1)	3	0	0	12
Mark Reber	Wigan	1999-2000	9(9)	5	0	0	20
Alan Reddicliffe	Warrington	2001	1	0	0	0	0
Tahi Reihana	Bradford	1997-98	17(21)	0	0	0	0
Paul Reilly	Wakefield	2008	5(2)	1	0	0	4
	Huddersfield	1999-2001, 2003-07	150(8)	35	1	0	142
Robert Relf	Widnes	2002-04	68(2)	5	0	0	20
Steve Renouf	Wigan	2000-01	55	40	0	0	160
Steele Retchless	London	1998-2004	177(6)	13	0	0	52
Ben Reynolds	Castleford	2013-14	1(3)	0	0	0	0
Scott Rhodes	Hull	2000	2	0	0	0	0
Phillipe Ricard	Paris	1996-97	2	0	0	0	0
Andy Rice	Huddersfield	2000-01	2(13)	1	0	0	4
Basil Richards	Huddersfield	1998-99	28(17)	1	0	0	4
Craig Richards	Oldham	1996	1	0	0	0	0
Greg Richards	St Helens	2013-14	4(10)	0	0	0	0
Pat Richards	Wigan	2006-13	199	147	759	4	2110
Andy Richardson	Hudds-Sheff	2000	(2)	0	0	0	0
Sean Richardson	Widnes	2002	2(18)	1	0	0	4
	Wakefield	1999	5(1)	0	0	0	0
	Castleford	1996-97	3(8)	1	0	0	4
Mark Riddell	Wigan	2009-10	45(11)	5	2	0	24
Neil Rigby	St Helens	2006	(1)	0	0	0	0
Shane Rigon	Bradford	2001	14(11)	12	0	0	48
Craig Rika	Halifax	1996	2	0	0	0	0
Chris Riley	Wakefield	2014	23	8	0	0	32
	Warrington	2005-14	146(10)	102	0	0	408
	Harlequins	2011	3	2	0	0	8
Glenn Riley	Warrington	2013-14	(15)	0	0	0	0
Peter Riley	Workington	1996	7(5)	0	0	0	0
Julien Rinaldi	London	2012	4(16)	1	0	0	4
	Wakefield	2002, 2010-11	27(9)	6	0	0	24
	Bradford	2009	(7)	1	0	0	4
	Harlequins	2007-08	4(43)	9	0	0	36
	Catalans	2006	16(6)	3	1	0	14
Dean Ripley	Castleford	2004	3(4)	1	0	0	4
Leroy Rivett	Warrington	2002	9	1	0	0	4
	Hudds-Sheff	2000	5(1)	1	0	0	4
	Leeds	1996-2000	39(15)	21	0	0	84
Jason Roach	Warrington	1998-99	29(7)	15	0	0	60
	Castleford	1997	7	4	0	0	16
Ben Roarty	Castleford	2006	11(6)	2	0	0	8
	Huddersfield	2003-05	52	5	0	0	20
Amos Roberts	Wigan	2009-11	47(2)	27	5	0	118
Mark Roberts	Wigan	2003	(3)	0	0	0	0
Oliver Roberts	Bradford	2013-14	(5)	0	0	0	0
Robert Roberts	Huddersfield	2001	(1)	0	0	0	0
	Halifax	2000	(3)	0	0	0	0
	Hull	1999	24(2)	4	13	4	46
Michael Robertson	London	2012-13	35	17	0	0	68
Chad Robinson	Harlequins	2009	13(1)	2	0	0	8
Connor Robinson	Hull KR	2014	(1)	0	0	0	0
Craig Robinson	Wakefield	2005	(1)	0	0	0	0
Jason Robinson	Wigan	1996-2000	126(1)	87	0	1	349
Jeremy Robinson	Paris	1997	10(3)	1	21	0	46
John Robinson	Widnes	2003-04	7	1	0	0	4
Luke Robinson	Huddersfield	2008-14	169(14)	43	4	0	180
	Salford	2005-07	79	28	10	2	134
	Wigan	2002-04	17(25)	9	6	1	49
	Castleford	2004	9	4	3	0	22
Will Robinson	Hull	2000	22	4	0	0	16
	Gateshead	1999	28	9	0	0	36
James Roby	St Helens	2004-14	163(115)	74	1	0	298
Mike Roby	St Helens	2004	(1)	0	0	0	0
Carl Roden	Warrington	1997	1	0	0	0	0
Shane Rodney	London	2012-13	28	3	12	0	36
Matt Rodwell	Warrington	2002	10	3	0	0	12
Darren Rogers	Castleford	1999-2004	162(1)	81	0	0	324
	Salford	1997-98	42	16	0	0	64
Jamie Rooney	Wakefield	2003-09	113(7)	60	321	21	903
	Castleford	2001	2(1)	0	6	0	12
Jonathan Roper	Castleford	2001	13	7	12	0	52
	Salford	2000	1(4)	1	3	0	10
	London	2000	4	0	0	0	0
	Warrington	1996-2000	75(8)	33	71	0	274
Scott Roskell	London	1996-97	30(2)	16	0	0	64
Steve Rosolen	London	1996-98	25(9)	10	0	0	40
Adam Ross	London	1996	(1)	0	0	0	0
Paul Round	Castleford	1996	(3)	0	0	0	0
Steve Rowlands	Widnes	2004-05	18(3)	2	15	0	38
	St Helens	2003	(1)	0	0	0	0

PLAYER	CLUB	YEAR	APP	TRIES	GOALS	FG	PTS
Paul Rowley	Leigh	2005	15(7)	3	0	0	12
	Huddersfield	2001	24	3	0	0	12
	Halifax	1996-2000	107(3)	27	1	3	113
Nigel Roy	London	2001-04	100	39	0	0	156
Nicky Royle	Widnes	2004	13	7	0	0	28
Shad Royston	Bradford	2011	17(1)	10	0	0	40
Chris Rudd	Warrington	1996-98	31(17)	10	16	0	72
Sean Rudder	Catalans	2006	22(1)	6	0	0	24
	Castleford	2004	9(3)	2	0	0	8
James Rushforth	Halifax	1997	(4)	0	0	0	0
Danny Russell	Huddersfield	1998-2000	50(13)	8	0	0	32
Ian Russell	Oldham	1997	1(3)	1	0	0	4
	Paris	1996	3	0	0	0	0
Matthew Russell	Warrington	2014	21(4)	3	0	0	12
	Hull	2012	6	0	0	0	0
	Wigan	2012	3	3	0	0	12
Richard Russell	Castleford	1996-98	37(4)	2	0	0	8
Robert Russell	Salford	1998-99	2(1)	0	1	0	2
Sean Rutgerson	Salford	2004-06	60(9)	4	0	0	16
Chris Ryan	London	1998-99	44(3)	17	10	0	88
Matt Ryan	Wakefield	2014	15(6)	4	0	0	16
Sean Ryan	Castleford	2004	11(5)	2	0	0	8
	Hull	2002-03	53	8	0	0	32
Justin Ryder	Wakefield	2004	19(3)	11	0	0	44
Jason Ryles	Catalans	2009	19(2)	2	0	0	8
Setaimata Sa	Hull	2014	4(6)	3	0	0	12
	Catalans	2010-12	58(5)	21	0	0	84
Teddy Sadaoui	Catalans	2006	7	0	0	0	0
Liam Salter	Hull KR	2012-14	55	14	0	0	56
Matt Salter	London	1997-99	14(34)	0	0	0	0
Ben Sammut	Hull	2000	20	4	67	0	150
	Gateshead	1999	26(2)	6	17	0	58
Jarrod Sammut	Wakefield	2014	16(1)	8	52	0	136
	Bradford	2012-13	35(3)	28	47	1	207
	Crusaders	2010-11	17(16)	17	0	0	68
Dean Sampson	Castleford	1996-2003	124(28)	24	0	0	96
Paul Sampson	London	2004	1(2)	1	0	0	4
	Wakefield	2000	17	8	0	0	32
Lee Sanderson	London	2004	1(5)	1	7	0	18
Jason Sands	Paris	1996-97	28	0	0	0	0
Mitchell Sargent	Castleford	2008-10	37(21)	6	0	0	24
Dan Sarginson	Wigan	2014	25	9	0	0	36
	London	2012-13	35(1)	10	0	0	40
	Harlequins	2011	8	5	0	0	20
Junior Sa'u	Salford	2014	25	12	0	0	48
Andre Savelio	St Helens	2014	(3)	0	0	0	0
Lokeni Savelio	Halifax	2000	2(11)	0	0	0	0
	Salford	1997-98	18(20)	0	0	0	0
Tom Saxton	Salford	2007	5	0	0	0	0
	Wakefield	2006	9(6)	2	0	0	8
	Hull	2005	19(8)	3	0	0	12
	Castleford	2002-04	37(12)	11	0	0	44
Jonathan Scales	Halifax	2000	1	0	0	0	0
	Bradford	1996-98	46(4)	24	0	0	96
Andrew Schick	Castleford	1996-98	45(13)	10	0	0	40
Clinton Schifcofske	Crusaders	2010-11	44	5	115	0	250
Garry Schofield	Huddersfield	1998	(2)	0	0	0	0
Gary Schubert	Workington	1996	(1)	0	0	0	0
Matt Schultz	Hull	1998-99	23(9)	2	0	0	8
	Leeds	1996	2(4)	0	0	0	0
John Schuster	Halifax	1996-97	31	9	127	3	293
Nick Scruton	Wakefield	2014	19(1)	4	0	0	16
	Bradford	2009-14	70(27)	5	0	0	20
	Leeds	2002, 2004-08	11(53)	3	0	0	12
	Hull	2004	2(16)	3	0	0	12
Danny Sculthorpe	Huddersfield	2009	5(8)	0	0	0	0
	Wakefield	2007-09	14(28)	1	0	0	4
	Castleford	2006	18(1)	4	0	1	17
	Wigan	2002-05	13(49)	7	0	0	28
Paul Sculthorpe	St Helens	1998-2008	223(4)	94	356	7	1095
	Warrington	1996-97	40	6	0	0	24
Mick Seaby	London	1997	3(2)	1	0	0	4
Danny Seal	Halifax	1996-99	8(17)	3	0	0	12
Matt Seers	Wakefield	2003	11(1)	2	0	0	8
Anthony Seibold	London	1999-2000	33(19)	5	0	0	20
Keith Senior	Leeds	1999-2011	319(2)	159	0	0	636
	Sheffield	1996-99	90(2)	40	0	0	160
Fili Seru	Hull	1998-99	37(1)	13	0	0	52
Anthony Seuseu	Halifax	2003	1(11)	1	0	0	4
Jerry Seuseu	Wigan	2005-06	29(9)	1	0	0	4
Brett Seymour	Hull	2012-13	26(1)	7	0	0	28
Will Sharp	Hull	2011-12	27(8)	10	0	0	40
	Harlequins	2008-10	65(1)	19	0	0	76
Jamie Shaul	Hull	2013-14	33	23	0	0	92
Darren Shaw	Salford	2002	5(9)	1	0	0	4
	London	1996, 2002	22(8)	3	0	0	12
	Castleford	2000-01	50(6)	1	0	0	4
	Sheffield	1998-99	51(1)	3	0	1	13
Mick Shaw	Halifax	1999	5	1	0	0	4
	Leeds	1996	12(2)	7	0	0	28
Ryan Shaw	London	2013	2	1	2	0	8

Super League Players 1996-2014

PLAYER	CLUB	YEAR	APP	TRIES	GOALS	FG	PTS
Phil Shead	Paris	1996	3(2)	0	0	0	0
Richard Sheil	St Helens	1997	(1)	0	0	0	0
Kelly Shelford	Warrington	1996-97	25(3)	4	0	2	18
Michael Shenton	Castleford	2004, 2006, 2008-10, 2013-14	150(2)	69	0	0	276
	St Helens	2011-12	51	15	0	0	60
Ryan Sheridan	Castleford	2004	2	0	0	0	0
	Widnes	2003	14(3)	2	0	0	8
	Leeds	1997-2002	123(7)	46	0	1	185
	Sheffield	1996	9(3)	5	0	1	21
Louis Sheriff	Hull KR	2011-12	8	3	0	0	12
Rikki Sheriffe	Bradford	2009-10	51	14	0	0	56
	Harlequins	2006-08	35(1)	16	0	0	64
	Halifax	2003	6(1)	3	0	0	12
Ian Sherratt	Oldham	1996	5(3)	1	0	0	4
Brent Sherwin	Catalans	2010	12	1	0	1	5
	Castleford	2008-10	48(1)	4	0	3	19
Peter Shiels	St Helens	2001-02	44(3)	11	0	0	44
Gary Shillabeer	Huddersfield	1999	(2)	0	0	0	0
Mark Shipway	Salford	2004-05	30(12)	3	0	0	12
Ian Sibbit	Bradford	2011-12	11(7)	0	0	0	0
	Salford	2005-07, 2009-10	64(17)	11	0	0	44
	Warrington	1999-2001, 2003-04	63(18)	24	0	0	96
Mark Sibson	Huddersfield	1999	2	2	0	0	8
Adam Sidlow	Bradford	2013-14	20(22)	8	0	0	32
	Salford	2009-12	34(44)	14	0	0	56
Harry Siejka	Wakefield	2014	6(3)	1	0	0	4
Jon Simms	St Helens	2002	(1)	0	0	0	0
Craig Simon	Hull	2000	23(2)	8	0	0	32
	Gateshead	1999	25(4)	6	0	0	24
Mickael Simon	Catalans	2010-14	25(40)	2	0	0	8
Darren Simpson	Huddersfield	1998-99	17(1)	5	0	0	20
Jamie Simpson	Huddersfield	2011	8(1)	0	0	0	0
Robbie Simpson	London	1999	6(7)	0	0	0	0
Kevin Sinfield	Leeds	1997-2014	403(25)	67	1454	28	3204
Matt Sing	Hull	2007-08	41	14	0	0	56
Wayne Sing	Paris	1997	18(1)	2	0	0	8
Brad Singleton	Leeds	2011-14	18(21)	2	0	0	8
	Wakefield	2013	(1)	0	0	0	0
Fata Sini	Salford	1997	22	7	0	0	28
John Skandalis	Huddersfield	2007-08	37(5)	4	0	0	16
Dylan Skee	Harlequins	2008-09	(3)	0	0	0	0
Ben Skerrett	Castleford	2003	(1)	0	0	0	0
Kelvin Skerrett	Halifax	1997-99	31(6)	2	0	0	8
	Wigan	1996	1(8)	0	0	0	0
Troy Slattery	Wakefield	2002-03	33(5)	4	0	0	16
	Huddersfield	1999	3	1	0	0	4
Mick Slicker	Huddersfield	2001, 2003-05	17(48)	2	0	0	8
	Sheffield	1999	(3)	1	0	0	4
	Halifax	1997	2(5)	0	0	0	0
Nick Slyney	London	2014	20(4)	3	0	0	12
Ian Smales	Castleford	1996-97	10(8)	5	0	0	20
Aaron Smith	Castleford	2006	(2)	0	0	0	0
	Bradford	2003-04	12(1)	3	0	0	12
Andy Smith	Harlequins	2007	6(3)	3	0	0	12
	Bradford	2004-06	9(9)	4	0	0	16
	Salford	2005	4	1	0	0	4
Byron Smith	Castleford	2004	(9)	0	0	0	0
	Halifax	2003	6(1)	0	0	0	0
Chris Smith	Hull	2001-02	12	3	0	0	12
	St Helens	1998-2000	62(9)	26	0	0	104
	Castleford	1996-97	36(1)	12	0	0	48
Craig Smith	Wigan	2002-04	77(3)	10	0	0	40
Damien Smith	St Helens	1998	21(1)	8	0	0	32
Daniel Smith	Wakefield	2014	10(9)	3	0	0	12
Danny Smith	Paris	1996	10(2)	1	15	0	34
	London	1996	2(1)	1	0	0	4
Darren Smith	St Helens	2003	25(1)	14	0	0	56
Gary Smith	Castleford	2001	(1)	0	0	0	0
Hudson Smith	Bradford	2000	8(22)	2	0	0	8
	Salford	1999	23(2)	5	0	0	20
James Smith	Salford	2000	23(3)	6	0	0	24
Jamie Smith	Hull	1998-99	24(6)	6	12	0	48
	Workington	1996	5(3)	0	1	0	2
Jason Smith	Hull	2001-04	61(3)	17	0	1	69
Jeremy Smith	Wakefield	2011	9(1)	1	0	0	4
	Salford	2009-10	27(17)	2	0	0	8
Kris Smith	London	2001	(1)	0	0	0	0
	Halifax	2001	(1)	0	0	0	0
Lee Smith	Wakefield	2012-13	29(4)	15	54	2	170
	Leeds	2005-12	125(10)	60	34	1	309
Leigh Smith	Workington	1996	9	4	0	0	16
Mark Smith	Widnes	2005	12(15)	4	0	0	16
	Wigan	1999-2004	35(77)	8	0	0	32
Martyn Smith	Harlequins	2010	(2)	0	0	0	0
Matty Smith	Wigan	2012-14	60(3)	9	114	12	276
	Salford	2010-12	67(4)	13	6	1	65
	St Helens	2006-08, 2010	17(2)	3	10	1	33
	Celtic	2009	15(1)	3	2	1	17
Michael Smith	Hull KR	2007	(3)	1	0	0	4
	Castleford	1998, 2001-04	86(33)	32	0	0	128
	Hull	1999	12(6)	3	0	0	12
Paul Smith	Huddersfield	2004-06	52(17)	13	0	0	52
Paul Smith	Warrington	2001	(1)	0	0	0	0
	Castleford	1997-2000	6(37)	3	0	0	12
Paul Smith	London	1997	7(1)	2	0	0	8
Peter Smith	Oldham	1996	2	0	0	0	0
Richard Smith	Wakefield	2001	8(1)	1	0	0	4
	Salford	1997	1	1	0	0	4
Tim Smith	Wakefield	2012-14	61	10	0	0	40
	Salford	2014	12	2	7	0	22
	Wigan	2008-09	13(8)	2	0	0	8
Tony Smith	Hull	2001-03	43(5)	26	0	0	104
	Wigan	1997-2000	66(5)	46	0	0	184
	Castleford	1996-97	18(2)	10	0	0	40
Tony Smith	Workington	1996	9	1	0	0	4
Tyrone Smith	Harlequins	2006-07	49(3)	13	0	0	52
	London	2005	20(4)	11	0	0	44
Rob Smyth	Leigh	2005	15(1)	4	0	0	16
	Warrington	2000-03	65	35	20	0	180
	London	1998-2000	32(2)	9	15	0	66
	Wigan	1996	11(5)	16	0	0	64
Marc Sneyd	Castleford	2014	25(1)	6	100	2	226
	Salford	2010-13	33(12)	4	61	3	141
Steve Snitch	Castleford	2010-12	38(18)	10	0	0	40
	Wakefield	2002-05, 2009	33(55)	9	0	0	36
	Huddersfield	2006-08	24(35)	12	0	0	48
Bright Sodje	Wakefield	2000	15	4	0	0	16
	Sheffield	1996-99	54	34	0	0	136
Iosia Soliola	St Helens	2010-14	83(24)	27	0	0	108
David Solomona	Warrington	2010-12	8(49)	16	1	0	66
	Bradford	2007-09	44(9)	19	0	0	76
	Wakefield	2004-06	73(3)	26	0	0	104
Denny Solomona	London	2014	19(1)	8	0	0	32
Alfred Songoro	Wakefield	1999	8(5)	4	0	0	16
Romain Sort	Paris	1997	(1)	0	0	0	0
Paul Southern	Salford	1997-2002	79(33)	6	13	0	50
	St Helens	2002	1(1)	0	0	0	0
Steve Southern	Wakefield	2012	7(8)	3	0	0	12
Cain Southernwood	Bradford	2010	2	0	0	0	0
Roy Southernwood	Wakefield	1999	1	0	0	0	0
	Halifax	1996	2	0	0	0	0
Jason Southwell	Huddersfield	2004	(1)	0	0	0	0
Waisale Sovatabua	Wakefield	2001-03	44(3)	19	0	0	76
	Hudds-Sheff	2000	23(1)	8	0	0	32
	Sheffield	1996-99	56(17)	19	0	1	77
Jamie Soward	London	2013	6(1)	4	21	0	58
Yusef Sozi	London	2000-01	(5)	0	0	0	0
Scott Spaven	Hull KR	2010	(2)	0	0	0	0
Andy Speak	Castleford	2001	4(4)	0	0	0	0
	Wakefield	2000	6(5)	2	0	0	8
	Leeds	1999	4	1	0	0	4
Dom Speakman	St Helens	2013	(1)	0	0	0	0
Tim Spears	Castleford	2003	(3)	0	0	0	0
Ady Spencer	London	1996-99	8(36)	5	0	0	20
Jack Spencer	Salford	2009-11	(7)	0	0	0	0
Tom Spencer	Wigan	2012-13	(7)	0	0	0	0
Rob Spicer	Wakefield	2002-05	28(18)	4	0	0	16
Russ Spiers	Wakefield	2011	(2)	0	0	0	0
Gadwin Springer	Catalans	2014	(1)	0	0	0	0
Stuart Spruce	Widnes	2002-03	45(4)	19	0	0	76
	Bradford	1996-2001	107(2)	57	0	0	228
Lee St Hilaire	Castleford	1997	4(2)	0	0	0	0
Marcus St Hilaire	Bradford	2006-07	34(1)	12	0	0	48
	Huddersfield	2003-05	72(2)	30	0	0	120
	Leeds	1996-2002	59(33)	31	0	0	124
Cyril Stacul	Catalans	2007-12	61(1)	18	0	0	72
Dylan Stainton	Workington	1996	2(3)	0	0	0	0
Mark Stamper	Workington	1996	(1)	0	0	0	0
John Stankevitch	Widnes	2005	17(5)	0	0	0	0
	St Helens	2000-04	74(40)	25	0	0	100
Gareth Stanley	Bradford	2000	1	1	0	0	4
Craig Stapleton	Salford	2009	24	2	0	0	8
	Leigh	2005	27(1)	4	0	0	16
Graham Steadman	Castleford	1996-97	11(17)	5	0	0	20
Jon Steel	Hull KR	2007-08	18	6	0	0	24
Jamie Stenhouse	Warrington	2000-01	9(3)	3	0	0	12
Gareth Stephens	Sheffield	1997-99	23(6)	2	0	0	8
David Stephenson	Hull	1998	11(7)	3	0	0	12
	Oldham	1997	10(8)	2	0	0	8
Francis Stephenson	London	2002-05	42(34)	5	0	0	20
	Wigan	2001	2(9)	0	0	0	0
	Wakefield	1999-2000	50(1)	6	0	0	24
Paul Sterling	Leeds	1997-2000	79(12)	50	0	0	200
Paul Stevens	Oldham	1996	2(1)	0	0	0	0
	London	1996	(1)	0	0	0	0

PLAYER	CLUB	YEAR	APP	TRIES	GOALS	FG	PTS
Warren Stevens	Leigh	2005	4(14)	1	0	0	4
	Warrington	1996-99, 2002-05	17(66)	1	0	0	4
	Salford	2001	(8)	0	0	0	0
Anthony Stewart	Harlequins	2006	4	0	0	0	0
	Salford	2004-06	51(2)	15	0	0	60
	St Helens	1997-2003	93(23)	44	0	0	176
Troy Stone	Widnes	2002	18(6)	1	0	0	4
	Huddersfield	2001	12(1)	1	0	0	4
James Stosic	Wakefield	2009	8(10)	1	0	0	4
Lynton Stott	Wakefield	1999	21	4	6	1	29
	Sheffield	1996-98	40(4)	15	0	0	60
Mitchell Stringer	Salford	2005-06	12(4)	0	0	0	0
	London	2004-05	10(19)	0	0	0	0
Graham Strutton	London	1996	9(1)	2	0	0	8
Matt Sturm	Leigh	2005	8(19)	3	0	0	12
	Warrington	2002-04	1(18)	0	0	0	0
	Huddersfield	1998-99	46	8	0	0	32
Anthony Sullivan	St Helens	1996-2001	137(2)	105	0	0	420
Michael Sullivan	Warrington	2006-07	21(16)	8	1	0	34
Phil Sumner	Warrington	1996	(5)	0	0	0	0
Liam Sutcliffe	Leeds	2013-14	22(17)	17	8	0	84
	Bradford	2014	3(1)	1	0	0	4
Ryan Sutton	Wigan	2014	1(6)	0	0	0	0
Simon Svabic	Salford	1998-2000	13(5)	3	19	0	50
Luke Swain	Salford	2009-10	54	3	0	0	12
Richard Swain	Hull	2004-07	89	5	0	0	20
Anthony Swann	Warrington	2001	3	1	0	0	4
Logan Swann	Warrington	2005-06	49(1)	17	0	0	68
	Bradford	2004	25	6	0	0	24
Willie Swann	Warrington	1996-97	25(2)	6	0	0	24
Adam Swift	St Helens	2012-14	33	28	0	0	112
Nathan Sykes	Castleford	1996-2004	158(52)	3	0	0	12
Paul Sykes	Wakefield	2012-14	59(1)	12	135	6	324
	Bradford	1999-2002, 2008-12	99(4)	35	64	2	270
	Harlequins	2006-07	31(2)	15	47	1	155
	London	2001-05	95(1)	26	219	3	545
Wayne Sykes	London	1999	(2)	0	0	0	0
Ukuma Ta'ai	Huddersfield	2013-14	19(28)	12	0	0	48
Semi Tadulala	Wakefield	2004-07, 2011	92	37	0	0	148
	Bradford	2008-09	49	30	0	0	120
Whetu Taewa	Sheffield	1997-98	33(7)	8	0	0	32
Zeb Taia	Catalans	2013-14	52	23	0	0	92
Alan Tait	Leeds	1996	3(3)	1	0	0	4
Fetuli Talanoa	Hull	2014	27	10	0	0	40
Willie Talau	Salford	2009-10	22	4	0	0	16
	St Helens	2003-08	130(1)	50	0	0	200
Ian Talbot	Wakefield	1999	9(5)	2	31	0	70
	Wigan	1997	3	1	0	0	4
Albert Talipeau	Wakefield	2004	2(3)	0	0	0	0
Gael Tallec	Halifax	2000	5(19)	3	0	0	12
	Castleford	1998-99	19(21)	3	0	0	12
	Wigan	1996-97	8(12)	3	0	0	12
Joe Tamani	Bradford	1996	11(3)	4	0	0	16
Ryan Tandy	Hull KR	2007	8(4)	2	0	0	8
Andrew Tangata-Toa							
	Huddersfield	1999	15	2	0	0	8
David Tangata-Toa							
	Celtic	2009	1(18)	4	0	0	16
	Hull KR	2007	(17)	3	0	0	12
Jordan Tansey	Castleford	2013-14	32	9	0	0	36
	Crusaders	2011	14(4)	5	0	0	20
	Hull	2009-10	30	9	0	0	36
	Leeds	2006-08	18(32)	19	3	0	82
Lama Tasi	Salford	2014	23(1)	0	0	0	0
Kris Tassell	Wakefield	2002	24	10	0	0	40
	Salford	2000-01	35(10)	12	0	0	48
Shem Tatupu	Wigan	1996	(3)	0	0	0	0
Tony Tatupu	Wakefield	2000-01	20	2	0	0	8
	Warrington	1997	21(1)	6	0	0	24
Taulima Tautai	Wakefield	2013-14	6(19)	2	0	0	8
James Taylor	Leigh	2005	(4)	0	0	0	0
Joe Taylor	Paris	1997	9(5)	2	0	0	8
Lawrence Taylor	Sheffield	1996	(1)	0	0	0	0
Scott Taylor	Wigan	2013-14	18(29)	6	0	0	24
	Hull KR	2009-12	21(29)	8	0	0	32
Frederic Teixido	Sheffield	1999	(4)	0	0	0	0
	Paris	1996-97	2(3)	1	0	0	4
Lionel Teixido	Catalans	2006-07	11(13)	3	0	0	12
Karl Temata	London	2005, 2012	1(8)	1	0	0	4
	Harlequins	2006-11	94(22)	7	0	0	28
Jason Temu	Hull	1998	13(2)	1	0	0	4
	Oldham	1996-97	25(3)	1	0	0	4
Paul Terry	London	1997	(1)	0	0	0	0
Anthony Thackeray							
	Castleford	2008	3(6)	0	0	0	0
	Hull	2007	2	0	0	0	0
Jamie Thackray	Crusaders	2010	1(16)	2	0	0	8
	Hull	2005-06, 2008-09	37(45)	6	0	0	24
	Leeds	2006-07	5(27)	7	0	0	28
	Castleford	2003-04	7(11)	3	0	0	12
	Halifax	2000-02	10(38)	3	0	0	12
Adam Thaler	Castleford	2002	(1)	0	0	0	0
Gareth Thomas	Crusaders	2010-11	27(1)	6	0	0	24
Giles Thomas	London	1997-99	1(2)	0	0	0	0
Oscar Thomas	London	2014	4(2)	0	1	0	2
Rob Thomas	Harlequins	2011	(2)	0	0	0	0
Steve Thomas	London	2004	4(2)	0	0	0	0
	Warrington	2001	2	0	0	0	0
Alex Thompson	Warrington	2009	(1)	1	0	0	4
Alex Thompson	Sheffield	1997	4(11)	0	0	0	0
Bobby Thompson	Salford	1999	28	5	2	0	24
Jordan Thompson							
	Hull	2014	4(19)	4	0	0	16
	Castleford	2009-13	47(24)	25	0	0	100
Luke Thompson	St Helens	2013-14	8(16)	4	0	0	16
Sam Thompson	Harlequins	2009	(2)	0	0	0	0
	St Helens	2008	(5)	0	0	0	0
Chris Thorman	Hull	2009	19(2)	1	0	0	4
	Huddersfield	2000-01, 2005-08	126(20)	51	320	3	847
	London	2003	26(1)	7	81	1	191
	Sheffield	1999	5(13)	2	8	1	25
Tony Thorniley	Warrington	1997	(5)	0	0	0	0
Andy Thornley	Salford	2009	(1)	1	0	0	4
Iain Thornley	Wigan	2012-14	40	25	0	0	100
Danny Tickle	Widnes	2014	26	3	77	0	166
	Hull	2007-13	159(5)	45	528	1	1237
	Wigan	2002-06	94(36)	34	200	2	538
	Halifax	2000-02	25(17)	10	91	2	224
Kris Tickle	Warrington	2001	(1)	0	0	0	0
Lewis Tierney	Wigan	2013-14	4	2	0	0	8
James Tilley	St Helens	2013-14	(3)	0	0	0	0
John Timu	London	1998-2000	57(3)	11	0	0	44
Kerrod Toby	London	1997	2(2)	0	0	0	0
Tulsen Tollett	London	1996-2001	105(5)	38	49	1	251
Joel Tomkins	Wigan	2005-11, 2014	101(40)	48	0	0	192
Logan Tomkins	Salford	2014	8(9)	3	0	0	12
	Wigan	2012-14	8(25)	1	0	0	4
Sam Tomkins	Wigan	2009-13	124(5)	107	28	1	485
Glen Tomlinson	Wakefield	1999-2000	41(5)	8	0	0	32
	Hull	1998	5	1	0	0	4
	Bradford	1996-97	27(13)	12	0	0	48
Ryan Tongia	Wakefield	2011	4	2	0	0	8
Ian Tonks	Castleford	1996-2001	32(50)	11	13	0	70
Tony Tonks	Huddersfield	2012	(1)	0	0	0	0
Motu Tony	Wakefield	2011-12	7(3)	1	0	0	4
	Hull	2005-09	76(20)	25	0	0	100
	Castleford	2004	8(1)	1	0	0	4
Mark Tookey	Harlequins	2006	12(14)	1	0	0	4
	London	2005	13(14)	5	0	0	20
	Castleford	2004	2(8)	1	0	0	4
Clinton Toopi	Leeds	2006-08	40(3)	9	0	0	36
David Tootill	Harlequins	2008	(4)	0	0	0	0
Paul Topping	Oldham	1996-97	23(10)	1	19	0	42
Patrick Torreilles	Paris	1996	9(1)	1	25	0	54
Albert Torrens	Huddersfield	2006	7	5	0	0	20
Mat Toshack	London	1998-2004	120(21)	24	0	0	96
Julien Touxagas	Catalans	2006-11	14(45)	4	0	0	16
Darren Treacy	Salford	2002	24(1)	6	1	0	26
Dean Treister	Hull	2003	16(1)	3	0	0	12
Rocky Trimarchi	Crusaders	2010	16(8)	0	0	0	0
Steve Trindall	London	2003-05	40(20)	3	0	0	12
Shane Tronc	Wakefield	2010	8(3)	2	0	0	8
Kyle Trout	Wakefield	2012-14	6(15)	3	0	0	12
George Truelove	Wakefield	2002	2	1	0	0	4
	London	2000	5	1	0	0	4
Va'aiga Tuigamala							
	Wigan	1996	21	10	3	0	46
Fereti Tuilagi	St Helens	1999-2000	43(15)	21	0	0	84
	Halifax	1996-98	55(3)	27	0	0	108
Evarn Tuimavave	Hull KR	2013	11(12)	2	0	0	8
Sateki Tuipulotu	Leeds	1996	6(3)	1	2	0	8
Tame Tupou	Bradford	2007-08	10(7)	8	0	0	32
Neil Turley	Leigh	2005	6(3)	2	20	1	49
Darren Turner	Huddersfield	2000-01, 2003-04	42(13)	13	0	0	52
	Sheffield	1996-99	41(29)	15	0	0	60
Ian Turner	Paris	1996	1(1)	1	0	0	4
Jordan Turner	St Helens	2013-14	54	23	13	1	119
	Hull	2010-12	62(5)	28	0	0	112
	Salford	2006-07, 2009	22(10)	4	1	0	18
Chris Tuson	Hull	2014	10(1)	0	0	0	0
	Wigan	2008, 2010-13	24(49)	13	0	0	52
	Castleford	2010	3(5)	0	0	0	0
Gregory Tutard	Paris	1996	1(1)	0	0	0	0
Brendon Tuuta	Warrington	1998	18(2)	4	0	0	16
	Castleford	1996-97	41(1)	3	0	0	12
Steve Tyrer	Salford	2010	20	6	9	0	42
	Celtic	2009	8	2	5	0	18
	St Helens	2006-08	17(3)	12	42	0	132
Harry Tyson-Wilson							
	Hull	2014	(1)	0	0	0	0

179

Super League Players 1996-2014

PLAYER	CLUB	YEAR	APP	TRIES	GOALS	FG	PTS
Wayne Ulugia	Hull KR	2014	3	1	0	0	4
Mike Umaga	Halifax	1996-97	38(1)	16	5	0	74
Kava Utoikamanu	Paris	1996	6(3)	0	0	0	0
Frederic Vaccari	Catalans	2010-11, 2013-14	50	26	0	0	104
David Vaealiki	Wigan	2005-07	67(1)	17	0	0	68
Joe Vagana	Bradford	2001-08	176(44)	17	0	0	68
Nigel Vagana	Warrington	1997	20	17	0	0	68
Tevita Vaikona	Bradford	1998-2004	145(2)	89	0	0	356
Lesley Vainikolo	Bradford	2002-07	132(4)	136	1	0	546
Eric Van Brussell	Paris	1996	2	0	0	0	0
Jace Van Dijk	Celtic	2009	19	1	1	0	6
Richard Varkulis	Warrington	2004	4(1)	3	0	0	12
Marcus Vassilakopoulos	Sheffield	1997-99	15(11)	3	10	2	34
	Leeds	1996-97	1(3)	0	0	0	0
Atelea Vea	London	2014	19(3)	2	0	0	8
Josh Veivers	Salford	2012	5	2	0	0	8
	Wakefield	2011	10(2)	2	22	0	52
Phil Veivers	Huddersfield	1998	7(6)	1	0	0	4
	St Helens	1996	(1)	1	0	0	4
Michael Vella	Hull KR	2007-11	111(5)	13	0	0	52
Bruno Verges	Catalans	2006	25	6	0	0	24
Eric Vergniol	Paris	1996	14(1)	6	0	0	24
Gray Viane	Salford	2007	9	2	0	0	8
	Castleford	2006	20(7)	14	0	0	56
	Widnes	2005	20	13	0	0	52
	St Helens	2004	4	1	0	0	4
Joe Vickery	Leeds	2013	9	1	0	0	4
Adrian Vowles	Castleford	1997-2001, 2003	125(1)	29	1	1	119
	Wakefield	2002-03	24(3)	6	1	0	26
	Leeds	2002	14(3)	2	0	0	8
Michael Wainwright	Castleford	2008-10	70	22	0	0	88
	Wakefield	2004-05	21(10)	8	0	0	32
Mike Wainwright	Salford	2000-02, 2007	75(3)	9	0	0	36
	Warrington	1996-99, 2003-07	168(14)	23	0	0	92
Adam Walker	Hull KR	2013-14	32(14)	4	0	0	16
	Huddersfield	2010-12	1(5)	0	0	0	0
Alex Walker	London	2014	1	0	0	0	0
Anthony Walker	St Helens	2013-14	9(7)	2	0	0	8
Ben Walker	Leeds	2002	23(1)	8	100	0	232
Chev Walker	Bradford	2011-14	44(22)	5	0	0	20
	Hull KR	2008-09	24(7)	5	0	0	20
	Leeds	1999-2006	142(19)	77	0	0	308
Chris Walker	Catalans	2010	11	6	2	0	28
Jonathan Walker	Hull KR	2014	2(6)	0	0	0	0
	Castleford	2010-13	17(31)	4	0	0	16
Jonny Walker	Wigan	2010	(1)	0	0	0	0
Matt Walker	Huddersfield	2001	3(6)	0	0	0	0
Anthony Wall	Paris	1997	9	3	3	0	18
Jon Wallace	London	2014	4(12)	0	0	0	0
Mark Wallace	Workington	1996	14(1)	3	0	0	12
Alex Walmsley	St Helens	2013-14	19(29)	6	0	0	24
Adam Walne	Salford	2012-14	5(17)	1	0	0	4
Jordan Walne	Salford	2013-14	7(17)	2	0	0	8
Joe Walsh	Huddersfield	2009	1(1)	1	0	0	4
	Harlequins	2007-08	1(4)	0	0	0	0
Luke Walsh	St Helens	2014	16	5	66	1	153
Lucas Walshaw	Wakefield	2011-14	15(6)	3	0	0	12
Josh Walters	Leeds	2014	5(3)	3	0	0	12
Kerrod Walters	Gateshead	1999	10(12)	2	1	0	10
Kevin Walters	Warrington	2001	1	0	0	0	0
Jason Walton	Salford	2009, 2014	4(15)	1	0	0	4
Barry Ward	St Helens	2002-03	20(30)	4	0	0	16
Danny Ward	Harlequins	2008-11	89(7)	4	0	0	16
	Hull KR	2007	11(9)	0	0	0	0
	Castleford	2006	18(7)	2	0	0	8
	Leeds	1999-2005	70(48)	9	0	1	37
Robbie Ward	Leeds	2014	4(2)	1	0	0	4
Stevie Ward	Leeds	2012-14	26(22)	5	0	0	20
Joe Wardle	Huddersfield	2011-14	83	45	0	0	180
	Bradford	2010	1(1)	0	0	0	0
Phil Waring	Salford	1997-99	6(8)	2	0	0	8
Brett Warton	London	1999-2001	49(7)	14	133	0	322
Kyle Warren	Castleford	2002	13(14)	3	0	0	12
Danny Washbrook	Wakefield	2012-14	74(5)	11	0	0	44
	Hull	2005-11	92(30)	11	0	0	44
	Bradford	2006	(4)	0	0	0	0
Adam Watene	Wakefield	2006-08	45(8)	5	0	0	20
Frank Watene	Wakefield	1999-2001	24(37)	6	0	0	24
Trent Waterhouse	Warrington	2012-14	65(5)	15	0	0	60
Kallum Watkins	Leeds	2008-14	104(7)	64	0	0	256
Dave Watson	Sheffield	1998-99	41(4)	4	0	0	16
Ian Watson	Salford	1997, 2002	24(17)	8	3	5	43
	Workington	1996	4(1)	1	15	0	34
Kris Watson	Warrington	1996	11(2)	2	0	0	8
Anthony Watts	Widnes	2012	(1)	0	0	0	0
Brad Watts	Widnes	2005	6	3	0	0	12
Liam Watts	Hull	2012-14	43(11)	3	0	0	12
	Hull KR	2008, 2010-12	31(26)	6	0	0	24
Michael Watts	Warrington	2002	3	0	0	0	0
Brent Webb	Catalans	2013-14	10	2	0	0	8
	Leeds	2007-12	137(1)	73	0	0	292
Jason Webber	Salford	2000	25(1)	10	0	0	40
Ian Webster	St Helens	2006	1	0	0	0	0
Jake Webster	Castleford	2013-14	21(4)	10	0	0	40
	Hull KR	2008-12	95(1)	34	7	0	150
James Webster	Hull	2008	1	0	0	0	0
	Hull KR	2007-08	36	2	0	2	10
Pat Weisner	Hull KR	2007	(2)	0	0	0	0
	Harlequins	2006	10(6)	3	0	0	12
Taylor Welch	Warrington	2008	1	0	0	0	0
Kris Welham	Hull KR	2007-14	145(2)	83	1	0	334
Paul Wellens	St Helens	1998-2014	395(40)	198	34	1	861
Jon Wells	Harlequins	2006-09	66	10	0	0	40
	London	2004-05	42(2)	19	0	0	76
	Wakefield	2003	22(1)	1	0	0	4
	Castleford	1996-2002	114(14)	49	0	0	196
Dwayne West	St Helens	2000-02	8(16)	6	0	0	24
	Wigan	1999	1(1)	0	0	0	0
Joe Westerman	Hull	2011-14	88(10)	23	52	1	197
	Castleford	2008-10	68(7)	29	151	0	418
Craig Weston	Widnes	2002, 2004	23(9)	2	1	2	12
	Huddersfield	1998-99	46(1)	15	15	0	90
Ben Westwood	Warrington	2002-14	288(8)	101	62	0	528
	Wakefield	1999-2002	31(7)	8	1	0	34
Michael Weyman	Hull KR	2014	22(1)	7	0	0	28
Andrew Whalley	Workington	1996	(2)	0	0	0	0
Paul Whatuira	Huddersfield	2008-10	59	23	0	0	92
Scott Wheeldon	Castleford	2014	5(17)	4	0	0	16
	London	2012-13	27(4)	3	0	0	12
	Hull KR	2009-12	30(42)	4	0	0	16
	Hull	2006-08	2(60)	4	0	0	16
Gary Wheeler	St Helens	2008-14	48(10)	17	13	0	94
Matt Whitaker	Castleford	2006	8(2)	0	0	0	0
	Widnes	2004-05	10(20)	9	0	0	36
	Huddersfield	2003-04	3(14)	0	0	0	0
Ben White	Leeds	2014	1	0	0	0	0
David White	Wakefield	2000	(1)	0	0	0	0
Josh White	Salford	1998	18(3)	5	5	1	31
	London	1997	14(2)	8	0	1	33
Lloyd White	Widnes	2012-14	21(38)	11	0	1	45
	Crusaders	2010-11	13(11)	8	0	0	32
	Celtic	2009	6	1	0	0	4
Paul White	Salford	2009	1	1	0	0	4
	Wakefield	2006-07	24(12)	12	0	0	48
	Huddersfield	2003-05	11(32)	17	16	0	100
Elliott Whitehead	Catalans	2013-14	34(1)	19	0	0	76
	Bradford	2009-13	90(10)	30	0	0	120
Richard Whiting	Hull	2004-14	157(63)	66	19	2	304
Emmerson Whittel	Bradford	2014	(1)	0	0	0	0
Danny Whittle	Warrington	1998	(2)	0	0	0	0
David Whittle	St Helens	2002	1(2)	0	0	0	0
	Warrington	2001	1(2)	0	0	0	0
Jon Whittle	Wakefield	2006	8(2)	3	0	0	12
	Widnes	2005	13	2	0	0	8
	Wigan	2003	1	0	0	0	0
Joel Wicks	London	2013-14	3(10)	0	0	0	0
Dean Widders	Castleford	2009-11	25(32)	23	0	0	92
Stephen Wild	Salford	2011-13	71	4	0	0	16
	Huddersfield	2006-10	116(2)	33	0	0	132
	Wigan	2001-05	67(20)	24	0	0	96
Matty Wildie	Wakefield	2010-14	13(26)	3	0	0	12
Oliver Wilkes	Wakefield	2008-09, 2012-13	55(47)	10	0	0	40
	Harlequins	2010-11	39(13)	4	0	0	16
	Wigan	2006	1(5)	0	0	0	0
	Leigh	2005	13(1)	1	0	0	4
	Huddersfield	2000-01	1(6)	0	0	0	0
	Sheffield	1998	(1)	0	0	0	0
Jon Wilkin	St Helens	2003-14	242(27)	70	0	1	281
Alex Wilkinson	Hull	2003-04	11(4)	1	0	0	4
	Huddersfield	2003	8	4	0	0	16
	London	2002	5(1)	0	0	0	0
	Bradford	2000-01	3(3)	1	0	0	4
Bart Williams	London	1998	5(3)	1	0	0	4
Daley Williams	Salford	2006-07	9(2)	4	0	0	16
Danny Williams	Harlequins	2006	9(13)	4	0	0	16
	London	2005	1(16)	0	0	0	0
Danny Williams	Bradford	2014	7	2	0	0	8
	Salford	2011-14	54	31	0	0	124
	Leeds	2006, 2008	13(2)	7	0	0	28
	Hull	2008	3	0	0	0	0
Dave Williams	Harlequins	2008-11	1(17)	0	0	0	0
Desi Williams	Wigan	2004	2	0	0	0	0
George Williams	Wigan	2013-14	13(9)	6	8	0	40
Jonny Williams	London	2004	(4)	0	0	0	0
Lee Williams	Crusaders	2011	1(7)	0	0	0	0
Rhys Williams	Warrington	2010-13	23(1)	15	0	0	60
	Salford	2013	4	0	0	0	0
	Castleford	2012	8	4	0	0	16
	Crusaders	2011	6	3	0	0	12
Sam Williams	Catalans	2014	11(1)	4	21	0	58

PLAYER	CLUB	YEAR	APP	TRIES	GOALS	FG	PTS
Luke Williamson	Harlequins	2009-10	39	6	0	0	24
John Wilshere	Salford	2006-07,					
		2009	72(2)	32	142	0	412
	Leigh	2005	26	8	6	0	44
	Warrington	2004	5	2	0	0	8
Craig Wilson	Hull	2000	2(16)	1	0	1	5
	Gateshead	1999	17(11)	5	0	1	21
George Wilson	Paris	1996	7(2)	3	0	0	12
John Wilson	Catalans	2006-08	69	23	0	0	92
Richard Wilson	Hull	1998-99	(13)	0	0	0	0
Scott Wilson	Warrington	1998-99	23(2)	6	0	0	24
Johan Windley	Hull	1999	2(2)	1	0	0	4
Paul Wingfield	Warrington	1997	5(3)	6	1	0	26
Frank Winterstein							
	Widnes	2012-13	37(9)	16	0	0	64
	Crusaders	2010-11	26(19)	4	0	0	16
	Wakefield	2009	(5)	0	0	0	0
Lincoln Withers	Hull KR	2012-13	18(22)	10	0	0	40
	Crusaders	2010-11	47	4	0	0	16
	Celtic	2009	21	6	0	0	24
Michael Withers	Wigan	2007	6(1)	1	0	0	4
	Bradford	1999-2006	156(6)	94	15	4	410
Michael Witt	London	2012-13	37	10	89	1	219
	Crusaders	2010-11	39	13	47	4	150
Jeff Wittenberg	Huddersfield	1998	18(1)	1	0	0	4
	Bradford	1997	8(9)	4	0	0	16
Kyle Wood	Huddersfield	2011,					
		2013-14	21(17)	4	0	0	16
	Wakefield	2012-13	5(37)	9	0	0	36
	Castleford	2010	1(4)	0	0	0	0
Martin Wood	Sheffield	1997-98	24(11)	4	18	2	54
Nathan Wood	Warrington	2002-05	90	38	0	3	155
	Wakefield	2002	11	2	0	0	8
Paul Wood	Warrington	2000-14	138(171)	40	0	0	160
Phil Wood	Widnes	2004	2(1)	0	0	0	0
Sam Wood	Bradford	2013-14	7(1)	0	0	0	0
James Woodburn-Hall							
	London	2013-14	9(4)	2	0	0	8
Darren Woods	Widnes	2005	(1)	0	0	0	0
David Woods	Halifax	2002	18(2)	8	0	0	32
Simon Worrall	Leeds	2008-09	5(16)	1	0	0	4
Michael Worrincy	Bradford	2009-10	12(34)	12	0	0	48
	Harlequins	2006-08	20(12)	10	0	0	40
Rob Worrincy	Castleford	2004	1	0	0	0	0
Troy Wozniak	Widnes	2004	13(7)	1	0	0	4
Matthew Wray	Wakefield	2002-03	13(3)	2	0	0	8
David Wrench	Wakefield	2002-06	28(52)	6	0	0	24
	Leeds	1999-2001	7(17)	0	0	0	0
Callum Wright	Wigan	2014	(2)	0	0	0	0
Craig Wright	Castleford	2000	1(9)	0	0	0	0
Nigel Wright	Huddersfield	1999	4(6)	1	0	0	4
	Wigan	1996-97	5(5)	2	0	1	9
Ricky Wright	Sheffield	1997-99	2(13)	0	0	0	0
Vincent Wulf	Paris	1996	13(4)	4	0	0	16
Andrew Wynyard	London	1999-2000	34(6)	4	0	0	16
Bagdad Yaha	Paris	1996	4(4)	2	4	0	16
Malakai Yasa	Sheffield	1996	1(3)	0	0	0	0
Kirk Yeaman	Hull	2001-14	281(17)	149	0	0	596
Grant Young	London	1998-99	22(2)	2	0	0	8
Nick Youngquest	Castleford	2011-12	37	28	0	0	112
	Crusaders	2010	26(1)	9	0	0	36
Ronel Zenon	Paris	1996	(4)	0	0	0	0
Nick Zisti	Bradford	1999	6(1)	0	0	0	0
Freddie Zitter	Catalans	2006	1	0	0	0	0

NEW FACES - Players making their Super League debuts in 2014

PLAYER	CLUB	DEBUT vs	ROUND	DATE
Jordan Abdull	Hull	Wakefield (a)	18	29/6/14
Brad Adams	Bradford	Widnes (h)	26	7/9/14
Scott Anderson	Wakefield	Salford (a)	1	16/2/14
Roy Asotasi	Warrington	St Helens (h)	1	13/2/14
Jordan Atkins	London	Widnes (a)	1	16/2/14
Sam Bates	Bradford	Wigan (a)	10	21/4/14
Matt Bowen	Wigan	Huddersfield (h)	1	7/2/14
Luke Briscoe	Wakefield	Wigan (a)	3	2/3/14
Liam Carberry	Widnes	Warrington (h)	21	18/7/14
Neville Costigan	Hull KR	Leeds (h)	1	16/2/14
Jordan Crowther	Wakefield	Wigan (a)	3	2/3/14
Brad Day	Castleford	Warrington (a)	24	15/8/14
Jamie Doran	Wigan	St Helens (h)	18	27/6/14
Josh Drinkwater	London	Bradford (a)	3	2/3/14
Anthony England	Warrington	Leeds (a)	2	21/2/14
Sonny Esslemont	Hull KR	Catalans (h)	26	7/9/14
Toby Everett	London	Salford (a)	26	7/9/14
Connor Farrell	Wigan	Widnes (h)	2	18/6/14
Matty Fozard	St Helens	Widnes (a)	10	21/4/14
Danny Galea	Widnes	London (h)	1	16/2/14
Pita Godinet	Wakefield	Salford (a)	1	16/2/14
Ashton Golding	Leeds	London (a)	24	17/8/14
Joan Guasch	Catalans	Widnes (h)	8	12/4/14
(club debut: London (h), CCR4, 4/4/14)				
Macauley Hallett	Hull KR	Catalans (h)	26	7/9/14
Ash Handley	Leeds	London (a)	24	17/8/14
Adam Henry	Bradford	Castleford (h)	1	16/2/14
Maxime Herold	London	Catalans (MW)	13	17/5/14
Max Jowitt	Wakefield	St Helens (a)	24	15/8/14
Kris Keating	Hull KR	Leeds (h)	1	16/2/14
Joe Keyes	London	Widnes (h)	18	28/6/14
George King	Warrington	Bradford (h)	18	29/6/14
Toby King	Warrington	London (h)	20	13/7/14
Callum Lancaster	Hull	Leeds (a)	14	23/5/14
Kevin Locke	Salford	Huddersfield (a)	19	5/7/14
Jack Logan	Hull	Wigan (a)	21	18/7/14
Will Maher	Castleford	Warrington (a)	24	15/8/14
Mose Masoe	St Helens	Hull KR (h)	4	7/3/14
Nesiasi Mataitonga	London	Widnes (a)	1	16/2/14
Rob Mulhern	Leeds	London (h)	6	21/3/14
Jake Mullaney	Salford	Wakefield (h)	1	16/2/14
Michael Oldfield	Catalans	Hull (a)	1	14/2/14
Gene Ormsby	Warrington	Leeds (a)	2	21/2/14
Eddy Pettybourne	Wigan	Huddersfield (h)	1	7/2/14
Joe Philbin	Warrington	Hull KR (a)	16	13/6/14
Ben Pomeroy	Catalans	Hull (a)	1	14/2/14
Jordan Rankin	Hull	Catalans (h)	1	14/2/14
Steve Rapira	Salford	London (a)	2	22/2/14
Connor Robinson	Hull KR	London (a)	22	26/7/14
Matt Ryan	Wakefield	Salford (a)	1	16/2/14
Junior Sa'u	Salford	Wakefield (h)	1	16/2/14
Andre Savelio	St Helens	Leeds (h)	7	28/3/14
Harry Siejka	Wakefield	St Helens (h)	6	23/3/14
Nick Slyney	London	Bradford (a)	3	2/3/14
Daniel Smith	Wakefield	Salford (a)	1	16/2/14
Denny Solomona	London	Warrington (h)	4	9/3/14
Gadwin Springer	Catalans	St Helens (a)	5	14/3/14
Ryan Sutton	Wigan	Bradford (h)	10	21/4/14
Fetuli Talanoa	Hull	Catalans (h)	1	14/2/14
Lama Tasi	Salford	Wakefield (h)	1	16/2/14
Oscar Thomas	London	St Helens (h)	21	19/7/14
Harry Tyson-Wilson	Hull	Huddersfield (a)	26	7/9/14
Wayne Ulugia	Hull KR	Widnes (h)	11	4/5/14
Atelea Vea	London	Wakefield (h)	5	15/3/14
Alex Walker	London	Bradford (h)	27	13/9/14
Jon Wallace	London	Wigan (a)	8	11/4/14
Luke Walsh	St Helens	Warrington (a)	1	13/2/14
Josh Walters	Leeds	Huddersfield (h)	16	12/6/14
(club debut: Leigh (h), CCQF, 6/6/14)				
Robbie Ward	Leeds	Hull (h)	14	23/5/14
Michael Weyman	Hull KR	Leeds (h)	1	16/2/14
Ben White	Leeds	London (a)	24	17/8/14
Emmerson Whittel	Bradford	London (a)	27	13/9/14
Sam Williams	Catalans	Hull (h)	17	21/6/14
Callum Wright	Wigan	Widnes (h)	2	18/6/14

OLD FACES - Players making their Super League debuts for new clubs in 2014

PLAYER	CLUB	DEBUT vs	ROUND	DATE
Paul Aiton	Leeds	Hull KR (a)	1	16/2/14
Kyle Amor	St Helens	Warrington (a)	1	13/2/14
Joe Arundel	Bradford	Warrington (h)	11	4/5/14
Chris Bailey	Huddersfield	Wigan (a)	1	7/2/14
Jordan Baldwinson	Bradford	Catalans (a)	14	24/5/14
John Bateman	Wigan	Wakefield (h)	3	2/3/14
(club debut: Sydney Roosters, WCC, 22/2/14)				
Danny Bridge	Bradford	Castleford (h)	1	16/2/14
Luke Briscoe	Leeds	Huddersfield (h)	16	12/6/14
Tom Briscoe	Leeds	Hull KR (a)	1	16/2/14
Jodie Broughton	Huddersfield	Leeds (h)	4	7/3/14
Greg Burke	Bradford	Hull (a)	4	7/3/14
Garreth Carvell	Hull	Catalans (h) (D2)	1	14/2/14
	Castleford	Salford (h)	18	28/6/14
Mason Caton-Brown	Salford	Huddersfield (a)	19	5/7/14
Jason Chan	Hull KR	Salford (h)	21	20/7/14
Rangi Chase	Salford	Wakefield (h)	1	16/2/14
Paul Clough	Widnes	Huddersfield (h)	3	28/2/14
Tony Clubb	Wigan	Huddersfield (h)	1	7/2/14
Ben Cockayne	Hull KR	Leeds (h) (D2)	1	16/2/14
Liam Colbon	Hull	Castleford (a)	5	16/3/14
James Cunningham	London	Widnes (a)	1	16/2/14
Matty Dawson	St Helens	Wakefield (a)	6	23/3/14
Luke Dorn	Castleford	Bradford (a) (D2)	1	16/2/14
James Duckworth	London	Bradford (a)	3	2/3/14
Greg Eden	Salford	Catalans (a)	11	3/5/14
(club debut: Widnes (h), CCR5, 27/4/14)				
Ben Evans	Warrington	St Helens (h)	1	13/2/14
Jacob Fairbank	Wakefield	Hull (a)	11	4/5/14
Jamal Fakir	Bradford	Salford (h)	8	11/4/14
(club debut: Oldham (h), CCR4, 6/4/14)				
Ben Farrar	London	Bradford (a)	3	2/3/14
Dale Ferguson	Bradford	Salford (h)	8	11/4/14
(club debut: Oldham (h), CCR4, 6/4/14)				
Liam Finn	Castleford	Bradford (a)	1	16/2/14
Carl Forster	London	Widnes (a)	1	16/2/14
Alex Foster	London	Widnes (a)	1	16/2/14
Ade Gardner	Hull KR	Wigan (a)	5	14/3/14
Lee Gaskell	Bradford	Castleford (h)	1	16/2/14
Luke George	Bradford	Wakefield (a)	2	20/2/14
Ashley Gibson	Castleford	Warrington (h)	10	21/4/14
Tony Gigot	London	Widnes (a)	1	16/2/14
Lee Gilmour	Wakefield	Bradford (a)	15	1/6/14
James Greenwood	London	Bradford (a)	3	2/3/14
George Griffin	London	Widnes (a)	1	16/2/14
Josh Griffin	Salford	Castleford (a)	18	28/6/14
Harrison Hansen	Salford	Wakefield (h)	1	16/2/14
Gareth Hock	Salford	Wakefield (h)	1	16/2/14
Jordan James	Wigan	Castleford (a) (D2)	4	9/3/14
Lee Jewitt	Castleford	Wakefield (MW)	13	18/5/14
Greg Johnson	Salford	Wakefield (h)	1	16/2/14
Paul Johnson	Widnes	London (h)	1	16/2/14
Antonio Kaufusi	Huddersfield	Wigan (a)	1	7/2/14
	Bradford	Warrington (h)	11	4/5/14
Jimmy Keinhorst	Wakefield	Salford (a)	1	16/2/14
Jamie Langley	Hull KR	Leeds (h)	1	16/2/14
Kevin Larroyer	Hull KR	Leeds (h)	1	16/2/14
Tommy Lee	Salford	Wakefield (h)	1	16/2/14
Jeff Lima	Catalans	Hull (a)	1	14/2/14
Rhodri Lloyd	Widnes	Huddersfield (h)	3	28/2/14
Andy Lynch	Castleford	Bradford (a) (D2)	1	16/2/14
Dominic Manfredi	Salford	Warrington (h)	5	14/3/14
Frankie Mariano	Castleford	Bradford (a)	1	16/2/14
Shannon McDonnell	St Helens	Wakefield (h)	24	15/8/14
Paul McShane	Wakefield	Salford (a)	1	16/2/14
Francis Meli	Salford	Wakefield (h)	1	16/2/14
Thomas Minns	London	Widnes (a)	1	16/2/14
Richard Moore	Wakefield	Leeds (a)	8	11/4/14
(club debut: Leeds (h) (D2), CCR4, 6/4/14)				
Scott Moore	London	Widnes (a)	1	16/2/14
Adrian Morley	Salford	Wakefield (h)	1	16/2/14
Anthony Mullally	Bradford	Wakefield (a)	2	20/2/14
Richard Owen	Wakefield	Warrington (h)	14	25/5/14
Mickey Paea	Hull	Catalans (h)	1	14/2/14
Iafeta Palea'aesina	Hull	Catalans (h)	1	14/2/14
Kevin Penny	Warrington	Castleford (a) (D2)	10	21/4/14
Jay Pitts	Bradford	Warrington (h)	11	4/5/14
(club debut: Catalans (h), CCR5, 27/4/14)				
Michael Platt	Salford	Leeds (a) (D2)	10	21/4/14
Justin Poore	Hull KR	Leeds (h)	1	16/2/14
Tony Puletua	Salford	Wakefield (h)	1	16/2/14
Chris Riley	Wakefield	Catalans (h)	4	9/3/14
Matthew Russell	Warrington	London (a)	4	9/3/14
Setaimata Sa	Hull	Leeds (a)	14	23/5/14
Jarrod Sammut	Wakefield	Bradford (h)	2	20/2/14
Dan Sarginson	Wigan	Huddersfield (h)	1	7/2/14
Nick Scruton	Wakefield	Catalans (h)	4	9/3/14
Tim Smith	Salford	Wakefield (h)	1	16/2/14
	Wakefield	London (h) (D2)	16	13/6/14
Marc Sneyd	Castleford	Bradford (a)	1	16/2/14
Liam Sutcliffe	Bradford	Hull (a)	4	7/3/14
Jordan Thompson	Hull	Catalans (h)	1	14/2/14
Danny Tickle	Widnes	London (h)	1	16/2/14
Joel Tomkins	Wigan	Salford (h) (D2)	23	31/7/14
Logan Tomkins	Salford	Bradford (a)	8	11/4/14
Chris Tuson	Hull	Bradford (h)	4	7/3/14
Jonathan Walker	Hull KR	Leeds (h)	1	16/2/14
Jason Walton	Salford	Wakefield (h) (D2)	1	16/2/14
Scott Wheeldon	Castleford	Bradford (a)	1	16/2/14
Danny Williams	Bradford	Catalans (h)	19	6/7/14

SUPER LEAGUE XIX
Club by Club

29 October 2013 - Widnes Vikings' Samoan second-rower Frank Winterstein joins on 12-month contract.

1 November 2013 - Sydney Roosters sign teenager Curtis Naughton following his release by Bulls.

2 November 2013 - John Bateman signs for Wigan.

8 November 2013 - Michael Platt joins newly-promoted Championship side North Wales Crusaders.

11 November 2013 - Australian hooker Heath L'Estrange released on compassionate grounds with 12 months left on his contract.

12 November 2013 - Elliot Kear signs contract extension to end of 2015 season.

12 November 2013 - joint chairman and former general manager Ryan Whitcut announces he is leaving the club. Mark Moore becomes chairman.

14 November 2013 - teenage centre Sam Wood signs new three-year contract to end of 2016.

5 December 2013 - new board of directors tells fans forum they have "unearthed information which has proved detrimental to the stability of the club".

11 December 2013 - Matt Diskin to continue as Bulls' captain for 2014 season.

13 December 2013 - staff redundancies made as part of bid to slash £400,000 from budget. CEO Robbie Hunter-Paul says player sales cannot be ruled out.

24 December 2013 - new board of directors all stand down, citing former owner Omar Khan's refusal to transfer his shares to them and a request for directors' loan repayment.

30 December 2013 - directors who stood down on Christmas Eve agree to lead club while discussions over future of the Bulls continue.

6 January 2014 - Samoan international Frank Winterstein released by mutual consent after suffering pectoral injury in World Cup against New Zealand,

7 January 2014 - Warrington youngsters James Saltonstall, Joe Philbin and Tom Walker join on short-term loan deals.

31 January 2014 - OK Bulls Ltd placed into administration and club is purchased by Bradford Bulls 2014 Ltd

10 February 2014 - prop Adam Sidlow agrees two-year contract extension to end of 2016.

11 February 2014 - halfback Luke Gale ends speculation over his future by signing two-year contract extension to end of 2016.

12 February 2014 - Garreth Carvell signs for Hull FC after change of club ownership, Warrington back-row forward Danny Bridge joins on month's loan.

14 February 2014 - Jarrod Sammut requests release from the remainder of contract and joins Wakefield.

16 February 2014 - 36-18 round-one home defeat by Castleford.

18 February 2014 - Anthony Mullally signs on month's loan from Huddersfield Giants.

20 February 2014 - Lee Gaskell suffers knee injury in battling 23-10 win at Wakefield.

KEY DATES - BRADFORD BULLS

25 February 2014 - RFL Board of Directors deduct six league points from Bradford, and place club in special measures, meaning no new permanent signings, after the club's administration. New owners pull out of deal to buy club. RFL claim new buyers are lined up.

1 March 2014 - Nick Scruton joins Wakefield for an undisclosed fee agreed by the club's administrators.

4 March 2014 - Liam Sutcliffe arrives on short-term loan deal from Leeds Rhinos.

5 March 2014 - Wigan Warriors forward Greg Burke joins on month's loan.

13 March 2014 - Mandy Koukash, wife of Salford Red Devils owner Dr Marwan Koukash, makes bid for club.

26 March 2014 - Bradford-based businessman Marc Green confirmed as club's new owner.

28 March 2014 - Steve Ferres appointed managing director.

31 March 2014 - Leeds Rhinos recall stand-off Liam Sutcliffe.

1 April 2014 - Tom Olbison suspended for one match for placing undue pressure on the neck of Danny Tickle in 22-18 defeat at Widnes.

3 April 2014 - France international Jamal Fakir, released by Catalans, signs contract to end of 2014 season.

14 April 2014 - Bulls submit appeal against the points deduction handed down by the RFL Board of Directors.

15 April 2014 - Anthony Mullally recalled by Huddersfield.

22 April 2014 - managing director Steve Ferres makes public apology after humiliating Easter Monday 84-6 defeat at Wigan.

23 April 2014 - Danny Bridge recalled by Warrington.

25 April 2014 - Jay Pitts and Joe Arundel join on loan from Hull FC.

2 May 2014 - Antonio Kaufusi joins on month's loan from Huddersfield.

4 May 2014 - shock 34-28 home win over Warrington ends seven-game losing run. Brett Kearney ruled out for between eight and 10 weeks with fractured thumb.

11 May 2014 - 50-0 home defeat to St Helens

15 May 2014 - teenage forwards Jordan Baldwinson and Mason Tonks return from NZ Warriors and sign for the remainder of season, and will return to Rhinos for 2015 campaign.

1 June 2014 - Adrian Purtell scores two tries in vital 20-12 home victory over Wakefield, leaving Bulls six points adrift of the Wildcats.

8 June 2014 - 46-10 home defeat to Warrington Wolves in Tetley's Challenge Cup quarter-final. Jay Pitts accepts one-match ban early guilty plea for dangerous tackle.

9 June 2014 - Antonio Kaufusi opts to end loan spell and return to parent club Huddersfield.

11 June 2014 - appeal against six-point deduction rejected.

16 June 2014 - Francis Cummins and assistant coach Lee St Hilaire sacked. Matt Diskin takes over as caretaker.

24 June 2014 - James Lowes appointed head coach on two-and-a-half-year contract to end of 2016.

26 June 2014 - club officials confirm intention to challenge the RFL points deduction in the High Court.

1 July 2014 - Salford Red Devils winger Danny Williams joins on month loan deal.

20 July 2014 - 52-26 defeat at Huddersfield confirms relegation.

21 July 2014 - Bulls withdraw points appeal.

4 August 2014 - Brett Kearney confirms return to Australia at season end.

3 September 2014 - captain Matt Diskin announces he is to retire at end of season.

CLUB RECORDS
Highest score: 98-6 v Toulouse, 19/4/2008 **Highest score against:** 6-84 v Wigan, 21/4/2014 **Record attendance:** 69,429 v Huddersfield, 14/3/53

MATCH RECORDS
Tries: 6 Eric Batten v Leeds, 15/9/45 Trevor Foster v Wakefield, 10/4/48 Steve McGowan v Barrow, 8/11/92 Lesley Vainikolo v Hull, 2/9/2005 **Goals:** 15 Iestyn Harris v Toulouse, 15/4/2008 **Points:** 36 John Woods v Swinton, 13/10/85

SEASON RECORDS
Tries: 63 Jack McLean 1951-52 **Goals:** 213 *(inc 5fg)* Henry Paul 2001 **Points:** 457 Henry Paul 2001

CAREER RECORDS
Tries: 261 Jack McLean 1950-56 **Goals:** 1,165 *(inc 25fg)* Paul Deacon 1998-2009 **Points:** 2,605 Paul Deacon 1998-2009 **Appearances:** 588 Keith Mumby 1973-90; 1992-93

BRADFORD BULLS

DATE	FIXTURE	RESULT	SCORERS	LGE	ATT
16/2/14	Castleford (h)	L18-36	t:Addy,Foster,Purtell g:Foster(3)	11th	8,214
20/2/14	Wakefield (a)	W10-23	t:Purtell,Kearney,George,O'Brien g:Foster(3) fg:Gale	7th	4,049
2/3/14	London Broncos (h)	W25-12	t:Gale,Sidlow,Addy,Olbison g:Foster(4) fg:Gale	14th	5,410
7/3/14	Hull FC (a)	L44-16	t:Diskin,Purtell,Henry g:Foster(2)	14th	11,307
16/3/14	Huddersfield (h)	L18-66	t:Henry(2),O'Brien g:Foster(3)	14th	6,781
23/3/14	Hull KR (a)	L16-0		14th	7,008
30/3/14	Widnes (a)	L22-18	t:Sutcliffe,Kear,Kearney g:Gale(3)	14th	5,581
6/4/14	Oldham (h) (CCR4)	W60-6	t:Gale(3),Kearney,Kear(2),O'Brien,Addy,Henry,Foster,Ferguson g:Gale(8)	N/A	2,788
11/4/14	Salford (h)	L24-38	t:Purtell,Sidlow,Kear,Henry g:Foster(4)	14th	6,144
17/4/14	Leeds (h)	L6-46	t:Gaskell g:Gale	14th	10,106
21/4/14	Wigan (a)	L84-6	t:Gale g:Gale	14th	15,529
27/4/14	Catalan Dragons (h) (CCR5)	W33-20	t:Gaskell,Foster(2),Gale,Purtell g:Foster(6) fg:Gale	N/A	2,341
4/5/14	Warrington (h)	W34-28	t:Foster,Kearney,Olbison,Purtell(2),Kear g:Foster(5)	13th	6,173
11/5/14	St Helens (h)	L0-50		13th	6,311
18/5/14	Huddersfield (MW) ●	L16-54	t:Addy,Foster(2) g:Foster(2)	13th	N/A
24/5/14	Catalan Dragons (a)	L46-4	t:Foster	13th	6,890
1/6/14	Wakefield (h)	W20-12	t:Purtell,Olbison g:Gale(4)	13th	6,249
8/6/14	Warrington (h) (CCQF)	L10-46	t:Kear,George g:Gale	N/A	5,064
15/6/14	Salford (a)	L46-18	t:Kear,Olbison,O'Brien g:Gale(3)	13th	3,407
20/6/14	Hull KR (h)	L18-44	t:Kear,O'Brien,Addy g:Gale(3)	13th	5,601
29/6/14	Warrington (a)	L50-24	t:Kearney,Purtell,Olbison,Pitts g:Gale(4)	13th	9,003
6/7/14	Catalan Dragons (h)	L30-32	t:Olbison,Henry,Fakir,Gale(2) g:Gale(5)	13th	5,188
11/7/14	St Helens (a)	L46-22	t:Gale,Arundel,Purtell,Foster g:Foster(3)	13th	10,238
20/7/14	Huddersfield (a)	L52-26	t:George(2),O'Brien,Kearney(2) g:Foster(3)	13th	6,145
27/7/14	Wigan (h)	W16-8	t:Williams,Arundel,Blythe g:Gale(2)	13th	6,535
1/8/14	Leeds (h)	W14-20	t:Williams,Gale,Gaskell g:Gale(4)	13th	16,009
17/8/14	Hull FC (h)	W34-28	t:Foster,Arundel(2),Sidlow,Pitts,Addy g:Foster(5)	13th	6,337
31/8/14	Castleford (a)	L32-18	t:Gaskell(3) g:Gale(3)	13th	7,428
7/9/14	Widnes (h)	L12-32	t:Olbison,Walker g:Gale(2)	13th	7,438
13/9/14	London Broncos (a)	W36-46	t:Gale(4),Arundel,Kearney,Pitts,Manuokafoa g:Foster(7)	13th	1,402

● Played at Etihad Stadium, Manchester

		APP		TRIES		GOALS		FG		PTS	
	D.O.B.	ALL	SL	ALL	SL	ALL	SL	ALL	SL	ALL	SL
Brad Adams	31/3/95	1(1)	1(1)	0	0	0	0	0	0	0	0
Danny Addy	15/1/91	19(10)	16(10)	6	5	0	0	0	0	24	20
Joe Arundel	22/8/91	9(3)	9(3)	5	5	0	0	0	0	20	20
Jordan Baldwinson	10/11/94	2(4)	2(4)	0	0	0	0	0	0	0	0
Sam Bates	2/12/95	(2)	(2)	0	0	0	0	0	0	0	0
Matty Blythe	20/11/88	11(6)	9(6)	1	1	0	0	0	0	4	4
Danny Bridge	4/1/93	4(4)	4(4)	0	0	0	0	0	0	0	0
Greg Burke	12/2/93	(1)	(1)	0	0	0	0	0	0	0	0
Nathan Conroy	6/3/95	(4)	(3)	0	0	0	0	0	0	0	0
Matt Diskin	27/1/82	17	15	1	1	0	0	0	0	4	4
James Donaldson	14/9/91	22(3)	20(3)	0	0	0	0	0	0	0	0
Jamal Fakir	30/8/82	6(10)	5(8)	1	1	0	0	0	0	4	4
Dale Ferguson	13/4/88	4(3)	3(3)	1	0	0	0	0	0	4	0
Jamie Foster	27/7/90	15(1)	14	10	7	50	44	0	0	140	116
Luke Gale	22/6/88	29	26	14	10	44	35	3	2	147	112
Lee Gaskell	28/10/90	23	21	6	5	0	0	0	0	24	20
Luke George	30/10/87	11(1)	9(1)	4	3	0	0	0	0	16	12
Adam Henry	2/9/91	24(3)	23(1)	6	5	0	0	0	0	24	20
Antonio Kaufusi	27/11/84	4	4	0	0	0	0	0	0	0	0
Elliot Kear	29/11/88	20(2)	17(2)	8	5	0	0	0	0	32	20
Brett Kearney	29/9/83	22	20	8	7	0	0	0	0	32	28
Manase Manuokafoa	24/3/85	22(5)	19(5)	1	1	0	0	0	0	4	4
Alex Mellor	24/9/94	(8)	(8)	0	0	0	0	0	0	0	0
Anthony Mullally	28/6/91	1(5)	1(5)	0	0	0	0	0	0	0	0
Adam O'Brien	11/7/93	13(16)	12(14)	6	5	0	0	0	0	24	20
Tom Olbison	20/3/91	22(5)	21(4)	7	7	0	0	0	0	28	28
Jay Pitts	9/12/89	17(1)	15(1)	3	3	0	0	0	0	12	12
Adrian Purtell	31/1/85	24	21	11	10	0	0	0	0	44	40
Oliver Roberts	24/12/95	(4)	(3)	0	0	0	0	0	0	0	0
Nick Scruton	24/12/84	2	2	0	0	0	0	0	0	0	0
Adam Sidlow	25/10/87	16(9)	16(7)	3	3	0	0	0	0	12	12
Liam Sutcliffe	25/11/94	3(1)	3(1)	1	1	0	0	0	0	4	4
Chev Walker	9/10/82	15(6)	12(6)	1	1	0	0	0	0	4	4
Emmerson Whittel	13/9/94	(1)	(1)	0	0	0	0	0	0	0	0
Danny Williams	26/9/86	7	7	2	2	0	0	0	0	8	8
Sam Wood	23/12/93	5(1)	4(1)	0	0	0	0	0	0	0	0

Luke Gale

LEAGUE RECORD
P27-W8-D0-L19
(13th, SL)
F512, A984, Diff-472
10 points.
(Deducted six points for entering administration)

CHALLENGE CUP
Quarter Finalists

ATTENDANCES
Best - v Leeds (SL - 10,106)
Worst - v Catalan Dragons (CC - 2,341)
Total (SL only) - 86,487
Average (SL only) - 6,653
(Down by 1,922 on 2013)

24 October 2013 - Ryan Boyle signs two-year contract extension.

31 October 2013 - Jamie Ellis has surgery after tearing pectoral muscle in training.

21 November 2013 - partnership announced with Championship One club York.

19 December 2013 - Liam Finn joins Tigers after being released by Featherstone.

13 February 2014 - Kirk Dixon signs one-year contract extension to end of 2015.

16 February 2014 - Kirk Dixon scores try and six goals and passes 1,000 points for the club in 36-18 round-one win at Bradford.

20 February 2014 - Grant Millington signs one-year contract extension to end of 2015 season.

23 February 2014 - Justin Carney scores hat-trick in 32-6 home win over Catalans.

28 February 2014 - Richard Owen returns to side with a hat-trick in 30-10 win at Hull KR.

6 March 2014 - Australian scrum-half Brett Seymour released from trial period without playing a match.

9 March 2014 - last-second Luke Dorn try secures 36-31 home win over Wigan.

13 March 2014 - fresh plans unveiled for new stadium as part of £135million retail development at Glasshoughton.

14 March 2014 - back-row forward Charlie Martin released after six appearances.

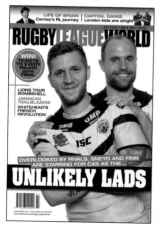

KEY DATES - CASTLEFORD TIGERS

16 March 2014 - late Frankie Mariano try and Marc Sneyd conversion see Tigers to 19-16 home win over Hull FC. Jordan Tansey given three-match ban for making deliberate physical contact with referee.

23 March 2014 - 23-16 defeat at Salford ends opening winning run at five matches

17 April 2014 - Oliver Holmes signs new deal to end of 2016.

18 April 2014 - Ryan Boyle out for season after knee reconstruction after rupturing ACL in the Tigers' win 43-20 win at Wakefield on Good Friday.

2 May 2014 - Lee Jewitt joins from Limoux.

15 May 2014 - Richard Owen moves to Wakefield for the remainder of the campaign.

16 May 2014 - Frankie Mariano signs new two-year deal to end of 2016.

23 May 2014 - Liam Finn signs two-year contract extension to end of 2016 season.

27 May 2014 - Lee Gilmour joins Wakefield on one-month loan deal.

27 May 2014 - Justin Carney banned for two matches for fighting in 34-22 home win over Widnes.

7 June 2014 - 16-4 win at Wigan moves Tigers into Challenge Cup semi-finals.

11 June 2014 - Melbourne's Samoan international Junior Moors signs three-year contract from 2015.

13 June 2014 - head coach Daryl Powell signs new five-year contract.

18 June 2014 - Garreth Carvell joins on loan for rest of season from Hull FC.

1 July 2014 - Marc Sneyd, on loan for 2014 from Salford, signs for Hull for 2015.

7 July 2014 - Ben Roberts signs from Melbourne Storm on two-year deal from 2015.

14 July 2014 - Denny Solomona signs from London Broncos on two-year deal from 2015.

16 July 2014 - Lee Jewitt signs two-year contract extension.

21 July 2014 - Matt Cook joins on two-year deal from London Broncos and Garreth Carvell extends until the end of 2014 season.

29 July 2014 - Weller Hauraki picks up two-game ban for reckless striking with knees in 18-all draw at Hull FC.

4 August 2014 - Featherstone prop Steve Crossley signs on two-year deal from 2015.

5 August 2014 - Justin Carney banned for two games for dangerous tackle in 64-18 home win over London.

10 August 2014 - 28-6 Challenge Cup semi-final win over Widnes Vikings.

23 August 2014 - 23-10 defeat by Leeds Rhinos in Challenge Cup final.

28 August 2014 - Bradford halfback Luke Gale joins on two-year deal.

11 September 2014 - Tigers confirm Craig Huby departure to Huddersfield, Weller Hauraki to Salford and Daryl Clark to Warrington. Richard Owen, Jamie Ellis, Lee Gilmour, Gareth Carvell and Dan Fleming not offered contracts.

11 September 2014 - London Broncos pair Scott Moore and Mike McMeeken sign on two-year deals.

11 September 2014 - James Clare extends contract to end of 2016 season.

11 September 2014 - Grant Millington extends contract until 2018 with an option for 2019.

19 September 2014 - 41-0 defeat at St Helens in Qualifying Play-off.

25 September 2014 - 30-14 home defeat by Warrington in Preliminary Semi-final.

1 October 2014 - Jamie Ellis signs for Huddersfield.

9 October 2014 - Daryl Clark named Steve Prescott Man of Steel.

CLUB RECORDS
Highest score: 106-0 v Rochdale, 9/9/2007 **Highest score against:** 12-76 v Leeds, 14/8/2009 **Record attendance:** 25,449 v Hunslet, 9/3/35

MATCH RECORDS
Tries: 5 Derek Foster v Hunslet, 10/11/72 John Joyner v Millom, 16/9/73 Steve Fenton v Dewsbury, 27/1/78 Ian French v Hunslet, 9/2/86 St John Ellis v Whitehaven, 10/12/89 **Goals:** 17 Sammy Lloyd v Millom, 16/9/73 **Points:** 43 Sammy Lloyd v Millom, 16/9/73

SEASON RECORDS
Tries: 40 St John Ellis 1993-94 **Goals:** 158 Sammy Lloyd 1976-77 **Points:** 334 Bob Beardmore 1983-84

CAREER RECORDS
Tries: 206 Alan Hardisty 1958-71 **Goals:** 875 Albert Lunn 1951-63 **Points:** 1,870 Albert Lunn 1951-63 **Appearances:** 613 John Joyner 1973-92

CASTLEFORD TIGERS

DATE	FIXTURE	RESULT	SCORERS	LGE	ATT
16/2/14	Bradford (a)	W18-36	t:Hauraki,Dixon,Clark,Carney,Dorn,Millington g:Dixon(6)	4th	8,214
23/2/14	Catalan Dragons (h)	W32-6	t:Carney(3),Dixon,Tansey,Clark g:Sneyd(4)	1st	5,104
28/2/14	Hull KR (a)	W10-30	t:Owen(3),Mariano,Holmes g:Sneyd(5)	2nd	7,022
9/3/14	Wigan (h)	W36-31	t:Dixon,Dorn(2),Milner,Clark,Channing g:Sneyd(6)	2nd	8,504
16/3/14	Hull FC (h)	W19-16	t:Shenton,Sneyd,Mariano g:Sneyd(3) fg:Sneyd	2nd	9,867
23/3/14	Salford (a)	L23-16	t:Carney,Hauraki,Dorn g:Sneyd(2)	3rd	5,823
27/3/14	London Broncos (a)	W6-54	t:Channing,Holmes,Shenton(2),Finn,Huby,Carney(2),Dorn g:Ellis(9)	2nd	1,036
6/4/14	Batley (a) (CCR4)	W10-48	t:Dorn(2),Carney(3),Ellis,Sneyd,Clare,Wheeldon g:Sneyd(6)	N/A	2,482
11/4/14	St Helens (h)	L28-30	t:Webster,Shenton(2),Millington,Carney g:Sneyd(4)	3rd	6,487
18/4/14	Wakefield (a)	W20-43	t:Carney,Clark(2),Owen(2),Wheeldon(2),Finn g:Sneyd(5) fg:Sneyd	3rd	5,159
21/4/14	Warrington (h)	W40-6	t:Clare(2),Shenton(3),Ellis,Owen g:Sneyd(6)	2nd	6,853
27/4/14	Sheffield (h) (CCR5)	W60-16	t:Carney,Millington(2),Dixon,Ellis(2),Clark,Tansey,Holmes g:Dixon(2),Sneyd(4)	N/A	4,648
4/5/14	Huddersfield (a)	L29-28	t:Shenton,Carney,Dixon,Webster,Clark g:Sneyd(4)	3rd	7,195
8/5/14	Leeds (h)	L14-22	t:Dixon,Sneyd g:Sneyd(3)	4th	9,208
18/5/14	Wakefield (MW) ●	W50-12	t:Clark(2),Carney(2),Tansey,Shenton,Sneyd(2),Mariano g:Sneyd(7)	3rd	N/A
25/5/14	Widnes (h)	W34-22	t:Shenton,Webster,Wheeldon,Dorn(2),Clark g:Sneyd(5)	3rd	5,576
1/6/14	Hull KR (h)	W54-12	t:Channing(2),Dorn(3),Millington,Dixon,Ellis,Webster,Huby,Clare g:Sneyd(5)	3rd	7,196
7/6/14	Wigan (a) (CCQF)	W4-16	t:Clare,Dixon,Jewitt g:Sneyd(2)	N/A	8,736
13/6/14	Wigan (a)	L46-6	t:Gibson g:Ellis	4th	11,914
22/6/14	St Helens (a)	L38-16	t:Dixon,Sneyd,Dorn g:Sneyd(2)	4th	12,648
28/6/14	Salford (h)	W14-10	t:Carney,Webster g:Sneyd(3)	4th	5,937
3/7/14	Widnes (a)	W20-40	t:Dorn,Holmes,Clark(3),Shenton(2) g:Sneyd(6)	4th	4,567
11/7/14	Huddersfield (h)	W44-30	t:Holmes,Carney,Finn(2),Milner,Dixon,Mariano,Millington g:Sneyd(6)	5th	5,310
17/7/14	Leeds (a)	D24-24	t:Shenton,Hauraki,Massey,Millington g:Sneyd(4)	4th	16,173
24/7/14	Hull FC (a)	D18-18	t:Shenton,Sneyd,Clare(2) g:Sneyd	4th	9,959
3/8/14	London Broncos (h)	W64-18	t:Dorn(2),Carney(3),Wheeldon,Shenton,Carvell,Mariano,Dixon(2),Milner g:Sneyd(8)	4th	5,233
10/8/14	Widnes (CCSF) ●●	W28-6	t:Finn,Clark,Dixon,Ellis,Webster g:Sneyd(4)	N/A	12,005
15/8/14	Warrington (a)	L48-10	t:Clare,Holmes g:Finn	5th	8,391
23/8/14	Leeds (CCF) ●●●	L10-23	t:Clark,Holmes g:Finn	N/A	77,914
31/8/14	Bradford (h)	W32-18	t:Lynch,Clare,Dorn,Shenton,Clark g:Sneyd(6)	2nd	7,428
7/9/14	Wakefield (h)	W26-22	t:Dorn,Clare(2),Dixon,Webster g:Sneyd(3)	2nd	9,182
13/9/14	Catalan Dragons (a)	L28-6	t:Dixon g:Sneyd	4th	9,223
19/9/14	St Helens (a) (QPO)	L41-0		N/A	7,548
25/9/14	Warrington (h) (PSF)	L14-30	t:Ellis,Dorn,Shenton g:Sneyd	N/A	6,219

● Played at Etihad Stadium, Manchester   ●● Played at Leigh Sports Village   ●●● Played at Wembley Stadium

		APP		TRIES		GOALS		FG		PTS	
	D.O.B.	ALL	SL	ALL	SL	ALL	SL	ALL	SL	ALL	SL
Ryan Boyle	17/10/87	(3)	(2)	0	0	0	0	0 0		0	0
Justin Carney	16/6/88	24	21	24	17	0	0	0 0		96	68
Garreth Carvell	21/4/80	1(5)	1(4)	1	1	0	0	0 0		4	4
Michael Channing	30/6/92	14(2)	13(2)	4	4	0	0	0 0		16	16
James Clare	13/4/91	17	14	11	9	0	0	0 0		44	36
Daryl Clark	10/2/93	22(8)	19(7)	16	13	0	0	0 0		64	52
Brad Day	23/9/94	(1)	(1)	0	0	0	0	0 0		0	0
Kirk Dixon	19/7/84	24(1)	20(1)	15	12	8	6	0 0		76	60
Luke Dorn	2/7/82	24	20	19	17	0	0	0 0		76	68
Jamie Ellis	4/10/89	11(10)	10(6)	7	3	10	10	0 0		48	32
Liam Finn	2/11/83	29	24	5	4	2	1	0 0		24	18
Daniel Fleming	8/7/92	(5)	(4)	0	0	0	0	0 0		0	0
Ashley Gibson	25/9/86	7	6	1	1	0	0	0 0		4	4
Weller Hauraki	18/2/85	28(2)	25(2)	3	3	0	0	0 0		12	12
Oliver Holmes	7/8/92	28(4)	23(4)	7	5	0	0	0 0		28	20
Craig Huby	21/5/86	25(4)	21(4)	2	2	0	0	0 0		8	8
Lee Jewitt	14/2/87	8(8)	7(6)	1	0	0	0	0 0		4	0
Andy Lynch	20/10/79	31	27	1	1	0	0	0 0		4	4
Will Maher	4/11/95	(1)	(1)	0	0	0	0	0 0		0	0
Frankie Mariano	10/5/87	8(22)	7(18)	5	5	0	0	0 0		20	20
Nathan Massey	11/7/89	10(13)	7(12)	1	1	0	0	0 0		4	4
Grant Millington	1/11/86	20(7)	19(6)	7	5	0	0	0 0		28	20
Adam Milner	19/12/91	12(13)	10(13)	3	3	0	0	0 0		12	12
Richard Owen	25/4/90	5	5	6	6	0	0	0 0		24	24
Ben Reynolds	15/1/94	1(1)	1(1)	0	0	0	0	0 0		0	0
Michael Shenton	22/7/86	32	27	18	18	0	0	0 0		72	72
Marc Sneyd	9/2/91	29(2)	25(1)	7	6	116	100	2 2		262	226
Jordan Tansey	9/9/86	7	6	3	2	0	0	0 0		12	8
Jake Webster	29/10/83	18(4)	14(4)	7	6	0	0	0 0		28	24
Scott Wheeldon	23/2/86	7(20)	5(17)	5	4	0	0	0 0		20	16

Michael Shenton

LEAGUE RECORD
P27-W17-D2-L8
(4th, SL/Preliminary Semi-Final)
F814, A583, Diff+231
36 points.

CHALLENGE CUP
Runners-Up

ATTENDANCES
Best - v Hull FC (SL - 9,867)
Worst - v Sheffield (CC - 4,648)
Total (SL, inc play-offs) - 98,104
Average (SL, inc play-offs) - 7,007
(Up by 715 on 2013)

19 October 2013 - centre Ben Pomeroy signs from Cronulla on two-year contract.

25 October 2013 - fee paid by Hull KR to take France international Kevin Larroyer on season-long loan.

5 November 2013 - South Sydney Rabbitohs' former Wigan prop Jeff Lima signs on a three-year contract.

5 December 2013 - Dragons fined £2,000 (half suspended to end 2014) by RFL after supporters verbally abused and intimidated match officials following Super League fixture against Hull Kingston Rover in Toulouse.

11 December 2013 - Manly winger Michael Oldfield joins on two-year deal.

12 December 2013 - fullback Morgan Escaré signs new three-year deal to end of 2016.

3 February 2014 - Jason Baitieri appointed co-captain along with Greg Mounis.

14 February 2014 - missed Thomas Bosc conversion to Zeb Taia try means 36-34 opening Super League defeat at the KC Stadium.

19 February 2014 - Olivier Elima suspended for four matches for twisting the legs of Hull FC hooker Aaron Heremaia during Hull defeat.

23 February 2014 - Julian Bousquet suspended for dangerous tackle in 32-6 defeat at Castleford Tigers. Scott Dureau suffers ruptured biceps

3 March 2014 - Ian Henderson breaks forearm in 40-12 home defeat by Leeds.

9 March 2014 - 56-14 away defeat by Wakefield Wildcats.

11 March 2014 - after fourth loss in a row Chairman Bernard Guasch cancels week in UK. Jamal Fakir dropped to reserve grade. Brent Webb to undergo medical tests to determine future.

13 March 2014 - Jamal Fakir refuses to play for Dragons reserve team Saint Estève XIII Catalan and turns down offers from other clubs.

14 March 2014 - improved showing in 40-22 defeat at table-toppers St Helens.

22 March 2014 - Louis Anderson scores two tries in 30-14 home win over Huddersfield.

17 April 2104 - 28-22 Easter Thursday win at London.

17 May 2014 - 24-22 defeat of London Broncos at Magic Weekend.

5 June 2014 - Eloi Pelissier ends speculation over his future by signing new two-year contract to end of 2016.

KEY DATES - CATALAN DRAGONS

7 June 2014 - Australian halfback Sam Williams signs from St George Illawarra Dragons to the end of the season.

14 June 2014 - Michael Oldfield scores hat-trick in 42-0 hammering of St Helens in Perpignan.

26 June 2014 - Scott Dureau to join Sydney Roosters on loan until end of 2014 season.

29 June 2014 - last second Liam Sutcliffe penalty goal means 32-31 defeat at Leeds.

1 July 2014 - Leon Pryce to leave for Hull FC at end of season.

3 July 2014 - head coach Laurent Frayssinous signs new two-year contract.

5 July 2014 - Louis Anderson signs 12-month contract extension.

9 July 2014 - former Australia Test centre Willie Tonga signs for 2015 from Parramatta on two-year deal.

12 July 2014 - 37-16 home defeat by Wigan. Vincent Duport gets three-match ban for making dangerous contact with England winger Josh Charnley; Gregory Mounis suspended for two matches for dangerous throw on John Bateman.

14 July 2014 - prop Mickael Simon signs for Wakefield for 2015.

16 July 2014 - assistant coach Jerome Guisset signs new two-year contract.

29 July 2014 - Olivier Elima extends contract for further two years.

1 August 2014 - fullback Brent Webb retires.

21 August 2014 - Thomas Bosc signs one-year contract with further 12-month option, keeping him at the Dragons until at least the end of the 2015 season.

22 August 2014 - Kevin Larroyer to remain on loan with Hull KR in 2015.

26 August 2014 - Leon Pryce dropped for rest of season after he signs for Hull FC for 2015.

29 August 2014 - Lopini Paea signs for Wakefield for 2015.

16 September 2014 - Australian star Todd Carney, sacked by Cronulla, signs three-year deal until end of 2017 season.

17 September 2014 - RFL announce they are to 'consider' Todd Carney registration.

17 September 2014 - Morgan Escaré signs new four-year deal until end of 2018.

18 September 2014 - Sam Williams joins Canberra Raiders for 2015.

20 September 2014 - Sam Williams scores last-second try in 24-20 win at Leeds in Elimination Play-off.

26 September 2014 - 18-16 win at Huddersfield in Preliminary Semi-final.

30 September 2014 - Remi Casty returns early from Sydney Roosters on four-year deal.

3 October 2014 - 30-12 Qualifying Semi-Final elimination by St Helens.

7 October 2014 - Michael Monaghan appointed assistant coach on two-year contract.

CLUB RECORDS

Highest score: 92-8 v York, 12/5/2013
Highest score against:
12-60 v Leeds, 15/9/2006
16-60 v Huddersfield, 28/6/2013
Record attendance: 18,150 v Warrington, 20/6/2009 *(Barcelona)*
11,500 v Warrington, 9/4/2012 *(Stade Gilbert Brutus)*

MATCH RECORDS

Tries:
4 Justin Murphy v Warrington, 13/9/2008
Damien Cardace v Widnes, 31/3/2012
Kevin Larroyer v York, 12/5/2013
Goals:
11 Thomas Bosc v Featherstone, 31/3/2007
Thomas Bosc v Batley, 29/5/2010
Scott Dureau v Widnes, 31/3/2012
Points:
26 Thomas Bosc v Featherstone, 31/3/2007

SEASON RECORDS

Tries: 29 Morgan Escare 2014
Goals: 134 Scott Dureau 2012
Points: 319 Scott Dureau 2012

CAREER RECORDS

Tries: 86 Clint Greenshields 2007-2012
Goals:
537 *(inc 12fg)* Thomas Bosc 2006-2014
Points: 1,270 Thomas Bosc 2006-2014
Appearances:
233 Gregory Mounis 2006-2014

CATALAN DRAGONS

DATE	FIXTURE	RESULT	SCORERS	LGE	ATT
14/2/14	Hull FC (a)	L36-34	t:Cardace(3),Whitehead,Taia(2),Escare g:Bosc(3)	8th	10,178
23/2/14	Castleford (a)	L32-6	t:Escare g:Dureau	12th	5,104
28/2/14	Leeds (h)	L12-40	t:Oldfield,Baile g:Barthau(2)	12th	6,300
9/3/14	Wakefield (a)	L56-14	t:Whitehead(2),Pryce g:Barthau	12th	4,190
14/3/14	St Helens (a)	L40-22	t:Garcia,Pelissier,Oldfield(2) g:Bosc(3)	12th	11,321
22/3/14	Huddersfield (h)	W30-14	t:Taia,Anderson(2),Escare,Whitehead g:Bosc(5)	12th	6,510
28/3/14	Wigan (a)	L22-16	t:Escare(2),Pomeroy g:Bosc(2)	12th	11,216
4/4/14	London Broncos (h) (CCR4)	W40-24	t:Pryce,Anderson(2),Bosc,Millard,Maria,Escare g:Bosc(6)	N/A	2,443
12/4/14	Widnes (h)	W42-20	t:Pomeroy(2),Whitehead(3),Escare,Duport(2),Millard g:Bosc(2),Escare	12th	9,588
17/4/14	London Broncos (a)	W22-28	t:Oldfield,Taia,Barthau,Pelissier,Duport g:Bosc(4)	11th	1,002
21/4/14	Hull KR (h)	W37-24	t:Escare,Whitehead(2),Oldfield(2),Millard g:Bosc(6) fg:Bosc	10th	9,863
27/4/14	Bradford (a) (CCR5)	L33-20	t:Millard,Duport,Elima,Oldfield g:Barthau(2)	N/A	2,341
3/5/14	Salford (h)	W37-24	t:Escare(3),Millard,Taia,Pryce g:Barthau(6) fg:Pelissier	9th	7,862
9/5/14	Warrington (a)	L42-10	t:Duport,Escare g:Barthau	10th	8,816
17/5/14	London Broncos (MW) ●	W24-22	t:Duport,Whitehead(2),Lima g:Bosc(4)	9th	N/A
24/5/14	Bradford (h)	W46-4	t:Escare(2),Taia,Oldfield,Simon,Millard,Pryce,Taia g:Bosc(7)	9th	6,890
30/5/14	Widnes (a)	D26-26	t:Millard,Duport,Escare,Pryce,Oldfield g:Bosc(3)	8th	4,745
14/6/14	St Helens (h)	W42-0	t:Duport(2),Oldfield(3),Henderson,Bosc,Millard g:Bosc(5)	7th	9,864
21/6/14	Hull FC (h)	W20-16	t:Escare,Oldfield,Garcia,Millard g:Bosc(2)	7th	9,275
29/6/14	Leeds (a)	L32-31	t:Escare,Taia(2),Pelissier,Millard g:Williams(5) fg:Escare	7th	13,888
6/7/14	Bradford (a)	W30-32	t:Escare,Duport,Pomeroy,Bousquet,Whitehead g:Williams(6)	7th	5,188
12/7/14	Wigan (h)	L16-37	t:Escare,Whitehead,Cardace g:Williams(2)	7th	9,505
19/7/14	Wakefield (h)	W40-6	t:Millard,Escare(2),Whitehead(3),Taia g:Williams(6)	7th	8,256
27/7/14	Huddersfield (a)	L38-16	t:Pelissier,Oldfield,Escare g:Williams(2)	7th	4,931
1/8/14	Warrington (h)	L24-26	t:Oldfield(3),Mounis g:Bosc(4)	7th	7,858
15/8/14	Salford (a)	L34-22	t:Oldfield,Mounis,Duport,Henderson g:Bosc(3)	7th	3,100
30/8/14	London Broncos (h)	W46-4	t:Duport,Escare(3),Pomeroy,Millard(2),Taia g:Bosc(7)	7th	7,067
7/9/14	Hull KR (a)	W14-32	t:Oldfield(3),Williams(2),Escare g:Bosc(4)	7th	6,412
13/9/14	Castleford (h)	W28-6	t:Escare(2),Taia,Henderson,Whitehead g:Bosc(4)	7th	9,223
20/9/14	Leeds (a) (EPO)	W20-24	t:Williams(2),Taia,Anderson g:Bosc(4)	N/A	7,112
26/9/14	Huddersfield (a) (PSF)	W16-18	t:Millard,Oldfield,Pomeroy g:Bosc(3)	N/A	6,900
2/10/14	St Helens (a) (QSF)	L30-12	t:Escare,Oldfield g:Bosc(2)	N/A	8,888

● Played at Etihad Stadium, Manchester

		APP		TRIES		GOALS		FG		PTS	
	D.O.B.	ALL	SL	ALL	SL	ALL	SL	ALL	SL	ALL	SL
Louis Anderson	27/6/85	15(8)	14(7)	5	3	0	0	0	0	20	12
Jean-Philippe Baile	7/6/87	2(5)	2(5)	1	1	0	0	0	0	4	4
Jason Baitieri	2/7/89	21(3)	19(3)	0	0	0	0	0	0	0	0
William Barthau	30/1/90	6	5	1	1	12	10	0	0	28	24
Thomas Bosc	5/8/83	21	20	2	1	83	77	1	1	175	159
Julian Bousquet	18/7/91	8(11)	7(11)	1	1	0	0	0	0	4	4
Damien Cardace	16/10/92	4	4	4	4	0	0	0	0	16	16
Vincent Duport	15/12/87	22	20	11	11	0	0	0	0	44	44
Scott Dureau	29/7/86	1	1	0	0	1	1	0	0	2	2
Olivier Elima	19/5/83	20(2)	18(2)	1	0	0	0	0	0	4	0
Morgan Escare	18/10/91	32	30	29	28	1	1	1	1	119	115
Jamal Fakir	30/8/82	(3)	(3)	0	0	0	0	0	0	0	0
Benjamin Garcia	5/4/93	(22)	(20)	2	2	0	0	0	0	8	8
Joan Guasch	5/7/93	(6)	(4)	0	0	0	0	0	0	0	0
Ian Henderson	23/4/83	17(1)	17(1)	3	3	0	0	0	0	12	12
Jeff Lima	4/7/82	20(5)	19(5)	1	1	0	0	0	0	4	4
Thibaut Margalet	3/1/93	(1)	(1)	0	0	0	0	0	0	0	0
Antoni Maria	21/3/87	(10)	(9)	1	0	0	0	0	0	4	0
Daryl Millard	20/2/85	25	23	14	12	0	0	0	0	56	48
Gregory Mounis	18/1/85	10(9)	10(9)	2	2	0	0	0	0	8	8
Michael Oldfield	24/11/90	31	29	23	22	0	0	0	0	92	88
Lopini Paea	19/4/84	3(20)	3(18)	0	0	0	0	0	0	0	0
Mathias Pala	14/6/89	5	5	0	0	0	0	0	0	0	0
Eloi Pelissier	18/6/91	14(16)	12(16)	4	4	0	0	1	1	17	17
Ben Pomeroy	10/1/84	29	27	7	6	0	0	0	0	28	24
Leon Pryce	9/10/81	25	23	5	4	0	0	0	0	20	16
Mickael Simon	2/4/87	9(3)	9(3)	1	1	0	0	0	0	4	4
Gadwin Springer	4/4/93	(1)	(1)	0	0	0	0	0	0	0	0
Zeb Taia	11/10/84	32	30	12	12	0	0	0	0	48	48
Frederic Vaccari	7/11/87	3	3	0	0	0	0	0	0	0	0
Brent Webb	8/11/80	2	2	0	0	0	0	0	0	0	0
Elliott Whitehead	4/9/89	28	27	18	18	0	0	0	0	72	72
Sam Williams	18/3/91	11(1)	11(1)	4	4	21	21	0	0	58	58

Morgan Escare

LEAGUE RECORD
P27-W14-D1-L12
(7th, SL/Qualifying Semi-Final)
F733, A667, Diff+66
29 points.

CHALLENGE CUP
Round Five

ATTENDANCES
Best - v St Helens (SL - 9,864)
Worst - v London Broncos
(CC - 2,443)
Total (SL only) - 108,061
Average (SL only) - 8,312
(Up by 133 on 2013)

7 February 2014 - Jermaine McGillvary scores hat-trick in comfortable 24-8 victory on opening night of season at Wigan. Former London Broncos forwards Chris Bailey and Antonio Kaufusi make debuts.

10 February 2014 - Larne Patrick set to miss three months after being carried off on a stretcher with dislocated his knee and damaged ligaments at Wigan.

18 February 2014 - Anthony Mullally goes to Bradford on month's loan.

23 February 2014 - A 24-12 lead with two minutes left ends in 24-all home draw with Hull KR.

28 February 2014 - two-score advantage again let slip in 22-20 defeat at Widnes.

7 March 2014 - 12-all home draw with Leeds.

6 April 2014 - controversial home Challenge Cup defeat by 17-16 by St Helens after Danny Bough's seemingly successful field goal is ruled out. Brett Ferres banned for five games after being sent off after 64 minutes for spear tackle on Jonny Lomax.

15 April 2014 - Scott Grix fined £300 after admitting striking Hull FC captain Gareth Ellis during 30-6 away defeat.

27 April 2014 - 20-year-old prop forward Josh Johnson signs contract extension to the end of 2016 season.

2 May 2014 - Antonio Kaufusi joins Bradford on loan.

4 May 2014 - late Danny Brough field goal secures 29-28 home win over Castleford.

23 May 2014 - 41-22 defeat at St Helens ends winning run at five games.

29 May 2014 - Joe Wardle scores twice in 31-22 home win over Wigan after trailing 12-0.

4 June 2014 - Ben Blackmore transferred to Featherstone Rovers with immediate effect for undisclosed fee.

9 June 2014 - Antonio Kaufusi returns from loan spell at Bradford.

12 June 2014 - 24-22 win at Leeds Rhinos.

16 June 2014 - Scott Grix signs new contract to end of 2016.

26 June 2014 - Larne Patrick scores two second-half tries to make it nine wins from last 10 matches with 26-22 away victory at Hull KR.

4 July 2014 - England youth captain Matthew English, 16, signs three-year professional contract.

5 July 2014 - 36-10 home defeat to Salford ends winning run at four matches.

KEY DATES - HUDDERSFIELD GIANTS

11 July 2014 - 44-30 defeat at Castleford.

29 August 2014 - Danny Brough field goal earns 24-all draw at Warrington.

11 September 2014 - Castleford prop Craig Huby signs on four-year deal from November.

12 September 2014 - late Leroy Cudjoe field goal earns 17-16 home win against St Helens and ensures third-placed finish.

18 September 2014 - injured Danny Brough misses 57-4 Qualifying Play-off defeat at Wigan as seven-game undefeated run ends.

26 September 2014 - Danny Brough returns in 18-16 Preliminary Semi-Final home defeat by Catalans.

27 September 2014 - David Faiumu to return to Australia.

1 October 2014 - Castleford halfback Jamie Ellis joins on two-year contract. Jack Miller and Peter Aspinall released.

6 October 2014 - Antonio Kaufusi to return to Australia.

13 October 2014 - Aaron Murphy extends contract to end of 2018 season.

15 October 2014 - Giants announce they are to run full-time Academy.

20 October 2014 - back-rower Oliver Roberts joins from Bradford for undisclosed fee on two-year contract.

5 November 2014 - Larne Patrick and Wigan back-rower Jack Hughes in one-year loan swap.

11 November 2014 - Danny Brough awarded Albert Goldthorpe Medal for record third time.

CLUB RECORDS

Highest score:
142-4 v Blackpool G, 26/11/94
Highest score against:
12-94 v Castleford, 18/9/88
Record attendance:
32,912 v Wigan, 4/3/50 *(Fartown)*
15,629 v Leeds, 10/2/2008
(McAlpine/Galpharm/John Smith's Stadium)

MATCH RECORDS

Tries:
10 Lionel Cooper v Keighley, 17/11/51
Goals: 18 Major Holland
v Swinton Park, 28/2/1914
Points: 39 Major Holland
v Swinton Park, 28/2/1914

SEASON RECORDS

Tries: 80 Albert Rosenfeld 1913-14
Goals: 156 *(inc 2fg)* Danny Brough 2013
Points: 346 Danny Brough 2013

CAREER RECORDS

Tries: 420 Lionel Cooper 1947-55
Goals: 958 Frank Dyson 1949-63
Points: 2,072 Frank Dyson 1949-63
Appearances: 485 Douglas Clark 1909-29

HUDDERSFIELD GIANTS

DATE	FIXTURE	RESULT	SCORERS	LGE	ATT
7/2/14	Wigan (a)	W8-24	t:Ferres,McGillvary(3),Grix g:Brough(2)	N/A	16,240
23/2/14	Hull KR (h)	D24-24	t:Brough,Robinson(2),Wood g:Brough(4)	5th	7,180
28/2/14	Widnes (a)	L22-20	t:McGillvary,Cudjoe,Crabtree g:Brough(4)	6th	5,577
7/3/14	Leeds (h)	D12-12	t:Broughton,Wardle g:Brough(2)	6th	8,759
16/3/14	Bradford (a)	W18-66	t:Grix(2),Wardle(2),Lawrence,Robinson,Chan,Ta'ai(2),McGillvary(2),Ferres g:Brough(9)	4th	6,781
22/3/14	Catalan Dragons (a)	L30-14	t:Grix,Ferres,Broughton g:Brough	5th	6,510
30/3/14	Warrington (h)	L14-33	t:Grix,Broughton g:Brough(3)	8th	7,068
6/4/14	St Helens (h) (CCR4)	L16-17	t:Lunt(2),Wardle g:Brough(2)	N/A	5,566
10/4/14	Hull FC (h)	L30-6	t:Broughton g:Brough	10th	9,515
18/4/14	Salford (a)	W22-42	t:Lunt,Murphy(3),Brough,McGillvary,Bailey g:Brough(7)	9th	5,068
21/4/14	Wakefield (h)	W36-16	t:Broughton,Lawrence,Ta'ai,Cudjoe,Chan,Lunt g:Brough(6)	7th	5,487
4/5/14	Castleford (h)	W29-28	t:Wardle,Cudjoe,McGillvary,Grix,Murphy g:Brough(4) fg:Brough	6th	7,195
10/5/14	London Broncos (a)	W16-30	t:Lunt,Ta'ai(2),Mullally,Cudjoe g:Brough(5)	5th	1,035
18/5/14	Bradford (MW) ●	W16-54	t:Wardle,Lunt,Robinson,Broughton,Brough,Grix,Ta'ai,Mullally,Patrick g:Brough(9)	5th	N/A
23/5/14	St Helens (a)	L41-22	t:Patrick,Blackmore(2),Ferres g:Brough(3)	6th	10,218
29/5/14	Wigan (h)	W31-22	t:Murphy,Lunt,Wardle(2),McGillvary g:Brough(5) fg:Brough	6th	6,198
12/6/14	Leeds (a)	W22-24	t:Wood,McGillvary,Crabtree,Wardle g:Brough(4)	6th	13,104
21/6/14	London Broncos (h)	W38-22	t:Grix,Ferres,McGillvary(2),Wardle(2),Broughton g:Brough(5)	6th	4,849
26/6/14	Hull KR (a)	W22-26	t:Cudjoe,Ta'ai,Crabtree,Patrick(2) g:Brough(3)	6th	8,953
5/7/14	Salford (h)	L10-36	t:Wardle,Patrick g:Cudjoe	6th	5,689
11/7/14	Castleford (a)	L44-30	t:Bailey(2),Cudjoe,Wardle,Crabtree g:Cudjoe(5)	6th	5,310
20/7/14	Bradford (h)	W52-26	t:Connor,Ta'ai(2),Robinson,Bailey,McGillvary(3),Ferres,Wardle g:Cudjoe(6)	6th	6,145
27/7/14	Catalan Dragons (h)	W38-16	t:Wood,Murphy,McGillvary(2),Wardle(2),Ferres g:Brough(5)	6th	4,931
3/8/14	Wakefield (a)	W18-36	t:Wardle,Crabtree,Lunt,Kopczak,Leeming,McGillvary,Connor g:Brough(4)	6th	4,317
17/8/14	Widnes (h)	W28-14	t:Patrick,Wardle,McGillvary,Kaufusi,Lunt g:Brough(4)	6th	5,346
28/8/14	Warrington (a)	D24-24	t:Bailey,Ta'ai,Lunt,Broughton g:Brough(3) fg:Brough(2)	5th	8,777
7/9/14	Hull FC (h)	W38-28	t:Connor(2),Faiumu,Broughton(2),Ferres,Mullally,McGillvary g:Brough(3)	5th	6,370
12/9/14	St Helens (h)	W17-16	t:Connor,Lunt,Cudjoe g:Connor(2) fg:Cudjoe	3rd	7,244
18/9/14	Wigan (a) (QPO)	L57-4	t:Cudjoe	N/A	8,652
26/9/14	Catalan Dragons (h) (PSF)	L16-18	t:Broughton,Murphy,Robinson g:Brough(2)	N/A	6,900

● Played at Etihad Stadium, Manchester

	D.O.B.	APP ALL	APP SL	TRIES ALL	TRIES SL	GOALS ALL	GOALS SL	FG ALL	FG SL	PTS ALL	PTS SL
Chris Bailey	5/7/82	13(13)	13(12)	5	5	0	0	0	0	20	20
Ben Blackmore	19/2/93	1	1	2	2	0	0	0	0	8	8
Danny Brough	15/1/83	27	26	3	3	100	98	4	4	216	212
Jodie Broughton	9/1/88	21	20	11	11	0	0	0	0	44	44
Jason Chan	26/1/84	14(2)	13(2)	2	2	0	0	0	0	8	8
Jake Connor	18/10/94	7	7	5	5	2	2	0	0	24	24
Eorl Crabtree	2/10/82	20(9)	19(9)	5	5	0	0	0	0	20	20
Leroy Cudjoe	7/4/88	23	23	8	8	12	12	1	1	57	57
Jacob Fairbank	4/3/90	(1)	(1)	0	0	0	0	0	0	0	0
David Faiumu	30/4/83	1(19)	1(18)	1	1	0	0	0	0	4	4
Brett Ferres	17/4/86	24	23	8	8	0	0	0	0	32	32
Scott Grix	1/5/84	24	23	8	8	0	0	0	0	32	32
Josh Johnson	25/7/94	5(5)	5(5)	0	0	0	0	0	0	0	0
Antonio Kaufusi	27/11/84	15(3)	15(2)	1	1	0	0	0	0	4	4
Craig Kopczak	20/12/86	16(12)	15(12)	1	1	0	0	0	0	4	4
Michael Lawrence	12/4/90	19(7)	18(7)	2	2	0	0	0	0	8	8
Kruise Leeming	7/9/95	(4)	(4)	1	1	0	0	0	0	4	4
Shaun Lunt	15/4/86	17(1)	16(1)	11	9	0	0	0	0	44	36
Jermaine McGillvary	16/5/88	27	26	20	20	0	0	0	0	80	80
Anthony Mullally	28/6/91	3(9)	3(9)	3	3	0	0	0	0	12	12
Aaron Murphy	26/11/88	20	19	7	7	0	0	0	0	28	28
Larne Patrick	3/11/88	11(10)	11(10)	6	6	0	0	0	0	24	24
Luke Robinson	25/7/84	27	26	6	6	0	0	0	0	24	24
Ukuma Ta'ai	17/1/87	11(16)	11(16)	10	10	0	0	0	0	40	40
Joe Wardle	22/9/91	28	27	18	17	0	0	0	0	72	68
Kyle Wood	18/6/89	16(7)	16(6)	3	3	0	0	0	0	12	12

Joe Wardle

LEAGUE RECORD
P27-W17-D3-L7
(3rd, SL/Preliminary Semi-Final)
F785, A626, Diff+159
37 points.

CHALLENGE CUP
Round Four

ATTENDANCES
Best - v Leeds (SL - 8,759)
Worst - v London Broncos (SL - 4,849)
Total (SL, inc play-offs) - 89,361
Average (SL, inc play-offs) - 6,383
(Up by 15 on 2013)

193

23 October 2013 - Daniel Holdsworth negotiates early exit from two-year deal to return to Australia.

8 November 2013 - Daniel Holdsworth signs for Cronulla Sharks.

9 November 2013 - Former fullback Steve Prescott MBE dies at the age of 39.

14 November 2013 - former South Sydney outside back Fetuli Talanoa joins on one-year contract with option for 2015.

21 November 2013 - former Australian Schoolboys captain Jordan Rankin joins from Gold Coast Titans on two-year deal.

22 January 2014 - teenage hooker James Cunningham joins London Broncos on loan for 2014 season.

12 February 2014 - prop Garreth Carvell returns from crisis club Bradford Bulls on initial one-year contract with option for further 12 months.

14 February 2014 - 36-34 home round one win over Catalans.

19 February 2014 - winger Liam Colbon joins on 12-month contract.

21 February 2014 - 34-22 defeat at St Helens in first leg of newly inaugurated Steve Prescott Cup.

7 March 2014 - winger Tom Lineham breaks ankle during 44-16 win over Bradford Bulls.

16 March 2014 - Micky Paea suspended for dangerous contact in 19-16 defeat at Castleford Tigers. Chairman Adam Pearson criticises disciplinary decision.

23 March 2014 - captain Gareth Ellis accepts early-guilty plea two-match ban for dangerous shoulder charge during 7-0 home defeat by Widnes Vikings.

28 March 2014 - 30-8 home win over Salford after midweek 'crisis' meeting.

3 April 2014 - last-second touchline conversion means 37-36 home Challenge Cup defeat by Salford.

4 April 2014 - offer to Bath winger Tom Biggs withdrawn when he is unable to agree early release.

10 April 2014 - 30-6 home win over Huddersfield.

11 April 2014 - chairman Adam Pearson fined £1,000 for publicly criticising the RFL Disciplinary Process and attempting to ridicule the role of a Tribunal Chairman.

17 April 2014 - field goal 46 seconds from time seals 21-20 defeat at Hull KR.

25 April 2014 - Jay Pitts and Joe Arundel go to Bradford on loan.

1 May 2014 - forward Josh Bowden signs new contract to end of 2016.

9 May 2014 - Aaron Heremaia signs for Widnes Vikings for 2015 after not being offered a contract.

9 May 2014 - fullback Jamie Shaul signs new four-and-a-half year contract.

17 May 2014 - Jason Crookes sent off in 38-24 defeat by Hull KR at Magic Weekend.

KEY DATES - HULL F.C.

20 May 2014 - Jason Crookes suspended for two games after being found guilty of making careless high tackle on Liam Salter.

21 May 2014 - former Catalan Dragons Setaimata Sa, after 18 months in rugby union with London Irish, signs to the end of the 2015 season.

23 May 2014 - 17-year-old Callum Lancaster makes debut in 20-6 defeat at Leeds.

2 June 2014 - Jason Crookes moves Featherstone Rovers for the rest of the season along with prop Chris Green on month-long loan deal.

13 June 2014 - Callum Lancaster and Jamie Shaul score hat-tricks in 56-6 win at Widnes.

21 June 2014 - Liam Watts misses 20-16 defeat at Catalans because of mis-laid passport.

26 June 2014 - Jordan Rankin returns temporarily to Australia on compassionate leave.

29 June 2014 - last-minute touchline Joe Westerman conversion to Kirk Yeaman try secures 20-all draw at Wakefield. Jordan Abdull makes debut.

1 July 2014 - Leon Pryce, two years, and Marc Sneyd, three with an option to extend for a transfer fee to Salford of 100,000 pounds, sign for 2015.

9 July 2014 - Fetuli Talanoa signs 12-month extension to end of 2015.

14 July 2014 - hooker James Cunningham recalled early from loan spell at relegated London Broncos.

18 July 2014 - Jack Logan makes debut in 56-10 defeat at Wigan.

29 July 2014 - forward Chris Tuson retires due to back injury.

30 July 2014 - Liam Watts signs three year extension.

1 August 2014 - Richard Horne, after being told the club will not renew his contract, stars in 19-12 home success over St Helens which ends run without a win at six games.

6 August 2014 - Richard Horne confirms retirement after 16 years with the club.

14 August 2014 - Dean Hadley signs extended deal until end of 2016 season.

15 August 2014 - Mark Minichiello signs from Gold Coast Titans on two-year deal.

20 August 2014 - captain Gareth Ellis signs contract extension to end of 2016.

22 August 2014 - Jordan Abdull signs new two-year contract. Academy teammates Jack Logan, Brad Fash, Jack Downs and Jansin Turgut also sign two-year deals.

29 August 2014 - 28-0 home win over Hull KR.

5 September 2014 - Gold Coast winger or centre Steve Michaels signs one-year deal, with option of second season.

12 September 2014 - 24-19 home win over Leeds means 11th-placed finish.

19 September 2014 - Ben Crooks released with a year left on contract to join Parramatta Eels.

1 October 2014 - Callum Lancaster signs first full-time contract until end of 2017.

2 October 2014 - former Bradford Bulls junior Curtis Naughton, who spent 2014 with Sydney Roosters reserve grade, signs initial 12-month deal with option for second year.

6 November 2014 - Jacob Miller released from last year of contract after not reporting back for pre-season training.

CLUB RECORDS

Highest score: 88-0 v Sheffield, 2/3/2003
Highest score against:
18-76 v Huddersfield, 19/9/2013
Record attendance:
28,798 v Leeds, 7/3/36 *(The Boulevard)*
23,004 v Hull KR, 2/9/2007 *(KC Stadium)*

MATCH RECORDS

Tries: 7 Clive Sullivan v Doncaster, 15/4/68
Goals: 14 Jim Kennedy v Rochdale, 7/4/21
Sammy Lloyd v Oldham, 10/9/78
Matt Crowther v Sheffield, 2/3/2003
Points: 36 Jim Kennedy v Keighley, 29/1/21

SEASON RECORDS

Tries: 52 Jack Harrison 1914-15
Goals: 170 Sammy Lloyd 1978-79
Points: 369 Sammy Lloyd 1978-79

CAREER RECORDS

Tries: 250 Clive Sullivan 1961-74; 1981-85
Goals: 687 Joe Oliver 1928-37; 1943-45
Points: 1,842 Joe Oliver 1928-37; 1943-45
Appearances: 500 Edward Rogers 1906-25

HULL F.C.

HULL F.C.

DATE	FIXTURE	RESULT	SCORERS	LGE	ATT
14/2/14	Catalan Dragons (h)	W36-34	t:Whiting,Yeaman(2),Rankin,Lineham,Thompson,Horne,Crooks g:Westerman(2)	7th	10,178
21/2/14	St Helens (a)	L34-22	t:Paea,Whiting,Ellis,Houghton g:Crooks(3)	8th	13,488
2/3/14	Warrington (a)	L18-16	t:Houghton,Lineham,Talanoa g:Crooks(2)	8th	10,276
7/3/14	Bradford (h)	W44-16	t:Ellis,Westerman,Shaul(2),Whiting,Heremaia,Houghton,Rankin g:Whiting(6)	5th	11,307
16/3/14	Castleford (a)	L19-16	t:Talanoa,Ellis,Colbon g:Crooks(2)	9th	9,867
23/3/14	Widnes (h)	L0-7		10th	10,286
28/3/14	Salford (h)	W30-8	t:Miller,Shaul,Crooks,Horne,Watts g:Crooks(5)	7th	9,821
3/4/14	Salford (h) (CCR4)	L36-37 (aet)	t:Arundel(2),Shaul(2),Talanoa,Rankin g:Crooks(6)	N/A	5,435
10/4/14	Huddersfield (h)	W30-6	t:Talanoa,Whiting,Rankin,Houghton,Miller,Hadley g:Whiting(3)	6th	9,515
17/4/14	Hull KR (a)	L21-20	t:Rankin,Bowden,Houghton,Talanoa g:Whiting(2)	8th	10,179
21/4/14	London Broncos (h)	W40-4	t:Shaul(2),Crooks,Thompson,Rankin(2),Miller g:Crooks(6)	6th	9,538
4/5/14	Wakefield (h)	L16-23	t:Houghton,Rankin,Crooks g:Crooks(2)	7th	10,088
9/5/14	Wigan (h)	L16-44	t:Ellis,Shaul,Talanoa g:Miller(2)	8th	10,539
17/5/14	Hull KR (MW) ●	L24-38	t:Hadley,Shaul,Houghton,Palea'aesina g:Miller(4)	10th	N/A
23/5/14	Leeds (a)	L20-6	t:Shaul g:Westerman	10th	15,247
31/5/14	London Broncos (a)	W12-50	t:Ellis,Lancaster(2),Westerman(2),Shaul,Houghton,Rankin,Talanoa g:Miller(3),Rankin(4)	10th	1,135
13/6/14	Widnes (a)	W6-56	t:Lancaster(3),Paea,Shaul(3),Horne,Rankin g:Rankin(10)	9th	5,014
21/6/14	Catalan Dragons (a)	L20-16	t:Ellis,Yeaman,Shaul g:Rankin(2)	10th	9,275
29/6/14	Wakefield (a)	D20-20	t:Sa,Horne,Yeaman(2) g:Abdull,Westerman	10th	5,168
4/7/14	Warrington (h)	L18-24	t:Lancaster(3) g:Abdull,Westerman(2)	10th	12,328
12/7/14	Salford (a)	L35-22	t:Hadley,Yeaman(2),Shaul g:Rankin(3)	11th	3,421
18/7/14	Wigan (a)	L56-10	t:Talanoa,Watts g:Rankin	12th	12,493
24/7/14	Castleford (h)	D18-18	t:Talanoa,Abdull,Yeaman g:Rankin(3)	12th	9,959
1/8/14	St Helens (h)	W19-12	t:Horne,Lineham,Paea g:Westerman(3) fg:Westerman	11th	10,214
17/8/14	Bradford (a)	L34-28	t:Shaul,Ellis(2),Sa,Lineham g:Westerman(4)	12th	6,337
29/8/14	Hull KR (h)	W28-0	t:Talanoa,Sa,Lineham(2),Thompson g:Rankin(4)	11th	18,103
7/9/14	Huddersfield (a)	L38-28	t:Houghton,Heremaia,Shaul,Thompson,Ellis g:Rankin(4)	12th	6,370
12/9/14	Leeds (h)	W24-19	t:Lineham,Ellis,Talanoa,Logan(2) g:Rankin(2)	11th	11,964

● Played at Etihad Stadium, Manchester

		APP		TRIES		GOALS		FG		PTS	
	D.O.B.	ALL	SL	ALL	SL	ALL	SL	ALL	SL	ALL	SL
Jordan Abdull	5/2/96	6(1)	6(1)	1	1	2	2	0	0	8	8
Joe Arundel	22/8/91	3	2	2	0	0	0	0	0	8	0
Josh Bowden	14/1/92	11(8)	10(8)	1	1	0	0	0	0	4	4
Garreth Carvell	21/4/80	6(1)	6(1)	0	0	0	0	0	0	0	0
Liam Colbon	30/9/84	8	8	1	1	0	0	0	0	4	4
Jason Crookes	21/4/90	3	3	0	0	0	0	0	0	0	0
Ben Crooks	15/6/93	12(1)	11(1)	4	4	26	20	0	0	68	56
James Cunningham	3/4/94	(2)	(2)	0	0	0	0	0	0	0	0
Gareth Ellis	3/5/81	24	24	10	10	0	0	0	0	40	40
Chris Green	3/1/90	2(6)	2(6)	0	0	0	0	0	0	0	0
Dean Hadley	5/8/92	11(4)	10(4)	3	3	0	0	0	0	12	12
Aaron Heremaia	19/9/82	7(18)	7(17)	2	2	0	0	0	0	8	8
Richard Horne	16/7/82	17(2)	17(2)	5	5	0	0	0	0	20	20
Danny Houghton	25/9/88	26(1)	25(1)	9	9	0	0	0	0	36	36
Callum Lancaster	13/10/96	5	5	8	8	0	0	0	0	32	32
Tom Lineham	21/9/91	14	14	7	7	0	0	0	0	28	28
Jack Logan	8/9/95	3	3	2	2	0	0	0	0	8	8
Jacob Miller	22/8/92	10	9	3	3	9	9	0	0	30	30
Mickey Paea	25/3/86	20(5)	19(5)	3	3	0	0	0	0	12	12
Iafeta Palea'aesina	10/2/82	(22)	(21)	1	1	0	0	0	0	4	4
Jay Pitts	9/12/89	2(1)	2(1)	0	0	0	0	0	0	0	0
Jordan Rankin	17/12/91	20(3)	19(3)	10	9	33	33	0	0	106	102
Setaimata Sa	14/9/87	4(6)	4(6)	3	3	0	0	0	0	12	12
Jamie Shaul	1/7/92	26	25	18	16	0	0	0	0	72	64
Fetuli Talanoa	23/11/87	28	27	11	10	0	0	0	0	44	40
Jordan Thompson	4/9/91	4(20)	4(19)	4	4	0	0	0	0	16	16
Chris Tuson	25/2/90	11(1)	10(1)	0	0	0	0	0	0	0	0
Harry Tyson-Wilson	29/12/96	(1)	(1)	0	0	0	0	0	0	0	0
Liam Watts	8/7/90	16(4)	16(3)	2	2	0	0	0	0	8	8
Joe Westerman	15/11/89	28	27	3	3	13	13	1	1	39	39
Richard Whiting	20/12/84	12(4)	12(4)	4	4	11	11	0	0	38	38
Kirk Yeaman	15/9/83	25	24	8	8	0	0	0	0	32	32

Jamie Shaul

LEAGUE RECORD
P27-W10-D2-L15
(11th, SL)
F653, A586, Diff+67
22 points.

CHALLENGE CUP
Round Four

ATTENDANCES
Best - v Hull KR (SL - 18,103)
Worst - v Salford (CC - 5,435)
Total (SL only) - 143,840
Average (SL only) - 11,065
(Down by 136 on 2013)

21 October 2013 - Papua New Guinea internationals Enoch Maki and Francis Paniu agree contracts.

25 October 2013 - fee paid for France international Kevin Larroyer to join on season-long loan from Catalan Dragons.

1 November 2013 - prop forward Evarn Tuimavave released from final year of contract on compassionate grounds.

8 November 2013 - Justin Poore joins on two-year deal from cash-strapped Wakefield.

12 November 2013 - Ben Cockayne returns from Wakefield after signing two-year deal.

23 December 2013 - Sean Gleeson breaks leg on final day of pre-season training camp in Tenerife.

13 January 2014 - George Griffin joins London Broncos.

17 January 2014 - Travis Burns and Josh Hodgson to be co-captains.

22 January 2014 - Enoch Maki and Francis Paniu released after they fail to gain work permits.

27 January 2014 - five-year naming rights agreement means Craven Park to be known as 'KC Lightstream Stadium'.

16 February 2014 - Michael Weyman banned for two matches on early guilty plea for dangerous contact on Jamie Peacock in 34-6 home defeat by Leeds in season opener in front of capacity crowd.

23 February 2014 - late tries from Josh Hodgson and Omari Caro earn 24-all draw at Huddersfield.

4 March 2014 - Sean Gleeson suffers serious injuries to his eye and eye socket in early-hours attack outside Wigan nightclub.

9 March 2014 - St Helens winger Ade Gardner joins on loan.

23 March 2014 - Justin Poore suspended for three matches for dangerous throw on Bradford's Matty Blythe in the 16-0 home win. Chairman Neil Hudgell describes RFL disciplinary as 'not fit for purpose'.

2 April 2014 - Ade Gardner loan extended to end of season.

10 April 2014 - chairman Neil Hudgell fined £1,000 for publicly criticising the RFL disciplinary process.

11 April 2014 - prop Adam Walker damages ankle in shock 25-12 win at Warrington Wolves.

16 April 2014 - former North Queensland Cowboy Wayne Ulugia arrives on contract until the end of 2015 season.

18 April 2014 - Craig Hall field goal 46 seconds from time earns 21-20 home win over Hull FC.

21 April 2014 - Justin Poore fractures kneecap in 37-24 Easter Monday defeat at Catalans

6 May 2014 - prop James Green signs two-year contract extension to end of 2016.

17 May 2014 - 38-24 Magic Weekend win over Hull FC.

KEY DATES - HULL KINGSTON ROVERS

30 May 2014 - Jordan Cox signs two-year contract extension to end of 2016.

1 June 2014 - Kevin Larroyer and Jordan Cox both suffer fractured ankles and Ben Cockayne a bad knee injury in 54-12 defeat at Castleford Tigers. Michael Weyman sent off.

2 June 2014 - Sean Gleeson announces retirement at age of 26 after failing to fully recover from street assault.

3 June 2014 - Michael Weyman gets second two-match ban of season after being found guilty of using foul and abusive language to referee Tim Roby during defeat at Castleford. Overturned on appeal.

6 June 2014 - fullback Greg Eden recalled from loan spell at Salford Red Devils.

12 June 2014 - independent tribunal rejects appeal by Rovers chairman Neil Hudgell against the £1,000 fine imposed in April for 'engaging in conduct which is prejudicial to the interests of the game'.

25 June 2014 - new North Stand at KC Lightstream Stadium named after club president and former coach and player Colin Hutton.

30 June 2014 - Wayne Ulugia sacked two months into 18-month contract for repeated breaches of club discipline.

30 June 2014 - Darrell Goulding signs from Wigan for 2015 on three-year contract.

3 July 2014 - coach Craig Sandercock sacked, assistant Chris Chester in charge to end of season.

5 July 2014 - prop forward Jonathan Walker released with immediate effect.

17 July 2014 - Jason Chan joins on loan to season end from Huddersfield.

29 July 2014 - Aaron Ollett and Steven Holker sign two-year contract extensions until end of 2016.

31 July 2014 - winger Ken Sio signs three-year deal from Parramatta Eels.

3 August 2014 - 28-10 defeat at Widnes scuppers play-off hopes.

4 August 2014 - Josh Hodgson to join Canberra Raiders at end of season.

11 August 2014 - Italy winger Josh Mantellato joins on three-year contract.

14 August 2014 - James Donaldson signs from Bradford on two-year contract.

19 August 2014 - London Broncos winger Kieran Dixon signs three-year contract from 2015.

22 August 2014 - Kevin Larroyer to remain on loan for second season.

23 August 2014 - Rhys Lovegrove released from final year of contract on compassionate grounds.

25 August 2014 - Chris Chester appointed head coach on permanent basis on three-year contract.

27 August 2014 - former Warrington forward Tyrone McCarthy signs two-year contract after year with Australian cub Northern Pride.

31 August 2014 - fullback Greg Eden released from final year of contract to enable move to Brisbane.

5 September 2014 - Willie Poching joins as assistant coach on one-year contract.

14 September 2014 - Omari Caro scores hat-trick in last-day 42-18 win at Wakefield, meaning a 9th-placed finish.

21 September 2014 - Travis Burns to join St Helens for 2015 for a transfer fee of 60,000 pounds.

23 September 2014 - homesick Australian halfback Kris Keating released 12 months into three-year contract.

26 September 2014 - Jamie Langley joins Sheffield Eagles.

1 October 2014 - assistant coach Stanley Gene leaves the club.

3 October 2014 - winger David Hodgson retires and joins coaching staff on two-year contract.

18 October 2014 - Gold Coast Titans release halfbacks Albert Kelly and Maurice Blair to sign two-year deals with the Robins.

21 October 2014 - French hooker John Boudebza signs from Lezignan on 12-month contract with option for second year.

25 October 2014 - Justin Poore announces retirement with immediate effect.

30 October 2014 - Neville Costigan quits the club halfway through two-year contract.

31 October 2014 - Leeds prop Ryan Bailey signs on two-year contract.

CLUB RECORDS

Highest score:
100-6 v Nottingham City, 19/8/90
Highest score against:
6-84 v Wigan, 1/4/2013
Record attendance:
27,670 v Hull FC, 3/4/53 *(Boothferry Park)*
11,526 v Leeds, 16/2/2014 *(Craven Park)*

MATCH RECORDS

Tries: 11 George West
v Brooklands Rovers, 4/3/1905
Goals:
14 Alf Carmichael v Merthyr, 8/10/1910
Mike Fletcher v Whitehaven, 18/3/90
Colin Armstrong v Nottingham City, 19/8/90
Damien Couturier v Halifax, 23/4/2006
Points: 53 George West
v Brooklands Rovers, 4/3/1905

SEASON RECORDS

Tries: 45 Gary Prohm 1984-85
Goals: 199 Mike Fletcher 1989-90
Points: 450 Mike Fletcher 1989-90

CAREER RECORDS

Tries: 207 Roger Millward 1966-80
Goals: 1,268 Mike Fletcher 1987-98
Points: 2,760 Mike Fletcher 1987-98
Appearances: 489 Mike Smith 1975-91

HULL KINGSTON ROVERS

DATE	FIXTURE	RESULT	SCORERS	LGE	ATT
16/2/14	Leeds (h)	L6-34	t:Keating g:Hall	12th	11,526
23/2/14	Huddersfield (a)	D24-24	t:Caro(2),Cox,J Hodgson g:Burns(4)	9th	7,180
28/2/14	Castleford (h)	L10-30	t:Green,Caro g:Burns	10th	7,022
7/3/14	St Helens (a)	L38-18	t:Larroyer,Eden,J Hodgson g:Burns(3)	11th	11,818
14/3/14	Wigan (a)	L34-20	t:Langley,Salter,Welham,Cockayne g:Burns(2)	11th	12,801
23/3/14	Bradford (h)	W16-0	t:Caro,Keating,Larroyer g:Burns(2)	11th	7,008
30/3/14	Wakefield (h)	W44-6	t:Costigan,Caro(2),J Hodgson(2),Welham(2),Keating g:Burns(6)	10th	6,983
6/4/14	Warrington (h) (CCR4)	L24-28	t:Cockayne,A Walker,Gardner,Caro g:Burns(4)	N/A	4,911
11/4/14	Warrington (a)	W12-25	t:Weyman(2),Burns,Keating g:Burns(4) fg:Burns	9th	8,778
17/4/14	Hull FC (h)	W21-20	t:Larroyer,Weyman,Horne(2) g:Burns(2) fg:Hall	7th	10,179
21/4/14	Catalan Dragons (a)	L37-24	t:Eden,Cox,Caro(2) g:Burns(4)	9th	9,863
4/5/14	Widnes (h)	L29-34	t:Weyman,Welham,Lovegrove,Cockayne,Gardner g:Burns(4) fg:Burns	10th	7,007
10/5/14	Salford (a)	D16-16	t:Welham,Larroyer,Costigan g:Burns(2)	9th	2,903
17/5/14	Hull FC (MW) ●	W24-38	t:Salter(2),Larroyer,Gardner(2),J Hodgson g:Burns(7)	8th	N/A
25/5/14	London Broncos (h)	W48-16	t:J Hodgson(2),Costigan,A Walker,Gardner(2),Larroyer,Hall(2) g:Burns(6)	8th	7,439
1/6/14	Castleford (a)	L54-12	t:Burns,Ulugia g:Burns(2)	9th	7,196
13/6/14	Warrington (h)	L4-34	t:Horne	10th	6,850
20/6/14	Bradford (a)	W18-44	t:Burns,J Hodgson,Welham,Hall(2),Eden(2),A Walker g:Burns(6)	9th	5,601
26/6/14	Huddersfield (h)	L22-26	t:D Hodgson(2),Welham,Gardner g:Burns(3)	9th	8,953
6/7/14	St Helens (h)	W40-10	t:Caro(3),Hall(3),Horne,Eden g:Burns(4)	9th	7,611
11/7/14	Leeds (a)	L30-6	t:J Hodgson g:Burns	9th	14,192
20/7/14	Salford (h)	L18-38	t:J Hodgson,Hall,Weyman g:Burns(3)	9th	8,213
26/7/14	London Broncos (a)	W10-62	t:J Hodgson,Eden(3),Larroyer,Salter(2),Weyman(2),Gardner,A Walker g:Burns(9)	9th	1,084
3/8/14	Widnes (a)	L28-10	t:Keating,Chan g:Burns	9th	5,345
14/8/14	Wigan (h)	D14-14	t:Hall,Chan,Cockayne g:Burns	9th	6,801
29/8/14	Hull FC (a)	L28-0		9th	18,103
7/9/14	Catalan Dragons (h)	L14-32	t:Salter,Hallett,Chan g:Burns	9th	6,412
14/9/14	Wakefield (a)	W18-42	t:Caro(3),Hallett(2),Eden(2),Carlile g:Hall(5)	9th	4,481

● Played at Etihad Stadium, Manchester

		APP		TRIES		GOALS		FG		PTS	
	D.O.B.	ALL	SL	ALL	SL	ALL	SL	ALL	SL	ALL	SL
Travis Burns	6/2/84	28	27	3	3	82	78	2	2	178	170
Keal Carlile	20/3/90	(13)	(12)	1	1	0	0	0	0	4	4
Omari Caro	7/3/91	13	12	15	14	0	0	0	0	60	56
Jason Chan	26/1/84	5(1)	5(1)	3	3	0	0	0	0	12	12
Ben Cockayne	20/7/83	17	16	4	3	0	0	0	0	16	12
Neville Costigan	16/3/85	25	24	3	3	0	0	0	0	12	12
Jordan Cox	27/5/92	5(13)	4(13)	2	2	0	0	0	0	8	8
Greg Eden	14/11/90	17	17	10	10	0	0	0	0	40	40
Sonny Esslemont	29/12/93	(1)	(1)	0	0	0	0	0	0	0	0
Ade Gardner	24/6/83	19	18	8	7	0	0	0	0	32	28
James Green	29/11/90	2(24)	2(23)	1	1	0	0	0	0	4	4
Craig Hall	21/2/88	15(3)	15(3)	9	9	6	6	1	1	49	49
Macauley Hallett	27/11/95	2	2	3	3	0	0	0	0	12	12
David Hodgson	8/8/81	9	9	2	2	0	0	0	0	8	8
Josh Hodgson	31/10/89	28	27	11	11	0	0	0	0	44	44
Graeme Horne	22/3/85	17(5)	17(5)	4	4	0	0	0	0	16	16
Kris Keating	26/11/88	24	23	5	5	0	0	0	0	20	20
Jamie Langley	21/12/83	6(5)	6(5)	1	1	0	0	0	0	4	4
Kevin Larroyer	19/6/89	20(5)	19(5)	7	7	0	0	0	0	28	28
Rhys Lovegrove	11/3/87	6(11)	6(10)	1	1	0	0	0	0	4	4
Jason Netherton	5/10/82	11(8)	11(7)	0	0	0	0	0	0	0	0
Aaron Ollett	19/11/92	2(4)	2(4)	0	0	0	0	0	0	0	0
Justin Poore	26/1/85	7	7	0	0	0	0	0	0	0	0
Connor Robinson	23/10/94	(1)	(1)	0	0	0	0	0	0	0	0
Liam Salter	14/6/93	22	21	6	6	0	0	0	0	24	24
Wayne Ulugia	8/5/92	3	3	1	1	0	0	0	0	4	4
Adam Walker	20/2/91	11(11)	10(11)	4	3	0	0	0	0	16	12
Jonathan Walker	20/2/91	2(6)	2(6)	0	0	0	0	0	0	0	0
Kris Welham	12/5/87	25	24	7	7	0	0	0	0	28	28
Michael Weyman	13/9/84	23(1)	22(1)	7	7	0	0	0	0	28	28

Travis Burns

LEAGUE RECORD
P27-W10-D3-L14
(9th, SL)
F627, A665, Diff-38
23 points.

CHALLENGE CUP
Round Four

ATTENDANCES
Best - v Leeds (SL - 11,526)
Worst - v Warrington (CC - 4,911)
Total (SL only) - 102,004
Average (SL only) - 7,846
(Up by 351 on 2013)

22 October 2013 - Richard Moore released.

24 October 2013 - Jimmy Keinhorst signs new three-year contract to end of 2016 season.

31 October 2013 - Leeds legend Lewis Jones inducted into RFL Hall of Fame.

1 November 2013 - 20-year-old forward Alex Foster signs new three-year contract.

3 November 2013 - hooker Paul McShane placed on transfer list after asking for release from last two years of contract.

5 November 2013 - PNG hooker Paul Aiton signs on three-year contract from cash-strapped Wakefield Trinity.

18 November 2013 - Richard Moore signs for Wakefield.

28 November 2013 - signing from Hunslet Andy Yates ruptures Achilles in training.

28 November 2013 - Paul McShane signs for Wakefield.

8 January 2014 - Jimmy Keinhorst and Luke Briscoe go to Wakefield on season-long loan deals.

14 January 2014 - Nineteen-year-olds James Duckworth and Thomas Minns and 20-year-old Alex Foster all to spend the 2014 season on loan at London Broncos.

24 January 2014 - Jamie Jones-Buchanan, 32, signs new three-year contract to end of 2016 season.

27 January 2014 - Jamie Peacock, 36, shelves retirement plans and signs new two-year contract to end of 2015.

12 February 2014 - Carl Ablett signs new five-year contract to end of 2018.

16 February 2014 - Tom Briscoe scores hat-trick on debut in 34-6 win at Hull KR.

21 February 2014 - Kallum Watkins stars in 100th game, 18-12 home win over Warrington.

28 February 2014 - Kevin Sinfield scores 16 points in 40-12 win over Catalans in Perpignan.

4 March 2014 - Liam Sutcliffe goes to Bradford on month's loan.

7 March 2014 - late Kallum Watkins try secures 12-all draw at Huddersfield.

18 March 2014 - Ryan Hall signs new five-year contract to end of 2018.

28 March 2014 - Jamie Jones-Buchanan tears biceps in round 7, 14-10 defeat, first of season, to St Helens.

KEY DATES - LEEDS RHINOS

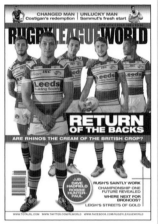

31 March 2014 - Liam Sutcliffe recalled from loan spell at Bradford Bulls.

7 April 2014 - Paul Aiton ruled out for three months to undergo treatment for virus.

11 April 2014 - 42-6 home win over Wakefield on 'Jamie Peacock Day' as he marks 500th career game with try.

26 April 2014 - Rob Burrow suffers broken collarbone during 32-12 home win over St Helens in fifth round of Tetley's Challenge Cup.

1 May 2014 - Joel Moon signs new five-year contract to end of 2018 season.

2 May 2014 - 28-12 home win over Wigan sees Rhinos top table.

8 May 2014 - Ben Jones-Bishop scores two tries in 22-14 derby win at third-placed Castleford Tigers to open up three-point lead at top of table.

10 May 2014 - Ben Jones-Bishop rejects offer of new deal and will leave club at end of season.

13 May 2014 - Ben Jones-Bishop signs for Salford Red Devils.

17 May 2014 - late Joel Moon try disallowed by VR in 18-14 Magic Weekend defeat by Wigan.

23 May 2014 - 18-year-old hooker Robbie Ward makes debut in 20-6 win over Hull FC at Headingley.

26 May 2014 - Newcastle Knights 29-year-old Australian prop Adam Cuthbertson signs four-year contract from 2015.

3 June 2014 - Carl Ablett submits Early Guilty Plea for a Grade C kicking offence in 24-6 defeat at Warrington and banned for two games.

6 June 2014 - late Robbie Ward try decisive in 25-12 home Challenge Cup quarter-final win over Leigh.

9 June 2014 - Jamie Peacock escapes with a fine for punching in the 43rd minute of the quarter-final.

10 June 2014 - Zak Hardaker gets five-match ban for homophobic abuse in defeat at Warrington 11 days before.

12 June 2014 - last-second Tom Briscoe try disallowed by VR in 24-22 home defeat by Huddersfield.

14 June 2014 - Kevin Sinfield awarded MBE.

25 June 2014 - threequarter Ash Handley, 18, handed new three-year contract.

29 June 2014 - last-second Liam Sutcliffe penalty secures 32-31 home win over Catalans.

4 July 2014 - Josh Walters signs new three-year contract.

17 July 2014 - Kevin Sinfield sent off for first time in career in 24-24 home draw with Castleford and banned for two games.

25 July 2014 - 22-18 victory at Salford keeps Rhinos two points behind leaders St Helens.

31 July 2014 - 36-year-old prop Kylie Leuluai extends his stay until the end of 2015.

1 August 2014 - 20-14 home defeat by Bradford begins five match losing league run.

9 August 2014 - 24-16 Challenge Cup semi-final victory over Warrington at Langtree Park, St Helens.

23 August 2014 - Ryan Hall wins Lance Todd Trophy in 23-10 Challenge Cup final win over Castleford.

29 August 2014 - RFL to investigate alleged homophobic abuse by Zak Hardaker in 13-12 home defeat by St Helens. CEO Gary Hetherington claims witchhunt and fined £1,000.

1 September 2014 - Kevin Sinfield MBE retires from international Rugby League.

3 September 2014 - RFL investigation into Zak Hardaker dropped.

12 September 2014 - 24-19 defeat at Hull FC means sixth place finish.

20 September 2014 - 24-20 home elimination by Catalans.

31 October 2014 - Ryan Bailey signs for Hull KR.

4 November 2014 - Ian Kirke signs for Wakefield.

CLUB RECORDS

Highest score:
106-10 v Swinton, 11/2/2001
Highest score against:
6-74 v Wigan, 20/5/92
Record attendance:
40,175 v Bradford, 21/5/47

MATCH RECORDS

Tries:
8 Fred Webster v Coventry, 12/4/1913
Eric Harris v Bradford, 14/9/31
Goals:
17 Iestyn Harris v Swinton, 11/2/2001
Points:
42 Iestyn Harris v Huddersfield, 16/7/99

SEASON RECORDS

Tries: 63 Eric Harris 1935-36
Goals: 173 *(inc 5fg)* Kevin Sinfield 2012
Points: 431 Lewis Jones 1956-57

CAREER RECORDS

Tries: 391 Eric Harris 1930-39
Goals:
1,691 *(inc 36fg)* Kevin Sinfield 1997-2014
Points: 3,678 Kevin Sinfield 1997-2014
Appearances: 625 John Holmes 1968-89

LEEDS RHINOS

DATE	FIXTURE	RESULT	SCORERS	LGE	ATT
16/2/14	Hull KR (a)	W6-34	t:Moon,T Briscoe(3),McGuire,Hardaker,Watkins g:Sinfield(3)	3rd	11,526
21/2/14	Warrington (h)	W18-12	t:Hardaker(2),T Briscoe g:Sinfield(3)	3rd	16,164
28/2/14	Catalan Dragons (a)	W12-40	t:Moon,Delaney,T Briscoe,Ablett,Hall(2),Sinfield g:Sinfield(6)	3rd	6,300
7/3/14	Huddersfield (a)	D12-12	t:S Ward,Watkins g:Sinfield(2)	3rd	8,759
14/3/14	Widnes (h)	W38-4	t:Jones-Bishop(2),Watkins,Bailey,Sinfield,Burrow,Jones-Buchanan g:Sinfield(5)	3rd	14,314
21/3/14	London Broncos (h)	W54-6	t:Singleton,Hall(3),Achurch,Jones-Bishop(2),Hardaker,Watkins,Burrow g:Hardaker(6),Burrow	2nd	12,870
28/3/14	St Helens (a)	L14-10	t:McGuire g:Sinfield(3)	3rd	13,788
6/4/14	Wakefield (a) (CCR4)	W6-60	t:Burrow(2),Ablett(2),McGuire,Hall(2),Achurch,Sutcliffe,T Briscoe,Moon g:Sinfield(8)	N/A	4,482
11/4/14	Wakefield (h)	W42-6	t:Sutcliffe,Hall,T Briscoe,Ablett,Peacock,Clarkson,Burrow g:Sinfield(7)	2nd	13,696
17/4/14	Bradford (a)	W6-46	t:Sinfield,Moon,McGuire,Hall(3),Sutcliffe,Watkins,Burrow g:Sinfield(3),Hardaker(2)	2nd	10,106
21/4/14	Salford (h)	W32-4	t:Sinfield,Hardaker,Burrow,Jones-Bishop,Hall,T Briscoe g:Sinfield(4)	1st	14,013
26/4/14	St Helens (h) (CCR5)	W32-12	t:Hardaker(2),Moon,McGuire,Peacock g:Sinfield(6)	N/A	12,194
2/5/14	Wigan (h)	W28-12	t:McGuire,Hardaker,T Briscoe,Hall,Sutcliffe g:Sinfield(4)	1st	18,139
8/5/14	Castleford (a)	W14-22	t:Jones-Bishop(2),Watkins(2) g:Sinfield(3)	1st	9,208
17/5/14	Wigan (MW) ●	L14-18	t:Hall(2),Ablett g:Sinfield	1st	N/A
23/5/14	Hull FC (h)	W20-6	t:Moon,Singleton,R Ward g:Sinfield(4)	1st	15,247
30/5/14	Warrington (a)	L24-6	t:Leuluai g:Sinfield	2nd	10,312
6/6/14	Leigh (h) (CCQF)	W25-12	t:Hall,S Ward,R Ward,Hardaker g:Sinfield(4) fg:Sinfield	N/A	7,145
12/6/14	Huddersfield (h)	L22-24	t:Watkins,Jones-Bishop,Bailey,Sutcliffe g:Sinfield(3)	2nd	13,104
22/6/14	Widnes (a)	W28-38	t:Watkins,McGuire(2),Sinfield,Sutcliffe,T Briscoe,Walters g:Sinfield(5)	2nd	5,543
29/6/14	Catalan Dragons (h)	W32-31	t:Hall,Jones-Bishop,Walters,Moon(2),Ablett g:Sutcliffe(4)	2nd	13,888
4/7/14	Wakefield (a)	L16-14	t:Watkins,Jones-Bishop,Hall g:Sutcliffe	2nd	4,634
11/7/14	Hull FC (h)	W30-6	t:Burrow(2),Sutcliffe,Ablett,McGuire g:Sinfield(5)	2nd	14,192
17/7/14	Castleford (h)	D24-24	t:T Briscoe,Bailey,Ablett(2) g:Sinfield(4)	3rd	16,173
25/7/14	Salford (a)	W18-22	t:Hardaker,Watkins,Ablett,S Ward g:Hardaker(3)	2nd	5,012
1/8/14	Bradford (h)	L14-20	t:Achurch,Delaney,L Briscoe g:Hardaker	3rd	16,009
9/8/14	Warrington (CCSF) ●●	W24-16	t:Hall(2),Moon,T Briscoe g:Sinfield(4)	N/A	12,132
17/8/14	London Broncos (a)	L40-36	t:Watkins,Walters,Sutcliffe(2),Achurch(2),Hardaker g:Hardaker,Watkins,Sutcliffe(3)	3rd	1,268
23/8/14	Castleford (CCF) ●●●	W10-23	t:T Briscoe,McGuire,Hall(2) g:Sinfield(3) fg:McGuire	N/A	77,914
29/8/14	St Helens (a)	L12-13	t:Sutcliffe g:Sinfield(4)	6th	17,682
5/9/14	Wigan (a)	L21-6	t:Sutcliffe g:Sinfield	6th	20,265
12/9/14	Hull FC (a)	L24-19	t:Ablett,McGuire,Hall g:Sinfield(3) fg:Sinfield	6th	11,964
20/9/14	Catalan Dragons (h) (EPO)	L20-24	t:Ablett,Watkins,Jones-Buchanan g:Sinfield(3),Hardaker	N/A	7,112

● Played at Etihad Stadium, Manchester
●● Played at Langtree Park, St Helens
●●● Played at Wembley Stadium

		APP		TRIES		GOALS		FG		PTS	
	D.O.B.	ALL	SL	ALL	SL	ALL	SL	ALL	SL	ALL	SL
Carl Ablett	19/12/85	28	24	12	10	0	0	0	0	48	40
Mitch Achurch	14/7/88	11(10)	10(9)	5	4	0	0	0	0	20	16
Paul Aiton	29/5/85	13(7)	13(5)	0	0	0	0	0	0	0	0
Ryan Bailey	11/11/83	8(14)	7(11)	3	3	0	0	0	0	12	12
Luke Briscoe	11/3/94	(3)	(3)	1	1	0	0	0	0	4	4
Tom Briscoe	19/3/90	31	26	13	10	0	0	0	0	52	40
Rob Burrow	26/9/82	15(5)	11(5)	9	7	1	1	0	0	38	30
Chris Clarkson	7/4/90	7(10)	7(8)	1	1	0	0	0	0	4	4
Brett Delaney	26/10/85	27(1)	22(1)	2	2	0	0	0	0	8	8
Ashton Golding	4/9/96	(1)	(1)	0	0	0	0	0	0	0	0
Ryan Hall	27/11/87	30	25	23	16	0	0	0	0	92	64
Ash Handley	16/2/96	1	1	0	0	0	0	0	0	0	0
Zak Hardaker	17/10/91	27	22	11	8	14	14	0	0	72	60
Ben Jones-Bishop	24/8/88	12	12	10	10	0	0	0	0	40	40
Jamie Jones-Buchanan	1/8/81	10(4)	8(4)	2	2	0	0	0	0	8	8
Jimmy Keinhorst	14/7/90	1	1	0	0	0	0	0	0	0	0
Ian Kirke	26/12/80	3(15)	2(11)	0	0	0	0	0	0	0	0
Kylie Leuluai	29/3/78	24(4)	19(4)	1	1	0	0	0	0	4	4
Danny McGuire	6/12/82	27	23	11	8	0	0	1	0	45	32
Elliot Minchella	28/1/96	(5)	(5)	0	0	0	0	0	0	0	0
Joel Moon	20/5/88	27	22	9	6	0	0	0	0	36	24
Rob Mulhern	18/10/94	(3)	(3)	0	0	0	0	0	0	0	0
Jamie Peacock	14/12/77	27	22	2	1	0	0	0	0	8	4
Kevin Sinfield	12/9/80	27	22	5	5	102	77	2	1	226	175
Brad Singleton	29/10/92	9(15)	9(13)	2	2	0	0	0	0	8	8
Liam Sutcliffe	25/11/94	12(14)	11(10)	11	10	8	8	0	0	60	56
Josh Walters	23/12/94	5(4)	5(3)	3	3	0	0	0	0	12	12
Robbie Ward	27/10/95	5(2)	4(2)	2	1	0	0	0	0	8	4
Stevie Ward	17/11/93	11(11)	10(10)	3	2	0	0	0	0	12	8
Kallum Watkins	12/3/91	30	25	13	13	0	0	0	0	52	52
Ben White	27/10/94	1	1	0	0	0	0	0	0	0	0

Ryan Hall

LEAGUE RECORD
P27-W15-D2-L10
(6th, SL/Elimination Play-Off)
F685, A421, Diff+264
32 points.

CHALLENGE CUP
Winners

ATTENDANCES
Best - v Wigan (SL - 18,139)
Worst - v Catalan Dragons
(EPO - 7,112)
Total (SL, inc play-offs) - 202,603
Average (SL, inc play-offs) - 14,472
(Down by 513 on 2013)

21 October 2013 - Kieran Dixon suffers serious knee injury in England Knights' game with Samoa.

27 October 2013 - Broncos hooker Ben Fisher announces he will retire at end of World Cup.

20 November 2013 - Broncos confirm intention to appoint administrators within ten days.

3 December 2013 - administration postponed for 10 working days as club states: "Negotiations to cement a permanent home for London Broncos and fulfil next season's fixtures are at a positive stage."

13 December 2013 - immediate future secured after ground-share with Barnet FC agreed.

14 January 2014 - Leeds Rhinos loan nineteen-year-olds James Duckworth and Thomas Minns and 20-year-old Alex Foster for season. George Griffin signs from Hull KR.

15 January 2014 - former St Helens, Widnes Vikings and Huddersfield Giants hooker Scott Moore signs after being released from second year of contract with North Queensland Cowboys

16 January 2014 - Melbourne winger Denny Solomona and Tonga's World Cup full-back Nesiasi Mataitonga signed.

18 January 2014 - veteran Australian prop Ben Ross denies he has come out of retirement despite Broncos release announcing his signing.

22 January 2014 - Wigan Warriors prop James Greenwood and Hull FC hooker James Cunningham arrive on loan for season.

30 January 2014 - Brisbane Broncos forward Nick Slyney signed.

4 February 2014 - Australian outside back Jordan Atkins signs.

6 February 2014 - Australian Joe Grima appointed assistant coach.

16 February 2014 - 64-10 away round-1 thashing at Widnes.

19 February 2014 - Sean Long ends short stint as coaching consultant.

22 February 2014 - 44-18 defeat to Salford Red Devils in first game at the Hive.

23 February 2014 - back-row forward Atelea Vea signs from St George Illawarra.

27 February 2014 - 21-year-old Australian halfback Josh Drinkwater signs from St George Illawarra.

2 March 2014 - 25-12 defeat at Bradford.

16 March 2014 - 50-22 home thrashing by Wakefield.

31 March 2014 - chief executive Gus Mackay leaves the club.

5 May 2014 - Tony Rea leaves his role as head coach with immediate effect to be replaced by Joe Grima.

7 May 2014 - Limoux prop forward Maxime Herold, 24, arrives on trial from Limoux.

KEY DATES - LONDON BRONCOS

10 May 2014 - 30-16 home defeat to Huddersfield in Joe Grima's first game in charge.

17 May 2014 - Josh Drinkwater can't convert his late try as Catalans edge Magic Weekend clash 24-22.

4 June 2014 - Jonathan Wallace re-signed on two-year deal to end of 2016 season.

13 June 2014 - 18-10 rain-sodden, round 16 defeat at Wakefield after leading 10-4 at half-time passes record set by Huddersfield in 2001 of 15 opening Super League losses.

17 June 2014 - Academy forward Toby Everett and stand-off Joe Keyes sign three-year contracts to end of 2017; outside back Harvey Burnett signs for 2015.

19 June 2014 - Australian prop Nick Slyney signs new two-year contract.

26 June 2014 - Liam Foran signs two-year deal from 2015.

4 July 2014 - Joel Wicks, Iliess Macani and James Woodburn-Hall sign new two-year deals to end of 2016 season.

8 July 2014 - Atelea Vea joins St Helens for 2015.

9 July 2014 - Italy World Cup hooker Ray Nasso signs two-year deal from 2015.

11 July 2014 - Andrew Henderson appointed assistant coach from 2015 on two-year deal.

13 July 2014 - 72-12 loss at Warrington is 20th straight defeat of season, guaranteeing relegation.

14 July 2014 - Denny Solomona signs for Castleford for 2015.

14 July 2014 - Broncos head coach Joey Grima announces club to remain full-time in Kingstone Press Championship in 2015.

17 July 2014 - Oscar Thomas rejoins club after spell in rugby union.

18 July 2014 - Manly loose forward Daniel Harrison joins on two-year deal.

25 July 2014 - former Hull FC forward Josh Cordoba joins on two-year deal.

30 July 2014 - under-19s halfback Alex Walker signs one-year deal.

1 August 2014 - former Warrington winger Rhys Williams signs on two-year deal from Central Queensland Capras.

7 August 2014 - Richard Mathers joins on two-year deal.

15 August 2014 - Catalan Dragons halfback William Barthau signs on two-year contract.

17 August 2014 - 40-36 round-25 home victory over Leeds is only win of season.

19 August 2014 - Kieran Dixon to join Hull KR at end of season.

27 August 2014 - Fiji World Cup centre Wes Naiqama signs from Penrith Panthers on two-year deal.

5 September 2014 - Rhys Lovegrove joins on two-year contract.

11 September 2014 - Scotland centre Ben Hellewell signs from Featherstone on two-year deal.

25 September 2014 - former Salford back-row forward Luke Adamson joins from Halifax on one-year deal.

5 November 2014 - Josh Drinkwater joins Wests Tigers.

CLUB RECORDS

Highest score: 82-0 v Highfield, 12/11/95
82-2 v Barrow, 20/5/2006
Highest score against:
6-82 v Warrington, 20/3/2011
10-82 v Warrington, 8/6/2013
Record attendance:
15,013 v Wakefield, 15/2/81

MATCH RECORDS

Tries:
5 Martin Offiah v Whitehaven, 14/3/99
Goals:
13 Rob Purdham v Barrow, 20/5/2006
Points:
34 Rob Purdham v Barrow, 20/5/2006

SEASON RECORDS

Tries: 43 Mark Johnson 1993-94
Goals: 159 John Gallagher 1993-94
Points: 384 John Gallagher 1993-94

CAREER RECORDS

Tries:
109 Luke Dorn 2005-2006; 2009-2013
Goals: 309 Steve Diamond 1981-84
Points: 772 Paul Sykes 2001-2007
Appearances:
202 Steele Retchless 1998-2004

LONDON BRONCOS

DATE	FIXTURE	RESULT	SCORERS	LGE	ATT
16/2/14	Widnes (a)	L64-10	t:Caton-Brown(2) g:Gigot	14th	5,327
22/2/14	Salford (h)	L18-44	t:Moore,Griffin,McMeeken g:Gigot(3)	14th	1,246
2/3/14	Bradford (a)	L25-12	t:Minns,Cunningham g:Drinkwater(2)	13th	5,410
9/3/14	Warrington (h)	L16-44	t:Slyney,Farrar,Minns g:Bishay(2)	13th	1,377
15/3/14	Wakefield (h)	L22-50	t:Minns,Solomona(2),Cook g:Drinkwater(3)	13th	1,017
21/3/14	Leeds (a)	L54-6	t:Caton-Brown g:Drinkwater	13th	12,870
27/3/14	Castleford (h)	L6-54	t:McMeeken g:Drinkwater	13th	1,036
4/4/14	Catalan Dragons (a) (CCR4)	L40-24	t:Solomona,Caton-Brown,Slyney(2) g:Drinkwater(4)	N/A	2,443
11/4/14	Wigan (a)	L36-14	t:O'Callaghan,McMeeken,Macani g:Drinkwater	13th	10,680
17/4/14	Catalan Dragons (h)	L22-28	t:Caton-Brown(2),Mataitonga,Solomona g:Drinkwater(3)	13th	1,002
21/4/14	Hull FC (a)	L40-4	t:Caton-Brown	13th	9,538
1/5/14	St Helens (a)	L48-18	t:Solomona,Minns,Bishay g:Drinkwater(3)	14th	9,408
10/5/14	Huddersfield (h)	L16-30	t:Vea,Foster,Solomona g:Drinkwater(2)	14th	1,035
17/5/14	Catalan Dragons (MW) ●	L24-22	t:Caton-Brown(2),Greenwood,Drinkwater g:Drinkwater(3)	14th	N/A
25/5/14	Hull KR (a)	L48-16	t:Caton-Brown,Foster(2) g:Drinkwater(2)	14th	7,439
31/5/14	Hull FC (h)	L12-50	t:Greenwood,Caton-Brown g:Drinkwater(2)	14th	1,135
13/6/14	Wakefield (a)	L18-10	t:Macani,Minns g:Drinkwater	14th	4,079
21/6/14	Huddersfield (a)	L38-22	t:Cunningham,Drinkwater,Solomona,Caton-Brown g:Drinkwater(3)	14th	4,849
28/6/14	Widnes (h)	L24-42	t:Solomona,Greenwood,Vea,Cook g:Drinkwater(4)	14th	1,422
5/7/14	Wigan (h)	L6-58	t:Minns g:Drinkwater	14th	2,013
13/7/14	Warrington (a)	L72-12	t:Keyes,Moore g:Drinkwater(2)	14th	9,318
19/7/14	St Helens (h)	L16-58	t:Woodburn-Hall,Lovell,Solomona g:Drinkwater(2)	14th	1,791
26/7/14	Hull KR (h)	L10-62	t:Atkins(2) g:Thomas	14th	1,084
3/8/14	Castleford (a)	L64-18	t:Krasniqi,Dollapi,McMeeken g:Drinkwater(3)	14th	5,233
17/8/14	Leeds (h)	W40-36	t:Atkins,Keyes(3),Dixon,McMeeken,Moore g:Drinkwater(6)	14th	1,268
30/8/14	Catalan Dragons (a)	L46-4	t:Dixon	14th	7,067
7/9/14	Salford (a)	L58-26	t:Atkins,Macani,Cook,Drinkwater,Slyney g:Drinkwater(3)	14th	3,268
13/9/14	Bradford (h)	L36-46	t:Cook,Keyes,Drinkwater(2),Dollapi,Slyney g:Drinkwater(6)	14th	1,402

● Played at Etihad Stadium, Manchester

		APP		TRIES		GOALS		FG		PTS	
	D.O.B.	ALL	SL	ALL	SL	ALL	SL	ALL	SL	ALL	SL
Jordan Atkins	22/1/83	13(1)	13(1)	4	4	0	0	0	0	16	16
Mike Bishay	8/2/93	4(7)	4(6)	1	1	2	2	0	0	8	8
Mason Caton-Brown	24/5/93	18	17	12	11	0	0	0	0	48	44
Matt Cook	14/11/86	26(2)	25(2)	4	4	0	0	0	0	16	16
James Cunningham	3/4/94	10(7)	10(7)	2	2	0	0	0	0	8	8
Kieran Dixon	22/8/92	4	4	2	2	0	0	0	0	8	8
Erjon Dollapi	16/3/93	(8)	(8)	2	2	0	0	0	0	8	8
Josh Drinkwater	15/6/92	24(1)	23(1)	5	5	58	54	0	0	136	128
James Duckworth	9/4/94	3	3	0	0	0	0	0	0	0	0
Toby Everett	22/12/95	(2)	(2)	0	0	0	0	0	0	0	0
Ben Farrar	2/12/86	23	22	1	1	0	0	0	0	4	4
Carl Forster	4/6/92	2(3)	2(3)	0	0	0	0	0	0	0	0
Alex Foster	25/9/93	21	20	3	3	0	0	0	0	12	12
Tony Gigot	27/12/90	2	2	0	0	4	4	0	0	8	8
James Greenwood	17/6/91	11(5)	10(5)	3	3	0	0	0	0	12	12
George Griffin	26/6/92	(20)	(19)	1	1	0	0	0	0	4	4
Maxime Herold	9/9/89	(2)	(2)	0	0	0	0	0	0	0	0
Joe Keyes	17/9/95	7	7	5	5	0	0	0	0	20	20
Olsi Krasniqi	26/6/92	19(8)	19(7)	1	1	0	0	0	0	4	4
Will Lovell	10/5/93	1(7)	1(7)	1	1	0	0	0	0	4	4
Iliess Macani	6/12/93	11(3)	10(3)	3	3	0	0	0	0	12	12
Nesiasi Mataitonga	25/2/93	11(1)	11(1)	1	1	0	0	0	0	4	4
Mike McMeeken	10/5/94	17(4)	17(3)	5	5	0	0	0	0	20	20
Thomas Minns	4/9/94	24	23	6	6	0	0	0	0	24	24
Scott Moore	23/1/88	27	26	3	3	0	0	0	0	12	12
Jamie O'Callaghan	21/9/90	12(1)	11(1)	1	1	0	0	0	0	4	4
Nick Slyney	11/2/88	21(4)	20(4)	5	3	0	0	0	0	20	12
Denny Solomona	27/10/93	20(1)	19(1)	9	8	0	0	0	0	36	32
Oscar Thomas	3/1/94	4(2)	4(2)	0	0	1	1	0	0	2	2
Atelea Vea	27/11/86	20(3)	19(3)	2	2	0	0	0	0	8	8
Alex Walker	4/9/95	1	1	0	0	0	0	0	0	0	0
Jon Wallace	8/10/94	4(12)	4(12)	0	0	0	0	0	0	0	0
Joel Wicks	27/10/94	1(6)	1(6)	0	0	0	0	0	0	0	0
James Woodburn-Hall	2/2/95	3(2)	3(2)	1	1	0	0	0	0	4	4

Matt Cook

LEAGUE RECORD
P27-W1-D0-L26
(14th, SL)
F438, A1237, Diff-799
2 points.

CHALLENGE CUP
Round Four

ATTENDANCES
Best - v Wigan (SL - 2,013)
Worst - v Catalan Dragons
(SL - 1,002)
Total (SL only) - 16,828
Average (SL only) - 1,294
(Down by 906 on 2013,
Twickenham Stoop)

13 December 2013 - Martin Vickers appointed new chief executive.

17 December 2013 - Harrison Hansen signs from Wigan for an undisclosed fee on four-year contract.

7 February 2014 - Jon Ford and Will Hope go to Sheffield Eagles on season-long loan deals.

16 February 2014 - Rangi Chase withdrawn injured in 18-14 round one home win over Wakefield.

20 February 2014 - hooker Gareth Owen joins Sheffield Eagles on season-long loan.

22 February 2014 - 44-18 win at London Broncos.

27 February 2014 - 38-0 home thrashing by St Helens.

10 March 2014 - Wigan Warriors utility back Dominic Manfredi joins on one-month loan.

11 March 2014 - Sean Long returns to backroom staff.

11 March 2014 - chairman Dr Marwan Koukash fined £1,000 for misconduct following comments made on social media website and for using foul and/or abusive language at a public event on February 4.

14 March 2014 - 28-12 home defeat to Warrington is third on a row.

23 March 2014 - Rangi Chase returns and kicks late field goal to secure 23-16 home win over unbeaten Castleford.

3 April 2014 - late touchline Jake Mullaney conversion secures thrilling 37-36 Challenge Cup win at Hull FC.

4 April 2014 - Wigan assistant Iestyn Harris takes over from Brian Noble as head coach. Noble turns down offer to stay on as football director.

8 April 2014 - Logan Tomkins joins on month's loan from Wigan.

11 April 2014 - 38-24 win at Bradford in Iestyn Harris's first game in charge.

17 April 2014 - Michael Platt signs from North Wales Crusaders; Niall Evalds, joins Barrow on season-long loan.

23 April 2014 - Logan Tomkins to remain on loan to end of season.

25 April 2014 - Hull KR fullback Greg Eden arrives on month's loan.

27 April 2014 - 30-20 home defeat to Widnes in fifth round of Challenge Cup.

2 May 2014 - New Zealand Warriors fullback Kevin Locke signs three-year contract from 2015.

13 May 2014 - Leeds Rhinos' Ben Jones-Bishop signs three-year contract from 2015.

10 May 2014 - 16-16 home draw with Hull KR halts four-match losing run.

16 May 2014 - assistant coach Andy Hay leaves to become coach at Featherstone.

6 June 2014 - Greg Eden recalled from loan by Hull KR.

KEY DATES - SALFORD RED DEVILS

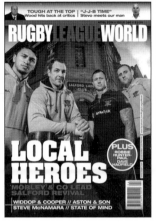

10 June 2014 - Kevin Locke secures early release from NZ Warriors, Tim Smith leaves on season loan to Wakefield and Shannan McPherson released for family reasons.

15 June 2014 - 46-18 home win over Bradford is first win in eight games

16 June 2014 - former Catalans, Wigan and Hull KR and current Newcastle Knights halfback Michael Dobson signs four-year contract from 2015.

23 June 2014 - London Broncos centre Mason Caton-Brown signs with immediate effect on two-and-a-half-year deal.

25 June 2014 - Batley threequarter Josh Griffin joins on contract to end of season.

28 June 2014 - last-second Jake Webster try means 14-10 loss at Castleford.

1 July 2014 - Marc Sneyd, on loan for 2014 at Castleford, signs for Hull FC for 2015 for £100,000 transfer fee.

1 July 2014 - winger Danny Williams joins Bradford on month loan deal.

5 July 2014 - Kevin Locke makes debut in 36-10 away win at Huddersfield. Lama Tasi sent off for high tackle on Danny Brough and accepts two-match ban.

15 July 2014 - Gareth Hock banned for seven matches for deliberate physical contact with referee during 35-22 home win over Hull FC.

18 July 2014 - Jason Walton and utility back Niall Evalds agree deals until end of 2017 season.

20 July 2014 - play-off hopes alive after 38-18 win at Hull KR.

25 July 2014 - narrow 22-18 home defeat to Leeds ends three-match winning run.

26 July 2014 - centre Michael Platt joins Leigh after three appearances in his second spell at Salford.

28 July 2014 - Jake Mullaney signs for Bradford Bulls.

4 August 2014 - Matty Ashurst signs for Wakefield for 2015.

15 August 2014 - former Leeds Rhinos hooker Liam Hood signs from Hunslet on one-year deal for 2015 season.

31 August 2014 - 42-6 humiliation at Wakefield ends play-off chances.

1 September 2014 - Danny Williams joins Bradford on a permanent basis.

2 September 2014 - Adrian Morley to play on in 2015 but hands captaincy to Harrison Hansen.

3 September 2014 - owner Marwan Koukash cancels team's end-of-year party after they fail to reach play-offs.

4 September 2014 - Gareth Hock makes transfer request.

5 September 2014 - teenage centre Brad England signs from Leeds Rhinos.

12 September 2014 - 36-6 home win over Widnes means 10th-placed finish

22 September 2014 - Marwan Koukash set to buy a NRL club to twin with Salford.

23 September 2014 - prop Carl Forster signs from St Helens.

1 October 2014 - Martin Gleeson retires and joins backroom staff as Academy coach.

14 October 2014 - Gareth Hock withdraws transfer request.

14 October 2014 - Tim Smith joins Wakefield on a permanent basis.

CLUB RECORDS

Highest score:
100-12 v Gateshead, 23/3/2003
Highest score against:
16-96 v Bradford, 25/6/2000
Record attendance:
26,470 v Warrington, 13/2/37 *(The Willows)*
7,102 v Wakefield, 16/2/2014
(AJ Bell Stadium)

MATCH RECORDS

Tries:
6 Frank Miles v Lees, 5/3/1898
Ernest Bone v Goole, 29/3/1902
Jack Hilton v Leigh, 7/10/39
Goals:
14 Steve Blakeley v Gateshead, 23/3/2003
Points:
39 Jim Lomas v Liverpool City, 2/2/1907

SEASON RECORDS

Tries: 46 Keith Fielding 1973-74
Goals: 221 David Watkins 1972-73
Points: 493 David Watkins 1972-73

CAREER RECORDS

Tries: 297 Maurice Richards 1969-83
Goals: 1,241 David Watkins 1967-79
Points: 2,907 David Watkins 1967-79
Appearances:
498 Maurice Richards 1969-83

SALFORD RED DEVILS

DATE	FIXTURE	RESULT	SCORERS	LGE	ATT
16/2/14	Wakefield (h)	W18-14	t:Hock,Hansen,Dixon g:Mullaney(3)	6th	7,102
22/2/14	London Broncos (a)	W18-44	t:Hansen(2),Williams,Fages(2),Smith,Mullaney,Meli		
			g:Mullaney(5),Smith	4th	1,246
27/2/14	St Helens (h)	L0-38		5th	6,353
6/3/14	Widnes (a)	L32-18	t:Johnson,Lee,Fages g:Mullaney(3)	8th	5,291
14/3/14	Warrington (h)	L12-28	t:Manfredi(2),Johnson	10th	6,260
23/3/14	Castleford (h)	W23-16	t:Gleeson,Johnson,Dixon(2) g:Mullaney(3) fg:Chase	8th	5,823
28/3/14	Hull FC (a)	L30-8	t:Johnson,Sa'u	9th	9,821
3/4/14	Hull FC (a) (CCR4)	W36-37			
		(aet)	t:Meli(3),Chase,Fages,Sa'u g:Mullaney(6) fg:Chase	N/A	5,435
11/4/14	Bradford (a)	W24-38	t:Mullaney,Sa'u,Smith,Ashurst,Puletua,Chase,Meli g:Mullaney(5)	8th	6,144
18/4/14	Huddersfield (h)	L22-42	t:Meli(3),Morley,Ashurst g:Mullaney	10th	5,068
21/4/14	Leeds (a)	L32-4	t:Tomkins	11th	14,013
27/4/14	Widnes (h) (CCR5)	L20-30	t:Hock(2),Sa'u,Tasi g:Lee(2)	N/A	2,630
3/5/14	Catalan Dragons (a)	L37-24	t:Meli,Williams,Eden,Hock g:Smith(4)	11th	7,862
10/5/14	Hull KR (h)	D16-16	t:Meli(2),Gleeson g:Mullaney(2)	11th	2,903
17/5/14	Widnes (MW) ●	L24-30	t:Sa'u,Chase,Ashurst,Williams,Meli g:Mullaney(2)	11th	N/A
22/5/14	Wigan (a)	L4-25	t:Meli	11th	3,706
30/5/14	St Helens (a)	L32-12	t:Evalds,Hock g:Smith(2)	11th	10,391
15/6/14	Bradford (h)	W46-18	t:Tomkins,Sa'u(2),Dixon,Chase(2),Meli,Evalds g:Chase(7)	11th	3,407
22/6/14	Warrington (a)	L36-20	t:Sa'u,Morley,Evalds(2) g:Chase(2)	12th	10,120
28/6/14	Castleford (a)	L14-10	t:Sa'u,Hock g:Chase	12th	5,937
5/7/14	Huddersfield (a)	W10-36	t:Chase,Ashurst,Caton-Brown,Fages,Johnson,Locke g:Locke(6)	12th	5,689
12/7/14	Hull FC (h)	W35-22	t:Chase,Caton-Brown(2),J Griffin,Johnson,D Griffin		
			g:J Griffin(4),Chase fg:Chase	12th	3,421
20/7/14	Hull KR (a)	W18-38	t:Caton-Brown,Evalds,Sa'u,J Griffin(2),Fages,Johnson g:J Griffin(5)	10th	8,213
25/7/14	Leeds (h)	L18-22	t:Sa'u,Fages,J Walne g:J Griffin(3)	11th	5,012
31/7/14	Wigan (a)	L45-4	t:J Griffin	12th	12,962
15/8/14	Catalan Dragons (h)	W34-22	t:Locke(2),Sa'u,Evalds,Fages,Puletua g:Locke(3),Chase(2)	10th	3,100
31/8/14	Wakefield (a)	L42-6	t:Hansen g:Locke	12th	4,016
7/9/14	London Broncos (h)	W58-26	t:Lee,J Walne,J Griffin(3),Johnson(3),Tomkins,Walton g:J Griffin(9)	10th	3,268
12/9/14	Widnes (h)	W36-6	t:Hansen,Sa'u(2),Puletua,Chase,J Griffin g:J Griffin(6)	10th	3,268

● Played at Etihad Stadium, Manchester

		APP		TRIES		GOALS		FG		PTS	
	D.O.B.	ALL	SL	ALL	SL	ALL	SL	ALL	SL	ALL	SL
Matty Ashurst	1/11/89	14(7)	14(7)	4	4	0	0	0	0	16	16
Mason Caton-Brown	24/5/93	8	8	4	4	0	0	0	0	16	16
Rangi Chase	11/4/86	25	23	8	7	13	13	3	2	61	56
Andrew Dixon	28/2/90	7(2)	7(2)	4	4	0	0	0	0	16	16
Greg Eden	14/11/90	5	4	1	1	0	0	0	0	4	4
Niall Evalds	26/8/93	11(2)	11(2)	6	6	0	0	0	0	24	24
Theo Fages	23/8/94	18(3)	17(2)	8	7	0	0	0	0	32	28
Martin Gleeson	28/5/80	13(1)	11(1)	2	2	0	0	0	0	8	8
Darrell Griffin	19/6/81	9(11)	9(10)	1	1	0	0	0	0	4	4
Josh Griffin	9/5/90	8	8	8	8	27	27	0	0	86	86
Harrison Hansen	26/10/85	23	21	5	5	0	0	0	0	20	20
Gareth Hock	5/9/83	15(1)	13(1)	6	4	0	0	0	0	24	16
Stuart Howarth	25/1/90	1(5)	1(5)	0	0	0	0	0	0	0	0
Greg Johnson	20/2/90	21	20	10	10	0	0	0	0	40	40
Tommy Lee	1/2/88	22(4)	20(4)	2	2	2	0	0	0	12	8
Kevin Locke	4/4/89	6	6	3	3	10	10	0	0	32	32
Dominic Manfredi	1/10/93	1	1	2	2	0	0	0	0	8	8
Shannan McPherson	12/12/85	(10)	(9)	0	0	0	0	0	0	0	0
Francis Meli	20/8/80	18	16	14	11	0	0	0	0	56	44
Adrian Morley	10/5/77	21(6)	19(6)	2	2	0	0	0	0	8	8
Jake Mullaney	28/5/90	13	12	2	2	30	24	0	0	68	56
Michael Platt	23/3/84	2(1)	1(1)	0	0	0	0	0	0	0	0
Tony Puletua	25/6/79	16(11)	16(9)	3	3	0	0	0	0	12	12
Steve Rapira	17/12/88	6(14)	5(13)	0	0	0	0	0	0	0	0
Junior Sa'u	18/4/87	27	25	14	12	0	0	0	0	56	48
Tim Smith	13/1/85	13(1)	12	2	2	7	7	0	0	22	22
Lama Tasi	3/5/90	25(1)	23(1)	1	0	0	0	0	0	4	0
Logan Tomkins	1/8/91	9(9)	8(9)	3	3	0	0	0	0	12	12
Adam Walne	3/10/90	(3)	(3)	0	0	0	0	0	0	0	0
Jordan Walne	28/12/92	7(13)	7(12)	2	2	0	0	0	0	8	8
Jason Walton	13/6/90	4(10)	4(10)	1	1	0	0	0	0	4	4
Danny Williams	26/9/86	9	9	3	3	0	0	0	0	12	12

Junior Sa'u

LEAGUE RECORD
P27-W11-D1-L15
(10th, SL)
F608, A695, Diff-87
23 points.

CHALLENGE CUP
Round Five

ATTENDANCES
Best - v Wakefield (SL - 7,102)
Worst - v Widnes (CC - 2,630)
Total (SL only) - 58,691
Average (SL only) - 4,515
(Up by 1,337 on 2013)

KEY DATES - ST HELENS

2 April 2014 - Ade Gardner loan to Hull KR extended to end of season.

11 April 2014 - three tries in last 13 minutes snatches 30-28 victory in top-of-the-table clash at Castleford.

12 April 2014 - Sia Soliola announces he is to return to Australia at end of season.

15 April 2014 - Willie Manu out for up to two months with a dislocated and broken thumb sustained in Saints' last-gasp 30-28 win at Castleford Tigers.

18 April 2014 - first defeat of season, by Wigan, at Langtree Park on Good Friday.

21 April 2014 - 40-26 Easter Monday defeat at Widnes.

26 April 2014 - 32-12 defeat at Leeds means Challenge Cup exit.

1 May 2014 - 48-18 home win over London ends three-match losing run.

2 June 2014 - Mark Percival, 20, Luke Thompson, 19, and Greg Richards, 18 all sign new deals to the end of 2018 season.

14 June 2014 - Jonny Lomax ruled out for rest of season with knee injury sustained in 42-0 defeat at Catalan Dragons.

22 June 2014 - Paul Wellens scores two tries in 38-16 home win over top-4 rivals Castleford.

27 June 2014 - Luke Walsh withdrawn with back injury in 16-12 win at Wigan.

3 July 2014 - free agent Shannon McDonnell signs to end of season.

8 July 2014 - second rower Atelea Vea signs from London on two-year deal from 2015.

22 July 2014 - forward Joe Greenwood signs three-year contract extension.

4 August 2014 - Sia Soliola to join Canberra Raiders at season end.

6 August 2014 - Jon Wilkin ruled out for remainder of season due to shoulder injury.

25 July 2014 - Luke Walsh stretchered off against Widnes Vikings with season-ending broken fibula.

14 August 2014 - Anthony Laffranchi to return to Australia at end of season.

4 September 2014 - Shannon McDonnell breaks jaw in 39-12 home defeat by Warrington.

13 September 2014 - Alex Walmsley sent off in 17-16 defeat at Huddersfield. But Saints win League Leaders' Shield when Castleford lose in Perpignan the day after.

16 September 2014 - Alex Walmsley found guilty of making a Grade B careless tackle on Luke Robinson and banned for one game.

19 September 2014 - 41-0 victory over Castleford at Langtree Park in Qualifying Play-off.

26 September 2014 - Saints choose Catalans in ClubCall.

2 October 2014 - 30-12 Qualifying Semi-Final win over Catalans.

3 October 2014 - coach Nathan Brown released from final year of contract to return home to Australia at end of season.

11 October 2014 - James Roby wins Harry Sunderland Trophy in 14-6 Grand Final win over Wigan.

14 October 2014 - prop Richard Beaumont released without making an appearance.

20 October 2014 - Keiron Cunningham appointed head coach on two-year contract; Jamahl Lolesi to continue as assistant.

23 October 2014 - Gary Wheeler joins Warrington.

9 November 2013 - former fullback Steve Prescott MBE dies at the age of 39.

3 December 2013 - James Roby signs new five-year contract.

24 January 2014 - Alex Walmsley, 23, signs three-year extension and winger Adam Swift extends his contract, both to end of 2017.

28 January 2014 - Louie McCarthy-Scarsbrook signs new contract until end of 2016.

6 February 2014 - Jonny Lomax, 23, signs new four-year deal up to end of 2017.

13 February 2014 - Luke Walsh scores late try and kicks eight goals in 38-8 win at Warrington.

18 February 2014 - Paul Clough joins Widnes on season-long loan deal.

21 February 2014 - 34-22 home win over Hull FC in first leg of newly inaugurated Steve Prescott Cup.

7 March 2014 - Mose Masoe makes debut in 38-18 home win over Hull KR.

9 March 2014 - Ade Gardner joins Hull KR on month's loan.

28 March 2014 - Tom Makinson scores two tries in the last 16 minutes to snatch a dramatic 14-10 home victory over Leeds Rhinos and maintain 100 per cent record.

CLUB RECORDS

Highest score:
112-0 v Carlisle, 14/9/86
Highest score against:
6-78 v Warrington, 12/4/1909
Record attendance:
35,695 v Wigan, 26/12/49 *(Knowsley Road)*
17,980 v Wigan, 6/4/2012
v Wigan, 18/4/2014 *(Langtree Park)*

MATCH RECORDS

Tries: 6 Alf Ellaby v Barrow, 5/3/32
Steve Llewellyn v Castleford, 3/3/56
Steve Llewellyn v Liverpool, 20/8/56
Tom van Vollenhoven v Wakefield, 21/12/57
Tom van Vollenhoven v Blackpool, 23/4/62
Frank Myler v Maryport, 1/9/69
Shane Cooper v Hull, 17/2/88
Goals: 16 Paul Loughlin v Carlisle, 14/9/86
Points:
40 Paul Loughlin v Carlisle, 14/9/86

SEASON RECORDS

Tries 62 Tom van Vollenhoven 1958-59
Goals: 214 Kel Coslett 1971-72
Points: 452 Kel Coslett 1971-72

CAREER RECORDS

Tries: 392 Tom van Vollenhoven 1957-68
Goals: 1,639 Kel Coslett 1962-76
Points: 3,413 Kel Coslett 1962-76
Appearances: 531 Kel Coslett 1962-76

ST HELENS

DATE	FIXTURE	RESULT	SCORERS	LGE	ATT
13/2/14	Warrington (a)	W8-38	t:Makinson,Roby,Amor,Laffranchi,Swift,Walsh g:Walsh(7)	2nd	13,157
21/2/14	Hull FC (h)	W34-22	t:Roby(2),Soliola,Lomax,Makinson,Percival g:Walsh(5)	2nd	13,488
27/2/14	Salford (a)	W0-38	t:Wilkin,Walsh,Percival(2),Amor,Laffranchi g:Walsh(7)	1st	6,353
7/3/14	Hull KR (h)	W38-18	t:Swift(2),Lomax,Walmsley,Soliola,Makinson,Wilkin g:Walsh(5)	1st	11,818
14/3/14	Catalan Dragons (h)	W40-22	t:Jones,Makinson(2),Turner,McCarthy-Scarsbrook,Hohaia,Swift g:Walsh(4),Lomax(2)	1st	11,321
23/3/14	Wakefield (a)	W16-24	t:Jones,Soliola,Dawson,Greenwood,Makinson g:Makinson(2)	1st	5,037
28/3/14	Leeds (h)	W14-10	t:Walker,Makinson(2) g:Makinson	1st	13,788
6/4/14	Huddersfield (a) (CCR4)	W16-17	t:Swift,Makinson(2) g:Walsh(2) fg:Walsh	N/A	5,566
11/4/14	Castleford (a)	W28-30	t:Soliola,Lomax,Makinson,Turner,Wellens,Swift g:Walsh(3)	1st	6,487
18/4/14	Wigan (h)	L14-33	t:Makinson(2),Turner g:Walsh	1st	17,980
21/4/14	Widnes (a)	L40-26	t:Soliola,Masoe,Wellens,Makinson,Hohaia g:Makinson(3)	3rd	7,706
26/4/14	Leeds (a) (CCR5)	L32-12	t:Swift,Jones g:Walsh(2)	N/A	12,194
1/5/14	London Broncos (h)	W48-18	t:Dawson,Walsh,Lomax,Makinson,Hohaia,Swift,Greenwood,Jones,Flanagan g:Walsh(6)	2nd	9,408
11/5/14	Bradford (a)	W0-50	t:Wilkin(2),Walsh,Lomax,Makinson,Swift,Soliola,McCarthy-Scarsbrook,Roby g:Walsh(7)	2nd	6,311
18/5/14	Warrington (MW) ●	L24-41	t:Walmsley,Turner,Hohaia,Dawson g:Walsh(4)	2nd	N/A
23/5/14	Huddersfield (h)	W41-22	t:Wheeler(2),Hohaia,Wellens,Dawson,Wilkin,Masoe g:Walsh(6) fg:Walsh	2nd	10,218
30/5/14	Salford (a)	W32-12	t:Wellens(2),Soliola,Hohaia,Wheeler g:Walsh(6)	1st	10,391
14/6/14	Catalan Dragons (a)	L42-0		1st	9,864
22/6/14	Castleford (h)	W38-16	t:Makinson,Wellens(2),Turner,Percival(2),Walsh g:Walsh(5)	1st	12,648
27/6/14	Wigan (a)	W12-16	t:Makinson(2),Wellens g:Percival(2)	1st	20,224
6/7/14	Hull KR (a)	L40-10	t:Percival,Masoe g:Percival	1st	7,611
11/7/14	Bradford (h)	W46-22	t:Roby,Wellens(2),Masoe,Percival,Swift,Hohaia,Makinson g:Percival(7)	1st	10,238
19/7/14	London Broncos (a)	W16-58	t:Percival(2),Amor,Turner(2),Wellens,Dawson(2),Thompson,Soliola,Laffranchi g:Percival(7)	1st	1,791
25/7/14	Widnes (h)	W44-22	t:Flanagan,Makinson(3),Masoe(2),Turner,Manu g:Percival(6)	1st	11,844
1/8/14	Hull FC (a)	L19-12	t:Makinson,Wellens g:Percival(2)	1st	10,214
15/8/14	Wakefield (h)	W40-16	t:Makinson(2),Jones(2),McDonnell(2),Soliola g:Percival(6)	1st	10,708
29/8/14	Leeds (a)	W12-13	t:McCarthy-Scarsbrook,Roby g:Percival,Makinson fg:Hohaia	1st	17,682
4/9/14	Warrington (h)	L12-39	t:McDonnell,Manu g:Makinson(2)	1st	12,854
12/9/14	Huddersfield (a)	L17-16	t:Makinson,Roby,Hohaia g:Percival(2)	1st	7,244
19/9/14	Castleford (h) (QPO)	W41-0	t:Roby(2),Turner,Swift,Makinson,Amor,Masoe g:Percival(6) fg:Turner	N/A	7,548
2/10/14	Catalan Dragons (h) (QSF)	W30-12	t:Turner,Swift,Manu,Masoe,Percival g:Percival(5)	N/A	8,888
11/10/14	Wigan (GF) ●●	W14-6	t:Soliola,Makinson g:Percival(3)	N/A	70,102

● Played at Etihad Stadium, Manchester
●● Played at Old Trafford, Manchester

	D.O.B.	APP ALL	APP SL	TRIES ALL	TRIES SL	GOALS ALL	GOALS SL	FG ALL	FG SL	PTS ALL	PTS SL
Kyle Amor	26/5/87	19	17	4	4	0	0	0	0	16	16
Matty Dawson	2/10/90	19	19	6	6	0	0	0	0	24	24
Mark Flanagan	4/12/87	17(5)	16(5)	2	2	0	0	0	0	8	8
Carl Forster	4/6/92	(1)	(1)	0	0	0	0	0	0	0	0
Matty Fozard	3/3/95	1	1	0	0	0	0	0	0	0	0
Joe Greenwood	2/4/93	3(9)	3(7)	2	2	0	0	0	0	8	8
Jordan Hand	13/5/93	(1)	(1)	0	0	0	0	0	0	0	0
Lance Hohaia	1/4/83	23	22	8	8	0	0	1	1	33	33
Josh Jones	12/5/93	22(4)	20(4)	6	5	0	0	0	0	24	20
Anthony Laffranchi	16/11/80	5(11)	5(11)	3	3	0	0	0	0	12	12
Jonny Lomax	4/9/90	15	13	5	5	2	2	0	0	24	24
Tom Makinson	10/10/91	31	29	29	27	9	9	0	0	134	126
Willie Manu	20/3/80	12(10)	11(10)	3	3	0	0	0	0	12	12
Mose Masoe	17/5/89	10(19)	10(17)	8	8	0	0	0	0	32	32
Louie McCarthy-Scarsbrook	14/1/86	18(11)	17(11)	3	3	0	0	0	0	12	12
Shannon McDonnell	5/8/87	3	3	3	3	0	0	0	0	12	12
Mark Percival	29/5/94	17(1)	16(1)	10	10	48	48	0	0	136	136
Greg Richards	12/7/95	4(8)	4(7)	0	0	0	0	0	0	0	0
James Roby	22/11/85	31	29	9	9	0	0	0	0	36	36
Andre Savelio	21/3/95	(3)	(3)	0	0	0	0	0	0	0	0
Iosia Soliola	4/8/86	18(14)	16(14)	10	10	0	0	0	0	40	40
Adam Swift	20/2/93	20	18	12	10	0	0	0	0	48	40
Luke Thompson	27/4/95	5(12)	5(12)	1	1	0	0	0	0	4	4
James Tilley	11/11/93	(1)	(1)	0	0	0	0	0	0	0	0
Jordan Turner	9/1/89	27	25	10	10	0	0	1	1	41	41
Anthony Walker	28/12/91	5(3)	5(2)	1	1	0	0	0	0	4	4
Alex Walmsley	10/4/90	20(5)	18(5)	2	2	0	0	0	0	8	8
Luke Walsh	12/5/87	18	16	5	5	70	66	2	1	162	153
Paul Wellens	27/2/80	21(10)	21(8)	12	12	0	0	0	0	48	48
Gary Wheeler	30/9/89	12	12	3	3	0	0	0	0	12	12
Jon Wilkin	11/1/83	20	19	5	5	0	0	0	0	20	20

Tom Makinson

LEAGUE RECORD
P27-W19-D0-L8
(1st, SL/Grand Final Winners, Champions)
F796, A563, Diff+233
38 points.

CHALLENGE CUP
Round Five

ATTENDANCES
Best - v Wigan (SL - 17,980)
Worst - v Castleford (QPO - 7,548)
Total (SL, inc play-offs) - 173,140
Average (SL, inc play-offs) - 11,543
(Up by 402 on 2013)

5 November 2013 - hooker Paul Aiton joins Leeds.

8 November 2013 - prop Justin Poore signs for Hull KR.

12 November 2013 - Ben Cockayne re-signs for Hull KR.

15 November 2013 - Matty Wildie signs new one-year contract.

18 November 2013 - prop Richard Moore returns on one-year deal following his release by Leeds.

26 November 2013 - former Melbourne Storm prop Scott Anderson signs from Brisbane Broncos on 12-month deal.

28 November 2013 - Leeds Rhinos hooker Paul McShane signs two-year deal.

5 December 2013 - Parramatta release forward Matt Ryan to enable him to take up two-year contract.

20 December 2013 - Samoa World Cup halfback Pita Godinet signs two-year contract.

8 January 2014 - Leeds pair Jimmy Keinhorst and Luke Briscoe sign season-long loan deals.

30 January 2014 - ground capacity cut by more than half to 5,333 after annual review of the stadium's safety certificate.

10 February 2014 - Lee Smith released from remainder of contract to join rugby union side Newcastle Falcons.

14 February 2014 - Jarrod Sammut signs two-year deal after requesting release from Bradford Bulls. Scott Anderson, Pita Godinet and Matt Ryan arrive after finally getting visas.

16 February 2014 - 18-14 round-1 defeat at Salford.

20 February 2014 - 23-10 round-two home defeat to Bradford.

1 March 2014 - Nick Scruton signs one-year deal for an undisclosed fee agreed by Bulls' administrators.

2 March 2014 - 46-24 defeat at Wigan.

5 March 2014 - former Aussie Schoolboys halfback Harry Siejka signs one-year deal.

7 March 2014 - Jordan Crowther signs four-year contract.

7 March 2014 - Warrington Wolves winger Chris Riley joins on month's loan.

9 March 2014 - 56-14 round 4 home win over Catalans.

12 March 2014 - Lucas Walshaw joins Dewsbury Rams on month's loan.

15 March 2014 - Richard Mathers scores four tries in 50-22 away win at London Broncos.

9 April 2014 - Chris Riley to stay on week-by-week basis.

1 May 2014 - Jacob Fairbank arrives on month's loan from Huddersfield.

4 May 2014 - 23-16 win, after trailing 16-0, at Hull FC is first win in six games.

9 May 2014 - late Paul Sykes try secures 24-18 win at Widnes.

15 May 2014 - Richard Owen joins on season loan from Castleford Tigers.

KEY DATES - WAKEFIELD T WILDCATS

18 May 2014 - 50-12 humbling by Castleford at Magic Weekend.

23 May 2014 - Australian prop Scott Anderson extends contract by two years to end of 2016.

25 May 2014 - 36-4 home defeat to Warrington.

27 May 2014 - Lee Gilmour arrives from Castleford on loan deal.

28 May 2014 - Taulima Tautai signs for Wigan for 2015.

1 June 2014 - 20-12 defeat at Bradford.

2 June 2014 - head coach Richard Agar quits and is replaced by his assistant James Webster.

10 June 2014 - Tim Smith returns from Salford on season loan.

12 June 2014 - Harry Siejka goes to Featherstone on month's loan.

13 June 2014 - 18-10 waterlogged, home win over London in James Webster's first game in charge puts Wakefield eight points clear of 13th placed Bradford.

16 June 2014 - young winger Tom Johnstone signs contract to end of 2015.

22 June 2014 - stunning 36-28 home win over Wigan.

25 June 2014 - Jarrod Sammut joins neighbours Featherstone on dual-registration.

29 June 2014 - last minute converted Kirk Yeaman try gains Hull FC 20-all draw at Belle Vue.

4 July 2014 - Craig Hall signs from Hull KR on two-year contract from 2015.

9 July 2014 - Nick Scruton signs new two-year deal to end of 2016.

14 July 2014 - Catalans prop Mickael Simon signs two-year deal from 2015.

16 July 2014 - Reece Lyne signs to end of 2017 on new three-year contract.

19 July 2014 - 40-6 defeat in Perpignan to Catalans ends James Webster's unbeaten run.

21 July 2014 - Daniel Smith signs new three-year deal.

23 July 2014 - ever-present Matt Ryan out for season after shoulder operation.

29 July 2014 - Andy Raleigh confirms retirement at end of season.

4 August 2014 - Matty Ashurst joins from Salford on two-year deal.

6 August 2014 - Richard Mathers not offered new contract and joins London Broncos for 2015.

12 August 2014 - Richard Moore joins Hunslet with immediate effect.

15 August 2014 - Danny Washbrook signs new 12-month contract for 2015.

29 August 2014 - prop Lopini Paea signs from Catalans on 12-month contract.

3 September 2014 - Ali Lauitiiti signs new two-year contract.

4 September 2014 - Lee Gilmour appointed assistant coach on two-year contract, and will be available to play.

11 September 2014 - Chris Riley signs permanent deal for 2015.

14 September 2014 - 42-18 home defeat to Hulll KR means 12th placed finish.

22 September 2014 - Harry Siejka signs for Bradford.

9 October 2014 - Paul Sykes joins Featherstone.

14 October 2014 - Tim Smith signs permanent 12-month contract.

20 October 2014 - Richard Owen signs three-year permanent contract.

4 November 2014 - Ian Kirke signs from Leeds on 12-month deal.

CLUB RECORDS

Highest score:
90-12 v Highfield, 27/10/92
Highest score against:
0-86 v Castleford, 17/4/95
Record attendance:
30,676 v Huddersfield, 26/2/21

MATCH RECORDS

Tries:
7 Fred Smith v Keighley, 25/4/59
Keith Slater v Hunslet, 6/2/71
Goals:
13 Mark Conway v Highfield, 27/10/92
Points:
36 Jamie Rooney v Chorley, 27/2/2004

SEASON RECORDS

Tries: 38 Fred Smith 1959-60
David Smith 1973-74
Goals: 163 Neil Fox 1961-62
Points: 407 Neil Fox 1961-62

CAREER RECORDS

Tries: 272 Neil Fox 1956-69; 1970-74
Goals: 1,836 Neil Fox 1956-69; 1970-74
Points: 4,488 Neil Fox 1956-69; 1970-74
Appearances:
605 Harry Wilkinson 1930-49

WAKEFIELD T WILDCATS

DATE	FIXTURE	RESULT	SCORERS	LGE	ATT
16/2/14	Salford (a)	L18-14	t:Ryan,Godinet,Lauitiiti g:Sykes	9th	7,102
20/2/14	Bradford (h)	L10-23	t:Fox,Lauitiiti g:Sammut	11th	4,049
2/3/14	Wigan (a)	L46-24	t:Lauitiiti,Kirmond,Fox,Lyne g:Sammut(4)	11th	11,703
9/3/14	Catalan Dragons (h)	W56-14	t:Tautai(2),Molloy,Lyne(2),Godinet(2),D Smith,Sykes g:Sammut(10)	9th	4,190
15/3/14	London Broncos (a)	W22-50	t:Mathers(4),Sammut,Collis(2),Lyne,Godinet g:Sammut(7)	7th	1,017
23/3/14	St Helens (h)	L16-24	t:Kirmond,Lyne,McShane g:Sammut(2)	9th	5,037
30/3/14	Hull KR (a)	L44-6	t:Godinet g:Sammut	11th	6,983
6/4/14	Leeds (h) (CCR4)	L6-60	t:Godinet g:Sammut	N/A	4,482
11/4/14	Leeds (a)	L42-6	t:Sammut g:Sammut	11th	13,696
18/4/14	Castleford (h)	L20-43	t:McShane,Sammut(2),Lyne g:Sammut(2)	12th	5,159
21/4/14	Huddersfield (a)	L36-16	t:Sammut,Walshaw,Molloy g:Sammut(2)	12th	5,487
4/5/14	Hull FC (a)	W16-23	t:Mathers,D Smith,Walshaw,Sammut g:Sammut(3) fg:Sykes	12th	10,088
9/5/14	Widnes (a)	W18-24	t:Riley,Moore,Siejka,Sykes g:Sammut(4)	12th	5,186
18/5/14	Castleford (MW) ●	L50-12	t:Scruton,Sykes g:Sammut(2)	12th	N/A
25/5/14	Warrington (h)	L4-36	t:Walshaw	12th	3,698
1/6/14	Bradford (a)	L20-12	t:Ryan(2) g:Sammut(2)	12th	6,249
13/6/14	London Broncos (h)	W18-10	t:Kirmond,D Smith,Ryan g:Sykes(3)	12th	4,079
22/6/14	Wigan (h)	W36-28	t:Kirmond,T Smith,Owen,Moore,Washbrook,Lyne g:Sykes(6)	11th	4,096
29/6/14	Hull FC (h)	D20-20	t:Mathers,Riley,Lyne,Scruton g:Sykes(2)	11th	5,168
4/7/14	Leeds (h)	W16-14	t:Washbrook,Mathers,Owen g:Sykes(2)	11th	4,634
10/7/14	Widnes (h)	W12-10	t:T Smith,Scruton g:Sykes(2)	10th	3,932
19/7/14	Catalan Dragons (a)	L40-6	t:Lyne g:Sykes	11th	8,256
27/7/14	Warrington (a)	W26-40	t:Riley(3),Washbrook,Keinhorst,Mathers,Scruton g:Sammut(6)	10th	9,252
3/8/14	Huddersfield (h)	L18-36	t:Sammut(2),Sykes g:Sammut(3)	10th	4,317
15/8/14	St Helens (a)	L40-16	t:Washbrook,Owen,Gilmour g:Sammut(2)	11th	10,708
31/8/14	Salford (h)	W42-6	t:Raleigh,Washbrook,Riley,Collis,Lauitiiti,Owen(2),Godinet g:Sykes(5)	10th	4,016
7/9/14	Castleford (a)	L26-22	t:Gilmour,Riley,Anderson,Owen g:Sykes(3)	11th	9,182
14/9/14	Hull KR (h)	L18-42	t:Collis,Riley,Raleigh g:Sykes(3)	12th	4,481

● Played at Etihad Stadium, Manchester

		APP		TRIES		GOALS		FG		PTS	
	D.O.B.	ALL	SL	ALL	SL	ALL	SL	ALL	SL	ALL	SL
Scott Anderson	8/1/86	20(1)	19(1)	1	1	0	0	0	0	4	4
Chris Annakin	30/1/91	(5)	(5)	0	0	0	0	0	0	0	0
Luke Briscoe	11/3/94	2	2	0	0	0	0	0	0	0	0
Dean Collis	21/10/85	10	9	4	4	0	0	0	0	16	16
Jordan Crowther	19/2/97	(1)	(1)	0	0	0	0	0	0	0	0
Jacob Fairbank	4/3/90	1(3)	1(3)	0	0	0	0	0	0	0	0
Peter Fox	5/11/83	10	9	2	2	0	0	0	0	8	8
Lee Gilmour	12/3/78	10(3)	10(3)	2	2	0	0	0	0	8	8
Pita Godinet	21/12/87	13(10)	12(10)	7	6	0	0	0	0	28	24
Max Jowitt	6/5/97	1	1	0	0	0	0	0	0	0	0
Jimmy Keinhorst	14/7/90	7	7	1	1	0	0	0	0	4	4
Danny Kirmond	11/11/85	22	21	4	4	0	0	0	0	16	16
Ali Lauitiiti	13/7/79	9(8)	8(8)	4	4	0	0	0	0	16	16
Reece Lyne	2/12/92	20	19	9	9	0	0	0	0	36	36
Richard Mathers	24/10/83	21	20	8	8	0	0	0	0	32	32
Paul McShane	19/11/89	25(2)	24(2)	2	2	0	0	0	0	8	8
Jon Molloy	23/3/91	3(8)	3(8)	2	2	0	0	0	0	8	8
Richard Moore	2/2/81	3(13)	2(13)	2	2	0	0	0	0	8	8
Richard Owen	25/4/90	14	14	6	6	0	0	0	0	24	24
Andy Raleigh	17/3/81	9(6)	9(6)	2	2	0	0	0	0	8	8
Chris Riley	22/3/88	23	23	8	8	0	0	0	0	32	32
Matt Ryan	13/6/88	15(7)	15(6)	4	4	0	0	0	0	16	16
Jarrod Sammut	15/2/87	17(1)	16(1)	8	8	53	52	0	0	138	136
Nick Scruton	24/12/84	19(2)	19(1)	4	4	0	0	0	0	16	16
Harry Siejka	3/2/92	6(3)	6(3)	1	1	0	0	0	0	4	4
Daniel Smith	20/3/93	10(10)	10(9)	3	3	0	0	0	0	12	12
Tim Smith	13/1/85	12	12	2	2	0	0	0	0	8	8
Paul Sykes	11/8/81	23(1)	22(1)	4	4	28	28	1	1	73	73
Taulima Tautai	3/4/88	3(16)	3(15)	2	2	0	0	0	0	8	8
Kyle Trout	1/3/91	1	1	0	0	0	0	0	0	0	0
Lucas Walshaw	4/8/92	8(2)	8(2)	3	3	0	0	0	0	12	12
Danny Washbrook	18/9/85	24(2)	23(2)	5	5	0	0	0	0	20	20
Matty Wildie	25/10/90	3(8)	3(8)	0	0	0	0	0	0	0	0

Paul McShane

LEAGUE RECORD
P27-W10-D1-L16
(12th, SL)
F557, A750, Diff-193
21 points.

CHALLENGE CUP
Round Four

ATTENDANCES
Best - v Hull FC (SL - 5,168)
Worst - v Warrington (SL - 3,698)
Total (SL only) - 56,856
Average (SL only) - 4,373
(Down by 3,600 on 2013)

17 October 2013 - 20-year-old former Wigan fullback Matthew Russell joins from Gold Coast Titans on two-year deal.

30 October 2013 - Chris Hill agrees five-year contract to end of 2018.

8 November 2013 - Lee Briers announces retirement with immediate effect on medical advice due to a neck injury.

6 January 2014 - Wolves depart for 3-week training camp in Sydney.

7 January 2014 - youngsters James Saltonstall, Joe Philbin and Tom Walker join Bradford on short-term loan deals.

12 February 2014 - Danny Bridge joins Bradford on month's loan.

13 February 2014 - 38-8 round-1, Thursday night TV defeat to St Helens on tenth Halliwell Jones Stadium anniversary.

21 February 2014 - 18-12 defeat at Leeds.

2 March 2014 - off the mark with 18-16 home win over Hull FC.

7 March 2014 - winger Chris Riley joins Wakefield on month's loan.

14 March 2014 - 28-12 round five win at Salford.

20 March 2014 - 12-4 home defeat by Wigan.

30 March 2014 - 29 unanswered second-half points secure 33-14 win at Huddersfield.

9 April 2014 - Chris Riley to stay at Wakefield on week-by-week basis.

16 April 2014 - fullback Matthew Russell agrees four-year deal up to November 2017.

21 April 2014 - Kevin Penny makes second debut in 40-6 round 10 defeat at Castleford.

23 April 2014 - Danny Bridge recalled from loan at Bradford.

4 May 2014 - shock 34-28 defeat at Bradford.

Wolves revival stuns Giants

7 May 2014 - hooker Brad Dwyer signs new two-year contract to end of 2016.

9 May 2014 - Joel Monaghan scores 100-try milestone on his 100th appearance in 42-10 home win over Catalans.

18 May 2014 - Ben Westwood returns from six-match injury absence in 41-24 Magic Weekend win over St Helens.

30 May 2014 - James Laithwaite breaks foot in 24-6 home win over Leeds Rhinos.

31 May 2014 - Michael Monaghan announces he will retire at end of current season.

2 June 2014 - Danny Bridge goes to Featherstone Rovers on month-long loan.

8 June 2014 - 46-10 Challenge Cup quarter-final win at Bradford.

10 June 2014 - Tony Smith extends contract as head of coaching and rugby until end of 2016, ending speculation of return to Australia. Recently stepped-down Wakefield head coach Richard Agar joins as first-team coach on two-year contract from 2015 season. Willie Poching and Richard Marshall will leave at end of current season.

29 June 2014 - 50-24 home win over Bradford is seventh on a row.

1 July 2014 - Fiji international prop Ashton Sims signs from North Queensland on a two-year deal from 2015.

2 July 2014 - prop Chris Hill signs five-and-a-half-year deal to end of 2019.

8 July 2014 - Gene Ormsby and Anthony England sign contracts until November 2016. Rhys and Ben Evans and James Laithwaite sign until November 2017. George King signs full-time contract until end of 2016.

18 July 2014 - 28-14 defeat at Widnes ends winning run at nine games.

---

25 July 2014 - Academy halfback Declan Patton signs contract until November 2016.

9 August 2014 - 24-16 Challenge Cup semi-final defeat to Leeds at Langtree Park, St Helens.

27 August 2014 - Castleford hooker Daryl Clark joins on a four-year deal from 2015.

5 September 2014 - Simon Grix, broken ankle, and Ben Westwood, calf, out for season after 39-12 win at St Helens.

9 September 2014 - Trent Waterhouse to leave at end of season. Chris Riley, Glenn Riley, Jordan Burke, Danny Bridge, James Saltonstall and Gavin Bennion all released.

11 September 2014 - 24-20 round-27 defeat at Wigan means 5th placed finish.

12 September 2014 - Brad Dwyer, 12-month loan, and Glenn Riley sign for London Broncos.

20 September 2014 - 22-19 Elimination Play-off win over Widnes after trailing 18-0.

23 September 2014 - Stefan Ratchford signs new contract until November 2018.

25 September 2014 - 30-14 Preliminary Semi-Final win at Castleford.

3 October 2014 - last-gasp Joe Burgess try means 16-12 defeat and Qualifying Semi-Final exit at Wigan.

7 October 2014 - Michael Monaghan joins Catalans as assistant coach.

16 October 2014 - Gareth O'Brien signs new contract to end of 2016.

23 October 2014 - St Helens utility back Gary Wheeler joins on one-year deal.

CLUB RECORDS

Highest score:
112-0 v Swinton, 20/5/2011
Highest score against:
12-84 v Bradford, 9/9/2001
Record attendance:
34,404 v Wigan, 22/1/49 *(Wilderspool)*
15,000 v St Helens, 30/3/2012
(Halliwell Jones Stadium)

MATCH RECORDS

Tries:
7 Brian Bevan v Leigh, 29/3/48
Brian Bevan v Bramley, 22/4/53
Goals:
16 Lee Briers v Swinton, 20/5/2011
Points:
44 Lee Briers v Swinton, 20/5/2011

SEASON RECORDS

Tries: 66 Brian Bevan 1952-53
Goals: 170 Steve Hesford 1978-79
Points: 363 Harry Bath 1952-53

CAREER RECORDS

Tries: 740 Brian Bevan 1945-62
Goals: 1,159 Steve Hesford 1975-85
Points: 2,586 Lee Briers 1997-2013
Appearances: 620 Brian Bevan 1945-62

WARRINGTON WOLVES

DATE	FIXTURE	RESULT	SCORERS	LGE	ATT
13/2/14	St Helens (h)	L8-38	t:J Monaghan(2)	13th	13,157
21/2/14	Leeds (a)	L18-12	t:J Monaghan,Westwood g:Ratchford(2)	13th	16,164
2/3/14	Hull FC (h)	W18-16	t:Ratchford,Waterhouse,B Evans g:Ratchford(3)	9th	10,276
9/3/14	London Broncos (a)	W16-44	t:Asotasi,Bridge,R Evans(4),Ormsby,Atkins(2) g:Ratchford(4)	7th	1,377
14/3/14	Salford (a)	W12-28	t:Bridge,Higham,Ormsby,J Monaghan,Asotasi g:Ratchford(4)	6th	6,260
20/3/14	Wigan (h)	L4-12	t:Ormsby	7th	11,550
30/3/14	Huddersfield (a)	W14-33	t:R Evans,Myler,Westwood,Russell,Ormsby,J Monaghan g:Ratchford,Bridge(3) fg:Ratchford	6th	7,068
6/4/14	Hull KR (a) (CCR4)	W24-28	t:Atkins(2),J Monaghan,R Evans,Asotasi g:Bridge(4)	N/A	4,911
11/4/14	Hull KR (h)	L12-25	t:Myler(2) g:Bridge(2)	7th	8,778
18/4/14	Widnes (h)	W44-6	t:O'Brien,J Monaghan,M Monaghan,Bridge,R Evans(2),Currie,Atkins g:Bridge(4),Ratchford(2)	5th	10,500
21/4/14	Castleford (a)	L40-6	t:M Monaghan g:Ratchford	8th	6,853
27/4/14	Doncaster (h) (CCR5)	W68-0	t:Penny(3),Russell,Atkins,Bridge(4),Dwyer,J Monaghan,R Evans g:Bridge(10)	N/A	3,002
4/5/14	Bradford (a)	L34-28	t:England,Bridge,Penny,J Monaghan,Russell g:Bridge(4)	8th	6,173
9/5/14	Catalan Dragons (h)	W42-10	t:J Monaghan(2),England,Ratchford,Bridge,Higham,Laithwaite g:Bridge(7)	7th	8,816
18/5/14	St Helens (MW) ●	W24-41	t:Ormsby,R Evans(2),Hill,Atkins,J Monaghan(2),Russell g:Bridge(4) fg:Ratchford	7th	N/A
25/5/14	Wakefield (a)	W4-36	t:Ratchford,Currie(2),Ormsby,Bridge,Atkins,Myler g:Bridge(4)	5th	3,698
30/5/14	Leeds (h)	W24-6	t:Bridge(2),Hill,J Monaghan g:Bridge(4)	5th	10,312
8/6/14	Bradford (a) (CCQF)	W10-46	t:Myler(2),Atkins,Russell,Ormsby,J Monaghan(2),Currie g:Bridge(7)	N/A	5,064
13/6/14	Hull KR (a)	W4-34	t:Ormsby,Ratchford,J Monaghan(2),B Evans,Atkins g:Bridge(5)	5th	6,850
22/6/14	Salford (h)	W36-20	t:Ormsby,Atkins,Bridge,J Monaghan,R Evans,Currie g:Bridge(6)	5th	10,120
29/6/14	Bradford (h)	W50-24	t:Harrison,Atkins,O'Brien(2),J Monaghan(2),Westwood,Ormsby,R Evans g:Ratchford(7)	5th	9,003
4/7/14	Hull FC (a)	W18-24	t:Ratchford,Atkins,Harrison,Ormsby g:Bridge(4)	5th	12,328
13/7/14	London Broncos (h)	W72-12	t:J Monaghan(4),Hill(3),Currie(3),Wood,Ormsby,Harrison g:Bridge(10)	4th	9,318
18/7/14	Widnes (a)	L28-14	t:Atkins,Bridge,Currie g:Bridge	5th	7,158
27/7/14	Wakefield (h)	W26-40	t:R Evans(2),J Monaghan,Ratchford,Atkins g:Bridge,Ratchford(2)	5th	9,252
1/8/14	Catalan Dragons (a)	W24-26	t:M Monaghan,Ormsby,R Evans,J Monaghan g:Bridge(5)	5th	7,858
9/8/14	Leeds (CCSF) ●●	L24-16	t:Bridge,Ratchford,Westwood g:Bridge(2)	N/A	12,132
15/8/14	Castleford (h)	W48-10	t:Atkins,O'Brien,Bridge,R Evans(2),England,Ratchford,J Monaghan g:Bridge(3),Ratchford(5)	4th	8,391
28/8/14	Huddersfield (h)	D24-24	t:O'Brien,Atkins,Harrison(2) g:O'Brien(4)	4th	8,777
4/9/14	St Helens (a)	W12-39	t:Ratchford,M Monaghan,O'Brien,J Monaghan(2),Myler,Atkins g:Ratchford(4),O'Brien fg:Myler	4th	12,854
11/9/14	Wigan (a)	L24-20	t:J Monaghan(2),Myler g:Ratchford(4)	5th	15,686
20/9/14	Widnes (h) (EPO)	W22-19	t:J Monaghan(3),R Evans g:Ratchford(3)	N/A	7,229
25/9/14	Castleford (a) (PSF)	W14-30	t:Atkins,J Monaghan(2),O'Brien,R Evans g:Ratchford(5)	N/A	6,219
3/10/14	Wigan (a) (QSF)	L16-12	t:J Monaghan,O'Brien g:Ratchford,O'Brien	N/A	15,023

● Played at Etihad Stadium, Manchester
●● Played at Langtree Park, St Helens

	D.O.B.	APP ALL	APP SL	TRIES ALL	TRIES SL	GOALS ALL	GOALS SL	FG ALL	FG SL	PTS ALL	PTS SL
Roy Asotasi	6/1/82	12(17)	11(14)	3	2	0	0	0	0	12	8
Ryan Atkins	7/10/85	30	26	19	15	0	0	0	0	76	60
Chris Bridge	5/7/84	30	26	16	11	90	67	0	0	244	178
Ben Currie	15/7/94	14(12)	12(12)	9	8	0	0	0	0	36	32
Brad Dwyer	28/4/93	(10)	(9)	1	0	0	0	0	0	4	0
Anthony England	19/10/86	13(11)	10(11)	3	3	0	0	0	0	12	12
Ben Evans	30/10/92	4(14)	3(12)	2	2	0	0	0	0	8	8
Rhys Evans	30/10/92	29	25	20	18	0	0	0	0	80	72
Simon Grix	28/9/85	12(3)	11(1)	0	0	0	0	0	0	0	0
Ben Harrison	24/2/88	22(2)	20(2)	5	5	0	0	0	0	20	20
Mick Higham	18/9/80	17(14)	15(12)	2	2	0	0	0	0	8	8
Chris Hill	3/11/87	33	29	5	5	0	0	0	0	20	20
George King	24/2/95	(2)	(2)	0	0	0	0	0	0	0	0
Toby King	9/7/96	1	1	0	0	0	0	0	0	0	0
James Laithwaite	23/9/91	14(10)	13(9)	1	1	0	0	0	0	4	4
Joel Monaghan	22/4/82	31	27	38	34	0	0	0	0	152	136
Michael Monaghan	13/5/80	18(7)	16(6)	4	4	0	0	0	0	16	16
Richard Myler	21/5/90	18(3)	15(3)	8	6	0	0	1	1	33	25
Gareth O'Brien	31/10/91	22(1)	21(1)	8	8	6	6	0	0	44	44
Gene Ormsby	12/9/92	20	19	13	12	0	0	0	0	52	48
Kevin Penny	3/10/87	3	2	4	1	0	0	0	0	16	4
Joe Philbin	16/11/94	(3)	(3)	0	0	0	0	0	0	0	0
Stefan Ratchford	19/7/88	30	27	9	8	48	48	2	2	134	130
Chris Riley	22/2/88	1	1	0	0	0	0	0	0	0	0
Glenn Riley	21/9/92	(12)	(11)	0	0	0	0	0	0	0	0
Matthew Russell	6/6/93	25(4)	21(4)	5	3	0	0	0	0	20	12
Trent Waterhouse	8/1/81	21(2)	19(1)	1	1	0	0	0	0	4	4
Ben Westwood	25/7/81	20	18	4	3	0	0	0	0	16	12
Paul Wood	10/10/81	2(9)	2(7)	1	1	0	0	0	0	4	4

Joel Monaghan

LEAGUE RECORD
P27-W17-D1-L9
(5th, SL/Qualifying Semi-Final)
F793, A515, Diff+278
35 points.

CHALLENGE CUP
Semi-Finalists

ATTENDANCES
Best - v St Helens (SL - 13,157)
Worst - v Doncaster (CC - 3,002)
Total (SL, inc play-offs) - 135,479
Average (SL, inc play-offs) - 9,677
(Down by 788 on 2013)

209

KEY DATES - WIDNES VIKINGS

28 November 2013 - head coach Denis Betts signs two-year contract extension to end of 2016.

13 January 2014 - Wales International Rhodri Lloyd joins on year-long loan from Wigan.

19 January 2014 - new signing, 21-year-old hooker Liam Carberry breaks leg in warm-up game against North Wales.

24 January 2014 - Brett Hodgson appointed as coaching consultant.

16 February 2014 - Danny Tickle scores 24 points on debut in 64-10 home hammering of London in round one.

18 February 2014 - Paul Clough joins on season-long loan deal from St Helens.

28 February 2014 - late Joe Mellor and Rhys Hanbury tries secure 22-20 home win over Huddersfield.

7 March 2014 - Kevin Brown scores two late tries as 32-18 home win over Salford maintains perfect start.

14 March 2014 - 38-4 defeat at Leeds ends winning opening run at 3 matches.

24 March 2014 - Tom Gilmore field goal seals rain-soaked 7-0 away win at Hull FC.

3 April 2014 - Academy players Teddy and Jay Chaplehow, Matt Whitley and Ed Chamberlain, all 18, and 17-year-old Ryan Ince sign full-time contracts to end of 2015.

8 April 2014 - consultant Brett Hodgson to join full-time in November 2014 on two-year contract.

17 April 2014 - centre Stefan Marsh signs two-year contract extension to end of 2016.

21 April 2014 - late MacGraff Leuluai try secures 40-26 home Easter Monday win over St Helens.

22 April 2014 - prop forward Paul Johnson signs new two-year contract to end of 2016.

23 April 2014 - injured hooker Liam Carberry signs new 12-month contract.

29 April 2014 - prop Eamon O'Carroll signs new two-year contract to end of 2016.

30 April 2014 - prop Phil Joseph signs new two-year contract to end of 2016.

1 May 2014 - Wales international Lloyd White signs new two-year contract to end of 2016.

7 May 2014 - forward Ben Kavanagh signs new two-year contract to end of 2016.

9 May 2014 - Hull FC hooker Aaron Heremaia signs two-year deal from 2015.

16 May 2014 - Willie Isa signs new two-year contract to end of 2016.

20 May 2014 - prop forward Steve Pickersgill announces retirement at age of 28 because of recurring neck and knee injuries.

22 May 2014 - winger Paddy Flynn signs new two-year contract to end of 2016.

25 May 2014 - Paddy Flynn sin-binned and banned for two matches for punching in 34-22 defeat at Castleford.

3 June 2014 - captain Jon Clarke announces he will retire at end of current season.

5 June 2014 - scrum-half Tom Gilmore scores hat-trick in 56-6 Challenge Cup home win over Keighley to make first Challenge Cup semi-final for 18 years.

6 June 2014 - halfback Danny Craven signs new three-year contract to end of 2017 season.

13 June 2014 - 56-6 home defeat to Hull FC.

18 June 2014 - 48-4 defeat at Wigan in delayed round-2 match.

25 June 2014 - Tom Gilmore signs new two-year contract to end of 2016.

28 June 2014 - 42-24 win at London ends winless run at five games.

10 July 2014 - Hep Cahill signs two-year contract to end of 2016.

10 July 2014 - Phil Joseph gets one-match ban after early guilty plea for dangerous tackle in 12-10 defeat at Wakefield.

18 July 2014 - two tries from Jack Owens in 28-14 home win over Warrington.

23 July 2014 - prop Manase Manuokafoa signs on two-year deal from Bradford for 2015.

28 July 2014 - Adam Lawton granted 'sabbatical' from contract to go to Australia.

10 August 2014 - some Vikings fans invade pitch after 28-6 Challenge Cup semi-final defeat to Castleford.

28 August 2014 - Jon Clarke appointed Head of Strength and Conditioning.

29 August 2014 - 24-10 home win over Wigan secures play-off place.

10 September 2014 - Dave Allen and former Academy captain Kieran Butterworth released.

20 September 2014 - 22-19 Elimination play-off defeat at Warrington after leading 18-0.

26 September 2014 - Leeds forward Chris Clarkson joins on loan for 2015.

2 October 2014 - MacGraff Leuluai signs new two-year contract to end of 2016.

9 October 2014 - Alex Gerrard signs new three-year contract.

14 October 2014 - Chris Dean signs new three-year contract.

CLUB RECORDS

Highest score:
90-4 v Doncaster, 10/6/2007
Highest score against:
6-76 v Catalan Dragons, 31/3/2012
Record attendance:
24,205 v St Helens, 16/2/61

MATCH RECORDS

Tries: 7 Phil Cantillon v York, 18/2/2001
Goals: 14 Mark Hewitt v Oldham, 25/7/99
Tim Hartley v Saddleworth, 7/3/2009
Points:
38 Gavin Dodd v Doncaster, 10/6/2007

SEASON RECORDS

Tries: 58 Martin Offiah 1988-89
Goals: 161 Mick Nanyn 2007
Points: 434 Mick Nanyn 2007

CAREER RECORDS

Tries: 234 Mal Aspey 1964-80
Goals: 1,083 Ray Dutton 1966-78
Points: 2,195 Ray Dutton 1966-78
Appearances: 591 Keith Elwell 1970-86

WIDNES VIKINGS

DATE	FIXTURE	RESULT	SCORERS	LGE	ATT
16/2/14	London Broncos (h)	W64-10	t:Owens,Tickle,Brown(3),Marsh(2),Flynn,Dean(2),Mellor g:Tickle(10)	1st	5,327
28/2/14	Huddersfield (h)	W22-20	t:Hanbury(2),Clough,Mellor g:Tickle(3)	4th	5,577
6/3/14	Salford (h)	W32-18	t:Dean,Mellor,Hanbury,Brown(2) g:Tickle(6)	4th	5,291
14/3/14	Leeds (a)	L38-4	t:Hanbury	5th	14,314
23/3/14	Hull FC (a)	W0-7	t:Ah Van g:Ah Van fg:Gilmore	4th	10,286
30/3/14	Bradford (h)	W22-18	t:Owens,Brown(2),Ah Van g:Tickle(3)	4th	5,581
6/4/14	Halifax (a) (CCR4)	W10-34	t:Clarke,Brown(2),Flynn,Hulme,Joseph g:Tickle(5)	N/A	2,271
12/4/14	Catalan Dragons (a)	L42-20	t:Flynn,Owens,White g:Tickle(2)	5th	9,588
18/4/14	Warrington (a)	L44-6	t:Flynn g:Tickle	6th	10,500
21/4/14	St Helens (h)	W40-26	t:Hanbury(2),Isa,Gerrard,Flynn,Dean,Leuluai g:Tickle(5),Owens	5th	7,706
27/4/14	Salford (a) (CCR5)	W20-30	t:Galea,Brown,Hanbury(2),White g:Tickle(4),Owens	N/A	2,630
4/5/14	Hull KR (a)	W29-34	t:Owens,Allen,Brown(3),Clarke g:Tickle(5)	5th	7,007
9/5/14	Wakefield (h)	L18-24	t:Hulme(2),Flynn g:Tickle(3)	6th	5,186
17/5/14	Salford (MW) ●	W24-30	t:Flynn(2),Owens,Dean,White,Hanbury g:Tickle(3)	6th	N/A
25/5/14	Castleford (a)	L34-22	t:Brown,Marsh,Phelps,Gilmore g:Tickle(3)	7th	5,576
30/5/14	Catalan Dragons (h)	D26-26	t:Hanbury,White,Marsh,Owens,Gilmore g:Tickle(3)	7th	4,745
5/6/14	Keighley (h) (CCQF)	W56-6	t:Hulme,Gilmore(3),Brown(2),Owens,Marsh,Isa,Craven g:Tickle(3),Owens(5)	N/A	5,252
13/6/14	Hull FC (h)	L6-56	t:Flynn g:Tickle	8th	5,014
18/6/14	Wigan (a)	L48-4	t:Flynn	8th	11,638
22/6/14	Leeds (h)	L28-38	t:Dean,Hanbury,Ah Van,Gore,Mellor g:Ah Van(4)	8th	5,543
28/6/14	London Broncos (a)	W24-42	t:Ah Van,Cahill,Galea,Hanbury(2),Flynn(2) g:Tickle(5),Ah Van(2)	8th	1,422
3/7/14	Castleford (h)	L20-40	t:Flynn,Galea,Ah Van,Dean g:Tickle(2)	8th	4,567
10/7/14	Wakefield (a)	L12-10	t:Tickle,Marsh g:Tickle	8th	3,932
18/7/14	Warrington (h)	W28-14	t:Owens(2),Hanbury,Flynn,Phelps g:Tickle(4)	8th	7,158
25/7/14	St Helens (a)	L44-22	t:Phelps(2),Marsh,Hanbury g:Tickle(3)	8th	11,844
3/8/14	Hull KR (h)	W28-10	t:Owens,Dean,Mellor,Brown,Marsh,Hanbury g:Tickle(2)	8th	5,345
10/8/14	Castleford (CCSF) ●●	L28-6	t:Owens g:Owens	N/A	12,005
17/8/14	Huddersfield (a)	L28-14	t:Tickle,Hanbury g:Tickle(3)	8th	5,346
29/8/14	Wigan (h)	W24-10	t:Ah Van(2),Flynn g:Tickle(6)	8th	6,223
7/9/14	Bradford (a)	W12-32	t:Flynn(2),Marsh(3),Ah Van,White g:Phelps(2)	8th	7,438
12/9/14	Salford (a)	L36-6	t:Ah Van g:Owens	8th	3,268
20/9/14	Warrington (a) (EPO)	L22-19	t:Flynn(2),Hanbury g:Tickle(3) fg:Brown	N/A	7,229

● Played at Etihad Stadium, Manchester
●● Played at Leigh Sports Village

		APP		TRIES		GOALS		FG		PTS	
	D.O.B.	ALL	SL	ALL	SL	ALL	SL	ALL	SL	ALL	SL
Patrick Ah Van	17/3/88	13	13	9	9	7	7	0	0	50	50
Dave Allen	15/9/85	7(11)	7(8)	1	1	0	0	0	0	4	4
Kevin Brown	2/10/84	29	25	17	12	0	0	1	1	69	49
Hep Cahill	15/10/86	18(2)	16(2)	1	1	0	0	0	0	4	4
Liam Carberry	24/2/93	(5)	(5)	0	0	0	0	0	0	0	0
Jon Clarke	4/4/79	22	19	2	1	0	0	0	0	8	4
Paul Clough	27/9/87	5(10)	4(8)	1	1	0	0	0	0	4	4
Danny Craven	21/11/91	9(3)	8(2)	1	0	0	0	0	0	4	0
Chris Dean	17/1/88	27(2)	23(2)	8	8	0	0	0	0	32	32
Paddy Flynn	11/12/87	30	27	19	18	0	0	0	0	76	72
Danny Galea	20/9/83	25(1)	21(1)	3	2	0	0	0	0	12	8
Alex Gerrard	5/11/91	22(2)	18(2)	1	1	0	0	0	0	4	4
Tom Gilmore	2/2/94	7	6	5	2	0	0	1	1	21	9
Grant Gore	21/11/91	2(3)	2(3)	1	1	0	0	0	0	4	4
Rhys Hanbury	27/8/85	27	24	18	16	0	0	0	0	72	64
Declan Hulme	14/1/93	4	2	4	2	0	0	0	0	16	8
Willie Isa	1/1/89	1(25)	1(21)	2	1	0	0	0	0	8	4
Paul Johnson	13/3/88	6(11)	5(11)	0	0	0	0	0	0	0	0
Phil Joseph	10/1/85	10(9)	9(9)	1	0	0	0	0	0	4	0
Ben Kavanagh	4/3/88	12(8)	11(6)	0	0	0	0	0	0	0	0
Adam Lawton	13/6/93	1(2)	1(2)	0	0	0	0	0	0	0	0
Macgraff Leuluai	9/2/90	17(9)	15(9)	1	1	0	0	0	0	4	4
Rhodri Lloyd	22/7/93	1(4)	(4)	0	0	0	0	0	0	0	0
Stefan Marsh	3/9/90	19	17	11	10	0	0	0	0	44	40
Joe Mellor	28/11/90	17	16	5	5	0	0	0	0	20	20
Eamon O'Carroll	13/6/87	5(3)	5(1)	0	0	0	0	0	0	0	0
Jack Owens	3/6/94	22	18	12	10	9	2	0	0	66	44
Cameron Phelps	11/2/85	17	16	4	4	2	2	0	0	20	20
Danny Tickle	10/3/83	30	26	3	3	89	77	0	0	190	166
Lloyd White	9/8/88	11(18)	9(16)	5	4	0	0	0	0	20	16

Kevin Brown

LEAGUE RECORD
P27-W13-D1-L13
(8th, SL/Elimination Play-Off)
F611, A725, Diff-114
27 points.

CHALLENGE CUP
Semi-Finalists

ATTENDANCES
Best - v St Helens (SL - 7,706)
Worst - v Castleford (SL - 4,567)
Total (SL only) - 73,263
Average (SL only) - 5,636
(Down by 379 on 2013)

2 November 2013 - back-rower John Bateman signs three-year contract with option for fourth season on undisclosed transfer fee.

17 December 2013 - Harrison Hansen signs for Saford for an undisclosed fee.

13 January 2014 - Rhodri Lloyd joins Widnes on year-long loan.

22 January 2014 - coach Shaun Wane, out of contract at end of 2014, reveals he has verbally agreed new three-year deal after being linked with move to NZ Warriors .

22 January 2014 - prop James Greenwood goes to London Broncos on loan for season.

23 January 2014 - prop Epalahame Lauaki released from final year of contract.

24 January 2014 - Wales international Jordan James, who joined Warriors coaching staff at end of World Cup and had agreed two-year deal to play with Gloucestershire All Golds, given 12-month playing contract.

7 February 2014 - 24-8 home defeat to Huddersfield on opening night in game brought forward a week to enable Warriors to fly down under to prepare for World Club Challenge clash with Sydney Roosters.

22 February 2014 - Michael Jennings becomes first player to score hat-trick in the World Club Challenge as Sydney Roosters win 36-14 in front of 31,515 crowd at Sydney Football Stadium.

25 February 2014 - Eddy Pettybourne banned for one game after submitting early guilty plea for high tackle in the WCC.

2 March 2014 - 48-24 round-3 home win over Wakefield on return from Australia.

4 March 2014 - Michael McIlorum signs new four-year contract to end of 2017.

6 March 2014 - partnership with Workington Town announced.

9 March 2014 - Michael McIlorum suspended for three matches for reckless high tackle in last-minute 36-31 defeat at Castleford.

10 March 2014 - Dominic Manfredi joins Salford on one-month loan.

20 March 2014 - 12-4 round 6 win at Warrington.

4 April 2014 - Josh Charnley out for up to two months with a knee injury sustained in 58-6 Challenge Cup win at Dewsbury.

8 April 2014 - Logan Tomkins joins Salford on month's loan.

KEY DATES - WIGAN WARRIORS

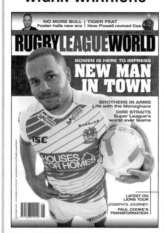

18 April 2014 - Iain Thornley tears pectoral muscle in 33-14 Good Friday victory at St Helens.

21 April 2014 - 84-6 home win over Bradford on Easter Monday.

23 April 2014 - Logan Tomkins to remain at Salford on loan to end of season.

2 May 2014 - 28-12 defeat at Leeds.

15 May 2014 - George Williams signs new four-year deal.

17 May 2014 - Blake Green tears biceps in 18-14 win over Leeds at Magic Weekend.

19 May 2014 - Blake Green sidelined for up to three months.

28 May 2014 - Wakefield forward Taulima Tautai signs three-year contract from 2015.

29 May 2014 - 31-22 defeat at Huddersfield after leading 12-0.

7 June 2014 - 16-4 home defeat by Castleford ends Cup run at quarter-final stage.

10 June 2014 - Blake Green to return to Australia end of season to join Melbourne.

13 June 2014 - 46-6 home league win over Castleford.

18 June 2014 - Connor Farrell makes debut in 48-4 home win over Widnes in postponed round two game. Michael McIlorum breaks arm.

18 June 2014 - re-signing of Joel Tomkins on four-and-a-half year contract for an undisclosed transfer fee to Saracens announced at half-time.

22 June 2014 - Liam Farrell gets one-match ban for dangerous tackle in 36-28 defeat at Wakefield.

27 June 2014 - 16-12 home defeat by St Helens.

6 July 2014 - Gil Dudson gets three-match ban for shoulder charge in 58-6 win at London Broncos.

15 July 2014 - Matty Bowen extends contract to end of 2015 season.

18 July 2014 - George Williams scores hat-trick in 56-10 home rout of Hull FC.

27 July 2014 - shock 16-8 defeat at relegated Bradford.

7 August 2014 - Academy forward Rhys Pugsley banned for two years for breaching RFL's anti-doping regulations.

29 August 2014 - 24-10 defeat at Widnes

1 September 2014 - Iain Thornley sustains season-ending knee injury in training.

11 September 2014 - 24-20 home win over Warrington secures second-placed finish.

18 September 2014 - 57-4 home Qualifying Play-off win over Huddersfield.

19 September 2014 - Matty Smith signs new four-year deal to end of 2018.

3 October 2014 - last-minute Joe Burgess try earns 16-12 home Qualifying Semi-final win over Warrington.

10 October 2014 - coach Shaun Wane and captain Sean O'Loughlin sign new three-year deals.

11 October 2014 - Ben Flower sent off less than two minutes into 14-6 Grand Final defeat by St Helens.

14 October 2014 - Ben Flower banned for six months, the longest initial suspension of the Super League era.

15 October 2014 - general manager Kris Radlinski promoted to board of directors.

5 November 2014 - Larne Patrick joins from Huddersfield on season-loan deal, with Jack Hughes heading the other way.

7 November 2014 - Greg Burke joins Hull KR on season loan.

11 November 2014 - Joe Burgess named Albert Goldthorpe Rookie of the Year.

CLUB RECORDS

Highest score:
116-0 v Flimby & Fothergill, 14/2/25
Highest score against:
0-75 v St Helens, 26/6/2005
Record attendance:
47,747 v St Helens, 27/3/59 *(Central Park)*
25,004 v St Helens, 25/3/2005
(JJB/DW Stadium)

MATCH RECORDS

Tries: 10 Martin Offiah v Leeds, 10/5/92
Shaun Edwards v Swinton, 29/9/92
Goals: 22 Jim Sullivan
v Flimby & Fothergill, 14/2/25
Points: 44 Jim Sullivan
v Flimby & Fothergill, 14/2/25

SEASON RECORDS

Tries: 62 Johnny Ring 1925-26
Goals: 186 Frano Botica 1994-95
Points: 462 Pat Richards 2010

CAREER RECORDS

Tries: 478 Billy Boston 1953-68
Goals: 2,317 Jim Sullivan 1921-46
Points: 4,883 Jim Sullivan 1921-46
Appearances: 774 Jim Sullivan 1921-46

WIGAN WARRIORS

DATE	FIXTURE	RESULT	SCORERS	LGE	ATT
7/2/14	Huddersfield (h)	L8-24	t:Thornley,Burgess	N/A	16,240
22/2/14	Sydney Roosters (WCC) ●	L36-14	t:Burgess,Charnley(2) g:Smith	N/A	31,515
2/3/14	Wakefield (h)	W46-24	t:Manfredi,Thornley,O'Loughlin(2),Hampshire,Bateman,Flower,Burgess, L Farrell g:Smith(5)	7th	11,703
9/3/14	Castleford (a)	L36-31	t:Bowen,Green,Smith,Clubb,Burgess,Charnley g:Smith(3) fg:Smith	10th	8,504
14/3/14	Hull KR (h)	W34-20	t:Thornley(3),Bowen,L Farrell,Flower g:Smith(5)	8th	12,801
20/3/14	Warrington (a)	W4-12	t:L Farrell,Green g:Smith(2)	6th	11,550
28/3/14	Catalan Dragons (h)	W22-16	t:Bowen,Charnley,L Farrell g:Smith(3)	5th	11,216
4/4/14	Dewsbury (a) (CCR4)	W6-58	t:Burgess(4),Sarginson,Thornley(2),Smith,Williams,Green g:Smith(6),Williams(3)	N/A	3,054
11/4/14	London Broncos (h)	W36-14	t:Clubb(2),Sarginson(2),Thornley(2),Bowen g:Williams(4)	4th	10,680
18/4/14	St Helens (a)	W14-33	t:O'Loughlin,Sarginson,L Farrell(2),Burgess g:Smith(6) fg:Smith	4th	17,980
21/4/14	Bradford (h)	W84-6	t:Green(2),Gelling(2),O'Loughlin,Hampshire(2),L Farrell,Hughes,Powell, Bateman,Goulding,Williams,Manfredi,Dudson g:Hampshire(8),Williams(4)	4th	15,529
27/4/14	Hunslet (h) (CCR5)	W52-8	t:Williams,Bowen(3),Smith(2),L Farrell,Sarginson,James g:Smith(8)	N/A	4,390
2/5/14	Leeds (a)	L28-12	t:Clubb,Taylor g:Smith(2)	4th	18,139
9/5/14	Hull FC (a)	W16-44	t:Sarginson(3),Gelling(2),Hughes,Burgess,Manfredi g:Smith(6)	3rd	10,539
17/5/14	Leeds (MW) ●●	W14-18	t:Gelling,Green,McIlorum g:Smith(3)	4th	N/A
22/5/14	Salford (h)	W4-25	t:Bateman,Powell,Burgess(2) g:Smith(4) fg:Smith	4th	3,706
29/5/14	Huddersfield (a)	L31-22	t:O'Loughlin,Bowen,Manfredi,Burgess g:Smith(3)	4th	6,198
7/6/14	Castleford (h) (CCQF)	L4-16	t:L Farrell	N/A	8,736
13/6/14	Castleford (h)	W46-6	t:Manfredi(2),Bowen,James,Burgess(2),L Farrell,McIlorum g:Smith(7)	3rd	11,914
18/6/14	Widnes (h)	W48-4	t:L Farrell(2),Charnley(5),O'Loughlin,C Farrell g:Smith(6)	1st	11,638
22/6/14	Wakefield (a)	L36-28	t:Hughes,L Farrell(2),Gelling,Sarginson g:Smith(4)	3rd	4,096
27/6/14	St Helens (h)	L12-16	t:Burgess,Charnley(2)	3rd	20,224
5/7/14	London Broncos (a)	W6-58	t:Charnley(3),Bowen,Bateman,Gelling,Taylor,Dudson,Burgess(2) g:Smith(9)	3rd	2,013
12/7/14	Catalan Dragons (a)	W16-37	t:Clubb,Bowen(2),Charnley,Taylor,Burgess g:Smith(6) fg:Smith	3rd	9,505
18/7/14	Hull FC (h)	W56-10	t:Tierney,Charnley,Williams(3),Smith,Powell,Manfredi(2),Taylor g:Smith(8)	2nd	12,493
27/7/14	Bradford (a)	L16-8	t:Manfredi(2)	3rd	6,535
31/7/14	Salford (h)	W45-4	t:Bowen,Gelling(3),Charnley,Williams,Clubb,Smith g:Smith(6) fg:Smith	2nd	12,962
14/8/14	Hull KR (a)	D14-14	t:Sarginson,O'Loughlin,Charnley g:Smith	2nd	6,801
29/8/14	Widnes (a)	L24-10	t:Manfredi,Charnley g:Smith	3rd	6,223
5/9/14	Leeds (a)	W21-6	t:Burgess,Smith,Flower g:Smith(4) fg:Smith	3rd	20,265
11/9/14	Warrington (h)	W24-20	t:Burgess(2),Charnley(2),Green g:Smith(2)	2nd	15,686
18/9/14	Huddersfield (h) (QPO)	W57-4	t:Charnley(2),Smith,Clubb,L Farrell,J Tomkins,Sarginson,Bowen, O'Loughlin,Burgess g:Smith(8) fg:Smith	N/A	8,652
3/10/14	Warrington (h) (QSF)	W16-12	t:J Tomkins,Gelling,Burgess g:Smith(2)	N/A	15,023
11/10/14	St Helens (GF) ●●●	L14-6	t:Burgess g:Smith	N/A	70,102

● Played at Allianz Stadium, Sydney ●● Played at Etihad Stadium, Manchester ●●● Played at Old Trafford, Manchester

		APP		TRIES		GOALS		FG		PTS	
	D.O.B.	ALL	SL	ALL	SL	ALL	SL	ALL	SL	ALL	SL
John Bateman	30/9/93	21(8)	19(7)	4	4	0	0	0	0	16	16
Matt Bowen	9/3/82	25	22	15	12	0	0	0	0	60	48
Joe Burgess	14/10/94	27	23	25	20	0	0	0	0	100	80
Greg Burke	12/2/93	1(5)	1(5)	0	0	0	0	0	0	0	0
Josh Charnley	26/6/91	21	19	23	21	0	0	0	0	92	84
Tony Clubb	12/6/87	9(14)	8(13)	7	7	0	0	0	0	28	28
Dominic Crosby	11/12/90	14(12)	14(9)	0	0	0	0	0	0	0	0
Jamie Doran	8/12/94	(2)	(2)	0	0	0	0	0	0	0	0
Gil Dudson	16/6/90	12(3)	10(3)	2	2	0	0	0	0	8	8
Connor Farrell	6/11/93	(2)	(2)	1	1	0	0	0	0	4	4
Liam Farrell	2/7/90	28	24	15	13	0	0	0	0	60	52
Ben Flower	19/10/87	23	20	3	3	0	0	0	0	12	12
Anthony Gelling	18/10/90	23	21	11	11	0	0	0	0	44	44
Darrell Goulding	3/3/88	14(2)	13(2)	1	1	0	0	0	0	4	4
Blake Green	19/9/86	21	19	7	6	0	0	0	0	28	24
Ryan Hampshire	29/12/94	4(4)	3(2)	3	3	8	8	0	0	28	28
Jack Hughes	4/1/92	12(11)	10(9)	3	3	0	0	0	0	12	12
Jordan James	24/5/80	2(15)	1(14)	2	1	0	0	0	0	8	4
Dominic Manfredi	1/10/93	14	12	11	11	0	0	0	0	44	44
Michael McIlorum	10/1/88	19(1)	16(1)	2	2	0	0	0	0	8	8
Jack Murphy	18/3/92	1	1	0	0	0	0	0	0	0	0
Sean O'Loughlin	24/11/82	23	20	8	8	0	0	0	0	32	32
Eddy Pettybourne	13/2/88	1(17)	1(15)	0	0	0	0	0	0	0	0
Sam Powell	3/7/92	15(7)	14(7)	3	3	0	0	0	0	12	12
Dan Sarginson	26/5/93	29	25	11	9	0	0	0	0	44	36
Matty Smith	23/7/87	32	28	8	5	122	107	7	7	283	241
Ryan Sutton	2/8/95	1(8)	1(6)	0	0	0	0	0	0	0	0
Scott Taylor	27/2/91	17(10)	15(9)	4	4	0	0	0	0	16	16
Iain Thornley	11/9/91	10	9	9	7	0	0	0	0	36	28
Lewis Tierney	20/10/94	1	1	1	1	0	0	0	0	4	4
Joel Tomkins	21/3/87	6(1)	6(1)	2	2	0	0	0	0	8	8
Logan Tomkins	1/8/91	3(2)	3(2)	0	0	0	0	0	0	0	0
George Williams	31/10/94	13(10)	11(9)	7	5	11	8	0	0	50	36
Callum Wright	18/10/94	(2)	(2)	0	0	0	0	0	0	0	0

Matty Smith

LEAGUE RECORD
P27-W18-D1-L8
(2nd, SL/Grand Final Runners-Up)
F834, A429, Diff+405
37 points.

CHALLENGE CUP
Quarter Finalists

ATTENDANCES
Best - v Leeds (SL - 20,265)
Worst - v Hunslet (CC - 4,390)
Total (SL, inc play-offs) - 207,026
Average (SL, inc play-offs) - 13,802
(Down by 747 on 2013)

SUPER LEAGUE XIX
Round by Round

ROUND 1

Friday 7th February 2014

WIGAN WARRIORS 8 HUDDERSFIELD GIANTS 24

WARRIORS: 1 Matt Bowen (D); 32 Joe Burgess; 3 Darrell Goulding; 23 Dan Sarginson (D); 4 Iain Thornley; 6 Blake Green; 7 Matty Smith (C); 8 Scott Taylor; 19 Sam Powell; 22 Eddy Pettybourne (D); 24 Tony Clubb (D); 12 Liam Farrell; 10 Ben Flower. Subs (all used): 9 Michael McIlorum; 14 Jack Hughes; 17 Dominic Crosby; 16 Gil Dudson.
Tries: Thornley (45), Burgess (51); **Goals:** Smith 0/2.
On report: Bowen (60) - alleged high tackle on Grix.
GIANTS: 1 Scott Grix; 2 Jermaine McGillvary; 3 Leroy Cudjoe; 4 Joe Wardle; 5 Aaron Murphy; 6 Danny Brough (C); 7 Luke Robinson; 8 Eorl Crabtree; 9 Shaun Lunt; 20 Antonio Kaufusi (D); 11 Brett Ferres; 15 Larne Patrick; 13 Chris Bailey (D). Subs (all used): 10 Craig Kopczak; 14 Michael Lawrence; 17 Ukuma Ta'ai; 18 Kyle Wood.
Tries: Ferres (6), McGillvary (17, 29, 53), Grix (71);
Goals: Brough 2/5.
Rugby Leaguer & League Express Men of the Match:
Warriors: Scott Taylor; *Giants:* Scott Grix.
Penalty count: 9-6; **Half-time:** 0-12;
Referee: Richard Silverwood; **Attendance:** 16,240.

Thursday 13th February 2014

WARRINGTON WOLVES 8 ST HELENS 38

WOLVES: 6 Stefan Ratchford; 5 Joel Monaghan; 3 Chris Bridge; 4 Ryan Atkins; 2 Chris Riley; 14 Michael Monaghan (C); 7 Richard Myler; 8 Chris Hill; 9 Mick Higham; 10 Roy Asotasi (D); 11 Trent Waterhouse; 12 Ben Westwood (C); 17 Ben Currie. Subs (all used): 20 Gareth O'Brien; 21 Glenn Riley; 23 James Laithwaite; 25 Ben Evans (D).
Tries: J Monaghan (2, 68);
Goals: Ratchford 0/1, O'Brien 0/1.
SAINTS: 1 Jonny Lomax; 2 Tom Makinson; 3 Jordan Turner; 22 Mark Percival; 5 Adam Swift; 24 Gary Wheeler; 7 Luke Walsh (D); 18 Alex Walmsley; 9 James Roby; 16 Kyle Amor (D); 12 Jon Wilkin; 13 Willie Manu; 10 Louie McCarthy-Scarsbrook. Subs (all used): 4 Josh Jones; 11 Iosia Soliola; 14 Anthony Laffranchi; 17 Paul Wellens (C).
Tries: Makinson (13), Roby (15), Amor (18), Laffranchi (41), Swift (72), Walsh (76); **Goals:** Walsh 7/7.
Rugby Leaguer & League Express Men of the Match:
Wolves: Joel Monaghan; *Saints:* Luke Walsh.
Penalty count: 9-7; **Half-time:** 4-20;
Referee: Phil Bentham; **Attendance:** 13,157.

Friday 14th February 2014

HULL FC 36 CATALAN DRAGONS 34

HULL: 20 Jamie Shaul; 5 Tom Lineham; 3 Ben Crooks; 4 Kirk Yeaman; 34 Fetuli Talanoa (D); 32 Jordan Rankin (D); 6 Richard Horne; 8 Mickey Paea (D); 9 Danny Houghton; 35 Garreth Carvell (D2); 11 Gareth Ellis (C); 14 Richard Whiting; 13 Joe Westerman. Subs (all used): 16 Jordan Thompson (D); 22 Josh Bowden; 26 Iafeta Palea'aesina (D); 33 Aaron Heremaia.
Tries: Whiting (24), Yeaman (36, 50), Rankin (53), Lineham (56), Thompson (63), Horne (66), Crooks (71);
Goals: Westerman 2/6, Crooks 0/2.
DRAGONS: 2 Morgan Escare; 5 Michael Oldfield (D); 4 Ben Pomeroy (D); 18 Daryl Millard; 26 Damien Cardace; 3 Leon Pryce; 6 Thomas Bosc; 23 Lopini Paea; 9 Ian Henderson; 10 Jeff Lima (D); 11 Zeb Taia; 17 Elliott Whitehead; 13 Gregory Mounis (C). Subs (all used): 8 Olivier Elima; 16 Eloi Pelissier; 22 Jamal Fakir; 24 Jason Baitieri (C).
Tries: Cardace (12, 28, 74), Whitehead (19), Taia (68, 80), Escare (77); **Goals:** Bosc 3/7.
On report:
Elima (48) - alleged dangerous contact on Heremaia.
Rugby Leaguer & League Express Men of the Match:
Hull: Jordan Rankin; *Dragons:* Damien Cardace.
Penalty count: 5-10; **Half-time:** 12-16;
Referee: Ben Thaler; **Attendance:** 10,178.

Sunday 16th February 2014

BRADFORD BULLS 18 CASTLEFORD TIGERS 36

BULLS: 1 Brett Kearney; 2 Elliot Kear; 21 Adam Henry (D); 3 Adrian Purtell; 5 Jamie Foster; 17 Lee Gaskell (D); 7 Luke Gale; 8 Nick Scruton; 9 Matt Diskin (C); 15 Adam Sidlow; 11 Tom Olbison; 16 Danny Addy; 18 James Donaldson. Subs (all used): 13 Chev Walker; 14 Manase Manuokafoa; 19 Adam O'Brien; 28 Danny Bridge (D).
Tries: Addy (4), Foster (43), Purtell (47);
Goals: Foster 3/3.
TIGERS: 6 Luke Dorn (D2); 2 Kirk Dixon; 23 Michael Channing; 3 Michael Shenton (C); 5 Justin Carney; 7 Marc Sneyd (D); 26 Liam Finn (D); 8 Andy Lynch (D2); 14 Daryl Clark; 10 Craig Huby; 16 Oliver Holmes; 12 Weller Hauraki; 11 Grant Millington. Subs (all used): 9 Adam Milner; 18 Frankie Mariano (D); 19 Scott Wheeldon (D); 25 Daniel Fleming.
Tries: Hauraki (34), Dixon (44), Clark (55), Carney (64), Dorn (73), Millington (78); **Goals:** Dixon 6/7.
Rugby Leaguer & League Express Men of the Match:
Bulls: Adrian Purtell; *Tigers:* Daryl Clark.
Penalty count: 6-9; **Half-time:** 6-6;
Referee: Robert Hicks; **Attendance:** 8,214.

HULL KINGSTON ROVERS 6 LEEDS RHINOS 34

ROVERS: 1 Greg Eden; 5 David Hodgson; 19 Craig Hall; 3 Kris Welham; 2 Ben Cockayne (D2); 6 Travis Burns (C); 7 Kris Keating (D); 10 Michael Weyman (D); 9 Josh Hodgson (C); 8 Justin Poore (D); 13 Jamie Langley (D); 11 Kevin Larroyer (D); 12 Neville Costigan (D). Subs (all used): 23 James Green; 14 Adam Walker; 17 Jonathan Walker (D); 15 Graeme Horne.
Try: Keating (21); **Goals:** Hall 1/1.
RHINOS: 1 Zak Hardaker; 20 Tom Briscoe (D); 3 Kallum Watkins; 4 Joel Moon; 5 Ryan Hall; 6 Danny McGuire; 13 Kevin Sinfield (C); 23 Brad Singleton; 7 Rob Burrow; 10 Jamie Peacock; 15 Brett Delaney; 12 Carl Ablett; 18 Chris Clarkson. Subs (all used): 8 Kylie Leuluai; 9 Paul Aiton (D); 16 Ryan Bailey; 21 Liam Sutcliffe.
Tries: Moon (4), T Briscoe (47, 56, 62), McGuire (64), Hardaker (68), Watkins (73); **Goals:** Sinfield 3/7.
Rugby Leaguer & League Express Men of the Match:
Rovers: Adam Walker; *Rhinos:* Kallum Watkins.
Penalty count: 8-5; **Half-time:** 6-6;
Referee: Richard Silverwood; **Attendance:** 11,526.

SALFORD RED DEVILS 18
WAKEFIELD TRINITY WILDCATS 14

RED DEVILS: 1 Jake Mullaney (D); 23 Greg Johnson (D); 22 Jason Walton (D2); 4 Junior Sa'u (D); 5 Francis Meli (D); 6 Rangi Chase (D); 7 Tim Smith (D); 8 Adrian Morley (C) (D); 9 Tommy Lee (D); 10 Lama Tasi (D); 13 Harrison Hansen (D); 12 Gareth Hock (D); 11 Tony Puletua (D). Subs (all used): 15 Darrell Griffin; 16 Andrew Dixon; 17 Shannan McPherson; 24 Stuart Howarth.
Tries: Hock (5), Hansen (28), Dixon (32);
Goals: Mullaney 3/3.
WILDCATS: 1 Richard Mathers; 2 Peter Fox; 3 Dean Collis; 19 Jimmy Keinhorst (D); 5 Reece Lyne; 6 Paul Sykes; 7 Pita Godinet (D); 8 Scott Anderson (D); 9 Paul McShane (D); 23 Daniel Smith (D); 11 Ali Lauitiiti; 12 Danny Kirmond (C); 13 Danny Washbrook. Subs (all used): 10 Andy Raleigh; 15 Matt Ryan (D); 17 Taulima Tautai; 22 Lucas Walshaw.
Tries: Ryan (44), Godinet (49), Lauitiiti (61);
Goals: Sykes 1/3.
Rugby Leaguer & League Express Men of the Match:
Red Devils: Tim Smith; *Wildcats:* Ali Lauitiiti.
Penalty count: 7-7; **Half-time:** 18-0;
Referee: James Child; **Attendance:** 7,102.

WIDNES VIKINGS 64 LONDON BRONCOS 10

VIKINGS: 1 Rhys Hanbury; 20 Paddy Flynn; 14 Chris Dean; 4 Stefan Marsh; 2 Jack Owens; 6 Kevin Brown (C); 7 Joe Mellor; 23 Phil Joseph; 15 Lloyd White; 25 Alex Gerrard; 17 Danny Galea (D); 12 Danny Tickle (D); 13 Hep Cahill. Subs (all used): 21 Danny Craven; 18 Paul Johnson (D); 16 Willie Isa; 24 Macgraff Leuluai.
Tries: Owens (11), Tickle (18), Brown (24, 33, 66), Marsh (29, 75), Flynn (43), Dean (49, 78), Mellor (61);
Goals: Tickle 10/11.
BRONCOS: 1 Nesiasi Mataitonga (D); 3 Jordan Atkins (D); 24 Mason Caton-Brown; 4 Thomas Minns (D); 27 Jamie O'Callaghan; 26 Tony Gigot (D); 14 Mike Bishay; 28 Carl Forster (D); 9 Scott Moore (D); 10 Olsi Krasniqi; 11 Mike McMeeken; 12 Matt Cook (C); 13 Alex Foster (D). Subs (all used): 20 James Cunningham (D); 17 Will Lovell; 18 George Griffin (D); 21 Joel Wicks.
Tries: Caton-Brown (5, 71); **Goals:** Gigot 1/2.
Rugby Leaguer & League Express Men of the Match:
Vikings: Kevin Brown; *Broncos:* Scott Moore.
Penalty count: 8-6; **Half-time:** 30-6;
Referee: Tim Roby; **Attendance:** 5,327.

ROUND 2

Thursday 20th February 2014

WAKEFIELD TRINITY WILDCATS 10
BRADFORD BULLS 23

WILDCATS: 1 Richard Mathers; 2 Peter Fox; 3 Dean Collis; 15 Matt Ryan; 5 Reece Lyne; 6 Paul Sykes; 7 Pita Godinet; 8 Scott Anderson; 9 Paul McShane; 23 Daniel Smith; 11 Ali Lauitiiti; 12 Danny Kirmond (C); 13 Danny Washbrook. Subs (all used): 10 Andy Raleigh; 17 Taulima Tautai; 20 Jarrod Sammut (D); 22 Lucas Walshaw.
Tries: Fox (22), Lauitiiti (55);
Goals: Sykes 0/1, Sammut 1/1.
BULLS: 1 Brett Kearney; 20 Luke George (D); 21 Adam Henry; 3 Adrian Purtell; 5 Jamie Foster; 17 Lee Gaskell; 7 Luke Gale; 8 Nick Scruton; 9 Matt Diskin (C); 15 Adam Sidlow; 28 Danny Bridge; 13 Chev Walker; 18 James Donaldson. Subs (all used): 14 Manase Manuokafoa; 19 Adam O'Brien; 16 Danny Addy; 29 Anthony Mullally (D).
Tries: Purtell (10), Kearney (32), George (44), O'Brien (65); **Goals:** Foster 3/5; **Field goal:** Gale (77).
On report:
Addy (54) - alleged dangerous tackle on Sammut.
Rugby Leaguer & League Express Men of the Match:
Wildcats: Ali Lauitiiti; *Bulls:* Matt Diskin.
Penalty count: 8-9; **Half-time:** 4-10;
Referee: Robert Hicks; **Attendance:** 4,049.

Friday 21st February 2014

LEEDS RHINOS 18 WARRINGTON WOLVES 12

RHINOS: 1 Zak Hardaker; 20 Tom Briscoe; 3 Kallum Watkins; 4 Joel Moon; 5 Ryan Hall; 13 Kevin Sinfield (C); 6 Danny McGuire; 8 Kylie Leuluai; 7 Rob Burrow; 10 Jamie Peacock; 12 Carl Ablett; 15 Brett Delaney; 18 Chris Clarkson. Subs (all used): 16 Ryan Bailey; 14 Stevie Ward; 9 Paul Aiton; 23 Brad Singleton.
Tries: Hardaker (21, 57), T Briscoe (36);
Goals: Sinfield 3/3.
WOLVES: 6 Stefan Ratchford; 5 Joel Monaghan; 3 Chris Bridge; 4 Ryan Atkins; 29 Gene Ormsby (D); 20 Gareth O'Brien; 7 Richard Myler; 8 Chris Hill; 9 Mick Higham; 10 Roy Asotasi; 11 Trent Waterhouse; 12 Ben Westwood (C); 13 Simon Grix. Subs (all used): 19 Anthony England (D); 14 Michael Monaghan (C); 17 Ben Currie; 25 Ben Evans.
Tries: J Monaghan (10), Westwood (76);
Goals: Ratchford 2/2.
Rugby Leaguer & League Express Men of the Match:
Rhinos: Zak Hardaker; *Wolves:* Chris Bridge.
Penalty count: 8-6; **Half-time:** 12-6;
Referee: Ben Thaler; **Attendance:** 16,164.

ST HELENS 34 HULL FC 22

SAINTS: 1 Jonny Lomax; 2 Tom Makinson; 3 Jordan Turner; 22 Mark Percival; 5 Adam Swift; 24 Gary Wheeler; 7 Luke Walsh; 18 Alex Walmsley; 9 James Roby; 16 Kyle Amor; 12 Jon Wilkin; 13 Willie Manu; 10 Louie McCarthy-Scarsbrook. Subs (all used): 4 Josh Jones; 11 Iosia Soliola; 14 Anthony Laffranchi; 17 Paul Wellens (C).
Tries: Roby (6, 58), Soliola (42), Lomax (51), Makinson (68), Percival (76); **Goals:** Walsh 5/6.
HULL: 20 Jamie Shaul; 5 Tom Lineham; 3 Ben Crooks; 15 Joe Arundel; 34 Fetuli Talanoa; 32 Jordan Rankin; 6 Richard Horne; 8 Mickey Paea; 9 Danny Houghton; 35 Garreth Carvell; 11 Gareth Ellis (C); 14 Richard Whiting; 13 Joe Westerman. Subs (all used): 16 Jordan Thompson; 22 Josh Bowden; 26 Iafeta Palea'aesina; 33 Aaron Heremaia.
Tries: Paea (2), Whiting (22), Ellis (62), Houghton (79);
Goals: Westerman 0/1, Crooks 3/3.
Rugby Leaguer & League Express Men of the Match:
Saints: Kyle Amor; *Hull:* Joe Westerman.
Penalty count: 6-6; **Half-time:** 6-10;
Referee: Richard Silverwood; **Attendance:** 13,488.

Saturday 22nd February 2014

LONDON BRONCOS 18 SALFORD RED DEVILS 44

BRONCOS: 1 Nesiasi Mataitonga; 3 Jordan Atkins; 4 Thomas Minns; 24 Mason Caton-Brown; 17 Will Lovell; 26 Tony Gigot; 14 Mike Bishay; 10 Olsi Krasniqi; 9 Scott Moore; 28 Carl Forster; 12 Matt Cook (C); 11 Mike McMeeken; 13 Alex Foster. Subs (all used): 20 James Cunningham; 27 Jamie O'Callaghan; 21 Joel Wicks; 18 George Griffin.
Tries: Moore (11), Griffin (70), McMeeken (74);
Goals: Gigot 3/3.
RED DEVILS: 1 Jake Mullaney; 23 Greg Johnson; 3 Martin Gleeson (C); 5 Francis Meli; 2 Danny Williams; 14 Theo Fages; 7 Tim Smith; 15 Darrell Griffin; 9 Tommy Lee; 10 Lama Tasi; 13 Harrison Hansen; 12 Gareth Hock; 18 Steve Rapira (D). Subs (all used): 22 Jason Walton; 17 Shannan McPherson; 19 Matty Ashurst; 21 Jordan Walne.
Tries: Hansen (16, 26), Williams (18), Fages (36, 73), Smith (39), Mullaney (57), Meli (62);
Goals: Mullaney 5/7, Smith 1/1.
Sin bin: Hock (46) - late challenge on Cunningham.
Rugby Leaguer & League Express Men of the Match:
Broncos: Scott Moore; *Red Devils:* Theo Fages.
Penalty count: 7-4; **Half-time:** 6-26;
Referee: James Child; **Attendance:** 1,246.

Sunday 23rd February 2014

HUDDERSFIELD GIANTS 24
HULL KINGSTON ROVERS 24

GIANTS: 1 Scott Grix; 2 Jermaine McGillvary; 3 Leroy Cudjoe; 4 Joe Wardle; 5 Aaron Murphy; 6 Danny Brough (C); 7 Luke Robinson; 8 Eorl Crabtree; 18 Kyle Wood; 20 Antonio Kaufusi; 11 Brett Ferres; 12 Jason Chan; 13 Chris Bailey. Subs (all used): 10 Craig Kopczak; 14 Michael Lawrence; 17 Ukuma Ta'ai; 28 Kruise Leeming.
Tries: Brough (12), Robinson (15, 40), Wood (24);
Goals: Brough 4/5.
Sin bin: Chan (19) - fighting;
Wardle (20) - professional foul.
ROVERS: 1 Greg Eden; 2 Ben Cockayne; 3 Kris Welham; 18 Liam Salter; 24 Omari Caro; 6 Travis Burns (C); 7 Kris Keating; 8 Justin Poore; 9 Josh Hodgson (C); 17 Jonathan Walker; 11 Kevin Larroyer; 13 Jamie Langley; 12 Neville Costigan. Subs (all used): 14 Adam Walker; 23 James Green; 22 Rhys Lovegrove; 20 Jordan Cox.
Tries: Caro (31, 80), Cox (44), J Hodgson (78);
Goals: Burns 4/4.
Sin bin: Poore (19) - fighting.
Rugby Leaguer & League Express Men of the Match:
Giants: Kyle Wood; *Rovers:* Josh Hodgson.
Penalty count: 5-11; **Half-time:** 24-6;
Referee: Phil Bentham; **Attendance:** 7,180.

CASTLEFORD TIGERS 32 CATALAN DRAGONS 6

TIGERS: 1 Jordan Tansey; 2 Kirk Dixon; 23 Michael Channing; 3 Michael Shenton (C); 5 Justin Carney; 7 Marc Sneyd; 26 Liam Finn; 8 Andy Lynch; 14 Daryl Clark; 10 Craig Huby; 16 Oliver Holmes; 12 Weller Hauraki; 11 Grant Millington. Subs (all used): 9 Adam Milner; 18 Frankie Mariano; 19 Scott Wheeldon; 25 Daniel Fleming.
Tries: Carney (8, 39, 79), Dixon (24), Tansey (45), Clark (70); **Goals:** Dixon 0/3, Sneyd 4/4.
Sin bin: Wheeldon (34) - fighting.
DRAGONS: 1 Brent Webb; 2 Morgan Escare; 26 Damien Cardace; 4 Ben Pomeroy; 5 Michael Oldfield; 3 Leon Pryce; 7 Scott Dureau; 10 Jeff Lima; 9 Ian Henderson; 21 Julian Bousquet; 11 Zeb Taia; 17 Elliott Whitehead; 13 Gregory Mounis (C). Subs (all used): 16 Eloi Pelissier; 15 Antoni Maria; 23 Lopini Paea; 24 Jason Baitieri (C).
Try: Escare (32); **Goals:** Dureau 1/1.
Sin bin: Pelissier (34) - fighting.
On report:
Bousquet (8) - alleged dangerous contact on Sneyd.
Rugby Leaguer & League Express Men of the Match:
Tigers: Daryl Clark; *Dragons:* Leon Pryce.
Penalty count: 12-4; **Half-time:** 12-6;
Referee: Tim Roby; **Attendance:** 5,104.

ROUND 3

Thursday 27th February 2014

SALFORD RED DEVILS 0 ST HELENS 38

RED DEVILS: 1 Jake Mullaney; 23 Greg Johnson; 3 Martin Gleeson; 5 Francis Meli; 2 Danny Williams; 14 Theo Fages; 7 Tim Smith; 11 Tony Puletua; 9 Tommy Lee; 10 Lama Tasi; 13 Harrison Hansen; 12 Gareth Hock; 16 Andrew Dixon. Subs (all used): 8 Adrian Morley (C); 19 Matty Ashurst; 17 Shannan McPherson; 24 Stuart Howarth.
SAINTS: 1 Jonny Lomax; 2 Tom Makinson; 3 Jordan Turner; 22 Mark Percival; 5 Adam Swift; 6 Lance Hohaia; 7 Luke Walsh; 16 Kyle Amor; 9 James Roby; 18 Alex Walmsley; 13 Willie Manu; 12 Jon Wilkin; 4 Josh Jones. Subs (all used): 10 Louie McCarthy-Scarsbrook; 14 Anthony Laffranchi; 11 Iosia Soliola; 17 Paul Wellens (C).
Tries: Wilkin (5), Walsh (12), Percival (51, 80), Amor (54), Laffranchi (73); **Goals:** Walsh 7/7.
Rugby Leaguer & League Express Men of the Match: *Red Devils:* Andrew Dixon; *Saints:* Luke Walsh.
Penalty count: 6-5; **Half-time:** 0-12;
Referee: Phil Bentham; **Attendance:** 6,353.

Friday 28th February 2014

CATALAN DRAGONS 12 LEEDS RHINOS 40

DRAGONS: 2 Morgan Escare; 28 Frederic Vaccari; 19 Mathias Pala; 27 Jean-Philippe Baile; 5 Michael Oldfield; 3 Leon Pryce; 14 William Barthau; 10 Jeff Lima; 9 Ian Henderson; 23 Lopini Paea; 11 Zeb Taia; 17 Elliott Whitehead; 13 Gregory Mounis (C). Subs (all used): 15 Antoni Maria; 20 Mickael Simon; 22 Jamal Fakir; 24 Jason Baitieri (C).
Tries: Oldfield (7), Baile (52); **Goals:** Barthau 2/2.
RHINOS: 1 Zak Hardaker; 20 Tom Briscoe; 3 Kallum Watkins; 4 Joel Moon; 5 Ryan Hall; 6 Danny McGuire; 13 Kevin Sinfield (C); 8 Kylie Leuluai; 9 Paul Aiton; 10 Jamie Peacock; 14 Stevie Ward; 12 Carl Ablett; 15 Brett Delaney. Subs (all used): 7 Rob Burrow; 16 Ryan Bailey; 18 Chris Clarkson; 23 Brad Singleton.
Tries: Moon (22), Delaney (26), T Briscoe (32), Ablett (46), Hall (49, 80), Sinfield (66);
Goals: Sinfield 6/6, Burrow 0/1.
Rugby Leaguer & League Express Men of the Match: *Dragons:* Leon Pryce; *Rhinos:* Kevin Sinfield.
Penalty count: 3-7; **Half-time:** 6-18;
Referee: Richard Silverwood; **Attendance:** 6,300.

HULL KINGSTON ROVERS 10 CASTLEFORD TIGERS 30

ROVERS: 1 Greg Eden; 2 Ben Cockayne; 3 Kris Welham; 18 Liam Salter; 24 Omari Caro; 6 Travis Burns (C); 7 Kris Keating; 17 Jonathan Walker; 9 Josh Hodgson (C); 23 James Green; 11 Kevin Larroyer; 22 Rhys Lovegrove; 12 Neville Costigan. Subs (all used): 15 Graeme Horne; 20 Jordan Cox; 14 Adam Walker; 21 Keal Carlile.
Tries: Green (12), Caro (40); **Goals:** Burns 1/2.
TIGERS: 6 Luke Dorn; 22 Richard Owen; 23 Michael Channing; 3 Michael Shenton (C); 5 Justin Carney; 7 Marc Sneyd; 26 Liam Finn; 8 Andy Lynch; 14 Daryl Clark; 10 Craig Huby; 18 Frankie Mariano; 12 Weller Hauraki; 11 Grant Millington. Subs (all used): 9 Adam Milner; 16 Oliver Holmes; 19 Scott Wheeldon; 25 Daniel Fleming.
Tries: Owen (15, 22, 75), Mariano (27), Holmes (68);
Goals: Sneyd 5/5.
Sin bin: Finn (33) - dangerous contact on Welham.
Rugby Leaguer & League Express Men of the Match: *Rovers:* James Green; *Tigers:* Liam Finn.
Penalty count: 6-10; **Half-time:** 10-18;
Referee: Ben Thaler; **Attendance:** 7,022.

WIDNES VIKINGS 22 HUDDERSFIELD GIANTS 20

VIKINGS: 1 Rhys Hanbury; 20 Paddy Flynn; 14 Chris Dean; 4 Stefan Marsh; 2 Jack Owens; 21 Danny Craven; 7 Joe Mellor; 23 Phil Joseph; 15 Lloyd White; 25 Alex Gerrard; 17 Danny Galea; 12 Danny Tickle (C); 24 Macgraff Leuluai. Subs (all used): 35 Paul Clough (D); 18 Paul Johnson; 16 Willie Isa; 34 Rhodri Lloyd (D).
Tries: Hanbury (30, 73), Clough (37), Mellor (68);
Goals: Tickle 3/4.
On report: Isa (58) - alleged late challenge on Wood.
GIANTS: 1 Scott Grix; 2 Jermaine McGillvary; 3 Leroy Cudjoe; 4 Joe Wardle; 5 Aaron Murphy; 6 Danny Brough (C); 7 Luke Robinson; 8 Eorl Crabtree; 18 Kyle Wood; 10 Craig Kopczak; 11 Brett Ferres; 12 Jason Chan; 14 Michael Lawrence. Subs (all used): 13 Chris Bailey; 16 David Faiumu; 17 Ukuma Ta'ai; 20 Antonio Kaufusi.
Tries: McGillvary (9), Cudjoe (22), Crabtree (49);
Goals: Brough 4/6.
Rugby Leaguer & League Express Men of the Match: *Vikings:* Joe Mellor; *Giants:* Brett Ferres.
Penalty count: 7-11; **Half-time:** 12-10;
Referee: Robert Hicks; **Attendance:** 5,577.

Sunday 2nd March 2014

BRADFORD BULLS 25 LONDON BRONCOS 12

BULLS: 1 Brett Kearney; 20 Luke George; 21 Adam Henry; 3 Adrian Purtell; 5 Jamie Foster; 16 Danny Addy; 7 Luke Gale; 14 Manase Manuokafoa; 9 Matt Diskin (C); 15 Adam Sidlow; 13 Chev Walker; 28 Danny Bridge; 18 James Donaldson. Subs (all used): 2 Elliot Kear; 11 Tom Olbison; 19 Adam O'Brien; 29 Anthony Mullally.
Tries: Gale (10), Sidlow (25), Addy (62), Olbison (79);
Goals: Foster 4/4; **Field goal:** Gale (75).
BRONCOS: 1 Nesiasi Mataitonga; 5 James Duckworth (D); 24 Mason Caton-Brown; 4 Thomas Minns; 27 Jamie O'Callaghan; 6 Ben Farrar (D); 7 Josh Drinkwater (D); 10 Olsi Krasniqi; 9 Scott Moore; 16 Nick Slyney (D); 12 Matt Cook (C); 11 Mike McMeeken; 13 Alex Foster. Subs (all used): 28 Carl Forster; 15 James Greenwood (D); 20 James Cunningham; 18 George Griffin.
Tries: Minns (28), Cunningham (68);
Goals: Drinkwater 2/2.
Rugby Leaguer & League Express Men of the Match: *Bulls:* Tom Olbison; *Broncos:* Scott Moore.
Penalty count: 4-5; **Half-time:** 12-6;
Referee: Tim Roby; **Attendance:** 5,410.

WARRINGTON WOLVES 18 HULL FC 16

WOLVES: 6 Stefan Ratchford; 5 Joel Monaghan; 3 Chris Bridge; 4 Ryan Atkins; 29 Gene Ormsby; 20 Gareth O'Brien; 7 Richard Myler; 8 Chris Hill; 9 Mick Higham; 10 Roy Asotasi; 11 Trent Waterhouse; 12 Ben Westwood (C); 17 Ben Currie. Subs (all used): 14 Michael Monaghan (C); 19 Anthony England; 23 James Laithwaite; 25 Ben Evans.
Tries: Ratchford (5), Waterhouse (20), B Evans (37);
Goals: Ratchford 3/4.
HULL: 20 Jamie Shaul; 5 Tom Lineham; 3 Ben Crooks; 4 Kirk Yeaman; 34 Fetuli Talanoa; 32 Jordan Rankin; 6 Richard Horne; 8 Mickey Paea; 9 Danny Houghton; 22 Josh Bowden; 11 Gareth Ellis (C); 19 Jay Pitts; 13 Joe Westerman. Subs (all used): 14 Richard Whiting; 33 Aaron Heremaia; 16 Jordan Thompson; 26 Iafeta Palea'aesina.
Tries: Houghton (12), Lineham (60), Talanoa (78);
Goals: Crooks 2/3.
Sin bin: Shaul (28) - professional foul.
Rugby Leaguer & League Express Men of the Match: *Wolves:* Gareth O'Brien; *Hull:* Gareth Ellis.
Penalty count: 10-7; **Half-time:** 18-6;
Referee: James Child; **Attendance:** 10,276.

WIGAN WARRIORS 46
WAKEFIELD TRINITY WILDCATS 24

WARRIORS: 26 Ryan Hampshire; 32 Joe Burgess; 5 Anthony Gelling; 4 Iain Thornley; 31 Dominic Manfredi; 6 Blake Green; 7 Matty Smith; 10 Ben Flower; 9 Michael McIlorum; 8 Scott Taylor; 12 Liam Farrell; 25 John Bateman; 13 Sean O'Loughlin (C). Subs (all used): 15 Logan Tomkins; 17 Dominic Crosby; 20 Greg Burke; 24 Tony Clubb.
Tries: Manfredi (5), Thornley (16), O'Loughlin (19, 25), Hampshire (28), Bateman (31), Flower (50), Burgess (57), L Farrell (61); **Goals:** Smith 5/9.
WILDCATS: 1 Richard Mathers; 2 Peter Fox; 6 Paul Sykes; 28 Luke Briscoe (D); 5 Reece Lyne; 20 Jarrod Sammut; 7 Pita Godinet; 22 Lucas Walshaw; 9 Paul McShane; 23 Daniel Smith; 11 Ali Lauitiiti; 12 Danny Kirmond (C); 18 Kyle Trout. Subs (all used): 13 Danny Washbrook; 17 Taulima Tautai; 15 Matt Ryan; 24 Jordan Crowther (D).
Tries: Lauitiiti (14), Kirmond (36), Fox (45), Lyne (73);
Goals: Sammut 4/4.
Sin bin: Mathers (60) - professional foul.
Rugby Leaguer & League Express Men of the Match: *Warriors:* Liam Farrell; *Wildcats:* Jarrod Sammut.
Penalty count: 6-6; **Half-time:** 30-12;
Referee: Matthew Thomason; **Attendance:** 11,703.

ROUND 4

Thursday 6th March 2014

WIDNES VIKINGS 32 SALFORD RED DEVILS 18

VIKINGS: 1 Rhys Hanbury; 20 Paddy Flynn; 14 Chris Dean; 4 Stefan Marsh; 2 Jack Owens; 6 Kevin Brown; 7 Joe Mellor; 23 Phil Joseph; 9 Jon Clarke (C); 25 Alex Gerrard; 17 Danny Galea; 12 Danny Tickle; 24 Macgraff Leuluai. Subs (all used): 35 Paul Clough; 18 Paul Johnson; 16 Willie Isa; 15 Lloyd White.
Tries: Dean (14), Mellor (42), Hanbury (60), Brown (65, 75); **Goals:** Tickle 6/6.
RED DEVILS: 1 Jake Mullaney; 23 Greg Johnson; 3 Martin Gleeson; 4 Junior Sa'u; 2 Danny Williams; 14 Theo Fages; 7 Tim Smith; 8 Adrian Morley (C); 24 Stuart Howarth; 10 Lama Tasi; 13 Harrison Hansen; 19 Matty Ashurst; 18 Steve Rapira. Subs (all used): 9 Tommy Lee; 11 Tony Puletua; 22 Jason Walton; 17 Shannan McPherson.
Tries: Johnson (34), Lee (37), Fages (55);
Goals: Mullaney 3/3.
Rugby Leaguer & League Express Men of the Match: *Vikings:* Joe Mellor; *Red Devils:* Harrison Hansen.
Penalty count: 5-2; **Half-time:** 8-12;
Referee: Richard Silverwood; **Attendance:** 5,291.

Friday 7th March 2014

HUDDERSFIELD GIANTS 12 LEEDS RHINOS 12

GIANTS: 1 Scott Grix; 2 Jermaine McGillvary; 3 Leroy Cudjoe; 4 Joe Wardle; 19 Jodie Broughton (D); 6 Danny Brough (C); 7 Luke Robinson; 20 Antonio Kaufusi; 18 Kyle Wood; 10 Craig Kopczak; 11 Brett Ferres; 12 Jason Chan; 14 Michael Lawrence. Subs: 8 Eorl Crabtree; 13 Chris Bailey; 16 David Faiumu; 22 Jacob Fairbank (not used).
Tries: Broughton (32), Wardle (69); **Goals:** Brough 2/4.
RHINOS: 1 Zak Hardaker; 20 Tom Briscoe; 3 Kallum Watkins; 4 Joel Moon; 5 Ryan Hall; 6 Danny McGuire; 13 Kevin Sinfield (C); 8 Kylie Leuluai; 9 Paul Aiton; 10 Jamie Peacock; 14 Stevie Ward; 12 Carl Ablett; 15 Brett Delaney. Subs: 7 Rob Burrow; 11 Jamie Jones-Buchanan; 19 Mitch Achurch (not used); 23 Brad Singleton.
Tries: S Ward (6), Watkins (72); **Goals:** Sinfield 2/3.
Rugby Leaguer & League Express Men of the Match: *Giants:* Eorl Crabtree; *Rhinos:* Jamie Peacock.
Penalty count: 9-6; **Half-time:** 4-6;
Referee: James Child; **Attendance:** 8,759.

HULL FC 44 BRADFORD BULLS 16

HULL: 20 Jamie Shaul; 5 Tom Lineham; 14 Richard Whiting; 4 Kirk Yeaman; 34 Fetuli Talanoa; 33 Aaron Heremaia; 6 Richard Horne; 8 Mickey Paea; 9 Danny Houghton; 22 Josh Bowden; 11 Gareth Ellis (C); 12 Chris Tuson (D); 13 Joe Westerman. Subs (all used): 16 Jordan Thompson; 17 Liam Watts; 26 Iafeta Palea'aesina; 32 Jordan Rankin.
Tries: Ellis (6), Westerman (14), Shaul (16, 45), Whiting (30), Heremaia (33), Houghton (39), Rankin (58); **Goals:** Whiting 6/8.
BULLS: 1 Brett Kearney; 2 Elliot Kear; 21 Adam Henry; 3 Adrian Purtell; 5 Jamie Foster; 16 Danny Addy; 7 Luke Gale; 29 Anthony Mullally; 9 Matt Diskin (C); 15 Adam Sidlow; 11 Tom Olbison; 28 Danny Bridge; 18 James Donaldson. Subs (all used): 14 Manase Manuokafoa; 19 Adam O'Brien; 26 Liam Sutcliffe (D); 27 Greg Burke (D).
Tries: Diskin (2), Purtell (27), Henry (77);
Goals: Foster 2/3.
Rugby Leaguer & League Express Men of the Match: *Hull:* Joe Westerman; *Bulls:* Luke Gale.
Penalty count: 4-10; **Half-time:** 32-10;
Referee: Phil Bentham; **Attendance:** 11,307.

ST HELENS 38 HULL KINGSTON ROVERS 18

SAINTS: 1 Jonny Lomax; 2 Tom Makinson; 3 Jordan Turner; 24 Gary Wheeler; 5 Adam Swift; 6 Lance Hohaia; 7 Luke Walsh; 18 Alex Walmsley; 9 James Roby; 16 Kyle Amor; 12 Jon Wilkin; 13 Willie Manu; 4 Josh Jones. Subs (all used): 8 Mose Masoe (D); 10 Louie McCarthy-Scarsbrook; 11 Iosia Soliola; 17 Paul Wellens (C).
Tries: Swift (6, 52), Lomax (13), Walmsley (48), Soliola (55), Makinson (57), Wilkin (67); **Goals:** Walsh 5/7.
ROVERS: 1 Greg Eden; 2 Ben Cockayne; 3 Kris Welham; 18 Liam Salter; 19 Craig Hall; 6 Travis Burns (C); 7 Kris Keating; 8 Justin Poore; 9 Josh Hodgson (C); 10 Michael Weyman; 11 Kevin Larroyer; 13 Jamie Langley; 15 Graeme Horne. Subs (all used): 14 Adam Walker; 20 Jordan Cox; 22 Rhys Lovegrove; 23 James Green.
Tries: Larroyer (31), Eden (38), J Hodgson (74);
Goals: Burns 3/3.
Sin bin: Burns (77) - professional foul.
Rugby Leaguer & League Express Men of the Match: *Saints:* Alex Walmsley; *Rovers:* Josh Hodgson.
Penalty count: 3-3; **Half-time:** 12-12;
Referee: Tim Roby; **Attendance:** 11,818.

Sunday 9th March 2014

LONDON BRONCOS 16 WARRINGTON WOLVES 44

BRONCOS: 6 Ben Farrar; 3 Jordan Atkins; 24 Mason Caton-Brown; 4 Thomas Minns; 27 Jamie O'Callaghan; 20 James Cunningham; 14 Mike Bishay; 16 Nick Slyney; 9 Scott Moore; 10 Olsi Krasniqi; 13 Alex Foster; 11 Mike McMeeken; 12 Matt Cook (C). Subs (all used): 28 Carl Forster; 18 George Griffin; 25 Iliess Macani; 23 Denny Solomona (D).
Tries: Slyney (8), Farrar (18), Minns (23);
Goals: Bishay 2/3.
WOLVES: 6 Stefan Ratchford; 18 Rhys Evans; 3 Chris Bridge; 4 Ryan Atkins; 29 Gene Ormsby; 20 Gareth O'Brien; 7 Richard Myler; 8 Chris Hill; 14 Michael Monaghan (C); 10 Roy Asotasi; 11 Trent Waterhouse; 12 Ben Westwood (C); 17 Ben Currie. Subs (all used): 1 Matthew Russell (D); 21 Glenn Riley; 23 James Laithwaite; 25 Ben Evans.
Tries: Asotasi (4), Bridge (26), R Evans (32, 47, 70, 75), Ormsby (45), Atkins (67, 80);
Goals: Ratchford 4/7, O'Brien 0/2.
Rugby Leaguer & League Express Men of the Match: *Broncos:* Mike Bishay; *Wolves:* Chris Hill.
Penalty count: 5-4; **Half-time:** 16-14;
Referee: Matthew Thomason; **Attendance:** 1,377.

WAKEFIELD TRINITY WILDCATS 56
CATALAN DRAGONS 14

WILDCATS: 1 Richard Mathers; 2 Peter Fox; 6 Paul Sykes; 5 Reece Lyne; 31 Chris Riley (D); 20 Jarrod Sammut; 7 Pita Godinet; 30 Nick Scruton (D); 9 Paul McShane; 17 Taulima Tautai; 11 Ali Lauitiiti; 12 Danny Kirmond (C); 13 Danny Washbrook. Subs (all used): 14 Matty Wildie; 15 Matt Ryan; 26 Jon Molloy; 23 Daniel Smith.
Tries: Tautai (13, 21), Molloy (23), Lyne (27, 37), Godinet (47, 51), D Smith (72), Sykes (76);
Goals: Sammut 10/10.
DRAGONS: 1 Brent Webb; 28 Frederic Vaccari; 5 Michael Oldfield; 11 Zeb Taia; 2 Morgan Escare; 3 Leon Pryce; 14 William Barthau; 10 Jeff Lima; 13 Gregory Mounis (C); 23 Lopini Paea; 12 Louis Anderson; 17 Elliott Whitehead; 24 Jason Baitieri (C). Subs (all used): 16 Eloi Pelissier; 22 Jamal Fakir; 27 Jean-Philippe Baile; 29 Benjamin Garcia.
Tries: Whitehead (62, 79), Pryce (68); **Goals:** Barthau 1/3.
Rugby Leaguer & League Express Men of the Match: *Wildcats:* Taulima Tautai; *Dragons:* Elliott Whitehead.
Penalty count: 13-6; **Half-time:** 32-0;
Referee: Ben Thaler; **Attendance:** 4,190.

CASTLEFORD TIGERS 36 WIGAN WARRIORS 31

TIGERS: 6 Luke Dorn; 2 Kirk Dixon; 23 Michael Channing; 3 Michael Shenton (C); 5 Justin Carney; 7 Marc Sneyd; 26 Liam Finn; 8 Andy Lynch; 9 Adam Milner; 10 Craig Huby; 16 Oliver Holmes; 12 Weller Hauraki; 11 Grant Millington. Subs (all used): 13 Nathan Massey; 14 Daryl Clark; 18 Frankie Mariano; 19 Scott Wheeldon.
Tries: Dixon (4), Dorn (8, 80), Milner (14), Clark (27), Channing (58); **Goals:** Sneyd 6/7.
Sin bin: Carney (6) - punching Bateman.

WARRIORS: 1 Matt Bowen; 2 Josh Charnley; 23 Dan Sarginson; 4 Iain Thornley; 32 Joe Burgess; 6 Blake Green; 7 Matty Smith (C); 17 Dominic Crosby; 9 Michael McIlorum; 8 Scott Taylor; 12 Liam Farrell; 25 John Bateman; 10 Ben Flower. Subs (all used): 15 Logan Tomkins; 22 Eddy Pettybourne; 24 Tony Clubb; 28 Jordan James (D2).
Tries: Bowen (16), Green (18), Smith (20), Clubb (36), Burgess (39), Charnley (78); **Goals:** Smith 3/6;
Field goal: Smith (79).
Sin bin: Flower (61) - dangerous tackle.
Rugby Leaguer & League Express Men of the Match: *Tigers:* Craig Huby; *Warriors:* Matty Smith.
Penalty count: 10-6; **Half-time:** 22-24;
Referee: Robert Hicks; **Attendance:** 8,504.

ROUND 5

Friday 14th March 2014

LEEDS RHINOS 38 WIDNES VIKINGS 4

RHINOS: 1 Zak Hardaker; 2 Ben Jones-Bishop; 3 Kallum Watkins; 4 Joel Moon; 20 Tom Briscoe; 13 Kevin Sinfield (C); 6 Danny McGuire; 8 Kylie Leuluai; 7 Rob Burrow; 10 Jamie Peacock; 12 Carl Ablett; 14 Stevie Ward; 15 Brett Delaney. Subs (all used): 11 Jamie Jones-Buchanan; 16 Ryan Bailey; 9 Paul Aiton; 19 Mitch Achurch.
Tries: Jones-Bishop (18, 24), Watkins (43), Bailey (51), Sinfield (54), Burrow (61), Jones-Buchanan (67);
Goals: Sinfield 5/7.
VIKINGS: 1 Rhys Hanbury; 20 Paddy Flynn; 3 Cameron Phelps; 14 Chris Dean; 2 Jack Owens; 6 Kevin Brown; 7 Joe Mellor; 25 Alex Gerrard; 9 Jon Clarke (C); 35 Paul Clough; 17 Danny Galea; 12 Danny Tickle; 24 Macgraff Leuluai. Subs (all used): 10 Ben Kavanagh; 16 Willie Isa; 15 Lloyd White; 34 Rhodri Lloyd.
Try: Hanbury (75); **Goals:** Owens 0/1.
Rugby Leaguer & League Express Men of the Match: *Rhinos:* Brett Delaney; *Vikings:* Alex Gerrard.
Penalty count: 4-6; **Half-time:** 10-0;
Referee: Robert Hicks; **Attendance:** 14,314.

SALFORD RED DEVILS 12 WARRINGTON WOLVES 28

RED DEVILS: 1 Jake Mullaney; 23 Greg Johnson; 22 Jason Walton; 4 Junior Sa'u; 34 Dominic Manfredi (D); 14 Theo Fages; 7 Tim Smith; 8 Adrian Morley (C); 9 Tommy Lee; 10 Lama Tasi; 19 Matty Ashurst; 16 Andrew Dixon; 13 Harrison Hansen. Subs (all used): 3 Martin Gleeson; 11 Tony Puletua; 17 Shannan McPherson; 21 Jordan Walne.
Tries: Manfredi (31, 62), Johnson (69);
Goals: Mullaney 0/3.
WOLVES: 6 Stefan Ratchford; 29 Gene Ormsby; 3 Chris Bridge; 4 Ryan Atkins; 5 Joel Monaghan; 20 Gareth O'Brien; 7 Richard Myler; 8 Chris Hill; 9 Mick Higham; 10 Roy Asotasi; 12 Ben Westwood (C); 23 James Laithwaite; 13 Simon Grix. Subs (all used): 14 Michael Monaghan (C); 1 Matthew Russell; 21 Glenn Riley; 25 Ben Evans.
Tries: Bridge (19), Higham (22), Ormsby (27), J Monaghan (50), Asotasi (65); **Goals:** Ratchford 4/5.
Rugby Leaguer & League Express Men of the Match: *Red Devils:* Dominic Manfredi; *Wolves:* Gareth O'Brien.
Penalty count: 7-11; **Half-time:** 4-16;
Referee: Ben Thaler; **Attendance:** 6,260.

ST HELENS 40 CATALAN DRAGONS 22

SAINTS: 1 Jonny Lomax; 2 Tom Makinson; 3 Jordan Turner; 4 Josh Jones; 5 Adam Swift; 6 Lance Hohaia; 7 Luke Walsh; 18 Alex Walmsley; 9 James Roby; 16 Kyle Amor; 12 Jon Wilkin; 13 Willie Manu; 17 Paul Wellens (C). Subs (all used): 8 Mose Masoe; 10 Louie McCarthy-Scarsbrook; 11 Iosia Soliola; 14 Anthony Laffranchi.
Tries: Jones (8), Makinson (14, 26), Turner (18), McCarthy-Scarsbrook (44), Hohaia (64), Swift (75);
Goals: Walsh 4/4, Lomax 2/3.
DRAGONS: 2 Morgan Escare; 5 Michael Oldfield; 27 Jean-Philippe Baile; 19 Mathias Pala; 28 Frederic Vaccari; 3 Leon Pryce; 6 Thomas Bosc; 20 Mickael Simon; 16 Eloi Pelissier; 10 Jeff Lima; 11 Zeb Taia; 17 Elliott Whitehead; 24 Jason Baitieri (C). Subs (all used): 13 Gregory Mounis (C); 23 Lopini Paea; 29 Benjamin Garcia; 30 Gadwin Springer (D).
Tries: Garcia (33), Pelissier (37), Oldfield (60, 70);
Goals: Bosc 3/4.
Rugby Leaguer & League Express Men of the Match: *Saints:* James Roby; *Dragons:* Leon Pryce.
Penalty count: 7-8; **Half-time:** 24-12;
Referee: George Stokes; **Attendance:** 11,321.

WIGAN WARRIORS 34 HULL KINGSTON ROVERS 20

WARRIORS: 1 Matt Bowen; 2 Josh Charnley; 3 Darrell Goulding; 4 Iain Thornley; 32 Joe Burgess; 6 Blake Green; 7 Matty Smith (C); 17 Dominic Crosby; 15 Logan Tomkins; 8 Scott Taylor; 12 Liam Farrell; 14 Jack Hughes; 10 Ben Flower. Subs (all used): 22 Eddy Pettybourne; 25 John Bateman; 27 George Williams; 28 Jordan James.
Tries: Thornley (5, 32, 77), Bowen (10), L Farrell (44), Flower (65); **Goals:** Smith 5/7.
ROVERS: 1 Greg Eden; 32 Ade Gardner (D); 18 Liam Salter; 3 Kris Welham; 2 Ben Cockayne; 6 Travis Burns (C); 7 Kris Keating; 8 Justin Poore; 9 Josh Hodgson (C); 10 Michael Weyman; 11 Kevin Larroyer; 12 Neville Costigan; 13 Jamie Langley. Subs (all used): 14 Adam Walker; 15 Graeme Horne; 20 Jordan Cox; 23 James Green.
Tries: Langley (15), Salter (19), Welham (27), Cockayne (36); **Goals:** Burns 2/4.
Rugby Leaguer & League Express Men of the Match: *Warriors:* Matty Smith; *Rovers:* Kris Keating.
Penalty count: 8-7; **Half-time:** 14-20;
Referee: Richard Silverwood; **Attendance:** 12,801.

Saturday 15th March 2014

LONDON BRONCOS 22 WAKEFIELD TRINITY WILDCATS 50

BRONCOS: 6 Ben Farrar; 27 Jamie O'Callaghan; 4 Thomas Minns; 24 Mason Caton-Brown; 23 Denny Solomona; 20 James Cunningham; 7 Josh Drinkwater; 16 Nick Slyney; 9 Scott Moore; 10 Olsi Krasniqi; 11 Mike McMeeken; 12 Matt Cook (C); 13 Alex Foster. Subs (all used): 28 Carl Forster; 15 James Greenwood; 14 Mike Bishay; 8 Atelea Vea (D).
Tries: Minns (24), Solomona (55, 71), Cook (75);
Goals: Drinkwater 3/4.
WILDCATS: 1 Richard Mathers; 2 Peter Fox; 3 Dean Collis; 5 Reece Lyne; 31 Chris Riley; 20 Jarrod Sammut; 7 Pita Godinet; 8 Scott Anderson; 9 Paul McShane; 30 Nick Scruton; 11 Ali Lauitiiti; 12 Danny Kirmond (C); 17 Taulima Tautai. Subs (all used): 14 Matty Wildie; 15 Matt Ryan; 6 Paul Sykes; 23 Daniel Smith.
Tries: Mathers (7, 9, 47, 79), Sammut (26), Collis (31, 65), Lyne (35), Godinet (73);
Goals: Sammut 7/9.
Rugby Leaguer & League Express Men of the Match: *Broncos:* Matt Cook; *Wildcats:* Scott Anderson.
Penalty count: 4-4; **Half-time:** 6-30;
Referee: Phil Bentham; **Attendance:** 1,017.

Sunday 16th March 2014

BRADFORD BULLS 18 HUDDERSFIELD GIANTS 66

BULLS: 1 Brett Kearney; 20 Luke George; 21 Adam Henry; 3 Adrian Purtell; 5 Jamie Foster; 26 Liam Sutcliffe; 7 Luke Gale; 14 Manase Manuokafoa; 9 Matt Diskin (C); 13 Chev Walker; 11 Tom Olbison; 16 Danny Addy; 18 James Donaldson. Subs (all used): 23 Oliver Roberts; 28 Danny Bridge; 19 Adam O'Brien; 2 Elliot Kear.
Tries: Henry (8, 42), O'Brien (63); **Goals:** Foster 3/3.
GIANTS: 1 Scott Grix; 2 Jermaine McGillvary; 3 Leroy Cudjoe; 4 Joe Wardle; 19 Jodie Broughton; 6 Danny Brough (C); 7 Luke Robinson; 20 Antonio Kaufusi; 18 Kyle Wood; 10 Craig Kopczak; 11 Brett Ferres; 12 Jason Chan; 14 Michael Lawrence. Subs (all used): 8 Eorl Crabtree; 13 Chris Bailey; 16 David Faiumu; 17 Ukuma Ta'ai.
Tries: Grix (1, 27), Wardle (16, 53), Lawrence (18), Robinson (30), Chan (38), Ta'ai (50, 67), McGillvary (58, 72), Ferres (69); **Goals:** Brough 9/12.
Rugby Leaguer & League Express Men of the Match: *Bulls:* Adam Henry; *Giants:* Brett Ferres.
Penalty count: 11-10; **Half-time:** 6-32;
Referee: Chris Leatherbarrow; **Attendance:** 6,781.

CASTLEFORD TIGERS 19 HULL FC 16

TIGERS: 1 Jordan Tansey; 22 Richard Owen; 23 Michael Channing; 3 Michael Shenton (C); 5 Justin Carney; 7 Marc Sneyd; 26 Liam Finn; 8 Andy Lynch; 14 Daryl Clark; 10 Craig Huby; 16 Oliver Holmes; 12 Weller Hauraki; 11 Grant Millington. Subs (all used): 4 Jake Webster; 9 Adam Milner; 13 Nathan Massey; 18 Frankie Mariano.
Tries: Shenton (6), Sneyd (45), Mariano (74);
Goals: Sneyd 3/3; **Field goal:** Sneyd (77).
HULL: 20 Jamie Shaul; 27 Liam Colbon (D); 3 Ben Crooks; 4 Kirk Yeaman; 34 Fetuli Talanoa; 33 Aaron Heremaia; 6 Richard Horne; 8 Mickey Paea; 9 Danny Houghton; 22 Josh Bowden; 11 Gareth Ellis (C); 12 Chris Tuson; 13 Joe Westerman. Subs (all used): 17 Liam Watts; 14 Richard Whiting; 16 Jordan Thompson; 32 Jordan Rankin.
Tries: Talanoa (4), Ellis (29), Colbon (56);
Goals: Crooks 2/3.
Rugby Leaguer & League Express Men of the Match: *Tigers:* Marc Sneyd; *Hull:* Aaron Heremaia.
Penalty count: 7-6; **Half-time:** 6-12;
Referee: Tim Roby; **Attendance:** 9,867.

ROUND 6

Thursday 20th March 2014

WARRINGTON WOLVES 4 WIGAN WARRIORS 12

WOLVES: 6 Stefan Ratchford; 5 Joel Monaghan; 3 Chris Bridge; 4 Ryan Atkins; 29 Gene Ormsby; 20 Gareth O'Brien; 7 Richard Myler; 8 Chris Hill; 9 Mick Higham; 10 Roy Asotasi; 11 Trent Waterhouse; 12 Ben Westwood (C); 13 Simon Grix. Subs (all used): 23 James Laithwaite; 21 Glenn Riley; 1 Matthew Russell; 14 Michael Monaghan (C).
Try: Ormsby (60); **Goals:** Ratchford 0/1.
WARRIORS: 1 Matt Bowen; 2 Josh Charnley; 3 Darrell Goulding; 4 Iain Thornley; 32 Joe Burgess; 6 Blake Green (C); 7 Matty Smith; 8 Scott Taylor; 15 Logan Tomkins; 17 Dominic Crosby; 25 John Bateman; 12 Liam Farrell; 10 Ben Flower. Subs (all used): 14 Jack Hughes; 22 Eddy Pettybourne; 24 Tony Clubb; 27 George Williams.
Tries: L Farrell (12), Green (50); **Goals:** Smith 2/4.
Rugby Leaguer & League Express Men of the Match: *Wolves:* Ben Westwood; *Warriors:* Liam Farrell.
Penalty count: 10-8; **Half-time:** 0-8;
Referee: Phil Bentham; **Attendance:** 11,550.

Friday 21st March 2014

LEEDS RHINOS 54 LONDON BRONCOS 6

RHINOS: 1 Zak Hardaker; 2 Ben Jones-Bishop; 3 Kallum Watkins; 14 Stevie Ward; 5 Ryan Hall; 6 Danny McGuire; 7 Rob Burrow (C); 8 Kylie Leuluai; 9 Paul Aiton; 17 Ian Kirke; 11 Jamie Jones-Buchanan; 12 Carl Ablett; 23 Brad Singleton. Subs (all used): 19 Mitch Achurch; 18 Chris Clarkson; 27 Rob Mulhern (D); 26 Elliot Minchella.
Tries: Singleton (2), Hall (8, 16, 36), Achurch (26), Jones-Bishop (39, 69), Hardaker (42), Watkins (56), Burrow (78); **Goals:** Hardaker 6/9, Burrow 1/1.
BRONCOS: 25 Iliess Macani; 27 Jamie O'Callaghan; 4 Thomas Minns; 24 Mason Caton-Brown; 23 Denny Solomona; 6 Ben Farrar; 7 Josh Drinkwater; 16 Nick Slyney; 9 Scott Moore; 10 Olsi Krasniqi; 11 Mike McMeeken; 12 Matt Cook (C); 13 Alex Foster. Subs (all used): 15 James Greenwood; 8 Atelea Vea; 20 James Cunningham; 18 George Griffin.
Try: Caton-Brown (50); **Goals:** Drinkwater 1/1.
Rugby Leaguer & League Express Men of the Match: *Rhinos:* Ryan Hall; *Broncos:* Iliess Macani.
Penalty count: 6-3; **Half-time:** 34-0;
Referee: Chris Leatherbarrow; **Attendance:** 12,870.

Saturday 22nd March 2014

CATALAN DRAGONS 30 HUDDERSFIELD GIANTS 14

DRAGONS: 2 Morgan Escare; 5 Michael Oldfield; 4 Ben Pomeroy; 11 Zeb Taia; 19 Mathias Pala; 3 Leon Pryce; 6 Thomas Bosc; 8 Olivier Elima; 16 Eloi Pelissier; 20 Mickael Simon; 17 Elliott Whitehead; 12 Louis Anderson; 24 Jason Baitieri (C). Subs (all used): 13 Gregory Mounis (C); 23 Lopini Paea; 27 Jean-Philippe Baile; 29 Benjamin Garcia.
Tries: Taia (15), Anderson (19, 45), Escare (60), Whitehead (75); **Goals:** Bosc 5/7.
GIANTS: 1 Scott Grix; 2 Jermaine McGillvary; 3 Leroy Cudjoe; 4 Joe Wardle; 19 Jodie Broughton; 6 Danny Brough (C); 7 Luke Robinson; 20 Antonio Kaufusi; 18 Kyle Wood; 10 Craig Kopczak; 11 Brett Ferres; 12 Jason Chan; 13 Chris Bailey. Subs (all used): 8 Eorl Crabtree; 16 David Faiumu; 17 Ukuma Ta'ai; 23 Josh Johnson.
Tries: Grix (65), Ferres (68), Broughton (79);
Goals: Brough 1/3.
Rugby Leaguer & League Express Men of the Match: *Dragons:* Eloi Pelissier; *Giants:* Scott Grix.
Penalty count: 8-6; **Half-time:** 14-0;
Referee: Richard Silverwood; **Attendance:** 6,510.

Sunday 23rd March 2014

HULL FC 0 WIDNES VIKINGS 7

HULL: 32 Jordan Rankin; 27 Liam Colbon; 15 Joe Arundel; 4 Kirk Yeaman; 34 Fetuli Talanoa; 33 Aaron Heremaia; 6 Richard Horne; 17 Liam Watts; 9 Danny Houghton; 11 Gareth Ellis (C); 12 Chris Tuson; 14 Richard Whiting; 13 Joe Westerman. Subs: 26 Iafeta Palea'aesina; 16 Jordan Thompson; 3 Ben Crooks; 21 Dean Hadley (not used).
VIKINGS: 1 Rhys Hanbury; 20 Paddy Flynn; 14 Chris Dean; 3 Cameron Phelps; 5 Patrick Ah Van; 6 Kevin Brown; 27 Tom Gilmore; 10 Ben Kavanagh; 9 Jon Clarke (C); 23 Phil Joseph; 17 Danny Galea; 12 Danny Tickle; 25 Alex Gerrard. Subs (all used): 15 Lloyd White; 34 Rhodri Lloyd; 16 Willie Isa; 18 Paul Johnson.
Try: Ah Van (1); **Goals:** Ah Van 1/2, Tickle 0/1;
Field goal: Gilmore (76).
On report: Kavanagh (32) - alleged high tackle.
Rugby Leaguer & League Express Men of the Match: *Hull:* Gareth Ellis; *Vikings:* Phil Joseph.
Penalty count: 5-7; **Half-time:** 0-4;
Referee: Ben Thaler; **Attendance:** 10,286.

HULL KINGSTON ROVERS 16 BRADFORD BULLS 0

ROVERS: 2 Ben Cockayne; 24 Omari Caro; 18 Liam Salter; 3 Kris Welham; 32 Ade Gardner; 6 Travis Burns (C); 7 Kris Keating; 8 Justin Poore; 9 Josh Hodgson (C); 10 Michael Weyman; 11 Kevin Larroyer; 12 Neville Costigan; 13 Jamie Langley. Subs (all used): 14 Adam Walker; 20 Jordan Cox; 23 James Green; 21 Keal Carlile.
Tries: Caro (11), Keating (18), Larroyer (60);
Goals: Burns 2/3.
BULLS: 1 Brett Kearney; 2 Elliot Kear; 21 Adam Henry; 3 Adrian Purtell; 22 Sam Wood; 26 Liam Sutcliffe; 7 Luke Gale; 14 Manase Manuokafoa; 9 Matt Diskin (C); 15 Adam Sidlow; 11 Tom Olbison; 16 Danny Addy; 18 James Donaldson. Subs (all used): 4 Matty Blythe; 19 Adam O'Brien; 28 Danny Bridge; 29 Anthony Mullally.
Rugby Leaguer & League Express Men of the Match: *Rovers:* Travis Burns; *Bulls:* Matty Blythe.
Penalty count: 6-5; **Half-time:** 12-0;
Referee: Robert Hicks; **Attendance:** 7,008.

SALFORD RED DEVILS 23 CASTLEFORD TIGERS 16

RED DEVILS: 1 Jake Mullaney; 23 Greg Johnson; 3 Martin Gleeson; 4 Junior Sa'u; 5 Francis Meli; 6 Rangi Chase; 7 Tim Smith; 8 Adrian Morley (C); 9 Tommy Lee; 10 Lama Tasi; 13 Harrison Hansen; 16 Andrew Dixon; 11 Tony Puletua. Subs (all used): 14 Theo Fages; 20 Adam Walne; 21 Jordan Walne; 17 Shannan McPherson.
Tries: Gleeson (5), Johnson (18), Dixon (41, 58);
Goals: Mullaney 3/4; **Field goal:** Chase (73).
TIGERS: 6 Luke Dorn; 22 Richard Owen; 23 Michael Channing; 3 Michael Shenton (C); 5 Justin Carney; 7 Marc Sneyd; 26 Liam Finn; 8 Andy Lynch; 14 Daryl Clark; 10 Craig Huby; 16 Oliver Holmes; 12 Weller Hauraki; 11 Grant Millington. Subs (all used): 4 Jake Webster; 9 Adam Milner; 13 Nathan Massey; 18 Frankie Mariano.
Tries: Carney (22), Hauraki (63), Dorn (69);
Goals: Sneyd 2/3.
Sin bin: Milner (57) - off the ball tackle.
Rugby Leaguer & League Express Men of the Match: *Red Devils:* Rangi Chase; *Tigers:* Daryl Clark.
Penalty count: 10-10; **Half-time:** 10-6;
Referee: James Child; **Attendance:** 5,823.

WAKEFIELD TRINITY WILDCATS 16 ST HELENS 24

WILDCATS: 1 Richard Mathers; 2 Peter Fox; 19 Jimmy Keinhorst; 5 Reece Lyne; 31 Chris Riley; 20 Jarrod Sammut; 7 Pita Godinet; 8 Scott Anderson; 9 Paul McShane; 30 Nick Scruton; 11 Ali Lauitiiti; 12 Danny Kirmond (C); 17 Taulima Tautai. Subs (all used): 10 Andy Raleigh; 15 Matt Ryan; 23 Daniel Smith; 29 Harry Siejka (D).
Tries: Kirmond (30), Lyne (36), McShane (42);
Goals: Sammut 2/3.
On report: Lauitiiti (71) - alleged late challenge on Lomax.
SAINTS: 1 Jonny Lomax; 2 Tom Makinson; 4 Josh Jones; 26 Matty Dawson (D); 5 Adam Swift; 17 Paul Wellens (C); 12 Jon Wilkin; 16 Kyle Amor; 9 James Roby; 14 Anthony Laffranchi; 13 Willie Manu; 15 Mark Flanagan; 25 Anthony Walker. Subs (all used): 11 Iosia Soliola; 27 Greg Richards; 23 Joe Greenwood; 8 Mose Masoe.
Tries: Jones (23), Soliola (48), Dawson (54), Greenwood (57), Makinson (61); **Goals:** Makinson 2/5.
On report: Amor (77) - alleged high tackle on Ryan.
Rugby League & League Express Men of the Match: *Wildcats:* Taulima Tautai; *Saints:* Jon Wilkin.
Penalty count: 8-12; **Half-time:** 10-4;
Referee: Tim Roby; **Attendance:** 5,037.

ROUND 7

Thursday 27th March 2014

LONDON BRONCOS 6 CASTLEFORD TIGERS 54

BRONCOS: 23 Denny Solomona; 27 Jamie O'Callaghan; 24 Mason Caton-Brown; 11 Mike McMeeken; 25 Iliess Macani; 6 Ben Farrar; 7 Josh Drinkwater; 15 James Greenwood; 9 Scott Moore; 10 Olsi Krasniqi; 16 Nick Slyney; 12 Matt Cook (C); 13 Alex Foster. Subs (all used): 8 Atelea Vea; 22 James Woodburn-Hall; 18 George Griffin; 20 James Cunningham.
Try: McMeeken (78); **Goals:** Drinkwater 1/1.
Sin bin: Vea (32) - professional foul.
TIGERS: 6 Luke Dorn; 24 James Clare; 23 Michael Channing; 3 Michael Shenton (C); 5 Justin Carney; 20 Jamie Ellis; 26 Liam Finn; 8 Andy Lynch; 14 Daryl Clark; 10 Craig Huby; 16 Oliver Holmes; 12 Weller Hauraki; 11 Grant Millington. Subs (all used): 7 Marc Sneyd; 25 Daniel Fleming; 13 Nathan Massey; 18 Frankie Mariano.
Tries: Channing (11), Holmes (22), Shenton (30, 58), Finn (37), Huby (46), Carney (52, 66), Dorn (54);
Goals: Ellis 9/9.
Rugby League & League Express Men of the Match: *Broncos:* Mike McMeeken; *Tigers:* Michael Shenton.
Penalty count: 3-3; **Half-time:** 0-24;
Referee: Ben Thaler; **Attendance:** 1,036.

Friday 28th March 2014

HULL FC 30 SALFORD RED DEVILS 8

HULL: 20 Jamie Shaul; 27 Liam Colbon; 3 Ben Crooks; 4 Kirk Yeaman; 34 Fetuli Talanoa; 6 Richard Horne; 7 Jacob Miller; 17 Liam Watts; 9 Danny Houghton (C); 16 Jordan Thompson; 21 Dean Hadley; 12 Chris Tuson; 13 Joe Westerman. Subs (all used): 14 Richard Whiting; 19 Jay Pitts; 26 Iafeta Palea'aesina; 33 Aaron Heremaia.
Tries: Miller (15), Shaul (31), Crooks (43), Horne (48), Watts (79); **Goals:** Crooks 5/5.
RED DEVILS: 1 Jake Mullaney; 23 Greg Johnson; 3 Martin Gleeson; 4 Junior Sa'u; 5 Francis Meli; 6 Rangi Chase; 7 Tim Smith; 8 Adrian Morley (C); 9 Tommy Lee; 10 Lama Tasi; 13 Harrison Hansen; 16 Andrew Dixon; 11 Tony Puletua. Subs (all used): 14 Theo Fages; 18 Steve Rapira; 21 Jordan Walne; 17 Shannan McPherson.
Tries: Johnson (25), Sa'u (53); **Goals:** Mullaney 0/2.
On report: Morley (34) - alleged late challenge on Miller.
Rugby League & League Express Men of the Match: *Hull:* Jacob Miller; *Red Devils:* Rangi Chase.
Penalty count: 5-7; **Half-time:** 12-4;
Referee: Robert Hicks; **Attendance:** 9,821.

ST HELENS 14 LEEDS RHINOS 10

SAINTS: 1 Jonny Lomax; 2 Tom Makinson; 4 Josh Jones; 26 Matty Dawson; 5 Adam Swift; 6 Lance Hohaia; 17 Paul Wellens (C); 8 Mose Masoe; 9 James Roby; 27 Greg Richards; 15 Mark Flanagan; 11 Iosia Soliola; 25 Anthony Walker. Subs (all used): 14 Anthony Laffranchi; 23 Joe Greenwood; 28 Luke Thompson; 33 Andre Savelio (D).
Tries: Walker (24), Makinson (65, 78);
Goals: Makinson 1/3.
RHINOS: 1 Zak Hardaker; 20 Tom Briscoe; 3 Kallum Watkins; 14 Stevie Ward; 5 Ryan Hall; 6 Danny McGuire; 13 Kevin Sinfield (C); 8 Kylie Leuluai; 7 Rob Burrow; 10 Jamie Peacock; 11 Jamie Jones-Buchanan; 12 Carl Ablett; 15 Brett Delaney. Subs: 2 Ben Jones-Bishop (not used); 17 Ian Kirke; 18 Chris Clarkson; 23 Brad Singleton.
Try: McGuire (18); **Goals:** Sinfield 3/3.
Rugby League & League Express Men of the Match: *Saints:* James Roby; *Rhinos:* Kevin Sinfield.
Penalty count: 4-3; **Half-time:** 6-6;
Referee: Richard Silverwood; **Attendance:** 13,788.

WIGAN WARRIORS 22 CATALAN DRAGONS 16

WARRIORS: 1 Matt Bowen; 2 Josh Charnley; 3 Darrell Goulding; 4 Iain Thornley; 32 Joe Burgess; 6 Blake Green; 7 Matty Smith; 8 Scott Taylor; 9 Logan Tomkins; 10 Ben Flower; 12 Liam Farrell; 25 John Bateman; 13 Sean O'Loughlin (C). Subs (all used): 17 Dominic Crosby; 22 Eddy Pettybourne; 24 Tony Clubb; 27 George Williams.
Tries: Bowen (29, 79), Charnley (53), L Farrell (67);
Goals: Smith 3/5.
DRAGONS: 2 Morgan Escare; 5 Michael Oldfield; 4 Ben Pomeroy; 18 Daryl Millard; 19 Mathias Pala; 3 Leon Pryce; 6 Thomas Bosc; 8 Olivier Elima; 16 Eloi Pelissier; 21 Julian Bousquet; 11 Zeb Taia; 12 Louis Anderson; 13 Gregory Mounis (C). Subs (all used): 15 Antoni Maria; 23 Lopini Paea; 27 Jean-Philippe Baile; 29 Benjamin Garcia.
Tries: Escare (4, 45), Pomeroy (10); **Goals:** Bosc 2/3.
Rugby League & League Express Men of the Match: *Warriors:* Matt Bowen; *Dragons:* Morgan Escare.
Penalty count: 10-5; **Half-time:** 4-10;
Referee: Tim Roby; **Attendance:** 11,216.

Sunday 30th March 2014

HUDDERSFIELD GIANTS 14 WARRINGTON WOLVES 33

GIANTS: 1 Scott Grix; 2 Jermaine McGillvary; 3 Leroy Cudjoe; 11 Brett Ferres; 19 Jodie Broughton; 6 Danny Brough (C); 7 Luke Robinson; 8 Eorl Crabtree; 9 Shaun Lunt; 10 Craig Kopczak; 12 Jason Chan; 17 Ukuma Ta'ai; 14 Michael Lawrence. Subs: 16 David Faiumu; 18 Kyle Wood; 20 Antonio Kaufusi; 23 Josh Johnson (not used).
Tries: Grix (8), Broughton (37); **Goals:** Brough 3/3.
WOLVES: 1 Matthew Russell; 5 Joel Monaghan; 3 Chris Bridge; 18 Rhys Evans; 29 Gene Ormsby; 6 Stefan Ratchford; 7 Richard Myler; 8 Chris Hill; 9 Mick Higham; 10 Roy Asotasi; 11 Trent Waterhouse; 12 Ben Westwood (C); 13 Simon Grix. Subs (all used): 14 Michael Monaghan (C); 21 Glenn Riley; 23 James Laithwaite; 25 Ben Evans.
Tries: R Evans (34), Myler (44), Westwood (63), Russell (71), Ormsby (75), J Monaghan (78);
Goals: Ratchford 1/3, Bridge 3/3;
Field goal: Ratchford (73).
Rugby League & League Express Men of the Match: *Giants:* Scott Grix; *Wolves:* Matthew Russell.
Penalty count: 4-8; **Half-time:** 14-4;
Referee: James Child; **Attendance:** 7,068.

HULL KINGSTON ROVERS 44
WAKEFIELD TRINITY WILDCATS 6

ROVERS: 2 Ben Cockayne; 32 Ade Gardner; 18 Liam Salter; 3 Kris Welham; 24 Omari Caro; 6 Travis Burns (C); 7 Kris Keating; 14 Adam Walker; 9 Josh Hodgson (C); 10 Michael Weyman; 11 Kevin Larroyer; 20 Jordan Cox; 12 Neville Costigan. Subs (all used): 21 Keal Carlile; 23 James Green; 16 Jason Netherton; 22 Rhys Lovegrove.
Tries: Costigan (4), Caro (12, 50), J Hodgson (30, 62), Welham (38, 73), Keating (59); **Goals:** Burns 6/8.
On report: Burns (25) - alleged high tackle.
WILDCATS: 20 Jarrod Sammut; 2 Peter Fox; 3 Dean Collis; 5 Reece Lyne; 31 Chris Riley; 6 Paul Sykes; 7 Pita Godinet; 8 Scott Anderson; 9 Paul McShane; 30 Nick Scruton; 15 Matt Ryan; 12 Danny Kirmond (C); 13 Danny Washbrook. Subs (all used): 29 Harry Siejka; 10 Andy Raleigh; 11 Ali Lauitiiti; 17 Taulima Tautai.
Try: Godinet (76); **Goals:** Sammut 1/1.
Rugby League & League Express Men of the Match: *Rovers:* Omari Caro; *Wildcats:* Pita Godinet.
Penalty count: 3-9; **Half-time:** 22-0;
Referee: Phil Bentham; **Attendance:** 6,983.

WIDNES VIKINGS 22 BRADFORD BULLS 18

VIKINGS: 2 Jack Owens; 20 Paddy Flynn; 14 Chris Dean; 3 Cameron Phelps; 5 Patrick Ah Van; 6 Kevin Brown; 27 Tom Gilmore; 25 Alex Gerrard; 9 Jon Clarke (C); 23 Phil Joseph; 17 Danny Galea; 12 Danny Tickle; 13 Hep Cahill. Subs (all used): 35 Paul Clough; 18 Paul Johnson; 34 Rhodri Lloyd; 15 Lloyd White.
Tries: Owens (14), Brown (25, 35), Ah Van (51);
Goals: Tickle 3/4.
Sin bin: Dean (38) - interference.
BULLS: 1 Brett Kearney; 2 Elliot Kear; 21 Adam Henry; 3 Adrian Purtell; 22 Sam Wood; 26 Liam Sutcliffe; 7 Luke Gale (C); 14 Manase Manuokafoa; 19 Adam O'Brien; 13 Chev Walker; 11 Tom Olbison; 4 Matty Blythe; 18 James Donaldson. Subs (all used): 16 Danny Addy; 23 Oliver Roberts; 29 Anthony Mullally; 28 Danny Bridge.
Tries: Sutcliffe (39), Kear (48), Kearney (67);
Goals: Gale 3/3.
Rugby League & League Express Men of the Match: *Vikings:* Kevin Brown; *Bulls:* Brett Kearney.
Penalty count: 5-5; **Half-time:** 16-6;
Referee: George Stokes; **Attendance:** 5,581.

ROUND 8

Thursday 10th April 2014

HULL FC 30 HUDDERSFIELD GIANTS 6

HULL: 20 Jamie Shaul; 27 Liam Colbon; 14 Richard Whiting; 4 Kirk Yeaman; 34 Fetuli Talanoa; 32 Jordan Rankin; 7 Jacob Miller; 8 Mickey Paea; 9 Danny Houghton; 35 Garreth Carvell; 11 Gareth Ellis (C); 12 Chris Tuson; 13 Joe Westerman. Subs (all used): 16 Jordan Thompson; 21 Dean Hadley; 33 Aaron Heremaia; 22 Josh Bowden.
Tries: Talanoa (5), Whiting (7), Rankin (18), Houghton (20), Miller (50), Hadley (60);
Goals: Whiting 3/6.
Sin bin: Whiting (63) - fighting.
GIANTS: 1 Scott Grix; 2 Jermaine McGillvary; 5 Aaron Murphy; 4 Joe Wardle; 19 Jodie Broughton; 6 Danny Brough (C); 7 Luke Robinson; 20 Antonio Kaufusi; 9 Shaun Lunt; 10 Craig Kopczak; 12 Jason Chan; 17 Ukuma Ta'ai; 13 Chris Bailey. Subs (all used): 8 Eorl Crabtree; 14 Michael Lawrence; 18 Kyle Wood; 23 Josh Johnson.
Try: Broughton (28); **Goals:** Brough 1/1.
Sin bin: Brough (63) - fighting.
Rugby League & League Express Men of the Match: *Hull:* Gareth Ellis; *Giants:* Danny Brough.
Penalty count: 4-5; **Half-time:** 20-6;
Referee: Richard Silverwood; **Attendance:** 9,515.

Friday 11th April 2014

BRADFORD BULLS 24 SALFORD RED DEVILS 38

BULLS: 1 Brett Kearney; 2 Elliot Kear; 21 Adam Henry; 3 Adrian Purtell; 5 Jamie Foster; 17 Lee Gaskell; 7 Luke Gale; 14 Manase Manuokafoa; 9 Matt Diskin (C); 13 Chev Walker; 12 Dale Ferguson; 4 Matty Blythe; 18 James Donaldson. Subs (all used): 30 Jamal Fakir; 29 Anthony Mullally; 15 Adam Sidlow; 19 Adam O'Brien.
Tries: Purtell (20), Sidlow (43), Kear (69), Henry (77);
Goals: Foster 4/4.
RED DEVILS: 1 Jake Mullaney; 23 Greg Johnson; 3 Martin Gleeson; 4 Junior Sa'u; 5 Francis Meli; 6 Rangi Chase; 7 Tim Smith; 8 Adrian Morley (C); 9 Tommy Lee; 10 Lama Tasi; 13 Harrison Hansen; 12 Gareth Hock; 11 Tony Puletua. Subs (all used): 19 Matty Ashurst; 21 Jordan Walne; 35 Logan Tomkins (D); 17 Shannan McPherson.
Tries: Mullaney (4), Sa'u (25), Smith (33), Ashurst (38), Puletua (49), Chase (73), Meli (79); **Goals:** Mullaney 5/7.
Rugby League & League Express Men of the Match: *Bulls:* Elliot Kear; *Red Devils:* Rangi Chase.
Penalty count: 6-6; **Half-time:** 6-22;
Referee: Phil Bentham; **Attendance:** 6,144.

CASTLEFORD TIGERS 28 ST HELENS 30

TIGERS: 6 Luke Dorn; 24 James Clare; 4 Jake Webster; 3 Michael Shenton (C); 5 Justin Carney; 7 Marc Sneyd; 26 Liam Finn; 8 Andy Lynch; 14 Daryl Clark; 10 Craig Huby; 16 Oliver Holmes; 12 Weller Hauraki; 11 Grant Millington. Subs (all used): 9 Adam Milner; 13 Nathan Massey; 15 Ryan Boyle; 18 Frankie Mariano.
Tries: Webster (1), Shenton (12, 32), Millington (15), Carney (60); **Goals:** Sneyd 4/5.
SAINTS: 1 Jonny Lomax; 2 Tom Makinson; 3 Jordan Turner; 26 Matty Dawson; 5 Adam Swift; 12 Jon Wilkin; 7 Luke Walsh; 8 Mose Masoe; 9 James Roby; 10 Louie McCarthy-Scarsbrook; 11 Iosia Soliola; 13 Willie Manu; 4 Josh Jones. Subs (all used): 14 Anthony Laffranchi; 17 Paul Wellens (C); 18 Alex Walmsley; 23 Joe Greenwood.
Tries: Soliola (27), Lomax (47), Makinson (54), Turner (68), Wellens (74), Swift (78); **Goals:** Walsh 3/6.
Rugby League & League Express Men of the Match: *Tigers:* Marc Sneyd; *Saints:* Paul Wellens.
Penalty count: 4-5; **Half-time:** 24-6;
Referee: Ben Thaler; **Attendance:** 6,487.

LEEDS RHINOS 42 WAKEFIELD TRINITY WILDCATS 6

RHINOS: 2 Ben Jones-Bishop; 20 Tom Briscoe; 3 Kallum Watkins; 4 Joel Moon; 5 Ryan Hall; 13 Kevin Sinfield (C); 21 Liam Sutcliffe; 8 Kylie Leuluai; 7 Rob Burrow; 10 Jamie Peacock; 12 Carl Ablett; 19 Mitch Achurch; 17 Ian Kirke. Subs (all used): 16 Ryan Bailey; 14 Stevie Ward; 18 Chris Clarkson; 23 Brad Singleton.
Tries: Sutcliffe (7), Hall (13), T Briscoe (22), Ablett (38), Peacock (57), Clarkson (62), Burrow (77);
Goals: Sinfield 7/7.
WILDCATS: 20 Jarrod Sammut; 2 Peter Fox; 28 Luke Briscoe; 15 Matt Ryan; 31 Chris Riley; 6 Paul Sykes; 7 Pita Godinet; 8 Scott Anderson; 9 Paul McShane; 30 Nick Scruton; 11 Ali Lauitiiti; 12 Danny Kirmond (C); 13 Danny Washbrook. Subs (all used): 21 Chris Annakin; 10 Andy Raleigh; 16 Richard Moore; 29 Harry Siejka.
Try: Sammut (72); **Goals:** Sammut 1/1.
Rugby League & League Express Men of the Match: *Rhinos:* Ryan Hall; *Wildcats:* Danny Washbrook.
Penalty count: 8-6; **Half-time:** 24-0;
Referee: George Stokes; **Attendance:** 13,696.

WARRINGTON WOLVES 12
HULL KINGSTON ROVERS 25

WOLVES: 1 Matthew Russell; 18 Rhys Evans; 3 Chris Bridge; 4 Ryan Atkins; 5 Joel Monaghan; 6 Stefan Ratchford; 7 Richard Myler; 8 Chris Hill; 14 Michael Monaghan (C); 16 Paul Wood; 11 Trent Waterhouse; 23 James Laithwaite; 13 Simon Grix. Subs (all used): 15 Ben Harrison; 17 Ben Currie; 19 Anthony England; 22 Brad Dwyer.
Tries: Myler (62, 72); **Goals:** Bridge 2/2.
ROVERS: 2 Ben Cockayne; 32 Ade Gardner; 3 Kris Welham; 18 Liam Salter; 24 Omari Caro; 6 Travis Burns (C); 7 Kris Keating; 14 Adam Walker; 9 Josh Hodgson (C); 10 Michael Weyman; 11 Kevin Larroyer; 15 Graeme Horne; 12 Neville Costigan. Subs (all used): 19 Craig Hall; 23 James Green; 16 Jason Netherton; 22 Rhys Lovegrove.
Tries: Weyman (35, 69), Burns (45), Keating (58);
Goals: Burns 4/4; **Field goal:** Burns (65).
Rugby League & League Express Men of the Match: *Wolves:* Matthew Russell; *Rovers:* Travis Burns.
Penalty count: 5-3; **Half-time:** 0-6;
Referee: Robert Hicks; **Attendance:** 8,778.

WIGAN WARRIORS 36 LONDON BRONCOS 14

WARRIORS: 1 Matt Bowen; 32 Joe Burgess; 3 Darrell Goulding; 4 Iain Thornley; 23 Dan Sarginson; 6 Blake Green; 27 George Williams; 8 Scott Taylor; 9 Michael McIlorum; 16 Gil Dudson; 24 Tony Clubb; 25 John Bateman; 13 Sean O'Loughlin (C). Subs (all used): 14 Jack Hughes; 22 Eddy Pettybourne; 19 Sam Powell; 28 Jordan James.
Tries: Clubb (26, 63), Sarginson (31, 71), Thornley (37, 78), Bowen (80); **Goals:** Williams 4/7.
BRONCOS: 23 Denny Solomona; 25 Iliess Macani; 24 Mason Caton-Brown; 4 Thomas Minns; 27 Jamie O'Callaghan; 6 Ben Farrar; 7 Josh Drinkwater; 15 James Greenwood; 9 Scott Moore; 10 Olsi Krasniqi; 8 Atelea Vea; 11 Mike McMeeken; 13 Alex Foster. Subs (all used): 1 Nesiasi Mataitonga; 12 Matt Cook (C); 30 Jon Wallace (D); 20 James Cunningham.

Tries: O'Callaghan (3), McMeeken (8), Macani (75);
Goals: Drinkwater 1/3.
Rugby Leaguer & League Express Men of the Match:
Warriors: Tony Clubb; *Broncos:* Josh Drinkwater.
Penalty count: 9-4; **Half-time:** 16-10;
Referee: Matthew Thomason; **Attendance:** 10,680.

Saturday 12th April 2014

CATALAN DRAGONS 42 WIDNES VIKINGS 20

DRAGONS: 2 Morgan Escare; 26 Damien Cardace; 4 Ben Pomeroy; 25 Vincent Duport; 18 Daryl Millard; 3 Leon Pryce; 6 Thomas Bosc; 8 Olivier Elima; 16 Eloi Pelissier; 10 Jeff Lima; 11 Zeb Taia; 17 Elliott Whitehead; 24 Jason Baitieri (C). Subs (all used): 21 Julian Bousquet; 23 Lopini Paea; 29 Benjamin Garcia; 32 Joan Guasch.
Tries: Pomeroy (5, 57), Whitehead (10, 37, 60), Escare (17), Duport (47, 70), Millard (75);
Goals: Bosc 2/6, Escare 1/3.
VIKINGS: 1 Rhys Hanbury; 20 Paddy Flynn; 29 Declan Hulme; 14 Chris Dean; 2 Jack Owens; 6 Kevin Brown; 21 Danny Craven; 8 Eamon O'Carroll; 9 Jon Clarke (C); 10 Ben Kavanagh; 24 Macgraff Leuluai; 12 Danny Tickle; 13 Hep Cahill. Subs (all used): 15 Lloyd White; 18 Paul Johnson; 23 Phil Joseph; 35 Paul Clough.
Tries: Flynn (23), Owens (27, 79), White (66);
Goals: Tickle 2/4.
Rugby Leaguer & League Express Men of the Match:
Dragons: Morgan Escare; *Vikings:* Hep Cahill.
Penalty count: 4-3; **Half-time:** 18-10;
Referee: James Child; **Attendance:** 9,588.

ROUND 9

Thursday 17th April 2014

BRADFORD BULLS 6 LEEDS RHINOS 46

BULLS: 1 Brett Kearney; 2 Elliot Kear; 4 Matty Blythe; 3 Adrian Purtell; 21 Adam Henry; 17 Lee Gaskell; 7 Luke Gale (C); 14 Manase Manuokafoa; 19 Adam O'Brien; 30 Jamal Fakir; 12 Dale Ferguson; 28 Danny Bridge; 18 James Donaldson. Subs (all used): 16 Danny Addy; 15 Adam Sidlow; 13 Chev Walker; 11 Tom Olbison.
Try: Gaskell (23); **Goals:** Gale 1/1.
RHINOS: 1 Zak Hardaker; 20 Tom Briscoe; 3 Kallum Watkins; 4 Joel Moon; 5 Ryan Hall; 6 Danny McGuire; 13 Kevin Sinfield (C); 8 Kylie Leuluai; 7 Rob Burrow; 23 Brad Singleton; 19 Mitch Achurch; 12 Carl Ablett; 15 Brett Delaney. Subs (all used): 14 Stevie Ward; 17 Ian Kirke; 18 Chris Clarkson; 21 Liam Sutcliffe.
Tries: Sinfield (4), Moon (9), McGuire (12), Hall (14, 50, 55), Sutcliffe (66), Watkins (73), Burrow (78); **Goals:** Sinfield 3/6, Hardaker 2/3.
Rugby Leaguer & League Express Men of the Match:
Bulls: Brett Kearney; *Rhinos:* Joel Moon.
Penalty count: 4-4; **Half-time:** 6-20;
Referee: Robert Hicks; **Attendance:** 10,106.

HULL KINGSTON ROVERS 21 HULL FC 20

ROVERS: 2 Ben Cockayne; 32 Ade Gardner; 18 Liam Salter; 3 Kris Welham; 24 Omari Caro; 6 Travis Burns (C); 19 Craig Hall; 8 Justin Poore; 9 Josh Hodgson (C); 10 Michael Weyman; 11 Kevin Larroyer; 15 Graeme Horne; 12 Neville Costigan. Subs (all used): 16 Jason Netherton; 23 James Green; 22 Rhys Lovegrove; 20 Jordan Cox.
Tries: Larroyer (15), Weyman (35), Horne (57, 59);
Goals: Burns 2/4; **Field goal:** Hall (79).
HULL: 20 Jamie Shaul; 27 Liam Colbon; 14 Richard Whiting; 4 Kirk Yeaman; 34 Fetuli Talanoa; 32 Jordan Rankin; 7 Jacob Miller; 8 Mickey Paea; 9 Danny Houghton; 35 Garreth Carvell; 11 Gareth Ellis (C); 21 Dean Hadley; 13 Joe Westerman. Subs (all used): 16 Jordan Thompson; 22 Josh Bowden; 6 Richard Horne; 17 Liam Watts.
Tries: Rankin (10), Bowden (43), Houghton (63), Talanoa (75); **Goals:** Whiting 2/4.
Rugby Leaguer & League Express Men of the Match:
Rovers: Travis Burns; *Hull:* Danny Houghton.
Penalty count: 7-6; **Half-time:** 10-4;
Referee: James Child; **Attendance:** 10,179.

LONDON BRONCOS 22 CATALAN DRAGONS 28

BRONCOS: 1 Nesiasi Mataitonga; 5 James Duckworth; 23 Denny Solomona; 24 Mason Caton-Brown; 4 Thomas Minns; 6 Ben Farrar; 7 Josh Drinkwater; 15 James Greenwood; 9 Scott Moore; 10 Olsi Krasniqi; 8 Atelea Vea; 11 Mike McMeeken; 13 Alex Foster. Subs (all used): 16 Nick Slyney; 12 Matt Cook (C); 20 James Cunningham; 25 Iliess Macani.
Tries: Caton-Brown (38, 70), Mataitonga (73), Solomona (78); **Goals:** Drinkwater 3/4.
DRAGONS: 2 Morgan Escare; 5 Michael Oldfield; 4 Ben Pomeroy; 25 Vincent Duport; 19 Mathias Pala; 6 Thomas Bosc; 14 William Barthau; 8 Olivier Elima; 16 Eloi Pelissier; 10 Jeff Lima; 11 Zeb Taia; 17 Elliott Whitehead; 24 Jason Baitieri (C). Subs (all used): 21 Julian Bousquet; 23 Lopini Paea; 29 Benjamin Garcia; 32 Joan Guasch.
Tries: Oldfield (9), Taia (27), Barthau (32), Pelissier (49), Duport (65); **Goals:** Bosc 4/5.
Rugby Leaguer & League Express Men of the Match:
Broncos: Mason Caton-Brown; *Dragons:* William Barthau.
Penalty count: 3-6; **Half-time:** 4-18;
Referee: Chris Leatherbarrow; **Attendance:** 1,002.

Friday 18th April 2014

ST HELENS 14 WIGAN WARRIORS 33

SAINTS: 1 Jonny Lomax; 2 Tom Makinson; 3 Jordan Turner; 4 Josh Jones; 26 Matty Dawson; 6 Lance Hohaia; 7 Luke Walsh; 18 Alex Walmsley; 9 James Roby; 10 Louie McCarthy-Scarsbrook; 12 Jon Wilkin; 11 Iosia Soliola; 15 Mark Flanagan. Subs (all used): 8 Mose Masoe; 17 Paul Wellens (C); 23 Joe Greenwood; 27 Greg Richards.
Tries: Makinson (6, 28), Turner (34); **Goals:** Walsh 1/3.
WARRIORS: 1 Matt Bowen; 32 Joe Burgess; 3 Darrell Goulding; 4 Iain Thornley; 23 Dan Sarginson; 6 Blake Green; 7 Matty Smith; 8 Scott Taylor; 9 Michael McIlorum; 10 Ben Flower; 25 John Bateman; 12 Liam Farrell; 13 Sean O'Loughlin (C). Subs (all used): 22 Eddy Pettybourne; 24 Tony Clubb; 27 George Williams; 28 Jordan James.
Tries: O'Loughlin (3), Sarginson (16), L Farrell (23, 44), Burgess (49); **Goals:** Smith 6/7; **Field goal:** Smith (68).
On report:
O'Loughlin (53) - alleged shoulder charge on Richards.
Rugby Leaguer & League Express Men of the Match:
Saints: Luke Walsh; *Warriors:* Sean O'Loughlin.
Penalty count: 6-6; **Half-time:** 14-20;
Referee: Richard Silverwood; **Attendance:** 17,980.

WARRINGTON WOLVES 44 WIDNES VIKINGS 6

WOLVES: 1 Matthew Russell; 18 Rhys Evans; 3 Chris Bridge; 4 Ryan Atkins; 5 Joel Monaghan; 20 Gareth O'Brien; 6 Stefan Ratchford; 8 Chris Hill; 14 Michael Monaghan (C); 10 Roy Asotasi; 11 Trent Waterhouse; 23 James Laithwaite; 15 Ben Harrison. Subs (all used): 9 Mick Higham; 17 Ben Currie; 21 Glenn Riley; 25 Ben Evans.
Tries: O'Brien (3), J Monaghan (11), M Monaghan (16), Bridge (34), R Evans (43, 59), Currie (56), Atkins (80);
Goals: Bridge 4/5, Ratchford 2/3.
VIKINGS: 1 Rhys Hanbury; 20 Paddy Flynn; 3 Cameron Phelps; 14 Chris Dean; 2 Jack Owens; 6 Kevin Brown; 21 Danny Craven; 25 Alex Gerrard; 9 Jon Clarke (C); 23 Phil Joseph; 17 Danny Galea; 12 Danny Tickle; 13 Hep Cahill. Subs (all used): 16 Willie Isa; 35 Paul Clough; 15 Lloyd White; 10 Ben Kavanagh.
Try: Flynn (75); **Goals:** Tickle 1/1.
Rugby Leaguer & League Express Men of the Match:
Wolves: Chris Hill; *Vikings:* Paddy Flynn.
Penalty count: 9-5; **Half-time:** 24-0;
Referee: Ben Thaler; **Attendance:** 10,500.

WAKEFIELD TRINITY WILDCATS 20 CASTLEFORD TIGERS 43

WILDCATS: 20 Jarrod Sammut; 1 Richard Mathers; 3 Dean Collis; 5 Reece Lyne; 31 Chris Riley; 6 Paul Sykes; 29 Harry Siejka; 8 Scott Anderson; 9 Paul McShane; 30 Nick Scruton; 12 Danny Kirmond (C); 15 Matt Ryan; 13 Danny Washbrook. Subs (all used): 7 Pita Godinet; 16 Richard Moore; 21 Chris Annakin; 23 Daniel Smith.
Tries: McShane (16), Sammut (29, 48), Lyne (42);
Goals: Sammut 2/4.
TIGERS: 24 James Clare; 22 Richard Owen; 23 Michael Channing; 3 Michael Shenton (C); 5 Justin Carney; 7 Marc Sneyd; 26 Liam Finn; 8 Andy Lynch; 14 Daryl Clark; 10 Craig Huby; 16 Oliver Holmes; 12 Weller Hauraki; 11 Grant Millington. Subs (all used): 9 Adam Milner; 15 Ryan Boyle; 18 Frankie Mariano; 19 Scott Wheeldon.
Tries: Carney (4), Clark (11, 74), Owen (21, 34), Wheeldon (38, 79), Finn (62); **Goals:** Sneyd 5/8;
Field goal: Sneyd (73).
Rugby Leaguer & League Express Men of the Match:
Wildcats: Jarrod Sammut; *Tigers:* Daryl Clark.
Penalty count: 1-4; **Half-time:** 12-26;
Referee: Phil Bentham; **Attendance:** 5,159.

SALFORD RED DEVILS 22 HUDDERSFIELD GIANTS 42

RED DEVILS: 1 Jake Mullaney; 23 Greg Johnson; 3 Martin Gleeson; 4 Junior Sa'u; 5 Francis Meli; 6 Rangi Chase; 7 Tim Smith; 8 Adrian Morley (C); 9 Tommy Lee; 10 Lama Tasi; 13 Harrison Hansen; 12 Gareth Hock; 11 Tony Puletua. Subs (all used): 19 Matty Ashurst; 15 Darrell Griffin; 35 Logan Tomkins; 17 Shannan McPherson.
Tries: Meli (26, 45, 77), Morley (30), Ashurst (61);
Goals: Mullaney 1/5.
GIANTS: 1 Scott Grix; 2 Jermaine McGillvary; 3 Leroy Cudjoe; 4 Joe Wardle; 5 Aaron Murphy; 6 Danny Brough (C); 18 Kyle Wood; 8 Eorl Crabtree; 9 Shaun Lunt; 10 Craig Kopczak; 12 Jason Chan; 15 Larne Patrick; 14 Michael Lawrence. Subs (all used): 13 Chris Bailey; 17 Ukuma Ta'ai; 21 Anthony Mullally; 23 Josh Johnson.
Tries: Lunt (9), Murphy (11, 35, 70), Brough (13), McGillvary (51), Bailey (57); **Goals:** Brough 7/8.
Rugby Leaguer & League Express Men of the Match:
Red Devils: Rangi Chase; *Giants:* Danny Brough.
Penalty count: 8-3; **Half-time:** 10-22;
Referee: Tim Roby; **Attendance:** 5,068.

ROUND 10

Monday 21st April 2014

HUDDERSFIELD GIANTS 36 WAKEFIELD TRINITY WILDCATS 16

GIANTS: 1 Scott Grix; 19 Jodie Broughton; 3 Leroy Cudjoe; 4 Joe Wardle; 5 Aaron Murphy; 6 Danny Brough (C); 18 Kyle Wood; 8 Eorl Crabtree; 9 Shaun Lunt; 20 Antonio Kaufusi; 12 Jason Chan; 15 Larne Patrick; 14 Michael Lawrence. Subs (all used): 10 Craig Kopczak; 13 Chris Bailey; 17 Ukuma Ta'ai; 21 Anthony Mullally.
Tries: Broughton (7), Lawrence (21), Ta'ai (28), Cudjoe (36), Chan (50), Lunt (75); **Goals:** Brough 6/6.
On report: Kaufusi (59) - alleged high tackle.
WILDCATS: 20 Jarrod Sammut; 2 Peter Fox; 1 Richard Mathers (C); 22 Lucas Walshaw; 31 Chris Riley; 6 Paul Sykes; 29 Harry Siejka; 10 Andy Raleigh; 9 Paul McShane; 30 Nick Scruton; 15 Matt Ryan; 13 Danny Washbrook; 23 Daniel Smith. Subs (all used): 7 Pita Godinet; 8 Scott Anderson; 16 Richard Moore; 26 Jon Molloy.
Tries: Sammut (16), Walshaw (26), Molloy (68);
Goals: Sammut 2/3.
Rugby Leaguer & League Express Men of the Match:
Giants: Shaun Lunt; *Wildcats:* Jarrod Sammut.
Penalty count: 8-10; **Half-time:** 24-10;
Referee: Robert Hicks; **Attendance:** 5,487.

HULL FC 40 LONDON BRONCOS 4

HULL: 20 Jamie Shaul; 27 Liam Colbon; 3 Ben Crooks; 14 Richard Whiting; 34 Fetuli Talanoa; 32 Jordan Rankin; 7 Jacob Miller; 8 Mickey Paea; 33 Aaron Heremaia; 35 Garreth Carvell; 11 Gareth Ellis (C); 19 Jay Pitts; 13 Joe Westerman. Subs (all used): 9 Danny Houghton; 16 Jordan Thompson; 6 Richard Horne; 26 Iafeta Palea'aesina.
Tries: Shaul (10, 50), Crooks (20), Thompson (27), Rankin (34, 68), Miller (43); **Goals:** Crooks 6/7.
BRONCOS: 1 Nesiasi Mataitonga; 25 Iliess Macani; 4 Thomas Minns; 24 Mason Caton-Brown; 23 Denny Solomona; 6 Ben Farrar; 7 Josh Drinkwater; 15 James Greenwood; 9 Scott Moore; 10 Olsi Krasniqi; 8 Atelea Vea; 11 Mike McMeeken; 12 Matt Cook (C). Subs (all used): 16 Nick Slyney; 30 Jon Wallace; 14 Mike Bishay; 22 James Woodburn-Hall.
Try: Caton-Brown (55); **Goals:** Drinkwater 0/1.
Sin bin: Solomona (41) - holding down.
Rugby Leaguer & League Express Men of the Match:
Hull: Gareth Ellis; *Broncos:* Mason Caton-Brown.
Penalty count: 6-5; **Half-time:** 22-0;
Referee: George Stokes; **Attendance:** 9,538.

LEEDS RHINOS 32 SALFORD RED DEVILS 4

RHINOS: 2 Ben Jones-Bishop; 20 Tom Briscoe; 1 Zak Hardaker; 4 Joel Moon; 5 Ryan Hall; 13 Kevin Sinfield (C); 6 Danny McGuire; 8 Kylie Leuluai; 7 Rob Burrow; 10 Jamie Peacock; 12 Carl Ablett; 19 Mitch Achurch; 15 Brett Delaney. Subs (all used): 16 Ryan Bailey; 23 Brad Singleton; 21 Liam Sutcliffe; 18 Chris Clarkson.
Tries: Sinfield (6), Hardaker (43), Burrow (60), Jones-Bishop (66), Hall (74), T Briscoe (78);
Goals: Sinfield 4/6.
RED DEVILS: 1 Jake Mullaney; 2 Danny Williams; 36 Michael Platt (D2); 4 Junior Sa'u; 5 Francis Meli; 6 Rangi Chase (C); 14 Theo Fages; 15 Darrell Griffin; 35 Logan Tomkins; 10 Lama Tasi; 19 Matty Ashurst; 12 Gareth Hock; 9 Tommy Lee. Subs (all used): 18 Steve Rapira; 21 Jordan Walne; 24 Stuart Howarth; 20 Adam Walne.
Try: Tomkins (28); **Goals:** Mullaney 0/1.
Rugby Leaguer & League Express Men of the Match:
Rhinos: Kevin Sinfield; *Red Devils:* Rangi Chase.
Penalty count: 11-4; **Half-time:** 6-4;
Referee: Ben Thaler; **Attendance:** 14,013.

WIDNES VIKINGS 40 ST HELENS 26

VIKINGS: 1 Rhys Hanbury; 20 Paddy Flynn; 14 Chris Dean; 3 Cameron Phelps; 2 Jack Owens; 28 Grant Gore; 6 Kevin Brown (C); 10 Ben Kavanagh; 15 Lloyd White; 18 Paul Johnson; 12 Danny Tickle; 17 Danny Galea; 24 Macgraff Leuluai. Subs (all used): 13 Hep Cahill; 25 Alex Gerrard; 16 Willie Isa; 19 Adam Lawton.
Tries: Hanbury (3, 44), Isa (20), Gerrard (32), Flynn (52), Dean (66), Leuluai (78);
Goals: Tickle 5/6, Owens 1/1.
SAINTS: 6 Lance Hohaia; 2 Tom Makinson; 24 Gary Wheeler; 4 Josh Jones; 26 Matty Dawson; 17 Paul Wellens (C); 12 Jon Wilkin; 8 Mose Masoe; 36 Matty Fozard (D); 25 Anthony Walker; 23 Joe Greenwood; 11 Iosia Soliola; 28 Luke Thompson. Subs (all used): 31 James Tilley; 33 Andre Savelio; 29 Jordan Hand; 10 Louie McCarthy-Scarsbrook.
Tries: Soliola (25), Masoe (36), Wellens (38), Makinson (61), Hohaia (69);
Goals: Makinson 3/4, Hohaia 0/1.
Rugby Leaguer & League Express Men of the Match:
Vikings: Macgraff Leuluai; *Saints:* Andre Savelio.
Penalty count: 5-6; **Half-time:** 18-16;
Referee: James Child; **Attendance:** 7,706.

WIGAN WARRIORS 84 BRADFORD BULLS 6

WARRIORS: 26 Ryan Hampshire; 31 Dominic Manfredi; 3 Darrell Goulding; 5 Anthony Gelling; 23 Dan Sarginson; 6 Blake Green; 27 George Williams; 16 Gil Dudson; 9 Michael McIlorum; 28 Jordan James; 25 John Bateman; 12 Liam Farrell; 13 Sean O'Loughlin (C). Subs (all used): 14 Jack Hughes; 24 Tony Clubb; 19 Sam Powell; 37 Ryan Sutton (D).
Tries: Green (5, 50), Gelling (9, 59), O'Loughlin (15), Hampshire (21, 25), L Farrell (28), Hughes (35), Powell (40), Bateman (45), Goulding (48), Williams (54), Manfredi (61), Dudson (78);
Goals: Hampshire 8/9, Williams 4/6.
BULLS: 1 Brett Kearney; 2 Elliot Kear; 3 Adrian Purtell; 21 Adam Henry; 22 Sam Wood; 17 Lee Gaskell; 7 Luke Gale (C); 14 Manase Manuokafoa; 19 Adam O'Brien; 30 Jamal Fakir; 11 Tom Olbison; 13 Chev Walker; 16 Danny Addy. Subs (all used): 23 Oliver Roberts; 31 Sam Bates (D); 24 Alex Mellor; 25 Nathan Conroy.
Try: Gale (67); **Goals:** Gale 1/1.
Rugby Leaguer & League Express Men of the Match:
Warriors: Ryan Hampshire; *Bulls:* Sam Bates.
Penalty count: 3-5; **Half-time:** 46-0;
Referee: Tim Roby; **Attendance:** 15,529.

CASTLEFORD TIGERS 40 WARRINGTON WOLVES 6

TIGERS: 1 Jordan Tansey; 22 Richard Owen; 21 Ashley Gibson (D); 3 Michael Shenton (C); 24 James Clare; 7 Marc Sneyd; 20 Jamie Ellis; 8 Andy Lynch; 9 Adam Milner; 19 Scott Wheeldon; 18 Frankie Mariano; 4 Jake Webster; 13 Nathan Massey. Subs (all used): 10 Craig Huby; 11 Grant Millington; 12 Weller Hauraki; 14 Daryl Clark.
Tries: Clare (13, 50), Shenton (34, 38, 73), Ellis (55), Owen (59); **Goals:** Sneyd 6/7.
WOLVES: 1 Matthew Russell; 5 Joel Monaghan; 18 Rhys Evans; 4 Ryan Atkins; 24 Kevin Penny (D2); 20 Gareth O'Brien; 6 Stefan Ratchford; 8 Chris Hill; 14 Michael Monaghan (C); 10 Roy Asotasi; 11 Trent Waterhouse; 23 James Laithwaite; 15 Ben Harrison. Subs (all used): 9 Mick Higham; 17 Ben Currie; 19 Anthony England; 25 Ben Evans.
Try: M Monaghan (21); **Goals:** Ratchford 1/1.
Rugby Leaguer & League Express Men of the Match: *Tigers:* Marc Sneyd; *Wolves:* Matthew Russell.
Penalty count: 6-8; **Half-time:** 18-6;
Referee: Richard Silverwood; **Attendance:** 6,853.

CATALAN DRAGONS 37 HULL KINGSTON ROVERS 24

DRAGONS: 2 Morgan Escare; 5 Michael Oldfield; 4 Ben Pomeroy; 25 Vincent Duport; 18 Daryl Millard; 3 Leon Pryce; 6 Thomas Bosc; 8 Olivier Elima; 16 Eloi Pelissier; 10 Jeff Lima; 11 Zeb Taia; 17 Elliott Whitehead; 24 Jason Baitieri (C). Subs (all used): 13 Gregory Mounis (C); 15 Antoni Maria; 23 Lopini Paea; 29 Benjamin Garcia.
Tries: Escare (4), Whitehead (13, 60), Oldfield (18, 52), Millard (42); **Goals:** Bosc 6/9; **Field goal:** Bosc (79).
ROVERS: 1 Greg Eden; 32 Ade Gardner; 3 Kris Welham; 18 Liam Salter; 24 Omari Caro; 6 Travis Burns (C); 19 Craig Hall; 8 Justin Poore; 9 Josh Hodgson (C); 10 Michael Weyman; 11 Kevin Larroyer; 15 Graeme Horne; 12 Neville Costigan. Subs (all used): 16 Jason Netherton; 20 Jordan Cox; 21 Keal Carlile; 22 Rhys Lovegrove.
Tries: Eden (27), Cox (34), Caro (38, 47);
Goals: Burns 4/4.
On report: Weyman (15) - alleged high tackle.
Rugby Leaguer & League Express Men of the Match: *Dragons:* Leon Pryce; *Rovers:* Travis Burns.
Penalty count: 8-5; **Half-time:** 16-18;
Referee: Phil Bentham; **Attendance:** 9,863.

ROUND 11

Thursday 1st May 2014

ST HELENS 48 LONDON BRONCOS 18

SAINTS: 1 Jonny Lomax; 2 Tom Makinson; 4 Josh Jones; 26 Matty Dawson; 5 Adam Swift; 6 Lance Hohaia; 7 Luke Walsh; 18 Alex Walmsley; 9 James Roby; 10 Louie McCarthy-Scarsbrook; 12 Jon Wilkin (C); 11 Iosia Soliola; 28 Luke Thompson. Subs (all used): 8 Mose Masoe; 15 Mark Flanagan; 23 Joe Greenwood; 30 Carl Forster.
Tries: Dawson (6), Walsh (11), Lomax (24), Makinson (27), Hohaia (44), Swift (46), Greenwood (53), Jones (60), Flanagan (76);
Goals: Walsh 6/9.
BRONCOS: 6 Ben Farrar; 25 Iliess Macani; 23 Denny Solomona; 24 Mason Caton-Brown; 4 Thomas Minns; 7 Josh Drinkwater; 14 Mike Bishay; 10 Olsi Krasniqi; 20 James Cunningham; 15 James Greenwood; 12 Matt Cook (C); 8 Atelea Vea; 13 Alex Foster. Subs (all used): 3 Jordan Atkins; 11 Mike McMeeken; 16 Nick Slyney; 30 Jon Wallace.
Tries: Solomona (31), Minns (50), Bishay (73);
Goals: Drinkwater 3/3.
Rugby Leaguer & League Express Men of the Match: *Saints:* Alex Walmsley; *Broncos:* Mike Bishay.
Penalty count: 4-5; **Half-time:** 20-6;
Referee: Matthew Thomason; **Attendance:** 9,408.

Friday 2nd May 2014

LEEDS RHINOS 28 WIGAN WARRIORS 12

RHINOS: 1 Zak Hardaker; 20 Tom Briscoe; 3 Kallum Watkins; 4 Joel Moon; 5 Ryan Hall; 6 Danny McGuire; 12 Carl Ablett; 8 Kylie Leuluai; 13 Kevin Sinfield (C); 10 Jamie Peacock; 18 Chris Clarkson; 19 Mitch Achurch; 15 Brett Delaney. Subs (all used): 17 Ian Kirke; 23 Brad Singleton; 21 Liam Sutcliffe; 16 Ryan Bailey.
Tries: McGuire (2), Hardaker (12), T Briscoe (35), Hall (42), Sutcliffe (77); **Goals:** Sinfield 4/5.
WARRIORS: 1 Matt Bowen; 32 Joe Burgess; 3 Darrell Goulding; 23 Dan Sarginson; 5 Anthony Gelling; 6 Blake Green; 7 Matty Smith; 8 Scott Taylor; 9 Michael Mcllorum (C); 16 Gil Dudson; 25 John Bateman; 12 Liam Farrell; 24 Tony Clubb. Subs (all used): 17 Dominic Crosby; 28 Jordan James; 14 Jack Hughes; 27 George Williams.
Tries: Clubb (21), Taylor (76); **Goals:** Smith 2/2.
Rugby Leaguer & League Express Men of the Match: *Rhinos:* Zak Hardaker; *Warriors:* Anthony Gelling.
Penalty count: 5-1; **Half-time:** 16-6;
Referee: Phil Bentham; **Attendance:** 18,139.

Saturday 3rd May 2014

CATALAN DRAGONS 37 SALFORD RED DEVILS 24

DRAGONS: 2 Morgan Escare; 5 Michael Oldfield; 4 Ben Pomeroy; 25 Vincent Duport; 18 Daryl Millard; 3 Leon Pryce; 14 William Barthau; 21 Julian Bousquet; 16 Eloi Pelissier; 20 Mickael Simon; 11 Zeb Taia; 12 Louis Anderson; 24 Jason Baitieri (C). Subs: 15 Antoni Maria; 19 Mathias Pala (not used); 23 Lopini Paea; 29 Benjamin Garcia.
Tries: Escare (1, 19, 70), Millard (8), Taia (45), Pryce (63); **Goals:** Barthau 6/7; **Field goal:** Pelissier (79).
RED DEVILS: 37 Greg Eden; 2 Danny Williams; 3 Martin Gleeson; 4 Junior Sa'u; 5 Francis Meli; 6 Rangi Chase; 7 Tim Smith; 8 Adrian Morley (C); 9 Tommy Lee; 10 Lama Tasi; 12 Gareth Hock; 13 Harrison Hansen; 18 Steve Rapira. Subs (all used): 11 Tony Puletua; 15 Darrell Griffin; 20 Adam Walne; 35 Logan Tomkins.
Tries: Meli (26), Williams (28), Eden (39), Hock (50);
Goals: Smith 4/4.
Rugby Leaguer & League Express Men of the Match: *Dragons:* Leon Pryce; *Red Devils:* Rangi Chase.
Penalty count: 4-4; **Half-time:** 16-18;
Referee: Ben Thaler; **Attendance:** 7,862.

Sunday 4th May 2014

BRADFORD BULLS 34 WARRINGTON WOLVES 28

BULLS: 17 Lee Gaskell; 2 Elliot Kear; 34 Joe Arundel (D); 21 Adam Henry; 5 Jamie Foster; 1 Brett Kearney; 7 Luke Gale; 35 Antonio Kaufusi (D); 9 Matt Diskin (C); 15 Adam Sidlow; 3 Adrian Purtell; 33 Jay Pitts; 16 Danny Addy. Subs (all used): 11 Tom Olbison; 19 Adam O'Brien; 24 Alex Mellor; 31 Sam Bates.
Tries: Foster (11), Kearney (16), Olbison (28), Purtell (48, 72), Kear (68); **Goals:** Foster 5/7.
WOLVES: 1 Matthew Russell; 5 Joel Monaghan; 18 Rhys Evans; 4 Ryan Atkins; 24 Kevin Penny; 3 Chris Bridge; 20 Gareth O'Brien; 8 Chris Hill; 14 Michael Monaghan (C); 19 Anthony England; 11 Trent Waterhouse; 23 James Laithwaite; 25 Ben Evans. Subs (all used): 10 Roy Asotasi; 15 Ben Harrison; 17 Ben Currie; 9 Mick Higham.
Tries: England (6), Bridge (18), Penny (23), J Monaghan (34), Russell (58); **Goals:** Bridge 4/5.
Rugby Leaguer & League Express Men of the Match: *Bulls:* Lee Gaskell; *Wolves:* Chris Bridge.
Penalty count: 9-5; **Half-time:** 16-22;
Referee: Richard Silverwood; **Attendance:** 6,173.

HUDDERSFIELD GIANTS 29 CASTLEFORD TIGERS 28

GIANTS: 1 Scott Grix; 2 Jermaine McGillvary; 3 Leroy Cudjoe; 4 Joe Wardle; 5 Aaron Murphy; 6 Danny Brough (C); 7 Luke Robinson; 8 Eorl Crabtree; 9 Shaun Lunt; 10 Craig Kopczak; 12 Jason Chan; 17 Ukuma Ta'ai; 14 Michael Lawrence. Subs (all used): 13 Chris Bailey; 16 David Faiumu; 18 Kyle Wood; 21 Anthony Mullally.
Tries: Wardle (29), Cudjoe (34), McGillvary (41), Grix (53), Murphy (57); **Goals:** Brough 4/6;
Field goal: Brough (75).
TIGERS: 24 James Clare; 2 Kirk Dixon; 23 Michael Channing; 3 Michael Shenton (C); 5 Justin Carney; 7 Marc Sneyd; 20 Jamie Ellis; 8 Andy Lynch; 14 Daryl Clark; 10 Craig Huby; 16 Oliver Holmes; 12 Weller Hauraki; 11 Grant Millington. Subs (all used): 4 Jake Webster; 9 Adam Milner; 18 Frankie Mariano; 19 Scott Wheeldon.
Tries: Shenton (11), Carney (14), Dixon (46), Webster (65), Clark (71); **Goals:** Sneyd 4/5.
Rugby Leaguer & League Express Men of the Match: *Giants:* Danny Brough; *Tigers:* Justin Carney.
Penalty count: 4-7; **Half-time:** 12-12;
Referee: James Child; **Attendance:** 7,195.

HULL FC 16 WAKEFIELD TRINITY WILDCATS 23

HULL: 20 Jamie Shaul; 2 Jason Crookes; 3 Ben Crooks; 4 Kirk Yeaman; 34 Fetuli Talanoa; 32 Jordan Rankin; 7 Jacob Miller; 8 Mickey Paea; 9 Danny Houghton; 22 Josh Bowden; 11 Gareth Ellis (C); 21 Dean Hadley; 13 Joe Westerman. Subs (all used): 33 Aaron Heremaia; 16 Jordan Thompson; 26 Iafeta Palea'aesina; 12 Chris Tuson.
Tries: Houghton (20), Rankin (39), Crooks (50);
Goals: Crooks 2/4.
Sin bin: Crookes (60) - fighting.
WILDCATS: 20 Jarrod Sammut; 1 Richard Mathers; 15 Matt Ryan; 22 Lucas Walshaw; 31 Chris Riley; 6 Paul Sykes; 29 Harry Siejka; 8 Scott Anderson; 9 Paul McShane; 30 Nick Scruton; 12 Danny Kirmond (C); 13 Danny Washbrook; 23 Daniel Smith. Subs (all used): 7 Pita Godinet; 16 Richard Moore; 26 Jon Molloy; 32 Jacob Fairbank (D).
Tries: Mathers (55), D Smith (61), Walshaw (63), Sammut (74); **Goals:** Sammut 3/4;
Field goal: Sykes (76).
Sin bin: Riley (60) - fighting.
Rugby Leaguer & League Express Men of the Match: *Hull:* Gareth Ellis; *Wildcats:* Jarrod Sammut.
Penalty count: 8-7; **Half-time:** 12-0;
Referee: Tim Roby; **Attendance:** 10,088.

HULL KINGSTON ROVERS 29 WIDNES VIKINGS 34

ROVERS: 2 Ben Cockayne; 32 Ade Gardner; 33 Wayne Ulugia (D); 3 Kris Welham; 19 Craig Hall; 6 Travis Burns (C); 7 Kris Keating; 23 James Green; 9 Josh Hodgson (C); 10 Michael Weyman; 11 Kevin Larroyer; 20 Jordan Cox; 12 Neville Costigan. Subs (all used): 13 Jamie Langley; 17 Jonathan Walker; 15 Graeme Horne; 22 Rhys Lovegrove.
Tries: Weyman (15), Welham (36), Lovegrove (38), Cockayne (43), Gardner (60); **Goals:** Burns 4/5;
Field goal: Burns (65).
VIKINGS: 1 Rhys Hanbury; 20 Paddy Flynn; 14 Chris Dean; 3 Cameron Phelps; 2 Jack Owens; 6 Kevin Brown; 21 Danny Craven; 18 Paul Johnson; 9 Jon Clarke (C); 25 Alex Gerrard; 11 Dave Allen; 12 Danny Tickle; 24 Macgraff Leuluai. Subs (all used): 15 Lloyd White; 16 Willie Isa; 10 Ben Kavanagh; 35 Paul Clough.
Tries: Owens (10), Allen (17), Brown (21, 51, 75), Clarke (72); **Goals:** Tickle 5/6.
Rugby Leaguer & League Express Men of the Match: *Rovers:* Ben Cockayne; *Vikings:* Kevin Brown.
Penalty count: 3-4; **Half-time:** 16-18;
Referee: Robert Hicks; **Attendance:** 7,007.

ROUND 12

Thursday 8th May 2014

CASTLEFORD TIGERS 14 LEEDS RHINOS 22

TIGERS: 1 Jordan Tansey; 2 Kirk Dixon; 21 Ashley Gibson; 3 Michael Shenton (C); 5 Justin Carney; 7 Marc Sneyd; 26 Liam Finn; 8 Andy Lynch; 9 Adam Milner; 18 Frankie Mariano; 16 Oliver Holmes; 4 Jake Webster; 19 Scott Wheeldon. Subs (all used): 10 Craig Huby; 11 Grant Millington; 12 Weller Hauraki; 14 Daryl Clark.
Tries: Dixon (7), Sneyd (37); **Goals:** Sneyd 3/3.
RHINOS: 1 Zak Hardaker; 2 Ben Jones-Bishop; 3 Kallum Watkins; 4 Joel Moon; 20 Tom Briscoe; 6 Danny McGuire; 12 Carl Ablett; 8 Kylie Leuluai; 13 Kevin Sinfield (C); 10 Jamie Peacock; 19 Mitch Achurch; 18 Chris Clarkson; 15 Brett Delaney. Subs (all used): 14 Stevie Ward; 23 Brad Singleton; 21 Liam Sutcliffe; 16 Ryan Bailey.
Tries: Jones-Bishop (17, 45), Watkins (29, 52);
Goals: Sinfield 3/4.
Rugby Leaguer & League Express Men of the Match: *Tigers:* Marc Sneyd; *Rhinos:* Zak Hardaker.
Penalty count: 3-2; **Half-time:** 14-12;
Referee: Richard Silverwood; **Attendance:** 9,208.

Friday 9th May 2014

HULL FC 16 WIGAN WARRIORS 44

HULL: 20 Jamie Shaul; 2 Jason Crookes; 3 Ben Crooks; 4 Kirk Yeaman; 34 Fetuli Talanoa; 6 Richard Horne; 7 Jacob Miller; 8 Mickey Paea; 9 Danny Houghton; 35 Garreth Carvell; 11 Gareth Ellis (C); 14 Richard Whiting; 13 Joe Westerman. Subs (all used): 33 Aaron Heremaia; 16 Jordan Thompson; 22 Josh Bowden; 26 Iafeta Palea'aesina.
Tries: Ellis (27), Shaul (55), Talanoa (76);
Goals: Miller 2/3.
WARRIORS: 23 Dan Sarginson; 31 Dominic Manfredi; 3 Darrell Goulding; 5 Anthony Gelling; 32 Joe Burgess; 6 Blake Green; 7 Matty Smith; 8 Scott Taylor; 9 Michael Mcllorum (C); 16 Gil Dudson; 25 John Bateman; 14 Jack Hughes; 24 Tony Clubb. Subs (all used): 37 Ryan Sutton; 28 Jordan James; 27 George Williams; 17 Dominic Crosby.
Tries: Sarginson (7, 51, 71), Gelling (16, 70), Hughes (38), Burgess (46), Manfredi (62);
Goals: Smith 6/9.
Rugby Leaguer & League Express Men of the Match: *Hull:* Jamie Shaul; *Warriors:* Matty Smith.
Penalty count: 6-5; **Half-time:** 6-20;
Referee: Robert Hicks; **Attendance:** 10,539.

WARRINGTON WOLVES 42 CATALAN DRAGONS 10

WOLVES: 1 Matthew Russell; 29 Gene Ormsby; 5 Joel Monaghan; 4 Ryan Atkins; 18 Rhys Evans; 6 Stefan Ratchford; 3 Chris Bridge; 8 Chris Hill; 14 Michael Monaghan (C); 19 Anthony England; 11 Trent Waterhouse; 23 James Laithwaite; 15 Ben Harrison. Subs (all used): 9 Mick Higham; 10 Roy Asotasi; 17 Ben Currie; 25 Ben Evans.
Tries: J Monaghan (16, 29), England (21), Ratchford (36), Bridge (41), Higham (45), Laithwaite (54); **Goals:** Bridge 7/7.
DRAGONS: 2 Morgan Escare; 5 Michael Oldfield; 4 Ben Pomeroy; 25 Vincent Duport; 18 Daryl Millard; 3 Leon Pryce; 14 William Barthau; 20 Mickael Simon; 16 Eloi Pelissier; 10 Jeff Lima; 11 Zeb Taia; 12 Louis Anderson; 24 Jason Baitieri (C). Subs (all used): 15 Antoni Maria; 23 Lopini Paea; 29 Benjamin Garcia; 32 Joan Guasch.
Tries: Duport (66), Escare (78); **Goals:** Barthau 1/2.
Rugby Leaguer & League Express Men of the Match: *Wolves:* Chris Bridge; *Dragons:* Morgan Escare.
Penalty count: 8-4; **Half-time:** 24-0;
Referee: James Child; **Attendance:** 8,816.

WIDNES VIKINGS 18
WAKEFIELD TRINITY WILDCATS 24

VIKINGS: 2 Jack Owens; 20 Paddy Flynn; 14 Chris Dean; 4 Stefan Marsh; 29 Declan Hulme; 6 Kevin Brown; 21 Danny Craven; 18 Paul Johnson; 9 Jon Clarke (C); 25 Alex Gerrard; 11 Dave Allen; 12 Danny Tickle; 24 Macgraff Leuluai. Subs (all used): 16 Willie Isa; 10 Ben Kavanagh; 15 Lloyd White; 35 Paul Clough.
Tries: Hulme (21, 42), Flynn (39); **Goals:** Tickle 3/5.
WILDCATS: 20 Jarrod Sammut; 1 Richard Mathers; 15 Matt Ryan; 22 Lucas Walshaw; 31 Chris Riley; 6 Paul Sykes; 29 Harry Siejka; 8 Scott Anderson; 9 Paul McShane; 30 Nick Scruton; 13 Danny Washbrook; 12 Danny Kirmond (C); 23 Daniel Smith. Subs (all used): 7 Pita Godinet; 16 Richard Moore; 26 Jon Molloy; 32 Jacob Fairbank.
Tries: Riley (8), Moore (18), Siejka (48), Sykes (79);
Goals: Sammut 4/5.
Rugby Leaguer & League Express Men of the Match: *Vikings:* Jack Owens; *Wildcats:* Nick Scruton.
Penalty count: 5-3; **Half-time:** 12-12;
Referee: Ben Thaler; **Attendance:** 5,186.

Saturday 10th May 2014

LONDON BRONCOS 16 HUDDERSFIELD GIANTS 30

BRONCOS: 6 Ben Farrar; 23 Denny Solomona; 24 Mason Caton-Brown; 4 Thomas Minns; 25 Iliess Macani; 9 Scott Moore; 7 Josh Drinkwater; 15 James Greenwood; 20 James Cunningham; 10 Olsi Krasniqi; 8 Atelea Vea; 12 Matt Cook (C); 13 Alex Foster. Subs (all used): 16 Nick Slyney; 30 Jon Wallace; 18 George Griffin; 14 Mike Bishay.
Tries: Vea (16), Foster (32), Solomona (36);
Goals: Drinkwater 2/4.

GIANTS: 27 Jake Connor; 2 Jermaine McGillvary; 3 Leroy Cudjoe; 4 Joe Wardle; 19 Jodie Broughton; 6 Danny Brough (C); 18 Kyle Wood; 8 Eorl Crabtree; 9 Shaun Lunt; 10 Craig Kopczak; 12 Jason Chan; 17 Ukuma Ta'ai; 13 Chris Bailey. Subs (all used): 14 Michael Lawrence; 15 Larne Patrick; 16 David Faiumu; 21 Anthony Mullally.
Tries: Lunt (7), Ta'ai (25, 43), Mullally (41), Cudjoe (80);
Goals: Brough 5/6.
Rugby Leaguer & League Express Men of the Match:
Broncos: Josh Drinkwater; *Giants:* Ukuma Ta'ai.
Penalty count: 10-10; **Half-time:** 16-10;
Referee: Tim Roby; **Attendance:** 1,035.

SALFORD RED DEVILS 16 HULL KINGSTON ROVERS 16

RED DEVILS: 1 Jake Mullaney; 2 Danny Williams; 3 Martin Gleeson; 4 Junior Sa'u; 5 Francis Meli; 6 Rangi Chase; 14 Theo Fages; 15 Darrell Griffin; 35 Logan Tomkins; 10 Lama Tasi; 13 Harrison Hansen; 12 Gareth Hock; 11 Tony Puletua. Subs (all used): 19 Matty Ashurst; 8 Adrian Morley (C); 18 Steve Rapira; 24 Stuart Howarth.
Tries: Meli (21, 55), Gleeson (64); **Goals:** Mullaney 2/3.
ROVERS: 2 Ben Cockayne; 5 David Hodgson; 3 Kris Welham; 18 Liam Salter; 32 Ade Gardner; 6 Travis Burns (C); 7 Kris Keating; 16 Jason Netherton; 9 Josh Hodgson (C); 10 Michael Weyman; 11 Kevin Larroyer; 20 Jordan Cox; 12 Neville Costigan. Subs (all used): 13 Jamie Langley; 23 James Green; 22 Rhys Lovegrove; 19 Craig Hall.
Tries: Welham (25), Larroyer (28), Costigan (58);
Goals: Burns 2/3.
Rugby Leaguer & League Express Men of the Match:
Red Devils: Junior Sa'u; *Rovers:* Travis Burns.
Penalty count: 6-6; **Half-time:** 4-10;
Referee: Phil Bentham; **Attendance:** 2,903.

Sunday 11th May 2014

BRADFORD BULLS 0 ST HELENS 50

BULLS: 2 Elliot Kear; 22 Sam Wood; 21 Adam Henry; 34 Joe Arundel; 5 Jamie Foster; 16 Danny Addy; 17 Lee Gaskell; 35 Antonio Kaufusi; 9 Matt Diskin (C); 15 Adam Sidlow; 11 Tom Olbison; 3 Adrian Purtell; 33 Jay Pitts. Subs (all used): 13 Chev Walker; 19 Adam O'Brien; 20 Luke George; 24 Alex Mellor.
SAINTS: 1 Jonny Lomax; 2 Tom Makinson; 4 Josh Jones; 26 Matty Dawson; 5 Adam Swift; 6 Lance Hohaia; 7 Luke Walsh; 25 Anthony Walker; 9 James Roby; 18 Alex Walmsley; 12 Jon Wilkin; 23 Joe Greenwood; 10 Louie McCarthy-Scarsbrook. Subs (all used): 8 Mose Masoe; 11 Iosia Soliola; 28 Luke Thompson; 17 Paul Wellens (C).
Tries: Wilkin (11, 39), Walsh (19), Lomax (21), Makinson (47), Swift (51), Soliola (64), McCarthy-Scarsbrook (71), Roby (75); **Goals:** Walsh 7/9.
Rugby Leaguer & League Express Men of the Match:
Bulls: Elliot Kear; *Saints:* Luke Walsh.
Penalty count: 6-4; **Half-time:** 0-22;
Referee: Matthew Thomason; **Attendance:** 6,311.

ROUND 13 - MAGIC WEEKEND

Saturday 17th May 2014

CATALAN DRAGONS 24 LONDON BRONCOS 22

DRAGONS: 2 Morgan Escare; 5 Michael Oldfield; 4 Ben Pomeroy; 25 Vincent Duport; 18 Daryl Millard; 3 Leon Pryce; 6 Thomas Bosc; 8 Olivier Elima; 16 Eloi Pelissier; 10 Jeff Lima; 11 Zeb Taia; 17 Elliott Whitehead; 24 Jason Baitieri (C). Subs (all used): 12 Louis Anderson; 20 Mickael Simon; 23 Lopini Paea; 32 Joan Guasch.
Tries: Duport (32), Whitehead (38, 70), Lima (57);
Goals: Bosc 4/4.
BRONCOS: 6 Ben Farrar; 3 Jordan Atkins; 24 Mason Caton-Brown; 23 Denny Solomona; 4 Thomas Minns; 20 James Cunningham; 7 Josh Drinkwater; 16 Nick Slyney; 9 Scott Moore; 10 Olsi Krasniqi; 8 Atelea Vea; 12 Matt Cook (C); 13 Alex Foster. Subs (all used): 15 James Greenwood; 14 Mike Bishay; 31 Maxime Herold (D); 30 Jon Wallace.
Tries: Caton-Brown (23, 63), Greenwood (65), Drinkwater (24); **Goals:** Drinkwater 3/4.
Rugby Leaguer & League Express Men of the Match:
Dragons: Elliott Whitehead;
Broncos: Mason Caton-Brown.
Penalty count: 9-6; **Half-time:** 12-6;
Referee: Matthew Thomason.

SALFORD RED DEVILS 24 WIDNES VIKINGS 30

RED DEVILS: 37 Greg Eden; 2 Danny Williams; 3 Martin Gleeson; 4 Junior Sa'u; 5 Francis Meli; 6 Rangi Chase; 1 Jake Mullaney; 15 Darrell Griffin; 35 Logan Tomkins; 10 Lama Tasi; 13 Harrison Hansen; 12 Gareth Hock; 11 Tony Puletua. Subs (all used): 8 Adrian Morley (C); 18 Steve Rapira; 24 Stuart Howarth; 19 Matty Ashurst.
Tries: Sa'u (18), Chase (21), Ashurst (42), Williams (54), Meli (74); **Goals:** Mullaney 2/4, Sa'u 0/1.
VIKINGS: 1 Rhys Hanbury; 20 Paddy Flynn; 14 Chris Dean; 4 Stefan Marsh; 2 Jack Owens; 6 Kevin Brown; 21 Danny Craven; 10 Ben Kavanagh; 9 Jon Clarke (C); 23 Phil Joseph; 11 Dave Allen; 12 Danny Tickle; 25 Alex Gerrard. Subs (all used): 15 Lloyd White; 24 Macgraff Leuluai; 16 Willie Isa; 18 Paul Johnson.
Tries: Flynn (5, 78), Owens (24), Dean (29), White (51), Hanbury (58); **Goals:** Tickle 3/7.
Rugby Leaguer & League Express Men of the Match:
Red Devils: Harrison Hansen; *Vikings:* Kevin Brown.
Penalty count: 7-9; **Half-time:** 12-12; **Referee:** Tim Roby.

Hull KR duo Neville Costigan and Ben Cockayne attempt to stop Hull FC's Iafeta Palea'aesina at the Magic Weekend

HULL FC 24 HULL KINGSTON ROVERS 38

HULL: 20 Jamie Shaul; 27 Liam Colbon; 34 Fetuli Talanoa; 4 Kirk Yeaman; 2 Jason Crookes; 32 Jordan Rankin; 7 Jacob Miller; 8 Mickey Paea; 9 Danny Houghton; 17 Liam Watts; 11 Gareth Ellis (C); 21 Dean Hadley; 13 Joe Westerman. Subs (all used): 33 Aaron Heremaia; 35 Garreth Carvell; 22 Josh Bowden; 26 Iafeta Palea'aesina.
Tries: Hadley (27), Shaul (39), Houghton (56), Palea'aesina (60); **Goals:** Miller 4/4.
Dismissal: Crookes (48) - high tackle on Salter.
ROVERS: 2 Ben Cockayne; 5 David Hodgson; 3 Kris Welham; 18 Liam Salter; 32 Ade Gardner; 6 Travis Burns (C); 7 Kris Keating; 16 Jason Netherton; 9 Josh Hodgson (C); 10 Michael Weyman; 11 Kevin Larroyer; 15 Graeme Horne; 12 Neville Costigan. Subs (all used): 23 James Green; 22 Rhys Lovegrove; 13 Jamie Langley; 17 Jonathan Walker.
Tries: Salter (10, 23), Larroyer (20), Gardner (50, 70), J Hodgson (79); **Goals:** Burns 7/7.
Rugby Leaguer & League Express Men of the Match:
Hull: Joe Westerman; *Rovers:* Travis Burns.
Penalty count: 7-5; **Half-time:** 12-18;
Referee: Richard Silverwood.

LEEDS RHINOS 14 WIGAN WARRIORS 18

RHINOS: 1 Zak Hardaker; 2 Ben Jones-Bishop; 21 Liam Sutcliffe; 4 Joel Moon; 5 Ryan Hall; 6 Danny McGuire; 13 Kevin Sinfield (C); 8 Kylie Leuluai; 12 Carl Ablett; 10 Jamie Peacock; 19 Mitch Achurch; 18 Chris Clarkson; 15 Brett Delaney. Subs (all used): 14 Stevie Ward; 16 Ryan Bailey; 17 Ian Kirke; 23 Brad Singleton.
Tries: Hall (28, 64), Ablett (58); **Goals:** Sinfield 1/3.
Sin bin: Bailey (24) - fighting.
On report: Brawl (24).
WARRIORS: 1 Matt Bowen; 32 Joe Burgess; 23 Dan Sarginson; 5 Anthony Gelling; 31 Dominic Manfredi; 6 Blake Green; 7 Matty Smith; 8 Scott Taylor; 27 George Williams; 16 Gil Dudson; 25 John Bateman; 14 Jack Hughes; 9 Michael McIlorum (C). Subs (all used): 3 Darrell Goulding; 17 Dominic Crosby; 19 Sam Powell; 37 Ryan Sutton.
Tries: Gelling (16), Green (38), McIlorum (55);
Goals: Smith 3/4.
Sin bin: McIlorum (24) - high tackle on Peacock; Bateman (24) - fighting.
On report: Brawl (24);
Crosby (33) - alleged dangerous tackle on Hall.
Rugby Leaguer & League Express Men of the Match:
Rhinos: Zak Hardaker; *Warriors:* Michael McIlorum.
Penalty count: 4-6; **Half-time:** 4-12; **Referee:** Ben Thaler.

Attendance: 36,339 *(at Etihad Stadium, Manchester).*

Sunday 18th May 2014

**CASTLEFORD TIGERS 50
WAKEFIELD TRINITY WILDCATS 12**

TIGERS: 1 Jordan Tansey; 2 Kirk Dixon; 4 Jake Webster; 3 Michael Shenton (C); 5 Justin Carney; 7 Marc Sneyd; 26 Liam Finn; 8 Andy Lynch; 14 Daryl Clark; 10 Craig Huby; 16 Oliver Holmes; 12 Weller Hauraki; 11 Grant Millington. Subs (all used): 18 Frankie Mariano; 19 Scott Wheeldon; 20 Jamie Ellis; 32 Lee Jewitt (D).
Tries: Clark (13, 79), Carney (17, 52), Tansey (21), Shenton (30), Sneyd (48, 62), Mariano (66);
Goals: Sneyd 7/9.
WILDCATS: 20 Jarrod Sammut; 1 Richard Mathers; 3 Dean Collis; 22 Lucas Walshaw; 31 Chris Riley; 6 Paul Sykes; 29 Harry Siejka; 8 Scott Anderson; 9 Paul McShane; 30 Nick Scruton; 15 Matt Ryan; 12 Danny Kirmond (C); 23 Daniel Smith. Subs (all used): 7 Pita Godinet; 16 Richard Moore; 13 Danny Washbrook; 32 Jacob Fairbank.
Tries: Scruton (57), Sykes (71); **Goals:** Sammut 2/2.
Rugby Leaguer & League Express Men of the Match:
Tigers: Marc Sneyd; *Wildcats:* Pita Godinet.
Penalty count: 5-4; **Half-time:** 22-0;
Referee: James Child.

BRADFORD BULLS 16 HUDDERSFIELD GIANTS 54

BULLS: 17 Lee Gaskell; 2 Elliot Kear; 20 Luke George; 21 Adam Henry; 5 Jamie Foster; 16 Danny Addy; 7 Luke Gale; 13 Chev Walker; 9 Matt Diskin (C); 15 Adam Sidlow; 11 Tom Olbison; 3 Adrian Purtell; 33 Jay Pitts. Subs (all used): 34 Joe Arundel; 19 Adam O'Brien; 22 Sam Wood; 24 Alex Mellor.
Tries: Addy (5), Foster (18, 77); **Goals:** Foster 2/3.
GIANTS: 1 Scott Grix; 19 Jodie Broughton; 3 Leroy Cudjoe; 4 Joe Wardle; 5 Aaron Murphy; 6 Danny Brough (C); 7 Luke Robinson; 8 Eorl Crabtree; 9 Shaun Lunt; 10 Craig Kopczak; 11 Brett Ferres; 12 Jason Chan; 17 Ukuma Ta'ai; 18 Kyle Wood; 21 Anthony Mullally.
Tries: Wardle (14), Lunt (25), Robinson (36), Broughton (38), Brough (53), Grix (57), Ta'ai (61), Mullally (67), Patrick (70); **Goals:** Brough 9/9.
Rugby Leaguer & League Express Men of the Match:
Bulls: Adrian Purtell; *Giants:* Danny Brough.
Penalty count: 3-4; **Half-time:** 10-24;
Referee: Robert Hicks.

ST HELENS 24 WARRINGTON WOLVES 41

SAINTS: 1 Jonny Lomax; 2 Tom Makinson; 3 Jordan Turner; 4 Josh Jones; 26 Matty Dawson; 6 Lance Hohaia; 7 Luke Walsh; 18 Alex Walmsley; 9 James Roby;

25 Anthony Walker; 12 Jon Wilkin; 23 Joe Greenwood; 10 Louie McCarthy-Scarsbrook. Subs (all used): 8 Mose Masoe; 11 Iosia Soliola; 17 Paul Wellens (C); 28 Luke Thompson.
Tries: Walmsley (38), Turner (52), Hohaia (58), Dawson (65); **Goals:** Walsh 4/4.
WOLVES: 1 Matthew Russell; 29 Gene Ormsby; 5 Joel Monaghan; 4 Ryan Atkins; 18 Rhys Evans; 3 Chris Bridge; 6 Stefan Ratchford; 8 Chris Hill; 14 Michael Monaghan (C); 19 Anthony England; 11 Trent Waterhouse; 12 Ben Westwood (C); 15 Ben Harrison. Subs (all used): 9 Mick Higham; 10 Roy Asotasi; 23 James Laithwaite; 25 Ben Evans.
Tries: Ormsby (7), R Evans (9, 24), Hill (21), Atkins (43), J Monaghan (46, 72), Russell (49);
Goals: Bridge 4/8; **Field goal:** Ratchford (69).
Sin bin: Ormsby (35) - professional foul.
Rugby Leaguer & League Express Men of the Match: *Saints:* Paul Wellens; *Wolves:* Stefan Ratchford.
Penalty count: 5-7; **Half-time:** 6-18;
Referee: Phil Bentham.

Attendance: 28,214 *(at Etihad Stadium, Manchester).*

ROUND 14

Thursday 22nd May 2014

SALFORD RED DEVILS 4 WIGAN WARRIORS 25

RED DEVILS: 37 Greg Eden; 2 Danny Williams; 3 Martin Gleeson; 4 Junior Sa'u; 5 Francis Meli; 6 Rangi Chase; 7 Tim Smith; 11 Tony Puletua; 35 Logan Tomkins; 10 Lama Tasi; 13 Harrison Hansen; 12 Gareth Hock; 18 Steve Rapira. Subs (all used): 8 Adrian Morley (C); 15 Darrell Griffin; 9 Tommy Lee; 19 Matty Ashurst.
Try: Meli (79); **Goals:** Smith 0/1.
WARRIORS: 26 Ryan Hampshire; 32 Joe Burgess; 23 Dan Sarginson; 5 Anthony Gelling; 31 Dominic Manfredi; 19 Sam Powell; 7 Matty Smith; 8 Scott Taylor; 9 Michael McIlorum (C); 16 Gil Dudson; 25 John Bateman; 14 Jack Hughes; 37 Ryan Sutton. Subs (all used): 3 Darrell Goulding; 17 Dominic Crosby; 27 George Williams; 28 Jordan James.
Tries: Bateman (40), Powell (46), Burgess (53, 74);
Goals: Smith 4/4; **Field goal:** Smith (71).
Rugby Leaguer & League Express Men of the Match: *Red Devils:* Rangi Chase; *Warriors:* Matty Smith.
Penalty count: 11-8; **Half-time:** 0-6;
Referee: Phil Bentham; **Attendance:** 3,706.

Friday 23rd May 2014

LEEDS RHINOS 20 HULL FC 6

RHINOS: 1 Zak Hardaker; 20 Tom Briscoe; 3 Kallum Watkins; 4 Joel Moon; 5 Ryan Hall; 13 Kevin Sinfield (C); 6 Danny McGuire; 8 Kylie Leuluai; 29 Robbie Ward (D); 23 Brad Singleton; 12 Carl Ablett; 19 Mitch Achurch; 18 Chris Clarkson. Subs (all used): 17 Ian Kirke; 15 Brett Delaney; 21 Liam Sutcliffe; 14 Stevie Ward.
Tries: Moon (21), Singleton (54), R Ward (71);
Goals: Sinfield 4/5.
HULL: 20 Jamie Shaul; 27 Liam Colbon; 34 Fetuli Talanoa; 4 Kirk Yeaman; 36 Callum Lancaster (D); 32 Jordan Rankin; 7 Jacob Miller; 8 Mickey Paea; 9 Danny Houghton; 17 Liam Watts; 11 Gareth Ellis (C); 21 Dean Hadley; 13 Joe Westerman. Subs (all used): 16 Jordan Thompson; 26 Iafeta Palea'aesina; 33 Aaron Heremaia; 28 Setaimata Sa (D).
Try: Shaul (79); **Goals:** Westerman 1/1.
Rugby Leaguer & League Express Men of the Match: *Rhinos:* Mitch Achurch; *Hull:* Gareth Ellis.
Penalty count: 5-3; **Half-time:** 6-0;
Referee: James Child; **Attendance:** 15,247.

ST HELENS 41 HUDDERSFIELD GIANTS 22

SAINTS: 17 Paul Wellens (C); 2 Tom Makinson; 3 Jordan Turner; 24 Gary Wheeler; 26 Matty Dawson; 6 Lance Hohaia; 7 Luke Walsh; 8 Mose Masoe; 9 James Roby; 10 Louie McCarthy-Scarsbrook; 12 Jon Wilkin; 15 Mark Flanagan; 11 Iosia Soliola. Subs (all used): 23 Joe Greenwood; 25 Anthony Walker; 27 Greg Richards; 28 Luke Thompson.
Tries: Wheeler (6, 66), Hohaia (10), Wellens (14), Dawson (26), Wilkin (43), Masoe (54);
Goals: Walsh 6/7; **Field goal:** Walsh (78).
GIANTS: 1 Scott Grix; 26 Ben Blackmore; 3 Leroy Cudjoe; 4 Joe Wardle; 5 Aaron Murphy; 6 Danny Brough (C); 7 Luke Robinson; 8 Eorl Crabtree; 9 Shaun Lunt; 10 Craig Kopczak; 11 Brett Ferres; 12 Jason Chan; 15 Larne Patrick. Subs (all used): 16 David Faiumu; 17 Ukuma Ta'ai; 18 Kyle Wood; 21 Anthony Mullally.
Tries: Patrick (18), Blackmore (44, 71), Ferres (55);
Goals: Brough 3/4.
Rugby Leaguer & League Express Men of the Match: *Saints:* Paul Wellens; *Giants:* Eorl Crabtree.
Penalty count: 5-5; **Half-time:** 22-6;
Referee: Richard Silverwood; **Attendance:** 10,218.

Saturday 24th May 2014

CATALAN DRAGONS 46 BRADFORD BULLS 4

DRAGONS: 2 Morgan Escare; 5 Michael Oldfield; 4 Ben Pomeroy; 25 Vincent Duport; 18 Daryl Millard; 3 Leon Pryce; 6 Thomas Bosc; 20 Mickael Simon; 16 Eloi Pelissier; 10 Jeff Lima; 11 Zeb Taia; 17 Elliott Whitehead; 8 Olivier Elima (C). Subs (all used): 12 Louis Anderson; 21 Julian Bousquet; 23 Lopini Paea; 27 Jean-Philippe Baile.
Tries: Escare (1, 42), Whitehead (11), Oldfield (13), Simon (49), Millard (55), Pryce (63), Taia (77);
Goals: Bosc 7/8.
BULLS: 17 Lee Gaskell; 2 Elliot Kear; 34 Joe Arundel; 3 Adrian Purtell; 5 Jamie Foster; 16 Danny Addy; 7 Luke Gale (C); 15 Adam Sidlow; 19 Adam O'Brien; 35 Antonio Kaufusi; 11 Tom Olbison; 33 Jay Pitts; 18 James Donaldson. Subs (all used): 14 Manase Manuokafoa; 21 Adam Henry; 25 Nathan Conroy; 36 Jordan Baldwinson (D).
Try: Foster (52); **Goals:** Foster 0/1.
On report: Kaufusi (40) - alleged dangerous challenge.
Rugby Leaguer & League Express Men of the Match: *Dragons:* Morgan Escare; *Bulls:* Adam O'Brien.
Penalty count: 8-8; **Half-time:** 18-0;
Referee: Tim Roby; **Attendance:** 6,890.

Sunday 25th May 2014

HULL KINGSTON ROVERS 48 LONDON BRONCOS 16

ROVERS: 2 Ben Cockayne; 5 David Hodgson; 3 Kris Welham; 18 Liam Salter; 32 Ade Gardner; 6 Travis Burns (C); 7 Kris Keating; 16 Jason Netherton; 9 Josh Hodgson (C); 10 Michael Weyman; 11 Kevin Larroyer; 15 Graeme Horne; 12 Neville Costigan. Subs (all used): 19 Craig Hall; 14 Adam Walker; 13 Jamie Langley; 17 Jonathan Walker.
Tries: J Hodgson (15, 79), Costigan (18), A Walker (30), Gardner (32, 62), Larroyer (57), Hall (66, 75);
Goals: Burns 6/9.
BRONCOS: 6 Ben Farrar; 3 Jordan Atkins; 24 Mason Caton-Brown; 4 Thomas Minns; 23 Denny Solomona; 20 James Cunningham; 7 Josh Drinkwater; 16 Nick Slyney; 9 Scott Moore; 10 Olsi Krasniqi; 8 Atelea Vea; 12 Matt Cook (C); 13 Alex Foster. Subs (all used): 18 George Griffin; 14 Mike Bishay; 15 James Greenwood; 11 Mike McMeeken.
Tries: Caton-Brown (25), Foster (47, 55);
Goals: Drinkwater 2/3.
Rugby Leaguer & League Express Men of the Match: *Rovers:* Neville Costigan; *Broncos:* James Cunningham.
Penalty count: 4-6; **Half-time:** 22-4;
Referee: Robert Hicks; **Attendance:** 7,439.

WAKEFIELD TRINITY WILDCATS 4 WARRINGTON WOLVES 36

WILDCATS: 20 Jarrod Sammut; 1 Richard Mathers; 15 Matt Ryan; 22 Lucas Walshaw; 33 Richard Owen (D); 6 Paul Sykes; 29 Harry Siejka; 8 Scott Anderson; 14 Matty Wildie; 30 Nick Scruton; 13 Danny Washbrook; 12 Danny Kirmond (C); 32 Jacob Fairbank. Subs (all used): 7 Pita Godinet; 16 Richard Moore; 21 Chris Annakin; 26 Jon Molloy.
Try: Walshaw (54); **Goals:** Sammut 0/1.
WOLVES: 1 Matthew Russell; 29 Gene Ormsby; 17 Ben Currie; 4 Ryan Atkins; 18 Rhys Evans; 6 Stefan Ratchford; 3 Chris Bridge; 8 Chris Hill; 9 Mick Higham; 19 Anthony England; 23 James Laithwaite; 12 Ben Westwood (C); 15 Ben Harrison. Subs (all used): 7 Richard Myler; 10 Roy Asotasi; 22 Brad Dwyer; 25 Ben Evans.
Tries: Ratchford (9), Currie (33, 36), Ormsby (39), Bridge (47), Atkins (73), Myler (76); **Goals:** Bridge 4/7.
On report: Westwood (4) - alleged dangerous challenge on Anderson.
Rugby Leaguer & League Express Men of the Match: *Wildcats:* Matt Ryan; *Wolves:* Ben Currie.
Penalty count: 11-10; **Half-time:** 0-18;
Referee: George Stokes; **Attendance:** 3,698.

CASTLEFORD TIGERS 34 WIDNES VIKINGS 22

TIGERS: 6 Luke Dorn; 2 Kirk Dixon; 4 Jake Webster; 3 Michael Shenton (C); 5 Justin Carney; 7 Marc Sneyd; 26 Liam Finn; 8 Andy Lynch; 14 Daryl Clark; 10 Craig Huby; 16 Oliver Holmes; 12 Weller Hauraki; 11 Grant Millington. Subs (all used): 18 Frankie Mariano; 19 Scott Wheeldon; 20 Jamie Ellis; 32 Lee Jewitt.
Tries: Shenton (6), Webster (21), Wheeldon (44), Dorn (46, 48), Clark (72); **Goals:** Sneyd 5/6.
Sin bin: Carney (45) - fighting.
VIKINGS: 1 Rhys Hanbury; 2 Jack Owens; 4 Stefan Marsh; 3 Cameron Phelps; 20 Paddy Flynn; 6 Kevin Brown (C); 27 Tom Gilmore; 35 Paul Clough; 15 Lloyd White; 25 Alex Gerrard; 11 Dave Allen; 12 Danny Tickle; 24 Macgraff Leuluai. Subs (all used): 28 Grant Gore; 16 Willie Isa; 18 Paul Johnson; 10 Ben Kavanagh.
Tries: Brown (12), Marsh (29), Phelps (75), Gilmore (77); **Goals:** Tickle 3/4.
Sin bin: Flynn (45) - fighting.
Rugby Leaguer & League Express Men of the Match: *Tigers:* Luke Dorn; *Vikings:* Kevin Brown.
Penalty count: 8-3; **Half-time:** 10-12;
Referee: Ben Thaler; **Attendance:** 5,576.

ROUND 15

Thursday 29th May 2014

HUDDERSFIELD GIANTS 31 WIGAN WARRIORS 22

GIANTS: 1 Scott Grix; 2 Jermaine McGillvary; 3 Leroy Cudjoe; 4 Joe Wardle; 5 Aaron Murphy; 6 Danny Brough (C); 18 Kyle Wood; 16 David Faiumu; 7 Luke Robinson; 23 Josh Johnson; 11 Brett Ferres; 14 Michael Lawrence; 13 Chris Bailey. Subs (all used): 8 Eorl Crabtree; 9 Shaun Lunt; 15 Larne Patrick; 17 Ukuma Ta'ai.
Tries: Murphy (23), Lunt (30), Wardle (33, 50), McGillvary (68); **Goals:** Brough 5/5;
Field goal: Brough (52).
WARRIORS: 1 Matt Bowen; 31 Dominic Manfredi; 3 Darrell Goulding; 5 Anthony Gelling; 32 Joe Burgess; 19 Sam Powell; 7 Matty Smith; 16 Gil Dudson; 27 George Williams; 17 Dominic Crosby; 25 John Bateman; 14 Jack Hughes; 13 Sean O'Loughlin (C). Subs (all used): 8 Scott Taylor; 20 Greg Burke; 26 Ryan Hampshire; 28 Jordan James.
Tries: O'Loughlin (12), Bowen (19), Manfredi (61), Burgess (78); **Goals:** Smith 3/4.
Rugby Leaguer & League Express Men of the Match: *Giants:* Brett Ferres; *Warriors:* John Bateman.
Penalty count: 5-10; **Half-time:** 18-12;
Referee: Ben Thaler; **Attendance:** 6,198.

Friday 30th May 2014

ST HELENS 32 SALFORD RED DEVILS 12

SAINTS: 17 Paul Wellens (C); 2 Tom Makinson; 3 Jordan Turner; 24 Gary Wheeler; 26 Matty Dawson; 6 Lance Hohaia; 7 Luke Walsh; 8 Mose Masoe; 9 James Roby; 10 Louie McCarthy-Scarsbrook; 12 Jon Wilkin; 15 Mark Flanagan; 11 Iosia Soliola. Subs (all used): 23 Joe Greenwood; 25 Anthony Walker; 27 Greg Richards; 28 Luke Thompson.
Tries: Wellens (16, 61), Soliola (28), Hohaia (30), Wheeler (50); **Goals:** Walsh 6/7.
RED DEVILS: 37 Greg Eden; 2 Danny Williams; 4 Junior Sa'u; 5 Francis Meli; 26 Niall Evalds; 6 Rangi Chase; 7 Tim Smith; 11 Tony Puletua; 35 Logan Tomkins; 10 Lama Tasi; 16 Andrew Dixon; 12 Gareth Hock; 18 Steve Rapira. Subs (all used): 8 Adrian Morley (C); 9 Tommy Lee; 15 Darrell Griffin; 21 Jordan Walne.
Tries: Evalds (46), Hock (68); **Goals:** Smith 2/2.
Rugby Leaguer & League Express Men of the Match: *Saints:* Paul Wellens; *Red Devils:* Niall Evalds.
Penalty count: 4-6; **Half-time:** 16-0;
Referee: Robert Hicks; **Attendance:** 10,391.

WARRINGTON WOLVES 24 LEEDS RHINOS 6

WOLVES: 1 Matthew Russell; 18 Rhys Evans; 5 Joel Monaghan; 4 Ryan Atkins; 29 Gene Ormsby; 6 Stefan Ratchford; 3 Chris Bridge; 8 Chris Hill; 14 Michael Monaghan (C); 19 Anthony England; 23 James Laithwaite; 17 Ben Currie; 15 Ben Harrison. Subs (all used): 7 Richard Myler; 9 Mick Higham; 10 Roy Asotasi; 25 Ben Evans.
Tries: Bridge (18, 34), Hill (31), J Monaghan (73);
Goals: Bridge 4/5.
On report:
Ratchford (48) - alleged dangerous challenge on Ablett.
RHINOS: 1 Zak Hardaker; 20 Tom Briscoe; 3 Kallum Watkins; 4 Joel Moon; 5 Ryan Hall; 6 Danny McGuire; 13 Kevin Sinfield (C); 8 Kylie Leuluai; 29 Robbie Ward; 10 Jamie Peacock; 19 Mitch Achurch; 12 Carl Ablett; 18 Chris Clarkson. Subs (all used): 14 Stevie Ward; 17 Ian Kirke; 21 Liam Sutcliffe; 23 Brad Singleton.
Try: Leuluai (60); **Goals:** Sinfield 1/1.
On report:
Ablett (73) - alleged use of the knee on J Monaghan.
Rugby Leaguer & League Express Men of the Match: *Wolves:* Michael Monaghan; *Rhinos:* Zak Hardaker.
Penalty count: 5-3; **Half-time:** 18-0;
Referee: James Child; **Attendance:** 10,312.

WIDNES VIKINGS 26 CATALAN DRAGONS 26

VIKINGS: 1 Rhys Hanbury; 14 Chris Dean; 3 Cameron Phelps; 4 Stefan Marsh; 2 Jack Owens; 6 Kevin Brown (C); 27 Tom Gilmore; 10 Ben Kavanagh; 15 Lloyd White; 35 Paul Clough; 17 Danny Galea; 12 Danny Tickle; 24 Macgraff Leuluai. Subs (all used): 19 Adam Lawton; 16 Willie Isa; 21 Danny Craven; 18 Paul Johnson.
Tries: Hanbury (17), White (28), Marsh (33), Owens (60), Gilmore (77); **Goals:** Tickle 3/5.
DRAGONS: 2 Morgan Escare; 5 Michael Oldfield; 4 Ben Pomeroy; 25 Vincent Duport; 18 Daryl Millard; 3 Leon Pryce; 6 Thomas Bosc; 20 Mickael Simon; 16 Eloi Pelissier; 10 Jeff Lima; 11 Zeb Taia; 17 Elliott Whitehead; 8 Olivier Elima (C). Subs (all used): 12 Louis Anderson; 21 Julian Bousquet; 27 Jean-Philippe Baile; 23 Lopini Paea.
Tries: Millard (7), Duport (11), Escare (48), Pryce (51), Oldfield (55); **Goals:** Bosc 3/5.
On report: Pelissier (72) - alleged dangerous challenge.
Rugby Leaguer & League Express Men of the Match: *Vikings:* Willie Isa; *Dragons:* Leon Pryce.
Penalty count: 8-4; **Half-time:** 16-10;
Referee: Phil Bentham; **Attendance:** 4,745.

Saturday 31st May 2014

LONDON BRONCOS 12 HULL FC 50

BRONCOS: 6 Ben Farrar; 3 Jordan Atkins; 24 Mason Caton-Brown; 4 Thomas Minns; 23 Denny Solomona; 1 Nesiasi Mataitonga; 7 Josh Drinkwater; 16 Nick Slyney; 9 Scott Moore; 15 James Greenwood; 8 Atelea Vea; 12 Matt Cook (C); 13 Alex Foster. Subs (all used): 30 Jon Wallace; 14 Mike Bishay; 11 Mike McMeeken; 18 George Griffin.
Tries: Greenwood (7), Caton-Brown (46);
Goals: Drinkwater 2/2.
Dismissal: Moore (38) - high tackle on Lancaster.
HULL: 20 Jamie Shaul; 34 Fetuli Talanoa; 3 Ben Crooks; 4 Kirk Yeaman; 36 Callum Lancaster; 32 Jordan Rankin; 7 Jacob Miller; 8 Mickey Paea; 9 Danny Houghton; 17 Liam Watts; 11 Gareth Ellis (C); 12 Chris Tuson; 13 Joe Westerman. Subs (all used): 33 Aaron Heremaia; 26 Iafeta Palea'aesina; 16 Jordan Thompson; 22 Josh Bowden.
Tries: Ellis (11), Lancaster (22, 68), Westerman (25, 65), Shaul (35), Houghton (60), Rankin (75), Talanoa (78); **Goals:** Miller 3/4, Rankin 4/5.
Rugby Leaguer & League Express Men of the Match: *Broncos:* George Griffin; *Hull:* Joe Westerman.
Penalty count: 13-4; **Half-time:** 6-22;
Referee: George Stokes; **Attendance:** 1,135.

Sunday 1st June 2014

BRADFORD BULLS 20
WAKEFIELD TRINITY WILDCATS 12

BULLS: 17 Lee Gaskell; 2 Elliot Kear; 4 Matty Blythe; 3 Adrian Purtell; 20 Luke George; 16 Danny Addy; 7 Luke Gale; 14 Manase Manuokafoa; 9 Matt Diskin (C); 35 Antonio Kaufusi; 11 Tom Olbison; 33 Jay Pitts; 13 Chev Walker. Subs (all used): 15 Adam Sidlow; 12 Dale Ferguson; 18 James Donaldson; 30 Jamal Fakir.
Tries: Purtell (11, 31), Olbison (19); **Goals:** Gale 4/5.
WILDCATS: 1 Richard Mathers; 33 Richard Owen; 15 Matt Ryan; 22 Lucas Walshaw; 31 Chris Riley; 20 Jarrod Sammut; 7 Pita Godinet; 8 Scott Anderson; 14 Matty Wildie; 30 Nick Scruton; 23 Daniel Smith; 12 Danny Kirmond (C); 13 Danny Washbrook. Subs (all used): 9 Paul McShane; 16 Richard Moore; 34 Lee Gilmour (D); 26 Jon Molloy.
Tries: Ryan (45, 77); **Goals:** Sammut 2/2.
Sin bin: Moore (52) - punching.
Rugby Leaguer & League Express Men of the Match:
Bulls: Luke Gale; *Wildcats:* Pita Godinet.
Penalty count: 10-5; **Half-time:** 16-0;
Referee: Richard Silverwood; **Attendance:** 6,249.

CASTLEFORD TIGERS 54 HULL KINGSTON ROVERS 12

TIGERS: 6 Luke Dorn; 2 Kirk Dixon; 23 Michael Channing; 3 Michael Shenton (C); 24 James Clare; 7 Marc Sneyd; 20 Jamie Ellis; 8 Andy Lynch; 9 Adam Milner; 10 Craig Huby; 16 Oliver Holmes; 12 Weller Hauraki; 11 Grant Millington. Subs (all used): 4 Jake Webster; 14 Daryl Clark; 19 Scott Wheeldon; 18 Frankie Mariano.
Tries: Channing (4, 30), Dorn (11, 34, 58), Millington (22), Dixon (29), Ellis (53), Webster (66), Huby (68), Clare (73); **Goals:** Sneyd 5/11.
ROVERS: 2 Ben Cockayne; 32 Ade Gardner; 15 Graeme Horne; 3 Kris Welham; 33 Wayne Ulugia; 6 Travis Burns (C); 7 Kris Keating; 14 Adam Walker; 9 Josh Hodgson (C); 10 Michael Weyman; 11 Kevin Larroyer; 20 Jordan Cox; 12 Neville Costigan. Subs (all used): 17 Jonathan Walker; 13 Jamie Langley; 23 James Green; 22 Rhys Lovegrove.
Tries: Burns (46), Ulugia (79); **Goals:** Burns 2/2.
Dismissal: Weyman (62) - dissent.
Rugby Leaguer & League Express Men of the Match:
Tigers: Daryl Clark; *Rovers:* Travis Burns.
Penalty count: 8-6; **Half-time:** 28-0;
Referee: Tim Roby; **Attendance:** 7,196.

ROUND 16

Thursday 12th June 2014

LEEDS RHINOS 22 HUDDERSFIELD GIANTS 24

RHINOS: 2 Ben Jones-Bishop; 20 Tom Briscoe; 3 Kallum Watkins; 4 Joel Moon; 5 Ryan Hall; 21 Liam Sutcliffe; 13 Kevin Sinfield (C); 8 Kylie Leuluai; 29 Robbie Ward; 10 Jamie Peacock; 14 Stevie Ward; 15 Brett Delaney; 16 Ryan Bailey. Subs (all used): 17 Ian Kirke; 28 Josh Walters; 30 Luke Briscoe (D); 18 Chris Clarkson.
Tries: Watkins (5), Jones-Bishop (18), Bailey (61), Sutcliffe (65); **Goals:** Sinfield 3/4.
GIANTS: 1 Scott Grix; 2 Jermaine McGillvary; 5 Aaron Murphy; 4 Joe Wardle; 19 Jodie Broughton; 6 Danny Brough (C); 18 Kyle Wood; 8 Eorl Crabtree; 7 Luke Robinson; 23 Josh Johnson; 11 Brett Ferres; 14 Michael Lawrence; 13 Chris Bailey. Subs (all used): 17 Ukuma Ta'ai; 15 Larne Patrick; 12 Jason Chan; 16 David Faiumu.
Tries: Wood (8), McGillvary (47), Crabtree (56), Wardle (58); **Goals:** Brough 4/4.
Rugby Leaguer & League Express Men of the Match:
Rhinos: Robbie Ward; *Giants:* Danny Brough.
Penalty count: 8-6; **Half-time:** 12-6;
Referee: Richard Silverwood; **Attendance:** 13,104.

Friday 13th June 2014

HULL KINGSTON ROVERS 4 WARRINGTON WOLVES 34

ROVERS: 1 Greg Eden; 32 Ade Gardner; 18 Liam Salter; 19 Craig Hall; 33 Wayne Ulugia; 6 Travis Burns (C); 7 Kris Keating; 14 Adam Walker; 9 Josh Hodgson (C); 10 Michael Weyman; 15 Graeme Horne; 13 Jamie Langley; 12 Neville Costigan. Subs (all used): 25 Aaron Ollett; 16 Jason Netherton; 17 Jonathan Walker; 23 James Green.
Try: Horne (58); **Goals:** Burns 0/1.
WOLVES: 1 Matthew Russell; 18 Rhys Evans; 5 Joel Monaghan; 4 Ryan Atkins; 29 Gene Ormsby; 3 Chris Bridge; 6 Stefan Ratchford; 8 Chris Hill; 9 Mick Higham (C); 25 Ben Evans; 13 Simon Grix; 17 Ben Currie; 15 Ben Harrison. Subs (all used): 10 Roy Asotasi; 21 Glenn Riley; 22 Brad Dwyer; 31 Joe Philbin (D).
Tries: Ormsby (30), Ratchford (34), J Monaghan (38, 78), B Evans (69), Atkins (73); **Goals:** Bridge 5/6.
Rugby Leaguer & League Express Men of the Match:
Rovers: Josh Hodgson; *Wolves:* Mick Higham.
Penalty count: 6-7; **Half-time:** 0-18;
Referee: Ben Thaler; **Attendance:** 6,850.

WAKEFIELD TRINITY WILDCATS 18
LONDON BRONCOS 10

WILDCATS: 1 Richard Mathers; 33 Richard Owen; 15 Matt Ryan; 22 Lucas Walshaw; 31 Chris Riley; 6 Paul Sykes; 35 Tim Smith (D2); 8 Scott Anderson; 9 Paul McShane; 30 Nick Scruton; 13 Danny Washbrook; 12 Danny Kirmond (C); 23 Daniel Smith. Subs (all used): 7 Pita Godinet; 17 Taulima Tautai; 26 Jon Molloy; 34 Lee Gilmour.
Tries: Kirmond (9), D Smith (63), Ryan (74);
Goals: Sykes 3/4.
On report: Scruton (65) - alleged high tackle on Macani.
BRONCOS: 25 Iliess Macani; 1 Nesiasi Mataitonga; 24 Mason Caton-Brown; 4 Thomas Minns; 27 Jamie O'Callaghan; 20 James Cunningham; 7 Josh Drinkwater; 16 Nick Slyney; 9 Scott Moore; 15 James Greenwood; 8 Atelea Vea; 12 Matt Cook (C); 13 Alex Foster. Subs (all used): 18 George Griffin; 10 Olsi Krasniqi; 17 Will Lovell; 30 Jon Wallace.
Tries: Macani (19), Minns (21); **Goals:** Drinkwater 1/2.
Rugby Leaguer & League Express Men of the Match:
Wildcats: Taulima Tautai; *Broncos:* Atelea Vea.
Penalty count: 6-5; **Half-time:** 4-10;
Referee: Robert Hicks; **Attendance:** 4,079.

WIDNES VIKINGS 6 HULL FC 56

VIKINGS: 1 Rhys Hanbury; 2 Jack Owens; 14 Chris Dean; 4 Stefan Marsh; 20 Paddy Flynn; 6 Kevin Brown; 27 Tom Gilmore; 18 Paul Johnson; 9 Jon Clarke (C); 10 Ben Kavanagh; 17 Danny Galea; 12 Danny Tickle; 24 Macgraff Leuluai. Subs (all used): 15 Lloyd White; 23 Phil Joseph; 13 Hep Cahill; 11 Dave Allen.
Try: Flynn (5); **Goals:** Tickle 1/2.
HULL: 20 Jamie Shaul; 34 Fetuli Talanoa; 3 Ben Crooks; 4 Kirk Yeaman; 36 Callum Lancaster; 6 Richard Horne; 32 Jordan Rankin; 8 Mickey Paea; 9 Danny Houghton; 17 Liam Watts; 11 Gareth Ellis (C); 12 Chris Tuson; 13 Joe Westerman. Subs (all used): 33 Aaron Heremaia; 26 Iafeta Palea'aesina; 28 Setaimata Sa; 16 Jordan Thompson.
Tries: Lancaster (8, 43, 71), Paea (13), Shaul (57, 75, 78), Horne (59), Rankin (67);
Goals: Rankin 10/10.
Rugby Leaguer & League Express Men of the Match:
Vikings: Paddy Flynn; *Hull:* Gareth Ellis.
Penalty count: 7-7; **Half-time:** 6-14;
Referee: Matthew Thomason; **Attendance:** 5,014.

WIGAN WARRIORS 46 CASTLEFORD TIGERS 6

WARRIORS: 1 Matt Bowen; 31 Dominic Manfredi; 23 Dan Sarginson; 5 Anthony Gelling; 32 Joe Burgess; 7 Matty Smith; 19 Sam Powell; 10 Ben Flower; 9 Michael McIlorum; 8 Scott Taylor; 12 Liam Farrell; 14 Jack Hughes; 13 Sean O'Loughlin (C). Subs (all used): 26 Ryan Hampshire; 17 Dominic Crosby; 28 Jordan James; 37 Ryan Sutton.
Tries: Manfredi (12, 79), Bowen (22), James (29), Burgess (35, 70), L Farrell (48), McIlorum (64);
Goals: Smith 7/8.
TIGERS: 6 Luke Dorn; 2 Kirk Dixon; 21 Ashley Gibson; 5 Justin Carney; 24 James Clare; 20 Jamie Ellis; 26 Liam Finn (C); 32 Lee Jewitt; 9 Adam Milner; 10 Craig Huby; 18 Frankie Mariano; 12 Weller Hauraki; 19 Scott Wheeldon. Subs (all used): 11 Grant Millington; 13 Nathan Massey; 16 Oliver Holmes; 28 Ben Reynolds.
Try: Gibson (74); **Goals:** Ellis 1/1.
Rugby Leaguer & League Express Men of the Match:
Warriors: Anthony Gelling; *Tigers:* Justin Carney.
Penalty count: 7-4; **Half-time:** 22-0;
Referee: Phil Bentham; **Attendance:** 11,914.

Saturday 14th June 2014

CATALAN DRAGONS 42 ST HELENS 0

DRAGONS: 2 Morgan Escare; 5 Michael Oldfield; 4 Ben Pomeroy; 25 Vincent Duport; 18 Daryl Millard; 3 Leon Pryce; 6 Thomas Bosc; 8 Olivier Elima; 16 Eloi Pelissier; 10 Jeff Lima; 11 Zeb Taia; 17 Elliott Whitehead; 24 Jason Baitieri (C). Subs (all used): 9 Ian Henderson; 12 Louis Anderson; 23 Lopini Paea; 29 Benjamin Garcia.
Tries: Duport (8, 55), Oldfield (38, 70, 80), Henderson (62), Bosc (68), Millard (76); **Goals:** Bosc 5/8.
Sin bin: Pelissier (79) - fighting.
SAINTS: 1 Jonny Lomax; 2 Tom Makinson; 3 Jordan Turner; 4 Josh Jones; 26 Matty Dawson; 24 Gary Wheeler; 7 Luke Walsh; 8 Mose Masoe; 9 James Roby; 10 Louie McCarthy-Scarsbrook; 11 Iosia Soliola; 15 Mark Flanagan; 17 Paul Wellens (C). Subs (all used): 13 Willie Manu; 18 Alex Walmsley; 22 Mark Percival; 28 Luke Thompson.
Sin bin: Walmsley (79) - fighting.
On report: Roby (10) - alleged dangerous contact on Elima; Soliola (60) - alleged high tackle on Baitieri.
Rugby Leaguer & League Express Men of the Match:
Dragons: Leon Pryce; *Saints:* James Roby.
Penalty count: 8-3; **Half-time:** 8-0;
Referee: James Child; **Attendance:** 9,864.

Sunday 15th June 2014

SALFORD RED DEVILS 46 BRADFORD BULLS 18

RED DEVILS: 26 Niall Evalds; 23 Greg Johnson; 22 Jason Walton; 4 Junior Sa'u; 5 Francis Meli; 6 Rangi Chase; 14 Theo Fages; 15 Darrell Griffin; 35 Logan Tomkins; 10 Lama Tasi; 16 Andrew Dixon; 12 Gareth Hock; 21 Jordan Walne. Subs (all used): 8 Adrian Morley (C); 9 Tommy Lee; 18 Steve Rapira; 11 Tony Puletua.
Tries: Tomkins (3), Sa'u (5, 36), Dixon (8), Chase (13, 25), Meli (67), Evalds (70); **Goals:** Chase 7/8.
On report: Chase (63) - alleged punching.
BULLS: 17 Lee Gaskell; 2 Elliot Kear; 3 Adrian Purtell; 21 Adam Henry; 20 Luke George; 16 Danny Addy; 7 Luke Gale; 14 Manase Manuokafoa; 9 Matt Diskin (C); 13 Chev Walker; 4 Matty Blythe; 11 Tom Olbison; 18 James Donaldson. Subs (all used): 19 Adam O'Brien; 15 Adam Sidlow; 30 Jamal Fakir; 36 Jordan Baldwinson.
Tries: Kear (22), Olbison (39), O'Brien (59);
Goals: Gale 3/3.
Rugby Leaguer & League Express Men of the Match:
Red Devils: Rangi Chase; *Bulls:* Adam Henry.
Penalty count: 5-8; **Half-time:** 34-12;
Referee: George Stokes *(replaced by Robert Hicks, 66)*;
Attendance: 3,407.

ROUND 2

Wednesday 18th June 2014

WIGAN WARRIORS 48 WIDNES VIKINGS 4

WARRIORS: 23 Dan Sarginson; 2 Josh Charnley; 3 Darrell Goulding; 5 Anthony Gelling; 32 Joe Burgess; 7 Matty Smith; 19 Sam Powell; 10 Ben Flower; 9 Michael McIlorum; 8 Scott Taylor; 12 Liam Farrell; 25 John Bateman; 13 Sean O'Loughlin (C). Subs (all used): 16 Gil Dudson; 36 Connor Farrell (D); 28 Jordan James; 41 Callum Wright (D).
Tries: L Farrell (1, 61), Charnley (14, 30, 35, 40, 55), O'Loughlin (26), C Farrell (75); **Goals:** Smith 6/9.
VIKINGS: 2 Jack Owens; 5 Patrick Ah Van; 21 Danny Craven; 3 Cameron Phelps; 20 Paddy Flynn; 6 Kevin Brown; 28 Grant Gore; 35 Paul Clough; 9 Jon Clarke (C); 25 Alex Gerrard; 17 Danny Galea; 12 Danny Tickle; 13 Hep Cahill. Subs (all used): 16 Willie Isa; 24 Macgraff Leuluai; 11 Dave Allen; 15 Lloyd White.
Try: Flynn (10); **Goals:** Tickle 0/1.
Rugby Leaguer & League Express Men of the Match:
Warriors: Dan Sarginson; *Vikings:* Jon Clarke.
Penalty count: 7-3; **Half-time:** 32-4;
Referee: James Child; **Attendance:** 11,638.

ROUND 17

Friday 20th June 2014

BRADFORD BULLS 18 HULL KINGSTON ROVERS 44

BULLS: 17 Lee Gaskell; 2 Elliot Kear; 3 Adrian Purtell; 4 Matty Blythe; 20 Luke George; 16 Danny Addy; 7 Luke Gale; 36 Jordan Baldwinson; 9 Matt Diskin (C); 15 Adam Sidlow; 33 Jay Pitts; 11 Tom Olbison; 18 James Donaldson. Subs (all used): 14 Manase Manuokafoa; 19 Adam O'Brien; 30 Jamal Fakir; 13 Chev Walker.
Tries: Kear (20), O'Brien (56), Addy (66); **Goals:** Gale 3/3.
ROVERS: 1 Greg Eden; 32 Ade Gardner; 3 Kris Welham; 19 Craig Hall; 5 David Hodgson; 6 Travis Burns (C); 7 Kris Keating; 16 Jason Netherton; 9 Josh Hodgson (C); 10 Michael Weyman; 15 Graeme Horne; 22 Rhys Lovegrove; 12 Neville Costigan. Subs (all used): 25 Aaron Ollett; 14 Adam Walker; 21 Keal Carlile; 23 James Green.
Tries: Burns (15), J Hodgson (35), Welham (39), Hall (42, 71), Eden (51, 79), A Walker (64);
Goals: Burns 6/8.
Rugby Leaguer & League Express Men of the Match:
Bulls: Elliot Kear; *Rovers:* Travis Burns.
Penalty count: 9-3; **Half-time:** 6-18;
Referee: Robert Hicks; **Attendance:** 5,601.

Saturday 21st June 2014

HUDDERSFIELD GIANTS 38 LONDON BRONCOS 22

GIANTS: 1 Scott Grix; 2 Jermaine McGillvary; 3 Leroy Cudjoe; 4 Joe Wardle; 19 Jodie Broughton; 6 Danny Brough (C); 18 Kyle Wood; 8 Eorl Crabtree; 7 Luke Robinson; 10 Craig Kopczak; 11 Brett Ferres; 14 Michael Lawrence; 13 Chris Bailey. Subs (all used): 12 Jason Chan; 15 Larne Patrick; 17 Ukuma Ta'ai; 23 Josh Johnson.
Tries: Grix (4), Ferres (15), McGillvary (22, 46), Wardle (27, 65), Broughton (63); **Goals:** Brough 5/7.
BRONCOS: 25 Iliess Macani; 23 Denny Solomona; 24 Mason Caton-Brown; 4 Thomas Minns; 27 Jamie O'Callaghan; 20 James Cunningham; 7 Josh Drinkwater; 15 James Greenwood; 9 Scott Moore; 16 Nick Slyney; 8 Atelea Vea; 12 Matt Cook (C); 13 Alex Foster. Subs (all used): 19 Erjon Dollapi; 18 George Griffin; 17 Will Lovell; 10 Olsi Krasniqi.
Tries: Cunningham (38), Drinkwater (54), Solomona (58), Caton-Brown (77); **Goals:** Drinkwater 3/4.
Rugby Leaguer & League Express Men of the Match:
Giants: Brett Ferres; *Broncos:* James Cunningham.
Penalty count: 4-9; **Half-time:** 22-6;
Referee: Tim Roby; **Attendance:** 4,849.

CATALAN DRAGONS 20 HULL FC 16

DRAGONS: 2 Morgan Escare; 5 Michael Oldfield; 4 Ben Pomeroy; 25 Vincent Duport; 18 Daryl Millard; 3 Leon Pryce; 6 Thomas Bosc; 20 Mickael Simon; 9 Ian Henderson; 10 Jeff Lima; 11 Zeb Taia; 17 Elliott Whitehead; 24 Jason Baitieri (C). Subs (all used): 13 Gregory Mounis (C); 21 Julian Bousquet; 29 Benjamin Garcia; 34 Sam Williams (D).
Tries: Escare (12), Oldfield (17), Garcia (38), Millard (47);
Goals: Bosc 2/5.
HULL: 20 Jamie Shaul; 5 Tom Lineham; 3 Ben Crooks; 4 Kirk Yeaman; 34 Fetuli Talanoa; 32 Jordan Rankin; 6 Richard Horne; 8 Mickey Paea; 33 Aaron Heremaia; 22 Josh Bowden; 11 Gareth Ellis (C); 12 Chris Tuson; 13 Joe Westerman. Subs (all used): 16 Jordan Thompson; 21 Dean Hadley; 26 Iafeta Palea'aesina; 28 Setaimata Sa.
Tries: Ellis (33), Yeaman (61), Shaul (64);
Goals: Rankin 2/3.
Rugby Leaguer & League Express Men of the Match:
Dragons: Leon Pryce; *Hull:* Jamie Shaul.
Penalty count: 7-7; **Half-time:** 16-4;
Referee: Phil Bentham; **Attendance:** 9,275.

Sunday 22nd June 2014

ST HELENS 38 CASTLEFORD TIGERS 16

SAINTS: 17 Paul Wellens (C); 2 Tom Makinson; 3 Jordan Turner; 22 Mark Percival; 26 Matty Dawson; 6 Lance Hohaia; 7 Luke Walsh; 8 Mose Masoe; 9 James

Roby; 10 Louie McCarthy-Scarsbrook; 12 Jon Wilkin; 15 Mark Flanagan; 11 Iosia Soliola. Subs (all used): 13 Willie Manu; 27 Greg Richards; 28 Luke Thompson; 33 Andre Savelio.
Tries: Makinson (5), Wellens (25, 40), Turner (29), Percival (46, 66), Walsh (64); **Goals:** Walsh 5/8.
TIGERS: 6 Luke Dorn; 2 Kirk Dixon; 4 Jake Webster; 3 Michael Shenton (C); 24 James Clare; 7 Marc Sneyd; 26 Liam Finn; 8 Andy Lynch; 14 Daryl Clark; 10 Craig Huby; 16 Oliver Holmes; 12 Weller Hauraki; 11 Grant Millington. Subs (all used): 13 Nathan Massey; 18 Frankie Mariano; 20 Jamie Ellis; 32 Lee Jewitt.
Tries: Dixon (22), Sneyd (73), Dorn (75);
Goals: Sneyd 2/3.
Rugby Leaguer & League Express Men of the Match: *Saints:* Paul Wellens; *Tigers:* Marc Sneyd.
Penalty count: 6-4; **Half-time:** 22-4;
Referee: Richard Silverwood; **Attendance:** 12,648.

WAKEFIELD TRINITY WILDCATS 36 WIGAN WARRIORS 28

WILDCATS: 1 Richard Mathers; 33 Richard Owen; 15 Matt Ryan; 5 Reece Lyne; 31 Chris Riley; 6 Paul Sykes; 35 Tim Smith; 8 Scott Anderson; 9 Paul McShane; 30 Nick Scruton; 34 Lee Gilmour; 12 Danny Kirmond (C); 13 Danny Washbrook. Subs (all used): 7 Pita Godinet; 17 Taulima Tautai; 16 Richard Moore; 23 Daniel Smith.
Tries: Kirmond (15), T Smith (31), Owen (33), Moore (40), Washbrook (67), Lyne (75);
Goals: Sykes 6/7.
WARRIORS: 23 Dan Sarginson; 2 Josh Charnley; 3 Darrell Goulding; 5 Anthony Gelling; 39 Jack Murphy; 19 Sam Powell; 7 Matty Smith (C); 8 Scott Taylor; 27 George Williams; 10 Ben Flower; 14 Jack Hughes; 12 Liam Farrell; 20 Greg Burke. Subs (all used): 28 Jordan James; 36 Connor Farrell; 37 Ryan Sutton; 41 Callum Wright.
Tries: Hughes (18), L Farrell (21, 47), Gelling (25), Sarginson (60); **Goals:** Smith 4/5.
On report: L Farrell (28) - alleged dangerous challenge.
Rugby Leaguer & League Express Men of the Match: *Wildcats:* Paul Sykes; *Warriors:* Liam Farrell.
Penalty count: 9-8; **Half-time:** 24-18;
Referee: George Stokes; **Attendance:** 4,096.

WARRINGTON WOLVES 36 SALFORD RED DEVILS 20

WOLVES: 1 Matthew Russell; 29 Gene Ormsby; 5 Joel Monaghan; 4 Ryan Atkins; 18 Rhys Evans; 3 Chris Bridge; 6 Stefan Ratchford; 8 Chris Hill; 9 Mick Higham; 25 Ben Evans; 13 Simon Grix; 12 Ben Westwood (C); 15 Ben Harrison. Subs (all used): 10 Roy Asotasi; 21 Glenn Riley; 22 Brad Dwyer; 17 Ben Currie.
Tries: Ormsby (6), Atkins (18), Bridge (23), J Monaghan (37), R Evans (67), Currie (80);
Goals: Bridge 6/7.
RED DEVILS: 26 Niall Evalds; 23 Greg Johnson; 22 Jason Walton; 4 Junior Sa'u; 5 Francis Meli; 6 Rangi Chase; 9 Tommy Lee; 8 Adrian Morley (C); 35 Logan Tomkins; 10 Lama Tasi; 16 Andrew Dixon; 19 Matty Ashurst; 21 Jordan Walne. Subs (all used): 15 Darrell Griffin; 18 Steve Rapira; 11 Tony Puletua; 36 Michael Platt.
Tries: Sa'u (2), Morley (44), Evalds (57, 74);
Goals: Chase 2/4.
Rugby Leaguer & League Express Men of the Match: *Wolves:* Ben Harrison; *Red Devils:* Niall Evalds.
Penalty count: 8-6; **Half-time:** 22-6;
Referee: James Child; **Attendance:** 10,120.

WIDNES VIKINGS 28 LEEDS RHINOS 38

VIKINGS: 1 Rhys Hanbury; 20 Paddy Flynn; 14 Chris Dean; 4 Stefan Marsh; 5 Patrick Ah Van; 7 Joe Mellor (C); 21 Danny Craven; 10 Ben Kavanagh; 15 Lloyd White; 25 Alex Gerrard; 19 Adam Lawton; 11 Dave Allen; 24 Macgraff Leuluai. Subs (all used): 16 Willie Isa; 18 Paul Johnson; 23 Phil Joseph; 28 Grant Gore.
Tries: Dean (20), Hanbury (29), Ah Van (40), Gore (71), Mellor (79); **Goals:** Ah Van 4/5.
On report: Leuluai (12) - alleged late challenge.
RHINOS: 2 Ben Jones-Bishop; 20 Tom Briscoe; 3 Kallum Watkins; 4 Joel Moon; 5 Ryan Hall; 13 Kevin Sinfield (C); 6 Danny McGuire; 16 Ryan Bailey; 29 Robbie Ward; 23 Brad Singleton; 15 Brett Delaney; 12 Carl Ablett; 21 Liam Sutcliffe. Subs (all used): 11 Jamie Jones-Buchanan; 17 Ian Kirke; 28 Josh Walters; 9 Paul Aiton.
Tries: Watkins (2), McGuire (12, 66), Sinfield (47), Sutcliffe (50), T Briscoe (61), Walters (74);
Goals: Sinfield 5/7.
Rugby Leaguer & League Express Men of the Match: *Vikings:* Joe Mellor; *Rhinos:* Brett Delaney.
Penalty count: 9-6; **Half-time:** 16-10;
Referee: Ben Thaler; **Attendance:** 5,543.

ROUND 18

Thursday 26th June 2014

HULL KINGSTON ROVERS 22 HUDDERSFIELD GIANTS 26

ROVERS: 1 Greg Eden; 32 Ade Gardner; 3 Kris Welham; 19 Craig Hall; 5 David Hodgson; 6 Travis Burns (C); 7 Kris Keating; 14 Adam Walker; 9 Josh Hodgson (C); 16 Jason Netherton; 15 Graeme Horne; 22 Rhys Lovegrove; 25 Aaron Ollett. Subs (all used): 21 Keal Carlile; 20 Jordan Cox; 10 Michael Weyman; 23 James Green.
Tries: D Hodgson (2, 79), Welham (17), Gardner (27);
Goals: Burns 3/5.
GIANTS: 1 Scott Grix; 2 Jermaine McGillvary; 3 Leroy Cudjoe; 4 Joe Wardle; 19 Jodie Broughton; 6 Danny Brough (C); 18 Kyle Wood; 23 Josh Johnson; 7 Luke Robinson; 10 Craig Kopczak; 11 Brett Ferres; 17 Ukuma Ta'ai; 14 Michael Lawrence. Subs (all used): 8 Eorl Crabtree; 13 Chris Bailey; 15 Larne Patrick; 16 David Faiumu.
Tries: Cudjoe (7), Ta'ai (21), Crabtree (33), Patrick (54, 67); **Goals:** Brough 3/5.
Rugby Leaguer & League Express Men of the Match: *Rovers:* Greg Eden; *Giants:* Danny Brough.
Penalty count: 11-10; **Half-time:** 16-16;
Referee: Ben Thaler; **Attendance:** 8,953.

Friday 27th June 2014

WIGAN WARRIORS 12 ST HELENS 16

WARRIORS: 1 Matt Bowen; 2 Josh Charnley; 5 Anthony Gelling; 23 Dan Sarginson; 32 Joe Burgess; 19 Sam Powell; 7 Matty Smith; 10 Ben Flower; 27 George Williams; 16 Gil Dudson; 14 Jack Hughes; 25 John Bateman; 13 Sean O'Loughlin (C). Subs (all used): 8 Scott Taylor; 17 Dominic Crosby; 28 Jordan James; 42 Jamie Doran (D).
Tries: Burgess (9), Charnley (58, 78); **Goals:** Smith 0/3.
SAINTS: 17 Paul Wellens (C); 2 Tom Makinson; 3 Jordan Turner; 22 Mark Percival; 5 Adam Swift; 6 Lance Hohaia; 7 Luke Walsh; 27 Greg Richards; 9 James Roby; 18 Alex Walmsley; 12 Jon Wilkin; 15 Mark Flanagan; 11 Iosia Soliola. Subs (all used): 13 Willie Manu; 10 Louie McCarthy-Scarsbrook; 28 Luke Thompson; 8 Mose Masoe.
Tries: Makinson (22, 66), Wellens (44);
Goals: Makinson 0/1, Percival 2/3.
Rugby Leaguer & League Express Men of the Match: *Warriors:* Matt Bowen; *Saints:* Jon Wilkin.
Penalty count: 11-5; **Half-time:** 4-4;
Referee: Phil Bentham; **Attendance:** 20,224.

Saturday 28th June 2014

LONDON BRONCOS 24 WIDNES VIKINGS 42

BRONCOS: 25 Iliess Macani; 27 Jamie O'Callaghan; 22 James Woodburn-Hall; 23 Denny Solomona; 5 James Duckworth; 33 Joe Keyes (D); 7 Josh Drinkwater; 16 Nick Slyney; 9 Scott Moore; 15 James Greenwood; 8 Atelea Vea; 13 Alex Foster; 12 Matt Cook (C). Subs (all used): 10 Olsi Krasniqi; 17 Will Lovell; 18 George Griffin; 19 Erjon Dollapi.
Tries: Solomona (40), Greenwood (68), Vea (70), Cook (80); **Goals:** Drinkwater 4/5.
VIKINGS: 1 Rhys Hanbury; 5 Patrick Ah Van; 3 Cameron Phelps; 14 Chris Dean; 20 Paddy Flynn; 6 Kevin Brown; 7 Joe Mellor; 23 Phil Joseph; 9 Jon Clarke (C); 10 Ben Kavanagh; 17 Danny Galea; 12 Danny Tickle; 13 Hep Cahill. Subs (all used): 16 Willie Isa; 28 Grant Gore; 24 Macgraff Leuluai; 11 Dave Allen.
Tries: Ah Van (9), Cahill (27), Galea (36), Hanbury (44, 74), Flynn (51, 64);
Goals: Tickle 5/5, Ah Van 2/2.
Rugby Leaguer & League Express Men of the Match: *Broncos:* Alex Foster; *Vikings:* Kevin Brown.
Penalty count: 4-2; **Half-time:** 8-18;
Referee: George Stokes; **Attendance:** 1,422.

CASTLEFORD TIGERS 14 SALFORD RED DEVILS 10

TIGERS: 6 Luke Dorn; 2 Kirk Dixon; 4 Jake Webster; 3 Michael Shenton (C); 5 Justin Carney; 7 Marc Sneyd; 26 Liam Finn; 8 Andy Lynch; 14 Daryl Clark; 10 Craig Huby; 11 Grant Millington; 12 Weller Hauraki; 19 Scott Wheeldon. Subs (all used): 9 Adam Milner; 18 Frankie Mariano; 32 Lee Jewitt; 35 Garreth Carvell (D).
Tries: Carney (29), Webster (80); **Goals:** Sneyd 3/3.
RED DEVILS: 26 Niall Evalds; 39 Josh Griffin (D); 5 Francis Meli; 4 Junior Sa'u; 23 Greg Johnson; 6 Rangi Chase; 14 Theo Fages; 8 Adrian Morley (C); 9 Tommy Lee; 10 Lama Tasi; 19 Matty Ashurst; 12 Gareth Hock; 11 Tony Puletua. Subs (all used): 21 Jordan Walne; 18 Steve Rapira; 35 Logan Tomkins; 22 Jason Walton.
Tries: Sa'u (65), Hock (70); **Goals:** Chase 1/2.
Rugby Leaguer & League Express Men of the Match: *Tigers:* Daryl Clark; *Red Devils:* Niall Evalds.
Penalty count: 6-10; **Half-time:** 6-0;
Referee: Tim Roby; **Attendance:** 5,937.

Sunday 29th June 2014

LEEDS RHINOS 32 CATALAN DRAGONS 31

RHINOS: 2 Ben Jones-Bishop; 20 Tom Briscoe; 3 Kallum Watkins; 4 Joel Moon; 5 Ryan Hall; 6 Danny McGuire; 21 Liam Sutcliffe; 23 Brad Singleton; 9 Paul Aiton; 10 Jamie Peacock (C); 15 Brett Delaney; 12 Carl Ablett; 16 Ryan Bailey. Subs (all used): 19 Mitch Achurch; 28 Josh Walters; 14 Stevie Ward; 30 Luke Briscoe.
Tries: Hall (8), Jones-Bishop (19), Walters (37), Moon (52, 65), Ablett (58); **Goals:** Sutcliffe 4/7.
On report: Delaney (15) - alleged late challenge on Pryce.
DRAGONS: 2 Morgan Escare; 5 Michael Oldfield; 4 Ben Pomeroy; 25 Vincent Duport; 18 Daryl Millard; 3 Leon Pryce; 34 Sam Williams; 8 Olivier Elima; 9 Ian Henderson; 10 Jeff Lima; 11 Zeb Taia; 17 Elliott Whitehead; 24 Jason Baitieri (C). Subs (all used): 29 Benjamin Garcia; 12 Louis Anderson; 16 Eloi Pelissier; 13 Gregory Mounis (C).
Tries: Escare (2), Taia (23, 43), Pelissier (31), Millard (69); **Goals:** Williams 5/6; **Field goal:** Escare (76).
On report: Mounis (36) - alleged high tackle on Peacock.
Rugby Leaguer & League Express Men of the Match: *Rhinos:* Jamie Peacock; *Dragons:* Sam Williams.
Penalty count: 10-8; **Half-time:** 14-20;
Referee: Robert Hicks; **Attendance:** 13,888.

WAKEFIELD TRINITY WILDCATS 20 HULL FC 20

WILDCATS: 1 Richard Mathers; 33 Richard Owen; 15 Matt Ryan; 5 Reece Lyne; 31 Chris Riley; 6 Paul Sykes; 35 Tim Smith; 8 Scott Anderson; 9 Paul McShane; 30 Nick Scruton; 34 Lee Gilmour; 12 Danny Kirmond (C); 13 Danny Washbrook. Subs (all used): 7 Pita Godinet; 17 Taulima Tautai; 16 Richard Moore; 23 Daniel Smith.
Tries: Mathers (40), Riley (54), Lyne (59), Scruton (72);
Goals: Sykes 2/4.
HULL: 20 Jamie Shaul; 5 Tom Lineham; 28 Setaimata Sa; 4 Kirk Yeaman; 34 Fetuli Talanoa; 37 Jordan Abdull (D); 6 Richard Horne; 8 Mickey Paea; 9 Danny Houghton; 17 Liam Watts; 11 Gareth Ellis (C); 12 Chris Tuson; 13 Joe Westerman. Subs (all used): 26 Iafeta Palea'aesina; 16 Jordan Thompson; 33 Aaron Heremaia; 14 Richard Whiting.
Tries: Sa (34), Horne (48), Yeaman (57, 79);
Goals: Abdull 1/3, Westerman 1/1.
Rugby Leaguer & League Express Men of the Match: *Wildcats:* Pita Godinet; *Hull:* Aaron Heremaia.
Penalty count: 7-9; **Half-time:** 6-6;
Referee: Richard Silverwood; **Attendance:** 5,168.

WARRINGTON WOLVES 50 BRADFORD BULLS 24

WOLVES: 1 Matthew Russell; 29 Gene Ormsby; 5 Joel Monaghan; 4 Ryan Atkins; 18 Rhys Evans; 6 Stefan Ratchford; 20 Gareth O'Brien; 10 Roy Asotasi; 9 Mick Higham; 12 Ben Westwood (C); 13 Simon Grix; 17 Ben Currie; 15 Ben Harrison. Subs (all used): 19 Anthony England; 21 Glenn Riley; 22 Brad Dwyer; 33 George King (D).
Tries: Harrison (5), Atkins (7), O'Brien (13, 65), J Monaghan (41, 47), Westwood (45), Ormsby (50), R Evans (70); **Goals:** Ratchford 7/9.
BULLS: 1 Brett Kearney; 2 Elliot Kear; 21 Adam Henry; 3 Adrian Purtell; 4 Matty Blythe; 17 Lee Gaskell; 7 Luke Gale; 14 Manase Manuokafoa; 9 Matt Diskin (C); 15 Adam Sidlow; 11 Tom Olbison; 33 Jay Pitts; 16 Danny Addy. Subs (all used): 36 Jordan Baldwinson; 19 Adam O'Brien; 13 Chev Walker; 18 James Donaldson.
Tries: Kearney (35), Purtell (50), Olbison (74), Pitts (79);
Goals: Gale 4/4.
Rugby Leaguer & League Express Men of the Match: *Wolves:* Stefan Ratchford; *Bulls:* Brett Kearney.
Penalty count: 4-7; **Half-time:** 16-6;
Referee: Matthew Thomason; **Attendance:** 9,003.

ROUND 19

Thursday 3rd July 2014

WIDNES VIKINGS 20 CASTLEFORD TIGERS 40

VIKINGS: 1 Rhys Hanbury; 5 Patrick Ah Van; 3 Cameron Phelps; 14 Chris Dean; 20 Paddy Flynn; 6 Kevin Brown; 7 Joe Mellor; 25 Alex Gerrard; 9 Jon Clarke (C); 10 Ben Kavanagh; 17 Danny Galea; 12 Danny Tickle; 13 Hep Cahill. Subs (all used): 16 Willie Isa; 15 Lloyd White; 11 Dave Allen; 24 Macgraff Leuluai.
Tries: Flynn (14), Galea (32), Ah Van (50), Dean (76);
Goals: Tickle 2/3, Ah Van 0/1.
TIGERS: 6 Luke Dorn; 2 Kirk Dixon; 23 Michael Channing; 3 Michael Shenton (C); 5 Justin Carney; 7 Marc Sneyd; 20 Jamie Ellis; 8 Andy Lynch; 14 Daryl Clark; 10 Craig Huby; 16 Oliver Holmes; 12 Weller Hauraki; 11 Grant Millington. Subs (all used): 9 Adam Milner; 13 Nathan Massey; 32 Lee Jewitt; 35 Garreth Carvell.
Tries: Dorn (2), Holmes (4), Clark (10, 62, 74), Shenton (35, 67); **Goals:** Sneyd 6/7.
Rugby Leaguer & League Express Men of the Match: *Vikings:* Danny Tickle; *Tigers:* Daryl Clark.
Penalty count: 6-4; **Half-time:** 12-22;
Referee: Phil Bentham; **Attendance:** 4,567.

Friday 4th July 2014

HULL FC 18 WARRINGTON WOLVES 24

HULL: 20 Jamie Shaul; 36 Callum Lancaster; 28 Setaimata Sa; 4 Kirk Yeaman; 34 Fetuli Talanoa; 6 Richard Horne; 37 Jordan Abdull; 17 Liam Watts; 9 Danny Houghton; 22 Josh Bowden; 11 Gareth Ellis (C); 12 Chris Tuson; 13 Joe Westerman. Subs (all used): 33 Aaron Heremaia; 8 Mickey Paea; 16 Jordan Thompson; 26 Iafeta Palea'aesina.
Tries: Lancaster (17, 55, 77);
Goals: Abdull 1/2, Westerman 2/3.
WOLVES: 1 Matthew Russell; 29 Gene Ormsby; 5 Joel Monaghan; 4 Ryan Atkins; 18 Rhys Evans; 3 Chris Bridge; 20 Gareth O'Brien; 8 Chris Hill; 9 Mick Higham; 15 Ben Harrison; 12 Ben Westwood (C); 17 Ben Currie; 6 Stefan Ratchford. Subs (all used): 19 Anthony England; 10 Roy Asotasi; 22 Brad Dwyer; 33 George King.
Tries: Ratchford (30), Atkins (39), Harrison (59), Ormsby (66); **Goals:** Bridge 4/5.
Rugby Leaguer & League Express Men of the Match: *Hull:* Callum Lancaster; *Wolves:* Matthew Russell.
Penalty count: 7-8; **Half-time:** 8-12;
Referee: Ben Thaler; **Attendance:** 12,328.

WAKEFIELD TRINITY WILDCATS 16 LEEDS RHINOS 14

WILDCATS: 1 Richard Mathers (C); 33 Richard Owen; 5 Reece Lyne; 19 Jimmy Keinhorst; 31 Chris Riley; 6 Paul Sykes; 35 Tim Smith; 10 Andy Raleigh; 9 Paul McShane; 30 Nick Scruton; 34 Lee Gilmour; 15 Matt Ryan; 13 Danny Washbrook. Subs (all used): 7 Pita Godinet; 17 Taulima Tautai; 16 Richard Moore; 23 Daniel Smith.
Tries: Washbrook (16), Mathers (53), Owen (78);
Goals: Sykes 2/3.
RHINOS: 2 Ben Jones-Bishop; 20 Tom Briscoe; 3 Kallum Watkins; 4 Joel Moon; 5 Ryan Hall; 21 Liam Sutcliffe; 6 Danny McGuire (C); 16 Ryan Bailey; 9 Paul Aiton; 10 Jamie Peacock; 14 Stevie Ward; 15 Brett Delaney; 28 Josh Walters. Subs (all used): 23 Brad Singleton; 26 Elliot Minchella; 27 Rob Mulhern; 29 Robbie Ward.

Tries: Watkins (33), Jones-Bishop (38), Hall (69);
Goals: Sutcliffe 1/3.
Rugby Leaguer & League Express Men of the Match:
Wildcats: Richard Mathers; *Rhinos:* Ben Jones-Bishop.
Penalty count: 5-6; **Half-time:** 6-8;
Referee: Matthew Thomason; **Attendance:** 4,634.

Saturday 5th July 2014

HUDDERSFIELD GIANTS 10 SALFORD RED DEVILS 36

GIANTS: 1 Scott Grix; 2 Jermaine McGillvary; 3 Leroy
Cudjoe; 4 Joe Wardle; 19 Jodie Broughton; 6 Danny
Brough (C); 18 Kyle Wood; 10 Craig Kopczak; 7 Luke
Robinson; 23 Josh Johnson; 11 Brett Ferres; 17 Ukuma
Ta'ai; 14 Michael Lawrence. Subs (all used): 8 Eorl
Crabtree; 13 Chris Bailey; 15 Larne Patrick; 16 David
Faiumu.
Tries: Wardle (20), Patrick (72);
Goals: Brough 0/1, Cudjoe 1/1.
RED DEVILS: 38 Kevin Locke (D); 23 Greg Johnson; 4
Junior Sa'u; 40 Mason Caton-Brown (D); 39 Josh Griffin;
6 Rangi Chase; 14 Theo Fages; 8 Adrian Morley (C); 9
Tommy Lee; 10 Lama Tasi; 19 Matty Ashurst; 21 Jordan
Walne; 11 Tony Puletua. Subs (all used): 18 Steve Rapira;
22 Jason Walton; 15 Darrell Griffin; 26 Niall Evalds.
Tries: Chase (11), Ashurst (15), Caton-Brown (50),
Fages (63), Johnson (65), Locke (69); **Goals:** Locke 6/6.
Dismissal: Tasi (60) - late challenge on Brough.
Rugby Leaguer & League Express Men of the Match:
Giants: Brett Ferres; *Red Devils:* Rangi Chase.
Penalty count: 6-7; **Half-time:** 4-12;
Referee: Robert Hicks; **Attendance:** 5,689.

LONDON BRONCOS 6 WIGAN WARRIORS 58

BRONCOS: 6 Ben Farrar; 25 Iliess Macani; 4 Thomas
Minns; 23 Denny Solomona; 27 Jamie O'Callaghan; 20
James Cunningham; 7 Josh Drinkwater; 16 Nick Slyney;
9 Scott Moore; 10 Olsi Krasniqi; 8 Atelea Vea; 13 Alex
Foster; 12 Matt Cook (C). Subs (all used): 21 Joel Wicks;
30 Jon Wallace; 18 George Griffin; 31 Maxime Herold.
Try: Minns (38); **Goals:** Drinkwater 1/1.
WARRIORS: 1 Matt Bowen; 2 Josh Charnley; 23 Dan
Sarginson; 5 Anthony Gelling; 32 Joe Burgess; 7 Matty
Smith (C); 27 George Williams; 17 Dominic Crosby; 19
Sam Powell; 16 Gil Dudson; 25 John Bateman; 12 Liam
Farrell; 24 Tony Clubb. Subs (all used): 8 Scott Taylor;
14 Jack Hughes; 20 Greg Burke; 22 Eddy Pettybourne.
Tries: Charnley (15, 30, 66), Bowen (24), Bateman (27),
Gelling (46), Taylor (54), Dudson (59), Burgess (73, 76);
Goals: Smith 9/10.
Rugby Leaguer & League Express Men of the Match:
Broncos: James Cunningham; *Warriors:* Josh Charnley.
Penalty count: 11-3; **Half-time:** 6-22;
Referee: Joe Cobb; **Attendance:** 2,013.

Sunday 6th July 2014

BRADFORD BULLS 30 CATALAN DRAGONS 32

BULLS: 1 Brett Kearney; 38 Danny Williams (D); 21
Adam Henry; 3 Adrian Purtell; 4 Matty Blythe; 17 Lee
Gaskell; 7 Luke Gale; 14 Manase Manuokafoa; 9 Matt
Diskin (C); 15 Adam Sidlow; 33 Jay Pitts; 11 Tom
Olbison; 18 James Donaldson. Subs (all used): 19 Adam
O'Brien; 30 Jamal Fakir; 16 Danny Addy; 13 Chev Walker.
Tries: Olbison (8), Henry (22), Fakir (25), Gale (42, 70);
Goals: Gale 5/6.
DRAGONS: 2 Morgan Escare; 5 Michael Oldfield; 4 Ben
Pomeroy; 25 Vincent Duport; 18 Daryl Millard; 3 Leon
Pryce; 34 Sam Williams; 8 Olivier Elima; 9 Ian
Henderson; 10 Jeff Lima; 11 Zeb Taia; 17 Elliott
Whitehead; 24 Jason Baitieri (C). Subs (all used): 13
Gregory Mounis (C); 16 Eloi Pelissier; 21 Julian
Bousquet; 29 Benjamin Garcia.
Tries: Escare (14), Duport (35), Pomeroy (48),
Bousquet (55), Whitehead (76); **Goals:** Williams 6/6.
Rugby Leaguer & League Express Men of the Match:
Bulls: Luke Gale; *Dragons:* Leon Pryce.
Penalty count: 6-6; **Half-time:** 18-12;
Referee: George Stokes; **Attendance:** 5,188.

HULL KINGSTON ROVERS 40 ST HELENS 10

ROVERS: 1 Greg Eden; 24 Omari Caro; 3 Kris Welham; 19
Craig Hall; 5 David Hodgson; 6 Travis Burns (C); 7 Kris
Keating; 16 Jason Netherton; 9 Josh Hodgson (C); 10
Michael Weyman; 15 Graeme Horne; 22 Rhys Lovegrove;
25 Aaron Ollett. Subs (all used): 21 Keal Carlile; 11 Kevin
Larroyer; 20 Jordan Cox; 23 James Green.
Tries: Caro (6, 22, 60), Hall (32, 68, 71), Horne (55),
Eden (76); **Goals:** Burns 4/8.
SAINTS: 17 Paul Wellens (C); 2 Tom Makinson; 3 Jordan
Turner; 22 Mark Percival; 5 Adam Swift; 6 Lance Hohaia;
12 Jon Wilkin; 27 Greg Richards; 9 James Roby; 18 Alex
Walmsley; 13 Willie Manu; 15 Mark Flanagan; 11 Iosia
Soliola. Subs (all used): 8 Mose Masoe; 10 Louie
McCarthy-Scarsbrook; 4 Josh Jones; 28 Luke Thompson.
Tries: Percival (8), Masoe (35); **Goals:** Percival 1/2.
Rugby Leaguer & League Express Men of the Match:
Rovers: Travis Burns; *Saints:* Louie McCarthy-Scarsbrook.
Penalty count: 4-3; **Half-time:** 14-10;
Referee: James Child; **Attendance:** 7,611.

ROUND 20

Thursday 10th July 2014

WAKEFIELD TRINITY WILDCATS 12
WIDNES VIKINGS 10

WILDCATS: 1 Richard Mathers (C); 33 Richard Owen; 19

Castleford's Marc Sneyd takes on Huddersfield's Michael Lawrence

Jimmy Keinhorst; 5 Reece Lyne; 31 Chris Riley; 6 Paul
Sykes; 35 Tim Smith; 16 Richard Moore; 14 Matty
Wildie; 30 Nick Scruton; 34 Lee Gilmour; 15 Matt Ryan;
13 Danny Washbrook. Subs (all used): 9 Paul McShane;
17 Taulima Tautai; 11 Ali Lauititi; 10 Andy Raleigh.
Tries: T Smith (49), Scruton (55); **Goals:** Sykes 2/2.
VIKINGS: 1 Rhys Hanbury; 5 Patrick Ah Van; 14 Chris
Dean; 4 Stefan Marsh; 20 Paddy Flynn; 6 Kevin Brown; 7
Joe Mellor; 13 Hep Cahill; 9 Jon Clarke (C); 25 Alex
Gerrard; 17 Danny Galea; 12 Danny Tickle; 24 Macgraff
Leuluai. Subs (all used): 15 Lloyd White; 16 Willie Isa;
23 Phil Joseph; 11 Dave Allen.
Tries: Tickle (18), Marsh (68); **Goals:** Tickle 1/2.
Rugby Leaguer & League Express Men of the Match:
Wildcats: Paul McShane; *Vikings:* Rhys Hanbury.
Penalty count: 6-7; **Half-time:** 0-4;
Referee: Ben Thaler; **Attendance:** 3,932.

Friday 11th July 2014

CASTLEFORD TIGERS 44 HUDDERSFIELD GIANTS 30

TIGERS: 7 Marc Sneyd; 2 Kirk Dixon; 4 Jake Webster; 3
Michael Shenton (C); 5 Justin Carney; 20 Jamie Ellis; 26
Liam Finn; 8 Andy Lynch; 14 Daryl Clark; 10 Craig Huby;
16 Oliver Holmes; 18 Frankie Mariano; 11 Grant
Millington. Subs (all used): 9 Adam Milner; 13 Nathan
Massey; 19 Scott Wheeldon; 32 Lee Jewitt.
Tries: Holmes (9), Carney (25), Finn (40, 53), Milner (45),
Dixon (47), Mariano (67), Millington (78);
Goals: Sneyd 6/8.
GIANTS: 27 Jake Connor; 2 Jermaine McGillvary; 3 Leroy
Cudjoe; 4 Joe Wardle; 19 Jodie Broughton; 18 Kyle Wood;
7 Luke Robinson; 20 Antonio Kaufusi; 13 Chris Bailey; 21
Anthony Mullally; 11 Brett Ferres (C); 15 Larne Patrick; 14
Michael Lawrence. Subs (all used): 8 Eorl Crabtree; 10
Craig Kopczak; 17 Ukuma Ta'ai; 28 Kruise Leeming.
Tries: Bailey (4, 60), Cudjoe (12), Wardle (57),
Crabtree (72); **Goals:** Cudjoe 5/5.
Rugby Leaguer & League Express Men of the Match:
Tigers: Liam Finn; *Giants:* Joe Wardle.
Penalty count: 7-3; **Half-time:** 16-12;
Referee: Richard Silverwood; **Attendance:** 5,310.

LEEDS RHINOS 30 HULL KINGSTON ROVERS 6

RHINOS: 2 Ben Jones-Bishop; 20 Tom Briscoe; 3 Kallum
Watkins; 4 Joel Moon; 5 Ryan Hall; 13 Kevin Sinfield
(C); 6 Danny McGuire; 15 Brett Delaney; 9 Paul Aiton; 10
Jamie Peacock; 12 Carl Ablett; 14 Stevie Ward; 28 Josh
Walters. Subs (all used): 21 Liam Sutcliffe; 7 Rob
Burrow; 19 Mitch Achurch; 27 Rob Mulhern.
Tries: Burrow (59, 77), Sutcliffe (62), Ablett (65),
McGuire (74); **Goals:** Sinfield 5/5.
ROVERS: 1 Greg Eden; 24 Omari Caro; 3 Kris Welham;
19 Craig Hall; 18 Liam Salter; 6 Travis Burns (C); 7 Kris

Keating; 16 Jason Netherton; 9 Josh Hodgson (C); 10
Michael Weyman; 15 Graeme Horne; 22 Rhys Lovegrove;
12 Neville Costigan. Subs (all used): 11 Kevin Larroyer;
14 Adam Walker; 23 James Green; 21 Keal Carlile.
Try: J Hodgson (67); **Goals:** Burns 1/1.
Rugby Leaguer & League Express Men of the Match:
Rhinos: Kevin Sinfield; *Rovers:* Neville Costigan.
Penalty count: 4-1; **Half-time:** 0-0;
Referee: Phil Bentham; **Attendance:** 14,192.

ST HELENS 46 BRADFORD BULLS 22

SAINTS: 17 Paul Wellens (C); 2 Tom Makinson; 3 Jordan
Turner; 22 Mark Percival; 5 Adam Swift; 6 Lance Hohaia;
12 Jon Wilkin; 16 Kyle Amor; 9 James Roby; 18 Alex
Walmsley; 15 Mark Flanagan; 11 Iosia Soliola; 28 Luke
Thompson. Subs (all used): 8 Mose Masoe; 10 Louie
McCarthy-Scarsbrook; 13 Willie Manu; 14 Anthony
Laffranchi.
Tries: Roby (9), Wellens (16, 80), Masoe (30),
Percival (36), Swift (39), Hohaia (43), Makinson (50);
Goals: Percival 7/8.
BULLS: 1 Brett Kearney; 38 Danny Williams; 21 Adam
Henry; 3 Adrian Purtell; 5 Jamie Foster; 17 Lee Gaskell;
7 Luke Gale (C); 14 Manase Manuokafoa; 19 Adam
O'Brien; 15 Adam Sidlow; 11 Tom Olbison; 33 Jay Pitts;
18 James Donaldson. Subs (all used): 4 Matty Blythe;
16 Danny Addy; 30 Jamal Fakir; 34 Joe Arundel.
Tries: Gale (57), Arundel (62), Purtell (64), Foster (73);
Goals: Foster 3/4.
Rugby Leaguer & League Express Men of the Match:
Saints: Paul Wellens; *Bulls:* Luke Gale.
Penalty count: 6-7; **Half-time:** 28-0;
Referee: Robert Hicks; **Attendance:** 10,238.

Saturday 12th July 2014

SALFORD RED DEVILS 35 HULL FC 22

RED DEVILS: 26 Niall Evalds; 23 Greg Johnson; 4 Junior
Sa'u; 40 Mason Caton-Brown; 39 Josh Griffin; 6 Rangi
Chase; 14 Theo Fages; 8 Adrian Morley (C); 9 Tommy
Lee; 15 Darrell Griffin; 13 Harrison Hansen; 19 Matty
Ashurst; 11 Tony Puletua. Subs (all used): 12 Gareth
Hock; 18 Steve Rapira; 21 Jordan Walne; 22 Jason
Walton.
Tries: Chase (16), Caton-Brown (24, 80), J Griffin (53),
Johnson (67), D Griffin (70);
Goals: J Griffin 4/6, Chase 1/1; **Field goal:** Chase (40).
HULL: 20 Jamie Shaul; 36 Callum Lancaster; 4 Kirk
Yeaman; 34 Fetuli Talanoa; 5 Tom Lineham; 32 Jordan
Rankin; 6 Richard Horne; 17 Liam Watts; 9 Danny
Houghton (C); 22 Josh Bowden; 21 Dean Hadley; 25
Setaimata Sa; 13 Joe Westerman. Subs (all used): 10
Chris Green; 26 Iafeta Palea'aesina; 33 Aaron Heremaia;
37 Jordan Abdull.

225

Tries: Hadley (57), Yeaman (59, 72), Shaul (75);
Goals: Westerman 0/1, Rankin 3/3.
Sin bin: Rankin (47) - professional foul.
Rugby Leaguer & League Express Men of the Match:
Red Devils: Josh Griffin; *Hull:* Kirk Yeaman.
Penalty count: 12-9; **Half-time:** 13-0;
Referee: Matthew Thomason; **Attendance:** 3,421.

CATALAN DRAGONS 16 WIGAN WARRIORS 37

DRAGONS: 2 Morgan Escare; 5 Michael Oldfield; 4 Ben Pomeroy; 25 Vincent Duport; 26 Damien Cardace; 3 Leon Pryce; 34 Sam Williams; 8 Olivier Elima; 9 Ian Henderson; 10 Jeff Lima; 11 Zeb Taia; 17 Elliott Whitehead; 24 Jason Baitieri (C). Subs (all used): 12 Louis Anderson; 13 Gregory Mounis (C); 16 Eloi Pelissier; 29 Benjamin Garcia.
Tries: Escare (16), Whitehead (22), Cardace (77);
Goals: Williams 2/3.
Sin bin: Duport (42) - dangerous tackle on Charnley; Garcia (45) - late challenge on Powell.
WARRIORS: 1 Matt Bowen; 2 Josh Charnley; 5 Anthony Gelling; 23 Dan Sarginson; 32 Joe Burgess; 27 George Williams; 7 Matty Smith; 17 Dominic Crosby; 19 Sam Powell; 24 Tony Clubb; 25 John Bateman; 12 Liam Farrell; 13 Sean O'Loughlin (C). Subs (all used): 8 Scott Taylor; 14 Jack Hughes; 20 Greg Burke; 22 Eddy Pettybourne.
Tries: Clubb (11), Bowen (27, 40), Charnley (38), Taylor (47), Burgess (49); **Goals:** Smith 6/6;
Field goal: Smith (71).
Rugby Leaguer & League Express Men of the Match:
Dragons: Morgan Escare; *Warriors:* Matt Bowen.
Penalty count: 8-12; **Half-time:** 10-24;
Referee: James Child; **Attendance:** 9,505.

Sunday 13th July 2014

WARRINGTON WOLVES 72 LONDON BRONCOS 12

WOLVES: 1 Matthew Russell; 29 Gene Ormsby; 5 Joel Monaghan; 34 Toby King (D); 18 Rhys Evans; 3 Chris Bridge; 20 Gareth O'Brien; 8 Chris Hill; 9 Mick Higham; 19 Anthony England; 12 Ben Westwood (C); 17 Ben Currie; 15 Ben Harrison. Subs (all used): 16 Paul Wood; 21 Glenn Riley; 22 Brad Dwyer; 31 Joe Philbin.
Tries: J Monaghan (8, 13, 32, 68), Hill (22, 62, 79), Currie (25, 27, 45), Wood (56), Ormsby (58), Harrison (77); **Goals:** Bridge 10/13.
BRONCOS: 6 Ben Farrar; 3 Jordan Atkins; 20 James Cunningham; 4 Thomas Minns; 23 Denny Solomona; 33 Joe Keyes; 7 Josh Drinkwater; 16 Nick Slyney; 9 Scott Moore; 10 Olsi Krasniqi; 8 Atelea Vea; 13 Alex Foster; 12 Matt Cook (C). Subs (all used): 18 George Griffin; 17 Will Lovell; 30 Jon Wallace; 19 Erjon Dollapi.
Tries: Keyes (16), Moore (50); **Goals:** Drinkwater 2/2.
Rugby Leaguer & League Express Men of the Match:
Wolves: Joel Monaghan; *Broncos:* Scott Moore.
Penalty count: 6-2; **Half-time:** 32-6;
Referee: Chris Leatherbarrow; **Attendance:** 9,318.

ROUND 21

Thursday 17th July 2014

LEEDS RHINOS 24 CASTLEFORD TIGERS 24

RHINOS: 1 Zak Hardaker; 20 Tom Briscoe; 3 Kallum Watkins; 4 Joel Moon; 5 Ryan Hall; 13 Kevin Sinfield (C); 6 Danny McGuire; 8 Kylie Leuluai; 9 Paul Aiton; 10 Jamie Peacock; 12 Carl Ablett; 14 Stevie Ward; 15 Brett Delaney. Subs (all used): 16 Ryan Bailey; 7 Rob Burrow; 19 Mitch Achurch; 11 Jamie Jones-Buchanan.
Tries: T Briscoe (8), Bailey (15), Ablett (25, 59);
Goals: Sinfield 4/4.
Dismissal: Sinfield (73) - headbutt on Dorn.
TIGERS: 6 Luke Dorn; 2 Kirk Dixon; 4 Jake Webster; 3 Michael Shenton (C); 5 Justin Carney; 7 Marc Sneyd; 26 Liam Finn; 8 Andy Lynch; 9 Adam Milner; 32 Lee Jewitt; 16 Oliver Holmes; 12 Weller Hauraki; 11 Grant Millington. Subs (all used): 10 Craig Huby; 14 Daryl Clark; 18 Frankie Mariano; 13 Nathan Massey.
Tries: Shenton (2), Hauraki (18), Massey (33), Millington (75); **Goals:** Sneyd 4/4.
Rugby Leaguer & League Express Men of the Match:
Rhinos: Carl Ablett; *Tigers:* Luke Dorn.
Penalty count: 4-8; **Half-time:** 18-18;
Referee: Ben Thaler; **Attendance:** 16,173.

Friday 18th July 2014

WIDNES VIKINGS 28 WARRINGTON WOLVES 14

VIKINGS: 1 Rhys Hanbury; 2 Jack Owens; 3 Cameron Phelps; 4 Stefan Marsh; 20 Paddy Flynn; 6 Kevin Brown; 7 Joe Mellor; 13 Hep Cahill; 9 Jon Clarke (C); 25 Alex Gerrard; 17 Danny Galea; 12 Danny Tickle; 24 Macgraff Leuluai. Subs (all used): 16 Willie Isa; 22 Liam Carberry (D); 10 Ben Kavanagh; 11 Dave Allen.
Tries: Owens (9, 60), Hanbury (36), Flynn (38), Phelps (46); **Goals:** Tickle 4/6.
WOLVES: 1 Matthew Russell; 29 Gene Ormsby; 6 Stefan Ratchford; 4 Ryan Atkins; 18 Rhys Evans; 3 Chris Bridge; 20 Gareth O'Brien; 8 Chris Hill; 9 Mick Higham; 19 Anthony England; 12 Ben Westwood (C); 17 Ben Currie; 16 Paul Wood. Subs (all used): 10 Roy Asotasi; 21 Glenn Riley; 22 Brad Dwyer; 31 Joe Philbin.
Tries: Atkins (54), Bridge (57), Currie (69);
Goals: Bridge 1/3.
Rugby Leaguer & League Express Men of the Match:
Vikings: Rhys Hanbury; *Wolves:* Ryan Atkins.
Penalty count: 7-6; **Half-time:** 16-0;
Referee: Phil Bentham; **Attendance:** 7,158.

WIGAN WARRIORS 56 HULL FC 10

WARRIORS: 34 Lewis Tierney; 2 Josh Charnley; 5 Anthony Gelling; 23 Dan Sarginson; 31 Dominic Manfredi; 27 George Williams; 7 Matty Smith; 24 Tony Clubb; 19 Sam Powell; 10 Ben Flower; 14 Jack Hughes; 12 Liam Farrell; 13 Sean O'Loughlin (C). Subs (all used): 8 Scott Taylor; 20 Greg Burke; 25 John Bateman; 28 Jordan James.
Tries: Tierney (3), Charnley (26), Williams (31, 47, 60), Smith (36), Powell (58), Manfredi (65, 69), Taylor (79);
Goals: Smith 8/10.
HULL: 20 Jamie Shaul; 5 Tom Lineham; 14 Richard Whiting; 38 Jack Logan (D); 34 Fetuli Talanoa; 37 Jordan Abdull; 32 Jordan Rankin; 22 Josh Bowden; 9 Danny Houghton (C); 10 Chris Green; 13 Joe Westerman; 21 Dean Hadley; 17 Liam Watts. Subs (all used): 24 James Cunningham; 26 Iafeta Palea'aesina; 8 Mickey Paea; 16 Jordan Thompson.
Tries: Talanoa (7), Watts (74); **Goals:** Rankin 1/2.
Rugby Leaguer & League Express Men of the Match:
Warriors: George Williams; *Hull:* Liam Watts.
Penalty count: 6-4; **Half-time:** 22-4;
Referee: Richard Silverwood; **Attendance:** 12,493.

Saturday 19th July 2014

LONDON BRONCOS 16 ST HELENS 58

BRONCOS: 34 Oscar Thomas (D); 4 Thomas Minns; 6 Ben Farrar; 22 James Woodburn-Hall; 23 Denny Solomona; 33 Joe Keyes; 7 Josh Drinkwater; 16 Nick Slyney; 9 Scott Moore; 10 Olsi Krasniqi; 11 Mike McMeeken; 13 Alex Foster; 12 Matt Cook (C). Subs (all used): 17 Will Lovell; 30 Jon Wallace; 18 George Griffin; 21 Joel Wicks.
Tries: Woodburn-Hall (20), Lovell (51), Solomona (61);
Goals: Drinkwater 2/3.
SAINTS: 17 Paul Wellens (C); 26 Matty Dawson; 3 Jordan Turner; 22 Mark Percival; 5 Adam Swift; 6 Lance Hohaia; 12 Jon Wilkin; 16 Kyle Amor; 9 James Roby; 18 Alex Walmsley; 11 Iosia Soliola; 15 Mark Flanagan; 4 Josh Jones. Subs (all used): 14 Anthony Laffranchi; 8 Mose Masoe; 10 Louie McCarthy-Scarsbrook; 28 Luke Thompson.
Tries: Percival (7, 48), Amor (12), Turner (17, 23), Wellens (31), Dawson (65, 79), Thompson (70), Soliola (73), Laffranchi (76); **Goals:** Percival 7/11.
Rugby Leaguer & League Express Men of the Match:
Broncos: Josh Drinkwater; *Saints:* Alex Walmsley.
Penalty count: 6-3; **Half-time:** 6-28;
Referee: Tim Roby; **Attendance:** 1,791.

CATALAN DRAGONS 40
WAKEFIELD TRINITY WILDCATS 6

DRAGONS: 2 Morgan Escare; 5 Michael Oldfield; 4 Ben Pomeroy; 11 Zeb Taia; 18 Daryl Millard; 3 Leon Pryce; 34 Sam Williams; 20 Mickael Simon; 9 Ian Henderson; 21 Julian Bousquet; 12 Louis Anderson; 17 Elliott Whitehead; 24 Jason Baitieri (C). Subs (all used): 15 Antoni Maria; 16 Eloi Pelissier; 23 Lopini Paea; 33 Thibaut Margalet.
Tries: Millard (13), Escare (15, 46), Whitehead (21, 38, 58), Taia (25); **Goals:** Williams 6/7.
On report:
Anderson (20) - alleged late challenge on Mathers.
WILDCATS: 1 Richard Mathers; 31 Chris Riley; 5 Reece Lyne; 19 Jimmy Keinhorst; 33 Richard Owen; 6 Paul Sykes; 35 Tim Smith; 10 Andy Raleigh; 9 Paul McShane; 16 Richard Moore; 34 Lee Gilmour; 12 Danny Kirmond (C); 13 Danny Washbrook. Subs (all used): 11 Ali Lauitiiti; 15 Matt Ryan; 17 Taulima Tautai; 30 Nick Scruton.
Try: Lyne (73); **Goals:** Sykes 1/1.
Rugby Leaguer & League Express Men of the Match:
Dragons: Elliott Whitehead; *Wildcats:* Danny Kirmond.
Penalty count: 6-5; **Half-time:** 28-0;
Referee: Robert Hicks; **Attendance:** 8,256.

Sunday 20th July 2014

HUDDERSFIELD GIANTS 52 BRADFORD BULLS 26

GIANTS: 27 Jake Connor; 2 Jermaine McGillvary; 3 Leroy Cudjoe; 4 Joe Wardle; 19 Jodie Broughton; 6 Danny Brough (C); 7 Luke Robinson; 8 Eorl Crabtree; 18 Kyle Wood; 20 Antonio Kaufusi; 11 Brett Ferres; 17 Ukuma Ta'ai; 14 Michael Lawrence. Subs (all used): 10 Craig Kopczak; 13 Chris Bailey; 15 Larne Patrick; 21 Anthony Mullally.
Tries: Connor (9), Ta'ai (20, 79), Robinson (27), Bailey (36), McGillvary (40, 65, 73), Ferres (47), Wardle (62); **Goals:** Cudjoe 6/10.
BULLS: 1 Brett Kearney; 5 Jamie Foster; 34 Joe Arundel; 3 Adrian Purtell; 20 Luke George; 17 Lee Gaskell; 7 Luke Gale (C); 14 Manase Manuokafoa; 19 Adam O'Brien; 30 Jamal Fakir; 11 Tom Olbison; 13 Chev Walker; 18 James Donaldson. Subs (all used): 15 Adam Sidlow; 24 Alex Mellor; 33 Jay Pitts; 16 Danny Addy.
Tries: George (6, 24), O'Brien (16), Kearney (42, 75);
Goals: Foster 3/5.
Rugby Leaguer & League Express Men of the Match:
Giants: Brett Ferres; *Bulls:* Brett Kearney.
Penalty count: 4-4; **Half-time:** 26-16;
Referee: Chris Leatherbarrow; **Attendance:** 6,145.

HULL KINGSTON ROVERS 18 SALFORD RED DEVILS 38

ROVERS: 19 Craig Hall; 24 Omari Caro; 3 Kris Welham; 18 Liam Salter; 5 David Hodgson; 6 Travis Burns (C); 7 Kris Keating; 16 Jason Netherton; 9 Josh Hodgson (C); 10 Michael Weyman; 11 Kevin Larroyer; 15 Graeme Horne; 12 Neville Costigan. Subs (all used): 23 James Green; 14 Adam Walker; 25 Aaron Ollett; 34 Jason Chan (D).
Tries: J Hodgson (22), Hall (32), Weyman (77);
Goals: Burns 3/3.
Sin bin: Burns (58) - punching Lee.
RED DEVILS: 26 Niall Evalds; 23 Greg Johnson; 4 Junior Sa'u; 40 Mason Caton-Brown; 39 Josh Griffin; 6 Rangi Chase; 14 Theo Fages; 8 Adrian Morley (C); 9 Tommy Lee; 15 Darrell Griffin; 19 Matty Ashurst; 13 Harrison Hansen; 11 Tony Puletua. Subs: 18 Steve Rapira; 21 Jordan Walne; 22 Jason Walton; 5 Francis Meli (not used).
Tries: Caton-Brown (28), Evalds (42), Sa'u (48), J Griffin (56, 65), Fages (60), Johnson (70);
Goals: J Griffin 5/7.
Rugby Leaguer & League Express Men of the Match:
Rovers: Josh Hodgson; *Red Devils:* Rangi Chase.
Penalty count: 5-9; **Half-time:** 12-4;
Referee: James Child; **Attendance:** 8,213.

ROUND 22

Thursday 24th July 2014

HULL FC 18 CASTLEFORD TIGERS 18

HULL: 20 Jamie Shaul; 5 Tom Lineham; 14 Richard Whiting; 4 Kirk Yeaman; 34 Fetuli Talanoa; 37 Jordan Abdull; 32 Jordan Rankin; 10 Chris Green; 9 Danny Houghton; 17 Liam Watts; 11 Gareth Ellis (C); 21 Dean Hadley; 13 Joe Westerman. Subs (all used): 8 Mickey Paea; 16 Jordan Thompson; 33 Aaron Heremaia; 28 Setaimata Sa.
Tries: Talanoa (15), Abdull (30), Yeaman (43);
Goals: Rankin 3/3.
TIGERS: 6 Luke Dorn; 2 Kirk Dixon; 21 Ashley Gibson; 3 Michael Shenton (C); 24 James Clare; 7 Marc Sneyd; 26 Liam Finn; 8 Andy Lynch; 9 Adam Milner; 35 Garreth Carvell; 18 Frankie Mariano; 12 Weller Hauraki; 13 Nathan Massey. Subs (all used): 11 Grant Millington; 14 Daryl Clark; 16 Oliver Holmes; 19 Scott Wheeldon.
Tries: Shenton (25), Sneyd (68), Clare (74, 77);
Goals: Sneyd 1/4.
On report:
Hauraki (76) - alleged use of the knees on Abdull.
Rugby Leaguer & League Express Men of the Match:
Hull: Gareth Ellis; *Tigers:* Marc Sneyd.
Penalty count: 9-4; **Half-time:** 12-4;
Referee: James Child; **Attendance:** 9,959.

Friday 25th July 2014

SALFORD RED DEVILS 18 LEEDS RHINOS 22

RED DEVILS: 38 Kevin Locke; 23 Greg Johnson; 4 Junior Sa'u; 40 Mason Caton-Brown; 39 Josh Griffin; 6 Rangi Chase; 14 Theo Fages; 8 Adrian Morley (C); 35 Logan Tomkins; 15 Darrell Griffin; 13 Harrison Hansen; 19 Matty Ashurst; 11 Tony Puletua. Subs (all used): 21 Jordan Walne; 18 Steve Rapira; 26 Niall Evalds; 22 Jason Walton.
Tries: Sa'u (12), Fages (38), J Walne (58);
Goals: J Griffin 3/3.
RHINOS: 1 Zak Hardaker; 20 Tom Briscoe; 3 Kallum Watkins; 4 Joel Moon; 5 Ryan Hall; 6 Danny McGuire (C); 7 Rob Burrow; 8 Kylie Leuluai; 9 Paul Aiton; 10 Jamie Peacock; 11 Jamie Jones-Buchanan; 28 Josh Walters; 12 Carl Ablett. Subs (all used): 23 Brad Singleton; 21 Liam Sutcliffe; 26 Elliot Minchella; 14 Stevie Ward.
Tries: Hardaker (20), Watkins (22), Ablett (46), S Ward (52); **Goals:** Hardaker 3/5.
Rugby Leaguer & League Express Men of the Match:
Red Devils: Adrian Morley;
Rhinos: Jamie Jones-Buchanan.
Penalty count: 5-8; **Half-time:** 12-12;
Referee: Richard Silverwood; **Attendance:** 5,012.

ST HELENS 44 WIDNES VIKINGS 22

SAINTS: 17 Paul Wellens (C); 2 Tom Makinson; 3 Jordan Turner; 22 Mark Percival; 26 Matty Dawson; 24 Gary Wheeler; 7 Luke Walsh; 16 Kyle Amor; 9 James Roby; 18 Alex Walmsley; 13 Willie Manu; 11 Iosia Soliola; 15 Mark Flanagan. Subs (all used): 4 Josh Jones; 8 Mose Masoe; 10 Louie McCarthy-Scarsbrook; 14 Anthony Laffranchi.
Tries: Flanagan (8), Makinson (19, 42, 60), Masoe (27, 33), Turner (45), Manu (64);
Goals: Percival 6/8.
VIKINGS: 1 Rhys Hanbury; 20 Paddy Flynn; 3 Cameron Phelps; 4 Stefan Marsh; 5 Patrick Ah Van; 6 Kevin Brown; 7 Joe Mellor; 13 Hep Cahill; 9 Jon Clarke (C); 25 Alex Gerrard; 17 Danny Galea; 11 Dave Allen; 12 Danny Tickle. Subs (all used): 14 Chris Dean; 16 Willie Isa; 22 Liam Carberry; 24 Macgraff Leuluai.
Tries: Phelps (50, 52), Marsh (54), Hanbury (70);
Goals: Tickle 3/4.
Sin bin: Leuluai (37) - repeated team offences.
Rugby Leaguer & League Express Men of the Match:
Saints: Alex Walmsley; *Vikings:* Alex Gerrard.
Penalty count: 10-4; **Half-time:** 22-0;
Referee: Ben Thaler; **Attendance:** 11,844.

Saturday 26th July 2014

LONDON BRONCOS 10 HULL KINGSTON ROVERS 62

BRONCOS: 6 Ben Farrar; 3 Jordan Atkins; 4 Thomas Minns; 22 James Woodburn-Hall; 23 Denny Solomona; 34 Oscar Thomas; 21 Joel Wicks; 16 Nick Slyney; 9 Scott Moore; 10 Olsi Krasniqi; 11 Mike McMeeken; 8 Atelea Vea; 12 Matt Cook (C). Subs (all used): 7 Josh Drinkwater; 18 George Griffin; 17 Will Lovell; 30 Jon Wallace.
Tries: Atkins (47, 65); **Goals:** Thomas 1/2.

ROVERS: 1 Greg Eden; 32 Ade Gardner; 18 Liam Salter; 3 Kris Welham; 5 David Hodgson; 6 Travis Burns (C); 19 Craig Hall; 14 Adam Walker; 9 Josh Hodgson (C); 10 Michael Weyman; 11 Kevin Larroyer; 34 Jason Chan; 12 Neville Costigan. Subs (all used): 23 James Green; 29 Connor Robinson (D); 16 Jason Netherton; 25 Aaron Ollett.
Tries: J Hodgson (9), Eden (18, 32, 80), Larroyer (25), Salter (42, 75), Weyman (53, 73), Gardner (58), A Walker (63); **Goals:** Burns 9/12.
Rugby Leaguer & League Express Men of the Match: *Broncos:* Joel Wicks; *Rovers:* Greg Eden.
Penalty count: 4-5; **Half-time:** 0-26;
Referee: Matthew Thomason; **Attendance:** 1,084.

Sunday 27th July 2014

BRADFORD BULLS 16 WIGAN WARRIORS 8

BULLS: 1 Brett Kearney; 2 Elliot Kear; 21 Adam Henry; 34 Joe Arundel; 38 Danny Williams; 17 Lee Gaskell; 7 Luke Gale (C); 14 Manase Manuokafoa; 19 Adam O'Brien; 30 Jamal Fakir; 11 Tom Olbison; 33 Jay Pitts; 18 James Donaldson. Subs (all used): 15 Adam Sidlow; 24 Alex Mellor; 4 Matty Blythe; 16 Danny Addy.
Tries: Williams (29), Arundel (35), Blythe (61);
Goals: Gale 2/3.
WARRIORS: 1 Matt Bowen; 2 Josh Charnley; 3 Darrell Goulding; 23 Dan Sarginson; 31 Dominic Manfredi; 27 George Williams; 7 Matty Smith; 10 Ben Flower; 19 Sam Powell; 17 Dominic Crosby; 12 Liam Farrell; 25 John Bateman; 13 Sean O'Loughlin (C). Subs (all used): 8 Scott Taylor; 14 Jack Hughes; 24 Tony Clubb; 37 Ryan Sutton.
Tries: Manfredi (9, 67); **Goals:** Smith 0/2.
Rugby Leaguer & League Express Men of the Match: *Bulls:* Lee Gaskell; *Warriors:* Darrell Goulding.
Penalty count: 10-8; **Half-time:** 12-4;
Referee: Robert Hicks; **Attendance:** 6,535.

HUDDERSFIELD GIANTS 38 CATALAN DRAGONS 16

GIANTS: 1 Scott Grix; 2 Jermaine McGillvary; 5 Aaron Murphy; 4 Joe Wardle; 19 Jodie Broughton; 6 Danny Brough (C); 7 Luke Robinson; 8 Eorl Crabtree; 18 Kyle Wood; 20 Antonio Kaufusi; 11 Brett Ferres; 17 Ukuma Ta'ai; 13 Chris Bailey. Subs (all used): 10 Craig Kopczak; 14 Michael Lawrence; 15 Larne Patrick; 28 Kruise Leeming.
Tries: Wood (5), Murphy (13), McGillvary (19, 51), Wardle (45, 65), Ferres (69); **Goals:** Brough 5/7.
DRAGONS: 2 Morgan Escare; 5 Michael Oldfield; 4 Ben Pomeroy; 11 Zeb Taia; 18 Daryl Millard; 3 Leon Pryce; 34 Sam Williams; 20 Mickael Simon; 9 Ian Henderson; 21 Julian Bousquet; 12 Louis Anderson; 17 Elliott Whitehead; 24 Jason Baitieri (C). Subs (all used): 10 Jeff Lima; 15 Antoni Maria; 16 Eloi Pelissier; 23 Lopini Paea.
Tries: Pelissier (28), Oldfield (51), Escare (76);
Goals: Williams 2/3.
Rugby Leaguer & League Express Men of the Match: *Giants:* Danny Brough; *Dragons:* Eloi Pelissier.
Penalty count: 7-2; **Half-time:** 14-6;
Referee: Phil Bentham; **Attendance:** 4,931.

WARRINGTON WOLVES 26
WAKEFIELD TRINITY WILDCATS 40

WOLVES: 1 Matthew Russell; 29 Gene Ormsby; 5 Joel Monaghan; 4 Ryan Atkins; 18 Rhys Evans; 3 Chris Bridge; 20 Gareth O'Brien; 8 Chris Hill; 9 Mick Higham; 15 Ben Harrison; 12 Ben Westwood (C); 17 Ben Currie; 6 Stefan Ratchford. Subs (all used): 7 Richard Myler; 16 Paul Wood; 19 Anthony England; 23 James Laithwaite.
Tries: R Evans (1, 42), J Monaghan (32), Ratchford (55), Atkins (70); **Goals:** Bridge 1/3, Ratchford 2/2.
WILDCATS: 1 Richard Mathers; 33 Richard Owen; 5 Reece Lyne; 19 Jimmy Keinhorst; 31 Chris Riley; 20 Jarrod Sammut; 35 Tim Smith; 10 Andy Raleigh; 9 Paul McShane; 30 Nick Scruton; 34 Lee Gilmour; 12 Danny Kirmond (C); 13 Danny Washbrook. Subs (all used): 11 Ali Lauitiiti; 16 Richard Moore; 17 Taulima Tautai; 14 Matty Wildie.
Tries: Riley (8, 21, 49), Washbrook (18), Keinhorst (60), Mathers (73), Scruton (76); **Goals:** Sammut 6/8.
Rugby Leaguer & League Express Men of the Match: *Wolves:* Ben Currie; *Wildcats:* Chris Riley.
Penalty count: 9-5; **Half-time:** 10-16;
Referee: Tim Roby; **Attendance:** 9,252.

ROUND 23

Thursday 31st July 2014

WIGAN WARRIORS 45 SALFORD RED DEVILS 4

WARRIORS: 1 Matt Bowen; 2 Josh Charnley; 5 Anthony Gelling; 23 Dan Sarginson; 31 Dominic Manfredi; 27 George Williams; 7 Matty Smith; 10 Ben Flower; 19 Sam Powell; 24 Tony Clubb; 12 Liam Farrell; 25 John Bateman; 13 Sean O'Loughlin (C). Subs (all used): 8 Scott Taylor; 11 Joel Tomkins (D2); 16 Gil Dudson; 28 Jordan James.
Tries: Bowen (13), Gelling (31, 42, 70), Charnley (34), Williams (72), Clubb (75), Smith (78); **Goals:** Smith 6/8;
Field goal: Smith (66).
RED DEVILS: 26 Niall Evalds; 23 Greg Johnson; 4 Junior Sa'u; 40 Mason Caton-Brown; 39 Josh Griffin; 6 Rangi Chase; 14 Theo Fages; 8 Adrian Morley (C); 9 Tommy Lee; 15 Darrell Griffin; 13 Harrison Hansen; 19 Matty Ashurst; 11 Tony Puletua. Subs (all used): 10 Lama Tasi; 21 Jordan Walne; 18 Steve Rapira; 35 Logan Tomkins.
Try: J Griffin (63); **Goals:** J Griffin 0/1.
Rugby Leaguer & League Express Men of the Match: *Warriors:* Matty Smith; *Red Devils:* Niall Evalds.
Penalty count: 5-6; **Half-time:** 16-0;
Referee: Phil Bentham; **Attendance:** 12,962.

Friday 1st August 2014

CATALAN DRAGONS 24 WARRINGTON WOLVES 26

DRAGONS: 2 Morgan Escare; 5 Michael Oldfield; 4 Ben Pomeroy; 11 Zeb Taia; 18 Daryl Millard; 3 Leon Pryce; 6 Thomas Bosc; 21 Julian Bousquet; 9 Ian Henderson; 10 Jeff Lima; 12 Louis Anderson; 17 Elliott Whitehead; 24 Jason Baitieri (C). Subs (all used): 13 Gregory Mounis (C); 16 Eloi Pelissier; 20 Mickael Simon; 23 Lopini Paea.
Tries: Oldfield (15, 62, 72), Mounis (48); **Goals:** Bosc 4/4.
WOLVES: 6 Stefan Ratchford; 29 Gene Ormsby; 5 Joel Monaghan; 3 Chris Bridge; 18 Rhys Evans; 7 Richard Myler; 20 Gareth O'Brien; 8 Chris Hill; 14 Michael Monaghan (C); 19 Anthony England; 11 Trent Waterhouse; 17 Ben Currie; 15 Ben Harrison. Subs (all used): 10 Roy Asotasi; 13 Simon Grix; 16 Paul Wood; 22 Brad Dwyer.
Tries: M Monaghan (12), Ormsby (38), R Evans (54), J Monaghan (65); **Goals:** Bridge 5/5.
Rugby Leaguer & League Express Men of the Match: *Dragons:* Louis Anderson; *Wolves:* Michael Monaghan.
Penalty count: 5-6; **Half-time:** 6-12;
Referee: Richard Silverwood; **Attendance:** 7,858.

HULL FC 19 ST HELENS 12

HULL: 20 Jamie Shaul; 5 Tom Lineham; 14 Richard Whiting; 4 Kirk Yeaman; 34 Fetuli Talanoa; 37 Jordan Abdull; 6 Richard Horne; 8 Mickey Paea; 9 Danny Houghton; 17 Liam Watts; 11 Gareth Ellis (C); 21 Dean Hadley; 13 Joe Westerman. Subs (all used): 10 Chris Green; 26 Iafeta Palea'aesina; 33 Aaron Heremaia; 28 Setaimata Sa.
Tries: Horne (19), Lineham (36), Paea (58);
Goals: Westerman 3/4; **Field goal:** Westerman (76).
SAINTS: 17 Paul Wellens (C); 2 Tom Makinson; 4 Josh Jones; 22 Mark Percival; 26 Matty Dawson; 24 Gary Wheeler; 3 Jordan Turner; 16 Kyle Amor; 9 James Roby; 18 Alex Walmsley; 15 Mark Flanagan; 13 Willie Manu; 11 Iosia Soliola. Subs (all used): 8 Mose Masoe; 10 Louie McCarthy-Scarsbrook; 14 Anthony Laffranchi; 28 Luke Thompson.
Tries: Makinson (4), Wellens (48); **Goals:** Percival 2/2.
Rugby Leaguer & League Express Men of the Match: *Hull:* Richard Horne; *Saints:* James Roby.
Penalty count: 8-3; **Half-time:** 12-6;
Referee: Ben Thaler; **Attendance:** 10,214.

LEEDS RHINOS 14 BRADFORD BULLS 20

RHINOS: 1 Zak Hardaker; 20 Tom Briscoe; 21 Liam Sutcliffe; 28 Josh Walters; 2 Ben Jones-Bishop; 6 Danny McGuire (C); 7 Rob Burrow; 8 Kylie Leuluai; 9 Paul Aiton; 23 Brad Singleton; 11 Jamie Jones-Buchanan; 19 Mitch Achurch; 15 Brett Delaney. Subs (all used): 17 Ian Kirke; 30 Luke Briscoe; 26 Elliot Minchella; 29 Robbie Ward.
Tries: Achurch (19), Delaney (52), L Briscoe (71);
Goals: Hardaker 1/3.
BULLS: 2 Elliot Kear; 4 Matty Blythe; 21 Adam Henry; 34 Joe Arundel; 38 Danny Williams; 17 Lee Gaskell; 7 Luke Gale (C); 14 Manase Manuokafoa; 19 Adam O'Brien; 30 Jamal Fakir; 11 Tom Olbison; 33 Jay Pitts; 18 James Donaldson. Subs (all used): 15 Adam Sidlow; 12 Dale Ferguson; 16 Danny Addy; 24 Alex Mellor.
Tries: Williams (4), Gale (49), Gaskell (75);
Goals: Gale 4/5.
Sin bin: Sidlow (21) - professional foul.
Rugby Leaguer & League Express Men of the Match: *Rhinos:* Brett Delaney; *Bulls:* Luke Gale.
Penalty count: 5-5; **Half-time:** 4-4;
Referee: Tim Roby; **Attendance:** 16,009.

Sunday 3rd August 2014

WAKEFIELD TRINITY WILDCATS 18
HUDDERSFIELD GIANTS 36

WILDCATS: 20 Jarrod Sammut; 33 Richard Owen; 5 Reece Lyne; 19 Jimmy Keinhorst; 31 Chris Riley; 6 Paul Sykes; 35 Tim Smith; 10 Andy Raleigh; 9 Paul McShane; 30 Nick Scruton; 34 Lee Gilmour; 12 Danny Kirmond (C); 13 Danny Washbrook. Subs (all used): 11 Ali Lauitiiti; 17 Taulima Tautai; 16 Richard Moore; 14 Matty Wildie.
Tries: Sammut (45, 79), Sykes (56); **Goals:** Sammut 3/3.
GIANTS: 1 Scott Grix; 2 Jermaine McGillvary; 5 Aaron Murphy; 4 Joe Wardle; 27 Jake Connor; 6 Danny Brough (C); 7 Luke Robinson; 8 Eorl Crabtree; 9 Shaun Lunt; 21 Anthony Mullally; 11 Brett Ferres; 15 Larne Patrick; 14 Michael Lawrence. Subs (all used): 10 Craig Kopczak; 13 Chris Bailey; 16 David Faiumu; 28 Kruise Leeming.
Tries: Wardle (1), Crabtree (8), Lunt (18), Kopczak (25), Leeming (31), McGillvary (34), Connor (74);
Goals: Brough 4/7.
Rugby Leaguer & League Express Men of the Match: *Wildcats:* Taulima Tautai; *Giants:* Shaun Lunt.
Penalty count: 5-8; **Half-time:** 0-32;
Referee: James Child; **Attendance:** 4,317.

WIDNES VIKINGS 28 HULL KINGSTON ROVERS 10

VIKINGS: 1 Rhys Hanbury; 20 Paddy Flynn; 14 Chris Dean; 4 Stefan Marsh; 2 Jack Owens; 6 Kevin Brown; 7 Joe Mellor; 23 Phil Joseph; 9 Jon Clarke (C); 10 Ben Kavanagh; 17 Danny Galea; 12 Danny Tickle; 13 Hep Cahill. Subs (all used): 15 Lloyd White; 16 Willie Isa; 11 Dave Allen; 8 Eamon O'Carroll.
Tries: Owens (8), Dean (36), Mellor (41), Brown (44), Marsh (54), Hanbury (67); **Goals:** Tickle 2/4, Owens 0/2.
ROVERS: 1 Greg Eden; 32 Ade Gardner; 3 Kris Welham; 18 Liam Salter; 2 Ben Cockayne; 6 Travis Burns (C); 7 Kris Keating; 16 Jason Netherton; 9 Josh Hodgson (C); 14 Adam Walker; 11 Kevin Larroyer; 34 Jason Chan; 12 Neville Costigan. Subs (all used): 21 Keal Carlile; 15 Graeme Horne; 23 James Green; 20 Jordan Cox.
Tries: Keating (23), Chan (48); **Goals:** Burns 1/2.
Rugby Leaguer & League Express Men of the Match: *Vikings:* Kevin Brown; *Rovers:* Jason Chan.
Penalty count: 5-6; **Half-time:** 10-4;
Referee: Robert Hicks; **Attendance:** 5,345.

CASTLEFORD TIGERS 64 LONDON BRONCOS 18

TIGERS: 6 Luke Dorn; 2 Kirk Dixon; 21 Ashley Gibson; 3 Michael Shenton (C); 5 Justin Carney; 7 Marc Sneyd; 26 Liam Finn; 32 Lee Jewitt; 9 Adam Milner; 10 Craig Huby; 16 Oliver Holmes; 4 Jake Webster; 13 Nathan Massey. Subs (all used): 18 Frankie Mariano; 19 Scott Wheeldon; 20 Jamie Ellis; 35 Garreth Carvell.
Tries: Dorn (14, 72), Carney (25, 31, 34), Wheeldon (40), Shenton (46), Carvell (50), Mariano (58), Dixon (64, 74), Milner (77); **Goals:** Sneyd 8/12.
BRONCOS: 6 Ben Farrar; 3 Jordan Atkins; 4 Thomas Minns; 1 Nesiasi Mataitonga; 23 Denny Solomona; 33 Joe Keyes; 7 Josh Drinkwater; 16 Nick Slyney; 9 Scott Moore; 10 Olsi Krasniqi; 11 Mike McMeeken; 8 Atelea Vea; 12 Matt Cook (C). Subs (all used): 21 Joel Wicks; 18 George Griffin; 30 Jon Wallace; 19 Erjon Dollapi.
Tries: Krasniqi (9), Dollapi (20), McMeeken (78);
Goals: Drinkwater 3/3.
Rugby Leaguer & League Express Men of the Match: *Tigers:* Justin Carney; *Broncos:* Mike McMeeken.
Penalty count: 6-5; **Half-time:** 28-12;
Referee: Joe Cobb; **Attendance:** 5,233.

ROUND 24

Thursday 14th August 2014

HULL KINGSTON ROVERS 14 WIGAN WARRIORS 14

ROVERS: 1 Greg Eden; 32 Ade Gardner; 18 Liam Salter; 19 Craig Hall; 2 Ben Cockayne; 6 Travis Burns (C); 7 Kris Keating; 14 Adam Walker; 9 Josh Hodgson (C); 16 Jason Netherton; 34 Jason Chan; 15 Graeme Horne; 12 Neville Costigan. Subs (all used): 21 Keal Carlile; 20 Jordan Cox; 23 James Green; 11 Kevin Larroyer.
Tries: Hall (20), Chan (37), Cockayne (58);
Goals: Burns 1/3.
WARRIORS: 1 Matt Bowen; 2 Josh Charnley; 23 Dan Sarginson; 5 Anthony Gelling; 31 Dominic Manfredi; 6 Blake Green; 7 Matty Smith; 17 Dominic Crosby; 19 Sam Powell; 10 Ben Flower; 11 Joel Tomkins; 12 Liam Farrell; 13 Sean O'Loughlin (C). Subs (all used): 8 Scott Taylor; 14 Jack Hughes; 22 Eddy Pettybourne; 27 George Williams.
Tries: Sarginson (2), O'Loughlin (73), Charnley (80);
Goals: Smith 1/3.
Rugby Leaguer & League Express Men of the Match: *Rovers:* Jason Chan; *Warriors:* Blake Green.
Penalty count: 9-7; **Half-time:** 10-4;
Referee: Richard Silverwood; **Attendance:** 6,801.

Friday 15th August 2014

SALFORD RED DEVILS 34 CATALAN DRAGONS 22

RED DEVILS: 38 Kevin Locke; 23 Greg Johnson; 4 Junior Sa'u; 40 Mason Caton-Brown; 26 Niall Evalds; 6 Rangi Chase; 14 Theo Fages; 8 Adrian Morley (C); 9 Tommy Lee; 10 Lama Tasi; 13 Harrison Hansen; 19 Matty Ashurst; 21 Jordan Walne. Subs (all used): 11 Tony Puletua; 35 Logan Tomkins; 18 Steve Rapira; 22 Jason Walton.
Tries: Locke (11, 29), Sa'u (16), Evalds (39), Fages (50), Puletua (60); **Goals:** Locke 3/4, Chase 2/2.
DRAGONS: 2 Morgan Escare; 5 Michael Oldfield; 4 Ben Pomeroy; 25 Vincent Duport; 18 Daryl Millard; 3 Leon Pryce; 6 Thomas Bosc; 21 Julian Bousquet; 9 Ian Henderson; 10 Jeff Lima; 11 Zeb Taia; 17 Elliott Whitehead; 24 Jason Baitieri (C). Subs (all used): 8 Olivier Elima; 12 Louis Anderson; 13 Gregory Mounis (C); 16 Eloi Pelissier.
Tries: Oldfield (6), Mounis (45), Duport (72), Henderson (79); **Goals:** Bosc 3/4.
Rugby Leaguer & League Express Men of the Match: *Red Devils:* Rangi Chase; *Dragons:* Ben Pomeroy.
Penalty count: 4-4; **Half-time:** 22-4;
Referee: Ben Thaler; **Attendance:** 3,100.

ST HELENS 40 WAKEFIELD TRINITY WILDCATS 16

SAINTS: 38 Shannon McDonnell (D); 2 Tom Makinson; 4 Josh Jones; 22 Mark Percival; 26 Matty Dawson; 24 Gary Wheeler; 17 Paul Wellens (C); 16 Kyle Amor; 9 James Roby; 18 Alex Walmsley; 14 Anthony Laffranchi; 10 Louie McCarthy-Scarsbrook; 3 Jordan Turner. Subs (all used): 8 Mose Masoe; 11 Iosia Soliola; 13 Willie Manu; 15 Mark Flanagan.
Tries: Makinson (3, 80), Jones (27, 66), McDonnell (42, 59), Soliola (54); **Goals:** Percival 6/7.
WILDCATS: 25 Max Jowitt (D); 33 Richard Owen; 3 Dean Collis; 5 Reece Lyne; 31 Chris Riley; 20 Jarrod Sammut; 35 Tim Smith; 8 Scott Anderson; 9 Paul McShane; 10 Andy Raleigh; 11 Ali Lauitiiti; 12 Danny Kirmond (C); 13 Danny Washbrook. Subs (all used): 14 Matty Wildie; 17 Taulima Tautai; 26 Jon Molloy; 34 Lee Gilmour.
Tries: Washbrook (39), Owen (50), Gilmour (69);
Goals: Sammut 2/3.
Rugby Leaguer & League Express Men of the Match: *Saints:* Jordan Turner; *Wildcats:* Taulima Tautai.
Penalty count: 5-3; **Half-time:** 12-6;
Referee: Phil Bentham; **Attendance:** 10,708.

WARRINGTON WOLVES 48 CASTLEFORD TIGERS 10

WOLVES: 1 Matthew Russell; 5 Joel Monaghan; 4 Ryan Atkins; 3 Chris Bridge; 18 Rhys Evans; 6 Stefan Ratchford; 20 Gareth O'Brien; 8 Chris Hill; 14 Michael Monaghan (C); 15 Ben Harrison; 11 Trent Waterhouse; 12 Ben Westwood (C); 13 Simon Grix. Subs (all used): 9 Mick Higham; 16 Paul Wood; 19 Anthony England; 23 James Laithwaite.
Tries: Atkins (4), O'Brien (18), Bridge (23), R Evans (53, 78), England (59), Ratchford (66), J Monaghan (73); **Goals:** Bridge 3/3, Ratchford 5/5.
TIGERS: 28 Ben Reynolds; 1 Jordan Tansey; 23 Michael Channing; 21 Ashley Gibson; 24 James Clare; 20 Jamie Ellis; 26 Liam Finn; 8 Andy Lynch; 9 Adam Milner; 19 Scott Wheeldon; 18 Frankie Mariano; 12 Weller Hauraki (C); 32 Lee Jewitt. Subs (all used): 13 Nathan Massey; 16 Oliver Holmes; 31 Brad Day (D); 33 Will Maher (D).
Tries: Clare (27), Holmes (46); **Goals:** Finn 1/2.
Rugby Leaguer & League Express Men of the Match: *Wolves:* Michael Monaghan; *Tigers:* Liam Finn.
Penalty count: 7-4; **Half-time:** 18-4;
Referee: James Child; **Attendance:** 8,391.

Sunday 17th August 2014

BRADFORD BULLS 34 HULL FC 28

BULLS: 1 Brett Kearney; 5 Jamie Foster; 21 Adam Henry; 34 Joe Arundel; 38 Danny Williams; 17 Lee Gaskell; 7 Luke Gale (C); 14 Manase Manuokafoa; 19 Adam O'Brien; 15 Adam Sidlow; 11 Tom Olbison; 33 Jay Pitts; 18 James Donaldson. Subs (all used): 36 Jordan Baldwinson; 4 Matty Blythe; 12 Dale Ferguson; 16 Danny Addy.
Tries: Foster (26), Arundel (36, 48), Sidlow (44), Pitts (52), Addy (70); **Goals:** Foster 5/6.
HULL: 20 Jamie Shaul; 5 Tom Lineham; 14 Richard Whiting; 4 Kirk Yeaman; 34 Fetuli Talanoa; 37 Jordan Abdull; 6 Richard Horne; 8 Mickey Paea; 9 Danny Houghton; 17 Liam Watts; 11 Gareth Ellis (C); 21 Dean Hadley; 13 Joe Westerman. Subs (all used): 10 Chris Green; 26 Iafeta Palea'aesina; 32 Jordan Rankin; 28 Setaimata Sa.
Tries: Shaul (4), Ellis (17, 54), Sa (73), Lineham (79); **Goals:** Westerman 4/5.
Rugby Leaguer & League Express Men of the Match: *Bulls:* Lee Gaskell; *Hull:* Liam Watts.
Penalty count: 8-5; **Half-time:** 10-12;
Referee: Robert Hicks; **Attendance:** 6,337.

HUDDERSFIELD GIANTS 28 WIDNES VIKINGS 14

GIANTS: 1 Scott Grix; 2 Jermaine McGillvary; 5 Aaron Murphy; 4 Joe Wardle; 19 Jodie Broughton; 6 Danny Brough (C); 7 Luke Robinson; 8 Eorl Crabtree; 9 Shaun Lunt; 20 Antonio Kaufusi; 11 Brett Ferres; 17 Ukuma Ta'ai; 15 Larne Patrick. Subs (all used): 10 Craig Kopczak; 13 Chris Bailey; 14 Michael Lawrence; 21 Anthony Mullally.
Tries: Patrick (4), Wardle (39), McGillvary (63), Kaufusi (69), Lunt (78); **Goals:** Brough 4/5.
VIKINGS: 1 Rhys Hanbury; 20 Paddy Flynn; 14 Chris Dean; 4 Stefan Marsh; 5 Patrick Ah Van; 6 Kevin Brown (C); 7 Joe Mellor; 8 Eamon O'Carroll; 15 Lloyd White; 13 Hep Cahill; 11 Dave Allen; 17 Danny Galea; 12 Danny Tickle. Subs (all used): 24 Macgraff Leuluai; 18 Paul Johnson; 22 Liam Carberry; 23 Phil Joseph.
Tries: Tickle (20), Hanbury (73); **Goals:** Tickle 3/3.
Rugby Leaguer & League Express Men of the Match: *Giants:* Danny Brough; *Vikings:* Kevin Brown.
Penalty count: 9-11; **Half-time:** 12-8;
Referee: Matthew Thomason; **Attendance:** 5,346.

LONDON BRONCOS 40 LEEDS RHINOS 36

BRONCOS: 6 Ben Farrar; 2 Kieran Dixon; 1 Nesiasi Mataitonga; 23 Denny Solomona; 3 Jordan Atkins; 7 Josh Drinkwater; 33 Joe Keyes; 16 Nick Slyney; 9 Scott Moore; 30 Jon Wallace; 8 Atelea Vea; 11 Mike McMeeken; 12 Matt Cook (C). Subs (all used): 10 Olsi Krasniqi; 18 George Griffin; 19 Erjon Dollapi; 34 Oscar Thomas.
Tries: Atkins (19), Keyes (23, 71, 73), Dixon (48), McMeeken (52), Moore (61); **Goals:** Drinkwater 6/8.
RHINOS: 1 Zak Hardaker (C); 20 Tom Briscoe; 3 Kallum Watkins; 31 Ash Handley (D); 5 Ryan Hall; 21 Liam Sutcliffe; 32 Ben White (D); 23 Brad Singleton; 9 Paul Aiton; 16 Ryan Bailey; 14 Stevie Ward; 19 Mitch Achurch; 28 Josh Walters. Subs (all used): 17 Ian Kirke; 18 Chris Clarkson; 26 Elliot Minchella; 33 Ashton Golding (D).
Tries: Watkins (2), Walters (6), Sutcliffe (12, 43), Achurch (31, 55), Hardaker (36);
Goals: Hardaker 1/3, Sutcliffe 3/4.
Rugby Leaguer & League Express Men of the Match: *Broncos:* Joe Keyes; *Rhinos:* Kallum Watkins.
Penalty count: 6-4; **Half-time:** 8-24;
Referee: Tim Roby; **Attendance:** 1,268.

ROUND 25

Thursday 28th August 2014

WARRINGTON WOLVES 24 HUDDERSFIELD GIANTS 24

WOLVES: 1 Matthew Russell; 29 Gene Ormsby; 4 Ryan Atkins; 5 Joel Monaghan; 18 Rhys Evans; 20 Gareth O'Brien; 7 Richard Myler; 8 Chris Hill; 14 Michael Monaghan (C); 15 Ben Harrison; 11 Trent Waterhouse; 12 Ben Westwood (C); 13 Simon Grix. Subs (all used): 9 Mick Higham; 16 Paul Wood; 23 James Laithwaite; 19 Anthony England.
Tries: O'Brien (18), Atkins (55), Harrison (62, 66); **Goals:** O'Brien 4/4.
GIANTS: 1 Scott Grix; 2 Jermaine McGillvary; 3 Leroy Cudjoe; 5 Aaron Murphy; 19 Jodie Broughton; 6 Danny Brough (C); 7 Luke Robinson; 8 Eorl Crabtree; 9 Shaun Lunt; 20 Antonio Kaufusi; 15 Larne Patrick; 14 Michael Lawrence; 13 Chris Bailey. Subs (all used): 10 Craig Kopczak; 16 David Faiumu; 17 Ukuma Ta'ai; 22 Jacob Fairbank.
Tries: Bailey (22), Ta'ai (27), Lunt (31), Broughton (44); **Goals:** Brough 3/4; **Field goals:** Brough (40, 80).
Rugby Leaguer & League Express Men of the Match: *Wolves:* Michael Monaghan; *Giants:* Danny Brough.
Penalty count: 7-4; **Half-time:** 6-19;
Referee: Ben Thaler; **Attendance:** 8,777.

Friday 29th August 2014

HULL FC 28 HULL KINGSTON ROVERS 0

HULL: 20 Jamie Shaul; 5 Tom Lineham; 28 Setaimata Sa; 4 Kirk Yeaman; 34 Fetuli Talanoa; 6 Richard Horne; 32 Jordan Rankin; 17 Liam Watts; 9 Danny Houghton; 22 Josh Bowden; 11 Gareth Ellis (C); 16 Jordan Thompson; 13 Joe Westerman. Subs (all used): 10 Chris Green; 26 Iafeta Palea'aesina; 33 Aaron Heremaia; 8 Mickey Paea.
Tries: Talanoa (9), Sa (17), Lineham (53, 75), Thompson (56); **Goals:** Rankin 4/6.
ROVERS: 1 Greg Eden; 24 Omari Caro; 3 Kris Welham; 18 Liam Salter; 32 Ade Gardner; 6 Travis Burns (C); 7 Kris Keating; 16 Jason Netherton; 9 Josh Hodgson (C); 10 Michael Weyman; 15 Graeme Horne; 34 Jason Chan; 12 Neville Costigan. Subs (all used): 14 Adam Walker; 23 James Green; 11 Kevin Larroyer; 20 Jordan Cox.
Rugby Leaguer & League Express Men of the Match: *Hull:* Gareth Ellis; *Rovers:* Josh Hodgson.
Penalty count: 6-1; **Half-time:** 12-0;
Referee: James Child; **Attendance:** 18,103.

LEEDS RHINOS 12 ST HELENS 13

RHINOS: 1 Zak Hardaker; 20 Tom Briscoe; 3 Kallum Watkins; 4 Joel Moon; 5 Ryan Hall; 13 Kevin Sinfield (C); 21 Liam Sutcliffe; 16 Ryan Bailey; 9 Paul Aiton; 10 Jamie Peacock; 11 Jamie Jones-Buchanan; 12 Carl Ablett; 15 Brett Delaney. Subs: 8 Kylie Leuluai; 19 Mitch Achurch; 29 Robbie Ward (not used); 23 Brad Singleton (not used).
Try: Sutcliffe (29); **Goals:** Sinfield 4/4.
Dismissal: Moon (22) - shoulder charge on Percival.
SAINTS: 38 Shannon McDonnell; 2 Tom Makinson; 22 Mark Percival; 4 Josh Jones; 26 Matty Dawson; 6 Lance Hohaia; 17 Paul Wellens (C); 16 Kyle Amor; 9 James Roby; 18 Alex Walmsley; 10 Louie McCarthy-Scarsbrook; 14 Anthony Laffranchi; 3 Jordan Turner. Subs (all used): 8 Mose Masoe; 11 Iosia Soliola; 15 Mark Flanagan; 13 Willie Manu.
Tries: McCarthy-Scarsbrook (62), Roby (70);
Goals: Percival 1/1, Makinson 1/1, Turner 0/1;
Field goal: Hohaia (74).
Rugby Leaguer & League Express Men of the Match: *Rhinos:* Paul Aiton; *Saints:* Louie McCarthy-Scarsbrook.
Penalty count: 9-6; **Half-time:** 12-2;
Referee: Richard Silverwood; **Attendance:** 17,682.

WIDNES VIKINGS 24 WIGAN WARRIORS 10

VIKINGS: 1 Rhys Hanbury; 20 Paddy Flynn; 14 Chris Dean; 4 Stefan Marsh; 5 Patrick Ah Van; 6 Kevin Brown; 7 Joe Mellor; 8 Eamon O'Carroll; 9 Jon Clarke (C); 25 Alex Gerrard; 17 Danny Galea; 12 Danny Tickle; 13 Hep Cahill. Subs (all used): 24 Macgraff Leuluai; 15 Lloyd White; 11 Dave Allen; 23 Phil Joseph.
Tries: Ah Van (8, 43), Flynn (12); **Goals:** Tickle 6/6.
WARRIORS: 23 Dan Sarginson; 2 Josh Charnley; 5 Anthony Gelling; 4 Iain Thornley; 31 Dominic Manfredi; 6 Blake Green; 7 Matty Smith; 16 Gil Dudson; 9 Michael McIlorum; 17 Dominic Crosby; 25 John Bateman; 12 Liam Farrell; 13 Sean O'Loughlin (C). Subs (all used): 8 Scott Taylor; 22 Eddy Pettybourne; 24 Tony Clubb; 42 Jamie Doran.
Tries: Manfredi (30), Charnley (34); **Goals:** Smith 1/2.
Sin bin: Farrell (52) - late challenge on Mellor.
Rugby Leaguer & League Express Men of the Match: *Vikings:* Kevin Brown; *Warriors:* Dan Sarginson.
Penalty count: 15-12; **Half-time:** 14-10;
Referee: Phil Bentham; **Attendance:** 6,223.

Saturday 30th August 2014

CATALAN DRAGONS 46 LONDON BRONCOS 4

DRAGONS: 2 Morgan Escare; 5 Michael Oldfield; 4 Ben Pomeroy; 25 Vincent Duport; 18 Daryl Millard; 6 Thomas Bosc; 34 Sam Williams; 8 Olivier Elima; 9 Ian Henderson; 12 Louis Anderson; 11 Zeb Taia; 17 Elliott Whitehead; 13 Gregory Mounis (C). Subs (all used): 16 Eloi Pelissier; 21 Julian Bousquet; 23 Lopini Paea; 29 Benjamin Garcia.
Tries: Duport (4), Escare (13, 21, 38), Pomeroy (29), Millard (34, 74), Taia (69); **Goals:** Bosc 7/8.
BRONCOS: 6 Ben Farrar; 3 Jordan Atkins; 1 Nesiasi Mataitonga; 4 Thomas Minns; 2 Kieran Dixon; 33 Joe Keyes; 7 Josh Drinkwater; 16 Nick Slyney; 9 Scott Moore; 30 Jon Wallace; 8 Atelea Vea; 11 Mike McMeeken; 12 Matt Cook (C). Subs (all used): 10 Olsi Krasniqi; 18 George Griffin; 19 Erjon Dollapi; 34 Oscar Thomas.
Try: Dixon (44); **Goals:** Drinkwater 0/1.
Rugby Leaguer & League Express Men of the Match: *Dragons:* Morgan Escare; *Broncos:* Matt Cook.
Penalty count: 9-9; **Half-time:** 34-0;
Referee: Tim Roby; **Attendance:** 7,067.

Sunday 31st August 2014

WAKEFIELD TRINITY WILDCATS 42 SALFORD RED DEVILS 6

WILDCATS: 6 Paul Sykes; 33 Richard Owen; 3 Dean Collis; 5 Reece Lyne; 31 Chris Riley; 7 Pita Godinet; 35 Tim Smith; 8 Scott Anderson; 9 Paul McShane (C); 10 Andy Raleigh; 34 Lee Gilmour; 26 Jon Molloy; 13 Danny Washbrook. Subs (all used): 11 Ali Lauitiiti; 17 Taulima Tautai; 14 Matty Wildie; 23 Daniel Smith.
Tries: Raleigh (11), Washbrook (15), Riley (19), Collis (55), Lauitiiti (58), Owen (63, 80), Godinet (70);
Goals: Sykes 5/8.
RED DEVILS: 38 Kevin Locke; 23 Greg Johnson; 4 Junior Sa'u; 40 Mason Caton-Brown; 26 Niall Evalds; 6 Rangi Chase; 14 Theo Fages; 8 Adrian Morley (C); 9 Tommy Lee; 10 Lama Tasi; 13 Harrison Hansen; 19 Matty Ashurst; 21 Jordan Walne. Subs (all used): 11 Tony Puletua; 16 Andrew Dixon; 15 Darrell Griffin; 35 Logan Tomkins.
Try: Hansen (47); **Goals:** Locke 1/1.
Rugby Leaguer & League Express Men of the Match: *Wildcats:* Tim Smith; *Red Devils:* Harrison Hansen.
Penalty count: 7-4; **Half-time:** 16-0;
Referee: Robert Hicks; **Attendance:** 4,016.

CASTLEFORD TIGERS 32 BRADFORD BULLS 18

TIGERS: 6 Luke Dorn; 2 Kirk Dixon; 4 Jake Webster; 3 Michael Shenton (C); 24 James Clare; 7 Marc Sneyd; 26 Liam Finn; 32 Lee Jewitt; 14 Daryl Clark; 8 Andy Lynch; 16 Oliver Holmes; 12 Weller Hauraki; 13 Nathan Massey. Subs (all used): 18 Frankie Mariano; 19 Scott Wheeldon; 20 Jamie Ellis; 23 Michael Channing.
Tries: Lynch (5), Clare (14), Dorn (31), Shenton (40), Clark (65); **Goals:** Sneyd 6/6.
BULLS: 1 Brett Kearney; 20 Luke George; 21 Adam Henry; 34 Joe Arundel; 38 Danny Williams; 17 Lee Gaskell; 7 Luke Gale (C); 14 Manase Manuokafoa; 19 Adam O'Brien; 15 Adam Sidlow; 12 Dale Ferguson; 33 Jay Pitts; 18 James Donaldson. Subs (all used): 11 Tom Olbison; 4 Matty Blythe; 30 Jamal Fakir; 16 Danny Addy.
Tries: Gaskell (35, 42, 55); **Goals:** Gale 3/3.
Rugby Leaguer & League Express Men of the Match: *Tigers:* Daryl Clark; *Bulls:* Lee Gaskell.
Penalty count: 8-4; **Half-time:** 24-6;
Referee: George Stokes; **Attendance:** 7,428.

ROUND 26

Thursday 4th September 2014

ST HELENS 12 WARRINGTON WOLVES 39

SAINTS: 38 Shannon McDonnell; 2 Tom Makinson; 26 Matty Dawson; 4 Josh Jones; 5 Adam Swift; 6 Lance Hohaia; 17 Paul Wellens (C); 16 Kyle Amor; 9 James Roby; 18 Alex Walmsley; 14 Anthony Laffranchi; 10 Louie McCarthy-Scarsbrook; 3 Jordan Turner. Subs (all used); 8 Mose Masoe; 11 Iosia Soliola; 13 Willie Manu; 15 Mark Flanagan.
Tries: McDonnell (3), Manu (31); **Goals:** Makinson 2/2.
WOLVES: 1 Matthew Russell; 5 Joel Monaghan; 4 Ryan Atkins; 6 Stefan Ratchford; 18 Rhys Evans; 20 Gareth O'Brien; 7 Richard Myler; 8 Chris Hill; 14 Michael Monaghan (C); 15 Ben Harrison; 23 James Laithwaite; 12 Ben Westwood (C); 13 Simon Grix. Subs (all used): 9 Mick Higham; 10 Roy Asotasi; 11 Trent Waterhouse; 17 Ben Currie.
Tries: Ratchford (6), M Monaghan (19), O'Brien (23), J Monaghan (25, 52), Myler (45), Atkins (63);
Goals: Ratchford 4/5, O'Brien 1/1; **Field goal:** Myler (40).
Rugby Leaguer & League Express Men of the Match: *Saints:* Shannon McDonnell; *Wolves:* Chris Hill.
Penalty count: 3-6; **Half-time:** 12-23;
Referee: James Child; **Attendance:** 12,854.

Friday 5th September 2014

WIGAN WARRIORS 21 LEEDS RHINOS 6

WARRIORS: 1 Matt Bowen; 2 Josh Charnley; 14 Jack Hughes; 23 Dan Sarginson; 32 Joe Burgess; 6 Blake Green; 7 Matty Smith; 10 Ben Flower; 9 Michael McIlorum; 17 Dominic Crosby; 11 Joel Tomkins; 12 Liam Farrell; 13 Sean O'Loughlin (C). Subs (all used): 19 Sam Powell; 22 Eddy Pettybourne; 24 Tony Clubb; 25 John Bateman.
Tries: Burgess (13), Smith (25), Flower (70);
Goals: Smith 4/4; **Field goal:** Smith (80).
RHINOS: 1 Zak Hardaker; 20 Tom Briscoe; 3 Kallum Watkins; 22 Jimmy Keinhorst; 5 Ryan Hall; 13 Kevin Sinfield (C); 21 Liam Sutcliffe; 16 Ryan Bailey; 9 Paul Aiton; 10 Jamie Peacock; 15 Brett Delaney; 12 Carl Ablett; 11 Jamie Jones-Buchanan. Subs (all used): 8 Kylie Leuluai; 19 Mitch Achurch; 14 Stevie Ward; 23 Brad Singleton.
Try: Sutcliffe (44); **Goals:** Sinfield 1/1.
Rugby Leaguer & League Express Men of the Match: *Warriors:* Sean O'Loughlin; *Rhinos:* Liam Sutcliffe.
Penalty count: 7-7; **Half-time:** 14-0;
Referee: Ben Thaler; **Attendance:** 20,265.

Sunday 7th September 2014

BRADFORD BULLS 12 WIDNES VIKINGS 32

BULLS: 1 Brett Kearney; 21 Adam Henry; 39 Brad Adams (D); 13 Chev Walker; 38 Danny Williams; 17 Lee Gaskell; 7 Luke Gale (C); 14 Manase Manuokafoa; 19 Adam O'Brien; 15 Adam Sidlow; 11 Tom Olbison; 33 Jay Pitts; 16 Danny Addy. Subs (all used): 34 Joe Arundel; 4 Matty Blythe; 30 Jamal Fakir; 18 James Donaldson.
Tries: Olbison (11), Walker (24); **Goals:** Gale 2/2.
VIKINGS: 1 Rhys Hanbury; 20 Paddy Flynn; 4 Stefan Marsh; 3 Cameron Phelps; 5 Patrick Ah Van; 6 Kevin Brown (C); 7 Joe Mellor; 8 Eamon O'Carroll; 15 Lloyd White; 18 Paul Johnson; 17 Danny Galea; 12 Danny Tickle; 13 Hep Cahill. Subs (all used): 22 Liam Carberry; 24 Macgraff Leuluai; 23 Phil Joseph; 14 Chris Dean.

Tries: Flynn (2, 8), Marsh (52, 55, 69), Ah Van (76), White (78); **Goals:** Tickle 0/5, Phelps 2/2.
Rugby Leaguer & League Express Men of the Match: *Bulls:* Adam O'Brien; *Vikings:* Stefan Marsh.
Penalty count: 5-2; **Half-time:** 12-8;
Referee: Robert Hicks; **Attendance:** 7,438.

HUDDERSFIELD GIANTS 38 HULL FC 28

GIANTS: 27 Jake Connor; 2 Jermaine McGillvary; 5 Aaron Murphy; 4 Joe Wardle; 19 Jodie Broughton; 6 Danny Brough (C); 7 Luke Robinson; 8 Eorl Crabtree; 9 Shaun Lunt; 21 Anthony Mullally; 11 Brett Ferres; 15 Larne Patrick; 13 Chris Bailey. Subs (all used): 10 Craig Kopczak; 16 David Faiumu; 14 Michael Lawrence; 17 Ukuma Ta'ai.
Tries: Connor (12, 36), Faiumu (33), Broughton (54, 79), Ferres (56), Mullally (62), McGillvary (67);
Goals: Brough 3/8.
HULL: 20 Jamie Shaul; 5 Tom Lineham; 4 Kirk Yeaman; 38 Jack Logan; 34 Fetuli Talanoa; 32 Jordan Rankin; 33 Aaron Heremaia; 17 Liam Watts; 9 Danny Houghton; 22 Josh Bowden; 11 Gareth Ellis (C); 16 Jordan Thompson; 13 Joe Westerman. Subs (all used): 30 Harry Tyson-Wilson (D); 10 Chris Green; 8 Mickey Paea; 21 Dean Hadley.
Tries: Houghton (7), Heremaia (25), Shaul (28), Thompson (51), Ellis (73); **Goals:** Rankin 4/5.
Rugby Leaguer & League Express Men of the Match: *Giants:* Danny Brough; *Hull:* Danny Houghton.
Penalty count: 5-3; **Half-time:** 14-18;
Referee: Phil Bentham; **Attendance:** 6,370.

HULL KINGSTON ROVERS 14 CATALAN DRAGONS 32

ROVERS: 1 Greg Eden; 30 Macauley Hallett (D); 15 Graeme Horne; 19 Craig Hall; 18 Liam Salter; 6 Travis Burns (C); 7 Kris Keating; 14 Adam Walker; 9 Josh Hodgson (C); 10 Michael Weyman; 11 Kevin Larroyer; 34 Jason Chan; 12 Neville Costigan. Subs (all used): 21 Keal Carlile; 23 James Green; 16 Jason Netherton; 27 Sonny Esslemont (D).
Tries: Salter (8), Hallett (35), Chan (47);
Goals: Burns 1/3.
DRAGONS: 2 Morgan Escare; 5 Michael Oldfield; 4 Ben Pomeroy; 25 Vincent Duport; 18 Daryl Millard; 6 Thomas Bosc; 34 Sam Williams; 8 Olivier Elima; 9 Ian Henderson; 12 Louis Anderson; 11 Zeb Taia; 17 Elliott Whitehead; 13 Gregory Mounis (C). Subs (all used): 16 Eloi Pelissier; 21 Julian Bousquet; 23 Lopini Paea; 29 Benjamin Garcia.
Tries: Oldfield (19, 28, 70), Williams (53, 74), Escare (77); **Goals:** Bosc 4/7.
Rugby Leaguer & League Express Men of the Match: *Rovers:* Macauley Hallett; *Dragons:* Sam Williams.
Penalty count: 5-6; **Half-time:** 12-10;
Referee: Richard Silverwood; **Attendance:** 6,412.

SALFORD RED DEVILS 58 LONDON BRONCOS 26

RED DEVILS: 38 Kevin Locke; 23 Greg Johnson; 4 Junior Sa'u; 39 Josh Griffin; 26 Niall Evalds; 6 Rangi Chase; 14 Theo Fages; 8 Adrian Morley (C); 9 Tommy Lee; 10 Lama Tasi; 13 Harrison Hansen; 19 Matty Ashurst; 21 Jordan Walne. Subs (all used): 11 Tony Puletua; 15 Darrell Griffin; 22 Jason Walton; 35 Logan Tomkins.
Tries: Lee (7), J Walne (21), J Griffin (30, 50, 55), Johnson (34, 54, 79), Tomkins (39), Walton (48);
Goals: J Griffin 9/10.
BRONCOS: 6 Ben Farrar; 3 Jordan Atkins; 1 Nesiasi Mataitonga; 4 Thomas Minns; 2 Kieran Dixon; 34 Oscar Thomas; 7 Josh Drinkwater; 16 Nick Slyney; 9 Scott Moore; 30 Jon Wallace; 11 Mike McMeeken; 8 Atelea Vea; 12 Matt Cook (C). Subs (all used): 10 Olsi Krasniqi; 19 Erjon Dollapi; 25 Iliess Macani; 32 Toby Everett (D).
Tries: Atkins (26), Macani (43), Cook (60), Drinkwater (65), Slyney (68); **Goals:** Drinkwater 3/5.
Rugby Leaguer & League Express Men of the Match: *Red Devils:* Josh Griffin; *Broncos:* Matt Cook.
Penalty count: 4-10; **Half-time:** 30-4;
Referee: Matthew Thomason; **Attendance:** 3,268.

**CASTLEFORD TIGERS 26
WAKEFIELD TRINITY WILDCATS 22**

TIGERS: 6 Luke Dorn; 2 Kirk Dixon; 4 Jake Webster; 3 Michael Shenton (C); 24 James Clare; 7 Marc Sneyd; 26 Liam Finn; 8 Andy Lynch; 14 Daryl Clark; 32 Lee Jewitt; 16 Oliver Holmes; 12 Weller Hauraki; 13 Nathan Massey. Subs (all used): 9 Adam Milner; 18 Frankie Mariano; 19 Scott Wheeldon; 35 Garreth Carvell.
Tries: Dorn (6), Clare (16, 28), Dixon (33), Webster (63);
Goals: Sneyd 3/5.
WILDCATS: 6 Paul Sykes; 33 Richard Owen; 34 Lee Gilmour; 5 Reece Lyne; 31 Chris Riley; 7 Pita Godinet; 35 Tim Smith; 8 Scott Anderson; 9 Paul McShane (C); 10 Andy Raleigh; 13 Danny Washbrook; 26 Jon Molloy; 23 Daniel Smith. Subs (all used): 11 Ali Lauitiiti; 14 Matty Wildie; 17 Taulima Tautai; 21 Chris Annakin.
Tries: Gilmour (35), Riley (38), Anderson (69), Owen (73); **Goals:** Sykes 3/4.
Rugby Leaguer & League Express Men of the Match: *Tigers:* Andy Lynch; *Wildcats:* Paul Sykes.
Penalty count: 4-7; **Half-time:** 22-10;
Referee: James Child; **Attendance:** 9,182.

ROUND 27

Thursday 11th September 2014

WIGAN WARRIORS 24 WARRINGTON WOLVES 20

WARRIORS: 1 Matt Bowen; 2 Josh Charnley; 5 Anthony Gelling; 23 Dan Sarginson; 32 Joe Burgess; 6 Blake Green; 7 Matty Smith; 10 Ben Flower; 9 Michael McIlorum; 17 Dominic Crosby; 11 Joel Tomkins; 12 Liam Farrell; 13 Sean O'Loughlin (C). Subs (all used): 19 Sam Powell; 22 Eddy Pettybourne; 24 Tony Clubb; 25 John Bateman.
Tries: Burgess (7, 45), Charnley (52, 63), Green (67);
Goals: Smith 2/5.
Sin bin: Pettybourne (55) - fighting.
On report: McIlorum (76) - challenge on Laithwaite.
WOLVES: 1 Matthew Russell; 5 Joel Monaghan; 6 Stefan Ratchford; 3 Chris Bridge; 18 Rhys Evans; 20 Gareth O'Brien; 7 Richard Myler; 8 Chris Hill; 14 Michael Monaghan (C); 10 Roy Asotasi; 23 James Laithwaite; 11 Trent Waterhouse; 15 Ben Harrison. Subs (all used): 9 Mick Higham; 16 Paul Wood; 17 Ben Currie; 19 Anthony England.
Tries: J Monaghan (27, 39), Myler (35);
Goals: Ratchford 4/4.
Sin bin: Wood (55) - fighting.
Rugby Leaguer & League Express Men of the Match: *Warriors:* Josh Charnley; *Wolves:* Richard Myler.
Penalty count: 3-4; **Half-time:** 4-18;
Referee: Phil Bentham; **Attendance:** 15,686.

Friday 12th September 2014

HUDDERSFIELD GIANTS 17 ST HELENS 16

GIANTS: 5 Aaron Murphy; 2 Jermaine McGillvary; 3 Leroy Cudjoe; 4 Joe Wardle; 19 Jodie Broughton; 27 Jake Connor; 7 Luke Robinson (C); 20 Antonio Kaufusi; 9 Shaun Lunt; 23 Josh Johnson; 11 Brett Ferres; 14 Michael Lawrence; 15 Larne Patrick. Subs (all used): 10 Craig Kopczak; 13 Chris Bailey; 16 David Faiumu; 17 Ukuma Ta'ai.
Tries: Connor (36), Lunt (42), Cudjoe (57);
Goals: Connor 2/3; **Field goal:** Cudjoe (71).
SAINTS: 17 Paul Wellens (C); 2 Tom Makinson; 22 Mark Percival; 4 Josh Jones; 26 Matty Dawson; 6 Lance Hohaia; 24 Gary Wheeler; 16 Kyle Amor; 9 James Roby; 8 Mose Masoe; 13 Willie Manu; 14 Anthony Laffranchi; 3 Jordan Turner. Subs (all used): 11 Iosia Soliola; 18 Alex Walmsley; 15 Mark Flanagan; 10 Louie McCarthy-Scarsbrook.
Tries: Makinson (23), Roby (25), Hohaia (60);
Goals: Percival 2/3.
Dismissal: Walmsley (28) - late challenge on Robinson.
Rugby Leaguer & League Express Men of the Match: *Giants:* Jake Connor; *Saints:* James Roby.
Penalty count: 6-3; **Half-time:** 6-10;
Referee: Richard Silverwood; **Attendance:** 7,244.

HULL FC 24 LEEDS RHINOS 19

HULL: 32 Jordan Rankin; 5 Tom Lineham; 38 Jack Logan; 4 Kirk Yeaman; 34 Fetuli Talanoa; 33 Aaron Heremaia; 6 Richard Horne; 17 Liam Watts; 9 Danny Houghton; 8 Mickey Paea; 11 Gareth Ellis (C); 16 Jordan Thompson; 13 Joe Westerman. Subs (all used): 10 Chris Green; 21 Dean Hadley; 24 James Cunningham; 22 Josh Bowden.
Tries: Lineham (15), Ellis (61), Talanoa (64), Logan (70, 75); **Goals:** Rankin 2/5.
RHINOS: 1 Zak Hardaker; 20 Tom Briscoe; 3 Kallum Watkins; 21 Liam Sutcliffe; 5 Ryan Hall; 13 Kevin Sinfield (C); 6 Danny McGuire; 23 Brad Singleton; 9 Paul Aiton; 10 Jamie Peacock; 12 Carl Ablett; 15 Brett Delaney; 11 Jamie Jones-Buchanan. Subs (all used): 8 Kylie Leuluai; 17 Ian Kirke; 19 Mitch Achurch; 7 Rob Burrow.
Tries: Ablett (37), McGuire (43), Hall (55);
Goals: Sinfield 3/4; **Field goal:** Sinfield (39).
Rugby Leaguer & League Express Men of the Match: *Hull:* Richard Horne; *Rhinos:* Danny McGuire.
Penalty count: 5-6; **Half-time:** 4-7;
Referee: Tim Roby; **Attendance:** 11,964.

SALFORD RED DEVILS 36 WIDNES VIKINGS 6

RED DEVILS: 38 Kevin Locke; 26 Niall Evalds; 4 Junior Sa'u; 39 Josh Griffin; 40 Mason Caton-Brown; 6 Rangi Chase; 14 Theo Fages; 8 Adrian Morley (C); 9 Tommy Lee; 10 Lama Tasi; 13 Harrison Hansen; 19 Matty Ashurst; 21 Jordan Walne. Subs (all used): 11 Tony Puletua; 15 Darrell Griffin; 35 Logan Tomkins; 22 Jason Walton.
Tries: Hansen (4), Sa'u (10, 57), Puletua (36), Chase (39), J Griffin (52); **Goals:** J Griffin 6/6.
VIKINGS: 2 Jack Owens; 20 Paddy Flynn; 4 Stefan Marsh; 3 Cameron Phelps; 5 Patrick Ah Van; 27 Tom Gilmore; 7 Joe Mellor (C); 10 Ben Kavanagh; 15 Lloyd White; 13 Hep Cahill; 24 Macgraff Leuluai; 14 Chris Dean; 16 Willie Isa. Subs (all used): 35 Paul Clough; 22 Liam Carberry; 23 Phil Joseph; 17 Danny Galea.
Try: Ah Van (72); **Goals:** Owens 1/1.
Rugby Leaguer & League Express Men of the Match: *Red Devils:* Junior Sa'u; *Vikings:* Willie Isa.
Penalty count: 5-6; **Half-time:** 24-0;
Referee: James Child; **Attendance:** 3,268.

Saturday 13th September 2014

LONDON BRONCOS 36 BRADFORD BULLS 46

BRONCOS: 35 Alex Walker (D); 2 Kieran Dixon; 6 Ben Farrar; 34 Oscar Thomas; 3 Jordan Atkins; 33 Joe Keyes; 7 Josh Drinkwater; 16 Nick Slyney; 9 Scott Moore; 30 Jon Wallace; 11 Mike McMeeken; 8 Atelea Vea; 12 Matt Cook (C). Subs (all used): 32 Toby Everett; 10 Olsi Krasniqi; 21 Joel Wicks; 19 Erjon Dollapi.
Tries: Cook (17), Keyes (22), Drinkwater (25, 70), Dollapi (36), Slyney (53); **Goals:** Drinkwater 6/6.
BULLS: 1 Brett Kearney; 5 Jamie Foster; 34 Joe Arundel; 13 Chev Walker; 21 Adam Henry; 16 Danny Addy; 7 Luke Gale (C); 14 Manase Manuokafoa; 19 Adam O'Brien; 36 Jordan Baldwinson; 11 Tom Olbison; 33 Jay Pitts; 18 James Donaldson. Subs (all used): 24 Alex Mellor; 40 Emmerson Whittel (D); 25 Nathan Conroy; 39 Brad Adams.
Tries: Gale (4, 7, 67, 77), Arundel (12), Kearney (57), Pitts (63), Manuokafoa (80); **Goals:** Foster 7/8.
Rugby Leaguer & League Express Men of the Match: *Broncos:* Matt Cook; *Bulls:* Jay Pitts.
Penalty count: 6-7; **Half-time:** 24-16;
Referee: Joe Cobb; **Attendance:** 1,402.

CATALAN DRAGONS 28 CASTLEFORD TIGERS 6

DRAGONS: 2 Morgan Escare; 5 Michael Oldfield; 4 Ben Pomeroy; 25 Vincent Duport; 18 Daryl Millard; 6 Thomas Bosc; 34 Sam Williams; 8 Olivier Elima; 9 Ian Henderson; 12 Louis Anderson; 11 Zeb Taia; 17 Elliott Whitehead; 24 Jason Baitieri (C). Subs (all used): 10 Jeff Lima; 15 Antoni Maria; 16 Eloi Pelissier; 29 Benjamin Garcia.
Tries: Escare (31, 40), Taia (42), Henderson (59), Whitehead (65); **Goals:** Bosc 4/5.
TIGERS: 6 Luke Dorn; 2 Kirk Dixon; 4 Jake Webster; 3 Michael Shenton (C); 24 James Clare; 7 Marc Sneyd; 26 Liam Finn; 8 Andy Lynch; 14 Daryl Clark; 32 Lee Jewitt; 16 Oliver Holmes; 12 Weller Hauraki; 13 Nathan Massey. Subs (all used): 10 Craig Huby; 11 Grant Millington; 19 Scott Wheeldon; 20 Jamie Ellis.
Try: Dixon (45); **Goals:** Sneyd 1/1.
Rugby Leaguer & League Express Men of the Match: *Dragons:* Morgan Escare; *Tigers:* Daryl Clark.
Penalty count: 6-6; **Half-time:** 10-0;
Referee: Ben Thaler; **Attendance:** 9,223.

Sunday 14th September 2014

**WAKEFIELD TRINITY WILDCATS 18
HULL KINGSTON ROVERS 42**

WILDCATS: 6 Paul Sykes; 33 Richard Owen; 3 Dean Collis; 5 Reece Lyne; 31 Chris Riley; 7 Pita Godinet; 35 Tim Smith; 8 Scott Anderson; 9 Paul McShane (C); 10 Andy Raleigh; 34 Lee Gilmour; 13 Danny Washbrook; 26 Jon Molloy. Subs (all used): 14 Matty Wildie; 11 Ali Lauitiiti; 21 Chris Annakin; 23 Daniel Smith.
Tries: Collis (54), Riley (65), Raleigh (67);
Goals: Sykes 3/3.
ROVERS: 1 Greg Eden; 24 Omari Caro; 18 Liam Salter; 3 Kris Welham; 30 Macauley Hallett; 6 Travis Burns (C); 19 Craig Hall; 14 Adam Walker; 9 Josh Hodgson (C); 10 Michael Weyman; 22 Rhys Lovegrove; 15 Graeme Horne; 12 Neville Costigan. Subs (all used): 23 James Green; 20 Jordan Cox; 21 Keal Carlile; 11 Kevin Larroyer.
Tries: Caro (1, 27, 39), Hallett (17, 35), Eden (22, 57), Carlile (44); **Goals:** Burns 0/1, Hall 5/7.
Rugby Leaguer & League Express Men of the Match: *Wildcats:* Paul McShane; *Rovers:* Craig Hall.
Penalty count: 7-5; **Half-time:** 0-30;
Referee: Robert Hicks; **Attendance:** 4,481.

PLAY-OFFS

QUALIFYING PLAY-OFFS

Thursday 18th September 2014

WIGAN WARRIORS 57 HUDDERSFIELD GIANTS 4

WARRIORS: 1 Matt Bowen; 2 Josh Charnley; 5 Anthony Gelling; 23 Dan Sarginson; 32 Joe Burgess; 6 Blake Green; 7 Matty Smith; 10 Ben Flower; 9 Michael McIlorum; 17 Dominic Crosby; 11 Joel Tomkins; 12 Liam Farrell; 13 Sean O'Loughlin (C). Subs (all used): 19 Sam Powell; 22 Eddy Pettybourne; 24 Tony Clubb; 25 John Bateman.
Tries: Charnley (23, 58), Smith (25), Clubb (32), L Farrell (35), J Tomkins (47), Sarginson (51), Bowen (54), O'Loughlin (64), Burgess (73);
Goals: Smith 8/11; **Field goal:** Smith (80).
GIANTS: 1 Scott Grix; 2 Jermaine McGillvary; 3 Leroy Cudjoe; 4 Joe Wardle; 5 Aaron Murphy; 27 Jake Connor; 7 Luke Robinson; 8 Eorl Crabtree; 9 Shaun Lunt; 20 Antonio Kaufusi; 11 Brett Ferres (C); 15 Larne Patrick; 14 Michael Lawrence. Subs (all used): 10 Craig Kopczak; 16 David Faiumu; 17 Ukuma Ta'ai; 23 Josh Johnson.
Try: Cudjoe (42); **Goals:** Connor 0/1.
Rugby Leaguer & League Express Men of the Match: *Warriors:* Matty Smith; *Giants:* Brett Ferres.
Penalty count: 5-7; **Half-time:** 24-0;
Referee: Richard Silverwood; **Attendance:** 8,652.

Friday 19th September 2014

ST HELENS 41 CASTLEFORD TIGERS 0

SAINTS: 17 Paul Wellens (C); 2 Tom Makinson; 22 Mark Percival; 24 Gary Wheeler; 5 Adam Swift; 6 Lance Hohaia; 15 Mark Flanagan; 27 Greg Richards; 9 James Roby; 16 Kyle Amor; 10 Louie McCarthy-Scarsbrook; 28 Luke Thompson; 3 Jordan Turner. Subs (all used): 8 Mose Masoe; 11 Iosia Soliola; 13 Willie Manu; 14 Anthony Laffranchi.
Tries: Roby (19, 25), Turner (46), Swift (58), Makinson (64), Amor (68), Masoe (75);
Goals: Percival 6/7; **Field goal:** Turner (40).
TIGERS: 6 Luke Dorn; 2 Kirk Dixon; 4 Jake Webster; 3 Michael Shenton (C); 5 Justin Carney; 20 Jamie Ellis; 26 Liam Finn; 8 Andy Lynch; 9 Adam Milner; 10 Craig Huby; 16 Oliver Holmes; 12 Weller Hauraki; 11 Grant Millington. Subs (all used): 13 Nathan Massey; 14 Daryl Clark; 19 Scott Wheeldon; 23 Michael Channing.
Sin bin: Shenton (63) - professional foul.
Rugby Leaguer & League Express Men of the Match: *Saints:* James Roby; *Tigers:* Nathan Massey.
Penalty count: 8-5; **Half-time:** 13-0;
Referee: James Child; **Attendance:** 7,548.

Catalan Dragons' Louis Anderson breaks through the Leeds defensive line

ELIMINATION PLAY-OFFS

Saturday 20th September 2014

WARRINGTON WOLVES 22 WIDNES VIKINGS 19

WOLVES: 1 Matthew Russell; 5 Joel Monaghan; 3 Chris Bridge; 4 Ryan Atkins; 18 Rhys Evans; 20 Gareth O'Brien; 7 Richard Myler; 8 Chris Hill; 9 Mick Higham; 15 Ben Harrison; 23 James Laithwaite; 11 Trent Waterhouse; 6 Stefan Ratchford. Subs (all used): 14 Michael Monaghan (C); 10 Roy Asotasi; 17 Ben Currie; 19 Anthony England. **Tries:** J Monaghan (35, 45, 56), R Evans (48); **Goals:** Ratchford 3/4.
VIKINGS: 1 Rhys Hanbury; 20 Paddy Flynn; 14 Chris Dean; 3 Cameron Phelps; 5 Patrick Ah Van; 6 Kevin Brown; 7 Joe Mellor; 8 Eamon O'Carroll; 9 Jon Clarke (C); 13 Hep Cahill; 17 Danny Galea; 12 Danny Tickle; 24 Macgraff Leuluai. Subs (all used): 16 Willie Isa; 23 Phil Joseph; 15 Lloyd White; 25 Alex Gerrard.
Tries: Flynn (4, 9), Hanbury (29); **Goals:** Tickle 3/4; **Field goal:** Brown (38).
Rugby Leaguer & League Express Men of the Match: *Wolves:* Chris Bridge; *Vikings:* Kevin Brown.
Penalty count: 9-4; **Half-time:** 6-19.
Referee: Ben Thaler; **Attendance:** 7,229.

LEEDS RHINOS 20 CATALAN DRAGONS 24

RHINOS: 1 Zak Hardaker; 20 Tom Briscoe; 3 Kallum Watkins; 4 Joel Moon; 5 Ryan Hall; 13 Kevin Sinfield (C); 6 Danny McGuire; 8 Kylie Leuluai; 7 Rob Burrow; 10 Jamie Peacock; 11 Jamie Jones-Buchanan; 15 Brett Delaney; 12 Carl Ablett. Subs (all used): 19 Mitch Achurch; 16 Ryan Bailey; 9 Paul Aiton; 21 Liam Sutcliffe.
Tries: Ablett (16), Watkins (39), Jones-Buchanan (70); **Goals:** Sinfield 3/3, Hardaker 1/1.
DRAGONS: 2 Morgan Escare; 5 Michael Oldfield; 4 Ben Pomeroy; 25 Vincent Duport; 18 Daryl Millard; 6 Thomas Bosc; 34 Sam Williams; 8 Olivier Elima; 9 Ian Henderson; 12 Louis Anderson; 11 Zeb Taia; 17 Elliott Whitehead; 13 Gregory Mounis (C). Subs (all used): 10 Jeff Lima; 29 Benjamin Garcia; 16 Eloi Pelissier; 21 Julian Bousquet.
Tries: Williams (25, 79), Taia (46), Anderson (57); **Goals:** Bosc 4/4.
On report: Duport (35) - alleged late challenge on Sinfield.
Rugby Leaguer & League Express Men of the Match: *Rhinos:* Zak Hardaker; *Dragons:* Sam Williams.
Penalty count: 7-3; **Half-time:** 14-6;
Referee: Phil Bentham; **Attendance:** 7,112.

PRELIMINARY SEMI-FINALS

Thursday 25th September 2014

CASTLEFORD TIGERS 14 WARRINGTON WOLVES 30

TIGERS: 6 Luke Dorn; 24 James Clare; 23 Michael Channing; 3 Michael Shenton (C); 5 Justin Carney; 7 Marc Sneyd; 20 Jamie Ellis; 8 Andy Lynch; 14 Daryl Clark; 10 Craig Huby; 16 Oliver Holmes; 12 Weller Hauraki; 13 Nathan Massey. Subs (all used): 2 Kirk Dixon; 11 Grant Millington; 9 Adam Milner; 19 Scott Wheeldon.

Tries: Ellis (23), Dorn (56), Shenton (76);
Goals: Sneyd 1/3.
WOLVES: 6 Stefan Ratchford; 5 Joel Monaghan; 3 Chris Bridge; 4 Ryan Atkins; 18 Rhys Evans; 20 Gareth O'Brien; 7 Richard Myler; 8 Chris Hill; 14 Michael Monaghan (C); 19 Anthony England; 23 James Laithwaite; 11 Trent Waterhouse; 15 Ben Harrison. Subs (all used): 9 Mick Higham; 10 Roy Asotasi; 17 Ben Currie; 16 Paul Wood.
Tries: Atkins (3), J Monaghan (26, 72), O'Brien (62), R Evans (66); **Goals:** Ratchford 5/6.
Sin bin: R Evans (74) - holding down.
Rugby Leaguer & League Express Men of the Match: *Tigers:* Oliver Holmes; *Wolves:* Stefan Ratchford.
Penalty count: 5-8; **Half-time:** 4-10;
Referee: Phil Bentham; **Attendance:** 6,219.

Friday 26th September 2014

HUDDERSFIELD GIANTS 16 CATALAN DRAGONS 18

GIANTS: 5 Aaron Murphy; 2 Jermaine McGillvary; 3 Leroy Cudjoe; 4 Joe Wardle; 19 Jodie Broughton; 6 Danny Brough (C); 7 Luke Robinson; 10 Craig Kopczak; 9 Shaun Lunt; 20 Antonio Kaufusi; 11 Brett Ferres; 17 Ukuma Ta'ai; 13 Chris Bailey. Subs (all used): 8 Eorl Crabtree; 15 Larne Patrick; 16 David Faiumu; 21 Anthony Mullally.
Tries: Broughton (3), Murphy (26), Robinson (61);
Goals: Brough 2/3.
DRAGONS: 2 Morgan Escare; 5 Michael Oldfield; 4 Ben Pomeroy; 25 Vincent Duport; 18 Daryl Millard; 6 Thomas Bosc; 34 Sam Williams; 8 Olivier Elima; 9 Ian Henderson; 12 Louis Anderson; 11 Zeb Taia; 17 Elliott Whitehead; 13 Gregory Mounis (C). Subs (all used): 10 Jeff Lima; 16 Eloi Pelissier; 21 Julian Bousquet; 29 Benjamin Garcia.
Tries: Millard (12), Oldfield (20), Pomeroy (70);
Goals: Bosc 3/4.
Rugby Leaguer & League Express Men of the Match: *Giants:* Danny Brough; *Dragons:* Ian Henderson.
Penalty count: 4-6; **Half-time:** 10-10;
Referee: James Child; **Attendance:** 6,900.

QUALIFYING SEMI-FINALS

Thursday 2nd October 2014

ST HELENS 30 CATALAN DRAGONS 12

SAINTS: 17 Paul Wellens (C); 2 Tom Makinson; 22 Mark Percival; 4 Josh Jones; 5 Adam Swift; 6 Lance Hohaia; 15 Mark Flanagan; 16 Kyle Amor; 9 James Roby; 8 Mose Masoe; 10 Louie McCarthy-Scarsbrook; 28 Luke Thompson; 3 Jordan Turner. Subs (all used): 11 Iosia Soliola; 13 Willie Manu; 18 Alex Walmsley; 27 Greg Richards.
Tries: Turner (25), Swift (37), Manu (47), Masoe (59), Percival (63); **Goals:** Percival 5/7.
DRAGONS: 2 Morgan Escare; 5 Michael Oldfield; 4 Ben Pomeroy; 25 Vincent Duport; 18 Daryl Millard; 6 Thomas Bosc; 34 Sam Williams; 8 Olivier Elima; 9 Ian Henderson; 12 Louis Anderson; 11 Zeb Taia; 17 Elliott Whitehead; 13 Gregory Mounis. Subs (all used): 10 Jeff Lima; 16 Eloi Pelissier; 21 Julian Bousquet; 29 Benjamin Garcia.
Tries: Escare (21), Oldfield (67); **Goals:** Bosc 2/2.

Rugby Leaguer & League Express Men of the Match: *Saints:* James Roby; *Dragons:* Michael Oldfield.
Penalty count: 7-7; **Half-time:** 12-6;
Referee: Richard Silverwood; **Attendance:** 8,888.

Friday 3rd October 2014

WIGAN WARRIORS 16 WARRINGTON WOLVES 12

WARRIORS: 1 Matt Bowen; 2 Josh Charnley; 5 Anthony Gelling; 23 Dan Sarginson; 32 Joe Burgess; 6 Blake Green; 7 Matty Smith; 10 Ben Flower; 9 Michael McIlorum; 17 Dominic Crosby; 11 Joel Tomkins; 12 Liam Farrell; 13 Sean O'Loughlin (C). Subs (all used): 19 Sam Powell; 22 Eddy Pettybourne; 24 Tony Clubb; 25 John Bateman.
Tries: J Tomkins (24), Gelling (54), Burgess (79);
Goals: Smith 2/3, Bowen 0/1.
WOLVES: 6 Stefan Ratchford; 5 Joel Monaghan; 3 Chris Bridge; 4 Ryan Atkins; 18 Rhys Evans; 20 Gareth O'Brien; 7 Richard Myler; 8 Chris Hill; 14 Michael Monaghan (C); 19 Anthony England; 23 James Laithwaite; 11 Trent Waterhouse; 15 Ben Harrison. Subs (all used): 9 Mick Higham; 10 Roy Asotasi; 17 Ben Currie; 1 Matthew Russell.
Tries: J Monaghan (38), O'Brien (46);
Goals: Ratchford 1/2, O'Brien 1/1.
Rugby Leaguer & League Express Men of the Match: *Warriors:* Sean O'Loughlin; *Wolves:* Mick Higham.
Penalty count: 5-9; **Half-time:** 8-4;
Referee: Phil Bentham; **Attendance:** 15,023.

GRAND FINAL

Saturday 11th October 2014

ST HELENS 14 WIGAN WARRIORS 6

SAINTS: 17 Paul Wellens (C); 2 Tom Makinson; 22 Mark Percival; 4 Josh Jones; 5 Adam Swift; 15 Mark Flanagan; 6 Lance Hohaia; 16 Kyle Amor; 9 James Roby; 8 Mose Masoe; 10 Louie McCarthy-Scarsbrook; 11 Iosia Soliola; 3 Jordan Turner. Subs (all used): 28 Luke Thompson; 13 Willie Manu; 18 Alex Walmsley; 27 Greg Richards.
Tries: Soliola (54), Makinson (69); **Goals:** Percival 3/3.
WARRIORS: 1 Matt Bowen; 2 Josh Charnley; 5 Anthony Gelling; 23 Dan Sarginson; 32 Joe Burgess; 6 Blake Green; 7 Matty Smith; 10 Ben Flower; 19 Sam Powell; 17 Dominic Crosby; 11 Joel Tomkins; 12 Liam Farrell; 13 Sean O'Loughlin (C). Subs (all used): 22 Eddy Pettybourne; 24 Tony Clubb; 25 John Bateman; 27 George Williams.
Try: Burgess (40); **Goals:** Smith 1/3.
Dismissal: Flower (2) - punching Hohaia.
Rugby Leaguer & League Express Men of the Match: *Saints:* James Roby; *Warriors:* Liam Farrell.
Penalty count: 9-7; **Half-time:** 2-6;
Referee: Phil Bentham; **Attendance:** 70,102
(at Old Trafford, Manchester).

St Helens' Mose Masoe brought down by Wigan's Joel Tomkins during the Super League Grand Final

SUPER LEAGUE XIX
Opta Analysis

SUPER LEAGUE XIX
TOP PERFORMERS

TACKLES
James Roby	St Helens	1054
Danny Houghton	Hull FC	1044
Joe Westerman	Hull FC	916
Josh Hodgson	Hull KR	909
Scott Moore	London Broncos	856
Tommy Lee	Salford	837
Matt Cook	London Broncos	834
James Donaldson	Bradford	833
Danny Washbrook	Wakefield	801
Jamie Peacock	Leeds	780

OFFLOADS
Brett Ferres	Huddersfield	58
Zeb Taia	Catalan Dragons	53
Leon Pryce	Catalan Dragons	51
Jamie Peacock	Leeds	49
Adam Walker	Hull KR	44
Gareth Hock	Salford	43
Ryan Atkins	Warrington	42
Joe Westerman	Hull FC	41
Trent Waterhouse	Warrington	40
Adrian Purtell	Bradford	39

CARRIES
Jamie Peacock	Leeds	519
James Roby	St Helens	509
Joe Westerman	Hull FC	488
Chris Hill	Warrington	432
Ryan Hall	Leeds	423
Andy Lynch	Castleford	412
Zeb Taia	Catalan Dragons	406
Zak Hardaker	Leeds	400
Danny Tickle	Widnes	395
Josh Hodgson	Hull KR	392

CLEAN BREAKS
Joe Burgess	Wigan	27
Jermaine McGillvary	Huddersfield	26
Rhys Hanbury	Widnes	25
Daryl Clark	Castleford	24
Joe Wardle	Huddersfield	24
Morgan Escare	Catalan Dragons	23
Rangi Chase	Salford	22
Michael Shenton	Castleford	22
Kallum Watkins	Leeds	22
Greg Eden	Hull KR/Salford	21

ERRORS
Ryan Hall	Leeds	42
Joe Burgess	Wigan	38
Luke Gale	Bradford	37
Jamie Shaul	Hull FC	36
Rangi Chase	Salford	36
Morgan Escare	Catalan Dragons	35
Kallum Watkins	Leeds	34
Kevin Brown	Widnes	34
Marc Sneyd	Castleford	33
Greg Eden	Hull KR/Salford	32

MOST METRES - Matthew Russell

METRES
Matthew Russell	Warrington	3546
Chris Hill	Warrington	3258
Zak Hardaker	Leeds	3254
Jamie Peacock	Leeds	3248
Ryan Hall	Leeds	3190
Jamie Shaul	Hull FC	3067
Zeb Taia	Catalan Dragons	3037
James Roby	St Helens	2980
Daryl Clark	Castleford	2920
Tom Briscoe	Leeds	2877

METRES FROM SCOOTS
James Roby	St Helens	2523
Josh Hodgson	Hull KR	2054
Daryl Clark	Castleford	1868
Mick Higham	Warrington	1693
Danny Houghton	Hull FC	1600
Michael Monaghan	Warrington	1526
Scott Moore	London Broncos	1465
Rob Burrow	Leeds	1235
Matthew Russell	Warrington	1199
Lloyd White	Widnes	1134

MISSED TACKLES
Scott Moore	London Broncos	91
Danny Addy	Bradford	87
Josh Hodgson	Hull KR	80
Luke Gale	Bradford	76
Adam Henry	Bradford	76
Danny Tickle	Widnes	71
Joe Westerman	Hull FC	70
Tom Olbison	Bradford	68
Elliott Whitehead	Catalan Dragons	67
Travis Burns	Hull KR	65

SUPPORTED BREAKS
Morgan Escare	Catalan Dragons	18
Joel Monaghan	Warrington	11
Danny McGuire	Leeds	10
Jamie Shaul	Hull FC	10
Tom Makinson	St Helens	9
Daryl Clark	Castleford	8
Scott Grix	Huddersfield	7
Michael Oldfield	Catalan Dragons	6
Michael Shenton	Castleford	6
Paul Wellens	St Helens	6

QUICK PTBs
Tom Briscoe	Leeds	91
Dan Sarginson	Wigan	66
Taulima Tautai	Wakefield	63
Ryan Atkins	Warrington	61
Fetuli Talanoa	Hull FC	61
Ryan Hall	Leeds	60
Chris Hill	Warrington	59
Alex Gerrard	Widnes	53
Gareth Ellis	Hull FC	51
Iosia Soliola	St Helens	49

PENALTIES CONCEDED
Josh Hodgson	Hull KR	24
Scott Moore	London Broncos	23
Josh Drinkwater	London Broncos	22
Morgan Escare	Catalan Dragons	21
Travis Burns	Hull KR	20
Danny Kirmond	Wakefield	19
Hep Cahill	Widnes	18
Rangi Chase	Salford	18
Liam Farrell	Wigan	18
Joe Westerman	Hull FC	18

TACKLE BUSTS
Matthew Russell	Warrington	107
Zak Hardaker	Leeds	103
Morgan Escare	Catalan Dragons	102
Daryl Clark	Castleford	96
Rangi Chase	Salford	90
Matt Bowen	Wigan	89
Dan Sarginson	Wigan	89
Ryan Hall	Leeds	86
Rhys Hanbury	Widnes	84
Justin Carney	Castleford	81

All statistics in Opta Analysis include
Super League regular season games only

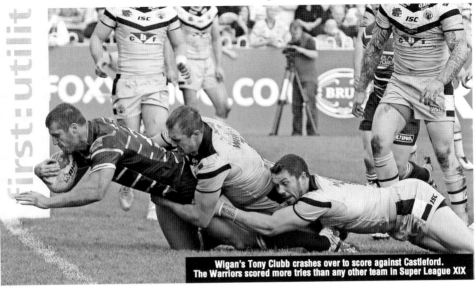

Wigan's Tony Clubb crashes over to score against Castleford. The Warriors scored more tries than any other team in Super League XIX

SUPER LEAGUE XIX AVERAGES PER MATCH

TACKLES		OFFLOADS		CLEAN BREAKS		ERRORS	
Leeds Rhinos	331.6	Warrington Wolves	13.4	Wigan Warriors	7.2	London Broncos	13.0
Widnes Vikings	319.1	Bradford Bulls	12.6	Castleford Tigers	7.1	Leeds Rhinos	12.9
Salford Red Devils	317.2	Leeds Rhinos	12.6	St Helens	7.0	Warrington Wolves	12.9
Huddersfield Giants	311.4	Catalan Dragons	12.3	Salford Red Devils	6.6	Castleford Tigers	12.7
London Broncos	309.9	Wakefield T Wildcats	11.4	Warrington Wolves	6.6	Hull FC	12.7
Hull FC	309.5	Castleford Tigers	10.9	Huddersfield Giants	6.4	Bradford Bulls	12.6
Bradford Bulls	308.3	Salford Red Devils	10.4	Catalan Dragons	6.3	Salford Red Devils	12.6
Warrington Wolves	304.1	Hull FC	10.3	Leeds Rhinos	6.2	Hull Kingston Rovers	12.4
Wakefield T Wildcats	302.3	Hull Kingston Rovers	10.1	Hull Kingston Rovers	6.1	St Helens	12.4
Wigan Warriors	298.3	Huddersfield Giants	9.5	Hull FC	5.4	Catalan Dragons	12.3
Castleford Tigers	297.9	St Helens	9.3	Widnes Vikings	5.3	Wigan Warriors	12.2
Hull Kingston Rovers	294.7	Wigan Warriors	7.7	Wakefield T Wildcats	5.2	Widnes Vikings	11.9
St Helens	294.4	Widnes Vikings	6.8	Bradford Bulls	4.4	Huddersfield Giants	11.3
Catalan Dragons	293.7	London Broncos	6.5	London Broncos	4.3	Wakefield T Wildcats	11.2

MISSED TACKLES		METRES		PASSES		KICKS IN GENERAL PLAY	
Bradford Bulls	35.6	Leeds Rhinos	1407.7	Leeds Rhinos	248.7	Leeds Rhinos	20.7
London Broncos	32.1	Warrington Wolves	1393.1	Wigan Warriors	238.4	Widnes Vikings	20.2
Wakefield T Wildcats	29.8	Wigan Warriors	1361.3	Salford Red Devils	221.1	Hull FC	19.2
Hull Kingston Rovers	28.6	Castleford Tigers	1327.6	St Helens	211.9	St Helens	18.9
Widnes Vikings	28.1	St Helens	1327.0	Castleford Tigers	210.4	Hull Kingston Rovers	18.7
Leeds Rhinos	27.8	Hull FC	1273.0	Huddersfield Giants	205.4	Wigan Warriors	18.7
Hull FC	27.0	Huddersfield Giants	1268.8	Widnes Vikings	201.9	Castleford Tigers	18.6
Salford Red Devils	26.2	Salford Red Devils	1246.3	Catalan Dragons	200.6	Warrington Wolves	18.4
Catalan Dragons	24.9	Hull Kingston Rovers	1244.9	Hull FC	198.4	Bradford Bulls	18.3
St Helens	24.6	Catalan Dragons	1244.3	Wakefield T Wildcats	197.2	Salford Red Devils	18.2
Huddersfield Giants	23.5	Widnes Vikings	1219.9	Hull Kingston Rovers	193.6	Huddersfield Giants	18.1
Castleford Tigers	21.2	Wakefield T Wildcats	1204.0	Warrington Wolves	193.4	Catalan Dragons	17.4
Wigan Warriors	20.7	Bradford Bulls	1088.0	Bradford Bulls	191.7	Wakefield T Wildcats	17.4
Warrington Wolves	20.6	London Broncos	1054.7	London Broncos	174.0	London Broncos	16.7

SUPER LEAGUE XIX TRIES SCORED/CONCEDED

TOTAL TRIES SCORED		TOTAL TRIES CONCEDED		SCORED FROM KICKS		CONCEDED FROM KICKS	
Wigan Warriors	151	London Broncos	222	Catalan Dragons	18	London Broncos	23
Castleford Tigers	145	Bradford Bulls	177	Castleford Tigers	17	Huddersfield Giants	17
St Helens	143	Wakefield T Wildcats	138	Warrington Wolves	17	Salford Red Devils	16
Warrington Wolves	142	Widnes Vikings	131	Widnes Vikings	16	Wakefield T Wildcats	16
Huddersfield Giants	140	Hull Kingston Rovers	122	Wigan Warriors	16	Bradford Bulls	14
Catalan Dragons	132	Salford Red Devils	121	Leeds Rhinos	15	Hull FC	13
Leeds Rhinos	123	Catalan Dragons	120	St Helens	13	Widnes Vikings	13
Hull FC	119	Huddersfield Giants	113	Wakefield T Wildcats	13	St Helens	12
Hull Kingston Rovers	114	Hull FC	106	Salford Red Devils	11	Castleford Tigers	11
Salford Red Devils	111	Castleford Tigers	104	Bradford Bulls	10	Warrington Wolves	11
Widnes Vikings	110	St Helens	101	Hull FC	10	Leeds Rhinos	10
Wakefield T Wildcats	99	Warrington Wolves	91	Huddersfield Giants	9	Hull Kingston Rovers	9
Bradford Bulls	88	Wigan Warriors	78	Hull Kingston Rovers	7	Wigan Warriors	8
London Broncos	79	Leeds Rhinos	72	London Broncos	7	Catalan Dragons	6

SUPER LEAGUE XIX TRIES SCORED/CONCEDED

TRIES SCORED FROM OWN HALF

Castleford Tigers	34
Catalan Dragons	30
Wigan Warriors	28
Leeds Rhinos	26
Huddersfield Giants	25
Warrington Wolves	22
Hull FC	21
St Helens	20
Salford Red Devils	15
Hull Kingston Rovers	14
Bradford Bulls	13
Wakefield T Wildcats	13
Widnes Vikings	13
London Broncos	6

TRIES CONCEDED FROM OVER 50M

London Broncos	43
Widnes Vikings	33
Wakefield T Wildcats	29
Hull Kingston Rovers	27
Bradford Bulls	25
Salford Red Devils	20
Catalan Dragons	19
St Helens	17
Huddersfield Giants	15
Hull FC	15
Warrington Wolves	13
Wigan Warriors	12
Castleford Tigers	10
Leeds Rhinos	2

TRIES SCORED FROM UNDER 10M

Huddersfield Giants	71
Warrington Wolves	68
Wigan Warriors	68
St Helens	65
Castleford Tigers	58
Hull Kingston Rovers	53
Leeds Rhinos	52
Catalan Dragons	50
Salford Red Devils	48
Wakefield T Wildcats	45
Hull FC	43
Widnes Vikings	42
Bradford Bulls	38
London Broncos	38

TRIES CONCEDED FROM UNDER 10M

London Broncos	83
Bradford Bulls	74
Catalan Dragons	57
Wakefield T Wildcats	57
Huddersfield Giants	55
Widnes Vikings	54
Salford Red Devils	52
Hull FC	50
Castleford Tigers	48
St Helens	48
Hull Kingston Rovers	46
Warrington Wolves	40
Wigan Warriors	40
Leeds Rhinos	35

TOTAL PENALTIES AWARDED

Wigan Warriors	199
Warrington Wolves	195
Bradford Bulls	189
Wakefield T Wildcats	183
Hull FC	179
Huddersfield Giants	172
Salford Red Devils	172
Castleford Tigers	170
Catalan Dragons	168
Widnes Vikings	165
Leeds Rhinos	162
Hull Kingston Rovers	159
London Broncos	153
St Helens	150

TOTAL PENALTIES CONCEDED

Catalan Dragons	200
Salford Red Devils	195
Huddersfield Giants	193
Wigan Warriors	187
Wakefield T Wildcats	181
Hull FC	179
Hull Kingston Rovers	179
Widnes Vikings	174
London Broncos	165
St Helens	161
Castleford Tigers	155
Warrington Wolves	155
Bradford Bulls	151
Leeds Rhinos	141

FOUL PLAY - AWARDED

Wakefield T Wildcats	38
Hull FC	33
Salford Red Devils	33
Castleford Tigers	32
Leeds Rhinos	30
Catalan Dragons	26
Widnes Vikings	26
Bradford Bulls	25
Warrington Wolves	25
Wigan Warriors	24
Hull Kingston Rovers	23
Huddersfield Giants	22
St Helens	22
London Broncos	21

FOUL PLAY CONCEDED

Wigan Warriors	43
Hull Kingston Rovers	39
Salford Red Devils	38
Catalan Dragons	37
Wakefield T Wildcats	29
Hull FC	27
Widnes Vikings	25
London Broncos	24
Castleford Tigers	23
Leeds Rhinos	20
St Helens	20
Bradford Bulls	19
Warrington Wolves	19
Huddersfield Giants	17

OFFSIDE - AWARDED

London Broncos	16
Salford Red Devils	13
Wigan Warriors	13
Bradford Bulls	11
Castleford Tigers	10
Hull FC	10
Leeds Rhinos	10
Warrington Wolves	10
Catalan Dragons	9
Hull Kingston Rovers	9
St Helens	9
Wakefield T Wildcats	9
Huddersfield Giants	8
Widnes Vikings	8

OFFSIDE - CONCEDED

Huddersfield Giants	15
St Helens	15
Hull FC	13
Hull Kingston Rovers	13
Widnes Vikings	11
Wigan Warriors	11
Castleford Tigers	10
London Broncos	10
Catalan Dragons	9
Leeds Rhinos	9
Wakefield T Wildcats	9
Bradford Bulls	8
Salford Red Devils	6
Warrington Wolves	6

SUPER LEAGUE XIX PENALTIES

INTERFERENCE - AWARDED

Wigan Warriors	85
Huddersfield Giants	83
Bradford Bulls	82
Warrington Wolves	79
Wakefield T Wildcats	78
Hull FC	74
Widnes Vikings	70
Leeds Rhinos	68
Salford Red Devils	65
Catalan Dragons	64
Castleford Tigers	63
Hull Kingston Rovers	59
St Helens	55
London Broncos	51

INTERFERENCE - CONCEDED

Widnes Vikings	84
Hull FC	83
Huddersfield Giants	82
Salford Red Devils	79
London Broncos	76
Wakefield T Wildcats	72
Bradford Bulls	67
St Helens	67
Warrington Wolves	66
Hull Kingston Rovers	65
Wigan Warriors	60
Leeds Rhinos	59
Castleford Tigers	58
Catalan Dragons	58

OBSTRUCTION - AWARDED

Bradford Bulls	31
Hull Kingston Rovers	22
Huddersfield Giants	21
Leeds Rhinos	21
Wakefield T Wildcats	21
London Broncos	20
Warrington Wolves	20
Wigan Warriors	20
Castleford Tigers	19
Catalan Dragons	18
Hull FC	17
Salford Red Devils	17
Widnes Vikings	13
St Helens	8

OBSTRUCTION - CONCEDED

Salford Red Devils	26
Wakefield T Wildcats	24
Wigan Warriors	24
Castleford Tigers	23
Huddersfield Giants	23
Warrington Wolves	21
Hull Kingston Rovers	20
Catalan Dragons	17
St Helens	17
Hull FC	16
Leeds Rhinos	16
Widnes Vikings	16
Bradford Bulls	14
London Broncos	11

BALL STEALING - AWARDED

St Helens	31
Catalan Dragons	25
Wigan Warriors	25
London Broncos	24
Salford Red Devils	22
Hull FC	21
Hull Kingston Rovers	21
Bradford Bulls	20
Warrington Wolves	20
Castleford Tigers	18
Huddersfield Giants	17
Leeds Rhinos	14
Wakefield T Wildcats	14
Widnes Vikings	14

BALL STEALING - CONCEDED

Catalan Dragons	43
Huddersfield Giants	29
Wakefield T Wildcats	24
Hull FC	22
Castleford Tigers	21
Hull Kingston Rovers	21
Warrington Wolves	19
Bradford Bulls	18
London Broncos	18
Wigan Warriors	17
Salford Red Devils	16
Widnes Vikings	14
St Helens	13
Leeds Rhinos	11

OFFSIDE MARKERS - AWARDED

Warrington Wolves	19
Castleford Tigers	13
Hull FC	10
Salford Red Devils	9
Catalan Dragons	8
St Helens	8
Bradford Bulls	6
Wigan Warriors	5
Leeds Rhinos	4
London Broncos	4
Wakefield T Wildcats	4
Huddersfield Giants	3
Hull Kingston Rovers	3
Widnes Vikings	1

OFFSIDE MARKERS - CONCEDED

St Helens	13
Huddersfield Giants	9
Catalan Dragons	8
Wakefield T Wildcats	8
London Broncos	7
Leeds Rhinos	7
Warrington Wolves	7
Widnes Vikings	7
Castleford Tigers	6
Wigan Warriors	6
Bradford Bulls	5
Hull Kingston Rovers	5
Salford Red Devils	5
Hull FC	4

OFFSIDE FROM KICK - AWARDED

Widnes Vikings	10
Hull Kingston Rovers	8
Catalan Dragons	7
Wakefield T Wildcats	7
Warrington Wolves	7
Huddersfield Giants	6
Wigan Warriors	6
Bradford Bulls	4
Hull FC	4
London Broncos	4
St Helens	4
Castleford Tigers	3
Leeds Rhinos	3
Salford Red Devils	3

OFFSIDE FROM KICK - CONCEDED

Leeds Rhinos	9
Wigan Warriors	9
Bradford Bulls	8
St Helens	6
Widnes Vikings	6
Huddersfield Giants	5
Hull Kingston Rovers	5
London Broncos	5
Wakefield T Wildcats	5
Catalan Dragons	4
Hull FC	4
Salford Red Devils	4
Castleford Tigers	3
Warrington Wolves	3

DISSENT - AWARDED

Widnes Vikings	4
Hull Kingston Rovers	3
Castleford Tigers	1
Catalan Dragons	1
Huddersfield Giants	1
Bradford Bulls	0
Hull FC	0
Leeds Rhinos	0
London Broncos	0
Salford Red Devils	0
St Helens	0
Wakefield T Wildcats	0
Warrington Wolves	0
Wigan Warriors	0

DISSENT - CONCEDED

Wigan Warriors	3
Hull Kingston Rovers	2
Bradford Bulls	1
Leeds Rhinos	1
Salford Red Devils	1
Wakefield T Wildcats	1
Warrington Wolves	1
Castleford Tigers	0
Catalan Dragons	0
Huddersfield Giants	0
Hull FC	0
London Broncos	0
St Helens	0
Widnes Vikings	0

BRADFORD BULLS

Adam Sidlow

MARKER TACKLES
James Donaldson 159
Adam Sidlow 130
Adam O'Brien 124
Danny Addy 108
Tom Olbison 99

METRES
Lee Gaskell 2249
Adam Sidlow 2201
Brett Kearney...............1918
Manase Manuokafoa 1787
Danny Addy 1761

CARRIES
Adam Sidlow 342
Danny Addy 324
Brett Kearney................305
Lee Gaskell 267
Luke Gale.......................262

Luke Gale

TACKLES
James Donaldson 833
Adam O'Brien 722
Adam Sidlow 667
Tom Olbison 640
Danny Addy 610

CLEAN BREAKS
Lee Gaskell 14
Tom Olbison 10
Jamie Foster 9
Elliot Kear 9
Adam Henry......................8

TACKLE BUSTS
Lee Gaskell 49
Elliot Kear 48
Luke Gale..........................46
Brett Kearney....................42
Adam Henry......................39

OFFLOADS
Adrian Purtell....................39
Matty Blythe 29
Luke Gale..........................29
Adam Sidlow 28
Adam Henry......................27

TRY ASSISTS
Lee Gaskell 19
Luke Gale..........................18
Adam Henry.......................5
Adam O'Brien 5
Danny Addy 4

TOTAL OPTA INDEX
Adam Sidlow 10491
Luke Gale.......................9913
Adam O'Brien 9057
Lee Gaskell 9047
Danny Addy 8924

CASTLEFORD TIGERS

Daryl Clark

MARKER TACKLES
Andy Lynch 108
Daryl Clark......................107
Oliver Holmes 106
Liam Finn..........................96
Craig Huby........................96

METRES
Daryl Clark.....................2920
Andy Lynch 2867
Justin Carney...............2578
Michael Shenton 2431
Weller Hauraki 2265

CARRIES
Andy Lynch 412
Weller Hauraki 348
Craig Huby......................345
Grant Millington..............296
Justin Carney..................294

Michael Shenton

TACKLES
Daryl Clark......................691
Andy Lynch 646
Oliver Holmes 614
Grant Millington..............611
Craig Huby......................569

CLEAN BREAKS
Daryl Clark........................24
Michael Shenton 22
Luke Dorn 20
Kirk Dixon 15
Justin Carney..................13

TACKLE BUSTS
Daryl Clark........................96
Justin Carney...................81
Luke Dorn 56
Marc Sneyd 56
Michael Shenton 55

OFFLOADS
Craig Huby........................38
Grant Millington...............33
Weller Hauraki 28
Andy Lynch 27
Daryl Clark........................20

TRY ASSISTS
Marc Sneyd 30
Liam Finn..........................20
Michael Shenton 17
Daryl Clark........................10
Jamie Ellis 8

TOTAL OPTA INDEX
Daryl Clark.................14730
Michael Shenton 12405
Andy Lynch 12285
Grant Millington..........10512
Craig Huby..................10452

235

CATALAN DRAGONS

Morgan Escare

TACKLES
Elliott Whitehead 768
Eloi Pelissier 691
Zeb Taia 648
Jason Baitieri................569
Jeff Lima 424

OFFLOADS
Zeb Taia 53
Leon Pryce 51
Ben Pomeroy.................29
Elliott Whitehead 27
Eloi Pelissier 18

CLEAN BREAKS
Morgan Escare 23
Daryl Millard 18
Michael Oldfield.............17
Ben Pomeroy.................16
Elliott Whitehead 16

TRY ASSISTS
Morgan Escare 16
Leon Pryce 15
Thomas Bosc..................13
Eloi Pelissier 10
Ben Pomeroy..................10

MARKER TACKLES
Elliott Whitehead 118
Eloi Pelissier 114
Jason Baitieri.................87
Zeb Taia 73
Olivier Elima 64

Elliott Whitehead

METRES
Zeb Taia 3037
Morgan Escare 2623
Jeff Lima 2108
Daryl Millard 2093
Michael Oldfield...........1953

CARRIES
Zeb Taia 406
Jeff Lima 307
Jason Baitieri................293
Morgan Escare 284
Elliott Whitehead 268

TACKLE BUSTS
Morgan Escare 102
Elliott Whitehead 59
Zeb Taia 54
Vincent Duport 51
Leon Pryce 51

TOTAL OPTA INDEX
Elliott Whitehead 13979
Morgan Escare 13606
Zeb Taia 12625
Eloi Pelissier 9587
Jason Baitieri...............9560

HUDDERSFIELD GIANTS

Danny Brough

TACKLES
Michael Lawrence 736
Eorl Crabtree 655
Ukuma Ta'ai..................616
Chris Bailey 596
Luke Robinson 546

OFFLOADS
Brett Ferres 58
Leroy Cudjoe 28
Danny Brough 20
David Faiumu..................20
Eorl Crabtree 16

CLEAN BREAKS
Jermaine McGillvary 26
Joe Wardle.....................24
Leroy Cudjoe 12
Ukuma Ta'ai...................12
Danny Brough 11

TRY ASSISTS
Danny Brough 32
Leroy Cudjoe 15
Brett Ferres 13
Luke Robinson 11
Shaun Lunt 8

MARKER TACKLES
Eorl Crabtree 114
Michael Lawrence 105
Ukuma Ta'ai...................104
Chris Bailey 90
Luke Robinson 89

Eorl Crabtree

METRES
Eorl Crabtree 2636
Jermaine McGillvary ...2624
Ukuma Ta'ai.................2262
Jodie Broughton 2208
Leroy Cudjoe 2158

CARRIES
Eorl Crabtree 374
Ukuma Ta'ai..................322
Danny Brough 321
Luke Robinson 307
Jermaine McGillvary 291

TACKLE BUSTS
Eorl Crabtree 69
Jermaine McGillvary 68
Ukuma Ta'ai.....................61
Danny Brough 58
Scott Grix 55

TOTAL OPTA INDEX
Eorl Crabtree 12900
Danny Brough 12464
Ukuma Ta'ai...............11954
Jermaine McGillvary ..10713
Leroy Cudjoe 9591

HULL F.C.

Danny Houghton

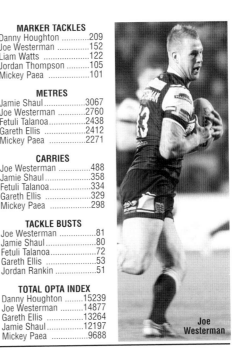

Joe Westerman

MARKER TACKLES
Danny Houghton 209
Joe Westerman 152
Liam Watts 122
Jordan Thompson 105
Mickey Paea 101

METRES
Jamie Shaul..................3067
Joe Westerman 2760
Fetuli Talanoa...............2438
Gareth Ellis 2412
Mickey Paea 2271

CARRIES
Joe Westerman 488
Jamie Shaul...................358
Fetuli Talanoa................334
Gareth Ellis 329
Mickey Paea 298

TACKLES
Danny Houghton 1044
Joe Westerman 916
Gareth Ellis 608
Jordan Thompson 538
Liam Watts 528

CLEAN BREAKS
Jamie Shaul.......................16
Kirk Yeaman 15
Gareth Ellis 11
Richard Horne 11
Ben Crooks 10

TACKLE BUSTS
Joe Westerman 81
Jamie Shaul.....................80
Fetuli Talanoa..................72
Gareth Ellis 53
Jordan Rankin 51

OFFLOADS
Joe Westerman 41
Liam Watts 25
Fetuli Talanoa...................23
Gareth Ellis 22
Danny Houghton 16

TRY ASSISTS
Jordan Rankin 13
Danny Houghton 11
Richard Horne 10
Aaron Heremaia.................9
Joe Westerman 9

TOTAL OPTA INDEX
Danny Houghton 15239
Joe Westerman 14877
Gareth Ellis 13264
Jamie Shaul...............12197
Mickey Paea 9688

HULL KINGSTON ROVERS

Josh Hodgson

Travis Burns

MARKER TACKLES
Kevin Larroyer 149
Josh Hodgson 129
Michael Weyman 104
Neville Costigan................99
Adam Walker 79

METRES
Josh Hodgson 2861
Greg Eden 2158
Ben Cockayne 2145
Michael Weyman 2035
Kris Welham 2027

CARRIES
Josh Hodgson 392
Travis Burns....................302
Adam Walker 289
Neville Costigan..............285
Michael Weyman 274

TACKLES
Josh Hodgson 909
Kevin Larroyer 693
Neville Costigan..............574
Michael Weyman 539
Adam Walker 526

CLEAN BREAKS
Greg Eden 21
Kris Welham 20
Josh Hodgson 17
Craig Hall..........................12
Ade Gardner 11

TACKLE BUSTS
Travis Burns.....................78
Greg Eden 73
Josh Hodgson 64
Kris Welham 51
Ben Cockayne 48

OFFLOADS
Adam Walker 44
Travis Burns.....................38
Josh Hodgson 29
James Green 23
Ben Cockayne 22

TRY ASSISTS
Travis Burns.....................21
Greg Eden 14
Josh Hodgson 11
Kris Keating 11
Kris Welham 6

TOTAL OPTA INDEX
Josh Hodgson 14762
Travis Burns...............10862
Kevin Larroyer 10054
Michael Weyman 9356
Adam Walker 8877

LEEDS RHINOS

Jamie Peacock

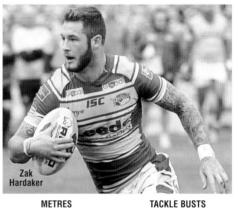

Zak Hardaker

TACKLES
Jamie Peacock................780
Brett Delaney.................751
Carl Ablett 660
Paul Aiton 557
Kevin Sinfield.................534

OFFLOADS
Jamie Peacock.................49
Ryan Hall 39
Joel Moon 34
Kallum Watkins 34
Tom Briscoe....................30

CLEAN BREAKS
Kallum Watkins 22
Tom Briscoe....................18
Ryan Hall 18
Liam Sutcliffe 15
Danny McGuire 13

TRY ASSISTS
Kallum Watkins 16
Danny McGuire 15
Joel Moon 15
Zak Hardaker 13
Liam Sutcliffe 6

MARKER TACKLES
Jamie Peacock................181
Brett Delaney 160
Brad Singleton...............111
Paul Aiton 106
Kevin Sinfield.................106

METRES
Zak Hardaker 3254
Jamie Peacock............3248
Ryan Hall 3190
Tom Briscoe.................2877
Kallum Watkins 2684

CARRIES
Jamie Peacock................519
Ryan Hall 423
Zak Hardaker 400
Tom Briscoe...................336
Kallum Watkins 327

TACKLE BUSTS
Zak Hardaker 103
Ryan Hall 86
Kallum Watkins 80
Tom Briscoe.....................70
Rob Burrow 61

TOTAL OPTA INDEX
Zak Hardaker 13381
Jamie Peacock...........12984
Kallum Watkins 12804
Ryan Hall 12669
Danny McGuire 11365

LONDON BRONCOS

Scott Moore

Matt Cook

TACKLES
Scott Moore.....................856
Matt Cook 834
Nick Slyney 717
Olsi Krasniqi 616
Alex Foster......................566

OFFLOADS
Scott Moore.....................23
Mike McMeeken 21
Atelea Vea 18
Josh Drinkwater 15
James Greenwood 12

CLEAN BREAKS
Mason Caton-Brown 10
Nick Slyney 9
Mike McMeeken 8
Denny Solomona 8
Atelea Vea 8

TRY ASSISTS
Josh Drinkwater 16
Scott Moore.....................15
Ben Farrar 9
James Cunningham...........4
Nesiasi Mataitonga 4

MARKER TACKLES
Matt Cook 179
Nick Slyney 147
Scott Moore....................146
Olsi Krasniqi 120
Alex Foster......................100

METRES
Matt Cook 2398
Olsi Krasniqi 1989
Scott Moore.................1801
Nick Slyney 1734
Atelea Vea 1730

CARRIES
Scott Moore.....................385
Matt Cook 317
Olsi Krasniqi 278
Ben Farrar 273
Nick Slyney 273

TACKLE BUSTS
Atelea Vea 59
Mason Caton-Brown 43
Matt Cook 30
Nick Slyney 28
Thomas Minns..................27

TOTAL OPTA INDEX
Matt Cook 12387
Scott Moore...............10535
Nick Slyney 9781
Olsi Krasniqi 8811
Atelea Vea 8433

SALFORD RED DEVILS

Rangi Chase

Junior Sa'u

MARKER TACKLES
Tommy Lee	161
Matty Ashurst	130
Adrian Morley	110
Harrison Hansen	90
Jordan Walne	79

METRES
Adrian Morley	2380
Junior Sa'u	2343
Rangi Chase	2137
Lama Tasi	1976
Greg Johnson	1856

CARRIES
Rangi Chase	372
Adrian Morley	336
Junior Sa'u	302
Lama Tasi	281
Harrison Hansen	255

TACKLES
Tommy Lee	837
Adrian Morley	670
Harrison Hansen	612
Matty Ashurst	610
Lama Tasi	549

CLEAN BREAKS
Rangi Chase	22
Theo Fages	17
Junior Sa'u	15
Niall Evalds	14
Greg Johnson	14

TACKLE BUSTS
Rangi Chase	90
Junior Sa'u	75
Greg Johnson	64
Gareth Hock	51
Jake Mullaney	42

OFFLOADS
Gareth Hock	43
Rangi Chase	32
Tony Puletua	21
Junior Sa'u	21
Theo Fages	17

TRY ASSISTS
Rangi Chase	25
Junior Sa'u	8
Jake Mullaney	7
Niall Evalds	6
Tim Smith	6

TOTAL OPTA INDEX
Rangi Chase	12185
Junior Sa'u	10395
Tommy Lee	10120
Adrian Morley	9364
Theo Fages	8996

ST HELENS

James Roby

Iosia Soliola

MARKER TACKLES
James Roby	210
Louie McCarthy-Scarsbrook	108
Iosia Soliola	94
Jon Wilkin	92
Anthony Laffranchi	81

METRES
James Roby	2980
Tom Makinson	2486
Alex Walmsley	2288
Louie McCarthy-Scarsbrook	2159
Iosia Soliola	2138

CARRIES
James Roby	509
Iosia Soliola	309
Louie McCarthy-Scarsbrook	307
Tom Makinson	299
Alex Walmsley	270

TACKLES
James Roby	1054
Iosia Soliola	601
Louie McCarthy-Scarsbrook	553
Mark Flanagan	489
Jon Wilkin	468

CLEAN BREAKS
Tom Makinson	19
Adam Swift	14
Paul Wellens	14
Iosia Soliola	12
Lance Hohaia	11

TACKLE BUSTS
Willie Manu	68
James Roby	62
Alex Walmsley	57
Tom Makinson	53
Mose Masoe	51

OFFLOADS
Louie McCarthy-Scarsbrook	24
James Roby	24
Mose Masoe	21
Iosia Soliola	21
Jordan Turner	17

TRY ASSISTS
James Roby	20
Paul Wellens	15
Jon Wilkin	14
Lance Hohaia	12
Luke Walsh	11

TOTAL OPTA INDEX
James Roby	18843
Iosia Soliola	10514
Tom Makinson	10018
Louie McCarthy-Scarsbrook	9634
Paul Wellens	9443

WAKEFIELD T WILDCATS

Danny Kirmond

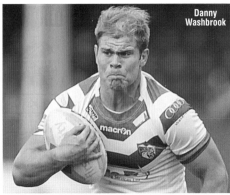

Danny Washbrook

TACKLES
Danny Washbrook	801
Danny Kirmond	687
Paul McShane	600
Scott Anderson	565
Nick Scruton	485

OFFLOADS
Taulima Tautai	38
Ali Lauitiiti	37
Danny Washbrook	23
Richard Moore	22
Daniel Smith	20

CLEAN BREAKS
Pita Godinet	17
Jarrod Sammut	16
Paul Sykes	11
Reece Lyne	10
Richard Mathers	8

TRY ASSISTS
Paul McShane	14
Tim Smith	13
Pita Godinet	9
Jarrod Sammut	9
Richard Mathers	5

METRES
Taulima Tautai	2112
Chris Riley	2050
Reece Lyne	1903
Scott Anderson	1745
Daniel Smith	1698

TACKLE BUSTS
Taulima Tautai	44
Jarrod Sammut	43
Reece Lyne	40
Paul Sykes	37
Pita Godinet	36

MARKER TACKLES
Danny Kirmond	133
Danny Washbrook	130
Scott Anderson	103
Paul McShane	94
Daniel Smith	89

CARRIES
Chris Riley	294
Taulima Tautai	277
Daniel Smith	265
Scott Anderson	256
Danny Washbrook	250

TOTAL OPTA INDEX
Danny Washbrook	10543
Danny Kirmond	9298
Paul McShane	8920
Taulima Tautai	8591
Scott Anderson	8333

WARRINGTON WOLVES

Stefan Ratchford

Chris Hill

TACKLES
Chris Hill	740
Mick Higham	593
Michael Monaghan	491
James Laithwaite	485
Ben Harrison	479

OFFLOADS
Ryan Atkins	42
Trent Waterhouse	40
Matthew Russell	28
Ben Westwood	27
Mick Higham	26

CLEAN BREAKS
Rhys Evans	20
Joel Monaghan	17
Ryan Atkins	15
Chris Bridge	14
Stefan Ratchford	14

TRY ASSISTS
Gareth O'Brien	20
Chris Bridge	17
Mick Higham	15
Michael Monaghan	11
Richard Myler	11

METRES
Matthew Russell	3546
Chris Hill	3258
Rhys Evans	2352
Joel Monaghan	2112
Stefan Ratchford	2077

TACKLE BUSTS
Matthew Russell	107
Ryan Atkins	59
Chris Bridge	58
Stefan Ratchford	58
Joel Monaghan	54

MARKER TACKLES
Chris Hill	112
James Laithwaite	107
Mick Higham	105
Ben Harrison	104
Ben Currie	90

CARRIES
Chris Hill	432
Matthew Russell	382
Chris Bridge	299
Stefan Ratchford	288
Mick Higham	275

TOTAL OPTA INDEX
Chris Hill	14632
Stefan Ratchford	11796
Ryan Atkins	11073
Matthew Russell	10982
Joel Monaghan	10808

WIDNES VIKINGS

WIDNES VIKINGS

Rhys
Hanbury

MARKER TACKLES
Alex Gerrard	126
Hep Cahill	111
Danny Galea	109
Danny Tickle	104
Macgraff Leuluai	95

METRES
Rhys Hanbury	2864
Danny Tickle	2592
Paddy Flynn	2534
Hep Cahill	1832
Kevin Brown	1614

CARRIES
Danny Tickle	395
Paddy Flynn	381
Kevin Brown	360
Rhys Hanbury	340
Hep Cahill	257

TACKLES
Danny Tickle	681
Willie Isa	626
Alex Gerrard	620
Danny Galea	585
Hep Cahill	582

CLEAN BREAKS
Rhys Hanbury	25
Paddy Flynn	20
Jack Owens	13
Stefan Marsh	8
Cameron Phelps	8

TACKLE BUSTS
Rhys Hanbury	84
Paddy Flynn	76
Phil Joseph	41
Jack Owens	39
Danny Tickle	36

OFFLOADS
Danny Tickle	28
Rhys Hanbury	21
Hep Cahill	18
Kevin Brown	14
Lloyd White	14

TRY ASSISTS
Kevin Brown	24
Rhys Hanbury	17
Joe Mellor	8
Lloyd White	8
Cameron Phelps	4

TOTAL OPTA INDEX
Rhys Hanbury	11519
Kevin Brown	11147
Paddy Flynn	10917
Danny Tickle	10358
Alex Gerrard	8861

Kevin
Brown

WIGAN WARRIORS

Liam
Farrell

MARKER TACKLES
John Bateman	123
Liam Farrell	102
Ben Flower	82
Jack Hughes	73
Dominic Crosby	71

METRES
Dan Sarginson	2708
Joe Burgess	2639
Liam Farrell	2608
Anthony Gelling	2532
Matt Bowen	2523

CARRIES
Dan Sarginson	385
Liam Farrell	350
Anthony Gelling	311
John Bateman	292
Matt Bowen	285

TACKLES
John Bateman	600
Liam Farrell	579
Scott Taylor	492
Sean O'Loughlin	480
Sam Powell	458

CLEAN BREAKS
Joe Burgess	27
Matt Bowen	18
Josh Charnley	18
Liam Farrell	17
Dan Sarginson	13

TACKLE BUSTS
Matt Bowen	89
Dan Sarginson	89
Anthony Gelling	64
Scott Taylor	57
John Bateman	55

OFFLOADS
Anthony Gelling	24
Sean O'Loughlin	21
Blake Green	20
John Bateman	17
Darrell Goulding	15

TRY ASSISTS
Matty Smith	25
Blake Green	16
Matt Bowen	12
Dan Sarginson	12
Anthony Gelling	11

TOTAL OPTA INDEX
Liam Farrell	13275
John Bateman	11693
Dan Sarginson	11172
Matt Bowen	10228
Matty Smith	9542

John
Bateman

241

CHAMPIONSHIP 2014
Club by Club

BARROW RAIDERS

DATE	FIXTURE	RESULT	SCORERS	LGE	ATT
16/2/14	North Wales (a)	L34-16	t:Grant(2),Wiper g:Mort(2)	12th	1,118
23/2/14	Leigh (h)	L8-52	t:Turner(2)	14th	1,252
2/3/14	Sheffield (a)	W18-24	t:Morrison,Toal(2),Harrison g:Mort(4)	11th	897
9/3/14	Workington (h)	L6-8	t:Shaw g:Mort	11th	1,512
16/3/14	Milford (a) (CCR3) ●	W10-18	t:Mort,Grant(2) g:Mort,Speakman(2)	N/A	1,000
23/3/14	Swinton (a) ●●	L44-26	t:Shaw(2),Grant,Campbell,Speakman g:Shaw(3)	12th	403
30/3/14	Whitehaven (h)	L37-12	t:Harrison,Burke g:Shaw(2)	13th	721
6/4/14	Keighley (a) (CCR4)	L54-28	t:Grant(2),Campbell(2),Dawson g:Mort(3),Shaw	N/A	823
13/4/14	Featherstone (h)	L18-38	t:Grant(2),Wiper,Shaw g:Shaw	14th	1,075
18/4/14	Halifax (h)	L18-32	t:Evalds(3) g:Shaw(3)	14th	1,169
4/5/14	Doncaster (a)	L30-28	t:Govin,Wiper,Evalds,Shaw(2) g:Shaw(4)	14th	573
11/5/14	Batley (h)	W18-14	t:Wiper,Toal(2) g:Shaw(3)	14th	940
18/5/14	Dewsbury (h)	L30-42	t:Toal,Grant,Campbell,Dawson,Evalds g:Shaw(5)	14th	914
25/5/14	Keighley (a)	L27-18	t:Toal(2),Grant g:Shaw(3)	14th	812
1/6/14	Rochdale (h)	W38-18	t:Wiper,Grant,Bullock,Campbell,Jones,Lloyd g:Shaw(7)	13th	1,058
8/6/14	Doncaster (h)	L10-22	t:Grant,Mort g:Shaw	13th	1,048
15/6/14	Leigh (a)	L60-0		14th	2,508
22/6/14	Swinton (h)	L24-38	t:Wiper,Campbell,Toal(2) g:Shaw(4)	14th	932
29/6/14	Batley (a)	L34-4	t:Wiper	14th	615
6/7/14	Whitehaven (h)	L18-30	t:Davies,Mossop(2) g:Shaw(3)	14th	1,105
13/7/14	Rochdale (a)	L54-22	t:Wiper,Mossop,Shaw,Grant g:Shaw(3)	14th	612
20/7/14	Sheffield (h)	L10-40	t:Grant(2) g:Shaw	14th	871
27/7/14	Dewsbury (a)	L34-14	t:Mossop,Briscoe,Grant g:Shaw	14th	575
3/8/14	Featherstone (a)	L62-12	t:Campbell,Shaw g:Shaw(2)	14th	1,626
10/8/14	Keighley (h)	L10-24	t:Wiper,Bradley Goulding g:Shaw	14th	668
17/8/14	Workington (a)	L32-18	t:Shaw,Grant,Davies g:Shaw(3)	14th	842
31/8/14	North Wales (a)	W36-16	t:Campbell,Dwyer,Davies,Lloyd,Toal,Mossop g:Shaw(5),Backhouse	14th	848
7/9/14	Halifax (a)	L30-24	t:Marwood,Shaw,Lloyd,Wiper g:Shaw(4)	14th	1,431

● Played at Headingley Carnegie, Leeds
●● Played at Park Lane, Sedgley Park

		APP		TRIES		GOALS		FG		PTS	
	D.O.B.	ALL	Ch	ALL	Ch	ALL	Ch	ALL	Ch	ALL	Ch
Mike Backhouse	14/6/82	10	9	0	0	1	1	0	0	2	2
Craig Briscoe	8/12/92	14(1)	14(1)	1	1	0	0	0	0	4	4
Ross Brookes	2/6/90	(1)	(1)	0	0	0	0	0	0	0	0
Joe Bullock	27/11/92	5(16)	4(16)	1	1	0	0	0	0	4	4
Joe Burke	18/5/90	9(12)	9(10)	1	1	0	0	0	0	4	4
Jamie Butler	29/8/80	2(14)	2(14)	0	0	0	0	0	0	0	0
Liam Campbell	5/6/86	24(2)	22(2)	8	6	0	0	0	0	32	24
Ben Davies	2/11/89	9(3)	9(3)	3	3	0	0	0	0	12	12
Andrew Dawson	12/3/89	16(4)	15(3)	2	1	0	0	0	0	8	4
Michael Dengate	22/6/91	(3)	(2)	0	0	0	0	0	0	0	0
Andrew Dixon	28/2/90	1	1	0	0	0	0	0	0	0	0
Connor Dwyer	29/12/93	9(1)	9(1)	1	1	0	0	0	0	4	4
Niall Evalds	26/8/93	5	5	5	5	0	0	0	0	20	20
Bobbie Goulding	4/2/72	3	3	0	0	0	0	0	0	0	0
Bradley Goulding	20/1/96	8	8	1	1	0	0	0	0	4	4
Mick Govin	5/11/84	5(2)	4(2)	1	1	0	0	0	0	4	4
Dalton Grant	21/4/90	28	26	18	14	0	0	0	0	72	56
Joe Hambley	2/12/95	4	4	0	0	0	0	0	0	0	0
Liam Harrison	3/12/82	28	26	2	2	0	0	0	0	8	8
Stuart Howarth	25/1/90	1	1	0	0	0	0	0	0	0	0
Danny Jones	12/11/92	18(8)	16(8)	1	1	0	0	0	0	4	4
Ben Karalius	6/12/91	6	6	0	0	0	0	0	0	0	0
Aaron Lloyd	28/6/92	2(13)	2(13)	3	3	0	0	0	0	12	12
Aaron Low	5/5/88	9(5)	8(5)	0	0	0	0	0	0	0	0
Brad Marwood	4/11/93	4(7)	4(5)	1	1	0	0	0	0	4	4
Jack Morrison	16/9/92	2(11)	1(10)	1	1	0	0	0	0	4	4
Ian Mort	21/6/88	11	9	2	1	11	7	0	0	30	18
Nathan Mossop	21/2/88	19(3)	18(3)	5	5	0	0	0	0	20	20
Ben Musolino	18/12/92	4	4	0	0	0	0	0	0	0	0
James Nixon	10/8/85	1	1	0	0	0	0	0	0	0	0
Matty Palmer	25/10/89	3(4)	2(4)	0	0	0	0	0	0	0	0
Michael Platt	23/3/84	2	2	0	0	0	0	0	0	0	0
Chris Rowe	8/2/94	(1)	0	0	0	0	0	0	0	0	0
Ryan Shaw	27/2/92	26	25	10	10	60	59	0	0	160	158
Dom Speakman	22/3/94	19	17	1	1	2	0	0	0	8	4
Dan Toal	22/9/89	20	18	10	10	0	0	0	0	40	40
Scott Turner	7/5/94	6	5	2	2	0	0	0	0	8	8
Adam Walne	3/10/90	1	1	0	0	0	0	0	0	0	0
Jason Walton	13/6/90	2	2	0	0	0	0	0	0	0	0
Max Wiper	18/9/90	28	26	10	10	0	0	0	0	40	40

Dalton Grant

LEAGUE RECORD
P26-W4-D0-L22-BP7
(14th, Championship)
F462, A870, Diff-408
19 points.

CHALLENGE CUP
Round Four

ATTENDANCES
Best - v Workington (Ch - 1,512)
Worst - v Keighley (Ch - 668)
Total (Championship only) - 13,392
Average (Championship only) - 1,030
(Down by 3 on 2013)

CLUB RECORDS
MATCH RECORDS Highest score: 138-0 v Nottingham City, 27/11/94 **Highest score against:** 0-90 v Leeds, 11/2/90 **Record attendance:** 21,651 v Salford, 15/4/38
Tries: 6 Val Cumberbatch v Batley, 21/11/36; Jim Thornburrow v Maryport, 19/2/38; Steve Rowan v Nottingham City, 15/11/92
Goals: 17 Darren Carter v Nottingham City, 27/11/94 **Points:** 42 Darren Carter v Nottingham City, 27/11/94
SEASON RECORDS Tries: 50 Jim Lewthwaite 1956-57 Goals: 135 Joe Ball 1956-57 Points: 323 Jamie Rooney 2010
CAREER RECORDS Tries: 352 Jim Lewthwaite 1943-57 Goals: 1,099 *(inc 63fg)* Darren Holt 1998-2002; 2004-2009; 2012
Points: 2,403 Darren Holt 1998-2002; 2004-2009; 2012 Appearances: 500 Jim Lewthwaite 1943-57

BATLEY BULLDOGS

DATE	FIXTURE	RESULT	SCORERS	LGE	ATT
16/2/14	Leigh (a)	L52-12	t:Greenwood,Connor g:Paterson(2)	14th	2,173
23/2/14	Workington (h)	W36-16	t:Finigan,Paterson,Leak,Smith,Bretherton,Gledhill g:Paterson(6)	9th	559
2/3/14	Halifax (a)	W8-10	t:Finigan(2) g:Paterson	6th	1,798
9/3/14	Doncaster (h)	L12-20	t:Greenwood,Bretherton g:Paterson(2)	8th	691
15/3/14	Kells (h) (CCR3)	W52-4	t:Leak,Rowe(2),Martin,Leatherbarrow(2),Scott,Finigan,Chandler,Leary g:Paterson(6)	N/A	365
23/3/14	Rochdale (a)	L14-10	t:Blackmore,Greenwood g:Paterson	9th	818
30/3/14	North Wales (h)	W14-26	t:Gledhill,Greenwood(2),Blake,Leak g:Paterson(3)	7th	906
6/4/14	Castleford (h) (CCR4)	L10-48	t:Griffin,Paterson g:Paterson	N/A	2,482
13/4/14	Keighley (h)	W29-20	t:Scott,Blackmore,Griffin,Leatherbarrow,Greenwood g:Paterson(4) fg:S Brown	7th	640
18/4/14	Dewsbury (a)	L43-10	t:Davies,A Brown g:Paterson	7th	1,999
4/5/14	Whitehaven (h)	L10-30	t:Paterson,Martin g:Paterson	8th	506
11/5/14	Barrow (h)	L18-14	t:Greenwood,Gledhill g:Paterson(3)	8th	940
18/5/14	Sheffield (h)	L12-16	t:Griffin,Bretherton g:Leatherbarrow(2)	10th	540
25/5/14	Swinton (a)	W18-33	t:Griffin,Bretherton,Leatherbarrow,Paterson,Nicholson,Blake g:Paterson,Leatherbarrow(3) fg:Leatherbarrow	10th	456
1/6/14	Featherstone (h)	L26-32	t:Blackmore(2),Paterson,Rowe g:Leatherbarrow(5)	8th	1,143
8/6/14	Rochdale (h)	W44-28	t:Bretherton,Griffin,Greenwood(2),Nicholson,Hirst,A Brown(2) g:Leatherbarrow(6)	9th	555
15/6/14	Keighley (a)	W24-28	t:Scott(2),Greenwood(2),Griffin g:Leatherbarrow(4)	8th	913
22/6/14	North Wales (h)	W55-12	t:Greenwood(3),Leatherbarrow,A Brown(2),Finigan,Scott,Blake,Smith g:Leatherbarrow(7) fg:Leatherbarrow	7th	563
29/6/14	Barrow (h)	W34-4	t:Greenwood(4),Davies,Finigan g:Leatherbarrow(5)	6th	615
6/7/14	Workington (a)	L22-16	t:Scott,Greenwood,Black g:Leatherbarrow(2)	5th	804
13/7/14	Halifax (h)	D22-22	t:A Brown(2),Martin,Black g:Leatherbarrow(3)	6th	1,155
20/7/14	Featherstone (a)	L52-6	t:Applegarth g:Paterson	6th	2,025
27/7/14	Sheffield (a)	W18-28	t:Reittie,Heaton,Fairbank,A Brown g:Leatherbarrow(6)	7th	763
3/8/14	Leigh (h)	L6-36	t:Greenwood g:Leatherbarrow	6th	976
10/8/14	Whitehaven (a)	L28-13	t:Greenwood(2) g:Leatherbarrow(2) fg:Leatherbarrow	9th	671
17/8/14	Dewsbury (h)	L14-16	t:Reittie,A Brown(2) g:Leatherbarrow	10th	1,159
31/8/14	Swinton (h)	W42-0	t:A Brown,Scott,Nicholson,Reittie,Black,Faal,Bretherton g:Leatherbarrow(7)	9th	664
7/9/14	Doncaster (a)	W10-34	t:Reittie(2),A Brown,Faal,Nicholson,Bretherton g:Leatherbarrow(5)	8th	1,160
13/9/14	Sheffield (a) (EPO) ●	L16-0		N/A	695

● Played at Keepmoat Stadium, Doncaster

	D.O.B.	APP		TRIES		GOALS		FG		PTS	
		ALL	Ch	ALL	Ch	ALL	Ch	ALL	Ch	ALL	Ch
Mark Applegarth	10/12/84	22(1)	20(1)	1	1	0	0	0	0	4	4
Peter Aspinall	4/4/94	(1)	(1)	0	0	0	0	0	0	0	0
Ben Black	29/4/81	15(1)	15(1)	3	3	0	0	0	0	12	12
Ben Blackmore	19/2/93	9	9	4	4	0	0	0	0	16	16
Luke Blake	10/8/89	28	26	3	3	0	0	0	0	12	12
Brad Brennan	18/1/93	1(6)	1(5)	0	0	0	0	0	0	0	0
Alex Bretherton	5/12/82	22(1)	21	7	7	0	0	0	0	28	28
Alex Brown	28/8/87	20	20	12	12	0	0	0	0	48	48
Simon Brown	23/6/89	3	3	0	0	0	0	1	1	1	1
Joe Chandler	2/11/88	15(11)	14(10)	1	0	0	0	0	0	4	0
Jake Connor	18/10/94	1	1	1	1	0	0	0	0	4	4
John Davies	8/1/91	21(4)	19(4)	2	2	0	0	0	0	8	8
Ayden Faal	12/12/86	6(2)	6(2)	2	2	0	0	0	0	8	8
Jacob Fairbank	4/3/90	(2)	(2)	1	1	0	0	0	0	4	4
Vinny Finigan	4/8/89	17	15	6	5	0	0	0	0	24	20
Adam Gledhill	15/2/93	18(7)	16(7)	3	3	0	0	0	0	12	12
Jordan Grayston	14/9/91	(1)	(1)	0	0	0	0	0	0	0	0
Miles Greenwood	30/7/87	25	24	22	22	0	0	0	0	88	88
Josh Griffin	9/5/90	10	9	6	5	0	0	0	0	24	20
Ben Heaton	12/3/90	7	7	1	1	0	0	0	0	4	4
Keegan Hirst	13/12/88	1(7)	1(7)	1	1	0	0	0	0	4	4
Josh Johnson	25/7/94	4(5)	4(5)	0	0	0	0	0	0	0	0
Alistair Leak	5/4/92	6(3)	5(2)	3	2	0	0	0	0	12	8
Jay Leary	8/9/92	1(4)	(3)	1	0	0	0	0	0	4	0
Scott Leatherbarrow	3/9/90	29	27	5	3	59	59	3	3	141	133
Charlie Martin	2/12/92	3(6)	1(6)	3	2	0	0	0	0	12	8
Nathan Mason	8/9/93	(2)	(2)	0	0	0	0	0	0	0	0
Anthony Mullally	28/6/91	1(1)	1(1)	0	0	0	0	0	0	0	0
Anthony Nicholson	28/11/90	6(19)	6(18)	4	4	0	0	0	0	16	16
Lee Paterson	20/7/82	24	22	5	4	33	26	0	0	86	68
Wayne Reittie	21/1/88	9(1)	9(1)	5	5	0	0	0	0	20	20
Alex Rowe	11/3/85	2(27)	2(25)	3	1	0	0	0	0	12	4
Sam Scott	5/6/90	23(1)	21(1)	7	6	0	0	0	0	28	24
Byron Smith	5/3/84	26(1)	24(1)	2	2	0	0	0	0	8	8
Kyle Trout	1/3/91	2(2)	2(2)	0	0	0	0	0	0	0	0

Scott Leatherbarrow

LEAGUE RECORD
P26-W12-D1-L13-BP7
(8th, Championship/Elimination Play-Off)
F582, A573, Diff+9
45 points.

CHALLENGE CUP
Round Four

ATTENDANCES
Best - v Castleford (CC - 2,482)
Worst - v Kells (CC - 365)
Total (Championship only) - 9,766
Average (Championship only) - 751
(Down by 2 on 2013)

CLUB RECORDS	
MATCH RECORDS	Highest score: 100-4 v Gateshead, 17/3/2010 **Highest score against:** 9-78 v Wakefield, 26/8/67 **Record attendance:** 23,989 v Leeds, 14/3/25
	Tries: 5 Joe Oakland v Bramley, 19/12/1908; Tommy Brannan v Swinton, 17/1/20; Jim Wale v Bramley, 4/12/26; Jim Wale v Cottingham, 12/2/27; Tommy Oldroyd v Highfield, 6/3/94; Ben Feehan v Halifax, 10/8/2008; Jermaine McGillvary v Whitehaven, 24/5/2009
	Goals: 16 Gareth Moore v Gateshead, 17/3/2010 **Points:** 40 Gareth Moore v Gateshead, 17/3/2010
SEASON RECORDS	**Tries:** 30 Johnny Campbell 2010 **Goals:** 144 Barry Eaton 2004 **Points:** 308 Richard Price 1997
CAREER RECORDS	**Tries:** 142 Craig Lingard 1998-2008 **Goals:** 463 Wharton 'Wattie' Davies 1897-1912 **Points:** 1,297 Wharton 'Wattie' Davies 1897-1912
	Appearances: 421 Wharton 'Wattie' Davies 1897-1912

DEWSBURY RAMS

DATE	FIXTURE	RESULT	SCORERS	LGE	ATT
16/2/14	Featherstone (h)	W11-10	t:Godwin,Thackeray g:Hyde fg:Thackeray	6th	2,096
23/2/14	Rochdale (a)	W12-42	t:Gallagher,Morton,Thackeray(2),Brown,Sheriff,Pryce g:Hemingway(3),Hyde(4)	2nd	817
2/3/14	Doncaster (a)	W12-20	t:Hale,Thackeray,Scott g:Hemingway,Hyde(3)	2nd	744
9/3/14	Whitehaven (h)	L16-23	t:Scott,Morton,Brown g:Hemingway,Grayston	3rd	903
16/3/14	West Hull (h) (CCR3)	W76-10	t:Morton,Gallagher,Aizue(2),Brown,Farrell(3),Robinson(3),Sheriff,Grady,Dowes g:Hemingway(10)	N/A	433
23/3/14	Sheffield (a)	L46-10	t:Godwin,Sheriff g:Grady	6th	911
30/3/14	Workington (h)	W38-16	t:Grady,Thackeray(2),Scott(2),Pryce,Morton g:Hemingway(3),Hyde(2)	6th	747
4/4/14	Wigan (h) (CCR4)	L6-58	t:Morton g:Hemingway	4th	3,054
13/4/14	Swinton (a)	L37-31	t:Grady(3),Godwin,Gallagher g:Hemingway(5) fg:Hyde	N/A	412
18/4/14	Batley (h)	W43-10	t:Grady,Scott(2),Godwin,Gallagher,Pryce,Hepworth g:Hemingway(7) fg:Hyde	6th	1,999
4/5/14	Keighley (a)	L40-20	t:Scott,Gallagher,Hyde,Nash g:Hemingway(2)	5th	817
11/5/14	Leigh (h)	L12-28	t:Hyde,Morton g:Grayston(2)	6th	1,193
18/5/14	Barrow (a)	W30-42	t:Thackeray(5),Hale,Morton g:Grayston(7)	6th	914
25/5/14	Halifax (h)	W20-18	t:Thackeray,Buchanan,Grady g:Grayston(4)	5th	1,213
1/6/14	North Wales (a) ●	W38-18	t:Thackeray(2),Hale,Buchanan,Hyde,Beckett g:Grayston(7)	5th	708
8/6/14	Featherstone (a)	L36-24	t:Morton,Thackeray,Hale,Aizue g:Grayston(2),Hemingway(2)	5th	2,110
15/6/14	Sheffield (h)	L12-28	t:Grady,Buchanan g:Hyde(2)	5th	867
22/6/14	Doncaster (h)	W24-8	t:Thackeray(2),Briggs,Beckett,Grady g:Hemingway(2)	5th	721
29/6/14	Leigh (a)	L30-22	t:Grady(2),Hale,Morton g:Hemingway(3)	7th	2,217
4/7/14	Swinton (h)	W48-6	t:Grady,Thackeray(2),Pryce,Wright,Morton,Buchanan,Briggs g:Hemingway(3),Hyde(5)	5th	749
13/7/14	Whitehaven (a)	L40-34	t:Thackeray,Grady,Pryce,Wood,Hale,Gallagher g:Hyde(5)	5th	843
20/7/14	North Wales (a) ●	W18-22	t:Sheriff,Wood,Pryce,Aizue g:Hemingway(3)	5th	686
27/7/14	Barrow (h)	W34-14	t:Dowes(2),Hyde(2),Spicer,Hellewell g:Hemingway(3),Hyde(2)	5th	575
3/8/14	Halifax (a)	L36-24	t:Grady(2),Gallagher,Wright g:Hemingway(2),Hyde(2)	5th	1,935
10/8/14	Rochdale (h)	W38-20	t:Gallagher,Hyde,Thackeray,Buchanan(2),Wood,Pryce g:Hemingway(3),Hyde(2)	5th	776
17/8/14	Batley (a)	W14-16	t:Hale,Farrell,Grady g:Hemingway(2)	5th	1,159
31/8/14	Keighley (h)	W24-12	t:Hellewell,Hepworth,Hyde,Thackeray g:Hemingway(3),Hyde	6th	1,028
7/9/14	Workington (a)	L23-4	t:Wood	6th	895
14/9/14	Workington (h) (EPO)	W50-6	t:Thackeray(3),Hale,Aizue,Hellewell,Hepworth,Gallagher g:Hemingway(3),Hyde(6)	N/A	805
21/9/14	Halifax (a) (PSF)	W0-25	t:Thackeray(2),Wood,Gallagher g:Hemingway(3),Hyde fg:Hyde	N/A	1,371
28/9/14	Leigh (a) (QSF)	L33-22	t:Thackeray,Hellewell,Farrell,Morton g:Hemingway(3)	N/A	2,828

● Played at The Rock, Wrexham

	D.O.B.	APP		TRIES		GOALS		FG		PTS	
		ALL	Ch	ALL	Ch	ALL	Ch	ALL	Ch	ALL	Ch
Makali Aizue	30/12/77	15(7)	14(7)	5	3	0	0	0	0	20	12
Callan Beckett	24/3/93	10	10	2	2	0	0	0	0	8	8
Kyle Briggs	7/12/87	3(1)	3(1)	2	2	0	0	0	0	8	8
Aaron Brown	27/7/92	8	6	3	2	0	0	0	0	12	8
Austin Buchanan	22/5/84	12	12	6	6	0	0	0	0	24	24
Ewan Dowes	4/3/81	17(2)	16(1)	3	2	0	0	0	0	12	8
Joel Farrell	15/3/94	1(10)	(10)	5	2	0	0	0	0	20	8
Tommy Gallagher	10/9/83	3(24)	2(24)	10	9	0	0	0	0	40	36
Wayne Godwin	13/3/82	13	12	4	4	0	0	0	0	16	16
Shane Grady	13/12/89	31	29	16	15	1	1	0	0	66	62
Jordan Grayston	14/9/91	7(2)	6(2)	0	0	23	23	0	0	46	46
Matthew Haggarty	8/1/91	7(21)	7(19)	0	0	0	0	0	0	0	0
Scott Hale	14/12/91	29	28	8	8	0	0	0	0	32	32
Ben Hellewell	30/1/92	10	10	4	4	0	0	0	0	16	16
Tom Hemingway	6/12/86	24(5)	23(4)	0	0	68	57	0	0	136	114
Ryan Hepworth	16/1/81	24(6)	23(6)	3	3	0	0	0	0	12	12
Kieran Hyde	10/10/89	25(6)	23(6)	7	7	36	36	3	3	103	103
Dale Morton	31/10/90	31	29	11	9	0	0	0	0	44	36
Jason Muranka	4/8/89	(3)	(3)	0	0	0	0	0	0	0	0
Jobe Murphy	16/10/92	16	16	0	0	0	0	0	0	0	0
Stephen Nash	14/1/86	4(15)	4(13)	1	1	0	0	0	0	4	4
Karl Pryce	27/7/86	24	23	7	7	0	0	0	0	28	28
Shaun Robinson	13/7/89	1	0	3	0	0	0	0	0	12	0
Jonathan Schofield	17/4/90	1	1	0	0	0	0	0	0	0	0
Greg Scott	21/6/91	12(1)	11	7	7	0	0	0	0	28	28
Louis Sheriff	6/9/92	9(1)	8(1)	4	3	0	0	0	0	16	12
Rob Spicer	22/9/84	17(4)	16(4)	1	1	0	0	0	0	4	4
Anthony Thackeray	19/2/86	29	28	28	28	0	0	1	1	113	113
Josh Tonks	14/8/91	3(1)	3(1)	0	0	0	0	0	0	0	0
Lucas Walshaw	4/8/92	4	2	0	0	0	0	0	0	0	0
Sam Wood	23/12/93	11	11	5	5	0	0	0	0	20	20
Ryan Wright	28/10/91	2(15)	1(14)	2	2	0	0	0	0	8	8

Anthony Thackeray

LEAGUE RECORD
P26-W15-D0-L11-BP6
(6th, Championship/
Qualifying Semi-Final)
F669, A585, Diff+84
51 points.

CHALLENGE CUP
Round Four

ATTENDANCES
Best - v Wigan (CC - 3,054)
Worst - v West Hull (CC - 433)
Total (Championship,
inc play-offs) - 14,380
Average (Championship,
inc play-offs) - 1,027
(Up by 141 on 2013)

CLUB RECORDS

MATCH RECORDS

SEASON RECORDS

CAREER RECORDS

Highest score: 90-5 v Blackpool, 4/4/93 Highest score against: 0-82 v Widnes, 30/11/86
Record attendance: 26,584 v Halifax, 30/10/20 *(Crown Flatt)*; 3,995 v Batley, 26/12/94; v Bradford, 18/4/2010 *(new ground)*
Tries: 8 Dai Thomas v Liverpool, 13/4/1907
Goals: 13 Greg Pearce v Blackpool Borough, 4/4/93; Francis Maloney v Hunslet, 25/3/2007 Points: 32 Les Holliday v Barrow, 11/9/94
Tries: 40 Dai Thomas 1906-07 Goals: 169 Barry Eaton 2000 Points: 394 Barry Eaton 2000
Tries: 144 Joe Lyman 1913-31 Goals: 863 Nigel Stephenson 1967-78; 1984-86 Points: 2,082 Nigel Stephenson 1967-78; 1984-86
Appearances: 454 Joe Lyman 1913-31

DONCASTER

DATE	FIXTURE	RESULT	SCORERS	LGE	ATT
16/2/14	Workington (a)	W12-22	t:Sanderson(2),Castle,Scott g:Sanderson(3)	4th	895
23/2/14	Keighley (h)	W30-12	t:Sanderson(2),Kelly,Scott,Welham,Morrison g:Sanderson(3)	3rd	647
2/3/14	Dewsbury (h)	L12-20	t:Spaven,Cooke g:Sanderson(2)	4th	744
9/3/14	Batley (a)	W12-20	t:Spaven(2),Morrison g:Sanderson(4)	4th	691
16/3/14	British Army (a) (CCR3) ●	W12-62	t:Cunningham(2),Scott(3),Waterman(3),Morrison(2),Wilkinson g:Sanderson(6),Scott(3)	N/A	357
23/3/14	Featherstone (h)	W22-16	t:Scott,Pitts,Cooke g:Sanderson(5)	2nd	1,317
30/3/14	Halifax (a)	L48-6	t:Arundel g:Sanderson	5th	1,482
6/4/14	Hemel (h) (CCR4)	W68-18	t:Waterman,Sanderson(2),Butterfield,Wilkinson(2),Emmett,Edwards,Wilson,Spurr,Welham,Cooke g:Sanderson(10)	N/A	348
13/4/14	North Wales (h)	W20-12	t:Morrison,Waterman,Crooks(2) g:Sanderson(2)	3rd	574
20/4/14	Sheffield (a)	W34-42	t:Wildie(2),Scott,Emmett,Edwards,Kent,Starling g:Sanderson(7)	3rd	1,018
27/4/14	Warrington (a) (CCR5)	L68-0		N/A	3,002
4/5/14	Barrow (a)	W30-28	t:Waterman(3),Scott(2) g:Sanderson(5)	2nd	573
11/5/14	Whitehaven (h)	L29-20	t:Hodson(2),Waterman,Sanderson g:Sanderson(2)	3rd	560
18/5/14	Leigh (a)	L50-20	t:Kent,Hodson,Scott,Cooke g:Sanderson(2)	4th	2,132
25/5/14	Rochdale (h)	W40-10	t:Kesik,Leaf,Castle,Hodson(2),Wilkinson,Spaven,Scott g:Scott(4)	3rd	600
1/6/14	Swinton (a)	W22-36	t:Robinson(2),Kesik,Hodson,Snitch g:Scott(6)	3rd	355
8/6/14	Barrow (a)	W10-22	t:Morrison,Wilkinson,Hodson,Colbon g:Scott(3)	3rd	1,048
15/6/14	Featherstone (a)	D22-22	t:Welham,Emmett,Whiting(2) g:Scott(3)	3rd	2,169
22/6/14	Dewsbury (a)	L24-8	t:Watts g:Scott(2)	4th	721
29/6/14	Whitehaven (h) ●●	W22-16	t:Kesik,Wilkinson,Cunningham,Hadley g:Scott(3)	4th	680
6/7/14	North Wales (a) ●●●	W24-28	t:Welham,Whiting,Spaven,Scott,Snitch g:Scott(4)	4th	538
13/7/14	Leigh (h)	W24-16	t:Hodson(2),Spaven,Crooks(2) g:Scott(2)	4th	1,113
20/7/14	Swinton (h)	W36-34	t:Morrison,Hodson,Kesik,Waterman,Wilkinson(2) g:Sanderson(6)	4th	617
27/7/14	Keighley (a)	L44-32	t:Kesik,Wilkinson,Castle,Morrison,Sanderson,Crooks g:Sanderson(4)	4th	723
3/8/14	Sheffield (h)	L22-26	t:Robinson,Morrison,Snitch g:Sanderson(5)	4th	954
10/8/14	Workington (h)	W36-10	t:Miller(2),Snitch,Dunn,Cunningham,Leaf g:Sanderson(6)	4th	504
17/8/14	Rochdale (a)	W16-22	t:Snitch(2),Hodson,Sanderson g:Sanderson(3)	4th	571
31/8/14	Halifax (h)	W39-18	t:Emmett,Cooke(2),Scott(2),Snitch(2) g:Sanderson(5) fg:Cooke	3rd	980
7/9/14	Batley (h)	L10-34	t:Hodson,Waterman g:Sanderson	4th	1,160
14/9/14	Leigh (a) (QPO)	L41-14	t:Cooke,Wilkinson g:Sanderson(3)	N/A	1,903
21/9/14	Sheffield (h) (PSF)	L24-58	t:Scott,Spaven,Hodson,Emmett g:Sanderson(4)	N/A	825

● Played at Aldershot Military Stadium ●● Played at Castle Park ●●● Played at The Rock, Wrexham

	D.O.B.	APP ALL	APP Ch	TRIES ALL	TRIES Ch	GOALS ALL	GOALS Ch	FG ALL	FG Ch	PTS ALL	PTS Ch
Joe Arundel	22/8/91	4	4	1	1	0	0	0	0	4	4
Mick Butterfield	5/12/84	4(1)	3	1	0	0	0	0	0	4	0
Matt Carbutt	3/10/85	24(5)	22(4)	0	0	0	0	0	0	0	0
Mark Castle	19/2/86	1(17)	1(17)	3	3	0	0	0	0	12	12
Liam Colbon	30/9/84	7(2)	7(2)	1	1	0	0	0	4	4	4
Paul Cooke	17/4/81	28	26	7	6	0	0	1	1	29	25
Jason Crookes	21/4/90	1	1	0	0	0	0	0	0	0	0
Ben Crooks	15/6/93	3	3	5	5	0	0	0	0	20	20
Liam Cunningham	28/10/89	9(1)	8(1)	4	2	0	0	0	0	16	8
Pasqualle Dunn	23/3/94	1(6)	1(6)	1	1	0	0	0	0	4	4
Grant Edwards	22/3/87	1(5)	(3)	2	1	0	0	0	0	8	4
Mike Emmett	13/5/87	26(1)	25	5	4	0	0	0	0	20	16
Chris Green	3/1/90	4	3	0	0	0	0	0	0	0	0
Dean Hadley	5/8/92	2(2)	2(2)	1	1	0	0	0	0	4	4
Tom Hodson	27/9/90	16	16	14	14	0	0	0	0	56	56
Michael Kelly	23/5/89	11(4)	11(4)	1	1	0	0	0	0	4	4
Liam Kent	9/4/91	11	10	2	2	0	0	0	0	8	8
Kyle Kesik	3/6/89	20(1)	19(1)	5	5	0	0	0	0	20	20
Shaun Leaf	10/2/84	12(2)	9(2)	2	2	0	0	0	0	8	8
Jacob Miller	22/8/92	5	5	2	2	0	0	0	0	8	8
Nev Morrison	27/5/90	20	17	9	7	0	0	0	0	36	28
Danny Nicklas	29/6/91	6	5	0	0	0	0	0	0	0	0
Jay Pitts	9/12/89	4	4	1	1	0	0	0	0	4	4
Craig Robinson	30/7/85	20(8)	18(7)	3	3	0	0	0	0	12	12
Stewart Sanderson	10/4/85	26	24	9	7	89	73	0	0	214	174
Dave Scott	8/6/93	29	27	15	12	30	27	0	0	120	102
Steve Snitch	22/2/83	10(5)	10(5)	8	8	0	0	0	0	32	32
Scott Spaven	6/3/90	11(16)	10(15)	7	7	0	0	0	0	28	28
Russ Spiers	28/4/91	8(20)	7(18)	0	0	0	0	0	0	0	0
Chris Spurr	7/7/80	(1)	0	1	0	0	0	0	0	4	0
Alex Starling	14/10/93	16(3)	13(3)	1	1	0	0	0	0	4	4
Lee Waterman	13/4/87	10(9)	7(9)	11	7	0	0	0	0	44	28
Liam Watts	8/7/90	3	3	1	1	0	0	0	0	4	4
Liam Welham	11/11/88	23(1)	21(1)	4	3	0	0	0	0	16	12
Richard Whiting	20/12/84	3	3	3	3	0	0	0	0	12	12
Matty Wildie	25/10/90	6(1)	5(1)	2	2	0	0	0	0	8	8
Richard Wilkinson	26/10/93	16(2)	13(2)	10	7	0	0	0	0	40	28
Ryan Wilson	21/12/93	2(11)	1(9)	1	0	0	0	0	0	4	0

Mike Emmett

LEAGUE RECORD
P26-W17-D1-L8-BP4
(4th, Championship/
Preliminary Semi-Final)
F643, A599, Diff+44
57 points.

CHALLENGE CUP
Round Five

ATTENDANCES
Best - v Featherstone (Ch - 1,317)
Worst - v Hemel (CC - 348)
Total (Championship,
inc play-offs) - 11,288
Average (Championship,
inc play-offs) - 806
(Up by 88 on 2013)

CLUB RECORDS
Highest score: 96-0 v Highfield, 20/3/94 **Highest score against:** 4-90 v Widnes, 10/6/2007
Record attendance: 10,000 v Bradford, 16/2/52 *(York Road)*; 6,528 v Castleford, 12/4/2007 *(Keepmoat Stadium)*

MATCH RECORDS
Tries: 6 Kane Epati v Oldham, 30/7/2006; Lee Waterman v Sharlston, 24/3/2012
Goals: 12 Tony Zelei v Nottingham City, 1/9/91; Robert Turner v Highfield, 20/3/94
Points: 32 Tony Zelei v Nottingham City, 1/9/91; Lee Waterman v Sharlston, 24/3/2012

SEASON RECORDS
Tries: 36 Lee Waterman 2012 Goals: 129 Jonny Woodcock 2002 Points: 306 Jonny Woodcock 2002

CAREER RECORDS
Tries: 112 Mark Roache 1985-97 Goals: 850 David Noble 1976-77; 1980-89; 1992 Points: 1,751 David Noble 1976-77; 1980-89; 1992
Appearances: 327 Audley Pennant 1980-83; 1985-97

FEATHERSTONE ROVERS

DATE	FIXTURE	RESULT	SCORERS	LGE	ATT
16/2/14	Dewsbury (a)	L11-10	t:Lockwood,Bussey g:Moore	7th	2,096
23/2/14	Halifax (h)	W28-20	t:Chisholm,Worthington,Sharp,Cording,Mendeika g:Moore(4)	4th	2,583
2/3/14	North Wales (a)	W6-36	t:Sharp(3),Briggs,Moore,Flanagan g:Moore(6)	3rd	1,418
9/3/14	Rochdale (h)	W56-6	t:Uaisele(3),Hardman(2),Ellis,Sharp(2),Worthington,Hellewell g:Moore(8)	2nd	2,323
23/3/14	Doncaster (a)	L22-16	t:Hardman(2),Worthington g:Moore(2)	3rd	1,317
30/3/14	Swinton (h)	W36-22	t:Uaisele(2),Sharp(2),Worthington,Mendeika(2) g:Moore(4)	2nd	2,020
6/4/14	North Wales (h) (CCR4)	W66-0	t:Crossley(2),Mendeika(3),Cording(2),Kain,Worthington,Dale,Sharp,Flanagan g:Moore(9)	N/A	1,312
13/4/14	Barrow (a)	W18-38	t:Moore,Kain,James,Worthington,Hardman(2),Sharp,Ellis g:Moore(3)	2nd	1,075
18/4/14	Keighley (h)	W36-12	t:Uaisele,Worthington,Hardman,Kain,Sharp,Mendeika(2) g:Moore(4)	2nd	2,056
27/4/14	Leigh (a) (CCR5)	L26-16	t:Sharp(2),Mendeika(2)	N/A	3,664
4/5/14	Leigh (h)	L10-29	t:Hellewell,Kain g:Briggs	3rd	3,230
11/5/14	Sheffield (a)	W22-36	t:Hellewell(2),Worthington,James,Mendeika,Briggs g:Briggs(6)	2nd	1,279
18/5/14	Workington (h)	W32-20	t:Moore,Trout,Hellewell,Hardman,Mendeika,Bussey g:Briggs(2),Moore(2)	2nd	2,016
25/5/14	Whitehaven (h)	W50-14	t:Mendeika(3),Sharp(3),Worthington(2),Smith,Cording g:Moore(5)	2nd	1,726
1/6/14	Batley (a)	W26-32	t:Worthington,Hellewell,Dale,Bridge,Hardman,Bussey g:Moore(4)	2nd	1,143
8/6/14	Dewsbury (h)	W36-24	t:Kain(3),Blackmore(2),Hardman g:Briggs,Bussey(5)	2nd	2,110
15/6/14	Doncaster (h)	D22-22	t:Blackmore,Bridge,Bostock,Bussey g:Siejka(3)	2nd	2,169
22/6/14	Workington (a)	L20-18	t:Lockwood,Sharp(2),Bostock g:Siejka	2nd	776
29/6/14	North Wales (h)	W56-18	t:Kain,Mendeika(3),Blackmore,Ellis,Kent,Flanagan,Sharp g:Sammut(10)	2nd	1,653
6/7/14	Rochdale (a)	L38-34	t:Crookes(2),Kain,Crossley,Uaisele,Hardman g:Moore(5)	2nd	735
13/7/14	Swinton (a) ●	W24-48	t:Trout,Dale,Mendeika,Kain,Sharp,Crookes(2),Ellis,Annakin g:Moore(3),Kain(3)	2nd	469
20/7/14	Batley (h)	W52-6	t:Worthington(2),Ellis,Flanagan,Crookes(2),Mendeika,James,Moore,Kain g:Moore(5),Sharp	2nd	2,025
27/7/14	Whitehaven (a)	W24-35	t:Moore,Sharp,Hardman,Crookes,Bostock,Worthington g:Moore(5) fg:Rooney	2nd	901
3/8/14	Barrow (h)	W62-12	t:Ellis(2),Sharp(2),Moore(2),Flanagan,Worthington(2),Annakin,Crookes,Crossley g:Moore,Rooney(6)	2nd	1,626
8/8/14	Leigh (a)	L48-18	t:Ellis,Crookes,Worthington g:Moore(3)	3rd	3,565
17/8/14	Halifax (a)	W4-20	t:Crookes(3),Pick g:Moore(2)	2nd	3,022
31/8/14	Sheffield (h)	L28-40	t:Kain,Teasdale(2),Sharp,Annakin g:Bussey(4)	2nd	2,085
7/9/14	Keighley (h)	W24-26	t:Hardman,Sharp,Pick,Crookes,Blackmore g:Moore(3)	2nd	1,919
14/9/14	Halifax (h) (QPO)	W34-16	t:Spears,Teasdale,Moore,Trout,James,Crookes g:Moore(5)	N/A	1,478
28/9/14	Sheffield (h) (QSF)	W21-12	t:Blackmore,Lockwood,Moore g:Moore(4) fg:Moore	N/A	1,730
5/10/14	Leigh (GF) ●●	L12-36	t:Sharp(2) g:Moore(2)	N/A	9,164

● Played at Park Lane, Sedgley Park   ●● Played at Headingley Carnegie, Leeds

		APP		TRIES		GOALS		FG		PTS	
	D.O.B.	ALL	Ch	ALL	Ch	ALL	Ch	ALL	Ch	ALL	Ch
Chris Annakin	30/1/91	2(9)	2(9)	3	3	0	0	0	0	12	12
Gavin Bennion	31/12/93	(1)	(1)	0	0	0	0	0	0	0	0
Ben Blackmore	19/2/93	11(1)	11(1)	6	6	0	0	0	0	24	24
Andrew Bostock	25/2/85	1(12)	1(11)	3	3	0	0	0	0	12	12
Danny Bridge	4/1/93	3(1)	3(1)	2	2	0	0	0	0	8	8
Kyle Briggs	7/12/87	8(4)	8(2)	2	2	10	10	0	0	28	28
Jack Bussey	17/8/92	8(15)	8(15)	4	4	9	9	0	0	34	34
Jamel Chisholm	7/11/92	1	1	1	1	0	0	0	0	4	4
Jamie Cording	30/12/89	17(1)	15(1)	4	2	0	0	0	0	16	8
Jason Crookes	21/4/90	15	15	14	14	0	0	0	0	56	56
Steve Crossley	28/11/89	27	26	4	2	0	0	0	0	16	8
Matty Dale	10/10/86	4(14)	4(12)	3	2	0	0	0	0	12	8
Andy Ellis	15/12/84	28	26	8	8	0	0	0	0	32	32
George Flanagan	8/10/86	2(17)	2(15)	5	4	0	0	0	0	20	16
Chris Green	3/1/90	3(2)	3(2)	0	0	0	0	0	0	0	0
Ian Hardman	8/12/84	27	25	13	13	0	0	0	0	52	52
Ben Hellewell	30/1/92	10	10	6	6	0	0	0	0	24	24
Keegan Hirst	13/12/88	9(11)	7(11)	0	0	0	0	0	0	0	0
Matt James	26/3/87	11(13)	10(12)	4	4	0	0	0	0	16	16
Andy Kain	1/9/85	24(2)	22(2)	12	11	3	3	0	0	54	50
Liam Kent	9/4/91	3(1)	3(1)	1	1	0	0	0	0	4	4
James Lockwood	21/3/86	29	27	3	3	0	0	0	0	12	12
James Mendeika	16/12/91	18(2)	16(2)	20	15	0	0	0	0	80	60
Gareth Moore	3/6/89	24	22	9	9	90	81	1	1	217	199
Shaun Pick	21/9/93	11(2)	11(2)	2	2	0	0	0	0	8	8
Colton Roche	23/6/93	(1)	(1)	0	0	0	0	0	0	0	0
Jamie Rooney	17/3/80	1(2)	1(2)	0	0	6	6	1	1	13	13
Jarrod Sammut	15/2/87	1	1	0	0	10	10	0	0	20	20
Tom Saxton	3/10/83	1	1	0	0	0	0	0	0	0	0
Will Sharp	12/5/86	30(1)	28(1)	27	24	1	1	0	0	110	98
Harry Siejka	3/2/92	3	3	0	0	4	4	0	0	8	8
Sam Smeaton	26/10/88	2	2	0	0	0	0	0	0	0	0
Daniel Smith	20/3/93	(1)	(1)	1	1	0	0	0	0	4	4
Tim Spears	27/7/84	20	18	1	1	0	0	0	0	4	4
Luke Teasdale	8/6/94	(7)	(7)	3	3	0	0	0	0	12	12
Kyle Trout	1/3/91	12(3)	12(3)	3	3	0	0	0	0	12	12
Etuate Uaisele	8/12/84	10	8	7	7	0	0	0	0	28	28
Greg Worthington	17/7/90	27	25	17	16	0	0	0	0	68	64

Gareth Moore

LEAGUE RECORD
P26-W18-D1-L7-BP5
(2nd, Championship/
Grand Final Runners-Up)
F871, A532, Diff+339
61 points.

CHALLENGE CUP
Round Five
(received bye in Round Three)

ATTENDANCES
Best - v Leigh (Ch - 3,230)
Worst - v North Wales (CC - 1,312)
Total (Championship,
inc play-offs) - 30,830
Average (Championship,
inc play-offs) - 2,055
(Down by 348 on 2013)

CLUB RECORDS
MATCH RECORDS
Highest score: 96-0 v Castleford Lock Lane, 8/2/2004 Highest score against: 14-80 v Bradford, 3/4/2005 Record attendance: 17,531 v St Helens, 21/3/59
Tries: 6 Mike Smith v Doncaster, 13/4/68; Chris Bibb v Keighley, 17/9/89
Goals: 13 Mark Knapper v Keighley, 17/9/89; Liam Finn v Hunslet Old Boys, 25/3/2012; Liam Finn v Swinton, 12/8/2012
Points: 40 Martin Pearson v Whitehaven, 26/11/95

SEASON RECORDS
CAREER RECORDS
Tries: 48 Paul Newlove 1992-93 Goals: 183 (inc 2fg) Liam Finn 2012 Points: 436 Liam Finn 2012
Tries: 162 Don Fox 1953-66 Goals: 1,210 Steve Quinn 1975-88 Points: 2,654 Steve Quinn 1975-88 Appearances: 440 Jim Denton 1921-34

HALIFAX

DATE	FIXTURE	RESULT	SCORERS	LGE	ATT
16/2/14	Swinton (h)	W28-18	t:Brown,Johnston,Reittie(2),Robinson g:Tyrer(4)	5th	1,587
23/2/14	Featherstone (a)	L28-20	t:Johnston,Kaye,Divorty g:Tyrer(4)	5th	2,583
2/3/14	Batley (h)	L8-10	t:Tyrer,Heaton	7th	1,798
9/3/14	Sheffield (h)	W30-28	t:Tyrer,Saxton(2),Potts,Ambler g:Tyrer(5)	5th	1,327
16/3/14	Hull Dockers (a) (CCR3) ●	W6-70	t:Worrincy(5),Johnston(2),Robinson(3),Tonks,Manning,Brooks g:Tyrer(9)	N/A	600
23/3/14	Whitehaven (a)	W14-36	t:Manning(3),Johnston,Potts,Saxton,Mennell g:Tyrer(4)	4th	751
30/3/14	Doncaster (h)	W48-6	t:Potts(2),Divorty,Manning(2),Murrell,Saxton,Fieldhouse,Davies g:Tyrer(5),Murrell	3rd	1,482
6/4/14	Widnes (h) (CCR4)	L10-34	t:Fieldhouse,Potts g:Tyrer	N/A	2,271
13/4/14	Leigh (h)	L28-36	t:Bracek,Divorty,Fieldhouse(2),Heaton g:Tyrer(4)	4th	2,282
18/4/14	Barrow (a)	W18-32	t:Cowling(2),Johnston,Fieldhouse(2),Mennell g:Tyrer(4)	4th	1,169
4/5/14	Workington (a)	D20-20	t:Johnston,Holden,Tyrer,Bracek g:Tyrer(2)	4th	732
11/5/14	North Wales (h)	L6-12	t:Murrell g:Tyrer	4th	1,444
18/5/14	Rochdale (h)	W12-28	t:Reittie(2),Tyrer(2),Fieldhouse(2) g:Tyrer(2)	3rd	721
25/5/14	Dewsbury (a)	L20-18	t:Saxton,Fieldhouse,Casey g:Tyrer(3)	4th	1,213
1/6/14	Keighley (a)	W14-28	t:Divorty,Fieldhouse,Manning,Ambler,Mennell g:Tyrer(4)	4th	1,217
11/6/14	Leigh (a)	L26-24	t:Potts,Tyrer,Ambler,Casey g:Tyrer(4)	4th	2,571
15/6/14	Workington (h)	W18-10	t:Divorty,Adamson,Fieldhouse g:Tyrer(3)	4th	1,658
22/6/14	Rochdale (h)	W42-24	t:Divorty(4),Fieldhouse,Ambler(2),Adamson g:Tyrer(2),Brown(2),Murrell	3rd	1,425
29/6/14	Sheffield (a)	W14-32	t:Fox(2),Casey(2),Fieldhouse,Adamson g:Brown(2),Murrell(2)	3rd	955
3/7/14	Keighley (h)	W38-6	t:Spencer,Tonks,Robinson,Ambler,Murrell,Divorty,Saxton g:Murrell(4),Mennell	3rd	1,519
13/7/14	Batley (a)	D22-22	t:Holden,Ambler,Saxton,Fieldhouse g:Murrell(3)	3rd	1,155
20/7/14	Whitehaven (h)	W52-12	t:Saxton,Ambler(2),Divorty,Tyrer(2),Adamson,Cowling,Murrell g:Tyrer(8)	3rd	1,317
27/7/14	Swinton (a)	W30-48	t:Mennell,Saxton,Potts,Johnston(2),Murrell,Adamson,Divorty g:Tyrer(8)	3rd	569
3/8/14	Dewsbury (h)	W36-24	t:Ambler,Johnston,Divorty,Cowling,Fieldhouse,Potts g:Tyrer(6)	3rd	1,935
10/8/14	North Wales (a)	W17-20	t:Tyrer,Casey,Ambler,Potts g:Tyrer(2)	2nd	704
17/8/14	Featherstone (h)	L4-20	t:Johnston	3rd	3,022
31/8/14	Doncaster (h)	L39-18	t:Bracek,Adamson,Mennell g:Tyrer,Brown(2)	4th	980
7/9/14	Barrow (h)	W30-24	t:Saxton(2),Fieldhouse,Tonks,Adamson,Casey g:Murrell(3)	3rd	1,431
14/9/14	Featherstone (a) (QPO)	L34-16	t:Kaye,Potts(2) g:Murrell(2)	N/A	1,478
21/9/14	Dewsbury (h) (PSF)	L0-25		N/A	1,371

● Played at KC Lightstream Stadium, Hull

		APP		**TRIES**		**GOALS**		**FG**		**PTS**	
	D.O.B.	ALL	Ch	ALL	Ch	ALL	Ch	ALL	Ch	ALL	Ch
Luke Adamson	17/11/87	28(1)	27(1)	7	7	0	0	0	0	28	28
Luke Ambler	18/12/89	28(1)	26(1)	11	11	0	0	0	0	44	44
Andy Bracek	21/3/84	17(10)	16(10)	3	3	0	0	0	0	12	12
Sam Brooks	29/9/93	6(8)	6(7)	1	0	0	0	0	0	4	0
Simon Brown	23/6/89	10(2)	8(2)	1	1	6	6	0	0	16	16
Callum Casey	6/6/90	11(15)	10(14)	6	6	0	0	0	0	24	24
Danny Cowling	20/12/92	15(1)	13(1)	4	4	0	0	0	0	16	16
Ben Davies	2/11/89	1(13)	(12)	1	1	0	0	0	0	4	4
Ross Divorty	27/11/88	24(5)	23(4)	13	13	0	0	0	0	52	52
Ryan Fieldhouse	10/4/88	25	23	16	15	0	0	0	0	64	60
Peter Fox	5/11/83	10	10	2	2	0	0	0	0	8	8
Ben Heaton	12/3/90	7(2)	7(2)	2	2	0	0	0	0	8	8
Keith Holden	23/6/93	1(16)	1(15)	2	2	0	0	0	0	8	8
Ben Johnston	8/3/88	19(5)	18(5)	11	9	0	0	0	0	44	36
Ben Kaye	19/12/88	22	21	2	2	0	0	0	0	8	8
Dane Manning	15/4/89	19	17	7	6	0	0	0	0	28	24
Joe Martin	28/3/95	1	1	0	0	0	0	0	0	0	0
Paul Mennell	26/10/86	14(12)	13(11)	5	5	1	1	0	0	22	22
Scott Murrell	5/9/85	25(1)	24(1)	5	5	16	16	0	0	52	52
Gareth Potts	25/7/90	20	19	11	10	0	0	0	0	44	40
Wayne Reittie	21/1/88	6	5	4	4	0	0	0	0	16	16
Adam Robinson	8/4/87	12(2)	11(2)	5	2	0	0	0	0	20	8
Tom Saxton	3/10/83	24	23	11	11	0	0	0	0	44	44
Jack Spencer	21/12/90	(16)	(16)	1	1	0	0	0	0	4	4
Tony Tonks	27/4/85	19(10)	19(8)	3	2	0	0	0	0	12	8
Steve Tyrer	16/3/89	25	23	9	9	86	76	0	0	208	188
Rob Worrincy	9/7/85	1	0	5	0	0	0	0	0	20	0

Ryan Fieldhouse

LEAGUE RECORD
P26-W16-D2-L8-BP6
(3rd, Championship/
Preliminary Semi-Final)
F714, A504, Diff+210
58 points.

CHALLENGE CUP
Round Four

ATTENDANCES
Best - v Featherstone (Ch - 3,022)
Worst - v Whitehaven (Ch - 1,317)
Total (Championship,
inc play-offs) - 23,598
Average (Championship,
inc play-offs) - 1,686
(Down by 21 on 2013)

CLUB RECORDS	
	Highest score: 94-4 v Myton, 25/3/2012 **Highest score against:** 6-88 v Hull KR, 23/4/2006
	Record attendance: 29,153 v Wigan, 21/3/59 *(Thrum Hall)*; 9,827 v Bradford, 12/3/2000 *(The Shay)*
MATCH RECORDS	**Tries:** 8 Keith Williams v Dewsbury, 9/11/57 **Goals:** 14 Bruce Burton v Hunslet, 27/8/72 **Points:** 32 John Schuster v Doncaster, 9/10/94
SEASON RECORDS	**Tries:** 48 Johnny Freeman 1956-57 **Goals:** 156 Graham Holroyd 2008 **Points:** 362 John Schuster 1994-95
CAREER RECORDS	**Tries:** 290 Johnny Freeman 1954-67 **Goals:** 1,028 Ronnie James 1961-71 **Points:** 2,191 Ronnie James 1961-71 **Appearances:** 482 Stan Kielty 1948-58

KEIGHLEY COUGARS

DATE	FIXTURE	RESULT	SCORERS	LGE	ATT
16/2/14	Whitehaven (h)	W36-14	t:Hesketh,Law,March,Cosgrove,Lynam,White g:Handforth(6)	2nd	1,061
23/2/14	Doncaster (a)	L30-12	t:Williams,White(2)	8th	647
2/3/14	Rochdale (a)	W14-40	t:Handforth,White(4),March,Graham,Craven g:Handforth(4)	5th	726
9/3/14	Leigh (h)	L26-28	t:Barnett,Craven,Williams,Lee g:Jones(5)	6th	1,309
15/3/14	Wath Brow (h) (CCR3)	W42-0	t:Lawton,Lynam,Craven,White(2),Handforth,Lee,Graham g:Jones(5)	N/A	488
23/3/14	Workington (a)	W22-24	t:Hesketh,Craven,Lynam(2),Cosgrove g:Jones,Handforth	5th	746
30/3/14	Sheffield (h)	L24-42	t:Law(2),Lynam,Shickell g:Jones(4)	8th	927
6/4/14	Barrow (h) (CCR4)	W54-28	t:Barnett(2),Lawton,White,Craven,Law,March,Rawlins,Peltier,Hesketh g:Jones(7)	N/A	823
13/4/14	Batley (a)	L29-20	t:White(2),Graham,Haley g:Jones(2)	8th	640
18/4/14	Featherstone (a)	L36-12	t:White,Jones g:Jones(2)	8th	2,056
26/4/14	Swinton (a) (CCR5)	W20-33	t:Lawton,Jode Sheriffe,Barnett(2),Craven,Williams g:Jones(4) fg:Handforth	N/A	468
4/5/14	Dewsbury (h)	W40-20	t:Barnett(3),Haigh(2),Peltier,White g:Jones(6)	7th	817
11/5/14	Swinton (h)	W20-12	t:Williams,White,Law,Barnett g:Jones(2)	7th	673
18/5/14	North Wales (a)	W14-16	t:Haley,Rawlins,Hesketh g:Jones(2)	7th	811
25/5/14	Barrow (h)	W27-18	t:White,Lawton(2),Barnett,Hesketh g:Jones(3) fg:Jones	6th	812
1/6/14	Halifax (h)	L14-28	t:Jode Sheriffe,Haley,Feather g:Jones	6th	1,217
5/6/14	Widnes (a) (CCQF)	L56-6	t:Williams g:Stead	N/A	5,252
10/6/14	Whitehaven (h)	L28-18	t:Feather,Lawton,White g:Jones(3)	8th	741
15/6/14	Batley (h)	L24-28	t:Jones(2),Williams,Barnett(2) g:Jones(2)	9th	913
22/6/14	Sheffield (a)	W16-29	t:Haley,Lynam,Craven,Hesketh g:Jones(6) fg:Jones	8th	743
29/6/14	Rochdale (h)	W48-6	t:Handforth(2),Haley(2),Lawton,Lynam,Craven(2),White g:Handforth(6)	6th	811
3/7/14	Halifax (a)	L38-6	t:Feather g:Lawton	7th	1,519
13/7/14	Workington (h)	L12-16	t:Rawlins,March g:Handforth(2)	9th	811
19/7/14	Leigh (a)	L30-0		10th	2,143
27/7/14	Doncaster (h)	W44-32	t:Haley(3),Law(2),Craven,Jones,Barnett g:Jones(6)	9th	723
3/8/14	Swinton (a) ●	W10-17	t:Barnett,White(3) fg:Handforth	8th	360
10/8/14	Barrow (a)	W10-24	t:Handforth(2),White,Craven g:Jones(4)	7th	668
17/8/14	North Wales (h)	L18-30	t:White,Jones,Lynam g:Jones(3)	8th	893
31/8/14	Dewsbury (a)	L24-12	t:Jones,Handforth g:Jones(2)	8th	1,028
7/9/14	Featherstone (h)	L24-26	t:Craven,Cosgrove,White,Shickell g:Jones(4)	10th	1,919

● Played at Park Lane, Sedgley Park

		APP		TRIES		GOALS		FG		PTS	
	D.O.B.	ALL	Ch	ALL	Ch	ALL	Ch	ALL	Ch	ALL	Ch
Matthew Bailey	1/12/91	(1)	(1)	0	0	0	0	0	0	0	0
Richie Barnett	26/4/81	27	24	14	10	0	0	0	0	56	40
Neil Cherryholme	20/12/86	1(24)	1(22)	0	0	0	0	0	0	0	0
Elliott Cosgrove	31/3/91	7(3)	7(3)	3	3	0	0	0	0	12	12
James Craven	14/10/88	23	20	12	9	0	0	0	0	48	36
Gavin Duffy	9/4/87	1	0	0	0	0	0	0	0	0	0
Charlie Eccleston	26/12/90	1	0	0	0	0	0	0	0	0	0
James Feather	15/4/84	16(2)	16(2)	3	3	0	0	0	0	12	12
Lewis Graham	3/10/93	4(7)	3(5)	3	2	0	0	0	0	12	8
Luke Haigh	24/7/87	11(11)	9(9)	2	2	0	0	0	0	8	8
James Haley	2/7/85	19	18	9	9	0	0	0	0	36	36
Paul Handforth	6/10/81	28	25	7	6	19	19	2	1	68	63
Sean Hesketh	17/8/86	28(1)	25(1)	6	5	0	0	0	0	24	20
Danny Jones	6/3/86	25	22	6	6	74	58	2	2	174	142
Sean Kelly	2/4/91	1	0	0	0	0	0	0	0	0	0
Scott Law	19/2/85	5(10)	3(9)	7	6	0	0	0	0	28	24
Danny Lawton	10/3/90	25	21	7	4	1	1	0	0	30	18
Jack Lee	19/12/92	1(13)	(11)	2	1	0	0	0	0	8	4
Ashley Lindsay	31/7/83	20	19	0	0	0	0	0	0	0	0
Josh Lynam	16/2/93	27(2)	24(1)	8	7	0	0	0	0	32	28
Paul March	25/7/79	9(7)	7(7)	4	3	0	0	0	0	16	12
Ryan Patchett	7/10/92	(1)	0	0	0	0	0	0	0	0	0
Ross Peltier	24/4/92	1(10)	(8)	2	1	0	0	0	0	8	4
Oliver Pursglove	18/1/86	7	6	0	0	0	0	0	0	0	0
Brendan Rawlins	28/1/86	26	23	3	2	0	0	0	0	12	8
Ben Sagar	19/12/89	5(7)	3(7)	0	0	0	0	0	0	0	0
Jesse Sheriffe	12/1/90	6	5	0	0	0	0	0	0	0	0
Jode Sheriffe	4/7/86	4(20)	4(17)	2	1	0	0	0	0	8	4
Andy Shickell	9/5/81	20(1)	18(1)	2	2	0	0	0	0	8	8
Ben Stead	13/10/92	1	0	0	0	1	0	0	0	2	0
Paul White	7/12/82	28	25	24	21	0	0	0	0	96	84
Daley Williams	15/5/86	13	10	6	4	0	0	0	0	24	16

Richie Barnett

LEAGUE RECORD
P26-W12-D0-L14-BP8
(10th, Championship)
F587, A601, Diff-14
44 points.

CHALLENGE CUP
Quarter Finalists

ATTENDANCES
Best - v Featherstone (Ch - 1,919)
Worst - v Wath Brow (CC - 488)
Total (Championship only) - 12,886
Average (Championship only) - 991
(Up by 188 on 2013)

CLUB RECORDS	Highest score: 104-4 v Highfield, 23/4/95 Highest score against: 2-92 v Leigh, 30/4/86 Record attendance: 14,500 v Halifax, 3/3/51
MATCH RECORDS	Tries: 6 Jason Critchley v Widnes, 18/8/96
	Goals: 15 John Wasyliw v Nottingham City, 1/11/92; Martyn Wood v Lancashire Lynx, 1/5/2000 Points: 36 John Wasyliw v Nottingham City, 1/11/92
SEASON RECORDS	Tries: 45 Nick Pinkney 1994-95 Goals: 187 John Wasyliw 1992-93 Points: 490 John Wasyliw 1992-93
CAREER RECORDS	Tries: 155 Sam Stacey 1904-20 Goals: 967 Brian Jefferson 1965-77 Points: 2,116 Brian Jefferson 1965-77
	Appearances: 372 Hartley Tempest 1902-15; David McGoun 1925-38

LEIGH CENTURIONS

DATE	FIXTURE	RESULT	SCORERS	LGE	ATT
16/2/14	Batley (h)	W52-12	t:Littler,Brierley(3),Beswick,Spencer(2),Higson,Sarsfield g:Ridyard(5),Brierley(3)	1st	2,173
23/2/14	Barrow (a)	W8-52	t:Brierley(5),Beswick,Goulden,McNally,Spencer g:Ridyard(8)	1st	1,252
2/3/14	Whitehaven (h)	W52-0	t:Armstrong(2),McNally,Goulden,Brierley(3),Kay,Emmitt g:Ridyard(6),Brierley(2)	1st	2,006
9/3/14	Keighley (a)	W26-28	t:Beswick,Armstrong,Brierley,Higson(2) g:Ridyard(4)	1st	1,309
14/3/14	Wigan St Patricks (a) (CCR3) ●	W6-74	t:Higson(2),Goulden(2),Duffy,Penkywicz(2),Haggerty,Pownall(2),McNally(2),Hankinson g:Brierley(11)	N/A	994
23/3/14	North Wales (h)	W35-22	t:Higson(3),Brierley,Wilkes,Kay,Penkywicz g:Ridyard(3) fg:Ridyard	1st	2,135
30/3/14	Rochdale (h)	W34-22	t:Kay(2),McNally,Brierley(2),Armstrong g:Ridyard(5)	1st	1,756
6/4/14	Rochdale (a) (CCR4)	W22-28	t:Wilkes(2),Ridyard,Brierley,McNally g:Ridyard(4)	N/A	1,007
13/4/14	Halifax (a)	W28-36	t:Barlow,Goulden,Sarsfield,Brierley(2),Armstrong g:Ridyard(6)	1st	2,282
18/4/14	Swinton (h)	W60-24	t:McNally(2),Armstrong(2),Hopkins,Haggerty(2),Kay(3),Pitman g:Ridyard(8)	1st	2,219
27/4/14	Featherstone (h) (CCR5)	W26-16	t:Brierley(3),Kay,Haggerty g:Ridyard(2),Brierley	N/A	3,664
4/5/14	Featherstone (a)	W10-29	t:Kay(2),Pitman,McNally,Brierley g:Ridyard(4) fg:Brierley	1st	3,230
11/5/14	Dewsbury (a)	W12-28	t:Kay,Brierley(2),Spencer,Haggerty g:Ridyard(4)	1st	1,193
18/5/14	Doncaster (h)	W50-20	t:Pitman,Beswick,McNally,Higson,Brierley,Sarsfield,Haggerty,Goulden,Armstrong g:Ridyard(7)	1st	2,132
25/5/14	Sheffield (a)	W12-54	t:Kay(4),Beswick,McNally,Brierley,Goulden,Penkywicz g:Ridyard(8),Brierley	1st	1,151
1/6/14	Workington (a)	W16-28	t:Kay,Penkywicz,Sarsfield(2),Brierley g:Ridyard(4)	1st	814
6/6/14	Leeds (a) (CCQF)	L25-12	t:Spencer,Armstrong g:Ridyard(2)	N/A	7,145
11/6/14	Halifax (h)	W26-24	t:Pownall,Wilkes(2),McNally g:Ridyard(5)	1st	2,571
15/6/14	Barrow (h)	W60-0	t:Kay(5),Thornley,Brierley(2),Hopkins,Penkywicz,Pownall g:Ridyard(8)	1st	2,508
22/6/14	Whitehaven (a)	W10-24	t:Goulden,Pownall,McNally,Brierley g:Ridyard(4)	1st	959
29/6/14	Dewsbury (h)	W30-22	t:Brierley,Kay(2),Goulden,Pownall(2) g:Ridyard(3)	1st	2,217
6/7/14	Sheffield (h)	W32-24	t:Brierley,Beswick,Hankinson,Sarsfield,Hopkins,Armstrong g:Brierley(4)	1st	2,166
13/7/14	Doncaster (a)	L24-16	t:Aspinwall,Brierley,Penkywicz g:Brierley,Haggerty	1st	1,113
19/7/14	Keighley (h)	W30-0	t:Armstrong,Beswick,Wilkes,McNally,Ridyard g:Ridyard(5)	1st	2,143
27/7/14	Rochdale (a)	W22-72	t:Barlow,McNally(2),Kay,Sarsfield,Hopkins,Armstrong(2),Pitman(3),Brierley g:Ridyard(12)	1st	1,211
3/8/14	Batley (a)	W6-36	t:Brierley,Sarsfield,Higson,Kay,Armstrong,McNally g:Ridyard(6)	1st	976
8/8/14	Featherstone (h)	W48-18	t:Armstrong(3),Penkywicz,Barlow,Acton,Higson g:Ridyard(10)	1st	3,565
17/8/14	Swinton (a)	W6-62	t:Barlow,Kay,Ridyard,Armstrong(2),Brierley,Platt,McNally(2),Bate,Higson g:Ridyard(9)	1st	1,342
30/8/14	Workington (h)	W22-12	t:Brierley(2),Higson,Kay g:Ridyard(3)	1st	3,375
7/9/14	North Wales (a)	W16-28	t:Walker,Armstrong,Hopkins,Brierley(2) g:Ridyard(4)	1st	1,206
14/9/14	Doncaster (h) (QPO)	W41-14	t:Haggerty,Platt(2),Brierley(2),McNally,Armstrong(2) g:Ridyard(4) fg:Haggerty	N/A	1,903
28/9/14	Dewsbury (h) (QSF)	W33-22	t:Higson(3),Platt,McNally g:Ridyard(6) fg:Ridyard	N/A	2,828
5/10/14	Featherstone (GF) ●●	W12-36	t:Sarsfield,McNally,Armstrong,Higson,Barlow,Brierley g:Ridyard(6)	N/A	9,164

● Played at Leigh Sports Village   ●● Played at Headingley Carnegie, Leeds

		APP		TRIES		GOALS		FG		PTS	
	D.O.B.	ALL	Ch	ALL	Ch	ALL	Ch	ALL	Ch	ALL	Ch
Jamie Acton	4/4/92	4(19)	3(18)	1	1	0	0	0	0	4	4
Tom Armstrong	12/9/89	28	25	23	22	0	0	0	0	92	88
Martin Aspinwall	21/10/81	4(8)	4(8)	1	1	0	0	0	0	4	4
Sam Barlow	7/3/88	24(4)	22(3)	5	5	0	0	0	0	20	20
Anthony Bate	28/4/93	3(6)	2(6)	1	1	0	0	0	0	4	4
Bob Beswick	8/12/84	19(13)	19(10)	7	7	0	0	0	0	28	28
Ryan Brierley	12/3/92	33	29	43	39	23	11	1	1	219	179
Alex Brown	28/8/87	2	2	0	0	0	0	0	0	0	0
Ryan Duffy	13/5/93	4(1)	2	1	0	0	0	0	0	4	0
Jake Emmitt	4/10/88	14(18)	14(15)	1	1	0	0	0	0	4	4
Lewis Foster	21/12/93	(1)	(1)	0	0	0	0	0	0	0	0
Tommy Goulden	30/6/81	21(3)	19(2)	9	7	0	0	0	0	36	28
Kurt Haggerty	8/1/89	19(7)	16(6)	7	5	1	1	1	1	31	23
Chris Hankinson	30/11/93	5(2)	5(1)	2	1	0	0	0	0	8	4
Adam Higson	19/5/87	25(1)	21(1)	17	15	0	0	0	0	68	60
Sam Hopkins	17/2/90	15(5)	14(4)	5	5	0	0	0	0	20	20
Liam Kay	17/12/91	30(2)	26(2)	27	26	0	0	0	0	108	104
Stuart Littler	19/2/79	7	5	1	1	0	0	0	0	4	4
Steve Maden	13/9/82	1	1	0	0	0	0	0	0	0	0
Gregg McNally	2/1/91	32	28	22	19	0	0	0	0	88	76
Sean Penkywicz	18/5/82	16(14)	12(14)	8	6	0	0	0	0	32	24
Cameron Pitman	9/7/89	15	13	6	6	0	0	0	0	24	24
Michael Platt	23/3/84	6	6	4	4	0	0	0	0	16	16
Jonathan Pownall	22/8/91	11	9	7	5	0	0	0	0	28	20
Martyn Ridyard	25/7/86	30	27	3	2	165	157	2	2	344	324
Matt Sarsfield	10/9/91	26(1)	23(1)	9	9	0	0	0	0	36	36
Tom Spencer	2/1/91	20(5)	18(3)	5	4	0	0	0	0	20	16
Andy Thornley	1/3/89	3(2)	3(1)	1	1	0	0	0	0	4	4
Jonathan Walker	20/2/91	(5)	(5)	1	1	0	0	0	0	4	4
Oliver Wilkes	2/5/80	12(15)	9(15)	6	4	0	0	0	0	24	16

Martyn Ridyard

LEAGUE RECORD
P26-W25-D0-L1-BP1
(1st, Championship/
Grand Final Winners, Champions)
F1024, A396, Diff+628
76 points.

CHALLENGE CUP
Quarter Finalists

ATTENDANCES
Best - v Featherstone (CC - 3,664)
Worst - v Rochdale (Ch - 1,756)
Total (Championship,
inc play-offs) - 35,697
Average (Championship,
inc play-offs) - 2,380
(Up by 824 on 2013)

CLUB RECORDS

MATCH RECORDS

SEASON RECORDS

CAREER RECORDS

Highest score: 92-2 v Keighley, 30/4/86 Highest score against: 4-94 v Workington, 26/2/95
Record attendance: 31,326 v St Helens, 14/3/53 (Hilton Park); 5,290 v Leeds, 11/5/2012 (Leigh Sports Village)
Tries: 6 Jack Wood v York, 4/10/47; Neil Turley v Workington, 31/1/2001
Goals: 15 Mick Stacey v Doncaster, 28/3/76 Points: 42 Neil Turley v Chorley, 4/4/2004
Tries: 55 Neil Turley 2001 Goals: 187 Neil Turley 2004 Points: 468 Neil Turley 2004
Tries: 189 Mick Martyn 1954-67 Goals: 1,043 Jimmy Ledgard 1948-58 Points: 2,492 John Woods 1976-85; 1990-92
Appearances: 503 Albert Worrall 1920-38

NORTH WALES CRUSADERS

DATE	FIXTURE	RESULT	SCORERS	LGE	ATT
16/2/14	Barrow (h)	W34-16	t:Reardon,Massam,K Ashall,Johnson,C Ashall,Adamson g:Johnson(5)	3rd	1,118
2/3/14	Featherstone (h)	L6-36	t:Gilmore g:Johnson	10th	1,418
9/3/14	Swinton (a)	W16-20	t:Smith,C Ashall,Johnson,Clay g:Johnson(2)	9th	587
16/3/14	Pilkington Recs (h) (CCR3)	W58-18	t:Wilde,Dallimore(2),Griffiths,Bannister(2),C Ashall,Clay(2),Johnson,Reid g:Johnson(7)	N/A	544
23/3/14	Leigh (a)	L35-22	t:Massam,Lawton,Johnson,Offerdahl g:Johnson(3)	10th	2,135
30/3/14	Batley (h)	L14-26	t:Johnson,Birkett,Adamson g:Johnson	10th	906
6/4/14	Featherstone (a) (CCR4)	L66-0		N/A	1,312
13/4/14	Doncaster (a)	L20-12	t:Middlehurst(2) g:Johnson(2)	11th	574
18/4/14	Rochdale (h)	L16-42	t:Johnson,Offerdahl,K Ashall g:Johnson(2)	13th	835
27/4/14	Whitehaven (a)	W0-34	t:Massam(3),Durbin,Reardon,Clay g:Johnson(5)	9th	621
4/5/14	Sheffield (h)	L6-56	t:Griffiths g:Johnson	12th	785
11/5/14	Halifax (a)	W6-12	t:Massam,Offerdahl g:Johnson(2)	12th	1,444
18/5/14	Keighley (h)	L14-16	t:Wild,C Ashall,Roets g:Johnson	11th	811
25/5/14	Workington (a)	W10-11	t:Reardon,Bannister g:Johnson fg:Durbin	10th	627
1/6/14	Dewsbury (a)	L38-18	t:Johnson,C Ashall,Massam g:Johnson(3)	11th	708
8/6/14	Swinton (h) ●	L24-42	t:Offerdahl,Bannister,Middlehurst(2),Lawton g:Johnson(2)	11th	715
15/6/14	Whitehaven (h) ●	W22-21	t:Birkett,Offerdahl,Smith,Middlehurst g:Johnson(3)	10th	621
22/6/14	Batley (a)	L55-12	t:Birkett,Adamson g:Johnson(2)	11th	563
29/6/14	Featherstone (h)	L56-18	t:Dallimore,Massam,Walker g:Johnson(2),Bannister	12th	1,653
6/7/14	Doncaster (h) ●	L24-28	t:Wilde,Reardon,Birkett,Martins g:Johnson(4)	11th	538
13/7/14	Sheffield (a)	L24-16	t:Smith(2),Martins g:Johnson(2)	11th	671
20/7/14	Dewsbury (h) ●	L18-22	t:Hudson,Adamson,Massam g:Johnson(3)	11th	686
27/7/14	Workington (h)	L8-12	t:Speakman,Smith	11th	658
3/8/14	Rochdale (a)	L30-28	t:Thornley,Johnson,Dallimore,Smith(2) g:Johnson(4)	11th	654
10/8/14	Halifax (h)	L17-20	t:Wilde,Roets,K Ashall g:Johnson(2) fg:Dallimore	11th	704
17/8/14	Keighley (a)	W18-30	t:Wild,Massam,Turner,Adamson,Smith g:Johnson(5)	11th	893
31/8/14	Barrow (a)	L36-16	t:Middlehurst(2),Reid g:Johnson(2)	11th	848
7/9/14	Leigh (h)	L16-28	t:Johnson,Duffy(2) g:Johnson(2)	11th	1,206

● Played at The Rock, Wrexham

Jono Smith

		APP		TRIES		GOALS		FG		PTS	
	D.O.B.	ALL	Ch	ALL	Ch	ALL	Ch	ALL	Ch	ALL	Ch
Toby Adamson	28/5/90	17(5)	17(5)	5	5	0	0	0	0	20	20
Craig Ashall	26/9/85	14	13	5	4	0	0	0	0	20	16
Karl Ashall	3/11/89	18(6)	16(6)	3	3	0	0	0	0	12	12
Steve Bannister	10/10/87	14(3)	12(3)	4	2	1	1	0	0	18	10
Dan Birkett	29/2/88	9	8	4	4	0	0	0	0	16	16
Jamie Clarke	15/11/84	(4)	(3)	0	0	0	0	0	0	0	0
Adam Clay	7/10/90	11	9	4	2	0	0	0	0	16	8
Jamie Dallimore	20/8/88	24(1)	22(1)	4	2	0	0	1	1	17	9
Alex Davidson	1/11/92	1(2)	1(2)	0	0	0	0	0	0	0	0
Ryan Duffy	13/5/93	1(8)	1(8)	2	2	0	0	0	0	8	8
Jamie Durbin	7/9/84	5	5	1	1	0	0	1	1	5	5
Harry Files	6/2/95	(2)	(2)	0	0	0	0	0	0	0	0
Matt Gee	12/12/94	5(1)	5(1)	0	0	0	0	0	0	0	0
Tom Gilmore	2/2/94	2	2	1	1	0	0	0	0	4	4
Grant Gore	21/11/91	1	1	0	0	0	0	0	0	0	0
Mick Govin	5/11/84	3(2)	3(2)	0	0	0	0	0	0	0	0
Owain Griffiths	18/7/91	(8)	(6)	2	1	0	0	0	0	8	4
Lee Hudson	28/9/90	9(5)	9(5)	1	1	0	0	0	0	4	4
Declan Hulme	14/1/93	3	3	0	0	0	0	0	0	0	0
Tommy Johnson	19/4/91	27(1)	26	9	8	69	62	0	0	174	156
Adam Lawton	13/6/93	2(1)	2(1)	2	2	0	0	0	0	8	8
Ryan MacDonald	24/2/78	(2)	(1)	0	0	0	0	0	0	0	0
Sebastien Martins	18/11/84	10(8)	10(8)	2	2	0	0	0	0	8	8
Rob Massam	29/11/87	21	21	10	10	0	0	0	0	40	40
Gary Middlehurst	24/10/83	18(2)	18(2)	7	7	0	0	0	0	28	28
David Mills	1/6/81	4(4)	3(4)	0	0	0	0	0	0	0	0
Andy Moulsdale	22/1/87	5	5	0	0	0	0	0	0	0	0
Mark Offerdahl	15/10/87	13(2)	12(1)	5	5	0	0	0	0	20	20
Michael Platt	23/3/84	3	3	0	0	0	0	0	0	0	0
Stuart Reardon	13/10/81	24	22	4	4	0	0	0	0	16	16
Matt Reid	16/9/92	4(8)	3(7)	2	1	0	0	0	0	8	4
Christiaan Roets	5/9/80	18(4)	16(4)	2	2	0	0	0	0	8	8
Jono Smith	12/11/88	5(18)	5(18)	8	8	0	0	0	0	32	32
Jonathan Soum	22/5/91	(4)	(4)	0	0	0	0	0	0	0	0
Dom Speakman	22/3/94	4	4	1	1	0	0	0	0	4	4
Simon Stephens	11/10/83	1(8)	(8)	1	0	0	0	0	0	4	0
Andy Thornley	1/3/89	1(1)	1(1)	1	1	0	0	0	0	4	4
Scott Turner	7/5/94	6	6	1	1	0	0	0	0	4	4
Jonny Walker	26/9/86	22(2)	21(1)	1	1	0	0	0	0	4	4
Craig White	13/1/88	4	2	0	0	0	0	0	0	0	0
Stephen Wild	26/4/81	26	24	2	2	0	0	0	0	8	8
Greg Wilde	22/12/93	9	7	3	2	0	0	0	0	12	8

LEAGUE RECORD
P26-W7-D0-L19-BP10
(11th, Championship)
F468, A709, Diff-241
31 points.

CHALLENGE CUP
Round Four

ATTENDANCES
Best - v Featherstone (Ch - 1,418)
Worst - v Doncaster (Ch - 538)
Total (Championship only) - 11,001
Average (Championship only) - 846
(Down by 50 on 2013,
Championship One)

CLUB RECORDS Highest score: 82-6 v West Hull, 6/4/2013 Highest score against: 4-98 v Wigan, 15/4/2012 Record attendance: 1,562 v South Wales, 1/9/2013
MATCH RECORDS Tries: 5 Rob Massam v Rochdale, 30/6/2013 Goals: 11 Tommy Johnson v West Hull, 6/4/2013 Points: 30 Tommy Johnson v West Hull, 6/4/2013
SEASON RECORDS Tries: 25 Rob Massam 2013 Goals: 101 Tommy Johnson 2013 Points: 246 Tommy Johnson 2013
CAREER RECORDS Tries: 46 Rob Massam 2012-2014 Goals: 211 Tommy Johnson 2012-2014 Points: 514 Tommy Johnson 2012-2014
Appearances: 69 Tommy Johnson 2012-2014

ROCHDALE HORNETS

DATE	FIXTURE	RESULT	SCORERS	LGE	ATT
23/2/14	Dewsbury (h)	L12-42	t:Dawson,Greenwood g:Crook(2)	13th	817
2/3/14	Keighley (h)	L14-40	t:Langley(2),Dawson g:Crook	13th	726
9/3/14	Featherstone (a)	L56-6	t:Walker g:Crook	14th	2,323
16/3/14	Gloucestershire All Golds (h) (CCR3)	W76-4	t:Baines(2),Langley(3),Te'o(3),Millard(3),Case,Llewellyn(2),Crook g:Crook(8)	N/A	307
23/3/14	Batley (h)	W14-10	t:Ratu,Crook,Te'o g:Crook	14th	818
30/3/14	Leigh (a)	L34-22	t:Langley,Bowman,Baines,Davies g:Crook(3)	14th	1,756
6/4/14	Leigh (h) (CCR4)	L22-28	t:Casey,English(2),Case g:Crook(3)	N/A	1,007
13/4/14	Whitehaven (h)	W20-16	t:Langley(2),Sheridan,Millard g:Crook(2)	13th	770
18/4/14	North Wales (a)	W16-42	t:Crook,Baines,Ratu(2),Bowman,Langley g:Crook(9)	11th	835
4/5/14	Swinton (h)	W31-16	t:Robinson,Casey,Case,Davies,Langley g:Crook(5) fg:Crook	9th	842
11/5/14	Workington (h)	L6-10	t:English g:Crook	11th	790
18/5/14	Halifax (h)	L12-28	t:Galbraith,Millard g:Baines(2)	12th	721
25/5/14	Doncaster (a)	L40-10	t:Robinson,Dandy g:Crook	12th	600
1/6/14	Barrow (a)	L38-18	t:Millard,Galbraith,Cookson g:Crook(3)	12th	1,058
8/6/14	Batley (a)	L44-28	t:Cookson,Robinson,Millard(2),English g:Crook(4)	14th	555
13/6/14	Swinton (a)	L39-18	t:Robinson(2),Millard g:Crook(3)	13th	430
22/6/14	Halifax (a)	L42-24	t:Llewellyn,Sheridan,Crook,Baines g:Crook(4)	13th	1,425
29/6/14	Keighley (a)	L48-6	t:Millard g:Crook	13th	811
6/7/14	Featherstone (h)	W38-34	t:Crook,Littler,Millard,Casey,Dawson,Dandy,Thompson g:Crook(5)	13th	735
13/7/14	Barrow (h)	W54-22	t:Sheridan,Millard,Dawson,McClurg(2),Case(2),Crook,Cookson g:Crook(7),Sheridan(2)	13th	612
20/7/14	Workington (a)	L30-18	t:Llewellyn,Dandy,Sheridan g:Crook(3)	13th	707
27/7/14	Leigh (a)	L22-72	t:Langley,Swift,Case,Walker g:Crook(3)	13th	1,211
3/8/14	North Wales (h)	W30-28	t:Swift(2),McDonnell,Sheridan(2) g:Crook(4),Langley	12th	654
10/8/14	Dewsbury (a)	L38-20	t:Littler,Baines,Langley g:Crook(4)	13th	776
17/8/14	Doncaster (a)	L16-22	t:Sheridan,Littler,Crook g:Crook(2)	12th	571
20/8/14	Sheffield (a) ●	L48-0		12th	560
31/8/14	Whitehaven (a)	L48-12	t:Baines(2) g:Crook(2)	12th	756
7/9/14	Sheffield (h)	L16-58	t:English,Crook,Dandy g:Crook(2)	12th	662

● Played at Sheffield Hallam University Sports Park

		APP		TRIES		GOALS		FG		PTS	
	D.O.B.	ALL	Ch	ALL	Ch	ALL	Ch	ALL	Ch	ALL	Ch
Chris Baines	25/9/84	19(2)	17(2)	8	6	2	2	0	0	36	28
Joe Bate	24/10/92	(1)	0	0	0	0	0	0	0	0	0
Richard Beaumont	2/2/88	2(2)	2(2)	0	0	0	0	0	0	0	0
Adam Bowman	12/11/87	(6)	(5)	2	2	0	0	0	0	8	8
Jordan Case	10/4/93	9(13)	8(12)	6	4	0	0	0	0	24	16
Sean Casey	26/2/93	13(2)	12(2)	3	2	0	0	0	0	12	8
Alex Clare	3/11/93	5(3)	4(3)	0	0	0	0	0	0	0	0
John Cookson	12/12/84	14(10)	12(10)	3	3	0	0	0	0	12	12
Paul Crook	28/8/86	28	26	8	7	84	73	1	1	201	175
James Dandy	23/5/90	12(5)	11(5)	4	4	0	0	0	0	16	16
Daniel Davies	14/7/87	15(1)	14(1)	2	2	0	0	0	0	8	8
Matty Dawson	2/10/90	5	5	4	4	0	0	0	0	16	16
Connor Dwyer	29/12/93	(2)	(2)	0	0	0	0	0	0	0	0
Wayne English	8/3/80	24	22	5	3	0	0	0	0	20	12
Mark Flanagan	4/12/87	3	3	0	0	0	0	0	0	0	0
Lewis Galbraith	1/2/95	5	5	2	2	0	0	0	0	8	8
Liam Gilchrist	28/3/89	2(9)	2(8)	0	0	0	0	0	0	0	0
Joe Greenwood	2/4/93	14(1)	14(1)	1	1	0	0	0	0	4	4
Josh Jones	12/5/93	2	2	0	0	0	0	0	0	0	0
Ryan King	23/1/92	6	6	0	0	0	0	0	0	0	0
Gareth Langley	24/10/84	15	14	12	9	1	1	0	0	50	38
Stuart Littler	19/2/79	11(1)	11(1)	3	3	0	0	0	0	12	12
Dave Llewellyn	3/12/82	14(2)	13(2)	4	2	0	0	0	0	16	8
Steve Marsh	2/11/86	1(10)	1(8)	0	0	0	0	0	0	0	0
Alex McClurg	28/8/89	3(10)	3(10)	2	2	0	0	0	0	8	8
Shannon McDonnell	5/8/87	3	3	1	1	0	0	0	0	4	4
Ryan Millard	13/3/87	22	20	12	9	0	0	0	0	48	36
Mark Percival	29/5/94	1	1	0	0	0	0	0	0	0	0
Mike Ratu	16/10/87	6	4	3	3	0	0	0	0	12	12
Greg Richards	12/7/95	(3)	(3)	0	0	0	0	0	0	0	0
Shaun Robinson	13/7/89	14	14	5	5	0	0	0	0	20	20
Steve Roper	10/11/86	1	1	0	0	0	0	0	0	0	0
Lewis Sheridan	14/1/94	12(12)	11(11)	7	7	2	2	0	0	32	32
Tony Suffolk	7/11/86	17(3)	16(3)	0	0	0	0	0	0	0	0
Adam Swift	20/2/93	3	3	3	3	0	0	0	0	12	12
Sam Te'o	30/7/88	5	4	4	1	0	0	0	0	16	4
Warren Thompson	24/2/90	20(2)	18(2)	1	1	0	0	0	0	4	4
James Tilley	11/11/93	10(6)	8(6)	0	0	0	0	0	0	0	0
Alex Trumper	5/4/91	11(2)	11(2)	0	0	0	0	0	0	0	0
Chris Tyrer	10/10/85	(2)	(1)	0	0	0	0	0	0	0	0
Anthony Walker	28/12/91	15(2)	15(2)	2	2	0	0	0	0	8	8
Gary Wheeler	30/9/89	2	2	0	0	0	0	0	0	0	0

Wayne English

LEAGUE RECORD
P26-W7-D0-L19-BP4
(12th, Championship)
F509, A919, Diff-410
25 points.

CHALLENGE CUP
Round Four

ATTENDANCES
Best - v Leigh (Ch - 1,211)
Worst - v Gloucestershire All Golds
(CC - 307)
Total (Championship only) - 9,929
Average (Championship only) - 764
(Up by 191 on 2013,
Championship One)

CLUB RECORDS Highest score: 120-4 v Illingworth, 13/3/2005 Highest score against: 0-106 v Castleford, 13/9/2007
Record attendance: 26,664 v Oldham, 25/3/22 *(Athletic Grounds)*; 8,061 v Oldham, 26/12/89 *(Spotland)*

MATCH RECORDS Tries: 5 Jack Corsi v Barrow, 31/12/21; Jack Corsi v Broughton Moor, 25/2/22; Jack Williams v St Helens, 4/4/33; Norman Brelsford v Whitehaven, 3/9/73;
Marlon Billy v York, 8/4/2001 Goals: 18 Lee Birdseye v Illingworth, 13/3/2005 Points: 44 Lee Birdseye v Illingworth, 13/3/2005

SEASON RECORDS Tries: 31 Marlon Billy 2001 Goals: 150 Martin Strett 1994-95 Points: 350 Mick Nanyn 2003

CAREER RECORDS Tries: 103 Jack Williams 1931-37 Goals: 741 Walter Gowers 1922-36 Points: 1,497 Walter Gowers 1922-36 Appearances: 456 Walter Gowers 1922-36

SHEFFIELD EAGLES

DATE	FIXTURE	RESULT	SCORERS	LGE	ATT
23/2/14	Swinton (a)	W16-30	t:Turner(3),Owen,Ford g:Brambani(4),Walker	7th	548
2/3/14	Barrow (h)	L18-24	t:Turner(2),Owen,Walker g:Brambani	8th	897
9/3/14	Halifax (a)	L30-28	t:Yere,Garside(2),Turner,Brambani g:Brambani(4)	10th	1,327
16/3/14	East Leeds (h) (CCR3)	W54-0	t:Yere,Turner,Owen,Brambani(2),Garside,Laulu-Togagae,Knowles,Aston,Squires g:Brambani(7)	N/A	619
23/3/14	Dewsbury (h)	W46-10	t:Taulapapa(2),Yere,Knowles(2),Owen,Garside,Turner g:Brambani(7)	7th	911
30/3/14	Keighley (a)	W24-42	t:Straugheir,Laulu-Togagae(2),Knowles,Turner,Yere,Walker,Garside g:Brambani(5)	6th	927
5/4/14	London Skolars (h) (CCR4)	W70-28	t:Knowles,Taulapapa,Davey,Blagbrough(3),Laulu-Togagae(2),Tagaloa,Burke,Walker,Garside g:Brambani(11)	N/A	505
13/4/14	Workington (a)	W14-24	t:Brambani,Garside(2),Straugheir g:Brambani(4)	5th	451
20/4/14	Doncaster (h)	L34-42	t:Straugheir(2),Brambani,Garside(2),Tagaloa g:Brambani(5)	6th	1,018
27/4/14	Castleford (a) (CCR5)	L60-16	t:Turner,Straugheir,Ashton g:Brambani(2)	N/A	4,648
4/5/14	North Wales (a)	W6-56	t:Laulu-Togagae(3),Turner(3),Taulapapa,Owen,Walker,Yere g:Brambani(8)	5th	785
11/5/14	Featherstone (h)	L22-36	t:Laulu-Togagae(2),Owen,Burke g:Brambani(3)	5th	1,279
18/5/14	Batley (a)	W12-16	t:Taulapapa,Turner,Aspinall g:Brambani(2)	5th	540
25/5/14	Leigh (h)	L12-54	t:Tagaloa,Taulapapa g:Brambani,Walker	7th	1,151
1/6/14	Whitehaven (a)	L24-22	t:Tagaloa,Yere(2),Turner g:Brambani(2),Knowles	7th	644
8/6/14	Workington (h)	W37-30	t:Turner(2),Taulapapa,Laulu-Togagae(2),Henderson g:Walker(6) fg:Brambani	6th	712
15/6/14	Dewsbury (a)	W12-28	t:Taulapapa(2),Turner,Yere,Walker g:Walker(4)	5th	867
22/6/14	Keighley (h)	L16-29	t:Laulu-Togagae,Straugheir,Knowles g:Walker(2)	7th	743
29/6/14	Halifax (h)	L14-32	t:Laulu-Togagae,Brambani,Yere g:Brambani	8th	955
6/7/14	Leigh (a)	L32-24	t:Turner(3),Davey g:Brambani(4)	9th	2,166
13/7/14	North Wales (h)	W24-16	t:Yere,Turner,Taulapapa,Tagaloa,Laulu-Togagae g:Brambani(2)	8th	671
20/7/14	Barrow (a)	W10-40	t:Briggs,Laulu-Togagae(2),Walker,Straugheir,Tagaloa,Taulapapa g:Brambani(6)	6th	871
27/7/14	Batley (h)	L18-28	t:Hope,Yere(2) g:Brambani(2),Walker	8th	763
3/8/14	Doncaster (a)	W22-26	t:Uaisele,Garside,Laulu-Togagae,Yere,Turner g:Brambani(3)	7th	954
10/8/14	Swinton (h)	W31-30	t:Yere,Laulu-Togagae(2),Uaisele(3) g:Brambani(3) fg:Knowles	6th	600
17/8/14	Whitehaven (h)	W36-28	t:Garside,Briggs,Yere,Walker,Laulu-Togagae(2) g:Brambani(6)	6th	644
20/8/14	Rochdale (h) ●	W48-0	t:Straugheir,Aston(3),Davey,Tagaloa,Yere,Turner,Laulu-Togagae g:Walker(4),Briggs(2)	5th	560
31/8/14	Featherstone (h)	W28-40	t:Briggs(3),Taulapapa,Laulu-Togagae(2),Straugheir g:Brambani(5),Walker	5th	2,085
7/9/14	Rochdale (a)	W16-58	t:Yere(2),Laulu-Togagae(5),Briggs,Uaisele,Turner,Stringer g:Brambani(7)	5th	662
13/9/14	Batley (h) (EPO) ●●	W16-0	t:Uaisele(2),Laulu-Togagae g:Brambani(2)	N/A	695
21/9/14	Doncaster (a) (PSF)	W24-58	t:Battye,Uaisele,Walker,Yere,Garside,Turner,Briggs,Laulu-Togagae(2),Straugheir g:Brambani(6),Walker,Briggs(2)	N/A	825
28/9/14	Featherstone (a) (QSF)	L21-12	t:Green,Laulu-Togagae g:Brambani(2)	N/A	1,730

● Played at Sheffield Hallam University Sports Park   ●● Played at Keepmoat Stadium, Doncaster

		APP		TRIES		GOALS		FG		PTS	
	D.O.B.	ALL	Ch	ALL	Ch	ALL	Ch	ALL	Ch	ALL	Ch
Tom Ashton	20/6/92	2(5)	2(4)	1	0	0	0	0	0	4	0
Peter Aspinall	4/4/94	4(7)	3(6)	1	1	0	0	0	0	4	4
Cory Aston	1/3/95	6(2)	5(2)	4	3	0	0	0	0	16	12
Eddie Battye	24/7/91	13(6)	13(6)	1	1	0	0	0	0	4	4
Jack Blagbrough	18/1/94	4(7)	4(5)	3	0	0	0	0	0	12	0
Dominic Brambani	10/5/85	30(1)	27(1)	6	4	115	95	1	1	255	207
Kyle Briggs	7/12/87	12	12	7	7	4	4	0	0	36	36
Jordan Burke	16/11/91	3(4)	2(3)	2	1	0	0	0	0	8	4
James Davey	21/8/89	1(16)	(14)	3	2	0	0	0	0	12	8
Jonathan Ford	1/11/93	3(1)	3(1)	1	0	0	0	0	0	4	0
Matt Garside	1/10/90	16(12)	13(12)	13	11	0	0	0	0	52	44
Theo Gonzalez-Trique	11/1/91	(2)	(2)	0	0	0	0	0	0	0	0
Peter Green	2/12/81	16(11)	14(11)	1	1	0	0	0	0	4	4
Corey Hanson	11/8/92	2	1	0	0	0	0	0	0	0	0
Andrew Henderson	17/6/79	28	27	1	1	0	0	0	0	4	4
Will Hope	2/6/93	8(4)	8(3)	1	1	0	0	0	0	4	4
Ben Jones	8/10/88	(3)	(3)	0	0	0	0	0	0	0	0
Michael Knowles	2/5/87	26(1)	24(1)	6	4	1	1	1	1	27	19
Quentin Laulu-Togagae	1/12/84	32	29	34	31	0	0	0	0	136	124
Tom Lillycrop	29/11/91	13(11)	11(11)	0	0	0	0	0	0	0	0
Gareth Owen	3/7/92	3(12)	2(11)	6	5	0	0	0	0	24	20
Alex Palmer	22/4/91	1(1)	1(1)	0	0	0	0	0	0	0	0
Connor Scott	27/5/93	2(2)	2(2)	0	0	0	0	0	0	0	0
Shaun Squires	20/3/90	1(1)	(1)	1	0	0	0	0	0	4	0
Duane Straugheir	29/9/89	27(1)	24(1)	10	9	0	0	0	0	40	36
Mitchell Stringer	1/11/83	29(1)	27(1)	1	1	0	0	0	0	4	4
Lelauloto Tagaloa	26/12/86	6(15)	5(13)	7	6	0	0	0	0	28	24
Misi Taulapapa	25/1/82	32	29	12	11	0	0	0	0	48	44
Scott Turner	15/4/88	31	28	26	24	0	0	0	0	104	96
Etuate Uaisele	8/12/84	7(1)	7(1)	8	8	0	0	0	0	32	32
Pat Walker	24/3/86	28(1)	26	8	7	21	21	0	0	74	70
Menzie Yere	24/10/83	30	28	19	18	0	0	0	0	76	72

Quentin Laulu-Togagae

LEAGUE RECORD
P26-W16-D0-L10-BP6
(5th, Championship/
Qualifying Semi-Final)
F790, A605, Diff+185
54 points.

CHALLENGE CUP
Round Five

ATTENDANCES
Best - v Featherstone (Ch - 1,279)
Worst - v London Skolars (CC - 505)
Total (Championship,
inc play-offs) - 11,599
Average (Championship,
inc play-offs) - 829
(Down by 99 on 2013,
Don Valley Stadium)

CLUB RECORDS
MATCH RECORDS
Highest score: 112-6 v Leigh East, 7/4/2013 Highest score against: 0-88 v Hull, 2/3/2003 Record attendance: 10,603 v Bradford, 16/8/97
Tries: 5 Daryl Powell v Mansfield, 2/1/89; Menzie Yere v Leigh East, 7/4/2013; Quentin Laulu-Togagae v Rochdale, 7/9/2014
Goals: 14 Dominic Brambani v Leigh East, 7/4/2013 Points: 32 Roy Rafferty v Fulham, 21/9/86
SEASON RECORDS
CAREER RECORDS
Tries: 46 Menzie Yere 2013 Goals: 169 *(inc 1fg)* Dominic Brambani 2013 Points: 361 Dominic Brambani 2013
Tries: 137 Menzie Yere 2009-2014 Goals: 986 Mark Aston 1986-2004 Points: 2,142 Mark Aston 1986-2004 Appearances: 389 Mark Aston 1986-2004

SWINTON LIONS

DATE	FIXTURE	RESULT	SCORERS	LGE	ATT
16/2/14	Halifax (a)	L28-18	t:Penny,Ackers(2) g:Nanyn(3)	9th	1,587
23/2/14	Sheffield (h)	L16-30	t:Nanyn,Brown,Penny g:Nanyn(2)	10th	548
2/3/14	Workington (a)	L18-6	t:Penny g:Nanyn	12th	663
9/3/14	North Wales (h)	L16-20	t:Nanyn,Menzies,Penny g:Nanyn(2)	12th	587
16/3/14	Gateshead (h) (CCR3)	W66-6	t:Bowman,Walker(2),Warrilow,Watkins(2),R Hawkyard(2),Nanyn(2),D Hawkyard, Barlow g:Nanyn(9)	N/A	249
23/3/14	Barrow (h) ●	W44-26	t:Dwyer,Currie(3),Thomas,Wood,Penny,Evans g:Nanyn(6)	11th	403
30/3/14	Featherstone (a)	L36-22	t:Nanyn,Barlow,Lewis Hulme,Penny g:Nanyn(2),Watson	11th	2,020
6/4/14	York (h) (CCR4)	W31-28	t:D Hawkyard(2),Watkins,Peet,Atkin g:Peet(5) fg:Atkin	N/A	427
13/4/14	Dewsbury (h)	W37-31	t:Halliwell,Brown,Penny(2),Ackers,Menzies g:O'Brien(6) fg:O'Brien	9th	412
18/4/14	Leigh (a)	L60-24	t:Penny(2),D Hawkyard,R Hawkyard g:Watson(4)	12th	2,219
26/4/14	Keighley (h) (CCR5)	L20-33	t:Bowman(3),Lewis g:Peet(2)	N/A	468
4/5/14	Rochdale (a)	L31-16	t:Worthington,D Hawkyard,Bowman g:Peet,Watson	13th	842
11/5/14	Keighley (a)	L20-12	t:D Hawkyard,Atkin g:O'Brien(2)	13th	673
18/5/14	Whitehaven (a)	L22-18	t:R Hawkyard,Nanyn,Brown g:O'Brien(3)	13th	801
25/5/14	Batley (h)	L18-33	t:O'Brien,Atkin,Philbin g:O'Brien(3)	13th	456
1/6/14	Doncaster (h)	L22-36	t:Atkin,Watson,R Hawkyard,D Hawkyard g:O'Brien(3)	14th	355
8/6/14	North Wales (a) ●●	W24-42	t:Watson,Burke,Ackers(2),Menzies,O'Brien,Atkin,Dwyer g:O'Brien(5)	12th	715
13/6/14	Rochdale (h)	W39-18	t:Ackers(2),Nanyn,Atkin,Barber(2) g:O'Brien(7) fg:O'Brien	12th	430
22/6/14	Barrow (a)	W24-38	t:Morrison,Bowman,Nanyn,Barber(3),R Hawkyard g:O'Brien(5)	12th	932
29/6/14	Workington (h) ●	L24-32	t:D Hawkyard,Atkin,Bennion,Warrilow g:Nanyn(4)	11th	405
4/7/14	Dewsbury (a)	L48-6	t:Johnson g:Nanyn	12th	749
13/7/14	Featherstone (h) ●	L24-48	t:Barber,Atkin,Ainscough,Morrison g:Nanyn(4)	12th	469
20/7/14	Doncaster (a)	L36-34	t:Nanyn,Bridge,R Hawkyard,Ackers,Brown,Barber g:Nanyn(5)	12th	617
27/7/14	Halifax (h)	L30-48	t:Barber,Dwyer,Penny,Menzies,Morrison g:Nanyn(5)	12th	569
3/8/14	Keighley (h) ●	L10-17	t:Ainscough,Barber g:Nanyn	12th	360
10/8/14	Sheffield (a)	L31-30	t:Burke,Dwyer(3),Atkin g:Nanyn(5)	12th	600
17/8/14	Leigh (h)	L6-62	t:Ackers g:Nanyn	13th	1,342
31/8/14	Batley (a)	L42-0		13th	664
7/9/14	Whitehaven (h)	L18-44	t:Ainscough,Penny,R Hawkyard g:Nanyn(3)	13th	549

● Played at Park Lane, Sedgley Park ●● Played at The Rock, Wrexham

		APP		TRIES		GOALS		FG		PTS	
	D.O.B.	ALL	Ch	ALL	Ch	ALL	Ch	ALL	Ch	ALL	Ch
Andy Ackers	25/12/93	21(4)	18(4)	9	9	0	0	0	0	36	36
Martin Ainscough	23/10/85	7	7	3	3	0	0	0	0	12	12
Martin Aspinwall	21/10/81	3	3	0	0	0	0	0	0	0	0
Chris Atkin	7/2/93	16(2)	14(2)	9	8	0	0	1	0	37	32
Ed Barber	26/4/90	10(3)	10(3)	9	9	0	0	0	0	36	36
Josh Barlow	15/5/91	13(6)	12(6)	2	1	0	0	0	0	8	4
Gavin Bennion	31/12/93	4(7)	4(7)	1	1	0	0	0	0	4	4
Anthony Bowman	18/3/92	10(1)	8(1)	6	2	0	0	0	0	24	8
Danny Bridge	4/1/93	8	8	1	1	0	0	0	0	4	4
James Brown	6/5/88	16(12)	14(11)	4	4	0	0	0	0	16	16
Jordan Burke	16/11/91	18	18	2	2	0	0	0	0	8	8
Jack Cooper	23/9/90	3(1)	3(1)	0	0	0	0	0	0	0	0
Ben Currie	15/7/94	2	2	3	3	0	0	0	0	12	12
Brad Dwyer	28/4/93	9(2)	9(2)	6	6	0	0	0	0	24	24
Anthony England	19/10/86	(1)	(1)	0	0	0	0	0	0	0	0
Rhys Evans	30/10/92	3	3	1	1	0	0	0	0	4	4
Liam Fishwick	19/2/93	3	3	0	0	0	0	0	0	0	0
Danny Halliwell	23/3/81	6	4	1	1	0	0	0	0	4	4
Darren Hawkyard	14/10/84	27	24	8	5	0	0	0	0	32	20
Ritchie Hawkyard	21/1/86	23(1)	20(1)	8	6	0	0	0	0	32	24
Lewis Hulme	1/7/94	(18)	(15)	1	1	0	0	0	0	4	4
Liam Hulme	28/10/91	1	1	0	0	0	0	0	0	0	0
Zach Johnson	9/3/91	2(1)	2(18)	1	1	0	0	0	0	4	4
Steve Lewis	22/10/86	4(1)	4	1	0	0	0	0	0	4	0
Steve Maden	13/9/82	1	1	0	0	0	0	0	0	0	0
Ryan Maneely	19/10/94	(1)	(1)	0	0	0	0	0	0	0	0
Luke Menzies	29/6/88	14(11)	11(11)	4	4	0	0	0	0	16	16
Mike Morrison	9/9/87	25(3)	22(3)	3	3	0	0	0	0	12	12
Mick Nanyn	3/6/82	22	21	9	7	54	45	0	0	144	118
Gareth O'Brien	31/10/91	8	8	2	2	34	34	2	2	78	78
Gene Ormsby	12/9/92	2	2	0	0	0	0	0	0	0	0
Jacque Peet	2/5/94	10(6)	8(6)	1	0	8	1	0	0	20	2
Kevin Penny	3/10/87	14	14	12	12	0	0	0	0	48	48
Joe Philbin	16/11/94	3	2	1	1	0	0	0	0	4	4
Chris Riley	22/2/88	1	1	0	0	0	0	0	0	0	0
Glenn Riley	21/9/92	9(3)	9(3)	0	0	0	0	0	0	0	0
Mark Thomas	22/10/89	(7)	(5)	1	1	0	0	0	0	4	4
Andy Thornley	1/3/89	4(1)	4(1)	0	0	0	0	0	0	0	0
Freddie Walker	11/10/92	16	14	2	0	0	0	0	0	8	0
Ben Warrilow	26/1/94	6(1)	3(1)	2	1	0	0	0	0	8	4
Kash Watkins	20/6/88	7(1)	5(1)	3	0	0	0	0	0	12	0
Ian Watson	27/10/76	19	16	2	2	6	6	0	0	20	20
Paul Wood	10/10/81	1(1)	1(1)	1	1	0	0	0	0	4	4
Joe Worthington	16/5/91	5(1)	4	1	1	0	0	0	0	4	4

Andy Ackers

LEAGUE RECORD
P26-W5-D0-L21-BP9
(13th, Championship)
F570, A865, Diff-295
24 points.

CHALLENGE CUP
Round Five

ATTENDANCES
Best - v Leigh (Ch - 1,342)
Worst - v Gateshead (CC - 249)
Total (Championship only) - 6,885
Average (Championship only) - 530
(Down by 122 on 2013)

CLUB RECORDS — Highest score: 94-0 v Gateshead, 22/8/2010 Highest score against: 0-112 v Warrington, 20/5/2011

MATCH RECORDS — Record attendance: 26,891 v Wigan, 12/2/64 *(Station Road)*; 1,796 v Leigh, 2/9/2012 *(Leigh Sports Village)*
Points: 30 Greg Pearce v Prescot, 11/8/96; Mick Nanyn v York, 25/3/2001; Gavin Dodd v Gateshead, 22/8/2010; Ian Mort v South Wales, 17/4/2011
Tries: 6 Mark Riley v Prescot, 11/8/96 Goals: 12 Ken Gowers v Liverpool City, 3/10/59

SEASON RECORDS — Tries: 42 John Stopford 1963-64 Goals: 128 Albert Blan 1960-61 Points: 338 Ian Mort 2011

CAREER RECORDS — Tries: 197 Frank Evans 1921-31 Goals: 970 Ken Gowers 1954-73 Points: 2,105 Ken Gowers 1954-73 Appearances: 601 Ken Gowers 1954-73

WHITEHAVEN

DATE	FIXTURE	RESULT	SCORERS	LGE	ATT
16/2/14	Keighley (a)	L36-14	t:Gardner,Nandye g:Southernwood(3)	13th	1,061
2/3/14	Leigh (a)	L52-0		14th	2,006
9/3/14	Dewsbury (a)	W16-23	t:Ainscough,Burns(2),Mitchell g:Southernwood(3) fg:Southernwood	13th	903
16/3/14	York (a) (CCR3)	L34-32	t:Tahraoui(2),Southernwood,Burns(2),Crellin g:Southernwood(4)	N/A	403
23/3/14	Halifax (h)	L14-36	t:Ainscough,Smith,Calvert g:Southernwood	13th	751
30/3/14	Barrow (h)	W37-12	t:Carr(2),Doran,Nandye,Calvert,Ainscough(2) g:Southernwood(3),Carr fg:Taylor	12th	721
13/4/14	Rochdale (a)	L20-16	t:Mitchell,Southernwood,Calvert g:Southernwood(2)	12th	770
18/4/14	Workington (h)	W22-16	t:Doran,Marabe,Nandye(2) g:Southernwood(3)	10th	1,401
27/4/14	North Wales (h)	L0-34		12th	621
4/5/14	Batley (a)	W10-30	t:Ainscough(2),Taylor,Calvert,Hand g:Southernwood(5)	10th	506
11/5/14	Doncaster (h)	W29-20	t:Nandye,Mitchell,Burns,McAvoy,Taylor g:Southernwood(4) fg:Southernwood	8th	560
18/5/14	Swinton (h)	W22-18	t:Southernwood,Calvert,Burns,Marabe g:Southernwood(3)	8th	801
25/5/14	Featherstone (a)	L50-14	t:Nandye(2),Burns g:Southernwood	9th	1,726
1/6/14	Sheffield (h)	W24-22	t:Nandye,Newton,Farrer,Calvert g:Carr(4)	8th	644
10/6/14	Keighley (h)	W28-18	t:Taylor,Nandye,McAvoy,Forster,Ainscough g:Carr(4)	7th	741
15/6/14	North Wales (a) ●	L22-21	t:Taylor,Nandye(2) g:Carr(2) fg:Seymour	8th	621
22/6/14	Leigh (h)	L10-24	t:Calvert,Nandye g:Southernwood	9th	959
29/6/14	Doncaster (a) ●●	L22-16	t:Taylor,Carr,Mitchell g:Southernwood(2)	9th	680
6/7/14	Barrow (a)	W18-30	t:Southernwood,Calvert(2),Ainscough,Mitchell,Nandye g:Southernwood(2),Carr	8th	1,105
13/7/14	Dewsbury (h)	W40-34	t:Carr(2),Ainscough(2),Calvert(3) g:Southernwood(5),Carr	7th	843
20/7/14	Halifax (a)	L52-12	t:Taylor(2) g:Southernwood(2)	9th	1,317
27/7/14	Featherstone (h)	L24-35	t:Calvert(2),McAvoy,Forster g:Carr(4)	10th	901
3/8/14	Workington (a)	L20-18	t:Nandye,Ainscough,Calvert g:Southernwood(3)	10th	1,939
10/8/14	Batley (h)	W28-13	t:Calvert,Carr,Burns,Nandye g:Southernwood(6)	10th	671
17/8/14	Sheffield (a)	L36-28	t:Nandye,Burns,Ainscough(2),Southernwood g:Southernwood(4)	9th	644
31/8/14	Rochdale (h)	W48-12	t:Thorman(2),Nandye,Hand,Burns(2),Crellin,Newton g:Seymour(7),Newton	10th	756
7/9/14	Swinton (a)	W18-44	t:McAvoy,Forster,Burns,Nandye,Southernwood,Mitchell,Newton g:Seymour(8)	9th	549

● Played at The Rock, Wrexham
●● Played at Castle Park, Doncaster

		APP		TRIES		GOALS		FG		PTS	
	D.O.B.	ALL	Ch	ALL	Ch	ALL	Ch	ALL	Ch	ALL	Ch
Shaun Ainscough	27/11/89	22	21	13	13	0	0	0	0	52	52
Jordan Burns	2/9/95	12(2)	11(2)	12	10	0	0	0	0	48	40
Craig Calvert	10/2/84	22	22	16	16	0	0	0	0	64	64
Tom Carr	16/7/91	23	22	6	6	17	17	0	0	58	58
Bradd Crellin	2/7/89	3(21)	3(20)	2	1	0	0	0	0	8	4
Paul Cullnean	8/1/77	1(3)	1(2)	0	0	0	0	0	0	0	0
Lee Doran	23/3/81	27	26	2	2	0	0	0	0	8	8
Callum Farrer	5/7/96	(2)	(2)	1	1	0	0	0	0	4	4
Carl Forster	4/6/92	13(6)	13(6)	3	3	0	0	0	0	12	12
Steve Fox	13/2/90	1	1	0	0	0	0	0	0	0	0
Ade Gardner	24/6/83	1	1	1	1	0	0	0	0	4	4
Jon Grayshon	10/5/83	(5)	(5)	0	0	0	0	0	0	0	0
Jordan Hand	13/5/93	15(5)	15(5)	2	2	0	0	0	0	8	8
Paul Jackson	29/9/78	16(1)	15(1)	0	0	0	0	0	0	0	0
Larsen Marabe	9/6/86	8(3)	7(3)	2	2	0	0	0	0	8	8
Scott McAvoy	9/4/86	27	26	4	4	0	0	0	0	16	16
Lee Mitchell	8/9/88	27	26	6	6	0	0	0	0	24	24
Jessie Joe Nandye	22/8/85	25(1)	24(1)	18	18	0	0	0	0	72	72
James Newton	20/12/91	26(1)	25(1)	3	3	1	1	0	0	14	14
Kurtis Quinn	12/1/96	(5)	(5)	0	0	0	0	0	0	0	0
James Robinson	4/3/79	2(17)	2(16)	0	0	0	0	0	0	0	0
Brett Seymour	27/9/84	19	19	0	0	15	15	1	1	31	31
Chris Smith	21/1/90	1(2)	1(2)	1	1	0	0	0	0	4	4
Cain Southernwood	4/5/92	23(2)	22(2)	7	6	57	53	2	2	144	132
Samir Tahraoui	28/12/90	7(10)	6(10)	2	0	0	0	0	0	8	0
Chris Taylor	25/10/93	26	25	7	7	0	0	1	1	29	29
Neil Thorman	4/6/84	4(21)	4(20)	2	2	0	0	0	0	8	8
Anthony Walker	28/12/91	(1)	(1)	0	0	0	0	0	0	0	0

Scott McAvoy

LEAGUE RECORD
P26-W13-D0-L13-BP6
(9th, Championship)
F592, A666, Diff-74
45 points.

CHALLENGE CUP
Round Three

ATTENDANCES
Best - v Workington (Ch - 1,401)
Worst - v Doncaster (Ch - 560)
Total (Championship only) - 10,370
Average (Championship only) - 798
(Up by 40 on 2013)

CLUB RECORDS	**Highest score:** 86-6 v Highfield, 25/1/95 **Highest score against:** 8-106 v Wigan, 12/5/2008 **Record attendance:** 18,500 v Wakefield, 19/3/60
MATCH RECORDS	**Tries:** 6 Vince Gribbin v Doncaster, 18/11/84 **Goals:** 13 Lee Anderson v Highfield, 25/1/95 **Points:** 32 Mick Nanyn v Batley, 22/8/2004
SEASON RECORDS	**Tries:** 34 Mike Pechey 1994-95 **Goals:** 141 John McKeown 1956-57 **Points:** 398 Mick Nanyn 2004
CAREER RECORDS	**Tries:** 248 David Seeds 1993-2007 **Goals:** 1,050 John McKeown 1948-61 **Points:** 2,133 John McKeown 1948-61
	Appearances: 417 John McKeown 1948-61

WORKINGTON TOWN

DATE	FIXTURE	RESULT	SCORERS	LGE	ATT
16/2/14	Doncaster (h)	L12-22	t:Miller,Tierney g:Connor(2)	8th	895
23/2/14	Batley (a)	L36-16	t:Mossop,Carter,Connor g:Connor(2)	11th	559
2/3/14	Swinton (h)	W18-6	t:Olstrum,Carter,Mattinson g:Connor(2),Forber	9th	663
9/3/14	Barrow (a)	W6-8	t:Hopkins g:Connor(2)	7th	1,512
15/3/14	Normanton (a) (CCR3) ●	W12-38	t:Morris(3),Forber,Carter(2),B Phillips g:Connor(5)	N/A	713
23/3/14	Keighley (h)	L22-24	t:Morris,Mossop,C Phillips,James g:Connor(3)	8th	746
30/3/14	Dewsbury (a)	L38-16	t:Dudson,Morris(2) g:Connor(2)	9th	747
6/4/14	Hunslet (a) (CCR4)	L27-10	t:Carter(2) g:Connor	N/A	504
13/4/14	Sheffield (h)	L14-24	t:Farrell,Mossop(2) g:Connor	10th	451
18/4/14	Whitehaven (a)	L22-16	t:Forber,Farrell,Mossop g:Forber(2)	9th	1,401
4/5/14	Halifax (h)	D20-20	t:Murphy,Manfredi,Shackley g:Forber(4)	11th	732
11/5/14	Rochdale (a)	W6-10	t:B Phillips,Morris g:Forber	9th	790
18/5/14	Featherstone (a)	L32-20	t:B Phillips,Stack(2),Connor g:Forber(2)	9th	2,016
25/5/14	North Wales (h)	L10-11	t:Farrell,B Phillips g:Forber	11th	627
1/6/14	Leigh (h)	L16-28	t:Forber,B Phillips,Stack g:Forber(2)	10th	814
8/6/14	Sheffield (a)	L37-30	t:C Phillips,B Phillips(2),Stack,Burke g:Forber(5)	10th	712
15/6/14	Halifax (a)	L18-10	t:Mossop,Carter g:Forber	10th	1,658
22/6/14	Featherstone (h)	W20-18	t:Mattinson,Forber,Morris g:Forber(4)	10th	776
29/6/14	Swinton (a) ●●	W24-32	t:Carter(2),Mossop(2),Lucock,Forber g:Forber(4)	10th	405
6/7/14	Batley (a)	W22-16	t:Lupton(2),Olstrum,Mossop g:Forber(3)	10th	804
13/7/14	Keighley (a)	W12-16	t:Tierney(2),Murphy g:Forber(2)	10th	811
20/7/14	Rochdale (h)	W30-18	t:Carter,Hulme(2),Forber,Mossop g:Forber(5)	8th	707
27/7/14	North Wales (a)	W8-12	t:B Phillips,Mattinson g:Forber(2)	7th	658
3/8/14	Whitehaven (h)	W20-18	t:Hulme,Lupton,Tierney g:Forber(4)	6th	1,939
10/8/14	Doncaster (h)	L36-10	t:Coward,L McAvoy g:Forber	8th	504
17/8/14	Barrow (h)	W32-18	t:Forber(2),Lupton,Patrick,Shackley,Farrell g:Forber(4)	7th	842
30/8/14	Leigh (a)	L22-12	t:Forber,Mossop g:Forber(2)	7th	3,375
7/9/14	Dewsbury (h)	W23-4	t:C Phillips,B Phillips(2),Lupton g:Forber(3) fg:Murphy	7th	895
14/9/14	Dewsbury (a) (EPO)	L50-6	t:Murphy g:Forber	N/A	805

● Played at Big Fellas Stadium, Featherstone ●● Played at Park Lane, Sedgley Park

		APP		TRIES		GOALS		FG		PTS	
	D.O.B.	ALL	Ch	ALL	Ch	ALL	Ch	ALL	Ch	ALL	Ch
Greg Burke	12/2/93	5(6)	5(6)	1	1	0	0	0	0	4	4
Brett Carter	9/7/88	24	22	10	6	0	0	0	0	40	24
Kayle Connor	8/1/90	16	14	2	2	20	14	0	0	48	36
Kris Coward	1/10/81	26(1)	24(1)	1	1	0	0	0	0	4	4
Jack Dawson	12/1/93	(1)	(1)	0	0	0	0	0	0	0	0
Gil Dudson	16/6/90	1(1)	1(1)	1	1	0	0	0	0	4	4
James Duerden	9/10/91	2(9)	2(8)	0	0	0	0	0	0	0	0
Connor Farrell	6/11/93	16(2)	15(2)	4	4	0	0	0	0	16	16
Carl Forber	17/3/85	27(1)	25(1)	9	8	54	54	0	0	144	140
Jack Gaskell	21/1/95	(2)	(1)	0	0	0	0	0	0	0	0
Anthony Gelling	18/10/90	1	1	0	0	0	0	0	0	0	0
Lee Haney	11/6/88	1	1	0	0	0	0	0	0	0	0
Sam Hopkins	17/2/90	(1)	(1)	1	1	0	0	0	0	4	4
Jack Hughes	4/1/92	1	1	0	0	0	0	0	0	0	0
Declan Hulme	14/1/93	7	7	3	3	0	0	0	0	12	12
Jordan James	24/5/80	1(4)	1(4)	1	1	0	0	0	0	4	4
Matthew Johnson	18/3/82	1	1	0	0	0	0	0	0	0	0
Rob Lever	13/7/95	1(4)	(4)	0	0	0	0	0	0	0	0
Nathan Lucock	2/10/93	2(11)	1(10)	1	1	0	0	0	0	4	4
Peter Lupton	7/3/82	19(5)	18(5)	5	5	0	0	0	0	20	20
Dominic Manfredi	1/10/93	2	2	1	1	0	0	0	0	4	4
Graeme Mattinson	24/4/85	24	23	3	3	0	0	0	0	12	12
Kieran McAvoy	4/9/92	(1)	(1)	0	0	0	0	0	0	0	0
Liam McAvoy	24/9/93	23(2)	22(2)	1	1	0	0	0	0	4	4
Ruairi McGoff	5/1/85	(1)	(1)	0	0	0	0	0	0	0	0
Elliott Miller	14/9/90	1	1	1	1	0	0	0	0	4	4
Andy Morris	15/5/93	6(3)	5(2)	8	5	0	0	0	0	32	20
Jason Mossop	12/9/85	28	26	11	11	0	0	0	0	44	44
Jack Murphy	18/3/92	26	24	3	3	0	0	1	1	13	13
Karl Olstrum	21/9/91	8(9)	8(8)	2	2	0	0	0	0	8	8
John Patrick	29/11/82	5	5	1	1	0	0	0	0	4	4
Brett Phillips	25/10/88	25(2)	24(1)	10	9	0	0	0	0	40	36
Callum Phillips	19/2/92	17(9)	16(9)	3	3	0	0	0	0	12	12
Sam Powell	3/7/92	1	1	0	0	0	0	0	0	0	0
Theerapol Ritson	7/1/96	2	2	0	0	0	0	0	0	0	0
Daniel Rooney	6/1/90	3(15)	2(15)	0	0	0	0	0	0	0	0
Jay Rossi	26/6/93	3	3	0	0	0	0	0	0	0	0
Callum Rowlandson	7/2/91	1(15)	1(13)	0	0	0	0	0	0	0	0
Marc Shackley	14/1/89	19(5)	17(5)	2	2	0	0	0	0	8	8
Jarrad Stack	13/2/88	17(2)	16(2)	4	4	0	0	0	0	16	16
Alex Szostak	4/3/86	4(1)	4(1)	0	0	0	0	0	0	0	0
Lewis Tierney	20/10/94	11	10	4	4	0	0	0	0	16	16

Jason Mossop

LEAGUE RECORD
P26-W12-D1-L13-BP10
(7th, Championship/
Elimination Play-Off)
F467, A524, Diff-57
48 points.

CHALLENGE CUP
Round Four

ATTENDANCES
Best - v Whitehaven (Ch - 1,939)
Worst - v Sheffield (Ch - 451)
Total (Championship only) - 10,891
Average (Championship only) - 838
(Up by 55 on 2013)

CLUB RECORDS
MATCH RECORDS

SEASON RECORDS
CAREER RECORDS

Highest score: 94-4 v Leigh, 26/2/95 Highest score against: 0-92 v Bradford, 14/2/99 Record attendance: 17,741 v Wigan, 3/3/65
Tries: 7 Ike Southward v Blackpool, 17/9/55 Goals: 14 Darren Holt v Gateshead, 12/6/2011
Points: 42 Dean Marwood v Highfield, 1/11/92; Dean Marwood v Leigh, 26/2/95
Tries: 49 Johnny Lawrenson 1951-52 Goals: 186 Lyn Hopkins 1981-82 Points: 438 Lyn Hopkins 1981-82
Tries: 274 Ike Southward 1952-68 Goals: 809 Iain MacCorquodale 1972-80 Points: 1,800 Iain MacCorquodale 1972-80
Appearances: 419 Paul Charlton 1961-69; 1975-80

CHAMPIONSHIP 2014
Round by Round

ROUND 1

Sunday 16th February 2014

NORTH WALES CRUSADERS 34 BARROW RAIDERS 16

CRUSADERS: 1 Tommy Johnson; 22 Adam Clay; 4 Michael Platt; 17 Stuart Reardon; 5 Rob Massam; 6 Andy Moulsdale; 7 Jamie Dallimore; 8 Jonny Walker; 9 Craig Ashall; 15 David Mills; 12 Gary Middlehurst; 14 Stephen Wild; 11 Toby Adamson. Subs (all used): 19 Karl Ashall; 10 Mark Offerdahl; 21 Simon Stephens; 13 Jono Smith.
Tries: Reardon (13), Massam (22), K Ashall (39), Johnson (50), C Ashall (66), Adamson (72);
Goals: Johnson 5/6.
Dismissal: Platt (46) - punching Grant.
RAIDERS: 1 Ian Mort; 21 Mike Backhouse; 3 Aaron Low; 4 Max Wiper; 5 Dalton Grant; 6 Dom Speakman; 7 Liam Campbell; 24 Joe Bullock; 9 Nathan Mossop; 17 Andrew Dawson; 11 Liam Harrison; 25 Craig Briscoe; 13 Dan Toal. Subs (all used): 19 Brad Marwood; 8 Joe Burke; 15 Danny Jones; 18 Jack Morrison.
Tries: Grant (17, 30), Wiper (43); **Goals:** Mort 2/3.
Rugby Leaguer & League Express Men of the Match: *Crusaders:* Mark Offerdahl; *Raiders:* Dalton Grant.
Penalty count: 10-6; **Half-time:** 18-12;
Referee: Gareth Hewer; **Attendance:** 1,118.

DEWSBURY RAMS 11 FEATHERSTONE ROVERS 10

RAMS: 1 Louis Sheriff; 2 Dale Morton; 3 Karl Pryce; 4 Shane Grady; 5 Greg Scott; 6 Tom Hemingway; 7 Anthony Thackeray; 8 Stephen Nash; 9 Wayne Godwin; 10 Ryan Hepworth; 11 Rob Spicer; 12 Scott Hale; 13 Aaron Brown. Subs (all used): 31 Kieran Hyde; 15 Tommy Gallagher; 17 Matthew Haggarty; 32 Makali Aizue.
Tries: Godwin (57), Thackeray (73);
Goals: Hemingway 0/1, Hyde 1/2;
Field goal: Thackeray (78).
ROVERS: 22 James Mendeika; 2 Will Sharp; 4 Ben Hellewell; 3 Greg Worthington; 26 Tom Saxton; 6 Jack Bussey; 7 Gareth Moore; 8 Steve Crossley; 9 Andy Ellis; 10 Keegan Hirst; 11 James Lockwood; 12 Tim Spears; 13 Matt James. Subs (all used): 14 George Flanagan; 15 Matty Dale; 16 Andrew Bostock; 18 Jamie Cording.
Tries: Lockwood (49), Bussey (69); **Goals:** Moore 1/2.
On report: Flanagan (37) - alleged punching.
Rugby Leaguer & League Express Men of the Match: *Rams:* Anthony Thackeray; *Rovers:* Matt James.
Penalty count: 9-8; **Half-time:** 0-0;
Referee: Chris Leatherbarrow; **Attendance:** 2,096.

HALIFAX 28 SWINTON LIONS 18

HALIFAX: 1 Ryan Fieldhouse; 5 Wayne Reittie; 3 Steve Tyrer; 4 Ben Heaton; 25 Gareth Potts; 7 Simon Brown; 18 Ben Johnston; 8 Tony Tonks; 9 Ben Kaye; 12 Andy Bracek; 23 Callum Casey; 13 Luke Adamson; 6 Scott Murrell. Subs (all used): 14 Paul Mennell; 15 Adam Robinson; 17 Ben Davies; 27 Ross Divorty.
Tries: Brown (11), Johnston (14), Reittie (33, 47), Robinson (52); **Goals:** Tyrer 4/5.
LIONS: 23 Jordan Burke; 22 Kevin Penny; 24 Rhys Evans; 4 Mick Nanyn; 21 Joe Worthington; 14 Liam Fishwick; 7 Ian Watson; 8 Luke Menzies; 9 Andy Ackers; 10 Jack Cooper; 3 Kash Watkins; 12 Darren Hawkyard; 15 Josh Barlow. Subs (all used): 6 Anthony Bowman; 16 Mike Morrison; 17 Zach Johnson; 13 James Brown.
Tries: Penny (40), Ackers (73, 76); **Goals:** Nanyn 3/3.
Rugby Leaguer & League Express Men of the Match: *Halifax:* Ben Johnston; *Lions:* Josh Barlow.
Penalty count: 10-8; **Half-time:** 18-6;
Referee: Joe Cobb; **Attendance:** 1,587.

KEIGHLEY COUGARS 36 WHITEHAVEN 14

COUGARS: 1 James Craven; 2 Richie Barnett; 22 Daley Williams; 3 Elliott Cosgrove; 5 Paul White; 14 Paul March; 7 Paul Handforth; 8 Andy Shickell; 9 James Feather; 10 Sean Hesketh; 11 Josh Lynam; 12 Brendan Rawlins; 17 Ben Sagar. Subs (all used): 15 Scott Law; 18 Neil Cherryholme; 27 Jack Lee; 32 Ross Peltier.
Tries: Hesketh (18), Law (25), March (29), Cosgrove (51), Lynam (68), White (76); **Goals:** Handforth 6/6.
WHITEHAVEN: 1 Tom Carr; 2 Craig Calvert; 4 Scott McAvoy; 16 Steve Fox; 29 Ade Gardner; 6 Chris Taylor; 7 Cain Southernwood; 19 Paul Cullnean; 9 James Newton; 10 Paul Jackson; 8 Samir Tahraoui; 12 Lee Mitchell; 11 Lee Doran. Subs (all used): 3 Jessie Joe Nandye; 14 Neil Thorman; 30 Jordan Hand; 21 Larsen Marabe.
Tries: Gardner (31), Nandye (59);
Goals: Southernwood 3/3.
Rugby Leaguer & League Express Men of the Match: *Cougars:* Paul Handforth; *Whitehaven:* Samir Tahraoui.
Penalty count: 6-4; **Half-time:** 18-8;
Referee: George Stokes; **Attendance:** 1,061.

LEIGH CENTURIONS 52 BATLEY BULLDOGS 12

CENTURIONS: 1 Gregg McNally; 22 Adam Higson; 3 Stuart Littler; 4 Tom Armstrong; 5 Alex Brown; 6 Martyn Ridyard; 7 Ryan Brierley; 8 Tom Spencer; 9 Bob Beswick; 26 Ryan Duffy; 11 Matt Sarsfield; 12 Tommy Goulden; 13 Sam Barlow. Subs (all used): 15 Liam Kay; 10 Oliver Wilkes; 30 Kurt Haggerty; 29 Jake Emmitt.
Tries: Littler (15), Brierley (23, 34, 69), Beswick (30), Spencer (53, 78), Higson (62), Sarsfield (76);
Goals: Ridyard 5/6, Brierley 3/3.
BULLDOGS: 1 Miles Greenwood; 26 Ben Blackmore; 3 Alex Bretherton; 17 Lee Paterson; 27 Jase Connor; 11 John Davies; 7 Scott Leatherbarrow; 8 Byron Smith; 14 Alistair Leak; 20 Adam Gledhill; 19 Joe Chandler; 12 Sam Scott; 13 Mark Applegarth. Subs (all used): 9 Anthony Nicholson; 10 Alex Rowe; 25 Nathan Mason; 15 Jay Leary.
Tries: Greenwood (8), Connor (59); **Goals:** Paterson 2/2.
Rugby Leaguer & League Express Men of the Match: *Centurions:* Matt Sarsfield; *Bulldogs:* Miles Greenwood.
Penalty count: 11-8; **Half-time:** 22-6;
Referee: Matthew Thomason; **Attendance:** 2,173.

WORKINGTON TOWN 12 DONCASTER 22

TOWN: 30 Lewis Tierney; 2 Elliott Miller; 14 Kayle Connor; 34 Jack Murphy; 5 Lee Haney; 6 Peter Lupton; 7 Callum Phillips; 8 Kris Coward; 9 Graeme Mattinson; 17 Liam McAvoy; 11 Brett Phillips; 12 Jarrad Stack; 13 Karl Olstrum. Subs (all used): 4 Andy Morris; 10 Marc Shackley; 15 Daniel Rooney; 31 Rob Lever.
Tries: Miller (7), Tierney (14); **Goals:** Connor 2/2.
DONCASTER: 1 Mick Butterfield; 5 Dave Scott; 24 Joe Arundel; 3 Liam Welham; 2 Stewart Sanderson; 6 Paul Cooke; 7 Danny Nicklas; 28 Jay Pitts; 9 Kyle Kesik; 14 Russ Spiers; 16 Craig Robinson; 12 Michael Kelly; 13 Mike Emmett. Subs (all used): 15 Scott Spaven; 29 Dean Hadley; 21 Matt Carbutt; 8 Mark Castle.
Tries: Sanderson (25, 71), Castle (49), Scott (54);
Goals: Sanderson 3/4.
On report: Pitts (3) - alleged dangerous tackle.
Rugby Leaguer & League Express Men of the Match: *Town:* Lewis Tierney; *Doncaster:* Paul Cooke.
Penalty count: 5-7; **Half-time:** 12-4;
Referee: Jamie Bloem; **Attendance:** 895.

ROUND 2

Sunday 23rd February 2014

BARROW RAIDERS 8 LEIGH CENTURIONS 52

RAIDERS: 1 Ian Mort; 2 Scott Turner; 26 Ryan Shaw; 4 Max Wiper; 5 Dalton Grant; 6 Dom Speakman; 7 Liam Campbell; 8 Joe Burke; 9 Nathan Mossop; 17 Andrew Dawson; 11 Liam Harrison; 3 Aaron Low; 15 Danny Jones. Subs (all used): 19 Brad Marwood; 16 Matty Palmer; 10 Jamie Butler; 18 Jack Morrison.
Tries: Turner (11, 59); **Goals:** Mort 0/2.
CENTURIONS: 1 Gregg McNally; 22 Adam Higson; 3 Stuart Littler; 4 Tom Armstrong; 5 Alex Brown; 6 Martyn Ridyard; 7 Ryan Brierley; 8 Tom Spencer; 9 Bob Beswick; 26 Ryan Duffy; 11 Matt Sarsfield; 12 Tommy Goulden; 13 Sam Barlow. Subs (all used): 10 Oliver Wilkes; 15 Liam Kay; 18 Jamie Acton; 29 Jake Emmitt.
Tries: Brierley (2, 17, 47, 52, 66), Beswick (28), Goulden (33), McNally (35), Spencer (63);
Goals: Ridyard 8/9.
Rugby Leaguer & League Express Men of the Match: *Raiders:* Andrew Dawson; *Centurions:* Ryan Brierley.
Penalty count: 8-7; **Half-time:** 4-30;
Referee: Chris Leatherbarrow; **Attendance:** 1,252.

BATLEY BULLDOGS 36 WORKINGTON TOWN 16

BULLDOGS: 1 Miles Greenwood; 26 Ben Blackmore; 3 Alex Bretherton; 17 Lee Paterson; 2 Vinny Finigan; 14 Alistair Leak; 7 Scott Leatherbarrow; 8 Byron Smith; 18 Luke Blake; 20 Adam Gledhill; 11 John Davies; 12 Sam Scott; 13 Mark Applegarth. Subs (all used): 9 Anthony Nicholson; 16 Brad Brennan; 10 Alex Rowe; 19 Joe Chandler.
Tries: Finigan (36), Paterson (45), Leak (52), Smith (57), Bretherton (66), Gledhill (69);
Goals: Paterson 6/6.
TOWN: 30 Lewis Tierney; 34 Jack Murphy; 14 Kayle Connor; 3 Jason Mossop; 1 Brett Carter; 6 Peter Lupton; 7 Callum Phillips; 8 Kris Coward; 9 Graeme Mattinson; 20 Callum Rowlandson; 11 Brett Phillips; 12 Jarrad Stack; 13 Karl Olstrum. Subs (all used): 10 Marc Shackley; 31 Rob Lever; 16 Carl Forber; 17 Liam McAvoy.
Tries: Mossop (9), Carter (30), Connor (48);
Goals: Connor 2/3.
Rugby Leaguer & League Express Men of the Match: *Bulldogs:* Scott Leatherbarrow; *Town:* Kayle Connor.
Penalty count: 9-7; **Half-time:** 6-10;
Referee: George Stokes; **Attendance:** 559.

DONCASTER 30 KEIGHLEY COUGARS 12

DONCASTER: 1 Mick Butterfield; 2 Stewart Sanderson; 3 Liam Welham; 4 Nev Morrison; 5 Dave Scott; 6 Paul Cooke; 7 Danny Nicklas; 14 Russ Spiers; 9 Kyle Kesik; 28 Jay Pitts; 16 Craig Robinson; 12 Michael Kelly; 13 Mike Emmett. Subs (all used): 8 Mark Castle; 15 Scott Spaven; 21 Matt Carbutt; 29 Dean Hadley.
Tries: Sanderson (2, 44), Kelly (13), Scott (29), Welham (51), Morrison (80); **Goals:** Sanderson 3/6.
Sin bin: Hadley (39) - fighting.
COUGARS: 1 James Craven; 2 Richie Barnett; 3 Elliott Cosgrove; 22 Daley Williams; 5 Paul White; 14 Paul March; 7 Paul Handforth; 8 Andy Shickell; 13 Ashley Lindsay; 10 Sean Hesketh; 11 Josh Lynam; 12 Brendan Rawlins; 17 Ben Sagar. Subs (all used): 16 Jode Sheriffe; 25 Lewis Graham; 27 Jack Lee; 32 Ross Peltier.
Tries: Williams (16), White (39, 61);
Goals: Handforth 0/3.
Sin bin: March (39) - fighting, (75) - dissent.
Rugby Leaguer & League Express Men of the Match: *Doncaster:* Mike Emmett; *Cougars:* Paul White.
Penalty count: 14-6; **Half-time:** 14-8;
Referee: Gareth Hewer; **Attendance:** 647.

FEATHERSTONE ROVERS 28 HALIFAX 20

ROVERS: 22 James Mendeika; 2 Will Sharp; 4 Ben Hellewell; 3 Greg Worthington; 5 Jamel Chisholm; 6 Jack Bussey; 7 Gareth Moore; 8 Steve Crossley; 9 Andy Ellis; 10 Keegan Hirst; 11 James Lockwood; 12 Tim Spears; 18 Jamie Cording. Subs (all used): 14 George Flanagan; 16 Andrew Bostock; 15 Matty Dale; 13 Matt James.
Tries: Chisholm (5), Worthington (16), Sharp (65), Cording (68), Mendeika (77); **Goals:** Moore 4/5.
HALIFAX: 25 Gareth Potts; 5 Wayne Reittie; 3 Steve Tyrer; 16 Danny Cowling; 4 Ben Heaton; 6 Scott Murrell; 18 Ben Johnston; 8 Tony Tonks; 9 Ben Kaye; 10 Luke Ambler; 11 Dane Manning; 13 Luke Adamson; 12 Andy Bracek. Subs (all used): 7 Simon Brown; 14 Paul Mennell; 17 Ben Davies; 27 Ross Divorty.
Tries: Johnston (20), Kaye (36), Divorty (46);
Goals: Tyrer 4/4.
Sin bin: Kaye (14) - holding down.
Rugby Leaguer & League Express Men of the Match: *Rovers:* Andy Ellis; *Halifax:* Ben Johnston.
Penalty count: 8-8; **Half-time:** 12-12;
Referee: Matthew Thomason; **Attendance:** 2,583.

ROCHDALE HORNETS 12 DEWSBURY RAMS 42

HORNETS: 14 Sean Casey; 1 Wayne English; 18 Matty Dawson; 4 Daniel Davies; 2 Gareth Langley; 6 Paul Crook; 7 Steve Roper; 8 John Cookson; 23 James Dandy; 10 Warren Thompson; 24 Tony Suffolk; 20 Mark Flanagan; 28 Anthony Walker. Subs (all used): 13 Jordan Case; 30 Greg Richards; 26 Adam Bowman; 22 Joe Greenwood.
Tries: Dawson (38), Greenwood (58); **Goals:** Crook 2/2.
RAMS: 1 Louis Sheriff; 2 Dale Morton; 3 Karl Pryce; 4 Shane Grady; 5 Greg Scott; 6 Tom Hemingway; 7 Anthony Thackeray; 8 Stephen Nash; 9 Wayne Godwin; 10 Ryan Hepworth; 11 Rob Spicer; 12 Scott Hale; 13 Aaron Brown. Subs (all used): 31 Kieran Hyde; 15 Tommy Gallagher; 32 Makali Aizue; 17 Matthew Haggarty.
Tries: Gallagher (29), Morton (50), Thackeray (52, 79), Brown (71), Sheriff (73), Pryce (77);
Goals: Hemingway 3/4, Hyde 4/5.
Rugby Leaguer & League Express Men of the Match: *Hornets:* Tony Suffolk; *Rams:* Aaron Brown.
Penalty count: 7-8; **Half-time:** 6-4;
Referee: Jamie Bloem; **Attendance:** 817.

SWINTON LIONS 16 SHEFFIELD EAGLES 30

LIONS: 23 Jordan Burke; 21 Joe Worthington; 24 Rhys Evans; 4 Mick Nanyn; 22 Kevin Penny; 14 Liam Fishwick; 7 Ian Watson; 10 Jack Cooper; 9 Andy Ackers; 8 Luke Menzies; 3 Kash Watkins; 12 Darren Hawkyard; 15 Josh Barlow. Subs (all used): 1 Ritchie Hawkyard; 16 Mike Morrison; 17 Zach Johnson; 13 James Brown.
Tries: Nanyn (4), Brown (40), Penny (66);
Goals: Nanyn 2/3.
EAGLES: 1 Quentin Laulu-Togagae; 2 Scott Turner; 3 Menzie Yere; 23 Jonathan Ford; 5 Misi Taulapapa; 6 Pat Walker; 7 Dominic Brambani; 20 Connor Scott; 9 Andrew Henderson; 10 Mitchell Stringer; 12 Peter Green; 22 Will Hope; 11 Michael Knowles. Subs (all used): 24 Gareth Owen; 15 Matt Garside; 21 Jack Blagbrough; 17 Ben Jones.
Tries: Turner (15, 57, 77), Owen (47), Ford (55);
Goals: Brambani 4/4, Walker 1/1.
Rugby Leaguer & League Express Men of the Match: *Lions:* Ian Watson; *Eagles:* Scott Turner.
Penalty count: 3-6; **Half-time:** 10-6;
Referee: Warren Turley; **Attendance:** 548.

ROUND 3

Sunday 2nd March 2014

SHEFFIELD EAGLES 18 BARROW RAIDERS 24

EAGLES: 1 Quentin Laulu-Togagae; 2 Scott Turner; 3 Menzie Yere; 25 Corey Hanson; 5 Misi Taulapapa; 6 Pat Walker; 7 Dominic Brambani; 21 Jack Blagbrough; 9 Andrew Henderson; 10 Mitchell Stringer; 11 Michael Knowles; 12 Peter Green; 22 Will Hope. Subs (all used): 24 Gareth Owen; 20 Connor Scott; 15 Matt Garside; 23 Jonathan Ford.
Tries: Turner (11, 55), Owen (42), Walker (46);
Goals: Brambani 1/4.
RAIDERS: 1 Ian Mort; 2 Scott Turner; 3 Aaron Low; 4 Max Wiper; 5 Dalton Grant; 26 Ryan Shaw; 7 Liam Campbell; 24 Joe Bullock; 6 Dom Speakman; 17 Andrew Dawson; 11 Liam Harrison; 25 Craig Briscoe; 13 Dan Toal. Subs (all used): 9 Nathan Mossop; 8 Joe Burke; 10 Jamie Butler; 18 Jack Morrison.
Tries: Morrison (27), Toal (33, 62), Harrison (69);
Goals: Mort 4/5.
Sin bin: Mossop (32) - professional foul.
Rugby Leaguer & League Express Men of the Match: *Eagles:* Scott Turner; *Raiders:* Liam Campbell.
Penalty count: 5-9; **Half-time:** 4-12;
Referee: Joe Cobb; **Attendance:** 897.

NORTH WALES CRUSADERS 6 FEATHERSTONE ROVERS 36

CRUSADERS: 1 Tommy Johnson; 22 Adam Clay; 4 Michael Platt; - Declan Hulme; 2 Dan Birkett; 7 Jamie Dallimore; 37 Tom Gilmore; 15 David Mills; 9 Craig Ashall; 8 Jonny Walker; 29 Steve Bannister; 11 Toby Adamson; 14 Stephen Wild. Subs (all used): 19 Karl Ashall; 27 Jamie Clarke; 21 Simon Stephens; 13 Jono Smith.
Try: Gilmore (20); **Goals:** Johnson 1/1.
ROVERS: 22 James Mendeika; 27 Etuate Uaisele; 3 Greg Worthington; 4 Ben Hellewell; 2 Will Sharp; 19 Kyle Briggs; 7 Gareth Moore; 8 Steve Crossley; 14 George Flanagan; 10 Keegan Hirst; 11 James Lockwood; 12 Tim Spears; 18 Jamie Cording. Subs (all used): 6 Jack Bussey; 15 Matty Dale; 16 Andrew Bostock; 20 Colton Roche.
Tries: Sharp (8, 54, 77), Briggs (43), Moore (61), Flanagan (66); **Goals:** Moore 6/6.
Rugby Leaguer & League Express Men of the Match: *Crusaders:* Stephen Wild; *Rovers:* Gareth Moore.
Penalty count: 7-11; **Half-time:** 6-6;
Referee: Warren Turley; **Attendance:** 1,418.

DONCASTER 12 DEWSBURY RAMS 20

DONCASTER: 1 Mick Butterfield; 2 Stewart Sanderson; 3 Liam Welham; 4 Nev Morrison; 5 Dave Scott; 6 Paul Cooke; 7 Danny Nicklas; 21 Matt Carbutt; 15 Scott Spaven; 28 Dean Hadley; 16 Craig Robinson; 12 Michael Kelly; 13 Mike Emmett. Subs (all used): 8 Mark Castle; 18 Ryan Wilson; 25 Alex Starling; 20 Shaun Leaf.
Tries: Spaven (44), Cooke (57); **Goals:** Sanderson 2/3.
RAMS: 1 Louis Sheriff; 2 Dale Morton; 3 Karl Pryce; 4 Shane Grady; 5 Greg Scott; 6 Tom Hemingway; 7 Anthony Thackeray; 8 Stephen Nash; 9 Wayne Godwin; 10 Ryan Hepworth; 11 Rob Spicer; 12 Scott Hale; 13 Aaron Brown. Subs (all used): 31 Kieran Hyde; 15 Tommy Gallagher; 32 Makali Aizue; 17 Matthew Haggarty.
Tries: Hale (50), Thackeray (60), Scott (72);
Goals: Hemingway 1/2, Hyde 3/3.
Rugby Leaguer & League Express Men of the Match:
Doncaster: Stewart Sanderson; *Rams:* Kieran Hyde.
Penalty count: 5-9; **Half-time:** 0-0;
Referee: George Stokes; **Attendance:** 744.

HALIFAX 8 BATLEY BULLDOGS 10

HALIFAX: 25 Gareth Potts; 21 Tom Saxton; 3 Steve Tyrer; 23 Callum Casey; 4 Ben Heaton; 7 Simon Brown; 18 Ben Johnston; 8 Tony Tonks; 9 Ben Kaye; 12 Andy Bracek; 11 Dane Manning; 13 Luke Adamson; 6 Scott Murrell. Subs (all used): 10 Luke Ambler; 14 Paul Mennell; 17 Ben Davies; 27 Ross Divorty.
Tries: Tyrer (44), Heaton (71); **Goals:** Tyrer 0/2.
BULLDOGS: 1 Miles Greenwood; 26 Ben Blackmore; 3 Alex Bretherton; 17 Lee Paterson; 2 Vinny Finigan; 14 Alistair Leak; 7 Scott Leatherbarrow; 8 Byron Smith; 18 Luke Blake; 20 Adam Gledhill; 11 John Davies; 12 Sam Scott; 13 Mark Applegarth. Subs (all used): 9 Anthony Nicholson; 10 Alex Rowe; 16 Brad Brennan; 19 Joe Chandler.
Tries: Finigan (56, 79); **Goals:** Paterson 1/2.
Rugby Leaguer & League Express Men of the Match:
Halifax: Ben Heaton; *Bulldogs:* Ben Blackmore.
Penalty count: 5-4; **Half-time:** 0-0;
Referee: Chris Leatherbarrow; **Attendance:** 1,798.

LEIGH CENTURIONS 52 WHITEHAVEN 0

CENTURIONS: 1 Gregg McNally; 22 Adam Higson; 3 Stuart Littler; 4 Tom Armstrong; 15 Liam Kay; 6 Martyn Ridyard; 7 Ryan Brierley; 8 Tom Spencer; 9 Bob Beswick; 16 Martin Aspinwall; 11 Matt Sarsfield; 12 Tommy Goulden; 13 Sam Barlow. Subs (all used): 14 Sean Penkywicz; 10 Oliver Wilkes; 29 Jake Emmitt; 30 Kurt Haggerty.
Tries: Armstrong (11, 14), McNally (20), Goulden (24), Brierley (30, 41, 58), Kay (37), Emmitt (64);
Goals: Ridyard 6/6, Brierley 2/3.
Sin bin: Barlow (75) - punching Doran.
On report: Spencer (65) - alleged late challenge on Taylor.
WHITEHAVEN: 1 Tom Carr; 2 Craig Calvert; 3 Jessie Joe Nandye; 4 Scott McAvoy; 5 Shaun Ainscough; 6 Chris Taylor; 7 Cain Southernwood; 8 Samir Tahraoui; 9 James Newton; 30 Jordan Hand; 11 Lee Doran; 12 Lee Mitchell; 10 Paul Jackson. Subs (all used): 14 Neil Thorman; 21 Larsen Marabe; 19 Paul Cullnean; 13 Bradd Crellin.
Rugby Leaguer & League Express Men of the Match:
Centurions: Tom Armstrong; *Whitehaven:* Larsen Marabe.
Penalty count: 5-9; **Half-time:** 36-0;
Referee: Dave Merrick; **Attendance:** 2,006.

ROCHDALE HORNETS 14 KEIGHLEY COUGARS 40

HORNETS: 14 Sean Casey; 2 Gareth Langley; 4 Daniel Davies; 18 Matty Dawson; 29 Sam Te'o; 6 Paul Crook; 17 Ryan Millard; 28 Anthony Walker; 23 James Dandy; 10 Warren Thompson; 22 Joe Greenwood; 20 Mark Flanagan; 24 Tony Suffolk. Subs (all used): 26 Connor Dwyer; 13 Jordan Case; 8 John Cookson; 25 Steve Marsh.
Tries: Langley (1, 8), Dawson (23); **Goals:** Crook 1/3.
Sin bin: Dandy (66) - late challenge.
COUGARS: 1 James Craven; 2 Richie Barnett; 3 Elliott Cosgrove; 19 Danny Lawton; 5 Paul White; 6 Danny Jones; 7 Paul Handforth; 8 Andy Shickell; - Luke Haigh; 10 Sean Hesketh; 11 Josh Lynam; 12 Brendan Rawlins; 13 Ashley Lindsay. Subs (all used): 14 Paul March; 16 Jode Sheriffe; 18 Neil Cherryholme; 25 Lewis Graham.
Tries: Handforth (20), White (38, 45, 52, 65), March (63), Graham (70), Craven (80);
Goals: Handforth 4/8.
Rugby Leaguer & League Express Men of the Match:
Hornets: Tony Suffolk; *Cougars:* Paul White.
Penalty count: 8-9; **Half-time:** 14-10;
Referee: Tom Crashley; **Attendance:** 726.

WORKINGTON TOWN 18 SWINTON LIONS 6

TOWN: 30 Lewis Tierney; 34 Jack Murphy; 14 Kayle Connor; 3 Jason Mossop; 1 Brett Carter; 16 Carl Forber; 7 Callum Phillips; 8 Kris Coward; 9 Graeme Mattinson; 10 Marc Shackley; 17 Liam McAvoy; 12 Jarrad Stack; 13 Karl Olstrum. Subs (all used): 6 Peter Lupton; 15 Daniel Rooney; 20 Callum Rowlandson; 31 Rob Lever.
Tries: Olstrum (10), Carter (18), Mattinson (25);
Goals: Connor 2/3, Forber 1/1.
LIONS: 1 Ritchie Hawkyard; 24 Chris Riley; 3 Kash Watkins; 4 Mick Nanyn; 22 Kevin Penny; 23 Jordan Burke; 7 Ian Watson; 10 Jack Cooper; - Brad Dwyer; 8 Luke Menzies; 12 Darren Hawkyard; 11 Danny Halliwell; 15 Josh Barlow. Subs (all used): 20 Mark Thomas; 16 Mike Morrison; 17 Zach Johnson; 13 James Brown.
Try: Penny (29); **Goals:** Nanyn 1/1.
Dismissal: Morrison (47) - high tackle on C Phillips.
Sin bin: Watkins (43) - late challenge on C Phillips.
Rugby Leaguer & League Express Men of the Match:
Town: Liam McAvoy; *Lions:* Darren Hawkyard.
Penalty count: 13-6; **Half-time:** 16-6;
Referee: Gareth Hewer; **Attendance:** 663.

ROUND 4

Sunday 9th March 2014

BATLEY BULLDOGS 12 DONCASTER 20

BULLDOGS: 1 Miles Greenwood; 26 Ben Blackmore; 3 Alex Bretherton; 17 Lee Paterson; 2 Vinny Finigan; 14 Alistair Leak; 7 Scott Leatherbarrow; 8 Byron Smith; 18 Luke Blake; 16 Brad Brennan; 12 Sam Scott; 19 Joe Chandler; 13 Mark Applegarth. Subs (all used): 23 Josh Johnson; 9 Anthony Nicholson; 10 Alex Rowe; 24 Peter Aspinall.
Tries: Greenwood (25), Bretherton (54);
Goals: Paterson 2/2.
DONCASTER: 5 Dave Scott; 24 Liam Colbon; 4 Nev Morrison; 3 Liam Welham; 2 Stewart Sanderson; 6 Paul Cooke; 7 Danny Nicklas; 14 Russ Spiers; 15 Scott Spaven; 21 Matt Carbutt; 25 Alex Starling; 12 Michael Kelly; 13 Mike Emmett. Subs (all used): 19 Liam Cunningham; 20 Shaun Leaf; 8 Mark Castle; 16 Craig Robinson.
Tries: Spaven (46, 76), Morrison (67);
Goals: Sanderson 4/4.
Rugby Leaguer & League Express Men of the Match:
Bulldogs: Alex Bretherton; *Doncaster:* Scott Spaven.
Penalty count: 7-6; **Half-time:** 6-0;
Referee: Warren Turley; **Attendance:** 691.

BARROW RAIDERS 6 WORKINGTON TOWN 8

RAIDERS: 1 Ian Mort; 2 Scott Turner; 3 Aaron Low; 4 Max Wiper; 5 Dalton Grant; 26 Ryan Shaw; 7 Liam Campbell; 24 Joe Bullock; 6 Dom Speakman; 17 Andrew Dawson; 11 Liam Harrison; 25 Craig Briscoe; 13 Dan Toal. Subs (all used): 8 Joe Burke; 9 Nathan Mossop; 15 Danny Jones; 18 Jack Morrison.
Try: Shaw (63); **Goals:** Mort 1/1.
TOWN: 30 Lewis Tierney; 34 Jack Murphy; 14 Kayle Connor; 3 Jason Mossop; 1 Brett Carter; 16 Carl Forber; 7 Callum Phillips; 8 Kris Coward; 9 Graeme Mattinson; 10 Marc Shackley; 17 Liam McAvoy; 12 Jarrad Stack; 13 Karl Olstrum. Subs (all used): 6 Peter Lupton; 21 Ruairi McGoff; 31 Rob Lever; 32 Sam Hopkins.
Try: Hopkins (22); **Goals:** Connor 2/2.
Rugby Leaguer & League Express Men of the Match:
Raiders: Joe Bullock; *Town:* Lewis Tierney.
Penalty count: 9-6; **Half-time:** 0-6;
Referee: Tom Crashley; **Attendance:** 1,512.

DEWSBURY RAMS 16 WHITEHAVEN 23

RAMS: 22 Jordan Grayston; 2 Dale Morton; 3 Karl Pryce; 4 Shane Grady; 5 Greg Scott; 6 Tom Hemingway; 7 Anthony Thackeray; 8 Stephen Nash; 9 Wayne Godwin; 10 Ryan Hepworth; 11 Rob Spicer; 12 Scott Hale; 13 Aaron Brown. Subs (all used): 31 Kieran Hyde; 15 Tommy Gallagher; 17 Matthew Haggarty; 16 Josh Tonks.
Tries: Scott (22), Morton (59), Brown (75);
Goals: Hemingway 1/2, Grayston 1/1.
WHITEHAVEN: 1 Tom Carr; 5 Shaun Ainscough; 4 Scott McAvoy; 3 Jessie Joe Nandye; 18 Jordan Burns; 6 Chris Taylor; 7 Cain Southernwood; 30 Jordan Hand; 9 James Newton; 10 Paul Jackson; 11 Lee Doran; 12 Lee Mitchell; 21 Larsen Marabe. Subs (all used): 14 Neil Thorman; 13 Bradd Crellin; 19 Paul Cullnean; 8 Samir Tahraoui.
Tries: Ainscough (6), Burns (13, 24), Mitchell (38);
Goals: Southernwood 3/5;
Field goal: Southernwood (77).
Rugby Leaguer & League Express Men of the Match:
Rams: Aaron Brown; *Whitehaven:* Shaun Ainscough.
Penalty count: 8-6; **Half-time:** 4-20;
Referee: Joe Cobb; **Attendance:** 903.

FEATHERSTONE ROVERS 56 ROCHDALE HORNETS 6

ROVERS: 1 Ian Hardman; 2 Will Sharp; 4 Ben Hellewell; 3 Greg Worthington; 27 Etuate Uaisele; 19 Kyle Briggs; 7 Gareth Moore; 8 Steve Crossley; 9 Andy Ellis; 15 Matty Dale; 11 James Lockwood; 12 Tim Spears; 6 Jack Bussey. Subs (all used): 14 George Flanagan; 10 Keegan Hirst; 16 Andrew Bostock; 23 Andy Kain.
Tries: Uaisele (9, 50, 55), Hardman (16, 42), Ellis (22), Sharp (28, 78), Worthington (35), Hellewell (44);
Goals: Moore 8/10.
HORNETS: 1 Wayne English; 2 Gareth Langley; 4 Daniel Davies; 28 Matty Dawson; 29 Sam Te'o; 17 Ryan Millard; 6 Paul Crook; 8 John Cookson; 18 James Tilley; 24 Tony Suffolk; 20 Mark Flanagan; 22 Joe Greenwood; 27 Anthony Walker. Subs (all used): 13 Jordan Case; 12 Alex Trumper; 10 Warren Thompson; 25 Steve Marsh.
Try: Walker (72); **Goals:** Crook 1/1.
Rugby Leaguer & League Express Men of the Match:
Rovers: Etuate Uaisele; *Hornets:* Wayne English.
Penalty count: 4-8; **Half-time:** 28-0;
Referee: Jamie Bloem; **Attendance:** 2,323.

HALIFAX 30 SHEFFIELD EAGLES 28

HALIFAX: 1 Ryan Fieldhouse; 21 Tom Saxton; 3 Steve Tyrer; 4 Ben Heaton; 25 Gareth Potts; 6 Scott Murrell; 18 Ben Johnston; 10 Luke Ambler; 9 Ben Kaye; 12 Andy Bracek; 11 Dane Manning; 15 Adam Robinson; 13 Luke Adamson. Subs (all used): 7 Simon Brown; 8 Tony Tonks; 17 Ben Davies; 27 Ross Divorty.
Tries: Tyrer (3), Saxton (17, 57), Potts (22), Ambler (76); **Goals:** Tyrer 5/6.
EAGLES: 1 Quentin Laulu-Togagae; 2 Scott Turner; 3 Menzie Yere; 23 Jonathan Ford; 5 Misi Taulapapa; 6 Pat Walker; 7 Dominic Brambani; 20 Connor Scott; 9 Andrew Henderson; 10 Mitchell Stringer; 11 Michael Knowles; 12 Peter Green; 16 Duane Straugheir. Subs (all used): 24 Gareth Owen; 29 Alex Palmer; 15 Matt Garside; 30 Shaun Squires.
Tries: Yere (9), Garside (26, 70), Turner (73), Brambani (78); **Goals:** Brambani 4/5.
Rugby Leaguer & League Express Men of the Match:
Halifax: Adam Robinson; *Eagles:* Shaun Squires.
Penalty count: 8-6; **Half-time:** 16-10;
Referee: George Stokes; **Attendance:** 1,327.

KEIGHLEY COUGARS 26 LEIGH CENTURIONS 28

COUGARS: 1 James Craven; 2 Richie Barnett; 19 Danny Lawton; 22 Daley Williams; 5 Paul White; 6 Danny Jones; 7 Paul Handforth; 8 Andy Shickell; - Luke Haigh; 10 Sean Hesketh; 11 Josh Lynam; 12 Brendan Rawlins; 13 Ashley Lindsay. Subs (all used): 16 Jode Sheriffe; 18 Neil Cherryholme; 25 Lewis Graham; 27 Jack Lee.
Tries: Barnett (9), Craven (37), Williams (50), Lee (63);
Goals: Jones 5/5.
CENTURIONS: 1 Gregg McNally; 22 Adam Higson; 3 Stuart Littler; 4 Tom Armstrong; 15 Liam Kay; 6 Martyn Ridyard; 7 Ryan Brierley; 8 Tom Spencer; 9 Bob Beswick; 16 Martin Aspinwall; 11 Matt Sarsfield; 12 Tommy Goulden; 13 Sam Barlow. Subs (all used): 10 Oliver Wilkes; 14 Sean Penkywicz; 29 Jake Emmitt; 30 Kurt Haggerty.
Tries: Beswick (2), Armstrong (17), Brierley (32), Higson (59, 78); **Goals:** Ridyard 4/7.
On report: Wilkes (21) - alleged use of the knee on Haigh.
Rugby Leaguer & League Express Men of the Match:
Cougars: Paul Handforth; *Centurions:* Jake Emmitt.
Penalty count: 10-11; **Half-time:** 12-20;
Referee: Chris Leatherbarrow; **Attendance:** 1,309.

SWINTON LIONS 16 NORTH WALES CRUSADERS 20

LIONS: 23 Jordan Burke; 5 Freddie Walker; 3 Kash Watkins; 4 Mick Nanyn; 22 Kevin Penny; 14 Liam Fishwick; 7 Ian Watson; 16 Mike Morrison; 24 Brad Dwyer; 8 Luke Menzies; 11 Danny Halliwell; 12 Darren Hawkyard; 15 Josh Barlow. Subs (all used): 9 Andy Ackers; 17 Zach Johnson; 10 Jack Cooper; 13 James Brown.
Tries: Nanyn (26), Menzies (60), Penny (62);
Goals: Nanyn 2/3.
On report:
Nanyn (26) - alleged use of the elbow on Smith.
CRUSADERS: 1 Tommy Johnson; 22 Adam Clay; 17 Stuart Reardon; 4 Michael Platt; 2 Dan Birkett; 37 Tom Gilmore; 7 Jamie Dallimore; 8 Jonny Walker; 9 Craig Ashall; 15 David Mills; 13 Jono Smith; 14 Stephen Wild; 11 Toby Adamson. Subs (all used): 21 Simon Stephens; 19 Karl Ashall; 12 Gary Middlehurst; 27 Jamie Clarke.
Tries: Smith (4), C Ashall (15), Johnson (44), Clay (53);
Goals: Johnson 2/4.
Rugby Leaguer & League Express Men of the Match:
Lions: Ian Watson; *Crusaders:* Jamie Dallimore.
Penalty count: 2-9; **Half-time:** 6-12;
Referee: Dave Merrick; **Attendance:** 587.

ROUND 5

Sunday 23rd March 2014

SHEFFIELD EAGLES 46 DEWSBURY RAMS 10

EAGLES: 1 Quentin Laulu-Togagae; 2 Scott Turner; 3 Menzie Yere; 16 Duane Straugheir; 5 Misi Taulapapa; 6 Pat Walker; 7 Dominic Brambani; 18 Tom Lillycrop; 9 Andrew Henderson; 10 Mitchell Stringer; 11 Michael Knowles; 12 Peter Green; 22 Will Hope. Subs (all used): 24 Gareth Owen; 20 Connor Scott; 4 Lelauloto Tagaloa; 15 Matt Garside.
Tries: Taulapapa (14, 20), Yere (30), Knowles (44, 67), Owen (52), Garside (56), Turner (78);
Goals: Brambani 7/8.
RAMS: 1 Louis Sheriff; 2 Dale Morton; 12 Scott Hale; 4 Shane Grady; 5 Greg Scott; 31 Kieran Hyde; 7 Anthony Thackeray; 32 Makali Aizue; 9 Wayne Godwin; 10 Ryan Hepworth; 11 Rob Spicer; 26 Lucas Walshaw; 13 Aaron Brown. Subs (all used): 14 Ryan Wright; 17 Matthew Haggarty; 29 Ewan Dowes; 25 Joel Farrell.
Tries: Godwin (60), Sheriff (63); **Goals:** Grady 1/2.
Rugby Leaguer & League Express Men of the Match:
Eagles: Michael Knowles; *Rams:* Ryan Wright.
Penalty count: 9-11; **Half-time:** 16-0;
Referee: Warren Turley; **Attendance:** 911.

DONCASTER 22 FEATHERSTONE ROVERS 16

DONCASTER: 5 Dave Scott; 4 Nev Morrison; 3 Liam Welham; 20 Shaun Leaf; 2 Stewart Sanderson; 6 Paul Cooke; 15 Scott Spaven; 14 Russ Spiers; 13 Mike Emmett; 21 Matt Carbutt; 24 Liam Kent; 12 Michael Kelly; 29 Jay Pitts. Subs (all used): 16 Craig Robinson; 11 Lee Waterman; 23 Richard Wilkinson; 18 Ryan Wilson.
Tries: Scott (18), Pitts (29), Cooke (70);
Goals: Sanderson 5/6.
ROVERS: 1 Ian Hardman; 2 Will Sharp; 3 Greg Worthington; 4 Ben Hellewell; 27 Etuate Uaisele; 19 Kyle Briggs; 7 Gareth Moore; 8 Steve Crossley; 14 George Flanagan; 13 Matt James; 11 James Lockwood; 12 Tim Spears; 6 Jack Bussey. Subs (all used): 23 Andy Kain; 15 Matty Dale; 10 Keegan Hirst; 16 Andrew Bostock.
Tries: Hardman (40, 56), Worthington (64);
Goals: Moore 2/2, Briggs 0/1.
Rugby Leaguer & League Express Men of the Match:
Doncaster: Dave Scott; *Rovers:* Ian Hardman.
Penalty count: 9-10; **Half-time:** 12-6;
Referee: Matthew Thomason; **Attendance:** 1,317.

LEIGH CENTURIONS 35
NORTH WALES CRUSADERS 22

CENTURIONS: 1 Gregg McNally; 22 Adam Higson; 3 Stuart Littler; 4 Tom Armstrong; 15 Liam Kay; 6 Martyn Ridyard; 7 Ryan Brierley; 8 Tom Spencer; 9 Bob Beswick; 16 Martin Aspinwall; 11 Matt Sarsfield; 12 Tommy Goulden; 13 Sam Barlow. Subs (all used): 10 Oliver Wilkes; 14 Sean Penkywicz; 29 Jake Emmitt; 30 Kurt Haggerty.
Tries: Higson (16, 22, 31), Brierley (51), Wilkes (61), Kay (70), Penkywicz (77); **Goals:** Ridyard 3/7;
Field goal: Ridyard (79).
CRUSADERS: 1 Tommy Johnson; 22 Adam Clay; 17 Stuart Reardon; 36 Declan Hulme; 5 Rob Massam; 6 Andy Moulsdale; 7 Jamie Dallimore; 8 Jonny Walker; 9 Craig Ashall; 10 Mark Offerdahl; 29 Steve Bannister; 30 Adam Lawton; 14 Stephen Wild. Subs (all used): 21 Simon Stephens; 15 David Mills; 26 Matt Reid; 19 Karl Ashall.
Tries: Massam (8), Lawton (46), Johnson (58), Offerdahl (66); **Goals:** Johnson 3/4.
Rugby Leaguer & League Express Men of the Match: *Centurions:* Tommy Goulden; *Crusaders:* Adam Lawton.
Penalty count: 7-10; **Half-time:** 12-6;
Referee: George Stokes; **Attendance:** 2,135.

ROCHDALE HORNETS 14 BATLEY BULLDOGS 10

HORNETS: 1 Wayne English; 2 Gareth Langley; 19 Dave Llewellyn; 22 Mike Ratu; 29 Sam Te'o; 17 Ryan Millard; 6 Paul Crook; 8 John Cookson; 14 Sean Casey; 10 Warren Thompson; 11 Chris Baines; 24 Tony Suffolk; 13 Jordan Case. Subs (all used): 25 Steve Marsh; 26 Adam Bowman; 4 Daniel Davies; 9 Lewis Sheridan.
Tries: Ratu (10), Crook (19), Te'o (70); **Goals:** Crook 1/3.
BULLDOGS: 1 Miles Greenwood; 26 Ben Blackmore; 3 Alex Bretherton; 17 Lee Paterson; 2 Vinny Finigan; 14 Alistair Leak; 7 Scott Leatherbarrow; 8 Byron Smith; 18 Luke Blake; 20 Adam Gledhill; 11 John Davies; 12 Sam Scott; 19 Joe Chandler. Subs (all used): 10 Alex Rowe; 9 Anthony Nicholson; 16 Brad Brennan; 30 Charlie Martin.
Tries: Blackmore (29), Greenwood (35);
Goals: Paterson 1/2.
Rugby Leaguer & League Express Men of the Match: *Hornets:* Chris Baines; *Bulldogs:* Alex Rowe.
Penalty count: 9-6; **Half-time:** 8-10;
Referee: Gareth Hewer; **Attendance:** 818.

SWINTON LIONS 44 BARROW RAIDERS 26

LIONS: 1 Ritchie Hawkyard; 5 Freddie Walker; 24 Rhys Evans; 4 Mick Nanyn; 22 Kevin Penny; 6 Anthony Bowman; 7 Ian Watson; 16 Mike Morrison; 28 Brad Dwyer; 8 Luke Menzies; 23 Ben Currie; 13 James Brown; 15 Josh Barlow. Subs (all used): 27 Lewis Hulme; 25 Paul Wood; 20 Mark Thomas; 17 Zach Johnson.
Tries: Dwyer (7), Currie (18, 25, 73), Thomas (34), Wood (48), Penny (68), Evans (76); **Goals:** Nanyn 6/8.
RAIDERS: 26 Ryan Shaw; 2 Scott Turner; 3 Aaron Low; 4 Max Wiper; 5 Dalton Grant; 6 Dom Speakman; 7 Liam Campbell; 15 Danny Jones; 14 Aaron Lloyd; 17 Andrew Dawson; 11 Liam Harrison; 16 Matty Palmer; 13 Dan Toal. Subs (all used): 19 Brad Marwood; 20 Ross Brookes; 18 Jack Morrison; 10 Jamie Butler.
Tries: Shaw (12, 58), Grant (40), Campbell (44), Speakman (52); **Goals:** Shaw 3/5.
Rugby Leaguer & League Express Men of the Match: *Lions:* Ben Currie; *Raiders:* Dom Speakman.
Penalty count: 3-4; **Half-time:** 24-10; **Referee:** Jamie Bloem; **Attendance:** 403 *(at Park Lane, Sedgley Park).*

WHITEHAVEN 14 HALIFAX 36

WHITEHAVEN: 1 Tom Carr; 5 Shaun Ainscough; 4 Scott McAvoy; 3 Jessie Joe Nandye; 2 Craig Calvert; 14 Neil Thorman; 7 Cain Southernwood; 30 Jordan Hand; 15 Chris Smith; 10 Paul Jackson; 11 Lee Doran; 12 Lee Mitchell; 21 Larsen Marabe. Subs (all used): 9 James Newton; 8 Samir Tahraoui; 18 Jordan Burns; 13 Bradd Crellin.
Tries: Ainscough (21), Smith (25), Calvert (80);
Goals: Southernwood 1/3.
HALIFAX: 1 Ryan Fieldhouse; 21 Tom Saxton; 3 Steve Tyrer; 11 Dane Manning; 25 Gareth Potts; 6 Scott Murrell; 18 Ben Johnston; 10 Luke Ambler; 9 Ben Kaye; 12 Andy Bracek; 27 Ross Divorty; 15 Adam Robinson; 13 Luke Adamson. Subs (all used): 14 Paul Mennell; 8 Tony Tonks; 17 Ben Davies; 23 Callum Casey.
Tries: Manning (8, 44, 62), Johnston (13), Potts (47), Saxton (53), Mennell (59); **Goals:** Tyrer 4/7.
Rugby Leaguer & League Express Men of the Match: *Whitehaven:* Jessie Joe Nandye; *Halifax:* Scott Murrell.
Penalty count: 11-9; **Half-time:** 10-10;
Referee: Tom Crashley; **Attendance:** 751.

WORKINGTON TOWN 22 KEIGHLEY COUGARS 24

TOWN: 34 Jack Murphy; 3 Jason Mossop; 12 Jarrad Stack; 4 Andy Morris; 14 Kayle Connor; 16 Carl Forber; 7 Callum Phillips; 33 Gil Dudson; 6 Peter Lupton; 10 Marc Shackley; 11 Brett Phillips; 31 Connor Farrell; 17 Liam McAvoy. Subs (all used): 18 James Duerden; 19 Nathan Lucock; 32 Jordan James; 8 Kris Coward.
Tries: Morris (24), Mossop (31), C Phillips (34), James (48); **Goals:** Connor 3/4.
COUGARS: 1 James Craven; 2 Richie Barnett; 3 Elliott Cosgrove; 19 Danny Lawton; 5 Paul White; 6 Danny Jones; 7 Paul Handforth; 8 Andy Shickell; - Luke Haigh; 10 Sean Hesketh; 11 Josh Lynam; 12 Brendan Rawlins; 13 Ashley Lindsay. Subs (all used): 16 Jode Sheriffe; 18 Neil Cherryholme; 25 Lewis Graham; 27 Jack Lee.
Tries: Hesketh (17), Craven (61), Lynam (67, 76), Cosgrove (73); **Goals:** Jones 1/4, Handforth 1/1.
Rugby Leaguer & League Express Men of the Match: *Town:* Callum Phillips; *Cougars:* Josh Lynam.
Penalty count: 11-11; **Half-time:** 16-4;
Referee: Joe Cobb; **Attendance:** 746.

ROUND 6

Sunday 30th March 2014

NORTH WALES CRUSADERS 14 BATLEY BULLDOGS 26

CRUSADERS: 1 Tommy Johnson; 22 Adam Clay; 17 Stuart Reardon; 36 Declan Hulme; 2 Dan Birkett; 28 Craig White; 7 Jamie Dallimore; 8 Jonny Walker; 19 Karl Ashall; 10 Mark Offerdahl; 14 Stephen Wild; 30 Adam Lawton; 11 Toby Adamson. Subs (all used): 25 Owain Griffiths; 29 Steve Bannister; 16 Ryan MacDonald; 15 David Mills.
Tries: Johnson (15), Birkett (61), Adamson (77);
Goals: Johnson 1/3.
BULLDOGS: 1 Miles Greenwood; 26 Ben Blackmore; 28 Josh Griffin; 17 Lee Paterson; 29 Alex Brown; 11 John Davies; 7 Scott Leatherbarrow; 8 Byron Smith; 18 Luke Blake; 20 Adam Gledhill; 30 Charlie Martin; 12 Sam Scott; 13 Mark Applegarth. Subs (all used): 10 Alex Rowe; 14 Alistair Leak; 25 Nathan Mason; 31 Kyle Trout.
Tries: Gledhill (4), Greenwood (8, 22), Blake (45), Leak (68); **Goals:** Paterson 3/5.
Rugby Leaguer & League Express Men of the Match: *Crusaders:* Jonny Walker; *Bulldogs:* Alex Rowe.
Penalty count: 13-12; **Half-time:** 6-16;
Referee: Matthew Thomason; **Attendance:** 906.

DEWSBURY RAMS 38 WORKINGTON TOWN 16

RAMS: 31 Kieran Hyde; 2 Dale Morton; 3 Karl Pryce; 4 Shane Grady; 5 Greg Scott; 13 Aaron Brown; 7 Anthony Thackeray; 29 Ewan Dowes; 6 Tom Hemingway; 10 Ryan Hepworth; 12 Scott Hale; 26 Lucas Walshaw; 11 Rob Spicer. Subs (all used): 14 Ryan Wright; 32 Makali Aizue; 15 Tommy Gallagher; 8 Stephen Nash.
Tries: Grady (4), Thackeray (6, 77), Scott (35, 49), Pryce (38), Morton (43);
Goals: Hemingway 3/3, Hyde 2/5.
TOWN: 34 Jack Murphy; 3 Jason Mossop; 12 Jarrad Stack; 35 Jack Hughes; 14 Kayle Connor; 16 Carl Forber; 7 Callum Phillips; 8 Kris Coward; 6 Peter Lupton; 32 Jordan James; 11 Brett Phillips; 31 Connor Farrell; 17 Liam McAvoy. Subs (all used): 4 Andy Morris; 15 Daniel Rooney; 10 Marc Shackley; 33 Gil Dudson.
Tries: Dudson (22), Morris (55, 59); **Goals:** Connor 2/3.
Rugby Leaguer & League Express Men of the Match: *Rams:* Kieran Hyde; *Town:* Andy Morris.
Penalty count: 12-5; **Half-time:** 22-6;
Referee: Tom Crashley; **Attendance:** 747.

FEATHERSTONE ROVERS 36 SWINTON LIONS 22

ROVERS: 1 Ian Hardman; 2 Will Sharp; 4 Ben Hellewell; 3 Greg Worthington; 27 Etuate Uaisele; 19 Kyle Briggs; 7 Gareth Moore; 8 Steve Crossley; 23 Andy Kain; 10 Keegan Hirst; 18 Jamie Cording; 12 Tim Spears; 11 James Lockwood. Subs (all used): 30 Luke Teasdale; 15 Matty Dale; 13 Matt James; 22 James Mendeika.
Tries: Uaisele (9, 72), Sharp (39, 43), Worthington (46), Mendeika (50, 61); **Goals:** Moore 4/7.
LIONS: 5 Freddie Walker; 22 Kevin Penny; 4 Mick Nanyn; 12 Darren Hawkyard; 2 Ben Warrilow; 6 Anthony Bowman; 7 Ian Watson; 23 Paul Wood; 28 Brad Dwyer; 8 Luke Menzies; 13 James Brown; 24 Ben Currie; 15 Josh Barlow. Subs (all used): 27 Lewis Hulme; 25 Anthony England; 17 Zach Johnson; 19 Jacque Peet.
Tries: Nanyn (14), Barlow (22), Lewis Hulme (34), Penny (75); **Goals:** Nanyn 2/3, Watson 1/1.
Rugby Leaguer & League Express Men of the Match: *Rovers:* James Mendeika; *Lions:* Brad Dwyer.
Penalty count: 5-5; **Half-time:** 10-16;
Referee: Gareth Hewer; **Attendance:** 2,020.

HALIFAX 48 DONCASTER 6

HALIFAX: 1 Ryan Fieldhouse; 21 Tom Saxton; 3 Steve Tyrer; 16 Danny Cowling; 25 Gareth Potts; 6 Scott Murrell; 18 Ben Johnston; 10 Luke Ambler; 9 Ben Kaye; 12 Andy Bracek; 11 Dane Manning; 27 Ross Divorty; 13 Luke Adamson. Subs (all used): 14 Paul Mennell; 8 Tony Tonks; 17 Ben Davies; 23 Callum Casey.
Tries: Potts (13, 46), Divorty (23), Manning (33, 48), Murrell (44), Saxton (55), Fieldhouse (61), Davies (77);
Goals: Tyrer 5/8, Murrell 1/1.
DONCASTER: 5 Dave Scott; 4 Nev Morrison; 3 Liam Welham; 24 Joe Arundel; 2 Stewart Sanderson; 6 Paul Cooke; 7 Danny Nicklas; 14 Russ Spiers; 15 Scott Spaven; 21 Matt Carbutt; 29 Liam Kent; 12 Michael Kelly; 13 Mike Emmett. Subs (all used): 26 Matty Wildie; 11 Lee Waterman; 8 Mark Castle; 18 Ryan Wilson.
Try: Arundel (5); **Goals:** Sanderson 1/2.
Sin bin: Morrison (53) - shoulder charge.
Rugby Leaguer & League Express Men of the Match: *Halifax:* Ben Johnston; *Doncaster:* Joe Arundel.
Penalty count: 9-6; **Half-time:** 16-6;
Referee: Joe Cobb; **Attendance:** 1,482.

KEIGHLEY COUGARS 24 SHEFFIELD EAGLES 42

COUGARS: 21 Jesse Sheriffe; 2 Richie Barnett; 3 Elliott Cosgrove; 19 Danny Lawton; 5 Paul White; 6 Danny Jones; 7 Paul Handforth; 8 Andy Shickell; - Luke Haigh; 10 Sean Hesketh; 11 Josh Lynam; 12 Brendan Rawlins; 15 Scott Law. Subs (all used): 16 Jode Sheriffe; 18 Neil Cherryholme; 27 Jack Lee; 32 Ross Peltier.
Tries: Law (13, 80), Lynam (47), Shickell (65);
Goals: Jones 4/4.
EAGLES: 1 Quentin Laulu-Togagae; 2 Scott Turner; 3 Menzie Yere; 16 Duane Straugheir; 5 Misi Taulapapa; 6 Pat Walker; 7 Dominic Brambani; 18 Tom Lillycrop; 24 Gareth Owen; 10 Mitchell Stringer; 11 Michael Knowles; 12 Peter Green; 22 Will Hope. Subs (all used): 14 James Davey; 15 Matt Garside; 4 Lelauloto Tagaloa; 26 Jordan Burke.
Tries: Straugheir (4), Laulu-Togagae (17, 50), Knowles (21), Turner (42), Yere (44), Walker (53), Garside (70); **Goals:** Brambani 5/8.
Rugby Leaguer & League Express Men of the Match: *Cougars:* Ross Peltier; *Eagles:* Pat Walker.
Penalty count: 7-6; **Half-time:** 6-14;
Referee: Dave Merrick; **Attendance:** 927.

LEIGH CENTURIONS 34 ROCHDALE HORNETS 22

CENTURIONS: 1 Gregg McNally; 22 Adam Higson; 31 Cameron Pitman; 4 Tom Armstrong; 15 Liam Kay; 6 Martyn Ridyard; 7 Ryan Brierley; 8 Tom Spencer; 9 Bob Beswick; 18 Jamie Acton; 30 Kurt Haggerty; 12 Tommy Goulden; 13 Sam Barlow. Subs (all used): 10 Oliver Wilkes; 14 Sean Penkywicz; 20 Andy Thornley; 29 Jake Emmitt.
Tries: Kay (1, 15), McNally (26), Brierley (37, 53), Armstrong (78); **Goals:** Ridyard 5/7.
Sin bin: Acton (60) - fighting.
HORNETS: 1 Wayne English; 2 Gareth Langley; 4 Daniel Davies; 22 Mike Ratu; 29 Sam Te'o; 6 Paul Crook; 17 Ryan Millard; 8 John Cookson; 18 James Tilley; 10 Warren Thompson; 11 Chris Baines; 13 Jordan Case; 24 Tony Suffolk. Subs (all used): 9 Lewis Sheridan; 25 Steve Marsh; 26 Adam Bowman; 28 Alex Clare.
Tries: Langley (31), Bowman (48), Baines (64), Davies (70); **Goals:** Crook 3/4.
Sin bin: Suffolk (60) - fighting.
On report: Langley (79) - alleged tripping.
Rugby Leaguer & League Express Men of the Match: *Centurions:* Tommy Goulden; *Hornets:* James Tilley.
Penalty count: 10-4; **Half-time:** 22-4;
Referee: Jamie Bloem; **Attendance:** 1,756.

WHITEHAVEN 37 BARROW RAIDERS 12

WHITEHAVEN: 1 Tom Carr; 5 Shaun Ainscough; 3 Jessie Joe Nandye; 4 Scott McAvoy; 2 Craig Calvert; 6 Chris Taylor; 7 Cain Southernwood; 20 Jordan Hand; 9 James Newton; 10 Paul Jackson; 11 Lee Doran; 12 Lee Mitchell; 21 Larsen Marabe. Subs (all used): 15 Chris Smith; 8 Samir Tahraoui; 29 Carl Forster; 13 Bradd Crellin.
Tries: Carr (13, 71), Doran (23), Nandye (30), Calvert (52), Ainscough (62, 72);
Goals: Southernwood 3/6, Carr 1/1;
Field goal: Taylor (79).
RAIDERS: 26 Ryan Shaw; 2 Scott Turner; 3 Aaron Low; 4 Max Wiper; 5 Dalton Grant; 6 Dom Speakman; 7 Liam Campbell; 18 Jack Morrison; 14 Aaron Lloyd; 17 Andrew Dawson; 11 Liam Harrison; 13 Dan Toal; 15 Danny Jones. Subs (all used): 9 Nathan Mossop; 24 Joe Bullock; 8 Joe Burke; 10 Jamie Butler.
Tries: Harrison (37), Burke (68); **Goals:** Shaw 2/2.
Rugby Leaguer & League Express Men of the Match: *Whitehaven:* Tom Carr; *Raiders:* Liam Harrison.
Penalty count: 4-9; **Half-time:** 16-6;
Referee: Chris Leatherbarrow; **Attendance:** 721.

ROUND 7

Sunday 13th April 2014

BATLEY BULLDOGS 29 KEIGHLEY COUGARS 20

BULLDOGS: 1 Miles Greenwood; 26 Ben Blackmore; 17 Lee Paterson; 28 Josh Griffin; 29 Alex Brown; - Simon Brown; 7 Scott Leatherbarrow; 8 Byron Smith; 18 Luke Blake; 20 Adam Gledhill; 11 John Davies; 12 Sam Scott; 13 Mark Applegarth. Subs (all used): 31 Kyle Trout; 10 Alex Rowe; - Jacob Fairbank; 19 Joe Chandler.
Tries: Scott (34), Blackmore (40), Griffin (45), Leatherbarrow (56), Greenwood (76);
Goals: Paterson 4/5; **Field goal:** S Brown (67).
COUGARS: 1 James Craven; 2 Richie Barnett; 3 Elliott Cosgrove; 4 James Haley; 5 Paul White; 6 Danny Jones; 7 Paul Handforth; 15 Scott Law; - Luke Haigh; 10 Sean Hesketh; 11 Josh Lynam; 25 Lewis Graham; 12 Brendan Rawlins. Subs (all used): 14 Paul March; 24 Matthew Bailey; 18 Neil Cherryholme; 32 Ross Peltier.
Tries: White (14, 51), Graham (22), Haley (80);
Goals: Jones 2/4.
Rugby Leaguer & League Express Men of the Match: *Bulldogs:* Miles Greenwood; *Cougars:* James Haley.
Penalty count: 8-9; **Half-time:** 10-12;
Referee: Warren Turley; **Attendance:** 640.

BARROW RAIDERS 18 FEATHERSTONE ROVERS 38

RAIDERS: 26 Ryan Shaw; 22 James Nixon; 4 Max Wiper; 3 Aaron Low; 5 Dalton Grant; 6 Dom Speakman; 7 Liam Campbell; 23 Adam Walne; - Mick Govin; 15 Danny Jones; 11 Liam Harrison; 13 Dan Toal; 20 Stuart Howarth. Subs (all used): 17 Andrew Dawson; 24 Joe Bullock; 12 Michael Dengate; 18 Jack Morrison.
Tries: Grant (24, 44), Wiper (36), Shaw (77);
Goals: Shaw 1/4.
ROVERS: 1 Ian Hardman; 27 Etuate Uaisele; 3 Greg Worthington; 22 James Mendeika; 2 Will Sharp; 23 Andy Kain; 7 Gareth Moore; 8 Steve Crossley; 9 Andy Ellis; 10 Keegan Hirst; 18 Jamie Cording; 12 Tim Spears; 11 James Lockwood. Subs (all used): 14 George Flanagan; 15 Matty Dale; 13 Matt James; 19 Kyle Briggs.
Tries: Moore (5), Kain (13), James (31), Worthington (46), Hardman (57, 62), Sharp (66), Ellis (75); **Goals:** Moore 3/8.

Championship 2014 - Round by Round

Rugby Leaguer & League Express Men of the Match: *Raiders:* Stuart Howarth; *Rovers:* Gareth Moore.
Penalty count: 6-7; **Half-time:** 10-12;
Referee: Jamie Bloem; **Attendance:** 1,075.

DONCASTER 20 NORTH WALES CRUSADERS 12

DONCASTER: 5 Dave Scott; 4 Nev Morrison; 22 Ben Crooks; 24 Joe Arundel; 2 Stewart Sanderson; 6 Paul Cooke; 23 Richard Wilkinson; 14 Russ Spiers; 26 Matty Wildie; 28 Jay Pitts; 29 Liam Kent; 25 Alex Starling; 13 Mike Emmett. Subs (all used): 16 Craig Robinson; 8 Mark Castle; 11 Lee Waterman; 17 Grant Edwards.
Tries: Morrison (37), Waterman (44), Crooks (63, 73);
Goals: Sanderson 2/4.
CRUSADERS: 1 Tommy Johnson; 22 Adam Clay; 17 Stuart Reardon; 3 Christiaan Roets; 5 Rob Massam; 7 Jamie Dallimore; 28 Craig White; 8 Jonny Walker; 9 Craig Ashall; 10 Mark Offerdahl; 12 Gary Middlehurst; 13 Jono Smith; 14 Stephen Wild. Subs (all used): 15 David Mills; 19 Karl Ashall; 21 Simon Stephens; 26 Matt Reid.
Tries: Middlehurst (55, 66); **Goals:** Johnson 2/2.
Sin bin: Smith (62) - professional foul.
Rugby Leaguer & League Express Men of the Match: *Doncaster:* Lee Waterman; *Crusaders:* Gary Middlehurst.
Penalty count: 11-6; **Half-time:** 6-0;
Referee: Dave Merrick; **Attendance:** 574.

HALIFAX 28 LEIGH CENTURIONS 36

HALIFAX: 1 Ryan Fieldhouse; 21 Tom Saxton; 3 Steve Tyrer; 4 Ben Heaton; 25 Gareth Potts; 6 Scott Murrell; 14 Paul Mennell; 10 Luke Ambler; 9 Ben Kaye; 12 Andy Bracek; 11 Dane Manning; 27 Ross Divorty; 13 Luke Adamson. Subs (all used): 19 Keith Holden; 8 Tony Tonks; 17 Ben Davies; 23 Callum Casey.
Tries: Bracek (15), Divorty (21), Fieldhouse (24, 27), Heaton (75); **Goals:** Tyrer 4/5.
Sin bin: Bracek (29) - fighting; Tonks (37) - fighting.
CENTURIONS: 1 Gregg McNally; 22 Adam Higson; 31 Cameron Pitman; 4 Tom Armstrong; 15 Liam Kay; 6 Martyn Ridyard; 7 Ryan Brierley; 8 Tom Spencer; 14 Sean Penkywicz; 10 Oliver Wilkes; 11 Matt Sarsfield; 12 Tommy Goulden; 35 Sam Hopkins. Subs (all used): 9 Bob Beswick; 18 Jamie Acton; 13 Sam Barlow; 29 Jake Emmitt.
Tries: Barlow (39), Goulden (43), Sarsfield (51), Brierley (56, 69), Armstrong (66); **Goals:** Ridyard 6/6.
Dismissal: Barlow (51) - punching Potts.
Sin bin: Barlow (29) - fighting; Acton (37) - fighting.
Rugby Leaguer & League Express Men of the Match: *Halifax:* Paul Mennell; *Centurions:* Ryan Brierley.
Penalty count: 6-6; **Half-time:** 24-6;
Referee: Chris Leatherbarrow; **Attendance:** 2,282.

ROCHDALE HORNETS 20 WHITEHAVEN 16

HORNETS: 1 Wayne English; 2 Gareth Langley; 4 Daniel Davies; - Gary Wheeler; 9 Lewis Sheridan; 14 Sean Casey; 17 Ryan Millard; 28 Anthony Walker; 6 Paul Crook; 24 Tony Suffolk; 11 Chris Baines; 29 Alex Clare; 18 James Tilley. Subs (all used): 8 John Cookson; 30 Greg Richards; 13 Jordan Case; 23 James Dandy.
Tries: Langley (28, 58), Sheridan (46), Millard (62);
Goals: Crook 2/4.
WHITEHAVEN: 1 Tom Carr; 5 Shaun Ainscough; 4 Scott McAvoy; 18 Jordan Burns; 2 Craig Calvert; 6 Chris Taylor; 7 Cain Southernwood; 10 Paul Jackson; 9 James Newton; 20 Jordan Hand; 11 Lee Doran; 12 Lee Mitchell; 21 Larsen Marabe. Subs (all used): 8 Samir Tahraoui; 13 Bradd Crellin; 14 Neil Thorman; 30 Carl Forster.
Tries: Mitchell (20), Southernwood (42), Calvert (78);
Goals: Southernwood 2/3.
Rugby Leaguer & League Express Men of the Match: *Hornets:* Wayne English; *Whitehaven:* Samir Tahraoui.
Penalty count: 5-5; **Half-time:** 4-6;
Referee: George Stokes; **Attendance:** 770.

SWINTON LIONS 37 DEWSBURY RAMS 31

LIONS: 1 Ritchie Hawkyard; 22 Kevin Penny; 19 Jacque Peet; 11 Danny Halliwell; 2 Ben Warrilow; 23 Gareth O'Brien; 7 Ian Watson; 16 Mike Morrison; 9 Andy Ackers; 8 Luke Menzies; 3 Kash Watkins; 12 Darren Hawkyard; 13 James Brown. Subs (all used): 27 Lewis Hulme; 17 Zach Johnson; 24 Glenn Riley; 15 Josh Barlow.
Tries: Halliwell (7), Brown (20), Penny (27, 51), Ackers (64), Menzies (79); **Goals:** O'Brien 6/6;
Field goal: O'Brien (76).
RAMS: 31 Kieran Hyde; 2 Dale Morton; 3 Karl Pryce; 4 Shane Grady; 5 Greg Scott; 6 Tom Hemingway; 7 Anthony Thackeray; 32 Makali Aizue; 9 Wayne Godwin; 29 Ewan Dowes; 10 Ryan Hepworth; 12 Scott Hale; 11 Rob Spicer. Subs (all used): 15 Tommy Gallagher; 14 Ryan Wright; 8 Stephen Nash; 17 Matthew Haggarty.
Tries: Grady (4, 17, 46), Godwin (13), Gallagher (58);
Goals: Hemingway 5/6; **Field goal:** Hyde (72).
Rugby Leaguer & League Express Men of the Match: *Lions:* James Brown; *Rams:* Shane Grady.
Penalty count: 5-8; **Half-time:** 18-16;
Referee: Andrew Sweet; **Attendance:** 412.

WORKINGTON TOWN 14 SHEFFIELD EAGLES 24

TOWN: 34 Jack Murphy; 3 Jason Mossop; 32 Anthony Gelling; 14 Kayle Connor; 1 Brett Carter; 30 Lewis Tierney; 16 Carl Forber; 8 Kris Coward; 9 Graeme Mattinson; 10 Marc Shackley; 11 Brett Phillips; 31 Connor Farrell; 17 Liam McAvoy. Subs: 13 Karl Olstrum; 15 Daniel Rooney; 12 Jarrad Stack; 18 James Duerden (not used).
Tries: Farrell (19), Mossop (58, 66); **Goals:** Connor 1/3.
EAGLES: 1 Quentin Laulu-Togagae; 5 Misi Taulapapa; 4 Lelauloto Tagaloa; 3 Menzie Yere; 2 Scott Turner; 6 Pat Walker; 7 Dominic Brambani; 18 Tom Lillycrop; 9 Andrew Henderson; 10 Mitchell Stringer; 12 Peter Green; 15 Matt Garside; 11 Michael Knowles. Subs (all used): 24 Gareth Owen; 26 Jordan Burke; 16 Duane Straugheir; 27 Peter Aspinall.
Tries: Brambani (2), Garside (28, 79), Straugheir (62);
Goals: Brambani 4/4.
Sin bin: Owen (42) - professional foul.
Rugby Leaguer & League Express Men of the Match: *Town:* Anthony Gelling; *Eagles:* Matt Garside.
Penalty count: 9-10; **Half-time:** 6-12;
Referee: Peter Brooke; **Attendance:** 451.

ROUND 8

Friday 18th April 2014

LEIGH CENTURIONS 60 SWINTON LIONS 24

CENTURIONS: 1 Gregg McNally; 22 Adam Higson; 31 Cameron Pitman; 4 Tom Armstrong; 15 Liam Kay; 6 Martyn Ridyard; 7 Ryan Brierley; 29 Jake Emmitt; 14 Sean Penkywicz; 18 Jamie Acton; 30 Kurt Haggerty; 12 Tommy Goulden; 13 Sam Barlow. Subs (all used): 8 Tom Spencer; 9 Bob Beswick; 10 Oliver Wilkes; 35 Sam Hopkins.
Tries: McNally (6, 14), Armstrong (17, 51), Hopkins (27), Haggerty (30, 76), Kay (36, 61, 68), Pitman (64); **Goals:** Ridyard 8/11.
Dismissal: Higson (75) - fighting.
On report: Brawl (75).
LIONS: 1 Ritchie Hawkyard; 22 Kevin Penny; 23 Gene Ormsby; 11 Danny Halliwell; 5 Freddie Walker; 6 Anthony Bowman; 7 Ian Watson; 8 Luke Menzies; 9 Andy Ackers; 16 Mike Morrison; 13 James Brown; 12 Darren Hawkyard; 29 Liam Hulme. Subs (all used): 27 Lewis Hulme; 20 Mark Thomas; 17 Zach Johnson; 3 Kash Watkins.
Tries: Penny (11, 34), D Hawkyard (74), R Hawkyard (79); **Goals:** Watson 4/4.
Dismissal: Johnson (75) - fighting.
On report: Brawl (75).
Rugby Leaguer & League Express Men of the Match: *Centurions:* Gregg McNally; *Lions:* Kevin Penny.
Penalty count: 10-6; **Half-time:** 34-12;
Referee: Adam Gill; **Attendance:** 2,219.

NORTH WALES CRUSADERS 16 ROCHDALE HORNETS 42

CRUSADERS: 1 Tommy Johnson; 22 Adam Clay; 17 Stuart Reardon; 3 Christiaan Roets; 5 Rob Massam; 6 Andy Moulsdale; 7 Jamie Dallimore; 8 Jonny Walker; 9 Craig Ashall; 10 Mark Offerdahl; 11 Toby Adamson; 12 Gary Middlehurst; 14 Stephen Wild. Subs (all used): 13 Jono Smith; 19 Karl Ashall; 21 Simon Stephens; 15 David Mills.
Tries: Johnson (19), Offerdahl (40), K Ashall (48);
Goals: Johnson 2/3.
Sin bin: Walker (27) - dissent; Smith (48) - fighting.
HORNETS: 1 Wayne English; 2 Gareth Langley; 4 Daniel Davies; 22 Mike Ratu; 29 Shaun Robinson; 6 Paul Crook; 17 Ryan Millard; 10 Warren Thompson; 14 Sean Casey; 25 Steve Marsh; 11 Chris Baines; 24 Tony Suffolk; 13 Jordan Case. Subs (all used): 26 Adam Bowman; 16 Liam Gilchrist; 9 Lewis Sheridan; 28 Connor Dwyer.
Tries: Crook (10), Baines (28), Ratu (35, 58), Bowman (45), Langley (64); **Goals:** Crook 9/9.
Sin bin: Bowman (48) - fighting.
Rugby Leaguer & League Express Men of the Match: *Crusaders:* Tommy Johnson; *Hornets:* Paul Crook.
Penalty count: 12-12; **Half-time:** 10-20;
Referee: Joe Cobb; **Attendance:** 835.

BARROW RAIDERS 18 HALIFAX 32

RAIDERS: - Niall Evalds; 21 Mike Backhouse; 26 Ryan Shaw; 4 Max Wiper; 5 Dalton Grant; 6 Dom Speakman; 7 Liam Campbell; 17 Andrew Dawson; - Mick Govin; 24 Joe Bullock; 11 Liam Harrison; 13 Dan Toal; 15 Danny Jones. Subs (all used): 3 Aaron Low; 12 Michael Dengate; 16 Matty Palmer; 18 Jack Morrison.
Tries: Evalds (12, 21, 77); **Goals:** Shaw 3/3.
HALIFAX: 1 Ryan Fieldhouse; 25 Gareth Potts; 16 Danny Cowling; 3 Steve Tyrer; 21 Tom Saxton; 6 Scott Murrell; 18 Ben Johnston; 8 Tony Tonks; 9 Ben Kaye; 10 Luke Ambler; 27 Ross Divorty; 11 Dane Manning; 13 Luke Adamson. Subs (all used): 14 Paul Mennell; 17 Ben Davies; 12 Andy Bracek; 24 Sam Brooks.
Tries: Cowling (17, 26), Johnston (38), Fieldhouse (43, 55), Mennell (57); **Goals:** Tyrer 4/6.
Rugby Leaguer & League Express Men of the Match: *Raiders:* Mick Govin; *Halifax:* Ben Johnston.
Penalty count: 5-8; **Half-time:** 12-16;
Referee: Jamie Bloem; **Attendance:** 1,169.

WHITEHAVEN 22 WORKINGTON TOWN 16

WHITEHAVEN: 1 Tom Carr; 5 Shaun Ainscough; 4 Scott McAvoy; 3 Jessie Joe Nandye; 2 Craig Calvert; 6 Chris Taylor; 7 Cain Southernwood; 8 Samir Tahraoui; 9 James Newton; 10 Paul Jackson; 11 Lee Doran; 12 Lee Mitchell; 21 Larsen Marabe. Subs (all used): 15 Chris Smith; 18 Jordan Burns; 22 James Robinson; 13 Bradd Crellin.
Tries: Doran (6), Marabe (31), Nandye (74, 78);
Goals: Southernwood 3/4.
Sin bin: Tahraoui (28) - late challenge on Mattinson.
TOWN: 30 Lewis Tierney; 34 Jack Murphy; 3 Jason Mossop; 14 Kayle Connor; 1 Brett Carter; 16 Carl Forber; 7 Callum Phillips; 8 Kris Coward; 9 Graeme Mattinson; 10 Marc Shackley; 11 Brett Phillips; 31 Connor Farrell; 13 Karl Olstrum. Subs (all used): 17 Liam McAvoy; 15 Daniel Rooney; 12 Jarrad Stack; 6 Peter Lupton.
Tries: Forber (18), Farrell (33), Mossop (36);
Goals: Connor 0/1, Forber 2/2.
Sin bin: Mattinson (28) - retaliation.
Rugby Leaguer & League Express Men of the Match: *Whitehaven:* Samir Tahraoui; *Town:* Connor Farrell.
Penalty count: 9-8; **Half-time:** 12-16;
Referee: Dave Merrick; **Attendance:** 1,401.

DEWSBURY RAMS 43 BATLEY BULLDOGS 10

RAMS: 31 Kieran Hyde; 2 Dale Morton; 3 Karl Pryce; 4 Shane Grady; 5 Greg Scott; 6 Tom Hemingway; 7 Anthony Thackeray; 29 Ewan Dowes; 9 Wayne Godwin; 10 Ryan Hepworth; 11 Rob Spicer; 12 Scott Hale; 16 Josh Tonks. Subs (all used): 22 Jordan Grayston; 8 Stephen Nash; 17 Matthew Haggarty; 15 Tommy Gallagher.
Tries: Grady (2), Scott (28, 51), Godwin (33), Gallagher (37), Pryce (69), Hepworth (75);
Goals: Hemingway 7/9; **Field goal:** Hyde (39).
BULLDOGS: 1 Miles Greenwood; 2 Vinny Finigan; 17 Lee Paterson; 28 Josh Griffin; 29 Alex Brown; - Simon Brown; 7 Scott Leatherbarrow; 8 Byron Smith; 18 Luke Blake; 20 Adam Gledhill; 11 John Davies; 12 Sam Scott; 31 Kyle Trout. Subs (all used): 14 Alistair Leak; 10 Alex Rowe; 16 Brad Brennan; 19 Joe Chandler.
Tries: Davies (10), A Brown (23); **Goals:** Paterson 1/2.
Rugby Leaguer & League Express Men of the Match: *Rams:* Tom Hemingway; *Bulldogs:* Alex Rowe.
Penalty count: 10-5; **Half-time:** 25-10;
Referee: Matthew Thomason; **Attendance:** 1,999.

FEATHERSTONE ROVERS 36 KEIGHLEY COUGARS 12

ROVERS: 1 Ian Hardman; 2 Will Sharp; 22 James Mendeika; 3 Greg Worthington; 27 Etuate Uaisele; 23 Andy Kain; 7 Gareth Moore; 8 Steve Crossley; 9 Andy Ellis; 10 Keegan Hirst; 18 Jamie Cording; 12 Tim Spears; 11 James Lockwood. Subs (all used): 14 George Flanagan; 15 Matty Dale; 13 Matt James; 19 Kyle Briggs.
Tries: Uaisele (16), Worthington (23), Hardman (25), Kain (28), Sharp (43), Mendeika (54, 64);
Goals: Moore 4/7.
COUGARS: 21 Jesse Sheriffe; 2 Richie Barnett; 19 Danny Lawton; 4 James Haley; 5 Paul White; 6 Danny Jones; 7 Paul Handforth; 16 Jode Sheriffe; - Luke Haigh; 10 Sean Hesketh; 11 Josh Lynam; 12 Brendan Rawlins; 14 Paul March. Subs (all used): 27 Jack Lee; 15 Scott Law; 18 Neil Cherryholme; 3 Elliott Cosgrove.
Tries: White (33), Jones (78); **Goals:** Jones 2/2.
On report: March (36) - alleged dangerous contact.
Rugby Leaguer & League Express Men of the Match: *Rovers:* James Mendeika; *Cougars:* Jack Lee.
Penalty count: 5-7; **Half-time:** 22-6;
Referee: Dave Sharpe; **Attendance:** 2,056.

Sunday 20th April 2014

SHEFFIELD EAGLES 34 DONCASTER 42

EAGLES: 1 Quentin Laulu-Togagae; 23 Jonathan Ford; 2 Scott Turner; 16 Duane Straugheir; 5 Misi Taulapapa; 6 Pat Walker; 7 Dominic Brambani; 21 Jack Blagbrough; 9 Andrew Henderson; 10 Mitchell Stringer; 15 Matt Garside; 27 Peter Aspinall; 12 Peter Green. Subs (all used): 18 Tom Lillycrop; 26 Jordan Burke; 28 Tom Ashton; 4 Lelauloto Tagaloa.
Tries: Straugheir (3, 27), Brambani (20), Garside (34, 37), Tagaloa (68); **Goals:** Brambani 5/6.
DONCASTER: 5 Dave Scott; 22 Jason Crookes; 24 Joe Arundel; 3 Liam Welham; 2 Stewart Sanderson; 6 Paul Cooke; 26 Matty Wildie; 28 Chris Green; 9 Kyle Kesik; 14 Russ Spiers; 29 Liam Kent; 25 Alex Starling; 13 Mike Emmett. Subs (all used): 16 Craig Robinson; 8 Mark Castle; 11 Lee Waterman; 17 Grant Edwards.
Tries: Wildie (10, 45), Scott (23), Emmett (48), Edwards (58), Kent (61), Starling (73);
Goals: Sanderson 7/7.
Sin bin: Emmett (32) - obstruction.
Rugby Leaguer & League Express Men of the Match: *Eagles:* Quentin Laulu-Togagae; *Doncaster:* Paul Cooke.
Penalty count: 3-3; **Half-time:** 28-12;
Referee: Gareth Hewer; **Attendance:** 1,018.

ROUND 2

Sunday 27th April 2014

WHITEHAVEN 0 NORTH WALES CRUSADERS 34

WHITEHAVEN: 1 Tom Carr; 5 Shaun Ainscough; 4 Scott McAvoy; 3 Jessie Joe Nandye; 2 Craig Calvert; 26 Brett Seymour; 7 Cain Southernwood; 8 Samir Tahraoui; 9 James Newton; 10 Paul Jackson; 11 Lee Doran; 12 Lee Mitchell; 6 Chris Taylor. Subs (all used): 14 Neil Thorman; 30 Carl Forster; 13 Bradd Crellin; 20 Jordan Hand.
CRUSADERS: 1 Tommy Johnson; 22 Adam Clay; 17 Stuart Reardon; 3 Christiaan Roets; 5 Rob Massam; 6 Andy Moulsdale; 20 Jamie Durbin; 8 Jonny Walker; 19 Karl Ashall; 10 Mark Offerdahl; 12 Gary Middlehurst; 14 Stephen Wild; 9 Craig Ashall. Subs (all used): 25 Owain Griffiths; 29 Steve Bannister; 30 Sebastien Martins; 13 Jono Smith.
Tries: Massam (17, 23, 54), Durbin (20), Reardon (43), Clay (76); **Goals:** Johnson 5/8.
Rugby Leaguer & League Express Men of the Match: *Whitehaven:* James Newton; *Crusaders:* Jamie Durbin.
Penalty count: 6-6; **Half-time:** 0-20;
Referee: Tom Crashley; **Attendance:** 621.

ROUND 9

Sunday 4th May 2014

BATLEY BULLDOGS 10 WHITEHAVEN 30

BULLDOGS: 1 Miles Greenwood; 26 Ben Blackmore; 17 Lee Paterson; 3 Alex Bretherton; 29 Alex Brown; - Simon

Brown; 7 Scott Leatherbarrow; 10 Alex Rowe; 18 Luke Blake; 20 Adam Gledhill; 19 Joe Chandler; 11 John Davies; 31 Kyle Trout. Subs (all used): 8 Byron Smith; 9 Anthony Nicholson; 30 Charlie Martin; 6 Ben Black.
Tries: Paterson (3), Martin (71); **Goals:** Paterson 1/2.
WHITEHAVEN: 5 Shaun Ainscough; 18 Jordan Burns; 6 Chris Taylor; 3 Jessie Joe Nandye; 2 Craig Calvert; 26 Brett Seymour; 7 Cain Southernwood; 10 Paul Jackson; 9 James Newton; 20 Jordan Hand; 12 Lee Mitchell; 4 Scott McAvoy; 11 Lee Doran. Subs (all used): 14 Neil Thorman; 13 Bradd Crellin; 8 Samir Tahraoui; 22 James Robinson.
Tries: Ainscough (9, 46), Taylor (19), Calvert (32), Hand (60); **Goals:** Southernwood 5/5.
Rugby Leaguer & League Express Men of the Match: *Bulldogs:* Alex Brown; *Whitehaven:* Paul Jackson.
Penalty count: 6-7; **Half-time:** 4-18;
Referee: Dave Merrick; **Attendance:** 506.

NORTH WALES CRUSADERS 6 SHEFFIELD EAGLES 56

CRUSADERS: 1 Tommy Johnson; 22 Adam Clay; 17 Stuart Reardon; 3 Christiaan Roets; 5 Rob Massam; 6 Andy Moulsdale; 20 Jamie Durbin; 8 Jonny Walker; 19 Karl Ashall; 10 Mark Offerdahl; 12 Garry Middlehurst; 14 Stephen Wild; 9 Craig Ashall. Subs (all used): 13 Jono Smith; 30 Sebastien Martins; 29 Steve Bannister; 25 Owain Griffiths.
Try: Griffiths (42); **Goals:** Johnson 1/1.
EAGLES: 1 Quentin Laulu-Togagae; 2 Scott Turner; 3 Menzie Yere; 5 Misi Taulapapa; 26 Jordan Burke; 6 Pat Walker; 7 Dominic Brambani; 18 Tom Lillycrop; 9 Andrew Henderson; 10 Mitchell Stringer; 15 Matt Garside; 27 Peter Aspinall; 16 Duane Straugheir. Subs (all used): 24 Gareth Owen; 12 Peter Green; 28 Tom Ashton; 21 Jack Blagbrough.
Tries: Laulu-Togagae (6, 56, 70), Turner (29, 36, 48), Taulapapa (32), Owen (61), Walker (63), Yere (77);
Goals: Brambani 8/10.
Rugby Leaguer & League Express Men of the Match: *Crusaders:* Christiaan Roets;
Eagles: Quentin Laulu-Togagae.
Penalty count: 8-4; **Half-time:** 0-22;
Referee: Chris Kendall; **Attendance:** 785.

DONCASTER 30 BARROW RAIDERS 28

DONCASTER: 5 Dave Scott; 4 Nev Morrison; 2 Stewart Sanderson; 11 Lee Waterman; 3 Liam Welham; 6 Paul Cooke; 26 Matty Wildie; 28 Liam Watts; 9 Kyle Kesik; 21 Matt Carbutt; 29 Liam Kent; 25 Alex Starling; 13 Mike Emmett. Subs (all used): 16 Craig Robinson; 18 Ryan Wilson; 17 Grant Edwards; 15 Scott Spaven.
Tries: Waterman (20, 34, 38), Scott (67, 77);
Goals: Sanderson 5/5.
RAIDERS: 29 Niall Evalds; 21 Mike Backhouse; 26 Ryan Shaw; 4 Max Wiper; 5 Dalton Grant; 6 Dom Speakman; 7 Liam Campbell; 8 Joe Burke; 27 Mick Govin; 17 Andrew Dawson; 11 Liam Harrison; 13 Dan Toal; 15 Danny Jones. Subs (all used): 14 Aaron Lloyd; 3 Aaron Low; 18 Jack Morrison; 24 Joe Bullock.
Tries: Govin (7), Wiper (14), Evalds (27), Shaw (42, 51);
Goals: Shaw 4/5.
Rugby Leaguer & League Express Men of the Match: *Doncaster:* Lee Waterman; *Raiders:* Mick Govin.
Penalty count: 10-3; **Half-time:** 18-16;
Referee: Jamie Bloem; **Attendance:** 573.

FEATHERSTONE ROVERS 10 LEIGH CENTURIONS 29

ROVERS: 1 Ian Hardman; 2 Will Sharp; 22 James Mendeika; 3 Greg Worthington; 4 Ben Hellewell; 19 Kyle Briggs; 23 Andy Kain; 8 Steve Crossley; 9 Andy Ellis; 10 Keegan Hirst; 18 Jamie Cording; 12 Tim Spears; 11 James Lockwood. Subs (all used): 14 George Flanagan; 6 Jack Bussey; 25 Gavin Bennion; 31 Shaun Pick.
Tries: Hellewell (11), Kain (76); **Goals:** Briggs 1/2.
Dismissal: Sharp (69) - fighting.
On report: Spears (60) - alleged high tackle on McNally; Brawl (69).
CENTURIONS: 1 Gregg McNally; 22 Adam Higson; 31 Cameron Pitman; 4 Tom Armstrong; 15 Liam Kay; 6 Martyn Ridyard; 7 Ryan Brierley; 8 Tom Spencer; 9 Bob Beswick; 35 Sam Hopkins; 11 Matt Sarsfield; 30 Kurt Haggerty; 29 Jake Emmitt. Subs (all used): 14 Sean Penkywicz; 18 Jamie Acton; 10 Oliver Wilkes; 13 Sam Barlow.
Tries: Kay (18, 61), Pitman (48), McNally (51), Brierley (67); **Goals:** Ridyard 4/5;
Field goal: Brierley (65).
Dismissal: Sarsfield (69) - fighting.
On report: Brawl (69).
Rugby Leaguer & League Express Men of the Match: *Rovers:* Jamie Cording; *Centurions:* Kurt Haggerty.
Penalty count: 5-8; **Half-time:** 4-4;
Referee: Chris Leatherbarrow; **Attendance:** 3,230.

KEIGHLEY COUGARS 40 DEWSBURY RAMS 20

COUGARS: 1 James Craven; 2 Richie Barnett; 19 Danny Lawton; 22 Daley Williams; 5 Paul White; 6 Danny Jones; 7 Paul Handforth; 16 Jode Sheriffe; 34 Luke Haigh; 10 Sean Hesketh; 11 Josh Lynam; 12 Brendan Rawlins; 14 Paul March. Subs (all used): 15 Scott Law; 18 Neil Cherryholme; 27 Jack Lee; 32 Ross Peltier.
Tries: Barnett (8, 26, 48), Haigh (14, 80), Peltier (30), White (63); **Goals:** Jones 6/9.
RAMS: 31 Kieran Hyde; 2 Dale Morton; 3 Karl Pryce; 4 Shane Grady; 5 Greg Scott; 6 Tom Hemingway; 7 Anthony Thackeray; 29 Ewan Dowes; 9 Wayne Godwin; 10 Ryan Hepworth; 11 Rob Spicer; 12 Scott Hale; 16 Josh Tonks. Subs (all used): 8 Stephen Nash; 15 Tommy Gallagher; 17 Matthew Haggarty; 22 Jordan Grayston.
Tries: Scott (38), Gallagher (52), Hyde (55), Nash (78);
Goals: Hemingway 2/4.
Rugby Leaguer & League Express Men of the Match: *Cougars:* Richie Barnett; *Rams:* Kieran Hyde.
Penalty count: 6-3; **Half-time:** 24-6;
Referee: Tom Crashley; **Attendance:** 817.

ROCHDALE HORNETS 31 SWINTON LIONS 16

HORNETS: 1 Wayne English; 2 Gareth Langley; 4 Daniel Davies; 22 Mike Ratu; 29 Shaun Robinson; 14 Sean Casey; 17 Ryan Millard; 10 Warren Thompson; 6 Paul Crook; 28 Anthony Walker; 11 Chris Baines; 24 Tony Suffolk; 13 Jordan Case. Subs (all used): 18 James Tilley; 26 Adam Bowman; 16 Liam Gilchrist; 9 Lewis Sheridan.
Tries: Robinson (13), Casey (16), Case (23), Davies (29), Langley (71); **Goals:** Crook 5/7; **Field goal:** Crook (75).
LIONS: 1 Ritchie Hawkyard; 24 Gene Ormsby; 23 Steve Lewis; 6 Anthony Bowman; 21 Joe Worthington; 28 Chris Atkin; 7 Ian Watson; 16 Mike Morrison; 9 Andy Ackers; 8 Luke Menzies; 19 Jacque Peet; 12 Darren Hawkyard; 13 James Brown. Subs (all used): 22 Brad Dwyer; 25 Glenn Riley; 26 Andy Thornley; 20 Mark Thomas.
Tries: Worthington (43), D Hawkyard (50), Bowman (64); **Goals:** Peet 1/2, Watson 1/1.
Rugby Leaguer & League Express Men of the Match: *Hornets:* Paul Crook; *Lions:* Ritchie Hawkyard.
Penalty count: 9-7; **Half-time:** 22-0;
Referee: Warren Turley; **Attendance:** 842.

WORKINGTON TOWN 20 HALIFAX 20

TOWN: 34 Jack Murphy; 35 Dominic Manfredi; 3 Jason Mossop; 14 Kayle Connor; 1 Brett Carter; 30 Sam Powell; 16 Carl Forber; 8 Kris Coward; 9 Graeme Mattinson; 10 Marc Shackley; 12 Jarrad Stack; 31 Connor Farrell; 17 Liam McAvoy. Subs: 7 Callum Phillips (not used); 15 Daniel Rooney; 11 Brett Phillips; 6 Peter Lupton.
Tries: Murphy (14), Manfredi (65), Shackley (74);
Goals: Forber 4/4.
HALIFAX: 1 Ryan Fieldhouse; 21 Tom Saxton; 3 Steve Tyrer; 16 Danny Cowling; 5 Wayne Reittie; 14 Paul Mennell; 18 Ben Johnston; 10 Luke Ambler; 9 Ben Kaye; 12 Andy Bracek; 11 Dane Manning; 27 Ross Divorty; 13 Luke Adamson. Subs (all used): 19 Keith Holden; 4 Ben Heaton; 17 Ben Davies; 23 Callum Casey.
Tries: Johnston (21), Holden (34), Tyrer (51), Bracek (77); **Goals:** Tyrer 2/4.
Rugby Leaguer & League Express Men of the Match: *Town:* Jack Murphy; *Halifax:* Paul Mennell.
Penalty count: 10-6; **Half-time:** 6-10;
Referee: Joe Cobb; **Attendance:** 732.

ROUND 10

Sunday 11th May 2014

SHEFFIELD EAGLES 22 FEATHERSTONE ROVERS 36

EAGLES: 1 Quentin Laulu-Togagae; 2 Scott Turner; 3 Menzie Yere; 5 Misi Taulapapa; 26 Jordan Burke; 6 Pat Walker; 7 Dominic Brambani; 18 Tom Lillycrop; 9 Andrew Henderson; 10 Mitchell Stringer; 15 Matt Garside; 12 Peter Green; 16 Duane Straugheir. Subs (all used): 24 Gareth Owen; 11 Michael Knowles; 28 Tom Ashton; 27 Peter Aspinall.
Tries: Laulu-Togagae (16, 37), Owen (27), Burke (34);
Goals: Brambani 3/4.
ROVERS: 1 Ian Hardman; 2 Will Sharp; 22 James Mendeika; 3 Greg Worthington; 4 Ben Hellewell; 19 Kyle Briggs; 23 Andy Kain; 8 Steve Crossley; 9 Andy Ellis; 13 Matt James; 18 Jamie Cording; 12 Tim Spears; 11 James Lockwood. Subs (all used): 6 Jack Bussey; 14 George Flanagan; 38 Chris Annakin; 10 Keegan Hirst.
Tries: Hellewell (6, 75), Worthington (31), James (52), Mendeika (59), Briggs (70); **Goals:** Briggs 6/7.
Rugby Leaguer & League Express Men of the Match: *Eagles:* Dominic Brambani; *Rovers:* Andy Ellis.
Penalty count: 6-14; **Half-time:** 22-10;
Referee: Joe Cobb; **Attendance:** 1,279.

BARROW RAIDERS 18 BATLEY BULLDOGS 14

RAIDERS: 29 Niall Evalds; 21 Mike Backhouse; 4 Max Wiper; 26 Ryan Shaw; 5 Dalton Grant; 6 Dom Speakman; 7 Liam Campbell; 8 Joe Burke; 27 Mick Govin; 17 Andrew Dawson; 11 Liam Harrison; 13 Dan Toal; 15 Danny Jones. Subs (all used): 10 Jamie Butler; 3 Aaron Low; 14 Aaron Lloyd; 24 Joe Bullock.
Tries: Wiper (23), Toal (28, 47); **Goals:** Shaw 3/3.
BULLDOGS: 1 Miles Greenwood; 2 Vinny Finigan; 3 Alex Bretherton; 17 Lee Paterson; 29 Alex Brown; 6 Ben Black; 7 Scott Leatherbarrow; 8 Byron Smith; 18 Luke Blake; 10 Alex Rowe; 11 John Davies; 19 Joe Chandler; 23 Josh Johnson. Subs (all used): 20 Adam Gledhill; 9 Anthony Nicholson; 16 Brad Brennan; 30 Charlie Martin.
Tries: Greenwood (34), Gledhill (37); **Goals:** Paterson 3/3.
Rugby Leaguer & League Express Men of the Match: *Raiders:* Joe Bullock; *Bulldogs:* Alex Rowe.
Penalty count: 7-6; **Half-time:** 12-12;
Referee: Warren Turley; **Attendance:** 940.

DEWSBURY RAMS 12 LEIGH CENTURIONS 28

RAMS: 22 Jordan Grayston; 2 Dale Morton; 19 Callan Beckett; 4 Shane Grady; 5 Greg Scott; 31 Kieran Hyde; 7 Anthony Thackeray; 29 Ewan Dowes; 9 Wayne Godwin; 32 Makali Aizue; 11 Rob Spicer; 12 Scott Hale; 16 Josh Tonks. Subs (all used): 1 Louis Sheriff; 10 Ryan Hepworth; 17 Matthew Haggarty; 15 Tommy Gallagher.
Tries: Hyde (13), Morton (73); **Goals:** Grayston 2/4.
Dismissal: Haggarty (40) - high tackle on Brierley.
CENTURIONS: 1 Gregg McNally; 22 Adam Higson; 31 Cameron Pitman; 4 Tom Armstrong; 15 Liam Kay; 6 Martyn Ridyard; 7 Ryan Brierley; 8 Tom Spencer; 9 Bob Beswick; 29 Jake Emmitt; 30 Kurt Haggerty; 12 Tommy Goulden; 35 Sam Hopkins. Subs (all used): 14 Sean Penkywicz; 18 Jamie Acton; 13 Sam Barlow; 10 Oliver Wilkes.
Tries: Kay (42), Brierley (45, 68), Spencer (56), Haggerty (60); **Goals:** Ridyard 4/5.
Sin bin: Haggerty (71) - dissent; Acton (80) - fighting.
On report:
Higson (36) - alleged shoulder charge on Beckett.
Rugby Leaguer & League Express Men of the Match: *Rams:* Scott Hale; *Centurions:* Bob Beswick.
Penalty count: 9-4; **Half-time:** 8-0;
Referee: Dave Merrick; **Attendance:** 1,193.

HALIFAX 6 NORTH WALES CRUSADERS 12

HALIFAX: 1 Ryan Fieldhouse; 21 Tom Saxton; 3 Steve Tyrer; 16 Danny Cowling; 25 Gareth Potts; 6 Scott Murrell; 18 Ben Johnston; 10 Luke Ambler; 9 Ben Kaye; 8 Tony Tonks; 11 Dane Manning; 27 Ross Divorty; 12 Andy Bracek. Subs (all used): 19 Keith Holden; 4 Ben Heaton; 17 Ben Davies; 13 Luke Adamson.
Try: Murrell (48); **Goals:** Tyrer 1/1.
CRUSADERS: 1 Tommy Johnson; 17 Stuart Reardon; 29 Steve Bannister; 3 Christiaan Roets; 5 Rob Massam; 20 Jamie Durbin; 7 Jamie Dallimore; 8 Jonny Walker; 24 Lee Hudson; 10 Mark Offerdahl; 12 Gary Middlehurst; 14 Stephen Wild; 9 Craig Ashall. Subs (all used): 13 Jono Smith; 30 Sebastien Martins; 11 Toby Adamson; 25 Owain Griffiths.
Tries: Massam (24), Offerdahl (33); **Goals:** Johnson 2/2.
Rugby Leaguer & League Express Men of the Match: *Halifax:* Scott Murrell; *Crusaders:* Craig Ashall.
Penalty count: 7-3; **Half-time:** 0-12;
Referee: Chris Leatherbarrow; **Attendance:** 1,444.

KEIGHLEY COUGARS 20 SWINTON LIONS 12

COUGARS: 1 James Craven; 2 Richie Barnett; 19 Danny Lawton; 22 Daley Williams; 5 Paul White; 6 Danny Jones; 7 Paul Handforth; 16 Jode Sheriffe; 34 Luke Haigh; 10 Sean Hesketh; 11 Josh Lynam; 12 Brendan Rawlins; 15 Scott Law. Subs (all used): 9 James Feather; 18 Neil Cherryholme; 27 Jack Lee; 32 Ross Peltier.
Tries: Williams (19), White (39), Law (54), Barnett (64);
Goals: Jones 2/4.
LIONS: 1 Ritchie Hawkyard; 21 Joe Worthington; 4 Mick Nanyn; 6 Anthony Bowman; 5 Freddie Walker; 22 Gareth O'Brien; 7 Ian Watson; 16 Mike Morrison; 9 Andy Ackers; 23 Glenn Riley; 24 Andy Thornley; 12 Darren Hawkyard; 13 James Brown. Subs (all used): 8 Luke Menzies; 17 Zach Johnson; 20 Mark Thomas; 25 Chris Atkin.
Tries: D Hawkyard (4), Atkin (36); **Goals:** O'Brien 2/2.
Rugby Leaguer & League Express Men of the Match: *Cougars:* Paul Handforth; *Lions:* Darren Hawkyard.
Penalty count: 9-9; **Half-time:** 10-12;
Referee: Tom Crashley; **Attendance:** 673.

ROCHDALE HORNETS 6 WORKINGTON TOWN 10

HORNETS: 1 Wayne English; - Lewis Galbraith; 4 Daniel Davies; 28 Alex Clare; 29 Shaun Robinson; 6 Paul Crook; 17 Ryan Millard; 8 John Cookson; 14 Sean Casey; 10 Warren Thompson; 11 Chris Baines; 13 Jordan Case; 24 Tony Suffolk. Subs (all used): 16 Liam Gilchrist; 9 Lewis Sheridan; 25 Steve Marsh; 18 James Tilley.
Try: English (77); **Goals:** Crook 1/1.
TOWN: 34 Jack Murphy; 3 Jason Mossop; 4 Andy Morris; 14 Kayle Connor; 1 Brett Carter; 16 Carl Forber; 7 Callum Phillips; 8 Kris Coward; 9 Graeme Mattinson; 10 Marc Shackley; 12 Jarrad Stack; 11 Brett Phillips; 17 Liam McAvoy. Subs (all used): 13 Karl Olstrum; 15 Daniel Rooney; 20 Callum Rowlandson; 6 Peter Lupton.
Tries: B Phillips (46), Morris (54); **Goals:** Forber 1/2.
Rugby Leaguer & League Express Men of the Match: *Hornets:* Lewis Sheridan; *Town:* Brett Phillips.
Penalty count: 5-2; **Half-time:** 0-0;
Referee: Jamie Bloem; **Attendance:** 790.

WHITEHAVEN 29 DONCASTER 20

WHITEHAVEN: 5 Shaun Ainscough; 18 Jordan Burns; 6 Chris Taylor; 3 Jessie Joe Nandye; 2 Craig Calvert; 26 Brett Seymour; 7 Cain Southernwood; 30 Carl Forster; 9 James Newton; 20 Jordan Hand; 12 Lee Mitchell; 4 Scott McAvoy; 11 Lee Doran. Subs (all used): 14 Neil Thorman; 21 Larsen Marabe; 22 James Robinson; 13 Bradd Crellin.
Tries: Nandye (11), Mitchell (17), Burns (27), McAvoy (37), Taylor (49); **Goals:** Southernwood 4/5;
Field goal: Southernwood (76).
Sin bin: Burns (58) - dissent.
DONCASTER: 5 Dave Scott; 22 Tom Hodson; 4 Nev Morrison; 11 Lee Waterman; 2 Stewart Sanderson; 6 Paul Cooke; 26 Matty Wildie; 29 Chris Green; 15 Scott Spaven; 28 Liam Watts; 24 Liam Kent; 16 Craig Robinson; 13 Mike Emmett. Subs (all used): 9 Kyle Kesik; 21 Matt Carbutt; 25 Alex Starling; 14 Russ Spiers.
Tries: Hodson (40, 46), Waterman (59), Sanderson (79);
Goals: Sanderson 2/4.
Rugby Leaguer & League Express Men of the Match: *Whitehaven:* Brett Seymour; *Doncaster:* Mike Emmett.
Penalty count: 11-11; **Half-time:** 24-6;
Referee: Andrew Sweet; **Attendance:** 560.

ROUND 11

Sunday 18th May 2014

BATLEY BULLDOGS 12 SHEFFIELD EAGLES 16

BULLDOGS: 17 Lee Paterson; 2 Vinny Finigan; 3 Alex Bretherton; 28 Josh Griffin; 29 Alex Brown; 6 Ben Black; 7 Scott Leatherbarrow; 8 Byron Smith; 18 Luke Blake;

20 Adam Gledhill; 11 John Davies; 19 Joe Chandler; 13 Mark Applegarth. Subs (all used): 9 Anthony Nicholson; 10 Alex Rowe; 31 Keegan Hirst; 23 Josh Johnson.
Tries: Griffin (9), Bretherton (51);
Goals: Leatherbarrow 2/3.
EAGLES: 1 Quentin Laulu-Togagae; 2 Scott Turner; 3 Menzie Yere; 4 Lelauloto Tagaloa; 5 Misi Taulapapa; 6 Pat Walker; 7 Dominic Brambani; 18 Tom Lillycrop; 9 Andrew Henderson; 10 Mitchell Stringer; 15 Matt Garside; 16 Duane Straugheir; 11 Michael Knowles. Subs (all used): 24 Gareth Owen; 12 Peter Green; 27 Peter Aspinall; 8 Eddie Battye.
Tries: Taulapapa (16), Turner (34), Aspinall (46);
Goals: Brambani 2/3.
Rugby Leaguer & League Express Men of the Match: *Bulldogs:* Ben Black; *Eagles:* Eddie Battye.
Penalty count: 6-3; **Half-time:** 6-10;
Referee: Dave Merrick; **Attendance:** 540.

NORTH WALES CRUSADERS 14 KEIGHLEY COUGARS 16

CRUSADERS: 1 Tommy Johnson; 17 Stuart Reardon; 29 Steve Bannister; 3 Christiaan Roets; 5 Rob Massam; 7 Jamie Dallimore; 19 Karl Ashall; 8 Jonny Walker; 24 Lee Hudson; 10 Mark Offerdahl; 12 Gary Middlehurst; 14 Stephen Wild; 9 Craig Ashall. Subs (all used): 13 Jono Smith; 30 Sebastien Martins; 11 Toby Adamson; 25 Owain Griffiths.
Tries: Wild (16), C Ashall (56), Roets (79);
Goals: Johnson 1/3.
Dismissal: Martins (80) - dissent.
COUGARS: 21 Jesse Sheriffe; 25 Lewis Graham; 19 Danny Lawton; 4 James Haley; 5 Paul White; 6 Danny Jones; 7 Paul Handforth; 8 Andy Shickell; 34 Luke Haigh; 10 Sean Hesketh; 12 Brendan Rawlins; 11 Josh Lynam; 13 Ashley Lindsay. Subs (all used): 9 James Feather; 16 Jode Sheriffe; 18 Neil Cherryholme; 17 Ben Sagar.
Tries: Haley (8), Rawlins (42), Hesketh (75);
Goals: Jones 2/3.
Rugby Leaguer & League Express Men of the Match: *Crusaders:* Gary Middlehurst; *Cougars:* Brendan Rawlins.
Penalty count: 8-9; **Half-time:** 4-6;
Referee: George Stokes; **Attendance:** 811.

BARROW RAIDERS 30 DEWSBURY RAMS 42

RAIDERS: 29 Niall Evalds; 1 Ian Mort; 4 Max Wiper; 26 Ryan Shaw; 5 Dalton Grant; 6 Dom Speakman; 7 Liam Campbell; 10 Jamie Butler; 9 Nathan Mossop; 17 Andrew Dawson; 11 Liam Harrison; 13 Dan Toal; 15 Danny Jones. Subs (all used): 8 Joe Burke; 24 Joe Bullock; 3 Aaron Low; 27 Mick Govin.
Tries: Toal (3), Grant (10), Campbell (22), Dawson (63), Evalds (66); **Goals:** Shaw 5/5.
RAMS: 22 Jordan Grayston; 2 Dale Morton; 19 Callan Beckett; 4 Shane Grady; 5 Greg Scott; 31 Kieran Hyde; 7 Anthony Thackeray; 29 Ewan Dowes; 9 Wayne Godwin; 32 Makali Aizue; 10 Ryan Hepworth; 12 Scott Hale; 1 Louis Sheriff. Subs (all used): 6 Tom Hemingway; 8 Stephen Nash; 17 Matthew Haggarty; 15 Tommy Gallagher.
Tries: Thackeray (17, 30, 32, 56, 67), Hale (43), Morton (80); **Goals:** Grayston 7/8.
Rugby Leaguer & League Express Men of the Match: *Raiders:* Liam Harrison; *Rams:* Anthony Thackeray.
Penalty count: 6-4; **Half-time:** 18-20;
Referee: Joe Cobb; **Attendance:** 914.

FEATHERSTONE ROVERS 32 WORKINGTON TOWN 20

ROVERS: 1 Ian Hardman; 2 Will Sharp; 22 James Mendeika; 3 Greg Worthington; 4 Ben Hellewell; 19 Kyle Briggs; 7 Gareth Moore; 8 Steve Crossley; 9 Andy Ellis; 37 Kyle Trout; 18 Jamie Cording; 12 Tim Spears; 11 James Lockwood. Subs (all used): 14 George Flanagan; 6 Jack Bussey; 38 Chris Annakin; 13 Matt James.
Tries: Moore (6), Trout (21), Hellewell (32), Hardman (54), Mendeika (70), Bussey (79);
Goals: Briggs 2/3, Moore 2/3.
TOWN: 34 Jack Murphy; 3 Jason Mossop; 12 Jarrad Stack; 14 Kayle Connor; 1 Brett Carter; 16 Carl Forber; 6 Peter Lupton; 8 Kris Coward; 9 Graeme Mattinson; 10 Marc Shackley; 11 Brett Phillips; 17 Liam McAvoy; 32 Greg Burke. Subs (all used): 7 Callum Phillips; 15 Daniel Rooney; 20 Callum Rowlandson; 18 James Duerden.
Tries: B Phillips (14), Stack (22, 77), Connor (28);
Goals: Forber 2/4.
Rugby Leaguer & League Express Men of the Match: *Rovers:* Jack Bussey; *Town:* Peter Lupton.
Penalty count: 5-7; **Half-time:** 16-14;
Referee: Andrew Sweet; **Attendance:** 2,016.

LEIGH CENTURIONS 50 DONCASTER 20

CENTURIONS: 1 Gregg McNally; 22 Adam Higson; 31 Cameron Pitman; 4 Tom Armstrong; 15 Liam Kay; 6 Martyn Ridyard; 7 Ryan Brierley; 8 Tom Spencer; 9 Bob Beswick; 29 Jake Emmitt; 11 Matt Sarsfield; 12 Tommy Goulden; 35 Sam Hopkins. Subs (all used): - Lewis Foster; 10 Oliver Wilkes; 18 Jamie Acton; 30 Kurt Haggerty.
Tries: Pitman (12), Beswick (14), McNally (25), Higson (34), Brierley (50), Sarsfield (53), Haggerty (67), Goulden (69), Armstrong (80); **Goals:** Ridyard 7/9.
DONCASTER: 5 Dave Scott; 22 Tom Hodson; 20 Shaun Leaf; 11 Lee Waterman; 2 Stewart Sanderson; 6 Paul Cooke; 26 Matty Wildie; 21 Matt Carbutt; 9 Kyle Kesik; 16 Craig Robinson; 28 Liam Kent; 12 Michael Kelly; 13 Mike Emmett. Subs (all used): 25 Alex Starling; 18 Ryan Wilson; 14 Russ Spiers; 15 Scott Spaven.
Tries: Kent (20), Hodson (29), Scott (40), Cooke (58);
Goals: Sanderson 2/4.
Rugby Leaguer & League Express Men of the Match: *Centurions:* Sam Hopkins; *Doncaster:* Mike Emmett.
Penalty count: 7-8; **Half-time:** 22-14;
Referee: Tom Crashley; **Attendance:** 2,132.

ROCHDALE HORNETS 12 HALIFAX 28

HORNETS: 1 Wayne English; 29 Lewis Galbraith; 19 Dave Llewellyn; 4 Daniel Davies; 24 Shaun Robinson; 14 Sean Casey; 17 Ryan Millard; 8 John Cookson; 6 Paul Crook; 10 Warren Thompson; 11 Chris Baines; 18 James Tilley; 13 Jordan Case. Subs (all used): 9 Lewis Sheridan; 25 Steve Marsh; 16 Liam Gilchrist; 28 Alex Clare.
Tries: Galbraith (76), Millard (79); **Goals:** Baines 2/2.
HALIFAX: 1 Ryan Fieldhouse; 5 Wayne Reittie; 11 Dane Manning; 3 Steve Tyrer; 21 Tom Saxton; 6 Scott Murrell; 18 Ben Johnston; 8 Tony Tonks; 14 Paul Mennell; 10 Luke Ambler; 13 Luke Adamson; 27 Ross Divorty; 24 Sam Brooks. Subs (all used): - Jack Spencer; 12 Andy Bracek; 23 Callum Casey; 19 Keith Holden.
Tries: Reittie (12, 27), Tyrer (16, 33), Fieldhouse (38, 56); **Goals:** Tyrer 2/6.
Rugby Leaguer & League Express Men of the Match: *Hornets:* Sean Casey; *Halifax:* Ross Divorty.
Penalty count: 6-5; **Half-time:** 0-22;
Referee: Michael Woodhead; **Attendance:** 721.

WHITEHAVEN 22 SWINTON LIONS 18

WHITEHAVEN: 1 Tom Carr; 18 Jordan Burns; 6 Chris Taylor; 3 Jessie Joe Nandye; 2 Craig Calvert; 26 Brett Seymour; 7 Cain Southernwood; 20 Jordan Hand; 9 James Newton; 21 Larsen Marabe; 4 Scott McAvoy; 12 Lee Mitchell; 11 Lee Doran. Subs (all used): 14 Neil Thorman; 30 Carl Forster; 22 James Robinson; 13 Bradd Crellin.
Tries: Southernwood (5), Calvert (48), Burns (52), Marabe (67); **Goals:** Southernwood 3/4.
LIONS: 1 Ritchie Hawkyard; 23 Steve Lewis; 4 Mick Nanyn; 19 Jacque Peet; 5 Freddie Walker; 22 Gareth O'Brien; 7 Ian Watson; 16 Mike Morrison; 9 Andy Ackers; 25 Glenn Riley; 24 Joe Philbin; 12 Darren Hawkyard; 15 Josh Barlow. Subs (all used): 8 Luke Menzies; 17 Zach Johnson; 13 James Brown; 28 Chris Atkin.
Tries: R Hawkyard (12), Nanyn (19), Brown (33);
Goals: O'Brien 3/4.
Rugby Leaguer & League Express Men of the Match: *Whitehaven:* Jessie Joe Nandye; *Lions:* James Brown.
Penalty count: 13-3; **Half-time:** 6-16;
Referee: Chris Kendall; **Attendance:** 801.

ROUND 12

Sunday 25th May 2014

SHEFFIELD EAGLES 12 LEIGH CENTURIONS 54

EAGLES: 1 Quentin Laulu-Togagae; 2 Scott Turner; 3 Menzie Yere; 4 Lelauloto Tagaloa; 5 Misi Taulapapa; 6 Pat Walker; 7 Dominic Brambani; 18 Tom Lillycrop; 9 Andrew Henderson; 10 Mitchell Stringer; 15 Matt Garside; 16 Duane Straugheir; 11 Michael Knowles. Subs (all used): 14 James Davey; 27 Peter Aspinall; 22 Will Hope; 8 Eddie Battye.
Tries: Tagaloa (12), Taulapapa (77);
Goals: Brambani 1/1, Walker 1/1.
CENTURIONS: 1 Gregg McNally; 23 Jonathan Pownall; 31 Cameron Pitman; 4 Tom Armstrong; 15 Liam Kay; 6 Martyn Ridyard; 7 Ryan Brierley; 8 Tom Spencer; 9 Bob Beswick; 13 Sam Barlow; 30 Kurt Haggerty; 12 Tommy Goulden; 27 Anthony Bate. Subs (all used): 14 Sean Penkywicz; 18 Jamie Acton; 29 Jake Emmitt; 10 Oliver Wilkes.
Tries: Kay (2, 19, 58, 66), Beswick (6), McNally (23), Brierley (47), Goulden (63), Penkywicz (74);
Goals: Ridyard 8/9, Brierley 1/2.
Rugby Leaguer & League Express Men of the Match: *Eagles:* Lelauloto Tagaloa; *Centurions:* Liam Kay.
Penalty count: 7-11; **Half-time:** 6-26;
Referee: Matthew Thomason; **Attendance:** 1,151.

DEWSBURY RAMS 20 HALIFAX 18

RAMS: 22 Jordan Grayston; 2 Dale Morton; 19 Callan Becket; 4 Shane Grady; 21 Austin Buchanan; 31 Kieran Hyde; 7 Anthony Thackeray; 29 Ewan Dowes; 9 Wayne Godwin; 32 Makali Aizue; 10 Ryan Hepworth; 12 Scott Hale; 20 Jobe Murphy. Subs (all used): 6 Tom Hemingway; 8 Stephen Nash; 17 Matthew Haggarty; 15 Tommy Gallagher.
Tries: Thackeray (36), Buchanan (43), Grady (76);
Goals: Grayston 4/5.
HALIFAX: 1 Ryan Fieldhouse; 5 Wayne Reittie; 11 Dane Manning; 3 Steve Tyrer; 21 Tom Saxton; 6 Scott Murrell; 18 Ben Johnston; 8 Tony Tonks; 14 Paul Mennell; 10 Luke Ambler; 13 Luke Adamson; 27 Ross Divorty; 24 Sam Brooks. Subs (all used): 12 Andy Bracek; 19 Keith Holden; 23 Callum Casey; - Jack Spencer.
Tries: Saxton (4), Fieldhouse (57), Casey (71);
Goals: Tyrer 3/8.
Sin bin: Saxton (49) - professional foul.
Rugby Leaguer & League Express Men of the Match: *Rams:* Anthony Thackeray; *Halifax:* Scott Murrell.
Penalty count: 8-8; **Half-time:** 6-8;
Referee: Joe Cobb; **Attendance:** 1,213.

DONCASTER 40 ROCHDALE HORNETS 10

DONCASTER: 5 Dave Scott; 4 Nev Morrison; 3 Liam Welham; 20 Shaun Leaf; 22 Tom Hodson; 6 Paul Cooke; 23 Richard Wilkinson; 8 Mark Castle; 9 Kyle Kesik; 29 Chris Green; 28 Liam Kent; 25 Alex Starling; 13 Mike Emmett. Subs (all used): 15 Scott Spaven; 14 Russ Spiers; 21 Matt Carbutt; 24 Steve Snitch.
Tries: Kesik (3), Leaf (9), Castle (24), Hodson (36, 44), Wilkinson (57), Spaven (62), Scott (76);
Goals: Scott 4/7, Hodson 0/1.
HORNETS: 1 Wayne English; - Lewis Galbraith; 19 Dave Llewellyn; 12 Alex Trumper; 28 Shaun Robinson; 6 Paul Crook; 17 Ryan Millard; 8 John Cookson; 23 James Dandy; 10 Warren Thompson; 11 Chris Baines; 27 Alex Clare; 18 James Tilley. Subs (all used): 9 Lewis Sheridan; 13 Jordan Case; 25 Steve Marsh; 21 Chris Tyrer.
Tries: Robinson (20), Dandy (73); **Goals:** Crook 1/2.
Rugby Leaguer & League Express Men of the Match: *Doncaster:* Paul Cooke; *Hornets:* Ryan Millard.
Penalty count: 8-9; **Half-time:** 22-6;
Referee: Gareth Hewer; **Attendance:** 600.

FEATHERSTONE ROVERS 50 WHITEHAVEN 14

ROVERS: 1 Ian Hardman; 2 Will Sharp; 3 Greg Worthington; 27 Etuate Uaisele; 22 James Mendeika; 23 Andy Kain; 7 Gareth Moore; 8 Steve Crossley; 9 Andy Ellis; 37 Kyle Trout; 18 Jamie Cording; 12 Tim Spears; 11 James Lockwood. Subs (all used): 14 George Flanagan; 6 Jack Bussey; 38 Daniel Smith; 13 Matt James.
Tries: Mendeika (8, 10, 30), Sharp (35, 56, 77), Worthington (44, 58), Smith (52), Cording (67);
Goals: Moore 5/10.
WHITEHAVEN: 1 Tom Carr; 18 Jordan Burns; 6 Chris Taylor; 3 Jessie Joe Nandye; 2 Craig Calvert; 26 Brett Seymour; 7 Cain Southernwood; 20 Jordan Hand; 9 James Newton; 10 Paul Jackson; 4 Scott McAvoy; 12 Lee Mitchell; 11 Lee Doran. Subs (all used): 14 Neil Thorman; 30 Carl Forster; 13 Bradd Crellin; 22 James Robinson.
Tries: Nandye (19, 48), Burns (38);
Goals: Southernwood 1/3.
Rugby Leaguer & League Express Men of the Match: *Rovers:* Greg Worthington; *Whitehaven:* Jessie Joe Nandye.
Penalty count: 10-6; **Half-time:** 22-8;
Referee: Tom Crashley; **Attendance:** 1,726.

KEIGHLEY COUGARS 27 BARROW RAIDERS 18

COUGARS: 1 James Craven; 2 Richie Barnett; 19 Danny Lawton; 4 James Haley; 5 Paul White; 6 Danny Jones; 7 Paul Handforth; 18 Neil Cherryholme; 9 James Feather; 10 Sean Hesketh; 11 Josh Lynam; 12 Brendan Rawlins; 17 Ben Sagar. Subs (all used): 16 Jode Sheriffe; 25 Lewis Graham; 27 Jack Lee; 32 Ross Peltier.
Tries: White (4), Lawton (9, 78), Barnett (60), Hesketh (64); **Goals:** Jones 3/5; **Field goal:** Jones (40).
RAIDERS: 29 Niall Evalds; 26 Ryan Shaw; 30 Jason Walton; 4 Max Wiper; 5 Dalton Grant; 6 Dom Speakman; 7 Liam Campbell; 17 Andrew Dawson; 9 Nathan Mossop; 15 Danny Jones; 11 Liam Harrison; 13 Dan Toal; 32 Andrew Dixon. Subs: 3 Aaron Low (not used); 10 Jamie Butler; 24 Joe Bullock; 27 Mick Govin.
Tries: Toal (29, 76), Grant (57); **Goals:** Shaw 3/3.
Rugby Leaguer & League Express Men of the Match: *Cougars:* Danny Lawton; *Raiders:* Dan Toal.
Penalty count: 4-6; **Half-time:** 13-6;
Referee: Warren Turley; **Attendance:** 812.

SWINTON LIONS 18 BATLEY BULLDOGS 33

LIONS: 1 Ritchie Hawkyard; 30 Steve Lewis; 19 Jacque Peet; 23 Andy Thornley; 5 Freddie Walker; 22 Gareth O'Brien; 28 Chris Atkin; 16 Mike Morrison; 7 Ian Watson; 25 Glenn Riley; 12 Darren Hawkyard; 24 Joe Philbin; 15 Josh Barlow. Subs (all used): 9 Andy Ackers; 17 Zach Johnson; 8 Luke Menzies; 13 James Brown.
Tries: O'Brien (33), Atkin (51), Philbin (71);
Goals: O'Brien 3/3.
Sin bin: Peet (75) - dissent.
BULLDOGS: 1 Miles Greenwood; 2 Vinny Finigan; 17 Lee Paterson; 28 Josh Griffin; 29 Alex Brown; 6 Ben Black; 7 Scott Leatherbarrow; 8 Byron Smith; 18 Luke Blake; 20 Adam Gledhill; 3 Alex Bretherton; 19 Joe Chandler; 11 John Davies. Subs (all used): 9 Anthony Nicholson; 10 Alex Rowe; 31 Keegan Hirst; 15 Jay Leary.
Tries: Griffin (4), Bretherton (10), Leatherbarrow (24), Paterson (58), Nicholson (63), Blake (75);
Goals: Paterson 1/3, Leatherbarrow 3/4;
Field goal: Leatherbarrow (80).
Rugby Leaguer & League Express Men of the Match: *Lions:* Gareth O'Brien; *Bulldogs:* Scott Leatherbarrow.
Penalty count: 2-9; **Half-time:** 6-16;
Referee: Chris Kendall; **Attendance:** 456.

WORKINGTON TOWN 10 NORTH WALES CRUSADERS 11

TOWN: 34 Jack Murphy; 3 Jason Mossop; 16 Carl Forber; 14 Kayle Connor; 1 Brett Carter; 6 Peter Lupton; 7 Callum Phillips; 8 Kris Coward; 9 Graeme Mattinson; 10 Marc Shackley; 11 Brett Phillips; 31 Connor Farrell; 17 Liam McAvoy. Subs (all used): 19 Nathan Lucock; 15 Daniel Rooney; 32 Greg Burke; 20 Callum Rowlandson.
Tries: Farrell (32), B Phillips (64); **Goals:** Forber 1/2.
On report: Mattinson (9) - alleged late challenge.
CRUSADERS: 1 Tommy Johnson; 17 Stuart Reardon; 29 Steve Bannister; 3 Christiaan Roets; 5 Rob Massam; 20 Jamie Durbin; 7 Jamie Dallimore; 10 Mark Offerdahl; 9 Craig Ashall; 8 Jonny Walker; 12 Gary Middlehurst; 14 Stephen Wild; 13 Jono Smith. Subs (all used): 30 Sebastien Martins; 11 Toby Adamson; 26 Matt Reid; 24 Lee Hudson.
Tries: Reardon (10), Bannister (37); **Goals:** Johnson 1/2;
Field goal: Durbin (77).
Rugby Leaguer & League Express Men of the Match: *Town:* Brett Phillips; *Crusaders:* Jamie Dallimore.
Penalty count: 7-5; **Half-time:** 6-10;
Referee: Chris Leatherbarrow; **Attendance:** 627.

ROUND 13

Sunday 1st June 2014

BATLEY BULLDOGS 26 FEATHERSTONE ROVERS 32

BULLDOGS: 1 Miles Greenwood; 2 Vinny Finigan; 17 Lee Paterson; 28 Josh Griffin; 26 Ben Blackmore; 6 Ben Black; 7 Scott Leatherbarrow; 8 Byron Smith; 18 Luke Blake; 31 Anthony Mullally; 3 Alex Bretherton; 19 Joe Chandler; 11 John Davies. Subs (all used): 9 Anthony Nicholson; 10 Alex Rowe; 20 Adam Gledhill; 15 Jay Leary.
Tries: Blackmore (24, 56), Paterson (72), Rowe (80);
Goals: Leatherbarrow 5/5.
ROVERS: 1 Ian Hardman; 2 Will Sharp; 22 James Mendeika; 3 Greg Worthington; 4 Ben Hellewell; 23 Andy Kain; 7 Gareth Moore; 8 Steve Crossley; 9 Andy Ellis; 39 Chris Green; 18 Jamie Cording; 12 Tim Spears; 11 James Lockwood. Subs (all used): 6 Jack Bussey; 40 Danny Bridge; 37 Kyle Trout; 15 Matty Dale.
Tries: Worthington (5), Hellewell (18), Dale (37), Bridge (42), Hardman (51), Bussey (62);
Goals: Moore 4/6.
Rugby Leaguer & League Express Men of the Match: *Bulldogs:* John Davies; *Rovers:* Andy Ellis.
Penalty count: 7-6; **Half-time:** 8-16;
Referee: Joe Cobb; **Attendance:** 1,143.

BARROW RAIDERS 38 ROCHDALE HORNETS 18

RAIDERS: 1 Ian Mort; 26 Ryan Shaw; 32 Michael Platt; 4 Max Wiper; 5 Dalton Grant; 6 Dom Speakman; 34 Bobbie Goulding; 10 Jamie Butler; 9 Nathan Mossop; 15 Danny Jones; 11 Liam Harrison; 30 Jason Walton; 13 Dan Toal. Subs (all used): 14 Aaron Lloyd; 7 Liam Campbell; 8 Joe Burke; 24 Joe Bullock.
Tries: Wiper (3), Grant (18), Bullock (33), Campbell (58), Jones (78), Lloyd (80); **Goals:** Shaw 7/7.
HORNETS: 1 Wayne English; - Lewis Galbraith; 4 Daniel Davies; 26 Mark Percival; 18 Shaun Robinson; 6 Paul Crook; 17 Ryan Millard; 16 Liam Gilchrist; 23 James Dandy; 10 Warren Thompson; 12 Alex Trumper; 20 Josh Jones; 11 Chris Baines. Subs (all used): 14 Sean Casey; 8 John Cookson; 25 Steve Marsh; 28 Stuart Littler.
Tries: Millard (17), Galbraith (62), Cookson (74);
Goals: Crook 3/3.
Rugby Leaguer & League Express Men of the Match: *Raiders:* Jason Walton; *Hornets:* Ryan Millard.
Penalty count: 8-4; **Half-time:** 20-6;
Referee: Tom Crashley; **Attendance:** 1,058.

DEWSBURY RAMS 38 NORTH WALES CRUSADERS 18

RAMS: 22 Jordan Grayston; 2 Dale Morton; 19 Callan Beckett; 4 Shane Grady; 21 Austin Buchanan; 31 Kieran Hyde; 7 Anthony Thackeray; 29 Ewan Dowes; 14 Ryan Wright; 32 Makali Aizue; 10 Ryan Hepworth; 12 Scott Hale; 20 Jobe Murphy. Subs (all used): 6 Tom Hemingway; 8 Stephen Nash; 17 Matthew Haggarty; 15 Tommy Gallagher.
Tries: Thackeray (4, 35), Hale (14), Buchanan (19), Hyde (38), Beckett (72); **Goals:** Grayston 7/7.
CRUSADERS: 1 Tommy Johnson; 17 Stuart Reardon; 29 Steve Bannister; 3 Christiaan Roets; 5 Rob Massam; 20 Jamie Durbin; 7 Jamie Dallimore; 10 Mark Offerdahl; 9 Craig Ashall; 8 Jonny Walker; 12 Gary Middlehurst; 14 Stephen Wild; 13 Jono Smith. Subs (all used): 21 Simon Stephens; 11 Toby Adamson; 26 Matt Reid; 24 Lee Hudson.
Tries: Johnson (12), C Ashall (24), Massam (75);
Goals: Johnson 3/3.
Rugby Leaguer & League Express Men of the Match: *Rams:* Anthony Thackeray; *Crusaders:* Tommy Johnson.
Penalty count: 9-7; **Half-time:** 32-12;
Referee: Matthew Thomason; **Attendance:** 708.

KEIGHLEY COUGARS 14 HALIFAX 28

COUGARS: 21 Jesse Sheriffe; 2 Richie Barnett; 19 Danny Lawton; 4 James Haley; 5 Paul White; 6 Danny Jones; 7 Paul Handforth; 8 Andy Shickell; 9 James Feather; 10 Sean Hesketh; 11 Josh Lynam; 12 Brendan Rawlins; 13 Ashley Lindsay. Subs (all used): 16 Jode Sheriffe; 17 Ben Sagar; 18 Neil Cherryholme; 34 Luke Haigh.
Tries: Jode Sheriffe (35), Haley (49), Feather (66);
Goals: Jones 1/3.
HALIFAX: 1 Ryan Fieldhouse; 26 Peter Fox; 11 Dane Manning; 3 Steve Tyrer; 21 Tom Saxton; 6 Scott Murrell; 18 Ben Johnston; 8 Tony Tonks; 9 Ben Kaye; 10 Luke Ambler; 12 Andy Bracek; 27 Ross Divorty; 13 Luke Adamson. Subs (all used): 14 Paul Mennell; 17 Ben Davies; 23 Callum Casey; 28 Jack Spencer.
Tries: Divorty (10), Fieldhouse (16), Manning (43), Ambler (70), Mennell (80); **Goals:** Tyrer 4/5.
Rugby Leaguer & League Express Men of the Match: *Cougars:* James Feather; *Halifax:* Ross Divorty.
Penalty count: 6-8; **Half-time:** 6-12;
Referee: Chris Kendall; **Attendance:** 1,217.

SWINTON LIONS 22 DONCASTER 36

LIONS: 28 Chris Atkin; 23 Jordan Burke; 30 Steve Lewis; 19 Jacque Peet; 1 Ritchie Hawkyard; 22 Gareth O'Brien; 7 Ian Watson; 16 Mike Morrison; 24 Brad Dwyer; 26 Glenn Riley; 25 Andy Thornley; 12 Darren Hawkyard; 9 Andy Ackers. Subs (all used): 8 Luke Menzies; 17 Zach Johnson; - Ed Barber; 27 Lewis Hulme.
Tries: Atkin (2), Watson (15), R Hawkyard (30), D Hawkyard (43); **Goals:** O'Brien 3/4.
DONCASTER: 5 Dave Scott; 4 Nev Morrison; 20 Shaun Leaf; 3 Liam Welham; 22 Tom Hodson; 6 Paul Cooke; 23 Richard Wilkinson; 21 Matt Carbutt; 9 Kyle Kesik; 16 Craig Robinson; 28 Liam Kent; 25 Alex Sterling; 13 Mike Emmett. Subs (all used): 15 Scott Spaven; 8 Mark Castle; 14 Russ Spiers; 24 Steve Snitch.
Tries: Robinson (6, 78), Kesik (23), Hodson (50, 65), Snitch (60); **Goals:** Scott 6/6.
Rugby Leaguer & League Express Men of the Match: *Lions:* Andy Thornley; *Doncaster:* Dave Scott.
Penalty count: 5-8; **Half-time:** 16-12;
Referee: Adam Gill; **Attendance:** 355.

WHITEHAVEN 24 SHEFFIELD EAGLES 22

WHITEHAVEN: 1 Tom Carr; 18 Jordan Burns; 3 Jessie Joe Nandye; 4 Scott McAvoy; 2 Craig Calvert; 26 Brett Seymour; 6 Chris Taylor; 22 James Robinson; 9 James Newton; 20 Jordan Hand; 21 Larsen Marabe; 12 Lee Mitchell; 11 Lee Doran. Subs (all used): 14 Neil Thorman; 13 Bradd Crellin; 27 Kurtis Quinn; 28 Callum Farrer.
Tries: Nandye (14), Newton (23), Farrer (40), Calvert (51); **Goals:** Carr 4/5.
EAGLES: 1 Quentin Laulu-Togagae; 2 Scott Turner; 3 Menzie Yere; 4 Lelauloto Tagaloa; 5 Misi Taulapapa; 19 Cory Aston; 7 Dominic Brambani; 21 Jack Blagbrough; 24 Gareth Owen; 10 Mitchell Stringer; 11 Michael Knowles; 29 Alex Palmer; 16 Duane Straugheir. Subs (all used): 14 James Davey; 12 Peter Green; 15 Matt Garside; 8 Eddie Battye.
Tries: Tagaloa (3), Yere (26, 36), Turner (71);
Goals: Brambani 2/3, Knowles 1/1.
Rugby Leaguer & League Express Men of the Match: *Whitehaven:* Lee Doran; *Eagles:* Menzie Yere.
Penalty count: 10-6; **Half-time:** 18-16;
Referee: Chris Leatherbarrow; **Attendance:** 644.

WORKINGTON TOWN 16 LEIGH CENTURIONS 28

TOWN: 34 Jack Murphy; 3 Jason Mossop; 12 Jarrad Stack; 14 Kayle Connor; 1 Brett Carter; 6 Peter Lupton; 16 Carl Forber; 17 Liam McAvoy; 9 Graeme Mattinson; 10 Marc Shackley; 11 Brett Phillips; 31 Connor Farrell; 13 Karl Olstrum. Subs (all used): 22 Jack Gaskell; 7 Callum Phillips; 20 Callum Rowlandson; 18 James Duerden.
Tries: Forber (4), B Phillips (43), Stack (69);
Goals: Forber 2/3.
On report: McAvoy (19) - alleged late challenge; Mattinson (61) - alleged dangerous contact.
CENTURIONS: 1 Gregg McNally; 23 Jonathan Pownall; 31 Cameron Pitman; 4 Tom Armstrong; 15 Liam Kay; 6 Martyn Ridyard; 7 Ryan Brierley; 8 Tom Spencer; 14 Sean Penkywicz; 27 Anthony Bate; 11 Matt Sarsfield; 12 Tommy Goulden; 13 Sam Barlow. Subs (all used): 9 Bob Beswick; 10 Oliver Wilkes; 29 Jake Emmitt; 18 Jamie Acton.
Tries: Kay (8), Penkywicz (15), Sarsfield (20, 62), Brierley (28); **Goals:** Ridyard 4/5.
On report: Acton (46) - alleged biting.
Rugby Leaguer & League Express Men of the Match: *Town:* Brett Phillips; *Centurions:* Sam Barlow.
Penalty count: 9-6; **Half-time:** 4-22;
Referee: Gareth Hewer; **Attendance:** 814.

ROUND 14

Sunday 8th June 2014

BATLEY BULLDOGS 44 ROCHDALE HORNETS 28

BULLDOGS: 1 Miles Greenwood; 2 Vinny Finigan; 17 Lee Paterson; 28 Josh Griffin; 29 Alex Brown; 6 Ben Black; 7 Scott Leatherbarrow; 8 Byron Smith; 18 Luke Blake; 20 Adam Gledhill; 11 John Davies; 3 Alex Bretherton; 13 Mark Applegarth. Subs (all used): 9 Anthony Nicholson; 10 Alex Rowe; 31 Keegan Hirst; 12 Sam Scott.
Tries: Bretherton (1), Griffin (31), Greenwood (33, 56), Nicholson (39), Hirst (44), A Brown (46, 60);
Goals: Leatherbarrow 6/8.
HORNETS: 1 Wayne English; 7 Lewis Galbraith; 4 Daniel Davies; 18 Stuart Littler; 29 Shaun Robinson; 6 Paul Crook; 17 Ryan Millard; 8 John Cookson; 23 James Dandy; 10 Warren Thompson; 11 Chris Baines; - Alex Trumper; 28 Joe Greenwood. Subs (all used): 9 Lewis Sheridan; 16 Anthony Walker; 19 Dave Llewellyn; 13 Jordan Case.
Tries: Cookson (4), Robinson (10), Millard (20, 53), English (75); **Goals:** Crook 4/5.
Rugby Leaguer & League Express Men of the Match: *Bulldogs:* Keegan Hirst; *Hornets:* Ryan Millard.
Penalty count: 9-7; **Half-time:** 22-16;
Referee: Matthew Thomason; **Attendance:** 555.

SHEFFIELD EAGLES 37 WORKINGTON TOWN 30

EAGLES: 1 Quentin Laulu-Togagae; 2 Scott Turner; 3 Menzie Yere; 4 Lelauloto Tagaloa; 5 Misi Taulapapa; 6 Pat Walker; 19 Cory Aston; 21 Jack Blagbrough; 9 Andrew Henderson; 10 Mitchell Stringer; 15 Matt Garside; 27 Peter Aspinall; 11 Michael Knowles. Subs (all used): 7 Dominic Brambani; 17 Ben Jones; 28 Tom Ashton; 12 Peter Green.
Tries: Turner (3, 40), Taulapapa (31), Laulu-Togagae (47, 50), Henderson (80);
Goals: Walker 6/6; **Field goal:** Brambani (79).
Sin bin: Taulapapa (58) - dissent.
TOWN: 30 Jack Murphy; 1 Brett Carter; 14 Kayle Connor; 12 Jarrad Stack; 3 Jason Mossop; 16 Carl Forber; 7 Callum Phillips; 8 Kris Coward; 9 Graeme Mattinson; 10 Marc Shackley; 11 Brett Phillips; 31 Connor Farrell; 17 Liam McAvoy. Subs (all used): 19 Nathan Lucock; 18 James Duerden; 32 Greg Burke; 20 Callum Rowlandson.
Tries: C Phillips (17), B Phillips (25, 63), Stack (68), Burke (75); **Goals:** Forber 5/5.
Rugby Leaguer & League Express Men of the Match: *Eagles:* Quentin Laulu-Togagae; *Town:* Brett Phillips.
Penalty count: 8-12; **Half-time:** 18-12;
Referee: Warren Turley; **Attendance:** 712.

NORTH WALES CRUSADERS 24 SWINTON LIONS 42

CRUSADERS: 1 Tommy Johnson; 17 Stuart Reardon; 29 Steve Bannister; 3 Christiaan Roets; 5 Rob Massam; 37 Grant Gore; 7 Jamie Dallimore; 8 Jonny Walker; 9 Craig Ashall; 10 Mark Offerdahl; 12 Gary Middlehurst; 14 Stephen Wild; 13 Jono Smith. Subs (all used): 11 Toby Adamson; 30 Sebastien Martins; 36 Jonathan Soum; - Adam Lawton.
Tries: Offerdahl (13), Bannister (24), Middlehurst (56, 72), Lawton (69); **Goals:** Johnson 2/5.
LIONS: 28 Chris Atkin; 1 Ritchie Hawkyard; 4 Mick Nanyn; 25 Andy Thornley; 18 Jordan Burke; 22 Gareth O'Brien; 7 Ian Watson; 16 Mike Morrison; 23 Brad Dwyer; 26 Glenn Riley; 12 Darren Hawkyard; 13 James Brown; 24 Martin Aspinwall. Subs (all used): 9 Andy Ackers; 17 Zach Johnson; 8 Luke Menzies; - Ed Barber.
Tries: Watson (7), Burke (20), Ackers (33, 37), Menzies (41), O'Brien (47), Atkin (50), Dwyer (61);
Goals: O'Brien 5/8.
Rugby Leaguer & League Express Men of the Match: *Crusaders:* Gary Middlehurst; *Lions:* Gareth O'Brien.
Penalty count: 6-9; **Half-time:** 8-20; **Referee:** Tom Crashley; **Attendance:** 715 *(at The Rock, Wrexham).*

BARROW RAIDERS 10 DONCASTER 22

RAIDERS: 1 Ian Mort; 26 Ryan Shaw; 32 Michael Platt; 4 Max Wiper; 5 Dalton Grant; 6 Dominic Speakman; 34 Bobbie Goulding; 8 Joe Burke; 9 Nathan Mossop; 15 Danny Jones; 11 Liam Harrison; 25 Craig Briscoe; 13 Dan Toal. Subs (all used): 14 Aaron Lloyd; 7 Liam Campbell; 10 Jamie Butler; 24 Joe Bullock.
Tries: Grant (31), Mort (80); **Goals:** Shaw 1/2.
Dismissal: Goulding (80) - dissent.
Sin bin: Toal (77) - fighting.
DONCASTER: 5 Dave Scott; 4 Nev Morrison; 29 Richard Whiting; 3 Liam Welham; 22 Tom Hodson; 6 Paul Cooke; 23 Richard Wilkinson; 21 Matt Carbutt; 9 Kyle Kesik; 16 Craig Robinson; 28 Liam Kent; 25 Alex Starling; 13 Mike Emmett. Subs (all used): 15 Scott Spaven; 24 Steve Snitch; 14 Russ Spiers; - Liam Colbon.
Tries: Morrison (8), Wilkinson (20), Hodson (70), Colbon (77); **Goals:** Scott 3/4.
Sin bin: Emmett (77) - fighting.
Rugby Leaguer & League Express Men of the Match: *Raiders:* Liam Harrison; *Doncaster:* Paul Cooke.
Penalty count: 8-7; **Half-time:** 6-10;
Referee: Gareth Hewer; **Attendance:** 1,048.

FEATHERSTONE ROVERS 36 DEWSBURY RAMS 24

ROVERS: 1 Ian Hardman; 36 Jason Crookes; 35 Ben Blackmore; 22 James Mendeika; 2 Will Sharp; 19 Kyle Briggs; 23 Andy Kain; 39 Chris Green; 9 Andy Ellis; 38 Kyle Trout; 18 Jamie Cording; 40 Danny Bridge; 11 James Lockwood. Subs (all used): 6 Jack Bussey; 16 Andrew Bostock; 15 Matty Dale; 14 George Flanagan.
Tries: Kain (22, 48, 60), Blackmore (28, 56), Hardman (75); **Goals:** Briggs 1/1, Bussey 5/6.
RAMS: 22 Jordan Grayston; 2 Dale Morton; 3 Karl Pryce; 19 Callan Beckett; 21 Austin Buchanan; 31 Kieran Hyde; 7 Anthony Thackeray; 29 Ewan Dowes; 9 Wayne Godwin; 32 Makali Aizue; 4 Shane Grady; 12 Scott Hale; 10 Ryan Hepworth. Subs (all used): 6 Tom Hemingway; 15 Tommy Gallagher; 8 Stephen Nash; 17 Matthew Haggarty.
Tries: Morton (6), Thackeray (9), Hale (25), Aizue (70);
Goals: Grayston 2/3, Hemingway 2/2.
Rugby Leaguer & League Express Men of the Match: *Rovers:* Andy Kain; *Rams:* Makali Aizue.
Penalty count: 10-10; **Half-time:** 14-16;
Referee: George Stokes; **Attendance:** 2,110.

Tuesday 10th June 2014

WHITEHAVEN 28 KEIGHLEY COUGARS 18

WHITEHAVEN: 1 Tom Carr; 5 Shaun Ainscough; 3 Jessie Joe Nandye; 6 Chris Taylor; 2 Craig Calvert; 26 Brett Seymour; 7 Cain Southernwood; 8 Samir Tahraoui; 9 James Newton; 30 Carl Forster; 4 Scott McAvoy; 12 Lee Mitchell; 11 Lee Doran. Subs (all used): 14 Neil Thorman; 13 Bradd Crellin; 27 Kurtis Quinn; 22 James Robinson.
Tries: Taylor (14), Nandye (29), McAvoy (54), Forster (73), Ainscough (75); **Goals:** Carr 4/5.
COUGARS: 21 Jesse Sheriffe; 2 Richie Barnett; 19 Danny Lawton; 4 James Haley; 5 Paul White; 6 Danny Jones; 7 Paul Handforth; 8 Andy Shickell; 9 James Feather; 10 Sean Hesketh; 11 Josh Lynam; 12 Brendan Rawlins; 13 Ashley Lindsay. Subs (all used): 16 Jode Sheriffe; 17 Ben Sagar; 18 Neil Cherryholme; 34 Luke Haigh.
Tries: Feather (4), Lawton (33), White (65);
Goals: Jones 3/3.
Rugby Leaguer & League Express Men of the Match: *Whitehaven:* Carl Forster; *Cougars:* Danny Jones.
Penalty count: 10-8; **Half-time:** 10-12;
Referee: Jamie Bloem; **Attendance:** 741.

Wednesday 11th June 2014

LEIGH CENTURIONS 26 HALIFAX 24

CENTURIONS: 1 Gregg McNally; 23 Jonathan Pownall; 36 Chris Hankinson; 30 Kurt Haggerty; 15 Liam Kay; 6 Martyn Ridyard; 7 Ryan Brierley; 8 Tom Spencer; 9 Bob Beswick; 10 Oliver Wilkes; 11 Matt Sarsfield; 12 Tommy Goulden; 13 Sam Barlow. Subs (all used): 14 Sean Penkywicz; 18 Jamie Acton; 27 Anthony Bate; 29 Jake Emmitt.
Tries: Pownall (6), Wilkes (10, 73), McNally (20);
Goals: Ridyard 5/5.
Dismissal: Haggerty (56) - fighting.
On report: Brawl (56).

HALIFAX: 1 Ryan Fieldhouse; 26 Peter Fox; 16 Danny Cowling; 3 Steve Tyrer; 25 Gareth Potts; 7 Simon Brown; 14 Paul Mennell; 8 Tony Tonks; 19 Keith Holden; 10 Luke Ambler; 11 Dane Manning; 27 Ross Divorty; 13 Luke Adamson. Subs (all used): 12 Andy Bracek; 18 Ben Johnston; 23 Callum Casey; 28 Jack Spencer.
Tries: Potts (17), Tyrer (38), Ambler (64), Casey (71);
Goals: Tyrer 4/4.
Dismissal: Manning (56) - late challenge on Barlow.
On report: Brawl (56).
Rugby Leaguer & League Express Men of the Match: *Centurions:* Tommy Goulden; *Halifax:* Ross Divorty.
Penalty count: 9-6; **Half-time:** 18-12;
Referee: Chris Leatherbarrow; **Attendance:** 2,571.

ROUND 15

Friday 13th June 2014

SWINTON LIONS 39 ROCHDALE HORNETS 18

LIONS: 28 Chris Atkin; 18 Jordan Burke; 4 Mick Nanyn; 6 Anthony Bowman; 1 Ritchie Hawkyard; 22 Gareth O'Brien; 7 Ian Watson; 23 Gavin Bennion; 9 Andy Ackers; 16 Mike Morrison; 13 James Brown; 12 Darren Hawkyard; 24 Martin Aspinwall. Subs (all used): 17 Zach Johnson; 8 Luke Menzies; - Ed Barber; 27 Lewis Hulme.
Tries: Ackers (2, 27), Nanyn (21), Atkin (37), Barber (54, 80); **Goals:** O'Brien 7/7; **Field goal:** O'Brien (70).
HORNETS: 1 Wayne English; 9 Lewis Sheridan; 4 Daniel Davies; 20 Stuart Littler; 28 Shaun Robinson; 6 Paul Crook; 17 Ryan Millard; 8 John Cookson; 23 James Dandy; 10 Warren Thompson; 11 Chris Baines; 24 Tony Suffolk; 27 Joe Greenwood. Subs (all used): 26 Alex McClurg; 16 Anthony Walker; 33 Dave Llewellyn; 18 James Tilley.
Tries: Robinson (11, 32), Millard (42); **Goals:** Crook 3/3.
Rugby Leaguer & League Express Men of the Match: *Lions:* Andy Ackers; *Hornets:* Shaun Robinson.
Penalty count: 10-5; **Half-time:** 24-12;
Referee: Gareth Hewer; **Attendance:** 430.

Sunday 15th June 2014

NORTH WALES CRUSADERS 22 WHITEHAVEN 21

CRUSADERS: 1 Tommy Johnson; 2 Dan Birkett; 29 Steve Bannister; 17 Stuart Reardon; 5 Rob Massam; 7 Jamie Dallimore; 19 Karl Ashall; 8 Jonny Walker; 24 Lee Hudson; 10 Mark Offerdahl; 12 Gary Middlehurst; 14 Stephen Wild; 11 Toby Adamson. Subs (all used): 13 Jono Smith; 30 Sebastien Martins; 3 Christiaan Roets; 25 Owain Griffiths.
Tries: Birkett (13), Offerdahl (18), Smith (44), Middlehurst (77); **Goals:** Johnson 3/5.
WHITEHAVEN: 1 Tom Carr; 2 Craig Calvert; 3 Jessie Joe Nandye; 6 Chris Taylor; 5 Shaun Ainscough; 26 Brett Seymour; 7 Cain Southernwood; 30 Carl Forster; 9 James Newton; 8 Samir Tahraoui; 4 Scott McAvoy; 12 Lee Mitchell; 11 Lee Doran. Subs (all used): 14 Neil Thorman; 27 Kurtis Quinn; 22 James Robinson; 13 Bradd Crellin.
Tries: Taylor (26), Nandye (49, 79), Southernwood (53);
Goals: Carr 2/5; **Field goal:** Seymour (69).
Rugby Leaguer & League Express Men of the Match: *Crusaders:* Gary Middlehurst; *Whitehaven:* Jessie Joe Nandye.
Penalty count: 7-11; **Half-time:** 8-6;
Referee: Chris Leatherbarrow; **Attendance:** 621 *(at The Rock, Wrexham).*

DEWSBURY RAMS 12 SHEFFIELD EAGLES 28

RAMS: 3 Karl Pryce; 2 Dale Morton; 19 Callan Beckett; 4 Shane Grady; 21 Austin Buchanan; 31 Kieran Hyde; 7 Anthony Thackeray; 29 Ewan Dowes; 6 Tom Hemingway; 32 Makali Aizue; 10 Ryan Hepworth; 12 Scott Hale; 15 Tommy Gallagher. Subs (all used): 14 Ryan Wright; 8 Stephen Nash; 17 Matthew Haggarty; - Kyle Briggs.
Tries: Grady (11), Buchanan (51);
Goals: Hemingway 0/1, Hyde 2/2.
On report: Nash (57) - alleged punching.
EAGLES: 1 Quentin Laulu-Togagae; 2 Scott Turner; 3 Menzie Yere; 15 Matt Garside; 5 Misi Taulapapa; 19 Cory Aston; 7 Dominic Brambani; 18 Tom Lillycrop; 9 Andrew Henderson; 10 Mitchell Stringer; 11 Michael Knowles; 22 Will Hope; 6 Pat Walker. Subs (all used): 24 Gareth Owen; 8 Eddie Battye; 12 Peter Green; 17 Ben Jones.
Tries: Taulapapa (20, 66), Turner (33), Yere (69), Walker (75); **Goals:** Walker 4/6.
On report: Stringer (57) - alleged punching.
Rugby Leaguer & League Express Men of the Match: *Rams:* Scott Hale; *Eagles:* Dominic Brambani.
Penalty count: 9-9; **Half-time:** 4-10;
Referee: Jamie Bloem; **Attendance:** 867.

FEATHERSTONE ROVERS 22 DONCASTER 22

ROVERS: 1 Ian Hardman; 36 Jason Crookes; 3 Greg Worthington; 35 Ben Blackmore; 2 Will Sharp; 23 Andy Kain; 33 Harry Siejka; 39 Chris Green; 9 Andy Ellis; 38 Kyle Trout; 18 Jamie Cording; 40 Danny Bridge; 11 James Lockwood. Subs: 6 Jack Bussey; 16 Andrew Bostock; 15 Matty Dale; 22 James Mendeika (not used).
Tries: Blackmore (22), Bridge (28), Bostock (44), Bussey (51); **Goals:** Siejka 3/4.
DONCASTER: 5 Dave Scott; 4 Nev Morrison; 3 Liam Welham; 29 Richard Whiting; 22 Tom Hodson; 6 Paul Cooke; 23 Richard Wilkinson; 16 Craig Robinson; 9 Kyle Kesik; 21 Matt Carbutt; 28 Liam Colbon; 25 Alex Starling; 13 Mike Emmett. Subs (all used): 14 Russ Spiers; 15 Scott Spaven; 24 Steve Snitch; 12 Michael Kelly.
Tries: Welham (8), Emmett (17), Whiting (35, 79);
Goals: Scott 3/4.
Rugby Leaguer & League Express Men of the Match: *Rovers:* Andy Kain; *Doncaster:* Paul Cooke.
Penalty count: 5-10; **Half-time:** 10-18;
Referee: Joe Cobb; **Attendance:** 2,169.

HALIFAX 18 WORKINGTON TOWN 10

HALIFAX: 1 Ryan Fieldhouse; 26 Peter Fox; 3 Steve Tyrer; 4 Ben Heaton; 21 Tom Saxton; 7 Simon Brown; 18 Ben Johnston; 10 Luke Ambler; 23 Callum Casey; 8 Tony Tonks; 11 Dane Manning; 27 Ross Divorty; 13 Luke Adamson. Subs (all used): 12 Andy Bracek; 19 Keith Holden; 24 Sam Brooks; 28 Jack Spencer.
Tries: Divorty (40), Adamson (55), Fieldhouse (62);
Goals: Tyrer 3/3.
TOWN: 23 Lewis Tierney; 1 Brett Carter; 4 Andy Morris; 30 Jack Murphy; 3 Jason Mossop; 6 Peter Lupton; 16 Carl Forber; 8 Kris Coward; 9 Graeme Mattinson; 10 Marc Shackley; 11 Brett Phillips; 12 Jarrad Stack; 13 Karl Olstrum. Subs (all used): 19 Nathan Lucock; 18 James Duerden; 7 Callum Phillips; 15 Daniel Rooney.
Tries: Mossop (2), Carter (30); **Goals:** Forber 1/3.
Rugby Leaguer & League Express Men of the Match: *Halifax:* Ben Johnston; *Town:* Lewis Tierney.
Penalty count: 4-10; **Half-time:** 6-10;
Referee: Warren Turley; **Attendance:** 1,658.

KEIGHLEY COUGARS 24 BATLEY BULLDOGS 28

COUGARS: 1 James Craven; 5 Paul White; 4 James Haley; 22 Daley Williams; 2 Richie Barnett; 6 Danny Jones; 7 Paul Handforth; 8 Andy Shickell; 9 James Feather; 10 Sean Hesketh; 25 Lewis Graham; 12 Brendan Rawlins; 13 Ashley Lindsay. Subs (all used): 34 Luke Haigh; 16 Jode Sheriffe; 32 Ross Peltier; 27 Jack Lee.
Tries: Jones (16, 56), Williams (45), Barnett (53, 76);
Goals: Jones 2/5.
BULLDOGS: 1 Miles Greenwood; 2 Vinny Finigan; 17 Lee Paterson; 28 Josh Griffin; 29 Alex Brown; 6 Ben Black; 7 Scott Leatherbarrow; 8 Byron Smith; 18 Luke Blake; 31 Keegan Hirst; 12 Sam Scott; 3 Alex Bretherton; 13 Mark Applegarth. Subs (all used): 9 Anthony Nicholson; 10 Alex Rowe; - Anthony Mullally; 19 Joe Chandler.
Tries: Scott (5, 20), Greenwood (37, 79), Griffin (68);
Goals: Leatherbarrow 4/6.
Rugby Leaguer & League Express Men of the Match: *Cougars:* Danny Jones; *Bulldogs:* Sam Scott.
Penalty count: 11-8; **Half-time:** 6-18;
Referee: Andrew Sweet; **Attendance:** 913.

LEIGH CENTURIONS 60 BARROW RAIDERS 0

CENTURIONS: 1 Gregg McNally; 23 Jonathan Pownall; 36 Chris Hankinson; 20 Andy Thornley; 15 Liam Kay; 6 Martyn Ridyard; 7 Ryan Brierley; 8 Tom Spencer; 9 Bob Beswick; 10 Oliver Wilkes; 11 Matt Sarsfield; 12 Tommy Goulden; 35 Sam Hopkins. Subs (all used): 14 Sean Penkywicz; 18 Jamie Acton; 27 Anthony Bate; 29 Jake Emmitt.
Tries: Kay (4, 17, 40, 48, 79), Thornley (35), Brierley (37, 65), Hopkins (56), Penkywicz (63), Pownall (74); **Goals:** Ridyard 8/11.
RAIDERS: 1 Ian Mort; 21 Mike Backhouse; 26 Ryan Shaw; 4 Max Wiper; 5 Dalton Grant; 7 Liam Campbell; 34 Bobbie Goulding; 8 Joe Burke; 9 Nathan Mossop; 15 Danny Jones; 11 Liam Harrison; - Ben Musolino; 13 Dan Toal. Subs (all used): 14 Aaron Lloyd; 3 Aaron Low; 10 Jamie Butler; 31 Ben Davies.
Rugby Leaguer & League Express Men of the Match: *Centurions:* Sean Penkywicz; *Raiders:* Dan Toal.
Penalty count: 9-5; **Half-time:** 24-0;
Referee: Dave Merrick; **Attendance:** 2,508.

ROUND 16

Sunday 22nd June 2014

BATLEY BULLDOGS 55 NORTH WALES CRUSADERS 12

BULLDOGS: 1 Miles Greenwood; 2 Vinny Finigan; 17 Lee Paterson; 28 Josh Griffin; 29 Alex Brown; 6 Ben Black; 7 Scott Leatherbarrow; 8 Byron Smith; 18 Luke Blake; 20 Adam Gledhill; 12 Sam Scott; 3 Alex Bretherton; 13 Mark Applegarth. Subs (all used): 4 Ayden Faal; 9 Anthony Nicholson; 10 Alex Rowe; 31 Keegan Hirst.
Tries: Greenwood (3, 42, 48), Leatherbarrow (8), A Brown (11, 78), Finigan (28), Scott (45), Blake (68), Smith (72); **Goals:** Leatherbarrow 7/10;
Field goal: Leatherbarrow (80).
CRUSADERS: 1 Tommy Johnson; 2 Dan Birkett; 17 Stuart Reardon; 29 Steve Bannister; 5 Rob Massam; 19 Karl Ashall; 7 Jamie Dallimore; 8 Jonny Walker; 24 Lee Hudson; 30 Sebastien Martins; 12 Gary Middlehurst; 14 Stephen Wild; 11 Toby Adamson. Subs (all used): 3 Christiaan Roets; 21 Simon Stephens; 37 Jonathan Soum; 27 Jamie Clarke.
Tries: Birkett (40), Adamson (60); **Goals:** Johnson 2/2.
Rugby Leaguer & League Express Men of the Match: *Bulldogs:* Miles Greenwood; *Crusaders:* Jonny Walker.
Penalty count: 6-8; **Half-time:** 20-6;
Referee: Tom Crashley; **Attendance:** 563.

SHEFFIELD EAGLES 16 KEIGHLEY COUGARS 29

EAGLES: 1 Quentin Laulu-Togagae; 2 Scott Turner; 3 Menzie Yere; 15 Matt Garside; 5 Misi Taulapapa; 7 Dominic Brambani; 19 Cory Aston; 18 Tom Lillycrop; 9 Andrew Henderson; 10 Mitchell Stringer; 11 Michael Knowles; 16 Duane Straugheir; 6 Pat Walker. Subs (all used): 24 Gareth Owen; 8 Eddie Battye; 12 Peter Green; 31 Theo Gonzalez-Trique.
Tries: Laulu-Togagae (1), Straugheir (22), Knowles (73);
Goals: Walker 2/3.
COUGARS: 1 James Craven; 2 Richie Barnett; 4 James Haley; 19 Danny Lawton; 22 Daley Williams; 6 Danny Jones; 7 Paul Handforth; 10 Sean Hesketh; 9 James Feather; 12 Brendan Rawlins; 11 Josh Lynam; 33 Oliver Pursglove; 13 Ashley Lindsay. Subs (all used): 16 Jode Sheriffe; 17 Ben Sagar; 18 Neil Cherryholme; 34 Luke Haigh.
Tries: Haley (12), Lynam (19), Craven (54), Hesketh (64); **Goals:** Jones 6/6; **Field goal:** Jones (76).
Rugby Leaguer & League Express Men of the Match: *Eagles:* Michael Knowles; *Cougars:* Danny Jones.
Penalty count: 7-5; **Half-time:** 10-14;
Referee: Joe Cobb; **Attendance:** 743.

BARROW RAIDERS 24 SWINTON LIONS 38

RAIDERS: 1 Ian Mort; 26 Ryan Shaw; 3 Aaron Low; 4 Max Wiper; 5 Dalton Grant; 6 Dom Speakman; 7 Liam Campbell; 31 Ben Davies; 9 Nathan Mossop; 15 Danny Jones; 11 Liam Harrison; - Ben Musolino; 13 Dan Toal. Subs (all used): 14 Aaron Lloyd; 17 Andrew Dawson; 24 Joe Bullock; 25 Craig Briscoe.
Tries: Wiper (6), Campbell (46), Toal (50, 66);
Goals: Shaw 4/4.
LIONS: 1 Ritchie Hawkyard; 18 Jordan Burke; 4 Mick Nanyn; 6 Anthony Bowman; 23 Steve Maden; 22 Gareth O'Brien; 7 Ian Watson; 13 James Brown; 9 Andy Ackers; 16 Mike Morrison; - Ed Barber; 12 Darren Hawkyard; 24 Martin Aspinwall. Subs (all used): 17 Zach Johnson; 8 Luke Menzies; 15 Josh Barlow; 27 Lewis Hulme.
Tries: Morrison (19), Bowman (23), Nanyn (32), Barber (37, 55, 70), R Hawkyard (57); **Goals:** O'Brien 5/7.
Rugby Leaguer & League Express Men of the Match: *Raiders:* Dan Toal; *Lions:* Ian Watson.
Penalty count: 5-5; **Half-time:** 6-22;
Referee: Chris Leatherbarrow; **Attendance:** 932.

DEWSBURY RAMS 24 DONCASTER 8

RAMS: 3 Karl Pryce; 2 Dale Morton; 19 Callan Beckett; 4 Shane Grady; 21 Austin Buchanan; - Kyle Briggs; 7 Anthony Thackeray; 29 Ewan Dowes; 6 Tom Hemingway; 32 Makali Aizue; 10 Ryan Hepworth; 12 Scott Hale; 20 Jobe Murphy. Subs (all used): 31 Kieran Hyde; 8 Stephen Nash; 11 Rob Spicer; 17 Matthew Haggarty.
Tries: Thackeray (30, 78), Briggs (39), Beckett (47), Grady (53); **Goals:** Hemingway 2/4, Hyde 0/1.
Sin bin: Spicer (59) - late challenge.
On report: Nash (26) - alleged late challenge on Spiers.
DONCASTER: 5 Dave Scott; 4 Nev Morrison; 19 Liam Cunningham; 3 Liam Welham; 2 Stewart Sanderson; 6 Paul Cooke; 26 Jacob Miller; 21 Matt Carbutt; 9 Kyle Kesik; 28 Liam Watts; 29 Liam Colbon; 25 Alex Starling; 24 Steve Snitch. Subs (all used): 14 Russ Spiers; 15 Scott Spaven; 18 Ryan Wilson; 12 Michael Kelly.
Try: Watts (65); **Goals:** Scott 2/2.
Rugby Leaguer & League Express Men of the Match: *Rams:* Dale Morton; *Doncaster:* Liam Watts.
Penalty count: 4-8; **Half-time:** 8-2;
Referee: Gareth Hewer; **Attendance:** 721.

HALIFAX 42 ROCHDALE HORNETS 24

HALIFAX: 1 Ryan Fieldhouse; 26 Peter Fox; 3 Steve Tyrer; 4 Ben Heaton; 21 Tom Saxton; 7 Simon Brown; 18 Ben Johnston; 10 Luke Ambler; 9 Ben Kaye; 8 Tony Tonks; 13 Luke Adamson; 27 Ross Divorty; 12 Andy Bracek. Subs (all used): 6 Scott Murrell; 14 Paul Mennell; 23 Callum Casey; 24 Sam Brooks.
Tries: Divorty (10, 25, 60, 70), Fieldhouse (28), Ambler (46, 53), Adamson (75);
Goals: Tyrer 2/3, Brown 2/3, Murrell 1/2.
HORNETS: 1 Wayne English; 5 Ryan King; 4 Daniel Davies; 28 Stuart Littler; 18 Shaun Robinson; 6 Paul Crook; 9 Lewis Sheridan; 27 Anthony Walker; 23 James Dandy; 10 Warren Thompson; 33 Dave Llewellyn; 20 Josh Jones; 24 Tony Suffolk. Subs (all used): 8 John Cookson; 11 Chris Baines; 21 Alex McClurg; 18 James Tilley.
Tries: Llewellyn (33), Sheridan (42), Crook (57), Baines (64); **Goals:** Crook 4/4.
Rugby Leaguer & League Express Men of the Match: *Halifax:* Ross Divorty; *Hornets:* Dave Llewellyn.
Penalty count: 9-4; **Half-time:** 16-6;
Referee: Jamie Bloem; **Attendance:** 1,425.

WHITEHAVEN 10 LEIGH CENTURIONS 24

WHITEHAVEN: 1 Tom Carr; 5 Shaun Ainscough; 3 Jessie Joe Nandye; 6 Chris Taylor; 2 Craig Calvert; 26 Brett Seymour; 7 Cain Southernwood; 20 Jordan Hand; 9 James Newton; 30 Carl Forster; 4 Scott McAvoy; 12 Lee Mitchell; 11 Lee Doran. Subs (all used): 14 Neil Thorman; 13 Bradd Crellin; 22 James Robinson; 8 Samir Tahraoui.
Tries: Calvert (3), Nandye (46); **Goals:** Southernwood 1/2.
Sin bin: Carr (35) - interference; Seymour (36) - dissent.
CENTURIONS: 1 Gregg McNally; 23 Jonathan Pownall; 31 Cameron Pitman; 20 Andy Thornley; 15 Liam Kay; 6 Martyn Ridyard; 7 Ryan Brierley; 8 Tom Spencer; 9 Bob Beswick; 10 Oliver Wilkes; 11 Matt Sarsfield; 12 Tommy Goulden; 35 Sam Hopkins. Subs (all used): 14 Sean Penkywicz; 36 Chris Hankinson; 18 Jamie Acton; 29 Jake Emmitt.
Tries: Goulden (8), Pownall (26), McNally (51), Brierley (70); **Goals:** Ridyard 4/4.
Rugby Leaguer & League Express Men of the Match: *Whitehaven:* Scott McAvoy; *Centurions:* Tom Spencer.
Penalty count: 6-16; **Half-time:** 4-12;
Referee: Chris Kendall; **Attendance:** 959.

WORKINGTON TOWN 20 FEATHERSTONE ROVERS 18

TOWN: 30 Lewis Tierney; 24 Matthew Johnson; 3 Jason Mossop; 4 Andy Morris; 1 Brett Carter; 7 Callum Phillips; 16 Carl Forber; 8 Kris Coward; 9 Graeme

Mattinson; 15 Daniel Rooney; 11 Brett Phillips; 12 Jarrad Stack; 18 James Duerden. Subs: 14 Kayle Connor (not used); 19 Nathan Lucock; 20 Callum Rowlandson; 32 Kieran McAvoy.
Tries: Mattinson (1), Forber (23), Morris (73);
Goals: Forber 4/4.
ROVERS: 1 Ian Hardman; 35 Jason Crookes; 36 Ben Blackmore; 3 Greg Worthington; 2 Will Sharp; 23 Andy Kain; 33 Harry Siejka; 16 Andrew Bostock; 9 Andy Ellis; 38 Kyle Trout; 18 Jamie Cording; 11 James Lockwood; 15 Matty Dale. Subs (all used): 6 Jack Bussey; 39 Chris Green; 37 Liam Kent; 22 James Mendeika.
Tries: Lockwood (30), Sharp (55, 78), Bostock (60);
Goals: Siejka 1/4.
Rugby Leaguer & League Express Men of the Match: *Town:* Brett Phillips; *Rovers:* Andrew Bostock.
Penalty count: 6-7; **Half-time:** 12-4;
Referee: Dave Merrick; **Attendance:** 776.

ROUND 17

Sunday 29th June 2014

BATLEY BULLDOGS 34 BARROW RAIDERS 4

BULLDOGS: 1 Miles Greenwood; 2 Vinny Finigan; 17 Lee Paterson; 19 Joe Chandler; 29 Alex Brown; 6 Ben Black; 7 Scott Leatherbarrow; 8 Byron Smith; 18 Luke Blake; 20 Adam Gledhill; 12 Sam Scott; 11 John Davies; 13 Mark Applegarth. Subs (all used): 4 Ayden Faal; 9 Anthony Nicholson; 10 Alex Rowe; 31 Keegan Hirst.
Tries: Greenwood (5, 14, 66, 71), Davies (22), Finigan (73); **Goals:** Leatherbarrow 5/6.
RAIDERS: 26 Ryan Shaw; 21 Mike Backhouse; 33 Ben Musolino; 4 Max Wiper; 5 Dalton Grant; 6 Dom Speakman; 19 Brad Marwood; 31 Ben Davies; 9 Nathan Mossop; 15 Danny Jones; 11 Liam Harrison; 25 Craig Briscoe; 13 Dan Toal. Subs (all used): 14 Aaron Lloyd; 17 Andrew Dawson; 24 Joe Bullock; 30 Connor Dwyer.
Try: Wiper (46); **Goals:** Shaw 0/1.
Rugby Leaguer & League Express Men of the Match: *Bulldogs:* Miles Greenwood; *Raiders:* Dom Speakman.
Penalty count: 4-3; **Half-time:** 18-0;
Referee: Chris Leatherbarrow; **Attendance:** 615.

SHEFFIELD EAGLES 14 HALIFAX 32

EAGLES: 1 Quentin Laulu-Togagae; 28 Tom Ashton; 3 Menzie Yere; 16 Duane Straugheir; 5 Misi Taulapapa; 6 Pat Walker; 7 Dominic Brambani; 8 Eddie Battye; 9 Andrew Henderson; 10 Mitchell Stringer; 15 Matt Garside; 22 Will Hope; 11 Michael Knowles. Subs (all used): 24 Gareth Owen; 18 Tom Lillycrop; 12 Peter Green; 4 Lelauloto Tagaloa.
Tries: Laulu-Togagae (55), Brambani (76), Yere (80);
Goals: Walker 0/1, Brambani 1/2.
HALIFAX: 1 Ryan Fieldhouse; 26 Peter Fox; 15 Adam Robinson; 23 Callum Casey; 21 Tom Saxton; 7 Simon Brown; 6 Scott Murrell; 8 Tony Tonks; 9 Ben Kaye; 10 Luke Ambler; 13 Luke Adamson; 27 Ross Divorty; 12 Andy Bracek. Subs (all used): 14 Paul Mennell; 18 Ben Johnston; 24 Sam Brooks; 28 Jack Spencer.
Tries: Fox (14, 36), Casey (21, 60), Fieldhouse (43), Adamson (71); **Goals:** Brown 2/3, Murrell 2/3.
Rugby Leaguer & League Express Men of the Match: *Eagles:* Eddie Battye; *Halifax:* Scott Murrell.
Penalty count: 8-6; **Half-time:** 0-16;
Referee: Tom Crashley; **Attendance:** 955.

DONCASTER 22 WHITEHAVEN 16

DONCASTER: 5 Dave Scott; 2 Stewart Sanderson; 3 Liam Welham; 19 Liam Cunningham; 22 Tom Hodson; 6 Paul Cooke; 23 Richard Wilkinson; 21 Matt Carbutt; 9 Kyle Kesik; 16 Craig Robinson; 28 Dean Hadley; 29 Liam Colbon; 13 Mike Emmett. Subs (all used): 15 Scott Spaven; 14 Russ Spiers; 24 Steve Snitch; 12 Michael Kelly.
Tries: Kesik (25), Wilkinson (37), Cunningham (43), Hadley (78); **Goals:** Scott 3/4.
WHITEHAVEN: 1 Tom Carr; 5 Shaun Ainscough; 6 Chris Taylor; 3 Jessie Joe Nandye; 2 Craig Calvert; 26 Brett Seymour; 7 Cain Southernwood; 20 Jordan Hand; 9 James Newton; 30 Carl Forster; 4 Scott McAvoy; 12 Lee Mitchell; 11 Lee Doran. Subs (all used): 14 Neil Thorman; 13 Bradd Crellin; 27 Jon Grayshon; 22 James Robinson.
Tries: Taylor (10), Carr (50), Mitchell (56);
Goals: Southernwood 2/3.
Rugby Leaguer & League Express Men of the Match: *Doncaster:* Richard Wilkinson; *Whitehaven:* Lee Doran.
Penalty count: 5-2; **Half-time:** 10-6;
Referee: Dave Merrick; **Attendance:** 680 *(at Castle Park).*

FEATHERSTONE ROVERS 56 NORTH WALES CRUSADERS 18

ROVERS: 34 Jarrod Sammut; 2 Will Sharp; 22 James Mendeika; 3 Greg Worthington; 36 Ben Blackmore; 23 Andy Kain; 33 Harry Siejka; 8 Steve Crossley; 9 Andy Ellis; 38 Kyle Trout; 37 Liam Kent; 40 Danny Bridge; 11 James Lockwood. Subs (all used): 6 Jack Bussey; 14 George Flanagan; 13 Matt James; 39 Chris Green.
Tries: Kain (1), Mendeika (14, 29, 31), Blackmore (20), Ellis (25), Kent (55), Flanagan (62), Sharp (76);
Goals: Sammut 10/10.
Dismissal: Lockwood (68) - fighting.
CRUSADERS: 1 Tommy Johnson; 5 Rob Massam; 29 Steve Bannister; 17 Stuart Reardon; 23 Greg Wilde; 19 Karl Ashall; 7 Jamie Dallimore; 8 Jonny Walker; 24 Lee Hudson; 30 Sebastien Martins; 12 Gary Middlehurst; 14 Stephen Wild; 11 Toby Adamson. Subs (all used): 37 Jonathan Soum; - Mick Govin; 3 Christiaan Roets; 13 Jono Smith.
Tries: Dallimore (7), Massam (51), Walker (70);
Goals: Johnson 2/2, Bannister 1/1.
Sin bin: Johnson (68) - fighting.
Rugby Leaguer & League Express Men of the Match: *Rovers:* James Mendeika; *Crusaders:* Mick Govin.
Penalty count: 8-10; **Half-time:** 38-6;
Referee: Andrew Sweet; **Attendance:** 1,653.

KEIGHLEY COUGARS 48 ROCHDALE HORNETS 6

COUGARS: 1 James Craven; 2 Richie Barnett; 19 Danny Lawton; 4 James Haley; 5 Paul White; 6 Danny Jones; 7 Paul Handforth; 12 Brendan Rawlins; 9 James Feather; 10 Sean Hesketh; 11 Josh Lynam; 33 Oliver Pursglove; 13 Ashley Lindsay. Subs (all used): 16 Jode Sheriffe; 17 Ben Sagar; 18 Neil Cherryholme; 34 Luke Haigh.
Tries: Handforth (18, 79), Haley (40, 73), Lawton (42), Lynam (47), Craven (53, 70), White (63);
Goals: Handforth 6/9.
HORNETS: 1 Wayne English; 12 Alex Trumper; 4 Daniel Davies; 20 Stuart Littler; 9 Lewis Sheridan; 28 Gary Wheeler; 17 Ryan Millard; 16 Anthony Walker; 6 Paul Crook; 10 Warren Thompson; 11 Chris Baines; 33 Dave Llewellyn; 24 Joe Greenwood. Subs (all used): 8 John Cookson; 13 Jordan Case; 21 Alex McClurg; 27 Richard Beaumont.
Try: Millard (58); **Goals:** Crook 1/1.
Rugby Leaguer & League Express Men of the Match: *Cougars:* Paul Handforth; *Hornets:* Ryan Millard.
Penalty count: 9-3; **Half-time:** 10-0;
Referee: Michael Woodhead; **Attendance:** 811.

LEIGH CENTURIONS 30 DEWSBURY RAMS 22

CENTURIONS: 1 Gregg McNally; 23 Jonathan Pownall; 36 Chris Hankinson; 20 Andy Thornley; 15 Liam Kay; 6 Martyn Ridyard; 7 Ryan Brierley; 8 Tom Spencer; 9 Bob Beswick; 35 Sam Hopkins; 11 Matt Sarsfield; 12 Tommy Goulden; 13 Sam Barlow. Subs (all used): 14 Sean Penkywicz; 10 Oliver Wilkes; 27 Anthony Bate; 29 Jake Emmitt.
Tries: Brierley (12), Kay (22, 42), Goulden (67), Pownall (74, 78); **Goals:** Ridyard 3/6.
Sin bin: Kay (72) - interference.
RAMS: 3 Karl Pryce; 2 Dale Morton; 19 Callan Beckett; 4 Shane Grady; 21 Austin Buchanan; - Kyle Briggs; 7 Anthony Thackeray; 29 Ewan Dowes; 6 Tom Hemingway; 32 Makali Aizue; 20 Jobe Murphy; 12 Scott Hale; 15 Tommy Gallagher. Subs (all used): 31 Kieran Hyde; 10 Ryan Hepworth; 8 Stephen Nash; 17 Matthew Haggarty.
Tries: Grady (16, 72), Hale (38), Morton (70);
Goals: Hemingway 3/4.
Rugby Leaguer & League Express Men of the Match: *Centurions:* Tommy Goulden; *Rams:* Anthony Thackeray.
Penalty count: 8-5; **Half-time:** 10-10;
Referee: Joe Cobb; **Attendance:** 2,217.

SWINTON LIONS 24 WORKINGTON TOWN 32

LIONS: 1 Ritchie Hawkyard; 2 Ben Warrilow; 6 Anthony Bowman; 4 Mick Nanyn; 5 Freddie Walker; 28 Chris Atkin; 18 Jordan Burke; 23 Gavin Bennion; 9 Andy Ackers; 16 Mike Morrison; 31 Ed Barber; 12 Darren Hawkyard; 13 James Brown. Subs (all used): 22 Ryan Maneely; 15 Josh Barlow; 17 Zach Johnson; 8 Luke Menzies.
Tries: D Hawkyard (58), Atkin (62), Bennion (70), Warrilow (78); **Goals:** Nanyn 4/4.
TOWN: 30 Jack Murphy; 3 Jason Mossop; 12 Jarrad Stack; 4 Andy Morris; 1 Brett Carter; 7 Callum Phillips; 16 Carl Forber; 8 Kris Coward; 9 Graeme Mattinson; 15 Daniel Rooney; 11 Brett Phillips; 24 Connor Farrell; 18 James Duerden. Subs (all used): 20 Callum Rowlandson; 32 Greg Burke; 13 Karl Olstrum; 19 Nathan Lucock.
Tries: Carter (19, 27), Mossop (22, 46), Lucock (43), Forber (51); **Goals:** Forber 4/7.
Rugby Leaguer & League Express Men of the Match: *Lions:* Mike Morrison; *Town:* Jarrad Stack.
Penalty count: 8-3; **Half-time:** 0-16; **Referee:** Jamie Bloem; **Attendance:** 405 *(at Park Lane, Sedgley Park).*

ROUND 18

Thursday 3rd July 2014

HALIFAX 38 KEIGHLEY COUGARS 6

HALIFAX: 1 Ryan Fieldhouse; 26 Peter Fox; 15 Adam Robinson; 23 Callum Casey; 21 Tom Saxton; 6 Scott Murrell; 14 Paul Mennell; 10 Luke Ambler; 9 Ben Kaye; 8 Tony Tonks; 13 Luke Adamson; 27 Ross Divorty; 12 Andy Bracek. Subs (all used): 18 Ben Johnston; 19 Keith Holden; 24 Sam Brooks; 28 Jack Spencer.
Tries: Spencer (35), Tonks (49), Robinson (53), Ambler (57), Murrell (60), Divorty (69), Saxton (76);
Goals: Murrell 4/5, Mennell 1/2.
COUGARS: 1 James Craven; 2 Richie Barnett; 19 Danny Lawton; 4 James Haley; 22 Daley Williams; 5 Paul White; 7 Paul Handforth; 12 Brendan Rawlins; 9 James Feather; 10 Sean Hesketh; 11 Josh Lynam; 33 Oliver Pursglove; 13 Ashley Lindsay. Subs (all used): 16 Jode Sheriffe; 17 Ben Sagar; 8 Andy Shickell; 34 Luke Haigh.
Try: Feather (14); **Goals:** Handforth 0/1, Lawton 1/1.
On report:
Lynam (65) - alleged high tackle on Fieldhouse.
Rugby Leaguer & League Express Men of the Match: *Halifax:* Luke Ambler; *Cougars:* Paul Handforth.
Penalty count: 6-5; **Half-time:** 6-4;
Referee: Chris Kendall; **Attendance:** 1,519.

Friday 4th July 2014

DEWSBURY RAMS 48 SWINTON LIONS 6

RAMS: 3 Karl Pryce; 2 Dale Morton; 19 Callan Beckett; 34 Ben Hellewell; 21 Austin Buchanan; 31 Kieran Hyde; 7 Anthony Thackeray; 29 Ewan Dowes; 6 Tom Hemingway; 32 Makali Aizue; 4 Shane Grady; 20 Jobe Murphy; 33 Kyle Briggs. Subs (all used): 14 Ryan Wright; 10 Ryan Hepworth; 17 Matthew Haggarty; 15 Tommy Gallagher.
Tries: Grady (2), Thackeray (31, 50), Pryce (37), Wright (43), Morton (60), Buchanan (73), Briggs (76);
Goals: Hemingway 3/3, Hyde 5/5.
LIONS: 1 Ritchie Hawkyard; 19 Jacque Peet; 31 Ed Barber; 4 Mick Nanyn; 5 Freddie Walker; 28 Chris Atkin; 22 Jordan Burke; 16 Mike Morrison; 9 Andy Ackers; 17 Zach Johnson; 23 Danny Bridge; 12 Darren Hawkyard; 13 James Brown. Subs (all used): 15 Josh Barlow; 24 Gavin Bennion; 25 Glenn Riley; 27 Lewis Hulme.
Try: Johnson (12); **Goals:** Nanyn 1/1.
Rugby Leaguer & League Express Men of the Match: *Rams:* Shane Grady; *Lions:* Zach Johnson.
Penalty count: 10-5; **Half-time:** 18-6;
Referee: Peter Brooke; **Attendance:** 749.

Sunday 6th July 2014

NORTH WALES CRUSADERS 24 DONCASTER 28

CRUSADERS: 1 Tommy Johnson; 2 Dan Birkett; 3 Christiaan Roets; 17 Stuart Reardon; 23 Greg Wilde; 19 Karl Ashall; 7 Jamie Dallimore; 8 Jonny Walker; 24 Lee Hudson; 30 Sebastien Martins; 29 Steve Bannister; 14 Stephen Wild; 11 Toby Adamson. Subs (all used): 13 Jono Smith; 37 Jonathan Soum; - Ryan Duffy; - Alex Davidson.
Tries: Wilde (21), Reardon (36), Birkett (48), Martins (62); **Goals:** Johnson 4/4.
DONCASTER: 5 Dave Scott; 2 Stewart Sanderson; 3 Liam Welham; 11 Lee Waterman; 22 Tom Hodson; 6 Paul Cooke; 23 Richard Wilkinson; 21 Matt Carbutt; 9 Kyle Kesik; 24 Steve Snitch; 29 Richard Whiting; 12 Michael Kelly; 13 Mike Emmett. Subs (all used): 15 Scott Spaven; 14 Russ Spiers; 16 Craig Robinson; 28 Liam Colbon.
Tries: Welham (13), Whiting (17), Spaven (57), Scott (66), Snitch (70); **Goals:** Scott 4/5.
Rugby Leaguer & League Express Men of the Match: *Crusaders:* Sebastien Martins; *Doncaster:* Mike Emmett.
Penalty count: 6-5; **Half-time:** 12-10;
Referee: Dave Merrick; **Attendance:** 538
(at The Rock, Wrexham).

BARROW RAIDERS 18 WHITEHAVEN 30

RAIDERS: 26 Ryan Shaw; 21 Mike Backhouse; 25 Craig Briscoe; 4 Max Wiper; 5 Dalton Grant; 6 Dom Speakman; 19 Brad Marwood; 31 Ben Davies; 9 Nathan Mossop; 17 Andrew Dawson; 11 Liam Harrison; 30 Connor Dwyer; 15 Danny Jones. Subs (all used): 14 Aaron Lloyd; 10 Jamie Butler; 24 Joe Bullock; 8 Joe Burke.
Tries: Davies (9), Mossop (15, 65); **Goals:** Shaw 3/3.
WHITEHAVEN: 1 Tom Carr; 5 Shaun Ainscough; 6 Chris Taylor; 3 Jessie Joe Nandye; 2 Craig Calvert; 26 Brett Seymour; 7 Cain Southernwood; 30 Carl Forster; 9 James Newton; 10 Paul Jackson; 4 Scott McAvoy; 12 Lee Mitchell; 11 Lee Doran. Subs (all used): 14 Neil Thorman; 13 Bradd Crellin; 29 Jon Grayshon; 22 James Robinson.
Tries: Southernwood (19), Calvert (23, 56), Ainscough (44), Mitchell (50), Nandye (73);
Goals: Southernwood 2/4, Carr 1/2.
Rugby Leaguer & League Express Men of the Match: *Raiders:* Nathan Mossop;
Whitehaven: Cain Southernwood.
Penalty count: 5-3; **Half-time:** 12-10;
Referee: Tim Roby; **Attendance:** 1,105.

LEIGH CENTURIONS 32 SHEFFIELD EAGLES 24

CENTURIONS: 1 Gregg McNally; 23 Jonathan Pownall; 36 Chris Hankinson; 4 Tom Armstrong; 15 Liam Kay; 9 Bob Beswick; 7 Ryan Brierley; 8 Tom Spencer; 14 Sean Penkywicz; 18 Jamie Acton; 11 Matt Sarsfield; 12 Tommy Goulden; 13 Sam Barlow. Subs (all used): 30 Kurt Haggerty; 35 Sam Hopkins; 29 Jake Emmitt; 16 Martin Aspinwall.
Tries: Brierley (3), Beswick (22), Hankinson (33), Sarsfield (37), Hopkins (39), Armstrong (80);
Goals: Brierley 4/6.
EAGLES: 1 Quentin Laulu-Togagae; 2 Scott Turner; 3 Menzie Yere; 16 Duane Straugheir; 5 Misi Taulapapa; 6 Pat Walker; 7 Dominic Brambani; 8 Eddie Battye; 9 Andrew Henderson; 10 Mitchell Stringer; 15 Matt Garside; 22 Will Hope; 11 Michael Knowles. Subs (all used): 14 James Davey; 4 Lelauloto Tagaloa; 27 Peter Aspinall; 31 Theo Gonzalez-Trique.
Tries: Turner (12, 50, 63), Davey (55);
Goals: Brambani 4/4.
On report:
Garside (21) - alleged late challenge on McNally.
Rugby Leaguer & League Express Men of the Match: *Centurions:* Sean Penkywicz; *Eagles:* James Davey.
Penalty count: 11-6; **Half-time:** 26-6;
Referee: Warren Turley; **Attendance:** 2,166.

ROCHDALE HORNETS 38 FEATHERSTONE ROVERS 34

HORNETS: 1 Wayne English; 29 Matty Dawson; 19 Dave Llewellyn; 20 Stuart Littler; 14 Sean Casey; 9 Lewis Sheridan; 17 Ryan Millard; 25 Anthony Walker; 6 Paul Crook; 10 Warren Thompson; 13 Jordan Case; 12 Alex Trumper; 28 Joe Greenwood. Subs (all used): 23 James Dandy; 7 Alex McClurg; - Richard Beaumont; 8 John Cookson.
Tries: Crook (4), Littler (10), Millard (14), Casey (43), Dawson (46), Dandy (57), Thompson (75);
Goals: Crook 5/5, Casey 0/2.
ROVERS: 1 Ian Hardman; 35 Jason Crookes; 27 Etuate Uaisele; 22 James Mendeika; 36 Ben Blackmore; 23 Andy Kain; 7 Gareth Moore; 8 Steve Crossley; 9 Andy Ellis; 38 Kyle Trout; 11 James Lockwood; 37 Liam Kent; 6 Jack Bussey. Subs (all used): 14 George Flanagan; 31 Shaun Pick; 13 Matt James; 2 Will Sharp.

Championship 2014 - Round by Round

Tries: Crookes (17, 51), Kain (20), Crossley (26), Uaisele (62), Hardman (69); **Goals:** Moore 5/6.
Rugby Leaguer & League Express Men of the Match: *Hornets:* Ryan Millard; *Rovers:* Andy Ellis.
Penalty count: 8-4; **Half-time:** 18-18;
Referee: Jamie Bloem; **Attendance:** 735.

WORKINGTON TOWN 22 BATLEY BULLDOGS 16

TOWN: 30 Jack Murphy; 34 Dominic Manfredi; 3 Jason Mossop; 24 Declan Hulme; 1 Brett Carter; 6 Peter Lupton; 16 Carl Forber; 8 Kris Coward; 9 Graeme Mattinson; 17 Liam McAvoy; 11 Brett Phillips; 12 Jarrad Stack; 31 Connor Farrell. Subs (all used): 13 Karl Olstrum; 32 Alex Szostak; 20 Callum Rowlandson; 7 Callum Phillips.
Tries: Lupton (18, 46), Olstrum (26), Mossop (59); **Goals:** Forber 3/5.
BULLDOGS: 1 Miles Greenwood; 32 Wayne Reittie; 4 Ayden Faal; 19 Joe Chandler; 29 Alex Brown; 6 Ben Black; 7 Scott Leatherbarrow; 8 Byron Smith; 18 Luke Blake; 20 Adam Gledhill; 3 Alex Bretherton; 12 Sam Scott; 13 Mark Applegarth. Subs (all used): 9 Anthony Nicholson; 10 Alex Rowe; 31 Keegan Hirst; 30 Charlie Martin.
Tries: Scott (31), Greenwood (39), Black (78); **Goals:** Leatherbarrow 2/3.
Rugby Leaguer & League Express Men of the Match: *Town:* Peter Lupton; *Bulldogs:* Scott Leatherbarrow.
Penalty count: 9-5; **Half-time:** 12-12;
Referee: Chris Leatherbarrow; **Attendance:** 804.

ROUND 19

Sunday 13th July 2014

SHEFFIELD EAGLES 24 NORTH WALES CRUSADERS 16

EAGLES: 1 Quentin Laulu-Togagae; 2 Scott Turner; 3 Menzie Yere; 16 Duane Straugheir; 5 Misi Taulapapa; 6 Pat Walker; 7 Dominic Brambani; 8 Eddie Battye; 9 Andrew Henderson; 10 Mitchell Stringer; 11 Michael Knowles; 22 Will Hope; 32 Kyle Briggs. Subs (all used): 14 James Davey; 18 Tom Lillycrop; 27 Peter Aspinall; 4 Lelauloto Tagaloa.
Tries: Yere (5), Turner (11), Taulapapa (38), Tagaloa (57), Laulu-Togagae (63); **Goals:** Brambani 2/5.
CRUSADERS: 1 Tommy Johnson; 2 Dan Birkett; 3 Christiaan Roets; 17 Stuart Reardon; 23 Greg Wilde; 19 Karl Ashall; 7 Jamie Dallimore; 8 Jonny Walker; 24 Lee Hudson; 30 Sebastien Martins; - Alex Davidson; 29 Steve Bannister; 11 Toby Adamson. Subs (all used): 13 Jono Smith; - Ryan Duffy; 26 Matt Reid; - Andy Thornley.
Tries: Smith (45, 78), Martins (70); **Goals:** Johnson 2/3.
Rugby Leaguer & League Express Men of the Match: *Eagles:* Michael Knowles; *Crusaders:* Jono Smith.
Penalty count: 7-9; **Half-time:** 14-0;
Referee: Chris Kendall; **Attendance:** 671.

BATLEY BULLDOGS 22 HALIFAX 22

BULLDOGS: 17 Lee Paterson; 32 Wayne Reittie; 4 Ayden Faal; 19 Joe Chandler; 29 Alex Brown; 6 Ben Black; 7 Scott Leatherbarrow; 8 Byron Smith; 18 Luke Blake; 20 Adam Gledhill; 12 Sam Scott; 11 John Davies; 13 Mark Applegarth. Subs (all used): 30 Charlie Martin; 9 Anthony Nicholson; 10 Alex Rowe; 31 Keegan Hirst.
Tries: A Brown (15, 80), Martin (57), Black (64); **Goals:** Leatherbarrow 3/5.
HALIFAX: 1 Ryan Fieldhouse; 26 Peter Fox; 15 Adam Robinson; 23 Callum Casey; 21 Tom Saxton; 6 Scott Murrell; 14 Paul Mennell; 8 Tony Tonks; 9 Ben Kaye; 10 Luke Ambler; 13 Luke Adamson; 27 Ross Divorty; 12 Andy Bracek. Subs (all used): 18 Ben Johnston; 19 Keith Holden; 24 Sam Brooks; 28 Jack Spencer.
Tries: Holden (30), Ambler (43), Saxton (46), Fieldhouse (53); **Goals:** Murrell 3/4.
Rugby Leaguer & League Express Men of the Match: *Bulldogs:* Alex Brown; *Halifax:* Paul Mennell.
Penalty count: 8-6; **Half-time:** 8-6;
Referee: Warren Turley; **Attendance:** 1,155.

DONCASTER 24 LEIGH CENTURIONS 16

DONCASTER: 5 Dave Scott; 2 Stewart Sanderson; 3 Liam Welham; - Ben Crooks; 22 Tom Hodson; 26 Jacob Miller; 23 Richard Wilkinson; 21 Matt Carbutt; 9 Kyle Kesik; 16 Craig Robinson; 25 Alex Starling; 24 Steve Snitch; 13 Mike Emmett. Subs (all used): 15 Scott Spaven; 14 Russ Spiers; 18 Ryan Wilson; 11 Lee Waterman.
Tries: Hodson (3, 67), Spaven (50), Crooks (63, 80); **Goals:** Scott 2/5.
CENTURIONS: 1 Gregg McNally; 23 Jonathan Pownall; 36 Chris Hankinson; 4 Tom Armstrong; 15 Liam Kay; 9 Bob Beswick; 7 Ryan Brierley; 8 Tom Spencer; 14 Sean Penkywicz; 16 Martin Aspinwall; 30 Kurt Haggerty; 12 Tommy Goulden; 13 Sam Barlow. Subs (all used): 22 Adam Higson; 35 Sam Hopkins; 10 Oliver Wilkes; 29 Jake Emmitt.
Tries: Aspinwall (6), Brierley (22), Penkywicz (30); **Goals:** Brierley 1/2, Haggerty 1/1.
Rugby Leaguer & League Express Men of the Match: *Doncaster:* Steve Snitch; *Centurions:* Sam Barlow.
Penalty count: 4-5; **Half-time:** 6-16;
Referee: Tom Crashley; **Attendance:** 1,113.

KEIGHLEY COUGARS 12 WORKINGTON TOWN 16

COUGARS: 1 James Craven; 2 Richie Barnett; 22 Daley Williams; 4 James Haley; 5 Paul White; 14 Paul March; 7 Paul Handforth; 8 Andy Shickell; 9 James Feather; 12 Brendan Rawlins; 11 Josh Lynam; 33 Oliver Pursglove; 13 Ashley Lindsay. Subs (all used): 10 Sean Hesketh; 15 Scott Law; 18 Neil Cherryholme; 27 Jack Lee.
Tries: Rawlins (72), March (77); **Goals:** Handforth 2/2.
TOWN: 24 Lewis Tierney; 3 Jason Mossop; 30 Jack Murphy; 12 Jarrad Stack; 1 Brett Carter; 6 Peter Lupton; 16 Carl Forber; 8 Kris Coward; 9 Graeme Mattinson; 17 Liam McAvoy; 11 Brett Phillips; - Alex Szostak; 13 Karl Olstrum. Subs (all used): 7 Callum Phillips; 15 Daniel Rooney; 18 James Duerden; 20 Callum Rowlandson.
Tries: Tierney (21, 37), Murphy (32); **Goals:** Forber 2/3.
Rugby Leaguer & League Express Men of the Match: *Cougars:* Oliver Pursglove; *Town:* Lewis Tierney.
Penalty count: 6-6; **Half-time:** 0-16;
Referee: Tim Roby; **Attendance:** 811.

ROCHDALE HORNETS 54 BARROW RAIDERS 22

HORNETS: 18 Shannon McDonnell; 14 Sean Casey; 29 Matty Dawson; 20 Stuart Littler; 5 Ryan King; 9 Lewis Sheridan; 17 Ryan Millard; 10 Warren Thompson; 6 Paul Crook; 15 Richard Beaumont; 19 Dave Llewellyn; 12 Alex Trumper; 28 Joe Greenwood. Subs (all used): 8 John Cookson; 13 Jordan Case; 24 Tony Suffolk; 7 Alex McClurg.
Tries: Sheridan (14), Millard (20), Dawson (29), McClurg (33, 49), Case (38, 52), Crook (56), Cookson (78); **Goals:** Crook 7/7, Sheridan 2/2.
RAIDERS: 26 Ryan Shaw; 32 Bradley Goulding; 25 Craig Briscoe; 4 Max Wiper; 5 Dalton Grant; - Ben Karalius; 7 Liam Campbell; 31 Ben Davies; 9 Nathan Mossop; 17 Andrew Dawson; 11 Liam Harrison; 33 Ben Musolino; 30 Connor Dwyer. Subs (all used): 19 Brad Marwood; 15 Danny Jones; 24 Joe Bullock; 18 Jack Morrison.
Tries: Wiper (1), Mossop (7), Shaw (43), Grant (73); **Goals:** Shaw 3/4.
Rugby Leaguer & League Express Men of the Match: *Hornets:* Lewis Sheridan; *Raiders:* Liam Harrison.
Penalty count: 5-7; **Half-time:** 30-10;
Referee: Joe Cobb; **Attendance:** 612.

SWINTON LIONS 24 FEATHERSTONE ROVERS 48

LIONS: 1 Ritchie Hawkyard; 5 Freddie Walker; 4 Mick Nanyn; 31 Ed Barber; 18 Jordan Burke; 28 Chris Atkin; 32 Martin Ainscough; 16 Mike Morrison; 9 Andy Ackers; 17 Zach Johnson; 12 Darren Hawkyard; 23 Danny Bridge; 15 Josh Barlow. Subs (all used): 27 Lewis Hulme; 8 Luke Menzies; 13 James Brown; 24 Gavin Bennion.
Tries: Barber (10), Atkin (33), Ainscough (49), Morrison (68); **Goals:** Nanyn 4/4.
Sin bin: Brown (43) - dangerous contact.
ROVERS: 1 Ian Hardman; 2 Will Sharp; 3 Greg Worthington; 22 James Mendeika; 35 Jason Crookes; 23 Andy Kain; 7 Gareth Moore; 8 Steve Crossley; 9 Andy Ellis; 38 Kyle Trout; 37 Liam Kent; 31 Shaun Pick; 6 Jack Bussey. Subs (all used): 14 George Flanagan; 15 Matty Dale; 13 Matt James; 42 Chris Annakin.
Tries: Trout (23), Dale (25), Mendeika (28), Kain (33), Sharp (42), Crookes (53, 70), Ellis (64), Annakin (75); **Goals:** Moore 3/3, Kain 3/6.
Rugby Leaguer & League Express Men of the Match: *Lions:* Mike Morrison; *Rovers:* Andy Kain.
Penalty count: 8-7; **Half-time:** 12-24;
Referee: Andrew Sweet; **Attendance:** 469
(at Park Lane, Sedgley Park).

WHITEHAVEN 40 DEWSBURY RAMS 34

WHITEHAVEN: 1 Tom Carr; 5 Shaun Ainscough; 3 Jessie Joe Nandye; 6 Chris Taylor; 2 Craig Calvert; 26 Brett Seymour; 7 Cain Southernwood; 10 Paul Jackson; 9 James Newton; 30 Carl Forster; 4 Scott McAvoy; 12 Lee Mitchell; 11 Lee Doran. Subs (all used): 14 Neil Thorman; 20 Jordan Hand; 22 James Robinson; 27 Jon Grayshon.
Tries: Carr (10, 55), Ainscough (22, 57), Calvert (36, 51, 70); **Goals:** Southernwood 5/6, Carr 1/1.
RAMS: 1 Louis Sheriff; 2 Dale Morton; 19 Callan Beckett; 3 Karl Pryce; 40 Sam Wood; 31 Kieran Hyde; 7 Anthony Thackeray; 29 Ewan Dowes; 6 Tom Hemingway; 32 Makali Aizue; 4 Shane Grady; 12 Scott Hale; 20 Jobe Murphy. Subs (all used): 14 Ryan Wright; 10 Ryan Hepworth; 15 Tommy Gallagher; 8 Stephen Nash.
Tries: Thackeray (26), Grady (29), Pryce (42), Wood (62), Hale (73), Gallagher (78); **Goals:** Hyde 5/6.
Rugby Leaguer & League Express Men of the Match: *Whitehaven:* Tom Carr; *Rams:* Kieran Hyde.
Penalty count: 5-7; **Half-time:** 16-12;
Referee: George Stokes; **Attendance:** 843.

ROUND 20

Saturday 19th July 2014

LEIGH CENTURIONS 30 KEIGHLEY COUGARS 0

CENTURIONS: 1 Gregg McNally; 22 Adam Higson; 31 Cameron Pitman; 4 Tom Armstrong; 15 Liam Kay; 6 Martyn Ridyard; 7 Ryan Brierley; 10 Oliver Wilkes; 9 Bob Beswick; 29 Jake Emmitt; 11 Matt Sarsfield; 30 Kurt Haggerty; 13 Sam Barlow. Subs (all used): 14 Sean Penkywicz; 16 Martin Aspinwall; 18 Jamie Acton; 35 Sam Hopkins.
Tries: Armstrong (9), Beswick (17), Wilkes (23), McNally (56), Ridyard (70); **Goals:** Ridyard 5/5.
On report: Brawl (79).
COUGARS: 1 James Craven; 2 Richie Barnett; 19 Danny Lawton; 4 James Haley; 5 Paul White; 6 Danny Jones; 14 Paul March; 8 Andy Shickell; 9 James Feather; 10 Sean Hesketh; 33 Oliver Pursglove; 12 Brendan Rawlins; 13 Ashley Lindsay. Subs (all used): 11 Josh Lynam; 15 Scott Law; 17 Ben Sagar; 18 Neil Cherryholme.
On report: Hesketh (61) - alleged bite on Emmitt; Brawl (79).
Rugby Leaguer & League Express Men of the Match: *Centurions:* Liam Kay; *Cougars:* Andy Shickell.
Penalty count: 9-10; **Half-time:** 18-0;
Referee: Adam Gill; **Attendance:** 2,143.

Sunday 20th July 2014

NORTH WALES CRUSADERS 18 DEWSBURY RAMS 22

CRUSADERS: 1 Tommy Johnson; 36 Scott Turner; 3 Christiaan Roets; 17 Stuart Reardon; 5 Rob Massam; 19 Karl Ashall; 37 Mick Govin; 8 Jonny Walker; 24 Lee Hudson; 30 Sebastien Martins; 26 Matt Reid; 14 Stephen Wild; 11 Toby Adamson. Subs (all used): 13 Jono Smith; 7 Jamie Dallimore; - Ryan Duffy; - Alex Davidson.
Tries: Hudson (27), Adamson (35), Massam (75); **Goals:** Johnson 3/4.
RAMS: 1 Louis Sheriff; 2 Dale Morton; 3 Karl Pryce; 40 Sam Wood; 21 Austin Buchanan; 31 Kieran Hyde; 7 Anthony Thackeray; 29 Ewan Dowes; 6 Tom Hemingway; 32 Makali Aizue; 4 Shane Grady; 12 Scott Hale; 20 Jobe Murphy. Subs (all used): 11 Rob Spicer; 10 Ryan Hepworth; 17 Matthew Haggarty; 15 Tommy Gallagher.
Tries: Sheriff (13), Wood (20), Pryce (44), Aizue (64); **Goals:** Hemingway 3/4.
Rugby Leaguer & League Express Men of the Match: *Crusaders:* Lee Hudson; *Rams:* Makali Aizue.
Penalty count: 9-8; **Half-time:** 14-10;
Referee: Gareth Hewer; **Attendance:** 686
(at The Rock, Wrexham).

BARROW RAIDERS 10 SHEFFIELD EAGLES 40

RAIDERS: 26 Ryan Shaw; 32 Bradley Goulding; 25 Craig Briscoe; 4 Max Wiper; 5 Dalton Grant; 7 Liam Campbell; - Ben Karalius; 31 Ben Davies; 9 Nathan Mossop; 17 Andrew Dawson; 11 Liam Harrison; 15 Danny Jones; 30 Connor Dwyer. Subs (all used): 16 Matty Palmer; 10 Jamie Butler; 24 Joe Bullock; 8 Joe Burke.
Tries: Grant (8, 22); **Goals:** Shaw 1/2.
Sin bin: Shaw (68) - obstruction.
EAGLES: 1 Quentin Laulu-Togagae; 2 Scott Turner; 3 Menzie Yere; 16 Duane Straugheir; 5 Misi Taulapapa; 6 Pat Walker; 7 Dominic Brambani; 8 Eddie Battye; 9 Andrew Henderson; 10 Mitchell Stringer; 11 Michael Knowles; 12 Peter Green; 32 Kyle Briggs. Subs (all used): 14 James Davey; 18 Tom Lillycrop; 22 Will Hope; 4 Lelauloto Tagaloa.
Tries: Briggs (7), Laulu-Togagae (19, 55), Walker (34), Straugheir (36), Tagaloa (70), Taulapapa (75); **Goals:** Brambani 6/7.
Rugby Leaguer & League Express Men of the Match: *Raiders:* Liam Campbell; *Eagles:* Mitchell Stringer.
Penalty count: 6-10; **Half-time:** 10-24;
Referee: Matthew Thomason; **Attendance:** 871.

DONCASTER 36 SWINTON LIONS 34

DONCASTER: 22 Tom Hodson; 2 Stewart Sanderson; 3 Liam Welham; 11 Lee Waterman; 4 Nev Morrison; 6 Paul Cooke; 26 Jacob Miller; 21 Matt Carbutt; 9 Kyle Kesik; 18 Ryan Wilson; 24 Steve Snitch; 25 Alex Starling; 13 Mike Emmett. Subs (all used): 8 Mark Castle; 16 Craig Robinson; 23 Richard Wilkinson; 33 Pasqualle Dunn.
Tries: Morrison (16), Hodson (25), Kesik (32), Waterman (39), Wilkinson (47, 55); **Goals:** Sanderson 6/6.
Sin bin: Waterman (43) - fighting.
LIONS: 1 Ritchie Hawkyard; 22 Jordan Burke; 31 Ed Barber; 4 Mick Nanyn; 19 Jacque Peet; 32 Martin Ainscough; 28 Chris Atkin; 16 Mike Morrison; 9 Andy Ackers; 8 Luke Menzies; 23 Danny Bridge; 12 Darren Hawkyard; 13 James Brown. Subs (all used): 15 Josh Barlow; 17 Zach Johnson; 24 Gavin Bennion; 27 Lewis Hulme.
Tries: Nanyn (13), Bridge (50), R Hawkyard (64), Ackers (68), Brown (73), Barber (78); **Goals:** Nanyn 5/6.
Dismissal: Johnson (43) - punching Miller.
Sin bin: Barlow (43) - fighting.
Rugby Leaguer & League Express Men of the Match: *Doncaster:* Steve Snitch; *Lions:* Ed Barber.
Penalty count: 4-6; **Half-time:** 24-6;
Referee: Jamie Bloem; **Attendance:** 617.

FEATHERSTONE ROVERS 52 BATLEY BULLDOGS 6

ROVERS: 22 James Mendeika; 2 Will Sharp; 3 Greg Worthington; 1 Ian Hardman; 35 Jason Crookes; 23 Andy Kain; 7 Gareth Moore; 8 Steve Crossley; 9 Andy Ellis; 13 Matt James; 38 Kyle Trout; 31 Shaun Pick; 15 Matty Dale. Subs (all used): 14 George Flanagan; 42 Chris Annakin; 16 Andrew Bostock; 10 Keegan Hirst.
Tries: Worthington (2, 28), Ellis (11), Flanagan (31), Crookes (39, 74), Mendeika (48), James (65), Moore (69), Kain (76); **Goals:** Moore 5/8, Sharp 1/2.
BULLDOGS: 17 Lee Paterson; 2 Vinny Finigan; 4 Ayden Faal; 19 Joe Chandler; 29 Alex Brown; 6 Ben Black; 7 Scott Leatherbarrow; 8 Byron Smith; 18 Luke Blake; 13 Mark Applegarth; 12 Sam Scott; 3 Alex Bretherton; 11 John Davies. Subs (all used): 32 Wayne Reittie; 9 Anthony Nicholson; 10 Alex Rowe; 30 Charlie Martin.
Try: Applegarth (52); **Goals:** Paterson 1/1.
Rugby Leaguer & League Express Men of the Match: *Rovers:* Andrew Bostock; *Bulldogs:* Scott Leatherbarrow.
Penalty count: 8-3; **Half-time:** 24-0;
Referee: George Stokes; **Attendance:** 2,025.

HALIFAX 52 WHITEHAVEN 12

HALIFAX: 25 Gareth Potts; 26 Peter Fox; 16 Danny Cowling; 3 Steve Tyrer; 21 Tom Saxton; 6 Scott Murrell; 18 Ben Johnston; 10 Luke Ambler; 14 Paul Mennell; 8 Tony Tonks; 15 Adam Robinson; 27 Ross Divorty; 13 Luke Adamson. Subs (all used): 12 Andy Bracek; 19 Keith Holden; 23 Callum Casey; 28 Jack Spencer.
Tries: Saxton (15), Ambler (20, 62), Divorty (23), Tyrer (30, 39), Adamson (32), Cowling (44), Murrell (58); **Goals:** Tyrer 8/9.

WHITEHAVEN: 1 Tom Carr; 5 Shaun Ainscough; 3 Jessie Joe Nandye; 6 Chris Taylor; 2 Craig Calvert; 26 Brett Seymour; 7 Cain Southernwood; 10 Paul Jackson; 9 James Newton; 30 Carl Forster; 4 Scott McAvoy; 12 Lee Mitchell; 11 Lee Doran. Subs (all used): 14 Neil Thorman; 31 Anthony Walker; 22 James Robinson; 27 Jon Grayshon.
Tries: Taylor (74, 78); **Goals:** Southernwood 2/2.
Rugby Leaguer & League Express Men of the Match: *Halifax:* Scott Murrell; *Whitehaven:* Chris Taylor.
Penalty count: 3-5; **Half-time:** 34-0;
Referee: Warren Turley; **Attendance:** 1,317.

WORKINGTON TOWN 30 ROCHDALE HORNETS 18

TOWN: 30 Jack Murphy; 7 Callum Phillips; 3 Jason Mossop; 24 Declan Hulme; 1 Brett Carter; 6 Peter Lupton; 16 Carl Forber; 8 Kris Coward; 9 Graeme Mattinson; 10 Marc Shackley; 11 Brett Phillips; 31 Alex Szostak; 17 Liam McAvoy. Subs (all used): 19 Nathan Lucock; 15 Daniel Rooney; 18 James Duerden; 20 Callum Rowlandson.
Tries: Carter (12), Hulme (17, 30), Forber (57), Mossop (61); **Goals:** Forber 5/6.
HORNETS: 18 Shannon McDonnell; 29 Shaun Robinson; 33 Dave Llewellyn; 20 Stuart Littler; 5 Ryan King; 14 Sean Casey; 9 Lewis Sheridan; 10 Warren Thompson; 6 Paul Crook; 27 Richard Beaumont; 12 Alex Trumper; 28 Joe Greenwood; 23 James Dandy. Subs (all used): 21 Alex McClurg; 24 Tony Suffolk; 8 John Cookson; 13 Jordan Case.
Tries: Llewellyn (26), Dandy (44), Sheridan (76);
Goals: Crook 3/3.
Rugby Leaguer & League Express Men of the Match: *Town:* Jack Murphy; *Hornets:* Joe Greenwood.
Penalty count: 8-6; **Half-time:** 16-6;
Referee: Chris Kendall; **Attendance:** 707.

ROUND 21

Sunday 27th July 2014

SHEFFIELD EAGLES 18 BATLEY BULLDOGS 28

EAGLES: 1 Quentin Laulu-Togagae; 2 Scott Turner; 3 Menzie Yere; 16 Duane Straugheir; 5 Misi Taulapapa; 6 Pat Walker; 7 Dominic Brambani; 8 Eddie Battye; 9 Andrew Henderson; 10 Mitchell Stringer; 11 Michael Knowles; 12 Peter Green; 32 Kyle Briggs. Subs (all used): 14 James Davey; 18 Tom Lillycrop; 22 Will Hope; 33 Etuate Uaisele.
Tries: Hope (26), Yere (48, 69);
Goals: Brambani 2/2, Walker 1/1.
BULLDOGS: 1 Miles Greenwood; 32 Wayne Reittie; 17 Lee Paterson; - Ben Heaton; 29 Alex Brown; 6 Ben Black; 7 Scott Leatherbarrow; 8 Byron Smith; 9 Anthony Nicholson; 13 Mark Applegarth; 11 John Davies; 12 Sam Scott; 18 Luke Blake. Subs (all used): 10 Alex Rowe; 23 Josh Johnson; 22 Jacob Fairbank; 19 Joe Chandler.
Tries: Reittie (4), Heaton (7), Fairbank (56), A Brown (77);
Goals: Leatherbarrow 6/8.
Rugby Leaguer & League Express Men of the Match: *Eagles:* Duane Straugheir; *Bulldogs:* Miles Greenwood.
Penalty count: 7-10; **Half-time:** 6-12;
Referee: George Stokes; **Attendance:** 763.

NORTH WALES CRUSADERS 8 WORKINGTON TOWN 12

CRUSADERS: 1 Tommy Johnson; 36 Scott Turner; 23 Greg Wilde; 3 Christiaan Roets; 5 Rob Massam; 19 Karl Ashall; 37 Dom Speakman; - Ryan Duffy; 24 Lee Hudson; 30 Sebastien Martins; 26 Matt Reid; 14 Stephen Wild; 11 Toby Adamson. Subs (all used): - Harry Files; 13 Jono Smith; 12 Gary Middlehurst; - Matt Gee.
Tries: Speakman (12), Smith (72); **Goals:** Johnson 0/2.
TOWN: 30 Jack Murphy; 7 Callum Phillips; 3 Jason Mossop; 24 Declan Hulme; 1 Brett Carter; 6 Peter Lupton; 16 Carl Forber; 8 Kris Coward; 9 Graeme Mattinson; 10 Marc Shackley; 11 Brett Phillips; 33 Alex Szostak; 17 Liam McAvoy. Subs (all used): 32 Greg Burke; 20 Callum Rowlandson; 31 Connor Farrell; 19 Nathan Lucock.
Tries: B Phillips (57), Mattinson (80); **Goals:** Forber 2/2.
Rugby Leaguer & League Express Men of the Match: *Crusaders:* Rob Massam; *Town:* Graeme Mattinson.
Penalty count: 10-13; **Half-time:** 4-0;
Referee: Andrew Sweet; **Attendance:** 658.

DEWSBURY RAMS 34 BARROW RAIDERS 14

RAMS: 3 Karl Pryce; 2 Dale Morton; 34 Ben Hellewell; 4 Shane Grady; 24 Sam Wood; 31 Kieran Hyde; 7 Anthony Thackeray; 29 Ewan Dowes; 6 Tom Hemingway; 32 Makali Aizue; 12 Scott Hale; 11 Rob Spicer; 20 Jobe Murphy. Subs (all used): 25 Joel Farrell; 10 Ryan Hepworth; 8 Stephen Nash; 15 Tommy Gallagher.
Tries: Dowes (10, 76), Hyde (15, 53), Spicer (25), Hellewell (48); **Goals:** Hemingway 3/3, Hyde 2/3.
RAIDERS: 26 Ryan Shaw; 32 Bradley Goulding; - Joe Hambley; 4 Max Wiper; 5 Dalton Grant; 7 Liam Campbell; 37 Ben Karalius; 31 Ben Davies; 9 Nathan Mossop; 17 Andrew Dawson; 11 Liam Harrison; 25 Craig Briscoe; 30 Connor Dwyer. Subs (all used): 19 Brad Marwood; 8 Joe Burke; 10 Jamie Butler; 24 Joe Bullock.
Tries: Mossop (19), Briscoe (33), Grant (72);
Goals: Shaw 1/3.
Rugby Leaguer & League Express Men of the Match: *Rams:* Kieran Hyde; *Raiders:* Nathan Mossop.
Penalty count: 7-4; **Half-time:** 18-10;
Referee: Dave Merrick; **Attendance:** 575.

KEIGHLEY COUGARS 44 DONCASTER 32

COUGARS: 1 James Craven; 2 Richie Barnett; 19 Danny Lawton; 4 James Haley; 5 Paul White; 6 Danny Jones; 7 Paul Handforth; 8 Andy Shickell; 9 James Feather; 10 Sean Hesketh; 11 Josh Lynam; 12 Brendan Rawlins; 13 Ashley Lindsay. Subs (all used): 14 Paul March; 15 Scott Law; 18 Neil Cherryholme; 34 Luke Haigh.
Tries: Haley (22, 59, 75), Law (32, 37), Craven (55), Jones (63), Barnett (73); **Goals:** Jones 6/8.
DONCASTER: 5 Dave Scott; 4 Nev Morrison; 3 Liam Welham; 34 Ben Crooks; 2 Stewart Sanderson; 15 Scott Spaven; 23 Richard Wilkinson; 21 Matt Carbutt; 9 Kyle Kesik; 16 Craig Robinson; 25 Alex Starling; 22 Steve Snitch; 13 Mike Emmett. Subs (all used): 14 Russ Spiers; 8 Mark Castle; 11 Lee Waterman; 33 Pasqualle Dunn.
Tries: Kesik (8), Wilkinson (25), Castle (45), Morrison (51), Sanderson (67), Crooks (79);
Goals: Sanderson 4/7.
Rugby Leaguer & League Express Men of the Match: *Cougars:* James Haley; *Doncaster:* Kyle Kesik.
Penalty count: 4-5; **Half-time:** 18-12;
Referee: Peter Brooke; **Attendance:** 723.

ROCHDALE HORNETS 22 LEIGH CENTURIONS 72

HORNETS: 29 Adam Swift; 2 Gareth Langley; 19 Dave Llewellyn; 5 Ryan King; 18 Shaun Robinson; 6 Paul Crook; 9 Lewis Sheridan; 10 Warren Thompson; 7 Alex McClurg; 16 Anthony Walker; 12 Alex Trumper; 20 Joe Greenwood; 24 Tony Suffolk. Subs (all used): 8 John Cookson; 11 Chris Baines; 13 Jordan Case; 23 James Dandy.
Tries: Langley (7), Swift (9), Case (66), Walker (78);
Goals: Crook 3/4.
Sin bin: Greenwood (12) - fighting.
On report: Brawl (12).
CENTURIONS: 1 Gregg McNally; 22 Adam Higson; 31 Cameron Pitman; 4 Tom Armstrong; 15 Liam Kay; 6 Martyn Ridyard; 7 Ryan Brierley; 29 Jake Emmitt; 14 Sean Penkywicz; 35 Sam Hopkins; 11 Matt Sarsfield; 30 Kurt Haggerty; 13 Sam Barlow. Subs (all used): 9 Bob Beswick; 12 Tommy Goulden; 16 Martin Aspinwall; 18 Jamie Acton.
Tries: Barlow (17), McNally (19, 59), Kay (25), Sarsfield (32), Hopkins (35), Armstrong (44, 69), Pitman (52, 73, 80), Brierley (55); **Goals:** Ridyard 12/12.
Sin bin: Sarsfield (12) - fighting.
On report: Brawl (12).
Rugby Leaguer & League Express Men of the Match: *Hornets:* Joe Greenwood; *Centurions:* Martyn Ridyard.
Penalty count: 13-7; **Half-time:** 12-30;
Referee: Chris Leatherbarrow; **Attendance:** 1,211.

SWINTON LIONS 30 HALIFAX 48

LIONS: 1 Ritchie Hawkyard; 5 Freddie Walker; 31 Ed Barber; 4 Mick Nanyn; 22 Kevin Penny; 18 Jordan Burke; 32 Martin Ainscough; 16 Mike Morrison; 21 Brad Dwyer; 23 Gavin Bennion; 24 Danny Bridge; 15 Josh Barlow; 8 Luke Menzies. Subs (all used): 9 Andy Ackers; 17 Zach Johnson; 13 James Brown; 19 Jacque Peet.
Tries: Barber (6), Dwyer (23), Penny (52), Menzies (70), Morrison (76); **Goals:** Nanyn 5/5.
HALIFAX: 25 Gareth Potts; 26 Peter Fox; 16 Danny Cowling; 3 Steve Tyrer; 21 Tom Saxton; 6 Scott Murrell; 18 Ben Johnston; 8 Tony Tonks; 14 Paul Mennell; 10 Luke Ambler; 15 Adam Robinson; 27 Ross Divorty; 13 Luke Adamson. Subs (all used): 12 Andy Bracek; 19 Keith Holden; 23 Callum Casey; 28 Jack Spencer.
Tries: Mennell (2), Saxton (10), Potts (14), Johnston (36, 41), Murrell (48), Adamson (56), Divorty (61); **Goals:** Tyrer 8/8.
Rugby Leaguer & League Express Men of the Match: *Lions:* Brad Dwyer; *Halifax:* Ben Johnston.
Penalty count: 5-4; **Half-time:** 12-24;
Referee: Tom Crashley; **Attendance:** 569.

WHITEHAVEN 24 FEATHERSTONE ROVERS 35

WHITEHAVEN: 1 Tom Carr; 5 Shaun Ainscough; 6 Chris Taylor; 3 Jessie Joe Nandye; 2 Craig Calvert; 26 Brett Seymour; 14 Neil Thorman; 22 James Robinson; 9 James Newton; 13 Bradd Crellin; 4 Scott McAvoy; 12 Lee Mitchell; 11 Lee Doran. Subs (all used): 7 Cain Southernwood; 31 Jon Grayshon; 30 Carl Forster; 10 Paul Jackson.
Tries: Calvert (13, 32), McAvoy (29), Forster (36);
Goals: Carr 4/6.
Sin bin: Doran (50) - dissent.
ROVERS: 22 James Mendeika; 2 Will Sharp; 3 Greg Worthington; 1 Ian Hardman; 35 Jason Crookes; 23 Andy Kain; 7 Gareth Moore; 8 Steve Crossley; 9 Andy Ellis; 13 Matt James; 11 James Lockwood; 31 Shaun Pick; 15 Matty Dale. Subs (all used): 34 Jamie Rooney; 42 Chris Annakin; 10 Keegan Hirst; 16 Andrew Bostock.
Tries: Moore (11), Sharp (17), Hardman (25), Crookes (41), Bostock (49), Worthington (60);
Goals: Moore 5/6; **Field goal:** Rooney (64).
Rugby Leaguer & League Express Men of the Match: *Whitehaven:* Scott McAvoy; *Rovers:* Andrew Bostock.
Penalty count: 15-5; **Half-time:** 22-16;
Referee: Joe Cobb; **Attendance:** 901.

ROUND 22

Sunday 3rd August 2014

BATLEY BULLDOGS 6 LEIGH CENTURIONS 36

BULLDOGS: 1 Miles Greenwood; 32 Wayne Reittie; 17 Lee Paterson; 33 Ben Heaton; 2 Vinny Finigan; 11 John Davies; 7 Scott Leatherbarrow; 8 Byron Smith; 9 Anthony Nicholson; 13 Mark Applegarth; 12 Sam Scott; 3 Alex Bretherton; 18 Luke Blake. Subs (all used): 10 Alex Rowe; 19 Joe Chandler; 20 Adam Gledhill; 23 Josh Johnson.
Try: Greenwood (42); **Goals:** Leatherbarrow 1/1.
Dismissal: Paterson (74) - verbal abuse.
CENTURIONS: 1 Gregg McNally; 22 Adam Higson; 31 Cameron Pitman; 4 Tom Armstrong; 15 Liam Kay; 6 Martyn Ridyard; 7 Ryan Brierley; 29 Jake Emmitt; 14 Sean Penkywicz; 35 Sam Hopkins; 11 Matt Sarsfield; 30 Kurt Haggerty; 13 Sam Barlow. Subs (all used): 9 Bob Beswick; 12 Tommy Goulden; 16 Martin Aspinwall; 18 Jamie Acton.
Tries: Brierley (1), Sarsfield (26), Higson (54), Kay (58), Armstrong (60), McNally (78); **Goals:** Ridyard 6/8.
Sin bin: Acton (75) - dangerous challenge.
Rugby Leaguer & League Express Men of the Match: *Bulldogs:* Miles Greenwood; *Centurions:* Martyn Ridyard.
Penalty count: 7-7; **Half-time:** 0-16;
Referee: Chris Kendall; **Attendance:** 976.

DONCASTER 22 SHEFFIELD EAGLES 26

DONCASTER: 5 Dave Scott; 2 Stewart Sanderson; 3 Liam Welham; 19 Liam Cunningham; 4 Nev Morrison; 6 Paul Cooke; 15 Scott Spaven; 21 Matt Carbutt; 9 Kyle Kesik; 16 Craig Robinson; 25 Alex Starling; 12 Michael Kelly; 24 Steve Snitch. Subs (all used): 14 Russ Spiers; 8 Mark Castle; 11 Lee Waterman; 33 Pasqualle Dunn.
Tries: Robinson (14), Morrison (45), Snitch (49);
Goals: Sanderson 5/5.
Sin bin: Scott (3) - professional foul;
Cooke (13) - dissent.
EAGLES: 1 Quentin Laulu-Togagae; 2 Scott Turner; 3 Menzie Yere; 33 Etuate Uaisele; 5 Misi Taulapapa; 32 Kyle Briggs; 7 Dominic Brambani; 8 Eddie Battye; 9 Andrew Henderson; 18 Tom Lillycrop; 11 Michael Knowles; 12 Peter Green; 16 Duane Straugheir. Subs (all used): 4 Lelauloto Tagaloa; 14 James Davey; 15 Matt Garside; 21 Jack Blagbrough.
Tries: Uaisele (4), Garside (24), Laulu-Togagae (59), Yere (68), Turner (71); **Goals:** Brambani 3/5.
Rugby Leaguer & League Express Men of the Match: *Doncaster:* Craig Robinson; *Eagles:* Kyle Briggs.
Penalty count: 11-9; **Half-time:** 10-12;
Referee: Chris Leatherbarrow; **Attendance:** 954.

FEATHERSTONE ROVERS 62 BARROW RAIDERS 12

ROVERS: 1 Ian Hardman; 2 Will Sharp; 3 Greg Worthington; 28 Sam Smeaton; 35 Jason Crookes; 7 Gareth Moore; 34 Jamie Rooney; 8 Steve Crossley; 9 Andy Ellis; 13 Matt James; 31 Shaun Pick; 38 Kyle Trout; 11 James Lockwood. Subs (all used): 14 George Flanagan; 42 Chris Annakin; 16 Andrew Bostock; 36 Ben Blackmore.
Tries: Ellis (2, 63), Sharp (16, 40), Moore (24, 35), Flanagan (32), Worthington (43, 80), Annakin (50), Crookes (58), Crossley (76);
Goals: Moore 1/3, Rooney 6/9.
RAIDERS: 26 Ryan Shaw; 36 Bradley Goulding; 31 Joe Hambley; 4 Max Wiper; 5 Dalton Grant; 7 Liam Campbell; 37 Ben Karalius; 8 Joe Burke; 9 Nathan Mossop; 35 Ben Davies; 11 Liam Harrison; 25 Craig Briscoe; 30 Connor Dwyer. Subs (all used): 14 Aaron Lloyd; 10 Jamie Butler; 15 Danny Jones; 24 Joe Bullock.
Tries: Campbell (28), Shaw (66); **Goals:** Shaw 2/2.
Rugby Leaguer & League Express Men of the Match: *Rovers:* Andy Ellis; *Raiders:* Liam Campbell.
Penalty count: 9-10; **Half-time:** 30-6;
Referee: Tom Crashley; **Attendance:** 1,626.

HALIFAX 36 DEWSBURY RAMS 24

HALIFAX: 1 Ryan Fieldhouse; 25 Gareth Potts; 16 Danny Cowling; 3 Steve Tyrer; 21 Tom Saxton; 6 Scott Murrell; 18 Ben Johnston; 8 Tony Tonks; 9 Ben Kaye; 10 Luke Ambler; 15 Adam Robinson; 27 Ross Divorty; 13 Luke Adamson. Subs (all used): 12 Andy Bracek; 14 Paul Mennell; 23 Callum Casey; 28 Jack Spencer.
Tries: Ambler (19), Johnston (31), Divorty (36), Cowling (42), Fieldhouse (59), Potts (65);
Goals: Tyrer 6/6.
RAMS: 3 Karl Pryce; 2 Dale Morton; 34 Ben Hellewell; 24 Sam Wood; 21 Austin Buchanan; 31 Kieran Hyde; 7 Anthony Thackeray; 10 Ryan Hepworth; 6 Tom Hemingway; 11 Rob Spicer; 12 Scott Hale; 4 Shane Grady; 20 Jobe Murphy. Subs (all used): 25 Joel Farrell; 14 Ryan Wright; 17 Matthew Haggarty; 15 Tommy Gallagher.
Tries: Grady (7, 54), Gallagher (52), Wright (79);
Goals: Hemingway 2/2, Hyde 2/2.
Rugby Leaguer & League Express Men of the Match: *Halifax:* Luke Ambler; *Rams:* Kieran Hyde.
Penalty count: 7-9; **Half-time:** 18-6;
Referee: Jamie Bloem; **Attendance:** 1,935.

ROCHDALE HORNETS 30 NORTH WALES CRUSADERS 28

HORNETS: 14 Shannon McDonnell; 2 Gareth Langley; 29 Stuart Littler; 5 Ryan King; 1 Wayne English; - Adam Swift; 17 Ryan Millard; 8 John Cookson; 6 Paul Crook; 16 Anthony Walker; 19 Dave Llewellyn; 18 Joe Greenwood; 24 Tony Suffolk. Subs (all used): 9 Lewis Sheridan; 7 Alex McClurg; 10 Warren Thompson; 13 Jordan Case.
Tries: Swift (10, 25), McDonnell (20), Sheridan (51, 61);
Goals: Crook 4/5, Langley 1/1.
CRUSADERS: 1 Tommy Johnson; 36 Scott Turner; - Andy Thornley; 3 Christiaan Roets; 5 Rob Massam; 19 Karl Ashall; 7 Jamie Dallimore; 11 Toby Adamson; 37 Dom Speakman; 30 Sebastien Martins; - Matt Gee; 14 Stephen Wild; 12 Gary Middlehurst. Subs (all used): 20 Mick Govin; 13 Jono Smith; 26 Matt Reid; - Ryan Duffy.
Tries: Thornley (2), Johnson (31), Dallimore (53), Smith (75, 78); **Goals:** Johnson 4/5.
Rugby Leaguer & League Express Men of the Match: *Hornets:* Adam Swift; *Crusaders:* Jono Smith.
Penalty count: 7-9; **Half-time:** 20-10;
Referee: George Stokes; **Attendance:** 654.

SWINTON LIONS 10 KEIGHLEY COUGARS 17

LIONS: 21 Jordan Burke; 5 Freddie Walker; 4 Mick Nanyn; 31 Ed Barber; 22 Kevin Penny; 32 Martin Ainscough; 28 Chris Atkin; 16 Mike Morrison; 9 Andy Ackers; 26 Glenn Riley; 23 Danny Bridge; 12 Darren Hawkyard; 13 James Brown. Subs (all used): 8 Luke Menzies; 24 Gavin Bennion; 27 Lewis Hulme; 19 Jacque Peet.
Tries: Ainscough (2), Barber (63); **Goals:** Nanyn 1/2.
COUGARS: 14 Paul March; 2 Richie Barnett; 19 Danny Lawton; 4 James Haley; 5 Paul White; 6 Danny Jones; 7 Paul Handforth; 8 Andy Shickell; 9 James Feather; 10 Sean Hesketh; 11 Josh Lynam; 12 Brendan Rawlins; 13 Ashley Lindsay. Subs (all used): 34 Luke Haigh; 18 Neil Cherryholme; 15 Scott Law; 16 Jode Sheriffe.
Tries: Barnett (5), White (13, 29, 49); **Goals:** Jones 0/4; **Field goal:** Handforth (75).
Rugby Leaguer & League Express Men of the Match: *Lions:* Mike Morrison; *Cougars:* Scott Law.
Penalty count: 5-6; **Half-time:** 4-12;
Referee: Warren Turley; **Attendance:** 360
(at Park Lane, Sedgley Park).

WORKINGTON TOWN 20 WHITEHAVEN 18

TOWN: 23 Lewis Tierney; 3 Jason Mossop; 30 Jack Murphy; 24 Declan Hulme; 1 Brett Carter; 6 Peter Lupton; 16 Carl Forber; 8 Kris Coward; 9 Graeme Mattinson; 10 Marc Shackley; 11 Brett Phillips; 33 Alex Szostak; 17 Liam McAvoy. Subs (all used): 7 Callum Phillips; 13 Karl Olstrum; 31 Connor Farrell; 32 Greg Burke.
Tries: Hulme (17), Lupton (23), Tierney (57);
Goals: Forber 4/4.
WHITEHAVEN: 1 Tom Carr; 5 Shaun Ainscough; 6 Chris Taylor; 3 Jessie Joe Nandye; 2 Craig Calvert; 26 Brett Seymour; 7 Cain Southernwood; 30 Carl Forster; 9 James Newton; 10 Paul Jackson; 4 Scott McAvoy; 12 Lee Mitchell; 11 Lee Doran. Subs (all used): 14 Neil Thorman; 22 James Robinson; 13 Bradd Crellin; 20 Jordan Hand.
Tries: Nandye (1), Ainscough (46), Calvert (53);
Goals: Southernwood 3/4.
Rugby Leaguer & League Express Men of the Match: *Town:* Brett Carter; *Whitehaven:* Carl Forster.
Penalty count: 11-9; **Half-time:** 12-4;
Referee: Matthew Thomason; **Attendance:** 1,939.

ROUND 23

Friday 8th August 2014

LEIGH CENTURIONS 48 FEATHERSTONE ROVERS 18

CENTURIONS: 1 Gregg McNally; 22 Adam Higson; 31 Cameron Pitman; 4 Tom Armstrong; 15 Liam Kay; 6 Martyn Ridyard; 7 Ryan Brierley; 35 Sam Hopkins; 14 Sean Penkywicz; 29 Jake Emmitt; 11 Matt Sarsfield; 12 Tommy Goulden; 13 Sam Barlow. Subs (all used): 8 Tom Spencer; 9 Bob Beswick; 10 Oliver Wilkes; 18 Jamie Acton.
Tries: Armstrong (6, 24, 44), Penkywicz (17), Barlow (55), Acton (77), Higson (80);
Goals: Ridyard 10/10.
ROVERS: 1 Ian Hardman; 2 Will Sharp; 3 Greg Worthington; 28 Sam Smeaton; 35 Jason Crookes; 23 Andy Kain; 7 Gareth Moore; 8 Steve Crossley; 9 Andy Ellis; 13 Matt James; 38 Kyle Trout; 31 Shaun Pick; 11 James Lockwood. Subs (all used): 34 Jamie Rooney; 6 Jack Bussey; 15 Matty Dale; 42 Chris Annakin.
Tries: Ellis (30), Crookes (36), Worthington (53);
Goals: Moore 3/3.
Sin bin: Moore (70) - punching; Hardman (78) - dissent.
On report:
Crookes (6) - alleged late challenge on McNally.
Rugby Leaguer & League Express Men of the Match: *Centurions:* Martyn Ridyard; *Rovers:* Andy Ellis.
Penalty count: 10-7; **Half-time:** 22-12;
Referee: Tim Roby; **Attendance:** 3,565.

Sunday 10th August 2014

SHEFFIELD EAGLES 31 SWINTON LIONS 30

EAGLES: 1 Quentin Laulu-Togagae; 2 Scott Turner; 3 Menzie Yere; 33 Etuate Uaisele; 5 Misi Taulapapa; 32 Kyle Briggs; 7 Dominic Brambani; 8 Eddie Battye; 9 Andrew Henderson; 18 Tom Lillycrop; 11 Michael Knowles; 12 Peter Green; 16 Duane Straugheir. Subs (all used): 14 James Davey; 4 Lelauloto Tagaloa; 15 Matt Garside; 10 Mitchell Stringer.
Tries: Yere (9), Laulu-Togagae (27, 42), Uaisele (37, 46, 53); **Goals:** Brambani 3/6;
Field goal: Knowles (67).
Sin bin: Green (18) - fighting.
LIONS: 3 Jordan Burke; 5 Freddie Walker; 31 Ed Barber; 4 Mick Nanyn; 22 Kevin Penny; 28 Chris Atkin; 32 Martin Ainscough; 16 Mike Morrison; 21 Brad Dwyer; 25 Glenn Riley; 23 Danny Bridge; 12 Darren Hawkyard; 13 James Brown. Subs (all used): 8 Luke Menzies; 24 Gavin Bennion; 19 Jacque Peet; 27 Lewis Hulme.
Tries: Burke (5), Dwyer (13, 64, 69), Atkin (33);
Goals: Nanyn 5/5.
Sin bin: G Riley (18) - fighting.
Rugby Leaguer & League Express Men of the Match: *Eagles:* Etuate Uaisele; *Lions:* Brad Dwyer.
Penalty count: 9-5; **Half-time:** 16-18;
Referee: Jamie Bloem; **Attendance:** 600.

NORTH WALES CRUSADERS 17 HALIFAX 20

CRUSADERS: 1 Tommy Johnson; 36 Scott Turner; 23 Greg Wilde; 3 Christiaan Roets; 5 Rob Massam; - Dom Speakman; 7 Jamie Dallimore; 30 Sebastien Martins; 19 Karl Ashall; 11 Toby Adamson; 21 Matt Gee; 14 Stephen Wild; 12 Gary Middlehurst. Subs (all used): 13 Jono Smith; 20 Harry Files; - Ryan Duffy; 26 Matt Reid.
Tries: Wilde (2), Roets (10), K Ashall (21);
Goals: Johnson 2/3; **Field goal:** Dallimore (68).
On report: Middlehurst (65) - alleged high tackle.
HALIFAX: 1 Ryan Fieldhouse; 25 Gareth Potts; 16 Danny Cowling; 3 Steve Tyrer; 21 Tom Saxton; 6 Scott Murrell; 18 Ben Johnston; 8 Tony Tonks; 9 Ben Kaye; 10 Luke Ambler; 15 Adam Robinson; 27 Ross Divorty; 13 Luke Adamson. Subs (all used): 19 Keith Holden; 23 Callum Casey; 24 Sam Brooks; 28 Jack Spencer.
Tries: Tyrer (18), Casey (56), Ambler (61), Potts (73);
Goals: Tyrer 2/4.
Sin bin: Saxton (66) - late challenge on Dallimore.
Rugby Leaguer & League Express Men of the Match: *Crusaders:* Karl Ashall; *Halifax:* Luke Ambler.
Penalty count: 5-5; **Half-time:** 16-6;
Referee: Tom Crashley; **Attendance:** 704.

BARROW RAIDERS 10 KEIGHLEY COUGARS 24

RAIDERS: 26 Ryan Shaw; 36 Bradley Goulding; 31 Joe Hambley; 4 Max Wiper; 5 Dalton Grant; 37 Ben Karalius; 7 Liam Campbell; 8 Joe Burke; 9 Nathan Mossop; 35 Ben Davies; 25 Craig Briscoe; 11 Liam Harrison; 30 Connor Dwyer. Subs (all used): 14 Aaron Lloyd; 15 Danny Jones; 16 Matty Palmer; 24 Joe Bullock.
Tries: Wiper (62), Bradley Goulding (78);
Goals: Shaw 1/2.
COUGARS: 1 James Craven; 2 Richie Barnett; 19 Danny Lawton; 4 James Haley; 5 Paul White; 6 Danny Jones; 7 Paul Handforth; 8 Andy Shickell; 9 James Feather; 10 Sean Hesketh; 11 Josh Lynam; 12 Brendan Rawlins; 13 Ashley Lindsay. Subs (all used): 14 Paul March; 18 Neil Cherryholme; 16 Jode Sheriffe; 34 Luke Haigh.
Tries: Handforth (18, 73), White (26), Craven (58);
Goals: Jones 4/4.
Rugby Leaguer & League Express Men of the Match: *Raiders:* Liam Campbell; *Cougars:* Paul Handforth.
Penalty count: 5-8; **Half-time:** 0-12;
Referee: Joe Cobb; **Attendance:** 668.

DEWSBURY RAMS 38 ROCHDALE HORNETS 20

RAMS: 3 Karl Pryce; 2 Dale Morton; 34 Ben Hellewell; 24 Sam Wood; 21 Austin Buchanan; 31 Kieran Hyde; 7 Anthony Thackeray; 10 Ryan Hepworth; 6 Tom Hemingway; 17 Matthew Haggarty; 12 Scott Hale; 4 Shane Grady; 20 Jobe Murphy. Subs (all used): 25 Joel Farrell; 14 Ryan Wright; 11 Rob Spicer; 15 Tommy Gallagher.
Tries: Gallagher (23), Hyde (31), Thackeray (33), Buchanan (52, 69), Wood (59), Pryce (72);
Goals: Hemingway 3/4, Hyde 2/3.
HORNETS: 1 Wayne English; 2 Gareth Langley; 5 Ryan King; 28 Stuart Littler; 14 Sean Casey; 6 Paul Crook; 7 Lewis Sheridan; 8 John Cookson; 23 James Dandy; 15 Anthony Walker; 11 Chris Baines; 13 Jordan Case; 24 Tony Suffolk. Subs (all used): 7 Alex McClurg; 12 Alex Trumper; 16 Liam Gilchrist; 18 James Tilley.
Tries: Littler (13), Baines (40), Langley (42);
Goals: Crook 4/4.
Rugby Leaguer & League Express Men of the Match: *Rams:* Kieran Hyde; *Hornets:* Wayne English.
Penalty count: 7-5; **Half-time:** 18-12;
Referee: Michael Woodhead; **Attendance:** 776.

DONCASTER 36 WORKINGTON TOWN 10

DONCASTER: 5 Dave Scott; 22 Tom Hodson; 20 Shaun Leaf; 19 Liam Cunningham; 2 Stewart Sanderson; 6 Paul Cooke; 26 Jacob Miller; 21 Matt Carbutt; 9 Kyle Kesik; 16 Craig Robinson; 11 Lee Waterman; 12 Michael Kelly; 24 Steve Snitch. Subs (all used): 15 Scott Spaven; 14 Russ Spiers; 8 Mark Castle; 33 Pasqualle Dunn.
Tries: Miller (11, 19), Snitch (49), Dunn (58), Cunningham (62), Leaf (79); **Goals:** Sanderson 6/6.
TOWN: 30 Theerapol Ritson; 7 Callum Phillips; 3 Jason Mossop; 33 John Patrick; 1 Brett Carter; 6 Peter Lupton; 16 Carl Forber; 8 Kris Coward; 9 Graeme Mattinson; 10 Marc Shackley; 11 Brett Phillips; 31 Connor Farrell; 17 Liam McAvoy. Subs (all used): 19 Nathan Lucock; 15 Daniel Rooney; 20 Callum Rowlandson; 32 Greg Burke.
Tries: Coward (71), L McAvoy (76); **Goals:** Forber 1/2.
Rugby Leaguer & League Express Men of the Match: *Doncaster:* Jacob Miller; *Town:* Graeme Mattinson.
Penalty count: 5-7; **Half-time:** 12-0;
Referee: Chris Kendall; **Attendance:** 504.

WHITEHAVEN 28 BATLEY BULLDOGS 13

WHITEHAVEN: 1 Tom Carr; 18 Jordan Burns; 3 Jessie Joe Nandye; 6 Chris Taylor; 2 Craig Calvert; 26 Brett Seymour; 7 Cain Southernwood; 10 Paul Jackson; 9 James Newton; 30 Carl Forster; 4 Scott McAvoy; 12 Lee Mitchell; 11 Lee Doran. Subs (all used): 14 Neil Thorman; 20 Jordan Hand; 8 Samir Tahraoui; 13 Bradd Crellin.
Tries: Calvert (5), Carr (46), Burns (53), Nandye (70);
Goals: Southernwood 6/6.
BULLDOGS: 1 Miles Greenwood; 32 Wayne Reittie; 3 Alex Bretherton; 33 Ben Heaton; 29 Alex Brown; 17 Lee Paterson; 7 Scott Leatherbarrow; 8 Byron Smith; 18 Luke Blake; 23 Josh Johnson; 13 Mark Applegarth; 12 Sam Scott; 11 John Davies. Subs (all used): 10 Alex Rowe; 19 Joe Chandler; 20 Adam Gledhill; 9 Anthony Nicholson.
Tries: Greenwood (27, 39); **Goals:** Leatherbarrow 2/2;
Field goal: Leatherbarrow (36).
Dismissal: Rowe (68) - shoulder charge on Forster.
Rugby Leaguer & League Express Men of the Match: *Whitehaven:* Carl Forster; *Bulldogs:* Miles Greenwood.
Penalty count: 9-7; **Half-time:** 6-13;
Referee: Dave Merrick; **Attendance:** 671.

ROUND 24

Sunday 17th August 2014

SHEFFIELD EAGLES 36 WHITEHAVEN 28

EAGLES: 1 Quentin Laulu-Togagae; 2 Scott Turner; 3 Menzie Yere; 33 Etuate Uaisele; 5 Misi Taulapapa; 32 Kyle Briggs; 7 Dominic Brambani; 8 Eddie Battye; 9 Andrew Henderson; 10 Mitchell Stringer; 16 Duane Straugheir; 15 Matt Garside; 6 Pat Walker. Subs (all used): 14 James Davey; 18 Tom Lillycrop; 4 Lelauloto Tagaloa; 21 Jack Blagbrough.
Tries: Garside (1), Briggs (4), Yere (14), Walker (29), Laulu-Togagae (42, 69); **Goals:** Brambani 6/6.
WHITEHAVEN: 1 Tom Carr; 5 Shaun Ainscough; 6 Chris Taylor; 3 Jessie Joe Nandye; 18 Jordan Burns; 26 Brett Seymour; 7 Cain Southernwood; 30 Carl Forster; 9 James Newton; 20 Jordan Hand; 4 Scott McAvoy; 12 Lee Mitchell; 11 Lee Doran. Subs (all used): 14 Neil Thorman; 13 Bradd Crellin; 8 Samir Tahraoui; 22 James Robinson.
Tries: Nandye (11), Burns (25), Ainscough (35, 77), Southernwood (48); **Goals:** Southernwood 4/5.
Rugby Leaguer & League Express Men of the Match: *Eagles:* Quentin Laulu-Togagae; *Whitehaven:* Shaun Ainscough.
Penalty count: 7-8; **Half-time:** 24-16;
Referee: Dave Merrick; **Attendance:** 644.

BATLEY BULLDOGS 14 DEWSBURY RAMS 16

BULLDOGS: 1 Miles Greenwood; 32 Wayne Reittie; 33 Ben Heaton; 4 Ayden Faal; 29 Alex Brown; 18 Luke Blake; 7 Scott Leatherbarrow; 8 Byron Smith; 9 Anthony Nicholson; 20 Adam Gledhill; 3 Alex Bretherton; 12 Sam Scott; 19 Joe Chandler. Subs (all used): 23 Josh Johnson; 10 Alex Rowe; 13 Mark Applegarth; 11 John Davies.
Tries: Reittie (39), A Brown (44, 73);
Goals: Leatherbarrow 1/3.
RAMS: 3 Karl Pryce; 2 Dale Morton; 34 Ben Hellewell; 40 Sam Wood; 21 Austin Buchanan; 31 Kieran Hyde; 7 Anthony Thackeray; 10 Ryan Hepworth; 6 Tom Hemingway; 17 Matthew Haggarty; 12 Scott Hale; 4 Shane Grady; 20 Jobe Murphy. Subs (all used): 25 Joel Farrell; 14 Ryan Wright; 11 Rob Spicer; 15 Tommy Gallagher.
Tries: Hale (52), Farrell (58), Grady (77);
Goals: Hemingway 2/4.
Rugby Leaguer & League Express Men of the Match: *Bulldogs:* Byron Smith; *Rams:* Joel Farrell.
Penalty count: 8-5; **Half-time:** 6-0;
Referee: Joe Cobb; **Attendance:** 1,159.

HALIFAX 4 FEATHERSTONE ROVERS 20

HALIFAX: 1 Ryan Fieldhouse; 25 Gareth Potts; 16 Danny Cowling; 3 Steve Tyrer; 21 Tom Saxton; 6 Scott Murrell; 7 Simon Brown; 8 Tony Tonks; 9 Ben Kaye; 10 Luke Ambler; 13 Luke Adamson; 27 Ross Divorty; 12 Andy Bracek. Subs (all used): 14 Paul Mennell; 18 Ben Johnston; 23 Callum Casey; 28 Jack Spencer.
Try: Johnston (56); **Goals:** Tyrer 0/1.
ROVERS: 1 Ian Hardman; 2 Will Sharp; 3 Greg Worthington; 36 Ben Blackmore; 35 Jason Crookes; 23 Andy Kain; 7 Gareth Moore; 8 Steve Crossley; 9 Andy Ellis; 6 Jack Bussey; 42 Chris Annakin; 31 Shaun Pick; 11 James Lockwood. Subs (all used): 13 Matt James; 16 Andrew Bostock; 10 Keegan Hirst; 30 Luke Teasdale.
Tries: Crookes (3, 13, 21), Pick (16); **Goals:** Moore 2/4.
Rugby Leaguer & League Express Men of the Match: *Halifax:* Scott Murrell; *Rovers:* Will Sharp.
Penalty count: 6-4; **Half-time:** 0-20;
Referee: George Stokes; **Attendance:** 3,022.

KEIGHLEY COUGARS 18
NORTH WALES CRUSADERS 30

COUGARS: 1 James Craven; 2 Richie Barnett; 19 Danny Lawton; 4 James Haley; 5 Paul White; 6 Danny Jones; 7 Paul Handforth; 8 Andy Shickell; 9 James Feather; 10 Sean Hesketh; 11 Josh Lynam; 33 Oliver Pursglove; 13 Ashley Lindsay. Subs (all used): 3 Elliott Cosgrove; 14 Paul March; 16 Jode Sheriffe; 18 Neil Cherryholme.
Tries: White (20), Jones (42), Lynam (51);
Goals: Jones 3/4.
CRUSADERS: 1 Tommy Johnson; 36 Scott Turner; 23 Greg Wilde; 17 Stuart Reardon; 5 Rob Massam; 37 Mick Govin; 7 Jamie Dallimore; 11 Toby Adamson; 19 Karl Ashall; 30 Sebastien Martins; 21 Matt Gee; 14 Stephen Wild; 12 Gary Middlehurst. Subs (all used): 3 Christiaan Roets; 13 Jono Smith; 24 Lee Hudson; - Ryan Duffy.
Tries: Wild (1), Massam (10), Turner (14), Adamson (25), Smith (77); **Goals:** Johnson 5/5.
Rugby Leaguer & League Express Men of the Match: *Cougars:* Danny Jones; *Crusaders:* Mick Govin.
Penalty count: 8-8; **Half-time:** 4-24;
Referee: Tom Crashley; **Attendance:** 893.

ROCHDALE HORNETS 16 DONCASTER 22

HORNETS: 1 Wayne English; 2 Gareth Langley; 28 Stuart Littler; 12 Alex Trumper; 29 Shaun Robinson; 6 Paul Crook; 9 Lewis Sheridan; 24 Tony Suffolk; 23 James Dandy; 15 Anthony Walker; 11 Chris Baines; 18 James Tilley; 27 Joe Greenwood. Subs (all used): 7 Alex McClurg; 16 Liam Gilchrist; 26 Greg Richards; 14 Sean Casey.
Tries: Sheridan (15), Littler (48), Crook (78);
Goals: Crook 2/3.
DONCASTER: 5 Dave Scott; 22 Tom Hodson; 20 Shaun Leaf; 19 Liam Cunningham; 2 Stewart Sanderson; 6 Paul Cooke; 26 Jacob Miller; 21 Matt Carbutt; 15 Scott Spaven; 16 Craig Robinson; 24 Steve Snitch; 11 Lee Waterman; 13 Mike Emmett. Subs (all used): 14 Russ Spiers; 8 Mark Castle; 3 Liam Welham; 33 Pasqualle Dunn.

Tries: Snitch (29, 64), Hodson (40), Sanderson (59);
Goals: Sanderson 3/4.
Rugby Leaguer & League Express Men of the Match:
Hornets: Lewis Sheridan; *Doncaster:* Steve Snitch.
Penalty count: 2-4; **Half-time:** 6-12;
Referee: Peter Brooke; **Attendance:** 571.

SWINTON LIONS 6 LEIGH CENTURIONS 62

LIONS: 3 Jordan Burke; 5 Freddie Walker; 31 Ed Barber; 4 Mick Nanyn; 22 Kevin Penny; 28 Chris Atkin; 1 Ritchie Hawkyard; 16 Mike Morrison; 23 Brad Dwyer; 24 Gavin Bennion; 15 Josh Barlow; 12 Darren Hawkyard; 9 Andy Ackers. Subs (all used): 13 James Brown; 19 Jacque Peet; 2 Ben Warrilow; 27 Lewis Hulme.
Try: Ackers (77); **Goals:** Nanyn 1/1.
CENTURIONS: 1 Gregg McNally; 22 Adam Higson; 36 Michael Platt; 4 Tom Armstrong; 15 Liam Kay; 6 Martyn Ridyard; 7 Ryan Brierley; 35 Sam Hopkins; 14 Sean Penkywicz; 29 Jake Emmitt; 11 Matt Sarsfield; 30 Kurt Haggerty; 13 Sam Barlow. Subs (all used): 9 Bob Beswick; 27 Anthony Bate; 16 Martin Aspinwall; 8 Tom Spencer.
Tries: Barlow (9), Kay (20), Ridyard (26), Armstrong (45, 63), Brierley (48), Platt (52), McNally (55, 69), Bate (75), Higson (80);
Goals: Ridyard 9/11.
Rugby Leaguer & League Express Men of the Match:
Lions: Mike Morrison; *Centurions:* Martyn Ridyard.
Penalty count: 6-7; **Half-time:** 0-16;
Referee: Chris Leatherbarrow; **Attendance:** 1,342.

WORKINGTON TOWN 32 BARROW RAIDERS 18

TOWN: 1 Brett Carter; 30 Jay Rossi; 3 Jason Mossop; 24 Declan Hulme; 33 John Patrick; 6 Peter Lupton; 16 Carl Forber; 8 Kris Coward; 9 Graeme Mattinson; 32 Greg Burke; 11 Brett Phillips; 31 Connor Farrell; 17 Liam McAvoy. Subs (all used): 7 Callum Phillips; 15 Daniel Rooney; 10 Marc Shackley; 13 Karl Olstrum.
Tries: Forber (10, 33), Lupton (20), Patrick (27), Shackley (49), Farrell (53); **Goals:** Forber 4/6.
RAIDERS: 36 Bradley Goulding; 21 Mike Backhouse; 26 Ryan Shaw; 4 Max Wiper; 5 Dalton Grant; 7 Liam Campbell; 37 Ben Karalius; 11 Liam Harrison; 9 Nathan Mossop; 8 Joe Burke; 16 Matty Palmer; 25 Craig Briscoe; 30 Connor Dwyer. Subs (all used): 14 Aaron Lloyd; 15 Danny Jones; 18 Jack Morrison; 35 Ben Davies.
Tries: Shaw (14), Grant (45), Davies (56);
Goals: Shaw 3/3.
Rugby Leaguer & League Express Men of the Match:
Town: Carl Forber; *Raiders:* Craig Briscoe.
Penalty count: 7-10; **Half-time:** 20-6;
Referee: Jamie Bloem; **Attendance:** 842.

ROUND 1

Wednesday 20th August 2014

SHEFFIELD EAGLES 48 ROCHDALE HORNETS 0

EAGLES: 1 Quentin Laulu-Togagae; 2 Scott Turner; 3 Menzie Yere; 33 Etuate Uaisele; 5 Misi Taulapapa; 32 Kyle Briggs; 19 Cory Aston; 8 Eddie Battye; 9 Andrew Henderson; 10 Mitchell Stringer; 16 Duane Straugheir; 28 Tom Ashton; 6 Pat Walker. Subs (all used): 14 James Davey; 18 Tom Lillycrop; 4 Lelauloto Tagaloa; 12 Peter Green.
Tries: Straugheir (4), Aston (30, 35, 76), Davey (38), Tagaloa (42), Yere (58), Turner (70), Laulu-Togagae (78);
Goals: Walker 4/6, Briggs 2/3.
HORNETS: 1 Wayne English; 2 Gareth Langley; 11 Chris Baines; 18 James Tilley; 28 Adam Swift; 17 Ryan Millard; 6 Paul Crook; 24 Tony Suffolk; 21 Alex McClurg; 4 Anthony Walker; 33 Dave Llewellyn; 27 Joe Greenwood; 12 Alex Trumper. Subs (all used): 9 Lewis Sheridan; 16 Liam Gilchrist; 8 John Cookson; 23 James Dandy.
Rugby Leaguer & League Express Men of the Match:
Eagles: Cory Aston; *Hornets:* Wayne English.
Penalty count: 7-8; **Half-time:** 22-0;
Referee: Matthew Thomason; **Attendance:** 560
(at Sheffield Hallam University Sports Park).

ROUND 25

Saturday 30th August 2014

LEIGH CENTURIONS 22 WORKINGTON TOWN 12

CENTURIONS: 1 Gregg McNally; 22 Adam Higson; 33 Michael Platt; 4 Tom Armstrong; 15 Liam Kay; 6 Martyn Ridyard; 7 Ryan Brierley; 29 Jake Emmitt; 14 Sean Penkywicz; 35 Sam Hopkins; 11 Matt Sarsfield; 30 Kurt Haggerty; 10 Oliver Wilkes. Subs (all used): 9 Bob Beswick; 36 Jonathan Walker; 27 Anthony Bate; 16 Martin Aspinwall.
Tries: Brierley (12, 56), Higson (32), Kay (40);
Goals: Ridyard 3/4.
TOWN: 30 Jack Murphy; 33 John Patrick; 3 Jason Mossop; 24 Declan Hulme; 1 Brett Carter; 6 Peter Lupton; 16 Carl Forber; 32 Greg Burke; 9 Graeme Mattinson; 10 Marc Shackley; 11 Brett Phillips; 31 Connor Farrell; 17 Liam McAvoy. Subs (all used): - Jordan James; 15 Daniel Rooney; 13 Karl Olstrum; 7 Callum Phillips.
Tries: Forber (15), Mossop (63); **Goals:** Forber 2/2.
On report:
Farrell (58) - alleged shoulder charge on McNally.
Rugby Leaguer & League Express Men of the Match:
Centurions: Jake Emmitt; *Town:* Brett Phillips.
Penalty count: 6-7; **Half-time:** 16-6;
Referee: Michael Woodhead; **Attendance:** 3,375.

Sunday 31st August 2014

BARROW RAIDERS 36 NORTH WALES CRUSADERS 16

RAIDERS: 36 Bradley Goulding; 21 Mike Backhouse; 26 Ryan Shaw; 4 Max Wiper; 5 Dalton Grant; 7 Liam Campbell; 19 Brad Marwood; 8 Joe Burke; 9 Nathan Mossop; 11 Liam Harrison; 25 Craig Briscoe; 13 Dan Toal; 30 Connor Dwyer. Subs (all used): 14 Aaron Lloyd; 15 Danny Jones; 35 Ben Davies; 10 Jamie Butler.
Tries: Campbell (17), Dwyer (21), Davies (31), Lloyd (74), Toal (76), Mossop (80); **Goals:** Shaw 5/5, Backhouse 1/1.
CRUSADERS: 1 Tommy Johnson; 5 Rob Massam; 17 Stuart Reardon; 23 Greg Wilde; 2 Dan Birkett; 37 Mick Govin; 7 Jamie Dallimore; 11 Toby Adamson; 19 Karl Ashall; 30 Sebastien Martins; 21 Matt Gee; 26 Matt Reid; 12 Gary Middlehurst. Subs (all used): 24 Lee Hudson; 13 Jono Smith; 8 Jonny Walker; - Ryan Duffy.
Tries: Middlehurst (5, 39), Reid (47); **Goals:** Johnson 2/3.
Sin bin: Massam (30) - holding down.
On report:
Dallimore (68) - alleged high tackle on Campbell.
Rugby Leaguer & League Express Men of the Match:
Raiders: Liam Harrison; *Crusaders:* Gary Middlehurst.
Penalty count: 9-5; **Half-time:** 18-12;
Referee: Adam Gill; **Attendance:** 848.

BATLEY BULLDOGS 42 SWINTON LIONS 0

BULLDOGS: 1 Miles Greenwood; 32 Wayne Reittie; 33 Ben Heaton; 4 Ayden Faal; 29 Alex Brown; 6 Ben Black; 7 Scott Leatherbarrow; 23 Josh Johnson; 9 Anthony Nicholson; 13 Mark Applegarth; 3 Alex Bretherton; 12 Sam Scott; 18 Luke Blake. Subs (all used): 19 Joe Chandler; 20 Adam Gledhill; 10 Alex Rowe; 11 John Davies.
Tries: A Brown (5), Scott (14), Nicholson (23), Reittie (51), Black (61), Faal (65), Bretherton (72);
Goals: Leatherbarrow 7/9.
LIONS: 1 Ritchie Hawkyard; 18 Jordan Burke; 31 Ed Barber; 4 Mick Nanyn; 22 Kevin Penny; 32 Martin Ainscough; 28 Chris Atkin; 16 Mike Morrison; 9 Andy Ackers; 25 Glenn Riley; 12 Darren Hawkyard; 23 Danny Bridge; 15 Josh Barlow. Subs (all used): 13 James Brown; 24 Gavin Bennion; 27 Lewis Hulme; 19 Jacque Peet.
Rugby Leaguer & League Express Men of the Match:
Bulldogs: Alex Rowe; *Lions:* Ritchie Hawkyard.
Penalty count: 9-8; **Half-time:** 14-0;
Referee: Chris Kendall; **Attendance:** 664.

DEWSBURY RAMS 24 KEIGHLEY COUGARS 12

RAMS: 3 Karl Pryce; 2 Dale Morton; 34 Ben Hellewell; 4 Shane Grady; 24 Sam Wood; 31 Kieran Hyde; 7 Anthony Thackeray; 17 Matthew Haggarty; 6 Tom Hemingway; 10 Ryan Hepworth; 12 Scott Hale; 11 Rob Spicer; 20 Jobe Murphy. Subs (all used): 14 Ryan Wright; 33 Jason Muranka; 25 Joel Farrell; 15 Tommy Gallagher.
Tries: Hellewell (7), Hepworth (23), Hyde (39), Thackeray (70); **Goals:** Hemingway 3/4, Hyde 1/1.
COUGARS: 1 James Craven; 2 Richie Barnett; 19 Danny Lawton; 4 James Haley; 5 Paul White; 6 Danny Jones; 7 Paul Handforth; 8 Andy Shickell; 9 James Feather; 10 Sean Hesketh; 11 Josh Lynam; 3 Elliott Cosgrove; 13 Ashley Lindsay. Subs (all used): 14 Paul March; 15 Scott Law; 16 Jode Sheriffe; 18 Neil Cherryholme.
Tries: Jones (57), Handforth (76); **Goals:** Jones 2/2.
Rugby Leaguer & League Express Men of the Match:
Rams: Kieran Hyde; *Cougars:* Danny Jones.
Penalty count: 7-7; **Half-time:** 18-0;
Referee: Matthew Thomason; **Attendance:** 1,028.

DONCASTER 39 HALIFAX 18

DONCASTER: 5 Dave Scott; 22 Tom Hodson; 20 Shaun Leaf; 19 Liam Cunningham; 2 Stewart Sanderson; 6 Paul Cooke; 23 Richard Wilkinson; 21 Matt Carbutt; 15 Scott Spaven; 16 Craig Robinson; 24 Steve Snitch; 34 Liam Colbon; 13 Mike Emmett. Subs (all used): 14 Russ Spiers; 8 Mark Castle; 11 Lee Waterman; 33 Pasqualle Dunn.
Tries: Emmett (3), Cooke (16, 50), Scott (40, 70), Snitch (74, 80); **Goals:** Sanderson 5/7;
Field goal: Cooke (39).
HALIFAX: 1 Ryan Fieldhouse; 25 Gareth Potts; 23 Callum Casey; 3 Steve Tyrer; 26 Peter Fox; 6 Scott Murrell; 7 Simon Brown; 10 Luke Ambler; 14 Paul Mennell; 24 Sam Brooks; 13 Luke Adamson; 27 Ross Divorty; 12 Andy Bracek. Subs (all used): 8 Tony Tonks; 16 Danny Cowling; 19 Keith Holden; 28 Jack Spencer.
Tries: Bracek (8), Adamson (59), Mennell (67);
Goals: Tyrer 1/1, Brown 2/2.
Rugby Leaguer & League Express Men of the Match:
Doncaster: Paul Cooke; *Halifax:* Ross Divorty.
Penalty count: 8-4; **Half-time:** 19-6;
Referee: Joe Cobb; **Attendance:** 980.

FEATHERSTONE ROVERS 28 SHEFFIELD EAGLES 40

ROVERS: 2 Will Sharp; 36 Ben Blackmore; 1 Ian Hardman; 3 Greg Worthington; 35 Jason Crookes; 6 Jack Bussey; 23 Andy Kain; 8 Steve Crossley; 9 Andy Ellis; 42 Chris Annakin; 31 Shaun Pick; 12 Tim Spears; 11 James Lockwood. Subs (all used): 30 Luke Teasdale; 13 Matt James; 38 Kyle Trout; 10 Keegan Hirst.
Tries: Kain (9), Teasdale (43, 55), Sharp (50), Annakin (70); **Goals:** Bussey 4/5.
EAGLES: 1 Quentin Laulu-Togagae; 2 Scott Turner; 3 Menzie Yere; 16 Duane Straugheir; 5 Misi Taulapapa; 32 Kyle Briggs; 7 Dominic Brambani; 8 Eddie Battye; 9 Andrew Henderson; 10 Mitchell Stringer; 11 Michael Knowles; 12 Peter Green; 6 Pat Walker. Subs (all used): 14 James Davey; 15 Matt Garside; 18 Tom Lillycrop; 4 Lelauloto Tagaloa.
Tries: Briggs (14, 65, 76), Taulapapa (27), Laulu-Togagae (31, 37), Straugheir (46);
Goals: Brambani 5/6, Walker 1/1.
Rugby Leaguer & League Express Men of the Match:
Rovers: Luke Teasdale; *Eagles:* Kyle Briggs.
Penalty count: 8-7; **Half-time:** 4-22;
Referee: Warren Turley; **Attendance:** 2,085.

WHITEHAVEN 48 ROCHDALE HORNETS 12

WHITEHAVEN: 5 Shaun Ainscough; 18 Jordan Burns; 3 Jessie Joe Nandye; 6 Chris Taylor; 13 Bradd Crellin; 26 Brett Seymour; 14 Neil Thorman; 30 Carl Forster; 9 James Newton; 20 Jordan Hand; 4 Scott McAvoy; 12 Lee Mitchell; 11 Lee Doran. Subs (all used): 22 James Robinson; 8 Samir Tahraoui; 16 Kurtis Quinn; 28 Callum Farrer.
Tries: Thorman (3, 27), Nandye (7), Hand (19), Burns (23, 56), Crellin (63), Newton (78);
Goals: Seymour 7/8, Newton 1/1.
HORNETS: 1 Wayne English; 2 Gareth Langley; 33 Dave Llewellyn; 20 Stuart Littler; 28 Shaun Robinson; 17 Ryan Millard; 6 Paul Crook; 8 John Cookson; 21 Alex McClurg; 4 Anthony Walker; 11 Chris Baines; 27 Joe Greenwood; 23 James Dandy. Subs (all used): 9 Lewis Sheridan; 16 Liam Gilchrist; 18 Alex Clare; 25 James Tilley.
Tries: Baines (71, 75); **Goals:** Crook 2/2.
Rugby Leaguer & League Express Men of the Match:
Whitehaven: Neil Thorman; *Hornets:* Chris Baines.
Penalty count: 9-8; **Half-time:** 30-0;
Referee: Chris Leatherbarrow; **Attendance:** 756.

ROUND 26

Sunday 7th September 2014

**NORTH WALES CRUSADERS 16
LEIGH CENTURIONS 28**

CRUSADERS: 1 Tommy Johnson; 36 Scott Turner; 17 Stuart Reardon; 3 Christiaan Roets; 5 Rob Massam; 37 Dom Speakman; 7 Jamie Dallimore; 8 Jonny Walker; 19 Karl Ashall; 11 Toby Adamson; 21 Matt Gee; 14 Stephen Wild; 12 Gary Middlehurst. Subs (all used): 13 Jono Smith; 24 Lee Hudson; - Ryan Duffy; 30 Sebastien Martins.
Tries: Johnson (8), Duffy (65, 75); **Goals:** Johnson 2/3.
CENTURIONS: 23 Jonathan Pownall; 22 Adam Higson; 34 Michael Platt; 4 Tom Armstrong; 2 Steve Maden; 6 Martyn Ridyard; 7 Ryan Brierley; 29 Jake Emmitt; 9 Bob Beswick; 35 Sam Hopkins; 10 Oliver Wilkes; 30 Kurt Haggerty; 13 Sam Barlow. Subs (all used): 14 Sean Penkywicz; 11 Matt Sarsfield; 33 Jonathan Walker; 18 Jamie Acton.
Tries: Walker (29), Armstrong (31), Hopkins (51), Brierley (63, 71); **Goals:** Ridyard 4/5.
On report: Beswick (30) - alleged punching.
Rugby Leaguer & League Express Men of the Match:
Crusaders: Ryan Duffy; *Centurions:* Ryan Brierley.
Penalty count: 10-6; **Half-time:** 6-10;
Referee: Jamie Bloem; **Attendance:** 1,206.

DONCASTER 10 BATLEY BULLDOGS 34

DONCASTER: 5 Dave Scott; 2 Stewart Sanderson; 20 Shaun Leaf; 19 Liam Cunningham; 22 Tom Hodson; 6 Paul Cooke; 23 Richard Wilkinson; 21 Matt Carbutt; 15 Scott Spaven; 16 Craig Robinson; 24 Steve Snitch; 29 Liam Colbon; 13 Mike Emmett. Subs (all used): 8 Mark Castle; 14 Russ Spiers; 12 Michael Kelly; 11 Lee Waterman.
Tries: Hodson (22), Waterman (54);
Goals: Sanderson 1/3.
BULLDOGS: 1 Miles Greenwood; 32 Wayne Reittie; 33 Ben Heaton; 4 Ayden Faal; 29 Alex Brown; 6 Ben Black; 7 Scott Leatherbarrow; 23 Josh Johnson; 9 Anthony Nicholson; 13 Mark Applegarth; 3 Alex Bretherton; 12 Sam Scott; 18 Luke Blake. Subs (all used): 10 Alex Rowe; 11 John Davies; 19 Joe Chandler; 20 Adam Gledhill.
Tries: Reittie (3, 77), A Brown (18), Faal (35), Nicholson (71), Bretherton (80);
Goals: Leatherbarrow 5/7.
Rugby Leaguer & League Express Men of the Match:
Doncaster: Mike Emmett; *Bulldogs:* Wayne Reittie.
Penalty count: 10-4; **Half-time:** 6-18;
Referee: Dave Merrick; **Attendance:** 1,160.

HALIFAX 30 BARROW RAIDERS 24

HALIFAX: 1 Ryan Fieldhouse; 25 Gareth Potts; 16 Danny Cowling; 23 Callum Casey; 21 Tom Saxton; 6 Scott Murrell; 14 Paul Mennell; 24 Sam Brooks; 9 Ben Kaye; 10 Luke Ambler; 11 Dane Manning; 15 Adam Robinson; 13 Luke Adamson. Subs (all used): 8 Tony Tonks; 12 Andy Bracek; 19 Keith Holden; 28 Jack Spencer.
Tries: Saxton (14, 35), Fieldhouse (42), Tonks (46), Adamson (52), Casey (75);
Goals: Murrell 3/6, Holden 0/1.
RAIDERS: 36 Bradley Goulding; 26 Ryan Shaw; 31 Joe Hambley; 4 Max Wiper; 5 Dalton Grant; 19 Brad Marwood; 7 Liam Campbell; 11 Liam Harrison; 9 Nathan Mossop; 35 Ben Davies; 25 Craig Briscoe; 13 Dan Toal; 30 Connor Dwyer. Subs (all used): 14 Aaron Lloyd; 10 Jamie Butler; 8 Joe Burke; 15 Danny Jones.
Tries: Marwood (23), Shaw (31), Lloyd (59), Wiper (66);
Goals: Shaw 4/4.
Rugby Leaguer & League Express Men of the Match:
Halifax: Scott Murrell; *Raiders:* Liam Campbell.
Penalty count: 8-4; **Half-time:** 8-12;
Referee: Tom Crashley; **Attendance:** 1,431.

KEIGHLEY COUGARS 24 FEATHERSTONE ROVERS 26

COUGARS: 1 James Craven; 22 Daley Williams; 19 Danny Lawton; 4 James Haley; 5 Paul White; 6 Danny Jones; 7

Paul Handforth; 8 Andy Shickell; 9 James Feather; 10 Sean Hesketh; 11 Josh Lynam; 13 Ashley Lindsay; 16 Jode Sheriffe. Subs (all used): 3 Elliott Cosgrove; 14 Paul March; 15 Scott Law; 18 Neil Cherryholme.
Tries: Craven (17), Cosgrove (32), White (57), Shickell (62); **Goals:** Jones 4/5.
Sin bin: Handforth (79) - dissent.
ROVERS: 2 Will Sharp; 36 Ben Blackmore; 3 Greg Worthington; 1 Ian Hardman; 35 Jason Crookes; 23 Andy Kain; 7 Gareth Moore; 8 Steve Crossley; 9 Andy Ellis; 38 Kyle Trout; 31 Shaun Pick; 12 Tim Spears; 11 James Lockwood. Subs (all used): 6 Jack Bussey; 10 Keegan Hirst; 13 Matt James; 30 Luke Teasdale.
Tries: Hardman (10), Sharp (21), Pick (67), Crookes (70), Blackmore (76); **Goals:** Moore 3/6.
Rugby Leaguer & League Express Men of the Match: *Cougars:* Danny Jones; *Rovers:* Shaun Pick.
Penalty count: 5-7; **Half-time:** 12-12;
Referee: Joe Cobb; **Attendance:** 1,919.

ROCHDALE HORNETS 16 SHEFFIELD EAGLES 58

HORNETS: 9 Lewis Sheridan; 1 Wayne English; 26 Alex Clare; 19 Dave Llewellyn; 29 Shaun Robinson; 6 Paul Crook; 17 Ryan Millard; 15 Anthony Walker; 28 James Tilley; 16 Liam Gilchrist; 11 Chris Baines; 12 Alex Trumper; 18 Joe Greenwood. Subs (all used): 23 James Dandy; 13 Jordan Case; 24 Tony Suffolk; 7 Alex McClurg.
Tries: English (2), Crook (7), Dandy (52);
Goals: Crook 2/3.
EAGLES: 1 Quentin Laulu-Togagae; 2 Scott Turner; 3 Menzie Yere; 33 Etuate Uaisele; 5 Misi Taulapapa; 32 Kyle Briggs; 7 Dominic Brambani; 12 Peter Green; 9 Andrew Henderson; 10 Mitchell Stringer; 11 Michael Knowles; 16 Duane Straugheir; 6 Pat Walker. Subs (all used): 14 James Davey; 15 Matt Garside; 8 Eddie Battye; 18 Tom Lillycrop.
Tries: Yere (11, 69), Laulu-Togagae (22, 37, 40, 74, 79), Briggs (27), Uaisele (31), Turner (33), Stringer (66);
Goals: Brambani 7/11.
Rugby Leaguer & League Express Men of the Match: *Hornets:* Joe Greenwood; *Eagles:* Quentin Laulu-Togagae.
Penalty count: 7-8; **Half-time:** 10-36;
Referee: Gareth Hewer; **Attendance:** 662.

SWINTON LIONS 18 WHITEHAVEN 44

LIONS: 1 Ritchie Hawkyard; 3 Jordan Burke; 19 Jacque Peet; 4 Mick Nanyn; 22 Kevin Penny; 32 Martin Ainscough; 28 Chris Atkin; 16 Mike Morrison; 9 Andy Ackers; 25 Glenn Riley; 12 Darren Hawkyard; 23 Danny Bridge; 15 Josh Barlow. Subs (all used): 24 Gavin Bennion; 13 James Brown; 27 Lewis Hulme; 21 Brad Dwyer.
Tries: Ainscough (5), Penny (59), R Hawkyard (71);
Goals: Nanyn 3/3.
WHITEHAVEN: 5 Shaun Ainscough; 18 Jordan Burns; 6 Chris Taylor; 3 Jessie Joe Nandye; 13 Bradd Crellin; 26 Brett Seymour; 14 Neil Thorman; 30 Carl Forster; 9 James Newton; 20 Jordan Hand; 4 Scott McAvoy; 12 Lee Mitchell; 11 Lee Doran. Subs (all used): 7 Cain Southernwood; 8 Samir Tahraoui; 22 James Robinson; 16 Kurtis Quinn.
Tries: McAvoy (12), Forster (20), Burns (40), Nandye (43), Southernwood (47), Mitchell (63), Newton (78); **Goals:** Seymour 8/9.
Rugby Leaguer & League Express Men of the Match: *Lions:* Mick Nanyn; *Whitehaven:* Lee Mitchell.
Penalty count: 6-9; **Half-time:** 6-18;
Referee: Chris Leatherbarrow; **Attendance:** 549.

WORKINGTON TOWN 23 DEWSBURY RAMS 4

TOWN: 30 Jack Murphy; 33 John Patrick; 3 Jason Mossop; 24 Declan Hulme; 34 Jay Rossi; 6 Peter Lupton; 16 Carl Forber; 8 Kris Coward; 7 Callum Phillips; - Greg Burke; 11 Brett Phillips; 32 Connor Farrell; 17 Liam McAvoy. Subs (all used): - Jordan James; 10 Marc Shackley; 13 Karl Olstrum; 19 Nathan Lucock.
Tries: C Phillips (4), B Phillips (43, 59), Lupton (55);
Goals: Forber 3/4; **Field goal:** Murphy (80).
RAMS: 1 Louis Sheriff; 21 Austin Buchanan; 34 Ben Hellewell; 24 Sam Wood; 2 Dale Morton; 31 Kieran Hyde; 23 Jonathan Schofield; 17 Matthew Haggarty; 6 Tom Hemingway; 10 Ryan Hepworth; 4 Shane Grady; 12 Scott Hale; 20 Jobe Murphy. Subs (all used): 25 Joel Farrell; 33 Jason Muranka; 14 Ryan Wright; 32 Makali Aizue.
Try: Wood (75); **Goals:** Hemingway 0/1.
Rugby Leaguer & League Express Men of the Match: *Town:* Brett Phillips; *Rams:* Tom Hemingway.
Penalty count: 8-3; **Half-time:** 6-0;
Referee: Warren Turley; **Attendance:** 895.

PLAY-OFFS

QUALIFYING PLAY-OFFS

Sunday 14th September 2014

LEIGH CENTURIONS 41 DONCASTER 14

CENTURIONS: 1 Gregg McNally; 22 Adam Higson; 34 Michael Platt; 4 Tom Armstrong; 15 Liam Kay; 6 Martyn Ridyard; 7 Ryan Brierley; 29 Jake Emmitt; 14 Sean Penkywicz; 35 Sam Hopkins; 11 Matt Sarsfield; 30 Kurt Haggerty; 13 Sam Barlow. Subs (all used): 9 Bob Beswick; 16 Martin Aspinwall; 18 Jamie Acton; 33 Jonathan Walker.
Tries: Haggerty (2), Platt (31, 36), Brierley (38, 65), McNally (40), Armstrong (70, 79); **Goals:** Ridyard 4/8;
Field goal: Haggerty (60).
DONCASTER: 5 Dave Scott; 22 Tom Hodson; 3 Liam Welham; 4 Nev Morrison; 2 Stewart Sanderson; 6 Paul Cooke; 23 Richard Wilkinson; 21 Matt Carbutt; 9 Kyle Kesik; 16 Craig Robinson; 33 Pasqualle Dunn; 34 Liam Colbon; 13 Mike Emmett. Subs (all used): 8 Mark Castle; 14 Russ Spiers; 15 Scott Spaven; 18 Ryan Wilson.
Tries: Cooke (10), Wilkinson (15); **Goals:** Sanderson 3/3.
Rugby Leaguer & League Express Men of the Match: *Centurions:* Jamie Acton; *Doncaster:* Matt Carbutt.
Penalty count: 7-11; **Half-time:** 24-14;
Referee: Matthew Thomason; **Attendance:** 1,903.

FEATHERSTONE ROVERS 34 HALIFAX 16

ROVERS: 2 Will Sharp; 36 Ben Blackmore; 3 Greg Worthington; 1 Ian Hardman; 35 Jason Crookes; 23 Andy Kain; 7 Gareth Moore; 8 Steve Crossley; 9 Andy Ellis; 13 Matt James; 12 Tim Spears; 31 Shaun Pick; 11 James Lockwood. Subs (all used): 30 Luke Teasdale; 6 Jack Bussey; 38 Kyle Trout; 10 Keegan Hirst.
Tries: Spears (12), Teasdale (33), Moore (56), Trout (60), James (74), Crookes (80); **Goals:** Moore 5/6.
HALIFAX: 1 Ryan Fieldhouse; 25 Gareth Potts; 16 Danny Cowling; 23 Callum Casey; 15 Adam Robinson; 6 Scott Murrell; 14 Paul Mennell; 10 Luke Ambler; 9 Ben Kaye; 24 Sam Brooks; 11 Dane Manning; 27 Ross Divorty; 13 Luke Adamson. Subs (all used): 8 Tony Tonks; 17 Ben Davies; 19 Keith Holden; 28 Jack Spencer.
Tries: Kaye (21), Potts (27, 31); **Goals:** Murrell 2/3.
Rugby Leaguer & League Express Men of the Match: *Rovers:* Gareth Moore; *Halifax:* Scott Murrell.
Penalty count: 8-5; **Half-time:** 12-16;
Referee: George Stokes; **Attendance:** 1,478.

ELIMINATION PLAY-OFFS

Saturday 13th September 2014

SHEFFIELD EAGLES 16 BATLEY BULLDOGS 0

EAGLES: 1 Quentin Laulu-Togagae; 2 Scott Turner; 3 Menzie Yere; 33 Etuate Uaisele; 5 Misi Taulapapa; 32 Kyle Briggs; 7 Dominic Brambani; 8 Eddie Battye; 9 Andrew Henderson; 10 Mitchell Stringer; 11 Michael Knowles; 16 Duane Straugheir; 6 Pat Walker. Subs (all used): 14 James Davey; 15 Matt Garside; 4 Lelauloto Tagaloa; 12 Peter Green.
Tries: Uaisele (69, 76), Laulu-Togagae (73);
Goals: Brambani 2/4.
BULLDOGS: 1 Miles Greenwood; 32 Wayne Reittie; 33 Ben Heaton; 19 Joe Chandler; 29 Alex Brown; 6 Ben Black; 7 Scott Leatherbarrow; 8 Byron Smith; 9 Anthony Nicholson; 13 Mark Applegarth; 3 Alex Bretherton; 12 Sam Scott; 18 Luke Blake. Subs (all used): 10 Alex Rowe; 20 Adam Gledhill; 11 John Davies; 34 Jordan Grayston.
Goals: Leatherbarrow 0/2.
Rugby Leaguer & League Express Men of the Match: *Eagles:* Andrew Henderson; *Bulldogs:* Byron Smith.
Penalty count: 8-7; **Half-time:** 0-0;
Referee: Dave Merrick; **Attendance:** 695
(at Keepmoat Stadium, Doncaster).

Sunday 14th September 2014

DEWSBURY RAMS 50 WORKINGTON TOWN 6

RAMS: 3 Karl Pryce; 2 Dale Morton; 34 Ben Hellewell; 4 Shane Grady; 24 Sam Wood; 31 Kieran Hyde; 7 Anthony Thackeray; 17 Matthew Haggarty; 6 Tom Hemingway; 10 Ryan Hepworth; 11 Rob Spicer; 12 Scott Hale; 20 Jobe Murphy. Subs (all used): 14 Ryan Wright; 32 Makali Aizue; 25 Joel Farrell; 15 Tommy Gallagher.
Tries: Thackeray (8, 30, 56), Hale (34), Aizue (42), Hellewell (52), Hepworth (67), Gallagher (75);
Goals: Hemingway 3/3, Hyde 6/7.
Sin bin: Wood (63) - punching.
On report: Aizue (26) - alleged high tackle on Burke.
TOWN: 30 Jack Murphy; 35 Theerapol Ritson; 3 Jason Mossop; 33 John Patrick; 34 Jay Rossi; 6 Peter Lupton; 16 Carl Forber; 8 Kris Coward; 19 Nathan Lucock; 32 Greg Burke; 11 Brett Phillips; 31 Connor Farrell; 17 Liam McAvoy. Subs (all used): - Jordan James; - Jack Dawson; 18 James Duerden; 7 Callum Phillips.
Try: Murphy (64); **Goals:** Forber 1/1.
Rugby Leaguer & League Express Men of the Match: *Rams:* Anthony Thackeray; *Town:* Jack Murphy.
Penalty count: 8-7; **Half-time:** 20-0;
Referee: Chris Leatherbarrow; **Attendance:** 805.

PRELIMINARY SEMI-FINALS

Sunday 21st September 2014

HALIFAX 0 DEWSBURY RAMS 25

HALIFAX: 30 Joe Martin; 25 Gareth Potts; 3 Steve Tyrer; 23 Callum Casey; 21 Tom Saxton; 6 Scott Murrell; 14 Paul Mennell; 24 Sam Brooks; 9 Ben Kaye; 10 Luke Ambler; 11 Dane Manning; 27 Ross Divorty; 13 Luke Adamson. Subs (all used): 8 Tony Tonks; 15 Adam Robinson; 19 Keith Holden; 12 Andy Bracek.
RAMS: 3 Karl Pryce; 2 Dale Morton; 34 Ben Hellewell; 4 Shane Grady; 24 Sam Wood; 31 Kieran Hyde; 7 Anthony Thackeray; 17 Matthew Haggarty; 6 Tom Hemingway; 10 Ryan Hepworth; 11 Rob Spicer; 12 Scott Hale; 20 Jobe Murphy. Subs (all used): 14 Ryan Wright; 33 Jason Muranka; 25 Joel Farrell; 15 Tommy Gallagher.
Tries: Thackeray (16, 74), Wood (48), Gallagher (58);
Goals: Hemingway 3/4, Hyde 1/2; **Field goal:** Hyde (39).
Rugby Leaguer & League Express Men of the Match: *Halifax:* Joe Martin; *Rams:* Anthony Thackeray.
Penalty count: 8-6; **Half-time:** 0-9;
Referee: Joe Cobb; **Attendance:** 1,371.

DONCASTER 24 SHEFFIELD EAGLES 58

DONCASTER: 5 Dave Scott; 22 Tom Hodson; 3 Liam Welham; 20 Shaun Leaf; 2 Stewart Sanderson; 6 Paul Cooke; 23 Richard Wilkinson; 21 Matt Carbutt; 9 Kyle Kesik; 16 Craig Robinson; 19 Liam Cunningham; 12 Michael Kelly; 13 Mike Emmett. Subs (all used): 14 Russ Spiers; 8 Mark Castle; 15 Scott Spaven; 18 Ryan Wilson.
Tries: Scott (16), Spaven (59), Hodson (72), Emmett (79); **Goals:** Sanderson 4/4.
Dismissal: Cunningham (27) - kicking Knowles.
EAGLES: 1 Quentin Laulu-Togagae; 2 Scott Turner; 3 Menzie Yere; 33 Etuate Uaisele; 5 Misi Taulapapa; 32 Kyle Briggs; 7 Dominic Brambani; 8 Eddie Battye; 9 Andrew Henderson; 10 Mitchell Stringer; 11 Michael Knowles; 16 Duane Straugheir; 6 Pat Walker. Subs (all used): 12 Peter Green; 15 Matt Garside; 18 Tom Lillycrop; 19 Cory Aston.
Tries: Battye (6), Uaisele (11), Walker (21), Yere (34), Garside (37), Turner (39), Briggs (41), Laulu-Togagae (44, 62), Straugheir (66);
Goals: Brambani 6/7, Walker 1/1, Briggs 2/2.
Rugby Leaguer & League Express Men of the Match: *Doncaster:* Richard Wilkinson; *Eagles:* Quentin Laulu-Togagae.
Penalty count: 5-5; **Half-time:** 6-34;
Referee: Matthew Thomason; **Attendance:** 825.

QUALIFYING SEMI-FINALS

Sunday 28th September 2014

LEIGH CENTURIONS 33 DEWSBURY RAMS 22

CENTURIONS: 1 Gregg McNally; 22 Adam Higson; 34 Michael Platt; 4 Tom Armstrong; 15 Liam Kay; 6 Martyn Ridyard; 7 Ryan Brierley; 29 Jake Emmitt; 9 Bob Beswick; 10 Oliver Wilkes; 11 Matt Sarsfield; 30 Kurt Haggerty; 13 Sam Barlow. Subs (all used): 14 Sean Penkywicz; 18 Jamie Acton; 27 Anthony Bate; 33 Jonathan Walker.
Tries: Higson (3, 14, 60), Platt (32), McNally (55);
Goals: Ridyard 6/7; **Field goal:** Ridyard (40).
Sin bin: Kay (24) - fighting.
RAMS: 3 Karl Pryce; 2 Dale Morton; 34 Ben Hellewell; 4 Shane Grady; 24 Sam Wood; 31 Kieran Hyde; 7 Anthony Thackeray; 17 Matthew Haggarty; 6 Tom Hemingway; 10 Ryan Hepworth; 11 Rob Spicer; 12 Scott Hale; 20 Jobe Murphy. Subs (all used): 14 Ryan Wright; 15 Tommy Gallagher; 25 Joel Farrell; 32 Makali Aizue.
Tries: Thackeray (28), Hellewell (43), Farrell (49), Morton (65); **Goals:** Hemingway 3/4.
Sin bin: Murphy (24) - fighting.
Rugby Leaguer & League Express Men of the Match: *Centurions:* Bob Beswick; *Rams:* Anthony Thackeray.
Penalty count: 5-8; **Half-time:** 21-6;
Referee: Matthew Thomason; **Attendance:** 2,828.

FEATHERSTONE ROVERS 21 SHEFFIELD EAGLES 12

ROVERS: 1 Ian Hardman; 2 Will Sharp; 31 Shaun Pick; 36 Ben Blackmore; 35 Jason Crookes; 23 Andy Kain; 7 Gareth Moore; 8 Steve Crossley; 9 Andy Ellis; 13 Matt James; 18 Jamie Cording; 12 Tim Spears; 11 James Lockwood. Subs (all used): 30 Luke Teasdale; 6 Jack Bussey; 42 Chris Annakin; 10 Keegan Hirst.
Tries: Blackmore (9), Lockwood (20), Moore (21);
Goals: Moore 4/5; **Field goal:** Moore (34).
EAGLES: 1 Quentin Laulu-Togagae; 2 Scott Turner; 3 Menzie Yere; 15 Matt Garside; 5 Misi Taulapapa; 32 Kyle Briggs; 7 Dominic Brambani; 8 Eddie Battye; 9 Andrew Henderson; 10 Mitchell Stringer; 11 Michael Knowles; 16 Duane Straugheir; 6 Pat Walker. Subs (all used): 19 Cory Aston; 12 Peter Green; 21 Jack Blagbrough; 18 Tom Lillycrop.
Tries: Green (45), Laulu-Togagae (48);
Goals: Brambani 2/2.
Rugby Leaguer & League Express Men of the Match: *Rovers:* Gareth Moore; *Eagles:* Kyle Briggs.
Penalty count: 13-10; **Half-time:** 21-0;
Referee: Joe Cobb; **Attendance:** 1,730.

GRAND FINAL

Sunday 5th October 2014

FEATHERSTONE ROVERS 12 LEIGH CENTURIONS 36

ROVERS: 2 Will Sharp; 35 Jason Crookes; 1 Ian Hardman; 18 Jamie Cording; 36 Ben Blackmore; 23 Andy Kain; 7 Gareth Moore; 8 Steve Crossley; 9 Andy Ellis; 13 Matt James; 31 Shaun Pick; 11 James Lockwood; 12 Tim Spears. Subs (all used): 30 Luke Teasdale; 6 Jack Bussey; 42 Chris Annakin; 10 Keegan Hirst.
Tries: Sharp (27, 51); **Goals:** Moore 2/2.
Sin bin: Crookes (68) - high tackle on Armstrong.
CENTURIONS: 1 Gregg McNally; 22 Adam Higson; 34 Michael Platt; 4 Tom Armstrong; 15 Liam Kay; 6 Martyn Ridyard; 7 Ryan Brierley; 29 Jake Emmitt; 14 Sean Penkywicz; 10 Oliver Wilkes; 11 Matt Sarsfield; 30 Kurt Haggerty; 13 Sam Barlow. Subs (all used): 9 Bob Beswick; 18 Jamie Acton; 16 Martin Aspinwall; 33 Jonathan Walker.
Tries: Sarsfield (5), McNally (17), Armstrong (22), Higson (65), Barlow (70), Brierley (80);
Goals: Ridyard 6/8.
Sin bin: Penkywicz (68) - retaliation.
Rugby Leaguer & League Express Men of the Match: *Rovers:* Jack Bussey; *Centurions:* Tom Armstrong.
Penalty count: 6-8; **Half-time:** 6-20;
Referee: Matthew Thomason; **Attendance:** 9,164
(at Headingley Carnegie, Leeds).

Leigh duo Martin Aspinwall and Jamie Acton combine to halt Featherstone's Keegan Hirst
during the Championship Grand Final

CHAMPIONSHIP ONE 2014
Club by Club

GATESHEAD THUNDER

DATE	FIXTURE	RESULT	SCORERS	LGE	ATT
9/3/14	Oxford (h)	W47-28	t:Capper,Brown(2),S Lynch,Payne(3),Beharrell,Heil g:Puckering(5) fg:Puckering	5th	254
16/3/14	Swinton (a) (CCR3)	L66-6	t:Capper g:Puckering	N/A	249
23/3/14	Hemel (a)	L37-24	t:Beharrell,Heil(2),Blades g:Puckering(4)	6th	200
30/3/14	Gloucestershire All Golds (h)	L20-28	t:Heil(2),Beharrell,Booth g:Beharrell(2)	6th	248
13/4/14	Oldham (a)	L52-16	t:Esslemont,Hough,Payne g:Puckering(2)	8th	436
18/4/14	York (h)	L26-30	t:Barron,Capper,Payne(2),Blades g:Puckering(2),Beharrell	8th	257
4/5/14	South Wales (a)	W16-50	t:Payne(2),Beharrell,Caro(2),Heil,Rooney,Ollett,Bowring,Carlile g:Beharrell(5)	6th	258
11/5/14	London Skolars (h)	W24-16	t:Bowring,Beharrell(2),Payne,Hough g:Rooney(2)	5th	209
18/5/14	Hunslet (a)	L52-6	t:Payne g:Beharrell	7th	566
1/6/14	Hemel (a)	W22-26	t:Sheriff,Payne,Caro,Mapals g:Beharrell(3),Rooney(2)	6th	126
8/6/14	Oxford (a)	W22-36	t:Sheriff,Blades,Brown,Rooney,Stamp,Mapals g:Beharrell(6)	6th	310
15/6/14	York (a)	L42-16	t:Blades,Esslemont,Payne g:Beharrell(2)	6th	495
22/6/14	Oldham (h)	L14-32	t:Heil,Stamp,Payne g:Beharrell	6th	253
29/6/14	London Skolars (a) ●	W6-66	t:Esslemont,Stamp,Farrell,Rooney(2),Payne,Butterfield,Sheriff(3),G Clarke, Hough,Meads g:Rooney(4),Meads(2),Stamp	5th	206
4/7/14	Hunslet (h)	L6-45	t:Meads g:Meads	6th	457
20/7/14	Gloucestershire All Golds (a)	W22-28	t:Stamp(2),Brown,R Clarke(2) g:Hardcastle(3),Beharrell	6th	126
27/7/14	Oxford (h)	W48-28	t:Brown,Hardcastle(2),Payne(2),Stoker,Esslemont,Hodgson g:Hardcastle(8)	5th	153
3/8/14	Hemel (h)	W34-26	t:Beharrell,Blades(2),Capper(2),Heil,R Clarke g:Hardcastle(3)	4th	166
10/8/14	York (a)	L34-30	t:Welham,Payne,Brown,Meads,Barron,Mapals g:Beharrell(3)	4th	571
17/8/14	South Wales (h)	W58-24	t:Beharrell,Meads(3),Hardcastle(2),Esslemont,Heil,Capper(2),Bowring(2) g:Hardcastle(7)	4th	161
31/8/14	Oldham (h)	W40-14	t:Meads(2),Capper,Mapals,R Clarke,Payne,Heil,Fewlass g:Beharrell(4)	4th	401
14/9/14	Hemel (h) (EPO) ●●	W15-14 *(aet)*	t:Brown,Mapals,Esslemont g:Beharrell fg:Beharrell	N/A	557
21/9/14	Hunslet (a) (ESF)	L50-6	t:Stamp g:Beharrell	N/A	463

● Played at Queen Elizabeth II Stadium, Enfield
●● Played at Kingston Park, Newcastle

	D.O.B.	APP ALL	Ch1	TRIES ALL	Ch1	GOALS ALL	Ch1	FG ALL	Ch1	PTS ALL	Ch1
Matt Barron	17/11/86	18(3)	18(2)	2	2	0	0	0	0	8	8
Matty Beharrell	29/3/94	20	20	8	8	31	31	1	1	95	95
Jacob Blades	9/8/93	15(2)	14(2)	6	6	0	0	0	0	24	24
Carl Booth	8/10/84	4	3	1	1	0	0	0	0	4	4
Sam Bowring	1/7/91	8(9)	8(9)	4	4	0	0	0	0	16	16
Joe Brown	24/4/87	23	22	7	7	0	0	0	0	28	28
Mick Butterfield	5/12/84	2	2	1	1	0	0	0	0	4	4
Tom Capper	10/10/92	15	14	8	7	0	0	0	0	32	28
Keal Carlile	20/3/90	3	3	1	1	0	0	0	0	4	4
Omari Caro	7/3/91	5	5	3	3	0	0	0	0	12	12
George Clarke	25/2/93	1(1)	1(1)	1	1	0	0	0	0	4	4
Rhys Clarke	12/3/91	14(5)	13(5)	4	4	0	0	0	0	16	16
Callum Cockburn	20/5/89	(6)	(5)	0	0	0	0	0	0	0	0
Connor Condron	29/11/91	(3)	(3)	0	0	0	0	0	0	0	0
Jordan Cox	27/5/92	(1)	(1)	0	0	0	0	0	0	0	0
Greg Eden	14/11/90	2	2	0	0	0	0	0	0	0	0
Sonny Esslemont	29/12/93	16	16	6	6	0	0	0	0	24	24
Joel Farrell	15/3/94	4(1)	4(1)	1	1	0	0	0	0	4	4
Lee Fewlass	29/4/89	12(8)	11(8)	1	1	0	0	0	0	4	4
Benn Hardcastle	4/1/90	4	4	4	4	21	21	0	0	58	58
Chris Heil	18/8/92	20(1)	19(1)	10	10	0	0	0	0	40	40
Joe Hodgson	11/8/94	(7)	(7)	1	1	0	0	0	0	4	4
Ricky Hough	22/8/95	17(5)	16(5)	3	3	0	0	0	0	12	12
Rhys Lovegrove	11/3/87	(1)	(1)	0	0	0	0	0	0	0	0
Sam Luckley	29/11/95	(1)	(1)	0	0	0	0	0	0	0	0
Sam Lynch	21/6/90	4	3	1	1	0	0	0	0	4	4
Tom Lynch	6/11/86	3	2	1	1	0	0	0	0	4	4
Ryan MacDonald	24/2/78	(1)	(1)	0	0	0	0	0	0	0	0
Lee Mapals	17/7/85	10	10	5	5	0	0	0	0	20	20
Joe Martin	28/3/95	2	2	0	0	0	0	0	0	0	0
Jordan Meads	16/2/92	9(1)	9(1)	7	7	3	3	0	0	34	34
Iain Murray	9/5/90	(5)	(5)	0	0	0	0	0	0	0	0
Aaron Ollett	19/11/92	8	8	1	1	0	0	0	0	4	4
Jason Payne	20/1/88	23	22	18	18	0	0	0	0	72	72
Nathan Powley	15/8/91	(3)	(2)	0	0	0	0	0	0	0	0
Carl Puckering	4/10/86	5	4	0	0	14	13	1	1	29	27
Jamie Rooney	17/3/80	8	8	4	4	8	8	0	0	32	32
Alex Ruff	1/5/95	(2)	(2)	0	0	0	0	0	0	0	0
Louis Sheriff	6/9/92	6	6	5	5	0	0	0	0	20	20
Paul Stamp	25/1/89	15(6)	14(6)	6	6	1	1	0	0	26	26
Josh Stoker	26/7/92	1(19)	1(18)	1	1	0	0	0	0	4	4
Kris Welham	12/5/87	2	2	1	1	0	0	0	0	4	4

Jason Payne

LEAGUE RECORD
P20-W11-D0-L9-BP3
(4th, Championship 1/
Elimination Semi-Final)
F615, A576, Diff+39
36 points.

CHALLENGE CUP
Round Three

ATTENDANCES
Best - v Hemel (EPO - 557)
Worst - v Oxford (Ch1 - 153)
Total (Championship 1,
inc play-offs) - 3,116
Average (Championship 1,
inc play-offs) - 283
(Up by 97 on 2013)

CLUB RECORDS	**Highest score:** 66-6 v Wakefield, 5/9/99; 66-6 v London Skolars, 29/6/2014 **Highest score against:** 0-132 v Blackpool Panthers, 16/5/2010
	Record attendance: 6,631 v Bradford, 16/5/99
MATCH RECORDS	**Tries:** 5 Andy Walker v London Skolars, 22/6/2003 **Goals:** 11 Ian Herron v Wakefield, 5/9/99 **Points:** 26 Ian Herron v Wakefield, 5/9/99
SEASON RECORDS	**Tries:** 25 Matt Daylight 1999 **Goals:** 129 *(inc 1fg)* Dan Russell 2008 **Points:** 293 Dan Russell 2008
CAREER RECORDS	**Tries:** 74 Kevin Neighbour 2001-2006; 2008-2010 **Goals:** 151 Paul Thorman 2001-2004 **Points:** 387 Paul Thorman 2001-2004
	Appearances: 218 Robin Peers 2002-2012

GLOUCESTERSHIRE ALL GOLDS

ALL GOLDS

DATE	FIXTURE	RESULT	SCORERS	LGE	ATT
2/3/14	York (a)	L26-16	t:Thomas,Elliott,Jenkins g:Jenkins(2)	6th	648
9/3/14	South Wales (h)	W29-17	t:Walter,Cook,Cowburn,Thomas(2) g:Jenkins(4) fg:Cook	4th	186
16/3/14	Rochdale (a) (CCR3)	L76-4	t:Elliott	N/A	307
30/3/14	Gateshead (a)	W20-28	t:Elliott,Thomas(2),Barlow,Cowburn g:Jenkins(4)	5th	248
13/4/14	Hunslet (h)	L4-44	t:Cowburn	5th	306
18/4/14	Oxford (a)	L38-24	t:Cowburn,Jenkins,Cook,Elliott g:Roper(4)	7th	240
4/5/14	Hemel (h)	L20-21	t:Smith,Ward,Thomas,Te'o g:Jenkins(2)	8th	126
18/5/14	London Skolars (a) ●	W24-34	t:Spencer-Tonks,Jenkins,Muranka(2),Canterbury(2),Duffy g:Jenkins(3)	6th	398
25/5/14	Oldham (h)	L22-30	t:Fairbank,Claridge,Canterbury,Cook g:Jenkins(3)	6th	264
1/6/14	South Wales (a)	W36-38	t:Cowburn,Jenkins,White,Francis(2),Cook(2) g:Jenkins(5)	5th	320
8/6/14	York (h)	W24-22	t:Cowburn,Jones,Muranka,Thomas g:Bradley(4)	5th	318
22/6/14	Oxford (h)	W36-20	t:Cook,Bradley,White,Fairbank,Foster,Thomas g:Bradley(6)	4th	323
29/6/14	Hunslet (a)	W16-23	t:Jones,Cook,White,Te'o g:Bradley(3) fg:Cook	4th	430
6/7/14	Hemel (h)	L14-22	t:Jenkins(2),Cowburn g:Bradley	4th	168
13/7/14	Oldham (a)	L46-6	t:White g:Bradley	4th	516
20/7/14	Gateshead (h)	L22-28	t:Claridge,Te'o,Ward(2) g:Bradley(3)	5th	126
3/8/14	York (h)	L18-42	t:Fairbank,Ward,White g:Bradley(3)	6th	184
9/8/14	South Wales (a)	W16-28	t:Cowburn,White,Duffy,Parry,Fairbank g:Bradley(4)	5th	177
17/8/14	London Skolars (h)	L12-36	t:Canterbury,Cowburn g:Cowburn(2)	5th	108
31/8/14	Hemel (a)	L44-24	t:Cook,Crowther,Cowburn,Fairbank g:Bradley(4)	6th	305
7/9/14	Oldham (a)	L68-24	t:Fairbank(2),Bradley,White g:Bradley(4)	6th	437

● Played at Queen Elizabeth II Stadium, Enfield

		APP		TRIES		GOALS		FG		PTS	
	D.O.B.	ALL	Ch1	ALL	Ch1	ALL	Ch1	ALL	Ch1	ALL	Ch1
Mark Barlow	16/2/84	6(3)	5(3)	1	1	0	0	0	0	4	4
Matt Bradley	2/8/91	11	11	2	2	38	38	0	0	84	84
Danny Cahill	11/3/94	1	0	0	0	0	0	0	0	0	0
Casey Canterbury	1/1/94	3(9)	3(9)	4	4	0	0	0	0	16	16
Harry Chapman-Walker	7/10/89	4(7)	4(7)	0	0	0	0	0	0	0	0
Scott Claridge	22/1/91	15	15	2	2	0	0	0	0	8	8
Craig Cook	26/5/83	20	19	8	8	0	0	2	2	34	34
Phil Cowburn	15/10/90	18(2)	17(2)	10	10	2	2	0	0	44	44
Jamie Crowther	28/10/92	3	3	1	1	0	0	0	0	4	4
Izaak Duffy	16/2/89	18	17	2	2	0	0	0	0	8	8
Marcus Elliott	8/3/94	6	5	4	3	0	0	0	0	16	12
Miles Fairbank	28/8/92	14(1)	14(1)	7	7	0	0	0	0	28	28
Danny Fallon	26/7/95	1(2)	1(1)	0	0	0	0	0	0	0	0
James Fisher	25/8/89	2(1)	2	0	0	0	0	0	0	0	0
Frankie Foster	17/1/96	(8)	(8)	1	1	0	0	0	0	4	4
Jack Francis	17/12/92	1(3)	1(3)	2	2	0	0	0	0	8	8
James Greene	27/3/87	2	2	0	0	0	0	0	0	0	0
Corey Hanson	11/8/92	3	3	0	0	0	0	0	0	0	0
Ash Haynes	11/3/94	3(3)	3(2)	0	0	0	0	0	0	0	0
Aidan Jenkins	7/3/90	13	12	6	6	18	18	0	0	60	60
Richard Jones	7/7/89	4(2)	4(2)	2	2	0	0	0	0	8	8
Joe McClean	10/8/89	3(15)	2(15)	0	0	0	0	0	0	0	0
Jason Muranka	18/7/94	16	15	3	3	0	0	0	0	12	12
Connor Nolan	18/7/94	(4)	4(8)	0	0	0	0	0	0	0	0
Steve Parry	19/10/88	(3)	(3)	1	1	0	0	0	0	4	4
Reece Rance	17/7/93	3	2	0	0	0	0	0	0	0	0
Steve Roper	10/11/86	1(2)	1(2)	0	0	4	0	0	0	8	0
Brendan Smith	6/9/89	17(2)	16(2)	1	1	0	0	0	0	4	4
Daniel Spencer-Tonks	18/1/95	3(3)	3(3)	1	1	0	0	0	0	4	4
Mike Stewart	14/2/89	2(3)	2(3)	0	0	0	0	0	0	0	0
Callum Stonier	21/5/91	(3)	(3)	0	0	0	0	0	0	0	0
Sam Te'o	30/7/88	15	15	3	3	0	0	0	0	12	12
Danny Thomas	21/12/83	18	17	8	8	0	0	0	0	32	32
James Tutuila	19/6/90	5(1)	4(1)	0	0	0	0	0	0	0	0
Chris Tyrer	10/10/85	1	1	0	0	0	0	0	0	0	0
Bobby Tyson-Wilson	6/11/94	(1)	(1)	0	0	0	0	0	0	0	0
Chris Vitalini	5/5/87	3	3	0	0	0	0	0	0	4	4
James Walter	11/9/91	6(3)	6(3)	1	1	0	0	0	0	16	16
Jarrod Ward	21/10/93	15	15	4	4	0	0	0	0	28	28
Ben White	27/10/94	12	12	7	7	0	0	0	0	28	28

Phil Cowburn

LEAGUE RECORD
P20-W8-D0-L12-BP5
(6th, Championship 1)
F446, A616, Diff-170
29 points.

CHALLENGE CUP
Round Three

ATTENDANCES
Best - v Oxford (Ch1 - 323)
Worst - v London Skolars (Ch1 - 108)
Total (Championship 1 only) - 2,109
Average (Championship 1 only) - 211
(Up by 16 on 2013)

CLUB RECORDS — Highest score: 38-36 v South Wales, 1/6/2014 **Highest score against:** 6-82 v Salford, 21/4/2013 **Record attendance:** 867 v Salford, 21/4/2013
MATCH RECORDS — Tries: 2 *(14 players)* **Goals:** 6 Matt Bradley v Oxford, 22/6/2014 **Points:** 16 Matt Bradley v Oxford, 22/6/2014
SEASON RECORDS — Tries: 10 Phil Cowburn 2014 **Goals:** 39 Matt Bradley 2013 **Points:** 84 Matt Bradley 2014
CAREER RECORDS — Tries: 16 Phil Cowburn 2013-2014 **Goals:** 77 Matt Bradley 2013-2014 **Points:** 166 Matt Bradley 2013-2014 **Appearances:** 38 Phil Cowburn 2013-2014

HEMEL STAGS

DATE	FIXTURE	RESULT	SCORERS	LGE	ATT
2/3/14	Hunslet (h)	L0-28		9th	210
9/3/14	Oldham (a)	D20-20	t:Swindells,Small,Al-Zubeidi,Hill g:Swindells(2)	7th	508
16/3/14	South Wales (a) (CCR3)	W12-38	t:Ljazouli,Al-Zubeidi,Jy-mel Coleman,Thorburn,Barbera,Hill,Swindells g:Swindells(2),Young(3)	N/A	213
23/3/14	Gateshead (h)	W37-24	t:Swindells,Small(2),Barbera(3),Brown g:Swindells(4) fg:Jy-mel Coleman	4th	200
30/3/14	South Wales (a)	W16-34	t:Swindells,Small,Brown,Cameron,Hill,Patchett,Hudson g:Swindells(2),Young	4th	193
6/4/14	Doncaster (a) (CCR4)	L68-18	t:Al-Zubeidi,Ingarfield,Hill g:Swindells(3)	N/A	348
18/4/14	London Skolars (h)	L24-27	t:Swindells,Barbera,Mbaraga,Small g:Swindells(4)	4th	284
4/5/14	Gloucestershire All Golds (a)	W20-21	t:Ljazouli,Ingarfield,Brown g:Swindells(4) fg:Jy-mel Coleman	4th	126
11/5/14	York (a)	L22-14	t:Brown,Simons g:Swindells(3)	4th	457
25/5/14	Oxford (h)	W30-24	t:Swindells,Mbaraga(2),Hill,Brown g:Swindells(5)	4th	170
1/6/14	Gateshead (h)	L22-26	t:Small,Mbaraga,Ljazouli,Cameron g:Swindells(3)	4th	126
8/6/14	Oldham (h)	W44-32	t:Simons,Hill(2),Morgan,Clement-Pascall,Ljazouli,Brown g:Jy-mel Coleman(8)	4th	233
15/6/14	Hunslet (a)	L26-6	t:Jy-mel Coleman g:Swindells	4th	450
29/6/14	York (h)	L22-46	t:Cook,Chester,Mbaraga,Hill g:Swindells(2),Cook	6th	227
6/7/14	Gloucestershire All Golds (a)	W14-22	t:Swindells,Cameron,Mbaraga,Hill g:Swindells(3)	5th	168
13/7/14	London Skolars (a) ●	L34-28	t:Cameron(2),Simons,Hill(2),Navarrete g:Swindells(2)	5th	378
20/7/14	South Wales (h)	W40-10	t:Tebb,Hill(2),Cook,Morgan(2),Jy-mel Coleman g:Swindells(6)	4th	176
3/8/14	Gateshead (a)	L34-26	t:Ingarfield,Cameron,Simons,Swindells,Jermaine Coleman g:Swindells(2),Jy-mel Coleman	5th	166
10/8/14	Hunslet (h)	L16-34	t:Swindells,Jy-mel Coleman,Bannister g:Swindells,Jy-mel Coleman	6th	254
17/8/14	Oldham (a)	L38-10	t:Jy-mel Coleman,Small g:Swindells	6th	438
31/8/14	Gloucestershire All Golds (h)	W44-24	t:Brown(2),Jy-mel Coleman,Ingarfield,Cook,Clement-Pascall,Cameron g:Swindells(7),Jy-mel Coleman	5th	305
6/9/14	Oxford (a)	D22-22	t:Cook,Chisholm,Mbaraga,Jy-mel Coleman g:Swindells(2),Jy-mel Coleman	5th	205
14/9/14	Gateshead (a) (EPO) ●●	L15-14 *(aet)*	t:Clement-Pascall,Jy-mel Coleman g:Swindells(3)	N/A	557

● Played at Queen Elizabeth II Stadium, Enfield
●● Played at Kingston Park, Newcastle

		APP		TRIES		GOALS		FG		PTS	
	D.O.B.	ALL	Ch1	ALL	Ch1	ALL	Ch1	ALL	Ch1	ALL	Ch1
Essad Al-Zubeidi	2/10/94	4	2	3	1	0	0	0	0	12	4
Guy Aldam	3/9/89	(5)	(3)	0	0	0	0	0	0	0	0
Matthew Bailey	1/12/91	1(9)	1(8)	0	0	0	0	0	0	0	0
Steve Bannister	10/10/87	3	3	1	1	0	0	0	0	4	4
Mitch Barbera	12/7/91	5(1)	4	5	4	0	0	0	0	20	16
Michael Brown	9/9/86	22	20	8	8	0	0	0	0	32	32
James Cameron	15/3/88	23	21	7	7	0	0	0	0	28	28
Ryan Chester	19/3/92	(13)	(13)	1	1	0	0	0	0	4	4
Jamel Chisholm	7/11/92	4	4	1	1	0	0	0	0	4	4
Cariern Clement-Pascall	28/9/90	8(4)	8(3)	3	3	0	0	0	0	12	12
Chris Clough	20/1/87	5(1)	5(1)	0	0	0	0	0	0	0	0
Jermaine Coleman	17/6/82	6(1)	6(1)	1	1	0	0	0	0	4	4
Jy-mel Coleman	13/10/88	21	20	8	7	12	12	2	2	58	54
Mathew Cook	28/6/94	9	9	4	4	1	1	0	0	18	18
Kieran Dixon	22/8/92	1(1)	1(1)	0	0	0	0	0	0	0	0
Owain Griffiths	18/7/91	(3)	(3)	0	0	0	0	0	0	0	0
Maxime Herold	9/9/89	(2)	(2)	0	0	0	0	0	0	0	0
James Hill	11/6/93	19	17	13	11	0	0	0	0	52	44
James Howitt	2/3/83	15(2)	13(2)	0	0	0	0	0	0	0	0
Lee Hudson	28/9/90	(7)	(6)	1	1	0	0	0	0	4	4
Alex Ingarfield	18/10/91	15(3)	13(3)	4	3	0	0	0	0	16	12
Ben Kavanagh	20/8/94	(5)	(5)	0	0	0	0	0	0	0	0
Dan Ljazouli	14/8/89	20(1)	18(1)	4	3	0	0	0	0	16	12
Malikhi Lloyd-Jones	29/8/94	(4)	(4)	0	0	0	0	0	0	0	0
Dominic Maloney	12/3/87	14(3)	12(3)	0	0	0	0	0	0	0	0
Eddie Mbaraga	9/9/87	12(8)	12(7)	7	7	0	0	0	0	28	28
Miles McLeod	9/11/92	1(4)	1(4)	0	0	0	0	0	0	0	0
Mike McMeeken	10/5/94	2	2	0	0	0	0	0	0	0	0
Jimmy Morgan	1/6/93	11	11	3	3	0	0	0	0	12	12
Romaine Navarrete	30/6/94	1(5)	1(5)	1	1	0	0	0	0	4	4
Ryan Patchett	7/10/92	1(2)	1(2)	1	1	0	0	0	0	4	4
Evan Simons	11/10/91	21(2)	20(1)	4	4	0	0	0	0	16	16
Aaron Small	28/10/91	17	15	7	7	0	0	0	0	28	28
Barry-John Swindells	6/4/82	22	20	9	8	62	57	0	0	160	146
Matthew Tebb	4/9/90	1(3)	1(3)	1	1	0	0	0	0	4	4
Joel Thomas	11/11/94	(2)	(2)	0	0	0	0	0	0	0	0
Ben Thorburn	6/4/91	5	4	1	1	0	0	0	0	4	4
Ben Young	16/9/93	10(1)	8(1)	0	0	4	1	0	0	8	2

James Cameron

LEAGUE RECORD
P20-W8-D2-L10-BP5
(5th, Championship 1/
Elimination Play-Off)
F482, A521, Diff-39
33 points.

CHALLENGE CUP
Round Four

ATTENDANCES
Best - v Gloucestershire All Golds
(Ch1 - 305)
Worst - v Gateshead (Ch1 - 126)
Total (Championship 1 only) - 2,185
Average (Championship 1 only) - 219
(Down by 80 on 2013)

CLUB RECORDS
MATCH RECORDS
Highest score: 52-24 v South Wales, 26/5/2013 Highest score against: 18-68 v Doncaster, 6/4/2014 Record attendance: 679 v Oldham, 12/5/2013
Tries: 3 Mitch Barbera v Gateshead, 23/3/2014 Goals: 8 Mike Bishay v South Wales, 26/5/2013; Jy-mel Coleman v Oldham, 8/6/2014
Points: 16 Mike Bishay v South Wales, 26/5/2013; Jy-mel Coleman v Oldham, 8/6/2014
SEASON RECORDS
CAREER RECORDS
Tries: 13 James Hill 2014 Goals: 62 Barry-John Swindells 2014 Points: 160 Barry-John Swindells 2014
Tries: 16 Barry-John Swindells 2013-2014 Goals: 109 Barry-John Swindells 2013-2014 Points: 282 Barry-John Swindells 2013-2014
Appearances: 42 Barry-John Swindells 2013-2014

HUNSLET HAWKS

DATE	FIXTURE	RESULT	SCORERS	LGE	ATT
2/3/14	Hemel (a)	W0-28	t:Kain,Mackay,Houston(2),Ballard g:Ballard(4)	1st	210
9/3/14	York (h)	L26-28	t:Wilson(2),Hood(2),Ballard g:Ballard(3)	3rd	409
16/3/14	Oxford (h) (CCR3)	W68-6	t:Hood,Maun(2),Broughton,Tebb,March(2),Reed,Mapals(2),T Coyle,Stenchion g:Ballard(10)	N/A	278
23/3/14	Oxford (a)	W20-46	t:Mapals(2),Kain,Ballard(2),Oakes g:Ballard(5),Mapals(2)	3rd	301
30/3/14	London Skolars (h)	W60-4	t:Akaidere(3),Houston,Mapals(2),Reed,Cook,Kain(2),Stenchion g:March,Ansell(7)	1st	289
6/4/14	Workington (h) (CCR4)	W27-10	t:Maun(2),Grimshaw,Mackay,Kain g:Ansell(3) fg:Ansell	N/A	504
13/4/14	Gloucestershire All Golds (a)	W4-44	t:Houston(3),Akaidere,Mapals,Ansell,Grimshaw,Maun g:Ansell(6)	1st	306
18/4/14	Oldham (h)	W38-12	t:Grimshaw,Broughton,Oakes,Tebb,Mackay,Watson,Akaidere g:Ansell(5)	1st	598
27/4/14	Wigan (a) (CCR5)	L52-8	t:Grimshaw,Mapals	N/A	4,390
11/5/14	South Wales (a) ●	W6-20	t:Ballard,Stenchion,Brickwood,Watson g:Ballard(2)	1st	255
18/5/14	Gateshead (h)	W52-6	t:Brickwood(5),Ballard(2),Wilson(2),Hood,Oakes,Grimshaw g:Ballard(6)	1st	566
25/5/14	York (a)	L40-0		2nd	837
1/6/14	Oxford (h)	W32-12	t:Stenchion,Maun(2),Watson(2),Akaidere g:Ansell(4)	1st	417
15/6/14	Hemel (h)	W26-6	t:Oakes(2),Akaidere,Mackay,Kain g:Ansell(3)	1st	450
29/6/14	Gloucestershire All Golds (h)	L16-23	t:Maun,Hood,Oakes g:Ansell(2)	3rd	430
4/7/14	Gateshead (a)	W6-45	t:Maun,Hood,Stenchion,Ballard,Watson,Mackay,Haley g:Ballard(8) fg:T Coyle	3rd	457
13/7/14	South Wales (h)	W74-0	t:Watson(3),Hood(2),Wilson(2),March,Mackay,Oakes(2),Reed,Houston g:Ballard(11)	3rd	456
27/7/14	Oldham (h)	L24-23	t:Grimshaw,Brickwood,Watson,Houston g:Ballard(3) fg:T Coyle	3rd	678
3/8/14	Oxford (h)	W48-6	t:Clarkson,March,Grimshaw(2),Mackay,Duffy(2),Watson g:March(4),T Coyle(4)	3rd	474
10/8/14	Hemel (a)	W16-34	t:Duffy(3),Maun,Broughton,Grimshaw g:March(4),T Coyle	2nd	254
17/8/14	York (h)	L18-20	t:Hood,Moore,T Coyle g:T Coyle,March(2)	3rd	796
22/8/14	London Skolars (a) ●●	W10-36	t:Briscoe,Maun,Stenchion,Mackay,Watson,Duffy g:March(6)	2nd	1,325
7/9/14	South Wales (a) ●●●	W6-50	t:Duffy(5),Maun,Stenchion,Watson,Haley,Brickwood g:T Coyle(5)	2nd	363
12/9/14	Oldham (h) (QPO)	L24-25	t:J Coyle,Oakes,March,Duffy g:March(4)	N/A	748
21/9/14	Gateshead (h) (ESF)	W50-6	t:Duffy(2),Duckworth,Watson(2),March,Hood(2),Moore g:Ansell,March(6)	N/A	463
28/9/14	York (a) (FE)	W24-32	t:Watson,Hood(2),Maun,Duffy,Duckworth g:March(4)	N/A	759
5/10/14	Oldham (GF) ●●●●	W17-16 *(aet)*	t:Watson,Duckworth,T Coyle g:March(2) fg:T Coyle	N/A	N/A

● Played at Glan-Yr-Afon Park, Blackwood ●● Played at Queen Elizabeth II Stadium, Enfield
●●● Played at Mountain Ash RFC ●●●● Played at Headingley Carnegie, Leeds

		APP		TRIES		GOALS		FG		PTS	
	D.O.B.	ALL	Ch1	ALL	Ch1	ALL	Ch1	ALL	Ch1	ALL	Ch1
Jamaine Akaidere	19/5/91	6	5	7	7	0	0	0	0	28	28
Danny Ansell	9/10/91	15(1)	13(1)	1	1	31	28	1	0	67	60
Ryan Bailey	11/11/83	1	1	0	0	0	0	0	0	0	0
Andy Ballard	10/5/86	10	9	8	8	52	42	0	0	136	116
Lee Brickwood	20/7/91	20	19	6	6	0	0	0	0	24	24
Luke Briscoe	11/3/94	4(3)	4(3)	1	1	0	0	0	0	4	4
Brooke Broughton	30/10/90	13(5)	10(5)	3	2	0	0	0	0	12	8
Casey Canterbury	1/1/94	(1)	(1)	0	0	0	0	0	0	0	0
George Clarke	25/2/93	1(3)	1(1)	0	0	0	0	0	0	0	0
Chris Clarkson	7/4/90	2	2	1	1	0	0	0	0	4	4
Chris Clough	20/1/87	(2)	(2)	0	0	0	0	0	0	0	0
Mathew Cook	28/6/94	(2)	(2)	1	1	0	0	0	0	4	4
James Coyle	28/12/85	9(1)	9(1)	1	1	0	0	0	0	4	4
Thomas Coyle	10/5/88	19	18	3	2	11	11	3	3	37	33
James Davies	25/5/93	(2)	(1)	0	0	0	0	0	0	0	0
James Duckworth	9/4/94	7	7	3	3	0	0	0	0	12	12
Gavin Duffy	9/4/87	12	12	15	15	0	0	0	0	60	60
Danny Grimshaw	25/2/86	18(1)	15(1)	9	7	0	0	0	0	36	28
Michael Haley	19/9/87	14(7)	13(7)	2	2	0	0	0	0	8	8
Luke Hardbottle	17/9/88	(1)	(1)	0	0	0	0	0	0	0	0
Liam Hood	6/1/92	4(13)	2(13)	13	12	0	0	0	0	52	48
James Houston	28/12/82	21(1)	19(1)	8	8	0	0	0	0	32	32
Stuart Kain	18/9/85	14(4)	12(4)	6	5	0	0	0	0	24	20
Aaron Lyons	14/11/90	8(9)	8(7)	0	0	0	0	0	0	0	0
Liam Mackay	26/10/90	22(2)	21(1)	8	7	0	0	0	0	32	28
Lee Mapals	17/7/85	9	6	8	5	2	2	0	0	36	24
David March	25/7/79	24	21	8	6	33	33	0	0	98	90
Danny Maun	5/1/81	25	22	13	9	0	0	0	0	52	36
Richard Moore	2/2/81	7	7	2	2	0	0	0	0	8	8
John Oakes	12/2/88	27	24	9	9	0	0	0	0	36	36
Ross Peltier	24/4/92	(5)	(5)	0	0	0	0	0	0	0	0
Lewis Reed	24/3/91	1(17)	1(14)	3	2	0	0	0	0	12	8
Luke Stenchion	15/2/86	9(11)	6(11)	7	6	0	0	0	0	28	24
Matthew Tebb	4/9/90	(9)	(6)	2	1	0	0	0	0	8	4
Liam Walmsley	27/3/89	(1)	(1)	0	0	0	0	0	0	0	0
Jimmy Watson	9/9/91	24	21	16	16	0	0	0	0	64	64
Aston Wilson	23/10/90	5(6)	4(6)	6	6	0	0	0	0	24	24
Andy Yates	23/2/90	(1)	(1)	0	0	0	0	0	0	0	0

Jimmy Watson

LEAGUE RECORD
P20-W15-D0-L5-BP4
(2nd, Championship 1/
Grand Final Winners, Champions)
F716, A249, Diff+467
49 points.

CHALLENGE CUP
Round Five

ATTENDANCES
Best - v York (Ch1 - 796)
Worst - v Oxford (CC - 278)
Total (Championship 1,
inc play-offs) - 6,096
Average (Championship 1,
inc play-offs) - 508
(Down by 74 on 2013,
Championship)

CLUB RECORDS		Highest score: 82-0 v Highfield, 21/1/96 **Highest score against:** 0-82 v Bradford, 2/3/2003
		Record attendance: 24,700 v Wigan, 15/3/24 *(Parkside)*; 2,454 v Wakefield, 13/4/98 *(South Leeds Stadium)*
MATCH RECORDS		Tries: 7 George Dennis v Bradford, 20/1/34 **Goals:** 12 Billy Langton v Keighley, 18/8/59 **Points:** 30 Simon Wilson v Highfield, 21/1/96
SEASON RECORDS		Tries: 34 Alan Snowden 1956-57 **Goals:** 181 Billy Langton 1958-59 **Points:** 380 Billy Langton 1958-59
CAREER RECORDS		Tries: 154 Fred Williamson 1943-55 **Goals:** 1,044 Billy Langton 1955-66 **Points:** 2,202 Billy Langton 1955-66 **Appearances:** 579 Geoff Gunney 1951-73

279

LONDON SKOLARS

DATE	FIXTURE	RESULT	SCORERS	LGE	ATT
2/3/14	Oxford (a)	L19-12	t:Smith,Carty g:Bradley(2)	5th	435
23/3/14	Oldham (h)	L16-18	t:Worrincy(2),Mvududu g:Bradley(2)	8th	479
30/3/14	Hunslet (a)	L60-4	t:Greenhalgh	8th	289
5/4/14	Sheffield (a) (CCR4)	L70-28	t:Davies,Robinson,Smith(2),O'Connor g:Bradley(4)	N/A	505
13/4/14	South Wales (h)	W66-14	t:Tuffour(2),Woodburn-Hall(3),Bishay(3),Williams,Pelo,Greenhalgh,Smith g:Bradley(9)	7th	417
18/4/14	Hemel (a)	W24-27	t:Smith(2),Robinson,Greenhalgh g:Bradley(5) fg:Bradley	6th	284
4/5/14	York (a)	L36-16	t:Wellings,Greenhalgh,Smith g:Bradley,Davies	7th	451
11/5/14	Gateshead (a)	L24-16	t:McMeeken,Greenhalgh,Mvududu g:Druce(2)	7th	209
18/5/14	Gloucestershire All Golds (h) ●	L24-34	t:Tuffour,Smith,Worrincy,Woodburn-Hall g:Druce(2),Bradley(2)	8th	398
1/6/14	Oldham (a)	L46-16	t:Greenhalgh,Kelly,Pelo g:Kelly(2)	8th	486
7/6/14	South Wales (h) ●	L18-46	t:Lovell(2),Mvududu,Smith g:Davies	8th	362
15/6/14	Oxford (a)	W28-52	t:Bishay(2),Williams(2),Duckworth,Solomona(3),Bryan g:Davies(8)	7th	316
29/6/14	Gateshead (h) ●	L6-66	t:Druce g:Davies	8th	206
6/7/14	York (h) ●	L20-30	t:Duckworth,Greenhalgh,Mvududu,Yates g:Davies(2)	8th	465
13/7/14	Hemel (h) ●	W34-28	t:Cox(2),Mvududu,Davies,Bishay,MacDonald g:Davies,Bishay(4)	7th	378
27/7/14	South Wales (a) ●●	L19-18	t:Davies,MacDonald,Williams g:Davies(3)	7th	486
3/8/14	Oldham (h) ●	L28-38	t:Lovell(2),Pelo,Macani g:Davies(4)	7th	419
9/8/14	Oxford (h) ●●●	L24-31	t:Davies,Mvududu,Bryan,Macani g:Davies(4)	7th	186
17/8/14	Gloucestershire All Golds (a)	W12-36	t:Mvududu(2),Yates,Macani(2),Bishay,Purslow g:Bishay(3),Druce	7th	108
22/8/14	Hunslet (h) ●	L10-36	t:Mvududu(2) g:Bishay	7th	1,325
7/9/14	York (a)	L38-28	t:Smith(2),Fatouri(2),Mvududu g:Yates(4)	7th	643

● Played at Queen Elizabeth II Stadium, Enfield
●● Played at Cardiff Arms Park
●●● Played at Pennine Way, Hemel

			APP		TRIES		GOALS		FG		PTS	
	D.O.B.		ALL	Ch1	ALL	Ch1	ALL	Ch1	ALL	Ch1	ALL	Ch1
Mike Bishay	8/2/93		7(4)	7(4)	7	7	8	8	0	0	44	44
Matt Bradley	2/8/91		7(1)	6(1)	0	0	25	21	1	1	51	43
Lamont Bryan	12/4/88		12(3)	12(3)	2	2	0	0	0	0	8	8
James Carty	13/9/91		1	1	1	1	0	0	0	0	4	4
Dion Chapman	16/2/92		1(2)	1(2)	0	0	0	0	0	0	0	0
Anthony Cox	19/1/94		11(5)	10(5)	2	2	0	0	0	0	8	8
Courtney Davies	1/7/94		16	15	4	3	25	25	0	0	66	62
Erjon Dollapi	16/3/93		3(3)	3(3)	0	0	0	0	0	0	0	0
Sam Druce	23/9/93		3(9)	3(9)	1	1	5	5	0	0	14	14
James Duckworth	9/4/94		6	6	2	2	0	0	0	0	8	8
Kazeem Fatouri	22/10/93		6(1)	5(1)	2	2	0	0	0	0	8	8
Tony Gigot	27/12/90		1	1	0	0	0	0	0	0	0	0
Judd Greenhalgh	16/1/93		15	14	7	7	0	0	0	0	28	28
Ibrahim Kabia	2/1/92		2	1	0	0	0	0	0	0	0	0
James Kelly	3/9/92		2	2	1	1	2	2	0	0	8	8
Will Lovell	10/5/93		8	8	4	4	0	0	0	0	16	16
Iliess Macani	6/12/93		9	9	4	4	0	0	0	0	16	16
Ryan MacDonald	24/2/78		2(13)	2(13)	2	2	0	0	0	0	8	8
Mike McMeeken	10/5/94		3	3	1	1	0	0	0	0	4	4
Mufaro Mvududu	29/8/91		17	16	12	12	0	0	0	0	48	48
Jamie O'Callaghan	21/9/90		3	3	0	0	0	0	0	0	0	0
Lloyd O'Connor	12/1/86		3	2	1	0	0	0	0	0	4	0
Martin Olima	1/11/81		2	2	0	0	0	0	0	0	0	0
John Paxton	20/4/85		21	20	0	0	0	0	0	0	0	0
Teli Pelo	22/7/84		19(1)	18(1)	3	3	0	0	0	0	12	12
Oliver Purslow	17/9/87		11(1)	11(1)	1	1	0	0	0	0	4	4
Louis Robinson	9/1/91		(14)	(13)	2	1	0	0	0	0	8	4
Martyn Smith	27/2/92		16(5)	16(4)	11	9	0	0	0	0	44	36
Denny Solomona	27/10/93		1	1	3	3	0	0	0	0	12	12
Josh Sunley	22/9/93		1	1	0	0	0	0	0	0	0	0
Michael Sykes	10/12/86		9(7)	9(6)	0	0	0	0	0	0	0	0
Thomas Tabb	7/1/86		1	1	0	0	0	0	0	0	0	0
Rob Thomas	9/10/90		(8)	(7)	0	0	0	0	0	0	0	0
Dennis Tuffour	17/2/89		11	11	3	3	0	0	0	0	12	12
Sam Wellings	13/12/89		4(6)	3(6)	1	1	0	0	0	0	4	4
Dave Williams	29/1/87		18(1)	17(1)	4	4	0	0	0	0	16	16
James Woodburn-Hall	2/2/95		2	2	4	4	0	0	0	0	16	16
Michael Worrincy	16/2/86		10	9	3	3	0	0	0	0	12	12
Danny Yates	28/5/94		9	9	2	2	4	4	0	0	16	16

Martyn Smith

LEAGUE RECORD
P20-W5-D0-L15-BP9
(7th, Championship 1)
F471, A647, Diff-176
24 points.

CHALLENGE CUP
Round Four
(received bye in Round Three)

ATTENDANCES
Best - v Hunslet (Ch1 - 1,325)
Worst - v Oxford (Ch1 - 186)
Total (Championship 1 only) - 4,635
Average (Championship 1 only) - 464
(Down by 9 on 2013)

CLUB RECORDS **MATCH RECORDS**	**Highest score:** 70-28 v St Albans, 19/3/2006 **Highest score against:** 4-98 v Sheffield, 3/8/2003 **Record attendance:** 1,427 v Keighley, 29/8/2008 **Tries:** 5 Mark Cantoni v Gateshead, 27/6/2004 **Goals:** 10 Jake Johnstone v Gateshead, 24/8/2003; Dylan Skee v South Wales, 29/7/2012; Dylan Skee v Rochdale, 5/8/2012 **Points:** 28 Dylan Skee v South Wales, 29/7/2012
SEASON RECORDS **CAREER RECORDS**	**Tries:** 20 Mark Cantoni 2004; James Anthony 2013 **Goals:** 100 Dylan Skee 2013 **Points:** 248 Dylan Skee 2013 **Tries:** 57 Austen Aggrey 2004-2012 **Goals:** 230 *(inc 1fg)* Dylan Skee 2011-2013 **Points:** 579 Dylan Skee 2011-2013 **Appearances:** 198 Gareth Honor 2003-2011

OLDHAM

DATE	FIXTURE	RESULT	SCORERS	LGE	ATT
2/3/14	South Wales (a) ▲	W4-18	t:Bloomfield,Files,Nield g:Gee(2),Palfrey	2nd	358
9/3/14	Hemel (h)	D20-20	t:Whitmore,Boults,Bloomfield,Hughes g:Gee(2)	2nd	508
15/3/14	Egremont (a) (CCR3) ●	W24-42	t:Agoro,Hughes,Nield(2),Langtree,Files,Crowley(2) g:Palfrey(5)	N/A	340
23/3/14	London Skolars (a)	W16-18	t:Ward,Okanga-Ajwang,Robinson g:Palfrey(3)	2nd	479
6/4/14	Bradford (a) (CCR4)	L60-6	t:Hughes g:Palfrey	N/A	2,788
13/4/14	Gateshead (h)	W52-16	t:Bloomfield(3),Gee,Crowley,Langtree(2),Hughes,Wood,Boults g:Palfrey(6)	2nd	436
18/4/14	Hunslet (a)	L38-12	t:Agoro,Davidson g:Palfrey(2)	3rd	598
4/5/14	Oxford (h)	W48-28	t:Ward(2),Whitmore,Langtree(2),Tyson,Agoro,Cookson g:Palfrey(8)	3rd	504
18/5/14	York (h)	W31-30	t:Bloomfield(3),Agoro,Cookson,Nield g:Palfrey(3) fg:Robinson	3rd	579
25/5/14	Gloucestershire All Golds (a)	W22-30	t:Crowley,Bloomfield,Ford(2),Ward,Agoro g:Roper(3)	3rd	264
1/6/14	London Skolars (h)	W46-16	t:Agoro(2),Crowley(2),Cookson,Ford,Mason,Bloomfield g:Roper(7)	3rd	486
8/6/14	Hemel (a)	L44-32	t:Roper,Ford(2),Crowley,Tyson,Agoro g:Palfrey(4)	3rd	233
15/6/14	South Wales (h)	W58-2	t:Nield,Wood(2),Agoro(3),Hughes,Bloomfield,Palfrey,Ford g:Palfrey(9)	3rd	408
22/6/14	Gateshead (a)	W14-32	t:Bloomfield,Crowley,Agoro(2),Palfrey,Ford g:Palfrey(4)	2nd	253
29/6/14	Oxford (a)	W22-38	t:Agoro,Crowley,Langtree(2),Bloomfield(2),Wood,Cookson g:Palfrey(3)	2nd	256
13/7/14	Gloucestershire All Golds (h)	W46-6	t:Joy,Palfrey(2),Agoro,Bloomfield(3),Ward,Wood g:Palfrey(5)	2nd	516
20/7/14	York (a)	L54-12	t:Cookson,Bloomfield g:Palfrey(2)	2nd	1,006
27/7/14	Hunslet (h)	W24-23	t:Clay,Nield,Robinson,Langtree,Crowley g:Palfrey(2)	2nd	678
3/8/14	London Skolars (a) ●●	W28-38	t:Ford,Agoro(3),Clay,Crowley,Langtree g:Palfrey,Roper(4)	2nd	419
17/8/14	Hemel (a)	W38-10	t:Joy,Clay(2),Cookson,Hughes,Tyson,Roper g:Roper(5)	2nd	438
31/8/14	Gateshead (a)	L40-14	t:Mason,Ford(2) g:Roper	3rd	401
7/9/14	Gloucestershire All Golds (h)	W68-24	t:Ford(2),Crowley(2),Joy,Langtree(2),Wood(2),Ward,Mooney,Bloomfield g:Roper(8),Nield(2)	3rd	437
12/9/14	Hunslet (a) (QPO)	W24-25	t:Ford,Bloomfield,Langtree,Ward g:Roper(4) fg:Crowley	N/A	748
21/9/14	York (a) (QSF)	W12-31	t:Thompson,Cookson,Nield,Langtree,Tyson g:Roper(5) fg:Roper	N/A	663
5/10/14	Hunslet (GF) ●●●	L17-16 (aet)	t:Roper,Bloomfield,Langtree g:Roper(2)	N/A	N/A

▲ *Abandoned after 72 minutes due to weather conditions*

● Played at Copeland Stadium, Whitehaven
●● Played at Queen Elizabeth II Stadium, Enfield
●●● Played at Headingley Carnegie, Leeds

		APP		TRIES		GOALS		FG		PTS	
	D.O.B.	ALL	Ch1	ALL	Ch1	ALL	Ch1	ALL	Ch1	ALL	Ch1
Mo Agoro	29/1/93	18	16	18	17	0	0	0	0	72	68
Dale Bloomfield	24/10/87	21	19	21	21	0	0	0	0	84	84
Jason Boults	7/9/83	20	18	2	2	0	0	0	0	8	8
Adam Clay	7/10/90	9	9	4	4	0	0	0	0	16	16
David Cookson	1/10/88	19	19	7	7	0	0	0	0	28	28
Josh Crowley	24/9/91	25	23	13	11	0	0	1	1	53	45
Alex Davidson	1/11/92	(7)	(6)	1	1	0	0	0	0	4	4
Adam Files	7/1/93	(4)	(3)	2	1	0	0	0	0	8	4
Jonathan Ford	1/11/93	16	16	13	13	0	0	0	0	52	52
Sam Gee	28/2/87	15(2)	13(2)	1	1	4	4	0	0	12	12
Mark Hobson	14/1/87	4(1)	2(1)	0	0	0	0	0	0	0	0
Kenny Hughes	30/3/90	4(18)	3(17)	6	4	0	0	0	0	24	16
Phil Joy	4/9/91	20(3)	20(1)	3	3	0	0	0	0	12	12
Danny Langtree	18/2/91	24	22	14	13	0	0	0	0	56	52
Nathan Mason	8/9/93	(16)	(16)	2	2	0	0	0	0	8	8
Paddy Mooney	28/3/94	1(6)	1(5)	1	1	0	0	0	0	4	4
Steven Nield	20/11/90	19	18	7	5	2	2	0	0	32	24
Edwin Okanga-Ajwang	29/11/94	3(1)	3	1	1	0	0	0	0	4	4
Gareth Owen	3/7/92	8	8	0	0	0	0	0	0	0	0
Lewis Palfrey	25/2/90	20(2)	18(2)	4	4	59	53	0	0	134	122
Brett Robinson	9/11/89	13(2)	11(2)	2	2	0	0	1	1	9	9
Steve Roper	10/11/86	16	16	3	3	39	39	1	1	91	91
Liam Thompson	3/1/92	12	12	1	1	0	0	0	0	4	4
George Tyson	1/10/93	2(14)	2(13)	4	4	0	0	0	0	16	16
Michael Ward	10/2/91	9(16)	7(16)	7	7	0	0	0	0	28	28
Tom Whitehead	13/9/91	6	5	0	0	0	0	0	0	0	0
Danny Whitmore	22/12/88	14(1)	13(1)	2	2	0	0	0	0	8	8
Ben Wood	10/6/89	7(7)	5(7)	7	7	0	0	0	0	28	28

Josh Crowley

LEAGUE RECORD
P20-W15-D1-L4-BP1
(3rd, Championship 1/
Grand Final Runners-Up)
F675, A457, Diff+218
48 points.

CHALLENGE CUP
Round Four

ATTENDANCES
Best - v Hunslet (Ch1 - 678)
Worst - v South Wales (Ch1 - 408)
Total (Championship 1 only) - 4,990
Average (Championship 1 only) - 499
(Down by 138 on 2013)

CLUB RECORDS	
	Highest score: 80-6 v Blackwood, 7/3/2010 Highest score against: 0-84 v Widnes, 25/7/99
	Record attendance: 28,000 v Huddersfield, 24/2/1912 *(Watersheddings)*; 1,275 v York, 12/9/2010 *(Whitebank Stadium)*
MATCH RECORDS	Tries: 7 James Miller v Barry, 31/10/1908
	Goals: 14 Bernard Ganley v Liverpool City, 4/4/59 Points: 34 Andy Ballard v London Skolars, 2/5/2009; Chris Baines v Hunslet, 20/9/2009
SEASON RECORDS	Tries: 49 Reg Farrar 1921-22 Goals: 200 Bernard Ganley 1957-58 Points: 412 Bernard Ganley 1957-58
CAREER RECORDS	Tries: 174 Alan Davies 1950-61 Goals: 1,358 Bernard Ganley 1951-61 Points: 2,761 Bernard Ganley 1951-61 Appearances: 627 Joe Ferguson 1899-1923

OXFORD

DATE	FIXTURE	RESULT	SCORERS	LGE	ATT
2/3/14	London Skolars (h)	W19-12	t:S Morris(2),Mulkeen g:Rowland(3) fg:Rowland	4th	435
9/3/14	Gateshead (a)	L47-28	t:Clarke,Rice,Hoggins,S Morris(2) g:Rowland(4)	6th	254
16/3/14	Hunslet (a) (CCR3)	L68-6	t:Thompson g:Rowland	N/A	278
23/3/14	Hunslet (h)	L20-46	t:Rice,Crabtree(3) g:Rowland(2)	7th	301
13/4/14	York (a)	W16-24	t:S Morris(2),Baird,Mulkeen,Rowland g:Rowland(2)	6th	574
18/4/14	Gloucestershire All Golds (h)	W38-24	t:Mulkeen,Thompson,Baird(2),Crabtree(2),Parker g:Rowland(5)	5th	240
4/5/14	Oldham (a)	L48-28	t:Thompson(2),Mulkeen,Brooker,Sharratt g:Rowland(4)	5th	504
18/5/14	South Wales (h)	W40-24	t:Thompson(2),S Morris(2),Mulkeen,Rowland,Hadden g:Rowland(4),Connick(2)	5th	236
25/5/14	Hemel (a)	L30-24	t:S Morris(2),Blaney,Sharratt g:Thompson,Connick(3)	5th	170
1/6/14	Hunslet (a)	L32-12	t:Connick,Parker g:Connick(2)	7th	417
8/6/14	Gateshead (h)	L22-36	t:Sharratt,Mulkeen,S Morris(2) g:Connick(3)	7th	310
15/6/14	London Skolars (h)	L28-52	t:Thompson,Connick,Blaney,S Morris,Briggs g:Connick(4)	8th	316
22/6/14	Gloucestershire All Golds (a)	L36-20	t:Connick,Briggs(2),Davies g:Connick,Rowland	8th	323
29/6/14	Oldham (h)	L22-38	t:Crabtree(2),S Morris,Hoggins g:Rowland(3)	7th	256
5/7/14	South Wales (a)	W16-36	t:Hoggins,Rowland,Brooker,Briggs,Osborn,Parker,Thompson g:Rowland,Connick(3)	7th	150
13/7/14	York (h) ●	L16-58	t:Egerton,Thompson(2) g:Connick(2)	8th	172
27/7/14	Gateshead (a)	L48-28	t:Thompson,Crabtree,Rowland,Brooker,S Morris,Parker g:Rowland(2)	8th	153
3/8/14	Hunslet (a)	L48-6	t:S Morris g:Rowland	8th	474
9/8/14	London Skolars (a) ●●	W24-31	t:Connick(2),Rowland,Hoggins,S Morris g:Rowland(4),Connick fg:Rice	8th	186
31/8/14	South Wales (h)	W29-22	t:Sharratt,Hoggins,Hadden,Brooker,Blaney g:Rowland(4) fg:Rowland	8th	240
6/9/14	Hemel (h)	D22-22	t:Rowland(2),Parker,Brooker g:Rowland(3)	8th	205

● Played at Dry Leas, Henley
●● Played at Pennine Way, Hemel

		APP		TRIES		GOALS		FG		PTS	
	D.O.B.	ALL	Ch1	ALL	Ch1	ALL	Ch1	ALL	Ch1	ALL	Ch1
John James Baird	30/10/88	15	14	3	3	0	0	0	0	12	12
Valu Bentley	9/10/82	5(1)	5(1)	0	0	0	0	0	0	0	0
Sam Blaney	4/12/89	7(9)	7(8)	3	3	0	0	0	0	12	12
Jack Briggs	2/2/89	9	9	4	4	0	0	0	0	16	16
Marcus Brooker	2/9/89	21	20	5	5	0	0	0	0	20	20
Chris Clarke	29/3/89	8(1)	7(1)	1	1	0	0	0	0	4	4
Tommy Connick	19/1/90	21	20	5	5	21	21	0	0	62	62
Michael Crabtree	24/4/91	14	13	8	8	0	0	0	0	32	32
Tom Davies	14/4/89	9(8)	8(8)	1	1	0	0	0	0	4	4
Sam Egerton	27/12/91	2	2	1	1	0	0	0	0	4	4
Dave Ellison	2/4/82	1(11)	1(10)	0	0	0	0	0	0	0	0
Luke Evans	9/5/90	5(4)	5(4)	0	0	0	0	0	0	0	0
Matty Hadden	7/6/90	12(2)	11(2)	2	2	0	0	0	0	8	8
Ed Hayles	10/6/83	2(12)	2(12)	0	0	0	0	0	0	0	0
Andrew Hoggins	7/8/88	16(2)	15(2)	5	5	0	0	0	0	20	20
Ryan McGoldrick	12/1/81	2		0	0	0	0	0	0	0	0
Jonny Morris	7/5/92	3(1)	3(1)	0	0	0	0	0	0	0	0
Sean Morris	6/5/89	17	17	17	17	0	0	0	0	68	68
Callum Mulkeen	10/12/90	20	19	6	6	0	0	0	0	24	24
Wes Newton	26/2/90	(5)	(4)	0	0	0	0	0	0	0	0
Graham O'Keeffe	13/5/91	5(2)	4(2)	0	0	0	0	0	0	0	0
Glenn Osborn	17/8/83	3(5)	3(4)	1	1	0	0	0	0	4	4
Yannic Parker	29/12/90	12	12	5	5	0	0	0	0	20	20
Jordan Rice	9/5/90	17(4)	16(4)	2	2	0	0	1	1	9	9
Jimmy Rowland	8/4/94	16(1)	15(1)	7	7	44	43	2	2	118	116
Rory Sharratt	26/3/92	8(12)	8(12)	4	4	0	0	0	0	16	16
Karl Temata	12/7/78	4	4	0	0	0	0	0	0	0	0
Alex Thompson	11/2/90	19(1)	18(1)	11	10	1	1	0	0	46	42
Edd Vickers	7/3/89	(3)	(3)	0	0	0	0	0	0	0	0

Tommy Connick

LEAGUE RECORD
P20-W7-D1-L12-BP1
(8th, Championship 1)
F493, A679, Diff-186
24 points.

CHALLENGE CUP
Round Three

ATTENDANCES
Best - v London Skolars (Ch1 - 435)
Worst - v York (Ch1 - 172)
Total (Championship 1 only) - 2,711
Average (Championship 1 only) - 271
(Down by 41 on 2013)

CLUB RECORDS
Highest score: 40-30 v Gloucestershire All Golds, 29/3/2013; 40-24 v South Wales, 18/5/2014 Highest score against: 6-68 v Hunslet, 16/3/2014
Record attendance: 435 v London Skolars, 2/3/2014

MATCH RECORDS
Tries: 3 John Clough v Gloucestershire All Golds, 29/3/2013; Michael Crabtree v Hunslet, 23/3/2014
Goals: 6 Jonny Leather v Gloucestershire All Golds, 29/3/2013 Points: 16 Jonny Leather v Gloucestershire All Golds, 29/3/2013

SEASON RECORDS
Tries: 17 Sean Morris 2014 Goals: 46 (inc 2fg) Jimmy Rowland 2014 Points: 118 Jimmy Rowland 2014

CAREER RECORDS
Tries: 24 Sean Morris 2013-2014 Goals: 49 (inc 2fg) Jimmy Rowland 2013-2014 Points: 124 Jimmy Rowland 2013-2014
Appearances: 38 Tommy Connick 2013-2014

SOUTH WALES SCORPIONS

DATE	FIXTURE	RESULT	SCORERS	LGE	ATT
				8th	358
2/3/14	Oldham (h) ▲	L4-18	t:Jones		
9/3/14	Gloucestershire All Golds (a)	L29-17	t:Farrer,Newbury,Leyshon g:Emanuelli(2) fg:Emanuelli	9th	186
				N/A	213
16/3/14	Hemel (h) (CCR3)	L12-38	t:Farrer,Hellard g:Emanuelli(2)	9th	638
23/3/14	York (a)	L76-0		9th	193
30/3/14	Hemel (h)	L16-34	t:O Phillips,Vitalini,Carleton g:Emanuelli(2)	9th	417
13/4/14	London Skolars (a)	L66-14	t:Farrer,Pope,Carter g:Emanuelli	9th	258
4/5/14	Gateshead (h)	L16-50	t:Wilde,Vitalini(2) g:Emanuelli(2)	9th	255
11/5/14	Hunslet (h) ●	L6-20	t:Sheridan g:Emanuelli	9th	236
18/5/14	Oxford (a)	L40-24	t:Farrer(3),Wilcox g:Emanuelli(4)		
1/6/14	Gloucestershire All Golds (h)	L36-38	t:Vitalini,Wilde(2),Sheridan,Farrer(2) g:Emanuelli(6)	9th	320
7/6/14	London Skolars (a) ●●	W18-46	t:Wilcox,Connor(2),Scrivens,Vitalini,Emanuelli,Wilde,Farrer g:Emanuelli(7)	9th	362
15/6/14	Oldham (a)	L58-2	g:Emanuelli	9th	408
21/6/14	York (h) ●	L10-48	t:Pring,Connor g:Emanuelli	9th	225
5/7/14	Oxford (h)	L16-36	t:Owens,B Phillips,Leyshon g:Emanuelli(2)	9th	150
13/7/14	Hunslet (a)	L74-0		9th	456
20/7/14	Hemel (a)	L40-10	t:O'Connor,Scrivens g:Emanuelli	9th	176
27/7/14	London Skolars (h) ●●●	W19-18	t:Vitalini,Sheridan,Pring g:Emanuelli(3) fg:Emanuelli	9th	486
9/8/14	Gloucestershire All Golds (h)	L16-28	t:Owens,Leyshon,Newbury g:Emanuelli(2)	9th	177
				9th	161
17/8/14	Gateshead (a)	L58-24	t:Newbury(2),Farrer(2),Elliott g:Elliott(2)	9th	240
31/8/14	Oxford (a)	L29-22	t:Elliott,O'Connor,Newbury,Edwards g:Emanuelli(3)	9th	363
7/9/14	Hunslet (h) ●●●●	L6-50	t:Emanuelli g:Emanuelli		

▲ *Abandoned after 72 minutes due to weather conditions*

● Played at Glan-Yr-Afon Park, Blackwood
●● Played at Queen Elizabeth II Stadium, Enfield
●●● Played at Cardiff Arms Park
●●●● Played at Mountain Ash RFC

		APP		TRIES		GOALS		FG		PTS	
	D.O.B.	ALL	Ch1	ALL	Ch1	ALL	Ch1	ALL	Ch1	ALL	Ch1
Scott Amber	27/2/92	1	1	0	0	0	0	0	0	0	0
Ashley Bateman	11/2/90	14(6)	13(6)	0	0	0	0	0	0	0	0
Scott Britton	20/10/88	1(1)	1	0	0	0	0	0	0	0	0
Phil Carleton	2/5/83	17	16	1	1	0	0	0	0	4	4
Daryl Carter	23/4/83	(1)	(1)	1	1	0	0	0	0	4	4
Harry Cartwright	15/4/95	1(2)	1(2)	0	0	0	0	0	0	0	0
Mike Connor	27/3/94	10(4)	10(3)	3	3	0	0	0	0	12	12
Neil Dallimore	24/2/81	2(4)	2(4)	0	0	0	0	0	0	0	0
Owain Davies	9/7/92	3(2)	3(2)	0	0	0	0	0	0	0	0
Richard East	22/11/84	9(7)	9(7)	0	0	0	0	0	0	0	0
Paul Edwards	18/5/96	3	3	1	1	0	0	0	0	4	4
Harrison Elliott	16/3/92	11(6)	11(6)	2	2	2	2	0	0	12	12
Paul Emanuelli	3/1/84	20	19	2	2	41	39	2	2	92	88
Morgan Evans	23/3/92	1(3)	1(3)	0	0	0	0	0	0	0	0
Connor Farrer	6/6/95	17(2)	17(1)	11	10	0	0	0	0	44	40
Rhys Fitzgerald	16/8/95	2(2)	1(2)	0	0	0	0	0	0	0	0
Scott Giles	5/7/86	1(8)	1(8)	0	0	0	0	0	0	0	0
Dafydd Hellard	21/2/85	8(3)	7(3)	1	0	0	0	0	0	4	4
Alex Jones	28/9/93	1	1	1	1	0	0	0	0	4	4
Chris Leyshon	24/12/94	20	19	3	3	0	0	0	0	12	12
Martin Luckwell	19/12/87	(2)	(2)	0	0	0	0	0	0	0	0
Ian Newbury	17/9/86	12	11	5	5	0	0	0	0	20	20
Lloyd O'Connor	1/12/86	1(3)	1(3)	2	2	0	0	0	0	8	8
Shaun Owens	29/11/88	5(2)	4(2)	2	2	0	0	0	0	8	8
Dan Parry	9/4/93	2(3)	2(3)	0	0	0	0	0	0	0	0
Barrie Phillips	27/5/86	16	15	1	1	0	0	0	0	4	4
Osian Phillips	2/5/94	7(6)	7(6)	1	1	0	0	0	0	4	4
Alan Pope	1/4/85	1(3)	1(3)	1	1	0	0	0	0	4	4
Jack Pring	25/1/93	16(1)	15(1)	2	2	0	0	0	0	8	8
Alex Randall	2/3/92	1	1	0	0	0	0	0	0	0	0
Kyle Scrivens	7/8/88	19(1)	19	2	2	0	0	0	0	8	8
Jordan Sheridan	19/7/94	20	19	3	3	0	0	0	0	12	12
Yousif Suliman	26/10/90	1	1	0	0	0	0	0	0	0	0
Chris True	21/6/83	(2)	(2)	0	0	0	0	0	0	0	0
Chris Vitalini	5/5/87	17	16	6	6	0	0	0	0	24	24
Matthew Wilcox	26/9/90	8(4)	7(4)	2	2	0	0	0	0	8	8
Greg Wilde	22/12/93	7	7	4	4	0	0	0	0	16	16

Connor Farrer

LEAGUE RECORD
P20-W2-D0-L18-BP4
(9th, Championship 1)
F304, A828, Diff-524
10 points.

CHALLENGE CUP
Round Three

ATTENDANCES
Best - v London Skolars (Ch1 - 486)
Worst - v Oxford (Ch1 - 150)
Total (Championship 1 only) - 2,785
Average (Championship 1 only) - 279
(Down by 64 on 2013)

CLUB RECORDS
Highest score: 70-22 v London Skolars, 23/5/2010; 70-16 v Gateshead, 11/7/2010 Highest score against: 28-84 v Halifax, 14/4/2012
Record attendance: 890 v Swinton, 13/6/2010
MATCH RECORDS Tries: 4 Dalton Grant v Gateshead, 22/5/2011 Goals: 11 Lewis Reece v Gateshead, 11/7/2010 Points: 30 Lewis Reece v Gateshead, 11/7/2010
SEASON RECORDS Tries: 19 Steve Parry 2010 Goals: 55 Lewis Reece 2011 Points: 130 Lewis Reece 2011
CAREER RECORDS Tries: 43 Steve Parry 2010-2013 Goals: 72 Lewis Reece 2010-2013 Points: 188 Lewis Reece 2010-2013 Appearances: 101 Ashley Bateman 2010-2014

283

YORK CITY KNIGHTS

DATE	FIXTURE	RESULT	SCORERS	LGE	ATT
2/3/14	Gloucestershire All Golds (h)	W26-16	t:B Dent,Joynt,B Hardcastle,P Smith,Golden g:B Hardcastle(3)	3rd	648
9/3/14	Hunslet (a)	W26-28	t:Minikin,E Smith,P Smith,Presley,Paterson,B Dent g:Reynolds,B Hardcastle	1st	409
16/3/14	Whitehaven (h) (CCR3)	W34-32	t:Morland,Mallinder,Presley,B Dent,Minikin,Elliott g:Crane,Haynes(4)	N/A	403
23/3/14	South Wales (h)	W76-0	t:B Hardcastle,B Dent,Presley(4),Aldous,Haynes(2),E Smith,Carter,Elliott,Ford,Mallinder g:B Hardcastle(10)	1st	638
6/4/14	Swinton (a) (CCR4)	L31-28	t:Lee,Paterson,B Hardcastle,P Smith,B Dent g:Haynes(4)	N/A	427
13/4/14	Oxford (h)	L16-24	t:Iley,Reynolds,Lee g:Reynolds,B Hardcastle	3rd	574
18/4/14	Gateshead (a)	W26-30	t:Presley,Lee,B Dent,P Smith,E Smith g:B Hardcastle(5)	2nd	257
4/5/14	London Skolars (h)	W36-16	t:Mallinder,A Dent,Lee,Saltonstall,E Smith,Haynes g:B Hardcastle(6)	2nd	451
11/5/14	Hemel (h)	W22-14	t:B Dent(2),Paterson,A Dent g:B Hardcastle,Reynolds(2)	2nd	457
18/5/14	Oldham (a)	L31-30	t:Lee(3),Aldous,Reynolds,Mallinder,Saltonstall g:Haynes	2nd	579
25/5/14	Hunslet (h)	W40-0	t:Morland,Lee(2),Presley,Mallinder,B Dent,Reynolds g:Reynolds(6)	1st	837
8/6/14	Gloucestershire All Golds (a)	L24-22	t:Morland,Presley,B Dent,Lee g:Reynolds(3)	2nd	318
15/6/14	Gateshead (h)	W42-16	t:Bell,Roche,Lee,Craig,Aldous,E Smith,Pickets g:B Hardcastle(7)	2nd	495
21/6/14	South Wales (a) ●	W10-48	t:B Dent(3),Roche,Ford(2),Lee,Haynes,Reynolds g:Reynolds(6)	1st	225
29/6/14	Hemel (a)	W22-46	t:Backhouse,Lee(2),P Smith(2),Mallinder,Morland,Minikin g:Reynolds(7)	1st	227
6/7/14	London Skolars (a) ●●	W20-30	t:Lee,P Smith,Day(2),Roche g:Reynolds(5)	1st	465
13/7/14	Oxford (a) ●●●	W16-58	t:B Dent(2),Day(3),Lee,Brining,Saltonstall,Ford,E Smith g:Reynolds(9)	1st	172
20/7/14	Oldham (h)	W54-12	t:P Smith(3),Lee,Saltonstall,B Dent,Reynolds,Aldous,Pickets g:Reynolds(9)	1st	1,006
3/8/14	Gloucestershire All Golds (a)	W18-42	t:B Dent(2),Craig(2),Lee,Ford,Mallinder,Haynes g:Reynolds(5)	1st	184
10/8/14	Gateshead (h)	W34-30	t:B Dent,Saltonstall(2),Tonks,Aldous,Backhouse g:Reynolds(5)	1st	571
17/8/14	Hunslet (a)	W18-20	t:Ford,Saltonstall,Roche g:Haynes(4)	1st	796
7/9/14	London Skolars (h)	W38-28	t:B Hardcastle,Reynolds(2),Minikin,E Smith,Brining,Saltonstall g:Reynolds(5)	1st	643
21/9/14	Oldham (h) (QSF)	L12-31	t:Saltonstall,Paterson g:Reynolds(2)	N/A	663
28/9/14	Hunslet (h) (FE)	L24-32	t:B Dent,P Smith,Lee,Backhouse g:Reynolds(4)	N/A	759

● Played at Glan-Yr-Afon Park, Blackwood
●● Played at Queen Elizabeth II Stadium, Enfield
●●● Played at Dry Leas, Henley

		APP		TRIES		GOALS		FG		PTS	
	D.O.B.	ALL	Ch1	ALL	Ch1	ALL	Ch1	ALL	Ch1	ALL	Ch1
Jack Aldous	3/4/91	21(1)	19(1)	5	5	0	0	0	0	20	20
Ryan Backhouse	8/9/93	5(10)	5(10)	3	3	0	0	0	0	12	12
Austin Bell	6/9/91	6(5)	4(5)	1	1	0	0	0	0	4	4
Brad Brennan	18/1/93	7(6)	7(6)	0	0	0	0	0	0	0	0
Kris Brining	16/11/93	(13)	(12)	2	2	0	0	0	0	8	8
Harry Carter	10/2/94	(7)	(6)	1	1	0	0	0	0	4	4
Tyler Craig	4/7/93	7(2)	7(2)	3	3	0	0	0	0	12	12
Ben Crane	30/12/91	1(2)	(2)	0	0	1	0	0	0	2	0
Brad Day	23/9/94	3(1)	3(1)	5	5	0	0	0	0	20	20
Adam Dent	2/11/93	2	2	2	2	0	0	0	0	8	8
Ben Dent	27/9/91	23	21	20	18	0	0	0	0	80	72
George Elliott	21/9/91	6	4	2	1	0	0	0	0	8	4
Daniel Fleming	8/7/92	(1)	(1)	0	0	0	0	0	0	0	0
James Ford	29/9/82	13(1)	12(1)	6	6	0	0	0	0	24	24
Nathan Freer	21/5/89	1(6)	1(5)	0	0	0	0	0	0	0	0
Jason Golden	6/11/85	3(2)	2(2)	1	1	0	0	0	0	4	4
Benn Hardcastle	4/1/90	8(2)	8(1)	4	3	34	34	0	0	84	80
Luke Hardcastle	12/8/92	2	2	0	0	0	0	0	0	0	0
Nathan Harper	31/1/92	(3)	(3)	0	0	0	0	0	0	0	0
James Haynes	22/3/89	17	15	5	5	13	5	0	0	46	30
Jack Iley	26/5/90	(2)	(2)	1	1	0	0	0	0	4	4
Jake Joynt	24/10/92	3(4)	3(2)	1	1	0	0	0	0	4	4
Jay Leary	8/9/92	1(2)	1(2)	0	0	0	0	0	0	0	0
Jack Lee	1/11/88	24	22	19	18	0	0	0	0	76	72
Ryan Mallinder	17/7/88	16(4)	15(3)	7	6	0	0	0	0	28	24
Greg Minikin	29/3/95	12	11	4	3	0	0	0	0	16	12
James Morland	29/6/95	8	6	4	3	0	0	0	0	16	12
Iain Morrison	6/5/83	(5)	(4)	0	0	0	0	0	0	0	0
Josh Nathaniel	24/5/91	1	1	0	0	0	0	0	0	0	0
Lee Paterson	5/7/81	15(3)	14(3)	4	3	0	0	0	0	16	12
Joe Pickets	27/11/90	6(3)	6(3)	2	2	0	0	0	0	8	8
Jack Pickles	3/6/92	2	2	0	0	0	0	0	0	0	0
Jon Presley	8/7/84	11	9	9	8	0	0	0	0	36	32
Ben Reynolds	15/1/94	16	16	7	7	70	70	0	0	168	168
Colton Roche	23/6/93	10(3)	10(3)	4	4	0	0	0	0	16	16
James Saltonstall	27/9/93	18	18	9	9	0	0	0	0	36	36
Ed Smith	12/11/92	23	21	7	7	0	0	0	0	28	28
Pat Smith	4/3/90	19(4)	17(4)	11	10	0	0	0	0	44	40
Josh Tonks	14/8/91	1(4)	1(4)	1	1	0	0	0	0	4	4
Jake Webster	29/10/83	1	1	0	0	0	0	0	0	0	0

Jack Lee

LEAGUE RECORD
P20-W17-D0-L3-BP3
(1st, Championship 1/
Final Eliminator)
F738, A367, Diff+371
54 points.

CHALLENGE CUP
Round Four

ATTENDANCES
Best - v Oldham (Ch1 - 1,006)
Worst - v Whitehaven (CC - 403)
Total (Championship 1,
inc play-offs) - 7,742
Average (Championship 1,
inc play-offs) - 645
(Down by 70 on 2013,
Championship)

CLUB RECORDS	**Highest score:** 132-0 v Northumbria University, 6/3/2011 **Highest score against:** 0-98 v Rochdale, 8/4/2001
MATCH RECORDS	**Record attendance:** 14,689 v Swinton, 10/2/34 *(Clarence Street)*, 4,977 v Halifax, 5/1/90 *(Ryedale/Huntington Stadium)* **Tries:** 7 Brad Davis v Highfield, 17/9/95 **Goals:** 20 Chris Thorman v Northumbria University, 6/3/2011 **Points:** 56 Chris Thorman v Northumbria University, 6/3/2011
SEASON RECORDS	**Tries:** 35 John Crossley 1980-81 **Goals:** 178 *(inc 4fg)* Danny Brough 2004 **Points:** 412 Danny Brough 2004
CAREER RECORDS	**Tries:** 167 Peter Foster 1955-67 **Goals:** 1,060 Vic Yorke 1954-67 **Points:** 2,159 Vic Yorke 1954-67 **Appearances:** 449 Willie Hargreaves 1952-65

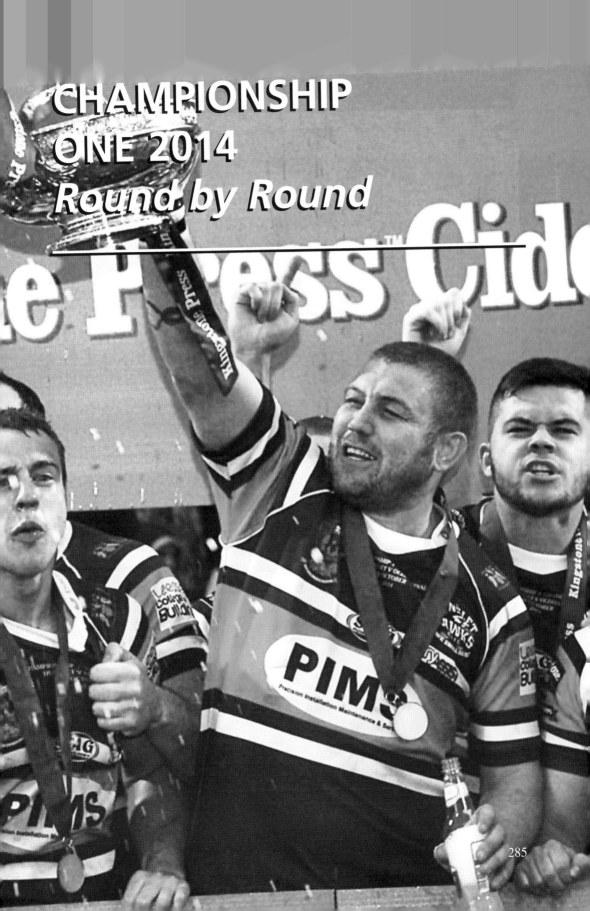

CHAMPIONSHIP
ONE 2014
Round by Round

ROUND 1

Sunday 2nd March 2014

HEMEL STAGS 0 HUNSLET HAWKS 28

STAGS: 1 Mitch Barbera; 2 James Cameron; 3 Aaron Small; 4 Michael Brown; 5 James Hill; 9 Ben Thorburn; 7 Ben Young; 21 Ryan Patchett; 14 Evan Simons; 10 Dan Ljazouli; 11 Barry-John Swindells; 23 Eddie Mbaraga; 13 Alex Ingarfield. Subs (all used): 18 Dominic Maloney; 16 Lee Hudson; 17 Matthew Bailey; 12 Cariern Clement-Pascall.
HAWKS: 1 Stuart Kain; 5 Lee Mapals; 3 Lee Brickwood; 4 Danny Maun; 28 Andy Ballard; 6 Thomas Coyle; 20 Danny Ansell; 10 James Houston; 9 David March; 15 Luke Stenchion; 11 John Oakes; 12 Aaron Lyons; 26 Liam Mackay. Subs (all used): 27 Liam Hood; 18 Brooke Broughton; 16 Lewis Reed; 8 Michael Haley.
Tries: Kain (28), Mackay (40), Houston (58, 67), Ballard (63); **Goals:** Ballard 4/5.
Rugby Leaguer & League Express Men of the Match: *Stags:* Ben Young; *Hawks:* Danny Maun.
Penalty count: 3-7; **Half-time:** 0-10;
Referee: Chris Kendall; **Attendance:** 210.

OXFORD 19 LONDON SKOLARS 12

OXFORD: 1 Sean Morris; 5 Callum Mulkeen; 12 Andrew Hoggins; 3 Marcus Brooker; 2 Michael Crabtree; 7 Jimmy Rowland; 6 Tommy Connick; 8 Chris Clarke; 9 Alex Thompson; 10 Matty Hadden; 11 John James Baird; 22 Graham O'Keeffe; 13 Valu Bentley. Subs (all used): 18 Jordan Rice; 15 Glenn Osborn; 14 Dave Ellison; 17 Rory Sharratt.
Tries: S Morris (2, 42), Mulkeen (79);
Goals: Rowland 3/3; **Field goal:** Rowland (31).
Sin bin: Clarke (71) - interference.
SKOLARS: 1 John Paxton; 2 Iliess Macani; 4 Dennis Tuffour; 3 Thomas Tabb; 5 James Carty; 6 Tony Gigot; 7 Matt Bradley; 22 Dave Williams; 14 Lloyd O'Connor; 10 Oliver Purslow; 11 Teli Pelo; 12 Lamont Bryan; 13 Michael Worrincy. Subs (all used): 9 Martyn Smith; 21 Rob Thomas; 20 Michael Sykes; 8 Ryan MacDonald.
Tries: Smith (40), Carty (72); **Goals:** Bradley 2/2.
Rugby Leaguer & League Express Men of the Match: *Oxford:* Sean Morris; *Skolars:* Lamont Bryan.
Penalty count: 8-11; **Half-time:** 7-6;
Referee: Andrew Sweet; **Attendance:** 435.

SOUTH WALES SCORPIONS 4 OLDHAM 18
(abandoned after 72 minutes due to weather conditions)

SCORPIONS: 1 Jordan Sheridan; 19 Alex Jones; 23 Alex Randall; 4 Kyle Scrivens; 5 Chris Leyshon; 6 Paul Emanuelli; 13 Ashley Bateman; 18 Harrison Elliott; 9 Connor Farrer; 14 Mike Connor; 11 Barrie Phillips; 12 Phil Carleton; 10 Chris Vitalini. Subs (all used): 21 Dan Parry; 15 Owain Davies; 22 Matthew Wilcox; 17 Rhys Fitzgerald.
Try: Jones (44); **Goals:** Emanuelli 0/1.
OLDHAM: 1 Tom Whitehead; 4 Steven Nield; 21 David Cookson; 9 Sam Gee; 5 Dale Bloomfield; 7 Brett Robinson; 16 Kenny Hughes; 19 Michael Ward; 17 Danny Whitmore; 10 Jason Boults; 11 Josh Crowley; 12 Danny Langtree; 22 Liam Thompson. Subs (all used): 14 Adam Files; 15 Paddy Mooney; 18 Alex Davidson; 6 Lewis Palfrey.
Tries: Bloomfield (20), Files (36), Nield (55);
Goals: Gee 2/2, Palfrey 1/2.
Rugby Leaguer & League Express Men of the Match: *Scorpions:* Chris Vitalini; *Oldham:* Jason Boults.
Penalty count: 3-6; **Half-time:** 0-12;
Referee: Adam Gill; **Attendance:** 358.

YORK CITY KNIGHTS 26
GLOUCESTERSHIRE ALL GOLDS 16

CITY KNIGHTS: 25 Luke Hardcastle; 5 Ben Dent; 30 James Morland; 4 Greg Minikin; 2 George Elliott; 6 Pat Smith; 23 Benn Hardcastle; 19 Jake Joynt; 9 Jack Lee; 18 Austin Bell; 15 Jason Golden; 12 Ed Smith; 13 Lee Paterson. Subs (all used): 14 Kris Brining; 16 Iain Morrison; 22 Ben Crane; 11 Ryan Mallinder.
Tries: B Dent (10), Joynt (20), B Hardcastle (23), P Smith (68), Golden (79); **Goals:** B Hardcastle 3/5.
On report: Paterson (62) - alleged punching.
ALL GOLDS: 20 Marcus Elliott; 2 Reece Rance; 3 James Greene; 4 Aidan Jenkins; 5 James Fisher; 6 Mark Barlow; 7 Danny Thomas; 15 Harry Chapman-Walker; 19 Craig Cook; 10 Izaak Duffy; 11 Jason Muranka; 12 James Tutuila; 13 Ash Haynes. Subs (all used): 8 Bobby Tyson-Wilson; 17 Connor Nolan; 16 Phil Cowburn; 1 Joe McClean.
Tries: Thomas (17), Elliott (44), Jenkins (54);
Goals: Jenkins 2/3.
Rugby Leaguer & League Express Men of the Match: *City Knights:* Lee Paterson; *All Golds:* Craig Cook.
Penalty count: 8-7; **Half-time:** 16-6;
Referee: Michael Woodhead; **Attendance:** 648.

ROUND 2

Sunday 9th March 2014

GATESHEAD THUNDER 47 OXFORD 28

THUNDER: 1 Sam Lynch; 2 Tom Capper; 3 Jacob Blades; 4 Joe Brown; 5 Carl Booth; 26 Matty Beharrell; 7 Carl Puckering; 8 Tom Lynch; 6 Paul Stamp; 10 Lee Fewlass; 24 Chris Heil; 12 Jason Payne; 13 Aaron Ollett. Subs (all used): 19 Josh Stoker; 28 Nathan Powley; 23 Callum Cockburn; 29 Rhys Clarke.
Tries: Capper (8), Brown (18, 69), S Lynch (51), Payne (61, 66, 73), Beharrell (64), Heil (77);
Goals: Puckering 5/10; **Field goal:** Puckering (35).
OXFORD: 1 Sean Morris; 5 Callum Mulkeen; 12 Andrew Hoggins; 3 Marcus Brooker; 2 Michael Crabtree; 7 Jimmy Rowland; 6 Tommy Connick; 8 Chris Clarke; 9 Alex Thompson; 10 Matty Hadden; 11 John James Baird; 22 Graham O'Keeffe; 13 Valu Bentley. Subs (all used): 18 Jordan Rice; 15 Glenn Osborn; 14 Dave Ellison; 17 Rory Sharratt.
Tries: Clarke (4), Rice (28), Hoggins (43), S Morris (54, 79); **Goals:** Rowland 4/6.
Rugby Leaguer & League Express Men of the Match: *Thunder:* Matty Beharrell; *Oxford:* John James Baird.
Penalty count: 12-9; **Half-time:** 13-14;
Referee: Michael Woodhead; **Attendance:** 254.

GLOUCESTERSHIRE ALL GOLDS 29
SOUTH WALES SCORPIONS 17

ALL GOLDS: 20 Marcus Elliott; 2 James Fisher; 3 James Greene; 4 Aidan Jenkins; 5 Reece Rance; 6 Mark Barlow; 7 Danny Thomas; 15 Harry Chapman-Walker; 19 Craig Cook; 10 Izaak Duffy; 11 Jason Muranka; 12 James Tutuila; 14 Ash Haynes. Subs (all used): 13 Brendan Smith; 1 Phil Cowburn; 16 Connor Nolan; 18 James Walter.
Tries: Walter (10), Cook (26), Cowburn (48), Thomas (65, 71); **Goals:** Jenkins 4/5; **Field goal:** Cook (77).
SCORPIONS: 1 Jordan Sheridan; 2 Ian Newbury; 22 Dafydd Hellard; 4 Kyle Scrivens; 5 Chris Leyshon; 6 Paul Emanuelli; 7 Shaun Owens; 11 Barrie Phillips; 9 Connor Farrer; 10 Chris Vitalini; 12 Phil Carleton; 15 Owain Davies; 13 Ashley Bateman. Subs (all used): 14 Mike Connor; 8 Alan Pope; 24 Matthew Wilcox; 17 Rhys Fitzgerald.
Tries: Farrer (14), Newbury (18), Leyshon (45);
Goals: Emanuelli 2/4; **Field goal:** Emanuelli (79).
Rugby Leaguer & League Express Men of the Match: *All Golds:* Harry Chapman-Walker; *Scorpions:* Matthew Wilcox.
Penalty count: 12-4; **Half-time:** 10-10;
Referee: Dave Sharpe; **Attendance:** 186.

HUNSLET HAWKS 26 YORK CITY KNIGHTS 28

HAWKS: 1 Stuart Kain; 5 Lee Mapals; 24 Aston Wilson; 4 Danny Maun; 28 Andy Ballard; 13 Danny Grimshaw; 6 Thomas Coyle; 10 James Houston; 9 David March; 15 Luke Stenchion; 11 John Oakes; 12 Aaron Lyons; 26 Liam Mackay. Subs (all used): 27 Liam Hood; 18 Brooke Broughton; 16 Lewis Reed; 8 Michael Haley.
Tries: Wilson (33, 75), Hood (39, 53), Ballard (80);
Goals: Ballard 3/5.
CITY KNIGHTS: 26 Ben Reynolds; 2 George Elliott; 24 Jake Webster; 4 Greg Minikin; 5 Ben Dent; 6 Pat Smith; 7 Jon Presley; 18 Austin Bell; 9 Jack Lee; 10 Jack Aldous; 15 Jason Golden; 12 Ed Smith; 13 Lee Paterson. Subs (all used): 23 Benn Hardcastle; 11 Ryan Mallinder; 8 Nathan Freer; 19 Jake Joynt.
Tries: Minikin (5), E Smith (9), P Smith (16), Presley (26), Paterson (50), B Dent (72);
Goals: Reynolds 1/5, B Hardcastle 1/1.
Sin bin: Reynolds (38) - professional foul.
Rugby Leaguer & League Express Men of the Match: *Hawks:* Aston Wilson; *City Knights:* Lee Paterson.
Penalty count: 6-2; **Half-time:** 8-18;
Referee: Adam Gill; **Attendance:** 409.

OLDHAM 20 HEMEL STAGS 20

OLDHAM: 1 Tom Whitehead; 4 Steven Nield; 3 Ben Wood; 9 Sam Gee; 5 Dale Bloomfield; 16 Kenny Hughes; 7 Brett Robinson; 10 Jason Boults; 17 Danny Whitmore; 19 Michael Ward; 11 Josh Crowley; 12 Danny Langtree; 22 Liam Thompson. Subs (all used): 14 Adam Files; 6 Lewis Palfrey; 18 Alex Davidson; 15 Paddy Mooney.
Tries: Whitmore (3), Boults (20), Bloomfield (28), Hughes (71); **Goals:** Gee 2/3, Palfrey 0/1.
STAGS: 2 James Cameron; 20 Essad Al-Zubeidi; 3 Aaron Small; 4 Michael Brown; 5 James Hill; 6 Jy-mel Coleman; 7 Ben Young; 23 Eddie Mbaraga; 14 Evan Simons; 10 Dan Ljazouli; 11 Barry-John Swindells; 13 Alex Ingarfield; 9 Ben Thorburn. Subs (all used): 15 Dominic Maloney; 18 Lee Hudson; 17 Matthew Bailey; 16 Guy Aldam.
Tries: Swindells (55), Small (58), Al-Zubeidi (78), Hill (80); **Goals:** Swindells 2/2, Young 0/2.
Sin bin: Cameron (62) - dangerous contact.
Rugby Leaguer & League Express Men of the Match: *Oldham:* Josh Crowley; *Stags:* Ben Young.
Penalty count: 10-9; **Half-time:** 16-0;
Referee: Peter Brooke; **Attendance:** 508.

ROUND 3

Sunday 23rd March 2014

HEMEL STAGS 37 GATESHEAD THUNDER 24

STAGS: 1 Mitch Barbera; 2 James Cameron; 3 Aaron Small; 4 Michael Brown; 5 James Hill; 6 Jy-mel Coleman; 7 Ben Young; 25 James Howitt; 14 Evan Simons; 10 Dan Ljazouli; 11 Barry-John Swindells; 13 Alex Ingarfield; 9 Ben Thorburn. Subs (all used): 17 Matthew Bailey; 18 Lee Hudson; 21 Ryan Patchett; 23 Eddie Mbaraga.
Tries: Swindells (10), Small (14, 33), Barbera (18, 36, 80), Brown (74); **Goals:** Swindells 4/7;
Field goal: Jy-mel Coleman (79).
THUNDER: 1 Sam Lynch; 3 Jacob Blades; 24 Chris Heil; 4 Joe Brown; 5 Carl Booth; 26 Matty Beharrell; 7 Carl Puckering; 11 Rhys Clarke; 9 Ricky Hough; 10 Lee Fewlass; 29 Sonny Esslemont; 12 Jason Payne; 23 Aaron Ollett. Subs (all used): 6 Paul Stamp; 19 Josh Stoker; 13 Sam Bowring; 14 Matt Barron.
Tries: Beharrell (6), Heil (45, 55), Blades (67);
Goals: Puckering 4/4.
Sin bin: Booth (28) - punching.
Rugby Leaguer & League Express Men of the Match: *Stags:* Jy-mel Coleman; *Thunder:* Chris Heil.
Penalty count: 7-3; **Half-time:** 26-6;
Referee: Dave Sharpe; **Attendance:** 200.

LONDON SKOLARS 16 OLDHAM 18

SKOLARS: 1 John Paxton; 5 Dennis Tuffour; 4 Teli Pelo; 3 Mufaro Mvududu; 25 Judd Greenhalgh; 6 Courtney Davies; 7 Matt Bradley; 10 Dave Williams; 9 Martyn Smith; 31 Ryan MacDonald; 12 Michael Worrincy; 11 Lamont Bryan; 13 Oliver Purslow. Subs (all used): 20 Mike Bishay; 8 Rob Thomas; 30 Michael Sykes; 15 Sam Wellings.
Tries: Worrincy (11, 65), Mvududu (37);
Goals: Bradley 2/4.
OLDHAM: 1 Tom Whitehead; 2 Mo Agoro; 3 Ben Wood; 24 Edwin Okanga-Ajwang; 5 Dale Bloomfield; 6 Lewis Palfrey; 7 Brett Robinson; 10 Jason Boults; 17 Danny Whitmore; 19 Michael Ward; 11 Josh Crowley; 12 Danny Langtree; 9 Sam Gee. Subs (all used): 16 Kenny Hughes; 13 Mark Hobson; 15 Paddy Mooney; 8 Phil Joy.
Tries: Ward (2), Okanga-Ajwang (21), Robinson (51);
Goals: Palfrey 3/3.
Rugby Leaguer & League Express Men of the Match: *Skolars:* Michael Worrincy; *Oldham:* Lewis Palfrey.
Penalty count: 10-11; **Half-time:** 12-12;
Referee: Chris Kendall; **Attendance:** 479.

OXFORD 20 HUNSLET HAWKS 46

OXFORD: 1 Sean Morris; 20 Yannic Parker; 5 Callum Mulkeen; 3 Marcus Brooker; 2 Michael Crabtree; 18 Jordan Rice; 6 Tommy Connick; 8 Chris Clarke; 17 Rory Sharratt; 10 Matty Hadden; 11 John James Baird; 12 Andrew Hoggins; 16 Sam Blaney. Subs (all used): 24 Tom Davies; 14 Dave Ellison; 9 Alex Thompson; 7 Jimmy Rowland.
Tries: Rice (45), Crabtree (63, 76, 80);
Goals: Rowland 2/4.
HAWKS: 1 Stuart Kain; 5 Lee Mapals; 2 Jimmy Watson; 4 Danny Maun; 28 Andy Ballard; 13 Danny Grimshaw; 6 Thomas Coyle; 22 George Clarke; 9 David March; 8 Michael Haley; 11 John Oakes; 18 Brooke Broughton; 26 Liam Mackay. Subs (all used): 14 Matthew Tebb; 16 Lewis Reed; 17 James Davies; 12 Aaron Lyons.
Tries: Mapals (11, 53), Kain (28), Ballard (30, 40), March (33, 69), Oakes (36);
Goals: Ballard 5/6, March 0/1, Mapals 2/2.
Rugby Leaguer & League Express Men of the Match: *Oxford:* Michael Crabtree; *Hawks:* David March.
Penalty count: 6-8; **Half-time:** 0-34;
Referee: Peter Brooke; **Attendance:** 301.

YORK CITY KNIGHTS 76 SOUTH WALES SCORPIONS 0

CITY KNIGHTS: 1 James Haynes; 2 George Elliott; 3 James Ford; 30 James Morland; 5 Ben Dent; 23 Benn Hardcastle; 7 Jon Presley; 18 Austin Bell; 9 Jack Lee; 10 Jack Aldous; 11 Ryan Mallinder; 12 Ed Smith; 13 Lee Paterson. Subs (all used): 15 Jason Golden; 16 Iain Morrison; 20 Harry Carter; 8 Nathan Freer.
Tries: B Hardcastle (6), B Dent (8), Presley (10, 42, 61, 74), Aldous (14), Haynes (30, 78), E Smith (35), Carter (39), Elliott (53), Ford (66), Mallinder (72); **Goals:** B Hardcastle 10/14.
SCORPIONS: 1 Jordan Sheridan; 5 Chris Leyshon; 22 Dafydd Hellard; 3 Jack Pring; 4 Kyle Scrivens; 6 Paul Emanuelli; 13 Ashley Bateman; 11 Barrie Phillips; 9 Connor Farrer; 17 Rhys Fitzgerald; 12 Phil Carleton; 14 Mike Connor; 10 Chris Vitalini. Subs (all used): 8 Alan Pope; 18 Harrison Elliott; 21 Matthew Wilcox; 16 Osian Phillips.
Rugby Leaguer & League Express Men of the Match: *City Knights:* Jon Presley; *Scorpions:* Chris Vitalini.
Penalty count: 10-4; **Half-time:** 40-0;
Referee: Andrew Sweet; **Attendance:** 638.

ROUND 4

Sunday 30th March 2014

GATESHEAD THUNDER 20
GLOUCESTERSHIRE ALL GOLDS 28

THUNDER: 3 Jacob Blades; 5 Carl Booth; 4 Joe Brown; 24 Chris Heil; 2 Tom Capper; 6 Paul Stamp; 26 Matty Beharrell; 11 Rhys Clarke; 9 Ricky Hough; 19 Josh Stoker; 12 Jason Payne; 13 Sam Bowring; 28 Sonny Esslemont. Subs (all used): 10 Lee Fewlass; 23 Callum Cockburn; 14 Matt Barron; 25 Nathan Powley.
Tries: Heil (6, 50), Beharrell (24), Booth (30);
Goals: Beharrell 2/4.
Dismissal: Powley (79) - dangerous tackle on Thomas.
On report: Brawl (79).
ALL GOLDS: 2 Marcus Elliott; 4 Aidan Jenkins; 18 Corey Hanson; 1 Phil Cowburn; 5 Scott Claridge; 6 Mark Barlow; 7 Danny Thomas; 10 Izaak Duffy; 19 Craig Cook; 15 Harry Chapman-Walker; 11 Jason Muranka; 12 James Tutuila; 13 Brendan Smith. Subs (all used): 8 Steve Roper; 14 Joe McClean; 16 Connor Nolan; 17 Callum Stonier.
Tries: Elliott (12), Thomas (16, 34), Barlow (55), Cowburn (60); **Goals:** Jenkins 4/6.
On report: Brawl (79).
Rugby Leaguer & League Express Men of the Match: *Thunder:* Chris Heil; *All Golds:* James Tutuila.
Penalty count: 5-14; **Half-time:** 16-16;
Referee: Adam Gill; **Attendance:** 248.

HUNSLET HAWKS 60 LONDON SKOLARS 4

HAWKS: 1 Stuart Kain; 5 Lee Mapals; 2 Jimmy Watson; 11 John Oakes; 21 Jamaine Akaidere; 13 Danny Grimshaw; 20 Danny Ansell; 10 James Houston; 9 David March; 29 Ryan Bailey; 18 Brooke Broughton; 12 Aaron Lyons; 26 Liam Mackay. Subs (all used): 14 Matthew Tebb; 16 Lewis Reed; 15 Luke Stenchion; 25 Mathew Cook.
Tries: Akaidere (2, 29, 79), Houston (21), Mapals (40, 42), Reed (46), Cook (53), Kain (62, 74), Stenchion (68); **Goals:** March 1/3, Ansell 7/8.
SKOLARS: 1 Dennis Tuffour; 5 John Paxton; 4 Kazeem Fatouri; 3 Mufaro Mvududu; 22 Judd Greenhalgh; 7 Matt Bradley; 6 Courtney Davies; 10 Dave Williams; 15 Mike Bishay; 21 Michael Sykes; 11 Michael Worrincy; 12 Teli Pelo; 13 Oliver Purslow. Subs (all used): 8 Rob Thomas; 9 Martyn Smith; 14 Anthony Cox; 20 Sam Wellings.
Try: Greenhalgh (8); **Goals:** Bradley 0/1.
Rugby Leaguer & League Express Men of the Match: *Hawks:* Danny Ansell; *Skolars:* Teli Pelo.
Penalty count: 12-4; **Half-time:** 20-4;
Referee: Andrew Sweet; **Attendance:** 289.

SOUTH WALES SCORPIONS 16 HEMEL STAGS 34

SCORPIONS: 1 Jordan Sheridan; 22 Dafydd Hellard; 3 Jack Pring; 4 Kyle Scrivens; 5 Chris Leyshon; 6 Paul Emanuelli; 7 Dan Parry; 16 Osian Phillips; 9 Connor Farrer; 10 Chris Vitalini; 11 Barrie Phillips; 12 Phil Carleton; 13 Ashley Bateman. Subs (all used): 21 Matthew Wilcox; 2 Martin Luckwell; 8 Alan Pope; 18 Harrison Elliott.
Tries: O Phillips (18), Vitalini (66), Carleton (79);
Goals: Emanuelli 2/3.
STAGS: 1 Mitch Barbera; 2 James Cameron; 3 Aaron Small; 4 Michael Brown; 5 James Hill; 6 Jy-mel Coleman; 7 Ben Young; 25 James Howitt; 14 Evan Simons; 10 Dan Ljazouli; 11 Barry-John Swindells; 13 Alex Ingarfield; 9 Ben Thorburn. Subs (all used): 23 Eddie Mbaraga; 15 Miles McLeod; 18 Lee Hudson; 17 Ryan Patchett.
Tries: Swindells (23), Small (26), Brown (32), Cameron (43), Hill (51), Patchett (58), Hudson (59);
Goals: Swindells 2/6, Young 1/1.
Rugby Leaguer & League Express Men of the Match: *Scorpions:* Connor Farrer; *Stags:* James Cameron.
Penalty count: 7-10; **Half-time:** 6-14;
Referee: Michael Woodhead; **Attendance:** 193.

ROUND 5

Sunday 13th April 2014

**GLOUCESTERSHIRE ALL GOLDS 4
HUNSLET HAWKS 44**

ALL GOLDS: 20 Marcus Elliott; 2 Scott Claridge; 1 Phil Cowburn; 16 Corey Hanson; 5 Sam Te'o; 6 Mark Barlow; 7 Danny Thomas; 18 Chris Tyrer; 19 Craig Cook; 10 Izaak Duffy; 11 Jason Muranka; 12 James Tutuila; 13 Brendan Smith. Subs (all used): 9 Steve Roper; 17 Callum Stonier; 14 Joe McClean; 15 Connor Nolan.
Try: Cowburn (35); **Goals:** Cowburn 0/1.
HAWKS: 1 Stuart Kain; 5 Lee Mapals; 2 Jimmy Watson; 4 Danny Maun; 21 Jamaine Akaidere; 7 James Coyle; 20 Danny Ansell; 10 James Houston; 9 David March; 15 Luke Stenchion; 18 Brooke Broughton; 11 John Oakes; 13 Danny Grimshaw. Subs (all used): 16 Lewis Reed; 12 Aaron Lyons; 19 Casey Canterbury; 25 Mathew Cook.
Tries: Houston (6, 39, 61), Akaidere (19), Mapals (27), Ansell (52), Grimshaw (57), Maun (80); **Goals:** Ansell 6/8.
Rugby Leaguer & League Express Men of the Match: *All Golds:* Phil Cowburn; *Hawks:* James Houston.
Penalty count: 5-3; **Half-time:** 4-24;
Referee: Dave Sharpe; **Attendance:** 306.

LONDON SKOLARS 66 SOUTH WALES SCORPIONS 14

SKOLARS: 1 Dennis Tuffour; 5 John Paxton; 4 Mufaro Mvududu; 3 James Woodburn-Hall; 25 Judd Greenhalgh; 6 Courtney Davies; 7 Matt Bradley; 30 Sam Wellings; 9 Lloyd O'Connor; 10 Teli Pelo; 29 Michael Worrincy; 11 Anthony Cox; 20 Martyn Smith. Subs (all used): 13 Louis Robinson; 8 Rob Thomas; 21 Dave Williams; 23 Mike Bishay.
Tries: Tuffour (13, 26), Woodburn-Hall (39, 64, 74), Bishay (45, 55, 66), Williams (49), Pelo (57), Greenhalgh (72), Smith (77); **Goals:** Bradley 9/12.
SCORPIONS: 5 Chris Leyshon; 2 Ian Newbury; 3 Jack Pring; 22 Dafydd Hellard; 8 Alan Pope; 6 Paul Emanuelli; 1 Scott Amber; 20 Scott Britton; 9 Connor Farrer; 23 Richard East; 12 Phil Carleton; 4 Kyle Scrivens; 10 Chris Vitalini. Subs: 7 Daryl Carter; 21 Matthew Wilcox (not used); 25 Scott Giles; - Mike Grady (not used).
Tries: Farrer (1), Pope (22), Carter (33);
Goals: Emanuelli 1/3.
Rugby Leaguer & League Express Men of the Match: *Skolars:* Dennis Tuffour; *Scorpions:* Paul Emanuelli.
Penalty count: 11-8; **Half-time:** 16-14;
Referee: Michael Woodhead; **Attendance:** 417.

OLDHAM 52 GATESHEAD THUNDER 16

OLDHAM: 1 Tom Whitehead; 2 Mo Agoro; 3 Ben Wood; 9 Sam Gee; 5 Dale Bloomfield; 6 Lewis Palfrey; 7 Brett Robinson; 8 Phil Joy; 17 Danny Whitmore; 10 Jason Boults; 11 Josh Crowley; 12 Danny Langtree; 13 Mark Hobson. Subs (all used): 16 Kenny Hughes; 18 Alex Davidson; 20 George Tyson; 19 Michael Ward.
Tries: Bloomfield (4, 55, 79), Gee (8), Crowley (28), Langtree (32, 41), Hughes (37), Wood (48), Boults (67);
Goals: Palfrey 6/10.
THUNDER: 29 Greg Eden; 1 Sam Lynch; 4 Joe Brown; 24 Chris Heil; 3 Jacob Blades; 7 Carl Puckering; 26 Matty Beharrell; 10 Lee Fewlass; 9 Ricky Hough; 28 Sonny Esslemont; 30 Aaron Ollett; 12 Jason Payne; 13 Sam Bowring. Subs (all used): 20 Connor Condron; 19 Josh Stoker; 23 Callum Cockburn; 17 Alex Ruff.
Tries: Esslemont (13), Hough (74), Payne (77);
Goals: Puckering 2/3.
Rugby Leaguer & League Express Men of the Match: *Oldham:* Kenny Hughes; *Thunder:* Sonny Esslemont.
Penalty count: 12-4; **Half-time:** 24-6;
Referee: Chris Kendall; **Attendance:** 436.

YORK CITY KNIGHTS 16 OXFORD 24

CITY KNIGHTS: 26 Ben Reynolds; 25 Luke Hardcastle; 3 James Ford; 28 Josh Nathaniel; 5 Ben Dent; 23 Benn Hardcastle; 7 Jon Presley; 8 Nathan Freer; 9 Jack Lee; 10 Jack Aldous; 11 Ryan Mallinder; 12 Ed Smith; 13 Lee Paterson. Subs (all used): 6 Pat Smith; 29 Daniel Fleming; 22 Ben Crane; 21 Jack Iley.
Tries: Iley (19), Reynolds (40), Lee (60);
Goals: Reynolds 1/2, B Hardcastle 1/1.
OXFORD: 1 Sean Morris; 20 Yannic Parker; 5 Callum Mulkeen; 3 Marcus Brooker; 2 Michael Crabtree; 7 Jimmy Rowland; 6 Tommy Connick; 8 Chris Clarke; 9 Alex Thompson; 10 Matty Hadden; 11 John James Baird; 16 Sam Blaney; 18 Jordan Rice. Subs (all used): 14 Dave Ellison; 24 Tom Davies; 17 Rory Sharratt; 32 Ed Hayles.
Tries: S Morris (29, 45), Baird (38), Mulkeen (53), Rowland (80); **Goals:** Rowland 2/5.
Rugby Leaguer & League Express Men of the Match: *City Knights:* Jack Lee; *Oxford:* Sean Morris.
Penalty count: 6-4; **Half-time:** 10-10;
Referee: Adam Gill; **Attendance:** 574.

ROUND 6

Friday 18th April 2014

HUNSLET HAWKS 38 OLDHAM 12

HAWKS: 1 Stuart Kain; 5 Lee Mapals; 2 Jimmy Watson; 4 Danny Maun; 21 Jamaine Akaidere; 7 James Coyle; 20 Danny Ansell; 10 James Houston; 9 David March; 15 Luke Stenchion; 18 Brooke Broughton; 11 John Oakes; 13 Danny Grimshaw. Subs (all used): 14 Matthew Tebb; 16 Lewis Reed; 12 Aaron Lyons; 26 Liam Mackay.
Tries: Grimshaw (21), Broughton (32), Oakes (41), Tebb (56), Mackay (63), Watson (74), Akaidere (79);
Goals: Ansell 5/8.
OLDHAM: 1 Tom Whitehead; 2 Mo Agoro; 21 David Cookson; 3 Ben Wood; 5 Dale Bloomfield; 6 Lewis Palfrey; 16 Kenny Hughes; 8 Phil Joy; 17 Danny Whitmore; 10 Jason Boults; 11 Josh Crowley; 12 Danny Langtree; 13 Mark Hobson. Subs (all used): 9 Sam Gee; 18 Alex Davidson; 20 George Tyson; 19 Michael Ward.
Tries: Agoro (24), Davidson (52); **Goals:** Palfrey 2/2.
Rugby Leaguer & League Express Men of the Match: *Hawks:* Danny Grimshaw; *Oldham:* Tom Whitehead.
Penalty count: 3-4; **Half-time:** 12-6;
Referee: Peter Brooke; **Attendance:** 598.

HEMEL STAGS 24 LONDON SKOLARS 27

STAGS: 2 James Cameron; 20 Essad Al-Zubeidi; 3 Aaron Small; 4 Michael Brown; 5 James Hill; 6 Jy-mel Coleman; 1 Mitch Barbera; 8 Dominic Maloney; 14 Evan Simons; 25 James Howitt; 11 Barry-John Swindells; 13 Alex Ingarfield; 10 Dan Ljazouli. Subs (all used): 18 Lee Hudson; 16 Guy Aldam; 15 Miles McLeod; 23 Eddie Mbaraga.
Tries: Swindells (11), Barbera (24), Mbaraga (69), Small (77); **Goals:** Swindells 4/4.
SKOLARS: 1 Dennis Tuffour; 5 John Paxton; 19 Kazeem Fatouri; 11 Anthony Cox; 25 Judd Greenhalgh; 6 Courtney Davies; 7 Matt Bradley; 34 Teli Pelo; 9 Martyn Smith; 30 Michael Sykes; 13 Michael Worrincy; 10 Dave Williams; 21 Sam Wellings. Subs (all used): 29 Louis Robinson; 8 Rob Thomas; 31 Ryan MacDonald; 32 Dion Chapman.
Tries: Smith (2, 36), Robinson (43), Greenhalgh (62);
Goals: Bradley 5/5; **Field goal:** Bradley (79).
Dismissal: Wellings (61) - high tackle on Barbera.
Rugby Leaguer & League Express Men of the Match: *Stags:* James Howitt; *Skolars:* Matt Bradley.
Penalty count: 6-6; **Half-time:** 12-12;
Referee: Andrew Sweet; **Attendance:** 284.

OXFORD 38 GLOUCESTERSHIRE ALL GOLDS 24

OXFORD: 1 Sean Morris; 20 Yannic Parker; 5 Callum Mulkeen; 3 Marcus Brooker; 2 Michael Crabtree; 7 Jimmy Rowland; 6 Tommy Connick; 8 Chris Clarke; 9 Alex Thompson; 10 Matty Hadden; 11 John James Baird; 16 Sam Blaney; 18 Jordan Rice. Subs (all used): 24 Tom Davies; 14 Dave Ellison; 34 Ed Hayles; 17 Rory Sharratt.
Tries: Mulkeen (20), Thompson (26), Baird (35, 67), Crabtree (44, 64), Parker (57); **Goals:** Rowland 5/7.
ALL GOLDS: 2 Marcus Elliott; 4 Aidan Jenkins; 17 Corey Hanson; 1 Phil Cowburn; 5 Scott Claridge; 3 Steve Roper; 7 Danny Thomas; 10 Izaak Duffy; 19 Craig Cook; 18 James Walter; 11 Jason Muranka; 8 Sam Te'o; 13 Brendan Smith. Subs (all used): 6 Mark Barlow; 14 Joe McClean; 15 Connor Nolan; 16 Callum Stonier.
Tries: Cowburn (10), Jenkins (14), Cook (31), Elliott (78); **Goals:** Roper 4/5.
Rugby Leaguer & League Express Men of the Match: *Oxford:* Alex Thompson; *All Golds:* Danny Thomas.
Penalty count: 5-4; **Half-time:** 18-18;
Referee: Michael Woodhead; **Attendance:** 240.

GATESHEAD THUNDER 26 YORK CITY KNIGHTS 30

THUNDER: 3 Jacob Blades; 13 Sam Bowring; 24 Chris Heil; 4 Joe Brown; 5 Tom Capper; 26 Matty Beharrell; 7 Carl Puckering; 8 Tom Lynch; 9 Ricky Hough; 14 Matt Barron; 28 Sonny Esslemont; 12 Jason Payne; 29 Aaron Ollett. Subs (all used): 6 Paul Stamp; 11 Rhys Clarke; 10 Lee Fewlass; 19 Josh Stoker.
Tries: Barron (22), Capper (34), Payne (49, 67), Blades (74); **Goals:** Puckering 2/3, Beharrell 1/2.
Sin bin: Heil (77) - dissent.
CITY KNIGHTS: 1 James Haynes; 2 George Elliott; 26 James Saltonstall; 28 James Morland; 5 Ben Dent; 23 Benn Hardcastle; 7 Jon Presley; 19 Jake Joynt; 9 Jack Lee; 10 Jack Aldous; 11 Ryan Mallinder; 12 Ed Smith; 13 Lee Paterson. Subs (all used): 6 Pat Smith; 8 Nathan Freer; 24 Nathan Harper; 35 Ryan Backhouse.
Tries: Presley (10), Lee (15), B Dent (25), P Smith (38), E Smith (44); **Goals:** B Hardcastle 5/5.
Sin bin: P Smith (54) - delaying restart.
Rugby Leaguer & League Express Men of the Match: *Thunder:* Jason Payne; *City Knights:* James Haynes.
Penalty count: 4-9; **Half-time:** 10-24;
Referee: Chris Kendall; **Attendance:** 257.

ROUND 7

Sunday 4th May 2014

**SOUTH WALES SCORPIONS 16
GATESHEAD THUNDER 50**

SCORPIONS: 1 Jordan Sheridan; 2 Ian Newbury; 24 Matthew Wilcox; 4 Kyle Scrivens; 5 Chris Leyshon; 6 Paul Emanuelli; 7 Greg Wilde; 16 Osian Phillips; 9 Connor Farrer; 10 Chris Vitalini; 18 Harrison Elliott; 12 Phil Carleton; 14 Mike Connor. Subs (all used): 23 Richard East; 25 Scott Giles; 22 Dafydd Hellard; 13 Ashley Bateman.
Tries: Wilde (27), Vitalini (39, 42); **Goals:** Emanuelli 2/3.
THUNDER: 3 Jacob Blades; 2 Omari Caro; 24 Chris Heil; 4 Joe Brown; 13 Sam Bowring; 21 Jamie Rooney; 26 Matty Beharrell; 29 Aaron Ollett; 27 Keal Carlile; 14 Matt Barron; 28 Sonny Esslemont; 12 Jason Payne; 9 Ricky Hough. Subs (all used): 10 Lee Fewlass; 11 Rhys Clarke; 6 Paul Stamp; 25 Callum Cockburn.
Tries: Payne (16, 25), Beharrell (18), Caro (48, 80), Heil (54), Rooney (59), Ollett (61), Bowring (71), Carlile (78); **Goals:** Beharrell 5/10.
Rugby Leaguer & League Express Men of the Match: *Scorpions:* Chris Vitalini; *Thunder:* Matty Beharrell.
Penalty count: 4-6; **Half-time:** 12-16;
Referee: Chris Campbell; **Attendance:** 258.

GLOUCESTERSHIRE ALL GOLDS 20 HEMEL STAGS 21

ALL GOLDS: 1 Phil Cowburn; 5 Scott Claridge; 11 Sam Te'o; 2 Jarrod Ward; 4 Aidan Jenkins; 7 Danny Thomas; 6 Mark Barlow; 18 James Walter; 19 Craig Cook; 10 Izaak Duffy; 12 Connor Nolan; 17 Jason Muranka; 13 Brendan Smith. Subs (all used): 14 Joe McClean; 8 Jack Francis; 16 Miles Fairbank; 15 Richard Jones.
Tries: Smith (12), Ward (17), Thomas (66), Te'o (69);
Goals: Jenkins 2/4.
STAGS: 2 James Cameron; 17 Jimmy Morgan; 3 Aaron Small; 4 Michael Brown; 5 James Hill; 6 Jy-mel Coleman; 7 Ben Young; 25 James Howitt; 14 Evan Simons; 10 Dan Ljazouli; 11 Barry-John Swindells; 13 Alex Ingarfield; 23 Eddie Mbaraga. Subs (all used): 18 Lee Hudson; 15 Miles McLeod; 16 Chris Clough; 20 Matthew Bailey.
Tries: Ljazouli (4), Ingarfield (26), Brown (28);
Goals: Swindells 4/4; **Field goal:** Jy-mel Coleman (79).
Rugby Leaguer & League Express Men of the Match: *All Golds:* Brendan Smith; *Stags:* Lee Hudson.
Penalty count: 8-4; **Half-time:** 12-18;
Referee: Tom Grant; **Attendance:** 126.

OLDHAM 48 OXFORD 28

OLDHAM: 4 Steven Nield; 2 Mo Agoro; 21 David Cookson; 25 Edwin Okanga-Ajwang; 5 Dale Bloomfield; 6 Lewis Palfrey; 7 Brett Robinson; 8 Phil Joy; 17 Danny Whitmore; 19 Michael Ward; 11 Josh Crowley; 12 Danny Langtree; 9 Sam Gee. Subs (all used): 16 Kenny Hughes; 18 Alex Davidson; 20 George Tyson; 28 Nathan Mason.
Tries: Ward (6, 20), Whitmore (12), Langtree (37, 45), Tyson (42), Agoro (54), Cookson (60); **Goals:** Palfrey 8/9.
OXFORD: 1 Sean Morris; 5 Callum Mulkeen; 31 Ryan McGoldrick; 3 Marcus Brooker; 20 Yannic Parker; 7 Jimmy Rowland; 6 Tommy Connick; 8 Chris Clarke; 9 Alex Thompson; 10 Matty Hadden; 11 John James Baird; 16 Sam Blaney; 18 Jordan Rice. Subs (all used): 12 Andrew Hoggins; 14 Dave Ellison; 17 Rory Sharratt; 24 Tom Davies.
Tries: Thompson (16, 51), Mulkeen (33), Brooker (71), Sharratt (77); **Goals:** Rowland 4/5.
Rugby Leaguer & League Express Men of the Match: *Oldham:* Lewis Palfrey; *Oxford:* Jimmy Rowland.
Penalty count: 9-9; **Half-time:** 26-12;
Referee: Michael Woodhead; **Attendance:** 504.

YORK CITY KNIGHTS 36 LONDON SKOLARS 16

CITY KNIGHTS: 1 James Haynes; 28 Adam Dent; 26 James Saltonstall; 4 Greg Minikin; 5 Ben Dent; 23 Benn Hardcastle; 7 Jon Presley; 19 Jake Joynt; 9 Jack Lee; 10 Jack Aldous; 11 Ryan Mallinder; 12 Ed Smith; 13 Lee Paterson. Subs (all used): 15 Jason Golden; 20 Harry Carter; 8 Nathan Freer; 6 Pat Smith.
Tries: Mallinder (6), A Dent (26), Lee (28), Saltonstall (62), E Smith (64), Haynes (78);
Goals: B Hardcastle 6/6.

SKOLARS: 1 Dennis Tuffour; 14 Judd Greenhalgh; 4 Mufaro Mvududu; 3 John Paxton; 5 Ibrahim Kabia; 6 Courtney Davies; 7 Matt Bradley; 20 Teli Pelo; 9 Martyn Smith; 21 Ryan MacDonald; 11 Sam Wellings; 12 Anthony Cox; 10 Dave Williams. Subs (all used): 13 Louis Robinson; 8 Rob Thomas; 16 Sam Druce; 22 Michael Sykes.
Tries: Wellings (12), Greenhalgh (17), Smith (76); **Goals:** Bradley 1/1, Davies 1/2.
Rugby Leaguer & League Express Men of the Match: *City Knights:* James Saltonstall; *Skolars:* Dennis Tuffour.
Penalty count: 6-6; **Half-time:** 18-10; **Referee:** Adam Gill; **Attendance:** 451.

ROUND 8

Sunday 11th May 2014

GATESHEAD THUNDER 24 LONDON SKOLARS 16

THUNDER: 3 Jacob Blades; 5 Tom Capper; 4 Joe Brown; 13 Sam Bowring; 25 Omari Caro; 1 Jamie Rooney; 26 Matty Beharrell; 14 Matt Barron; 27 Keal Carlile; 30 Aaron Ollett; 12 Jason Payne; 11 Rhys Clarke; 9 Ricky Hough. Subs (all used): 19 Josh Stoker; 6 Paul Stamp; 22 Callum Cockburn; 21 Joe Hodgson.
Tries: Bowring (6), Beharrell (9, 60), Payne (56), Hough (73); **Goals:** Beharrell 0/2, Rooney 2/3.
SKOLARS: 1 John Paxton; 14 Judd Greenhalgh; 4 Mufaro Mvududu; 3 Lamont Bryan; 5 Jamie O'Callaghan; 6 Courtney Davies; 19 Sam Druce; 10 Dave Williams; 9 Martyn Smith; 20 Teli Pelo; 12 Michael Worrincy; 16 Mike McMeeken; 22 Oliver Purslow. Subs (all used): 21 Ryan MacDonald; 11 Louis Robinson; 13 Sam Wellings; 8 Rob Thomas.
Tries: McMeeken (39), Greenhalgh (64), Mvududu (76); **Goals:** Druce 2/3.
On report: Davies (55) - alleged dangerous challenge.
Rugby Leaguer & League Express Men of the Match: *Thunder:* Jason Payne; *Skolars:* Sam Druce.
Penalty count: 3-10; **Half-time:** 8-6; **Referee:** Michael Woodhead; **Attendance:** 209.

SOUTH WALES SCORPIONS 6 HUNSLET HAWKS 20

SCORPIONS: 1 Jordan Sheridan; 24 Matthew Wilcox; 3 Jack Pring; 4 Kyle Scrivens; 5 Chris Leyshon; 6 Paul Emanuelli; 7 Greg Wilde; 16 Osian Phillips; 9 Connor Farrer; 10 Chris Vitalini; 11 Barrie Phillips; 12 Phil Carleton; 23 Richard East. Subs: 13 Ashley Bateman; 14 Mike Connor; 21 Ian Newbury (not used); 25 Scott Giles.
Try: Sheridan (36); **Goals:** Emanuelli 1/1.
Sin bin: Farrer (47) - fighting.
HAWKS: 13 Danny Grimshaw; 2 Jimmy Watson; 3 Lee Brickwood; 4 Danny Maun; 28 Andy Ballard; 6 Thomas Coyle; 7 James Coyle; 8 Michael Haley; 9 David March; 10 James Houston; 11 John Oakes; 18 Brooke Broughton; 26 Liam Mackay. Subs (all used): 27 Liam Hood; 15 Luke Stenchion; 1 Stuart Kain; 22 George Clarke.
Tries: Ballard (7), Stenchion (26), Brickwood (47), Watson (73); **Goals:** Ballard 2/4.
Sin bin: Hood (47) - fighting.
Rugby Leaguer & League Express Men of the Match: *Scorpions:* Richard East; *Hawks:* Danny Maun.
Penalty count: 4-7; **Half-time:** 6-10; **Referee:** Adam Gill; **Attendance:** 255 *(at Glan-Yr-Afon Park, Blackwood).*

YORK CITY KNIGHTS 22 HEMEL STAGS 14

CITY KNIGHTS: 26 Ben Reynolds; 28 Adam Dent; 25 James Saltonstall; 4 Greg Minikin; 5 Ben Dent; 23 Benn Hardcastle; 7 Jon Presley; 17 Jack Pickles; 9 Jack Lee; 10 Jack Aldous; 11 Ryan Mallinder; 12 Ed Smith; 13 Lee Paterson. Subs (all used): 6 Pat Smith; 3 James Ford; 8 Nathan Freer; 19 Jake Joynt.
Tries: B Dent (37, 69), Paterson (39), A Dent (73); **Goals:** B Hardcastle 1/2, Reynolds 2/2.
STAGS: 2 James Cameron; 5 James Hill; 4 Michael Brown; 3 Aaron Small; 17 Jimmy Morgan; 6 Jy-mel Coleman; 7 Ben Young; 25 James Howitt; 14 Evan Simons; 10 Dan Ljazouli; 11 Barry-John Swindells; 16 Chris Clough; 13 Alex Ingarfield. Subs (all used): 23 Eddie Mbaraga; 21 Ben Kavanagh; 15 Matthew Bailey; 19 Malikhi Lloyd-Jones.
Tries: Brown (14), Simons (48); **Goals:** Swindells 3/4.
Rugby Leaguer & League Express Men of the Match: *City Knights:* James Saltonstall; *Stags:* James Cameron.
Penalty count: 15-11; **Half-time:** 10-6; **Referee:** Chris Kendall; **Attendance:** 457.

ROUND 9

Sunday 18th May 2014

HUNSLET HAWKS 52 GATESHEAD THUNDER 6

HAWKS: 1 Stuart Kain; 3 Lee Brickwood; 2 Jimmy Watson; 24 Aston Wilson; 28 Andy Ballard; 6 Thomas Coyle; 20 Danny Ansell; 10 James Houston; 9 David March; 8 Michael Haley; 18 Brooke Broughton; 11 John Oakes; 26 Liam Mackay. Subs (all used): 13 Danny Grimshaw; 27 Liam Hood; 12 Aaron Lyons; 16 Lewis Reed.
Tries: Brickwood (8, 12, 59), Ballard (40, 47), Wilson (41, 76), Hood (50), Oakes (62), Grimshaw (67); **Goals:** Ballard 6/10.
THUNDER: 3 Jacob Blades; 28 Omari Caro; 4 Joe Brown; 24 Chris Heil; 5 Tom Capper; 26 Matty Beharrell; 1 Jamie Rooney; 29 Aaron Ollett; 27 Keal Carlile; 14 Matt Barron; 12 Jason Payne; 13 Sam Bowring; 9 Ricky Hough. Subs (all used): 6 Paul Stamp; 10 Lee Fewlass; 19 Josh Stoker; 21 Joe Hodgson.
Try: Payne (24); **Goals:** Beharrell 1/1.
Rugby Leaguer & League Express Men of the Match: *Hawks:* Andy Ballard; *Thunder:* Matt Barron.
Penalty count: 7-2; **Half-time:** 16-6; **Referee:** Peter Brooke; **Attendance:** 566.

LONDON SKOLARS 24 GLOUCESTERSHIRE ALL GOLDS 34

SKOLARS: 1 Dennis Tuffour; 20 Judd Greenhalgh; 3 John Paxton; 31 Lamont Bryan; 5 Jamie O'Callaghan; 6 James Woodburn-Hall; 4 Sam Druce; 10 Dave Williams; 9 Martyn Smith; 34 Teli Pelo; 11 Michael Worrincy; 12 Will Lovell; 13 Oliver Purslow. Subs (all used): 8 Ryan MacDonald; - Erjon Dollapi; 29 Louis Robinson; 7 Matt Bradley.
Tries: Tuffour (4), Smith (24), Worrincy (58), Woodburn-Hall (68); **Goals:** Druce 2/2, Bradley 2/2.
ALL GOLDS: 1 Phil Cowburn; 4 Aidan Jenkins; 2 Jarrod Ward; 11 Sam Te'o; 8 Daniel Spencer-Tonks; 3 Danny Fallon; 7 Danny Thomas; 18 James Walter; 19 Craig Cook; 10 Izaak Duffy; 16 Jason Muranka; 12 Miles Fairbank; 13 Brendan Smith. Subs (all used): 14 Joe McClean; 15 Harry Chapman-Walker; 17 Jack Francis; 5 Casey Canterbury.
Tries: Spencer-Tonks (3), Jenkins (9), Muranka (27, 46), Canterbury (35, 78), Duffy (74); **Goals:** Fallon 0/1, Jenkins 3/6.
Rugby Leaguer & League Express Men of the Match: *Skolars:* James Woodburn-Hall; *All Golds:* Jason Muranka.
Penalty count: 10-7; **Half-time:** 12-18; **Referee:** Jamie Bloem; **Attendance:** 398 *(at Queen Elizabeth II Stadium, Enfield).*

OLDHAM 31 YORK CITY KNIGHTS 30

OLDHAM: 4 Steven Nield; 2 Mo Agoro; 21 David Cookson; 25 Jonathan Ford; 5 Dale Bloomfield; 6 Lewis Palfrey; 7 Brett Robinson; 8 Phil Joy; 17 Danny Whitmore; 19 Michael Ward; 11 Josh Crowley; 12 Danny Langtree; 20 George Tyson. Subs (all used): 16 Kenny Hughes; 18 Alex Davidson; 14 Adam Files; 28 Nathan Mason.
Tries: Bloomfield (7, 19, 27), Agoro (12), Cookson (16), Nield (77); **Goals:** Palfrey 3/6; **Field goal:** Robinson (24).
CITY KNIGHTS: 1 James Haynes; 25 James Saltonstall; 3 James Ford; 4 Greg Minikin; 5 Ben Dent; 6 Pat Smith; 26 Ben Reynolds; 17 Jack Pickles; 9 Jack Lee; 10 Jack Aldous; 11 Ryan Mallinder; 12 Ed Smith; 13 Lee Paterson. Subs (all used): 21 Jack Iley; 32 Brad Brennan; 35 Ryan Backhouse; 28 Tyler Craig.
Tries: Lee (35, 40, 56), Aldous (38), Reynolds (41), Mallinder (52), Saltonstall (69); **Goals:** Haynes 1/4, Reynolds 0/3.
Rugby Leaguer & League Express Men of the Match: *Oldham:* Dale Bloomfield; *City Knights:* Jack Lee.
Penalty count: 11-5; **Half-time:** 27-14; **Referee:** Adam Gill; **Attendance:** 579.

OXFORD 40 SOUTH WALES SCORPIONS 24

OXFORD: 1 Sean Morris; 5 Callum Mulkeen; 32 Ryan McGoldrick; 3 Marcus Brooker; 30 Jack Briggs; 7 Jimmy Rowland; 6 Tommy Connick; 24 Tom Davies; 9 Alex Thompson; 10 Matty Hadden; 11 John James Baird; 12 Andrew Hoggins; 18 Jordan Rice. Subs (all used): 8 Chris Clarke; 35 Luke Evans; 16 Sam Blaney; 17 Rory Sharratt.
Tries: Thompson (12, 77), S Morris (18, 50), Mulkeen (26), Rowland (37), Hadden (48); **Goals:** Rowland 4/5, Connick 2/2.
SCORPIONS: 1 Jordan Sheridan; 4 Kyle Scrivens; 3 Jack Pring; 24 Matthew Wilcox; 5 Chris Leyshon; 6 Paul Emanuelli; 7 Greg Wilde; 16 Osian Phillips; 9 Connor Farrer; 23 Richard East; 11 Barrie Phillips; 12 Phil Carleton; 10 Chris Vitalini. Subs (all used): 14 Mike Connor; 13 Ashley Bateman; 18 Harrison Elliott; 25 Scott Giles.
Tries: Farrer (4, 15, 65), Wilcox (70); **Goals:** Emanuelli 4/4.
Rugby Leaguer & League Express Men of the Match: *Oxford:* Matty Hadden; *Scorpions:* Connor Farrer.
Penalty count: 5-5; **Half-time:** 22-12; **Referee:** Gareth Hewer; **Attendance:** 236.

ROUND 10

Sunday 25th May 2014

HEMEL STAGS 30 OXFORD 24

STAGS: 2 James Cameron; 17 Jimmy Morgan; 3 Aaron Small; 4 Michael Brown; 5 James Hill; 6 Jy-mel Coleman; 13 Alex Ingarfield; 25 James Howitt; 14 Evan Simons; 10 Dan Ljazouli; 16 Chris Clough; 11 Barry-John Swindells; 23 Eddie Mbaraga. Subs (all used): 8 Dominic Maloney; 21 Ben Kavanagh; 15 Matthew Bailey; 19 Romaine Navarrete.
Tries: Swindells (14), Mbaraga (24, 64), Hill (31), Brown (58); **Goals:** Swindells 5/7.
OXFORD: 1 Sean Morris; 30 Jack Briggs; 12 Andrew Hoggins; 3 Marcus Brooker; 2 Michael Crabtree; 18 Jordan Rice; 6 Tommy Connick; 24 Tom Davies; 9 Alex Thompson; 10 Matty Hadden; 11 John James Baird; 16 Sam Blaney; 8 Chris Clarke. Subs (all used): 14 Dave Ellison; 34 Ed Hayles; 31 Luke Evans; 17 Rory Sharratt.
Tries: S Morris (42, 54), Blaney (46), Sharratt (78); **Goals:** Thompson 1/1, Connick 3/3.
Rugby Leaguer & League Express Men of the Match: *Stags:* Jy-mel Coleman; *Oxford:* Tommy Connick.
Penalty count: 7-8; **Half-time:** 20-0; **Referee:** Adam Gill; **Attendance:** 170.

GLOUCESTERSHIRE ALL GOLDS 22 OLDHAM 30

ALL GOLDS: 7 Danny Thomas; 2 Jarrod Ward; 17 Sam Te'o; 4 Aidan Jenkins; 5 Scott Claridge; - Ben White; 9 Casey Canterbury; 15 Harry Chapman-Walker; 19 Craig Cook; 10 Izaak Duffy; 11 Miles Fairbank; 12 Jason Muranka; 13 Brendan Smith. Subs (all used): 14 Joe McClean; 18 Frankie Foster; 16 Daniel Spencer-Tonks; 3 Danny Fallon.
Tries: Fairbank (24), Claridge (56), Canterbury (65), Cook (77); **Goals:** Jenkins 3/4.
OLDHAM: 4 Steven Nield; 2 Mo Agoro; 21 David Cookson; 26 Jonathan Ford; 5 Dale Bloomfield; - Steve Roper; 7 Brett Robinson; 8 Phil Joy; 17 Danny Whitmore; 10 Jason Boults; 11 Josh Crowley; 12 Danny Langtree; 9 Sam Gee. Subs (all used): 20 George Tyson; 19 Michael Ward; 16 Kenny Hughes; 28 Nathan Mason.
Tries: Crowley (13), Bloomfield (28), Ford (37, 46), Ward (61), Agoro (74); **Goals:** Roper 3/6.
Rugby Leaguer & League Express Men of the Match: *All Golds:* Sam Te'o; *Oldham:* Jonathan Ford.
Penalty count: 7-7; **Half-time:** 6-14; **Referee:** Michael Woodhead; **Attendance:** 264.

YORK CITY KNIGHTS 40 HUNSLET HAWKS 0

CITY KNIGHTS: 25 Ben Reynolds; 26 James Saltonstall; 3 James Ford; 27 James Morland; 5 Ben Dent; 6 Pat Smith; 7 Jon Presley; 32 Brad Brennan; 9 Jack Lee; 10 Jack Aldous; 11 Ryan Mallinder; 12 Ed Smith; 28 Joe Pickets. Subs (all used): 20 Harry Carter; 18 Austin Bell; 29 Ryan Backhouse; 30 Colton Roche.
Tries: Morland (3), Lee (19, 74), Presley (37), Mallinder (57), B Dent (63), Reynolds (71); **Goals:** Reynolds 6/8.
HAWKS: 13 Danny Grimshaw; 3 Lee Brickwood; 2 Jimmy Watson; 4 Danny Maun; 28 Andy Ballard; 6 Thomas Coyle; 7 James Coyle; 10 James Houston; 27 Liam Hood; 8 Michael Haley; 18 Brooke Broughton; 11 John Oakes; 26 Liam Mackay. Subs (all used): 14 Matthew Tebb; 24 Aston Wilson; 15 Luke Stenchion; 12 Aaron Lyons.
Rugby Leaguer & League Express Men of the Match: *City Knights:* Pat Smith; *Hawks:* Danny Grimshaw.
Penalty count: 10-5; **Half-time:** 20-0; **Referee:** Dave Merrick; **Attendance:** 837.

ROUND 11

Sunday 1st June 2014

HEMEL STAGS 22 GATESHEAD THUNDER 26

STAGS: 2 James Cameron; 17 Jimmy Morgan; 13 Alex Ingarfield; 3 Aaron Small; 5 James Hill; 4 Michael Brown; 6 Jy-mel Coleman; 25 James Howitt; 14 Evan Simons; 10 Dan Ljazouli; 16 Chris Clough; 11 Barry-John Swindells; 23 Eddie Mbaraga. Subs (all used): 21 Ben Kavanagh; 19 Malikhi Lloyd-Jones; 15 Romaine Navarrete; 20 Ryan Chester.
Tries: Small (11), Mbaraga (23), Ljazouli (61), Cameron (80); **Goals:** Swindells 3/3 *(last conversion attempt declined).*
THUNDER: 1 Louis Sheriff; 27 Lee Mapals; 24 Chris Heil; 4 Joe Brown; 2 Omari Caro; 26 Matty Beharrell; - Jamie Rooney; 14 Matt Barron; 6 Paul Stamp; 29 Aaron Ollett; 12 Jason Payne; 11 Rhys Clarke; 28 Sonny Esslemont. Subs (all used): 3 Jacob Blades; 10 Lee Fewlass; 13 Sam Bowring; 30 Ricky Hough.
Tries: Sheriff (8), Payne (19), Caro (37), Mapals (47); **Goals:** Beharrell 3/3, Rooney 2/2.
Rugby Leaguer & League Express Men of the Match: *Stags:* Eddie Mbaraga; *Thunder:* Matty Beharrell.
Penalty count: 9-9; **Half-time:** 12-18; **Referee:** Chris Campbell; **Attendance:** 126.

HUNSLET HAWKS 32 OXFORD 12

HAWKS: 1 Stuart Kain; 3 Lee Brickwood; 2 Jimmy Watson; 4 Danny Maun; 21 Jamaine Akaidere; 13 Danny Grimshaw; 20 Danny Ansell; 10 James Houston; 9 David March; 16 Lewis Reed; 18 Brooke Broughton; 11 John Oakes; 26 Liam Mackay. Subs (all used): 8 Michael Haley; 15 Luke Stenchion; 24 Aston Wilson; 27 Liam Hood.
Tries: Stenchion (33), Maun (51, 68), Watson (55, 62), Akaidere (78); **Goals:** Ansell 4/6.
OXFORD: 2 Michael Crabtree; 30 Jack Briggs; 5 Callum Mullkeen; 3 Marcus Brooker; 20 Yannic Parker; 18 Jordan Rice; 6 Tommy Connick; 24 Tom Davies; 9 Alex Thompson; 10 Matty Hadden; 11 John James Baird; 13 Valu Bentley; 34 Karl Temata. Subs (all used): 14 Dave Ellison; 36 Ed Hayles; 31 Luke Evans; 17 Rory Sharratt.
Tries: Connick (29), Parker (39); **Goals:** Connick 2/2.
Rugby Leaguer & League Express Men of the Match: *Hawks:* David March; *Oxford:* Yannic Parker.
Penalty count: 11-7; **Half-time:** 6-12; **Referee:** Michael Woodhead; **Attendance:** 417.

OLDHAM 46 LONDON SKOLARS 16

OLDHAM: 4 Steven Nield; 2 Mo Agoro; 21 David Cookson; 25 Jonathan Ford; 5 Dale Bloomfield; 26 Steve Roper; 7 Brett Robinson; 8 Phil Joy; 17 Danny Whitmore; 10 Jason Boults; 11 Josh Crowley; 12 Danny Langtree; 9 Sam Gee. Subs (all used): 16 Kenny Hughes; 19 Michael Ward; 20 George Tyson; 28 Nathan Mason.
Tries: Agoro (10, 37), Crowley (19, 67), Cookson (40), Ford (48), Mason (57), Bloomfield (79); **Goals:** Roper 7/9.
Sin bin: Langtree (28) - fighting; Mason (28) - fighting; Whitmore (71) - fighting.
SKOLARS: 1 Iliess Macani; 31 Judd Greenhalgh; 3 John Paxton; 34 Martin Olima; 14 Jamie O'Callaghan; 7 Courtney Davies; 6 James Kelly; 10 Dave Williams; 9

Martyn Smith; 20 Teli Pelo; 12 Michael Worrincy; 11 Will Lovell; 13 Oliver Purslow. Subs (all used): 8 Ryan MacDonald; 22 Erjon Dollapi; 27 Anthony Cox; 4 Sam Druce.
Tries: Greenhalgh (3), Kelly (24), Pelo (53);
Goals: Kelly 2/3.
Sin bin: Pelo (28) - fighting; Smith (28) - fighting; Davies (71) - fighting.
Rugby Leaguer & League Express Men of the Match: *Oldham:* Mo Agoro; *Skolars:* Courtney Davies.
Penalty count: 9-5; **Half-time:** 22-10;
Referee: Dave Sharpe; **Attendance:** 486.

SOUTH WALES SCORPIONS 36 GLOUCESTERSHIRE ALL GOLDS 38

SCORPIONS: 1 Jordan Sheridan; 4 Kyle Scrivens; 3 Jack Pring; 24 Matthew Wilcox; 5 Chris Leyshon; 6 Paul Emanuelli; 7 Greg Wilde; 23 Richard East; 9 Connor Farrer; 18 Harrison Elliott; 11 Barrie Phillips; 12 Phil Carleton; 10 Chris Vitalini. Subs (all used): 13 Ashley Bateman; 21 Martin Luckwell; 22 Neil Dallimore; 25 Scott Giles.
Tries: Vitalini (11), Wilde (19, 59), Sheridan (42), Farrer (75, 79); **Goals:** Emanuelli 6/6.
ALL GOLDS: 7 Danny Thomas; 2 Jarrod Ward; 3 Phil Cowburn; 4 Aidan Jenkins; 5 Scott Claridge; 6 Ben White; 9 Matt Bradley; 18 James Walter; 19 Craig Cook; 10 Izaak Duffy; 11 Jason Muranka; 12 Miles Fairbank; 13 Brendan Smith. Subs (all used): 14 Joe McClean; 20 Casey Canterbury; 16 Richard Jones; 17 Jack Francis.
Tries: Cowburn (7), Jenkins (24), White (27), Francis (46, 53), Cook (68, 70); **Goals:** Jenkins 0/2, Bradley 5/7.
Rugby Leaguer & League Express Men of the Match: *Scorpions:* Connor Farrer; *All Golds:* Jack Francis.
Penalty count: 6-7; **Half-time:** 12-14;
Referee: Jamie Bloem; **Attendance:** 320.

ROUND 12

Saturday 7th June 2014

LONDON SKOLARS 18 SOUTH WALES SCORPIONS 46

SKOLARS: 1 Iliess Macani; 21 Judd Greenhalgh; 4 Mufaro Mvududu; 34 Martin Olima; 3 John Paxton; 7 Courtney Davies; 6 James Kelly; 31 Teli Pelo; 9 Martyn Smith; 10 Dave Williams; 11 Will Lovell; 12 Michael Worrincy; 13 Oliver Purslow. Subs (all used): 5 Sam Druce; 8 Ryan MacDonald; 20 Erjon Dollapi; 14 Lamont Bryan.
Tries: Lovell (8, 80), Mvududu (31), Smith (47);
Goals: Davies 1/4.
SCORPIONS: 1 Jordan Sheridan; 4 Kyle Scrivens; 3 Jack Pring; 24 Matthew Wilcox; 5 Chris Leyshon; 6 Paul Emanuelli; 7 Greg Wilde; 23 Richard East; 9 Connor Farrer; 18 Harrison Elliott; 14 Mike Connor; 11 Barrie Phillips; 10 Chris Vitalini. Subs (all used): 15 Owain Davies; 22 Neil Dallimore; 13 Ashley Bateman; 16 Osian Phillips.
Tries: Wilcox (5), Connor (15, 73), Scrivens (19), Vitalini (57), Emanuelli (60), Wilde (64), Farrer (76);
Goals: Emanuelli 7/8.
Rugby Leaguer & League Express Men of the Match: *Skolars:* Martyn Smith; *Scorpions:* Paul Emanuelli.
Penalty count: 10-7; **Half-time:** 8-18;
Referee: Michael Woodhead; **Attendance:** 362
(at Queen Elizabeth II Stadium, Enfield).

Sunday 8th June 2014

HEMEL STAGS 44 OLDHAM 32

STAGS: 2 James Cameron; 17 Jimmy Morgan; 3 Aaron Small; 4 Michael Brown; 5 James Hill; 23 Eddie Mbaraga; 6 Jy-mel Coleman; 8 Dominic Maloney; 14 Evan Simons; 25 James Howitt; 12 Cariern Clement-Pascall; 16 Chris Clough; 10 Dan Ljazouli. Subs (all used): 21 Ben Kavanagh; 18 Romaine Navarrete; 15 Matthew Bailey; 20 Ryan Chester.
Tries: Simons (13), Hill (15, 75), Morgan (26), Clement-Pascall (42), Ljazouli (56), Brown (65);
Goals: Jy-mel Coleman 8/9.
OLDHAM: 4 Steven Nield; 2 Mo Agoro; 21 David Cookson; 25 Jonathan Ford; 5 Dale Bloomfield; 26 Steve Roper; 6 Lewis Palfrey; 10 Jason Boults; 17 Danny Whitmore; 8 Phil Joy; 11 Josh Crowley; 12 Danny Langtree; 9 Sam Gee. Subs (all used): 20 George Tyson; 19 Michael Ward; 16 Kenny Hughes; 28 Nathan Mason.
Tries: Roper (7), Ford (20, 50), Crowley (33), Tyson (53), Agoro (61); **Goals:** Palfrey 4/6.
Rugby Leaguer & League Express Men of the Match: *Stags:* Jy-mel Coleman; *Oldham:* Lewis Palfrey.
Penalty count: 6-4; **Half-time:** 18-16;
Referee: Dave Merrick; **Attendance:** 233.

GLOUCESTERSHIRE ALL GOLDS 24 YORK CITY KNIGHTS 22

ALL GOLDS: 7 Danny Thomas; 4 Aidan Jenkins; 11 Miles Fairbank; 3 Phil Cowburn; 5 Jarrod Ward; 6 Ben White; 9 Matt Bradley; 18 James Walter; 19 Craig Cook; 10 Izaak Duffy; 12 Jason Muranka; 16 Richard Jones; 17 Jack Francis. Subs (all used): 14 Casey Canterbury; 15 Harry Chapman-Walker; 8 Daniel Spencer-Tonks; 13 Frankie Foster.
Tries: Cowburn (25), Jones (39), Muranka (52), Thomas (55); **Goals:** Bradley 4/5.
CITY KNIGHTS: 25 Ben Reynolds; 26 James Saltonstall; 3 Tyler Craig; 4 James Morland; 5 Ben Dent; 6 Pat Smith; 7 Jon Presley; 32 Brad Brennan; 9 Jack Lee; 10 Jack Aldous; 12 Ed Smith; 11 Ryan Mallinder; 28 Joe Pickets. Subs (all used): 29 Ryan Backhouse; 18 Austin Bell; 20 Harry Carter; 35 Colton Roche.
Tries: Morland (9), Presley (14), B Dent (22), Lee (68);
Goals: Reynolds 3/4.
Rugby Leaguer & League Express Men of the Match: *All Golds:* Danny Thomas; *City Knights:* Jon Presley.
Penalty count: 8-6; **Half-time:** 12-16;
Referee: Peter Brooke; **Attendance:** 318.

OXFORD 22 GATESHEAD THUNDER 36

OXFORD: 1 Sean Morris; 30 Jack Briggs; 5 Callum Mulkeen; 3 Marcus Brooker; 2 Michael Crabtree; 7 Jimmy Rowland; 6 Tommy Connick; 34 Karl Temata; 17 Rory Sharratt; 10 Matty Hadden; 11 John James Baird; 12 Andrew Hoggins; 18 Jordan Rice. Subs (all used): 14 Dave Ellison; 15 Glenn Osborn; 13 Valu Bentley; 36 Ed Hayles.
Tries: Sharratt (19), Mulkeen (43), S Morris (57, 75);
Goals: Connick 3/4.
Sin bin: Rowland (48) - fighting.
THUNDER: 22 Louis Sheriff; 1 Lee Mapals; 4 Joe Brown; 24 Chris Heil; 3 Jacob Blades; 26 Matty Beharrell; 27 Jamie Rooney; 14 Matt Barron; 6 Paul Stamp; 30 Ricky Hough; 12 Jason Payne; 13 Sam Bowring; 29 Sonny Esslemont. Subs (all used): 19 Josh Stoker; 18 Iain Murray; 28 Joel Farrell; 21 Joe Hodgson.
Tries: Sheriff (10), Blades (23), Brown (29), Rooney (51), Stamp (61), Mapals (64); **Goals:** Beharrell 6/6.
Sin bin: Barron (48) - fighting.
Rugby Leaguer & League Express Men of the Match: *Oxford:* Sean Morris; *Thunder:* Louis Sheriff.
Penalty count: 6-4; **Half-time:** 4-18;
Referee: Chris Kendall; **Attendance:** 310.

ROUND 13

Sunday 15th June 2014

HUNSLET HAWKS 26 HEMEL STAGS 6

HAWKS: 1 Stuart Kain; 21 Jamaine Akaidere; 2 Jimmy Watson; 4 Danny Maun; 3 Lee Brickwood; 13 Danny Grimshaw; 20 Danny Ansell; 10 James Houston; 9 David March; 15 Luke Stenchion; 18 Brooke Broughton; 11 John Oakes; 26 Liam Mackay. Subs (all used): 8 Michael Haley; 33 Andy Yates; 27 Liam Hood; 24 Aston Wilson.
Tries: Oakes (1, 34), Akaidere (7), Mackay (42), Kain (59); **Goals:** Ansell 3/5.
Sin bin: Ansell (74) - fighting.
STAGS: 2 James Cameron; 17 Jimmy Morgan; 3 Aaron Small; 11 Barry-John Swindells; 5 James Hill; 23 Eddie Mbaraga; 6 Jy-mel Coleman; 25 James Howitt; 14 Evan Simons; 18 Romaine Navarrete; 12 Cariern Clement-Pascall; 15 Matthew Bailey; 10 Dan Ljazouli. Subs (all used): 21 Maxime Herold; 16 Guy Aldam; 20 Ryan Chester; 7 Ben Young.
Try: Jy-mel Coleman (52); **Goals:** Swindells 1/1.
Sin bin: Navarrete (74) - fighting.
Rugby Leaguer & League Express Men of the Match: *Hawks:* John Oakes; *Stags:* Evan Simons.
Penalty count: 8-6; **Half-time:** 14-0;
Referee: Dave Sharpe; **Attendance:** 450.

OLDHAM 58 SOUTH WALES SCORPIONS 2

OLDHAM: 4 Steven Nield; 2 Mo Agoro; 21 David Cookson; 25 Jonathan Ford; 5 Dale Bloomfield; 26 Steve Roper; 6 Lewis Palfrey; 8 Phil Joy; 17 Danny Whitmore; 10 Jason Boults; 11 Josh Crowley; 20 George Tyson; 9 Sam Gee. Subs (all used): 16 Kenny Hughes; 19 Michael Ward; 3 Ben Wood; 28 Nathan Mason.
Tries: Nield (14), Wood (27, 77), Agoro (32, 58, 62), Hughes (44), Bloomfield (51), Palfrey (67), Ford (73);
Goals: Palfrey 9/10.
SCORPIONS: 1 Jordan Sheridan; 4 Kyle Scrivens; 12 Phil Carleton; 24 Matthew Wilcox; 5 Chris Leyshon; 6 Paul Emanuelli; 7 Greg Wilde; 25 Scott Giles; 9 Connor Farrer; 18 Harrison Elliott; 14 Mike Connor; 11 Barrie Phillips; 10 Chris Vitalini. Subs (all used): 13 Ashley Bateman; 23 Richard East; 16 Osian Phillips; 22 Dafydd Hellard.
Goals: Emanuelli 1/1.
Rugby Leaguer & League Express Men of the Match: *Oldham:* George Tyson; *Scorpions:* Connor Farrer.
Penalty count: 2-3; **Half-time:** 18-2;
Referee: Chris Campbell; **Attendance:** 408.

OXFORD 28 LONDON SKOLARS 52

OXFORD: 1 Sean Morris; 30 Jack Briggs; 5 Callum Mulkeen; 3 Marcus Brooker; 2 Michael Crabtree; 18 Jordan Rice; 6 Tommy Connick; 34 Karl Temata; 9 Alex Thompson; 10 Matty Hadden; 11 John James Baird; 12 Andrew Hoggins; 13 Valu Bentley. Subs (all used): 17 Rory Sharratt; 15 Glenn Osborn; 36 Ed Hayles; 16 Sam Blaney.
Tries: Thompson (13), Connick (31), Blaney (43), S Morris (57), Briggs (61); **Goals:** Connick 4/6.
SKOLARS: 1 John Paxton; 34 Judd Greenhalgh; 4 Mufaro Mvududu; 14 Denny Solomona; 30 James Duckworth; 6 Courtney Davies; 7 Mike Bishay; 10 Dave Williams; 9 Martyn Smith; 20 Erjon Dollapi; 12 Mike McMeeken; 11 Anthony Cox; 13 Oliver Purslow. Subs (all used): 8 Ryan MacDonald; 19 Sam Druce; 21 Michael Sykes; 22 Lamont Bryan.
Tries: Bishay (10, 46), Williams (18, 74), Duckworth (27), Solomona (35, 65, 71), Bryan (68);
Goals: Davies 8/10.
Rugby Leaguer & League Express Men of the Match: *Oxford:* Sean Morris; *Skolars:* Mike Bishay.
Penalty count: 7-10; **Half-time:** 12-22;
Referee: Peter Brooke; **Attendance:** 316.

YORK CITY KNIGHTS 42 GATESHEAD THUNDER 16

CITY KNIGHTS: 1 James Haynes; 25 James Saltonstall; 27 Tyler Craig; 12 Ed Smith; 5 Ben Dent; 6 Pat Smith; 23 Benn Hardcastle; 32 Brad Brennan; 9 Jack Lee; 18 Austin Bell; 11 Ryan Mallinder; 28 Colton Roche; 10 Jack Aldous. Subs (all used): 20 Harry Carter; 26 Joe Pickets; 29 Ryan Backhouse; 16 Iain Morrison.
Tries: Bell (16), Roche (24), Lee (34), Craig (48), Aldous (52), E Smith (61), Pickets (78);
Goals: B Hardcastle 7/7.
THUNDER: 27 Louis Sheriff; 1 Lee Mapals; 4 Joe Brown; 29 Kris Welham; 3 Jacob Blades; 26 Matty Beharrell; 7 Jamie Rooney; 14 Matt Barron; 6 Paul Stamp; 30 Ricky Hough; 12 Jason Payne; 16 Joel Farrell; 28 Sonny Esslemont. Subs (all used): 19 Josh Stoker; 10 Lee Fewlass; 24 Chris Heil; 13 Sam Bowring.
Tries: Blades (8), Esslemont (18), Payne (39);
Goals: Beharrell 2/3.
Rugby Leaguer & League Express Men of the Match: *City Knights:* Jack Aldous; *Thunder:* Jason Payne.
Penalty count: 8-9; **Half-time:** 18-16;
Referee: Adam Gill; **Attendance:** 495.

ROUND 14

Saturday 21st June 2014

SOUTH WALES SCORPIONS 10 YORK CITY KNIGHTS 48

SCORPIONS: 1 Jordan Sheridan; 2 Ian Newbury; 3 Jack Pring; 24 Matthew Wilcox; 4 Kyle Scrivens; 6 Paul Emanuelli; 21 Greg Wilde; 23 Richard East; 9 Connor Farrer; 10 Chris Vitalini; 15 Owain Davies; 14 Mike Connor; 13 Ashley Bateman. Subs (all used): 7 Shaun Owens; 18 Harrison Elliott; 16 Osian Phillips; 25 Harry Cartwright.
Tries: Pring (11), Connor (47); **Goals:** Emanuelli 1/2.
CITY KNIGHTS: 1 James Haynes; 25 James Saltonstall; 3 James Ford; 27 Tyler Craig; 5 Ben Dent; 26 Ben Reynolds; 6 Pat Smith; 34 Brad Brennan; 9 Jack Lee; 28 Colton Roche; 29 Ryan Backhouse; 12 Ed Smith; 30 Joe Pickets. Subs (all used): 14 Kris Brining; 20 Harry Carter; 16 Iain Morrison; 24 Nathan Harper.
Tries: B Dent (2, 25, 54), Roche (8), Ford (18, 61), Lee (35), Haynes (66), Reynolds (70);
Goals: Reynolds 6/9.
Rugby Leaguer & League Express Men of the Match: *Scorpions:* Mike Connor; *City Knights:* Ben Reynolds.
Penalty count: 8-5; **Half-time:** 4-24;
Referee: Dave Sharpe; **Attendance:** 225
(at Glan-Yr-Afon Park, Blackwood).

Sunday 22nd June 2014

GATESHEAD THUNDER 14 OLDHAM 32

THUNDER: 27 Louis Sheriff; 2 Lee Mapals; 4 Joe Brown; 24 Chris Heil; 3 Jacob Blades; 26 Matty Beharrell; 7 Jamie Rooney; 14 Matt Barron; 6 Paul Stamp; 10 Lee Fewlass; 29 Joel Farrell; 12 Jason Payne; 30 Ricky Hough. Subs (all used): 15 Jordan Meads; 17 Alex Ruff; 11 Rhys Clarke; 19 Josh Stoker.
Tries: Heil (6), Stamp (8), Payne (20);
Goals: Beharrell 1/3.
OLDHAM: 4 Steven Nield; 2 Mo Agoro; 21 David Cookson; 25 Jonathan Ford; 5 Dale Bloomfield; 6 Lewis Palfrey; 26 Steve Roper; 10 Jason Boults; 17 Danny Whitmore; 8 Phil Joy; 11 Josh Crowley; 12 Danny Langtree; 9 Sam Gee. Subs (all used): 16 Kenny Hughes; 3 Ben Wood; 19 Michael Ward; 28 Nathan Mason.
Tries: Bloomfield (2), Crowley (36), Agoro (50, 55), Palfrey (59), Ford (70); **Goals:** Palfrey 4/6.
Sin bin: Whitmore (17) - punching.
Rugby Leaguer & League Express Men of the Match: *Thunder:* Matt Barron; *Oldham:* Lewis Palfrey.
Penalty count: 7-8; **Half-time:** 14-12;
Referee: Andrew Sweet; **Attendance:** 253.

GLOUCESTERSHIRE ALL GOLDS 36 OXFORD 20

ALL GOLDS: 7 Danny Thomas; 2 Jarrod Ward; 3 Sam Te'o; 5 Phil Cowburn; 4 Aidan Jenkins; 6 Matt Bradley; 9 Ben White; 10 Izaak Duffy; 19 Craig Cook; 17 Miles Fairbank; 11 Richard Jones; 12 Jason Muranka; 13 Brendan Smith. Subs (all used): 14 Casey Canterbury; 15 Harry Chapman-Walker; 16 Joe McClean; 20 Frankie Foster.
Tries: Cook (9), Bradley (16), White (23), Fairbank (62), Foster (65), Thomas (71); **Goals:** Bradley 6/6.
OXFORD: 1 Sean Morris; 30 Jack Briggs; 5 Callum Mulkeen; 3 Marcus Brooker; 2 Michael Crabtree; 7 Jimmy Rowland; 6 Tommy Connick; 34 Karl Temata; 9 Alex Thompson; 15 Glenn Osborn; 11 John James Baird; 16 Sam Blaney; 13 Valu Bentley. Subs (all used): 17 Rory Sharratt; 12 Andrew Hoggins; 24 Tom Davies; 18 Jordan Rice.
Tries: Connick (30), Briggs (49, 78), Davies (56);
Goals: Connick 1/2, Rowland 1/2.
Rugby Leaguer & League Express Men of the Match: *All Golds:* Matt Bradley; *Oxford:* Rory Sharratt.
Penalty count: 4-5; **Half-time:** 18-6;
Referee: Adam Gill; **Attendance:** 323.

ROUND 15

Sunday 29th June 2014

LONDON SKOLARS 6 GATESHEAD THUNDER 66

SKOLARS: 1 John Paxton; 33 Courtney Davies; 4 Mufaro Mvududu; 3 Kazeem Fatouri; 32 Dennis Tuffour; 6 Danny

Yates; 7 Mike Bishay; 20 Teli Pelo; 9 Martyn Smith; 10 Dave Williams; 11 Anthony Cox; 12 Mike McMeeken; 13 Oliver Purslow. Subs (all used): 8 Ryan MacDonald; 16 Sam Druce; 31 Lamont Bryan; 22 Michael Sykes.
Try: Druce (42); **Goals:** Davies 1/1.
THUNDER: 1 Louis Sheriff; 30 Mick Butterfield; 24 Chris Heil; 4 Joe Brown; 5 Tom Capper; 15 Jordan Meads; 7 Jamie Rooney; 29 Ricky Hough; 6 Paul Stamp; 14 Matt Barron; 22 Joel Farrell; 12 Jason Payne; 28 Sonny Esslemont. Subs (all used): 11 Rhys Clarke; 26 George Clarke; 19 Josh Stoker; 10 Lee Fewlass.
Tries: Esslemont (3), Stamp (10), Farrell (17), Rooney (19, 31), Payne (21), Butterfield (39), Sheriff (48, 52, 75), G Clarke (56), Hough (72), Meads (80); **Goals:** Rooney 4/7, Meads 2/4, Stamp 1/2.
Rugby Leaguer & League Express Men of the Match: *Skolars:* Martyn Smith; *Thunder:* Paul Stamp.
Penalty count: 6-11; **Half-time:** 0-36;
Referee: Tom Grant; **Attendance:** 206
(at Queen Elizabeth II Stadium, Enfield).

HEMEL STAGS 22 YORK CITY KNIGHTS 46

STAGS: 2 James Cameron; 17 Jimmy Morgan; 3 Mathew Cook; 4 Michael Brown; 5 James Hill; 6 Jy-mel Coleman; 23 Eddie Mbaraga; 8 Dominic Maloney; 14 Evan Simons; 25 James Howitt; 12 Cariern Clement-Pascall; 11 Barry-John Swindells; - Chris Clough. Subs (all used): 16 Maxime Herold; 15 Matthew Bailey; 20 Ryan Chester; 18 Matthew Tebb.
Tries: Cook (10), Chester (49), Mbaraga (75), Hill (80);
Goals: Swindells 2/2, Cook 1/1, Jy-mel Coleman 0/1.
CITY KNIGHTS: 1 James Haynes; 4 Greg Minikin; 3 James Ford; 27 James Morland; 25 James Saltonstall; 26 Ben Reynolds; 6 Pat Smith; 34 Brad Brennan; 9 Jack Lee; 10 Jack Aldous; 28 Ryan Backhouse; 12 Ed Smith; 30 Joe Pickets. Subs (all used): 14 Kris Brining; 11 Ryan Mallinder; 29 Tyler Craig; 24 Nathan Harper.
Tries: Backhouse (5), Lee (17, 70), P Smith (45, 60), Mallinder (53), Morland (56), Minikin (63);
Goals: Reynolds 7/8.
Rugby Leaguer & League Express Men of the Match: *Stags:* Jy-mel Coleman; *City Knights:* Pat Smith.
Penalty count: 5-4; **Half-time:** 6-12;
Referee: Chris Campbell; **Attendance:** 227.

HUNSLET HAWKS 16 GLOUCESTERSHIRE ALL GOLDS 23

HAWKS: 1 Stuart Kain; 36 Gavin Duffy; 24 Aston Wilson; 4 Danny Maun; 3 Lee Brickwood; 7 James Coyle; 20 Danny Ansell; 10 James Houston; 6 Thomas Coyle; 8 Michael Haley; 18 Brooke Broughton; 11 John Oakes; 26 Liam Mackay. Subs (all used): 27 Liam Hood; 12 Aaron Lyons; 16 Lewis Reed; 38 Liam Walmsley.
Tries: Maun (21), Hood (49), Oakes (60);
Goals: Ansell 2/3.
ALL GOLDS: 7 Danny Thomas; 5 Scott Claridge; 4 Phil Cowburn; 3 Sam Te'o; 2 Jarrod Ward; 9 Ben White; 6 Matt Bradley; 17 Miles Fairbank; 19 Craig Cook; 10 Izaak Duffy; 12 Jason Muranka; 11 Richard Jones; 13 Brendan Smith. Subs (all used): 8 Mike Stewart; 18 James Walter; 16 Joe McClean; 20 Frankie Foster.
Tries: Jones (14), Cook (26), White (32), Te'o (56);
Goals: Bradley 3/4; **Field goal:** Cook (75).
Rugby Leaguer & League Express Men of the Match: *Hawks:* Stuart Kain; *All Golds:* Craig Cook.
Penalty count: 5-6; **Half-time:** 6-16;
Referee: Dave Sharpe; **Attendance:** 430.

OXFORD 22 OLDHAM 38

OXFORD: 1 Sean Morris; 30 Jack Briggs; 5 Callum Mulkeen; 3 Marcus Brooker; 2 Michael Crabtree; 7 Jimmy Rowland; 6 Tommy Connick; 14 Dave Ellison; 9 Alex Thompson; 15 Glenn Osborn; 11 John James Baird; 12 Andrew Hoggins; 18 Jordan Rice. Subs (all used): 24 Tom Davies; 17 Rory Sharratt; 36 Ed Hayles; 16 Sam Blaney.
Tries: Crabtree (14, 71), S Morris (31), Hoggins (51);
Goals: Rowland 3/4.
OLDHAM: 4 Steven Nield; 2 Mo Agoro; 21 David Cookson; 25 Jonathan Ford; 5 Dale Bloomfield; 6 Lewis Palfrey; 26 Steve Roper; 10 Jason Boults; 17 Danny Whitmore; 8 Phil Joy; 11 Josh Crowley; 12 Danny Langtree; 9 Sam Gee. Subs (all used): 16 Kenny Hughes; 3 Ben Wood; 19 Michael Ward; 28 Nathan Mason.
Tries: Agoro (7), Crowley (21), Langtree (24, 57), Bloomfield (41, 76), Wood (43), Cookson (65);
Goals: Palfrey 3/8.
Rugby Leaguer & League Express Men of the Match: *Oxford:* John James Baird; *Oldham:* Danny Langtree.
Penalty count: 7-5; **Half-time:** 10-14;
Referee: Peter Brooke; **Attendance:** 256.

ROUND 16

Friday 4th July 2014

GATESHEAD THUNDER 6 HUNSLET HAWKS 45

THUNDER: 27 Louis Sheriff; 30 Mick Butterfield; 4 Joe Brown; 24 Chris Heil; 5 Tom Capper; 15 Jordan Meads; 6 Paul Stamp; 14 Matt Barron; 29 Ricky Hough; 10 Lee Fewlass; 22 Joel Farrell; 12 Jason Payne; 11 Rhys Clarke. Subs (all used): 20 Connor Condron; 18 Iain Murray; 19 Josh Stoker; 3 Jacob Blades.
Try: Meads (63); **Goals:** Meads 1/1.
HAWKS: 2 Jimmy Watson; 36 Gavin Duffy; 3 Lee Brickwood; 4 Danny Maun; 28 Andy Ballard; 13 Danny Grimshaw; 7 James Coyle; 10 James Houston; 6 Thomas Coyle; 8 Michael Haley; 26 Liam Mackay; 11 John Oakes; 9 David March. Subs (all used): 27 Liam Hood; 16 Lewis Reed; 24 Aston Wilson; 15 Luke Stenchion.
Tries: Maun (6), Hood (34), Stenchion (36), Ballard (48), Watson (70), Mackay (73), Haley (76);
Goals: Ballard 8/8; **Field goal:** T Coyle (80).
Rugby Leaguer & League Express Men of the Match: *Thunder:* Jordan Meads; *Hawks:* Danny Grimshaw.
Penalty count: 5-9; **Half-time:** 0-18;
Referee: Andrew Sweet; **Attendance:** 457.

Saturday 5th July 2014

SOUTH WALES SCORPIONS 16 OXFORD 36

SCORPIONS: 1 Jordan Sheridan; 2 Ian Newbury; 3 Jack Pring; 4 Kyle Scrivens; 5 Chris Leyshon; 6 Paul Emanuelli; 12 Phil Carleton; 23 Richard East; 9 Connor Farrer; 15 Owain Davies; 11 Barrie Phillips; 14 Mike Connor; 13 Ashley Bateman. Subs (all used): 22 Neil Dallimore; 7 Shaun Owens; 18 Harrison Elliott; 24 Morgan Evans.
Tries: Owens (24), B Phillips (37), Leyshon (45);
Goals: Emanuelli 2/5.
OXFORD: 2 Michael Crabtree; 30 Jack Briggs; 3 Marcus Brooker; 20 Yannic Parker; 5 Callum Mulkeen; 6 Tommy Connick; 7 Jimmy Rowland; 24 Tom Davies; 9 Alex Thompson; 15 Glenn Osborn; 36 Ed Hayles; 12 Andrew Hoggins; 18 Jordan Rice. Subs (all used): 14 Dave Ellison; 16 Sam Blaney; 17 Rory Sharratt; 31 Edd Vickers.
Tries: Hoggins (10), Rowland (16), Brooker (21), Briggs (28), Osborn (62), Parker (67), Thompson (75);
Goals: Rowland 1/3, Connick 3/5.
Rugby Leaguer & League Express Men of the Match: *Scorpions:* Chris Leyshon; *Oxford:* Alex Thompson.
Penalty count: 6-9; **Half-time:** 12-18;
Referee: Dave Sharpe; **Attendance:** 150.

Sunday 6th July 2014

GLOUCESTERSHIRE ALL GOLDS 14 HEMEL STAGS 22

ALL GOLDS: 7 Danny Thomas; 2 Scott Claridge; 3 Jarrod Ward; 5 Phil Cowburn; 4 Aidan Jenkins; 6 Ben White; 9 Matt Bradley; 10 Izaak Duffy; 19 Craig Cook; 12 Miles Fairbank; 11 Jason Muranka; 17 Sam Te'o; 13 Brendan Smith. Subs (all used): 14 Casey Canterbury; 8 Mike Stewart; 16 Frankie Foster; 18 James Walter.
Tries: Jenkins (25, 37), Cowburn (33);
Goals: Bradley 1/3.
STAGS: 2 James Cameron; 17 Jimmy Morgan; 3 Mathew Cook; 4 Michael Brown; 5 James Hill; 6 Jy-mel Coleman; - Jermaine Coleman; 25 James Howitt; 14 Evan Simons; 8 Dominic Maloney; - Mike McMeeken; 11 Barry-John Swindells; 23 Eddie Mbaraga. Subs (all used): 16 Romaine Navarrete; 10 Dan Ljazouli; 20 Ryan Chester; 18 Matthew Tebb.
Tries: Swindells (8), Cameron (14), Mbaraga (21), Hill (57); **Goals:** Swindells 3/5.
Rugby Leaguer & League Express Men of the Match: *All Golds:* Aidan Jenkins; *Stags:* Jy-mel Coleman.
Penalty count: 10-3; **Half-time:** 14-16;
Referee: Adam Gill; **Attendance:** 168.

LONDON SKOLARS 20 YORK CITY KNIGHTS 30

SKOLARS: 1 John Paxton; 3 Courtney Davies; 21 Judd Greenhalgh; 4 Mufaro Mvududu; 34 James Duckworth; 6 Danny Yates; 7 Mike Bishay; 22 Michael Sykes; 16 Sam Druce; 20 Teli Pelo; 11 Anthony Cox; 31 Lamont Bryan; 10 Dave Williams. Subs (all used): 8 Ryan MacDonald; 13 Louis Robinson; 9 Martyn Smith; 12 Dion Chapman.
Tries: Duckworth (50), Greenhalgh (56), Mvududu (78), Yates (80); **Goals:** Davies 2/4.
CITY KNIGHTS: 1 James Haynes; 5 Ben Dent; 3 James Ford; 4 Greg Minikin; 25 James Saltonstall; 6 Pat Smith; 26 Ben Reynolds; 34 Brad Brennan; 9 Jack Lee; 10 Jack Aldous; 11 Ryan Mallinder; 31 Ryan Backhouse; 28 Joe Pickets. Subs (all used): 14 Kris Brining; 29 Colton Roche; 13 Lee Paterson; 30 Brad Day.
Tries: Lee (19), P Smith (28), Day (38, 44), Roche (41);
Goals: Reynolds 5/5.
Rugby Leaguer & League Express Men of the Match: *Skolars:* Louis Robinson; *City Knights:* James Haynes.
Penalty count: 9-5; **Half-time:** 0-18;
Referee: Michael Woodhead; **Attendance:** 465
(at Queen Elizabeth II Stadium, Enfield).

ROUND 17

Sunday 13th July 2014

HUNSLET HAWKS 74 SOUTH WALES SCORPIONS 0

HAWKS: 2 Jimmy Watson; 3 Lee Brickwood; 24 Aston Wilson; 4 Danny Maun; 28 Andy Ballard; 13 Danny Grimshaw; 20 Danny Ansell; 10 James Houston; 27 Liam Hood; 8 Michael Haley; 9 David March; 11 John Oakes; 26 Liam Mackay. Subs (all used): 1 Stuart Kain; 15 Luke Stenchion; 16 Lewis Reed; 18 Brooke Broughton.
Tries: Watson (2, 52, 55), Hood (11, 40), Wilson (30, 49), March (34), Mackay (42), Oakes (46, 80), Reed (57), Houston (78); **Goals:** Ballard 11/13.
SCORPIONS: 1 Jordan Sheridan; 2 Ian Newbury; 3 Jack Pring; 22 Dafydd Hellard; 5 Chris Leyshon; 6 Paul Emanuelli; 12 Phil Carleton; 18 Harrison Elliott; 9 Connor Farrer; 10 Chris Vitalini; 11 Barrie Phillips; 4 Kyle Scrivens; 13 Ashley Bateman. Subs (all used): 21 Dan Parry; 25 Morgan Evans; 23 Richard East; 24 Harry Cartwright.
Rugby Leaguer & League Express Men of the Match: *Hawks:* Jimmy Watson; *Scorpions:* Kyle Scrivens.
Penalty count: 6-4; **Half-time:** 26-0;
Referee: Adam Gill; **Attendance:** 456.

LONDON SKOLARS 34 HEMEL STAGS 28

SKOLARS: 1 John Paxton; 32 Iliess Macani; 21 Judd Greenhalgh; 4 Mufaro Mvududu; 34 James Duckworth; 6 Courtney Davies; 7 Danny Yates; 22 Michael Sykes; 9 Martyn Smith; 20 Teli Pelo; 12 Dion Chapman; 31 Lamont Bryan; 10 Dave Williams. Subs (all used): 8 Ryan MacDonald; 13 Louis Robinson; 16 Mike Bishay; 11 Anthony Cox.
Tries: Cox (20, 32), Mvududu (28), Davies (36), Bishay (40), MacDonald (41);
Goals: Davies 1/3, Bishay 4/4.
STAGS: 2 James Cameron; 17 Jimmy Morgan; 4 Michael Brown; 3 Mathew Cook; 5 James Hill; - Jermaine Coleman; 6 Jy-mel Coleman; 25 James Howitt; 14 Evan Simons; 8 Dominic Maloney; 11 Barry-John Swindells; 15 Mike McMeeken; 10 Dan Ljazouli. Subs (all used): 18 Matthew Tebb; 20 Ryan Chester; 21 Romaine Navarrete; 12 Cariern Clement-Pascall.
Tries: Cameron (5, 69), Simons (14), Hill (25, 62), Navarrete (50); **Goals:** Swindells 2/6.
Rugby Leaguer & League Express Men of the Match: *Skolars:* Anthony Cox; *Stags:* Evan Simons.
Penalty count: 7-6; **Half-time:** 26-14;
Referee: Gareth Hewer; **Attendance:** 378
(at Queen Elizabeth II Stadium, Enfield).

OLDHAM 46 GLOUCESTERSHIRE ALL GOLDS 6

OLDHAM: 4 Steven Nield; 2 Mo Agoro; 21 David Cookson; 25 Jonathan Ford; 5 Dale Bloomfield; 26 Steve Roper; 6 Lewis Palfrey; 8 Phil Joy; 9 Sam Gee; 10 Jason Boults; 11 Josh Crowley; 12 Danny Langtree; 22 Liam Thompson. Subs (all used): 16 Kenny Hughes; 19 Michael Ward; 3 Ben Wood; 28 Nathan Mason.
Tries: Joy (14), Palfrey (32, 79), Agoro (40), Bloomfield (42, 60, 68), Ward (53), Wood (77);
Goals: Palfrey 5/9.
ALL GOLDS: 7 Danny Thomas; 2 Jarrod Ward; 16 Sam Te'o; 1 Phil Cowburn; 5 Scott Claridge; 6 Ben White; 9 Matt Bradley; 18 James Walter; 19 Craig Cook; 12 Miles Fairbank; 11 Jason Muranka; 17 Richard Jones; 13 Brendan Smith. Subs (all used): 20 Casey Canterbury; 8 Frankie Foster; 15 Harry Chapman-Walker; 14 Joe McClean.
Try: White (37); **Goals:** Bradley 1/1.
Rugby Leaguer & League Express Men of the Match: *Oldham:* Josh Crowley; *All Golds:* Jarrod Ward.
Penalty count: 6-6; **Half-time:** 14-6;
Referee: Jamie Bloem; **Attendance:** 516.

OXFORD 16 YORK CITY KNIGHTS 58

OXFORD: 31 Sam Egerton; 20 Yannic Parker; 5 Callum Mulkeen; 3 Marcus Brooker; 30 Jack Briggs; 18 Jordan Rice; 6 Tommy Connick; 16 Sam Blaney; 17 Rory Sharratt; 24 Tom Davies; 11 John James Baird; 12 Andrew Hoggins; 9 Alex Thompson. Subs (all used): 36 Ed Hayles; 27 Wes Newton; 32 Edd Vickers; 34 Luke Evans.
Tries: Egerton (6), Thompson (56, 68);
Goals: Connick 2/3.
CITY KNIGHTS: 1 James Haynes; 25 James Saltonstall; 3 James Ford; 28 Brad Day; 5 Ben Dent; 26 Ben Reynolds; 6 Pat Smith; 29 Colton Roche; 9 Jack Lee; 10 Jack Aldous; 11 Ryan Mallinder; 12 Ed Smith; 30 Joe Pickets. Subs (all used): 14 Kris Brining; 13 Lee Paterson; 34 Jay Leary; 31 Ryan Backhouse.
Tries: B Dent (3, 36), Day (12, 28, 76), Lee (16), Brining (44), Saltonstall (50), Ford (58), E Smith (63);
Goals: Reynolds 9/10.
Rugby Leaguer & League Express Men of the Match: *Oxford:* Alex Thompson; *City Knights:* Ben Reynolds.
Penalty count: 4-4; **Half-time:** 4-28;
Referee: Dave Merrick; **Attendance:** 172
(at Dry Leas, Henley).

ROUND 18

Sunday 20th July 2014

HEMEL STAGS 40 SOUTH WALES SCORPIONS 10

STAGS: 2 James Cameron; 5 James Hill; 4 Michael Brown; 3 Mathew Cook; 17 Jimmy Morgan; - Jermaine Coleman; 6 Jy-mel Coleman; 8 Dominic Maloney; 18 Matthew Tebb; 10 Dan Ljazouli; 11 Barry-John Swindells; 12 Cariern Clement-Pascall; 13 Alex Ingarfield. Subs (all used): 14 Evan Simons; 20 Ryan Chester; 25 James Howitt; 19 Malikhi Lloyd-Jones.
Tries: Tebb (2), Hill (9, 59), Cook (13), Morgan (28, 75), Jy-mel Coleman (40); **Goals:** Swindells 6/7.
SCORPIONS: 1 Jordan Sheridan; 5 Chris Leyshon; 3 Jack Pring; 22 Dafydd Hellard; 4 Kyle Scrivens; 21 Dan Parry; 6 Paul Emanuelli; 10 Chris Vitalini; 25 Harry Cartwright; 18 Harrison Elliott; 11 Barrie Phillips; 12 Phil Carleton; 13 Ashley Bateman. Subs (all used): 19 Neil Dallimore; 14 Lloyd O'Connor; 23 Richard East; 24 Morgan Evans.
Tries: O'Connor (43), Scrivens (51); **Goals:** Emanuelli 1/2.
Rugby Leaguer & League Express Men of the Match: *Stags:* Jimmy Morgan; *Scorpions:* Lloyd O'Connor.
Penalty count: 11-9; **Half-time:** 28-0;
Referee: Michael Woodhead; **Attendance:** 176.

GLOUCESTERSHIRE ALL GOLDS 22 GATESHEAD THUNDER 28

ALL GOLDS: 7 Danny Thomas; 2 Scott Claridge; 3 Phil Cowburn; 4 Aidan Jenkins; 5 Jarrod Ward; 6 Ben White; 9 Matt Bradley; - Joe McClean; 19 Craig Cook; 12 Miles Fairbank; 11 Jason Muranka; 17 Sam Te'o; 13 Brendan Smith. Subs (all used): 14 Casey Canterbury; 15 Harry Chapman-Walker; 8 Mike Stewart; 18 Daniel Spencer-Tonks.

Tries: Claridge (40), Te'o (50), Ward (53, 71);
Goals: Bradley 3/4.
THUNDER: 27 Greg Eden; 2 Lee Mapals; 24 Chris Heil; 4 Joe Brown; 5 Tom Capper; 26 Matty Beharrell; 7 Benn Hardcastle; 14 Matt Barron; 6 Paul Stamp; 28 George Clarke; 11 Rhys Clarke; 12 Jason Payne; 30 Sonny Esslemont. Subs: 29 Ricky Hough; 18 Iain Murray; 19 Josh Stoker; 15 Jordan Meads (not used).
Tries: Stamp (5, 28), Brown (60), R Clarke (63, 78);
Goals: Hardcastle 3/4, Beharrell 1/1.
Rugby Leaguer & League Express Men of the Match:
All Golds: Sam Te'o; *Thunder:* Rhys Clarke.
Penalty count: 6-4; **Half-time:** 6-12;
Referee: Dave Sharpe; **Attendance:** 126.

YORK CITY KNIGHTS 54 OLDHAM 12

CITY KNIGHTS: 1 James Haynes; 25 James Saltonstall; 3 James Ford; 27 Brad Day; 5 Ben Dent; 6 Pat Smith; 26 Ben Reynolds; 34 Jay Leary; 9 Jack Lee; 10 Jack Aldous; 11 Ryan Mallinder; 12 Ed Smith; 29 Colton Roche. Subs (all used): 14 Kris Brining; 13 Lee Paterson; 28 Joe Pickets; 30 Ryan Backhouse.
Tries: P Smith (3, 43, 53), Lee (7), Saltonstall (19), B Dent (24), Reynolds (29), Aldous (38), Pickets (73);
Goals: Reynolds 9/9.
OLDHAM: 4 Steven Nield; 27 Adam Clay; 21 David Cookson; 24 Edwin Okanga-Ajwang; 5 Dale Bloomfield; 6 Lewis Palfrey; 26 Steve Roper; 8 Phil Joy; 9 Sam Gee; 10 Jason Boults; 11 Josh Crowley; 12 Danny Langtree; 22 Liam Thompson. Subs (all used): 17 Danny Whitmore; 19 Michael Ward; 3 Ben Wood; 20 George Tyson.
Tries: Cookson (33), Bloomfield (79); **Goals:** Palfrey 2/2.
Rugby Leaguer & League Express Men of the Match:
City Knights: Ben Reynolds; *Oldham:* Danny Langtree.
Penalty count: 7-4; **Half-time:** 36-6;
Referee: Tom Crashley; **Attendance:** 1,006.

ROUND 19

Sunday 27th July 2014

GATESHEAD THUNDER 48 OXFORD 28

THUNDER: 15 Jordan Meads; 2 Lee Mapals; 24 Chris Heil; 4 Joe Brown; 3 Jacob Blades; 26 Matty Beharrell; 9 Benn Hardcastle; 14 Matt Barron; 6 Paul Stamp; 29 Ricky Hough; 12 Jason Payne; 11 Rhys Clarke; 30 Sonny Esslemont. Subs (all used): 10 Lee Fewlass; 19 Josh Stoker; 13 Sam Bowring; 21 Joe Hodgson.
Tries: Brown (21), Hardcastle (25, 40), Payne (47, 74), Stoker (52), Esslemont (55), Hodgson (80);
Goals: Hardcastle 8/8.
OXFORD: 1 Sean Morris; 20 Yannic Parker; 5 Callum Mulkeen; 3 Marcus Brooker; 2 Michael Crabtree; 7 Jimmy Rowland; 6 Tommy Connick; 24 Tom Davies; 17 Rory Sharratt; 34 Luke Evans; 12 Andrew Hoggins; 9 Alex Thompson; 18 Jordan Rice. Subs (all used): 27 Wes Newton; 30 Jonny Morris; 31 Edd Vickers; 36 Ed Hayles.
Tries: Thompson (13), Crabtree (30), Rowland (37), Brooker (58), S Morris (65), Parker (74);
Goals: Rowland 2/5, Connick 0/1.
Rugby Leaguer & League Express Men of the Match:
Thunder: Matty Beharrell; *Oxford:* Jimmy Rowland.
Penalty count: 2-6; **Half-time:** 18-14;
Referee: Jamie Bloom; **Attendance:** 153.

OLDHAM 24 HUNSLET HAWKS 23

OLDHAM: 4 Steven Nield; 2 Mo Agoro; 21 David Cookson; 25 Jonathan Ford; 27 Adam Clay; 26 Steve Roper; 6 Lewis Palfrey; 8 Phil Joy; - Gareth Owen; 10 Jason Boults; 11 Josh Crowley; 12 Danny Langtree; 22 Liam Thompson. Subs (all used): 7 Brett Robinson; 19 Michael Ward; 3 Ben Wood; 20 George Tyson.
Tries: Clay (4), Nield (26), Robinson (33), Langtree (72), Crowley (77); **Goals:** Palfrey 2/5.
Sin bin: Tyson (68) - fighting.
On report: Ward (59) - alleged late tackle; Langtree (68) - challenge on Haley.
HAWKS: 2 Jimmy Watson; 36 Gavin Duffy; 3 Lee Brickwood; 4 Danny Maun; 28 Andy Ballard; 13 Danny Grimshaw; 6 Thomas Coyle; 10 James Houston; 9 David March; 8 Michael Haley; 12 Aaron Lyons; 11 John Oakes; 26 Liam Mackay. Subs (all used): 23 Chris Clough; 15 Luke Stenchion; 16 Lewis Reed; 14 Matthew Tebb.
Tries: Grimshaw (17), Brickwood (50), Watson (60), Houston (63); **Goals:** Ballard 3/4;
Field goal: T Coyle (71).
Sin bin: Haley (68) - fighting.
On report: Haley (68) - alleged retaliation.
Rugby Leaguer & League Express Men of the Match:
Oldham: Lewis Palfrey; *Hawks:* Jimmy Watson.
Penalty count: 10-6; **Half-time:** 16-6;
Referee: Warren Turley; **Attendance:** 678.

SOUTH WALES SCORPIONS 19 LONDON SKOLARS 18

SCORPIONS: 1 Jordan Sheridan; 2 Ian Newbury; 3 Jack Pring; 12 Phil Carleton; 5 Chris Leyshon; 6 Paul Emanuelli; 7 Shaun Owens; 25 Neil Dallimore; 13 Ashley Bateman; 18 Harrison Elliott; 11 Barrie Phillips; 14 Mike Connor; 10 Chris Vitalini. Subs (all used): 21 Dan Parry; 23 Richard East; 16 Osian Phillips; 22 Morgan Evans.
Tries: Vitalini (15), Sheridan (28), Pring (65);
Goals: Emanuelli 3/4; **Field goal:** Emanuelli (76).
Sin bin: Bateman (9) - dissent.
SKOLARS: 1 Josh Sunley; 14 James Duckworth; 3 John Paxton; 4 Mufaro Mvududu; 5 Iliess Macani; 6 Courtney Davies; 7 Danny Yates; 22 Erjon Dollapi; 9 Martyn Smith; 21 Michael Sykes; 11 Anthony Cox; 31 Lamont Bryan; 10 Dave Williams. Subs (all used): 13 Louis Robinson; 8 Ryan MacDonald; 16 Mike Bishay; 20 Teli Pelo.
Tries: Davies (21), MacDonald (51), Williams (59);
Goals: Davies 3/3.
Sin bin: Sunley (36) - high tackle.
Rugby Leaguer & League Express Men of the Match:
Scorpions: Paul Emanuelli; *Skolars:* Dave Williams.
Penalty count: 7-12; **Half-time:** 12-6;
Referee: Adam Gill; **Attendance:** 486
(at Cardiff Arms Park).

ROUND 20

Sunday 3rd August 2014

GATESHEAD THUNDER 34 HEMEL STAGS 26

THUNDER: 15 Jordan Meads; 3 Jacob Blades; 24 Chris Heil; 4 Joe Brown; 5 Tom Capper; 26 Matty Beharrell; 7 Benn Hardcastle; 14 Matt Barron; 6 Paul Stamp; 10 Lee Fewlass; 11 Rhys Clarke; 12 Jason Payne; 29 Ricky Hough. Subs (all used): 21 Joe Hodgson; 13 Sam Bowring; 19 Josh Stoker; 18 Iain Murray.
Tries: Beharrell (4), Blades (19, 36), Capper (42, 52), Heil (62), R Clarke (66); **Goals:** Hardcastle 3/7.
STAGS: 2 James Cameron; 17 Jimmy Morgan; 3 Mathew Cook; 4 Michael Brown; 5 James Hill; 22 Jermaine Coleman; 6 Jy-mel Coleman; 8 Dominic Maloney; 14 Evan Simons; 25 James Howitt; 11 Barry-John Swindells; 12 Cariern Clement-Pascall; 13 Alex Ingarfield. Subs (all used): 20 Ryan Chester; 23 Eddie Mbaraga; 19 Malikhi Lloyd-Jones; 18 Kieran Dixon.
Tries: Ingarfield (24), Cameron (46), Simons (57), Swindells (68), Jermaine Coleman (75);
Goals: Swindells 2/4, Jy-mel Coleman 1/1.
Sin bin: Simons (35) - repeated team offences.
Rugby Leaguer & League Express Men of the Match:
Thunder: Tom Capper; *Stags:* Jy-mel Coleman.
Penalty count: 14-10; **Half-time:** 14-6;
Referee: Gareth Hewer; **Attendance:** 166.

GLOUCESTERSHIRE ALL GOLDS 18 YORK CITY KNIGHTS 42

ALL GOLDS: 7 Danny Thomas; 2 Scott Claridge; 3 Phil Cowburn; 18 Sam Te'o; 5 Jarrod Ward; 6 Ben White; 9 Matt Bradley; 10 Joe McClean; 19 Craig Cook; 8 Mike Stewart; 11 Miles Fairbank; 12 Daniel Spencer-Tonks; 13 Brendan Smith. Subs (all used): 14 Casey Canterbury; 15 Harry Chapman-Walker; 16 Frankie Foster; 17 Connor Nolan.
Tries: Fairbank (21), Ward (45), White (48);
Goals: Bradley 3/3.
Sin bin: Smith (62) - fighting.
CITY KNIGHTS: 1 James Haynes; 25 James Saltonstall; 3 James Ford; 31 Tyler Craig; 5 Ben Dent; 6 Pat Smith; 26 Ben Reynolds; 28 Colton Roche; 9 Jack Lee; 10 Jack Aldous; 11 Ryan Mallinder; 12 Ed Smith; 13 Lee Paterson. Subs (all used): 14 Kris Brining; 29 Ryan Backhouse; 30 Joe Pickets; 35 Brad Brennan.
Tries: B Dent (1, 71), Craig (12, 63), Lee (15), Ford (50), Mallinder (67), Haynes (79); **Goals:** Reynolds 5/9.
Dismissal: E Smith (62) - fighting.
Sin bin: Pickets (62) - fighting.
Rugby Leaguer & League Express Men of the Match:
All Golds: Ben White; *City Knights:* Jack Aldous.
Penalty count: 4-9; **Half-time:** 6-16;
Referee: Adam Gill; **Attendance:** 184.

HUNSLET HAWKS 48 OXFORD 6

HAWKS: 2 Jimmy Watson; 36 Gavin Duffy; 3 Lee Brickwood; 4 Danny Maun; 1 Stuart Kain; 13 Danny Grimshaw; 6 Thomas Coyle; 10 James Houston; 9 David March; 8 Michael Haley; 11 John Oakes; 30 Chris Clarkson; 26 Liam Mackay. Subs (all used): 14 Matthew Tebb; 15 Luke Stenchion; 23 Chris Clough; 24 Aston Wilson.
Tries: Clarkson (7), March (15), Grimshaw (24, 36), Mackay (41), Duffy (47, 75), Watson (56);
Goals: March 4/4, T Coyle 4/4.
OXFORD: 1 Sean Morris; 20 Yannic Parker; 5 Callum Mulkeen; 3 Marcus Brooker; 30 Jonny Morris; 7 Jimmy Rowland; 6 Tommy Connick; 24 Tom Davies; 17 Rory Sharratt; 34 Luke Evans; 36 Ed Hayles; 12 Andrew Hoggins; 9 Alex Thompson. Subs (all used): 16 Sam Blaney; 18 Jordan Rice; 22 Graham O'Keeffe; 27 Wes Newton.
Try: S Morris (52); **Goals:** Rowland 1/1.
Rugby Leaguer & League Express Men of the Match:
Hawks: David March; *Oxford:* Sean Morris.
Penalty count: 8-6; **Half-time:** 24-0;
Referee: Michael Woodhead; **Attendance:** 474.

LONDON SKOLARS 28 OLDHAM 38

SKOLARS: 1 John Paxton; 16 Iliess Macani; 22 Judd Greenhalgh; 3 Mufaro Mvududu; 34 James Duckworth; 6 Courtney Davies; 7 Danny Yates; 20 Teli Pelo; 33 Mike Bishay; 21 Michael Sykes; 31 Lamont Bryan; 12 Will Lovell; 10 Dave Williams. Subs (all used): 8 Ryan MacDonald; 9 Martyn Smith; 13 Louis Robinson; 11 Anthony Cox.
Tries: Lovell (15, 32), Pelo (29), Macani (39), Mvududu (72); **Goals:** Davies 4/5.
OLDHAM: 4 Steven Nield; 2 Mo Agoro; 3 Ben Wood; 25 Jonathan Ford; 27 Adam Clay; 6 Lewis Palfrey; 26 Steve Roper; 8 Phil Joy; - Gareth Owen; 19 Michael Ward; 11 Josh Crowley; 12 Danny Langtree; 22 Liam Thompson. Subs (all used): 7 Brett Robinson; 28 Nathan Mason; 15 Paddy Mooney; 20 George Tyson.
Tries: Ford (3), Agoro (10, 12, 78), Clay (39), Crowley (42), Langtree (49);
Goals: Palfrey 1/3, Roper 4/4.
Rugby Leaguer & League Express Men of the Match:
Skolars: Will Lovell; *Oldham:* Josh Crowley.
Penalty count: 9-5; **Half-time:** 22-20;
Referee: Dave Sharpe; **Attendance:** 419
(at Queen Elizabeth II Stadium, Enfield).

ROUND 21

Saturday 9th August 2014

LONDON SKOLARS 24 OXFORD 31

SKOLARS: 1 John Paxton; 3 Iliess Macani; 32 Kazeem Fatouri; 33 Mufaro Mvududu; 34 James Duckworth; 7 Danny Yates; 6 Courtney Davies; 21 Michael Sykes; 9 Martyn Smith; 20 Teli Pelo; 31 Lamont Bryan; 12 Will Lovell; 10 Dave Williams. Subs (all used): 16 Sam Druce; 11 Anthony Cox; 13 Louis Robinson; 8 Ryan MacDonald.
Tries: Davies (21), Mvududu (51), Bryan (69), Macani (74); **Goals:** Davies 4/4.
OXFORD: 1 Sean Morris; 20 Yannic Parker; 5 Callum Mulkeen; 3 Marcus Brooker; 21 Sam Egerton; 7 Jimmy Rowland; 6 Tommy Connick; 24 Tom Davies; 17 Rory Sharratt; 34 Luke Evans; 9 Alex Thompson; 12 Andrew Hoggins; 18 Jordan Rice. Subs (all used): 16 Sam Blaney; 36 Ed Hayles; 22 Graham O'Keeffe; 27 Wes Newton.
Tries: Connick (9, 80), Rowland (17), Hoggins (30), S Morris (37); **Goals:** Rowland 4/4, Connick 1/1;
Field goal: Rice (73).
Rugby Leaguer & League Express Men of the Match:
Skolars: Mufaro Mvududu; *Oxford:* Rory Sharratt.
Penalty count: 4-3; **Half-time:** 6-24;
Referee: Peter Brooke; **Attendance:** 186
(at Pennine Way, Hemel).

SOUTH WALES SCORPIONS 16 GLOUCESTERSHIRE ALL GOLDS 28

SCORPIONS: 1 Jordan Sheridan; 2 Ian Newbury; 3 Jack Pring; 4 Kyle Scrivens; 5 Chris Leyshon; 6 Paul Emanuelli; 7 Shaun Owens; 25 Neil Dallimore; - Lloyd O'Connor; 10 Chris Vitalini; 11 Barrie Phillips; 14 Mike Connor; 13 Ashley Bateman. Subs (all used): 9 Connor Farrer; 16 Osian Phillips; 18 Harrison Elliott; 23 Richard East.
Tries: Owens (16), Leyshon (43), Newbury (70);
Goals: Emanuelli 2/3.
ALL GOLDS: 7 Danny Thomas; 2 Jarrod Ward; 18 Sam Te'o; 4 Phil Cowburn; 5 Scott Claridge; 1 Ben White; 3 Matt Bradley; 8 Mike Stewart; 14 Casey Canterbury; 10 Izaak Duffy; 11 Miles Fairbank; 12 Connor Nolan; 13 Brendan Smith. Subs (all used): 9 Steve Parry; 15 Harry Chapman-Walker; 16 Joe McClean; 17 Frankie Foster.
Tries: Cowburn (8), White (13), Duffy (24), Parry (37), Fairbank (66); **Goals:** Bradley 4/5.
Sin bin: Smith (75) - high tackle on Farrer.
Rugby Leaguer & League Express Men of the Match:
Scorpions: Shaun Owens; *All Golds:* Izaak Duffy.
Penalty count: 7-8; **Half-time:** 6-22;
Referee: Dave Sharpe; **Attendance:** 177.

Sunday 10th August 2014

HEMEL STAGS 16 HUNSLET HAWKS 34

STAGS: 2 James Cameron; 5 James Hill; 4 Michael Brown; 3 Aaron Small; 18 Kieran Dixon; 6 Jy-mel Coleman; 7 Ben Young; 8 Dominic Maloney; 14 Evan Simons; 10 Dan Ljazouli; 11 Barry-John Swindells; - Steve Bannister; 13 Alex Ingarfield. Subs (all used): 20 Ryan Chester; 15 Joel Thomas; 23 Eddie Mbaraga; 22 Jermaine Coleman.
Tries: Swindells (49), Jy-mel Coleman (52), Bannister (63); **Goals:** Swindells 1/3, Jy-mel Coleman 1/1.
HAWKS: 2 Jimmy Watson; 1 Stuart Kain; 3 Lee Brickwood; 4 Danny Maun; 36 Gavin Duffy; 13 Danny Grimshaw; 6 Thomas Coyle; 10 James Houston; 9 David March; 15 Luke Stenchion; 30 Chris Clarkson; 11 John Oakes; 26 Liam Mackay. Subs (all used): 7 James Coyle; 39 Ross Peltier; 31 Luke Briscoe; 18 Brooke Broughton.
Tries: Duffy (10, 19, 39), Maun (27), Broughton (44), Grimshaw (67); **Goals:** March 4/5, T Coyle 1/2.
Rugby Leaguer & League Express Men of the Match:
Stags: Eddie Mbaraga; *Hawks:* Gavin Duffy.
Penalty count: 6-5; **Half-time:** 0-22; **Referee:** Adam Gill *(replaced by John McMullen, 12)*; **Attendance:** 254.

YORK CITY KNIGHTS 34 GATESHEAD THUNDER 30

CITY KNIGHTS: 1 James Haynes; 25 James Saltonstall; 28 Tyler Craig; 27 Brad Day; 5 Ben Dent; 6 Pat Smith; 26 Ben Reynolds; 29 Colton Roche; 9 Jack Lee; 10 Jack Aldous; 30 Ryan Backhouse; 12 Ed Smith; 13 Lee Paterson. Subs (all used): 14 Kris Brining; 34 Brad Brennan; 35 Jay Leary; 31 Josh Tonks.
Tries: B Dent (11), Saltonstall (17, 65), Tonks (36), Aldous (43), Backhouse (51); **Goals:** Reynolds 5/7.
THUNDER: 3 Jacob Blades; 2 Lee Mapals; 4 Joe Brown; 28 Kris Welham; 5 Tom Capper; 26 Matty Beharrell; 15 Jordan Meads; 14 Matt Barron; 6 Paul Stamp; 10 Lee Fewlass; 12 Jason Payne; 11 Rhys Clarke; 23 Sonny Esslemont. Subs (all used): 29 Ricky Hough; 18 Rhys Lovegrove; 30 Jordan Cox; 13 Sam Bowring.
Tries: Welham (5), Payne (22), Brown (59), Meads (69), Barron (76), Mapals (79); **Goals:** Beharrell 3/6.
Sin bin: Lovegrove (43) - holding down.
Rugby Leaguer & League Express Men of the Match:
City Knights: Pat Smith; *Thunder:* Lee Fewlass.
Penalty count: 12-10; **Half-time:** 16-10;
Referee: Gareth Hewer; **Attendance:** 571.

Championship One 2014 - Round by Round

ROUND 22

Sunday 17th August 2014

GATESHEAD THUNDER 58
SOUTH WALES SCORPIONS 24

THUNDER: 15 Jordan Meads; 13 Sam Bowring; 24 Chris Heil; 4 Joe Brown; 5 Tom Capper; 26 Matty Beharrell; 7 Benn Hardcastle; 14 Matt Barron; 6 Paul Stamp; 10 Lee Fewlass; 11 Rhys Clarke; 12 Jason Payne; 2 Sonny Esslemont. Subs (all used): 19 Josh Stoker; 21 Joe Hodgson; 29 Ricky Hough; 30 Ryan MacDonald.
Tries: Beharrell (2), Meads (7, 64), Hardcastle (15, 77), Esslemont (33), Heil (35), Capper (37, 61), Bowring (54, 74); **Goals:** Hardcastle 7/11.
SCORPIONS: 5 Chris Leyshon; 2 Ian Newbury; 3 Jack Pring; 24 Paul Edwards; 21 Yousif Suliman; 13 Ashley Bateman; 1 Jordan Sheridan; 23 Richard East; 9 Connor Farrer; 16 Osian Phillips; 11 Barrie Phillips; 4 Kyle Scrivens; 18 Harrison Elliott. Subs (all used): 14 Lloyd O'Connor; 19 Chris True; 22 Dafydd Hellard; 25 Scott Giles.
Tries: Newbury (13, 80), Farrer (24, 29), Elliott (50); **Goals:** Elliott 2/5.
Sin bin:
B Phillips (73) - dangerous challenge on MacDonald.
Rugby Leaguer & League Express Men of the Match: *Thunder:* Benn Hardcastle; *Scorpions:* Harrison Elliott.
Penalty count: 4-4; **Half-time:** 32-16;
Referee: Jonathan Roberts; **Attendance:** 161.

GLOUCESTERSHIRE ALL GOLDS 12
LONDON SKOLARS 36

ALL GOLDS: 1 Phil Cowburn; 2 Jarrod Ward; 3 Jamie Crowther; 17 Sam Te'o; 5 Scott Claridge; 13 Brendan Smith; 20 Casey Canterbury; 10 Izaak Duffy; 19 Craig Cook; 18 Chris Vitalini; 11 Daniel Spencer-Tonks; 12 Connor Nolan; 15 Miles Fairbank. Subs (all used): 9 Steve Parry; 6 Mark Barlow; 16 Joe McClean; 14 Ash Haynes.
Tries: Canterbury (30), Cowburn (54);
Goals: Cowburn 2/2.
SKOLARS: 1 John Paxton; 2 Iliess Macani; 11 Anthony Cox; 4 Mufaro Mvududu; 5 Dennis Tuffour; 7 Danny Yates; 6 Mike Bishay; 20 Teli Pelo; 9 Martyn Smith; 8 Michael Sykes; 10 Lamont Bryan; 12 Will Lovell; 21 Oliver Purslow. Subs (all used): 16 Sam Druce; 17 Kazeem Fatouri; 22 Sam Wellings; 13 Louis Robinson.
Tries: Mvududu (14, 42), Yates (34), Macani (45, 73), Bishay (67), Purslow (71); **Goals:** Bishay 3/6, Druce 1/1.
Rugby Leaguer & League Express Men of the Match: *All Golds:* Phil Cowburn; *Skolars:* Will Lovell.
Penalty count: 6-5; **Half-time:** 6-10;
Referee: Sam Ansell; **Attendance:** 108.

HUNSLET HAWKS 18 YORK CITY KNIGHTS 20

HAWKS: 2 Jimmy Watson; 36 Gavin Duffy; 3 Lee Brickwood; 4 Danny Maun; 37 James Duckworth; 13 Danny Grimshaw; 6 Thomas Coyle; 38 Richard Moore; 9 David March; 8 Michael Haley; 31 Luke Briscoe; 11 John Oakes; 26 Liam Mackay. Subs (all used): 27 Liam Hood; 1 Stuart Kain; 18 Brooke Broughton; 39 Ross Peltier.
Tries: Hood (32), Moore (60), T Coyle (64);
Goals: T Coyle 1/1, March 2/2.
Sin bin: March (71) - dissent.
CITY KNIGHTS: 1 James Haynes; 25 James Saltonstall; 3 James Ford; 4 Greg Minikin; 5 Ben Dent; 6 Pat Smith; 7 Jon Presley; 29 Colton Roche; 9 Jack Lee; 10 Jack Aldous; 11 Ryan Mallinder; 12 Ed Smith; 13 Lee Paterson. Subs (all used): 14 Kris Brining; 34 Brad Brennan; 35 Josh Tonks; 30 Ryan Backhouse.
Tries: Ford (40), Saltonstall (71), Roche (75);
Goals: Haynes 4/4.
Rugby Leaguer & League Express Men of the Match: *Hawks:* Richard Moore; *City Knights:* Ryan Backhouse.
Penalty count: 3-8; **Half-time:** 6-6;
Referee: Chris Kendall; **Attendance:** 796.

OLDHAM 38 HEMEL STAGS 10

OLDHAM: 6 Lewis Palfrey; 2 Mo Agoro; 21 David Cookson; 25 Jonathan Ford; 1 Adam Clay; 26 Steve Roper; 7 Brett Robinson; 8 Phil Joy; 14 Gareth Owen; 10 Jason Boults; 11 Josh Crowley; 12 Danny Langtree; 22 Liam Thompson. Subs (all used): 16 Kenny Hughes; 28 Nathan Mason; 19 Michael Ward; 20 George Tyson.
Tries: Joy (3), Clay (25, 79), Cookson (31), Hughes (38), Tyson (50), Roper (65); **Goals:** Roper 5/7.
STAGS: 2 James Cameron; 3 Aaron Small; 4 Michael Brown; 17 Mathew Cook; 5 Jamel Chisholm; 6 Jy-mel Coleman; 7 Ben Young; 8 Dominic Maloney; 14 Evan Simons; 10 Dan Ljazouli; 11 Barry-John Swindells; 12 Cariern Clement-Pascall; 13 Alex Ingarfield. Subs (all used): 20 Ryan Chester; 15 Joel Thomas; 19 Eddie Mbaraga; 18 Owain Griffiths.
Tries: Jy-mel Coleman (9), Small (76);
Goals: Swindells 1/2.
Rugby Leaguer & League Express Men of the Match: *Oldham:* Phil Joy; *Stags:* Jy-mel Coleman.
Penalty count: 4-6; **Half-time:** 20-6;
Referee: Dave Sharpe; **Attendance:** 438.

ROUND 14

Friday 22nd August 2014

LONDON SKOLARS 10 HUNSLET HAWKS 36

SKOLARS: 1 John Paxton; 16 Iliess Macani; 3 Anthony Cox; 33 Mufaro Mvududu; 34 Dennis Tuffour; 6 Mike Bishay; 7 Danny Yates; 20 Teli Pelo; 9 Martyn Smith; - Erjon Dollapi; 31 Lamont Bryan; 12 Will Lovell; 13 Oliver Purslow. Subs (all used): 21 Michael Sykes; - Louis Robinson; 10 Sam Wellings; - Sam Druce.
Tries: Mvududu (57, 76); **Goals:** Bishay 1/2.
HAWKS: 2 Jimmy Watson; 37 James Duckworth; 3 Lee Brickwood; 4 Danny Maun; 36 Gavin Duffy; 6 Thomas Coyle; 7 James Coyle; 38 Richard Moore; 9 David March; 8 Michael Haley; 31 Luke Briscoe; 11 John Oakes; 26 Liam Mackay. Subs (all used): 20 Danny Ansell; 15 Luke Stenchion; 39 Ross Peltier; 24 Aston Wilson.
Tries: Briscoe (12), Maun (23), Stenchion (27), Mackay (29), Watson (33), Duffy (52); **Goals:** March 6/6.
Rugby Leaguer & League Express Men of the Match: *Skolars:* Mufaro Mvududu; *Hawks:* Richard Moore.
Penalty count: 7-6; **Half-time:** 0-30;
Referee: Tom Crashley; **Attendance:** 1,325
(at Queen Elizabeth II Stadium, Enfield).

ROUND 23

Sunday 31st August 2014

HEMEL STAGS 44 GLOUCESTERSHIRE ALL GOLDS 24

STAGS: 2 James Cameron; 3 Aaron Small; 4 Michael Brown; 17 Mathew Cook; 5 Jamel Chisholm; - Jermaine Coleman; 6 Jy-mel Coleman; 8 Dominic Maloney; 14 Evan Simons; 10 Dan Ljazouli; 11 Barry-John Swindells; 15 Steve Bannister; 19 Eddie Mbaraga. Subs (all used): 12 Cariern Clement-Pascall; 13 Alex Ingarfield; 18 Owain Griffiths; 20 Ryan Chester.
Tries: Brown (10, 24), Jy-mel Coleman (33), Ingarfield (43), Cook (49), Clement-Pascall (51), Cameron (55); **Goals:** Swindells 7/7, Jy-mel Coleman 1/1.
ALL GOLDS: 4 Phil Cowburn; 2 Jarrod Ward; 3 Jamie Crowther; 17 Sam Te'o; 5 Scott Claridge; 8 Ben White; 9 Matt Bradley; 10 Izaak Duffy; 19 Craig Cook; 18 Chris Vitalini; 12 Connor Nolan; 15 Miles Fairbank; 16 Ash Haynes. Subs (all used): 13 Brendan Smith; 20 Casey Canterbury; 6 Mark Barlow; 14 Joe McClean.
Tries: Cook (4), Crowther (58), Cowburn (63), Fairbank (78); **Goals:** Bradley 4/4.
On report: Fairbank (10) - alleged late challenge.
Rugby Leaguer & League Express Men of the Match: *Stags:* Michael Brown; *All Golds:* Phil Cowburn.
Penalty count: 6-3; **Half-time:** 18-6;
Referee: Gareth Hewer; **Attendance:** 305.

GATESHEAD THUNDER 40 OLDHAM 14

THUNDER: 1 Joe Martin; 2 Lee Mapals; 24 Chris Heil; 4 Joe Brown; 5 Tom Capper; 26 Matty Beharrell; 15 Jordan Meads; 14 Matt Barron; 6 Paul Stamp; 10 Lee Fewlass; 11 Rhys Clarke; 12 Jason Payne; 28 Sonny Esslemont. Subs (all used): 19 Josh Stoker; 13 Sam Bowring; 18 Iain Murray; 29 Ricky Hough.
Tries: Meads (4, 72), Capper (11), Mapals (19), R Clarke (30), Payne (46), Heil (68), Fewlass (78);
Goals: Beharrell 4/8.
Sin bin: Heil (54) - professional foul.
OLDHAM: 6 Lewis Palfrey; 2 Mo Agoro; 21 David Cookson; 25 Jonathan Ford; 1 Adam Clay; 26 Steve Roper; 7 Brett Robinson; 8 Phil Joy; 14 Gareth Owen; 19 Michael Ward; 11 Josh Crowley; 12 Danny Langtree; 22 Liam Thompson. Subs (all used): 28 Nathan Mason; 15 Paddy Mooney; 16 Kenny Hughes; 9 Sam Gee.
Tries: Mason (52), Ford (55, 65); **Goals:** Roper 1/3.
On report: Langtree (77) - alleged high tackle.
Rugby Leaguer & League Express Men of the Match: *Thunder:* Jordan Meads; *Oldham:* Sam Gee.
Penalty count: 4-4; **Half-time:** 20-0;
Referee: Dave Merrick; **Attendance:** 401.

OXFORD 29 SOUTH WALES SCORPIONS 22

OXFORD: 1 Sean Morris; 20 Yannic Parker; 3 Marcus Brooker; 30 Jonny Morris; 5 Callum Mulkeen; 6 Tommy Connick; 7 Jimmy Rowland; 22 Graham O'Keeffe; 17 Rory Sharratt; 34 Luke Evans; 9 Alex Thompson; 12 Andrew Hoggins; 18 Jordan Rice. Subs (all used): 10 Matty Hadden; 16 Sam Blaney; 24 Tom Davies; 36 Ed Hayles.
Tries: Sharratt (11), Hoggins (29), Hadden (55), Brooker (77), Blaney (80); **Goals:** Rowland 4/5;
Field goal: Rowland (80).
SCORPIONS: 1 Jordan Sheridan; 2 Ian Newbury; 22 Dafydd Hellard; 24 Paul Edwards; 5 Chris Leyshon; 6 Paul Emanuelli; 7 Shaun Owens; 18 Harrison Elliott; 9 Connor Farrer; 16 Osian Phillips; 4 Kyle Scrivens; 12 Phil Carleton; 13 Ashley Bateman. Subs (all used): 14 Lloyd O'Connor; 3 Jack Pring; 23 Richard East; 25 Scott Giles.
Tries: Elliott (15), O'Connor (36), Newbury (49), Edwards (73); **Goals:** Emanuelli 3/4.
Rugby Leaguer & League Express Men of the Match: *Oxford:* Jimmy Rowland; *Scorpions:* Osian Phillips.
Penalty count: 9-8; **Half-time:** 12-12;
Referee: Andrew Sweet; **Attendance:** 240.

ROUND 24

Saturday 6th September 2014

OXFORD 22 HEMEL STAGS 22

OXFORD: 1 Sean Morris; 20 Yannic Parker; 3 Marcus Brooker; 30 Jonny Morris; 5 Callum Mulkeen; 6 Tommy Connick; 7 Jimmy Rowland; 22 Graham O'Keeffe; 17 Rory Sharratt; 34 Luke Evans; 9 Alex Thompson; 12 Andrew Hoggins; 18 Jordan Rice. Subs (all used): 10 Matty Hadden; 16 Sam Blaney; 24 Tom Davies; 36 Ed Hayles.
Tries: Rowland (8, 57), Parker (27), Brooker (69);
Goals: Rowland 3/5.
STAGS: 2 James Cameron; 3 Aaron Small; 4 Michael Brown; 18 Mathew Cook; 5 Jamel Chisholm; 19 Eddie Mbaraga; 6 Jy-mel Coleman; 8 Dominic Maloney; 14 Evan Simons; 10 Dan Ljazouli; 11 Barry-John Swindells; 12 Cariern Clement-Pascall; - Steve Bannister. Subs (all used): 13 Alex Ingarfield; 15 Miles McLeod; 17 Owain Griffiths; 20 Ryan Chester.
Tries: Cook (6), Chisholm (16), Mbaraga (51), Jy-mel Coleman (71);
Goals: Swindells 2/3, Jy-mel Coleman 1/1.
Rugby Leaguer & League Express Men of the Match: *Oxford:* Jimmy Rowland; *Stags:* Eddie Mbaraga.
Penalty count: 4-4; **Half-time:** 12-10;
Referee: Michael Woodhead; **Attendance:** 205.

Sunday 7th September 2014

OLDHAM 68 GLOUCESTERSHIRE ALL GOLDS 24

OLDHAM: 4 Steven Nield; 1 Adam Clay; 21 David Cookson; 25 Jonathan Ford; 5 Dale Bloomfield; 26 Steve Roper; 7 Brett Robinson; 8 Phil Joy; 14 Gareth Owen; 15 Paddy Mooney; 11 Josh Crowley; 12 Danny Langtree; 22 Liam Thompson. Subs (all used): 16 Kenny Hughes; 28 Nathan Mason; 19 Michael Ward; 3 Ben Wood.
Tries: Ford (2, 77), Crowley (12, 34), Joy (25), Langtree (28, 58), Wood (32, 40), Ward (52), Mooney (75), Bloomfield (79);
Goals: Roper 8/10, Nield 2/2.
ALL GOLDS: 1 Phil Cowburn; 2 Jarrod Ward; 11 Sam Te'o; 4 Jamie Crowther; 5 Scott Claridge; 8 Ben White; 7 Matt Bradley; 10 Izaak Duffy; 19 Craig Cook; 17 Chris Vitalini; 18 Miles Fairbank; 16 Ash Haynes; 13 Brendan Smith. Subs (all used): 15 Connor Nolan; 14 Joe McClean; 12 James Tutuila; 9 Steve Parry.
Tries: Fairbank (19, 62), Bradley (45), White (71);
Goals: Bradley 4/4.
Rugby Leaguer & League Express Men of the Match: *Oldham:* Steve Roper; *All Golds:* Matt Bradley.
Penalty count: 9-4; **Half-time:** 42-6;
Referee: Andrew Sweet; **Attendance:** 437.

SOUTH WALES SCORPIONS 6 HUNSLET HAWKS 50

SCORPIONS: 1 Jordan Sheridan; 2 Ian Newbury; 3 Jack Pring; 24 Paul Edwards; 5 Chris Leyshon; 6 Paul Emanuelli; 12 Phil Carleton; 18 Harrison Elliott; 9 Connor Farrer; 16 Osian Phillips; 4 Kyle Scrivens; 14 Mike Connor; 13 Ashley Bateman. Subs: 21 Dan Parry (not used); 22 Chris True; 23 Richard East; 25 Scott Giles.
Try: Emanuelli (26); **Goals:** Emanuelli 1/1.
HAWKS: 2 Jimmy Watson; 37 James Duckworth; 3 Lee Brickwood; 4 Danny Maun; 36 Gavin Duffy; 6 Thomas Coyle; 7 James Coyle; 8 Michael Haley; 20 Danny Ansell; 38 Richard Moore; 11 John Oakes; 31 Luke Briscoe; 26 Liam Mackay. Subs (all used): 12 Aaron Lyons; 15 Luke Stenchion; 16 Lewis Reed; 39 Ross Peltier.
Tries: Duffy (6, 48, 76, 78, 80), Maun (19), Stenchion (36), Watson (58), Haley (62), Brickwood (70);
Goals: Ansell 0/2, T Coyle 5/8.
Rugby Leaguer & League Express Men of the Match: *Scorpions:* Paul Emanuelli; *Hawks:* Gavin Duffy.
Penalty count: 2-7; **Half-time:** 6-14; **Referee:** Adam Gill;
Attendance: 363 *(at Mountain Ash RFC).*

YORK CITY KNIGHTS 38 LONDON SKOLARS 28

CITY KNIGHTS: 26 Ben Reynolds; 25 James Saltonstall; 27 Tyler Craig; 4 Greg Minikin; 5 Ben Dent; 6 Pat Smith; 23 Benn Hardcastle; 34 Brad Brennan; 9 Jack Lee; 28 Colton Roche; 29 Ryan Backhouse; 12 Ed Smith; 13 Lee Paterson. Subs (all used): 14 Kris Brining; 10 Jack Aldous; 18 Austin Bell; 35 Josh Tonks.
Tries: B Hardcastle (1), Reynolds (16, 37), Minikin (27), E Smith (33), Brining (52), Saltonstall (78);
Goals: Reynolds 5/7.
SKOLARS: 1 John Paxton; 31 Judd Greenhalgh; 19 Kazeem Fatouri; 4 Mufaro Mvududu; 5 Dennis Tuffour; 7 Danny Yates; 22 Lamont Bryan; 20 Teli Pelo; 9 Martyn Smith; 8 Michael Sykes; 11 Anthony Cox; 12 Will Lovell; 10 Dave Williams. Subs (all used): 14 Louis Robinson; 13 Oliver Purslow; 21 Sam Wellings; 6 Sam Druce.
Tries: Smith (7, 48), Fatouri (23, 64), Mvududu (58);
Goals: Yates 4/5.
Rugby Leaguer & League Express Men of the Match: *City Knights:* James Saltonstall; *Skolars:* Danny Yates.
Penalty count: 5-4; **Half-time:** 26-10;
Referee: Dave Sharpe; **Attendance:** 643.

PLAY-OFFS

QUALIFYING PLAY-OFF

Friday 12th September 2014

HUNSLET HAWKS 24 OLDHAM 25

HAWKS: 2 Jimmy Watson; 36 Gavin Duffy; 4 Danny Maun; 3 Lee Brickwood; 37 James Duckworth; 6 Thomas Coyle; 7 James Coyle; 38 Richard Moore; 9 David March; 8 Michael Haley; 11 John Oakes; 12 Aaron Lyons; 26 Liam Mackay. Subs (all used): 15 Luke Stenchion; 10 James Houston; 27 Liam Hood; 39 Ross Peltier.
Tries: J Coyle (10), Oakes (23), March (69), Duffy (72);
Goals: March 4/5.
OLDHAM: 4 Steven Nield; 1 Adam Clay; 21 David Cookson; 25 Jonathan Ford; 5 Dale Bloomfield; 6 Lewis Palfrey; 26 Steve Roper; 8 Phil Joy; 14 Gareth Owen; 10 Jason Boults; 11 Josh Crowley; 12 Danny Langtree; 22 Liam Thompson. Subs (all used): 19 Michael Ward; 28 Nathan Mason; 16 Kenny Hughes; 20 George Tyson.
Tries: Ford (36), Bloomfield (42), Langtree (48), Ward (58); **Goals:** Roper 4/5; **Field goal:** Crowley (40).

Hunslet's Liam Hood on the charge against Oldham during the Championship One Grand Final

Rugby Leaguer & League Express Men of the Match:
Hawks: David March; *Oldham:* Steven Nield.
Penalty count: 5-6; **Half-time:** 12-7;
Referee: Chris Kendall; **Attendance:** 748.

ELIMINATION PLAY-OFF

Sunday 14th September 2014

GATESHEAD THUNDER 15 HEMEL STAGS 14
(after golden point extra-time)

THUNDER: 1 Joe Martin; 2 Lee Mapals; 24 Chris Heil; 4 Joe Brown; 5 Tom Capper; 26 Matty Beharrell; 15 Jordan Meads; 14 Matt Barron; 29 Ricky Hough; 10 Lee Fewlass; 12 Jason Payne; 11 Rhys Clarke; 28 Sonny Esslemont. Subs (all used): 20 Connor Condron; 19 Josh Stoker; - Sam Luckley; 13 Sam Bowring.
Tries: Brown (12), Mapals (40), Esslemont (53);
Goals: Beharrell 1/4; **Field goal:** Beharrell (83).
STAGS: 2 James Cameron; 15 Miles McLeod; 4 Michael Brown; 3 Mathew Cook; 5 Jamel Chisholm; - Jermaine Coleman; 6 Jy-mel Coleman; 8 Dominic Maloney; 14 Evan Simons; 10 Dan Ljazouli; 11 Barry-John Swindells; 12 Cariern Clement-Pascall; 19 Eddie Mbaraga. Subs (all used): 13 Alex Ingarfield; 21 Ben Kavanagh; 20 Ryan Chester; 25 James Howitt.
Tries: Clement-Pascall (23), Jy-mel Coleman (60);
Goals: Swindells 3/3.
Rugby Leaguer & League Express Men of the Match:
Thunder: Matty Beharrell; *Stags:* Jermaine Coleman.
Penalty count: 11-10; **Half-time:** 8-6;
Referee: Tom Crashley; **Attendance:** 557
(at Kingston Park, Newcastle).

QUALIFYING SEMI-FINAL

Sunday 21st September 2014

YORK CITY KNIGHTS 12 OLDHAM 31

CITY KNIGHTS: 1 James Haynes; 25 James Saltonstall; 3 James Ford; 4 Greg Minikin; 5 Ben Dent; 6 Pat Smith; 26 Ben Reynolds; 28 Colton Roche; 9 Jack Lee; 10 Jack Aldous; 11 Ryan Mallinder; 12 Ed Smith; 13 Lee Paterson. Subs (all used): 14 Kris Brining; 34 Brad Brennan; 18 Austin Bell; 35 Josh Tonks.
Tries: Saltonstall (48), Paterson (63);
Goals: Reynolds 2/2.
On report: Lee (76) - alleged biting.

OLDHAM: 4 Steven Nield; 1 Adam Clay; 21 David Cookson; 25 Jonathan Ford; 5 Dale Bloomfield; 6 Lewis Palfrey; 26 Steve Roper; 8 Phil Joy; 14 Gareth Owen; 10 Jason Boults; 11 Josh Crowley; 12 Danny Langtree; 22 Liam Thompson. Subs (all used): 19 Michael Ward; 28 Nathan Mason; 16 Kenny Hughes; 20 George Tyson.
Tries: Thompson (11), Cookson (20), Nield (22), Langtree (40), Tyson (69); **Goals:** Roper 5/6;
Field goal: Roper (68).
Rugby Leaguer & League Express Men of the Match:
City Knights: James Saltonstall; *Oldham:* Danny Langtree.
Penalty count: 5-5; **Half-time:** 0-24;
Referee: George Stokes; **Attendance:** 663.

ELIMINATION SEMI-FINAL

Sunday 21st September 2014

HUNSLET HAWKS 50 GATESHEAD THUNDER 6

HAWKS: 2 Jimmy Watson; 36 Gavin Duffy; 4 Danny Maun; 3 Lee Brickwood; 37 James Duckworth; 6 Thomas Coyle; 20 Danny Ansell; 38 Richard Moore; 9 David March; 8 Michael Haley; 16 Lewis Reed; 31 Luke Briscoe. Subs (all used): 27 Liam Hood; 8 Michael Haley; 26 Liam Mackay. Subs (all used): 27 Liam Hood; 8 Michael Haley; 26 Liam Mackay.
Tries: Duffy (8, 57), Duckworth (15), Watson (22, 63), March (38), Hood (48, 80), Moore (68);
Goals: Ansell 1/1, March 6/8.
THUNDER: 2 Lee Mapals; - Omari Caro; 24 Chris Heil; 4 Joe Brown; 5 Tom Capper; 15 Jordan Meads; 26 Matty Beharrell; 14 Matt Barron; 29 Ricky Hough; 10 Lee Fewlass; 11 Rhys Clarke; 12 Jason Payne; 28 Sonny Esslemont. Subs (all used): 6 Paul Stamp; 19 Josh Stoker; 21 Joe Hodgson; 13 Sam Bowring.
Try: Stamp (42); **Goals:** Beharrell 1/1.
Sin bin: Heil (72) - dissent; Beharrell (74) - dissent.
Rugby Leaguer & League Express Men of the Match:
Hawks: David March; *Thunder:* Matty Beharrell.
Penalty count: 9-6; **Half-time:** 24-0;
Referee: Chris Leatherbarrow; **Attendance:** 463.

FINAL ELIMINATOR

Sunday 28th September 2014

YORK CITY KNIGHTS 24 HUNSLET HAWKS 32

CITY KNIGHTS: 1 James Haynes; 25 James Saltonstall; 29 Tyler Craig; 4 Greg Minikin; 5 Ben Dent; 6 Pat Smith;

26 Ben Reynolds; 28 Colton Roche; 9 Jack Lee; 10 Jack Aldous; 35 Josh Tonks; 12 Ed Smith; 13 Lee Paterson. Subs (all used): 14 Kris Brining; 18 Austin Bell; 27 Ryan Backhouse; 34 Brad Brennan.
Tries: B Dent (17), P Smith (40), Lee (62), Backhouse (79); **Goals:** Reynolds 4/4.
HAWKS: 2 Jimmy Watson; 37 James Duckworth; 3 Lee Brickwood; 4 Danny Maun; 36 Gavin Duffy; 6 Thomas Coyle; 20 Danny Ansell; 10 James Houston; 9 David March; 38 Richard Moore; 11 John Oakes; 12 Aaron Lyons; 26 Liam Mackay. Subs (all used): 27 Liam Hood; 8 Michael Haley; 16 Lewis Reed; 31 Luke Briscoe.
Tries: Watson (56), Hood (59, 74), Maun (67), Duffy (77), Duckworth (80); **Goals:** March 4/6.
Sin bin: Duffy (78) - interference.
Rugby Leaguer & League Express Men of the Match:
City Knights: Josh Tonks; *Hawks:* Liam Hood.
Penalty count: 6-7; **Half-time:** 12-0;
Referee: George Stokes; **Attendance:** 759.

GRAND FINAL

Sunday 5th October 2014

HUNSLET HAWKS 17 OLDHAM 16
(after golden point extra-time)

HAWKS: 2 Jimmy Watson; 36 Gavin Duffy; 4 Danny Maun; 3 Lee Brickwood; 37 James Duckworth; 6 Thomas Coyle; 20 Danny Ansell; 38 Richard Moore; 9 David March; 10 James Houston; 11 John Oakes; 12 Aaron Lyons; 31 Luke Briscoe. Subs (all used): 27 Liam Hood; 8 Michael Haley; 1 Stuart Kain; 40 Luke Hardbottle.
Tries: Watson (22), Duckworth (45), T Coyle (53);
Goals: March 2/3; **Field goal:** T Coyle (85).
OLDHAM: 4 Steven Nield; 29 Adam Clay; 21 David Cookson; 25 Jonathan Ford; 5 Dale Bloomfield; 6 Lewis Palfrey; 26 Steve Roper; 8 Phil Joy; 30 Gareth Owen; 10 Jason Boults; 11 Josh Crowley; 12 Danny Langtree; 22 Liam Thompson. Subs (all used): 19 Michael Ward; 28 Nathan Mason; 16 Kenny Hughes; 20 George Tyson.
Tries: Roper (5), Bloomfield (31), Langtree (74);
Goals: Roper 2/3.
Rugby Leaguer & League Express Men of the Match:
Hawks: Liam Hood; *Oldham:* Jonathan Ford.
Penalty count: 4-3; **Half-time:** 6-10; **Referee:** Joe Cobb.
(at Headingley Carnegie, Leeds).

293

CHALLENGE CUP 2014
Round by Round

ROUND 3

Friday 14th March 2014

WIGAN ST PATRICKS 6 LEIGH CENTURIONS 74

ST PATRICKS: 1 Jayden Sandford; 2 Zac Cotton; 3 Liam Gannon; 4 Brad Hargreaves; 5 James Noon; 6 Ryan Smith; 7 Brad Smith; 8 Jonny Brown; 9 Anthony Griffiths; 10 Kieron Harrison; 11 Tom Atherton; 12 Ricky Murphy; 13 Simon Atherton. Subs (all used): 16 Jamie Winstanley-Bristow; 17 Phil Mitchell; 18 Tom Woodcock; 20 Dean Hatton.
Try: Sandford (14); **Goals:** B Smith 1/1.
CENTURIONS: 1 Gregg McNally; 22 Adam Higson; 3 Stuart Littler; 4 Tom Armstrong; 23 Jonathan Pownall; 15 Liam Kay; 7 Ryan Brierley; 18 Jamie Acton; 14 Sean Penkywicz; 26 Ryan Duffy; 30 Kurt Haggerty; 12 Tommy Goulden; 27 Anthony Bate. Subs (all used): - Chris Hankinson; 8 Tom Spencer; 13 Sam Barlow; 29 Jake Emmitt.
Tries: Higson (5, 22), Goulden (8, 60), Duffy (19), Penkywicz (35, 70), Haggerty (39), Pownall (42, 48), McNally (43, 77), Hankinson (52); **Goals:** Brierley 11/13.
Rugby League & League Express Men of the Match: *St Patricks:* Simon Atherton; *Centurions:* Sean Penkywicz.
Penalty count: 5-5; **Half-time:** 6-34; **Referee:** Michael Woodhead; **Attendance:** 994 *(at Leigh Sports Village).*

Saturday 15th March 2014

BATLEY BULLDOGS 52 KELLS 4

BULLDOGS: 7 Scott Leatherbarrow; 17 Lee Paterson; 30 Charlie Martin; 19 Joe Chandler; 2 Vinny Finigan; 11 John Davies; 14 Alistair Leak; 8 Byron Smith; 18 Luke Blake; 20 Adam Gledhill; 12 Sam Scott; 13 Mark Applegarth; 15 Jay Leary. Subs (all used): 3 Alex Bretherton; 9 Anthony Nicholson; 10 Alex Rowe; 16 Brad Brennan.
Tries: Leak (7), Rowe (23, 63), Martin (30), Leatherbarrow (45, 78), Scott (51), Finigan (57), Chandler (60), Leary (75); **Goals:** Paterson 6/10.
KELLS: 1 Lewis Smith; 2 Reece O'Neill; 3 Craig Benson; 4 Scott Lofthouse; 5 Dan Joyce; 6 Tyrone Dalton; 7 Ross Crawford; 8 David Lowery; 9 Carl Sice; 10 Lewis White; 11 Barry Boyd; 12 Ryan Watson; 13 Tony Burns. Subs (all used): 14 Troy Armstrong; 15 Ross Ainley; 16 Paul Lowery; 17 Martin O'Neill.
Try: Burns (15); **Goals:** Crawford 0/1.
On report: Sice (23) - alleged high tackle on Rowe.
Rugby League & League Express Men of the Match: *Bulldogs:* Scott Leatherbarrow; *Kells:* Carl Sice.
Penalty count: 14-3; **Half-time:** 14-4;
Referee: Jamie Bloem; **Attendance:** 365.

NORMANTON KNIGHTS 12 WORKINGTON TOWN 38

KNIGHTS: 1 Lee Maskill; 2 Aaron Butterfield; 3 Steve Lewis; 4 Paul Greaves; 5 Joe Crossland; 6 Tom Alexander; 7 Adrian Mulcahy; 8 Patrick Waterton; 9 Chris Woolford; 10 Dave Evans; 11 Jordan Ratcliffe; 12 Paul Seal; 14 Tom Carroll. Subs (all used): 13 Jonny Kirk; 15 Ryan Kelsy; 16 Ian Hoult; 20 Clarke Thompson.
Tries: Woolford (23, 61); **Goals:** Mulcahy 2/2.
TOWN: 1 Brett Carter; 34 Jack Murphy; 3 Jason Mossop; 4 Andy Morris; 14 Kayle Connor; 16 Carl Forber; 7 Callum Phillips; 8 Kris Coward; 9 Graeme Mattinson; 10 Marc Shackley; 17 Liam McAvoy; 12 Jarrad Stack; 31 Rob Lever. Subs (all used): 13 Karl Olstrum; 19 Nathan Lucock; 20 Callum Rowlandson; 11 Brett Phillips.
Tries: Morris (19, 27, 64), Forber (33), Carter (47, 71), B Phillips (78); **Goals:** Connor 5/7.
Rugby League & League Express Men of the Match: *Knights:* Chris Woolford; *Town:* Callum Phillips.
Penalty count: 4-16; **Half-time:** 6-16;
Referee: Peter Brooke; **Attendance:** 713
(at Big Fellas Stadium, Featherstone).

EGREMONT RANGERS 24 OLDHAM 42

RANGERS: 1 Anthony Leak; 2 Ryan Barnes; 3 Rhys Davies; 4 Keiron Glenn; 5 Jack Stainton; 6 Paul Corkhill; 7 Lewis Beckwith; 22 Richard Farrer; 9 Daniel Telford; 10 Brad Hailes; 11 Matthew Bewsher; 12 Gary Elliott; 13 Matthew Henson. Subs (all used): 15 John-Paul Brocklebank; 16 Patrick Wells; 17 Kevin Brown; 14 James Newton.
Tries: Beckwith (34), Brocklebank (43), Farrer (58), Glenn (68); **Goals:** Bewsher 2/2, Beckwith 2/2.
OLDHAM: 4 Steven Nield; 2 Mo Agoro; 3 Ben Wood; 9 Sam Gee; 5 Dale Bloomfield; 6 Lewis Palfrey; 7 Brett Robinson; 10 Jason Boults; 16 Kenny Hughes; 19 Michael Ward; 11 Josh Crowley; 12 Danny Langtree; 13 Mark Hobson. Subs (all used): 14 Adam Files; 24 Edwin Okanga-Ajwang; 8 Phil Joy; 18 Alex Davidson.
Tries: Agoro (5), Hughes (9), Nield (20, 25), Langtree (37), Files (54), Crowley (75, 77); **Goals:** Palfrey 5/8.
Rugby League & League Express Men of the Match: *Rangers:* Lewis Beckwith; *Oldham:* Josh Crowley.
Penalty count: 10-6; **Half-time:** 6-24;
Referee: Andrew Sweet; **Attendance:** 340
(at Copeland Stadium, Whitehaven).

KEIGHLEY COUGARS 42 WATH BROW HORNETS 0

COUGARS: 1 James Craven; 2 Richie Barnett; 19 Danny Lawton; 22 Daley Williams; 5 Paul White; 6 Danny Jones; 7 Paul Handforth; 8 Andy Shickell; - Luke Haigh; 10 Sean Hesketh; 11 Josh Lynam; 12 Brendan Rawlins; 13 Ashley Lindsay. Subs (all used): 16 Jode Sheriffe; 18 Neil Cherryholme; 25 Lewis Graham; 27 Jack Lee.
Tries: Lawton (16), Lynam (22), Craven (32), White (39, 48), Handforth (57), Lee (70), Graham (73);
Goals: Jones 5/8.
HORNETS: 1 Jamie Devine; 2 Luke Davison; 3 Peter Caddy; 4 Francis King; 5 Scott Pink; 6 Karl Dixon; 7 Mark Watson; 8 James Dixon; 9 Ryan Doran; 10 Richard Huby; 11 Adam Ramsden; 12 Matty Huby; 13 Charlie Tomlinson. Subs (all used): 14 Ben Agnew; 15 Jamie Martin; 16 Lewis McCarron; 17 Liam Martin.
Rugby Leaguer & League Express Men of the Match: *Cougars:* Paul Handforth; *Hornets:* Matty Huby.
Penalty count: 7-7; **Half-time:** 20-0;
Referee: Dave Sharpe; **Attendance:** 488.

Sunday 16th March 2014

HULL DOCKERS 6 HALIFAX 70

DOCKERS: 1 Danny Patrick; 2 David Palmer; 3 Jonathon Long; 4 Tom Oates; 5 Robbie Smith; 6 Chris Stephenson; 7 Craig Skelton; 14 Richard Dougal; 9 Matty Johnson; 10 Matthew McNee; 11 Andrew Taylor; 12 Jon Eccles; 13 Craig Render. Subs (all used): 8 Kallum Birch; 23 Mike Jarvis; 18 Mike Ayers; 16 Paul Fletcher.
Try: Jarvis (36); **Goals:** Stephenson 1/1.
HALIFAX: 1 Ryan Fieldhouse; 2 Rob Worrincy; 3 Steve Tyrer; 16 Danny Cowling; 5 Wayne Reittie; 7 Simon Brown; 18 Ben Johnston; 10 Luke Ambler; 14 Paul Mennell; 17 Ben Davies; 11 Dane Manning; 8 Adam Robinson; 23 Callum Casey. Subs (all used): 8 Tony Tonks; 19 Keith Holden; 24 Sam Brooks; 27 Ross Divorty.
Tries: Worrincy (10, 54, 57, 62, 80), Johnston (15, 63), Robinson (33, 68, 73), Tonks (40), Manning (44), Brooks (50); **Goals:** Tyrer 9/13.
Rugby Leaguer & League Express Men of the Match: *Dockers:* Chris Stephenson; *Halifax:* Ben Johnston.
Penalty count: 6-2; **Half-time:** 6-22; **Referee:** Tom Grant; **Attendance:** 600 *(at KC Lightstream Stadium, Hull).*

NORTH WALES CRUSADERS 58 PILKINGTON RECS 18

CRUSADERS: 1 Tommy Johnson; 22 Adam Clay; 23 Greg Wilde; 17 Stuart Reardon; 3 Christiaan Roets; 28 Craig White; 7 Jamie Dallimore; 21 Simon Stephens; 19 Karl Ashall; 8 Jonny Walker; 29 Steve Bannister; 14 Stephen Wild; 9 Craig Ashall. Subs (all used): 25 Owain Griffiths; 27 Jamie Clarke; 10 Mark Offerdahl; 26 Matt Reid.
Tries: Wilde (7), Dallimore (17, 27), Griffiths (25), Bannister (32, 34), C Ashall (39), Clay (58, 73), Johnson (62), Reid (75); **Goals:** Johnson 7/11.
PILKINGTON RECS: 1 Ryan Hilliard; 2 Danny Filson; 3 Mark Fishton; 4 Ian Stanley; 5 Andrew Knapper; 6 Greg Smith; 7 Danny Lynch; 11 Steve Charlson; 9 Ryan Liptrot; 10 Richard Rafferty; 12 Mark Briody; 8 Danny Hallsall; 13 Tom Roughley. Subs (all used): 15 Ben Gravner; 19 John Rees; 16 Barry Pope; 17 Liam Bostock.
Tries: Knapper (14), Filson (45, 79), Rafferty (50);
Goals: Lynch 1/4.
Rugby Leaguer & League Express Men of the Match: *Crusaders:* Jamie Dallimore;
Pilkington Recs: Richard Rafferty.
Penalty count: 10-4; **Half-time:** 36-4;
Referee: Jamie Callaghan; **Attendance:** 544.

SHEFFIELD EAGLES 54 EAST LEEDS 0

EAGLES: 1 Quentin Laulu-Togagae; 2 Scott Turner; 3 Menzie Yere; 30 Shaun Squires; 5 Misi Taulapapa; 19 Cory Aston; 7 Dominic Brambani; 12 Peter Green; 24 Gareth Owen; 10 Mitchell Stringer; 16 Duane Straugheir; 15 Matt Garside; 11 Michael Knowles. Subs (all used): 6 Pat Walker; 22 Will Hope; 4 Lelauloto Tagaloa; 14 James Davey.
Tries: Yere (5), Turner (14), Owen (16), Brambani (23, 61), Garside (32), Laulu-Togagae (41), Knowles (56), Aston (66), Squires (80);
Goals: Brambani 7/10.
EAST LEEDS: 1 Tom Sheldrake; 2 Kyle Quinlan; 3 Dean Langton; 4 Declan Tomlinson; 5 Jason Priestley; 6 Nathan Conroy; 7 Ryan Gaunt; 8 Lee Fisher; 9 Luke Tomlinson; 16 Dale Pattison; 11 Ben Walker; 12 David Nurse; 13 Jake Normington. Subs (all used): 14 John Carter; 15 Ashley James; 10 Tom Idle; 17 Joey Walkin.
Rugby Leaguer & League Express Men of the Match: *Eagles:* Misi Taulapapa; *East Leeds:* Ben Walker.
Penalty count: 12-6; **Half-time:** 24-0;
Referee: Dave Merrick; **Attendance:** 619.

MILFORD MARLINS 10 BARROW RAIDERS 18

MARLINS: 1 Ryan Oxtoby; 2 Elliott Watmough; 3 Aaron Jones-Bishop; 4 Whetu Austin; 5 Sam Hood; 6 Sam Clayton; 7 Josh Parle; 8 David Yates; 9 James Coates; 10 John Elkington; 11 Joe Ramsden; 12 Luke Reeves; 13 Sam Wilson. Subs (all used): 14 John Plunkett; 15 Matthew Brockson; 16 Travis Stolk; 17 Anthony Ward.
Tries: Watmough (13), Oxtoby (16); **Goals:** Oxtoby 1/2.
RAIDERS: 1 Ian Mort; 21 Mike Backhouse; 3 Aaron Low; 4 Max Wiper; 5 Dalton Grant; 6 Dom Speakman; 7 Liam Campbell; 15 Danny Jones; 9 Nathan Mossop; 17 Andrew Dawson; 11 Liam Harrison; 16 Matty Palmer; 13 Dan Toal. Subs (all used): 19 Brad Marwood; 8 Joe Burke; 18 Jack Morrison; 23 Chris Rowe.
Tries: Mort (5), Grant (31, 61);
Goals: Mort 1/1, Speakman 2/2.
Rugby Leaguer & League Express Men of the Match: *Marlins:* Josh Parle; *Raiders:* Dalton Grant.
Penalty count: 4-11; **Half-time:** 10-12;
Referee: Chris Campbell; **Attendance:** 1,000
(at Headingley Carnegie, Leeds).

BRITISH ARMY 12 DONCASTER 62

BRITISH ARMY: 1 Matt Curgenven; 5 Zac Yabia; 3 Colin Marangon; 4 Sonoma Veikune; 2 Scott Watkins; 6 Rob Martin; 7 Tony Lawless; 8 Tom Howley; 9 Danny Hunter; 10 Bruce Francis; 11 Andre Zwijnen; 12 Chris Brand; 13 Aaron Morfitt. Subs (all used): 14 Liam Garside; 15 Lagdia Buluilakeba; 17 Andy Parkin; 16 Casey Shaw.
Tries: Veikune (10), Curgenven (62); **Goals:** Lawless 2/2.
DONCASTER: 5 Dave Scott; 4 Nev Morrison; 20 Shaun Leaf; 11 Lee Waterman; 2 Stewart Sanderson; 6 Paul Cooke; 23 Richard Wilkinson; 16 Craig Robinson; 7 Danny Nicklas; 21 Matt Carbutt; 19 Liam Cunningham; 25 Alex Starling; 13 Mike Emmett. Subs (all used): 14 Russ Spiers; 18 Ryan Wilson; 17 Grant Edwards; 1 Mick Butterfield.
Tries: Cunningham (5, 21), Scott (12, 46, 67), Waterman (26, 43, 56), Morrison (30, 73), Wilkinson (39); **Goals:** Sanderson 6/7, Scott 3/4.
Rugby Leaguer & League Express Men of the Match: *British Army:* Andre Zwijnen; *Doncaster:* Lee Waterman.
Penalty count: 1-7; **Half-time:** 6-34;
Referee: Chris Kendall; **Attendance:** 357
(at Aldershot Military Stadium).

DEWSBURY RAMS 76 WEST HULL 10

RAMS: 1 Louis Sheriff; 2 Dale Morton; 4 Shane Grady; 22 Jordan Grayston; 18 Shaun Robinson; 31 Kieran Hyde; 6 Tom Hemingway; 15 Tommy Gallagher; 14 Ryan Wright; 32 Makali Aizue; 26 Lucas Walshaw; 25 Joel Farrell; 13 Aaron Brown. Subs (all used): 5 Greg Scott; 8 Stephen Nash; 17 Matthew Haggarty; 29 Ewan Dowes.
Tries: Morton (5), Gallagher (11), Aizue (15, 18), Brown (26), Farrell (32, 67, 73), Robinson (47, 51, 56), Sheriff (51), Grady (70), Dowes (75);
Goals: Hemingway 10/14.
WEST HULL: 1 Ash Rout; 2 Kristian Parker; 3 Tom Radley; 4 Ryan Langton; 5 Josh Hart; 6 Dean Thompson; 7 Ian Kerman; 8 James Garmston; 9 Callum Windley; 10 Brian Newby; 11 Sam Radford; 12 Paul Shaw; 13 Lewis Brown. Subs (all used): 14 Louis Crowther; 15 Karl Arnott; 16 Aaron Hickingbotham; 17 Scott Howlett.
Tries: Parker (21), Crowther (30); **Goals:** Kerman 1/2.
Rugby Leaguer & League Express Men of the Match: *Rams:* Joel Farrell; *West Hull:* Ian Kerman.
Penalty count: 10-6; **Half-time:** 32-10;
Referee: Adam Gill; **Attendance:** 433.

HUNSLET HAWKS 68 OXFORD 6

HAWKS: 2 Jimmy Watson; 5 Lee Mapals; 24 Aston Wilson; 4 Danny Maun; 28 Andy Ballard; 13 Danny Grimshaw; 6 Thomas Coyle; 8 Michael Haley; 27 Liam Hood; 15 Luke Stenchion; 11 John Oakes; 18 Brooke Broughton; 9 David March. Subs (all used): 14 Matthew Tebb; 22 George Clarke; 16 Lewis Reed; 17 James Davies.
Tries: Hood (2), Maun (7, 34), Broughton (10), Tebb (26), March (29, 32), Reed (38), Mapals (40, 70), T Coyle (57), Stenchion (62); **Goals:** Ballard 10/12.
OXFORD: 7 Jimmy Rowland; 5 Callum Mulkeen; 12 Andrew Hoggins; 3 Marcus Brooker; 2 Michael Crabtree; 18 Jordan Rice; 6 Tommy Connick; 24 Tom Davies; 9 Alex Thompson; 10 Matty Hadden; 11 John James Baird; 22 Graham O'Keeffe; 8 Chris Clarke. Subs (all used): 16 Sam Blaney; 15 Glenn Osborn; 14 Dave Ellison; 27 Wes Newton.
Try: Thompson (67); **Goals:** Rowland 1/1.
Rugby Leaguer & League Express Men of the Match: *Hawks:* Andy Ballard; *Oxford:* Alex Thompson.
Penalty count: 11-7; **Half-time:** 52-0;
Referee: Matthew Thomason; **Attendance:** 278.

ROCHDALE HORNETS 76
GLOUCESTERSHIRE ALL GOLDS 4

HORNETS: 1 Wayne English; 2 Gareth Langley; 19 Dave Llewellyn; 22 Mike Ratu; 29 Sam Te'o; 17 Ryan Millard; 6 Paul Crook; 8 John Cookson; 18 James Tilley; 10 Warren Thompson; 11 Chris Baines; 24 Tony Suffolk; 13 Jordan Case. Subs (all used): 25 Steve Marsh; 21 Chris Tyrer; 20 Joe Bate; 9 Lewis Sheridan.
Tries: Baines (2, 16), Langley (8, 49, 51), Te'o (22, 28, 46), Millard (30, 38, 69), Case (42), Llewellyn (63, 75), Crook (72); **Goals:** Crook 8/15.
ALL GOLDS: 20 Marcus Elliott; 2 Danny Cahill; 4 Aidan Jenkins; 1 Phil Cowburn; 5 Reece Rance; 6 Mark Barlow; 7 Danny Thomas; 10 Izaak Duffy; 19 Craig Cook; 14 Joe McClean; 11 Jason Muranka; 12 James Tutuila; 13 Brendan Smith. Subs (all used): 8 Connor Nolan; 15 Ash Haynes; 16 James Fisher; 17 Danny Fallon.
Try: Elliott (57); **Goals:** Jenkins 0/1.
Rugby Leaguer & League Express Men of the Match: *Hornets:* Ryan Millard; *All Golds:* Izaak Duffy.
Penalty count: 7-3; **Half-time:** 36-0;
Referee: Joe Cobb; **Attendance:** 307.

SOUTH WALES SCORPIONS 12 HEMEL STAGS 38

SCORPIONS: 1 Jordan Sheridan; 2 Ian Newbury; 3 Jack Pring; 22 Dafydd Hellard; 5 Chris Leyshon; 6 Paul Emanuelli; 13 Ashley Bateman; 17 Rhys Fitzgerald; 7 Shaun Owens; 12 Phil Carleton; 11 Barrie Phillips; 21 Matthew Wilcox; 10 Chris Vitalini. Subs (all used): 14 Mike Connor; 9 Connor Farrer; 4 Kyle Scrivens; 20 Scott Britton.
Tries: Farrer (40), Hellard (58); **Goals:** Emanuelli 2/2.
STAGS: 2 James Cameron; 20 Essad Al-Zubeidi; 3 Aaron Small; 4 Michael Brown; 5 James Hill; 6 Jy-mel Coleman; 7 Ben Young; 25 James Howitt; 9 Ben Thorburn; 8 Dominic Maloney; 11 Barry-John Swindells; 13 Alex Ingarfield; 10 Dan Ljazouli. Subs (all used): 14 Evan Simons; 12 Cariern Clement-Pascall; 16 Guy Aldam; 1 Mitch Barbera.
Tries: Ljazouli (13), Al-Zubeidi (22), Jy-mel Coleman (32), Thorburn (61), Barbera (65), Hill (69), Swindells (72);
Goals: Swindells 2/3, Young 3/4.
Rugby Leaguer & League Express Men of the Match: *Scorpions:* Connor Farrer; *Stags:* Dominic Maloney.
Penalty count: 5-5; **Half-time:** 6-16;
Referee: Warren Turley; **Attendance:** 213.

SWINTON LIONS 66 GATESHEAD THUNDER 6

LIONS: 1 Ritchie Hawkyard; 2 Ben Warrilow; 11 Danny Halliwell; 4 Mick Nanyn; 5 Freddie Walker; 6 Anthony Bowman; 7 Ian Watson; 8 Luke Menzies; 9 Andy Ackers; 16 Mike Morrison; 3 Kash Watkins; 12 Darren Hawkyard; 15 Josh Barlow. Subs (all used): 27 Lewis Hulme; 13 James Brown; 17 Zach Johnson; 20 Mark Thomas.
Tries: Bowman (5), Walker (11, 19), Warrilow (15), Watkins (27, 61), R Hawkyard (35, 42), Nanyn (37, 80), D Hawkyard (46), Barlow (73); **Goals:** Nanyn 9/12.
Sin bin: Morrison (66) - fighting.
THUNDER: 1 Sam Lynch; 5 Carl Booth; 3 Jacob Blades; 4 Joe Brown; 2 Tom Capper; 6 Paul Stamp; 7 Carl Puckering; 8 Tom Lynch; 9 Ricky Hough; 10 Lee Fewlass; 24 Chris Heil; 12 Jason Payne; 29 Rhys Clarke. Subs (all used): 25 Nathan Powley; 19 Josh Stoker; 23 Callum Cockburn; 14 Matt Barron.
Try: Capper (2); **Goals:** Puckering 1/1.
Sin bin: T Lynch (66) - fighting.
Rugby League & League Express Men of the Match:
Lions: Ian Watson; *Thunder:* Tom Capper.
Penalty count: 6-5; **Half-time:** 40-6;
Referee: Gareth Hewer; **Attendance:** 249.

YORK CITY KNIGHTS 34 WHITEHAVEN 32

CITY KNIGHTS: 1 James Haynes; 2 George Elliott; 30 James Morland; 4 Greg Minikin; 5 Ben Dent; 6 Pat Smith; 7 Jon Presley; 18 Austin Bell; 9 Jack Lee; 10 Jack Aldous; 11 Ryan Mallinder; 12 Ed Smith; 22 Ben Crane. Subs (all used): 14 Kris Brining; 19 Jake Joynt; 20 Harry Carter; 8 Nathan Freer.
Tries: Morland (24), Mallinder (29), Presley (33), B Dent (39), Minikin (62), Elliott (69);
Goals: Crane 1/1, Haynes 4/6.
WHITEHAVEN: 1 Tom Carr; 5 Shaun Ainscough; 4 Scott McAvoy; 3 Jessie Joe Nandye; 18 Jordan Burns; 6 Chris Taylor; 7 Cain Southernwood; 10 Paul Jackson; 9 James Newton; 8 Samir Tahraoui; 11 Lee Doran; 12 Lee Mitchell; 21 Larsen Marabe. Subs (all used): 14 Neil Thorman; 19 Paul Cullnean; 22 James Robinson; 13 Bradd Crellin.
Tries: Tahraoui (10, 78), Southernwood (12), Burns (21, 64), Crellin (59); **Goals:** Southernwood 4/6.
Rugby League & League Express Men of the Match:
City Knights: Nathan Freer;
Whitehaven: Cain Southernwood.
Penalty count: 7-8; **Half-time:** 22-16;
Referee: Tom Crashley; **Attendance:** 403.

ROUND 4

Thursday 3rd April 2014

HULL FC 36 SALFORD RED DEVILS 37
(after golden point extra-time)

HULL: 20 Jamie Shaul; 15 Joe Arundel; 3 Ben Crooks; 4 Kirk Yeaman; 34 Fetuli Talanoa; 32 Jordan Rankin; 7 Jacob Miller; 8 Mickey Paea; 9 Danny Houghton (C); 22 Josh Bowden; 21 Dean Hadley; 12 Chris Tuson; 13 Joe Westerman. Subs (all used): 17 Liam Watts; 16 Jordan Thompson; 26 Iafeta Palea'aesina; 33 Aaron Heremaia.
Tries: Arundel (5, 22), Shaul (38, 65), Talanoa (42), Rankin (54); **Goals:** Crooks 6/7.
RED DEVILS: 1 Jake Mullaney; 23 Greg Johnson; 3 Martin Gleeson; 4 Junior Sa'u; 5 Francis Meli; 6 Rangi Chase; 7 Tim Smith; 8 Adrian Morley (C); 9 Tommy Lee; 10 Lama Tasi; 13 Harrison Hansen; 12 Gareth Hock; 18 Steve Rapira. Subs (all used): 14 Theo Fages; 11 Tony Puletua; 21 Jordan Walne; 17 Shannan McPherson.
Tries: Meli (7, 31, 79), Chase (10), Fages (57), Sa'u (69);
Goals: Mullaney 6/6; **Field goal:** Chase (88).
Rugby League & League Express Men of the Match:
Hull: Joe Westerman; *Red Devils:* Rangi Chase.
Penalty count: 10-4; **Half-time:** 16-18;
Referee: Ben Thaler; **Attendance:** 5,435.

Friday 4th April 2014

CATALAN DRAGONS 40 LONDON BRONCOS 24

DRAGONS: 2 Morgan Escare; 5 Michael Oldfield; 4 Ben Pomeroy; 25 Vincent Duport; 18 Daryl Millard; 3 Leon Pryce; 6 Thomas Bosc; 8 Olivier Elima; 16 Eloi Pelissier; 10 Jeff Lima; 11 Zeb Taia; 12 Louis Anderson; 24 Jason Baitieri (C). Subs (all used): 15 Antoni Maria; 23 Lopini Paea; 29 Benjamin Garcia; 32 Joan Guasch (D).
Tries: Pryce (4), Anderson (12, 55), Bosc (22), Millard (47), Maria (50), Escare (75); **Goals:** Bosc 6/7.
BRONCOS: 23 Denny Solomona; 25 Iliess Macani; 24 Mason Caton-Brown; 4 Thomas Minns; 27 Jamie O'Callaghan; 6 Ben Farrar; 7 Josh Drinkwater; 15 James Greenwood; 9 Scott Moore; 16 Nick Slyney; 8 Atelea Vea; 12 Matt Cook (C); 13 Alex Foster. Subs (all used): 10 Olsi Krasniqi; 11 Mike McMeeken; 14 Mike Bishay; 18 George Griffin.
Tries: Solomona (27), Caton-Brown (60), Slyney (72, 80);
Goals: Drinkwater 4/4.
Rugby League & League Express Men of the Match:
Dragons: Leon Pryce; *Broncos:* Josh Drinkwater.
Penalty count: 9-8; **Half-time:** 16-6;
Referee: Robert Hicks; **Attendance:** 2,443.

DEWSBURY RAMS 6 WIGAN WARRIORS 58

RAMS: 31 Kieran Hyde; 2 Dale Morton; 3 Karl Pryce; 4 Shane Grady; 5 Greg Scott; 13 Aaron Brown; 7 Anthony Thackeray; 10 Ryan Hepworth; 9 Wayne Godwin; 29 Ewan Dowes; 12 Scott Hale; 26 Lucas Walshaw; 11 Rob Spicer. Subs (all used): 14 Ryan Wright; 6 Tom Hemingway; 8 Stephen Nash; 17 Matthew Haggarty.
Try: Morton (44); **Goals:** Hemingway 1/1.
WARRIORS: 26 Ryan Hampshire; 2 Josh Charnley; 23 Dan Sarginson; 4 Iain Thornley; 32 Joe Burgess; 6 Blake Green; 7 Matty Smith; 8 Scott Taylor; 9 Michael McIlorum; 10 Ben Flower; 24 Tony Clubb; 12 Liam Farrell; 13 Sean O'Loughlin (C). Subs (all used): 14 Jack Hughes; 22 Eddy Pettybourne; 27 George Williams; 28 Jordan James.
Tries: Burgess (5, 9, 50, 59), Sarginson (56), Thornley (64, 74), Smith (66), Williams (72), Green (80);
Goals: Smith 6/7, Williams 3/3.
Rugby League & League Express Men of the Match:
Rams: Anthony Thackeray; *Warriors:* Joe Burgess.
Penalty count: 8-10; **Half-time:** 0-12;
Referee: Joe Cobb; **Attendance:** 3,054.

Saturday 5th April 2014

SHEFFIELD EAGLES 70 LONDON SKOLARS 28

EAGLES: 1 Quentin Laulu-Togagae; 2 Scott Turner; 3 Menzie Yere; 4 Lelauloto Tagaloa; 5 Misi Taulapapa; 6 Pat Walker; 7 Dominic Brambani; 18 Tom Lillycrop; 14 James Davey; 10 Mitchell Stringer; 15 Matt Garside; 16 Duane Straugheir; 11 Michael Knowles. Subs (all used): 24 Gareth Owen; 21 Jack Blagbrough; 26 Jordan Burke; 27 Peter Aspinall.
Tries: Knowles (4), Taulapapa (10), Davey (22), Blagbrough (32, 50, 75), Laulu-Togagae (39, 57), Tagaloa (44), Burke (67), Walker (69), Garside (78);
Goals: Brambani 11/12.
SKOLARS: 1 John Paxton; 5 Ibrahim Kabia; 3 Mufaro Mvududu; 4 Kazeem Fatouri; 22 Judd Greenhalgh; 6 Courtney Davies; 7 Matt Bradley; 14 Teli Pelo; 16 Lloyd O'Connor; 10 Dave Williams; 11 Michael Worrincy; 12 Anthony Cox; 20 Sam Wellings. Subs (all used): 15 Martyn Smith; 8 Rob Thomas; 13 Louis Robinson; 21 Michael Sykes.
Tries: Davies (28), Robinson (34), Smith (54, 62), O'Connor (71); **Goals:** Bradley 4/5.
Rugby League & League Express Men of the Match:
Eagles: Jack Blagbrough; *Skolars:* Martyn Smith.
Penalty count: 5-4; **Half-time:** 30-12;
Referee: Peter Brooke; **Attendance:** 505.

Sunday 6th April 2014

BATLEY BULLDOGS 10 CASTLEFORD TIGERS 48

BULLDOGS: 1 Miles Greenwood; 17 Lee Paterson; 3 Alex Bretherton; 28 Josh Griffin; 2 Vinny Finigan; 11 John Davies; 7 Scott Leatherbarrow; 8 Byron Smith; 18 Luke Blake; 20 Adam Gledhill; 30 Charlie Martin; 12 Sam Scott; 13 Mark Applegarth. Subs (all used): 10 Alex Rowe; 14 Alistair Leak; 15 Jay Leary; 19 Joe Chandler.
Tries: Griffin (24), Paterson (80); **Goals:** Paterson 1/2.
TIGERS: 6 Luke Dorn; 24 James Clare; 23 Michael Channing; 3 Michael Shenton (C); 5 Justin Carney; 7 Marc Sneyd; 26 Liam Finn; 8 Andy Lynch; 9 Adam Milner; 19 Scott Wheeldon; 16 Oliver Holmes; 12 Weller Hauraki; 13 Nathan Massey. Subs (all used): 15 Ryan Boyle; 18 Frankie Mariano; 20 Jamie Ellis; 25 Daniel Fleming.
Tries: Dorn (5, 59), Carney (18, 47, 70), Ellis (63), Sneyd (65), Clare (73), Wheeldon (79); **Goals:** Sneyd 6/9.
Rugby League & League Express Men of the Match:
Bulldogs: John Davies; *Tigers:* Marc Sneyd.
Penalty count: 5-8; **Half-time:** 6-12;
Referee: George Stokes; **Attendance:** 2,482.

BRADFORD BULLS 60 OLDHAM 6

BULLS: 1 Brett Kearney; 2 Elliot Kear; 21 Adam Henry; 3 Adrian Purtell; 22 Sam Wood; 16 Danny Addy; 7 Luke Gale (C); 14 Manase Manuokafoa; 19 Adam O'Brien; 13 Chev Walker; 4 Matty Blythe; 12 Dale Ferguson (D); 18 James Donaldson. Subs (all used): 5 Jamie Foster; 23 Oliver Roberts; 25 Nathan Conroy; 30 Jamal Fakir (D).
Tries: Gale (6, 20, 77), Kearney (17), Kear (40, 59), O'Brien (43), Addy (46), Henry (56), Foster (70), Ferguson (79); **Goals:** Gale 8/11.
OLDHAM: 1 Tom Whitehead; 2 Mo Agoro; 3 Ben Wood; 9 Sam Gee; 5 Dale Bloomfield; 6 Lewis Palfrey; 7 Brett Robinson; 19 Michael Ward; 17 Danny Whitmore; 10 Jason Boults; 11 Josh Crowley; 12 Danny Langtree; 13 Mark Hobson. Subs (all used): 8 Phil Joy; 15 Paddy Mooney; 16 Kenny Hughes; 20 George Tyson.
Try: Hughes (24); **Goals:** Palfrey 1/1.
Rugby League & League Express Men of the Match:
Bulls: Luke Gale; *Oldham:* Lewis Palfrey.
Penalty count: 12-6; **Half-time:** 24-6; **Referee:** Chris Leatherbarrow *(replaced by Scott Mikalauskas, 60)*;
Attendance: 2,788.

DONCASTER 68 HEMEL STAGS 18

DONCASTER: 1 Mick Butterfield; 4 Nev Morrison; 3 Liam Welham; 11 Lee Waterman; 2 Stewart Sanderson; 6 Paul Cooke; 23 Richard Wilkinson; 21 Matt Carbutt; 15 Scott Spaven; 18 Ryan Wilson; 20 Shaun Leaf; 25 Alex Starling; 17 Grant Edwards. Subs (all used): 16 Craig Robinson; 14 Russ Spiers; 13 Mike Emmett; 24 Chris Spurr.
Tries: Waterman (5), Sanderson (9, 72), Butterfield (13), Wilkinson (17, 45), Emmett (32), Edwards (39), Wilson (66), Spurr (69), Welham (74), Cooke (78);
Goals: Sanderson 10/12.
STAGS: 2 James Cameron; 5 James Hill; 4 Michael Brown; 3 Aaron Small; 20 Essad Al-Zubeidi; 1 Mitch Barbera; 7 Ben Young; 8 Dominic Maloney; 14 Evan Simons; 25 James Howitt; 11 Barry-John Swindells; 13 Alex Ingarfield; 10 Dan Ljazouli. Subs (all used): 18 Lee Hudson; 15 Matthew Bailey; 23 Eddie Mbaraga; 16 Guy Aldam.
Tries: Al-Zubeidi (20), Ingarfield (22), Hill (29);
Goals: Swindells 3/3.
Rugby League & League Express Men of the Match:
Doncaster: Richard Wilkinson; *Stags:* Mitch Barbera.
Penalty count: 7-5; **Half-time:** 34-18;
Referee: Chris Kendall; **Attendance:** 348.

FEATHERSTONE ROVERS 66
NORTH WALES CRUSADERS 0

ROVERS: 1 Ian Hardman; 2 Will Sharp; 22 James Mendeika; 3 Greg Worthington; 27 Etuate Uaisele; 23 Andy Kain; 7 Gareth Moore; 8 Steve Crossley; 9 Andy Ellis; 10 Keegan Hirst; 18 Jamie Cording; 12 Tim Spears; 11 James Lockwood. Subs (all used): 14 George Flanagan; 15 Matty Dale; 13 Matt James; 19 Kyle Briggs.
Tries: Crossley (2, 18), Mendeika (15, 42, 78), Cording (21, 56), Kain (32), Worthington (48), Dale (60), Sharp (70), Flanagan (75); **Goals:** Moore 9/12.
CRUSADERS: 23 Greg Wilde; 2 Dan Birkett; 17 Stuart Reardon; 3 Christiaan Roets; 22 Adam Clay; 28 Craig White; 7 Jamie Dallimore; 10 Mark Offerdahl; 19 Karl Ashall; 15 David Mills; 26 Matt Reid; 29 Steve Bannister; 14 Stephen Wild. Subs (all used): 16 Ryan MacDonald; 8 Jonny Walker; 25 Owain Griffiths; 1 Tommy Johnson.
Rugby League & League Express Men of the Match:
Rovers: Andy Kain; *Crusaders:* Craig White.
Penalty count: 6-4; **Half-time:** 26-0;
Referee: Gareth Hewer; **Attendance:** 1,312.

HALIFAX 10 WIDNES VIKINGS 34

HALIFAX: 1 Ryan Fieldhouse; 21 Tom Saxton; 3 Steve Tyrer; 16 Danny Cowling; 25 Gareth Potts; 6 Scott Murrell; 7 Simon Brown; 10 Luke Ambler; 9 Ben Kaye; 12 Andy Bracek; 11 Dane Manning; 27 Ross Divorty; 13 Luke Adamson. Subs (all used): 14 Paul Mennell; 8 Tony Tonks; 17 Ben Davies; 23 Callum Casey.
Tries: Fieldhouse (10), Potts (17); **Goals:** Tyrer 1/2.
VIKINGS: 2 Jack Owens; 20 Paddy Flynn; 14 Chris Dean; 34 Rhodri Lloyd; 29 Declan Hulme; 6 Kevin Brown; 15 Lloyd White; 25 Alex Gerrard; 9 Jon Clarke (C); 23 Phil Joseph; 17 Danny Galea; 12 Danny Tickle; 13 Hep Cahill. Subs (all used): 35 Paul Clough; 11 Dave Allen; 16 Willie Isa; 8 Eamon O'Carroll.
Tries: Clarke (22), Brown (50, 75), Flynn (57), Hulme (63), Joseph (69); **Goals:** Tickle 5/6.
Rugby League & League Express Men of the Match:
Halifax: Scott Murrell; *Vikings:* Kevin Brown.
Penalty count: 8-9; **Half-time:** 10-6;
Referee: Matthew Thomason; **Attendance:** 2,271.

HULL KINGSTON ROVERS 24
WARRINGTON WOLVES 28

ROVERS: 2 Ben Cockayne; 32 Ade Gardner; 18 Liam Salter; 3 Kris Welham; 24 Omari Caro; 6 Travis Burns (C); 7 Kris Keating; 14 Adam Walker; 9 Josh Hodgson (C); 10 Michael Weyman; 11 Kevin Larroyer; 20 Jordan Cox; 12 Neville Costigan. Subs (all used): 21 Keal Carlile; 23 James Green; 16 Jason Netherton; 22 Rhys Lovegrove.
Tries: Cockayne (13), A Walker (18), Gardner (53), Caro (75); **Goals:** Burns 4/5.
WOLVES: 1 Matthew Russell; 5 Joel Monaghan; 3 Chris Bridge; 4 Ryan Atkins; 18 Rhys Evans; 6 Stefan Ratchford; 7 Richard Myler; 8 Chris Hill; 9 Mick Higham; 10 Roy Asotasi; 11 Trent Waterhouse; 12 Ben Westwood (C); 13 Simon Grix. Subs (all used): 14 Michael Monaghan (C); 16 Paul Wood; 23 James Laithwaite; 25 Ben Evans.
Tries: Atkins (21, 60), J Monaghan (32), R Evans (43), Asotasi (73); **Goals:** Bridge 4/5.
Rugby League & League Express Men of the Match:
Rovers: Adam Walker; *Wolves:* Richard Myler.
Penalty count: 8-6; **Half-time:** 14-10;
Referee: Richard Silverwood; **Attendance:** 4,911.

HUNSLET HAWKS 27 WORKINGTON TOWN 10

HAWKS: 1 Stuart Kain; 5 Lee Mapals; 2 Jimmy Watson; 4 Danny Maun; 21 Jamaine Akaidere; 13 Danny Grimshaw; 20 Danny Ansell; 10 James Houston; 9 David March; 15 Luke Stenchion; 11 John Oakes; 18 Brooke Broughton; 26 Liam Mackay. Subs (all used): 14 Matthew Tebb; 16 Lewis Reed; 12 Aaron Lyons; 22 George Clarke.
Tries: Maun (6, 68), Grimshaw (26), Mackay (33), Kain (77); **Goals:** Ansell 3/6; **Field goal:** Ansell (40).
TOWN: 30 Lewis Tierney; 34 Jack Murphy; 3 Jason Mossop; 14 Kayle Connor; 1 Brett Carter; 6 Peter Lupton; 16 Carl Forber; 8 Kris Coward; 19 Nathan Lucock; 10 Marc Shackley; 11 Brett Phillips; 31 Connor Farrell; 15 Daniel Rooney. Subs (all used): 4 Andy Morris; 22 Jack Gaskell; 20 Callum Rowlandson; 18 James Duerden.
Tries: Carter (53, 61); **Goals:** Connor 1/2.
Rugby League & League Express Men of the Match:
Hawks: David March; *Town:* Brett Carter.
Penalty count: 6-5; **Half-time:** 17-0;
Referee: Warren Turley; **Attendance:** 504.

KEIGHLEY COUGARS 54 BARROW RAIDERS 28

COUGARS: 1 James Craven; 2 Richie Barnett; 19 Danny Lawton; 4 James Haley; 5 Paul White; 6 Danny Jones; 7 Paul Handforth; 8 Andy Shickell; - Luke Haigh; 10 Sean Hesketh; 11 Josh Lynam; 12 Brendan Rawlins; 14 Paul March. Subs (all used): 15 Scott Law; 16 Jode Sheriffe; 27 Jack Lee; 32 Ross Peltier.
Tries: Barnett (13, 74), Lawton (28), White (31), Craven (37), Law (48), March (56), Rawlins (59), Peltier (62), Hesketh (71); **Goals:** Jones 7/10.
RAIDERS: 1 Ian Mort; 2 Scott Turner; 26 Ryan Shaw; 4 Max Wiper; 5 Dalton Grant; 6 Dom Speakman; 7 Liam Campbell; 15 Danny Jones; - Mick Govin; 18 Jack Morrison; 11 Liam Harrison; 24 Joe Bullock; 13 Dan Toal. Subs (all used): 8 Joe Burke; 17 Andrew Dawson; 19 Brad Marwood; 12 Michael Dengate.
Tries: Grant (17, 80), Campbell (22, 70), Dawson (53);
Goals: Mort 3/3, Shaw 1/3.
Rugby League & League Express Men of the Match:
Cougars: Paul March; *Raiders:* Liam Campbell.
Penalty count: 7-5; **Half-time:** 20-14;
Referee: Dave Merrick; **Attendance:** 823.

ROCHDALE HORNETS 22 LEIGH CENTURIONS 28

HORNETS: 1 Wayne English; 14 Sean Casey; 4 Daniel Davies; 22 Mike Ratu; 9 Lewis Sheridan; 6 Paul Crook; 17 Ryan Millard; 8 John Cookson; 23 James Dandy; 10 Warren Thompson; 11 Chris Baines; 29 Alex Clare; 18 James Tilley. Subs (all used): 16 Liam Gilchrist; 25 Steve Marsh; 26 Adam Bowman; 13 Jordan Case.
Tries: Casey (27), English (32, 59), Case (52);
Goals: Crook 3/4.
CENTURIONS: 1 Gregg McNally; 22 Adam Higson; 31 Cameron Pitman; 3 Stuart Littler; 15 Liam Kay; 6 Martyn Ridyard; 7 Ryan Brierley; 8 Tom Spencer; 14 Sean Penkywicz; 10 Oliver Wilkes; 11 Matt Sarsfield; 30 Kurt Haggerty; 35 Sam Hopkins. Subs (all used): 9 Bob Beswick; 20 Andy Thornley; 18 Jamie Acton; 29 Jake Emmitt.
Tries: Wilkes (5, 7), Ridyard (24), Brierley (47), McNally (51); **Goals:** Ridyard 4/6.
Sin bin: Littler (64) - holding down.
Rugby Leaguer & League Express Men of the Match: *Hornets:* Wayne English; *Centurions:* Jake Emmitt.
Penalty count: 7-12; **Half-time:** 10-18;
Referee: Dave Sharpe; **Attendance:** 1,007.

SWINTON LIONS 31 YORK CITY KNIGHTS 28

LIONS: 1 Ritchie Hawkyard; 2 Ben Warrilow; 19 Jacque Peet; 11 Danny Halliwell; 5 Freddie Walker; 28 Chris Atkin; 7 Ian Watson; 8 Luke Menzies; 9 Andy Ackers; 16 Mike Morrison; 3 Kash Watkins; 12 Darren Hawkyard; 13 James Brown. Subs: 27 Lewis Hulme; 17 Zach Johnson; 21 Joe Worthington; 4 Mick Nanyn (not used).
Tries: D Hawkyard (13, 39), Watkins (33), Peet (35), Atkin (60); **Goals:** Peet 5/6; **Field goal:** Atkin (80).
CITY KNIGHTS: 1 James Haynes; 2 George Elliott; 3 James Ford; 4 James Morland; 5 Ben Dent; 6 Pat Smith; 7 Jon Presley; 18 Austin Bell; 9 Jack Lee; 10 Jack Aldous; 15 Jason Golden; 12 Ed Smith; 13 Lee Paterson. Subs (all used): 23 Benn Hardcastle; 11 Ryan Mallinder; 16 Iain Morrison; 19 Jake Joynt.
Tries: Lee (2), Paterson (26), B Hardcastle (48), P Smith (53), B Dent (72); **Goals:** Haynes 4/5.
Rugby Leaguer & League Express Men of the Match: *Lions:* James Brown; *City Knights:* Benn Hardcastle.
Penalty count: 5-7; **Half-time:** 22-12;
Referee: Jamie Bloem; **Attendance:** 427.

WAKEFIELD TRINITY WILDCATS 6 LEEDS RHINOS 60

WILDCATS: 1 Richard Mathers; 2 Peter Fox; 3 Dean Collis; 6 Paul Sykes; 5 Reece Lyne; 20 Jarrod Sammut; 7 Pita Godinet; 8 Scott Anderson; 9 Paul McShane; 16 Richard Moore (D2); 11 Ali Lauitiiti; 12 Danny Kirmond (C); 13 Danny Washbrook. Subs (all used): 23 Daniel Smith; 17 Taulima Tautai; 30 Nick Scruton; 15 Matt Ryan.
Try: Godinet (36); **Goals:** Sammut 1/1.
RHINOS: 1 Zak Hardaker; 20 Tom Briscoe; 3 Kallum Watkins; 4 Joel Moon; 5 Ryan Hall; 6 Danny McGuire; 13 Kevin Sinfield (C); 8 Kylie Leuluai; 7 Rob Burrow; 10 Jamie Peacock; 15 Brett Delaney; 12 Carl Ablett; 17 Ian Kirke. Subs (all used): 14 Stevie Ward; 16 Ryan Bailey; 19 Mitch Achurch; 21 Liam Sutcliffe.
Tries: Burrow (18, 73), Ablett (22, 31), McGuire (25), Hall (28, 40), Achurch (45), Sutcliffe (50), T Briscoe (69), Moon (78); **Goals:** Sinfield 8/11.
Rugby Leaguer & League Express Men of the Match: *Wildcats:* Nick Scruton; *Rhinos:* Rob Burrow.
Penalty count: 3-5; **Half-time:** 6-32;
Referee: James Child; **Attendance:** 4,482.

HUDDERSFIELD GIANTS 16 ST HELENS 17

GIANTS: 1 Scott Grix; 2 Jermaine McGillvary; 5 Aaron Murphy; 4 Joe Wardle; 19 Jodie Broughton; 6 Danny Brough (C); 7 Luke Robinson; 8 Eorl Crabtree; 9 Shaun Lunt; 10 Craig Kopczak; 11 Brett Ferres; 12 Jason Chan; 14 Michael Lawrence. Subs (all used): 13 Chris Bailey; 16 David Faiumu; 18 Kyle Wood; 20 Antonio Kaufusi.
Tries: Lunt (27, 57), Wardle (38); **Goals:** Brough 2/3.
Dismissal: Ferres (64) - dangerous tackle on Lomax.
SAINTS: 1 Jonny Lomax; 2 Tom Makinson; 3 Jordan Turner; 4 Josh Jones; 5 Adam Swift; 6 Lance Hohaia; 7 Luke Walsh; 16 Kyle Amor; 9 James Roby; 18 Alex Walmsley; 13 Willie Manu; 15 Mark Flanagan; 11 Iosia Soliola. Subs (all used): 25 Anthony Walker; 17 Paul Wellens (C); 23 Joe Greenwood; 8 Mose Masoe.
Tries: Swift (9), Makinson (14, 66); **Goals:** Walsh 2/4;
Field goal: Walsh (80).
Rugby Leaguer & League Express Men of the Match: *Giants:* Shaun Lunt; *Saints:* Luke Walsh.
Penalty count: 5-13; **Half-time:** 10-8;
Referee: Phil Bentham; **Attendance:** 5,566.

ROUND 5

Saturday 26th April 2014

LEEDS RHINOS 32 ST HELENS 12

RHINOS: 1 Zak Hardaker; 20 Tom Briscoe; 3 Kallum Watkins; 4 Joel Moon; 5 Ryan Hall; 13 Kevin Sinfield (C); 6 Danny McGuire; 8 Kylie Leuluai; 7 Rob Burrow; 10 Jamie Peacock; 12 Carl Ablett; 19 Mitch Achurch; 15 Brett Delaney. Subs (all used): 17 Ian Kirke; 21 Liam Sutcliffe; 18 Chris Clarkson; 23 Brad Singleton.
Tries: Hardaker (4, 36), Moon (48), McGuire (73), Peacock (78); **Goals:** Sinfield 6/6.
SAINTS: 1 Jonny Lomax; 2 Tom Makinson; 3 Jordan Turner; 22 Mark Percival; 5 Adam Swift; 12 Jon Wilkin; 7 Luke Walsh; 16 Kyle Amor; 9 James Roby; 18 Alex Walmsley; 10 Louie McCarthy-Scarsbrook; 11 Iosia Soliola; 4 Josh Jones. Subs (all used): 8 Mose Masoe; 27 Greg Richards; 23 Joe Greenwood; 17 Paul Wellens (C).
Tries: Swift (12), Jones (52); **Goals:** Walsh 2/2.
Rugby Leaguer & League Express Men of the Match: *Rhinos:* Ryan Hall; *Saints:* James Roby.
Penalty count: 4-4; **Half-time:** 12-6;
Referee: Richard Silverwood; **Attendance:** 12,194.

SWINTON LIONS 20 KEIGHLEY COUGARS 33

LIONS: 1 Ritchie Hawkyard; 21 Joe Worthington; 6 Anthony Bowman; 19 Jacque Peet; 2 Ben Warrilow; 28 Chris Atkin; 7 Ian Watson; 16 Mike Morrison; 9 Andy Ackers; 8 Luke Menzies; 24 Joe Philbin; 12 Darren Hawkyard; 13 James Brown. Subs (all used): 27 Lewis Hulme; 17 Zach Johnson; 20 Mark Thomas; - Steve Lewis.
Tries: Bowman (7, 14, 59), Lewis (64); **Goals:** Peet 2/4.
Sin bin: R Hawkyard (39) - fighting.
COUGARS: 1 James Craven; 2 Richie Barnett; 19 Danny Lawton; 22 Daley Williams; 5 Paul White; 6 Danny Jones; 7 Paul Handforth; 15 Scott Law; 14 Paul March; 10 Sean Hesketh; 11 Josh Lynam; 12 Brendan Rawlins; 17 Ben Sagar. Subs (all used): 25 Lewis Graham; 16 Jode Sheriffe; 34 Luke Haigh; 32 Ross Peltier.
Tries: Lawton (2), Jode Sheriffe (25), Barnett (35, 55), Craven (45), Williams (67); **Goals:** Jones 4/7;
Field goal: Handforth (75).
Sin bin: Williams (39) - fighting.
Rugby Leaguer & League Express Men of the Match: *Lions:* Mike Morrison; *Cougars:* Paul March.
Penalty count: 4-8; **Half-time:** 10-16;
Referee: Tim Roby; **Attendance:** 468.

Sunday 27th April 2014

BRADFORD BULLS 33 CATALAN DRAGONS 20

BULLS: 1 Brett Kearney; 2 Elliot Kear; 20 Luke George; 3 Adrian Purtell; 5 Jamie Foster; 17 Lee Gaskell; 7 Luke Gale; 14 Manase Manuokafoa; 9 Matt Diskin (C); 30 Jamal Fakir; 33 Jay Pitts (D); 16 Danny Addy; 13 Chev Walker. Subs (all used): 15 Adam Sidlow; 19 Adam O'Brien; 11 Tom Olbison; 21 Adam Henry.
Tries: Gaskell (28), Foster (34, 37), Gale (43), Purtell (57); **Goals:** Foster 6/6; **Field goal:** Gale (79).
DRAGONS: 2 Morgan Escare; 5 Michael Oldfield; 4 Ben Pomeroy; 25 Vincent Duport; 18 Daryl Millard; 3 Leon Pryce; 14 William Barthau; 8 Olivier Elima; 16 Eloi Pelissier; 21 Julian Bousquet; 11 Zeb Taia; 17 Elliott Whitehead; 24 Jason Baitieri (C). Subs (all used): 12 Louis Anderson; 23 Lopini Paea; 29 Benjamin Garcia; 32 Joan Guasch.
Tries: Millard (2), Pomeroy (10), Elima (13), Oldfield (61); **Goals:** Barthau 2/4.
Rugby Leaguer & League Express Men of the Match: *Bulls:* Lee Gaskell; *Dragons:* Zeb Taia.
Penalty count: 9-5; **Half-time:** 18-16;
Referee: James Child; **Attendance:** 2,341.

LEIGH CENTURIONS 26 FEATHERSTONE ROVERS 16

CENTURIONS: 1 Gregg McNally; 22 Adam Higson; 31 Cameron Pitman; 4 Tom Armstrong; 15 Liam Kay; 6 Martyn Ridyard; 7 Ryan Brierley; 10 Oliver Wilkes; 14 Sean Penkywicz; 26 Ryan Duffy; 11 Matt Sarsfield; 12 Tommy Goulden; 13 Sam Barlow. Subs (all used): 9 Bob Beswick; 35 Sam Hopkins; 30 Kurt Haggerty; 8 Tom Spencer.
Tries: Brierley (1, 26, 72), Kay (57), Haggerty (63);
Goals: Ridyard 2/3, Brierley 1/2.
ROVERS: 1 Ian Hardman; 27 Etuate Uaisele; 3 Greg Worthington; 22 James Mendeika; 2 Will Sharp; 23 Andy Kain; 7 Gareth Moore; 13 Matt James; 9 Andy Ellis; 10 Keegan Hirst; 18 Jamie Cording; 12 Tim Spears; 11 James Lockwood. Subs (all used): 14 George Flanagan; 15 Matty Dale; 16 Andrew Bostock; 19 Kyle Briggs.
Tries: Sharp (6, 22), Mendeika (15, 77);
Goals: Moore 0/4, Briggs 0/1.
Rugby Leaguer & League Express Men of the Match: *Centurions:* Sam Barlow; *Rovers:* Keegan Hirst.
Penalty count: 9-6; **Half-time:** 12-12;
Referee: Ben Thaler; **Attendance:** 3,664.

SALFORD RED DEVILS 20 WIDNES VIKINGS 30

RED DEVILS: 37 Greg Eden (D); 36 Michael Platt; 3 Martin Gleeson; 4 Junior Sa'u; 5 Francis Meli; 6 Rangi Chase; 14 Theo Fages; 8 Adrian Morley (C); 35 Logan Tomkins; 10 Lama Tasi; 13 Harrison Hansen; 12 Gareth Hock; 9 Tommy Lee. Subs (all used): 7 Tim Smith; 15 Darrell Griffin; 18 Steve Rapira; 11 Tony Puletua.
Tries: Hock (26, 76), Sa'u (54), Tasi (74); **Goals:** Lee 2/4.
VIKINGS: 1 Rhys Hanbury; 2 Jack Owens; 3 Cameron Phelps; 14 Chris Dean; 20 Paddy Flynn; 6 Kevin Brown; 21 Danny Craven; 25 Alex Gerrard; 9 Jon Clarke (C); 18 Paul Johnson; 17 Danny Galea; 12 Danny Tickle; 24 Macgraff Leuluai. Subs (all used): 15 Lloyd White; 16 Willie Isa; 35 Paul Clough; 10 Ben Kavanagh.
Tries: Galea (11), Brown (16), Hanbury (36, 48), White (80); **Goals:** Tickle 4/4, Owens 1/1.
Rugby Leaguer & League Express Men of the Match: *Red Devils:* Gareth Hock; *Vikings:* Danny Craven.
Penalty count: 10-8; **Half-time:** 4-18;
Referee: Phil Bentham; **Attendance:** 2,630.

WARRINGTON WOLVES 68 DONCASTER 0

WOLVES: 1 Matthew Russell; 24 Kevin Penny; 4 Ryan Atkins; 18 Rhys Evans; 5 Joel Monaghan; 3 Chris Bridge; 20 Gareth O'Brien; 8 Chris Hill; 9 Mick Higham (C); 19 Anthony England; 17 Ben Currie; 23 James Laithwaite; 25 Ben Evans. Subs (all used): 10 Roy Asotasi; 11 Trent Waterhouse; 21 Glenn Riley; 22 Brad Dwyer.
Tries: Penny (9, 63, 67), Russell (15), Atkins (17), Bridge (35, 38, 59, 73), Dwyer (43), J Monaghan (55), R Evans (79); **Goals:** Bridge 10/12.
DONCASTER: 11 Lee Waterman; 5 Dave Scott; 20 Shaun Leaf; 3 Liam Welham; 4 Nev Morrison; 23 Richard Wilkinson; 26 Matty Wildie; 14 Russ Spiers; 9 Kyle Kesik; 29 Chris Green; 25 Alex Starling; 28 Liam Kent; 16 Craig Robinson. Subs (all used): 15 Scott Spaven; 17 Grant Edwards; 18 Ryan Wilson; 21 Matt Carbutt.
Rugby Leaguer & League Express Men of the Match: *Wolves:* Chris Bridge; *Doncaster:* Richard Wilkinson.
Penalty count: 7-3; **Half-time:** 30-0;
Referee: Matthew Thomason; **Attendance:** 3,002.

WIGAN WARRIORS 52 HUNSLET HAWKS 8

WARRIORS: 1 Matt Bowen; 31 Dominic Manfredi; 5 Anthony Gelling; 23 Dan Sarginson; 32 Joe Burgess; 19 Sam Powell; 7 Matty Smith; 8 Scott Taylor; 27 George Williams; 28 Jordan James; 25 John Bateman; 12 Liam Farrell (C); 14 Jack Hughes. Subs (all used): 17 Dominic Crosby; 24 Tony Clubb; 26 Ryan Hampshire; 37 Ryan Sutton.
Tries: Williams (3), Bowen (5, 17, 27), Smith (8, 24), L Farrell (11), Sarginson (47), James (73);
Goals: Smith 8/9.
HAWKS: 1 Stuart Kain; 5 Lee Mapals; 2 Jimmy Watson; 4 Danny Maun; 3 Lee Brickwood; 13 Danny Grimshaw; 20 Danny Ansell; 10 James Houston; 27 Liam Hood; 15 Luke Stenchion; 18 Brooke Broughton; 11 John Oakes; 9 David March. Subs (all used): 14 Matthew Tebb; 16 Lewis Reed; 12 Aaron Lyons; 26 Liam Mackay.
Tries: Grimshaw (13), Mapals (20); **Goals:** Ansell 0/2.
Rugby Leaguer & League Express Men of the Match: *Warriors:* Joe Burgess; *Hawks:* Danny Grimshaw.
Penalty count: 4-6; **Half-time:** 42-8;
Referee: George Stokes; **Attendance:** 4,390.

CASTLEFORD TIGERS 60 SHEFFIELD EAGLES 16

TIGERS: 1 Jordan Tansey; 2 Kirk Dixon; 21 Ashley Gibson; 3 Michael Shenton (C); 5 Justin Carney; 20 Jamie Ellis; 26 Liam Finn; 19 Scott Wheeldon; 9 Adam Milner; 10 Craig Huby; 16 Oliver Holmes; 4 Jake Webster; 11 Grant Millington. Subs (all used): 7 Marc Sneyd; 13 Nathan Massey; 14 Daryl Clark; 18 Frankie Mariano.
Tries: Carney (8, 12, 39, 75), Millington (17, 21), Dixon (30), Ellis (33, 53), Clark (36), Tansey (48), Holmes (58); **Goals:** Dixon 2/8, Sneyd 4/4.
EAGLES: 1 Quentin Laulu-Togagae; 2 Scott Turner; 25 Corey Hanson; 16 Duane Straugheir; 26 Jordan Burke; 6 Pat Walker; 7 Dominic Brambani; 18 Tom Lillycrop; 9 Andrew Henderson; 12 Peter Green; 15 Matt Garside; 27 Peter Aspinall; 5 Misi Taulapapa. Subs (all used): 14 James Davey; 21 Jack Blagbrough; 4 Lelauloto Tagaloa; 28 Tom Ashton.
Tries: Turner (3), Straugheir (43), Ashton (67);
Goals: Brambani 2/3.
Rugby Leaguer & League Express Men of the Match: *Tigers:* Justin Carney; *Eagles:* Quentin Laulu-Togagae.
Penalty count: 6-5; **Half-time:** 36-4;
Referee: Robert Hicks; **Attendance:** 4,648.

QUARTER FINALS

Thursday 5th June 2014

WIDNES VIKINGS 56 KEIGHLEY COUGARS 6

VIKINGS: 1 Rhys Hanbury; 29 Declan Hulme; 4 Stefan Marsh; 14 Chris Dean; 2 Jack Owens; 6 Kevin Brown (C); 27 Tom Gilmore; 35 Paul Clough; 15 Lloyd White; 25 Alex Gerrard; 17 Danny Galea; 12 Danny Tickle; 24 Macgraff Leuluai. Subs (all used): 21 Danny Craven; 10 Ben Kavanagh; 16 Willie Isa; 11 Dave Allen.
Tries: Hulme (2), Gilmore (6, 52, 68), Brown (9, 15), Owens (29), Marsh (34), Isa (41), Craven (60);
Goals: Tickle 3/4, Owens 5/6.
COUGARS: 21 Jesse Sheriffe; 19 Danny Lawton; 22 Daley Williams; 25 Lewis Graham; 20 Gavin Duffy; 23 Sean Kelly; 28 Ben Stead; 15 Scott Law; 27 Jack Lee; 32 Ross Peltier; 29 Charlie Eccleston; 33 Oliver Pursglove; 17 Ben Sagar. Subs (all used): 34 Luke Haigh; 26 Ryan Patchett; 18 Neil Cherryholme; 11 Josh Lynam.
Try: Williams (45); **Goals:** Stead 1/1.
Rugby Leaguer & League Express Men of the Match: *Vikings:* Kevin Brown; *Cougars:* Scott Law.
Penalty count: 2-3; **Half-time:** 32-0;
Referee: James Child; **Attendance:** 5,252.

Friday 6th June 2014

LEEDS RHINOS 25 LEIGH CENTURIONS 12

RHINOS: 1 Zak Hardaker; 20 Tom Briscoe; 3 Kallum Watkins; 4 Joel Moon; 5 Ryan Hall; 21 Liam Sutcliffe; 13 Kevin Sinfield (C); 8 Kylie Leuluai; 29 Robbie Ward; 10 Jamie Peacock; 14 Stevie Ward; 15 Brett Delaney; 16 Ryan Bailey. Subs (all used): 17 Ian Kirke; 18 Chris Clarkson; 23 Brad Singleton; 28 Josh Walters (D).
Tries: Hall (5), S Ward (30), R Ward (73), Hardaker (77);
Goals: Sinfield 4/4; **Field goal:** Sinfield (75).
Sin bin: Peacock (43) - retaliation.
CENTURIONS: 1 Gregg McNally; 23 Jonathan Pownall; 22 Adam Higson; 4 Tom Armstrong; 15 Liam Kay; 6 Martyn Ridyard; 7 Ryan Brierley; 8 Tom Spencer; 14 Sean Penkywicz; 10 Oliver Wilkes; 11 Matt Sarsfield; 30 Kurt Haggerty; 13 Sam Barlow. Subs (all used): 29 Jake Emmitt; 9 Bob Beswick; 26 Ryan Duffy; 12 Tommy Goulden.
Tries: Spencer (9), Armstrong (14); **Goals:** Ridyard 2/2.
Sin bin: Sarsfield (43) - use of the head.
Rugby Leaguer & League Express Men of the Match: *Rhinos:* Stevie Ward; *Centurions:* Tom Spencer.
Penalty count: 8-7; **Half-time:** 12-12;
Referee: Ben Thaler; **Attendance:** 7,145.

Wigan's Anthony Gelling takes on Castleford's James Clare and Michael Shenton

Saturday 7th June 2014

WIGAN WARRIORS 4 CASTLEFORD TIGERS 16

WARRIORS: 1 Matt Bowen; 31 Dominic Manfredi; 5 Anthony Gelling; 23 Dan Sarginson; 32 Joe Burgess; 27 George Williams; 7 Matty Smith; 10 Ben Flower; 9 Michael McIlorum; 16 Gil Dudson; 12 Liam Farrell; 25 John Bateman; 13 Sean O'Loughlin (C). Subs (all used): 14 Jack Hughes; 17 Dominic Crosby; 26 Ryan Hampshire; 37 Ryan Sutton.
Try: L Farrell (63); **Goals:** Smith 0/1.
TIGERS: 6 Luke Dorn; 2 Kirk Dixon; 4 Jake Webster; 3 Michael Shenton (C); 24 James Clare; 7 Marc Sneyd; 26 Liam Finn; 8 Andy Lynch; 14 Daryl Clark; 10 Craig Huby; 16 Oliver Holmes; 12 Weller Hauraki; 32 Lee Jewitt. Subs (all used): 11 Grant Millington; 18 Frankie Mariano; 19 Scott Wheeldon; 20 Jamie Ellis.
Tries: Clare (31), Dixon (70), Jewitt (78);
Goals: Sneyd 2/3.
Rugby Leaguer & League Express Men of the Match:
Warriors: Matt Bowen; *Tigers:* Marc Sneyd.
Penalty count: 10-8; **Half-time:** 0-6;
Referee: Richard Silverwood; **Attendance:** 8,736.

Sunday 8th June 2014

BRADFORD BULLS 10 WARRINGTON WOLVES 46

BULLS: 17 Lee Gaskell; 2 Elliot Kear; 4 Matty Blythe; 3 Adrian Purtell; 20 Luke George; 16 Danny Addy; 7 Luke Gale; 14 Manase Manuokafoa; 9 Matt Diskin (C); 13 Chev Walker; 33 Jay Pitts; 11 Tom Olbison; 18 James Donaldson. Subs (all used): 15 Adam Sidlow; 19 Adam O'Brien; 30 Jamal Fakir; 21 Adam Henry.
Tries: Kear (19), George (46); **Goals:** Gale 1/2.
WOLVES: 1 Matthew Russell; 18 Rhys Evans; 5 Joel Monaghan; 4 Ryan Atkins; 29 Gene Ormsby; 3 Chris Bridge; 7 Richard Myler; 8 Chris Hill; 14 Michael Monaghan (C); 19 Anthony England; 15 Ben Harrison; 17 Ben Currie; 6 Stefan Ratchford. Subs (all used): 13 Simon Grix; 9 Mick Higham; 10 Roy Asotasi; 25 Ben Evans.
Tries: Myler (15, 62), Atkins (22), Russell (25), Ormsby (52), J Monaghan (64, 71), Currie (73);
Goals: Bridge 7/8.

Rugby Leaguer & League Express Men of the Match:
Bulls: Luke Gale; *Wolves:* Stefan Ratchford.
Penalty count: 4-9; **Half-time:** 4-18;
Referee: Phil Bentham; **Attendance:** 5,064.

SEMI-FINALS

Saturday 9th August 2014

LEEDS RHINOS 24 WARRINGTON WOLVES 16

RHINOS: 1 Zak Hardaker; 20 Tom Briscoe; 3 Kallum Watkins; 4 Joel Moon; 5 Ryan Hall; 6 Danny McGuire; 13 Kevin Sinfield (C); 8 Kylie Leuluai; 7 Rob Burrow; 10 Jamie Peacock; 11 Jamie Jones-Buchanan; 12 Carl Ablett; 15 Brett Delaney. Subs (all used): 17 Ian Kirke; 9 Paul Aiton; 16 Ryan Bailey; 21 Liam Sutcliffe.
Tries: Hall (25, 36), Moon (52), T Briscoe (67);
Goals: Sinfield 4/5.
WOLVES: 1 Matthew Russell; 5 Joel Monaghan; 4 Ryan Atkins; 3 Chris Bridge; 18 Rhys Evans; 6 Stefan Ratchford; 7 Richard Myler; 8 Chris Hill; 14 Michael Monaghan (C); 19 Anthony England; 11 Trent Waterhouse; 12 Ben Westwood (C); 15 Ben Harrison. Subs (all used): 16 Paul Wood; 13 Simon Grix; 10 Roy Asotasi; 9 Mick Higham.
Tries: Bridge (43), Ratchford (59), Westwood (75);
Goals: Bridge 2/3.
Rugby Leaguer & League Express Men of the Match:
Rhinos: Danny McGuire; *Wolves:* Michael Monaghan.
Penalty count: 4-5; **Half-time:** 14-0;
Referee: Phil Bentham; **Attendance:** 12,132.
(at Langtree Park, St Helens).

Sunday 10th August 2014

CASTLEFORD TIGERS 28 WIDNES VIKINGS 6

TIGERS: 6 Luke Dorn; 2 Kirk Dixon; 4 Jake Webster; 3 Michael Shenton (C); 24 James Clare; 7 Marc Sneyd; 26 Liam Finn; 8 Andy Lynch; 14 Daryl Clark; 10 Craig Huby; 16 Oliver Holmes; 18 Frankie Mariano; 13 Nathan Massey. Subs (all used): 19 Scott Wheeldon; 20 Jamie Ellis; 32 Lee Jewitt; 35 Garreth Carvell.

Tries: Finn (4), Clark (8), Dixon (32), Ellis (47), Webster (69); **Goals:** Sneyd 4/6.
VIKINGS: 1 Rhys Hanbury; 20 Paddy Flynn; 14 Chris Dean; 4 Stefan Marsh; 2 Jack Owens; 6 Kevin Brown; 7 Joe Mellor; 25 Alex Gerrard; 9 Jon Clarke (C); 10 Ben Kavanagh; 17 Danny Galea; 12 Danny Tickle; 13 Hep Cahill. Subs (all used): 11 Dave Allen; 8 Eamon O'Carroll; 15 Lloyd White; 16 Willie Isa.
Try: Owens (74); **Goals:** Owens 1/1.
Rugby Leaguer & League Express Men of the Match:
Tigers: Daryl Clark; *Vikings:* Stefan Marsh.
Penalty count: 5-8; **Half-time:** 14-0;
Referee: Richard Silverwood; **Attendance:** 12,005
(at Leigh Sports Village).

FINAL

Saturday 23rd August 2014

CASTLEFORD TIGERS 10 LEEDS RHINOS 23

TIGERS: 6 Luke Dorn; 2 Kirk Dixon; 4 Jake Webster; 3 Michael Shenton (C); 24 James Clare; 7 Marc Sneyd; 26 Liam Finn; 8 Andy Lynch; 14 Daryl Clark; 10 Craig Huby; 16 Oliver Holmes; 12 Weller Hauraki; 13 Nathan Massey. Subs (all used): 18 Frankie Mariano; 19 Scott Wheeldon; 20 Jamie Ellis; 32 Lee Jewitt.
Tries: Clark (12), Holmes (47);
Goals: Sneyd 0/1, Finn 1/1.
RHINOS: 1 Zak Hardaker; 20 Tom Briscoe; 3 Kallum Watkins; 4 Joel Moon; 5 Ryan Hall; 13 Kevin Sinfield (C); 6 Danny McGuire; 8 Kylie Leuluai; 7 Rob Burrow; 10 Jamie Peacock; 15 Brett Delaney; 12 Carl Ablett; 11 Jamie Jones-Buchanan. Subs (all used): 9 Paul Aiton; 16 Ryan Bailey; 17 Ian Kirke; 21 Liam Sutcliffe.
Tries: T Briscoe (5), McGuire (17), Hall (25, 67);
Goals: Sinfield 3/4; **Field goal:** McGuire (77).
Rugby Leaguer & League Express Men of the Match:
Tigers: Lee Jewitt; *Rhinos:* Danny McGuire.
Penalty count: 2-2; **Half-time:** 4-16;
Referee: Phil Bentham; **Attendance:** 77,914
(at Wembley Stadium).

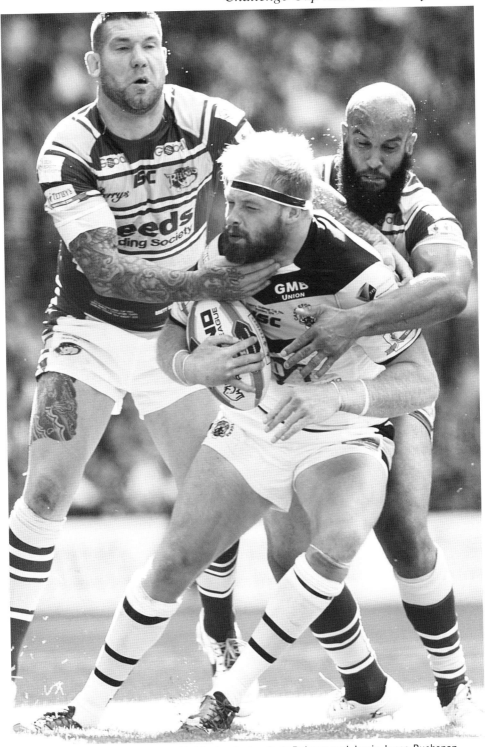

Castleford's Oliver Holmes tackled by Leeds duo Brett Delaney and Jamie Jones-Buchanan during the Challenge Cup Final

SUPER LEAGUE 2015 FIXTURES

ROUND 1

Thursday February 5
Widnes Vikings v Wigan Warriors................8.00pm
Friday February 6
St Helens v Catalans Dragons.....................8.00pm
Sunday February 8
Castleford Tigers
v Wakefield Trinity Wildcats 3.30pm
Huddersfield Giants v Hull FC 3.00pm
Hull KR v Leeds Rhinos 3.00pm
Warrington Wolves v Salford Red Devils 3.00pm

ROUND 2

Thursday February 12
Salford Red Devils v St Helens....................8.00pm
Friday February 13
Hull FC v Warrington Wolves 8.00pm
Leeds Rhinos v Widnes Vikings 8.00pm
Wigan Warriors v Huddersfield Giants 8.00pm
Saturday February 14
Catalans Dragons v Castleford Tigers 6.00pm
Sunday February 15
Wakefield Trinity Wildcats v Hull KR 3.00pm

WORLD CLUB CHALLENGE SERIES

Friday February 20
Warrington Wolves
v St George Illawarra Dragons 8.00pm
Saturday February 21
Wigan Warriors v Brisbane Broncos...........7.45pm
Sunday February 22
St Helens v South Sydney Rabbitohs 7.00pm

ROUND 3

Thursday February 26
Leeds Rhinos v Huddersfield Giants 8.00pm
Friday February 27
St Helens v Castleford Tigers 8.00pm
Saturday February 28
Catalans Dragons v Warrington Wolves 6.00pm
Sunday March 1
Hull KR v Wigan Warriors 3.00pm
Salford Red Devils v Hull FC 3.00pm
Widnes Vikings v Wakefield Trinity Wildcats 3.00pm

ROUND 4

Thursday March 5
Hull FC v Leeds Rhinos 8.00pm
Friday March 6
Wakefield Trinity Wildcats v St Helens 8.00pm
Saturday March 7
Catalans Dragons v Salford Red Devils........6.00pm
Sunday March 8
Castleford Tigers v Wigan Warriors 3.30pm
Huddersfield Giants v Widnes Vikings 3.00pm
Warrington Wolves v Hull KR 3.00pm

ROUND 5

Thursday March 12
Huddersfield Giants v Castleford Tigers 8.00pm
Friday March 13
Warrington Wolves v Leeds Rhinos 8.00pm
Wigan Warriors v Hull FC 8.00pm
Sunday March 15
Hull KR v Catalans Dragons 3.00pm
Salford Red Devils
v Wakefield Trinity Wildcats 3.00pm
Widnes Vikings v St Helens 3.00pm

ROUND 6

Thursday March 19
St Helens v Warrington Wolves...................8.00pm
Friday March 20
Hull FC v Catalans Dragons........................8.00pm
Leeds Rhinos v Wigan Warriors 8.00pm
Sunday March 22
Castleford Tigers v Salford Red Devils 3.30pm
Wakefield Trinity Wildcats
v Huddersfield Giants 3.00pm
Widnes Vikings v Hull KR 3.00pm

ROUND 7

Thursday March 26
Salford Red Devils v Widnes Vikings 8.00pm
Friday March 27
Castleford Tigers v Hull FC 8.00pm
Hull KR v St Helens....................................8.00pm
Warrington Wolves v Huddersfield Giants....8.00pm
Wigan Warriors v Wakefield Trinity Wildcats ..8.00pm
Saturday March 28
Catalans Dragons v Leeds Rhinos...............6.00pm

ROUND 8

Thursday April 2
Hull FC v Hull KR.......................................8.00pm
Wakefield Trinity Wildcats
v Catalans Dragons 8.00pm
Widnes Vikings v Warrington Wolves 8.00pm
Friday April 3
Castleford Tigers v Leeds Rhinos ....TBC
Huddersfield Giants v Salford Red Devils 6.00pm
Wigan Warriors v St Helens ....TBC

ROUND 9

Monday April 6
Catalans Dragons v Widnes Vikings ....TBC
Hull KR v Huddersfield Giants ....TBC
Leeds Rhinos v Wakefield Trinity Wildcats ..3.00pm
Salford Red Devils v Wigan Warriors ....TBC
St Helens v Hull FC ....TBC
Warrington Wolves v Castleford Tigers ....TBC

ROUND 10

Friday April 10
Hull FC v Widnes Vikings 8.00pm
Saturday April 11
Castleford Tigers v Hull KR...............................TBC
Sunday April 12
Huddersfield Giants v St Helens 3.00pm
Salford Red Devils v Leeds Rhinos 3.00pm
Warrington Wolves
v Wakefield Trinity Wildcats 3.00pm
Wigan Warriors v Catalans Dragons 3.00pm

ROUND 11

Thursday April 16
Wigan Warriors v Warrington Wolves..........8.00pm
Friday April 17
St Helens v Leeds Rhinos 8.00pm
Sunday April 19
Huddersfield Giants v Catalans Dragons 3.00pm
Hull KR v Salford Red Devils * ....TBC
Wakefield Trinity Wildcats v Hull FC * ....TBC
Widnes Vikings v Castleford Tigers 3.00pm

** Games to be re-arranged due to these teams
entering the Challenge Cup at the fifth round stage
on this weekend*

ROUND 12

Thursday April 23
Wakefield Trinity Wildcats v Wigan Warriors ..8.00pm
Friday April 24
Hull FC v Huddersfield Giants 8.00pm
Leeds Rhinos v Warrington Wolves 8.00pm
St Helens v Widnes Vikings 8.00pm
Saturday April 25
Catalans Dragons v Hull KR 6.00pm
Sunday April 26
Salford Red Devils v Castleford Tigers 3.00pm

ROUND 13

Thursday April 30
Huddersfield Giants v Leeds Rhinos 8.00pm
Friday May 1
Hull FC v Salford Red Devils 8.00pm
St Helens v Wakefield Trinity Wildcats 8.00pm
Wigan Warriors v Hull KR 8.00pm
Sunday May 3
Castleford Tigers v Catalans Dragons 3.30pm
Warrington Wolves v Widnes Vikings 3.00pm

ROUND 14

Thursday May 7
Hull KR v Wakefield Trinity Wildcats 8.00pm
Friday May 8
Wigan Warriors v Castleford Tigers 8.00pm
Saturday May 9
Catalans Dragons v St Helens 6.00pm
Sunday May 10
Salford Red Devils v Huddersfield Giants 3.00pm
Warrington Wolves v Hull FC 3.00pm
Widnes Vikings v Leeds Rhinos 3.00pm

---

*All kick-offs given as local time, and all fixtures are subject to change.
The RFL and Super League (Europe) Ltd will endeavour to keep them as accurate as possible*

CHALLENGE CUP ROUND 6

Weekend of May 16/17

ROUND 15

Thursday May 21
Castleford Tigers v Huddersfield Giants 8.00pm
Friday May 22
Hull FC v St Helens 8.00pm
Leeds Rhinos v Hull KR 8.00pm
Salford Red Devils v Warrington Wolves 8.00pm
Saturday May 23
Catalans Dragons v Wigan Warriors 6.00pm
Sunday May 24
Wakefield Trinity Wildcats v Widnes Vikings ..3.00pm

ROUND 16 - MAGIC WEEKEND

Saturday May 30
Salford Red Devils v Widnes Vikings 2.30pm
Hull FC v Hull KR.....................................4.45pm
Leeds Rhinos v Wigan Warriors 7.00pm
Sunday May 30
Catalans Dragons v Huddersfield Giants 1.00pm
St Helens v Warrington Wolves....................3.15pm
Castleford Tigers
v Wakefield Trinity Wildcats 5.30pm

ROUND 17

Thursday June 4
Widnes Vikings v Hull FC 8.00pm
Friday June 5
St Helens v Salford Red Devils 8.00pm
Sunday June 7
Huddersfield Giants v Wigan Warriors 3.00pm
Hull KR v Castleford Tigers 3.00pm
Wakefield Trinity Wildcats v Leeds Rhinos ..3.00pm
Warrington Wolves v Catalans Dragons 3.00pm

ROUND 18

Thursday June 11
Leeds Rhinos v Castleford Tigers 8.00pm
Friday June 12
St Helens v Wigan Warriors 8.00pm
Saturday June 13
Catalans Dragons v Hull FC........................6.00pm
Sunday June 14
Huddersfield Giants v Warrington Wolves....3.00pm
Hull KR v Widnes Vikings 3.00pm
Wakefield Trinity Wildcats
v Salford Red Devils 3.00pm

ROUND 19

Thursday June 18
Castleford Tigers v St Helens 8.00pm
Friday June 19
Wigan Warriors v Salford Red Devils 8.00pm
Saturday June 20
Catalans Dragons
v Wakefield Trinity Wildcats 6.00pm
Sunday June 21
Hull KR v Warrington Wolves 3.00pm
Leeds Rhinos v Hull FC 3.00pm
Widnes Vikings v Huddersfield Giants 3.00pm

CHALLENGE CUP QUARTER FINALS

Weekend of June 27/28

ROUND 20

Thursday July 2
Warrington Wolves v Wigan Warriors..........8.00pm
Friday July 3
Leeds Rhinos v St Helens 8.00pm
Sunday July 5
Castleford Tigers v Widnes Vikings.............3.30pm
Huddersfield Giants v Hull KR.....................3.00pm
Hull FC v Wakefield Trinity Wildcats 3.00pm
Salford Red Devils v Catalans Dragons........3.00pm

ROUND 21

Thursday July 9
Wigan Warriors v Leeds Rhinos 8.00pm
Friday July 10
Hull FC v Castleford Tigers 8.00pm
St Helens v Huddersfield Giants 8.00pm
Sunday July 12
Salford Red Devils v Hull KR......................3.00pm
Wakefield Trinity Wildcats
v Warrington Wolves...................................3.00pm
Widnes Vikings v Catalans Dragons 3.00pm

ROUND 22

Thursday July 16
Warrington Wolves v St Helens....................8.00pm
Friday July 17
Leeds Rhinos v Salford Red Devils 8.00pm
Wigan Warriors v Widnes Vikings................8.00pm
Saturday July 18
Catalans Dragons v Huddersfield Giants 6.00pm
Sunday July 19
Hull KR v Hull FC......................................3.00pm
Wakefield Trinity Wildcats
v Castleford Tigers 3.00pm

ROUND 23

Thursday July 23
Hull FC v Wigan Warriors 8.00pm
Friday July 24
St Helens v Hull KR...................................8.00pm
Sunday July 26
Castleford Tigers v Warrington Wolves........3.30pm
Huddersfield Giants
v Wakefield Trinity Wildcats 3.00pm
Leeds Rhinos v Catalans Dragons...............3.00pm
Widnes Vikings v Salford Red Devils 3.00pm

CHALLENGE CUP SEMI-FINALS

Weekend of August 1/2

CHALLENGE CUP FINAL

Saturday August 29 *(at Wembley Stadium)*

SUPER LEAGUE GRAND FINAL

Saturday October 10 *(at Old Trafford, Manchester)*

CHAMPIONSHIP 2015 FIXTURES

ROUND 1
Friday February 13
Dewsbury Rams v Sheffield Eagles.............8.00pm
Sunday February 15
Batley Bulldogs v Workington Town 3.00pm
Featherstone Rovers v Hunslet Hawks 3.00pm
Leigh Centurions v Bradford Bulls 3.00pm
London Broncos v Doncaster 3.00pm
Whitehaven v Halifax.................................3.00pm

ROUND 2
Sunday February 22
Bradford Bulls v Whitehaven 3.00pm
Doncaster v Featherstone Rovers ....TBC
Halifax v Leigh Centurions 3.00pm
Hunslet Hawks v Batley Bulldogs 3.00pm
Sheffield Eagles v London Broncos ....TBC
Workington Town v Dewsbury Rams 3.00pm

ROUND 3
Sunday March 1
Batley Bulldogs v Halifax...........................3.00pm
Featherstone Rovers v Bradford Bulls.........3.00pm
Hunslet Hawks v Dewsbury Rams 3.00pm
Leigh Centurions v London Broncos...........3.00pm
Whitehaven v Sheffield Eagles 3.00pm
Workington Town v Doncaster 3.00pm

ROUND 4
Sunday March 8
Bradford Bulls v Hunslet Hawks 3.00pm
Dewsbury Rams v Whitehaven 3.00pm
Doncaster v Leigh Centurions...........................TBC
Halifax v Featherstone Rovers....................3.00pm
London Broncos v Workington Town 3.00pm
Sheffield Eagles v Batley Bulldogs ....TBC

ROUND 5
Sunday March 15
Batley Bulldogs v Bradford Bulls................3.00pm
Featherstone Rovers v Leigh Centurions......3.00pm
Halifax v Dewsbury Rams 3.00pm
Hunslet Hawks v Doncaster 3.00pm
Whitehaven v London Broncos 3.00pm
Workington Town v Sheffield Eagles...........3.00pm

CHALLENGE CUP ROUND 4
Weekend of March 21/22

ROUND 6
Friday March 27
Dewsbury Rams v Featherstone Rovers 8.00pm
Saturday March 28
London Broncos v Halifax...........................3.00pm
Sunday March 29
Bradford Bulls v Workington Town 3.00pm
Doncaster v Batley Bulldogs ....TBC
Leigh Centurions v Whitehaven..................3.00pm
Sheffield Eagles v Hunslet Hawks....................TBC

ROUND 7
Friday April 3
Batley Bulldogs v Dewsbury Rams 7.30pm
Bradford Bulls v Halifax.............................8.00pm
Doncaster v Sheffield Eagles ....TBC
Featherstone Rovers v London Broncos ....TBC
Hunslet Hawks v Leigh Centurions 2.00pm
Workington Town v Whitehaven 3.00pm

ROUND 8
Monday April 6
Dewsbury Rams v Bradford Bulls 3.00pm
Featherstone Rovers v Sheffield Eagles 3.00pm
Halifax v Hunslet Hawks 3.00pm
Leigh Centurions v Workington Town 3.00pm
London Broncos v Batley Bulldogs 3.00pm
Whitehaven v Doncaster 3.00pm

ROUND 9
Sunday April 12
Batley Bulldogs v Featherstone Rovers 3.00pm
Bradford Bulls v London Broncos...............3.00pm
Doncaster v Dewsbury Rams ....TBC
Halifax v Workington Town 3.00pm
Hunslet Hawks v Whitehaven.....................3.00pm
Sheffield Eagles v Leigh Centurions ....TBC

CHALLENGE CUP ROUND 5
Weekend of April 18/19

ROUND 10
Sunday April 26
Doncaster v Bradford Bulls................................TBC
Leigh Centurions v Batley Bulldogs.............3.00pm
London Broncos v Dewsbury Rams 3.00pm
Sheffield Eagles v Halifax..................................TBC
Whitehaven v Featherstone Rovers 3.00pm
Workington Town v Hunslet Hawks 3.00pm

ROUND 11
Sunday May 3
Batley Bulldogs v Whitehaven....................3.00pm
Bradford Bulls v Sheffield Eagles 3.00pm
Dewsbury Rams v Leigh Centurions 3.00pm
Featherstone Rovers v Workington Town 3.00pm
Halifax v Doncaster 3.00pm
Hunslet Hawks v London Broncos 3.00pm

ROUND 12
Sunday May 10
Dewsbury Rams v Hunslet Hawks 3.00pm
Leigh Centurions v Halifax 3.00pm
London Broncos v Featherstone Rovers 3.00pm
Sheffield Eagles v Doncaster ....TBC
Whitehaven v Bradford Bulls......................3.00pm
Workington Town v Batley Bulldogs 3.00pm

ROUND 13
Sunday May 17
Batley Bulldogs v London Broncos 3.00pm
Bradford Bulls v Featherstone Rovers..........3.00pm
Doncaster v Workington Town ....TBC
Halifax v Whitehaven.................................3.00pm
Leigh Centurions v Hunslet Hawks 3.00pm
Sheffield Eagles v Dewsbury Rams ....TBC

CHALLENGE CUP ROUND 6
Weekend of May 16/17

ROUND 14 - SUMMER BASH
Weekend of May 23/24
(at Bloomfield Road, Blackpool)

ROUND 15
Friday May 29
Hunslet Hawks v Sheffield Eagles 8.00pm
Sunday May 31
Dewsbury Rams v Doncaster 3.00pm
Featherstone Rovers v Batley Bulldogs 3.00pm
London Broncos v Bradford Bulls................3.00pm
Whitehaven v Leigh Centurions..................3.00pm
Workington Town v Halifax.........................3.00pm

ROUND 16
Sunday June 7
Batley Bulldogs v Sheffield Eagles 3.00pm
Bradford Bulls v Doncaster 3.00pm
Dewsbury Rams v Workington Town 3.00pm
Featherstone Rovers v Halifax.....................3.00pm
London Broncos v Leigh Centurions............3.00pm
Whitehaven v Hunslet Hawks 3.00pm

ROUND 17
Friday June 12
Hunslet Hawks v Halifax 8.00pm
Sunday June 14
Batley Bulldogs v Leigh Centurions.............3.00pm
Bradford Bulls v Dewsbury Rams 3.00pm
Doncaster v London Broncos ....TBC
Sheffield Eagles v Whitehaven ....TBC
Workington Town v Featherstone Rovers 3.00pm

ROUND 18
Sunday June 21
Dewsbury Rams v Halifax 3.00pm
Featherstone Rovers v Doncaster 3.00pm
Leigh Centurions v Sheffield Eagles 3.00pm
London Broncos v Hunslet Hawks 3.00pm
Whitehaven v Batley Bulldogs....................3.00pm
Workington Town v Bradford Bulls..............3.00pm

ROUND 19
Sunday June 28
Bradford Bulls v Batley Bulldogs.................3.00pm
Doncaster v Whitehaven ....TBC
Halifax v London Broncos 3.00pm
Hunslet Hawks v Featherstone Rovers 3.00pm
Leigh Centurions v Dewsbury Rams 3.00pm
Sheffield Eagles v Workington Town...................TBC

CHALLENGE CUP QUARTER FINALS
Weekend of June 27/28

ROUND 20
Sunday July 5
Batley Bulldogs v Doncaster 3.00pm
Featherstone Rovers v Dewsbury Rams 3.00pm
Halifax v Sheffield Eagles 3.00pm
Hunslet Hawks v Bradford Bulls 3.00pm
London Broncos v Whitehaven 3.00pm
Workington Town v Leigh Centurions 3.00pm

ROUND 21
Sunday July 12
Dewsbury Rams v London Broncos 3.00pm
Doncaster v Hunslet Hawks ....TBC
Halifax v Batley Bulldogs............................3.00pm
Leigh Centurions v Featherstone Rovers.......3.00pm
Sheffield Eagles v Bradford Bulls ....TBC
Whitehaven v Workington Town 3.00pm

ROUND 22
Sunday July 19
Batley Bulldogs v Hunslet Hawks 3.00pm
Bradford Bulls v Leigh Centurions 3.00pm
Doncaster v Halifax..TBC
Sheffield Eagles v Featherstone Rovers ....TBC
Whitehaven v Dewsbury Rams 3.00pm
Workington Town v London Broncos 3.00pm

ROUND 23
Sunday July 26
Dewsbury Rams v Batley Bulldogs 3.00pm
Featherstone Rovers v Whitehaven 3.00pm
Halifax v Bradford Bulls..............................3.00pm
Hunslet Hawks v Workington Town 3.00pm
Leigh Centurions v Doncaster 3.00pm
London Broncos v Sheffield Eagles 3.00pm

CHALLENGE CUP SEMI-FINALS
Weekend of August 1/2

CHALLENGE CUP FINAL
Saturday August 29 *(at Wembley Stadium)*

All fixtures are subject to change. The RFL will endeavour to keep them as accurate as possible

LEAGUE ONE
2015 FIXTURES

LEAGUE ONE CUP ROUND 1
Weekend of February 28/March 1

CHALLENGE CUP ROUND 3
Weekend of March 7/8

LEAGUE ONE CUP ROUND 2
Weekend of March 14/15

CHALLENGE CUP ROUND 4
Weekend of March 21/22

LEAGUE ONE CUP SEMI-FINALS
Weekend of March 28/29

ROUND 1
Friday April 3
Coventry Bears v Oxford 3.00pm
Gateshead Thunder v Barrow Raiders 3.00pm
Keighley Cougars v York City Knights 3.00pm
London Skolars v Hemel Stags 3.00pm
Rochdale Hornets v Oldham 3.00pm
Swinton Lions v North Wales Crusaders 3.00pm
Gloucestershire v South Wales Scorpions 3.00pm

ROUND 2
Saturday April 11
Barrow Raiders v Swinton Lions 6.30pm
Sunday April 12
Hemel Stags v Keighley Cougars 2.30pm
North Wales Crusaders v Gateshead Thunder......2.30pm
Oldham v Coventry Bears 3.00pm
Oxford v York City Knights 3.00pm
South Wales Scorpions v London Skolars 3.00pm
Gloucestershire v Rochdale Hornets 3.00pm

ROUND 3
Saturday April 18
Rochdale Hornets v Barrow Raiders 5.30pm
Sunday April 19
Coventry Bears v Hemel Stags 3.00pm
Gateshead Thunder v Keighley Cougars 3.00pm
London Skolars v Gloucestershire........................3.00pm
South Wales Scorpions v Oldham.........................3.00pm
Swinton Lions v Oxford 3.00pm
York City Knights v North Wales Crusaders 3.00pm

ROUND 4
Saturday April 25
Barrow Raiders v South Wales Scorpions............6.30pm
Sunday April 26
Keighley Cougars v North Wales Crusaders 3.00pm
Oldham v London Skolars......................................3.00pm
Oxford v Hemel Stags 3.00pm
Rochdale Hornets v Gateshead Thunder 3.00pm
Gloucestershire v Swinton Lions..........................3.00pm
York City Knights v Coventry Bears 3.00pm

ROUND 5
Sunday May 3
Coventry Bears v Rochdale Hornets 3.00pm
Gateshead Thunder v Oxford................................3.00pm
Hemel Stags v South Wales Scorpions 2.30pm
London Skolars v Keighley Cougars 3.00pm
North Wales Crusaders v Barrow Raiders 2.30pm
Oldham v Gloucestershire.....................................3.00pm
Swinton Lions v York City Knights 3.00pm

ROUND 6
Saturday May 9
Barrow Raiders v Oldham 6.30pm
Rochdale Hornets v Swinton Lions.......................5.30pm
Sunday May 10
Hemel Stags v Gateshead Thunder 2.30pm
Keighley Cougars v Coventry Bears 3.00pm
Oxford v London Skolars 3.00pm
South Wales Scorpions
v North Wales Crusaders......................................3.00pm
Gloucestershire v York City Knights 3.00pm

ROUND 7
Saturday May 16
Rochdale Hornets v Oxford 5.30pm
Sunday May 17
London Skolars v Barrow Raiders.........................3.00pm
North Wales Crusaders v Hemel Stags 2.30pm
Oldham v Gateshead Thunder 3.00pm
Swinton Lions v Keighley Cougars 3.00pm
Gloucestershire v Coventry Bears 3.00pm
York City Knights v South Wales Scorpions 3.00pm

LEAGUE ONE CUP FINAL
Saturday May 23 *(at Bloomfield Road, Blackpool)*

ROUND 8
Friday May 29
Gateshead Thunder v York City Knights 8.00pm
Sunday May 31
Coventry Bears v Barrow Raiders 3.00pm
Hemel Stags v Swinton Lions 2.30pm
Keighley Cougars v Oldham 3.00pm
North Wales Crusaders v London Skolars...........2.30pm
Oxford v Gloucestershire......................................3.00pm
South Wales Scorpions v Rochdale Hornets.......3.00pm

ROUND 9
Sunday June 7
Barrow Raiders v Keighley Cougars 3.00pm
London Skolars v Coventry Bears 3.00pm
Oldham v North Wales Crusaders 3.00pm
Oxford v South Wales Scorpions 3.00pm
Swinton Lions v Gateshead Thunder 3.00pm
Gloucestershire v Hemel Stags 3.00pm
York City Knights v Rochdale Hornets..................3.00pm

ROUND 10
Sunday June 14
Coventry Bears v Swinton Lions 3.00pm
Gateshead Thunder v Gloucestershire..................3.00pm
Hemel Stags v Barrow Raiders 2.30pm
Keighley Cougars v South Wales Scorpions 3.00pm
North Wales Crusaders v Rochdale Hornets........2.30pm
Oldham v Oxford 3.00pm
York City Knights v London Skolars 3.00pm

ROUND 11
Saturday June 20
Barrow Raiders v Gloucestershire.........................6.30pm
Sunday June 21
Hemel Stags v York City Knights..........................2.30pm
Keighley Cougars v Rochdale Hornets..................3.00pm
London Skolars v Gateshead Thunder..................3.00pm
Oxford v North Wales Crusaders..........................3.00pm
South Wales Scorpions v Coventry Bears 3.00pm
Swinton Lions v Oldham 3.00pm

ROUND 12
Saturday June 27
Barrow Raiders v Gateshead Thunder...................6.30pm
Rochdale Hornets v Hemel Stags 5.30pm
Sunday June 28
London Skolars v South Wales Scorpions 3.00pm
North Wales Crusaders v Keighley Cougars 2.30pm
Oxford v Coventry Bears 3.00pm
Gloucestershire v Oldham 3.00pm
York City Knights v Swinton Lions 3.00pm

ROUND 13
Sunday July 5
Coventry Bears v North Wales Crusaders 3.00pm
Gateshead Thunder v Rochdale Hornets 3.00pm
Hemel Stags v London Skolars 2.30pm
Keighley Cougars v Oxford 3.00pm
Oldham v York City Knights 3.00pm
South Wales Scorpions v Gloucestershire 3.00pm
Swinton Lions v Barrow Raiders...........................3.00pm

ROUND 14
Saturday July 11
Barrow Raiders v London Skolars.........................6.30pm
Sunday July 12
Coventry Bears v Keighley Cougars 3.00pm
Gateshead Thunder v Hemel Stags 3.00pm
North Wales Crusaders
v South Wales Scorpions 2.30pm
Oldham v Rochdale Hornets 3.00pm
Oxford v Swinton Lions...3.00pm
York City Knights v Gloucestershire 3.00pm

ROUND 15
Saturday July 18
Barrow Raiders v North Wales Crusaders 6.30pm
Sunday July 19
Keighley Cougars v Swinton Lions 3.00pm
London Skolars v Oldham.....................................3.00pm
Rochdale Hornets v Coventry Bears 3.00pm
South Wales Scorpions v Hemel Stags 3.00pm
Gloucestershire v Oxford 3.00pm
York City Knights v Gateshead Thunder 3.00pm

ROUND 16
Sunday July 26
Hemel Stags v Coventry Bears 2.30pm
Keighley Cougars v Gateshead Thunder 3.00pm
North Wales Crusaders v Oldham 2.30pm
Oxford v Barrow Raiders.......................................3.00pm
South Wales Scorpions v York City Knights 3.00pm
Swinton Lions v Rochdale Hornets.......................3.00pm
Gloucestershire v London Skolars........................3.00pm

ROUND 17
Saturday August 1
Barrow Raiders v Hemel Stags 6.30pm
Sunday August 2
Coventry Bears v York City Knights 3.00pm
Gateshead Thunder v Swinton Lions 3.00pm
London Skolars v Oxford 3.00pm
North Wales Crusaders v Gloucestershire............2.30pm
Oldham v Keighley Cougars 3.00pm
Rochdale Hornets v South Wales Scorpions........3.00pm

ROUND 18
Saturday August 8
Barrow Raiders v Coventry Bears 6.30pm
Sunday August 9
Hemel Stags v Oldham 2.30pm
Rochdale Hornets v North Wales Crusaders 3.00pm
South Wales Scorpions v Keighley Cougars 3.00pm
Swinton Lions v London Skolars 3.00pm
Gloucestershire v Gateshead Thunder..................3.00pm
York City Knights v Oxford 3.00pm

ROUND 19
Sunday August 16
Coventry Bears v South Wales Scorpions............3.00pm
Gateshead Thunder v Oldham 3.00pm
Hemel Stags v Gloucestershire 2.30pm
Keighley Cougars v Barrow Raiders 3.00pm
London Skolars v York City Knights 3.00pm
North Wales Crusaders v Swinton Lions...............2.30pm
Oxford v Rochdale Hornets 3.00pm

ROUND 20
Sunday August 23
Gateshead Thunder v Coventry Bears 3.00pm
London Skolars v North Wales Crusaders.............3.00pm
Oldham v Barrow Raiders 3.00pm
Rochdale Hornets v Keighley Cougars 3.00pm
South Wales Scorpions v Oxford 3.00pm
Swinton Lions v Gloucestershire...........................3.00pm
York City Knights v Hemel Stags 3.00pm

ROUND 21
Saturday September 5
Barrow Raiders v Rochdale Hornets......................6.30pm
Sunday September 6
Coventry Bears v London Skolars 3.00pm
Hemel Stags v Oxford 2.30pm
North Wales Crusaders v York City Knights 2.30pm
Oldham v Swinton Lions 3.00pm
South Wales Scorpions
v Gateshead Thunder..3.00pm
Gloucestershire v Keighley Cougars 3.00pm

ROUND 22
Sunday September 13
Coventry Bears v Gloucestershire 3.00pm
Gateshead Thunder v North Wales Crusaders......3.00pm
Keighley Cougars v Hemel Stags..........................3.00pm
Oxford v Oldham 3.00pm
Rochdale Hornets v London Skolars.....................3.00pm
Swinton Lions v South Wales Scorpions 3.00pm
York City Knights v Barrow Raiders 3.00pm

GRAND FINALS
1998-2013

1998

DIVISION ONE GRAND FINAL

Saturday 26th September 1998

FEATHERSTONE ROVERS 22 WAKEFIELD TRINITY 24

ROVERS: 1 Steve Collins; 2 Carl Hall; 3 Shaun Irwin; 4 Danny Baker; 5 Karl Pratt; 6 Jamie Coventry; 7 Ty Fallins; 8 Chico Jackson; 9 Richard Chapman; 10 Stuart Dickens; 11 Gary Price; 12 Neil Lowe; 13 Richard Slater. Subs: 14 Paddy Handley for Coventry (70); 15 Asa Amone for Lowe (50); 16 Micky Clarkson for Jackson (50); 17 Steve Dooler (not used). **Tries:** Baker (15), Jackson (45), Collins (49), Hall (69); **Goals:** Chapman 3.
TRINITY: 1 Martyn Holland; 2 Josh Bostock; 3 Adam Hughes; 4 Martin Law; 5 Kevin Gray; 6 Garen Casey; 7 Roger Kenworthy; 8 Francis Stephenson; 9 Roy Southernwood; 10 Gary Lord; 11 Ian Hughes; 12 Sonny Whakarau; 13 Matt Fuller. Subs: 14 Sean Richardson for I Hughes (32); 15 Andy Fisher for Lord (26); 16 David Mycoe (not used); 17 Wayne McDonald for Whakarau (70); Lord for Stephenson (40); Stephenson for Lord (70). **Tries:** Southernwood (2), Bostock (7, 25), Casey (58), Stephenson (76); **Goals:** Casey 2.
League Express Men of the Match:
Rovers: Richard Chapman; *Trinity:* Garen Casey.
Penalty count: 8-3; **Half time:** 6-12;
Referee: Nick Oddy (Halifax); **Attendance:** 8,224
(at McAlpine Stadium, Huddersfield).

SUPER LEAGUE GRAND FINAL

Saturday 24th October 1998

LEEDS RHINOS 4 WIGAN WARRIORS 10

RHINOS: 1 Iestyn Harris (C); 22 Leroy Rivett; 3 Richie Blackmore; 4 Brad Godden; 5 Francis Cummins; 13 Daryl Powell; 7 Ryan Sheridan; 8 Martin Masella; 21 Terry Newton; 25 Darren Fleary; 11 Adrian Morley; 17 Anthony Farrell; 12 Marc Glanville. Subs: 20 Jamie Mathiou for Masella (25); 24 Marcus St Hilaire for Powell (40); 14 Graham Holroyd for Newton (49); 27 Andy Hay for Fleary (54); Powell for Godden (58); Masella for Mathiou (71).
Try: Blackmore (20).
WARRIORS: 1 Kris Radlinski; 2 Jason Robinson; 3 Danny Moore; 4 Gary Connolly; 5 Mark Bell; 6 Henry Paul; 7 Tony Smith; 16 Terry O'Connor; 9 Robbie McCormack; 10 Tony Mestrov; 20 Lee Gilmour; 17 Stephen Holgate; 13 Andy Farrell (C). Subs: 8 Neil Cowie for O'Connor (18BB, rev 48); 14 Mick Cassidy for McCormack (19BB, rev 27); 25 Paul Johnson for Moore (37); 12 Simon Haughton for Gilmour (27BB, rev 33); Haughton for Holgate (33); Cowie for Mestrov (54); Cassidy for Haughton (64); Holgate for Cowie (68); Haughton for Gilmour (71BB, rev 75); Mestrov for O'Connor (75BB).
Try: Robinson (37); **Goals:** Farrell 3.
League Express Men of the Match:
Rhinos: Iestyn Harris; *Warriors:* Jason Robinson.
Penalty count: 7-13; **Half-time:** 4-6;
Referee: Russell Smith (Castleford); **Attendance:** 43,553
(at Old Trafford, Manchester).

1999

NORTHERN FORD PREMIERSHIP GRAND FINAL

Saturday 25th September 1999

DEWSBURY RAMS 11 HUNSLET HAWKS 12

RAMS: 1 Nathan Graham; 2 Alex Godfrey; 3 Paul Evans; 4 Brendan O'Meara; 5 Adrian Flynn; 6 Richard Agar; 7 Barry Eaton; 8 Alan Boothroyd; 9 Paul Delaney; 10 Matthew Long; 11 Andy Spink; 12 Mark Haigh; 13 Damian Ball. Subs: 14 Brendan Williams for Eaton (5BB, rev 15); 15 Sean Richardson for Haigh (50); 16 Simon Hicks for Long (25); 17 Paul Medley for Spink (50); Williams for Evans (61); Long for Boothroyd (71); Spink for Long (78).
Tries: Flynn (27), Ball (54); **Goal:** Eaton; **Field goal:** Agar.

HAWKS: 1 Abraham Fatnowna; 2 Chris Ross; 3 Shaun Irwin; 4 Paul Cook; 5 Iain Higgins; 6 Marcus Vassilakopoulos; 7 Latham Tawhai; 8 Richard Hayes; 9 Richard Pachniuk; 10 Steve Pryce; 11 Rob Wilson; 12 Jamie Leighton; 13 Lee St Hilaire. Subs: 14 Mick Coyle for Wilson (57); 15 Phil Kennedy for Pryce (35); 16 Jamie Thackray for St Hilaire (25); 17 Richard Baker for Higgins (55); Higgins for Fatnowna (62); Pryce for Kennedy (65).
Tries: Cook (31), Higgins (46); **Goal:** Ross;
Field goals: Tawhai, Leighton.
League Express Men of the Match:
Rams: Barry Eaton; *Hawks:* Latham Tawhai.
Penalty count: 8-5; **Half-time:** 7-7;
Referee: Steve Ganson (St Helens); **Attendance:** 5,783
(at Headingley Stadium, Leeds).

SUPER LEAGUE GRAND FINAL

Saturday 9th October 1999

BRADFORD BULLS 6 ST HELENS 8

BULLS: 28 Stuart Spruce; 2 Tevita Vaikona; 20 Scott Naylor; 5 Michael Withers; 17 Leon Pryce; 6 Henry Paul; 1 Robbie Paul (C); 10 Paul Anderson; 9 James Lowes; 29 Stuart Fielden; 15 David Boyle; 23 Bernard Dwyer; 13 Steve McNamara. Subs: 14 Paul Deacon for R Paul (53); 4 Nathan McAvoy (not used); 12 Mike Forshaw for McNamara (18); 22 Brian McDermott for Anderson (18); Anderson for Fielden (61); Fielden for Dwyer (65); R Paul for Deacon (72).
Try: H Paul (18); **Goal:** H Paul.
SAINTS: 1 Paul Atcheson; 14 Chris Smith; 3 Kevin Iro; 4 Paul Newlove; 5 Anthony Sullivan; 13 Paul Sculthorpe; 20 Tommy Martyn; 8 Apollo Perelini; 9 Keiron Cunningham; 10 Julian O'Neill; 2 Fereti Tuilagi; 21 Sonny Nickle; 11 Chris Joynt (C). Subs: 26 Paul Wellens for Martyn (52); 6 Sean Hoppe for Newlove (43); 16 Vila Matautia for O'Neill (20); 7 Sean Long for Perelini (24); Perelini for Matautia (46); O'Neill for Perelini (69).
Tries: Iro (65); **Goals:** Long 2.
League Express Men of the Match:
Bulls: Henry Paul; *Saints:* Kevin Iro.
Penalty count: 4-7; **Half-time:** 6-2;
Referee: Stuart Cummings (Widnes); **Attendance:** 50,717
(at Old Trafford, Manchester).

2000

NORTHERN FORD PREMIERSHIP GRAND FINAL

Saturday 29th July 2000

DEWSBURY RAMS 13 LEIGH CENTURIONS 12

RAMS: 1 Nathan Graham; 2 Richard Baker; 4 Dan Potter; 3 Brendan O'Meara; 5 Adrian Flynn; 6 Richard Agar; 7 Barry Eaton; 8 Shayne Williams; 9 David Mycoe; 10 Mark Haigh; 11 Sean Richardson; 12 Daniel Frame; 13 Damian Ball. Subs: 14 Gavin Wood (not used); 15 Paul Delaney for Mycoe (53); 16 Ryan McDonald for Haigh (30); 17 Matthew Long for Williams (23); Haigh for McDonald (64).
Tries: Eaton (2), Long (23); **Goals:** Eaton 2; **Field goal:** Agar.
Sin bin: Williams (66) - use of the elbow.
On report: Richardson (20) - high tackle on Donlan.
CENTURIONS: 1 Stuart Donlan; 5 David Ingram; 3 Paul Anderson; 4 Andy Fairclough; 2 Alan Cross; 6 Liam Bretherton; 7 Kieron Purtill; 8 Tim Street; 9 Mick Higham; 10 Andy Leatham; 11 Simon Baldwin; 12 Heath Cruckshank; 13 Adam Bristow. Subs: 14 James Arkwright for Cross (68); 15 Paul Norman for Street (36); 16 Radney Bowker (not used); 17 David Whittle for Leatham (24); Street for Norman (62).
Tries: Higham (29, 69); **Goals:** Bretherton 2.
Sin bin: Whittle (66) - retaliation.
League Express Men of the Match:
Rams: Richard Agar; *Centurions:* Mick Higham.
Penalty count: 4-4; **Half-time:** 10-6;
Referee: Robert Connolly (Wigan); **Attendance:** 8,487
(at Gigg Lane, Bury).

SUPER LEAGUE GRAND FINAL

Saturday 14th October 2000

ST HELENS 29 WIGAN WARRIORS 16

SAINTS: 17 Paul Wellens; 24 Steve Hall; 3 Kevin Iro; 15 Sean Hoppe; 5 Anthony Sullivan; 20 Tommy Martyn; 7 Sean Long; 8 Apollo Perelini; 9 Keiron Cunningham; 10 Julian O'Neill; 11 Chris Joynt (C); 22 Tim Jonkers; 13 Paul Sculthorpe. Subs: 14 Fereti Tuilagi for O'Neill (20); 12 Sonny Nickle for Perelini (28); 26 John Stankevitch for Jonkers (50); 23 Scott Barrow (not used); Perelini for Nickle (52); Jonkers for Stankevitch (66); Stankevitch for Perelini (67BB); O'Neill for Hall (74). **Tries:** Hoppe (7), Joynt (28, 50), Tuilagi (69), Jonkers (80); **Goals:** Long 4; **Field goal:** Sculthorpe.
WARRIORS: 5 Jason Robinson; 2 Brett Dallas; 1 Kris Radlinski; 3 Steve Renouf; 26 David Hodgson; 6 Tony Smith; 7 Willie Peters; 8 Terry O'Connor; 9 Terry Newton; 10 Neil Cowie; 11 Mick Cassidy; 12 Denis Betts; 13 Andy Farrell (C). Subs: 23 Brady Malam for Cowie (30); 17 Tony Mestrov for O'Connor (43); 19 Chris Chester for Cassidy (47BB, rev 69); 14 Lee Gilmour for Betts (51); O'Connor for Mestrov (61); Cowie for Malam (67); Chester for Newton (75). **Tries:** Farrell (13), Hodgson (58), Smith (61); **Goals:** Farrell 2.
League Express Men of the Match:
Saints: Chris Joynt; *Warriors:* Andy Farrell.
Penalty count: 10-6; **Half-time:** 11-4;
Referee: Russell Smith (Castleford); **Attendance:** 58,132
(at Old Trafford, Manchester).

2001

NORTHERN FORD PREMIERSHIP GRAND FINAL

Saturday 28th July 2001

OLDHAM 14 WIDNES VIKINGS 24

OLDHAM: 1 Mark Sibson; 2 Joey Hayes; 3 Anthony Gibbons; 4 Pat Rich; 5 Joe McNicholas; 6 David Gibbons; 7 Neil Roden; 8 Leo Casey; 9 Keith Brennan; 10 Paul Norton; 11 Phil Farrell; 12 Bryan Henare; 13 Kevin Mannion. Subs: 14 Mike Ford for Mannion (27); 15 Jason Clegg for Casey (18); 16 John Hough for Brennan (44); 17 Danny Guest for Norton (40BB, rev 54); Mannion for Henare (66); Guest for Clegg (73). **Tries:** Brennan (9), Ford (74), Mannion (80); **Goal:** Rich.
VIKINGS: 1 Paul Atcheson; 2 Damian Munro; 3 Craig Weston; 4 Jason Demetriou; 5 Chris Percival; 6 Richard Agar; 7 Martin Crompton; 8 Simon Knox; 9 Phil Cantillon; 10 Stephen Holgate; 11 Steve Gee; 12 Sean Richardson; 13 Tommy Hodgkinson. Subs: 14 Andy Craig for Percival (65); 15 Chris McKinney for Gee (41); 16 Joe Faimalo for Knox (32); 17 Matthew Long for Holgate (23); Knox for Long (49BB, rev 61); Holgate for Long (74). **Tries:** Gee (17), Demetriou (38, 60), Cantillon (50), Munro (69); **Goals:** Weston 2.
League Express Men of the Match:
Oldham: Jason Clegg; *Vikings:* Phil Cantillon.
Penalty count: 8-5; **Half-time:** 4-10;
Referee: Steve Ganson (St Helens); **Attendance:** 8,974
(at Spotland, Rochdale).

SUPER LEAGUE GRAND FINAL

Saturday 13th October 2001

BRADFORD BULLS 37 WIGAN WARRIORS 6

BULLS: 5 Michael Withers; 2 Tevita Vaikona; 20 Scott Naylor; 23 Graham Mackay; 3 Leon Pryce; 6 Henry Paul; 1 Robbie Paul (C); 8 Joe Vagana; 9 James Lowes; 22 Brian McDermott; 11 Daniel Gartner; 19 Jamie Peacock; 12 Mike Forshaw. Subs: 29 Stuart Fielden for McDermott (21BB, rev 65); 10 Paul Anderson for Vagana (22); 15 Shane Rigon for Pryce (40); 7 Paul Deacon for R Paul (69); Vagana for Anderson (53); Fielden for Gartner (72); Anderson for Vagana (74). **Tries:** Lowes (9), Withers (11, 27, 31), Fielden (65), Mackay (72); **Goals:** H Paul 5, Mackay; **Field goal:** H Paul.

WARRIORS: 1 Kris Radlinski; 2 Brett Dallas; 4 Gary Connolly; 3 Steve Renouf; 5 Brian Carney; 6 Matthew Johns; 7 Adrian Lam; 8 Terry O'Connor; 9 Terry Newton; 20 Harvey Howard; 11 Mick Cassidy; 14 David Furner; 13 Andy Farrell (C). Subs: 15 Paul Johnson for Carney (12BB); 10 Neil Cowie for Howard (17); 12 Denis Betts for O'Connor (32); 19 Chris Chester for Farrell (59); O'Connor for Cowie (55); Howard for Newton (64); Cowie for Cassidy (72).
Try: Lam (63); **Goal:** Furner.
League Express Men of the Match:
Bulls: Michael Withers; *Warriors:* Adrian Lam.
Penalty count: 6-7; **Half-time:** 26-0;
Referee: Stuart Cummings (Widnes); **Attendance:** 60,164
(at Old Trafford, Manchester).

2002

NORTHERN FORD PREMIERSHIP GRAND FINAL

Saturday 12th October 2002

HUDDERSFIELD GIANTS 38 LEIGH CENTURIONS 16

GIANTS: 1 Ben Cooper; 2 Hefin O'Hare; 3 Eorl Crabtree; 4 Graeme Hallas; 5 Marcus St Hilaire; 6 Stanley Gene; 7 Chris Thorman; 8 Michael Slicker; 9 Paul March; 10 Jeff Wittenberg; 11 David Atkins; 12 Robert Roberts; 13 Steve McNamara. Subs: 14 Heath Cruckshank for Roberts (24BB); 15 Chris Molyneux for Slicker (53); 16 Darren Turner for March (21); 17 Andy Rice for Cruckshank (57); Roberts for Wittenberg (34); Wittenberg for Roberts (74). **Tries:** O'Hare (12, 78), St Hilaire (34, 53), Thorman (46), Gene (57); **Goals:** McNamara 7.
Sin bin: Roberts (47) - fighting.
CENTURIONS: 1 Neil Turley; 2 Leon Felton; 4 Jon Roper; 3 Dale Cardoza; 5 Oliver Marns; 6 Willie Swann; 7 Bobbie Goulding; 8 Vila Matautia; 9 Paul Rowley; 10 David Bradbury; 11 Simon Baldwin; 12 Andrew Isherwood; 13 Adam Bristow. Subs: 14 Gareth Price for Bradbury (24BB, rev 35); 15 John Duffy for Swann (32); 16 John Hamilton for Bristow (46BB, rev 57); 17 David Whittle for Matautia (22); Matautia for Bradbury (53BB); Swann for Goulding (58); Hamilton for Whittle (67); Bradbury for Turley (72); Goulding for Swann (75). **Tries:** Cardoza (9), Marns (18), Hamilton (70); **Goals:** Turley 2.
Sin bin: Whittle (47) - fighting; Bristow (74) - interference.
On report: Isherwood (66) - high tackle on Roberts.
Rugby Leaguer & League Express Men of the Match:
Giants: Chris Thorman; *Centurions:* Adam Bristow.
Penalty count: 11-11; **Half-time:** 14-10;
Referee: Karl Kirkpatrick (Warrington); **Attendance:** 9,051
(at Halton Stadium, Widnes).

SUPER LEAGUE GRAND FINAL

Saturday 19th October 2002

BRADFORD BULLS 18 ST HELENS 19

BULLS: 6 Michael Withers; 2 Tevita Vaikona; 20 Scott Naylor; 15 Brandon Costin; 5 Lesley Vainikolo; 1 Robbie Paul (C); 7 Paul Deacon; 8 Joe Vagana; 9 James Lowes; 29 Stuart Fielden; 11 Daniel Gartner; 12 Jamie Peacock; 13 Mike Forshaw. Subs: 14 Lee Gilmour for Gartner (21); 10 Paul Anderson for Vagana (25); 22 Brian McDermott for Fielden (34); 3 Leon Pryce for Vainikolo (53); Fielden for Anderson (55); Vainikolo for Paul (77). **Tries:** Naylor (3), Paul (44), Withers (47); **Goals:** Deacon 3.
SAINTS: 1 Paul Wellens; 5 Darren Albert; 3 Martin Gleeson; 4 Paul Newlove; 19 Anthony Stewart; 13 Paul Sculthorpe; 7 Sean Long; 8 Darren Britt; 9 Keiron Cunningham; 10 Barry Ward; 23 Mike Bennett; 15 Tim Jonkers; 11 Chris Joynt (C). Subs: 2 Sean Hoppe for Wellens (3); 12 Peter Shiels for Ward (27); 14 John Stankevitch for Britt (31BB, rev 58); 17 Mick Higham for Joynt (54); Stankevitch for Shiels (58); Joynt for Britt (75); Shiels for Jonkers (77). **Tries:** Bennett (24), Long (32), Gleeson (56); **Goals:** Long 3; **Field goal:** Long.
Rugby Leaguer & League Express Men of the Match:
Bulls: Paul Deacon; *Saints:* Mike Bennett.
Penalty count: 5-4; **Half-time:** 12-8;
Referee: Russell Smith (Castleford); **Attendance:** 61,138
(at Old Trafford, Manchester).

2003

NATIONAL LEAGUE TWO GRAND FINAL

Sunday 5th October 2003

KEIGHLEY COUGARS 13 SHEFFIELD EAGLES 11

COUGARS: 1 Matt Foster; 2 Max Tomlinson; 3 David Foster; 4 James Rushforth; 5 Andy Robinson; 6 Paul Ashton; 7 Matt Firth; 8 Phil Stephenson; 9 Simeon Hoyle; 10 Danny Ekis; 11 Oliver Wilkes; 12 Ian Sinfield; 13 Lee Patterson. Subs (all used): 14 Chris Wainwright; 15 Richard Mervill; 16 Mick Durham; 17 Jason Ramshaw.
Tries: M Foster (7), Robinson (74); **Goals:** Ashton 2;
Field goal: Firth.
EAGLES: 1 Andy Poynter; 2 Tony Weller; 3 Richard Goddard; 4 Tom O'Reilly; 5 Greg Hurst; 6 Gavin Brown; 7 Mark Aston; 8 Jack Howieson; 9 Gareth Stanley; 10 Dale Laughton; 11 Andy Raleigh; 12 Craig Brown; 13 Wayne Flynn. Subs (all used): 14 Peter Reilly; 15 Simon Tillyer; 16 Nick Turnbull; 17 Mitchell Stringer.
Try: O'Reilly (51); **Goals:** G Brown 3; **Field goal:** Reilly.
Rugby Leaguer & League Express Men of the Match: *Cougars:* Simeon Hoyle; *Eagles:* Andy Raleigh.
Penalty count: 6-8; **Half-time:** 9-4;
Referee: Peter Taberner (Wigan). *(at Halton Stadium, Widnes).*

NATIONAL LEAGUE ONE GRAND FINAL

Sunday 5th October 2003

LEIGH CENTURIONS 14 SALFORD CITY REDS 31

CENTURIONS: 1 Neil Turley; 2 Damian Munro; 3 Alan Hadcroft; 4 Danny Halliwell; 5 Leroy Rivett; 6 John Duffy; 7 Tommy Martyn; 8 Sonny Nickle; 9 Patrick Weisner; 10 Paul Norman; 11 Sean Richardson; 12 Willie Swann; 13 Adam Bristow. Subs (all used): 14 David Bradbury; 15 Lee Sanderson; 16 Bryan Henare; 17 Ricky Bibey.
Tries: Richardson (33), Halliwell (38), Swann (65); **Goal:** Turley.
On report: Nickle (60) - late tackle on Clinch.
CITY REDS: 1 Jason Flowers; 2 Danny Arnold; 3 Stuart Littler; 4 Alan Hunte; 5 Andy Kirk; 6 Cliff Beverley; 7 Gavin Clinch; 8 Neil Baynes; 9 Malcolm Alker; 10 Andy Coley; 11 Simon Baldwin; 12 Paul Highton; 13 Chris Charles. Subs (all used): 14 Steve Blakeley; 15 David Highton; 16 Martin Moana; 17 Gareth Haggerty.
Tries: Hunte (3, 52), Beverley (23), Littler (73);
Goals: Charles 6, Blakeley; **Field goal:** Blakeley.
Rugby Leaguer & League Express Men of the Match: *Centurions:* Willie Swann; *City Reds:* Gavin Clinch.
Penalty count: 10-10; **Half-time:** 10-16;
Referee: Richard Silverwood (Dewsbury); **Attendance:** 9,186 *(at Halton Stadium, Widnes).*

SUPER LEAGUE GRAND FINAL

Saturday 18th October 2003

BRADFORD BULLS 25 WIGAN WARRIORS 12

BULLS: 17 Stuart Reardon; 2 Tevita Vaikona; 6 Michael Withers; 4 Shontayne Hape; 5 Lesley Vainikolo; 15 Karl Pratt; 7 Paul Deacon; 8 Joe Vagana; 9 James Lowes; 29 Stuart Fielden; 11 Daniel Gartner; 12 Jamie Peacock; 13 Mike Forshaw. Subs (all used): 10 Paul Anderson; 18 Lee Radford; 3 Leon Pryce; 1 Robbie Paul (C).
Tries: Reardon (51), Hape (59), Lowes (75);
Goals: Deacon 6/6; **Field goal:** Deacon.
WARRIORS: 1 Kris Radlinski; 5 Brian Carney; 18 Martin Aspinwall; 14 David Hodgson; 2 Brett Dallas; 15 Sean O'Loughlin; 20 Luke Robinson; 30 Quentin Pongia; 9 Terry Newton; 10 Craig Smith; 11 Mick Cassidy; 12 Danny Tickle; 13 Andy Farrell (C). Subs (all used): 4 Paul Johnson; 8 Terry O'Connor; 23 Gareth Hock; 17 Mark Smith.
Tries: Tickle (17), Radlinski (72); **Goals:** Farrell 2/3.
Rugby Leaguer & League Express Men of the Match: *Bulls:* Stuart Reardon; *Warriors:* Kris Radlinski.
Penalty count: 7-6; **Half-time:** 4-6;
Referee: Karl Kirkpatrick (Warrington); **Attendance:** 65,537 *(at Old Trafford, Manchester).*

2004

NATIONAL LEAGUE ONE GRAND FINAL

Sunday 10th October 2004

LEIGH CENTURIONS 32 WHITEHAVEN 16
(after extra time)

CENTURIONS: 1 Neil Turley; 2 Rob Smyth; 3 Danny Halliwell; 4 Ben Cooper; 5 David Alstead; 6 John Duffy; 7 Tommy Martyn; 8 Simon Knox; 9 Paul Rowley; 10 Matt Sturm; 11 David Larder; 12 Oliver Wilkes; 13 Ian Knott. Subs (all used): 14 Dave McConnell; 15 Heath Cruckshank; 16 Richard Marshall; 17 Willie Swann.
Tries: Cooper (27, 83), Martyn (61), Turley (87);
Goals: Turley 6/8; **Field goals:** Turley 2, Rowley, Martyn.
WHITEHAVEN: 1 Gary Broadbent; 2 Craig Calvert; 3 David Seeds; 4 Mick Nanyn; 5 Wesley Wilson; 6 Leroy Joe; 7 Sam Obst; 8 Marc Jackson; 9 Aaron Lester; 10 David Fatialofa; 11 Paul Davidson; 12 Howard Hill; 13 Craig Walsh. Subs (all used): 14 Spencer Miller; 15 Carl Sice; 16 Chris McKinney; 17 Ryan Tandy.
Tries: Wilson (2, 71), Calvert (45); **Goals:** Nanyn 2/6.
Rugby Leaguer & League Express Men of the Match: *Centurions:* Neil Turley; *Whitehaven:* Aaron Lester.
Penalty count: 5-9; **Half-time:** 7-6; **Full-time:** 16-16;
Referee: Ronnie Laughton (Barnsley); **Attendance:** 11,005 *(at Halton Stadium, Widnes).*

SUPER LEAGUE GRAND FINAL

Saturday 16th October 2004

BRADFORD BULLS 8 LEEDS RHINOS 16

BULLS: 6 Michael Withers; 17 Stuart Reardon; 16 Paul Johnson; 4 Shontayne Hape; 5 Lesley Vainikolo; 18 Iestyn Harris; 7 Paul Deacon; 8 Joe Vagana; 1 Robbie Paul (C); 29 Stuart Fielden; 12 Jamie Peacock; 13 Logan Swann; 11 Lee Radford. Subs: 10 Paul Anderson for Vagana (14); 15 Karl Pratt for Paul (23); 27 Rob Parker for Anderson (24); 19 Jamie Langley for Peacock (32); Paul for Withers (ht); Peacock for Radford (48); Radford for Swann (54); Vagana for Parker (56); Parker for Fielden (63); Fielden for Vagana (67); Swann for Langley (68).
Tries: Vainikolo (7), Hape (43); **Goals:** Deacon 0/2.
RHINOS: 21 Richard Mathers; 18 Mark Calderwood; 5 Chev Walker; 4 Keith Senior; 22 Marcus Bai; 13 Kevin Sinfield (C); 6 Danny McGuire; 19 Danny Ward; 9 Matt Diskin; 8 Ryan Bailey; 3 Chris McKenna; 29 Ali Lauitiiti; 11 David Furner. Subs: 16 Willie Poching for Furner (19); 10 Barrie McDermott for Ward (22); Ward for Bailey (29); 7 Rob Burrow for Lauitiiti (30); Bailey for McDermott (41); 20 Jamie Jones-Buchanan for McKenna (48); Lauitiiti for Ward (50); Furner for Sinfield (60); McKenna for Poching (63); Sinfield for Diskin (67); Poching for McKenna (72); Ward for Bailey (73).
Tries: Diskin (15), McGuire (75); **Goals:** Sinfield 4/4.
Rugby Leaguer & League Express Men of the Match: *Bulls:* Lesley Vainikolo; *Rhinos:* Richard Mathers.
Penalty count: 5-5; **Half-time:** 4-10;
Referee: Steve Ganson (St Helens); **Attendance:** 65,547 *(at Old Trafford, Manchester).*

2005

NATIONAL LEAGUE ONE GRAND FINAL

Sunday 9th October 2005

CASTLEFORD TIGERS 36 WHITEHAVEN 8

TIGERS: 1 Michael Platt; 2 Waine Pryce; 3 Michael Shenton; 4 Jon Hepworth; 5 Damien Blanch; 6 Brad Davis; 7 Andrew Henderson; 8 Adam Watene; 9 Aaron Smith; 10 Richard Fletcher; 11 Tom Haughey; 12 Steve Crouch; 13 Deon Bird. Subs (all used): 14 Paul Handforth; 15 Craig Huby; 16 Adrian Vowles; 17 Frank Watene.
Tries: Huby (22), Crouch (24), Blanch (26), Davis (33, 45), Haughey (52); **Goals:** Fletcher 2/3, Huby 3/4, Hepworth 1/1.

WHITEHAVEN: 1 Gary Broadbent; 2 Craig Calvert; 3 David Seeds; 4 Mick Nanyn; 5 Wesley Wilson; 6 Leroy Joe; 7 Joel Penny; 8 Ryan Tandy; 9 Carl Sice; 10 David Fatialofa; 11 Spencer Miller; 12 Howard Hill; 13 Aaron Lester. Subs (all used): 14 Carl Rudd; 15 Aaron Summers; 16 Craig Chambers; 17 Marc Jackson.
Tries: Seeds (56), Calvert (78); **Goals:** Nanyn 0/2.
Sin bin: Joe (16) - late tackle on Davis.
On report: Joe (16) - late tackle on Davis;
Sice (40) - alleged biting.
Rugby Leaguer & League Express Men of the Match:
Tigers: Brad Davis; *Whitehaven:* Wesley Wilson.
Penalty count: 4-9; **Half-time:** 26-0;
Referee: Steve Ganson (St Helens); **Attendance:** 13,300
(at Halton Stadium, Widnes).

SUPER LEAGUE GRAND FINAL

Saturday 15th October 2005

BRADFORD BULLS 15 LEEDS RHINOS 6

BULLS: 6 Michael Withers; 3 Leon Pryce; 13 Ben Harris; 4 Shontayne Hape; 5 Lesley Vainikolo; 18 Iestyn Harris; 7 Paul Deacon; 12 Jamie Peacock (C); 9 Ian Henderson; 29 Stuart Fielden; 16 Paul Johnson; 10 Brad Meyers; 11 Lee Radford. Subs (all used): 24 Adrian Morley for Johnson (5); 19 Jamie Langley for Peacock (24); 8 Joe Vagana for Fielden (24); Johnson for Radford (24); 1 Robbie Paul for Henderson (31); Peacock for Vagana (45); Fielden for Morley (49); Henderson for Paul (54); Radford for Meyers (60); Morley for Peacock (62); Meyers for Langley (73); Peacock for Johnson (74).
Tries: L Pryce (29), Vainikolo (53); **Goals:** Deacon 3/5;
Field goal: I Harris.
RHINOS: 1 Richard Mathers; 2 Mark Calderwood; 3 Chev Walker; 12 Chris McKenna; 5 Marcus Bai; 6 Danny McGuire; 7 Rob Burrow; 8 Ryan Bailey; 14 Andrew Dunemann; 15 Danny Ward; 20 Gareth Ellis; 16 Willie Poching; 13 Kevin Sinfield (C). Subs (all used): 10 Barrie McDermott for Ward (17); 11 Ali Lauitiiti for Poching (21); 18 Jamie Jones-Buchanan for Bailey (31); Ward for McDermott (34); 9 Matt Diskin for Ellis (48); Poching for Lauitiiti (48); McDermott for Ward (54); Ellis for Poching (54); Lauitiiti for McDermott (61); Poching for Dunemann (65); Ward for Jones-Buchanan (68); Dunemann for Ellis (71).
Try: McGuire (22); **Goals:** Sinfield 1/2.
Rugby Leaguer & League Express Men of the Match:
Bulls: Leon Pryce; *Rhinos:* Danny McGuire.
Penalty count: 6-8; **Half-time:** 8-6;
Referee: Ashley Klein (Keighley); **Attendance:** 65,537
(at Old Trafford, Manchester).

2006

NATIONAL LEAGUE TWO GRAND FINAL

Sunday 8th October 2006

SHEFFIELD EAGLES 35 SWINTON LIONS 10

EAGLES: 1 Johnny Woodcock; 5 Greg Hurst; 4 Jimmy Walker; 3 James Ford; 2 Rob Worrincy; 6 Brendon Lindsay; 7 Gavin Brown; 8 Jack Howieson; 9 Paul Pickering; 10 Mitchell Stringer; 11 Andy Hay; 12 Dale Holdstock; 13 Andy Smith. Subs (all used): 14 Craig Poucher; 15 Martin Ostler; 16 Sean Dickinson; 17 Waisale Sovatabua.
Tries: Worrincy (21, 43), Lindsay (38), Woodcock (39), Walker (51), Hay (60); **Goals:** Woodcock 5/6;
Field goal: G Brown.
LIONS: 1 Wayne English; 2 Andy Saywell; 3 Darren Woods; 4 David Alstead; 5 Marlon Billy; 6 Martin Moana; 7 Chris Hough; 8 Bruce Johnson; 9 Phil Wood; 10 Dave Newton; 11 Kris Smith; 12 Ian Sinfield; 13 Lee Marsh. Subs (all used): 14 Liam McGovern; 15 Chris Morley; 16 Danny Aboushakra; 17 Ian Parry.
Tries: Saywell (35), Alstead (74); **Goals:** McGovern 1/2.
Rugby Leaguer & League Express Men of the Match:
Eagles: Johnny Woodcock; *Lions:* Wayne English.
Penalty count: 3-4; **Half-time:** 16-4;
Referee: Peter Taberner (Wigan).
(at Halliwell Jones Stadium, Warrington).

Dewsbury Rams were National League Two Champions in 2006. This game was to determine who took the second promotion place.

NATIONAL LEAGUE ONE GRAND FINAL

Sunday 8th October 2006

HULL KINGSTON ROVERS 29 WIDNES VIKINGS 16

ROVERS: 1 Ben Cockayne; 2 Leroy Rivett; 3 Gareth Morton; 4 Jon Goddard; 5 Byron Ford; 6 Scott Murrell; 7 James Webster; 8 Makali Aizue; 9 Ben Fisher; 10 David Tangata-Toa; 11 Iain Morrison; 12 Michael Smith; 13 Tommy Gallagher. Subs (all used): 14 Pat Weisner; 15 Dwayne Barker; 16 Jason Netherton; 17 Dave Wilson.
Tries: Ford (6), Goddard (18, 36), Murrell (24), Weisner (43); **Goals:** Morton 4/6; **Field goal:** Murrell.
VIKINGS: 1 Gavin Dodd; 2 Damien Blanch; 3 Sean Gleeson; 4 Daryl Cardiss; 5 John Kirkpatrick; 6 Dennis Moran; 7 Ian Watson; 8 Terry O'Connor; 9 Mark Smith; 10 Barrie McDermott; 11 Mick Cassidy; 12 David Allen; 13 Bob Beswick. Subs (all used): 14 Aaron Summers; 15 Oliver Wilkes; 16 Jordan James; 17 Ryan Tandy.
Tries: Dodd (32), Tandy (57), Blanch (70); **Goals:** Dodd 2/3.
Rugby Leaguer & League Express Men of the Match:
Rovers: James Webster; *Vikings:* Mark Smith.
Penalty count: 8-5; **Half-time:** 22-4;
Referee: Phil Bentham (Warrington); **Attendance:** 13,024
(at Halliwell Jones Stadium, Warrington).

SUPER LEAGUE GRAND FINAL

Saturday 14th October 2006

HULL FC 4 ST HELENS 26

HULL: 1 Shaun Briscoe; 14 Motu Tony; 4 Sid Domic; 3 Kirk Yeaman; 5 Gareth Raynor; 13 Paul Cooke; 7 Richard Horne; 8 Ewan Dowes; 9 Richard Swain (C); 10 Garreth Carvell; 11 Lee Radford; 12 Shayne McMenemy; 24 Danny Washbrook. Subs: 15 Paul King for Carvell (17); 19 Graeme Horne for Radford (23); 26 Scott Wheeldon for Dowes (27); 6 Richard Whiting for McMenemy (29); Dowes for Wheeldon (49); Carvell for King (49); Radford for G Horne (51); McMenemy for Whiting (54); King for Carvell (68); Wheeldon for Dowes (73); Whiting for Tony (76); G Horne for Radford (77).
Try: Domic (24); **Goals:** Cooke 0/1.
SAINTS: 1 Paul Wellens; 2 Ade Gardner; 3 Jamie Lyon; 4 Willie Talau; 5 Francis Meli; 6 Leon Pryce; 7 Sean Long (C); 17 Paul Anderson; 9 Keiron Cunningham; 10 Jason Cayless; 11 Lee Gilmour; 12 Jon Wilkin; 16 Jason Hooper. Subs: 23 Maurie Fa'asavalu for P Anderson (12); 19 James Graham for Cayless (25); 15 Mike Bennett for Fa'asavalu (28); 14 James Roby for Cunningham (31); P Anderson for Wilkin (33); Cunningham for Gilmour (49); Cayless for P Anderson (52); Wilkin for Hooper (56); Fa'asavalu for Cayless (58); Gilmour for Graham (66); Cayless for Fa'asavalu (72); P Anderson for Wilkin (75).
Tries: Meli (17), Pryce (29), Talau (49), Gardner (52), Cunningham (62); **Goals:** Lyon 3/5.
Rugby Leaguer & League Express Men of the Match:
Hull: Shaun Briscoe; *Saints:* Paul Wellens.
Penalty count: 4-2; **Half-time:** 4-10;
Referee: Karl Kirkpatrick (Warrington); **Attendance:** 72,582
(at Old Trafford, Manchester).

2007

NATIONAL LEAGUE TWO GRAND FINAL

Sunday 7th October 2007

FEATHERSTONE ROVERS 24 OLDHAM 6

ROVERS: 1 Loz Wildbore; 2 Danny Kirmond; 3 Jon Whittle; 4 Wayne McHugh; 5 Ade Adebisi; 6 Andy Kain; 7 Paul Handforth; 8 Gareth Handford; 9 Joe McLocklan; 10 Stuart Dickens; 11 Jamie Field; 12 Richard Blakeway; 13 Tom Haughey. Subs (all used): 14 Jamie Benn; 15 Ian Tonks; 16 James Houston; 17 Gavin Swinson.
Tries: McHugh (39, 49), Handforth (46); **Goals:** Dickens 5/6;
Field goals: Wildbore (66, 70).
Dismissal: Blakeway (64) – head butt on Roberts.

OLDHAM: 1 Gareth Langley; 2 Byron Ford; 3 Craig Littler; 4 Adam Hughes; 5 Lucas Onyango; 6 Neil Roden; 7 James Coyle; 8 Anthony Tonks; 9 Simeon Hoyle; 10 Richard Mervill; 11 Ian Sinfield; 12 Robert Roberts; 13 Geno Costin. Subs (all used): 14 Ian Hodson; 15 Alex Wilkinson; 16 Said Tamghart; 17 Matty Brooks.
Try: Hughes (31); **Goals:** Langley 1/2.
Rugby Leaguer & League Express Men of the Match:
Rovers: Paul Handforth; *Oldham:* Robert Roberts.
Penalty count: 9-5; **Half-time:** 10-6; **Referee:** Gareth Hewer.
(at Headingley Carnegie, Leeds).

Celtic Crusaders were National League Two Champions in 2007. This game was to determine who took the second promotion place.

NATIONAL LEAGUE ONE GRAND FINAL

Sunday 7th October 2007

CASTLEFORD TIGERS 42 WIDNES VIKINGS 10

TIGERS: 1 Stuart Donlan; 2 Danny Williams; 3 Michael Shenton; 4 Ryan McGoldrick; 5 Kirk Dixon; 6 Anthony Thackeray; 7 Danny Brough; 8 Liam Higgins; 9 Andrew Henderson; 10 Awen Guttenbeil; 11 Joe Westerman; 12 Ryan Clayton; 13 Peter Lupton. Subs (all used): 14 Mark Leafa; 15 Chris Charles; 16 Michael Wainwright; 17 Ryan Boyle.
Tries: Wainwright (20), McGoldrick (29), Guttenbeil (44, 76), M Shenton (52), Westerman (62), Clayton (66);
Goals: Brough 6/9; **Field goals:** Brough (25, 55).
VIKINGS: 1 Scott Grix; 2 Damien Blanch; 3 Toa Kohe-Love; 4 Mick Nanyn; 5 Gavin Dodd; 6 Dennis Moran; 7 Joel Penny; 8 Mick Cassidy; 9 Mark Smith; 10 Oliver Wilkes; 11 Joel Tomkins; 12 Paul Noone; 13 Bob Beswick. Subs (all used): 14 Aaron Summers; 15 Jordan James; 16 Ian Webster; 17 Lee Doran.
Tries: Nanyn (35), Wilkes (69); **Goals:** Nanyn 1/2.
Rugby Leaguer & League Express Men of the Match:
Tigers: Danny Brough; *Vikings:* Scott Grix.
Penalty count: 7-2; **Half-time:** 13-4; **Referee:** Phil Bentham; **Attendance:** 20,814 *(at Headingley Carnegie, Leeds).*

SUPER LEAGUE GRAND FINAL

Saturday 13th October 2007

LEEDS RHINOS 33 ST HELENS 6

RHINOS: 1 Brent Webb; 5 Lee Smith; 3 Clinton Toopi; 4 Keith Senior; 2 Scott Donald; 6 Danny McGuire; 7 Rob Burrow; 8 Kylie Leuluai; 9 Matt Diskin; 10 Jamie Peacock; 11 Jamie Jones-Buchanan; 12 Gareth Ellis; 13 Kevin Sinfield (C). Subs (all used): 14 Ali Lauitiiti for Diskin (23); 16 Ryan Bailey for Leuluai (18); 18 Ian Kirke for Jones-Buchanan (33); 22 Carl Ablett for Kirke (57); Leuluai for Bailey (55); Jones-Buchanan for Lauitiiti (60); Diskin for Ablett (63); Kirke for Leuluai (65); Bailey for Kirke (76).
Tries: Webb (19), Lauitiiti (50), Donald (52), Smith (69), Jones-Buchanan (80); **Goals:** Sinfield 6/7;
Field goal: Burrow (55).
SAINTS: 1 Paul Wellens; 2 Ade Gardner; 3 Matt Gidley; 4 Willie Talau; 5 Francis Meli; 6 Leon Pryce; 7 Sean Long; 8 Nick Fozzard; 9 Keiron Cunningham (C); 10 Jason Cayless; 11 Lee Gilmour; 30 Chris Flannery; 12 Jon Wilkin. Subs (all used): 17 James Graham for Cayless (15); 14 James Roby for Cunningham (23); 23 Maurie Fa'asavalu for Fozzard (23); 15 Mike Bennett for Wilkin (31); Cayless for Fa'asavalu (34); Cunningham for Flannery (51); Wilkin for Bennett (55); Fa'asavalu for Cayless (55); Fozzard for Graham (57); Cayless for Fozzard (68); Graham for Fa'asavalu (68); Bennett for Gilmour (72).
Try: Roby (27); **Goals:** Long 1/2.
Rugby Leaguer & League Express Men of the Match:
Rhinos: Rob Burrow; *Saints:* Sean Long.
Penalty count: 4-5; **Half-time:** 8-6; **Referee:** Ashley Klein; **Attendance:** 71,352 *(at Old Trafford, Manchester).*

2008

NATIONAL LEAGUE TWO GRAND FINAL

Sunday 28th September 2008

DONCASTER 18 OLDHAM 10

DONCASTER: 1 Zebastian Luisi; 2 Dean Colton; 3 Andreas Bauer; 4 Shaun Leaf; 5 Wayne Reittie; 6 Kyle Wood; 7 Luke Gale; 8 Nathan Freer; 9 Corey Lawrie; 10 Alex Benson; 11 Peter Green; 12 Craig Lawton; 13 Josh Weeden. Subs (all used): 14 Kyle Briggs; 15 Chris Buttery; 16 Michael Haley; 17 Mark Castle.
Tries: Buttery (44), Gale (49), Briggs (73); **Goals:** Gale 3/4.
OLDHAM: 1 Paul O'Connor; 2 Gareth Langley; 3 Marcus St Hilaire; 4 Mick Nanyn; 5 Daryl Cardiss; 6 Phil Joseph; 7 James Coyle; 8 Adam Robinson; 9 Matty Brooks; 10 Richard Mervill; 11 Tommy Goulden; 12 Danny Halliwell; 13 Robert Roberts. Subs (all used): 14 Ian Hodson; 15 Luke Menzies; 16 Chris Baines; 17 Said Tamghart.
Tries: Hodson (34), Nanyn (62); **Goals:** Nanyn 1/4.
Rugby Leaguer & League Express Men of the Match:
Doncaster: Luke Gale; *Oldham:* Adam Robinson.
Penalty count: 7-8; **Half-time:** 2-6; **Referee:** Ronnie Laughton.
(at Halliwell Jones Stadium, Warrington).

Gateshead Thunder were National League Two Champions in 2008. This game was to determine who took the second promotion place.

NATIONAL LEAGUE ONE GRAND FINAL

Sunday 28th September 2008

CELTIC CRUSADERS 18 SALFORD CITY REDS 36
(after extra time)

CRUSADERS: 1 Tony Duggan; 2 Luke Dyer; 3 Josh Hannay; 4 Mark Dalle Cort; 5 Anthony Blackwood; 6 Damien Quinn; 7 Jace Van Dijk; 8 Jordan James; 9 Neil Budworth; 10 David Tangata-Toa; 11 Chris Beasley; 12 Darren Mapp; 13 Terry Martin. Subs (all used): 14 Aaron Summers; 15 Ian Webster; 16 Mark Lennon; 17 Neale Wyatt.
Tries: Blackwood (38), Dyer (50), J James (54), Tangata-Toa (66); **Goals:** Hannay 0/1, Lennon 1/3.
CITY REDS: 1 Karl Fitzpatrick; 2 Matt Gardner; 3 Stuart Littler; 4 John Wilshere; 5 Paul White; 6 Robbie Paul; 7 Richard Myler; 8 Paul Highton; 9 Malcolm Alker; 10 Craig Stapleton; 11 Ian Sibbit; 12 Luke Adamson; 13 Jordan Turner. Subs (all used): 14 Stefan Ratchford; 15 Steve Bannister; 16 Lee Jewitt; 17 Phil Leuluai.
Tries: White (5, 86), Gardner (26), Fitzpatrick (63), Sibbit (83), Myler (99); **Goals:** Wilshere 6/7.
Rugby Leaguer & League Express Men of the Match:
Crusaders: Tony Duggan; *City Reds:* John Wilshere.
Penalty count: 5-5; **Half-time:** 4-10; **Full-time:** 18-18; **Referee:** Ben Thaler; **Attendance:** 7,104
(at Halliwell Jones Stadium, Warrington).

SUPER LEAGUE GRAND FINAL

Saturday 4th October 2008

LEEDS RHINOS 24 ST HELENS 16

RHINOS: 5 Lee Smith; 22 Ryan Hall; 19 Carl Ablett; 4 Keith Senior; 2 Scott Donald; 6 Danny McGuire; 7 Rob Burrow; 8 Kylie Leuluai; 9 Matt Diskin; 10 Jamie Peacock; 11 Jamie Jones-Buchanan; 12 Gareth Ellis; 13 Kevin Sinfield (C). Subs (all used): 17 Nick Scruton; 14 Ali Lauitiiti; 18 Ian Kirke; 16 Ryan Bailey.
Tries: Smith (23), Hall (37), McGuire (49, 63);
Goals: Sinfield 4/4.
SAINTS: 1 Paul Wellens; 2 Ade Gardner; 3 Matt Gidley; 4 Willie Talau; 5 Francis Meli; 6 Leon Pryce; 7 Sean Long; 18 Bryn Hargreaves; 9 Keiron Cunningham (C); 17 James Graham; 11 Lee Gilmour; 12 Jon Wilkin; 16 Chris Flannery. Subs (all used): 8 Nick Fozzard; 21 Paul Clough; 14 James Roby; 23 Maurie Fa'asavalu.
Tries: Graham (6), Gidley (43), Gardner (59); **Goals:** Long 2/3.
Rugby Leaguer & League Express Men of the Match:
Rhinos: Jamie Peacock; *Saints:* Sean Long.
Penalty count: 6-8; **Half-time:** 12-6; **Referee:** Ashley Klein; **Attendance:** 68,810 *(at Old Trafford, Manchester).*

2009

CHAMPIONSHIP ONE GRAND FINAL

Sunday 4th October 2009

KEIGHLEY COUGARS 28 OLDHAM 26

COUGARS: 1 George Rayner; 2 Sam Gardner; 3 Dan Potter; 4 Oliver Pursglove; 5 Gavin Duffy; 6 Jon Presley; 7 Danny Jones; 17 Scott Law; 14 Jamaine Wray; 8 Andy Shickell; 11 Will Cartledge; 18 Greg Nicholson; 13 Carl Hughes. Subs (all used): 21 Ryan Smith; 28 Ryan Benjafield; 9 James Feather; 16 Brendan Rawlins.
Tries: Gardner (24), Jones (42, 50), Presley (63), Pursglove (67); **Goals:** Jones 4/5.
OLDHAM: 4 Paul Reilly; 21 Lucas Onyango; 24 Marcus St Hilaire; 22 Phil Joseph; 1 Paul O'Connor; 18 Neil Roden; 7 Thomas Coyle; 15 Jason Boults; 30 Martin Roden; 16 Wayne Kerr; 23 Chris Baines; 12 Tommy Goulden; 28 Craig Lawton. Subs (all used): 10 Jamie I'Anson; 25 Luke Menzies; 27 Matt Ashe; 29 Ben Heaton.
Tries: Menzies (35, 76), N Roden (54), St Hilaire (70), Kerr (78); **Goals:** Baines 3/4, Ashe 0/1.
Rugby Leaguer & League Express Men of the Match:
Cougars: Danny Jones; *Oldham:* Luke Menzies.
Penalty count: 9-2; **Half-time:** 4-6; **Referee:** Ronnie Laughton. *(at Halliwell Jones Stadium, Warrington).*

Dewsbury Rams were Championship One Champions in 2009.
This game was to determine who took the second promotion place.

CHAMPIONSHIP GRAND FINAL

Sunday 4th October 2009

BARROW RAIDERS 26 HALIFAX 18

RAIDERS: 1 Gary Broadbent; 36 Andy Ballard; 32 Andreas Bauer; 4 Liam Harrison; 5 James Nixon; 24 Jamie Rooney; 31 James Coyle; 34 Rob Roberts; 9 Andy Ellis; 8 Brett McDermott; 33 Dave Allen; 22 Ned Catic; 26 Zebastian Luisi. Subs (all used): 15 Chris Young; 13 Andy Bracek; 35 Danny Halliwell; 14 Paul Noone.
Tries: Harrison (33), Ballard (37), Allen (61), Bauer (66, 78); **Goals:** Rooney 3/5.
HALIFAX: 4 Shad Royston; 5 James Haley; 15 Mark Roberts; 2 Lee Paterson; 23 Rob Worrincy; 19 Mick Govin; 7 Ben Black; 21 Neil Cherryholme; 9 Sean Penkywicz; 22 David Wrench; 11 David Larder; 27 Steve Bannister; 12 Paul Smith. Subs (all used): 13 Bob Beswick; 14 Mark Gleeson; 16 Said Tamghart; 26 Dominic Maloney.
Tries: Haley (12), Royston (31), Black (45), Govin (70); **Goals:** Paterson 1/5.
Rugby Leaguer & League Express Men of the Match:
Raiders: Gary Broadbent; *Halifax:* Mick Govin.
Penalty count: 8-5; **Half-time:** 10-10; **Referee:** Phil Bentham; **Attendance:** 11,398 *(at Halliwell Jones Stadium, Warrington).*

SUPER LEAGUE GRAND FINAL

Saturday 10th October 2009

LEEDS RHINOS 18 ST HELENS 10

RHINOS: 1 Brent Webb; 2 Scott Donald; 3 Lee Smith; 4 Keith Senior; 5 Ryan Hall; 6 Danny McGuire; 7 Rob Burrow; 8 Kylie Leuluai; 14 Matt Diskin; 10 Jamie Peacock; 11 Jamie Jones-Buchanan; 18 Carl Ablett; 13 Kevin Sinfield (C). Subs (all used): 16 Ryan Bailey for Leuluai (19); 19 Luke Burgess for Peacock (29); 17 Ian Kirke for Jones-Buchanan (29); 12 Ali Lauitiiti for Ablett (29); Jones-Buchanan for Lauitiiti (36); Peacock for Burgess (46); Leuluai for Bailey (53); Ablett for Kirke (57); Burgess for Diskin (62); Bailey for Leuluai (67); Diskin for Burgess (69); Kirke for Jones-Buchanan (76).
Tries: Diskin (30), Smith (37, 72); **Goals:** Sinfield 2/4;
Field goals: Sinfield (42), Burrow (78).

SAINTS: 1 Paul Wellens; 2 Ade Gardner; 3 Matt Gidley; 18 Kyle Eastmond; 5 Francis Meli; 6 Leon Pryce; 7 Sean Long; 10 James Graham; 9 Keiron Cunningham (C); 16 Tony Puletua; 12 Jon Wilkin; 11 Lee Gilmour; 13 Chris Flannery. Subs (all used): 14 James Roby for Cunningham (25); 15 Bryn Hargreaves for Puletua (24); 17 Paul Clough for Gilmour (31); 23 Maurie Fa'asavalu for Graham (31); Graham for Fa'asavalu (48); Puletua for Hargreaves (50); Gilmour for Wilkin (55); Cunningham for Clough (61); Wilkin for Roby (65); Roby for Flannery (73).
Try: Eastmond (13); **Goals:** Eastmond 3/3.
Rugby Leaguer & League Express Men of the Match:
Rhinos: Kevin Sinfield; *Saints:* James Graham.
Penalty count: 8-7; **Half-time:** 8-8; **Referee:** Steve Ganson; **Attendance:** 63,259 *(at Old Trafford, Manchester).*

2010

CHAMPIONSHIP ONE GRAND FINAL

Sunday 26th September 2010

OLDHAM 4 YORK CITY KNIGHTS 25

OLDHAM: 1 Paul O'Connor; 2 Lucas Onyango; 24 Marcus St Hilaire; 4 Mick Fogerty; 5 John Gillam; 6 Neil Roden; 28 Gregg McNally; 8 Jason Boults; 9 Martin Roden; 16 Wayne Kerr; 18 Chris Clarke; 13 Joe Chandler; 21 Valu Bentley. Subs (all used): 10 Dave Ellison; 19 Ben Heaton; 17 Danny Whitmore; 7 Matt Ashe.
Try: Fogerty (20); **Goals:** McNally 0/1.
CITY KNIGHTS: 31 James Haynes; 2 Wayne Reittie; 3 Mike Mitchell; 4 Lee Waterman; 28 Danny Wilson; 6 Chris Thorman; 1 Danny Ratcliffe; 17 Nathan Freer; 33 Jack Lee; 10 Alex Benson; 11 Jordan Ross; 29 Ryan Esders; 15 Luke Hardbottle. Subs (all used): 32 Paul Stamp; 36 Callum Dinsdale; 26 Steve Lewis; 30 Jack Stearman.
Tries: Reittie (7), Haynes (26), Thorman (64), Lewis (74); **Goals:** Waterman 2/3, Thorman 2/2; **Field goal:** Thorman (69).
Rugby Leaguer & League Express Men of the Match:
Oldham: Neil Roden; *City Knights:* Chris Thorman.
Penalty count: 2-7; **Half-time:** 4-10; **Referee:** Gareth Hewer. *(at Halliwell Jones Stadium, Warrington).*

Hunslet Hawks were Championship One Champions in 2010.
This game was to determine who took the second promotion place.

CHAMPIONSHIP GRAND FINAL

Sunday 26th September 2010

FEATHERSTONE ROVERS 22 HALIFAX 23
(after golden point extra time)

ROVERS: 1 Ian Hardman; 26 Zak Hardaker; 3 Sam Smeaton; 4 Liam Welham; 2 Tom Saxton; 6 Kyle Briggs; 9 Liam Finn; 17 Tony Tonks; 31 Ben Kaye; 10 Stuart Dickens; 18 Tim Spears; 13 Jamie Field; 11 Matty Dale. Subs (all used): 19 Ross Divorty; 16 Dane Manning; 12 Jon Grayshon; 7 Andy Kain.
Tries: Briggs (28), Hardaker (30, 52), Dale (45);
Goals: Briggs 3/4.
HALIFAX: 4 Shad Royston; 2 Lee Paterson; 6 Luke Branighan; 18 Dylan Nash; 23 Rob Worrincy; 26 Graham Holroyd; 7 Ben Black; 10 Neil Cherryholme; 13 Bob Beswick; 22 David Wrench; 11 David Larder; 22 David Wrench; 27 Sam Barlow. Subs (all used): 9 Sean Penkywicz; 17 Frank Watene; 19 Dominic Maloney; 24 Steve Bannister.
Tries: Worrincy (20), Black (58), Branighan (60), Bannister (75); **Goals:** Paterson 3/4; **Field goal:** Black (82).
On report: Barlow (35) - alleged high tackle on Divorty.
Rugby Leaguer & League Express Men of the Match:
Rovers: Tom Saxton; *Halifax:* Ben Black.
Penalty count: 6-3; **Half-time:** 12-4; **Full-time:** 22-22;
Referee: Robert Hicks; **Attendance:** 9,443
(at Halliwell Jones Stadium, Warrington).

SUPER LEAGUE GRAND FINAL

Saturday 2nd October 2010

ST HELENS 10 WIGAN WARRIORS 22

SAINTS: 1 Paul Wellens; 30 Jamie Foster; 3 Matt Gidley; 5 Francis Meli; 24 Jonny Lomax; 12 Jon Wilkin; 34 Matty Smith; 10 James Graham; 9 Keiron Cunningham (C); 15 Bryn Hargreaves; 4 Iosia Soliola; 13 Chris Flannery; 11 Tony Puletua. Subs (all used): 17 Paul Clough; 14 James Roby; 22 Andrew Dixon; 25 Jacob Emmitt.
Tries: Dixon (28), Meli (74); **Goals:** Foster 1/2.
WARRIORS: 6 Sam Tomkins; 24 Darrell Goulding; 3 Martin Gleeson; 4 George Carmont; 5 Pat Richards; 19 Paul Deacon; 7 Thomas Leuluai; 8 Stuart Fielden; 15 Michael McIlorum; 10 Andy Coley; 11 Harrison Hansen; 12 Joel Tomkins; 13 Sean O'Loughlin (C). Subs (all used): 9 Mark Riddell; 17 Iafeta Palea'aesina; 25 Liam Farrell; 14 Paul Prescott.
Tries: Gleeson (4, 16), Goulding (20), S Tomkins (53); **Goals:** Richards 2/3, Riddell 1/3, S Tomkins 0/1.
Rugby Leaguer & League Express Men of the Match: *Saints:* Tony Puletua; *Warriors:* Thomas Leuluai.
Penalty count: 6-11; **Half time:** 6-16;
Referee: Richard Silverwood; **Attendance:** 71,526 *(at Old Trafford, Manchester).*

2011

CHAMPIONSHIP ONE GRAND FINAL

Sunday 2nd October 2011

KEIGHLEY COUGARS 32 WORKINGTON TOWN 12

COUGARS: 18 James Haythornthwaite; 4 Danny Lawton; 22 Ben Sagar; 33 Jake Normington; 5 Gavin Duffy; 6 Jason Demetriou; 36 Jy-Mel Coleman; 17 Ryan Benjafield; 9 James Feather; 10 Scott Law; 11 Will Cartledge; 12 Oliver Pursglove; 21 Richard Jones. Subs (all used): 14 Jamaine Wray; 8 Andy Shickell; 16 Brendan Rawlins; 7 Ryan Smith.
Tries: Lawton (5), Feather (20), Rawlins (25), Pursglove (32), Normington (69, 77); **Goals:** Lawton 4/6.
TOWN: 1 Brett Carter; 2 Elliott Miller; 3 Jason Mossop; 4 Aaron Low; 5 Neil Frazer; 24 Darren Holt; 7 Scott Kaighan; 10 Kris Coward; 13 Karl Olstrum; 29 Dave Armitstead; 11 Mike Whitehead; 18 Joe McKenna; 12 Jarrad Stack. Subs (all used): 23 Marc Bainbridge; 15 Ruairi McGoff; 32 Chris Clough; 17 James Robinson.
Tries: Kaighan (65), Frazer (74); **Goals:** Holt 2/2.
Rugby Leaguer & League Express Men of the Match: *Cougars:* Jason Demetriou; *Town:* Jarrad Stack.
Penalty count: 7-5; **Half-time:** 22-0; **Referee:** Tim Roby. *(at Halliwell Jones Stadium, Warrington).*

Swinton Lions were Championship One Champions in 2011. This game was to determine who took the second promotion place.

CHAMPIONSHIP GRAND FINAL

Sunday 2nd October 2011

FEATHERSTONE ROVERS 40 SHEFFIELD EAGLES 4

ROVERS: 1 Ian Hardy; 33 Ben Cockayne; 3 Sam Smeaton; 17 Greg Worthington; 5 Tom Saxton; 6 Andy Kain; 7 Liam Finn; 8 Tony Tonks; 9 Ben Kaye; 10 Stuart Dickens; 11 Jon Grayshon; 12 Tim Spears; 28 Jon Hepworth. Subs (all used): 18 Ross Divorty; 13 Matty Dale; 4 Andrew Bostock; 30 Kirk Netherton.
Tries: Spears (4), Finn (7, 39), Hardman (42), Cockayne (56), Hepworth (59), Saxton (79); **Goals:** Finn 6/7.
Sin bin: Netherton (54) - fighting.
EAGLES: 6 Quentin Laulu-Togagae; 5 Tim Bergin; 26 Corey Hanson; 1 Misi Taulapapa; 16 Vinny Finigan; 13 Dane McDonald; 7 Simon Brown; 8 Jack Howieson; 9 Andrew Henderson; 10 Mitchell Stringer; 11 Alex Szostak; 12 Peter Green; 19 Joe Hirst. Subs (all used): 22 Ryan Hepworth; 30 Sam Scott; 20 Pat Smith; 14 Jonny Woodcock.
Try: McDonald (12); **Goals:** Brown 0/1.
Sin bin: Hirst (54) - fighting.

Rugby Leaguer & League Express Men of the Match: *Rovers:* Liam Finn; *Eagles:* Joe Hirst.
Penalty count: 7-11; **Half-time:** 18-4;
Referee: Matthew Thomason; **Attendance:** 7,263 *(at Halliwell Jones Stadium, Warrington).*

SUPER LEAGUE GRAND FINAL

Saturday 8th October 2011

LEEDS RHINOS 32 ST HELENS 16

RHINOS: 1 Brent Webb; 23 Ben Jones-Bishop; 27 Zak Hardaker; 12 Carl Ablett; 5 Ryan Hall; 13 Kevin Sinfield (C); 6 Danny McGuire; 8 Kylie Leuluai; 9 Danny Buderus; 10 Jamie Peacock; 11 Jamie Jones-Buchanan; 3 Brett Delaney; 21 Chris Clarkson. Subs (all used): 7 Rob Burrow; 16 Ryan Bailey; 17 Ian Kirke; 14 Ali Lauitiiti.
Tries: Burrow (34), Webb (65), Hall (70), Ablett (74), Hardaker (80); **Goals:** Sinfield 6/7.
SAINTS: 1 Paul Wellens (C); 28 Tom Makinson; 3 Michael Shenton; 5 Francis Meli; 22 Jamie Foster; 25 Lee Gaskell; 20 Jonny Lomax; 10 James Graham (C); 9 James Roby; 11 Tony Puletua; 12 Jon Wilkin; 4 Iosia Soliola; 16 Paul Clough. Subs (all used): 19 Andrew Dixon; 14 Scott Moore; 15 Louie McCarthy-Scarsbrook; 17 Gary Wheeler.
Tries: Makinson (50), Shenton (55); **Goals:** Foster 4/5.
Rugby Leaguer & League Express Men of the Match: *Rhinos:* Rob Burrow; *Saints:* Lee Gaskell.
Penalty count: 5-7; **Half-time:** 8-2; **Referee:** Phil Bentham; **Attendance:** 69,107 *(at Old Trafford, Manchester).*

2012

CHAMPIONSHIP ONE GRAND FINAL

Sunday 30th September 2012

BARROW RAIDERS 13 DONCASTER 16

RAIDERS: 1 Andy Ballard; 2 Lee Haney; 3 Chris Larkin; 4 Aaron Low; 5 James Nixon; 6 Scott Kaighan; 7 Liam Campbell; 8 Jamie Butler; 9 James Dandy; 10 Ryan Duffy; 11 Liam Harrison; 12 James Gordon; 13 Daniel Toal. Subs (all used): 14 Liam Finch; 15 Martin Ostler; 16 Ruairi McGoff; 17 Andrew Dawson.
Tries: Larkin (4), Low (77); **Goals:** Ballard 2/3;
Field goal: Kaighan (39).
DONCASTER: 1 Lee Waterman; 2 Tom Hodson; 3 Chris Spurr; 4 Danny Cowling; 5 Stewart Sanderson; 6 Kyle Kesik; 7 Craig Fawcett; 8 Mark Castle; 9 Mike Emmett; 10 Russ Spiers; 11 Lucas Walshaw; 12 Michael Kelly; 13 Carl Hughes. Subs (all used): 14 Nathan Powley; 15 Craig Robinson; 16 Grant Edwards; 17 Liam Cunningham.
Tries: Sanderson (11), Waterman (46), Fawcett (57); **Goals:** Hodson 2/3.
Rugby Leaguer & League Express Men of the Match: *Raiders:* Liam Harrison; *Doncaster:* Craig Fawcett.
Penalty count: 4-5; **Half-time:** 7-4; **Referee:** Jamie Leahy. *(at Halliwell Jones Stadium, Warrington).*

CHAMPIONSHIP GRAND FINAL

Sunday 30th September 2012

FEATHERSTONE ROVERS 16 SHEFFIELD EAGLES 20

ROVERS: 1 Ian Hardman; 2 Tangi Ropati; 3 Nathan Chappell; 4 Greg Worthington; 5 Tom Saxton; 6 Andy Kain; 7 Liam Finn; 8 Anthony England; 9 Ben Kaye; 10 James Lockwood; 11 Matty Dale; 12 Tim Spears; 13 Kyle Briggs. Subs (all used): 14 Dominic Maloney; 15 Stuart Dickens; 16 Andrew Bostock; 17 Jon Hepworth.
Tries: Hardman (17), Hepworth (51); **Goals:** Finn 4/4.
On report: Maloney (57) - alleged use of the elbow on Turner.
EAGLES: 1 Quentin Laulu-Togagae; 2 Misi Taulapapa; 3 Duane Straugheir; 4 Menzie Yere; 5 Scott Turner; 6 Simon Brown; 7 Dominic Brambani; 8 Jack Howieson; 9 Andrew Henderson; 10 Mitchell Stringer; 11 Michael Knowles; 12 Sam Scott; 13 Alex Szostak. Subs (all used): 14 James Davey; 15 Peter Green; 16 Dane McDonald; 17 Liam Higgins.

Tries: Turner (9), Laulu-Togagae (32), McDonald (46), Taulapapa (57); **Goals:** Brown 2/5.
Rugby Leaguer & League Express Men of the Match:
Rovers: Ian Hardman; *Eagles:* Michael Knowles.
Penalty count: 4-6; **Half-time:** 8-10; **Referee:** Tim Roby;
Attendance: 6,409 *(at Halliwell Jones Stadium, Warrington).*

SUPER LEAGUE GRAND FINAL

Saturday 6th October 2012

LEEDS RHINOS 26 WARRINGTON WOLVES 18

RHINOS: 4 Zak Hardaker; 2 Ben Jones-Bishop; 3 Kallum Watkins; 12 Carl Ablett; 5 Ryan Hall; 13 Kevin Sinfield (C); 6 Danny McGuire; 8 Kylie Leuluai; 7 Rob Burrow; 10 Jamie Peacock; 11 Jamie Jones-Buchanan; 15 Brett Delaney; 16 Ryan Bailey. Subs (all used): 17 Ian Kirke; 20 Darrell Griffin; 25 Stevie Ward; 31 Shaun Lunt.
Tries: Sinfield (19), Jones-Bishop (28), Ablett (59), Hall (72);
Goals: Sinfield 5/5.
WOLVES: 1 Brett Hodgson; 5 Joel Monaghan; 19 Stefan Ratchford; 4 Ryan Atkins; 2 Chris Riley; 6 Lee Briers; 7 Richard Myler; 20 Chris Hill; 14 Mick Higham; 13 Ben Harrison; 12 Ben Westwood; 11 Trent Waterhouse; 15 Simon Grix. Subs (all used): 8 Adrian Morley (C); 9 Michael Monaghan; 16 Paul Wood; 17 Michael Cooper.
Tries: Myler (4), J Monaghan (38), Atkins (45);
Goals: Hodgson 3/4.
Rugby Leaguer & League Express Men of the Match:
Rhinos: Kevin Sinfield; *Wolves:* Richard Myler.
Penalty count: 6-5; **Half-time:** 14-14;
Referee: Richard Silverwood; **Attendance:** 70,676
(at Old Trafford, Manchester).

2013

CHAMPIONSHIP ONE GRAND FINAL

Sunday 29th September 2013

OLDHAM 18 ROCHDALE HORNETS 32

OLDHAM: 1 Richard Lepori; 2 Mo Agoro; 21 David Cookson; 25 Jonathan Ford; 5 Dale Bloomfield; 23 Lewis Palfrey; 16 Kenny Hughes; 18 Phil Joy; 9 Sam Gee; 10 Jason Boults; 11 Josh Crowley; 12 Danny Langtree; 13 Mark Hobson. Subs (all used): 14 Adam Files; 19 Michael Ward; 22 Liam Thompson; 28 Matthew Haggarty.
Tries: Ford (12), Hughes (38), Cookson (44);
Goals: Palfrey 3/3.
HORNETS: 1 Wayne English; 2 Gareth Langley; 20 Daniel Davies; 23 Dave Hull; 17 Martin Waring; 6 Paul Crook; 7 Steve Roper; 29 Carl Forster; 31 Chris Hough; 10 Warren Thompson; 26 Dave Llewellyn; 14 Alex Trumper; 18 Joe Greenwood. Subs (all used): 8 John Cookson; 9 Alex McClurg; 11 Chris Baines; 13 Jordan Case.
Tries: Llewellyn (5), Davies (20), Hull (58), Cookson (71), English (78); **Goals:** Crook 6/6.
Rugby Leaguer & League Express Men of the Match:
Oldham: Lewis Palfrey; *Hornets:* Paul Crook.
Penalty count: 1-2; **Half-time:** 12-12;
Referee: Chris Leatherbarrow. *(at Leigh Sports Village).*

North Wales Crusaders were Championship One Champions in 2013. This game was to determine who took the second promotion place.

CHAMPIONSHIP GRAND FINAL

Sunday 29th September 2013

BATLEY BULLDOGS 12 SHEFFIELD EAGLES 19

BULLDOGS: 1 Miles Greenwood; 5 Johnny Campbell; 3 Jason Walton; 4 Danny Maun; 21 Greg Johnson; 6 Ben Black; 7 Gareth Moore; 8 Byron Smith; 9 Paul Mennell; 28 Anthony Mullally; 11 Alex Bretherton; 16 John Davies; 13 Ashley Lindsay. Subs (all used): 14 George Flanagan; 15 Keegan Hirst; 19 Alex Rowe; 17 Liam Walmsley.
Try: Campbell (13); **Goals:** Moore 4/5.
EAGLES: 1 Quentin Laulu-Togagae; 5 Misi Taulapapa; 4 Tom Armstrong; 3 Menzie Yere; 2 Scott Turner; 6 Pat Walker; 7 Dominic Brambani; 25 Eddie Battye; 9 Andrew Henderson; 10 Mitchell Stringer; 11 Michael Knowles; 15 Alex Szostak; 13 Joe Hirst. Subs (all used): 14 James Davey; 12 Peter Green; 16 Duane Straugheir; 21 Matt Garside.
Tries: Turner (56, 67), Yere (61), Laulu-Togagae (70);
Goals: Brambani 1/5; **Field goal:** Walker (74).
Rugby Leaguer & League Express Men of the Match:
Bulldogs: Keegan Hirst; *Eagles:* Dominic Brambani.
Penalty count: 6-7; **Half-time:** 12-0;
Referee: Matthew Thomason; **Attendance:** 6,374
(at Leigh Sports Village).

SUPER LEAGUE GRAND FINAL

Saturday 5th October 2013

WARRINGTON WOLVES 16 WIGAN WARRIORS 30

WOLVES: 19 Stefan Ratchford; 5 Joel Monaghan; 3 Chris Bridge; 4 Ryan Atkins; 2 Chris Riley; 6 Lee Briers; 7 Richard Myler; 16 Paul Wood; 14 Mick Higham; 18 Chris Hill; 13 Ben Harrison; 12 Ben Westwood; 15 Simon Grix. Subs (all used): 9 Michael Monaghan; 8 Adrian Morley (C); 17 Michael Cooper; 10 Garreth Carvell.
Tries: J Monaghan (20), Grix (24), Westwood (27);
Goals: Ratchford 2/3.
On report: Westwood (2) - alleged punch on Green.
WARRIORS: 1 Sam Tomkins; 2 Josh Charnley; 3 Darrell Goulding; 17 Iain Thornley; 5 Pat Richards; 6 Blake Green; 7 Matty Smith; 10 Lee Mossop; 9 Michael McIlorum; 20 Gil Dudson; 11 Harrison Hansen; 12 Liam Farrell; 13 Sean O'Loughlin (C). Subs (all used): 15 Ben Flower; 4 Jack Hughes; 26 Dominic Crosby; 21 Scott Taylor.
Tries: Goulding (37), McIlorum (47), Charnley (53), Green (65), Richards (74); **Goals:** Richards 5/6.
Rugby Leaguer & League Express Men of the Match:
Wolves: Chris Hill; *Warriors:* Michael McIlorum.
Penalty count: 7-10; **Half-time:** 16-6;
Referee: Richard Silverwood; **Attendance:** 66,281
(at Old Trafford, Manchester).

LONGEST SERVING PLAYERS 2014

SUPER LEAGUE

PLAYER	CLUB	DEBUT vs	COMP	DATE	APPS
Tom Olbison	Bradford Bulls	Warrington Wolves (h)	SL	17/4/09	86
Craig Huby	Castleford Tigers	Leeds Rhinos (a)	SL	7/6/03	241
Gregory Mounis	Catalan Dragons	Wigan Warriors (h)	SL	11/2/06	233
Eorl Crabtree	Huddersfield Giants	London Broncos (a)	SL	13/4/01	372
Richard Horne	Hull FC	Leeds Rhinos (a)	SL	16/4/99	387
Jason Netherton	Hull Kingston Rovers	Keighley Cougars (a)	NRC	13/2/05	182
Kevin Sinfield	Leeds Rhinos	Sheffield Eagles (h)	SL	22/8/97	491
Jamie O'Callaghan	London Broncos	Wigan Warriors (a) *(Harlequins)*	SL	27/6/08	111
Danny Williams	Salford Red Devils	Hull Kingston Rovers (a)	SL	17/7/11	56
		(finished the domestic season on loan with Bradford Bulls)			
Paul Wellens	St Helens	Halifax Blue Sox (h)	SL	30/8/98	491
Matty Wildie	Wakefield Trinity Wildcats	Huddersfield Giants (a)	SL	1/8/10	42
Paul Wood	Warrington Wolves	Wakefield Trinity Wildcats (a)	SL	10/9/00	339
Ben Kavanagh	Widnes Vikings	Blackpool Panthers (a)	NRC	3/2/08	161
Sean O'Loughlin	Wigan Warriors	Hull FC (h)	SL	5/4/02	343

Paul Wellens

CHAMPIONSHIP

PLAYER	CLUB	DEBUT vs	COMP	DATE	APPS
Liam Harrison	Barrow Raiders	Gateshead Thunder (a)	NRC	12/6/06	258
Byron Smith	Batley Bulldogs	Hunslet Hawks (a)	NRC	3/2/08	187
Austin Buchanan	Dewsbury Rams	Rochdale Hornets (h)	NL1	6/5/07	132
Kyle Kesik	Doncaster	Siddal (h) (D2)	CC	6/3/10	116
	Doncaster	Batley Bulldogs (a) (D) *(loan from Sheffield Eagles)*	Ch	19/7/09	7
Andy Kain	Featherstone Rovers	Celtic Crusaders (a)	NL2	2/6/07	210
Ryan Fieldhouse	Halifax	Oldham (h)	NRC	13/2/11	89
James Feather	Keighley Cougars	Oldham (a)	NRC	26/2/06	237
Steve Maden	Leigh Centurions	Barrow Raiders (h) (D2)	NRC	3/2/08	166
	Leigh Centurions	Swinton Lions (a) (D)	ATC	1/2/04	44
John Cookson	Rochdale Hornets	Oldham (a) (D2)	NRC	8/2/10	121
	Rochdale Hornets	Salford City Reds (a) (D) *(loan from Leigh Centurions)*	NRC	14/3/08	4
Wayne English	Rochdale Hornets	Oldham (a)	NRC	8/2/10	115
Mitchell Stringer	Sheffield Eagles	Gateshead Thunder (h) (D3)	NL2	12/5/06	245
	Sheffield Eagles	Batley Bulldogs (h) (D2) *(loan from London Broncos)*	NRC	4/3/05	1
	Sheffield Eagles	Hunslet Hawks (a) (D)	NFP	7/7/02	35
Ritchie Hawkyard	Swinton Lions	Oldham (a)	NRC	1/2/08	144
Craig Calvert	Whitehaven	Rochdale Hornets (h)	NL1	11/7/04	267
Kris Coward	Workington Town	Blackpool Panthers (h)	NL2	15/7/07	137

Mitchell Stringer

CHAMPIONSHIP ONE

PLAYER	CLUB	DEBUT vs	COMP	DATE	APPS
Jason Payne	Gateshead Thunder	Oldham (a)	NL2	1/7/07	151
Danny Grimshaw	Hunslet Hawks	London Skolars (a)	NRC	7/2/10	87
Stuart Kain	Hunslet Hawks	London Skolars (a)	NRC	7/2/10	100
John Oakes	Hunslet Hawks	London Skolars (a)	NRC	7/2/10	116
John Paxton	London Skolars	Dewsbury Rams (a)	Ch1	10/4/09	100
Jason Boults	Oldham	Rochdale Hornets (h)	NRC	11/2/07	193
Ashley Bateman	South Wales Scorpions	Workington Town (h)	Ch1	28/2/10	101
Jack Lee	York City Knights	Rochdale Hornets (h)	Ch1	25/4/10	116

Jason Payne

- *Player's continuous service, beginning with first team debut, and finishing the season as a registered player with that club.*
- *All information correct up to the end of the 2014 domestic season.*
- *If player has had more than one spell with club, all debuts and separate appearance totals are included.*

2014 SEASON
Stats round-up

Joel Monaghan

Matty Smith

TRIES *(play-offs in brackets, included in total)*

1	Joel Monaghan	Warrington Wolves	34 (6)
2	Morgan Escare	Catalan Dragons	28 (1)
3	Tom Makinson	St Helens	27 (2)
4	Michael Oldfield	Catalan Dragons	22 (2)
5	Josh Charnley	Wigan Warriors	21 (2)
6	Jermaine McGillvary	Huddersfield Giants	20 (0)
	Joe Burgess	Wigan Warriors	20 (3)
8	Michael Shenton	Castleford Tigers	18 (1)
	Elliott Whitehead	Catalan Dragons	18 (0)
	Rhys Evans	Warrington Wolves	18 (2)
	Paddy Flynn	Widnes Vikings	18 (2)

GOALS *(play-offs in brackets, included in total)*

1	Matty Smith	Wigan Warriors	107 (11)
2	Marc Sneyd	Castleford Tigers	100 (1)
3	Danny Brough	Huddersfield Giants	98 (2)
4	Travis Burns	Hull Kingston Rovers	78 (-)
5	Thomas Bosc	Catalan Dragons	77 (9)
	Kevin Sinfield	Leeds Rhinos	77 (3)
	Danny Tickle	Widnes Vikings	77 (3)
8	Chris Bridge	Warrington Wolves	67 (0)
9	Luke Walsh	St Helens	66 (0)
10	Josh Drinkwater	London Broncos	54 (-)

GOALS PERCENTAGE *(play-offs included)*

			G	Att	%
1	Jamie Ellis	Castleford Tigers	10	10	100.00
2	Kevin Locke	Salford Red Devils	10	11	90.90
3	Luke Gale	Bradford Bulls	35	39	89.74
4	Sam Williams	Catalan Dragons	21	25	84.00
5	Josh Griffin	Salford Red Devils	27	33	81.81
	Jacob Miller	Hull FC	9	11	81.81
7	Jarrod Sammut	Wakefield Trinity Wildcats	52	64	81.25
8	Kevin Sinfield	Leeds Rhinos	77	98	78.57
	Luke Walsh	St Helens	66	84	78.57
	Jamie Foster	Bradford Bulls	44	56	78.57
	Jordan Rankin	Hull FC	33	42	78.57

(10 minimum attempts to qualify)

POINTS *(play-offs in brackets, included in total)*

			T	G	FG	Pts
1	Matty Smith	Wigan Warriors	5	107	7	241 (27)
2	Marc Sneyd	Castleford Tigers	6	100	2	226 (2)
3	Danny Brough	Huddersfield Giants	3	98	4	212 (4)
4	Chris Bridge	Warrington Wolves	11	67	0	178 (0)
5	Kevin Sinfield	Leeds Rhinos	5	77	1	175 (6)
6	Travis Burns	Hull Kingston Rovers	3	78	2	170 (-)
7	Danny Tickle	Widnes Vikings	3	77	0	166 (6)
8	Thomas Bosc	Catalan Dragons	1	77	1	159 (18)
9	Luke Walsh	St Helens	5	66	1	153 (0)
10	Joel Monaghan	Warrington Wolves	34	0	0	136 (24)
	Mark Percival	St Helens	10	48	0	136 (32)
	Jarrod Sammut	Wakefield Trinity Wildcats	8	52	0	136 (-)

Joe Westerman

BEST ATTENDANCES

		Round	Date
70,102	St Helens v Wigan	GF	11/10/14
		(at Old Trafford, Manchester)	
20,265	Wigan v Leeds	26	5/9/14
20,224	Wigan v St Helens	18	27/6/14
18,139	Leeds v Wigan	11	2/5/14
18,103	Hull FC v Hull KR	25	29/8/14
17,980	St Helens v Wigan	9	18/4/14
17,682	Leeds v St Helens	25	29/8/14
16,240	Wigan v Huddersfield	1	7/2/14
16,173	Leeds v Castleford	21	17/7/14
16,164	Leeds v Warrington	2	21/2/14

WORST ATTENDANCES

		Round	Date
1,002	London Broncos v Catalan Dragons	9	17/4/14
1,017	London Broncos v Wakefield	5	15/3/14
1,035	London Broncos v Huddersfield	12	10/5/14
1,036	London Broncos v Castleford	7	27/3/14
1,084	London Broncos v Hull KR	22	26/7/14
1,135	London Broncos v Hull FC	15	31/5/14
1,246	London Broncos v Salford	2	22/2/14
1,268	London Broncos v Leeds	24	17/8/14
1,377	London Broncos v Warrington	4	9/3/14
1,402	London Broncos v Bradford	27	13/9/14

* Super League attendance figures include play-offs.

CHALLENGE CUP

TRIES

1	Justin Carney	Castleford Tigers	7
	Ryan Hall	Leeds Rhinos	7
3	James Mendeika	Featherstone Rovers	5
	Rob Worrincy	Halifax	5
	Chris Bridge	Warrington Wolves	5
	Kevin Brown	Widnes Vikings	5

GOALS

1	Kevin Sinfield	Leeds Rhinos	25
2	Chris Bridge	Warrington Wolves	23
3	Dominic Brambani		
		Sheffield Eagles	20
4	Danny Jones	Keighley Cougars	16
	Stewart Sanderson		
		Doncaster	16
	Marc Sneyd	Castleford Tigers	16

POINTS

			T	G	FG	Pts
1	Chris Bridge	Warrington Wolves	5	23	0	66
2	Kevin Sinfield	Leeds Rhinos	0	25	1	51
3	Dominic Brambani					
		Sheffield Eagles	2	20	0	48
4	Ryan Brierley	Leigh Centurions	4	12	0	40
	Stewart Sanderson					
		Doncaster	2	16	0	40
	Matty Smith	Wigan Warriors	3	14	0	40

BEST ATTENDANCES

		Round	Date
77,914	Castleford v Leeds	F	23/8/14
		(at Wembley Stadium)	
12,194	Leeds v St Helens	5	26/4/14
12,132	Leeds v Warrington	SF	9/8/14
		(at Langtree Park, St Helens)	
12,005	Castleford v Widnes	SF	10/8/14
		(at Leigh Sports Village)	
8,736	Wigan v Castleford	QF	7/6/14

WORST ATTENDANCES

		Round	Date
213	South Wales v Hemel	3	16/3/14
249	Swinton v Gateshead	3	16/3/14
278	Hunslet v Oxford	3	16/3/14
307	Rochdale v Gloucestershire All Golds	3	16/3/14
340	Egremont v Oldham	3	15/3/14
		(at Copeland Stadium, Whitehaven)	

CONSECUTIVE APPEARANCES
(Super League, including play-offs, and Challenge Cup)

1	Joe Westerman	Hull FC	44
2	Iosia Soliola	St Helens	37
3	Matt Cook	London Broncos	34
	Zeb Taia	Catalan Dragons	34
5	Morgan Escare	Catalan Dragons	32
6	Josh Hodgson	Hull Kingston Rovers	29
	Mose Masoe	St Helens	29
8	Travis Burns	Hull Kingston Rovers	28
	Rhys Evans	Warrington Wolves	28
	Fetuli Talanoa	Hull FC	28

FINAL TABLE

	P	W	D	L	F	A	D	Pts
St Helens	27	19	0	8	796	563	233	38
Wigan Warriors	27	18	1	8	834	429	405	37
Huddersfield Giants	27	17	3	7	785	626	159	37
Castleford Tigers	27	17	2	8	814	583	231	36
Warrington Wolves	27	17	1	9	793	515	278	35
Leeds Rhinos	27	15	2	10	685	421	264	32
Catalan Dragons	27	14	1	12	733	667	66	29
Widnes Vikings	27	13	1	13	611	725	-114	27
Hull Kingston Rovers	27	10	3	14	627	665	-38	23
Salford Red Devils	27	11	1	15	608	695	-87	23
Hull FC	27	10	2	15	653	586	67	22
Wakefield Trinity Wildcats	27	10	1	16	557	750	-193	21
Bradford Bulls *	27	8	0	19	512	984	-472	10
London Broncos	27	1	0	26	438	1237	-799	2

* Deducted six points for entering administration

AVERAGE ATTENDANCES

	2014 Avg	2013 Avg	Diff
Leeds Rhinos	14,472	14,985	-513
Wigan Warriors	13,802	14,549	-747
St Helens	11,543	11,141	+402
Hull FC	11,065	11,201	-136
Warrington Wolves	9,677	10,465	-788
Catalan Dragons	8,312	8,179	+133
Hull Kingston Rovers	7,846	7,495	+351
Castleford Tigers	7,007	6,292	+715
Bradford Bulls	6,653	8,575	-1,922
Huddersfield Giants	6,383	6,368	+15
Widnes Vikings	5,636	6,015	-379
Salford Red Devils	4,515	3,178	+1,337
Wakefield Trinity Wildcats	4,373	7,973	-3,600
London Broncos	1,294	2,200	-906
		(Twickenham Stoop)	

2014 Average	8,041	
2013 Average	8,473	
Difference	-432	

2014 Season - Stats round-up

CHAMPIONSHIP

Martyn Ridyard

TRIES *(play-offs in brackets, included in total)*

1	Ryan Brierley	Leigh Centurions	39 (3)
2	Quentin Laulu-Togagae	Sheffield Eagles	31 (4)
3	Anthony Thackeray	Dewsbury Rams	28 (6)
4	Liam Kay	Leigh Centurions	26 (0)
5	Will Sharp	Featherstone Rovers	24 (2)
	Scott Turner	Sheffield Eagles	24 (1)
7	Miles Greenwood	Batley Bulldogs	22 (0)
	Tom Armstrong	Leigh Centurions	22 (3)
9	Paul White	Keighley Cougars	21 (-)
10	Gregg McNally	Leigh Centurions	19 (3)

GOALS *(play-offs in brackets, included in total)*

1	Martyn Ridyard	Leigh Centurions	157 (16)
2	Dominic Brambani	Sheffield Eagles	95 (10)
3	Gareth Moore	Featherstone Rovers	81 (11)
4	Steve Tyrer	Halifax	76 (0)
5	Paul Crook	Rochdale Hornets	73 (-)
	Stewart Sanderson	Doncaster	73 (7)
7	Tommy Johnson	North Wales Crusaders	62 (-)
8	Scott Leatherbarrow	Batley Bulldogs	59 (0)
	Ryan Shaw	Barrow Raiders	59 (-)
10	Danny Jones	Keighley Cougars	58 (-)

POINTS *(play-offs in brackets, included in total)*

			T	G	FG	Pts
1	Martyn Ridyard	Leigh Centurions	2	157	2	324 (33)
2	Dominic Brambani	Sheffield Eagles	4	95	1	207 (20)
3	Gareth Moore	Featherstone Rovers	9	81	1	199 (31)
4	Steve Tyrer	Halifax	9	76	0	188 (0)
5	Ryan Brierley	Leigh Centurions	39	11	1	179 (12)
6	Paul Crook	Rochdale Hornets	7	73	1	175 (-)
7	Stewart Sanderson	Doncaster	7	73	0	174 (14)
8	Ryan Shaw	Barrow Raiders	10	59	0	158 (-)
9	Tommy Johnson	North Wales Crusaders	8	62	0	156 (-)
10	Danny Jones	Keighley Cougars	6	58	2	142 (-)

FINAL TABLE

	P	W	D	L	BP	F	A	D	Pts
Leigh Centurions	26	25	0	1	1	1024	396	628	76
Featherstone Rovers	26	18	1	7	5	871	532	339	61
Halifax	26	16	2	8	6	714	504	210	58
Doncaster	26	17	1	8	4	643	599	44	57
Sheffield Eagles	26	16	0	10	6	790	605	185	54
Dewsbury Rams	26	15	0	11	6	669	585	84	51
Workington Town	26	12	1	13	10	467	524	-57	48
Batley Bulldogs	26	12	1	13	7	582	573	9	45
Whitehaven	26	13	0	13	6	592	666	-74	45
Keighley Cougars	26	12	0	14	8	587	601	-14	44
North Wales Crusaders	26	7	0	19	10	468	709	-241	31
Rochdale Hornets	26	7	0	19	4	509	919	-410	25
Swinton Lions	26	5	0	21	9	570	865	-295	24
Barrow Raiders	26	4	0	22	7	462	870	-408	19

AVERAGE ATTENDANCES

	2014 Avg	2013 Avg	Diff
Leigh Centurions	2,380	1,556	+824
Featherstone Rovers	2,055	2,403	-348
Halifax	1,686	1,707	-21
Barrow Raiders	1,030	1,033	-3
Dewsbury Rams	1,027	886	+141
Keighley Cougars	991	803	+188
North Wales Crusaders	846	896	-50
		(Championship One)	
Workington Town	838	783	+55
Sheffield Eagles	829	928	-99
		(Don Valley Stadium)	
Doncaster	806	718	+88
Whitehaven	798	758	+40
Rochdale Hornets	764	573	+191
		(Championship One)	
Batley Bulldogs	751	753	-2
Swinton Lions	530	652	-122
2014 Average	1,095		
2013 Average	1,020		
Difference	+75		

BEST ATTENDANCES

		Round	Date
9,164	Featherstone v Leigh	GF	5/10/14
	(at Headingley Carnegie, Leeds)		
3,565	Leigh v Featherstone	23	8/8/14
3,375	Leigh v Workington	25	30/8/14
3,230	Featherstone v Leigh	9	4/5/14
3,022	Halifax v Featherstone	24	17/8/14
2,828	Leigh v Dewsbury	QSF	28/9/14
2,583	Featherstone v Halifax	2	23/2/14
2,571	Leigh v Halifax	14	11/6/14
2,508	Leigh v Barrow	15	15/6/14
2,323	Featherstone v Rochdale	4	9/3/14

WORST ATTENDANCES

		Round	Date
355	Swinton v Doncaster	13	1/6/14
360	Swinton v Keighley	22	3/8/14
	(at Park Lane, Sedgley Park)		
403	Swinton v Barrow	5	23/3/14
	(at Park Lane, Sedgley Park)		
405	Swinton v Workington	17	29/6/14
	(at Park Lane, Sedgley Park)		
412	Swinton v Dewsbury	7	13/4/14
430	Swinton v Rochdale	15	13/6/14
451	Workington v Sheffield	7	13/4/14
456	Swinton v Batley	12	25/5/14
469	Swinton v Featherstone	19	13/7/14
	(at Park Lane, Sedgley Park)		
504	Doncaster v Workington	23	10/8/14

* Championship attendance figures include play-offs, but not Challenge Cup.

CHAMPIONSHIP ONE

TRIES *(play-offs in brackets, included in total)*

1	Dale Bloomfield	Oldham	21 (2)
2	Jason Payne	Gateshead Thunder	18 (0)
	Ben Dent	York City Knights	18 (1)
	Jack Lee	York City Knights	18 (1)
5	Mo Agoro	Oldham	17 (0)
	Sean Morris	Oxford	17 (-)
7	Jimmy Watson	Hunslet Hawks	16 (4)
8	Gavin Duffy	Hunslet Hawks	15 (4)
9	Jonathan Ford	Oldham	13 (1)
	Danny Langtree	Oldham	13 (3)

GOALS *(play-offs in brackets, included in total)*

1	Ben Reynolds	York City Knights	70 (6)
2	Matt Bradley *	Gloucestershire All Golds	59 (-)
3	Barry-John Swindells	Hemel Stags	57 (3)
4	Benn Hardcastle **	York City Knights	55 (0)
5	Lewis Palfrey	Oldham	53 (0)
6	Steve Roper ***	Oldham	43 (11)
	Jimmy Rowland	Oxford	43 (-)
8	Andy Ballard	Hunslet Hawks	42 (0)
9	Paul Emanuelli	South Wales Scorpions	39 (-)
10	David March	Hunslet Hawks	33 (16)

* includes 21 for London Skolars (regular season)
** includes 21 for Gateshead Thunder (regular season)
*** includes 4 for Gloucestershire All Golds (regular season)

318

POINTS *(play-offs in brackets, included in total)*

			T	G	FG	Pts	
1	Ben Reynolds	York City Knights	7	70	0	168	(12)
2	Barry-John Swindells	Hemel Stags	8	57	0	146	(6)
3	Benn Hardcastle *	York City Knights	7	55	0	138	(0)
4	Matt Bradley **	Gloucestershire All Golds	2	59	1	127	(-)
5	Lewis Palfrey	Oldham	4	53	0	122	(0)
6	Andy Ballard	Hunslet Hawks	8	42	0	116	(0)
	Jimmy Rowland	Oxford	7	43	2	116	(-)
8	Steve Roper ***	Oldham	3	43	1	99	(27)
9	Matty Beharrell	Gateshead Thunder	8	31	1	95	(5)
10	David March	Hunslet Hawks	6	33	0	90	(40)

* includes 58 for Gateshead Thunder (regular season)
** includes 43 for London Skolars (regular season)
*** includes 8 for Gloucestershire All Golds (regular season)

FINAL TABLE

	P	W	D	L	BP	F	A	D	Pts
York City Knights	20	17	0	3	3	738	367	371	54
Hunslet Hawks	20	15	0	5	4	716	249	467	49
Oldham	20	15	1	4	1	675	457	218	48
Gateshead Thunder	20	11	0	9	3	615	576	39	36
Hemel Stags	20	8	2	10	5	482	521	-39	33
Gloucestershire All Golds	20	8	0	12	5	446	616	-170	29
London Skolars	20	5	0	15	9	471	647	-176	24
Oxford	20	7	1	12	1	493	679	-186	24
South Wales Scorpions	20	2	0	18	4	304	828	-524	10

AVERAGE ATTENDANCES

	2014 Avg	2013 Avg	Diff
York City Knights	645	715	-70
			(Championship)
Hunslet Hawks	508	582	-74
			(Championship)
Oldham	499	637	-138
London Skolars	464	473	-9
Gateshead Thunder	283	186	+97
South Wales Scorpions	279	343	-64
Oxford	271	312	-41
Hemel Stags	219	299	-80
Gloucestershire All Golds	211	195	+16
2014 Average	375		
2013 Average	435		
Difference	-60		

BEST ATTENDANCES *(figure unavailable for Grand Final)*

		Round	Date
1,325	London Skolars v Hunslet	14	22/8/14
	(at Queen Elizabeth II Stadium, Enfield)		
1,006	York v Oldham	18	20/7/14
837	York v Hunslet	10	25/5/14
796	Hunslet v York	22	17/8/14
759	York v Hunslet	FE	28/9/14
748	Hunslet v Oldham	QPO	12/9/14
678	Oldham v Hunslet	19	27/7/14
663	York v Oldham	QSF	21/9/14
648	York v Gloucestershire All Golds	1	2/3/14
643	York v London Skolars	24	7/9/14

WORST ATTENDANCES

		Round	Date
108	Gloucestershire All Golds v London Skolars	22	17/8/14
126	Gloucestershire All Golds v Hemel	7	4/5/14
126	Hemel v Gateshead	11	1/6/14
126	Gloucestershire All Golds v Gateshead	18	20/7/14
150	South Wales v Oxford	16	5/7/14
153	Gateshead v Oxford	19	27/7/14
161	Gateshead v South Wales	22	17/8/14
166	Gateshead v Hemel	20	3/8/14
168	Gloucestershire All Golds v Hemel	16	6/7/14
170	Hemel v Oxford	10	25/5/14

* Championship One attendance figures include play-offs,
but not Challenge Cup.

Ryan Brierley

TRIES

1	Ryan Brierley	Leigh Centurions	43
2	Joel Monaghan	Warrington Wolves	38
3	Quentin Laulu-Togagae	Sheffield Eagles	34
4	Morgan Escare	Catalan Dragons	29
	Tom Makinson	St Helens	29
6	Anthony Thackeray	Dewsbury Rams	28
7	Will Sharp	Featherstone Rovers	27
	Liam Kay	Leigh Centurions	27
9	Scott Turner	Sheffield Eagles	26
10	Joe Burgess	Wigan Warriors	25

GOALS

1	Martyn Ridyard	Leigh Centurions	165
2	Matty Smith	Wigan Warriors	122
3	Marc Sneyd	Castleford Tigers	116
4	Dominic Brambani	Sheffield Eagles	115
5	Kevin Sinfield	Leeds Rhinos	102
6	Danny Brough	Huddersfield Giants	100
7	Chris Bridge	Warrington Wolves	90
	Gareth Moore	Featherstone Rovers	90
9	Danny Tickle	Widnes Vikings	89
	Stewart Sanderson	Doncaster	89

POINTS

			T	G	FG	Pts
1	Martyn Ridyard	Leigh Centurions	3	165	2	344
2	Matty Smith	Wigan Warriors	8	122	7	283
3	Marc Sneyd	Castleford Tigers	7	116	2	262
4	Dominic Brambani	Sheffield Eagles	6	115	1	255
5	Chris Bridge	Warrington Wolves	16	90	0	244
6	Kevin Sinfield	Leeds Rhinos	5	102	2	226
7	Ryan Brierley	Leigh Centurions	43	23	1	219
8	Gareth Moore	Featherstone Rovers	9	90	1	217
9	Danny Brough	Huddersfield Giants	3	100	4	216
10	Stewart Sanderson	Doncaster	9	89	0	214

FIELD GOALS

1	Matty Smith	Wigan Warriors	7
2	Danny Brough	Huddersfield Giants	4
3	Luke Gale	Bradford Bulls	3
	Rangi Chase	Salford Red Devils	3
	Scott Leatherbarrow	Batley Bulldogs	3
	Kieran Hyde	Dewsbury Rams	3
	Thomas Coyle	Hunslet Hawks	3